SIMON'S TAX CASES

1991

EDITOR

RENGAN KRISHNAN

of Lincoln's Inn, Barrister

London

BUTTERWORTHS

United Kingdom	Butterworth & Co (Publishers) Ltd, 88 Kingsway, LONDON WC2B 6AB and 4 Hill Street, EDINBURGH EH2 3LZ
Australia	Butterworths Pty Ltd, SYDNEY, MELBOURNE, BRISBANE, ADELAIDE, PERTH, CANBERRA and HOBART
Canada	Butterworths Canada Ltd, MARKHAM and VANCOUVER
Ireland	Butterworth (Ireland) Ltd, DUBLIN
Malaysia	Malayan Law Journal Pte Ltd, KUALA LUMPUR
New Zealand	Butterworths of New Zealand Ltd, WELLINGTON and AUCKLAND
Puerto Rico	Equity de Puerto Rico Inc, HATO REY
Singapore	Malayan Law Journal Pte Ltd, SINGAPORE
USA	Butterworth Legal Publishers, AUSTIN, Texas, CLEARWATER, Florida, ORFORD, New Hampshire, ST PAUL, Minnesota, SALEM, New Hampshire

These reports should be cited thus:
[1991] STC

©
Butterworth & Co (Publishers) Ltd
1992

ISBN 0 406 009 058

Typeset by CCC, printed and bound in Great Britain by William Clowes Limited, Beccles and London.

CASES REPORTED

iv

SUBJECT INDEX

VALUE ADDED TAX

Packe v Johnson (Inspector of Taxes)

CHANCERY DIVISION
MILLETT J
19 JULY 1990

Appeal – Commissioners – Adjournment of appeal – Refusal of adjournment – Taxpayer appealing to commissioners against assessments to capital gains tax – Taxpayer not appearing at hearing but letter to commissioners' clerk from taxpayer setting out contentions and requesting adjournment – Commissioners refusing to adjourn and confirming assessments – Whether commissioners acted properly in refusing adjournment.

The taxpayer appealed to the General Commissioners against estimated assessments to capital gains tax for the years 1983–84 and 1984–85. The appeal was originally listed for hearing on 12 July 1988 but was adjourned to 13 September 1988 at the request of the taxpayer. When the appeal came on for hearing on 13 September the taxpayer did not appear and was not represented but a letter requesting a further adjournment was delivered to the commissioners' clerk from the taxpayer's agents. The letter stated that all the necessary information (ie the accounts) sufficient to justify the reduction of the assessments to nil had been supplied to the inspector of taxes. The commissioners refused the adjournment on the ground that it was a second hearing and confirmed the assessments stating that no evidence had been adduced to justify the discharging or varying of the assessments. The taxpayer appealed.

Held – If the commissioners had not given any reason for refusing an adjournment, their decision would stand unless the taxpayer could show that in all the circumstances no reasonable body of commissioners could have refused an adjournment. However, if the reason given by the commissioners was inadequate and other relevant considerations did not appear to have been taken into account, their decision could not be upheld unless the circumstances were such that no reasonable body of commissioners could have granted an adjournment. By refusing the adjournment and hence any opportunity for the taxpayer to put the accounts in evidence, and then by treating the accounts as not having been before them, the commissioners had deprived the taxpayer of any opportunity of putting forward his case in reliance on the accounts which had been professionally prepared. The commissioners were at fault either in refusing an adjournment, or having properly refused an adjournment, in refusing to admit the accounts in evidence. Accordingly, there was a miscarriage of justice. The taxpayer's appeal would therefore be allowed. *Noble v Wilkinson (Inspector of Taxes)* (1958) 38 TC 135 distinguished.

Notes

For adjournment of hearing of appeals by the commissioners, see Simon's Taxes A3.516.

Case referred to in judgment

Noble v Wilkinson (Inspector of Taxes) (1958) 38 TC 135.

Cases also cited

Banin v MacKinlay (Inspector of Taxes) [1985] STC 144, [1985] 1 All ER 842, 58 TC **a**
398, CA.
Ottley v Morris (Inspector of Taxes) [1978] STC 594, [1979] 1 All ER 65, 52 TC 375.
R v Blundeston Prison Board of Visitors, ex p Fox-Taylor [1982] 1 All ER 646.

Case stated
b

1. At a meeting of the Commissioners for the general purposes of the income tax for the division of Brighton held on 13 September 1988, Mr William James Packe (the taxpayer) appealed against two estimated assessments to capital gains tax for the years of assessment 1983–84 and 1984–85 respectively, both being in the sum of £40,000.

2. The appeals had originally been listed for hearing before the commissioners on **c** 12 July 1988, but were adjourned to 13 September 1988, at the request of the taxpayer's agents, transmitted to the commissioners by the Crown.

3. The question for the commissioners' determination was whether those assessments should have been confirmed or discharged.

4. The taxpayer was neither present nor represented at the hearing before the commissioners, but there was placed before the commissioners a letter to their clerk **d** from his agents, Atkinsons, which the commissioners decided to take into consideration. That letter stated that all necessary information had already been provided and that there seemed to be no reason why the assessments should not be reduced to a nil figure. The letter contained an undertaking by the agents to deal with any further inquiries from the inspector by return of post and a request that the appeals be adjourned. Mr J S Powell, an inspector of taxes from Brighton 2 tax **e** office, appeared for the Crown.

5. No evidence was given on either side, but Mr Powell gave a brief explanation of the background of the case.

6. The commissioners made no findings of fact.

7. The taxpayer's contentions were:
f
(a) that all the necessary information had been supplied to the Crown;
(b) that the information contained sufficient evidence to justify reducing the assessments to nil; and
(c) that in all the circumstances the hearing of the appeals ought to be adjourned.

8. The Crown's contentions were:
g
(a) that the accounts and computations submitted were too inconsistent among themselves to provide a satisfactory basis for the determination of the appeal;
(b) that the accounts and computations, being inconsistent with other information available to the Crown, ought not to be relied on in deciding how to deal with the assessments;
h
(c) that the burden of showing that an assessment should be discharged was on the taxpayer;
(d) that the taxpayer had adduced no evidence to show that the assessments should be discharged in the present case;
(e) that in all the circumstances the commissioners should not grant a further adjournment; and
j
(f) that the assessments ought to be confirmed.

9. No authorities were cited to the commissioners.

10. The commissioners who heard the appeals decided as follows:

(a) no evidence having been adduced on either side, the commissioners were not in a position to make any findings concerning the accounts, returns or other information supplied by the taxpayer to the Crown;

(b) no evidence had been adduced before the commissioners to justify the discharging or varying of the assessments;

(c) the commissioners would not grant a further adjournment as that was a second hearing; and

(d) the commissioners would confirm both assessments in the original figures.

11. By a letter dated 6 October 1988 the taxpayer declared his dissatisfaction with the commissioners' decision as being erroneous in point of law and required the commissioners to state a case for the opinion of the High Court pursuant to the Taxes Management Act 1970, s 56.

12. The questions of law for the opinion of the High Court were:

(i) whether the commissioners had been justified in refusing an adjournment; and

(ii) whether the commissioners had been justified in confirming the estimated assessments.

John Walters for the taxpayer.
Launcelot Henderson for the Crown.

MILLETT J. At a meeting of the General Commissioners for the division of Brighton held on 13 September 1988 the taxpayer, Mr William James Packe, appealed against two estimated assessments to capital gains tax for the years 1983–84 and 1984–85 respectively. Each assessment was in the sum of £40,000.

The appeal had originally been listed for hearing before the General Commissioners on 12 July 1988. On that occasion the taxpayer did not attend and was not represented. He had previously sought an adjournment by requesting the inspector of taxes to ask for an adjournment. The inspector had done so, and the commissioners had agreed. They had adjourned the hearing until 13 September 1988. No correspondence ensued between the taxpayer and the inspector between those two dates.

On 13 September 1988 the taxpayer was neither present nor represented before the commissioners. On that date his accountant had written a letter, which must have been delivered by hand to the inspector, requesting him to seek a further adjournment from the commissioners. A copy of that letter had also been written to (and, I infer, handed to) the clerk to the General Commissioners. It was before them. The letter was in these terms:

'We refer to the listed hearings against these assessments, and we have to advise you that we have written to the Inspector of Taxes . . . today suggesting that all necessary information has already been provided and there would seem to be no reason why these assessments should not be reduced to a nil figure. If, however, the Inspector has any further enquiries to make, we have undertaken to deal with these by return of post. In the circumstances, may we please request an adjournment of these appeals until the next meeting.'

The inspector opposed the application for an adjournment. The commissioners refused an adjournment and upheld the assessments on the grounds, inter alia, that no evidence had been adduced before them by either side. The burden was on the taxpayer to show that the assessments should be discharged or varied. In the absence of evidence, the assessments had to be upheld.

The appeal comes before me by way of case stated. In the case the commissioners have set out their reasons for refusing the adjournment and for confirming the assessments. As will appear, they are not entirely clear. The taxpayer submits that substantial injustice has been occasioned to him by reason of the refusal to adjourn and the inevitable determination of the case against him in the absence of evidence, and submits that there has been a miscarriage of justice.

The onus—and it is a heavy one—in such a case is on the taxpayer to show that there has been a miscarriage of justice.

The case stated records that there was placed before the commissioners the accountants' letter to their clerk which contained the grounds on which he sought *a* an adjournment and which the commissioners decided to take into consideration. The commissioners annexed the letter to the case. The case continues: 'No evidence was given on either side, but [the inspector] gave a brief explanation of the background of the case. We made no findings of fact'. It then recites the taxpayer's contentions, being those set out in the accountant's letter. They may be summarised as being (a) that all the necessary information had been supplied to the inspector; (b) *b* that such information contained sufficient evidence to justify reducing the assessments to nil; and (c) that in all the circumstances the hearing of the appeal ought to be adjourned. The case then sets out the inspector's contentions, which were that (a) the accounts and computations submitted were too inconsistent with one another to provide a satisfactory basis for the determination of the appeal; (b) the accounts and computations were inconsistent with other information available *c* to the inspector and ought not to be relied on in deciding how to deal with the assessments; (c) the burden of showing that an assessment should be discharged was on the taxpayer; (d) the taxpayer had adduced no evidence to show that the assessments should be discharged; and (e) in all the circumstances the commissioners should not grant a further adjournment and the assessments ought to be confirmed.

The commissioners then record their decision as follows: *d*

'(a) No evidence having been adduced on either side, we were not in a position to make any findings concerning the accounts, returns or other information supplied by [the taxpayer to the inspector]; (b) No evidence had been adduced before us to justify the discharging or varying of the assessments; (c) We would not grant a further adjournment as this was a second hearing; (d) We would confirm both assessments in the original figures . . . The questions of *e* law for the opinion of the High Court are: (i) whether we were justified in refusing an adjournment; (ii) whether we were justified in confirming the estimated assessments.'

In my judgment the commissioners were plainly correct in distinguishing the two questions which were before them. The first question was whether they ought to *f* allow or refuse an adjournment: if they decided to refuse the adjournment the second question would then arise, whether they should or should not confirm the estimated assessments. Those were two quite separate questions, and are correctly distinguished at the end of the case stated, but they had become confused both in the arguments of the inspector and in the reasons given by the commissioners for their decision. The only ground specifically given by the commissioners for their decision to refuse *g* an adjournment was that it was a second hearing. That was, of course, a relevant consideration; but it ignored other considerations of far greater relevance. Counsel for the Crown did not seek to support it as a sufficient ground for the commissioners' refusal of any adjournment.

This is not a case like *Noble v Wilkinson (Inspector of Taxes)* (1958) 38 TC 135, where the commissioners refused an adjournment in view of the past history of the *h* case, there having been lengthy delay and a failure on the part of the taxpayer to deal with questions from the inspector. The sole ground given by the commissioners in the present case was that it was a second hearing. A decision to grant or refuse an adjournment is a matter of discretion. In my judgment it would normally be for the taxpayer to show that in all the circumstances no reasonable body of commissioners could have refused an adjournment. Had the commissioners given no reason for *j* refusing an adjournment, but simply said that in all the circumstances they had decided to refuse it, that is what the taxpayer would have to show in order to support an appeal. But where the sole ground given for the refusal of an adjournment is inadequate and other relevant considerations do not appear to have been taken into account, then the decision cannot be supported unless the circumstances were such that no reasonable body of commissioners could have granted the adjournment.

In the present case the commissioners knew that there was a dispute as to the
a reliability of the accounts. They ought to have considered whether an adjournment
should be granted in order to enable the taxpayer to meet the criticisms of the
accounts which the inspector had made. At first sight, they do not appear to have
done so.

However, I am prepared to read the case as a whole and perhaps somewhat
benignly to infer from the recital in para 4 of the facts that the commissioners did
b take into account the contents of the letter from the taxpayer's accountants which
had been placed before them. I take their ground for refusing an adjournment to be
that, having considered the grounds on which it was sought and which were set out
in the letter, no adjournment should be granted especially as this was a second
hearing. In my judgment, if the commissioners had approached the question of an
adjournment on that basis then their decision to refuse an adjournment, at least,
c could not be criticised. The grounds for an adjournment set out in the accountants'
letter were that they had submitted information (ie the accounts) to the inspector,
those accounts justified reducing the assessment to a nil figure and therefore there
was no purpose in a hearing. They asked for an adjournment in order to enable the
inspector to consider the accounts and to agree them, but in case he did not, they
would wish to have an opportunity of placing the accounts before the commissioners.
d Had the commissioners taken those submissions into account, they might well have
come to the conclusion that, in all the circumstances, they should proceed then and
there to deal with the case on the basis of the accounts which could be treated as
before them. The only ground on which an adjournment was sought was to enable
the inspector to agree the accounts and the inspector had made it perfectly clear that
he was not prepared to do so. There was, therefore, no need for an adjournment. It
e would not have been a miscarriage of justice for the commissioners to proceed on the
basis of the accounts, to hear the inspector's criticisms of them, and to decide
whether the accounts justified varying or discharging the assessments. True, that
would have deprived the accountants of any opportunity of attending before the
commissioners and presenting arguments to meet the inspector's criticisms, but the
commissioners could properly have concluded that the accountants had taken a risk
f in neither turning up nor writing and asking for an adjournment until the last
moment, thus giving the inspector no opportunity of telling them that he would
oppose an adjournment. That was a risk which they could properly be treated as
having taken with their eyes open.

Had the commissioners gone through that process of reasoning, they could, in my
judgment, reasonably have refused an adjournment; but this would inevitably have
g involved regarding the accounts as before them, and they would then have had to
consider whether, having seen the accounts and considered the inspector's criticisms,
those accounts justified any variation or discharge of the assessment. Had they
approached the matter in that way, again I think they could not have been faulted.
But, as I understand the case (and the contrary was not contended by counsel for
the Crown) the commissioners did not adopt that approach. They refused an
h adjournment and then treated the accounts as not being in evidence at all. The case
stated expressly records that no evidence had been adduced on either side. The
second ground for the decision: 'No evidence had been adduced before us to justify
the discharging or varying of the assessments' must not, I think, be taken as a finding
that the accounts were insufficient to justify the discharging or varying of the
assessments since the commissioners had expressly stated that they could make no
j finding concerning the accounts because they had no evidence before them of any
kind.

In my judgment, by refusing the adjournment and hence any opportunity for the
taxpayer to put the accounts in evidence, for what they were worth, and then not
regarding the accounts as being before them, the commissioners deprived the
taxpayer of any opportunity of putting forward his case in reliance on accounts
which had been professionally prepared. The risk of injustice in adopting that

procedure may well have outweighed any inconvenience in a short adjournment, but the commissioners never took that risk into account. In my judgment, the commissioners were at fault, either in refusing an adjournment or, having properly refused an adjournment, in refusing to admit the accounts in evidence. In my judgment, there was a miscarriage of justice. Accordingly, I shall allow the appeal, set aside the determination of the commissioners and remit the case to another panel of General Commissioners under s 56(6) of the Taxes Management Act 1970.

Appeal allowed with no order as to costs.

Solicitors: *Dean-Wilson*, Brighton (for the taxpayer); *Solicitor of Inland Revenue.*

Siew Ling Choo   Barrister.

a   # Burford v Durkin (Inspector of Taxes)

COURT OF APPEAL, CIVIL DIVISION
SLADE, NICHOLLS AND FARQUHARSON LJJ
29, 30 OCTOBER 1990

b   *Assessment – Assessment out of time – Making of an assessment – Sub-contractors in the construction industry – Exemption certificates – Sub-contractors not holding valid exemption certificates – Contractor making gross payments to sub-contractors – Inspector raising assessment on contractor – Assessment certified as entered in assessment book by a different inspector – Whether assessment validly made – Income Tax (Sub-Contractors in the Construction Industry) Regulations 1975, reg 12.*

c

The taxpayer had paid his sub-contractors gross without ensuring that gross payments were to be made only against the production of valid tax exemption certificates issued under s 70(1) of the Finance (No 2) Act 1975. The irregularities came to the Revenue's attention and an inspector, having decided that a number of specific assessments pursuant to reg 12*ᵃ* of the Income Tax (Sub-Contractors in the

d Construction Industry) Regulations 1975 should be made against him, directed a second inspector to complete the making of those assessments. The taxpayer appealed against those assessments contending, inter alia, that an assessment was validly made only if all such acts as were necessary to constitute the making of the assessment were the acts of one and the same inspector and that, since, in the instant case, the second inspector was not the same inspector who exercised the discretion

e to make the assessments pursuant to reg 12, the assessments were not valid. The Crown contended that the assessments were validly made by the first inspector, for whom the second inspector merely acted as an agent. A Special Commissioner held that the second inspector had 'made' the assessments as the agent, and at the request, of the first, and upheld them. Mervyn Davies J dismissed the taxpayer's appeal on the ground that the process of making the assessments had been completed when

f the first inspector had decided to make them and computed their amounts, subsequent acts by the second inspector being purely ministerial or administrative in character. The taxpayer appealed.

Held – (1) Where a statute conferred a power on an official to exercise his discretion, only that official could exercise it; but once he had exercised it he could delegate

g purely ministerial tasks flowing from such exercise to others—the carrying out of such tasks being treated in law as his.

(2) The process of making an assessment, for the purpose of applying reg 12(1), was only complete when (a) an inspector had exercised his discretion as to its relevant details, and (b) those details had been entered on an assessment sheet or card, (c) that sheet or card had been bound into a folder constituting a volume of the

h assessment book, and (d) an inspector—whether the same or not—had signed an accompanying certificate in the assessment book recording the date of that entry in that book. The assessments in question had accordingly been validly 'made' by the first inspector, when the second inspector, as agent for the first, had carried out those last three ministerial tasks.

The taxpayer's appeal would therefore be dismissed.

j

Notes

For deductions on account of tax from payments to certain sub-contractors, see Simon's Taxes E5.502.

---

a   Regulation 12, so far as material, is set out at p 9 *d–f*, post

For the Finance (No 2) Act 1975, ss 69, 70 (now the Income and Corporation Taxes Act 1988, ss 561(5), 566), see ibid, Part G1.

For the Income Tax (Sub-Contractors in the Construction Industry) Regulations 1975, reg 12, see ibid, Part H2.

Cases referred to in judgments

Agricultural, Horticultural and Forestry Industry Training Board v Aylesbury Mushrooms Ltd [1972] 1 WLR 190, [1972] 1 All ER 280.

Craven (Inspector of Taxes) v White [1985] STC 531, [1985] 1 WLR 1024, [1985] 3 All ER 125; *affd* [1987] STC 297, [1987] 3 WLR 660, [1987] 3 All ER 27, CA; *affd* [1988] STC 476, [1989] AC 398, [1988] 3 All ER 495, HL.

Customs and Excise Comrs v Cure & Deeley Ltd [1962] 1 QB 340, [1961] 3 All ER 641.

Honig v Sarsfield (Inspector of Taxes) [1986] STC 246, 59 TC 337, CA.

Horder v Scott (1880) 5 QBD 552.

R v Commission for Racial Equality, ex p Cottrell and Rothon [1980] 1 WLR 1580, [1980] 3 All ER 265.

Cases also cited

Pickford v Quirke (Inspector of Taxes) (1927) 13 TC 251, CA.

Wakefield and District Light Railways Co v Wakefield Corp [1906] 2 KB 140.

Appeal

Derek Burford, the taxpayer, appealed against a decision of Mervyn Davies J (see [1989] STC 845) dated 25 October 1989 dismissing the taxpayer's appeal from a determination of a Special Commissioner dismissing his appeals against the inspector's refusal to grant the taxpayer's application for a sub-contractor's exemption certificate and also against six assessments raised under reg 12(1) of the Income Tax (Sub-Contractors in the Construction Industry) Regulations 1975, SI 1975/1960. The grounds of appeal were, inter alia, that the judge had erred in holding that an assessment could be made simply by a decision to assess and the calculation of the amount, without all relevant data being particularised in an assessment book and authorised by the signature of the officer charged with making the assessments.

Robin Mathew for the taxpayer.
Alan Moses QC for the Crown.

SLADE LJ. This is an appeal by a taxpayer, Mr Derek Burford, from an order made by Mervyn Davies J on 25 October 1989 (see [1989] STC 845) whereby he dismissed an appeal by the taxpayer on a case stated pursuant to s 56 of the Taxes Management Act 1970.

The taxpayer became an employee of a firm of contractors (Deedes) 30 or more years ago. In 1970 he was asked by his employers to become a self-employed labour-only contractor. He did that and obtained a sub-contractor's exemption certificate pursuant to s 70 of the Finance (No 2) Act 1975 (the 1975 Act).

The advantage of having an exemption certificate arose in this way. By virtue of ss 69 and 70 of the 1975 Act, when a sub-contractor does not possess a s 70 certificate, the contractor is under a duty to deduct a percentage of the wages paid and to hand the sum deducted to the Revenue to be held by them on account of the tax which should be paid by the sub-contractor. The taxpayer's exemption certificate entitled him to be paid by any contractor for whom he worked without having tax deducted from his pay by the contractor. In fact in the event he worked only for Deedes. In time his activities as a self-employed labour-only contractor were successful. It seems that he hired out to Deedes as sub-contractors, or sub-subcontractors, not

only himself but other workers who were in relation to himself sub-contractors. Not
a all the persons employed by him as sub-contractors possessed valid tax certificates.
In a number of cases over the years he appears to have paid sub-contractors of his
who did not produce valid s 70 certificates substantial gross sums, without making
the proper deductions required by s 69 of the 1975 Act.

In due course the failure to make proper deductions came to the attention of the
Revenue. As a result, the taxpayer's tax exemption certificate was cancelled on 29
b February 1984. In addition assessments were made on him pursuant to reg 12(1) of
the Income Tax (Sub-Contractors in the Construction Industry) Regulations 1975,
SI 1975/1960 (the 1975 regulations), which were made pursuant to powers conferred
by s 69 of the 1975 Act.

The amounts of the assessments were: 1978–79, £18,106·41; 1979–80, £60,430·53;
1980–81, £40,884·00; 1981–82, £56,460·00; 1982–83, £84,015·60; 1983–84,
c £97,941·00.

The taxpayer appealed to the Special Commissioners against the refusal of a s 70
certificate. That appeal failed and the matter was not pursued before Mervyn
Davies J.

The taxpayer also appealed against the assessments themselves. The amounts of
the assessments were not questioned before the judge. What was argued before him
d was the question whether, as the Special Commissioner had held, the assessments
had been validly 'made' within the meaning of reg 12(1) of the 1975 regulations
which, as amended by the Income Tax (Sub-Contractors in the Construction
Industry) Regulations 1982, SI 1982/1391, reads as follows:

'Where—

e (a) there is a dispute between a contractor and a sub-contractor as to the
amount, if any, deductible by the contractor under the principal section from
a payment to the sub-contractor or his nominee; or

(b) the Inspector has reason to believe, as a result of an inspection under
Regulation 11 or otherwise, that the amount which a contractor is liable to
pay to the Collector under these Regulations is greater than the amount, if
f any, which he has so paid, or

(c) the Inspector for any other reason sees fit to do so,

the Inspector may at his discretion make an assessment on the contractor in
the amount which, according to the best of his judgment, the contractor is
liable to pay under these Regulations, and such assessment shall be subject to
the provisions of Parts IV, V and VI of the Taxes Management Act 1970 as if
g it were an assessment to income tax and as if the amount assessed were income
tax charged on the contractor and those Parts of that Act shall apply accordingly
with any necessary modifications, except that the amount charged by the
assessment shall be due and payable fourteen days after the assessment is made.'

As counsel for the taxpayer has rightly pointed out in his skeleton argument, the
h sums falling to be deducted pursuant to s 69 of the 1975 Act are not themselves tax.
As they are not tax, the regulation had to be drafted in terms which deem the
amount assessed to be tax.

The essence of the submissions made by counsel for the taxpayer, both in this
court and in the court below, is that the assessments were not validly 'made' for the
purpose of reg 12(1), on the ground that in the Revenue offices the discretion
j conferred by reg 12(1) was exercised by one inspector, Mr Martin, while it was
another inspector, Mr McEnhill, who actually signed the certificate that assessments
had been entered in the assessment book and thus, it is said, 'made' the assessments.
In counsel's submission an assessment is validly made only if all such acts as are
necessary to constitute the making of the assessment are the acts of one and the same
inspector.

In order to consider these submissions further, it is necessary to look at the factual background as appearing from the case stated. In his decision annexed to the case the Special Commissioner said ([1989] STC 845 at 857):

'Mr Martin received information concerning the taxpayer's tax affairs relevant to his operation of the sub-contractors' tax deduction scheme, from Operations Division M4 of the Inland Revenue and that information included the Revenue's file relating to its investigation of the taxpayer's tax affairs. I infer that the file included reports from the Revenue officers who had interviewed the taxpayer concerning his alleged failure to operate correctly the provisions of the sub-contractors' tax deduction scheme. I also infer that by the time that the assessments were made in October 1984, Mr Martin had been seised of the taxpayer's tax affairs for several months at the least. Mr Martin confirmed in his evidence that he took all these matters into account when deciding to make the assessments, which are the subject of these appeals, on the taxpayer. In my judgment, Mr Martin applied his mind to the question of making the assessments on the taxpayer and according to the best of his judgment using all the information available to him and I find accordingly.'

The Special Commissioner continued:

'[Counsel for the taxpayer] submits that it was necessary for Mr Martin personally to make the assessments, which it is conceded, he did not do. He instructed or asked Mr McEnhill to do so and I infer that the assessments were made by Mr McEnhill as the agent and at the request of Mr Martin. That Mr McEnhill had power to do so is clear from s 113 of the Taxes Management Act 1970.'

The case itself contains this passage (at 846):

'[The commissioner made] the following additional findings of fact: (a) Mr Martin instructed Mr McEnhill to make the assessments on [the taxpayer]. (b) It was the practice in the Shepherds Bush tax office for assessments to be made in monthly batches. The assessment cards were signed usually by a management inspector and such cards were eventually bound up in the assessment book.'

As the judge said (at 862):

'Thus it was that Mr Martin was initially concerned with the assessments and that Mr McEnhill finally signed the assessment card or book [I think that should more accurately have read "certificate".] Before me, counsel for the taxpayer accepted that Mr McEnhill had been given by Mr Martin the amounts of the assessments and that Mr McEnhill had little to do save to "make" the assessments in the sense of signing them in the records of the Revenue, ie on the cards or in the appropriate book.'

As a formal matter it has been common ground in this court that an assessment under s 69 of the 1975 Act is finally 'made' when a certificate recording the entry of the relevant assessment in the assessment book is signed, and that it was Mr McEnhill who actually signed the certificate in the present case.

On the facts, however, the judge rejected the taxpayer's argument that it was Mr McEnhill who 'made' the assessment for the purpose of reg 12(1). He found that for that purpose the assessment was made by Mr Martin. His reasoning appears from the following passage of his judgment (at 863):

'There is nothing in the legislation which indicates the mechanics or formal steps that are to be taken when an assessment is made. As I see it, the process of making an assessment consists of (i) the decision to make the assessment, and (ii) a calculation of its amount. There is then the recording of the fact and of the amount of the assessment so that the appropriate notice of assessment and claim for payment can be made. Counsel for the Crown described the recording as a consequential process that was purely ministerial or administrative in character.

a Thus the assessment was "made" by Mr Martin when he alone exercised the discretion in reg 12(1), i e deciding whether or not to make an assessment and, having decided to do so, working on the figures to calculate the sum that ought to be claimed. I accept the submission that it was Mr Martin who made the assessment. It seems to me that once Mr Martin had decided to make an assessment and had calculated the amounts of the assessment then the

b assessments were "made" because there was no further step to be taken pursuant to the power impliedly given by the reg 12(1) discretion. The papers handed to Mr McEnhill were handed over for the purpose of processing. The fact that that processing involved Mr McEnhill in signing a card or book to record the assessment does not mean that Mr McEnhill made the assessment. On the facts before me, I regard the assessment as having been made by Mr Martin for the

c reasons that I have given.'

The first ground of appeal, as set out in the notice of appeal, is:

'The Learned Judge misdirected himself in finding that Mr [Martin] made the assessments upon the Plaintiff in that: (i) he did not do so and (ii) there being a finding of fact to the contrary in the Case Stated.'

d I shall revert later in this judgment to the question whether it was Mr Martin or Mr McEnhill who made the relevant assessment for the purpose of reg 12(1); this is, of course, the all-important question in the case.

However, in so far as reliance is based by the taxpayer on the Special Commissioner's findings of fact, I think this is a bad point. On a proper reading of his decision the Special Commissioner did no more than find that Mr McEnhill did

e the physical acts which were necessary to complete the assessment which Mr Martin had already determined to make. He further found that Mr McEnhill did so, 'as the agent and at the request of' Mr Martin.

Grounds 2 and 3 of the notice of appeal read as follows:

'2. The Learned Judge erred in holding that an assessment can be made

f simply by the decision to assess and calculation of the amount; without the amount and other relevant data being particularised in an assessment book or index authorised by signature of the Officer charged with making the assessment.

3. The Learned Judge misdirected himself in distinguishing *Honig v Sarsfield* on the basis that for "time limit purposes" an assessment is not made until it is appropriately particularised and signed by the authorised Officer in the Revenue

g records: In the instant matter the Learned Judge found that an Inspector made assessments at the time he instructed another to make assessments.'

In *Honig v Sarsfield (Inspector of Taxes)* [1986] STC 246, this court held that for the purpose of determining whether the statutory time limits have been complied with for the purpose of s 40(1) of the Taxes Management Act 1970, an assessment is made when the inspector who is authorised to make the assessment signs the

h certificate in the assessment book. This decision was subsequently followed and applied by this court in *Craven (Inspector of Taxes) v White* [1987] STC 297, [1987] 3 WLR 660.

The judge dealt with the *Honig* decision as follows (at 863):

'The question in that case was, in the context of time limits, whether the

j material date was the date of the making of the assessment or the date of service of a notice of assessment. No doubt for time limit purposes an assessment is not made until it is appropriately signed in the Revenue records. Any other approach to a time limit question would be impractical. But when, as here, one has to consider whether or not the assessments in question were made by Mr Martin alone it is, I think, right to approach the matter in the way that I have set out above.'

I find some difficulty in accepting the reasoning in this particular passage of the judge's judgment, and in the earlier passage referring to the time when the assessment *a* was made in the present case. It is true that the essential issue in the *Honig* case was *when* the assessments were made. In the instant case the more relevant question is *by whom* the assessments were made for the purpose of applying reg 12(1). Nevertheless I accept counsel for the taxpayer's submission that the nature of the act required to make an assessment must be the same in each case. The closing words of reg 12(1) themselves provide that the amount charged by the assessment shall be due and *b* payable 14 days after the assessment is 'made'. In my judgment this makes it clear that for the purpose of starting that period of 14 days an assessment cannot be said to be made until a certificate has been signed showing that the relevant assessment has been entered in the assessment book. It cannot have been the intention of the makers of the regulation that the mere decision to make the assessment could set the 14-day period running. The word 'make' at the beginning of reg 12(1) must, in my *c* judgment, bear a meaning corresponding with the word 'made' at the end of the regulation. In short, I accept counsel for the taxpayer's submission that the assessment in the present case was 'made' for the purpose of reg 12(1) when Mr McEnhill finally signed the certificate. I respectfully disagree with the judge's view that 'once Mr Martin had decided to make an assessment and had calculated the amounts of the assessment, then the assessments were "made"' for the purpose of *d* reg 12(1).

In my view, however, it does not follow that merely because the assessment was 'made' when Mr McEnhill finally signed the certificate, it was he who 'made' the assessment for the purpose of applying reg 12(1).

The Special Commissioner found as a fact that Mr McEnhill signed the document which completed the making of the assessment as the agent and at the request of Mr *e* Martin. The general principle of law is expressed in the old latin tag 'qui facit per alium facit per se'—acts done by an authorised agent are deemed to be the acts of the principal.

Counsel for the Crown advanced a general proposition of law to the following effect. Where a statute confers a power on an official to exercise his discretion, only that official can exercise it. But once he has exercised that discretion he may delegate *f* purely ministerial tasks which flow from the exercise of that discretion to another. If he does so, he has still properly exercised his statutory power; the carrying out of the ministerial task is treated in law as being his.

Counsel supported that general proposition of law by reference to the cases of *Horder v Scott* (1880) 5 QBD 552 and *R v Commission for Racial Equality, ex p Cottrell and Rothon* [1980] 1 WLR 1580, and to a case closer to the present case on *g* its facts, namely the decision of Sachs J in *Customs and Excise Comrs v Cure & Deeley Ltd* [1962] 1 QB 340.

Since that decision is relied on by both sides in this case, but for different purposes, I think I should refer to it in a little detail. It concerned reg 12 of the Purchase Tax Regulations 1945, SR & O 1945/517, which, so far as material for present purposes, provided as follows: *h*

> 'If any person fails to furnish a return as required by these Regulations or furnishes an incomplete return the commissioners may, without prejudice to any penalties which may be incurred by such person, determine the amount of tax appearing to them to be due from such person, and demand payment thereof . . .'
j

The regulation thus gave the commissioners two separate discretions, namely a discretion to determine the amount of the tax due and a discretion to demand payment thereof. The commissioners in that case made a determination pursuant to the regulation. It was signed by a Mr Seed, who was the assistant secretary to the commissioners. There was no objection to his signing the determination because he

was a person authorised to do so within the meaning of s 4(1) of the Customs and
a Excise Act 1952, which provided:

'Any act or thing required or authorised by or under any enactment to be
done by the Commissioners or any of them may be done—

    (a) by any one or more of the Commissioners; or
    (b) if the Commissioners so authorise, by a secretary or assistant secretary to
b   the Commissioners; or
    (c) by any other person authorised generally or specially in that behalf in
       writing by the Commissioners.'

That subsection would have authorised Mr Seed also to make the demand for
payment. Unfortunately, however, in the event he did not do so. The actual demand
was signed and sent in the course of ordinary routine by a chief executive officer, Mr
c Piper, who was not authorised, generally or specifically, to sign letters of demand.
The taxpayer company took the point, not dissimilar to the point taken in the
present case, that the demand was not signed by a properly authorised person and
that therefore no lawful demand had been made.

Sachs J in his judgment, having summarised the facts, dealt with this point as
d follows ([1962] 1 QB 340 at 371–372):

'It is, however, clear, as was rightly conceded for the commissioners, that
now wherever an act, other than a purely ministerial act, is by relevant
legislation authorised to be done by the commissioners, then that act can only
be done by a person duly authorised, as set out in section 4(1). At one stage it
was submitted that any demand for payment made by virtue of regulation 12
e was a purely ministerial act and thus, unlike the determination referred to in
that regulation, one to which section 4(1) did not apply: that submission,
however, was not pressed because even after a determination has been made it
is an important matter of discretion to decide whether and when there should
be issued the demand which has the effect mentioned in the regulation. In the
result the point at issue became an extremely narrow one. The defendants
f submitted that it was the act of demanding which had to be made by a duly
authorised person, and that the relevant words "any act . . . may be done" ought
not to be construed as if it read "any act may be authorised." For the
commissioners it was argued that in relation to a demand section 4(1) ought not
to be read as if it contained a provision that the demand must be signed by one
of the persons referred to in that subsection; and that the demand in the present
g case was really the act of Mr. Seed, so that it was not in point whether Mr. Seed
signed it or indeed if the document were sent off without any signature at all.
The commissioners relied on the maxim qui facit per alium facit per se, the
defendants on the maxim delegatus non potest delegare. On this narrow issue
my mind has fluctuated and my conclusions have been reached with hesitation.
It is to be noted that throughout the 321 sections of the Act of 1952 a careful
h distinction is drawn between those acts which only a commissioner can do and
those which can be done by an officer or other designated persons. The acts
which are reserved to the commissioners are all of importance but none the less
have in practice often to be performed in various parts of the country by others
than the commissioners personally. The provisions of section 4(1) thus seem to
be designed for the protection of those who may be affected by such acts. The
j demand upon which the present action is founded was one which both in terms
of pleading and in common parlance was made by the letter of August 16. That
demand was an act which cannot be said to have been done by the commissioners
personally. To have effect it must thus, having regard to section 4(1), be an act
which was in law that of Mr. Seed. Having read and re-read the letter, the act
to my mind was that of Mr. Piper, and though authorised by Mr. Seed was not

the act of Mr. Seed himself. On that basis it was not the act of any person nominated by section 4(1).'

From the point of view of the Crown the significance of this decision is that it was common ground in that case that there would have been no objection to Mr Seed's delegating to Mr Piper the signing of the demand if such signature had been a purely ministerial act; in those circumstances the act of signing the demand by Mr Piper would in law have been the act of Mr Seed himself. That contention, however, was unsustainable on the facts of that case because Mr Piper's function had not been purely ministerial; he had been left with an important matter of discretion, namely whether and when the demand should be issued.

In my judgment counsel for the Crown rightly distinguished that case from the present where, on the facts as found by the Special Commissioner, Mr McEnhill was left by Mr Martin with no discretion at all. Counsel for the taxpayer, for his part, expressly accepted the correctness of the general proposition of law advanced by counsel for the Crown which I have mentioned, but he submitted that on a proper reading of reg 12(1) it has no application in the present case, essentially for two reasons. First and foremost he pointed out that reg 12(1) gives the inspector power, as he put it, to impose a severe financial burden on the subject. He reminded us of the well-known principle expressed by Donaldson J in *Agricultural, Horticultural and Forestry Industry Training Board v Aylesbury Mushrooms Ltd* [1972] 1 WLR 190 at 196, in the words 'it is important that statutory powers which involve taxation should be strictly construed'.

Ground 4 of the notice of appeal submits:

'The Learned Judge failed to give due weight to the special character of the statutory deduction scheme found in Section 69 of [the 1975 Act] and administered via [the 1975 regulations]; in particular the Learned Judge did not give proper weight to the necessity for strict compliance with the provisions of Regulation 12 of the said Regulations.'

A very relevant example of this approach to the strict construction of taxing provisions is, in counsel for the taxpayer's submission, to be found in the strict and narrow construction of s 4(1) of the Customs and Excise Act 1952 adopted by Sachs J in the case of *Cure & Deeley*.

The power given by reg 12(1), he suggested, is exceptional and it should be followed to the letter. He pointed out that the wording of the regulation is: 'The inspector may at his discretion make' etc. By its terms it contemplates he suggested, that the same inspector who exercises his discretion by deciding to make the assessment will actually make it by arranging for the relevant entry in the assessment book and certifying that the entry has been made. If this course is followed, a taxpayer who wishes to question the reasonableness or otherwise of the exercise of the discretion will be in a better position to do so than he would be if one inspector exercised the discretion and another signed the certificate—so the argument runs. For the purpose of this regulation, he submitted, the signature on the certificate should not be regarded as a mere ministerial act; it is a fundamental part of the process of assessment authorised by the regulation.

Though this argument, like all counsel's submissions, was advanced with skill and force, I cannot for my part see that any contravention of the wording of reg 12(1), or any potential prejudice to taxpayers, is involved if the course which was followed in the present case is adopted provided only, as happened here, the person who has been instructed to arrange for the assessment to be entered in the assessment book and to sign the certificate, has not been asked to exercise any independent judgment of his own. It has not been suggested that there is any statutory requirement that the name of the individual inspector who has made the assessment should appear on the actual notice of assessment. A taxpayer who wishes to challenge the assessment and asks which inspector made it will, no doubt very properly, be given the name of a the inspector who *decided* to make it, as I understand indeed happened in the present case. It will neither improve nor harm the taxpayer's case if the inspector who made the relevant decision arranged for the relevant entry in the assessment book and signature of the certificate to be carried out by another inspector. The situation seems to me quite different from that which appertained in the case of *Cure & Deeley* because, as I have indicated already, Mr Seed had left it to Mr Piper to exercise an important discretion by deciding whether or not, and when, the demand

b should be issued. In the present case the function performed by Mr McEnhill was in my judgment in truth a purely ministerial act.

A second reason why counsel for the taxpayer suggested that the general proposition advanced by counsel for the Crown does not apply in the application of reg 12(1) on its proper construction turned on two sections of the Taxes Management Act 1970, namely ss 1(3) and 113(1B), primarily on the latter.

c I should perhaps read the sections. Section 1(3) provides:

> 'Any legal proceedings or administration act relating to any tax begun by one inspector or collector may be continued by another inspector or, as the case may be, another collector; and any inspector or collector may act for any division or other area.'

d Section 113(1B) reads:

> 'Where the Board or an inspector or other officer of the Board have in accordance with section 29 of this Act, or any other provision of the Taxes Acts, decided to make an assessment to tax, and have taken all other decisions needed for arriving at the amount of the assessment, they may entrust to some other officer of the Board responsibility for completing the assessing procedure,
e whether by means involving the use of a computer or otherwise, including responsibility for serving notice of the assessment on the person liable for tax.'

The first of these sections is included in Part I of the Taxes Management Act 1970; the second is included in Part XI. Counsel for the taxpayer pointed out that neither of them is expressly incorporated in reg 12. This, he suggested, is a further indication

f that inspectors carrying out their functions under the regulation were not intended to have any powers of delegation, even in respect of acts such as those now under consideration, which might ordinarily be regarded as purely ministerial.

For my part, I cannot accept this submission. As to s 1(3) this, in my judgment, is not a power to delegate at all. While s 113(1B) is in terms a power to delegate, its inclusion in the 1970 Act is in my judgment sufficiently explained, as counsel for the

g Crown explained it, by the need for the legislature to confer authority on inspectors and others to authorise others to use computerisation in completing the assessment procedure which, in the absence of express provision, might well be considered as going beyond a mere ministerial act. The omission to incorporate it in reg 12 (if there was indeed an omission to incorporate it by implication, which is denied by the Crown) does not in my judgment denote an intention on the part of the makers

h of the 1975 regulations that the inspector making a determination thereunder should have no power to delegate the merely ministerial acts necessary to give effect to a determination made by him pursuant to the regulation.

To sum up, the general proposition of law advanced by counsel for the Crown is in my judgment a correct one. I can see no reason why it should not apply on the facts of the present case, stressing, as I do, that the function performed by Mr

j McEnhill on the instructions of Mr Martin was purely ministerial and that, on the facts as found by the Special Commissioner, Mr McEnhill exercised no independent discretion of his own. As the judge thought, the relevant assessment was, for the purpose of applying reg 12, in law made by Mr Martin and no one else but Mr Martin. I agree and think that this suffices to dispose of the appeal.

It was argued before the judge that even if the relevant assessments were not to be treated as having been 'made' by Mr Martin under the general law, ss 1(3) and

113(1B) of the 1970 Act were, by necessary implication, incorporated in the
regulation and that one or both of these subsections would have had this effect.   *a*
These submissions on behalf of the Crown, which the judge himself rejected for the
reasons given in his judgment, are repeated in a respondent's notice. In view of my
conclusions already expressed, I do not consider that it is necessary to prolong this
judgment by expressing any obiter opinion on the submissions raised in the
respondent's notice one way or the other. I therefore refrain from doing so.

For the reasons which I have stated, I would for my part dismiss this appeal.   *b*

NICHOLLS LJ. I agree that this appeal fails. I make some observations of my own
only because, although reaching the same conclusion as the judge, we are doing so
by a slightly different route.

Regulation 12 of the Income Tax (Sub-Contractors in the Construction Industry)
Regulations 1975, SI 1975/1960, provides for the making of an assessment by an   *c*
inspector in the exercise of his discretion. Neither these regulations nor, more
generally, the Taxes Management Act 1970, in particular s 29, casts any illumination
on what the assessing procedure involves, beyond the requirement that in general
assessments are to be made by an inspector, and the fact that s 112 of the Taxes
Management Act 1970 envisages that an assessment is a document. In principle,
and having regard to the nature and functions of an assessment, it seems to me that   *d*
in this context making an assessment will normally involve: (a) a decision to make
an assessment in a particular amount; and (b) an appropriate documentary record
being made of that decision with the intention that that document shall take effect
as an assessment.

I have in mind that this appeal is by way of case stated. Understandably, the case
stated does not attempt to go, in the utmost detail, into precisely what happened in   *e*
the present case. But before turning to the facts found in this case, I can illustrate
my general observations on steps (a) and (b) by reference to what counsel for the
Crown told us was currently the normal practice of the Revenue in making
assessments. He told us that, in practice, step (b) involves the preparation of a
document, either in typed or manuscript form, which records the prescribed
essential ingredients of the proposed assessment to which step (a) relates: the   *f*
taxpayer, the amount of the assessment and so forth. That document, with similar
documents relating to other proposed assessments, is then inserted and bound into a
folder known as the assessment book. These sheets, or cards, form another volume
of that book. However, the completion of the physical process of inserting these
sheets or cards into the binder, so as thereby to form the book, does not of itself
complete the assessing procedure. That procedure is complete, and an assessment is   *g*
regarded by the Revenue as having been made when, and only when, an
accompanying certificate in the assessment book is signed. That certificate is to the
effect that on the date when the certificate is signed, which is stated, assessments as
set out in the accompanying sheets or cards in the book, which sheets or cards are
then identified, have been made. The signature and dating of the certificate are
intended to make operative as assessments the details recorded in the assessment   *h*
book to which the certificate relates.

Clearly, if an inspector, in the exercise of his discretion, decides to make an
assessment on a taxpayer in a particular amount, he is not required personally to
prepare the sheet or card for insertion into the assessment book. He can instruct
someone else to do that act for him and on his behalf. The preparation of that sheet
or card is important. The accuracy of what is recorded is important, not least to the   *j*
taxpayer. But, important as it is, the preparation of that document calls for no
exercise of discretion or judgment. It is a mechanical task. Likewise, in my view,
with the signing of the certificate. I can see no reason in principle why, if another
officer of the Board has been duly instructed or requested so to do by the inspector
who made the decision to assess, that other officer cannot sign a certificate on behalf

of the inspector just as much as he can prepare the sheet or card on the inspector's
a behalf. If in signing the certificate the other officer is doing no more than carrying
out the inspector's instruction or request, he is not exercising any discretion. He is
merely taking the final, formal, documentary step, albeit a very important one,
needed to give effect to the decision already made by the inspector. In such
circumstances the resultant assessment is an assessment 'made' by the inspector who
made the decision to assess, just as much as it would be in a case where that inspector
b had signed the relevant certificate himself.

In the present case the Special Commissioner found as facts that, having made his
decision to assess the taxpayer, Mr Martin gave instructions to the Sch D section in
the Shepherds Bush district tax office for the assessments to be made, and that the
assessment book was signed in due course by Mr McEnhill of that office. The Special
Commissioner inferred that the assessments were made by Mr McEnhill as agent
c for and on behalf of Mr Martin. By that I understand the Special Commissioner to
mean that in acting as he did, Mr McEnhill was acting as agent for and on behalf of
Mr Martin.

In those circumstances the proper conclusion as a matter of law is that the
assessments in question were 'made' by Mr Martin within the meaning of reg 12.
Thus there is no ground on which the taxpayer can impeach the assessments in this
d case as not having been made in accordance with reg 12.

Like my Lord, in these circumstances I do not consider that it is necessary to
express any view on the Crown's alternative arguments based on s 1(3) and s 113(1B)
of the Taxes Management Act 1970, and I shall not do so.

I too would dismiss this appeal.

e **FARQUHARSON LJ.** I agree with both judgments.

Appeal dismissed with costs. Application for leave to appeal to House of Lords refused.

*30 January. The Appeal Committee of the House of Lords (Lord Bridge of Harwich,
Lord Templeman and Lord Oliver of Aylmerton) refused to leave to appeal.*

Solicitors: *Fairchild Greig* (for the taxpayer); *Solicitor of Inland Revenue.*

Siew Ling Choo   Barrister.

Note

a

Wright v Field (Inspector of Taxes) and related appeal

CHANCERY DIVISION
VINELOTT J   b
27 NOVEMBER 1990

Emoluments from office or employment – Deduction of tax by employer on payment of income assessable to tax – Failure to deduct tax – Whether office worker employed or self-employed – Whether in determining tax due payments to worker without deduction of tax should have been taken into account – Income Tax (Employments) Regulations c
1973, reg 29.

Notes

For the deduction of tax under the PAYE scheme, see Simon's Taxes, Division E4.9.
For the Income Tax (Employments) Regulations 1973, reg 29, see ibid, Part H1.   d

Cases stated

Wright v Field (Inspector of Taxes)

1. On 21 and 22 November 1989, one of the Special Commissioners heard the   e
appeals of Mr P J A Wright (Mr Wright) against determinations made by the
inspector of taxes under reg 29 of the Income Tax (Employments) Regulations 1973,
SI 1973/334 (the 1973 regulations), to the effect that Mr Wright was liable, as an
employer, to pay £300 additional tax in respect of the year 1984–85 and £378
additional tax in respect of the year 1985–86.
2. The determinations related to certain payments made (without deduction of f
income tax under PAYE) to employees of Mr Wright (the employees' allowances).
During the course of the year 1985–86, Mr Wright's business was incorporated by
the name Devon Flat Roofing Ltd (the company); and such payments continued to
be made. Together with the appeals referred to in para 1 above, the commissioner
heard appeals by the company against similar determinations for 1985–86 and
1986–87.   g
3. None of the determinations related to payments made by Mr Wright (and
afterwards by the company) to a Mrs Carol Bews (Mrs Bews). The questions for the
commissioner's determination were, shortly, whether the determinations should
have included tax in respect of the payments to Mrs Bews (in addition to the
employees' allowances) and if so, whether the determinations under appeal must be
increased in amount. The unusual feature of the case was that these questions were h
raised not by the inspector but by Mr Wright.
4. Oral evidence was given by: Mr Wright; Catherine Vera Hurl (Mrs Hurl), a
collector of taxes at Exeter Collection; and the respondent inspector Mr Field, the
district inspector at Exeter 2 district.
[Paragraph 5 listed the documents placed in evidence before the commissioner.]
6. On the evidence the commissioner found the following facts: (a) At all material j
times Mr Wright was concerned in business in the construction industry, in
particular in connection with flat roofs. He had several employees directly engaged
in that business. During the tax year 1984–85 and up to December 1985 in the tax
year 1985–86 he was a sole trader. (b) In February 1985, Mr Wright engaged the
services of Mrs Bews as secretary/bookkeeper on a part-time basis. One of her
principal duties was to answer the telephone. She also kept the PAYE records.

a Initially, Mrs Bews was engaged as an employee at the rate of £2·50 per hour. The indications are that, at first, she received her wages net, after deduction of tax under PAYE. (c) A few weeks later, Mrs Bews asked Mr Wright whether she could become 'self-employed', so that she would receive payment without deduction of tax. Mr Wright was familiar with such a change (which is not uncommon in the construction industry) and he agreed, on the understanding that Mrs Bews would have accounts prepared by a qualified accountant. Mrs Bews' hourly rate was increased to £3 in

b recognition of the fact that Mrs Bews' liability to national insurance contribution would be increased (and Mr Wright's liability reduced) by the change. Evidence in Mr Wright's possession suggests that the tax previously deducted from Mrs Bews' wages (not yet remitted to the collector) was refunded to her by Mr Wright. (d) In May 1985 Mrs Bews obtained from an officer of the Department of Health and Social Security a form enabling her to be registered by that department as 'self-

c employed'. At or about the same time she obtained a similar form from the inspector of taxes. After completion, these forms were lodged with the department and the inspector respectively. Mrs Bews' answers to questions on the forms did not reveal her initial engagement as an employee of Mr Wright. (e) Mr Wright was not the only person for whom Mrs Bews did work during the years in question but her engagement with Mr Wright was her principal engagement. (f) Mrs Bews' secretarial

d functions ceased in September 1986 (that is to say, after the period with which the determinations directed to Mr Wright personally are concerned), but her bookkeeping functions continued. (g) Early in November 1986 the business cash book covering the period up to December 1985 was lost. It is common ground that the loss was accidental. (h) On 10 November 1986, Mrs Hurl attended Mr Wright's premises to conduct a routine audit for PAYE purposes. Mrs Bews (who had by

e then ceased acting as secretary) was not present during Mrs Hurl's visit. Inspection of the current cash book revealed the payment of allowances (without deduction of tax) to certain employees in respect of whom Mrs Hurl had records. Save as to amount, there is no issue on that score. Mr Wright immediately accepted Mrs Hurl's view that the employees' allowances were taxable under Sch E and that tax should have accordingly been deducted therefrom. (i) The current cash book also

f disclosed regular payments (without deduction of tax) to Mrs Bews, in respect of whom Mrs Hurl had no PAYE record. Mr Wright told Mrs Hurl that Mrs Bews 'sorted out her own tax', and that the gross payments were in order because Mrs Bews was self-employed. Mrs Hurl may have challenged that statement during her visit; but it is evident that she either then or shortly afterwards accepted it because the information which she had about the payments to Mrs Bews was noted only in

g an 'aide memoire' section of her audit report papers; and on her return to her office she put in train the calculation of the tax due in respect of the employees' allowances only. (That involved an element of estimation of the amounts of the payments in question, because of the loss of the previous cash book.) (j) On or about 10 December 1986 Mrs Hurl sent a report to the inspector to inform him of the existence of Mrs Bews as a potential Sch D taxpayer. The report included the information that Mrs

h Bews appeared to receive £50–£90 a week. That report was not immediately placed on the file for Mrs Bews (which had been created following receipt of her 'self-employed' form in or about May 1985). At or about the same time in December 1986 professionally-drawn accounts for Mrs Bews (in the name 'Bews Secretarial Services') for the period May 1985 to September 1986, were received by the inspector. The accounts were accepted by the inspector and Mrs Bews' accountant was so informed.

j When Mrs Hurl's report was attached to the file the accounts were reviewed in the light of the information in the report as to the level of Mrs Bews' receipts. The accounts were found to be consistent with the information. (k) At the time when Mrs Bews' accounts were reviewed the inspector had no evidence that Mrs Bews might have been employed by Mr Wright (or the company). On the contrary, such information as he had indicated that Mrs Bews was self-employed. (l) Mrs Bews' functions as the company's bookkeeper (as distinct from those of a secretarial nature) ceased in December 1986. (m) At the end of 1986 and early in 1987 Mr Wright or his advisers did some legal research and he formed the opinion that the payments *a* which had been made to Mrs Bews were truly assessable under Sch E, with the consequence that he and the company were indebted to the Crown under the 1973 regulations. He expressed this view in the course of a telephone conversation with a Revenue officer at Exeter 2 district. (n) On 27 April 1987 Mr Wright's and the company's solicitor wrote to the inspector on behalf of the company. Having set out shortly the circumstances surrounding the treatment by Mr Wright of Mrs Bews as *b* 'self-employed', the letter continued:

'Based on the facts given to me, I find it difficult to see how Mrs Bews could be regarded as being self-employed, when one applies the usual criteria. I can see, however, that such criteria are open to individual interpretation and that it is not possible to be categoric in all cases. Given that the Revenue accept that Mrs Bews was self-employed from February 1985 to December 1986, will you *c* please kindly confirm that no PAYE liability attaches to [the company] during that period.'

(o) On 13 May 1987 an inspector at Exeter 2 district replied:

'I refer to your letter dated 27 April 1987 and our subsequent telephone conversation on 11 May 1987 and confirm that no PAYE liability attaches to *d* [the company] during the period February 1985 to December 1986 in respect of Mrs Bews.'

Although the letters referred to the company only, it has never been in doubt that the inspector's letter expressed the Revenue's view of Mr Wright's personal position as well. (p) Notwithstanding the terms of the inspector's letter of 13 May 1987, no *e* agreement was reached with the collector on the basis proposed by the latter (namely that PAYE should be paid in respect of the employees' allowances). In consequence, on 26 August 1988 the inspector made the determinations now under appeal.

7. Mr Wright contended: (i) that Mrs Bews had clearly been an employee throughout, and that he should accordingly have deducted tax from her emoluments; (ii) that the determinations should accordingly have included amounts by reference *f* to those emoluments; (iii) that the inspector was well aware of his (Mr Wright's) liability in respect of the payments to Mrs Bews; and (iv) that the determinations should be altered to reflect that liability.

8. On behalf of the inspector it was not conceded that Mrs Bews had been an employee; but it was accepted that had Mrs Bews' status been subjected to inquiry in December 1986 (which it was not) it might well have been found that she was not *g* self-employed. It was conceded that the inspector was aware of that possibility before the determinations under appeal were made. It was, however, contended: (i) that since the inspector had informed Mrs Bews' accountant that she was assessable to tax under Sch D, he had correctly decided that no useful purpose would be served by reopening the question concerning status; (ii) that in the light of the correspondence it would be wrong now to reopen the matter; and therefore (iii) that *h* the determinations should not now be altered to include amounts referable to the payments made to Mrs Bews.

9. The commissioner gave his decision orally at the conclusion of the hearing. In the absence of any evidence from Mrs Bews, the commissioner was wholly unable to reach a definitive conclusion on her status (at least from May 1985 onwards); although on the evidence before the commissioner it seemed unlikely that the change *j* from 'employed' to 'self-employed' had been justified. However, even if Mr Wright's contention on that matter were correct, it did not follow that the inspector was under a positive duty to reopen the matter. The commissioner held that in the circumstances of the case he was under no such duty: and the considerations mentioned in the first of the contentions made on the inspector's behalf provided ample management grounds for his choosing not to take any steps in that direction.

a   Further, since the determinations under appeal were made in respect of the employees' allowances only, in the knowledge that a theoretical question in relation to Mrs Bews' position existed, the commissioner did not think that the inspector could now make a further determination (in respect of Mrs Bews' remuneration), even if he wished to: which he emphatically did not. In the commissioner's view, following (at the latest) the exchange of letters between the solicitor and the inspector in April–May 1987, the matter was closed, and that Mr Wright (and the company)

b   were no longer at risk. The commissioner pointed out to Mr Wright that the liability of a person as employer under the 1973 regulations was a secondary liability, in the sense that it was dependent on the primary liability of a third party to tax under Sch E; and that as the inspector had never alleged as against Mrs Bews that she was so liable, there could be no debt owed to the Crown by him (or the company) in respect of the payments made to Mrs Bews.

c   For those reasons the commissioner held that there was, in principle, nothing wrong with the determinations made.

    10. Mr Wright had offered revised figures for the employees' allowances, which the inspector had accepted. On the basis of those figures the parties agreed that the amounts of tax due were as follows: 1984–85, £80·40; 1985–86, £112·80, and the commissioner determined the appeals accordingly.

d   11. Mr Wright immediately declared his dissatisfaction with the determinations as being erroneous in point of law and on 18 December 1989 required the commissioners to state a case for the opinion of the High Court pursuant to the Taxes Management Act 1970, s 56.

    12. The question of law for the opinion of the court was whether, in the circumstances of the case, the commissioner was required to take the payments

e   made to Mrs Bews into account in arriving at the amounts of tax due in respect of the determinations under appeal.

Devon Flat Roofing Ltd v Field (Inspector of Taxes)

    1. On 21 and 22 November 1989, one of the Special Commissioners heard the

f   appeals of Devon Flat Roofing Ltd (the company) against determinations made by the inspector of taxes under reg 29 of the Income Tax (Employments) Regulations 1973, SI 1973/334 (the 1973 regulations), to the effect that the company was liable as an employer to pay £637·20 additional tax in respect of the year 1985–86 and £203·00 additional tax in respect of the year 1986–87.

    2. Together with the appeals the commissioner heard appeals by Mr P J A Wright

g   (Mr Wright) (a director of the company) against similar determinations directed to him personally for 1984–85 and 1985–86.

    The issue, facts and arguments in Mr Wright's appeals were substantially the same as those in the company's appeals: and the commissioner gave a single decision, to the same effect, in each.

    3. Paragraphs 2 to 9 (both inclusive) of the case referred to in the preceding

h   paragraph hereof are respectfully referred to, and, subject to the next paragraph hereof, form part of this case.

    4. (i) By way of addition to para 6(a) the commissioner found that in December 1985 the flat roofing business previously carried on by Mr Wright as a sole trader was transferred to the company which had been formed for that purpose; and that the company carried on the said business during the remainder of the tax year

j   1985–86 and in 1986–87. (ii) By way of amendment of para 6(p) the commissioner found that the determinations directed to the company in relation to the years 1985–86 and 1986–87 were made not on 26 August 1988 but on 14 April 1988.

    5. Mr Wright had offered a revised figure for the employees' allowances paid by the company in 1985–86, which the inspector had accepted. It was agreed that the 1986–87 figure was correct. On the basis of those figures it was agreed that the amount of tax due for 1985–86 was £247·20 and that the determined figure for

1986–87 (£203·00) should be confirmed, and the commissioner determined the appeals accordingly.

6. Mr Wright immediately declared, on behalf of the company, its dissatisfaction with the determinations as being erroneous in point of law and on 18 December 1989 required the commissioners to state a case for the opinion of the High Court pursuant to the Taxes Management Act 1970, s 56.

7. The question of law for the opinion of the court was whether, in the circumstances of the case, the commissioner was required to take the payments made to Mrs Bews into account in arriving at the amounts of tax due in respect of the determinations under appeal.

Mr Wright appeared in person representing both appellants.
Launcelot Henderson for the Crown.

VINELOTT J: These are appeals by way of case stated against a decision of one of the Special Commissioners. They must be the oddest tax appeals ever to have come before the court.

The facts are fully and carefully set out in the first of the two cases stated; that is, the case stated in relation to the appeal by Peter Jonathan Arthur Wright (Mr Wright). A brief summary of the background of the appeals will suffice for the purposes of this judgment.

Until December 1985 Mr Wright carried on business in the construction industry specialising in the installation of flat roofs. In December 1985 he formed or acquired a company Devon Flat Roofing Ltd (the company) and transferred his business to it. In February 1985 he engaged a Mrs Bews as secretary/bookkeeper. At first she was paid as an employee; that is, she was paid a net sum after deduction of tax under the PAYE scheme and national insurance contributions were paid by her and Mr Wright on the footing that she was engaged under a contract of employment.

After a few weeks she asked Mr Wright whether she could be engaged as a self-employed contractor. He was agreeable to the change on condition that she would have accounts prepared by a qualified accountant. Thereafter she was paid at an hourly rate of £3. Previously she had been paid at a rate of £2·50 less PAYE tax, but, of course, once she became self-employed Mr Wright was no longer liable to make national insurance contributions, so that the burden on him was not increased.

In May 1985 Mrs Bews was registered as self-employed by the DHSS and her status as a self-employed person taxable under Sch D was also recognised by the local inspector of taxes. In September 1986 Mrs Bews' functions as a secretary came to an end though she continued to work for the company as a bookkeeper until December 1986 or January 1987, when she ceased to do any work for the company at all.

In November 1986 a Mrs Hurl, a collector of taxes, attended at the company's premises to conduct a routine audit for PAYE purposes. Inspection of the cash books available (and one of them had been lost) revealed that allowances had been paid to employees without deduction of tax. Mr Wright accepted Mrs Hurl's view that tax should have been deducted under Sch E.

Although Mr Wright had agreed in principle at this meeting that tax should have been deducted from the allowances and accounted for to the Revenue, no agreement was reached as to the figures; and in April and August 1988 the local inspector made a determination under reg 29 of the Income Tax (Employments) Regulations 1973, SI 1973/334, of the tax due from Mr Wright in respect of the years 1984–85 and 1985–86 and from the company in respect of the years 1985–86 and 1986–87. The sums are not large: £300 and £378 for 1984–85 and 1985–86 respectively in the case of Mr Wright, and £637·20 and £203 for 1985–86 and 1986–87 respectively in the case of the company.

However, in the course of the audit and in subsequent correspondence a question

arose about the nature of Mrs Bews' engagement, whether she was an employee or
a self-employed. The history of this dispute is fully set out in the case stated in the
appeal by Mr Wright, and I do not need to repeat it. It is sufficient to say that it was
Mr Wright who contended that she was an employee.

In December 1986 accounts drawn up by a professionally qualified accountant for
Mrs Bews' business (which was carried on under the name 'Bews' Secretarial
Services') for the period May 1985 to September 1986 had been submitted on her
b behalf and accepted by the inspector. In April 1987 the solicitors acting for Mr
Wright and the company wrote to the inspector to say that they found it difficult to
see how Mrs Bews could be regarded as self-employed though 'it is not possible to be
categoric in all cases'. They asked for an assurance that the Revenue accepted that
Mrs Bews was self-employed from February 1985 to December 1986 and that no
PAYE liability attached to the company. That confirmation, which was clearly
c sought in relation to Mr Wright as well as the company (though not so expressed)
was given on 13 May 1987.

There one would have thought that the dispute about Mrs Bews would have
ended. But it did not. When the matter came before the Special Commissioner Mr
Wright, who appeared in person, contended that he and the company should have
deducted tax from Mrs Bews' emoluments under Sch E and should have accounted
d for the tax to the Revenue. The Revenue declined to accept the proffered opportunity
to make a further determination under reg 29, though in theory they could have
accepted the offer without reopening Mrs Bews' returns. They took the view—
understandably, I think—that they should not put themselves in that ambiguous
position.

Before the Special Commissioner figures were put forward and agreed concerning
e the allowances paid to the other employees. The determinations were then confirmed
by the Special Commissioner in the amounts of £80·40 and £112·80 for the years
1984–85 and 1985–86 in the case of Mr Wright, and £247·20 and £203 for 1985–86
and 1986–87 in the case of the company.

As to Mrs Bews' position, the Special Commissioner said:

'In the absence of any evidence from Mrs Bews, I was wholly unable to reach a
f definitive conclusion on her status (at least from May 1985 onwards); although
on the evidence before me it seemed unlikely that the change from "employed"
to "self-employed" had been justified. However, even if Mr Wright's contention
on that matter were correct, it did not follow that the inspector was under a
positive duty to reopen the matter. I held that in the circumstances of the case
he was under no such duty: and the considerations mentioned in the first of the
g contentions made on the inspector's behalf [that is, that since he had informed
Mrs Bews' accountant that he would assess her under Sch D he had correctly
decided that no useful purpose would be served by reopening the question
concerning her status] provided ample management grounds for his choosing
not to take any steps in that direction.'

h The Special Commissioner went on to express the opinion, first, that it was not
open to the inspector to make any further determination in respect of Mrs Bews'
remuneration because, following the exchange of letters in April/May 1987 to which
I have referred, the matter was closed, and that Mr Wright and the company were
no longer at risk, and second, that the liability of an employer under the PAYE
regulations was a secondary liability, and that as the inspector had never alleged that
j Mrs Bews was liable to be taxed as an employee under the PAYE regulations, Mr
Wright and the company could not themselves be so liable. These observations are
not, as I see it, necessary for the determination of the appeal before me, and I express
no opinion on them.

It is sufficient to say that under s 56(1) of the Taxes Management Act 1970 an
appeal by way of case stated lies if, and only if, the taxpayer or the Revenue is

dissatisfied with the determination of the commissioners as erroneous in point of law. There is no issue between Mr Wright and the company on the one hand and the Crown on the other hand in relation to which the commissioner could be said to have erred in law. The inspector had made no determination under reg 29 of the amount of tax payable in respect of Mrs Bews' emoluments. The only issue related to PAYE tax claimed in respect of payments to other employees, and those figures were agreed.

Mr Wright, who appeared before me and, as I have said, before the Special Commissioner in person, submitted that the Revenue, in failing to make any determination under reg 29 in relation to the emoluments paid to Mrs Bews, had connived at the suppression of a fraud. The claim that the Revenue were under a duty to make such a determination is not, in my judgment, a matter which can be raised in an appeal by way of case stated against a determination under the regulation in relation to emoluments paid to others. Such a contention can be raised, if at all, only by way of judicial review of the conduct of the Revenue. I do not wish to encourage Mr Wright to make such an application. I very much doubt whether Mr Wright or his company could claim to have any private interest within RSC Ord 53, r 3(7) in claiming that the Revenue ought to have made determinations against them under reg 29 in relation to Mrs Bews' remuneration. If they want to pay tax which has not been assessed there is of course nothing to prevent them making a donation.

Mr Wright submitted that he has an interest as a member of the public in ensuring that the tax laws are properly administered. It is, on the face of it, paradoxical and unreal that Mr Wright should be able to assert a public interest which conflicts with his private interest. But a claim for judicial review would face the further to my mind fatal objection that reg 29 is permissive and it was plainly within the Revenue's managerial power to decide to accept accounts from Mrs Bews on the footing that she was self-employed and to decline to make any determination under reg 29 against Mr Wright or the company.

The gravamen of Mr Wright's complaint is that Mrs Bews, when she first claimed as against the DHSS and the Revenue that she was self-employed, did not inform them that she had been initially engaged as an employee and that there had been no real change but only a cosmetic change when she became, as she represented to them, self-employed. However, the inspector was well aware of Mrs Bews' earlier history and of Mr Wright's contention that she had been an employee throughout when he wrote to Mr Wright's and the company's solicitors to confirm that no PAYE liability attached to him or the company. He was, in my judgment, at that stage plainly entitled to take the view that no purpose would be served in reopening Mrs Bews' tax affairs.

In my judgment these appeals are quite simply perverse, and they must be dismissed. The Revenue seek an order for costs, and in my judgment they are entitled to it. Mr Wright sought to have this matter adjourned so that he could make further submissions on costs. I think there is nothing more to be said on that topic, and I think it would be unjust to the Revenue to expose them to further delay and possible expense which they might not be able to recover.

Mr Wright, I should add, also asked me to give directions as to an appeal which he apparently proposes to prosecute in the Court of Appeal. I give no directions. If Mr Wright wants any directions for the acceleration of an appeal or for the submission of written cases on behalf of the Revenue he will have apply to the Court of Appeal.

Appeals dismissed with costs.

Solicitor: *Solicitor of Inland Revenue.*

Siew Ling Choo   Barrister.

a   # Holmes v Mitchell (Inspector of Taxes)

CHANCERY DIVISION
VINELOTT J
4 DECEMBER 1990

b   *Relief – Personal relief – Wife – Taxpayer and wife living in same house but as separate
households – Whether taxpayer living with his wife – Whether taxpayer's wife wholly
maintained by him during relevant years of assessment – Whether taxpayer entitled to
higher personal allowances – Income and Corporation Taxes Act 1970, s 8(1)(a).*

The taxpayer married H in 1959. From 1972, they lived in the same house but as
c   separate households. The taxpayer paid for all the outgoings and expenses on the
matrimonial home but otherwise, the taxpayer and H maintained themselves out of
their respective incomes and paid their own separately assessed proportion of tax.
On 14 December 1982, the taxpayer declared that he was seeking a divorce and in
February 1986, a divorce petition on the ground of two years separation by consent
was lodged with the county court. The petition specified 14 December 1982 as the
d   start of the separation. In September 1986, a decree nisi was granted and in March
1987, the decree was made absolute. The taxpayer's claims to higher personal
allowances for the years 1983–84 to 1986–87 inclusive were refused by the inspector
of taxes on the ground that he had not satisfied either of the requirements of s 8(1)(a)ᵃ
of the Income and Corporation Taxes Act 1970. The taxpayer appealed to the
General Commissioners contending (i) that he had been living with H during the
e   relevant years of assessment and that the separation date in the petition was a legal
fiction; and (ii) that H was wholly maintained by him during the relevant years of
assessment. The commissioners dismissed the appeal, finding that H had not been
wholly maintained by the taxpayer during the relevant years of assessment and that
during those years the taxpayer and H had in fact been separated in such
circumstances that the separation was likely to be permanent. The taxpayer
f   appealed.

Held – (1) On the facts, it could not be said that H had been wholly maintained by
the taxpayer during the relevant years of assessment and, accordingly, the
requirement in s 8(1)(a)(ii) had not been satisfied.
g   (2) A husband and wife might be separated even though they were living under
the same roof if they had ceased to be one household and had become two households.
From 1972, the taxpayer and H had lived as separate households under the same
roof and the taxpayer's declaration of his intention of seeking a divorce in December
1982 had made the circumstances of the separation such that it was likely to be
permanent. Accordingly, H could not be treated as living with the taxpayer during
h   the relevant years of assessment for the purposes of s 8(1)(a)(i); *Hopes v Hopes* [1949]
P 227 applied.
The appeal would therefore be dismissed.

Notes

j   For the circumstances in which a married man was entitled to a higher personal
relief, see Simon's Taxes E2.212.
For the Income and Corporation Taxes Act 1970, s 8(1)(a) (subsequently the
Income and Corporation Taxes Act 1988, s 257(1)(a), now spent), see ibid, Part G1.

---

a   Section 8(1)(a), so far as material, is set out at p 29 *fg*, post

Cases referred to in judgment

Hopes v Hopes [1949] P 227, [1948] 2 All ER 920, CA.
Santos v Santos [1972] Fam 247, [1972] 2 All ER 246, CA.
Wanbon v Wanbon [1946] 2 All ER 366.

Case also cited

Naylor v Naylor [1962] P 253, [1961] 2 All ER 129.

Case stated

1. At a meeting of the Commissioners for the general purposes of the income tax for the division of Derby held on 11 November 1987, R Holmes (the taxpayer) appealed as follows: (a) under the provisions of s 42(3) of the Taxes Management Act 1970 against the inspector's refusal to accept his claims to higher personal allowances under s 8(1)(a) of the Income and Corporation Taxes Act 1970, for the tax years 1983–84, 1984–85, 1985–86 and 1986–87, and (b) against the following Sch E income tax assessments:

Year	Amount
1983–84	£1,529·00
1984–85	£11,342·00
1985–86	£5,887·00
1986–87	£7,017·00

2. The taxpayer appeared in person and the inspector was represented by Mr A W Lewis, inspector of taxes, PD9 Tax District.

3. Shortly stated, the questions for the commissioners' decision were:

(a) whether the taxpayer's wife was to be treated for income tax purposes as living with the taxpayer between 5 April 1983 and 27 March 1987, and, if not
(b) whether she was wholly maintained by the taxpayer during the relevant years of assessment.

[Paragraph 4 listed the documents proved or admitted in evidence.]

5. No cases were referred to in argument, but the commissioners were referred to the provisions of ss 8(1) and 42(1) of the Income and Corporation Taxes Act 1970 (the 1970 Act).

6. The commissioners heard oral evidence from the taxpayer, Mr Mitchell (the inspector of taxes) and Mrs Joyce Winifred Holmes (the former wife of the taxpayer).

7. The following facts were proved or admitted before the commissioners: (a) The taxpayer had married Joyce Winifred Holmes (Mrs Holmes) on 31 March 1959. The taxpayer had been a civil servant, and Mrs Holmes a teacher, both had retired. (b) By approximately 1962, the taxpayer and Mrs Holmes were sleeping in separate beds, and by the mid-1960's they were separately assessed to income tax (in that the tax payable was apportioned between them by the Revenue). (c) From 1965, Mrs Holmes started not to cook or perform any household tasks for the taxpayer, and in 1972 she retired as a teacher. (d) From at least 1972, the financial arrangement was that the taxpayer paid the outgoings in respect of gas, electricity and rates on the matrimonial home, but otherwise the parties maintained themselves out of their respective incomes, and similarly paid their own separately assessed proportion of tax. They lived as separate households under the same roof from this time and in the words of the taxpayer 'more or less ignored each other'. (e) In September 1980, the taxpayer's work moved to Nottingham, and he took lodgings there rather than move house but returned to the matrimonial home most weekends. (f) In 1981, the taxpayer suffered a heart attack, and convalesced at home. (g) On 14 December

a 1982, the taxpayer declared that he was going to seek a divorce, and shortly afterwards consulted solicitors, and in early 1983 a divorce petition was filed on his behalf on the grounds of Mrs Holmes' alleged unreasonable behaviour. This petition was contested by Mrs Holmes, and not pursued to a hearing. (h) The financial and living arrangements between the taxpayer and Mrs Holmes continued after 14 December 1982 as they had done prior to that date. (i) The taxpayer retired finally on 4 January 1986, and, in February 1986, a second petition dated 12 February

b 1986, was presented to the Macclesfield County Court on the basis of two years separation by consent. This was the result of an agreement that had been reached between the respective parties' solicitors during 1985 to settle the matrimonial dispute. The solicitors agreed that 14 December 1982 was an appropriate date to specify as the start of the separation. (j) The taxpayer's address was stated in the second petition to be 5 Hallam Way, West Hallam, Derbyshire which is the address

c of his daughter and remained his address to the date of hearing of these appeals. (k) Decree nisi of divorce in respect of the second petition was pronounced on 10 September 1986, but the grant of decree absolute was held up, because the registrar declined to approve the proposed financial settlement. An order was finally made in March 1987, and decree absolute granted on 27 March 1987. (l) For the relevant tax years, the gross income of Mrs Holmes and the expenditure by the

d taxpayer on the outgoings at the former matrimonial home are tabulated below:

Tax year	Gross income of Mrs Holmes	Expenditure of the tax-payer
1983–84	£4,832·00	£1,212·00
1984–85	£5,082·00	£1,182·19
1985–86	£5,449·00	£1,234·00
1986–87	£5,881·00	£1,200·00 (approximate)

e

The expenditure figure for 1986–87 could only be given approximately, because Mrs Holmes started paying the gas and electricity bills with effect from December 1986, and the rates with effect from April 1987.

8. The taxpayer contended further to his grounds of appeal lodged on 11 March

f 1987, as follows: (1) The inspector's decision was incompetent and irrelevant, and the decision to disallow the claim for higher personal allowances had been made without any proper investigation. (2) The inspector refused to make out any grounds for the decision, or to introduce any documents. Since the 1970 Act itself did not define the word 'wholly' it was not shown that the definition being followed by the Revenue personnel had any relevance to law, or, indeed any authority from the Board of Inland Revenue. (3) The decision and activity carried out by the inspector

g was a further example of the incompetence which his staff had shown over the previous 20 years. Documentary evidence of this statement was offered to the commissioners but they declined to consider it.

9. The taxpayer pointed out that there was nothing in the 1970 Act which required that both limbs be satisfied simultaneously, however he submitted that he was

h entitled to higher personal allowances under s 8(1)(a) of the 1970 Act because he satisfied both limbs of the sub-paragraph. He submitted that he satisfied limb (i) in that he was to be regarded as having Mrs Holmes living with him for the relevant years of assessment because (by reference to s 42(1) of the 1970 Act) he was neither separated under an order of a court, nor by deed of separation, nor was he in fact separated in such circumstances that the separation was likely to be permanent. The

j separation date stated in the petition of 14 December 1982 was a legal fiction. As far as limb (ii) was concerned, he submitted that Mrs Holmes was wholly maintained by him during the years of assessment in exactly the same way in which she had been wholly maintained by him between 1965 and the decree absolute. Indeed the standard of maintenance was higher than was required by those laws which pertained to divorce, separation etc.

10. During the course of his submissions, the taxpayer indicated that he was aware of cases which would support his argument, but had failed to bring them with him. *a* As he appeared in person, the commissioners were inclined to grant a short adjournment of two weeks to enable the taxpayer to produce these cases. It then transpired that the taxpayer did not have these cases available at home, but that he would have to write to a friend in London for further advice, and he could not say what authorities he would quote, as this depended on the advice that he was given. The commissioners were not prepared to allow an adjournment for this purpose, *b* and accordingly proceeded to determine the appeals.

11. It was submitted by the inspector that the taxpayer was not entitled to the higher personal allowances because he failed to satisfy either of the limbs in s 8(1)(*a*) of the 1970 Act, in relation to the period covered by the assessments under appeal.

12. The commissioners who heard the appeals, decided: (a) The announcement by the taxpayer of his intention to seek a divorce on 14 December 1982 made the *c* circumstances of the separation described at para 7(d) above such that it was likely to be permanent, and therefore Mrs Holmes was not to be treated as living with the taxpayer from 14 December 1982 for the purposes of ss 42(1)(*b*) and 8(1)(*a*)(i) of the 1970 Act. (b) Whilst the commissioners had accepted that the taxpayer was contributing to the maintenance of Mrs Holmes by meeting the outgoings on the matrimonial home, and that, taken with her own pension and other income, such *d* contribution was sufficient to maintain her at an acceptable standard of living, such contribution did not satisfy the requirement for the taxpayer to have 'wholly maintained' Mrs Holmes during the relevant years of assessment as set out in s 8(1)(*a*)(ii) of the 1970 Act.

13. The commissioners accordingly dismissed the taxpayer's appeals against the refusal of higher personal allowances, and consequently confirmed the assessments *e* in the amounts assessed.

14. The taxpayer immediately after the determination of the appeal declared to the commissioners his dissatisfaction therewith as being erroneous in point of law, and required them to state a case for the opinion of the High Court pursuant to the Taxes Management Act 1970, s 56.

15. The question of law for the opinion of the High Court was whether on the *f* facts found by the commissioners their decision as set out in para 12 above was correct in law.

Addendum

16. During the course of the taxpayer's evidence, he stated that the separation date stated in the divorce petition of 14 December 1982 was a 'legal fiction', which *g* had been invented by the solicitors concerned, and had no basis in truth, because he had not separated from, nor left, Mrs Holmes on that date. The commissioners warned the taxpayer that he was in danger of suggesting that he had committed perjury in the course of the divorce proceedings, but he continued to maintain that the separation was a 'legal fiction', and furthermore that it had been 'connived at' by the registrar of the county court. Mrs Holmes in her evidence stated that the date of *h* 14 December 1982 had been decided on because it referred to a definite event, namely the taxpayer announcing his intention of commencing divorce proceedings. In the event, the commissioners heard sufficient direct evidence from the parties to enable them to determine the question of whether or not they were separated and it was not necessary for the commissioners to rely on the divorce petition in determining the appeal. *j*

17. The solicitors acting for the taxpayer at the time were Gadsby Coxon & Copestake of Derby. Shortly after the conclusion of the hearing it came to the commissioners' clerk's knowledge that it was Mr C P Hackney who had dealt with the taxpayer's divorce at Gadsby Coxon & Copestake. Mr Hackney had joined the clerk's firm as a partner on 1 January 1987 but the taxpayer had lodged a complaint

to the Solicitors' Complaints Bureau against Mr Hackney relating to the time when
a Mr Hackney had conduct of his affairs at Gadsby Coxon & Copestake.

18. The commissioners' clerk convened a meeting at short notice to explain the
circumstances to the commissioners and they, whilst being satisfied that the advice
given to them during the course of the hearing had not been in any way partial,
agreed that had the above circumstances been known prior to the hearing they
would probably have sought the parties' consent to the appeal being heard by a
b different division of commissioners. The commissioners, accordingly, instructed
their clerk to apply to the High Court for directions as to what should be done. The
taxpayer was notified of the circumstances and of the commissioners' actions by
letter dated 16 November 1987.

19. The clerk duly instructed counsel who, however, advised that a motion for
directions would be inappropriate and on 27 November 1987, the clerk wrote to the
c taxpayer informing him of counsel's opinion and explaining the required procedure.
The taxpayer responded with a formal request dated 2 December 1987 for a case to
be stated.

20. At a further meeting held on 26 April 1989, the clerk reported to the
commissioners on the progress which had been made in agreeing the form of the
case stated with the parties and they directed their clerk that they were not willing
d to agree to any further amendments to the case stated but that this addendum be
added.

The taxpayer appeared in person.
Launcelot Henderson for the Crown.
e

VINELOTT J. This is an appeal by way of case stated against a decision of the
General Commissioners for the division of Derby. The appeal is brought by the
taxpayer, Ronald Holmes. The issue before the commissioners was whether the
taxpayer was entitled to deduct personal allowances at the higher rate appropriate
f to a married man living with or maintaining his wife during the tax years 1983–84
up to and including the tax year 1986–87.

Under s 8(1)(*a*) of the Income and Corporation Taxes Act 1970 (the 1970 Act) a
taxpayer is entitled to the higher allowance if he can prove either:

'(i) that for the year of assessment he has his wife living with him, or

(ii) that his wife is wholly maintained by him during the year of assessment,
g   and that he is not entitled in computing the amount of his income for that year
for income tax purposes to make any deduction in respect of the sums paid for
the maintenance of his wife . . .'

Section 42(1) of the 1970 Act, which is headed, 'Construction of references to
married women living with their husbands, etc.', provides:
h
'A married woman shall be treated for income tax purposes as living with her
husband unless—

(*a*) they are separated under an order of a court of competent jurisdiction, or
by deed of separation, or

(*b*) they are in fact separated in such circumstances that the separation is
j   likely to be permanent.'

The commissioners found that the taxpayer's wife had not been wholly maintained
by him during the years of assessment and also that during those years the taxpayer
and his wife had been in fact separated in such circumstances that the separation
was likely to be permanent, although the marriage was not in fact dissolved until
1987.

In his submissions to me the taxpayer, who appeared in person, directed his submissions primarily to the requirement in sub-para (ii) of s 8(1)(*a*). He submitted *a* that at the hearing before the commissioners the inspector had wrongly refused to adhere to an internal practice of which he, the taxpayer, had been told in correspondence which was to the effect that 'wholly' is not to be construed as requiring a husband to show that his wife made no contribution to her maintenance but only that his contributions were sufficient to maintain her having regard to her own contributions to her household expenses. I myself would doubt whether 'wholly' *b* does fall to be construed literally as excluding any case where a wife makes any contribution, however small, to her maintenance. I find it quite unnecessary, however, to express any concluded opinion on the point or to endeavour to define what 'wholly' does mean in this context.

The claim that the taxpayer's wife was wholly maintained by him in the relevant years was in my judgment quite unsustainable on the evidence before the *c* commissioners. The joint incomes of the husband and the wife in those years varied from a little under £24,000 in the first year to a little under £16,000 in the year 1985–86. The wife's income, which consisted of a pension earned during the years when she had worked as a teacher, contributed just under £5,000 in the first year and just under £6,000 in the last year. She maintained herself out of that income save only that the taxpayer paid house insurance, rates, water rates, electricity, gas *d* and phone bills. The wife also had the benefit of living in the matrimonial home which the taxpayer says is his absolute property, together with its furniture, though I should mention in this connection that there is no evidence as to whether the wife had or claimed a beneficial interest in the matrimonial home.

It is to my mind quite impossible on that evidence to say that the taxpayer's wife was wholly maintained by him. In substance she maintained herself with the *e* assistance of the taxpayer, who allowed her to occupy the matrimonial home and paid the outgoings on it. I think the taxpayer has really confused two things: on the one hand whether his wife was wholly maintained by him and on the other whether he made contributions which were necessary so as to maintain the standard of living which she enjoyed. The latter test might well be satisfied, but it is not what the statutory provision requires. *f*

Before the commissioners the taxpayer sought an adjournment because he said he thought there were cases which would support his case. The commissioners were at first inclined to grant a short adjournment of two weeks, but when it transpired that a more extensive period was required and that some research was involved they declined to grant an adjournment. Before me the taxpayer has referred to the Matrimonial Causes Act 1973 (the 1973 Act), and he has referred (though without *g* citing them) to cases in which the general guidelines for the division of joint incomes between former spouses in the proportions of one-third to two-thirds have been laid down. The cases under the 1973 Act have no possible bearing on the issue which the commissioners had to decide and I cannot see that if they had been referred to it would have made any difference to the outcome.

I turn, then, to the other limb of s 8(1): was the taxpayer's wife living with him in *h* the relevant years of assessment; that is to say, referring to s 42(1), were they in fact separated in such circumstances that the separation was likely to be permanent? This provision first appeared in the Finance Act 1950 (the 1950 Act), which introduced a new code for the taxation of spouses who were living together but who might be separated by, amongst other things, the exigencies of work or war. The word 'separated' is not defined. However, it had been established before the 1950 *j* Act was passed that a husband and wife might be separated and that one might be said to have deserted the other even though they were living under the same roof. The cases are all considered in the case of *Hopes v Hopes* [1949] P 227. Bucknill LJ said (at 234):

'The cases to which I have referred establish that there may be desertion, although husband and wife are living in the same dwelling, if there is such a forsaking and abandonment by one spouse of the other that the court can say that the spouses were living lives separate and apart from one another.'

Denning LJ said (at 235):

'One of the essential elements of desertion is the fact of separation. Can that exist whilst the parties are living under the same roof? My answer is: "Yes". The husband who shuts himself up in one or two rooms of his house, and ceases to have anything to do with his wife, is living separately and apart from her as effectively as if they were separated by the outer door of a flat.'

He referred later to a decision of the Divorce Division, *Wanbon v Wanbon* [1946] 2 All ER 366, where the parties were said to be still living in one household, and he commented:

'If that means that, although living at arms length, they were still sharing the same living room, eating at the same table and sitting by the same fire, then I cannot agree with the finding of desertion. It is most important to draw a clear line between desertion, which is a ground for divorce, and gross neglect or chronic discord, which is not. That line is drawn at the point where the parties are living separately and apart. In cases where they are living under the same roof, that point is reached when they cease to be one household and become two households; or, in other words, when they are no longer residing with one another or cohabiting with one another.'

The 1973 Act introduced separation as a ground for divorce. Under s 1(2) a marriage may be said to have broken down irretrievably if '(d) ... the parties of the marriage have lived apart for a continuous period of at least two years immediately preceding the presentation of the petition ... and the respondent consents ...' or '(e) ... the parties to the marriage have lived apart for a continuous period of at least five years ...' whether or not the respondent consents.

In *Santos v Santos* [1972] Fam 247, the Court of Appeal had to decide whether for this purpose parties were living apart if they were physically separated and if not whether the intention to live apart had to be shared by both or whether it was enough that it was entertained by one and communicated to the other. The Court of Appeal held that it was necessary to show not only the factum of separation but also that one spouse had ceased to recognise the marriage as subsisting and intended never to return, albeit that that state of mind may not have been communicated.

The test stated by Denning LJ in *Hopes v Hopes* was accepted as correct where the question was whether the fact of separation had been shown. Sachs LJ (at 262), referring to s 2(5) of the Divorce Reform Act 1969 (the 1969 Act), said—

'... the subsection makes it clear beyond further debate that when two spouses are living in the same house, then, as regards living apart, a line is to be drawn, in accordance with the views of Denning L.J., and they are to be held to be living apart if not living in the same household.'

Section 2(5) of the 1969 Act is now s 2(6) of the 1973 Act, which provides that for the purposes of paras (d) and (e) of s 1(2)—

'... a husband and wife shall be treated as living apart unless they are living with each other in the same household, and references in this section to the parties to a marriage living with each other shall be construed as references to their living with each other in the same household.'

This of course is not directed to s 42(1) of the 1970 Act and its predecessor in the 1950 Act, but the principle that two spouses may be said to be living apart though

living in the same house if they are in this sense not living in the same household is
to my mind clearly applicable.   *a*

Turning to the evidence before the commissioners, the relevant findings are set
out in para 7, of which the following sub-paragraphs are material. In (d) the
commissioners, having referred to the arrangement under which the taxpayer paid
the outgoings on the house but otherwise the husband and wife maintained
themselves out of their own incomes and paid their own separately assessed
proportion of tax, commented: 'They lived as separate households under the same   *b*
roof from this time and in the words of the Taxpayer "more or less ignored each
other".' Before me the taxpayer complained that the words 'as separate households'
did not appear in the original draft of the case stated and were not mentioned at the
hearing. The purport is nonetheless to my mind clear, and I do not think that the
adoption of that phraseology, with its echo of the matrimonial legislation and of the
passage from Denning LJ, in any way detracts from their conclusion.   *c*

In sub-para (g) the commissioners refer to a declaration by the taxpayer on
14 December 1982 that he was going to seek a divorce and to the facts that afterwards
he consulted solicitors and that a divorce petition was filed. That petition was not
proceeded with and the parties went on living as before. Then in sub-para (i) the
commissioners refer to a second petition dated 12 February 1986 which was presented
on the basis of a two-year separation by consent. They add: *d*

> 'This was the result of an agreement that had been reached between the
> respective parties' Solicitors during 1985 to settle the matrimonial dispute. The
> Solicitors agreed that the 14th December 1982 was an appropriate date to
> specifiy as the start of the separation.'

The petition, I should add, was a petition by the taxpayer.   *e*
The conclusion which the commissioners drew was:

> 'The announcement by the Taxpayer of his intention of seeking a divorce on
> 14th December 1982 made the circumstances of the separation described in
> paragraph 7d above such that it was likely to be permanent, and therefore Mrs
> Holmes was not to be treated as living with the Taxpayer from 14th December
> 1982 for the purposes of Sections 42(1)(b) and 8(1)(a)(i) of the [1970 Act].'   *f*

I have dealt at some length with this aspect of the matter because the taxpayer
does not have the benefit of legal representation and because I thought it right to
look carefully at the legislation and the facts found to satisfy myself that it could not
be said that the commissioners had misunderstood the provisions or the principles
to be applied. I am quite satisfied that the decision they reached was one which it   *g*
was open to them to reach on the basis of their findings of primary fact; namely, that
the taxpayer and his wife for all practical purposes lived separately though under the
same roof from 1972 onwards. That situation having obtained for ten years the
commissioners were entitled to take the view that the decision and the statement by
the taxpayer of his decision that he was going to seek a divorce was the point at
which that de facto separation became one that was likely to be permanent. It follows *h*
that this appeal fails.

There is, however, one other matter which I should mention. The solicitors who
acted for the taxpayer at the time of his divorce were a firm called Gadsby Coxon &
Copestake. After the hearing before the commissioners it came to their clerk's
knowledge that a gentleman who dealt with the divorce whilst with Gadsby Coxon
& Copestake had joined the firm of which the clerk to the General Commissioners   *j*
was a partner. The gentleman who had been with Gadsby Coxon & Copestake
became a partner in the firm of which the clerk to the General Commissioners was a
partner on 1 January 1987. The taxpayer had lodged a complaint with the Solicitors'
Complaints Bureau against that gentleman relating to the conduct of his affairs
while he was with Gadsby Coxon & Copestake.

a The commissioners felt anxiety about this state of affairs and they instructed their clerk to apply to the High Court for directions; and they notified the taxpayer of the circumstances I have described and of the action they had taken. Counsel later advised the commissioners that the course which they had sought to take was wholly inappropriate—advice with which I should say I wholly concur—and it was after this that the case was finally stated. The case was finally stated some two years after the original hearing before the commissioners.

b Although I can understand the anxiety felt by the commissioners it has not been suggested by the taxpayer before me that the circumstances I have described introduced such an element of potential impartiality or bias as to invalidate the case stated, and I do not think, therefore, that I need say more about that aspect of the case.

c *Appeal dismissed with costs.*

Solicitor: *Solicitor of Inland Revenue.*

Siew Ling Choo   Barrister.

Fitzpatrick v Inland Revenue Commissioners and related appeals

a

FIRST DIVISION OF THE INNER HOUSE OF THE COURT OF SESSION AS THE COURT OF
EXCHEQUER IN SCOTLAND
THE LORD PRESIDENT (HOPE), LORD ALLANBRIDGE AND LORD MAYFIELD
28 SEPTEMBER 1990

b

*Case stated – Remission – Motion to remit – Omissions from cases stated – Setting out
findings of commissioners in the body of the case — Taxes Management Act 1970, s 56(7).*

The taxpayers, five journalists, were in 1985–86 employed by the owner of a morning
and evening newspaper. Each received in that year 'a newspaper allowance' which
formed part of his or her taxable emoluments for the purposes of s 183(1) of the
Income and Corporation Taxes Act 1970, and claimed to be entitled to deduct from
it an equivalent sum expended on buying newspapers and periodicals, as being
'necessarily obliged' to incur that expenditure 'in the performance of' the duties of
their employment, within s 189(1) of that Act. The inspector refused each claim and
the taxpayers appealed. The Special Commissioners, before whom the appeal came
on for hearing, held that (a) the pleasure each taxpayer derived from reading the
newspapers and periodicals was an incidental benefit, which did not in itself
disqualify the expenditure from deduction under s 189(1) of the 1970 Act; but (b) the
duties of each started when he or she arrived at the office (or set off for an outside
assignment, if that was the first task of the day) and finished when he or she left the
office (or completed the first assignment of the day); and (c) by reading papers and
periodicals they were merely preparing themselves to carry out the duties of their
employment, as distinct from preparing articles etc for publication. The Special
Commissioners accordingly upheld the rejection by the inspector of taxes of all the
claims. The taxpayers demanded cases to be stated for the opinion of the Court of
Session and responded to drafts sent to them by the commissioners by requesting
certain amendments and insertions to be made. None of those had been made by
the commissioners when they signed and stated five cases, each of which merely
summarised the proceedings, listed the documents produced, gave the outcome,
and had annexed to it a copy of their decision 'as part of this case' and put as the
question of law for the opinion of the court 'whether, on the facts found, we were
entitled to conclude that no deduction could be made ... for the expenditure in
question'. The taxpayers moved the court to remit the cases for amendment pursuant
to s 56(7) of the Taxes Management Act 1970 on the grounds that they were defective
in failing to include questions to focus sufficiently the issues of law and in failing to
set out their findings of fact as to the professional history of each taxpayer and the
use to which the newspapers and periodicals were put by them.

c

d

e

f

g

h

Held – The duty of the commissioners under s 56(4) of the Taxes Management Act
1970, when stating a case for the opinion of the court, was to 'set forth the facts', and
that duty was not fulfilled where all that was done was to annex a copy of the decision
which had led to the demand for a case: the proper practice was for the material facts
to be set out in the body of the case, introduced by the statement that they had been
found to be admitted or proved. Accordingly, since it was not clear from the instant
cases whether the facts contained in the commissioners' decision represented facts
which they had accepted as proved or admitted, or were a mere narrative of evidence
which had been led, and it appeared doubtful whether they had taken any account
at all of the taxpayers' proposed amendments and insertions, all the cases would be
remitted to them for further consideration of those proposed amendments and

j

insertions, and then for them to state in the body of each case what relevant facts
a they had found to have been admitted or proved.
   Dicta of Megarry J in *Fleming (Inspector of Taxes) v London Produce Co Ltd* (1968)
44 TC 582 at 592, approved.

Notes

b For expenses 'necessarily obliged to incur or defray', see Simon's Taxes E4.705.
   For the form of the case stated see ibid, A3.707.
   For the Income and Corporation Taxes Act 1970, s 189(1) (now the Income and
Corporation Taxes Act 1988, s 198(1)), see ibid, Part G1.
   For the Taxes Management Act 1970, s 56(7), see ibid, Part G2.

c **Case referred to in opinion**

Fleming (Inspector of Taxes) v London Produce Co Ltd [1968] 1 WLR 1013, [1968] 2
   All ER 975, 44 TC 582.

d **Motion to remit**

Five taxpayers—Thomas Fitzpatrick, Rosemary Long, Barclay McBain, Cameron
Simpson and James Traynor—moved the Court of Session to remit for amendment
by the Special Commissioners five cases which the commissioners had on 18 May
1989 signed and stated for the opinion of that court as the Court of Exchequer for
Scotland. The facts are stated in the opinion of the court.

e
R N M Anderson for the taxpayers.
J W McNeill for the Crown.

THE LORD PRESIDENT (HOPE). The taxpayers in these five cases are
journalists employed in different capacities by George Outram & Co Ltd. They
f appealed to the Special Commissioners against refusals by the inspector of taxes to
allow deductions from their assessable emoluments under s 189(1) of the Income and
Corporation Taxes Act 1970 for expenditure on the purchase of newspapers and
periodicals. They argued that they were entitled to these deductions because their
expenditure was incurred wholly and exclusively for the purposes of their respective
employments on the Glasgow Herald or the Evening Times and because they were
g necessarily obliged to incur the expenditure in the performance of the duties of their
employment. By agreement of the parties the appeals were heard together and the
Special Commissioners issued a single written decision on the matter on 18 May
1989. They held that the requirements of s 189(1) were not satisfied and they refused
the appeals. Each of the five taxpayers then declared dissatisfaction with the decision
as being erroneous in point of law and required the commissioners to state and sign
h a case for the opinion of this court.
   The appeals are now before us on the Single Bills on the motion of the taxpayers
for the cases which have been stated by the Special Commissioners to be sent back
to them for amendment. Their complaint is that the cases which have been stated
for our opinion under s 56 of the Taxes Management Act 1970 are defective in two
respects. They say that the commissioners have failed to include sufficient questions
j in each case to focus sufficiently the issues of law between the parties. And they say
that the commissioners have also failed to set out in each case their findings of fact as
to the professional history of the taxpayers and the use to which the newspapers and
periodicals were put by them. We have been provided with copies of a document
dated 25 June 1990 which contains various amendments and insertions which were
suggested on the taxpayers' behalf. It is apparent from the cases which were signed

by the commissioners on 28 August 1990 that none of the amendments and insertions
set out in this document were accepted by them. Normally that would be an end of a
the matter, but in this instance it is submitted that the cases are so patently defective
that they should be sent back at once to the commissioners for amendment in terms
of s 56(7) of the Taxes Management Act 1970. We were informed that these are test
cases and that it is particularly important that the facts should be fully stated in order
that the issues of law may be properly focused for our decision.

Counsel for the Crown did not dispute that it was appropriate for the cases to be b
sent back for amendment. In our opinion he was right not to do so. It is plain from
an examination of the cases that they are not in proper form. What the commissioners
have done is to provide in each case a narrative of the proceedings together with a
list of the documents produced and then to set out for our opinion the question
whether, on the facts found, they were entitled to conclude that no deduction could
be made under s 189(1) of the Income and Corporation Taxes Act 1970 for the c
expenditure in question. They have annexed to each case a copy of their decision
dated 18 May 1989, which is said to form part of the case. This opinion contains a
narrative of the material facts of each case before proceeding to discuss the questions
of law which were argued before the commissioners. But no attempt has been made
to set out in the cases themselves the facts on which we at this stage must now hear
and determine the question or questions of law which arise. There is a complete d
absence of any statement in the body of each stated case of the facts found by the
commissioners.

The taxpayers suggested in their document dated 25 June 1990 that the material
facts of each case should be put into numbered paragraphs for ease of reference by
the court. This suggestion was made under reference to *Fleming (Inspector of Taxes)
v London Produce Co Ltd* [1968] 1 WLR 1013 at 1022, 44 TC 582 at 592 in which e
Megarry J said—

> 'In preparing cases stated, it would be welcome if commissioners would
> remember that over-lengthy paragraphs are inconvenient, and a proper system
> of numbering or lettering each paragraph and sub-paragraph is warmly to be
> commended.'

f

We agree, but in this instance the point which has been raised goes beyond
considerations of convenience to the court. In our opinion the commissioners have
failed to fulfil their statutory duty in terms of s 56(4) to set forth in the cases stated
the facts on which the cases are being stated for our determination. The statutory
requirement is not fulfilled where all that is done is to annex to the case a copy of the
decision which was issued by the commissioners at the outset before the request was g
made for them to state a case for the opinion of this court. The normal and proper
practice is for the facts found by the commissioners to be set out in the body of the
case itself, introduced by the statement that they found the following facts to be
admitted or proved. No such statement appears in the cases which are before us
today. It is also usual for the contentions of the parties to be set out in the case in
separate and numbered paragraphs. This is of assistance to the court in focusing the h
points of law which may properly be argued in the appeal.

We appreciate that the decision which the commissioners issued in these cases
went far beyond a brief statement of the reasons for their determination of the
appeals. It is a full opinion, which extends to 14 pages and sets out with care and in
considerable detail the material facts. But it is not clear whether all the facts which
are set out in this opinion were accepted as proved by the commissioners, as distinct j
from being a narrative of the evidence which was led. In any event, it is plain from
the way in which the cases have been stated for our opinion that the commissioners
took no further steps to set out the facts found by them following the request for a
stated case, and the way in which they have proceeded raises a substantial doubt as
to whether they took into account at all the various points which were put to them
by the taxpayers in their document dated 25 June 1990.

In this situation we are in no doubt that the cases must be returned to the
a commissioners for amendment. We do not think that we can begin to answer the
question of law which has been put before us until we have been provided by the
commissioners with a clear and succinct statement of the facts which they found
admitted or proved in each case.

We shall, therefore, grant the motion which has been made by the taxpayers by
remitting each case to the commissioners for amendment in the following respects.
b First, they should set out in the body of each stated case in separate numbered
paragraphs the facts which they found admitted or proved, based on the evidence
which they have heard. Second, in carrying out this exercise, they should give
further consideration to the suggested amendments and insertions contained in the
taxpayers' document dated 25 June 1990, including the four questions of law which
are set out on the second page of that document. We wish to make it clear that, in
c making this request, it is entirely a matter for the commissioners whether to accept
or reject any of this material, and we are not to be taken as suggesting that any of it
is either appropriate or inappropriate for inclusion in the case. We also wish to make
it clear that in our opinion the single question of law which has already been stated
by the commissioners is sufficient for the disposal of these appeals, but the points
made in the three additional questions proposed by the taxpayers may be of assistance
d to the commissioners in deciding which, if any, of the proposed amendments or
insertions they should accept. Third, the commissioners should set out in the body
of each case, in separate numbered paragraphs, the contentions of each party to
these appeals.

Cases remitted to the Special Commissioners for amendment.

e
Solicitors: *Haig-Scott & Co, W S,* Edinburgh (instructed by *Berwin Leighton*) (for
the taxpayers); *Solicitor of Inland Revenue.*

Rengan Krishnan Esq   Barrister.

Note

R v Inspector of Taxes and another, ex parte Kelly

QUEEN'S BENCH DIVISION (CROWN OFFICE LIST)
VINELOTT J (SITTING AS AN ADDITIONAL JUDGE OF THE QUEEN'S BENCH DIVISION)
30 NOVEMBER 1990

Relief – Interest – Loan for purchase or improvement of land – Mortgage interest relief at source – Taxpayer taking up remortgage with second building society – Part of loan used to redeem first mortgage and balance used for living expenses – Whether taxpayer entitled to mortgage interest relief at source – Income and Corporation Taxes Act 1988, s 370(2)(b).

Notes

For mortgage interest relief at source in general, see Simon's Taxes A3.430.

For the Income and Corporation Taxes Act 1988, s 370, see ibid, Part G1.

Application for judicial review

Wilfred Kelly (the applicant) applied for judicial review of the decision of the inspector of taxes refusing to allow interest to be paid under the mortgage interest relief at source scheme on a remortgage taken up by the applicant. The grounds of the application and the facts are set out in the judgment.

The applicant appeared in person.
Launcelot Henderson for the Crown.

VINELOTT J. This is an application for judicial review. The background is shortly this. The taxpayer, who is known as Wilfred Kelly (the applicant), has, over the years, bought more than one house with the assistance of loans from building societies. The most recent is a house known as 44 Church Meadows in Wigan, which he bought some time after 1988. He borrowed £45,300 from Nationwide Anglia Building Society, and he was allowed to pay interest net of standard rate tax under the mortgage interest relief at source (MIRAS) scheme, which I will mention in a moment. In November 1989 a new mortgage was taken out with Leeds & Holbeck Building Society. The sum borrowed was £52,419, of which £45,300 was used to repay the loan to Nationwide Anglia.

The Revenue, at an interview with the applicant and his wife, understood him to say that the surplus of £7,119 had been used for living expenses. I was told by the applicant today that it was used for home improvement. However, there is no evidence as to that, and as this is the first time that it has been so asserted, I think I must disregard it for the purposes of this application. It would, as I understand it, be of no assistance to the applicant if he could show that the surplus moneys had been used for home improvement because home improvement is not now a qualifying purpose for the purpose of mortgage interest relief and has not been since 1988.

It is of importance to the applicant that interest on £30,000 of the loan, that being the maximum amount on which income tax relief can be obtained, should not only rank for relief against tax, but that it should be treated as within the MIRAS scheme so that he can pay the interest net of tax and without being liable to account for the tax to the Revenue. The reason, quite simply, is that neither the applicant nor his

wife, and the properties were purchased in the name of his wife, has an income
a sufficient to absorb personal allowances; so that an allowance of gross interest against
his income would not assist him or his wife at all.

If interest on the loan up to £30,000 can be brought within the MIRAS scheme,
then he pays smaller repayments and suffers no other disadvantage. The only
disadvantage is that suffered by the general body of taxpayers because the tax on the
interest in the case of a building society is in effect made good by the Crown.

b The Revenue found themselves compelled to refuse to allow interest to be paid
under the MIRAS system after deduction of tax because the loan is a mixed loan,
partly for a qualifying and partly for a non-qualifying purpose. I shall explain the
reasons for that in a moment.

The applicant was so informed by letter of 19 February 1990. The reason for
refusing relief under the MIRAS scheme is there explained, and the reasons are
c amplified in a further letter of 8 March 1990. In that letter, the Revenue pointed out
to the applicant that if the building society was prepared to divide the loan into two
separate loans, one covering the part used to discharge the earlier mortgage and the
other non-qualifying expenditure, he would be entitled (up to £30,000) to relief in
respect of interest on the first part of the loan.

That suggestion was not taken up for some considerable time. Instead, the
d applicant made the application which is now before me. He applied first to a judge
of the Queen's Bench Division for leave to apply for judicial review. The matter in
respect of which the application is made is described as a ruling in respect of a tax
matter concerning MIRAS allowance, and he refers to the letter of 19 February.
Popplewell J gave leave on 22 May, and the application for review was then made
on 23 May. The applicant has since applied to the building society to split the loan
e in the way suggested by the Revenue. I shall turn to that in a moment.

It is, to my mind, as plain as anything could well be that the Revenue were not
only right in the view they took in February but that no other view could have been
entertained. The law relating to the deduction or allowance for interest has got into
a Byzantine tangle. Broadly speaking, apart from the MIRAS scheme, the ordinary
taxpayer who pays interest on a loan for a qualifying purpose, now the purchase of
f residential property, is entitled to relief on interest paid on the first £30,000 of the
loan. He gets that relief by way of a deduction from or set off against his taxable
income, and it is reflected, if he is employed, in his coding.

So far, the matter is relatively straightforward. It has been the law since, I think,
1965 when the more general principle of relief for interest was modified in the case
of individuals. That, as I have said, gives no relief to a person who is not liable to tax
g because he has no income, or who has not sufficient income, to use up all his
allowances.

That exceptional relief, or more accurately in the case of a person who does not
pay standard rate tax subsidy, is given under the MIRAS scheme. The MIRAS
scheme has two aspects. First, it enables the taxpayer, having first obtained a
certificate certifying that the loan is within the MIRAS scheme, instead of paying
h the interest gross, to pay under deduction of tax so that the immediate impact on his
income is reduced. The tax deducted is then brought into account in the ordinary
way in calculating the tax on his income. If he has no income or insufficient income,
then he is not liable to account for the tax deducted in making the interest payment.
That is achieved by s 369(4) of the Income and Corporation Taxes Act 1988 (the
1988 Act).

j The payee is bound to accept the interest paid under deduction. He is compensated
by a payment of the sum treated as tax paid by him, and that payment is treated as
income received by him. That is provided for by s 369(6). But these provisions apply
only to a qualifying borrower making payment to a qualifying lender of relevant
loan interest, all these expressions being defined in the 1988 Act. Relevant loan
interest is interest paid to a qualifying lender, to which s 370(2) applies. Subsection

(2) requires that the interest must, amongst other things, be interest, the whole of which would be eligible for relief under s 353, or would be taken into account in a computation of profits or gains or losses for the purposes of Sch D Case I, II or VI.

The latter part of that subsection is irrelevant. What is important is that the whole of the interest must be eligible for relief. As I have said, interest on a mixed loan, of which this, on the face of it, is one, is outside that provision. It must follow that on the date when this application was made, there was no conceivable ground for criticising the Revenue. The Revenue had done no more than give effect to the legislation.

However, since that time there has been a further development. In July 1990, the applicant, or his wife, I think, wrote to the Leeds & Holbeck Building Society (the building society) and sent a cheque for arrears of mortgage instalments. The building society confirmed that the mortgage account was excluded from the MIRAS scheme because he had applied for a multi-purpose loan where the total was not specifically for house purchase. The society suggested that he should apply to the tax authorities and ask for a MIRAS form and a letter confirming that they had no objection to an application for tax relief if the mortgage was split, and they enclosed other forms for him to complete for the Revenue.

A note in the applicant's handwriting on that letter says 'wrote 2nd August'. That refers to a letter sent to the Revenue on 2 August in which he asked them to issue a MIRAS 4 form with a covering letter stating that they had no objection to the application for tax relief on his wife's mortgage on the split basis. Then he wrote to the building society on 8 August to tell them that he had written to the Revenue. The Revenue, however, I am told, never saw the letter from the taxpayer and were unaware that anything was required or was expected to be done by them in order to split the borrowing in the way suggested. Normally, of course, it would be for the taxpayer and the building society to make that arrangement. The Revenue are then only called to give effect to it on application for MIRAS relief in respect of the split part.

The Revenue were quite unaware of the difficulties raised by the building society until today. However, counsel for the Crown was able to tell me, on instructions, that the Revenue are prepared to do everything within their power to assist the applicant and are prepared themselves to take the responsibility of writing to the building society and to explain the situation that has been reached and to state that if the building society will now split the mortgage in the way that the applicant requires, they will issue the MIRAS 4 which will enable the loan interest on the first £30,000 to be paid under deduction of tax.

It is a pity that the applicant should have launched into hostile proceedings by way of judicial review before approaching the building society and asking for the borrowing to be split. I have no doubt at all that if this matter had been raised before, the Revenue would long since have taken the steps which they now propose to take.

The applicant, unfortunately, I think, feels that he has been unsympathetically treated by the Revenue. I see no grounds justifying that feeling in the documents that I have seen. More importantly, for the purposes of today, as I have said, the Revenue are prepared, by way of concession and to assist the applicant, to take the steps that I have indicated, which will resolve matters in the future. It will be for the Revenue to decide how far they can allow the MIRAS certificate, once issued, to apply to outstanding mortgage interest which has accrued before the issue of the certificate. It will be within their general managerial powers, I think, to make that concession. I can, of course, give no direction, and it would not be right for me to ask the Revenue now to say what course they propose to take. I have no doubt, however, that the Revenue will look sympathetically at the position as, in my experience, they are always prepared to do.

There is only one other matter that I need mention. Strictly, no application for judicial review can be entertained if there are statutory provisions which enable the matter complained of to be brought by way of appeal to some appropriate tribunal.

a   The regulations relating to MIRAS interest relief generally do provide (see SI 1982/1236, reg 19) for an appeal to the General Commissioners against, amongst other things, a refusal to issue a relevant certificate under the MIRAS scheme. The Revenue failed to notice that there is this provision to appeal and, in the circumstances, do not rely on it.

The applicant has complained that he had no right of appeal. I think the answer to that is that he had a right of appeal but there was nothing against which he could b   have appealed, because the view the Revenue took on the information available to the Revenue at the time, there being no application to split the mortgage, was plainly right. So an appeal would have been a waste of time. With the co-operation of the Revenue, things are likely to be put right in the future.

Application dismissed with costs.

c
Solicitor: *Solicitor of Inland Revenue.*

Siew Ling Choo   Barrister.

O'Leary v McKinlay (Inspector of Taxes)   *a*

CHANCERY DIVISION
VINELOTT J
5, 6, 7 DECEMBER 1990

Emoluments from office or employment – Interest-free loan – Interest-free loan made by   *b*
employer to trustee for benefit of employee – Money invested in bank with interest
accruing to employee – Source of income – Whether source of income taxpayer's
employment or bank deposit – Whether income emolument arising from employment –
Income and Corporation Taxes Act 1970, ss 109(2), 181(1).

The taxpayer was a professional footballer employed by Arsenal Football Club Ltd   *c*
(the club). He was resident and ordinarily resident in the United Kingdom, but
domiciled in Eire. Prior to entering into a new contract of employment on 1 August
1979, the taxpayer had informed the club that in addition to his agreed basic wage
and bonuses he wished to receive an additional annual sum of £28,985 in a tax
efficient manner. The club entered into an arrangement suggested by the taxpayer's
advisers which it was hoped would enable the taxpayer to receive that sum free of   *d*
income tax in the United Kingdom. Under the arrangement, a third party settled a
nominal sum of £10 on the taxpayer for life with remainder over. The trustee was
Hambros Channel Islands Trust Corp Ltd (the trustee) and the settlement took
effect under Jersey law. The club lent the trustee a sum of £266,000 free of interest
and repayable on demand. The money was then invested by the trustee in a deposit
account at a Jersey bank. The interest derived therefrom less the trustee's fee was   *e*
approximately equal to the stipulated sum. The employment contract between the
club and the taxpayer was terminable by mutual consent or if, on or before 31 July
1981, the club demanded repayment of the loan to the trustee. The taxpayer
appealed against assessments to income tax under Sch E for the years of assessment
1979–80 to 1986–87 inclusive. He contended that the source of the income was not   *f*
his employment with the club but the deposit account with the Jersey bank and that
accordingly it was not taxable under Sch E as an emolument of his employment but
under Sch D, Case V as income arising from foreign possessions on a remittance
basis. The Special Commissioner dismissed the appeal holding that the source of the
income was the taxpayer's employment with the club and that accordingly the
income was chargeable to tax under Sch E as an emolument of his employment on
an arising basis. The taxpayer appealed.   *g*

Held – The income arising from the settlement was in reality income provided by
the club and payable to the taxpayer for so long as he was employed with the club.
Accordingly, it was an emolument arising from the taxpayer's employment by the
club and as such was assessable to tax under Sch E to the exclusion of any charge   *h*
under Sch D, Case V. The appeal would therefore be dismissed.

Notes

For emoluments chargeable under Sch E, see Simon's Taxes Division E4.4.
     For the Income and Corporation Taxes Act 1970, ss 109, 181 (now the Income   *j*
and Corporation Taxes Act 1988, ss 18, 19), see ibid, Part G1.

Cases referred to in judgment

Bucks v Bowers (Inspector of Taxes) [1970] Ch 431, [1970] 2 All ER 202, 46 TC 267.

Dale v IRC [1954] AC 11, [1953] 2 All ER 671, 34 TC 468, HL.

a   *F S Securities Ltd v IRC* [1965] AC 631, [1964] 2 All ER 691, 41 TC 666, HL.

IRC v Westminster (Duke) [1936] AC 1, 19 TC 490, HL.

Laidler v Perry (Inspector of Taxes) [1966] AC 16, [1965] 2 All ER 121, 42 TC 351, HL.

Northend (Inspector of Taxes) v White & Leonard and Corbin Greener (a firm) and others [1975] STC 317, [1975] 1 WLR 1037, [1975] 2 All ER 481, 50 TC 121.

b   *Ramsay (W T) Ltd v IRC* [1981] STC 174, [1982] AC 300, [1981] 1 All ER 865, 54 TC 101, HL.

Recknell v IRC [1952] 2 All ER 147, 33 TC 201.

Salisbury House Estate Ltd v Fry (Inspector of Taxes) [1930] AC 432, 15 TC 266, HL.

White (Inspector of Taxes) v Franklin [1965] 1 WLR 492, [1965] 1 All ER 692, 42 TC

c   283, CA.

Cases also cited

Bray (Inspector of Taxes) v Best [1989] STC 159, [1989] 1 WLR 167, [1989] 1 All ER 969, HL.

d   *Brumby (Inspector of Taxes) v Milner* [1976] STC 534, [1976] 1 WLR 1096, [1976] 3 All ER 636, 51 TC 583, HL.

Hochstrasser (Inspector of Taxes) v Mayes [1960] AC 376, [1959] 3 All ER 817, 38 TC 673, HL.

Case stated

e

1. On 17 and 18 July 1989 a Special Commissioner heard the appeal of David Anthony O'Leary (the taxpayer) against assessments to income tax under Sch E in respect of the eight years of assessment 1979–80 to 1986–87 inclusive.

2. The question for determination was whether certain income from a large principal sum, of which income the taxpayer was the beneficial owner under the

f   terms of a settlement made in Jersey, Channel Islands on 1 August 1979, was chargeable to income tax under Sch E as emoluments of the taxpayer's employment with Arsenal Football Club.

3. No oral evidence was tendered, but there was supplied to the commissioner a statement of agreed facts and a folder of 36 documents all admitted and agreed and a document headed 'David O'Leary: summary of appellant's submissions'. The

g   commissioner referred to those documents in order to incorporate them in the case, but did not annex them thereto, although they would be available for the use of the court and the parties if required.

4. On 9 August 1989 the commissioner gave his decision in writing, dismissing the appeal having regard to the facts and for the reasons mentioned therein. The decision having been given in principle only, the parties subsequently agreed the

h   figures, and in consequence on 27 September 1989 the commissioner determined the appeals in the amounts set out in letters of that date sent from the office of the Special Commissioners of the Income Tax Acts to the solicitors for the taxpayer and the Crown.

5. The solicitors for the taxpayer having declared dissatisfaction and required the statement of a case for the opinion of the High Court, the Special Commissioners

j   have stated this case. The commissioner annexed thereto so as to form part thereof the decision above-mentioned.

6. The question of law for the opinion of the court was whether, on the agreed facts, the income arising under the above-mentioned settlement in the eight years of assessment under appeal constituted emoluments of the taxpayer's employment by Arsenal Football Club so as to be chargeable to income tax under Sch E.

DECISION

Mr David Anthony O'Leary (the taxpayer) appeals against income tax assessments *a*
under Sch E in respect of the eight years of assessment 1979–80 to 1986–87, during
which time he was an employee of Arsenal Football Club Ltd (the club) and was
resident and ordinarily resident in the United Kingdom, but domiciled in the
Republic of Ireland.

No oral evidence was tendered, but I have a statement of agreed facts, to which is
appended a folder containing copies of 36 documents all admitted and agreed. My *b*
decision is based on the agreed facts, but for convenience I make the following brief
summary. The taxpayer having previously been employed as a football player by
the club entered into a new employment contract with the club which is dated
1 August 1979, but was apparently executed on 8 August 1979, and terminated on
31 July 1981. Subsequently on 13 August 1981, 8 August 1985, 1 July 1986, and
16 February 1987, he entered into fresh employment contracts with the club. The *c*
express or implied terms of these further contracts are sufficiently similar to the
express terms of the first contract to justify my dealing primarily with the first
contract, it being my view and common ground that whatever decision is arrived at
in relation to the first contract covers the other four contracts also. During
discussions between the taxpayer and the club prior to August 1979 the taxpayer
stated that in addition to his agreed basic wages and bonuses he wished to receive an *d*
additional annual sum of £28,985 in a tax efficient manner. The advisers of the
taxpayer suggested to the club an arrangement which it was hoped would have the
effect that the taxpayer would receive that annual sum so that he would not be liable
to income tax thereon in the United Kingdom. The club agreed to take part in the
arrangement. Consequently a Mr Mulhall in practice as an accountant in the
Republic of Ireland, being approached by the taxpayer's advisers, settled the nominal *e*
sum of £10 on the taxpayer for life with a remainder over. The trustee was Hambros
Channel Islands Trust Corp Ltd, and the settlement took effect under Jersey law. I
am not told who paid the costs charges and expenses of drafting and executing the
settlement, but I assume it was not Mr Mulhall. This settlement was part of an
arrangement whereby the club was to lend free of interest and repayable on demand
the sum of £266,000 to the trustee, which sum the trustee would, it was envisaged, *f*
invest by depositing the same with Hambros Bank (Jersey) Ltd.

The employment agreement could be terminated by the taxpayer only 'in the
event of the club failing to fulfil the terms and conditions' thereof. However, the
following clause, numbered 10, dealt with the arrangement:

'(A) This agreement may be terminated at any time by mutual consent of
both club and player. *g*

(B) Without prejudice to the generality of sub-clause (A) above, if on or
before the 31 day of July 1981 the club demands repayment of the whole or any
part of the loan of £266,000 made from the first day of August 1979 by the club
to the trustees of a settlement made in Jersey Channel Islands on the first day of
August 1979 between Kevin Shane Mulhall of the one part and Hambros
Channel Islands Trust Corporation Ltd of the other part then upon the player *h*
giving written notice that this sub-clause should become operative, the club
and the player mutually agree that this agreement shall be terminated.

Copies of the settlement and the terms of the loan are attached hereto.'

The foregoing summary does not displace the statement of agreed facts. From
that statement and from the documents I conclude as follows. The arrangement was *j*
a tax avoidance scheme; but I consider it as it stands, without any prejudice for or
against it. It is for the taxpayer to establish the facts, which he has done by the
statement of agreed facts; it is for the Crown to establish the principles of law that
impose liability to tax by reference to those facts. It seems clear to me that the
taxpayer's advisers perceived that the income of the trust fund including the
£266,000 was chargeable to tax in the United Kingdom as income of the taxpayer

(subject to the proviso hereunder mentioned) only to the extent that it was remitted
a to the United Kingdom – and as it would never be remitted to the United Kingdom
it would in effect avoid United Kingdom income tax imposed on non-United
Kingdom income of persons resident in the United Kingdom by Sch D Case V.
Section 109 of the Income and Corporation Taxes Act 1970 (the 1970 Act) charges
tax under Sch D, Case V as 'tax in respect of income arising from possessions out of
the United Kingdom, not being income consisting of emoluments of any office or
b employment'. Thus, provided that the income under the settlement was not
'emoluments of any office or employment' ie was not chargeable under Sch E, it
could, by not being remitted to the United Kingdom, escape United Kingdom
income tax. If charged under Sch E, the income under the settlement would be
taken out of Sch D Case V, and would be charged in the year of assessment in which
it was emoluments irrespective of whether remitted to the United Kingdom or not.
c   It was therefore important that the additional annual sum that the taxpayer
wished to receive should not rank as emoluments from his employment. It was a
view widely held that if an employer, to reward an employee, made a loan repayable
on demand to the employee free of interest or at interest, then, while the value of the
loan at the date of its being made (if any) would rank as an emolument, nevertheless
profits that the employee might make by investing the moneys lent to him would
d not be chargeable as emoluments from the employment. It was to reduce tax
avoidance in respect of such loans that s 66 was enacted in the Finance Act 1976 (the
1976 Act). It was clearly in the mind of the taxpayer's advisers that, while a simple
loan by the club to the taxpayer would fall within s 66 of the 1976 Act, a loan to
trustees of a settlement under which the employee is the principal beneficiary is not
caught by the clear wording of s 66. Hence the structure of a loan to trustees outside
e the United Kingdom, the investment of the moneys lent so as to produce income
outside the United Kingdom. It was a perfectly legitimate tax avoidance scheme.
     I can deal shortly with s 66. Mr Butterfield, who appeared for the Crown,
submitted that that section made no difference whatever to this case; he would make
the same challenge on the same grounds whether that section existed or not. He did
not refer me to its wording, or rely on it at all. Mr Flesch QC, who appeared for the
f taxpayer, submitted that s 66 was not relevant. In view of Mr Butterfield's concession
I do not have to come to any decision as respects s 66.
     Mr Flesch and his junior Mr Baker kindly provided a type-written summary of
their submissions. I do not need therefore to set out fully their submissions as made
orally.
     Mr Butterfield relied on *Furniss (Inspector of Taxes) v Dawson* [1984] STC 153,
g [1984] AC 474 and I therefore take account of that decision, particularly of the
opinion of Lord Brightman ([1984] STC 153 at 165–167, [1984] AC 474 at 526–528).
Mr Butterfield submitted that there was in fact a commercial agreement between
the club and the taxpayer to pay the taxpayer, among other sums, £28,985 a year;
onto that agreement was superimposed, for tax avoidance purposes only, the
settlement, the loan of £266,000 by the club to the settlement trustee, and the
h deposit of those moneys by the trustee with the bank at interest. If one ignores those
three items, one is left with the club's obligation to pay £28,985, and the receipt by
the taxpayer of that sum year by year.
     I cannot accept that contention. Whatever facts might have emerged from cross-
examination of witnesses (perhaps the taxpayer, his advisers, managers of the club,
officers of the trustee and of the bank) I decline to make the inference from the
j agreed facts or from the admitted documents that there was a commercial agreement
to pay £28,985 or any sum. In fact, over the years, rather less was paid to the
taxpayer than had been expected (see cl 14 of the agreed facts). Nor can I perform
the mental gymnastic of ignoring the loan to the settlement or the investment of the
money by deposit with the bank, without ignoring also the consideration for that
investment namely the interest. Moreover this appears to me to be a case where
there were two ways or more of fashioning a transaction, and the parties chose to

fashion the transaction in a way they hoped would be tax-free (see *Craven (Inspector of Taxes) v White* [1988] STC 476 at 480, [1989] AC 398 at 479–480 per Lord Keith).   *a*

Mr Flesch relied on *IRC v Duke of Westminster* [1936] AC 1, 19 TC 490. Save as giving general guidance, to be viewed in the light of subsequent authorities, it is not on all fours with the present case. In that case the annual payments under covenant were made under a voluntary obligation outside the service contract. Here the loan and the settlement are contracted for in cl 10 of the contract of employment.

During the hearing, at my suggestion, the parties considered the correct taxation   *b* treatment of a loan which an employer makes to an employee repayable on demand free of interest in order to reward the employee; with the additional fact that the employee deposits the moneys at a bank to provide himself with interest. Mr Flesch submitted that while there is no reported authority directly in line, the principle is clear that the making of the loan itself, whether voluntary or contractual may be an emolument but, since the loan is repayable on demand, it is without value. If the use   *c* of the loan moneys provide income or capital gains or some other benefit to the employee, the source of that income or gain or benefit is not the employment but is the transaction of the employee whereby he turns the borrowed moneys to account. As a general proposition of law I accept that. It seems to me to be clearly supported by two decisions of the House of Lords, the first being *Tennant v Smith (Surveyor of Taxes)* [1892] AC 150 at 154, 3 TC 158 at 163. That was a case where under his   *d* contract of employment the taxpayer occupied a house owned by the employer. Adapting the reasoning of the House of Lords in that case to the present circumstance, it seems to me that the use of borrowed money, as opposed to the borrowing itself, is not an emolument from the employment. I also refer to *Heaton (Inspector of Taxes) v Bell* [1970] AC 728 at 741, 46 TC 211 at 238; there an employee had the use of a car provided by the employer. While I find the headnotes somewhat   *e* misleading, reasons given in the House of Lords [1970] AC 728 at 747, 755, 758, 760–762, 766, 46 TC 211 at 247, 255, 257, 260–261 and 265 support the view that the use of the car in itself was not an emolument from the employment, though the fact that the employee could in place of the car receive cash if he so wished brought the case to the other side of the line. The principle that I derive from those two authorities is corroborated by the fact, of which I take notice, that the practice of   *f* beneficial loans to employees has for many years been widespread, and is in practice not brought within the tax net save by the express enactment of ss 61 and 66 of the 1976 Act. I cannot accept Mr Butterfield's contention that a beneficial loan is chargeable under general Sch E principles if it is made pursuant to the employee's contract of employment, but not if made voluntarily. I therefore conclude that, had the club, pursuant to a contract with the taxpayer, lent him £266,000 interest-free   *g* repayable on demand with or without security, the source of any income or other profit or benefit that might accrue to the taxpayer from his exploitation of the cash would be that exploitation; the income or profit or benefit would not, on the true construction of s 181(1) of the 1970 Act, have been the employment of the taxpayer; the employment would have been simply the 'causa sine qua non' and not the 'causa causans', to adopt the test applied by the House of Lords in *Hochstrasser (Inspector*   *h* *of Taxes) v Mayes* [1960] AC 376, 38 TC 673.

Both parties claimed to find support from the definition of 'earned income' in s 530(1) of the 1970 Act. Under s 530(1)(c) there is included in 'earned income' 'any income . . . immediately derived by the individual from the carrying on or exercise by him of his trade, profession or vocation'. Reference was made to *Buck v Bowers (Inspector of Taxes)* [1970] Ch 431, 46 TC 267, where merchant bankers in the course   *j* of business held securities and investments, the income from which was taxed by deduction at source. It was held that such income was not 'immediately derived' from the carrying on of the trade, although it was certainly derived in the course of the trade. For my part I would limit that decision to the case of income taxed at source. The same is, however, not true of *Northend (Inspector of Taxes) v White & Lennard and Corbin Greener (a firm) and others* [1975] STC 317, [1975] 1 WLR 1037.

a Solicitors dealt with clients' money by placing it in clients' deposit account, with a
bank, on which account interest accrued to and was retained by the solicitor. It was
held that the interest was 'immediately derived' from the contract with the bank, not
from the profession. Those two authorities, it seems to me, albeit related to Sch D
not Sch E are some indication that where an employee himself deposits with the
bank moneys borrowed from his employer the source of the income on the deposit is
the deposit itself and not the employment.

b   However, I have to consider *White (Inspector of Taxes) v Franklin* [1965] 1 WLR
492, 42 TC 283, a decision of the Court of Appeal, dealing with earned income relief
by reference to s 530(1)(*a*), especially the words 'any income arising in respect of any
remuneration from any office or employment held by the individual . . .'. A voluntary
settlement of shares in a company made to induce an officer of the company to stay
with the company gave to him the income of certain shares in the company 'so long
c as he shall be engaged in the management of the company'. The General
Commissioners decided that the dividend income 'constituted remuneration of an
office or employment and was thus earned income' within s 525(1)(*a*) of the Income
Tax Act 1952, the predecessor of s 530(1)(*a*) of the 1970 Act. That decision was
confirmed on appeal to the High Court, then to the Court of Appeal. In the High
Court it was held that the employment was the causa causans of the payment to the
d beneficiary under the trust of the dividends, not simply the causa sine qua non.
    I think the reasoning of the Court of Appeal is well summarised in the following
passage from the judgment of Harman LJ ([1965] 1 WLR 492 at 516, 42 TC 283 at
297):

e   '. . . it is fair to say, therefore, that the payment arises out of the performance
    of his duties and is earned income in the sense that it is the product of the office
    of profit which he holds. It is not merely a limitation in a family settlement
    distributing income which arises from family property to persons with certain
    qualifications, although it can very plausibly be put in that guise. I think that it
    is "because" he holds office, and not merely "during the time that he does," that
    is the paramount consideration in the settlors' mind and that when he receives
    the money he is entitled to say: "This is part of my remuneration for doing this
f   particular job".'

    The Court of Appeal considered that the case was 'very near the line'. It is to be
noted that the dividends (Sch F being not yet law) were for tax purposes a
distribution of the taxed profits of the company deemed to be 'grossed up' for tax
purposes. They were thus received, like the interest in *Bucks v Bowers*, after tax.
g Nevertheless they were 'any remuneration from any office or employment'.
    I turn to the present case. I perceive no contract whereby the club was obliged to
provide an income of £28,985 or any other stipulated sum. That was the income
looked for, but what was agreed in cl 10 of the first service contract (and expressly or
impliedly agreed in subsequent contracts) was that the club should lend a lump sum
(in the first instance £266,000) to the trustees of the settlement by way of loan, the
h terms of the settlement and of the loan (free of interest and to be repayable on
demand) being agreed as part of his service agreement between the taxpayer and the
club. I observe that the trustee immediately deposited the £266,000 with Hambros
Bank (Jersey) Ltd so that that account bears interest at a rate of 11·5% with effect
from 15 August 1979 and matures on 30 July 1981.
    Under the service agreement the taxpayer is to be employed for two years, and,
j save in the case of breach of contract, it may (apart from cl 10) not be terminated
save by mutual consent. However, under cl 10(B) the club may not demand
repayment of any part of the £266,000 save at risk that the taxpayer will forthwith
terminate his employment. Had the club lent £266,000 to the taxpayer and he made
a contract of loan to the bank in Jersey, then I would consider it clear that the only
source of the bank interest would be the bank deposit. That is not the present case.
I also accept the principle that where, by deduction at source or otherwise, income

chargeable otherwise than under Sch E accrues to an employee, the circumstance
that the income is charged otherwise than under Sch E may perhaps oust Sch E. *a*
The Schedules are mutually exclusive (although as is well known the Cases within a
Schedule are not). As I understand the principle that justifies the decision in *White
v Franklin* it is that moneys received by an employee otherwise than from an
employer may be emoluments from the employment within the meaning of s 530
(and consequently within the meaning of Sch E), notwithstanding that they are,
before or after receipt by the employee, brought into charge to tax under some other *b*
Schedule or statutory provision than Sch E. In *Franklin* the other provision was
what would now be Sch F. The dividends were dividends, taxable as such, but were
also emoluments from the employment. What would have kept them out of Sch E
was the fact that they were dividends as well as emoluments. They could not be
taxed twice.

In the present case neither the taxpayer nor anybody as his agent made a contract *c*
of loan having its own vitality as a source of income. Nevertheless the trustee did
just that, using money provided by the employer, the club, under an arrangement
made between the club, the employee and the trustee whereby the equitable title to
Jersey Income vested in the employee.

Both the wording of Sch D, Case V and the judgments in *Franklin* make it clear
that income may accrue *from an employment* even if it also accrues from, say, *d*
dividends, or rents, or interest.

It seems to me that all the facts of this case point to the interest accruing to the
taxpayer from his employment with the club, being remuneration for his services.
Consequently the interest is chargeable to tax under Sch E as it arises. In particular
I note the following facts: the taxpayer, or his advisers, raised the question of an
annual sum of £28,985 'in a tax efficient manner' in the context of reward for his *e*
services—a tax efficient reward for services and for nothing else; the loan to the
settlement was agreed as part of the service agreement; the loan, and its yield of
income, was likely to last only as long as the employment contract; there was no
other factor (such as the house removal in *Hochstrasser v Mayes*) to which the loan
and interest related. It seems to me a reasonably plain case of emoluments chargeable
under Sch E. The *Franklin* decision fortifies me in that view. *f*

Mr Flesch made a passing reference to s 122(1), (2) and (3) of the 1970 Act. I
perceive an argument that the income tax under consideration, albeit chargeable
under Sch E, is also 'chargeable under Case IV or Case V of Schedule D', so that tax
is computed on income received in the United Kingdom (the amount of which was
nil) not on income arising. I would reject that argument, were it to be tendered,
because the wording of Sch D, Case V itself causes tax otherwise chargeable on the *g*
interest under Case V to cease to be so chargeable. Mr Flesch properly left it as a
passing reference.

The figures have apparently not been agreed, and I am asked to give my decision
in principle only. I decide the question presented to me against the taxpayer, and
adjourn the appeals so that, if possible, figures may be agreed so that a final
determination may be made. *h*

Michael Flesch QC and *Philip Baker* for the taxpayer.
Andrew Thornhill QC and *Nicholas Warren* for the Crown.

VINELOTT J. This is an appeal from a decision of one of the Special Commissioners.
He dismissed appeals by the taxpayer, David Anthony O'Leary, against assessments *j*
to income tax under Sch E for each of the years of assessment 1979–80 to 1986–87
inclusive. It is only necessary to consider the years of assessment 1979–80 and
1980–81. The arrangements which gave rise to the income which it is sought to tax
under Sch E were repeated with immaterial modifications in the subsequent years
of assessment.

The relevant facts can be shortly stated. The taxpayer is a well-known footballer.

He was born in and is domiciled in Eire, and he has played in international matches
a   for Eire. However, his life as a professional footballer has been spent with Arsenal
Football Club Ltd (the club). Prior to August 1979 there were discussions between
the taxpayer and the club and their respective advisers as to the terms on which he
would be employed for the future. He was anxious to ensure that he received an
annual sum of £28,985 in addition to his agreed basic wage and bonuses in what is
described as a 'tax efficient' way; that is, in such a way that it would not be liable to
b   United Kingdom tax.

The arrangement that was entered into is shortly this. A Mr Mulhall, an
accountant practising in Eire, settled a nominal sum of £10. The settlement is dated
1 August 1979, and the parties are Mr Mulhall and Hambros Channel Islands Trust
Corp Ltd (the trustee). There is a conventional definition of the expression 'the trust
fund' which is to include the sum of £10 and all other moneys coming into the hands
c   of the trustee as trustee of the settlement. The income of the trust fund is to be paid
to the taxpayer during his life with remainder (subject to a discretionary power to
pay capital to the taxpayer) to the Catholic Church in Eire. Income arising is to be
treated as accruing from day to day. The trustee is given express power to invest the
trust fund in making a deposit on loan to an associated company, Hambros Bank
(Jersey) Ltd (the bank) without being liable to account for any profit thereby made.
d   Subject to that the trustee has a very wide power of investment. However, this
power of investment is not to be exercised without the prior consent of the taxpayer.
The trustee is given the right to retain £1,000 p a out of the income of the trust fund
as its remuneration for a period of two years and thereafter is to be entitled to charge
such fees and other remuneration as it currently charges for its services as trustee of
similar trusts.

e   On 1 August the taxpayer also entered into an agreement with the club under
which he agreed to play for the club for a period of two years unless his employment
was previously determined or extended. The agreement is terminable (amongst
other things) by mutual consent or if before 31 July 1981 the club demands
repayment of 'the loan . . . made on 1st August 1979 by the club' to the trustee. A
copy of the settlement and of an undated letter from the club to the trustee recording
f   a loan of £266,000 free of interest and repayable on demand and an acknowledgement
of receipt of the loan by the trustee are attached to the agreement. The sum of
£266,000 was then placed on deposit by the trustee with the bank on a fixed account
maturing on 30 July 1981 at interest payable half-yearly at the rate of 11·5%. That
is £30,590 p a, leaving after deducting the trustee's fee £29,590.

The practical effect of these arrangements was that the taxpayer became entitled
g   to receive the interest on the deposit with the bank so long and only so long as he
continued to play for the club. Of course, in theory the club might have called on
the trustee to repay the loan during the currency of the agreement and the taxpayer
might nonetheless have decided not to terminate the agreement; and the club might
have left the loan outstanding even though the agreement expired or was terminated
by agreement on some ground other than a demand for repayment of the loan by
h   the club. But these possibilities are merely theoretical. The scheme was set up in
order to provide the taxpayer with additional income while he continued to play for
the club under the terms of the agreement and for no other purpose. Again, the
trustee might have invested the money (with the taxpayer's consent) in some other
way. It may be that the taxpayer would have agreed a reinvestment if his income
was not adversely affected. He would have been very unlikely to have agreed a
j   reinvestment made to enhance the capital of the trust fund which he could only
receive at the discretion of the trustee. Moreover, as the loan was repayable on
demand the trustee's freedom of investment was necessarily limited. It would expose
itself to considerable risk if it dealt with the money otherwise than by leaving it on
deposit with a reliable financial institution. But these possibilities are both remote
and irrelevant. The claim is that he was liable to tax on whatever benefit he derived
under the agreement while he was employed by the club; in the event that benefit

was provided in the form originally intended—the income less the management fee (representing the cost to the employer of providing the benefit) from the sum *a* deposited with the bank.

The case for the taxpayer is that the income received by the taxpayer was income 'arising from possessions out of the United Kingdom, not being income consisting of emoluments of any office or employment' within Sch D, Case V and that accordingly (the taxpayer being domiciled in Eire though resident and ordinarily resident in the United Kingdom) he was taxable only on the income remitted to the *b* United Kingdom. None has been remitted. The case for the Crown which succeeded before the Special Commissioner is that the income was taxable as an emolument of the taxpayer's employment by the club within Sch E, Case I.

I think the ordinary informed member of the public unversed in the niceties of tax law would say without hesitation that the income arising under the settlement was an emolument of the taxpayer's employment by the club. For in reality it was *c* income provided by the club and payable to him so long as he was employed by the club for his services to the club. The income was accordingly chargeable to tax under Sch E to the exclusion (by virtue of the excepting words at the end of Case V) of any charge under Case V.

Counsel for the taxpayer, submitted that a proper understanding of the structure of the income tax compels the conclusion that (apart from s 66 of the Finance Act *d* 1976) if an employer lends money to an employee the employee is taxable if and to the extent that a quantifiable benefit is conferred on him by the terms on which the loan is made. Any income which the taxpayer then derives from investing the moneys lent to him or from employing them in a trading adventure is taxable under the appropriate Schedule as income from the source from which it is directly derived; the income is not taxable under Sch E as income from his employment. If *e* the loan is repayable on demand there is no quantifiable benefit on which tax can be exacted under Sch E, though it might be otherwise if the loan were made for a specified period at a rate of interest less than the rate obtainable by the employee by depositing the money lent with a reputable financial institution for an equivalent period. If (as in the instant case) the employee is domiciled abroad he may deposit the money lent with a foreign bank and the interest though chargeable under Case V *f* then escapes tax so far as unremitted; so also if the employee uses the money lent to purchase a house or other non-income producing property. The position is the same if moneys are lent to trustees for an employee and the trustees use the money in a way which produces income or some other benefit for the employee. The growing practice whereby employers lent money free of interest or at a favourable rate of interest to employees repayable on demand though with the intention that the loan *g* should be used to purchase a house and that repayment would not be demanded while the employee continued to serve the employer led to an unacceptable loss of tax which was countered by s 66 of the Finance Act 1976 (the 1976 Act). Under that section, where a loan is made to a director or to a person in what is misleadingly described as higher-paid employment and which is either free of interest or which bears interest at less than a market rate, tax is payable for the period while the loan *h* is outstanding on an amount equal in effect to the difference between the interest payable and interest at an 'official' rate ascertained in accordance with the 1976 Act which is intended to reflect market rates for the time being in force. However, s 66 only applies if the loan is made to the employee or to a 'relative' of a defined class. It does not apply in the instant case where the loan was made to the trustee of a settlement under which the employee was entitled to the income. *j*

The Special Commissioner accepted counsel for the taxpayer's submission that—

> '... had the club, pursuant to a contract with the taxpayer, lent him £266,000 interest free repayable on demand with or without security, the source of any income or other profit or benefit that might accrue to the taxpayer from his exploitation of the cash would be that exploitation . . .'

Counsel for the taxpayer submitted that the Special Commissioner ought
a concurrently to have held that the source of the income which accrued from the
exploitation of the loan by the trustee was similarly the deposit with the bank and
not the taxpayer's contract of employment. That source having been a deposit with
a bank outside the United Kingdom it was taxable only under Sch D, Case V and as
the taxpayer was domiciled outside the United Kingdom the income from it was
taxable only so far as remitted to the United Kingdom.

b   The Special Commissioner rejected that submission and I think he was right to do
so. The fallacy which I think underlies counsel for the taxpayer's submission can be
shortly stated. If an employer lends money to an employee free of interest or at a
favourable rate of interest and if the employee is free to exploit the money in any
manner he chooses his employment cannot be said to have been the source of the
income derived from the exploitation; the employer is the source of the money and
c the taxpayer is assessable to tax under Sch E on the benefit to him of obtaining the
loan on the terms on which the loan was made; but if the loan is repayable on
demand that benefit cannot be quantified and form the basis of an assessment under
Sch E. By contrast, if an employer were to lend money to a bank on terms that
interest was paid to the employee until further order the interest paid to him while
he remained an employee would almost inevitably be taxable as an emolument of his
d employment—though no doubt there might be circumstances in which it could be
said that the enjoyment of the income did not arise from the employment but from
something else, for instance, from motives of benevolence towards an old and valued
employee in temporary difficulty (see *Laidler v Perry (Inspector of Taxes)* [1966] AC
16 at 31, 42 TC 351 at 363–364 per Lord Reid). So also I think if an employer were
to lend money to an employee free of interest but on terms that the loan would be
e employed by placing it on deposit at an agreed bank and charged as security for
repayment of the loan on demand. The benefit to the employee would then be the
interest earned on the deposit and nothing else.

      If that is right the instant case is a fortiori. The taxpayer never had the free
disposal of the £266,000. It is in fact very unlikely that the club would have been
willing to put a sum of that magnitude at his free disposal. The purpose and effect of
f the arrangement was to provide the taxpayer with the income derived from the
investment of £266,000 (calculated to be approximately equal to the stipulated sum
if put on deposit after deducting the trustee's fee) for so long as he continued to be
employed by the club; the £266,000 could not be otherwise invested without his
consent and if it had been the income (and I think any capital advanced to him)
would equally have been emoluments from his employment. To reach that
g conclusion it is not necessary to—

> '. . . brush aside deeds, disregard the legal rights and liabilities arising under a
> contract between parties, and decide the question of taxability or non-taxability
> upon the footing of the rights and liabilities of the parties being different from
> what in law they are . . .'

h (see *IRC v Duke of Westminster* [1936] AC 1 at 25, 19 TC 490 at 524, per Lord
Russell of Killowen). It is only necessary to construe the agreement and the
documents attached to it together and in their full context. The principle explained
in *IRC v Duke of Westminster*:

> 'While obliging the court to accept documents or transactions, found to be
> genuine, as such, . . . does not compel the court to look at a document or a
j > transaction in blinkers, isolated from any context to which it properly belongs.'

(See *W T Ramsay Ltd v IRC* [1981] STC 174 at 180, [1982] AC 300 at 323, per Lord
Wilberforce.)
      That is enough to decide this case. But I was referred by counsel for the taxpayer
to a number of authorities and I think that in deference to his careful argument I
should say something about them.

There are first two cases in which the question was whether a taxpayer was liable to pay the special contribution introduced by s 49 of the Finance Act 1948. The question was whether the income in question was 'investment income' which was defined as meaning 'income from any source other than a source of earned income'. In *Dale v IRC* [1954] AC 11, 34 TC 468, the income in question was an annuity under a will payable (free of tax) to the taxpayer in his capacity as one of the trustees of the will on whom onerous duties fell. In *Recknell v IRC* (1952) 33 TC 201, the income was income from shares in a company which had been made available to employees (of whom the taxpayer was one) selected according to their worth to the company. In both cases the income was held to be earned income. Counsel for the taxpayer relied on these cases as showing that the question whether income is earned income and the question whether income is taxable under Sch E are separate and distinct questions. He relied on observations by Lord Normand (in *Dale v IRC* [1954] AC 11 at 28, 29, 34 TC 468 at 491, 492) that 'the source of the sum and its character as a receipt in the hands of the trustee are two separate and unconnected things' and that 'the conception "investment income" cuts across the Schedules'. I shall return to this point in a moment.

Then there are three cases in which the question was whether income to which the taxpayer was entitled was earned income attracting earned income relief. In *Bucks v Bowers (Inspector of Taxes)* [1970] Ch 431, 46 TC 267, merchant bankers in the course of their business held securities and foreign investments, and, following the principles established in *F S Securities Ltd v IRC* [1965] AC 631, 41 TC 666, income taxed by deduction could not be brought into their trading account for the purposes of tax so as to form a component part of the trading profit charged under Sch D Case I and so as to constitute 'earned income' under that head. Pennycuick J held that the share of the income of the securities and investments to which the taxpayer was entitled did not fall within s 525(1) of the Income Tax Act 1952 (which is reproduced with immaterial exceptions in s 530(1) of the Income and Corporation Taxes Act 1970) para (c) of which defined earned income as including—

'... any income which is charged under ... Schedule D and is immediately derived by the individual from the carrying on or exercise by him of his trade, profession or vocation, either as an individual or, in the case of a partnership, as a partner personally acting therein.'

That decision was followed by Templeman J in *Northend (Inspector of Taxes) v White & Leonard and Corbin Greener (a firm) and others* [1975] STC 317, [1975] 1 WLR 1037, where the income in question was interest earned on a clients' deposit account maintained by the respondent firm of solicitors.

In *White (Inspector of Taxes) v Franklin* [1965] 1 WLR 492, 42 TC 283, the taxpayer was an assistant managing director of a company. His mother and brother, to induce him to stay with the company, transferred the income of certain shares to him so long as he should be engaged in the management of the company. It was held by Ungoed-Thomas J and by the Court of Appeal that the income was earned income being 'income arising in respect of any remuneration from any office or employment of profit held by' him within s 525(1)(a) of the Income Tax Act 1952. The Special Commissioner said of that case:

'As I understand the principle that justifies the decision in *White v Franklin* it is that moneys received by an employee otherwise than from an employer may be emoluments from the employment within the meaning of s 530 (and consequently within the meaning of Sch E), notwithstanding that they are, before or after receipt by the employee, brought into charge to tax under some other Schedule or statutory provision than Sch E. In *Franklin* the other provision was what would now be Sch F. The dividends were dividends, taxable as such, but were also emoluments from the employment. What would have kept them out of Sch E was the fact that they were dividends as well as emoluments. They could not be taxed twice.'

A little later, after having expressed the opinion that 'all the facts of this case point
to the interest accruing to the taxpayer from his employment with the club, being
a remuneration for his services', he added: 'It seems to me a reasonably plain case of
emoluments chargeable under Sch E. The *Franklin* decision fortifies me in that
view.'

Counsel for the taxpayer criticised these passages on two grounds. He submitted
that the Special Commissioner, when inferring from the principle that moneys
b received by an employee otherwise than from an employer may be emoluments from
the employment the consequence that they were 'consequently within the meaning
of Sch E', erred. The Special Commissioner overlooked the fact that in *White v
Franklin* the question was whether the income in question was earned income not
whether it was Sch E income, and overlooked the distinction clearly drawn in *Dale
v IRC* between the source of a payment and its character in the hands of the
c recipient. He submitted that while income which is Sch E income will almost
inevitably if not inevitably be earned income the converse, that earned income must
be Sch E income, is not true. In *White v Franklin* the dividends to which the
taxpayer became entitled and in respect of which he claimed to be entitled to earned
income relief would today be taxable under Sch F and (by virtue of s 87(3) of the
Finance Act 1972) chargeable only under Sch F.

d With the greatest respect to counsel for the taxpayer's argument I think this
criticism is captious. The question in *White v Franklin* was whether the income was
part of the taxpayer's remuneration for acting as assistant managing director or
whether 'he was being paid as a member of the family, and that, if he did not qualify,
the income would be paid to other members of the family, and that, therefore, truly
looked at, this was merely a family arrangement arising from the bounty of his
e mother and his elder brother' (see per Harman LJ [1965] 1 WLR 492 at 515, 42 TC
283 at 296). The Court of Appeal treated the question as whether the income was
remuneration and took the view that it was. That entailed the conclusion that it was
earned income. If it was remuneration then under the law as it then stood
(distributions by a company not falling within any of the Schedules) it was taxable
under Sch E alone.

f Counsel for the taxpayer's second criticism was that the Special Commissioner
placed too much emphasis on *White v Franklin* (which all the members of the Court
of Appeal regarded as a borderline case) and paid too little regard to *Bucks v Bowers*
and *Northend v White & Leonard and Corbin Greener*. I think there is a clear
distinction between these two cases. Income which arises in the course of carrying
on a trade ('in respect of' the trade) may arise incidentally and not directly or in the
words of s 525 of the Income Tax Act 1952 'immediately' from the trade. That was
g the character of the income in question in *Bucks v Bowers* and *Northend v White &
Leonard and Corbin Greener*. By contrast the charge under Sch E extends to all
emoluments accruing or arising to an employee in return for acting as an employee
and not for some other reason or 'for something else'. And income so arising attracts
earned income relief which is very widely defined in s 530(1)(a) of the 1970 Act.

h Difficult questions may arise as to the way in which income within the scope of
Sch E falls to be taxed if it also falls prima facie within the terms of another Schedule:
though now if it falls within Sch F, Sch E is excluded by s 87(3) of the Finance Act
1972. In *Dale v IRC*, Lord Normand specifically left open the question whether the
annuity in that case was taxable by deduction under Case III. In practice these
questions are unlikely to arise. Case V now specifically excludes 'income consisting
of emoluments of any office or employment'. Moreover, *Salisbury House Estate Ltd
j v Fry (Inspector of Taxes)* [1930] AC 432, 15 TC 267, is authority for the proposition
that Sch D is a residual Schedule providing for the taxation of income not dealt with
specifically (see per Lord Atkin [1930] AC 432 at 454–455, 15 TC 267 at 318–319).
So if emoluments of an office or employment are taxable under Sch E they are
excluded from Sch D. Thus in practice the only questions that are likely to arise are
whether income which falls within some other Schedule attracts earned income
relief and whether tax is deductible at source.

Counsel for the taxpayer took me through the history of Case V. Originally income from employment outside the United Kingdom was taxed under Case V. *a* Foreign employments were transferred to Sch E by the Finance Act 1956 and the words 'not being income consisting of emoluments of any office or employment' were then added to Case V. I cannot see that the history of these words advances counsel for the taxpayer's argument. Case V must be construed as it stands. Moreover, even if those words had not been included in Case V the *Salisbury House Estate* case is authority for the proposition that foreign employment having been *b* brought within Sch E the emoluments could not be taxable under Sch D.

In my judgment therefore the Special Commissioner reached the right conclusion and for the right reason. It follows that the appeal must be dismissed with costs.

Appeal dismissed with costs.

c

Solicitors: *Herbert Reeves & Co* (for the taxpayer); *Solicitor of Inland Revenue.*

Siew Ling Choo   Barrister.

Note
Napier v Griffiths (Inspector of Taxes)

COURT OF APPEAL, CIVIL DIVISION
RALPH GIBSON, NICHOLLS LJJ AND SIR DENYS BUCKLEY
12 DECEMBER 1990

Assessment – Estimated assessment – Burden of proof – Appeal against assessment – Failure of taxpayer to produce accounts – Taxpayer complaining that case stated did not set out certain matters in dispute – Whether case stated should be remitted for amendment.

Notes

For the power of the court to remit a case to the commissioners, see Simon's Taxes Division A3.710.

For expenses generally and travelling expenses, see ibid, Division E4.701–708.

Case referred to in judgment

Edwards (Inspector of Taxes) v Old Bushmill's Distillery Co Ltd (in liquidation) (1924) 10 TC 285, HL.

Appeal

Alec William Napier, the taxpayer, appealed against a decision of Vinelott J (see [1989] STC 811) dated 6 October 1989 whereby, on a case stated by a Special Commissioner, he dismissed the taxpayer's motion to remit the case for amendment and upheld the decision of the commissioner dismissing his appeal against assessments to income tax under Sch D for the years 1981–82 to 1983–84. The facts are set out in the judgment of Ralph Gibson LJ.

The taxpayer appeared in person.
Nicholas Warren for the Crown.

RALPH GIBSON LJ. This is an appeal by Mr Napier (the taxpayer) from the decision of Vinelott J of 6 October 1989 whereby, on a case stated by a Special Commissioner of the Income Tax Acts, pursuant to s 56 of the Taxes Management Act 1970, he dismissed the taxpayer's motion to remit the case for amendment and confirmed the determination of the commissioner. The judgment of Vinelott J is reported at [1989] STC 811, and it is not necessary, therefore, for me to set out the facts and history of this matter. The taxpayer has appeared in person before this court, as he did before Vinelott J.

I will say at once that, in my judgment, and for the reasons which follow, this appeal should be dismissed.

The appeal is concerned with assessments made by the inspector under Sch D for the years 1980–81 and for each of the years 1981–82, 1982–83 and 1983–84. The taxpayer produced no accounts for the years 1981–82 onwards. The appeals were first before the Special Commissioner on 3 June 1985. Assessments under Sch E for the years 1976–77 and up to 1979–80 which are irrelevant to this appeal were confirmed. An assessment under Sch D for the year 1980–81 was discharged as the taxpayer had no relevant earnings, and the Sch E assessment for 1980–81 relating to the period between 5 April and a date in May 1980 when the taxpayer's contract with Sperry Gyroscope ended was also confirmed.

The hearing of the appeals as to the assessments for the years 1981–82 onwards
was adjourned so that the taxpayer could produce accounts and figures and, if
possible, agree them with the inspector. No accounts, however, were provided
during the interim period to the inspector or produced at the resumed hearing on
5 December 1985.

After hearing the taxpayer and obtaining his answers to questions put to him and
from evidence about his work provided by the taxpayer at the hearing on 3 June
1985, the Special Commissioner found the facts set out in the case which is set out in
the report to which I have referred, and reached certain conclusions. I need refer
only to some of those conclusions for the purposes of this appeal.

In para 6.2 of the case it was found that, over the years, the contracts under which
the taxpayer had worked varied in length and there were long gaps between them.
He had no contract with anyone between May 1980, when he completed the three-
and-a-half year contract with Sperry Gyroscope, and May 1981 when he began
working for GEC Mechanical Handling.

Then, in para 6.3, paraphrasing what was there said, the taxpayer began work for
GEC on a date agreed to be 10 May 1981.

Finally in para 9.1, the Special Commissioner held ([1989] STC 811 at 812):

> '(1) that the taxpayer was assessable under Sch D for the years under appeal;
> (2) that, having been assessed under Sch E for the immediately preceding years,
> he was to be treated as having commenced a new business in May 1981.'

Questions of law for the opinion of the court are set out in the case (at 813) and
they were as follows:

> '(1) Whether the commissioner was correct in holding that for the years under
> appeal the taxpayer was assessable under Sch D.
> (2) Whether the commissioner was correct in holding that for the purpose of
> computing his liability to tax under Sch D the taxpayer was to be treated as if
> he had started a new business in May 1981.
> (3) Whether the commissioner was entitled to determine the assessments on
> the basis of the estimated figures proffered by the taxpayer and not dissented
> from by the inspector.
> (4) Whether the commissioner was correct in holding that no expenditure
> was deductible in respect of the flat at Welling.'

As to question 1, in the proceedings before Vinelott J no issue was raised by either
side as to it. The judge said (at 816): 'There is no doubt that the taxpayer was
assessable under Sch D. That much has always been common ground between him
and the Revenue'. In this court the taxpayer submitted that there was no evidence
before the Special Commissioner and no facts found in the case sufficient to support
the conclusion. Since the Crown had raised the question as a matter of law, and
since the taxpayer now thought that the conclusion might be wrong, the case should,
he said, be remitted so that specific findings of fact could be made. There is, in my
view, no ground of appeal in this point at all. The fact that the taxpayer was
assessable under Sch D was and had been common ground throughout, and it is, in
my view, far too late to put forward that point as an appeal in this court.

As to question 2 this was, as Vinelott J said, the central issue. The taxpayer accepts
that the judge correctly stated the substance of the importance of the point to his tax
liability. The judge rejected the point because, as he found, there was no evidence
adduced by the taxpayer at the hearing to support the claim advanced that he had
commenced his business in May 1980. The judge continued:

> 'The only evidence before the commissioner was that his engagement by
> GEC commenced on 10 May 1981 and that between that date and the earlier
> termination of his employment by Sperry Gyroscope he had not earned
> anything. There was no evidence that he was actively engaged in any business

activities, albeit not producing any profit, or in doing anything preparatory to
commencing a business.'

The taxpayer submitted that that was wrong. He referred us to a note of what was
said at the hearing before the Special Commissioner. The words on which he relied
read as follows:

'At the end of May 1980 [the taxpayer] ceased work under a contract with a
company called Centre Dynamics Ltd. and on 22 June 1980 he wrote to London
Provincial 20 informing them that he had returned to being self-employed.'

That was the passage to which we were referred.

That was not part of the evidence or of the submissions of the taxpayer to the
commissioner but was part of an explanation or account of the facts being given by
Mr Griffiths (the inspector). The letter of 22 June 1980 was, as we were told, in a
bundle before the Special Commissioner but it does not appear that any reference
was made to it, other than that to which I have referred, at any stage in the hearing.
The taxpayer intended to refer to the letter before Vinelott J but, as he showed us in
the transcript of the proceedings before the judge, the taxpayer got sidetracked in
his submissions and did not revert to it.

It was produced to us and we have looked at it. It contains that which the inspector
said it contained, namely information that he had returned to being self-employed,
and it contained a paragraph to which the taxpayer drew particular attention, which
reads as follows:

'I have at intervals reaffirmed my claims to have losses on some of my activities
set off against profits on others and/or be carried forward. This letter reaffirms
such claims.'

After the argument was concluded we were told by counsel for the Crown that it
appears from the documents before the court that that letter, although in the bundle
taken to the hearing by the inspector, was not among the documents retained by the
Special Commissioner for her further consideration of the case, and it is therefore
submitted that the probability is that she did not expressly consider it.

The taxpayer, on that factual basis, referred us to 23 Halsbury's Laws (4th edn)
para 1628, and in particular the passage which says, with reference to amendment
and remission of the case stated:

'If the facts stated as found are insufficient to enable the point of law to be
determined, the case may either be returned for amendment or remitted for the
appeal to be reheard without requiring the subsequent resubmission of the case
to the court.'

In the footnote there is a reference to the case of *Edwards (Inspector of Taxes) v Old
Bushmill's Distillery Co Ltd (in liquidation)* (1924) 10 TC 285, a decision of the House
of Lords, in a passage to which the taxpayer referred our attention.

The taxpayer's contention was that, since there was evidence before the Special
Commissioner which showed that he had started business in May 1980 and not in
May 1981, the judge was wrong to refuse to remit the case for the finding of further
facts on that issue and for amendment of the case.

For my part, I would reject that submission. Counsel for the Crown pointed out
that the Special Commissioner, in the passage in the case to which I have referred,
found that the taxpayer had no contract with anyone between May 1980 and May
1981. It is true that, although having no contract, the taxpayer might have been
carrying on a business, for example doing work on software with a view to earning a
profit therefrom at a later date. The taxpayer referred us to s 170(5) of the Income
and Corporation Taxes Act 1970. The taxpayer, however, gave no evidence to the
Special Commissioner to show that he had been doing anything to that effect.
Counsel for the Crown also pointed out that in the note of the proceedings there is a

passage which reads as follows. It is just towards the end of the minute-clerk's note
book.   *a*

'Miss Wix [the commissioner] proceeded with the assessments and reminded
[the taxpayer] that unless further evidence was forthcoming she would have to
confirm the amounts as assessed by the Revenue. She said that they would be
dealt with in year order and commenced with that of 1981/82 and asked [the
taxpayer] if he could demonstrate that it was excessive. [The taxpayer] replied
that he had only commenced working 15 days previous to this accounting year   *b*
and that was towards the end of May 1981.'

The taxpayer urged on us that that record is, or is probably, mistaken. He must,
he said, have said 'only commenced earning 15 days previous to this accounting year'
and not 'working', and in support of that contention he commented that the clerk
making the note was probably such as to draw no distinction between 'earning' and *c*
'working'.

For my part, I can find in these submissions no basis for departing from the
conclusion of Vinelott J on this point. I agree that, even with the letter of 22 June
1980, there is no evidence to support the claim that he commenced his business in
May 1980. The letter, even if regarded as evidence before the Special Commissioner,
did not constitute either a claim that he had been engaged in business since May   *d*
1980, or evidence to show that he had.

I turn to question 3. The judge (at 816) merely noted that no criticism was made
of the way in which the estimates were arrived at or of the computations based on
them. The taxpayer in this court repeated what he had said in his RSC Ord 53
proceedings, namely that he had been stopped before the Special Commissioner
from making any criticism. There is no ground of appeal in this court in these   *e*
proceedings on that contention. All criticisms of the conduct of the hearing by the
inspector have been considered and rejected. That is not to say that the taxpayer
was not or is not free in this court to advance the grounds of appeal addressed to the
contents of the case or to the absence of necessary facts. There is on the third
question, in my judgment, no basis for departing from the judgment of the judge.

As to question 4, the deductions of expenditure in respect of the flat at Welling, *f*
the taxpayer did not in this court pursue the point.

The further matter of capital allowances on the value of the taxpayer's car was
acknowledged by the taxpayer to be concerned with trivial sums and he did not
pursue that point either. He did, however, complain that the assessments had been
determined before he was given the opportunity to deal with allowances for the cost
of travel by car other than any capital allowances. He referred us to the note of the *g*
proceedings before the commissioner. There is a reference there by the commissioner
to her having determined the assessments and followed by the taxpayer inquiring as
to whether his car was an allowable expense. The taxpayer acknowledged that there
was no reference by him as recorded in the notes to any cost of running the car being
claimed as an allowance or an expense. He told us that he was stopped by the Special
Commissioner holding up her hand so that there was no note made by the notetaker *h*
of that means of stopping him. Having seen and heard the taxpayer, and read the
papers, I am, for my part, confident that, if the taxpayer had intended to put
forward evidence of costs of this nature, he would have done so and, if it had not
been received, he would have protested in a way which would not have escaped the
notice of anyone present. There is, in my view, nothing in that point either.

I have not mentioned every point that the taxpayer has advanced. For my part, I *j*
would uphold the judgment of Vinelott J for the reasons which he set out in it and I
would dismiss the appeal.

NICHOLLS LJ. I agree. I add only this on the principal matter of which the
taxpayer complains. I do not find it surprising that before the Special Commissioner

a there was no evidence directed at the taxpayer's contention, advanced before the judge and before this court, concerning the date on which he commenced the relevant business. The absence of such evidence is not surprising because, so far as I can see, before the Special Commissioner the taxpayer did not advance a case that he had commenced the relevant business in May 1980. Hence the lack of evidence directed at this point. It was not a live issue before the Special Commissioner.

For the reasons given by my Lord, I too would dismiss this appeal.

b **SIR DENYS BUCKLEY.** I agree with both judgments.

Appeal dismissed with costs. Leave to appeal to the House of Lords refused.

Solicitor: *Solicitor of Inland Revenue.*

Siew Ling Choo   Barrister.

Inland Revenue Commissioners v Spencer-Nairn   *a*

FIRST DIVISION OF THE INNER HOUSE OF THE COURT OF SESSION AS THE COURT OF
EXCHEQUER IN SCOTLAND
THE LORD PRESIDENT (HOPE), LORD ALLANBRIDGE AND LORD WYLIE
22, 23 NOVEMBER, 14 DECEMBER 1990   *b*

*Capital transfer tax – Disposition – Transfer of value – Disposition to a connected
person resulting in diminution of value of transferor's estate – Whether transferor
intended to confer gratuitous benefit on any person – Whether disposition such as might
be expected in transaction at arm's length between unconnected persons – Finance Act
1975, ss 20(2), (4).*   *c*

In 1975 the transferor, who owned a farm in Fife, at the request of his son and
relying exclusively on the advice of his family's factor, accountant and tax adviser
(B), let it to a Jersey-registered company at a rent less than its then fair rent, virtually
the whole of which was absorbed in its repair and maintenance. The tenant then
demanded that the transferor should at his own expense replace the piggery   *d*
buildings. B valued the farm at £177,730 and advised the transferor that since the
cost of such replacement and necessary repairs was £80,000 (which the transferor
could not spare) he should consider selling it for £97,730. B then handled all the
negotiations for its sale in 1976 for £101,350 to another Jersey-registered company
(Domaine). The farm was not advertised for sale and the transferor took no
professional advice other than from B. Neither the transferor nor B appreciated   *e*
until much later that Domaine was, in relation to the transferor, 'a connected person'
within the meaning of s 51(4) of the Finance Act 1975 (the 1975 Act). In due course
the market value of the farm, at the date missives for its sale to Domaine were
exchanged, was determined for the purposes of s 19(3) of the Capital Gains Tax Act
1979 at £199,000 by the Lands Tribunal for Scotland on the basis that on a true
construction of s 5 of the Argicultural Holdings (Scotland) Act 1949 the transferor   *f*
had been under no greater liability to the tenant in relation to the buildings than to
keep them in reasonable repair: so that to replace them would have constituted an
improvement. On 9 January 1989 the Revenue issued to the transferor a notice of
determination to capital transfer tax in respect of his sale to Domaine on the ground
that it constituted a chargeable transfer of value, within s 20(2)ᵃ of the 1975 Act, of
some £94,000. On appeal against that notice, a Special Commissioner found as facts: *g*
(a) that subjectively, the transferor had not intended, when selling the farm to
Domaine, to confer a gratuitous benefit on any person; (b) that the farm had not
then been an attractive proposition and was most unlikely to have been of interest to
an institutional purchaser; (c) that B's belief that the tenant could require the
transferor to spend about £80,000 on repairs and renewals had been reasonable; (d)
that it was not unusual for sellers not to employ professional advisers; (e) that   *h*
telephone calls to institutional investors would not have produced any result; and
(f) that in all the circumstances, B's advice to the transferor had been sound and the
transferor's actions reasonable. He therefore held that the transferor had discharged
the burden of proving, in the terms of s 20(4)(b)ᵇ of the 1975 Act, that the transferor's
disposition of the farm to Domaine had been 'such as might be expected to be
made in a transaction at arm's length between persons not connected with each   *j*
other' so that by virtue of that subsection it had not been 'a transfer of value'.
The Crown appealed to the Inner House, contending that the true and only

---

a   Section 20(2), so far as material, is set out at p 67 *g h*, post
b   Section 20(4), so far as material, is set out at p 67 *h j*, post

reasonable conclusion from the primary facts contradicted the determination of the
a commissioner.

Held – In deciding whether a transferor had discharged the burden imposed on him
by s 20(4)(*b*) of the 1975 Act of proving that a disposition of property by him to a
'connected person' within the meaning of s 51(4) of that Act had been such as might
be expected to be made in a transaction at arm's length between persons not
b connected with each other, the disparity between the price received by him and the
open market value of that property was no more than a single factor to be taken into
consideration; and that in all the circumstances the decision by the commissioner,
that the transferor had discharged that burden, was one he was entitled to make.
Accordingly, the Crown's appeal would be dismissed.

Dictum of Lord Reid in *Duke of Buccleuch v IRC* [1967] 1 AC 506 at 524
c considered.

Dictum of Lord Radcliffe in *Edwards (Inspector of Taxes) v Bairstow* (1954) 36
TC 207 at 229 applied.

Notes
d For transfer of value, see Foster: Inheritance Tax, Division C1.

For dispositions lacking gratuitous intent, see ibid, Division C1.43.

For arm's length transactions, see ibid, C1.44.

For the Finance Act 1975, s 20(2), (4) (now the Inheritance Tax Act 1984, ss 3(1),
10(1)), see ibid, Part S.

e

Cases referred to in opinions

Buccleuch (Duke) v IRC [1967] 1 AC 506, [1967] 1 All ER 129, HL.
Edwards (Inspector of Taxes) v Bairstow [1956] AC 14, [1955] 3 All ER 48, 36 TC
207, HL.

f

Case stated

I. On 20, 21 and 23 November 1989 a Special Commissioner heard the appeal of
Michael Alastair Spencer-Nairn of Baltilly, Ceres, By Cupar, Fife (the transferor)
against a determination of the Board of Inland Revenue (the Crown) in relation to
g capital transfer tax. That determination was dated 9 January 1989.

II. Shortly stated the question for the commissioner's decision was whether the
transferor's disposition dated 27 August 1976 of part of the estate of Over Rankeilour,
near Cupar, Fife effected a transfer of value which was a chargeable transfer for the
purposes of capital transfer tax.

III. The following witnesses gave evidence before the commissioner: the transferor
h and Mr John Burgess (witnesses of fact); Mr Colin Strang-Steele and Mr James
Gordon Menzies (expert witnesses).

[Paragraph IV listed the documents proved or admitted before the commissioner.]

V. The commissioner's findings of fact on the evidence adduced, the respective
contentions of Mr Brian Gill QC on behalf of the transferor and Mr D S Wishart on
behalf of the Crown and the commissioner's conclusions were set out in his reserved
j decision which was issued on 14 December 1989 and a copy of which was annexed
as part of the case.

VI. On 9 January 1990 the Crown required the Special Commissioners to state
and sign a case for the opinion of the Court of Session as the Court of Exchequer in
Scotland, which case the commissioner stated and signed accordingly.

VII. The question of law for the opinion of the court was whether on the facts as
found the commissioner had erred in holding that the disposition of part of the Over

Rankeilour Estate did not effect a transfer of value and consequently was not a chargeable transfer for the purposes of capital transfer tax.

DECISION

In 1976 Mr Michael Alastair Spencer-Nairn (the transferor) sold Over Rankeilour Farm, near Cupar, Fife (the farm) to a Jersey-registered company, namely Domaine de Herupe Société à Responsabilité Limitée (Domaine). Missives were exchanged on 6 April 1976, entry was granted to Domaine on 16 May 1976, the disposition in favour of Domaine was executed on 27 August 1976 and it was recorded in the Division of the Register of Sasines for the county of Fife on 8 October 1976. It is common ground between the parties that for the purposes of this appeal the relevant date in relation to the sale of the farm to Domaine was 16 May 1976. It is also common ground that the disposition by the transferor in favour of Domaine was a transaction between connected persons for the purposes of s 20(4)(*a*) of the Finance Act 1975 (the 1975 Act).

The Inland Revenue Commissioners (the Crown) contends that the disposition by the transferor of the farm in favour of Domaine constituted a transfer of value and have caused a notice of determination dated 9 January 1989 to be served on the transferor. It is against that notice which the transferor now appeals.

Section 20 of the 1975 Act (which was the relevant statute in relation to the events giving rise to this appeal) is as follows, where relevant:

'(1) The following provisions of this section shall have effect, subject to the other provisions of this Part of this Act, for determining for the purposes of capital transfer tax what is a chargeable transfer and what value is transferred by a chargeable transfer.

(2) Subject to subsections (3) and (4) below, a transfer of value is any disposition made by a person ("the transferor") as a result of which the value of his estate immediately after the disposition is less than it would be but for the disposition; and the amount by which it is less is the value transferred by the transfer . . .

(4) A disposition is not a transfer of value if it is shown that it was not intended, and was not made in a transaction intended, to confer any gratuitous benefit on any person and either—

(*a*) that it was made in a transaction at arm's length between persons not connected with each other, or

(*b*) that it was such as might be expected to be made in a transaction at arm's length between persons not connected with each other . . .'

Accordingly, the transferor has two hurdles to clear. First he must satisfy me that, subjectively, he did not intend to confer any gratuitous benefit on any person when selling the farm to Domaine. Second he must satisfy me that, objectively, the sale of the farm to Domaine was such as might be expected to be made in an arm's length transaction between unconnected persons. He must satisfy me on both counts. It is the Crown's case, as presented by Mr D S Wishart of the Scottish Inland Revenue Solicitor's Office, that the case for the transferor, as presented by Mr Brian Gill, fails on both counts.

The facts

The transferor was never a farmer. At the relevant time he owned heritable estate extending to some 950-odd acres part of which had been in his family since before the First World War and part of which had been purchased in or about the year 1950. The transferor, now aged 80 years and retired, was formerly a director in the family floor covering business. He had little or no experience of farming or estate management and relied heavily on the advice given to him by Mr John Burgess, a chartered accountant and actuary. Besides his accounting qualifications, Mr Burgess had acted as a factor for the Spencer-Nairn family for over 30 years until his retirement in or about 1980. Mr Burgess also acted as factor for third parties outside the Spencer-Nairn family to a limited extent. From 1946 onwards, however, his principal activities were acting on a day-to-day basis as factor, accountant and tax adviser to the Spencer-Nairn family. In that capacity he negotiated lettings to their tenants and also negotiated the sale of heritable property. By far the larger part of the Spencer-Nairn estate was let to agricultural tenants.

That estate consisted broadly of three farms; namely the farm, Westhall Farm (lying to the north of the farm) and Gathercauld Farm, with which latter farm this appeal is not concerned. The farm and Westhall Farm lay broadly within a ring fence although divided from each other by the Westhall ditch. Together those two farms amounted to some 746 acres, of which total the farm comprised some 600 acres.

At the relevant time the buildings on the farm consisted of Over Rankeilour House, a large and imposing mansion, the steading, the farm manager's house and two cottages. The steading included a substantial pig breeding unit, including a farrowing house, the condition of which became a matter of concern for the transferor in 1976.

In 1972 the transferor let the farm (with other heritable property) to his son who was at that time a student at the Royal Agricultural College at Cirencester. The transferor hoped that his son would run the estate in due course.

However, in 1974 the transferor's son abandoned his agricultural career and took up an accountancy appointment in the Channel Islands. At the same time he renounced the lease from his father and a new lease on the same terms was granted to a Jersey-registered company, Over Rankeilour Farms Ltd. The new lease to the company followed immediately on the renunciation of his lease by the transferor's son.

The oral evidence before me was to the effect that the rent payable for the farm both by the transferor's son and by Over Rankeilour Farms Ltd was £10 per acre but the minute of the lease to Over Rankeilour Farms Ltd shows the rent at £7,500 pa for the farm, Westhall Farm and Gathercauld Farm totalling some 960 acres. I infer therefore that the oral evidence in relation to the rent referred to the usable areas of the farm as it is clear that part of the farm constituted woodland. I accept the oral evidence of Mr C B Strang-Steele that a rent of £10 per acre was not a fair rent for the farm in 1975 and that it should have been higher. When granting the lease to Over Rankeilour Farms Ltd the transferor relied exclusively on the advice of Mr Burgess.

I infer that the transferor granted the lease to Over Rankeilour Farms Ltd at the request of his son.

Following the grant of the lease in 1975 the transferor found that virtually the whole of the rent which he received from his tenant was absorbed by the cost of repairs and maintenance of the let subjects. In addition the farm manager employed by the tenant was making insistent demands that the piggery buildings should be replaced at the landlord's expense. Faced with such demands Mr Burgess obtained a report from the Edinburgh and East of Scotland College of Agriculture on the state of the piggery and on the basis of that report and further advice from an architect he advised the transferor that the estimated cost of replacing the piggery and carrying out necessary repairs to the farm manager's house amounted to some £80,000.

The transferor was unable to fund such expenditure and therefore Mr Burgess advised him that he should consider the possibility of selling the farm and Westhall Farm. The transferor was unwilling to sell Westhall Farm as the farmhouse was his residence and he maintained a sentimental attachment to it. An alternative plan was therefore devised whereby the transferor would sell the farm, which comprised all the land to the south of the Westhall ditch. It included the mansion house, the farm manager's house, the farm cottages and the steading including the piggeries.

No advertising of the farm took place and no professional advice was taken by the transferor in relation to the sale other than that which he obtained from Mr Burgess.

The whole of the negotiations in connection with the sale of the farm were handled
by Mr Burgess alone.   a
  Mr Burgess first prepared a valuation of the farm using his own experience and
knowledge together with sales information published by the Scottish Landowner's
Federation showing average prices and trends. At that time in addition to acting as
accountant and factor to the transferor Mr Burgess also prepared the farm accounts
for the tenant. His valuation was therefore designed to be fair to both parties
although he was not acting for the transferor's tenant when negotiating the sale of b
the farm. Mr Burgess's valuation of the farm was in the sum of £177,730 gross from
which he deducted the estimated expenditure required on the piggery and the farm
manager's house of £80,000 leaving a net valuation of £97,730.
  Mr Burgess's approach to the tenant via the farm manager, to purchase at that
figure met with a rebuff. The tenant did not wish to purchase.
  A short while later Domaine offered to purchase the farm for £101,350. Mr c
Burgess's advice to the transferor was that as the offer exceeded his valuation it
should be accepted quickly and the transferor concurred.

The expert evidence

From the oral evidence given by Mr Strang-Steele for the transferor and by Mr
J G Menzies, district valuer for the Tyneside region, on behalf of the Crown, I d
accept the following propositions: (1) As I have noted previously, the rent reserved
in the letting to Over Rankeilour Farms Ltd in 1975 was too low. (2) There was a
gradually rising market for agricultural land offered for sale with vacant possession
in 1976. Prices of agricultural land rose much more sharply in 1977. (3) The farm
enjoyed no development potential and possessed no 'hope value' and there was no
prospect of obtaining early vacant possession from the tenant. (4) It was most e
unlikely that the farm would have been of interest to an institutional purchaser in
1976. (5) The farm was not an attractive proposition to a purchaser in the state and
condition in which it was in 1976. (6) Mr Burgess's belief that the tenant could
require the landlord to expend a sum in the region of £80,000 on repairs and
renewals and Mr Burgess's interpretation of the terms of the lease to Over Rankeilour
Farms Ltd and in particular his interpretation of s 5 of the Agricultural Holdings f
(Scotland) Act 1949 and the advice which he tendered to the transferor in the light
of his beliefs was reasonable. At that time the interpretation of s 5 was a matter for
argument which had not been settled finally by the courts and was looked on as a
'grey area'. (7) Accordingly it was reasonable for Mr Burgess to make a deduction
from his valuation of the farm in relation to repairs and renewals which he believed
the tenant could demand.   g

Conclusions

Mr Wishart, for the Crown, faced a difficult task in this appeal for although the
burden of proof lay on the transferor, knowledge of the circumstances surrounding
the disposal of the farm to Domaine lay almost entirely with the transferor, his
advisers and his family. Accordingly Mr Wishart has had to found his case on three h
known circumstances, namely: (1) that the rent payable under the lease between the
transferor and Over Rankeilour Farms Ltd was too low; (2) that the disposal of the
farm took place between connected persons; and (3) that in the opinion of Mr
Menzies and of the Lands Tribunal (the tribunal), whose opinion was sought in
relation to the transferor's capital gains tax appeal, the price paid by Domaine for
the farm was too low.   j
  From these three known circumstances Mr Wishart has invited me to make a
series of inferences and assumptions.
  I will deal first with the subjective test contained in the opening words of s 20(4)
of the 1975 Act. Did the transferor intend to confer a gratuitous benefit on any
person when selling the farm to Domaine?
  Having heard the evidence of the transferor and Mr Burgess, and having studied

their behaviour whilst giving evidence, I have come to the conclusion that the
transferor did not intend to confer any gratuitous benefit on any person when
disposing of Over Rankeilour Farm in 1976. The transferor's behaviour at the time
may have seemed unusual or unwise to the officious bystander but I have come to
the conclusion that despite his business experience as a director of his family floor
covering firm the transferor is a somewhat unworldly person. He was not a farmer
and did not mix with other farmers and appears to have had little knowledge of
agricultural practices and values. Mr Burgess had advised the transferor's father and
his family for many years and the transferor trusted him completely. Although in
some financial difficulty and wishing to obtain the best price for his land he relied
completely on the advice of Mr Burgess once the extent of the land to be sold had
been decided. The transferor's only difference of opinion with Mr Burgess arose
when he suggested that both Westhall Farm and the farm should be sold. That
difference of opinion arose not in relation to values or farming or estate management
practices but out of sentiment because the transferor did not wish to give up his
residence at Westhall Farm.

In my judgment the level of the rent paid by the tenant of the farm is a neutral
factor in this appeal. The level of the rent receivable by the landlord of the farm
affected the respective valuations made by the expert witnesses in the case but it was
not suggested that the valuation should adopt different (higher) rental values. In any
event, the rent payable by the tenant of the farm was determined by Mr Burgess,
who believed honestly, but wrongly, that it was a market rent. Finally, the tribunal
rejected the institutional method of valuation using rental values and arrived at their
valuation on the basis of capital values of tenanted land.

Mr Burgess's advice to the transferor was given honestly at the time and on the
evidence before me I take the view that neither the transferor nor Mr Burgess
appreciated that they were dealing with a connected person when agreeing the sale
of the farm to Domaine. Such knowledge came to them much later.

I now move on to the second, objective test contained in s 20(4)(b) of the 1975 Act.
Was the disposition such as might be expected to be made in a transaction at arm's
length between persons not connected with each other? Mr Wishart submits that I
should ignore completely what actually happened in 1976 and decide the matter on
the basis of what would have occurred between two hypothetical parties in a
hypothetical arm's length transaction at that time. It is, however, necessary to
compare what actually occurred with what is likely to have taken place objectively
between unconnected persons dealing with each other at arm's length, in relation to
the sale of the farm.

I had the benefit of hearing expert evidence from Mr Menzies for the Crown and
from Mr Strang-Steele for the transferor. Where the opinions of those two witnesses
differ I prefer the evidence of Mr Strang-Steele. Mr Menzies, although a most
experienced district valuer, had little experience relevant to the transaction which
was the subject of this appeal. He had no experience in private practice, no
experience of the sale of a farm to an institution and no experience of the sale of a let
farm other than to a sitting tenant. By contrast Mr Strang-Steele, as the senior
partner of a well-known firm of chartered surveyors had all the relevant experience
which Mr Menzies lacked, as he generously acknowledged.

Mr Wishart has contended that the transferor should have led evidence from an
expert witness as to the state of the law in relation to s 5 of the Agricultural Holdings
(Scotland) Act 1949 in 1976. I reject that submission and I am content to accept the
evidence of Mr Strang-Steele as a competent practitioner in the profession of
surveyor and land agent, whose business it was to apply or to attempt to apply that
legislation. He believed that the law in relation to s 5 was unclear and that differing
opinions were honestly held by practitioners as to the precise meaning of the section.
It was a 'grey area'.

Mr Strang-Steele stated that it was by no means unusual for sellers not to employ
professional advisers. He commended the advice and actions of Mr Burgess. His

initial approach to the tenant was correct. Once the tenant had decided not to purchase few options remained. In the opinion of Mr Strang-Steele institutional a investors would not have been interested in purchasing the farm in its state and condition in 1976 and bearing in mind that it was let to a corporate tenant. Mr Menzies suggested that telephone calls should have been made to some of the institutional investors, but on the evidence of Mr Strang-Steele I am prepared to accept that such telephone calls would not have produced any result at that time. There was also evidence that institutional investors take a considerable while to b reach a decision and whilst awaiting such a decision, which in any event was likely to be in the negative, Domaine might well have withdrawn its offer to purchase. Judged against the yardstick of the advice which Mr Strang-Steele would have given in an arm's length transaction, he believes that Mr Burgess's advice was sound and the actions of the transferor reasonable in all the circumstances.

Mr Wishart submitted that the hypothetical purchaser would have paid £199,000, c which is the value attributed to the farm by the tribunal in relation to the transferor's capital gains tax appeal. That valuation was, however, reached on the basis of the tribunal's ruling on the meaning and effect of s 5 of the Agricultural Holdings (Scotland) Act 1949. That ruling was not available to Mr Burgess in 1976 and I accept Mr Strang-Steele's opinion that Mr Burgess's view of the law was not an unreasonable one. In any event, the transferor was anxious to sell both to improve d his own financial position and to relieve himself of the liabilities which attached to ownership of the farm. He accepted Mr Burgess's valuation which has been shown to be one which could be honestly and reasonably held and therefore it is hardly surprising that when the transferor received an offer from Domaine which was higher than the figure contained in Mr Burgess's valuation, he accepted it.

On the evidence before me advertising the farm would have been to no avail and e it is highly probable that had the transferor not accepted the offer from Domaine, no sale of the farm would have taken place in 1976.

The appeal succeeds and I quash the notice of determination.

William C Galbraith QC and *J W McNeill* for the Crown.
W A Nimmo Smith QC and *Colin J Tyre* for the transferor. f

The court made avizandum.

14 December. The following opinions of the court were delivered.

THE LORD PRESIDENT (HOPE). The question for the decision of the Special g Commissioner (the commissioner) was whether the transferor's disposition of Over Rankeilour Farm (the farm) to a Jersey-registered company named Domaine de Herupe Société à Responsabilité Limitée (Domaine) was a transfer of value which was a chargeable transfer for the purposes of capital transfer tax.

Missives for the sale of the farm were exchanged between parties on 6 April 1976. Domaine took entry to the property on 16 May 1976, and a disposition in their h favour was executed on 27 August and recorded in the Register of Sasines on 8 October 1976. It is common ground that the date of the sale was 16 May 1976 and that this was the date of the disposition made by the transferor for the purposes of s 20 of the Finance Act 1975 (the 1975 Act). The price at which the farm was sold to Domaine was £101,350, but Domaine was connected with the transferor in accordance with s 63 of the Capital Gains Tax Act 1979 and, as regards capital j transfer tax, with s 51(4) of the 1975 Act. So the actual consideration was irrelevant for the purposes of calculating the capital gains tax liability, the transaction being deemed to have taken place at a price equal to the market value of the asset. The question of the open market value as at the valuation date, which was agreed for the purposes of capital gains tax to be 6 April 1976, was referred to the Lands Tribunal for Scotland (the tribunal) for their determination. On 11 December 1984 the

tribunal pronounced an order determining the open market value of the farm at that
a date to be £199,000 (see *Spencer-Nairn v IRC* 1985 SLT (Lands Tr) 46). That
decision then formed the basis of a determination by the Board of Inland Revenue
(the Crown) in relation to capital transfer tax which was dated 9 January 1989. This
was that there had been a chargeable transfer for the purposes of that tax and that
the net value transferred by the transferor was approximately £94,000. In the
hearing before the commissioner it was accepted that the transaction could not be
b described as one which was made at arm's length between persons not connected
with each other. He held that the transferor had nevertheless not made a transfer of
value. He was satisfied that the disposition was not intended to confer any gratuitous
benefit on Domaine and that it was such as might be expected to be made in a
transaction at arm's length between persons not connected with each other. The
affect of his decision was that the transferor was entitled to the benefit of s 20(4) of
c the 1975 Act and that there was no chargeable transfer.

The Crown has now appealed against this decision. The question of law which
the commissioner has now stated for our opinion is whether, on the facts as found
by him, he erred in holding that the disposition did not effect a transfer of value and
consequently was not a chargeable transfer for the purposes of capital transfer tax.

In opening the argument which we heard in support of the appeal, counsel for the
d Crown accepted that the commissioner had identified correctly the nature of the
questions to which he had to address his mind in applying s 20(4) to the facts. As the
commissioner put it, the transferor had to satisfy him first that, subjectively, he did
not intend to confer any gratuitous benefit on any person when selling the farm to
Domaine and second that, objectively, the sale of the farm to Domaine was such as
much be expected to be made in an arm's length transaction between connected
e persons. It was not contended that the commissioner had erred in his decision on
the first question, which was that the transferor did not intend to confer any
gratuitous benefit on any person when disposing of the farm in 1976. It should be
noted that the commissioner held that neither the transferor nor his factor, Mr
Burgess, appreciated that they were dealing with a connected person when they
agreed to sell the farm to Domaine. But it was submitted that the commissioner had
f failed properly to apply the second test, because he did not examine the question
objectively as to what might be expected to have happened had this been a
transaction at arm's length between persons who were not connected with each
other. It was also submitted that, even if the objective test had been correctly
applied, nevertheless his decision was contrary to the true and only reasonable
conclusion which was open to him on the facts as he found them to be, and that for
g this reason also his decision was erroneous in point of law.

The relevant provisions of s 20 of the 1975 Act, now to be found in ss 3(1) and
10(1) of the Inheritance Tax Act 1984, are as follows:

'(2) Subject to subsections (3) and (4) below, a transfer of value is any
disposition made by a person ("the transferor") as a result of which the value of
h his estate immediately after the disposition is less than it would be but for the
disposition; and the amount by which it is less is the value transferred by the
transfer . . .
(4) A disposition is not a transfer of value if it is shown that it was not intended,
and was not made in a transaction intended, to confer any gratuitous benefit on
any person and either—

j (a) that it was made in a transaction at arm's length between persons not
connected with each other, or
(b) that it was such as might be expected to be made in a transaction at arm's
length between persons not connected with each other . . .'

It is plain from an examination of these two subsections that sub-s (4) has no
function in cases where the disposition takes place at full value, with the result that

immediately after it there is no diminution in the value of the transferor's estate. Its only purpose is to deal with cases where the value of his estate is less than it was before the transfer because the disposition was for a price less than the open market value of the property as defined by s 38(1) of the 1975 Act. That being its purpose, it is also plain that transactions which are gratuitous or which were for less than the open market value of the property may nevertheless be taken out of charge if they satisfy the tests which it lays down. The fact that the transaction was for less than the open market value cannot be conclusive of the issue at this stage, otherwise the subsection would be deprived of its content. The gratuitous element in the transaction becomes therefore no more than a factor, which must be weighed in the balance with all the other facts and circumstances to see whether the onus which is on the transferor has been discharged. I mention this point at the outset because much emphasis was laid in the argument for the Crown on the fact that the diminution in value which had occurred in this case was very great. It was said that the fact that there was a sale at less than open market value was clear in this case, and that a very careful approach to the facts was required. But questions of value as such were not for the commissioner to decide (see para 7(4) of Sch 4 to the 1975 Act). His task was to apply the wording of s 20(4) to the facts which he found to be proved. Since it is inevitable in all these cases that there is a difference between the price paid and the open market value as defined by the 1975 Act, the weight to be attached to that factor was a matter for him in the light of such reasons for the shortfall as were established by the evidence.

It is appropriate, therefore, to look now at the facts as set forth by the commissioner. He did not enumerate in separate and distinct detail all the facts which he found to be proved. In para V of the case he tells us that his findings of fact on the evidence are set out in the reserved decision which he issued on 14 December 1989, a copy of which was annexed as part of the case. The decision contains a section which is headed '*The facts*' before going on to summarise the expert evidence and then to describe the conclusions reached by the commissioner. But it became clear in the course of the argument that the first section is not exhaustive of the primary facts found proved by him, and that it is necessary to refer to parts of the other two sections in order to arrive at a complete picture of what these were. Fortunately, counsel on both sides were agreed that this could be done, and in particular that propositions which the commissioner accepted from the expert evidence which are set out in the last section of the decision also formed part of the facts on which his determination was reached. Nevertheless it would have been preferable for the facts to be set out in the body of the case as stated by the commissioner so that we knew precisely what these were when we came to answer the question whether his decision was erroneous in point of law (see *Edwards (Inspector of Taxes) v Bairstow* [1956] AC 14 at 36, 36 TC 207 at 229 per Lord Radcliffe).

I do not need to set out again in this opinion the whole of the factual background which is described in the first of the three sections in the decision. The important points for present purposes are as follows: (a) The transferor had little or no experience of farming or estate management and relied heavily on the advice given to him by Mr John Burgess, a chartered accountant and actuary. Mr Burgess had acted as factor, accountant and tax adviser to the Spencer-Nairn family for many years, and he had also acted as factor for third parties outside the family to a limited extent. In the former capacity he negotiated lettings to tenants and also negotiated the sale of heritable property. (b) The farm was let to a Jersey-registered company, Over Rankeilour Farms Ltd. The lease was granted to the company in 1975, and the rent payable was £10 per acre which was not a fair rent for the farm at that date. When granting the lease to the company, the transferor had relied exclusively on the advice of Mr Burgess. (c) Virtually the whole of the rent which was payable by the company to the transferor was absorbed by the cost of repairs and maintenance of the let subjects. In addition the tenant's farm manager was making insistent demands that the piggery buildings on the farm should be replaced at the landlord's expense. Mr Burgess advised the transferor that the estimated cost of replacing the

piggery and carrying out necessary repairs to the farm manager's house amounted
to about £80,000. The transferor was unable to fund such expenditure, and he was
advised by Mr Burgess that he should consider the possibility of selling the farm.
(d) Mr Burgess prepared a valuation of the farm, using his own experience and
knowledge together with sales information published by the Scottish Landowners'
Federation showing average prices and yields. His valuation of the farm was in the
sum of £177,730 gross from which he deducted the estimated expenditure on the
piggery and the farm manager's house amounting to £80,000. This left a net
valuation of £97,730. His approach to the tenant via the farm manager to purchase
at that figure met with a rebuff because the tenant did not wish to purchase.
(e) A short while later Domaine offered to purchase the farm at £101,350. Mr
Burgess's advice to the transferor was that, as the offer exceeded his valuation, it
should be accepted quickly and the transferor concurred. No advertising of the farm
took place, and no professional advice was taken by the transferor in relation to the
sale other than that which he obtained from Mr Burgess. The whole of the
negotiations in connection with the sale of the farm were handled by Mr Burgess
alone.

The following additional facts are taken from the section headed '*The expert
evidence*': (f) The farm was not an attractive proposition to a purchaser in the state
and condition in which it was in 1976. It was most unlikely that it would have been
of interest to an institutional purchaser at that time. (g) Mr Burgess's belief that the
tenant could require the landlord to expend about £80,000 on repairs and renewals
and the advice which he tendered to the transferor in the light of his beliefs was
reasonable. This belief was based on his interpretation of the terms of the lease and
of s 5 of the Agricultural Holdings (Scotland) Act 1949, which was looked on at that
time as a 'grey area'.

The following further facts are taken from the final section headed '*Conclusions*':
(h) It was not unusual for sellers not to employ professional advisers. Mr Burgess's
initial approach to the tenant was correct, but once the tenant had decided not to
purchase few options remained. Telephone calls to institutional investors would not
have produced any result in view of the state and condition of the farm in 1976, and
bearing in mind that it was let to a corporate tenant. (i) Judged against the yardstick
of the advice which the transferor's expert witness Mr Strang-Steele would have
given in an arm's length transaction, Mr Burgess's advice was sound and the actions
of the transferor were reasonable in all the circumstances. (j) Neither the transferor
nor Mr Burgess appreciated that they were dealing with a connected person when
agreeing to the sale of the farm to Domaine.

Much emphasis was, as I have said, placed in the Crown's argument on the fact
that the tribunal had found that the open market value of the farm was almost twice
the price which was paid for it by Domaine. It was said that this fact was of crucial
importance in this case, and that this was the context in which the objective test in
s 20(4)(*b*) had to be applied. Reference was made to the concept of a sale in the open
market (as defined in s 38(1) of the 1975 Act), this being the basis on which property
was valued for the purposes of capital transfer tax. In *Duke of Buccleuch v IRC*
[1967] 1 AC 506 at 524, Lord Reid said, under reference to the meaning of 'in the
open market':

> 'In my view the phrase requires that the seller must take—or here be supposed
> to have taken—such steps as are reasonable to attract as much competition as
> possible for the particular piece of property which is to be sold.'

The fact that the tribunal had held that the open market value of the farm was so
far in excess of the price paid by Domaine showed that, looking at the matter
objectively, there was a market for the property at that price. This meant that there
were purchasers in that market who might be expected to be found if the normal
steps were taken to find them and to persuade them to bid. Under reference to
1 Dymond's Capital Taxes, para 7.132, it was submitted that the question of value,
which is crucial to the antecedent question whether there has been a diminution in

the value of the transferor's estate, provided the essential starting point which, in
this case, the commissioner had chosen to ignore. He had confined himself, it was
said, to a discussion of what Mr Burgess did or did not do and to the question
whether what he did or did not do was reasonable. What he should have done was to
compare what he did or did not do with what happens generally in a transaction at
arm's length. The implication of this argument was that, if the commissioner had
applied the objective test in the way in which the Crown said it should be applied,
he would have reached the view that the open market value and the price which was
to be expected to be obtained on the basis which s 20(4)(*b*) describes, were the same.

In my opinion this argument places too much weight on the background which
s 20(2) provides to s 20(4)(*b*) and it does not pay sufficient attention to the separate
test which s 20(4)(*b*) provides. I agree that the question of open market value is
crucial to the question whether there has been diminution in value of the transferor's
estate. This is the result of applying the provisions of s 38(1) to what s 20(2) lays
down for determining whether a transfer of value has taken place. But the purpose
of s 20(4) is to enable the transferor, if he can, to escape from a rigid application of
the open market test in cases where there was no intention on his part to confer a
gratuitous benefit on any person and one or other of the two further tests in the
subsection are also satisfied. This is necessary if the inevitable bad bargains which
occur from time to time are not to be subjected to tax and, so far as s 20(4)(*a*) is
concerned, if the great mass of transactions which take place every day at arm's
length between persons not connected with each other are to be exempted from
scrutiny. The fact that a price is less than that which meets the definition of open
market value is common to all cases which fall within s 20(4), but it cannot be right,
without introducing a purely circular argument, to treat the definition of open
market value, or a finding as to the open market value, as a test of what a transaction
must satisfy in order to meet what the subsection requires. This is to place too much
emphasis on the question of value and insufficient emphasis on the transaction itself
which is what sub-s (4) is about.

But there is another answer to the Crown's argument which arises on the facts of
this case. An examination of the determination by the tribunal shows that the major
difference between the competing valuations in that case arose from the different
approaches to the question of the landlord's obligation to replace and renew buildings
on the farm (see *Spencer-Nairn v IRC* 1985 SLT (Lands Tr) 46 at 51). Mr Burgess's
view was that a deduction should be made from his gross valuation in respect of the
estimated expenditure of £80,000 on the piggery and the farmhouse in order to
arrive at the open market value of the farm. Mr Strang-Steele, who gave the
principal valuation evidence for the transferor, used the investment approach to the
valuation of the farm. He also made a substantial deduction to take account of the
landlord's obligation for maintenance, management and insurance. The district
valuer who gave evidence for the Crown made no such deduction, on the view that
the landlord's obligation was only for fair wear and tear, and that to provide a new
pig unit would have involved a substantial improvement to the farm. The tribunal
held in favour of the Crown on this point. The relevant passage in their opinion (at
51) is as follows:

> 'With this background, we do not consider that a hypothetical purchaser in
> 1976 would then be legally obliged to provide modernised piggeries at his own
> expense as advised by the college of agriculture. This would have constituted a
> major improvement on which the tenant would also have been required to be
> rented. In our opinion his only obligation would have been to replace or renew
> the existing buildings which were adequate to the district and as might be
> rendered necessary by natural decay or by fair wear or tear.'

They also rejected the investment method of valuation which had been used by
Mr Strang-Steele for a reason which they expressed (at 52) in these terms:

a
'The tribunal do not consider, however, that an institutional investor would be interested in purchasing this 600-acre farm with a large mansion house in ill-repair and with the farmland already tenanted by a Jersey-registered company. It is noteworthy too that no comparable sale to a institutional investor in the locality has been proferred.'

b
They held that the best evidence as to the value of the subjects was to be derived from an analysis of actual sales of let farms in the surrounding area at or about the relevant date. In a passage which does not appear in the report of the decision but which is to be found in the opinion of the tribunal which was lodged as a production in the present case, the following summary is given of the district valuer's general evidence on this point:

c
'He submitted and spoke to a comparison of the sales of seven let farms and five vacant possession farms. The latter were all in Fife or Kinross and, of the let farms, six were in Fife and one was at Carnoustie. Two of the vacant possession sales were close to the valuation date while of the let farms, two were sold in 1975 and two in May 1976. He illustrated the relationship between tenanted and vacant possession. He said he had valued Over Rankeilour subject to tenancy and with vacant possession in the light of the sales evidence, from

d
which he had derived average values per acre for arable and pasture land. In his experience financial institutions were not interested in buying small let farms. Such farms were often bought by the sitting tenant and this accounted for the relatively low price at which many changed hands. He said that institutions were only active in purchasing large agricultural units around the valuation date and it was only the tenant of a large farm who had therefore to compete

e
with institutional purchasers content to leave a good tenant in possession. For this reason, larger let farms on sale were more likely to achieve a greater percentage of the vacant possession value.'

An examination of this decision tells us two things which are relevant to the argument presented by the Crown. The first is that most of the difference between

f
the price paid by Domaine in 1976 and the open market value which was determined by the tribunal in 1984 is accounted for by the view which Mr Burgess took in 1976 about the landlord's obligation in regard to the piggery. This point takes away much of the force of the argument based on a comparison between the two figures, one being almost twice that of the other. It shows that what is of importance for the purposes of s 20(4)(b) in this case is not the difference in value as such but whether

g
the advice which was given and relied on in 1976 was advice which might be expected to be given and relied on at that time in a transaction at arm's length between persons not connected with each other. The second thing is that the market which was envisaged by the calculations of the district valuer which were accepted by the tribunal was a market for the sale of small farms which were often bought by sitting tenants, and it was one which was of no interest to institutional investors.

h
The commissioner has found in this case that Mr Burgess's approach to the tenant met with a rebuff and that the tenant did not wish to purchase. He also found that it was most unlikely that the farm would have been of interest to an institutional purchaser in 1976. These findings provide the background to the question whether the sale to Domaine was one which might be expected to be made in a transaction at arm's length between persons not connected with each other. They show that

j
surrounding facts and circumstances may be such that, even although the price indicated by the tribunal was not achieved, the statutory test in s 20(4)(b) may nevertheless be capable of being satisfied. On this view the question becomes one of fact for the commissioner, and the weight to be attached to the tribunal's decision was a matter for him to assess.

For these reasons I consider that what I understood to be the Crown's primary argument, that the commissioner misdirected himself in law as to the effect of the finding about open market value in the context of s 20(2), must be rejected. It was also submitted that he misdirected himself by failing to apply the objective test which he set for himself in this passage of his decision:

> 'Mr Wishart submits that I should ignore completely what actually happened in 1976 and decide the matter on the basis of what would have occurred between two hypothetical parties in a hypothetical arm's length transaction at that time. It is, however, necessary to compare what actually occurred with what is likely to have taken place objectively between unconnected persons dealing with each other at arm's length, in relation to the sale of the farm.'

No criticism was made of the second sentence in this quotation as it stands, but it was said that he did not make that comparison and that, to use Lord Radcliffe's words in *Edwards v Bairstow* [1956] AC 14 at 36, 36 TC 207 at 229, the true and only reasonable conclusion on the facts found contradicted his determination.

In my opinion the facts which are of particular significance in the context of this argument are that at the time of the sale both the transferor and Mr Burgess were unaware that they were dealing with a connected person in selling the farm to Domaine and that, judged against the yardstick of the advice which Mr Strang-Steele would have given in an arm's length transaction, Mr Burgess's advice was sound and that the actions of the transferor were reasonable in all the circumstances. The first point is important because, in my view, a good way of testing the question whether the sale was such as might be expected to be made in a transaction between persons not connected with each other is to see what persons who were unaware that they were connected with each other actually did. That there was, in fact, a connection was of no significance in this case as to the way in which the sale was effected or the price which was achieved. The second point is important because, in my opinion, it goes a long way towards answering the Crown's argument that the commissioner did not apply an objective test to the facts. His decision is, I agree, open to the criticism that he did not in terms make the comparison which, at the outset of this part of his decision, he described. But I think that the conclusion to be drawn from the evidence which he accepted from Mr Strang-Steele is that the comparison with what might be expected to have taken place objectively is to be found in that evidence. If the yardstick of Mr Strang-Steele's advice in an arm's length transaction is applied, Mr Burgess's advice was not only sound and reasonable but it was advice which might be expected to be given in the circumstances in which the transferor was placed at the time. The two propositions seem to me to go hand in hand, if I may use that metaphor, since Mr Strang-Steele's test of what was sound and reasonable was what he would have done in a transaction at arm's length.

Various other detailed points were made in support of the argument that the commissioner erred in law in holding that the sale of Domaine was not such as might be expected to be made in a transaction at arm's length. I agree with what your Lordships say about them and I need add only a few words of my own. The fact that no advertising took place and that no professional advice was taken other than that which was given by Mr Burgess was said to be inconsistent with a transaction of that kind. It was pointed out that no legal advice was sought about the landlord's obligaton for renewal of the piggery, although this was obviously a matter of importance to the decision whether to sell and if so at what price. But I agree with counsel for the transferor that the facts found by the commissioner were sufficient to entitle him to decide the case as he did. The question which he had to resolve with reference to s 20(4)(b) was whether the sale to Domaine was such as might be expected to be made on the hypothesis which that paragraph describes. The only assumption which had to be made to compare what actually happened here with what might be expected to happen on the statutory hypothesis was that the seller and the purchaser were not connected with each other and that they were dealing at arm's length. The words 'might be expected' suggest that there may be no single answer to this question, and that in the end the question is one of fact for the

commissioner assuming that he was properly instructed as to the relevant law. I
think that he was entitled to conclude that the sale to Domaine at the price in
question was one which might be expected to be entered into on the statutory
hypothesis, given the circumstances in which the transferor found himself at the
time and that he acted on what has been judged to be sound advice.

In my opinion we should answer the question of law in this case in the negative
and dismiss the appeal.

LORD ALLANBRIDGE. On May 1976 the respondent (the transferor) sold Over
Rankeilour Farm (the farm) to a Jersey-registered company (Domaine). It was
agreed that the disposition by the transferor was a transaction between connected
persons for the purposes of s 20(4) of the Finance Act 1975 (the 1975 Act). The price
paid for the farm in May 1976 was £101,350.

The parts of s 20 which are relevant to this appeal are as follows:

'(1) The following provisions of this section shall have effect, subject to the
other provisions of this Part of this Act, for determining for the purposes of
capital transfer tax what is a chargeable transfer and what value is transferred
by a chargeable transfer.

(2) Subject to subsections (3) and (4) below, a transfer of value is any disposition
made by a person ("the transferor") as a result of which the value of his estate
immediately after the disposition is less that it would be but for the disposition;
and the amount by which it is less is the value transferred by the transfer . . .

(4) A disposition is not a transfer of value if it is shown that it was not intended,
and was not made in a transaction intended, to confer any gratuitous benefit on
any person and either—

(a) that it was made in a transaction at arm's length between persons not
connected with each other, or

(b) that it was such as might be expected to be made in a transaction at arm's
length between persons not connected with each other . . .'

Before capital transfer tax can be payable there must be a diminution in the value
of the transferor's estate immediately after the disposition. In this case the Crown
maintains that as the market value of the farm, as decided by the Lands Tribunal
for Scotland (the tribunal), was £199,000 as at 6 April 1976, then in terms of s 20(2)
the value transferred by the transferor was £199,000 less £101,350, namely, about
£94,000, after taking certain reliefs into account. It so happens that the tribunal
were valuing the farm for the purposes of the Capital Gains Tax Act 1979, and in
terms of s 19(3) thereof required to assess 'the market value' of the asset, but that
valuation approach is the same as for capital transfer tax, where s 38(1) of the 1975
Act states that the value of any property for the purposes of the latter tax is 'the open
market' price.

In the present case there is no doubt that there was a 'transfer of value' in May
1976 as far as the transferor's estate was concerned, unless he can satisfy the
conditions of s 20(4). The onus of proof is on him. The Special Commissioner (the
commissioner) has found in this case that the transferor has satisfied the first test
contained in the preamble of sub-s (4), namely, that the disposition was not intended,
and was not made in a transaction intending, to confer any gratuitous benefit on
Domaine. That was a subjective test based on the transferor's intention. The
transferor has succeeded in passing that test and counsel for the Crown submitted
no arguments to this court that the commissioner was wrong in his decision on this
aspect of the case.

Counsel for the Crown submitted that the commissioner was wrong in his decision
that the transferor has also passed the second test in terms of sub-s (4)(b), which was
objective in nature. The test is whether 'it [the disposition] was such as might be
expected to be made in a transaction at arm's length between persons not connected
with each other'. The unusual feature of this case is that whilst it is conceded that

the transferor and Domaine were 'connected persons' for the purposes of the legislation, the commissioner has found as a fact that not only did the transferor not intend to confer any gratuitous benefit on Domaine but that neither he nor his factor appreciated that they were dealing with a connected person when he agreed to sell the farm to Domaine in May 1976.

Before deciding whether the commissioner was right in his conclusion that the transferor had passed the second test, it is necessary to decide what was the question which he required to answer in terms of sub-s (4)(*b*). The stated case showed that the commissioner posed the question in two sentences. The question posed was:

> 'Was the disposition such as might be expected to be made in a transaction at arm's length between persons not connected with each other?... It is, however, necessary to compare what actually occurred with what is likely to have taken place objectively between unconnected persons dealing with each other at arm's length, in relation to the sale of the farm.'

In submitting its appeal, counsel for the Crown in this case accepted that the commissioner had asked the right question but argued that he had reached the wrong answer on the facts and also submitted that the question had been wrongly approached on a subjective basis.

As regards the proper question to be asked, I, for my part, accept that the commissioner asked the correct question. It can be put in various forms but the form used was appropriate and I agree it is necessary to ascertain what actually occurred and then compare such facts with what is likely to have occurred objectively between unconnected persons dealing with each other at arm's length. Another way of asking the question is suggested by 1 Dymond's Capital Taxes, para 7.130, namely 'Has [it been] shown that a similar transaction might have been expected to be made at arm's length ... by unconnected persons'? And that, in my view, is an equally valid way of putting the question.

However, it was argued by counsel for the Crown that the commissioner had wrongly applied a subjective approach in considering the question at issue. It was said that no consideration was given to whether the actings of the transferor and the advice given by Mr Burgess, his factor, were 'typical' of what would happen in an arm's length transaction. I have already said the situation in this case was unique in that neither of these two persons appreciated that the offer by Domaine came from 'a connected person'. The question was not whether this was a 'typical' transaction because this was an unusual situation which might have been very different had the transferor and Mr Burgess realised they were dealing with 'a connected person'. The question to be determined was whether what actually happened in this particular case was likely to have occurred between two unconnected persons dealing with each other at arm's length. I am therefore satisfied that the commissioner not only asked the correct question in this case but did so on an objective approach.

I now turn to consider whether or not the court can or should interfere with the decision of the commissioner in this case. Various versions of the proper approach to be adopted by an appellate court were put forward by Lord Radcliffe in the House of Lords in *Edwards (Inspector of Taxes) v Bairstow* [1956] AC 14 at 36, 36 TC 207 at 229. The test he preferred was whether or not 'the true and only reasonable conclusion contradicted the determination' of the Special Commissioners. I respectfully accept and adopt that test in the circumstances of this case.

On that basis the Crown in this appeal argued that two main features of the present case make the determination of the commissioner unreasonable. In the first place they say that the fact that the price paid for the farm was only about half its market value is a striking feature and requires close and careful examination. I agree. However, a close examination of the facts reveals how such a difference can reasonably be explained. It is found as a fact that the transferor's factor, Mr Burgess, advised him that the estimated cost of replacing the piggery and carrying out other necessary repairs amounted to some £80,000. Furthermore, Mr Burgess took the

view that the tenant could require the transferor to expend that sum in view of the
a terms of s 5 of the Agricultural Holdings (Scotland) Act 1949. That view was held to
be wrong by the tribunal in December 1984 when they decided there was no legal
obligation on the landlord to provide modernised piggeries (see *Spencer-Nairn v
IRC* 1985 SLT (Lands Tr) 46 at 51). As pointed out in the stated case in this appeal,
that decision was not available to Mr Burgess in 1976. Furthermore, it was held as a
fact in the stated case that Mr Burgess's view of the law as it stood in 1976 was not
b 'an unreasonable one'. Thus this striking feature of the case has a 'reasonable'
explanation.

   In the second place an argument was submitted on behalf of the Crown to the
effect that the transferor and Domaine were not acting 'at arm's length' in a number
of respects. We were informed that there was as yet no reported case on the proper
interpretation of s 20(4)(*b*) but, for example, the author of *Whiteman on Capital
c Gains Tax* (4th edn, 1988) p 203 in para 9–33, suggested one of several matters which
would be taken into account in considering whether a transaction was 'at arm's
length', was whether the parties had separate legal or other professional representation. I accept that can be a proper matter to investigate. As regards this matter,
counsel for the Crown suggested that Mr Burgess was only a chartered accountant
and actually could not be said to be a professional adviser as regards the sale of a
d farm. However, the facts found in the stated case answer this argument. It is stated
that besides his accounting qualifications, Mr Burgess had acted as a factor for the
Spencer-Nairn family for over 30 years until his retirement in about 1980, had acted
as a factor to other third parties to a limited extent and as the Spencer-Nairn factor
had negotiated lettings to their tenants and also negotiated the sale of heritable
property at a time when by far the larger part of the Spencer-Nairn estate was let to
e agricultural tenants. In these circumstances I do not consider that the qualifications
of Mr Burgess can be said to be such that he could not give professional advice to the
transferor regarding the sale of the farm and that it was 'reasonable' that the
transferor should accept that advice.

   Another matter, suggested by the author of *Whiteman on Capital Gains Tax* in the
same paragraph, to be taken into account in considering whether parties were 'at
f arm's length', was the presence or absence of bona fide negotiation. I accept that this
is also a proper matter for inquiry. Counsel for the Crown in looking at the
negotiations then said that the refusal of the tenant in this case to purchase, could be
discounted or disregarded because the tenant, namely, a Jersey-registered company
called Over Rankeilour Farms Ltd, was also, like Domaine, 'a connected person'. I
can find no facts set out in the stated case which satisfies me that such was the
g position. There is no evidence to suggest that the tenant company was controlled,
for example, by the transferor's son so as to make it 'a connected person' with the
transferor. All the stated case discloses is that the transferor's son was the original
tenant who renounced the lease and at his request it was then granted to the said
Jersey-registered company. That attack, which can only be based on a matter of
speculation, on the bona fide of the negotiations leading up to the sale of the farm,
h therefore fails.

   Another attack on the bona fide of these negotiations was that the transferor never
advertised the farm for sale nor made any inquiries to see if any other institutional
investors would have been interested in the purchase of it. All the transferor and his
factor did was to offer to sell the farm to the tenant at Mr Burgess's net valuation of
£97,730. The tenant did not wish to purchase. The transferor then quickly accepted
j the offer of £101,350 when it providentially arrived straight 'out of the blue'. I accept
that at first sight this does seem to have been a somewhat unusual course of
negotiations. However, the commissioner has found a reasonable explanation for it.
In the stated case, it is said that it was most unlikely that the farm would have been
of interest to an institutional purchaser in 1976 and that the farm was not an
attractive proposition to a purchaser in the state and condition in which it was in
1976. The circumstances of these negotiations to sell the farm were carefully

examined by the commissioner. The sentence at the end of the second last paragraph of the stated case sums up this matter succinctly. It is stated that the transferor—

> '... accepted Mr Burgess's valuation which has been shown to be one which could be honestly and reasonably held and therefore it is hardly surprising that when the transferor received an offer from Domaine which was higher than the figure contained in Mr Burgess's valuation, he accepted it.'

That is clearly an affirmative answer by the commissioner to the question already correctly posed, namely, was the disposition such as might be expected to be made in a transaction at arm's length between unconnected persons.

Having considered the arguments submitted by counsel for the Crown in this appeal and the answers to them by counsel for the transferor, I am satisfied that the commissioner asked the right question as regards the proper application of s 20(4)(b), and that his affirmative answer was a 'true and reasonable conclusion' based on the facts found in the stated case. As I have said earlier in this opinion, this was a unique case in that one of the facts found in it was that the transferor did not know he was selling the farm to 'a connected person'. This was, of course, a subjective matter as regards the transferor but when considering whether his actings at the time were objectively such as might have been expected to be made by an unconnected person, it explains to some considerable extent how an answer in favour of the transferor came to be made. In other words it is probably a highly unusual feature when contrasted with other cases which may fall to be determined under s 20(4)(b) of the 1975 Act.

On the whole matter I would therefore answer the question in the stated case in the negative and refuse the appeal.

LORD WYLIE. On 16 May 1976 the respondent (the transferor) sold part of the estate of Over Rankeilour in Fife, described as Over Rankeilour Farm, to a Jersey-registered company named Domaine de Herupe Société à Responsabilité Limitée (Domaine), at a purchase price of £101,350. It was tenanted by another Jersey-registered company named Over Rankeilour Farms Ltd in terms of a lease granted in July 1975. For the purpose of assessing capital gains tax liability the consideration passing is deemed not to be the sale price but the open market value of the asset as determined in terms of ss 19, 62 and 63 of the Capital Gains Tax Act 1979. Agreement could not be reached on this issue and on a reference to the Lands Tribunal for Scotland (the tribunal) the open market value was determined on 11 December 1984 at the figure of £199,000 (see *Spencer-Nairn v IRC* 1985 SLT (Lands Tr) 46). On the basis of this decision the Board of Inland Revenue (the Crown) made a determination for the purposes of capital transfer tax that there had been a transfer of value which was a chargeable transfer of approximately £94,000. On appeal the Special Commissioner (the commissioner) held that by virtue of the provisions of s 20(4) of the Finance Act 1975 (the 1975 Act) there had been no chargeable transfer and it is against that decision that this appeal has been taken.

The relevant provisions of s 20 of the 1975 Act have been fully set out by your Lordships and it is not necessary for me to set them out again. It is clear from the terms of sub-s (2) that a transfer of value can arise if, and only if, there is a diminution in the value of the estate as a consequence of the transaction. In this instance there clearly had been a diminution of value having regard to the determination of the market value of the asset by the tribunal on the one hand and the selling price on the other. It does not, however, necessarily follow that there has been a 'transfer of value' giving rise to liability to capital transfer tax. It is open to the transferor to establish, if he can, and the onus is on him, that he satisfies the criteria laid down in sub-s (4). The preamble in that subsection lays down a subjective test, namely that the 'disposition ... was not intended, and was not made in a transaction intended, to confer any gratuitous benefit'.

The commissioner held that the transferor did not intend to confer any gratuitous

benefit on any person when disposing of the farm and this finding is not being
a challenged. The transferor has accordingly satisfied this requirement, but in addition
he must satisfy one or other of two further tests. He must establish either—

'(a) that it was made in a transaction at arm's length between persons not
connected with each other, or
(b) that it was such as might be expected to be made in a transaction at arm's
length between persons not connected with each other. . .'
b

In the present case it is a matter of concession that the transferor cannot rely on
para (a) because he was in fact connected with the purchaser at the time of the
transaction for the purposes both of the Capital Gains Tax Act 1979 and the 1975
Act. There is, however, a significant finding in fact by the commissioner that—

c
'. . . neither the transferor nor Mr Burgess appreciated that they were dealing
with a connected person when agreeing the sale of the farm to Domaine. Such
knowledge came to them much later.'

While not of course capable of bringing the transferor within the provisions of
para (a) it is nevertheless a significant factor in any assessment of his claim to fall
under para (b). The connection which did exist between the parties could in no way
d influence the sale so far as the transferor was concerned when he was unaware of the
connection at the material time. In that respect this case is highly special.

The primary thrust of the argument advanced on behalf of the Crown, as I
understood it, was that the commissioner had failed to apply the objective test
prescribed for the purposes of para (b). On the contrary, notwithstanding his correct
formulation of the test, he had in fact applied a subjective test. He had considered
e whether, in all the circumstances, the advice offered by Mr Burgess was reasonable
and whether, in all the circumstances, the acceptance of that advice by the transferor
was reasonable. He ought to have considered objectively what, in a hypothetical
situation, would have been done by parties not connected with each other and acting
at arm's length with each other. He failed to do what he himself stated he was
required to do, namely, 'to compare what actually occurred with what is likely to
f have taken place objectively between unconnected persons dealing with each other
at arm's length, in relation to the sale of the farm'.

The starting point, it was submitted, had to be the determination of the tribunal
as the true market value of the asset, indicating the kind of price which could have
been obtained if the transferor had set about marketing the property in the
hypothetical circumstances desiderated. This would have involved obtaining a
g valuation from a professional valuer with a knowledge of the market instead of the
ready acceptance of the 'in-house' advice and valuation of an accountant who had
acted as his factor over a number of years. It would have involved taking legal advice
as to the meaning and effect of s 5 of the Agricultural Holdings (Scotland) Act 1949
(the 1949 Act) on the all-important question of an estimated expenditure of £80,000
on the piggery and the farm manager's house. It would certainly have involved
h advertising and properly testing the market instead of simply accepting an offer not
greatly in excess of the valuation made by Mr Burgess, an offer which had come in
'out of the blue'. No bona fide negotiation had taken place. The offer was simply
accepted as it stood, on the advice of Mr Burgess. These were the kind of relevant
circumstances which could be taken into account in deciding whether the transaction
would satisfy the test of being a bargain at arm's length, and they were conspicuously
j absent in this instance (see *Whiteman on Capital Gains Tax* (4th edn, 1988) p 203 in
para 9-33). If the market, which by definition was there to be tapped, had been
properly tested as it would have been in the hypothetical transaction 'at arm's length
between persons not connected with each other', presumably the market value, or
something at least approximating to the market value, would have been achieved.

It seems to me that the flaw in this line of argument is that it overlooks the essential
purpose of the provisions of the subsection. Section 20(4) only comes into play where

there has been a transfer of value by virtue of the fact that the disposition by the
transferor has resulted in a diminution in the value of the estate. Its purpose is to   *a*
relieve the transferor of a tax liability which would otherwise arise, provided he can
satisfy the criteria laid down in the subsection. The construction advanced on behalf
of the Crown seems to imply that one must look at the market value which a
hypothetical purchaser at arm's length would have paid and where he did not do so
the disposition was not such as might be expected in a transaction at arm's length.
Indeed it appears that it was submitted in terms to the commissioner that the   *b*
hypothetical purchaser would have paid the full market value as determined by the
tribunal. On that construction the exclusion from tax liability under para (*b*) would
never arise which cannot be right. The subsection operates, and can only operate,
in the context of a transaction in which the market value has not been achieved, and
it invites an examination of the whole circumstances of the transaction itself,
including the circumstances of the transferor at the material time, to ascertain   *c*
whether the statutory criteria are satisfied and exclusion from tax liability is justified.

Second, although the disparity between the market value as determined by the
tribunal and the price paid is indeed very wide, it was recognised by the tribunal
that the main difference between the two valuations advanced lay in the discount
which the hypothetical purchaser in 1976 would or would not have made for the cost
of providing new piggeries. Mr Burgess had made a gross valuation of £177,730   *d*
from which he deducted the estimated expenditure required on the piggery and the
manager's house, to produce a net valuation of £97,730. On a construction of s 5 of
the 1949 Act the tribunal declined to make such a discount in determining the
market value at the material time. Therein lies the explanation for the disparity
between the two sets of values. It is not, however, this disparity which is the critical
factor for the purposes of para (*b*). As I have already indicated, the question of value   *e*
has been resolved by the time one gets past sub-s (2). Subsection (4)(*b*) is not
concerned with value, an issue which has already been determined. What is relevant
for the purposes of this subsection is whether the factor's view as to the effect of s 5
of the 1949 Act was a view which prevailed at the material time and whether the
advice given on the basis of that view, and accepted, was the kind of advice which
might be expected to be given and accepted in an arm's length transaction between   *f*
unconnected persons at that time. On this critical issue the commissioner has made
significant findings in fact. He accepted Mr Strang-Steele's evidence that in 1976
the law was unclear and that the factor's view was not unreasonable. He concluded
that, judged against the yardstick of the advice which this witness would have given
in an arm's length transaction, the advice was sound and the acceptance of it was
reasonable.   *g*

In support of the commissioner's decision counsel for the transferor relied on a
number of other findings. Shortly stated they are as follows. The rent of £10 an acre
payable under the 1975 lease was below the market level and was totally absorbed by
the cost of repairs and maintenance. The tenant's farm manager was pressing for the
replacement of the piggery buildings, at a cost which the transferor was unable to
fund. An offer to sell to the tenant at the factor's net valuation of £97,730 had been   *h*
rejected. It was most unlikely that the farm would have been of interest to an
institutional investor, let as it was to a corporate tenant. Advertising would have
been to no avail in the absence of any indication in the evidence that there was a
purchaser around prepared to pay a sum anywhere in the region of the market value
as determined by the tribunal.

It is against these objective facts that the issue as to whether the disposition was   *j*
such as might be expected to be made, in 1976, in a transaction at arm's length
between persons not connected with each other has to be determined. In that factual
situation, including the transferor's ignorance of any connection with the purchaser
at the material time, I am satisfied that the commissioner was entitled to hold that
the requirements of s 20(4)(*b*) were satisfied. Nor could it be said, on the basis of
these findings, that Lord Radcliffe's preferred test in *Edwards (Inspector of Taxes) v*

Bairstow [1956] AC 14 at 36, 36 TC 207 at 229—that the decision was contrary to
a 'the true and only reasonable conclusion' which was open to him—was satisfied.
For these reasons I agree that the question of law should be answered in the
negative and the appeal refused.

Appeal dismissed with costs.

b Solicitors: *Solicitor of Inland Revenue*; *Morton Fraser Milligan, WS*, Edinburgh (for
the transferor).

Rengan Krishnan Esq   Barrister.

Margrie Holdings Ltd v Customs and Excise Commissioners

FIRST DIVISION OF THE INNER HOUSE OF THE COURT OF SESSION AS THE COURT OF
EXCHEQUER IN SCOTLAND
THE LORD PRESIDENT (HOPE), LORD MILLIGAN AND LORD GRIEVE
24 JULY, 9 AUGUST 1990

*Value added tax – Exemptions – Land – Disposition of major interest in land –
Disposition recording contract for sale of land to taxpayers by vendors and subsequent
sale to purchasers by vendor with taxpayers' consent – Whether taxpayers had supplied
a major interest in land to purchaser – Value Added Tax Act 1983, Sch 6, Group 1,
item 1.*

Margrie Holdings Ltd (the taxpayers) carried on business as a holding and
management company and Muirfield Farm Ltd (Muirfield) was one of its wholly-
owned subsidiaries. In 1983 the managing director of the taxpayers and of Muirfield
entered into a verbal agreement with T Boland & Co Ltd (Boland) for the sale of a
piece of land owned by Muirfield to Boland. Missives were subsequently entered
into between the taxpayers and Boland although the land remained heritably vested
in Muirfield. By a disposition dated 15 and 18 May 1984, the land was disponed by
Muirfield to Boland with the taxpayers' consent. It was common ground that no
disposition of the land was ever granted to the taxpayers and that the taxpayers
never took a recorded title to the land. Prior to 1 June 1984, the supply of services in
the course of construction, alteration or demolition of buildings was zero-rated for
value added tax purposes but with effect from that date, (a) under s 10 and para 3 of
Sch 6 to the Finance Act 1984, alterations to buildings became taxable at the
standard rate and (b) under Sch 6 to the Value Added Tax Act 1983 (the 1983 Act),
all supplies of reconstructed buildings became exempt supplies. Consequently, the
supply of reconstructed buildings no longer attracted any value added tax so that
there was no output tax on the supply which could be set against the input tax
incurred on the work of reconstruction. Transitional rules provided for input tax
incurred prior to 1 June 1984. Under those rules, a taxpayer's right to recover input
tax would be lost only if he had made an exempt supply after 31 March 1984. In
1983 and 1984, the taxpayers were engaged in the reconstruction of warehouse
premises and incurred costs on which they paid input tax. The taxpayers' entitlement
to recover input tax amounting to £223,556 depended on whether they had made
an exempt supply within item 1 of Group 1 of Sch 6[a] to the 1983 Act to Boland after
31 March 1984 in consequence of the transaction relating to the sale of the land in
question. The value added tax tribunal found that they had on the basis that the
taxpayers had supplied a major interest in the land to Boland when they took entry
to it and paid the price on 15 May 1984. The taxpayers appealed to the Inner House
of the Court of Session.

Held – On a proper construction of the disposition, in particular the dispositive
clause, it was plain that the disposition of the major interest in the land in question
was by Muirfield to Boland. The clause did not contain any words which could be
construed as amounting to a disposition of that interest to the taxpayers. The
taxpayers merely had a contractual right against Muirfield to demand performance
by Muirfield of their obligation to convey the land to them. There was no divestiture
by Muirfield of their major interest in the land until they delivered the disposition
to Boland and there was never a disposition of that interest at any stage to the

---

a   Sch 6, Group 1, item 1, so far as material, is set out at p 82 *g*, post

taxpayers. Accordingly, the taxpayers never had a major interest in the land and
a   there was no basis for there having been an exempt supply by the taxpayers to
Boland after 31 March 1984. The taxpayers' appeal would therefore be allowed.

Dicta of Lord President Emslie in *Gibson v Hunter Home Designs Ltd* 1976 SC 23
at 27 applied.

b **Notes**

For the meaning of 'exemptions', see De Voil: Value Added Tax A9.01.
For exemptions relating to transactions in land, see ibid, Division A9.11.
For the Value Added Tax Act 1983, Sch 6, Group 1, item 1, see ibid, Division C1.

c **Cases referred to in opinions**

Customs and Excise Comrs v Oliver [1980] STC 73, [1980] 1 All ER 353.
Embassy Picture House (Troon) Ltd v Cammo Developments Ltd (1970) SLT (Notes)
      85, CS.
Gibson v Hunter Home Designs Ltd 1976 SC 23, CS.
d *Orr v Mitchell* [1893] AC 238, HL.
Rodger (Builders) Ltd v Fawdry 1950 SC 483, CS.

Appeal

e   Margrie Holdings Ltd, the taxpayers, appealed against a decision of the Edinburgh
Value Added Tax Tribunal dismissing an appeal against an assessment by the
Customs and Excise Commissioners, the commissioners, to recover input tax which
the commissioners claimed had been wrongly recovered by the taxpayers. The facts
are set out in the opinion of Lord President Hope.

f   *M G Clarke* for the taxpayers.
C J Harris for the commissioners.

The court made avizandum.

9 August 1990. The following opinions were delivered.

g
THE LORD PRESIDENT (HOPE). This is an appeal from a decision of the
value added tax tribunal dated 29 July 1988 by which they refused an appeal against
an assessment by the Customs and Excise Commissioners (the commissioners) to
recover value added tax input tax which, it was alleged, had been wrongly claimed
by the taxpayers. The assessment was restricted to the sum of £11,599·74 claimed
h   by the taxpayers and paid by the commissioners for the period from 1 April 1984 to
30 June 1984. There was a further claim by the taxpayers for the period from 1 July
1984 to 30 September 1984 in the sum of £223,556·04 which has not yet been paid
by the commissioners. The taxpayers' entitlement to this sum depends on the result
of the appeal.

The taxpayers carry on business as a holding and management company. The
j   group includes a wholly-owned subsidiary of the taxpayers named Muirfield Farm
Ltd (Muirfield). The managing director of both companies at the material time was
Mr John McAvoy. During 1983 and 1984 the taxpayers were engaged in the
reconstruction of warehouse premises in Edinburgh and they incurred costs on
which they paid value added tax input tax. Prior to 1 June 1984 the supply of
services in the course of the construction, alteration or demolition of buildings was
zero-rated for value added tax, although any work of repair or maintenance was in

general taxable at the standard rate (see the Value Added Tax Act 1983 (the 1983
Act), Sch 5, Group 8). But with effect from 1 June 1984, alterations to buildings   *a*
became taxable at the standard rate (see the Finance Act 1984, Sch 6, Part II). From
that date also all supplies of reconstructed buildings ceased to be zero-rated and they
became exempt supplies. The consequence of these changes was that the supply of
a reconstructed building no longer attracted any value added tax, so there was no
output tax on the supply which under s 14 of the 1983 Act could be set against the
input tax incurred on the work of reconstruction. Transitional rules were made with   *b*
regard to input tax incurred prior to 1 June 1984. The details of these rules need not
be described, but their effect was that the right to recover the input tax depended
among other things on whether the taxpayer had made any exempt supplies after
31 March 1984. If he had made any exempt supplies after that date he fell into the
category of a partly exempt trader, and the benefit of the transitional provisions was
not available to him.   *c*
   This case is concerned with a transaction relating to a piece of land at Gullane. It
was owned by Muirfield who were the heritable proprietors. It was one of three
parcels of land which had been owned by that company, two of which had previously
been sold to T Boland & Co Ltd (Boland) in March 1982 and March 1983
respectively. In December 1983 Mr McAvoy made a verbal agreement with Mr
Thomas Boland, the managing director of Boland that the third parcel of land would   *d*
be sold to that company in March 1984 at a price of £60,525. In due course missives
were entered into dated 29 and 30 March 1984 between the taxpayers and Boland,
although the subjects remained heritably vested in Muirfield. The land was then
disponed by Muirfield with consent of the taxpayers to Boland by a disposition
dated 15 and 18 May 1984 which was recorded in the Register of Sasines on 25 June
1984. It is a matter of agreement that no disposition of the property which is the   *e*
subject matter of this appeal was ever granted in favour of the taxpayers and that the
taxpayers never took a recorded title to the subjects at any stage.
   Section 1 of the 1983 Act provides that a tax, to be known as value added tax, shall
be charged in accordance with the provisions of the 1983 Act on the supply of goods
and services in the United Kingdom. It is not obvious from that provision that the
1983 Act has anything to do with dispositions of heritable subjects, but para 4 of   *f*
Sch 2 to the 1983 Act provides: 'The granting, assignment or surrender of a major
interest in land is a supply of goods'. The expression 'major interest' in relation to
land is defined in s 48(1) as meaning in relation to Scotland inter alia 'the estate or
interest of the proprietor of the dominium utile'. There is no dispute in this case,
therefore, that what was supplied to Boland was a major interest in land within the
meaning of that definition and that this was a supply of goods for the purposes of the   *g*
1983 Act. The significance of this for the purposes of the transitional rules can be
seen from the fact that the supplies of goods and services which are exempt supplies
in terms of s 17 of the 1983 Act include 'the grant, assignment or surrender of any
interest in or right over land or of any licence to occupy land' (see Sch 6, Group 1,
item 1). So the supply of the interest of the proprietor of the dominium utile in the
land was not only a supply of goods but it was also an exempt supply within the   *h*
meaning of s 17, being a supply of goods of a description specified in Sch 6 to the
1983 Act. The question so far as the taxpayers are concerned, therefore, is whether
they were involved in the making of an exempt supply to Boland in consequence of
this transaction, which would deprive them of the benefit of the transitional
provisions.
   The parties were agreed that the taxpayers' entitlement to the input tax claimed   *j*
by them depended on whether, in regard to this transaction, they had made an
exempt supply after 31 March 1984. Answer 2 for the commissioners to the taxpayers'
grounds of appeal defines the issue in these terms:

   'All the Tribunal was asked to decide was whether there had been a supply,
   whether it was made by [the taxpayers], and at what time it was made. [The

taxpayers] conceded at the appeal before the Tribunal that [Boland] obtained a
supply of a major interest in land. It was not disputed that the said supply was
an exempt supply. Accordingly the only issue before the Tribunal was,
(a) who made the supply? and
(b) on what date?'

At the outset of his argument for the taxpayers, counsel informed us that the point
about the date was no longer insisted on by them. It was now accepted that the
transaction in question took place after 31 March 1984. The only remaining question
in the case, therefore, is, as the commissioners have put it in their answer, 'who
made the supply'? Counsel for the taxpayers' argument assumed that 'the supply' in
question was the supply of a major interest in land to Boland. I confess that this
seemed to me to be a reasonable reading of the commissioners' answer, and
throughout counsel for the taxpayers' address I thought this was the point at issue in
the case. It is also the basis of the decision by the tribunal, which is to be found in
the following passage taken from the penultimate paragraph of the decision:

> 'We concluded that the missives gave no personal rights to the parties other
> than the right to demand a disposition upon payment of the price, and, further,
> that in particular no possession or control of the land was given in terms of these
> missives. When we turn to the terms of the disposition, however, we find
> ourselves in agreement with [the commissioners'] solicitors' construction of it,
> and in particular, hold that by virtue thereof [the taxpayers] supplied a major
> interest in land to [Boland] when they took entry and paid the price on 15 May
> 1984.'

For reasons which I shall deal with briefly in a moment that approach does not stand
up to examination. But it is not necessary to deal with the point in detail because
counsel for the commissioners entirely disclaimed this argument. He informed us
that it had never been contended by the commissioners that the taxpayers had
supplied a major interest in land to Boland. It was conceded that that company had
acquired a major interest in land, but it had always been accepted by the
commissioners that the taxpayers did not have the major interest in the land at any
stage. As counsel for the commissioners put it, what they had was a personal interest
in the land, and it was that interest which was the subject of the exempt supply. It is
odd that the tribunal should have misunderstood the point at issue, to the extent
even of making no reference to s 3(2)(b) of the 1983 Act which provides an essential
step in the argument on this point. It is also odd that it should have been described
in the commissioners' answers in terms which are entirely consistent with the
approach by the tribunal and do not suggest that the supply in question in this case
was something different from the major interest in the land obtained by Boland. But
I need not dwell on this point, because it seems to me that the commissioners'
argument as now explained to us by counsel is just as unsound as the version of it
which was adopted by the tribunal.

The tribunal's view was that, on a proper construction of the disposition, the
taxpayers supplied a major interest in the land to Boland when they took entry to it
and paid the price. The major interest in the land is the proprietorship of the
dominium utile, which was previously vested in Muirfield and to which the
taxpayers never had a recorded title at any time. It was not, I think, necessary that
the taxpayers should have recorded a title to it to enable them to supply that interest
to Boland within the meaning of the legislation relating to value added tax. A
personal right to that interest would be sufficient to enable them, as the proprietors
of that right, to transmit it and thus supply it to the purchaser. So the question is
whether, on a proper construction of the disposition, the transaction which took
place can be analysed in this way. The relevant part of the disposition is as follows:

'WE, MUIRFIELD FARM LIMITED, incorporated under the Companies
Acts and having our Registered Office at Forty five Frederick Street, Edinburgh,

heritable proprietors of the subjects hereinafter disponed CONSIDERING
that we have sold the said subjects to MARGRIE HOLDINGS LIMITED, *a*
incorporated under the Companies Acts and having their Registered Office at
Forty five Frederick Street, Edinburgh, at the price of ONE THOUSAND
NINE HUNDRED AND THIRTY EIGHT POUNDS of which sum we
hereby acknowledge the receipt FURTHER CONSIDERING that the said
Margrie Holdings Limited have since sold the subjects hereinafter disponed to
T. BOLAND & CO. LIMITED, incorporated under the Companies Acts and *b*
having their Registered Office at Forty nine Northumberland Street, Edin-
burgh, at the price of SIXTY THOUSAND FIVE HUNDRED AND
TWENTY FIVE POUNDS: AND NOW SEEING that the said T. Boland
& Co. Limited have paid to the said Margrie Holdings Limited the said price
of Sixty Thousand Five Hundred and Twenty Five Pounds, of which sum the
said Margrie Holdings Limited hereby acknowledge the receipt and that the *c*
said Margrie Holdings Limited have requested us to grant these presents:
THEREFORE we the said Muirfield Farm Limited with consent of the said
Margrie Holdings Limited and we the said Margrie Holdings Limited for all
right, title and interest, present and future, competent to us in and to the said
subjects hereinafter disposed DO HEREBY . . . DISPONE to and in favour of
the said T. Boland & Co. Limited and their successors and assignees whomsoever *d*
heritably and irredeemably ALL and WHOLE those parts of the Lands of
Muirfield, Gullane, and other lands comprising both the *dominium directum*
and *dominium utile* thereof lying in the Parish of Dirleton and County of East
Lothian.'

It can be seen that the disposition follows the normal and familiar pattern in such
cases. It sets out first the narrative clause by which the parties and the consideration *e*
for the grant are identified, and it then proceeds to the dispositive clause which
describes the property and the person to whom it is conveyed. The most important
clause for present purposes is the dispositive clause which, if unambiguous, is
decisive of all questions relating to the matter with which it deals including the
extent of the land or interest in it which is conveyed and the identity of the grantee
(see *Orr v Mitchell* [1893] AC 238 at 254, per Lord Macnaghten). I do not think that *f*
there is any ambiguity in this case. It is perfectly clear from the dispositive clause
that the disposition of the major interest is by Muirfield in favour of Boland. The
clause does not contain any words of disposition which could be construed as
amounting to a disposition of that interest to the taxpayers, even as a first step in its
transmission to Boland. What the clause does is to narrate the consent of the
taxpayers for all right, title and interest competent to them in and to the subjects to *g*
the disposition by Muirfield. The explanation for that consent is to be found in the
previous narrative about the sale of the subjects by Muirfield to the taxpayers and
the subsequent sale to Boland, but this is a narrative of sales only, not of the
divestiture of the major interest from one party and its transmission to another. I
think that it is plain, therefore, on a proper reading of the disposition that the
taxpayers' position was simply that they had a right to demand performance by *h*
Muirfield of their contractual obligation to convey the land to them. But this was no
more than a jus crediti, a contractual right against Muirfield. In the words of Lord
President Emslie in *Gibson v Hunter Home Designs Ltd* 1976 SC 23 at 27:

'In the law of Scotland no right of property vests in a purchaser until there
has been delivered to him the relevant disposition. On delivery of the disposition *j*
the purchaser becomes vested in a personal right to the subjects in question and
his acquisition of a real right to the subjects is dependent upon recording the
disposition in the appropriate Register of Sasines. Putting the matter in another
way the seller of subjects under missives is not, in a question with the purchaser,
divested of any part of his right of property in the subjects of sale until, in

implement of his contractual obligation to do so, he delivers to the purchaser
a   the appropriate disposition.'

So there was no divestiture by Muirfield of their major interest in the land until they
delivered the disposition to Boland, and there never was a disposition of that interest
at any stage in favour of the taxpayers. The tribunal's approach to the matter must
therefore be rejected as unsound and, as I have said, counsel for the commissioners
did not seek to support it.

b   Counsel for the commissioners' approach assumed therefore that the major interest
in the land passed directly from Muirfield to Boland in terms of the disposition. He
contended that on a proper analysis of the disposition the taxpayers nevertheless had
a personal right in the land which was the subject of an exempt supply. He accepted
that the supply of a personal right in land was not a supply of goods having regard to
the terms of para 4 of Sch 2 to the 1983 Act which refers only to a major interest in
c   land. His argument was that there was here a supply of services. Section 3(2)(*b*)
provides—

'... anything which is not a supply of goods but is done for a consideration
(including, if so done, the granting, assignment or surrender of any right) is a
supply of services.'

d   He pointed to the fact that it is recorded in the disposition that the price of £60,525
was paid by Boland to the taxpayers. This showed, he said, that something had been
done by the taxpayers for which they had received consideration from Boland, and
that was enough for there to have been a supply of services within the meaning of
s 3(2)(*b*). I need not express an opinion on this stage of the argument, however,
because the crucial question is whether this was an exempt supply. This is the only
e   point of importance in the present case, because only an exempt supply could
deprive the taxpayers of the transitional relief.

Counsel for the commissioners' argument was that the taxpayers had a personal
right in the land, and this was an 'interest in' land within the meaning of item 1 of
Group 1 of Sch 6. This was said to be clear on a proper reading of the disposition.
He maintained that the question of title was not a governing factor in this matter.
f   We were referred to *Customs and Excise Comrs v Oliver* [1980] STC 73 in which it
was held that the sale by a second-hand car dealer at auction of cars which he had
either stolen or knew to be stolen was nevertheless a supply for the purposes of value
added tax on the proceeds arising from the sale. Griffiths J, as he then was, said (at
74) that it is clear from the language of the 1983 Act that 'supply' is a word of the
widest import. He adopted (at 75) the definition of 'supply' put forward by counsel
g   for the commissioners, to the effect that this was the passing of possession in goods
pursuant to an agreement whereunder the supplier agreed to part and the recipient
agreed to take possession. It was neither here nor there that the unfortunate
purchaser might at some later date have to part with his car because the contract of
sale was in fact void. Counsel for the commissioners invited us to take a practical
approach to the matter and on this analogy he said that the taxpayers had a sufficient
h   interest in the land for the purposes of the definition of the exempt supply.

In my opinion this argument must be rejected. I think that we can accept that the
word 'supply' is a word of wide import and that a title need not be demonstrated in
order to show that there was a supply. But that is not what this case is about. The
question here is whether the supply, if there was one, was an exempt supply, and for
that to be so it must be a supply of a description specified in Sch 6. This means in
j   the present case that it has to be capable of being described as 'the grant, assignment
or surrender of any interest in or right over land'. The crucial phrase is 'interest in
... land', and this is a phrase which must be construed according to the law of
Scotland since we are concerned with land in Scotland in this case and with a
transaction entered into in this country. If the supply was of a major interest in land
there would be no difficulty. That was the attraction of the argument which found

favour with the tribunal because plainly the phrase 'interest in . . . land' includes a major interest in land as defined in s 48(1) of the 1983 Act. But once it is accepted, as *a* it had to be, that the taxpayers never had a major interest in the land in question in this case, the basis for there being an exempt supply disappears. In my opinion the taxpayers never had an interest *in* the land at all, as the law of Scotland understands that expression. To return to the words of Lord President Emslie in *Gibson v Hunter Home Designs Ltd* 1976 SC 23 at 27—

> '. . . the seller of subjects under missives is not, in a question with the *b*
> purchaser, divested of any part of his right of property in the subjects of sale
> until, in implement of his contractual obligation to do so, he delivers to the
> purchaser the appropriate disposition. Until the moment of delivery the
> purchaser, even if he has paid the price and obtained occupation of the subjects,
> has no more than a right under the contract of sale, the missives, to demand
> performance by the seller of his contractual obligation to convey.' *c*

The taxpayers' position therefore was that they had a right under their contract with Muirfield to obtain a disposition in implement of the sale which is narrated in the disposition but they had nothing more than that. Their right was enough to prevent Muirfield in breach of their contract with the taxpayers from conveying the subjects to anyone else, but it was a personal right under their contract with Muirfield not an *d* interest in the land itself. No doubt it was necessary for their consent to be given to the disposition to Boland. This is in accordance with sound conveyancing practice, and it avoided the risks to the purchaser exemplified by the case of *Rodger (Builders) Ltd v Fawdry* 1950 SC 483. But the granting of consent is to be seen as no more than the surrender of the taxpayers' personal right against Muirfield. It cannot be inferred from the granting of this consent that the taxpayers had acquired a personal interest *e* in the land, especially as there is nothing in the narrative which the disposition contains to indicate any such interest was acquired by them. An interest in the land could only have been acquired by the taxpayers from Muirfield who were the heritable proprietors, and for that to be achieved there would have had to have been a divestiture by Muirfield of that interest in favour of the taxpayers. I can find nothing in the language of the disposition to that effect. *f*

Counsel for the commissioners stressed more than once that this was a case about interest in land and not about title. But I do not think that these concepts can be separated in this case. If the supply is to be an exempt supply it must be of the description specified in item 1 of Group 1 of Sch 6. This means that the subject of the supply must be identified and it must be an interest in land which has been either granted, assigned or surrendered. In the context of this case one must first find an *g* interest in the land which was capable of being granted, assigned or surrendered by the taxpayers. That, I think, takes one inevitably to the question of title, because it is not conceivable that the taxpayers, by consenting to the disposition, were granting, assigning or surrendering an interest in land which they had not acquired. But the only title which emerges from a study of the narrative clause in the disposition is a title to enforce a contract of sale. A right to enforce a contract is not an interest in *h* land in any sense recognised by Scots law. It is merely a right to become owner of the land on payment of the price and on fulfilment of such other conditions, if any, as the missives may contain (see *Embassy Picture House (Troon) Ltd v Cammo Developments Ltd* (1970) SLT (Notes) 85 per Clerk Grant LJ). I do not think that any assistance is to be derived in this case from *Customs and Excise Comrs v Oliver*, which was a case about the supply of moveable property and not what is necessary *j* to establish that there was an interest in land for the purposes of an exempt supply.

For these reasons I consider that the tribunal reached the wrong decision in this case. I would allow this appeal and set aside the assessment.

LORD MILLIGAN. I agree with the opinion of your Lordship in the Chair. There is nothing which I can usefully add.

LORD GRIEVE.   I entirely agree with the opinion of your Lordship in the Chair,
a and there is nothing I can usefully add to it.

Appeal allowed

Solicitors: *Brodies, WS*, Edinburgh (for the taxpayers); *Shepherd & Wedderburn,
WS*, Edinburgh (for the commissioners).

b
                                                              Siew Ling Choo   Barrister.

Shilton v Wilmshurst (Inspector of Taxes)   *a*

HOUSE OF LORDS

LORD BRIDGE OF HARWICH, LORD BRANDON OF OAKBROOK, LORD TEMPLEMAN, LORD
ACKNER AND LORD GOFF OF CHIEVELEY

16, 17, 21 JANUARY, 7 FEBRUARY 1991

b

*Emoluments from office or employment – Payments on retirement or removal from office
or employment – Inducement to enter into employment – Footballer transferred to new
club – Transfer package including payment to footballer by old club – Whether payment
an emolument from employment by new club – Income and Corporation Taxes Act 1970,
ss 181(1), 187.*   *c*

The taxpayer, a well-known footballer, was employed by Nottingham Forest
Football Club. In 1982 Nottingham Forest needed, to raise money and reduce the
wages bill. Accordingly they agreed to transfer the taxpayer, subject to his consent,
to Southampton Football Club; and after the manager of Nottingham Forest had   *d*
indicated to him that should he agree terms of employment with Southampton,
Nottingham Forest might be willing to make a payment to him for consenting to
the transfer, the taxpayer agreed such terms and so consented. Nottingham Forest
then paid him £75,000 for so consenting. The inspector assessed him to tax on that
sum for the year 1982–83, under Sch E, pursuant to s 181(1)[a] of the Income and
Corporation Taxes Act 1970 which provided that 'tax under this Schedule shall be   *e*
charged in respect of any office or employment on emoluments therefrom'. The
taxpayer appealed against the assessment, contending that it was a payment on
termination of employment, chargeable to tax under s 187 and was subject to the
reliefs in s 188. The General Commissioners determined that the payment by
Nottingham Forest to the taxpayer was an inducement to him to play football for
Southampton and, as such, an emolument flowing from the service which he was to   *f*
render to Southampton and consequently liable to tax under s 181(1). Morritt J
allowed the taxpayer's appeal on the ground that a payment by a third party to an
employee might be an emolument 'from' his employment where the payer had a
direct or indirect interest in the past or future performance of that employment,
that Nottingham Forest had no such interest and accordingly the payment by
Nottingham Forest did not fall to be taxed under s 181(1). The Court of Appeal   *g*
upheld Morritt J's decision on the ground that, to be chargeable under s 181(1), an
emolument had to be referable to the performance of services by the employee under
his contract of employment. The Crown appealed to the House of Lords.

Held – (1) Section 181(1) was not confined to 'emoluments from the employer' but   *h*
embraced all 'emoluments from employment' and it was not limited to emoluments
provided in the course of employment. Thus it comprehended emoluments provided
by a third party, a person who was not an employer, and it applied to emoluments
paid as an inducement to enter into a contract of employment and to perform
services in the future. Emoluments 'from employment' meant emoluments 'from
being or becoming an employee'. Accordingly, the payment of £75,000 by   *j*
Nottingham Forest was an emolument 'from employment' because it was an
emolument 'from becoming an employee'. It was paid to the taxpayer in return for
his agreement to act as or become an employee of Southampton.

---

a   Section 181(1), so far as material, is set out at p 90 *f*, post

Dicta of Lord Radcliffe in *Hochstrasser (Inspector of Taxes) v Mayes* (1957) 38 TC
a 673 at 707 applied.

(2) There was nothing in s 181(1) to justify the inference that an 'emolument from
employment' only applied to an emolument provided by a person who had an
interest in the performance by the employee of the services which he had become
bound to perform when he entered into the contract of employment.

Accordingly, the payment of £75,000 by Nottingham Forest to the taxpayer was
b chargeable to tax under s 181(1). The Crown's appeal would therefore be allowed.

Notes

For payments on termination or variation of employment, see Simon's Taxes E4.405.

c   For the Income and Corporation Taxes Act 1970, s 181(1) (now the Income and
Corporation Taxes Act 1988, s 19(1)), see ibid, Part G1.

Cases referred to in opinions

Bray (Inspector of Taxes) v Best [1989] STC 159, [1989] 1 WLR 167, [1989] 1 All
d   ER 969, HL.
Brumby (Inspector of Taxes) v Milner [1976] STC 534, [1976] 1 WLR 1096, [1976]
      3 All ER 636, 51 TC 583, HL; *affg* [1975] STC 644, [1976] 1 WLR 29, [1975] 3
      All ER 1004, CA; *affg* [1975] STC 215, [1975] 1 WLR 958, [1975] 2 All ER 773.
Glantre Engineering Ltd v Goodhand (Inspector of Taxes) [1983] STC 1, [1983] 1 All
      ER 542, 52 TC 165.
e   *Hamblett v Godfrey (Inspector of Taxes)* [1987] STC 60, [1987] 1 WLR 357, [1987]
      1 All ER 916, 59 TC 694, CA.
Hochstrasser (Inspector of Taxes) v Mayes [1960] AC 376, [1959] 3 All ER 817, 38 TC
      673, HL.
Laidler v Perry (Inspector of Taxes) [1966] AC 16, [1965] 2 All ER 121, 42 TC 351,
      HL.
f   *Pritchard (Inspector of Taxes) v Arundale* [1972] Ch 229, [1971] 3 All ER 1011,
      47 TC 680.

Appeal

g   The inspector of taxes (the Crown), appealed against an order of the Court of Appeal
(Sir Nicolas Browne-Wilkinson V-C, Staughton and Beldam LJJ) given on
6 December 1989 ([1990] STC 55), dismissing its appeal from a decision of Morritt J
dated 17 November 1988 ([1988] STC 868) allowing an appeal by Peter Leslie
Shilton (the taxpayer) from a determination of the General Commissioners that a
payment to him by the Nottingham Forest Football Club of £75,000 was chargeable
h   to tax under s 181 of the Income and Corporation Taxes Act 1970 as an emolument
his employment with the Southampton Football Club. The facts are set out in the
opinion of Lord Templeman.

Alan Moses QC for the Crown.
Andrew Thornhill QC and *David Ewart* for the taxpayer.
j
Their Lordships took time for consideration.

7 February 1991. The following opinions were delivered.

LORD BRIDGE OF HARWICH. My Lords, I have had the advantage of reading

in draft the speech of my noble and learned friend Lord Templeman. I agree with it
and for the reasons which he gives I, too, would allow the appeal.

LORD BRANDON OF OAKBROOK. My Lords, for the reasons given in the
speech to be delivered by my noble and learned friend, Lord Templeman, I would
allow the appeal.

LORD TEMPLEMAN. My Lords, in August 1982 the world-famous goalkeeper,
Mr Shilton (the taxpayer), was transferred from Nottingham Forest to Southampton.
There were three parts to the transfer. Nottingham Forest agreed with Southampton
to transfer the taxpayer to Southampton for a transfer fee of £325,000. Nottingham
Forest agreed with the taxpayer to pay £75,000 to the taxpayer if he agreed to be
transferred to Southampton. The taxpayer agreed with Southampton that he would
play for Southampton for four years on agreed terms as to salary and otherwise if
Southampton paid him £80,000. The Revenue assessed the sums of £75,000 and
£80,000 amounting in the aggregate to £155,000, to income tax under s 181(1) of
the Income and Corporation Taxes Act 1970 (the 1970 Act). The taxpayer agreed
the assessment so far as it applied to the sum of £80,000 paid by Southampton but
disputed the assessment so far as it applied to the sum of £75,000 paid by Nottingham
Forest.

Section 183 of the 1970 Act, now replaced by s 131 of the Income and Corporation
Taxes Act 1988 (the 1988 Act), provided that:

'(1) Tax under Case I, II or III of Schedule E shall . . . be chargeable on the
full amount of the emoluments falling under that Case . . . and the expression
"emoluments" shall include all salaries, fees, wages, perquisites and profits
whatsoever.'

It is common ground that the sum of £75,000 paid by Nottingham Forest to the
taxpayer was an emolument as defined by s 183.

Section 181 of the 1970 Act, as amended and now replaced, so far as material, by
s 19 of the 1988 Act, provided that tax under Sch E—

'. . . shall be charged in respect of any office or employment on emoluments
therefrom which fall under . . . Case I: where the person holding the office or
employment is resident and ordinarily resident in the United Kingdom . . .'

The commissioners found and it is not disputed that:

'Although there were three parts to the negotiations these parts should be
looked at as a whole as if agreement had not been reached between the
appropriate parties on each part, then the whole would have failed.'

On that finding the commissioners held that:

'The payment by Nottingham Forest to [the taxpayer] was an inducement to
him to play football for Southampton and as such an emolument flowing from
that service which he was to render to Southampton.'

The commissioners concluded that the payment of £75,000 by Nottingham Forest
to the taxpayer was chargeable to tax under s 181 of the 1970 Act as an emolument
of his employment with Southampton.

Morritt J allowed an appeal by the taxpayer on the grounds that the payment of
£75,000 by Nottingham Forest was an emolument 'for' but not 'from' his employment
with Southampton and that an emolument paid to an employee by a third party, ie
a person other than the employer, was only an emolument 'from' the employer's
employment if the third party had some interest in the performance by the employee
of his contract of employment (see [1988] STC 868 at 877–878). Nottingham Forest
had no interest in the performance by the taxpayer of his contract of employment
with Southampton. Once he had been transferred it did not matter to Nottingham

Forest whether the taxpayer fulfilled his contractual obligations to Southampton or
a not or whether he kept goal for Southampton well or badly. The Court of Appeal
(Sir Nicolas Browne-Wilkinson V-C, Staughton and Beldam LJJ) upheld the
decision of Morritt J holding that to be chargeable under s 181(1) an emolument
must be referable to the performance of services by the employee under his contract
of employment (see [1990] STC 55 at 62).

   If the emolument of £75,000 is not chargeable under s 181(1) it is chargeable
b under s 187 of the 1970 Act, now s 148 of the 1988 Act, but various reliefs and
allowances apply to the charge under s 187, so the impost of tax on the taxpayer
under s 181 will be heavier than the impost under s 187 which he has already paid.
The Crown takes the view that the result of this appeal will have substantial
repercussions on the ambit of s 181 and may have repercussions on other taxing
provisions. Accordingly the Crown now appeals and seeks to restore the decision of
c the General Commissioners and the assessment.

   I sympathise with the conclusion which absolves the taxpayer from part of the tax
claimed by the Revenue but if that conclusion is to be upheld it must be consistent
with the logical construction and application of the taxing statute. Section 181 is not
confined to 'emoluments from the employer' but embraces all 'emoluments from
employment'; the section must therefore comprehend an emolument provided by a
d third party, a person who is not the employer. Section 181 is not limited to
emoluments provided in the course of employment; the section must therefore apply
first to an emolument which is paid as a reward for past services and as an inducement
to continue to perform services and, second, to an emolument which is paid as an
inducement to enter into a contract of employment and to perform services in the
future. The result is that an emolument 'from employment' means an emolument
e 'from being or becoming an employee'. The authorities are consistent with this
analysis and are concerned to distinguish in each case between an emolument which
is derived 'from being or becoming an employee' on the one hand, and an emolument
which is attributable to something else on the other hand, for example, to a desire
on the part of the provider of the emolument to relieve distress or to provide
assistance to a home buyer. If an emolument is not paid as a reward for past services
f or as an inducement to enter into employment and provide future services but is
paid for some other reason, then the emolument is not received 'from the
employment'. The task of determining whether an emolument was paid for being
or becoming an employee or was paid for another reason, is frequently difficult and
gives rise to fine distinctions. In the present case, the £80,000 emolument provided
by Southampton was admittedly an emolument 'from becoming an employee' and is
g admitted to fall within s 181 because £80,000 was paid as an inducement to the
taxpayer to enter into a contract of employment under which he would perform
services for Southampton for the next four years. The £75,000 paid by Nottingham
Forest was also an inducement to the taxpayer to enter into a contract of employment
under which he would perform services for Southampton for the next four years.
True it is that unless Nottingham Forest and Southampton induced the taxpayer to
h enter the employment of Southampton, the sum of £325,000 would not be paid by
Southampton to Nottingham Forest. Thus Nottingham Forest had a powerful
motive for offering an inducement to the taxpayer to become an employee of
Southampton. This motive does not alter the fact that the £75,000 paid by
Nottingham Forest was an emolument 'from employment' because it was an
emolument 'from becoming an employee' indistinguishable from the £80,000 paid
j by Southampton for the like purpose. If the provider of the emolument is the
employer who has an interest in the performance of the contract, the court may find
difficulty in accepting that the emolument was not 'from the employment' but from
something else. The difficulty is not so great where a person who is not the employer
provides an emolument because such a person may well be activated by motives
other than desire to see that the employee enters into or continues in the employment
of another.

The authorities have been concerned with those cases in which it is not clear whether an emolument has been paid to an employee for acting or agreeing to act as *a* an employee or has been paid for some other reason.

In *Hochstrasser (Inspector of Taxes) v Mayes* [1960] AC 376, 38 TC 673, ICI operated a scheme under which ICI made a tax-free loan to an employee member of the scheme to enable the employee to purchase a house. Under the scheme, if the employee were transferred to another place of work and sold his house at a loss, ICI were bound to make good the loss. The employee purchased a house for £1,850 with *b* the help of an ICI loan of £300 and on transfer sold his house for £1,500. ICI duly paid the employee £350 and this House decided that the emolument of £350 was not an emolument 'from' employment. This was a case of an existing employee and Viscount Simonds decided that the emolument was not a reward for past services. Lord Radcliffe said ([1960] AC 376 at 391–392, 38 TC 676 at 707):

> '... it is not easy in any of these cases in which the holder of an office or *c* employment receives a benefit which he would not have received but for his holding of that office or employment to say precisely why one considers that the money paid in one instance is, in another instance is not, a "perquisite or profit ... therefrom." The test to be applied is the same for all. It is contained in the statutory requirement that the payment, if it is to be the subject of assessment, *d* must arise "from" the office or employment. In the past several explanations have been offered by judges of eminence as to the significance of the word "from" in this context. It has been said that the payment must have been made to the employee "as such." It has been said that it must have been made to him "in his capacity of employee." It has been said that it is assessable if paid "by way of remuneration for his services," and said further that this is what is meant by *e* payment to him "as such." These are all glosses, and they are all of value as illustrating the idea which is expressed by the words of the statute. But it is perhaps worth observing that they do not displace those words. For my part, I think that their meaning is adequately conveyed by saying that, while it is not sufficient to render a payment assessable that an employee would not have received it unless he had been an employee, it is assessable if it has been paid to *f* him in return for acting as or being an employee.'

Lord Radcliffe was dealing with an emolument paid to an existing employee. Applying his words to an emolument paid to a prospective employee 'it is assessable if it has been paid to him in return for his agreement to act as or become an employee'. Lord Radcliffe decided in that case that the emolument had not been paid to the employee in return for his acting as or being an employee. He said ([1960] *g* AC 376 at 392, 38 TC 673 at 708):

> 'The essential point is that what was paid to him was paid to him in respect of his personal situation as a house-owner, who had taken advantage of the housing scheme and had obtained a claim to indemnity accordingly. In my opinion, such a payment is no more taxable as a profit from his employment than would be a payment out of a provident or distress fund set up by an employer for the *h* benefit of employees whose personal circumstances might justify assistance.'

In the present case Nottingham Forest paid £75,000 as an emolument in return for the taxpayer agreeing to act as or become an employee of Southampton and for no other reason. The taxpayer accepted the emolument of £75,000 in return for agreeing to act as or become an employee of Southampton just as he accepted *j* £80,000 from Southampton for the same reason. The taxation consequences to the taxpayer should be and are the same. The taxpayer sought and obtained the aggregate sum of £155,000 for his agreement to enter the employment of Southampton. It did not matter to the taxpayer whether the £155,000 was paid wholly or partly by Southampton or Nottingham Forest or some other third party.

In *Laidler v Perry (Inspector of Taxes)* [1966] AC 16, 42 TC 351 a company gave each of its employees a gift voucher for £10 each Christmas. The gift was held to be taxable. Lord Reid said ([1966] AC 16 at 30, 42 TC 351 at 363):

> 'There is a wealth of authority on this matter and various glosses on or paraphrases of the words in the Act appear in judicial opinions, including speeches in this House. No doubt they were helpful in the circumstances of the cases in which they were used, but in the end we must always return to the words in the statute and answer the question—did this profit arise from the employment? The answer will be "no" if it arose from something else.'

The commissioners had held that the vouchers were made available in return for services rather than as gifts not constituting a reward for services. Lord Reid said ([1966] AC 16 at 32, 42 TC 351 at 364) that 'this finding does appear to me to negative mere personal gift, and it appears to me to be unassailable'. In the present case both the sums of £80,000 and £75,000 were made available in return for the taxpayer's agreement to render services.

Pritchard (Inspector of Taxes) v Arundale [1972] Ch 229, 47 TC 680 was a case dealing with a prospective employee. A senior partner in a firm of chartered accountants agreed to leave his firm and serve a company as managing director on terms inter alia that 4,000 shares in the company would be transferred to him by a shareholder. The Revenue claimed that the 4,000 shares constituted an emolument from the employment. The taxpayer claimed that the shares were an inducement to him to give up an established position and status and to compensate him for so doing. The commissioners accepted this claim and held that the transfer of the shares was not something in the nature of a reward for his future services with the company. Megarry J held that there was ample evidence on which the commissioners could reach their conclusion.

In the instant case counsel for the taxpayer, argued in the first place that for the purposes of s 181, an emolument must be 'for' employment and not merely 'from' that employment. If the argument were correct, no emolument provided by a third party would be taxable under s 181. The argument substitutes the words 'emolument from the employer' for the words 'emolument from the employment'. The courts below shrank from this conclusion and accepted that an emolument provided by a third party in the employ of another could be an emolument from the employment in some circumstances. The courts below said that the third party must have an interest in the performance of the contract and relied on the following passage from the judgment of Megarry J in *Pritchard v Arundale* [1972] Ch 229 at 240–241, 47 TC 680 at 689–690:

> 'Second, to return, as always one must, to the language of the statute, the payment must be an emolument "from" the office or employment; and I do not think "from" means "for." In other words, the payment must be made in reference to the services rendered under the office or employment, and as a reward for them, and so in that sense flow "from" the office or employment; and this is not the same as a payment made "for" undertaking the office or employment. I am not saying that merely because some benefit is, as it were, a premium or other initial payment in return for entering into a contract of employment it is not taxable. Remuneration for services is still remuneration for services, even if paid in a lump sum in advance. But whereas it will normally be very difficult to demonstrate that periodical payments made by an employer to an employee during the employment are anything but payments taxable under Schedule E, the fact that a payment is in the form of a lump sum paid at or before the commencement of the employment is a factor which, taken with other factors, may exclude Schedule E. If that Schedule is to apply, what the payments must relate to, and reward, is not the mere existence of a contract of service, nor merely entering into such contract, but the services rendered or to be rendered under the contract.'

This passage was unnecessary for the decision because on the finding of the commissioners in *Pritchard v Arundale* the emolument of 4,000 shares did not arise from employment but from something else, namely, as compensation for the taxpayer giving up an established position. In the present case the commissioners found that the payment of £75,000 by Nottingham Forest was an inducement to the taxpayer to play football for Southampton and nothing else. As Morritt J pointed out ([1988] STC 868 at 877), the commissioners rejected the contention that the payment was compensation for the loss of the rights he enjoyed under his existing contract with Nottingham Forest.

Morritt J, applying the passage which I have cited from the judgment of Megarry J in *Pritchard v Arundale* held in the instant case (at 877–878):

'A payment by a third party may nevertheless be an emolument from the employment where the payer has an interest direct or indirect in the performance of the contract of employment either in the past as in the case of tips or in the future as in the *Pritchard v Arundale* case itself.'

In the Court of Appeal Sir Nicolas Browne-Wilkinson V-C said ([1990] STC 55 at 62) that the essential characteristic required to make a payment an emolument 'from' the employment was that the payment must be 'referable to the performance of the services under the relevant contract of employment and nothing else'. Staughton LJ said (at 63) that the distinction between appointment and employment, ie the difference between becoming and remaining an employee 'is often of no consequence so far as a payment by the employer is concerned. The same may be true in the case of a payment by a third party, if he is interested in the services to be performed'.

There is nothing in s 181 or the authorities to justify the inference that an 'emolument from employment' only applies to an emolument provided by a person who has an interest in the performance by the employee of the services which he becomes bound to perform when he enteres into the contract of employment.

If s 181 applies only to an emolument provided by an employer or by a third party who has an interest in the performance by the employee of his contract of service with the employer, there are difficulties in defining the 'interest' which makes the employee liable to pay tax on the emoluments under s 181. Counsel for the taxpayer suggested that if the £75,000 had been paid by a shareholder in Southampton Football Club Ltd interested in the dividends and capital value of his shares or if the £75,000 had been paid by a sponsor of the Southampton football team interested in obtaining valuable publicity or if the £75,000 had been paid by a philanthropic millionaire supporter of Southampton sentimentally interested in the fortunes of the club, then the £75,000 would or might have been an emolument from the employment of the taxpayer by Southampton. But, he said, as the £75,000 was provided by Nottingham Forest, who were only interested in the £325,000 payable if the taxpayer agreed to play football for Southampton, s 181 does not apply. I prefer the simpler view that an emolument arises from employment if it is provided as a reward or inducement for the employee to remain or become an employee and not for something else.

I can find nothing in the 1970 Act which suggests the gloss which the courts below have put on the statute. In the present case both Southampton and Nottingham Forest were interested in the taxpayer becoming an employee of Southampton. Both Southampton and Nottingham Forest provided emoluments to induce the taxpayer to become an employee of Southampton. So far as the taxpayer is concerned, both the emoluments of £80,000 from Southampton and £75,000 from Nottingham Forest were paid to him for the same purpose and had the same effect, namely, as an inducement to him to agree to become an employee of Southampton. The actual performance of the terms of his contract of employment did not depend on either or both the emoluments. The taxpayer kept goal for Southampton because he had contracted to do so, not because he had received emoluments. The taxpayer made miraculous saves for Southampton because he was an honourable man and a

professional footballer and was contractually bound to do his best for Southampton.
Emoluments amounting to £155,000 may be expected to inspire a goalkeeper to
great achievements but that inspiration came as much from the £75,000 provided
by Nottingham Forest as it came from the £80,000 provided by Southampton.
Indirectly, the whole of the £155,000 can be said to have been provided by
Southampton. On the transfer of the taxpayer there will be shown in the accounts of
Nottingham Forest the receipt of the net sum of £250,000 from the transfer.
Nottingham Forest received £325,000 from Southampton and were enabled to pay
£75,000 to the taxpayer leaving them with £250,000.

In *Brumby (Inspector of Taxes) v Milner* [1976] STC 534, [1976] 1 WLR 1096
under a company profit-sharing scheme the trustees of a trust deed with the help of
a loan from the company purchased shares in the company to be held in trust for the
employees and former employees of the company. When the company merged with
a larger company the scheme became impracticable and the trustees reluctantly
resolved to determine the scheme, whereon the capital of the trust fund became
distributable between the current employees and former employees at the discretion
of the trustees and was distributed in amounts varying with length of service. It was
contended on behalf of an employee that the distribution was not made in order to
reward the employees but because the merger had made the continuation of the
scheme impracticable and that the distributions were not received by the employees
'from' this employment but were received as an incident of the merger. This
argument was rejected by Walton J ([1975] STC 215, [1975] 1 WLR 958), the Court
of Appeal ([1975] STC 644, [1976] 1 WLR 29) and this House ([1976] STC 534,
[1976] 1 WLR 1096). The tests suggested by Lord Radcliffe in *Hochstrasser v Mayes*
[1960] AC 376 at 391, 38 TC 673 at 707 and by Lord Reid in *Laidler v Perry* [1966]
AC 16 at 30, 42 TC 351 at 363 were applied and Lord Kilbrandon ([1976] STC 534
at 538, [1976] 1 WLR 1096 at 1101) said:

> 'It was submitted that the payment arose not from the taxpayer's employment
> but from the company's reluctant decision to wind up the profit-sharing scheme.
> I cannot agree with that. Certainly the money forming the payment became
> available in consequence of certain events and decisions connected with the
> structure of the company. But the sole reason for making the payment to the
> taxpayer was that he was an employee, and the payment arose from his
> employment. It arose from nothing else, as it would have done if, for example,
> it had been made to an employee for some compassionate reason.'

The fact that the emoluments were provided by the trustees and not by the
company and the fact that the trustees as trustees had no interest in the performance
by the taxpayers of their services as employees were not argued to make any
difference.

In *Glantre Engineering Ltd v Goodhand (Inspector Taxes)* [1983] STC 1, a company
appointed a financial director and paid him £10,000 which the company claimed
was to compensate him for his loss in leaving his previous employment. Warner J
declined to interfere with the finding of the commissioners who held that the
£10,000 was an inducement to the employee to enter the employment of the
company and was taxable.

This is an illustration of the fact that an emolument from employment may be an
emolument for agreeing to become an employee.

In *Hamblett v Godfrey (Inspector of Taxes)* [1987] STC 60, [1987] 1 WLR 357, a
sum of £1,000 paid to a civil servant for giving up her rights to join a trade union
was held to be taxable under s 181 of the 1970 Act. The taxpayer received the £1,000
in recognition of the loss of rights that were not personal rights but were directly
connected with her employment. The source of the payment was the employment.

In *Bray (Inspector of Taxes) v Best* [1989] STC 159, [1989] 1 WLR 167, this
House held that payments otherwise taxable under s 181 escaped taxation because
the distributions were found to be attributable to the fiscal year in which they were
made and after the termination of the taxpayer's employment and were not

attributable to any year of assessment during which the taxpayer's employment
subsisted.

In the instant case Staughton LJ ([1990] STC 55 at 63), treated the decisions in
Hamblett v Godfrey and *Bray v Best* as establishing that:

> 'If a payment is *not* made for being an employee, or does not arise from the
> existence of the employer-employee relationship, it is not an emolument from
> the employment. Specifically, I would hold that a payment made to induce a
> person to accept an office or enter into a contract of employment is not on that
> ground alone an emolument from the office or employment.'

But *Hamblett v Godfrey* only decided that the payment in that case arose from the
employment and not from 'something else'. *Bray v Best* was not concerned with the
present problem. Neither case is authority for the proposition advanced by the Lord
Justice.

My Lords, in August 1982 the taxpayer was transferred from Nottingham Forest
to Southampton. The transfer fee for Nottingham Forest was £250,000. The
signing-on fee for the taxpayer was £155,000. The rest of the transfer to Southampton
was £405,000. The signing-on fee is liable to tax in the hands of the taxpayer under
s 181 of the 1970 Act. I would allow the appeal and restore the assessment pursuant
to the findings and decision of the commissioners.

LORD ACKNER. My Lords, I have had the advantage of reading in draft the
speech of my noble and learned friend Lord Templeman. I agree with it and for the
reasons which he gives I, too, would allow the appeal.

LORD GOFF OF CHIEVELEY. My Lords, for the reasons given in the speech to
be delivered by my noble and learned friend, Lord Templeman, I would allow the
appeal.

Appeal allowed.

Solicitors: *Solicitor of Inland Revenue*; *Hempsons*, agents for *George Davies & Co*,
Manchester (for the taxpayer).

Siew Ling Choo   Barrister.

a
R v Inland Revenue Commissioners, ex parte T C Coombs & Co

HOUSE OF LORDS
LORD MACKAY OF CLASHFERN LC, LORD OLIVER OF AYLMERTON, LORD GOFF OF
b CHIEVELEY, LORD JAUNCEY OF TULLICHETTLE AND LORD LOWRY
5, 6, 9 NOVEMBER 1990, 14 FEBRUARY 1991

Judicial review – Information – Power to require information – Inspector's notice requiring stockbrokers to deliver documents containing entries concerning client companies and former employee – Whether inspector's notice valid – Taxes Management
c *Act 1970, s 20(3), (4), (7).*

An inspector, with the consent of a General Commissioner under s 20(7)[a] of the Taxes Management Act 1970, served two notices under s 20(3)[b] and (4)[c] of the Act requiring the applicants, a firm of stockbrokers, to deliver such documents as contained or might contain information relevant to the tax liability of a taxpayer.
d Between 1979 and 1984 the taxpayer had been employed by the applicants to trade only for certain specified clients. The first notice required the applicants to deliver or make available a long list of documents relating to all business transactions over the period 6 April 1980 to 5 April 1986 concerning 12 companies. Of the 12, four were the taxpayer's and the applicants' clients. Another company was not a client of the applicants and was unknown to them. A sixth company, Hereford Securities &
e Management SA (Hereford), acted on behalf of unknown principals. The remaining six companies were clients of the applicants but, according to affidavits sworn by the applicants, the taxpayer and the directors of those companies, had no connection with the taxpayer. The Revenue accepted that in response to the first notice the applicants had supplied all the documents in their power relating to the first four companies and did not pursue their inquiries in regard to the company which the
f applicants claimed was unknown to them. The Revenue did not accept however that the documents supplied in respect of Hereford represented all the documents in the applicants' possession. When the applicants applied by judicial review for a declaration that they had complied with the first notice the Revenue withdrew the notice and served on the applicants a second notice requiring the delivery of a list of documents relating to Hereford, the remaining six companies and the taxpayer.
g The applicants then obtained leave to apply by judicial review for (a) an order quashing the second notice in so far as it required the applicants to deliver documents relating to the affairs of the six companies; and (b) a declaration that the applicants had complied with the second notice in so far as it required them to deliver documents relating to the affairs of Hereford and the taxpayer. In the judicial review proceedings the applicants adduced evidence that the companies were not linked to
h the taxpayer and submitted that no inspector could have reasonably come to the conclusion that there had been such a connection. The Revenue refused, on grounds of confidentiality, to reveal to the court the information placed before the commissioner when seeking his consent for the notice under s 20(7). Schiemann J dismissed the application on the grounds that the applicants had failed to satisfy the court that, on the material before the inspector when issuing the notice, the inspector
j could not reasonably have come to the conclusion that the documents might contain

---
a Section 20(7), so far as material, is set out at p 102 *h–j*
b Section 20(3), so far as material, is set out at p 102 *d–f*
c Section 20(4), so far as material, is set out at p 102 *f–h*

relevant information and that no adverse inference could be drawn from the
Revenue's silence. The Court of Appeal by a majority (Parker and Taylor LJJ, *a*
Bingham LJ dissenting) reversed that decision allowing the applicants' appeal on
the grounds that the applicants' evidence stated facts which could not be reconciled
with the inspector's opinion being reasonable and that the Crown's failure to adduce
evidence in reply established a prima facie case that the inspector could not have
formed the reasonable opinion required. The Crown appealed to the House of
Lords.   *b*

Held – Parliament had designated the inspector as the decision-maker as regards
the issue of a notice under s 20(3) requiring a party to deliver documents which in
his reasonable opinion might contain information relevant to the tax liability of a
taxpayer. Parliament had also designated the commissioner as the monitor of the
decision by providing under s 20(7) that the commissioner consented to the *c*
inspector's decision to issue such a notice. A presumption of regularity applied to
both. No unfavourable inference could be drawn from the Revenue's silence because
there was an obvious explanation for it, and the presumption that the inspector
acted intra vires when giving the notice could only be displaced by evidence which
could not be reconciled with the inspector's having had the required reasonable
opinion. The applicants had failed to adduce that evidence. The Crown's appeal *d*
would therefore be allowed.
    Dicta of Lord Diplock in *IRC v Rossminster Ltd* [1980] STC 42 at 56 applied.
    Per Lord Mackay of Clashfern LC. When the consent of a General or Special
Commissioner was required to the giving of a notice by an inspector under s 20, the
obligation on the commissioner to consider all the circumstances implied a duty on
the inspector to lay before the commissioner all the information he had about the *e*
relevant circumstances including any which might be unfavourable to the giving of
the notice. Where an application for judicial review was made in circumstances such
as the instant case, it would be appropriate for the inspector's affidavit to include a
statement of the way in which the sitting before the commissioner had been
conducted with as much detail of the subject matter as was possible.
                                                                               f

Notes

For Taxes Management Act 1970, s 20, see Simon's Taxes Part G2.

Cases referred to in opinions

Derby (Earl) v Bury Improvement Comrs (1869) LR 4 Ex 222.   *g*
IRC v Rossminster Ltd [1980] STC 42, [1980] AC 952, [1980] 1 All ER 80, 52 TC
  160, HL.
R v Nat Bell Liquors Ltd [1922] 2 AC 128, HL.
R v Northumberland Compensation Appeal Tribunal, ex p Shaw [1952] 1 KB 338, CA.
R (Martin) v Mahony [1910] 2 IR 695.
                                                                               h

Appeal

The Commissioners of Inland Revenue (the Crown), appealed against an order of
the Court of Appeal (Parker, Taylor LJJ (Bingham LJ dissenting)) given on 26 May
1989 ([1989] STC 520) allowing an appeal by T C Coombs & Co (the applicants)
from a decision of Schiemann J ([1989] STC 104) dismissing an application by the *j*
applicants for judicial review and holding that the applicants had failed to satisfy the
court that on the material before the inspector at the time he took the decision he
could not have reasonably come to the conclusion that the documents might contain
the relevant information. The facts are set out in the opinion of Lord Lowry.

P I F Vallance QC and *Launcelot Henderson* for the Crown.

a *David Goldberg QC* and *Edward Bailey* for the applicants.

Their Lordships took time for consideration.

14 February 1991. The following opinions were delivered.

b **LORD MACKAY OF CLASHFERN LC.** My Lords, I have had the advantage of reading in draft the speech prepared by my noble and learned friend Lord Lowry. For the reasons he has given, I would allow the appeal and award to the Crown the costs of the second judicial review proceedings, both here and below, but allow the cost of the first judicial review proceedings to the applicants in these proceedings, the respondents here.

c   On two matters dealt with by my noble and learned friend, I wish to add my own comment. First, counsel for the Crown submitted that the recipient of a notice had the same task whether he was seeking judicial review or challenging, on the same grounds, the validity of the notice by way of defence to penalty proceedings. This question was not argued before your Lordships and, therefore, like my noble and learned friend I would be most reluctant to come to a definite conclusion on it.

d   A second issue to which I wish to turn is of great general importance. My noble and learned friend Lord Lowry has quoted the terms of s 20(7) of the Taxes Management Act 1970 (the 1970 Act) in which it is provided that consent of a General or Special Commissioner is required to the giving of a notice by an inspector under s 20 and that the commissioner is to give his consent only on being satisfied that in all the circumstances, and I emphasise 'all the circumstances', the inspector *e* is justified in proceeding under this section. Section 20B(1), which my noble and learned friend has also quoted, requires that the person who is to receive the notice must, before the notice is given, have been given a reasonable opportunity to deliver or make available the documents in question and the inspector must not apply to the commissioner for consent until the person has been given that opportunity. It follows that one of the circumstances into which the commissioner must inquire, *f* when an application is made to him, is whether such a reasonable opportunity has been given and any correspondence that passes in that connection between the inspector and the person to whom he wishes to give notice should be placed before the commissioner. The obligation on the commissioner to consider all the circumstances implies a duty on the officer of the Revenue who appears before the commissioner to lay before the commissioner all the information he has about the *g* relevant circumstances including any which might be unfavourable to the giving of the notice.

Where an application for judicial review is made in circumstances such as the present, I would regard it as appropriate for the Revenue affidavit to include a statement of the way in which the sitting before the commissioner was conducted, with as much detail of the subject matter placed before him as is possible. For *h* example, I cannot see any reason why it should not be stated that all correspondence passing between the Revenue and the person to whom the notice is proposed to be given relating to the notice was placed before the commissioner if that had taken place.

In enacting these provisions Parliament obviously placed great weight on the *j* position of the independent commissioner and the need for the commissioner's consent. It is important that this be given full effect. I do not wish to suggest in any way that the Revenue practice hitherto has not been consistent with this view but the affidavit in the present case relating to the proceedings before the commissioner could have dealt more explicitly than it did with some of the matters that have been

in issue. It would be a great benefit to the court in any similar proceedings for
judicial review in the future to have a full affidavit on this aspect of the matter.   *a*

LORD OLIVER OF AYLMERTON. My Lords, I have had the advantage of
reading in draft the speech prepared by my noble and learned friend, Lord Lowry.
I agree with it and would allow the appeal for the reasons which he has given.

LORD GOFF OF CHIEVELEY. My Lords, for the reasons given in the speech to   *b*
be delivered by my noble and learned friend, Lord Lowry, I would allow the appeal.

LORD JAUNCEY OF TULLICHETTLE. My Lords, I have had the advantage of
reading in draft the speech of my noble and learned friend Lord Lowry. I agree with
it and for the reasons which he gives therein I would allow the appeal. I wish only to   *c*
add a few words of my own on two matters.

Section 20B of the Taxes Management Act 1970 (the 1970 Act) (as amended)
provides that before a notice is served on a person under sub-ss (1) or (3) of s 20 the
person must be given a reasonable opportunity to deliver or make available the
documents in question. It follows that when an inspector seeks to obtain the consent
of a commissioner under s 20(7) the attitude of the person to the Revenue's request   *d*
for documents is likely to be known to the inspector. It is, in my view, essential that
at this stage the inspector places before the commissioner all the material which is
relevant to the application for consent including any observations made or
documents delivered by that person. Only when all such material is before the
commissioner can he properly exercise his statutory function.

The Revenue have a heavy responsibility when seeking to exercise their powers   *e*
under s 20 of the 1970 Act and they must only hide behind a cloak of confidence
when this is absolutely necessary and not as a matter of course. If a person to whom
a request for documents has been made asks reasonable questions or raises reasonable
objections the Revenue should deal with these matters unless there are compelling
reasons for adopting a wall of silence. In the case of Hereford the applicants
maintained that they had handed over all the documents which they possessed. By   *f*
letter of 27 January 1988 to the applicants' solicitors the Revenue stated that they
did not accept they had received all documents relating to Hereford. When the
solicitors asked the Revenue what documents they thought had not been delivered
the Revenue on 16 February 1988 gave the following singularly unhelpful reply:

> 'With regard to the second notice, it is for your clients to decide to what
> extent they have complied with their obligations in regard to Hereford Securities   *g*
> & Management SA (all accounts) and T P Ramsden and with respect the
> Revenue are entitled to receive their response under a notice the scope of which
> is not so far as I am aware challenged on grounds of construction.'

Counsel for the Crown agreed that in the event of the Revenue initiating penalty
proceedings in relation to the Hereford documents it would be necessary to establish
that there were such documents in the possession of the applicants which had not   *h*
been produced. In these circumstances it is very difficult to justify the unhelpful
attitude adopted by the Revenue in their letter of 16 February 1988. Indeed I
understood their counsel to accept that his clients were unreasonable to answer in
this manner. While my observations on this matter do not affect the result of this
appeal it is important that the Revenue should bear these observations in mind when
exercising their s 20 powers on other occasions.   *j*

LORD LOWRY. My Lords, this appeal arises out of the service by an inspector of
taxes on behalf of the Inland Revenue Commissioners (the Crown) on a firm of
stockbrokers, T C Coombs & Co (the applicants), of two notices under s 20 of the

Taxes Management Act 1970 (the 1970 Act) respectively dated 1 April 1987 (the first
a   notice) and 6 January 1988 (the second notice) requiring the applicants to deliver or
to make available for inspection such documents as were in their possession or power
and as '(in the inspector's reasonable opinion)' contained or might contain information
relevant to the tax liability of a businessman (the taxpayer) who was employed by
the applicants on a commission basis as a trader from 12 November 1979 until June
1984 on the terms that he would trade for certain specified clients only and would be
b   paid 20% of the net income generated by him through those clients.
The first notice required the applicants to deliver or make available:

'All client account files operated by [the taxpayer] to include all books of
account and accounting records and all other documents or records whatsoever
relating to any business operated covering the period 6 April 1980 to 5 April
1986 inclusive or which may contain entries within the period 6 April 1980 to
c   5 April 1986 inclusive and in particular for the period specified all client account
statements in account with [12 named companies] and in addition all
correspondence files, all commission statements, all contract notes, notification
forms to the Mutual Reference Society.'

Of the 12 companies, four, Gantillion (Hong Kong) Ltd, Hereford Securities
d   Account 99, Privatbank & Trust Co Zurich AG and DF Gaggiari & Co, were clients
of the taxpayer and of the applicants and shortly before he left the applicants, the
taxpayer became a principal in respect of Account 99. Another company, Inshala
Foundation was not a client of the applicants and, they stated, was unknown to
them. A sixth company, Hereford Securities & Management SA, acted on behalf of
undisclosed principals. The remaining six companies were clients of the applicants
e   but, according to the applicants, had no connection with the taxpayer.
In response to the first notice the applicants supplied what are taken to be all the
documents in their possession or power relating to the four companies which were
clients of the taxpayer. They also supplied documents relating to Hereford Securities
& Management SA (Hereford), but the Crown have not conceded that these
represented all the Hereford related documents in the applicants' possession or
f   power. The Revenue did not further pursue their inquiries in regard to Inshala
Foundation and so the second notice required production of:

'All client account statements, books of accounts, accounting records,
correspondence, commission statements, contract notes, notification forms to
the Mutual Reference Society and all other documents or records whatsoever
g   relating to all business transactions in the period 6 April 1980 to 5 April 1986
inclusive' [concerning the six remaining companies (the six companies),
Hereford and the taxpayer].

The first notice was signed by an authorised inspector Mr Price, who was a 'group
leader', and was given with the consent of a General Commissioner for the division
h   of Kensington. The second notice was signed by a different authorised inspector,
Mr Hopkins (who had succeeded Mr Price) and was given with the consent of
another General Commissioner for Kensington. The 'named officer' for the purpose
of s 20(3) was in each notice Mr Allcock.
The applicants were originally given leave on 6 November 1987 to apply by
judicial review for (1) a declaration that they had complied with the first notice and
j   (2) an order prohibiting the Revenue from commencing penalty proceedings for
alleged non-compliance. That notice, however, was then withdrawn and the second
notice was served, and, accordingly, after service of the second notice, the applicants
sought, and on 8 March 1988 obtained, leave to apply by judicial review for (1) an
order quashing the second notice in so far as it required the applicants to deliver

documents relating to the affairs of the six companies, (2) a declaration that the
applicants had complied with the second notice in so far as it required them to
deliver documents relating to the affairs of Hereford and the taxpayer and (3) an
order prohibiting the Revenue from commencing penalty proceedings for alleged
non-compliance with the second notice.

The judicial review proceedings in the High Court (see [1989] STC 104) were
heard by Schiemann J, who dismissed the application with costs. The Court of
Appeal (see [1989] STC 520) by a majority (Parker and Taylor LJJ, Bingham LJ
dissenting) allowing the applicants' appeal with costs, set aside the order of
Schiemann J, quashed the second notice 'in so far as it relates to the six companies'
and declared that, in relation to Hereford and the taxpayer, the applicants had
complied with that notice. Bingham LJ would have dismissed the appeal in so far as
it related to the six companies (and, by necessary implication, also to the taxpayer),
but agreed with the majority on Hereford. Schiemann J had refused to give the
applicants their costs of obtaining leave to seek judicial review of the first notice, but
the Court of Appeal unanimously reversed him on that point. By a subsequent order
the Court of Appeal refused the Crown leave to appeal to this House, but leave to
appeal was granted by your Lordships. There are, accordingly, three issues for
decision: (1) the validity of the second notice in relation to the six companies; (2) the
correctness of the Court of Appeal's declaration in regard to Hereford; and (3) the
question concerning the costs of challenging the first notice.

Section 20 of the 1970 Act (which was substituted by the Finance Act 1976 for the
original s 20), so far as directly material, provides:

> '(3) Subject to this section, an inspector may, for the purpose of enquiring
> into the tax liability of any person ("the taxpayer"), by notice in writing require
> any of the persons who in relation to the taxpayer are subject to this subsection
> to deliver to the inspector or, if the person to whom the notice is given so elects,
> to make available for inspection by a named officer of the Board, such documents
> as are in his possession or power and as (in the inspector's reasonable opinion)
> contain, or may contain, information relevant to any tax liability to which the
> taxpayer is or may be, or may have been, subject, or to the amount of any such
> liability.
>
> (4) The persons so subject are—
>
> (a) the taxpayer's spouse, and any son or daughter of his;
> (b) in so far as the inspector's enquiries relate to liability of the taxpayer in
> respect of income, profits or gains that were, or may have been, derived
> from—
>
> (i) any business (past or present) carried on by the taxpayer or his spouse,
> or
> (ii) any business (past or present) with whose management either of them
> was concerned at a material time,
>
> any person who is carrying on a business, or was doing so at a material time,
> and any company whether carrying on a business or not . . .
>
> (7) Notices under this section are not to be given by an inspector unless he is
> authorised by the Board for its purposes; and—
>
> (a) a notice is not to be given by him except with the consent of a General or
> Special Commissioner; and
> (b) the Commissioner is to give his consent only on being satisfied that in all
> the circumstances the inspector is justified in proceeding under this section.
>
> (8) The references in subsections (1), (2) and (3) above to documents are to
> those specified or described in the notice in question; and—

(*a*) the notice shall require them to be delivered or (as the case may be) made available within such time as may be there specified; and

(*b*) the person to whom they are delivered or made available may take copies of, or extracts from them;

and a notice under subsection (3) shall name the taxpayer with whose liability the inspector (or, as the case may be, the Board) is concerned.

(9) To the extent specified in section 20B below, the above provisions are subject to the restrictions of that section.'

Certain provisions of section 20B may also be noted:

'(1) Before a notice is given to a person by an inspector under section 20(1) or (3), or under section 20A, the person must have been given a reasonable opportunity to deliver (or, in the case of section 20(3), to deliver or make available) the documents in question; and the inspector must not apply for consent under section 20(7) or, as the case may be, section 20A(3), until the person has been given that opportunity . . .

(3) An inspector cannot under section 20(1) or (3) . . . give notice to a barrister, advocate or solicitor, but the notice must in any such case be given (if at all) by the Board . . .'

Subsection (4) permits the delivery of facsimile copies of documents instead of the originals, provided the originals are made available for inspection. Subsection (5) limits the obligation to deliver or make available any document to documents the whole of which originate not more than six years before the date of the notice. Subsection (6) provides:

'But subsection (5) does not apply where the notice is so expressed as to exclude the restrictions of that subsection; and it can only be so expressed where—

(*a*) the notice being given by an inspector with consent under section 20(7), the Commissioner giving consent has also given approval to the exclusion;

(*b*) the notice being given by the Board, they have applied to a General or Special Commissioner for, and obtained, that approval.

For this purpose the Commissioner gives approval only if satisfied, on the inspector's or the Board's application, that there is reasonable ground for believing that tax has, or may have been, lost to the Crown owing to the fraud of the taxpayer.'

Because they specified the period 6 April 1980 to 5 April 1986, both the first notice dated 1 April 1987 and the second notice dated 6 January 1988 were 'so expressed *as to exclude* the restrictions of [s 20B(5)]' (emphasis added). Therefore, no point having been taken, it can be assumed that the commissioner gave his approval to the notices in that form in accordance with s 20B(6)(*a*) cited above. It may be noted that for the purpose of sub-s (6) the commissioner gives approval—

'. . . only if satisfied, on the inspector's or the Board's application, that there is reasonable ground for believing that tax has, or may have been, lost to the Crown owing to the fraud of the taxpayer.'

It is fair to say that this point was not canvassed before your Lordships and I do not propose to attribute significance to it in favour of either party.

Subsection (8) requires the client's consent before a barrister, advocate or solicitor is obliged to deliver or make available a privileged document. Penalty proceedings for non-compliance with a notice under s 20 are dealt with in ss 98–100 of the 1970 Act.

Schiemann J, dismissing the entire application, pointed out ([1989] STC 104 at 106) that the main challenge to the second notice was based on a submission that there was no material available to the inspector on which he could form the reasonable opinion that the documents which the applicants admittedly had in their possession in relation to the six companies contained or might contain information relevant to any tax liability to which the taxpayer was or might be, or might have been, subject or to the amount of any such liability. Counsel for the applicants had accepted that the inspector was not obliged to state in the notice the factual basis for his opinion. Counsel for the Crown had, for his part, accepted that the inspector, before serving the notice, must be in possession of facts from which he could and did form the relevant opinion. The judge pointed out that a prerequisite of service of a notice is the consent of an independent commissioner, who needs to be satisfied that the inspector is justified in proceeding under s 20, which involves the commissioner being satisfied on the material placed before him that the inspector's opinion is reasonable. He further observed that the applicants' counsel accepted that the applicants had to put before the court some evidence from which the court could conclude that there was no material from which the inspector could form the 'reasonable opinion' which was needed to justify service of the notice. Counsel for the Crown, while conceding in principle that judicial review would lie, contended that the evidential requirements for quashing the notice were not satisfied. The judge continued (at 107):

'In my judgment the proper approach for the court to such a case as this is to consider whether the applicant has satisfied the court that on the material before the administrator, at the time when he took the decision (whether or not that material is before the court) the administrator could not reasonably have come to the conclusion to which he asserts he came. If the administrator puts before the court all the material which was before him, then no difficulty arises. If he puts before the court none or only some of the material before him, then the court must draw inferences as best it can from whatever material on either side it has before it. The court will, however, bear in mind that it is for the applicant to persuade the court that the administrator acted illegally.'

First pointing out the possible effect of non-disclosure by an administrator whose action is challenged and adverting to the reasons for confidentiality which could militate against disclosure, the judge reviewed (at 108–109) the evidence adduced on each side. He then posed the question: 'Have the applicants satisfied the court that on the material before the administrator the administrator could not reasonably have come to the conclusion to which he asserts he did come?' and answered that question in the negative. The following passage contains the judge's reasoning (at 110):

'Counsel for the applicants submitted that the Crown, by failing to set forth its evidential material, was in effect, though not in form, asserting that his clients had no right to have the reasonableness of the Crown's decision tested by judicial review. On the facts of this case, and on the ground of challenge I have so far examined in this judgment, that seems to me a justified submission. But the question I have to ask myself is whether the legislature intended the courts to have a wider power of review that I have recognised in this judgment. Counsel for the applicants submitted that the word "reasonable" in section 20(3) points to that conclusion. There is force in his point. However, it seems to me that the statutory requirement of the approval of the commissioners in private before the notice is issued and the general undesirability of the Revenue revealing a taxpayer's affairs to third parties—who may, as the taxpayer asserts a   in the present case, be totally unconnected with him, or may only be distantly connected, or may be trade competitors—reduce the force of counsel for the applicants' submission.'

As to Hereford (in relation to which the applicants had supplied documents, although not in such measure as to satisfy the Revenue), the applicants had submitted that there was no evidence of failure on their part to provide documents, but the judge held that so to declare would be inappropriate and that it should be left to the
b   Revenue to proceed for penalties under s 98, which would provide a means of deciding the point. He also refused to give the applicants their costs of challenging the first notice, because the substance of their objection to it was the same as their unsuccessful complaint against the second notice.

The majority in the Court of Appeal disagreed with Schiemann J on all issues, but Bingham LJ would have upheld him on the first, which related to the six companies.
c   The dispute depended, as Parker LJ put it ([1989] STC 520 at 523)—

'. . . partly on the construction of certain provisions of the Taxes Management Act 1970 as substituted by s 57 of and Sch 6 to the Finance Act 1976, partly on the application of such provisions to the evidence and partly on the extent of the burden on an applicant who seeks judicial review of action such as is
d   exemplified in the present case by the giving of the notices.'

Having commented on the width of the power conferred by s 20(3), Parker LJ listed (at 524) the safeguards provided by the 1970 Act and commented that the fact of the commissioner's consent to the giving of the notice was 'a significant matter when the effect of the evidence is being considered'.

e   Having reviewed the evidence on both sides and analysed the decision of this House in *IRC v Rossminster Ltd* [1980] STC 42, [1980] AC 952, on which the Crown had strongly relied and about which I shall have something to say presently, Parker LJ (at 530) stated his conclusions:

'That evidence, unanswered as it is, certainly establishes, in my view, a prima
f   facie case that Mr Hopkins cannot have formed the reasonable opinion required. Indeed, even without the support of any inference from the failure to give reasons, it states facts which cannot be reconciled with there having been the required reasonable opinion on the part of Mr Hopkins. I consider, however, that an inference can in this case be drawn. The Crown has not only declined to give reasons, it has not sought leave to cross-examine the applicants' affidavit evidence. It has, in addition, not given any evidence as to the basis on which it
g   is contended that the applicants are subject to s 20(3). It is not known whether its case is that its inquiries relate to income, profits or gains derived from a business carried on by the taxpayer or his spouse and, if so, what business or whether it is that they relate to profits etc from a business with whose management the taxpayer was associated. If it is the latter and the case is that
h   the taxpayer or his spouse was associated with the management of each of the six companies, the affidavits of the taxpayer and the representatives of the companies, being unanswered, establish that this was not the case and the application must succeed on that ground alone. No public immunity can, in my view, arise on this matter. It is not a question of opinion. It is a question of fact on which the onus is on the Crown. Furthermore, although I accept that the Crown is entitled to protect the identity of its sources, it by no means follows
j   that all information from all sources is confidential. An informant might, for example, in the case of an English company, advise the Revenue to make company searches in respect of six companies. If it did so and found that in each case the company was owned by a seventh of which the taxpayer was a

director, I can see no reason why they should not, when challenged, so state.
Here we are faced with a blank wall which impedes the administration of justice.
On judicial review the court is not, of course, a Court of Appeal. It is not,
therefore, entitled to look at the evidence and form its own view of the
conclusion to draw from it. Unless, however, it has access to that evidence, it
cannot carry out that which is its function, namely to see whether any inspector
could reasonably have formed the required opinion. In the case of a pending
prosecution and conflicting evidence of fact, it may temporarily be prevented
from doing so. In the present case, it is not, in my judgment, so prevented. I
would allow the appeal and quash the second notice in so far as it relates to the
six companies, and I would declare in relation to Hereford Securities &
Management SA (all accounts) and T S Ramsden that the applicants have
complied with the notice. I see no reason to grant any further relief. As to the
first notice it has not been pursued and, in the light of that fact alone, the
applicants should have the costs incurred in challenging it. This is the more so
when it follows from the above that it would, if pursued, have failed in respect
of all accounts save the four as to which there is not any issue.'

Taylor LJ concurred in regard to each issue. Observing that the presumption of
regularity applies to the commissioner's exercise of his function under s 20(7), he
continued (at 535):

'If, as is conceded, the inspector's decision can still be challenged despite the
commissioner's consent, then the court has in my view to conduct its review on
the same principles as it applies generally in its supervisory jurisdiction. The
commissioner's consent is one fact to be taken into account. But it must be
stressed that the hearing before the commissioner is ex parte. The recipient of
the notice is not heard nor does he have the opportunity to place any material
he might wish to adduce before the commissioner.'

Taylor LJ further said (at 535):

'Evidential problems are at the heart of this case. The applicants do not deny
the inspector held the opinion he claims to have held. Their challenge is to its
reasonableness. The burden is therefore on the applicants to show that the
inspector's opinion was not reasonable.'

And (at 536) he said:

'The issues here are (1) have the applicants by evidence raised a prima facie
case that the inspector's opinion was unreasonable; (2) if yes, what is the effect
of the Crown's failure to adduce evidence in reply?'

As to (1) he said, 'The burden on the applicants is accepted by both parties to be
that defined by Lord Diplock in [*Rossminster*]' and then cited the passage ([1980]
STC 42 at 56, [1980] AC 952 at 1013):

'Where Parliament has designated a public officer as decision-maker for a
particular class of decisions the High Court, acting as a reviewing court under
RSC Ord 53, is not a court of appeal. It must proceed on the presumption
omnia praesumuntur rite esse acta until that presumption can be displaced by
the applicant for review, on whom the onus lies of doing so. Since no reasons
have been given by the decision-maker and no unfavourable inference can be
drawn from this fact because there is obvious justification for his failure to do
so, the presumption that he acted intra vires can only be displaced by evidence
of facts which cannot be reconciled with there having been reasonable cause for
his belief that the documents might be required as evidence . . .'

He concluded, giving his reasons, that the applicants had satisfied that test.

a   Commenting on the Revenue's failure to answer the applicants' evidence by giving reasons for the opinion held by the inspector, Taylor LJ observed that ordinarily, if a prima facie case is made out by an applicant that a respondent has acted unreasonably or taken a decision without good reason, his failure to answer the case or give reasons may lead to the inference that he had no good reasons. He adverted to the Revenue's claim that their reticence was justified by the duty of confidentiality

b   and stated that, while no adverse inference adding weight to the applicants' case should be drawn from failure to disclose reasons where such failure is justified by confidentiality, the plea of justified silence is not a *positive answer* to the applicants' case, which, not having been rebutted, *retains* what weight it has on its own merits. He concluded that the applicants had made out a positive case that the inspector's opinion was not reasonable.

c   Bingham LJ dissented concerning the six companies and on this issue would have affirmed Schiemann J. In his view the case fell 'squarely within the principle laid down by Lord Diplock' in *Rossminster* ([1980] STC 42 at 56, [1980] AC 952 at 1013). He said (at 532):

'I do not think the right approach to this case is to ask whether the applicants have raised a prima facie case which causes the onus of rebutting it to shift to

d   the Crown, and then to ask whether the Crown has discharged the onus of rebutting it. If, as I think, the case is one in which the inspector could not be expected to give reasons for his opinion either at the time he gave the notice or when the reasonableness of his opinion was challenged, there is only one question to be asked. It is: Do the applicants show that the inspector did not hold the opinion he claims to have held or, if he did hold it, that that opinion

e   was not reasonable? In a case covered by Lord Diplock's ruling, the applicant must adduce evidence of facts which cannot be reconciled with there having been reasonable cause for the inspector's belief that the documents contained or might contain information relevant to the taxpayer's liability. The onus is on the applicant for judicial review. His task is, I think, the same whether he is seeking judicial review or challenging, on the same grounds, the validity of the

f   notice by way of defence to penalty proceedings.'

He then set out six facts or groups of facts to which he paid attention in reaching that conclusion. It is convenient to reproduce what he said under his fifth heading since it deals with matters which have been strongly relied on against the Crown (at 533):

g   '(5) When the inspector gave the second notice he knew that Mr Mahon for the applicants had deposed:

"We have raised the matter of the [first] Notice with the Managers/Directors of these six clients. They deny any involvement with Mr Ramsden and see no reason why the documents the Applicants have relating to their affairs

h   should be disclosed as part of an inquiry into the tax liability of Mr Ramsden."

We now have an affidavit from Mr Sum, the manager of Rosary, who deposes:

"I am able to state that to the best of my knowledge and belief, Mr T P Ramsden has never had any dealings with that Company. Furthermore I am aware who the beneficial owner of the account is and can confirm that it is not Mr Ramsden or any person connected with Mr Ramsden."

j   Similar statements are made on behalf of the remaining five companies, all Panamanian, by Swiss directors apparently resident in Geneva. These directors were also directors of Hereford, through one of whose accounts the taxpayer admittedly dealt. If these statements showed the beneficial ownership of the

companies in a manner which convincingly excluded any beneficial interest in
the taxpayer, that might be compelling evidence that the inspector could not
reasonably have held a contrary view when he gave the second notice. But the
means of knowledge and the degree of involvement of Mr Sum and the Swiss
directors are wholly unclear. No detail is disclosed of the beneficial ownership
of these companies. There is no reason why these companies, who are not
themselves the subject of any notice, should give this information, but in its
absence the possibility that the taxpayer has an interest in the companies
through agents, trusts, nominees or fronting companies cannot in my view be
excluded.'

Dealing with the 67 minute hearing at which the General Commissioner gave
consent to the second notice, Bingham LJ said (at 534):

'The Revenue are, in my view, entitled to rely on the rule that, where acts are
of an official nature, or require the concurrence of official persons, a presumption
arises in favour of their due execution: omnia praesumuntur rite et solenniter
esse acta donec probetur in contrarium (*Broom's Legal Maxims* (10th edn, 1939)
p 642). The contrary has not been proved. It has not been contended that, by
seeking to challenge the inspector's decision to give the notice rather than the
General Commissioner's decision to give his consent, the applicants have
adopted a wrong procedure. It does, however, as I think, make it very hard for
the applicants to show that the inspector's opinion must have been unreasonable
when a responsible commissioner who saw the material on which the inspector
relied plainly considered it to be reasonable.'

On Hereford and on the costs point Bingham LJ, without giving reasons, agreed
with the majority and differed from Schiemann J.

My Lords, I find myself in agreement with Schiemann J on the substantive issues.

The case for the validity of the second notice, or any s 20(3) notice, is supported
by the presumption of regularity, which is strong in relation to the function of the
commissioner under s 20(7). He is an independent person entrusted by Parliament
with the duty of supervising the exercise of the intrusive power conferred by s 20(3)
and 'in the absence of any proof to the contrary, credit ought to be given to public
officers, who have acted prima facie within the limits of their authority, for having
done so with honesty and discretion' (see *Earl of Derby v Bury Improvement Comrs*
(1869) LR 4 Ex 222 at 226). The commissioner must be taken to be satisfied that the
inspector was justified in proceeding under s 20 and hence that the inspector held,
and reasonably held, the opinion required by s 20(3). The presumption that that
opinion was reasonable and that the commissioner was right to be satisfied can be
displaced only by evidence showing that at the time of giving the second notice the
inspector could not reasonably have held that opinion. In order to decide whether
the applicants succeed in this task, the court must consider all the evidence on both
sides and all the available facts, one of which is that the commissioner, having heard
an application, consented to the giving of the notice.

Another fact is the sparseness of the evidence adduced by the Revenue. In our
legal system generally, the silence of one party in face of the other party's evidence
may convert that evidence into proof in relation to matters which are, or are likely
to be, within the knowledge of the silent party and about which that party could be
expected to give evidence. Thus, depending on the circumstances, a prima facie
case may become a strong or even an overwhelming case. But, if the silent party's
failure to give evidence (or to give the necessary evidence) can be credibly explained,
even if not entirely justified, the effect of his silence in favour of the other party may
be either reduced or nullified. Schiemann J and all the members of the Court of
Appeal have commented with varying emphasis on what appears to me also to be

the excessive degree of reticence of the Revenue in this case, but three comments
must in fairness be made:

a

1. Part of the evidence is that an express undertaking (the observance of which is
dictated by morality and expediency alike) was given to an important source not to
reveal either the source or the information obtained from it.

2. Without knowing the facts a court cannot tell what evidence, if given, may
indirectly betray a source.

b

3. The Revenue have relied on their general duty of confidentiality as a
justification for the reticence.

Provided they are not shown to be acting in bad faith, their attitude at least
explains, if it may not entirely *justify*, their reticence, and thereby reduces its effect
in favour of the applicants. I do not wish to discourage the Revenue from observing
due confidence, much less from keeping promises, once made, but even their

c

statutory declarations contemplate that officers will make disclosure for the purposes
of their duties. If, therefore, a strong case is made for quashing a s 20(3) notice, it
may be the *duty* of the Revenue to meet that case with something more cogent than
silence, however understandable or justifiable. They should, of course, maintain
silence if disclosure would be unnecessary or unavailing or if a promise of silence has
been given.

d

Applying the principles to the instant case, I consider the evidence summarised
in the judgments below. Does it show that the inspector's opinion, when he gave the
second notice, was unreasonable? I think not, for the following reasons:

(1) Possibly the best evidence for the applicants was that reviewed by Bingham
LJ under his fifth heading to which I have referred, but its reliability must not be
assumed when it cannot be tested against the information, some of it confidential,
which the inspector could have put before the commissioner.

e

(2) Even if I hazard a guess—and it can be little more—that the Revenue could,
and perhaps should, have made fuller disclosure, there was still evidence, obtained
from the informant and presumably given to the commissioner, which the Revenue
could not tell the court.

(3) The fact that the commissioner in these circumstances gave his consent is of
paramount importance.

f

(4) The applicants purport to prove facts about the six companies. What they
need to do is prove facts which are inconsistent (or irreconcilable) with the inspector's
having had a reasonable (not necessarily a correct) opinion when he gave the second
notice that the applicants had documents relating to the six companies which
contained *or might contain* information relevant to any tax liability to which the
taxpayer was *or might be or might have been* subject.

g

To support their case the applicants, as a reductio ad absurdum, submitted that,
if the Crown's arguments were sound, the quashing of a s 20(3) notice, though
available in theory, could never be achieved in practice. My Lords, this prospect
does not fill me with alarm when I reflect that Parliament has subjected an intrusive
and potentially oppressive (but presumably necessary) power to what I suggest to be
the effective supervision of s 20(7). Nor should the difficulty of achieving a remedy

h

cause surprise when one considers the following points:

1. The applicant has to prove a negative.

2. What he has to prove is not a fact within his own knowledge but the absence of
a reasonable opinion on the part of someone else, namely, the inspector.

3. The inspector's opinion has to have been reasonable but need not have been
correct.

j

4. The resolution of the question will usually depend in large measure on evidence
which is not before the court.

5. By reason of the principle of confidentiality (which the applicant concedes),
the general rule for taking account of a party's silence does not fully apply and, for

the same reason, the court cannot assess the extent to which in each case it does not apply.

6. Proceedings in which affidavit evidence is the general rule are not well suited to resolving factual questions.

I hope that these observations will also help to show how much better a position the commissioner is in to make a just appraisal under s 20(7) than a court conducting a judicial review. They may also illustrate what I regard as the fallacy of relying on readily understandable silence as a means of converting into proof an inconclusive prima facie case. It is idle to suggest, as the applicants have done, that the court should be able to police effectively the Revenue's power under s 20(3), if that involves abrogating accepted rules of evidence. Another suggestion was that the use of the word 'reasonable' in s 20(3) meant that the court must be put in a position to assess the reasonableness of the inspector's opinion by being given access to the relevant evidence and by having a wider power of review than is commonly recognised (see per Schiemann J [1989] STC 104 at 110). I can see no warrant for this proposition either on principle or in the words of the 1970 Act. I consider that the expression 'reasonable opinion' sets the standard for the commissioner and, like Schiemann J, that s 20(7) is the real and intended safeguard.

Parker LJ distinguished *Rossminster* on its facts both accurately and effectively, whereas Bingham LJ considered that the present case fell 'squarely within the principle laid down by Lord Diplock in that case'. (I have, when commenting on the judgment of Taylor LJ, already cited the passage in question in *Rossminster* [1980] STC 42 at 56, [1980] AC 952 at 1103.) While I appreciate the distinctions drawn between that case and the present, I agree with Bingham LJ on the principle. Parliament designated the inspector as the decision-maker and also designated the commissioner as the monitor of the decision. A presumption of regularity applied to both. No unfavourable inference can be drawn from the silence of the Revenue because there is (to put it no higher) an obvious explanation for their silence, and the presumption that the inspector acted intra vires when giving the notice can only be displaced by evidence which cannot be reconciled with the inspector's having had the required reasonable opinion.

Bingham LJ, however, agreed with the majority on Hereford. Taylor LJ went further and, having expressed a firm view about Hereford, made what he regarded as the Revenue's unreasonable approach on Hereford a touchstone of their attitude regarding the six companies. I have shared with some of your Lordships the temptation to endorse the Court of Appeal's view on Hereford, influenced by the uncommunicative intransigence of the Revenue in correspondence which, admittedly without knowing all the facts, I found difficult to reconcile with the reasonable attitude which ought to characterise a government department in its dealings with the public. But the question is the same about Hereford as about the six companies: Have the applicants proved that when giving the second notice the inspector's opinion that there remained in the applicants' power or possession relevant documents which they had not disclosed was not reasonable? On the same principles as those which I have tried to bring to my consideration of issue 1, my answer must be No. In this connection I have taken note of the contrast between the Revenue's attitude of acceptance towards the disclosure made in respect of four of the original 12 companies and their scepticism, for which I feel there is bound to be a rational explanation, with regard to Hereford. In my opinion your Lordships ought not to be satisfied on the evidence available at this stage that the inspector's opinion about Hereford on 6 January 1988 was unreasonable.

I would advert here to four points which were mentioned but not strenuously pursued.

(1) The group leader when the first notice was given was Mr Price and when the second notice was given was Mr Hopkins. It was their respective opinions, as the

inspectors giving the notice, which the commissioners must have found to be
a reasonable, but Mr Allcock was the officer who attended on the commissioner.
Parker LJ queried the validity of this procedure ([1989] STC 520 at 526), but with
respect I consider that the commissioner could properly be informed by Mr Allcock
of his superior officer's opinion and the grounds thereof. Conceivably the
commissioner might have required the requesting inspector to attend on him before
giving his consent to the notice, but I cannot see a parallel between the procedure
b under s 20(7) and, for example, the issue of a warrant by a magistrate on the sworn
information of a complainant who must attend before him.

(2) It was suggested that the Revenue could have applied to cross-examine the
applicants' witnesses on their affidavits, with the implication that failure to do so
weakened their case. With respect I do not consider that this suggestion amounts to
a significant argument, since the applicants' averments could be contradicted only
c by putting to the deponents material in the possession of the Revenue and this could
be done effectively only at the cost of the confidentiality which the Revenue wished,
and in one case had promised, to maintain. Moreover, it can with a greater show of
reason, be submitted that the applicants could have made a similar application in
order to find out how far the Revenue had informed the commissioner when seeking
consent for the second notice and what kind of link they were alleging between the
d taxpayer and the six companies.

(3) Another query was whether the applicants might have attacked the
commissioner's decision to give consent as well as or instead of the inspector's notice.
The point was not argued and did not become relevant but, for my own part, I
consider that the notice was the appropriate target. If the inspector's opinion was
not reasonable, then a condition precedent to giving the notice was lacking and the
e act of giving the notice was ultra vires. If the commissioner's consent could have
been quashed in this case, it would have been on the same ground that would have
caused the notice to be ultra vires but, assuming the commissioner's function under
s 20(7) to be judicial, a challenge to his decision would in addition have to meet the
argument that a judicial decision, if otherwise competent, will not be quashed for
unreasonableness or for want of evidence not apparent on the face of the record (see
f R (Martin) v Mahony [1910] 2 IR 695; R v Nat Bell Liquors Ltd [1922] 2 AC 128;
R v Northumberland Compensation Appeal Tribunal, ex p Shaw [1952] 1 KB 338). Of
course, different considerations could arise if the commissioner's decision were to be
attacked on other grounds, such as want of jurisdiction, bias or disregard of natural
justice.

(4) Reference was made from time to time to the penalty proceedings which the
g Revenue can bring under ss 98–100 of the 1970 Act before a General or Special
Commissioner or in the High Court for failure to comply with a s 20(3) notice.
Counsel for the Crown, with whom Bingham LJ appeared to concur ([1989] STC
520 at 532), submitted that the recipient of a notice had the same task whether he
was seeking judicial review or challenging, on the same grounds, the validity of the
notice by way of defence to penalty proceedings. The applicants had, for the purpose
h of this appeal, no particular interest in refuting this statement and the question was
not argued before your Lordships. I therefore do not propose to discuss the
proposition. It is, however, clear that the issue in penalty proceedings will be not, or
not only, whether the service of the notice on the recipient was intra vires but
whether the recipient (who may have no relevant documents despite the inspector's
opinion to the contrary) is in default. On that issue the Crown will have to produce
j enough evidence to prove their case: onus ei incumbit qui affirmat.

My Lords, despite the length of this opinion, I feel that I must mention before I
conclude a point which featured only briefly in the present appeal but which is of
general importance. The applicants asked the Court of Appeal to infer that the
proceedings before the General Commissioner may have been a formality, in which

case small reliance should be placed on his consent. The Crown then, pursuant to
leave, put in a new affidavit by Mr Allcock showing that on 1 April 1987 he attended   *a*
before a commissioner for 37 minutes and 'laid before him all the documentary
evidence to which I have referred'. He also deposed that he attended before a
different commissioner on 6 January 1988 and continued:

> 'Once again I laid all the documentary evidence, to which I have referred,
> before the Commissioner. He asked for clarification on a number of points, and
> after one hour and seven minutes [he] signed the Notice referred to as the   *b*
> "Second Notice" in these Judicial Review proceedings.'

The applicants contended in their printed case that the protection given by s 20(7)
should not be overstated, particularly because the Crown had not shown (as it was
said they ought to have done) that they had made full disclosure to the commissioner,
when seeking consent to the second notice, of what had already passed between   *c*
them and the applicants. Before your Lordships counsel for the applicants reinforced
and refined his argument by emphasising that the second application was made to a
different commissioner and by submitting that Mr Allcock's choice of language led
to the clear inference that in his second application he had relied exclusively on the
evidence tendered to the first commissioner and had not revealed the later
correspondence. Thus what had been an ancillary contention designed to weaken   *d*
the efficacy of the commissioner's consent was elevated into a new point of substance
to the effect that the commissioner's consent to the second notice (and consequently
the notice itself) had been vitiated by the Revenue's non-disclosure of vital facts.
Your Lordships, in order to clarify the issues, invited counsel for the applicants, if
he meant to rely on the new point, to apply for leave to amend his printed case; and,
counsel for the applicants having somewhat tentatively decided to seek, and then   *e*
having formulated, an amendment, your Lordships sought the views of counsel for
the Crown. He suggested that, if he had the opportunity to show counsel for the
applicants certain notes relating to the second hearing before the commissioner
(which presumably would provide an indication of what had been disclosed), the
application to amend might be abandoned. Counsel conferred but this step failed to
produce the result foreseen by counsel for the Crown and eventually your Lordships *f*
refused leave since to allow the amendment would open a new issue of fact which
had not played a part in any of the earlier proceedings.

In these circumstances it would seem that the only fair and practical course is
neither to draw the adverse inference from Mr Allcock's affidavit which counsel for
the applicants has pressed on your Lordships nor, on the other hand, to make the
assumption, which would greatly help the Crown, that they told the second   *g*
commissioner of everything which passed between the parties since the giving of the
first notice.

I suggest that, for the immediate purpose of this appeal, the point has now been
disposed of, but I take the opportunity of stating my clear view that, when seeking a
commissioner's consent under s 20(7), the Revenue are absolutely bound to make
full disclosure to the commissioner of all facts within their knowledge which could *h*
properly influence the commissioner against giving his consent to a s 20(3) notice. I
do not by any means wish to imply that the Revenue have heretofore proceeded on
any other basis, but it may be worth emphasising that failure to make full disclosure
will, if it comes to light, almost inevitably vitiate the consent and nullify the notice
given pursuant thereto.

It will be difficult for an applicant for judicial review to demonstrate such a failure *j*
if it should occur. Nevertheless, the principle of full disclosure being made and
being seen to be made, so far as those objects can be reconciled with the proper
claims of confidentiality, is important and may on appropriate occasions be
safeguarded by an application to cross-examine.

The last issue concerns the applicants' costs of challenging the first notice. On this

a point I agree with the Court of Appeal because the Revenue abandoned the first notice and thereby surrendered to the applicants in the proceedings arising from it. The fact that the Crown turned out to be right in principle is not a reason for refusing the applicants their costs of the earlier proceedings.

Accordingly, my Lords, I would allow the Crown's appeal and restore the order of Schiemann J except in regard to the costs of the first judicial review proceedings

b which I would award to the applicants.

Appeal allowed with costs of the second judicial review proceedings. Cost of the first judicial review proceedings to the applicant.

Solicitors: *Solicitor of Inland Revenue*; *Edwin Coe* (for the applicants).

c
                                                Rengan Krishnan Esq   Barrister.

Alexander v Inland Revenue Commissioners   a

COURT OF APPEAL, CIVIL DIVISION
RALPH GIBSON, NICHOLLS LJJ AND SIR DENYS BUCKLEY
13 DECEMBER 1990, 17 JANUARY 1991

Capital transfer tax – Valuation – Jurisdiction of Lands Tribunal – Valuation of   b
leasehold premises – Liability to repay proportion of statutory discount in the event of
disposal – Whether valuation of leasehold premises taking into account liability to repay
discount valuation of land within the exclusive jurisdiction of Lands Tribunal – Principles
applicable in valuation – Finance Act 1975, ss 22(1), 38, Sch 4, para 7(4).

In 1983, A (the deceased) acquired a leasehold interest in a flat for a consideration of   c
£35,400 pursuant to the 'right to buy' provisions of the Housing Act 1980 (the 1980
Act) at a discount of £24,600. The lease contained a covenant by the tenant to pay
the landlords the relevant percentage of the discount if, within five years of the grant
of the lease, there should be a disposal falling within the terms of the covenant. The
liability to pay was a charge on the leasehold. The amount so payable was to be
reduced by 20% of the discount for each complete year which elapsed after the grant   d
of the lease in 1983. On 17 January 1984, before the end of the first full year, the
deceased died. Under s 22(1)[a] of the Finance Act 1975 (the 1975 Act), on the death
of any person, 'tax shall be charged as if, immediately before his death, he had made
a transfer of value and the value transferred by it had been equal to the value of his
estate immediately before his death'. Under s 38(1)[b], the value of the property would,
for the purposes of capital transfer tax, be the price which the property might   e
reasonably be expected to fetch if sold in the open market at that time. In 1986, the
Crown gave notice to the deceased's son and executor of her estate (the executor)
that the value of the lease had been determined at £52,000. The executor appealed
to the Lands Tribunal (the tribunal) inviting them to determine two issues : (i) the
value of the leasehold interest at 17 January 1984 free from incumbrances; and (ii)
the amount of the deduction to be made from that value in respect of the liability of   f
the deceased to repay the relevant percentage of the discount. His case was that the
market value of the flat on 17 January was £60,000, the amount repayable to the
landlords on a sale on that date was £24,600 and consequently the net worth of the
flat was £35,400. The tribunal determined the open market value of the leasehold
interest immediately before the deceased's death as £63,000 but concluded that they
had no jurisdiction to decide the appropriate deduction to be made from that value   g
to allow for the liability to repay the discount. The Crown appealed by way of case
stated to the Court of Appeal contending, inter alia, (i) that the tribunal had
exclusive jurisdiction under para 7(4) of Sch 4[c] to the 1975 Act because the property
to be valued was land, being a lease of land subject to the incumbrance of the charge
securing repayment of the discount; (ii) that the principles exemplified in *IRC v
Crossman* [1937] AC 26 applied to the valuation process in s 38(1); and (iii) that   h
accordingly, the market value of the lease should be taken as the amount which a
person would be willing to pay to acquire the lease, subject to the obligation to make
a repayment to the landlords in the event of a disposal within the provisions of the
1980 Act but on the footing that his own acquisition did not give rise to such a
disposal.

    j

Held – (1) The liability to repay the discount, contained in a covenant in the lease
and secured by a charge on the lease, was an incumbrance on the property and fell

---

a   Section 22(1), so far as material, is set out at p 117 *f*, post
b   Section 38(1), so far as material, is set out at p 117 *g*, post
c   Sch 4, para 7(4), so far as material, is set out at p 118 *b*, post

a to be taken into account in determining the value of that property. The question as
to the value of the leasehold, taking into the account the liability to repay the
discount, was a question as to the value of land within the exclusive jurisdiction of
the tribunal under para 7(4) of Sch 4 to the 1975 Act.

(2) The entity to be valued was the lease taking into account the obligations of the
deceased and her successors in title to make repayment to the landlord under the
provisions of the 1980 Act.

b (3) In valuing the lease under s 38 of the 1975 Act, the tribunal were required to
determine the amount which, on a hypothetical sale, a person would be willing to
pay to acquire the lease held by the deceased subject to the obligation which would
fall on the hypothetical purchaser to make a repayment to the landlord in the event
of a disposal within s 8(3) of the 1980 Act, but on the footing that his own hypothetical
acquisition did not itself give rise to such a disposal. *IRC v Crossman* [1937] AC 26
c applied.

The Crown's appeal would therefore be allowed.

Notes

For jurisdiction of the Lands Tribunal, see Foster: Inheritance Tax L1.09.
d For valuation in the open market, see ibid, H2.01.

For the Finance Act 1975, ss 22, 38, Sch 4, para 7 (now the Inheritance Tax Act
1984, ss 4, 160, 222), see ibid, Part S.

Cases referred to in judgments

e *Buccleuch (Duke) v IRC* [1967] 1 AC 506, [1967] 1 All ER 129, HL.
IRC v Crossman [1937] AC 26, [1936] 1 All ER 762, HL.
Lynall v IRC [1972] AC 680, [1971] 3 All ER 914, 47 TC 375, HL.
Practice Direction (Appeals by Case Stated, RSC Ord 58A) [1956] 1 WLR 1112,
[1956] 3 All ER 117.
Sutherland (decd), Re [1960 Ch 611, [1959] 2 All ER 682, CA; *rvsd* [1963] AC 235,
f [1961] 3 All ER 855, HL.

Case stated

1. This was an appeal by A M K Alexander (the executor), executor of Mrs D E
Alexander (deceased), from a determination by the Inland Revenue Commissioners
g given on 18 February 1986 determining the principal value under para 7 of Sch 4 to
the Finance Act 1975 at £52,000 of the premises known as 44 Speed House,
Barbican, London EC2.

2. The members of the tribunal were duly selected by the President of the Lands
Tribunal under s 2 of the Lands Tribunal Act 1949, to deal with this case.

3. At the hearing before the Lands Tribunal the facts which were proved or
h admitted and the contentions put forward by the parties were contained in their
decision a signed copy of which was annexed to and formed part of the case.

4. The question on which the decision of the court was desired was whether the
tribunal had been correct in law in deciding that they had had no jurisdiction to
decide liabilities between the vendor and a third party which might well have been
a charge against the deceased's estate but which had not affected the open market
j value of the premises at the prescribed date.

DECISION

This is an appeal under para 7 of Sch 4 to the Finance Act 1975 (the 1975 Act)
against the determination of the Inland Revenue Commissioners that the leasehold
premises known as 44 Speed House, Barbican, London EC2 be valued at £52,000 as
at 17 January 1984.

Mr A M K Alexander (the executor), executor of Mrs D E Alexander (deceased), appeared in person and gave evidence. Mr A Sainer appeared for the Crown and called Mr J S Prisk FRICS, the district valuer, City of London.

The issues in dispute relate to the value of the premises within the terms of s 38 of the 1975 Act and the amount of deduction to be made therefrom under para 2 of Sch 10 to the 1975 Act in respect of the liability to repay a proportion of a discount in purchase price under the 'right to buy provisions' of the Housing Act 1980 and the provisions of the lease.

From an agreed statement of fact and the evidence we find the following: Speed House, completed in 1968, stands in the north-east corner of the Barbican development adjoining the main entrance to the Barbican Centre. No 44 is a self-contained flat on the sixth floor above podium level, equivalent to the ninth or tenth floor above street level. The accommodation of the flat comprises an entrance hall, living room, kitchen (fully fitted), bathroom, separate wc with hand basin and one bedroom with a total area of 626 square feet. The flat is known as a type 20 and there are 36 similar flats in Speed House. At the date of valuation, 17 January 1984, the internal decorations were in a neglected state but otherwise the flat was in good order. The estimated cost of redecoration (painting only) was £1,000. The premises were leased by the City Council to Doris Emily Alexander, the deceased, for 125 years from 1 July 1981 at a nominal rent of £10 pa. The deceased purchased the leasehold interest in the property on 4 March 1983 under the 'right to buy' provisions of the Housing Act 1980 at a discount of £24,600. The terms of the acquisition included a provision for repayment of all or part of the discount should the property be resold within five years. The lease provides for the proportion of the discount repayable to decrease by 20% for each complete year of ownership.

Mr Alexander had the premises valued at some time after the valuation date by a firm of estate agents dealing extensively with the purchase and sale of flats in the Barbican, but he did not call any witnesses from that firm. He referred to a type 20 flat at 38 Speed House offered for sale on the market by the City Corporation in July 1984 at £64,000 but not sold until 1986.

In his view, having regard to the state of decoration and repair, the leasehold interest in the subject premises was worth £60,000 at the valuation date. From this he deducted £24,600, being the amount of the rebate repayable to the City Council at that time, giving a net worth to the estate of the deceased of £35,400.

Mr Prisk, a valuer of considerable experience, referred to the fact that the long lease of the subject premises was granted to the deceased on 4 March 1983 for a consideration of £60,000 less £24,600 discount under the 'right to buy' provisions of the Housing Act 1980. The figure of £60,000 related to a valuation date of 8 August 1980.

He also referred to the sale of eight similar leasehold flats in the Barbican, (six of them being type 20 flats), between 8 March 1983 and 1 January 1985, at prices ranging between £62,000 and £64,500 with one exception at £67,500. Four were disposed of by the City Council and four were sold (assigned) by the leaseholders.

On the basis of this evidence he was of the opinion that the open market value of the subject premises as at 17 January 1984 was £64,000 on the assumption that the tenant had fully complied with the covenants in the lease, including those relating to internal decorations. Having regard to the actual state of the premises he reduced his figure to £63,000.

From this figure he deducted £13,136 representing the value in January 1984 of a deferred repayment of the rebate under s 8 of the Housing Act 1980 giving a figure, in round terms, of £50,000.

Mr Prisk justified his deduction thus: By virtue of s 8(3) of the Housing Act 1980, effect to which was given in clause 3 of the lease, the passing of the leasehold interest on death is not a 'trigger' for the repayment of a discount. Therefore anyone acquiring the leasehold interest on death (other than for value) would assume the potential liability for repayment. If the premises were not sold until after 4 March 1988 the liability for repayment would be nil.

He had analysed all the transactions relating to flats in Speed House and of 101 cases only three were resold within 18 months of purchase. Sixty-six purchasers retained ownership for two years or more and 22 still owned their flats having acquired them more than six years ago.

On the basis of this evidence he formed the view that the leaseholder of the subject premises would be unlikely to sell before 4 March 1984, when the repayment would have been reduced to £19,680, and would most probably defer sale until after 4 March 1985 when the repayment would be reduced to £14,760. The value of that repayment at 17 January 1984, deferred 14 months at 10%, was £13,136. Deducting this from the figure of £63,000 gave, in round figures, £50,000.

Decision

We have inspected the subject premises in the knowledge that their present condition today is not the same as that at the date of valuation. We have also viewed the Barbican development.

We have no hesitation, on the evidence before us, in accepting Mr Prisk's valuation of £63,000 as representing the open market value of the interest of the deceased in the subject premises immediately before her death on the material date taking account of their state of repair at that time.

We have had some difficulty in deciding the appropriate deduction to be made from the above market value to allow for the liability to repay to the City Council part of the rebate granted under the Housing Act 1980.

In the first instance we are in some doubt as to our authority to decide the matter, a view we expressed during the course of the hearing.

Disputes relating to the valuation of an interest in land may be referred to this tribunal for determination under para 7 of Sch 4 to the 1975 Act. The relevant part of para 7 is sub-para (4) which reads:

> 'Neither the Special Commissioners nor the High Court shall determine any question as to the value of land in the United Kingdom on any appeal under this paragraph, but on any such question the appeal shall be to the Lands Tribunal or, as the case may be, the Lands Tribunal for Scotland or for Northern Ireland.'

The Solicitor of Inland Revenue drew our attention to paras 1 and 2 of Sch 10 to the 1975 Act. Paragraph 1 deals with liabilities to be taken into account in determining the value of a transferor's estate and para 2 reads: 'A liability which is an incumbrance on any property shall, so far as possible, be taken to reduce the value of that property.' As we understand his argument the liability to repay a proportion of the rebate in the instant case is an incumbrance which is deemed to reduce the value of the property and therefore falls within the jurisdiction of this tribunal.

Paragraph 7 of Sch 4 to the 1975 Act clearly limits the authority of this tribunal to questions concerning the ascertainment of the value of land in accordance with s 38 of the 1975 Act, which reads as follows:

> '(1) Except as otherwise provided by this Part of this Act, the value at any time of any property shall for the purposes of capital transfer tax be the price which the property might reasonably be expected to fetch if sold in the open market at that time; but that price shall not be assumed to be reduced on the grounds that the whole property is to be placed on the market at one and the same time.
>
> (2) Schedule 10 to this Act shall have effect with respect to the valuation of property for the purposes of capital transfer tax and the determination of the value transferred by a transfer of value.'

The word 'incumbrance' in para 2 of Sch 10 is not defined but it seems to us that any charge on premises must be an incumbrance. In so far as an incumbrance affects the open market value of premises, that is already taken into account in ascertaining the value within the meaning of s 38 of the 1975 Act.

Therefore it seems to us that para 2 of Sch 10 to the 1975 Act is confined to those incumbrances, or parts of incumbrances, which have no effect on the open market value of premises but which nevertheless affect the value of the transferor's estate.

We have ascertained the open market value of the premises in this case and that figure is derived from evidence of open market transactions of similar premises where the vendor in some instances was under a liability to repay a discount to the council. Therefore, in so far as that situation has any effect on open market value that fact is reflected in the figure of £63,000.

Having ascertained that figure it is our view that this tribunal has no jurisdiction to decide the extent of any liability between the hypothetical statutory vendor and a third party which may well be a charge against the estate of the deceased but is not a matter which affects the open market of the premises.

For these reasons we determine that the open market value of the leasehold interest in the premises as at 17 January 1984 was £63,000.

Section 22 of the 1975 Act deems that the deceased made a transfer of value immediately before her death. If that had happened she would have been under an obligation under s 8(1) and (2) of the Housing Act 1980 to repay the whole of the discount. If she had failed to meet that obligation it would have resolved on the purchaser who would have been entitled to an indemnity under the consent implied in the assignment of the lease. It is reasonable to suppose that a purchaser in the open market would expect the vendor to repay the required sum to the council.

The figure of £63,000 in this case is derived from open market transactions of similar premises where the vendor was also under a liability to repay a discount to the council. Therefore, in so far as the situation had any effect on open market value it can be assumed that it is already reflected in the figure of £63,000.

Having ascertained the open market value of the property as between vendor and purchaser it is our view that this tribunal has no jurisdiction to decide the liabilities between the vendor and a third party which may well be a charge against the deceased's estate but does not affect the open market value of the premises.

It seems to us that para 2 of Sch 10 is concerned with the process of ascertaining the tax liability of a transferor's estate and not the open market value of the land.

For these reasons we confirm the open market value of the premises as at 17 January 1984 was £63,000.

We invited the parties to make written submissions as to costs, and this they have done. The Crown's costs of this determination are to be paid by the executor, if not agreed to be taxed by the registrar of the Lands Tribunal on the basis of scale 3 of the County Court scale of costs with certificate for expert witness, but the amount of costs receivable to be limited to 30% of those costs, having regard to the issues decided by this tribunal in relation to the totality of the matters argued.

Nicholas Warren for the Crown.
The executor appeared in person.

Cur adv vult

17 January 1991. The following judgments were delivered.

RALPH GIBSON LJ. This is an appeal by the Inland Revenue Commissioners pursuant to s 3(4) of the Lands Tribunal Act 1949 by way of case stated under RSC Ord 61, r 1. The appeal raises questions as to the determination of the value for the purposes of capital transfer tax, now inheritance tax, of an interest in land which had been acquired by the deceased under the 'right to buy' provisions in the Housing

Act 1980 (the 1980 Act) and was at the date of death subject to a charge to secure
a repayment of the relevant percentage of discount on early disposal. The right to buy
provisions are now contained in Part V of the Housing Act 1985.

The facts which led to the decision of the Lands Tribunal and the history of this
dispute can be summarised as follows.

Mrs Alexander, the deceased, who died on 17 January 1984, acquired on 4 March
1983 a long leasehold interest in a flat, 44 Speed House, Barbican. The landlords are
b the City of London. The lease was granted for a consideration of £35,400 pursuant
to the 'right to buy' provisions of the 1980 Act at a discount of £24,600 under s 7 of
that Act.

The lease contained covenants by the tenant to pay to the landlords the relevant
percentage of the discount if, within five years of the grant of the lease, there should
be a disposal falling within the terms of the covenant, which included an assignment
c of the lease or the grant of a sublease for more than 21 years otherwise than at a rack
rent. The covenant was required by s 8(3) of the 1980 Act. The liability to pay was
to be a charge on the leasehold premises. The amount so payable was provided to be
reduced by 20% of the discount for each complete year which elapsed after the grant
of the lease on 4 March 1983. The deceased died before the end of the first full year.
Details of the reducing sums repayable on early disposal were set out in Mr
d Alexander's submissions to the Lands Tribunal: before 3 March 1984, £24,600;
between 4 March 1984 and 3 March 1985, £19,680; between 4 March 1985 and
3 March 1986, £14,760; between 4 March 1986 and 3 March 1987, £9,840; between
4 March 1987 and 3 March 1988, £4,920; and after 4 March 1988, nothing.

The respondent to this appeal is Mr A M Alexander, the son of the deceased and
the executor of her estate (the executor). There has been, in fact, no disposal of the
e lease such as would give rise to the obligation to repay any part of the discount sum.
The vesting in the executor on death and the subsequent vesting in a beneficiary, if
any, are not disposals within the provision of s 8(3) of the 1980 Act and of the
covenant in the lease.

By s 22(1) of the Finance Act 1975 (the 1975 Act):

f 'On the death of any person . . . tax shall be charged as if, immediately before
his death, he had made a transfer of value and the value transferred by it had
been equal to the value of his estate immediately before his death . . .'

The value of the property to which the deceased was beneficially entitled (s 23(1) of
the 1975 Act) is to be determined by reference to s 38 of the 1975 Act. That section
provides:

g '(1) Except as otherwise provided by this Part of this Act, the value at any
time of any property shall for the purposes of capital transfer tax be the price
which the property might reasonably be expected to fetch if sold in the open
market at that time; but that price shall not be assumed to be reduced on the
grounds that the whole property is to be placed on the market at one and the
same time.
h (2) Schedule 10 to this Act shall have effect with respect to the valuation of
property for the purposes of capital transfer tax and the determination of the
value transferred by a transfer of value.'

The essential question may be described thus: is the value of the lease to be taken
as the value which the lease would have if transferred, on the basis that the transferee
j must pay the relevant percentage of repayable premium, or is the lease to be valued
as in the hands of the deceased immediately before her death when nothing had
happened to cause any proportion of premium to be payable?

On 18 February 1986 the Board of Inland Revenue gave notice to the executor
that they had determined the value of the leasehold interest held by the deceased on
17 January 1984 in the sum of £52,000. The executor appealed against that
determination by written notice under para 7(1) of Sch 4 to the 1975 Act.

The right of appeal is described thus in para 7:

'(1) A person on whom a notice under paragraph 6 above has been served   *a*
may . . . appeal against any determination specified in it . . . to the Board . . .
(2) Subject to the following provisions of this paragraph the appeal shall be to
the Special Commissioners . . .
(4) Neither the Special Commissioners nor the High Court shall determine any
question as to the value of land in the United Kingdom on any appeal under
this paragraph, but on any such question the appeal shall be to the Lands   *b*
Tribunal . . .'

By his appeal the executor invited the Lands Tribunal to determine two issues,
first, the value of the leasehold interest at 17 January 1984 free from incumbrances
and, second, the amount of the deduction to be made from that value in respect of
the liability of the deceased to repay the relevant percentage of the discount. His   *c*
case was that the worth of the flat to the executor on 17 January 1984 was £60,000,
the market value, less the amount repayable to the landlords on a sale on that date,
namely £24,600, showing a net worth of £35,400.

The district valuer, Mr Prisk, contended that the market value of the individual
flat, apart from the charge for repayment of discount, was £63,000 and that any
reduction in value by reason of liability to repay discount did not exceed £13,000.   *d*
That was his estimate of the deduction on which a willing buyer, wanting to place
himself in the same position as the deceased, would settle and he added that a
deduction of that amount represented a halfway point between 'best' and 'worst'
positions and that would commend it between willing buyer and willing seller.

The Lands Tribunal, Mr C R Mallett and Mr T Hoyes, both Fellows of the Royal
Institute of Chartered Surveyors, determined the open market value of the interest   *e*
of the deceased in the leasehold premises immediately before her death as £63,000,
that is to say the market price of the flat as assessed by Mr Prisk but without regard
to the charge in respect of repayment of discount.

The Lands Tribunal found difficulty in deciding the appropriate deduction to be
made from the market value to allow for the liability to repay discount and it was the
tribunal themselves which raised the question as to their jurisdiction to decide the   *f*
matter. They concluded that the tribunal had no jurisdiction to decide the question,
which they described as being:

'. . . the extent of any liability between the hypothetical statutory vendor and
a third party which may well be a charge against the estate of the deceased but
is not a matter which affects the open market value of the premises.'

                                                                                        g
Their decision, therefore, did no more than fix the open market value of the lease
without regard to the covenant for repayment.

The Crown asked the Lands Tribunal to state a case for this court. The Lands
Tribunal in stating the case annexed to it their decision of 11 April 1989 pursuant to
Practice Direction (Appeals by Case Stated, RSC Ord 58A) [1956] 1 WLR 1112. The
case stated is dated 4 June 1990. The question for the decision of the court is: *h*

'. . . whether the Tribunal was correct in law in deciding that it had no
jurisdiction to decide liabilities between the vendor and the third party which
may well be a charge against the deceased's estate but which do not affect the
open market value of the premises at the prescribed date.'

By letter of 25 August 1989 the Crown had applied to the Special Commissioners.   *j*
After stating the events which had occurred and the decision of the Lands Tribunal,
and after reference to s 38 of and Sch 10 and Sch 4 to the 1975 Act, the question was
posed thus:

'The question is whether the proper subject of valuation is the encumbered
leasehold (either on general principles or by virtue of paragraph 2 of Schedule
10 to the 1975 Act) in which case . . . the appeal as a whole falls within the

a   jurisdiction of the Lands Tribunal under paragraph 7(4) of Schedule 4; *or*
whether the statute requires the parties first to value the notionally unencum-
bered leasehold (a matter for the Lands Tribunal); second to value the liability
or charge (prima facie a matter for your Commissioners) and finally to establish
the value transferred (again, if there is any dispute, prima facie a matter for
your Commissioners).'

b   The Crown inquired whether the commissioners would be willing to assume
jurisdiction in the appeal.

Mr Widdows, Special Commissioner, heard the further appeal by the executor
and on 28 December 1989 issued his written decision. On 17 May 1990 he stated his
conclusions in the form of a special case (to which his written decision was annexed)
for the opinion of the High Court. He held that the issue as to the amount of the
deduction from the open market value to reflect the liability of the deceased to
c   refund the proportion of the discount on disposal of the premises was a question of
law only and not one of land valuation; and therefore within the jurisdiction of the
Special Commissioners under para 7 of Sch 4 to the 1975 Act; and, secondly, that,
as a matter of law, the liability to repay the relevant proportion of discount should
be taken into account in determining the value of the deceased's estate as a current
d   liability at the date of death under para 1(1) of Sch 10 and not as a liability falling to
be discharged at a future date under para 1(4) of that Schedule. No evidence was
required. He accordingly held that the market value of £63,000 as determined by
the Lands Tribunal must be reduced by £24,600, the amount of discount repayable
on disposal at the date of death, and that the value of the leasehold interest was
therefore reduced to £38,400.

e   *The appeal to this court*

The appeal before us is only that on the case stated by the Lands Tribunal. The
case stated by the Special Commissioner will be heard in the first place by a judge of
the High Court from which decision an appeal might come to this court. The
Crown's case on this appeal is that the Lands Tribunal were wrong in law to decline
f   jurisdiction to determine the amount by which the market value of the premises was
to be reduced by reference to the liability to repay the discount on disposal; that the
case should be remitted to the Lands Tribunal to determine the question; and that
this court should decide the principles in accordance with which that determination
is to be made. In effect, therefore, this court is asked to decide principles which will
be decisive of the questions raised by the decision of the Special Commissioner.
g   Application was made for leave to amend the case stated by adding the following
additional questions for the opinion of the court, namely: Whether the entity to be
valued is the lease taking into account the obligations of the tenant and her successors
in title to make repayments to the landlords under the provisions of the Housing Act
1980; and, if so, whether the principles exemplified in *IRC v Crossman* [1937] AC 26
are applicable. The executor did not resist the making of the amendment and leave
h   was granted.

The executor, who has appeared in person before this court, as he did below, in
effect adopted the reasoning of the Lands Tribunal and of the Special Commissioner
and invited this court to uphold their decisions. The reasoning of the Lands Tribunal
can, I think, be summarised as follows: (i) The Crown's contention, based on paras
1 and 2 of Sch 10, was that the liability to repay a proportion of the discount is an
j   incumbrance which is deemed to reduce the value of the property and therefore falls
within the jurisdiction of the Lands Tribunal. (ii) 'Incumbrance' in para 2 of Sch 10,
is not defined but any charge on the premises must be an incumbrance. (iii) In so far
as an incumbrance affects the open market value of premises, that is taken into
account in ascertaining value under s 38. (iv) Paragraph 2 of Sch 10 is confined to
those incumbrances which have no effect on the open market value of the premises
but which do affect the value of the transferor's estate. Further, that paragraph is
concerned with the process of ascertaining the tax liability of a transferor's estate

and not the open market value of the land. (v) The open market value of £63,000 covers any effect on price of the liability of the vendor to pay discount. (vi) Section 22 of the 1975 Act deems that the deceased made a transfer of value immediately before her death. If that had happened, she would have been under an obligation under s 8 of the 1980 Act to repay the whole of the discount. (vii) The figure of £63,000, the open market value of the flat immediately before the death, is derived from open market transactions of similar premises where the vendor was also under a liability to repay a discount to the council. Therefore, in so far as that liability had any effect on the open market value, it is already reflected in the figure of £63,000. (viii) Once the Lands Tribunal had ascertained the open market value of the property as between vendor and purchaser, the Lands Tribunal had no jurisdiction to decide the liabilities between the vendor and a third party, which liability may well be a charge against the deceased's estate but does not affect the open market value of the premises.

Next, although no appeal from the decision from the Special Commissioner is before this court, the executor submitted that his decision was correct and supports the conclusion of the Lands Tribunal. I will therefore set out in summary the careful reasoning of the Special Commissioner, which I found to be of the greatest assistance in understanding the problems raised in the application of the provisions of the 1975 Act to the facts of this particular case. As the Special Commissioner observed: 'It may be that an obligation of this nature (the obligation to repay discount) was in no one's contemplation when the 1975 Act was drafted.' The Special Commissioner proceeded by the following steps:

(i) Since the Lands Tribunal had declined, after determining the open market value of £63,000, to decide the further question as to the amount of any deduction to be made to reflect the deceased's liability to refund on disposal of the premises the relevant percentage of discount, the questions for decision by him were whether determination of the amount of that deduction fell within the jurisdiction of the commissioners under para 7(2) of Sch 4, and if it did, what the amount of the deduction should be.

(ii) The question of the amount of deduction was one of law and not one of land valuation and was accordingly within the jurisdiction of the Special Commissioners under para 7(2). As a matter of law the liability to repay the relevant percentage of discount must be taken into account in determining the value of the deceased's estate as a current liability at the date of death under para 1 of Sch 10 and not as a liability falling to be discharged at a future date under para 1(4) of that Schedule.

(iii) After reference to the submissions made for the Crown (based on the principles stated in *IRC v Crossman* [1937] AC 26 and *Duke of Buccleuch v IRC* [1967] 1 AC 506), the Special Commissioner held that the leasehold interest of the deceased could not have been put on the market subject to a continuing obligation to repay a proportion of the discount on a future sale because the completion of the first sale would trigger the covenant for repayment and the obligation would then be discharged.

(iv) The proper treatment of the liability to repay the relevant proportion of discount was not by valuation of it as a future contingent liability under para 1(4) of Sch 10 because the better view was that it was a current liability necessarily falling to be discharged on a disposal, in order to release the land charge, like a mortgage debt. The approach contended for by the Crown would lead to an over-statement of the value of the estate in terms of realisable value at the valuation date. Section 22 of the 1975 Act applies to the case of transfer on death, the general principle of the 1975 Act, namely that the tax is charged on the person who makes a gratuitous transfer by reference to the price which could have been obtained in the open market for the property transferred. Under para 1(1) of Sch 10 the deceased's 'liability' under the covenant to repay the relevant percentage of discount was to be taken account of as at the date of death, ie in the sum of £24,600. The value of the leasehold interest was therefore £38,400.

Counsel for the Crown's submissions were, in substance, as follows:

a   (i) The Lands Tribunal under para 7(4) of Sch 4 to the 1975 Act (the current provision is in s 222(4) of the Inheritance Tax Act 1984) had exclusive jurisdiction (and thus the Special Commissioner had no jurisdiction) first because the property to be valued is one item, namely land, being the lease subject to the incumbrance of the charge securing repayment of discount.

b   (ii) If that primary contention be rejected, then the obligation of the deceased to make a repayment to the landlord was a contingent liability which would arise if, but only if, there should be a disposal within s 8(3) of the 1980 Act; and that contingent liability falls within para 2 of Sch 10 to the 1975 Act: 'A liability which is an incumbrance on any property shall, so far as is possible, be taken to reduce the value of that property.'

It must therefore be taken to reduce the value of the lease. The reduced value is *c* the value of the lease for the purposes of capital transfer tax and is a question of valuation of land. It remains a question of valuation of land for the Lands Tribunal whether the Lands Tribunal proceed by fixing the open market value of the lease without regard to the obligation then deduct the appropriate sum in respect of the liability, or whether the Lands Tribunal value the property which the deceased had taking account of that liability.

d   (iii) If the primary contentions be right, the valuation of the lease, taking into account the obligations of the deceased to repay the discount, should be carried out by applying the principles stated in *IRC v Crossman* [1937] AC 26.

(iv) On that basis, the market value of the lease for these purposes should be taken as the amount which a person would be willing to pay to acquire the lease, subject to the obligation to make a repayment to the landlords in the event of a disposal within *e* s 8(3) of the 1980 Act but on the footing that his own acquisition did not give rise to such a disposal. There could be no further reduction under para 1 of Sch 10 to the 1975 Act in respect of that obligation because full account would have been taken of it in the valuation of the lease.

f *Conclusion*

For my part, I accept the primary submission made by counsel for the Crown. I have reached that conclusion for the following reasons.

The basis of charge is stated by s 19 of the 1975 Act: 'A tax, to be known as capital transfer tax, shall be charged on the value transferred by a chargeable transfer.' The administration and collection of the tax is to be governed by Sch 4. A 'chargeable *g* transfer' is defined in s 20, which proceeds by explaining what is a 'transfer of value' and by then providing that a chargeable transfer is any transfer of value made by an individual after 26 March 1974, excluding exempt transfers. By s 20(2), subject to sub-ss (3) and (4), a transfer of value is any disposition made by a transferor as a result of which the value of his estate immediately after the disposition is less than it would be but for the disposition; and *the amount by which it is less is the value* *h* *transferred by the transfer*. Emphasis has been added to the concluding words: they show that the value of what is transferred is fixed by the amount by which the value of the transferor's estate is reduced, and that means the value of the property in his hands.

A disposition, of course, is not a transfer of value if it is shown that it was not intended, and was not made in a transaction intended to confer a gratuitous benefit *j* on any person. For example, provided a sale is made in a transaction at arm's length between persons not connected with each other, capital transfer tax was not provided to be levied on an improvident sale which reduces the value of a vendor's estate by much more than the price received.

Capital transfer tax, chargeable on transfers of value as described, was applied to transfers on death by s 22(1) of the 1975 Act (subject to certain following provisions which are not relevant to this case):

'On the death of any person after the passing of this Act tax shall be charged
as if, immediately before his death, he had made a transfer of value and the *a*
*value transferred by it had been equal to the value of his estate immediately before
his death . . .'*

Again I have emphasised the concluding words: the value of the estate, and
therefore of each item of property of which it is made up, which is deemed to have
been transferred, is taken to be the value immediately before the death and again, as
I understand, that means the value of the property in his hands. *b*

The provisions on valuation contained in s 38 have been set out above.

The property of which the value is in question in this case is the leasehold interest
in the flat held by the deceased. The obligation to repay the relevant percentage of
discount was a charge on the property as well as an obligation contained in a
covenant in the lease. Paragraph 1 of Sch 10 directs that, in determining the value
of the transferor's estate at any time, his liabilities at that time (ie the date of death), *c*
shall be taken into account; para 2 directs that a liability that is an incumbrance on
any property shall, so far as possible, be taken to reduce the value of that property.

The liability to repay the discount, being charged on the leasehold premises, was,
in my judgment, an incumbrance on the property and should be taken into account
in ascertaining the value of that property. I therefore agree that on the appeal being
made to the Lands Tribunal by the executor from the determination by the Board *d*
of the value of the flat, the question as to the value of the flat, taking into account
the liability to repay discount, was a question as to the value of land for the Lands
Tribunal under para 7(4) of Sch 4. I would so answer the substance of the question
raised in the case, although the issue as to the value of the property of the deceased
in the flat was not correctly described by the Lands Tribunal, as a question of
'deciding liabilities between the vendor and a third party'. It was, in my judgment, *e*
a question of the value of the property in the hands of the deceased.

That seems to me to be the effect of the concluding words of s 22(1) as set out
above. Although, in the case of the deemed transfer on death, there can remain no
part of the estate which would be reduced by the amount transferred, the concluding
words of s 20(2) seems to me to be consistent with my view that, in determining the
value of a particular item of property, the relevant value is that which it had when *f*
held in the hands of the deceased.

As to the questions added to the case by amendment, namely whether the entity
to be valued is the lease taking into account the obligations of the deceased and her
successors in title to make repayment to the landlord under the provisions of the
1980 Act, it follows from what I have said that, in my judgment, it is.

The third question is whether the principles stated in *IRC v Crossman* are *g*
applicable, ie to be applied to the valuation of the lease taking into account the
obligations of the tenant to repay discount.

It is first necessary to examine what those principles are. In *Crossman*, a testator
at the time of his death owned a number of shares in a company the articles of
association of which imposed rigid restrictions on the alienation and transfer of the
shares. It was contended for the personal representatives of the testator that the *h*
value of the shares for the purposes of the Finance Act 1894 (the 1894 Act) was
limited to the restricted price fixed by the articles to be paid by any existing
shareholder exercising his right of pre-emption under the articles. Two of the
provisions in the 1894 Act must be noted: the first is s 1:

'In the case of every person dying after the commencement of this Part of this *j*
Act, there shall . . . be levied and paid, upon the principal value ascertained as
herein-after provided of all property real or personal . . . which passes on the
death of such person a duty, called "Estate duty" . . .'

Next, by s 7(5):

'The principal value of any property shall be estimated to be the price which,

in the opinion of the Commissioners, such property would fetch if sold in the
open market at the time of the death of the deceased.'

The contention of the personal representatives was rejected by the majority
decision of the House. Viscount Hailsham LC ([1937] AC 26 at 41) said—

'. . . it seems to me that this construction [contended for by the personal
representatives] involves treating the provisions of s. 7, sub-s. 5, as if their true
effect were to make the existence of an open market a condition of liability
instead of merely to prescribe the open market price as the measure of value.'

Later (at 42) he said—

'. . . the purpose of s. 7, sub-s. 5, is not to define the property in respect of
which estate duty is to be levied but merely to afford a method of ascertaining
its value.'

Lord Roche, to the like effect (at 74) said—

'. . . s. 7, sub-s. 5, . . . is simply a provision for estimating by means of an
hypothesis the value of property which has passed otherwise than by an actual
sale and transfer and may be incapable of so passing.'

In *Re Sutherland (decd)* [1963] AC 235 at 262 Lord Guest said:

'The purpose of section 7(5) . . . is to value the property. "It does not," as the
Master of the Rolls (Lord Evershed) [in the Court of Appeal, see [1960] Ch 611
at 624] said, "require you to assume that the sale . . . has occurred." It simply
prescribes as the criterion for value price in the open market as between a
willing seller and a willing buyer, which is a familiar basis of valuation.'

In *Lynall v IRC* [1972] AC 680, 47 TC 375 the correctness of the decision of the
majority in *Crossman* was challenged but approved by the House of Lords.

I have no doubt that the principles stated in *Crossman*'s case are applicable to s 38
of the 1975 Act which in substance is the same as s 7(5) of the 1894 Act with words
which were originally added to give statutory recognition to the decision of the
House of Lords in the *Duke of Buccleuch*'s case. It follows that, in valuing that which
passed from the deceased on the deceased's transfer of value immediately before her
death under s 22, in order to determine the amount by which the value of the estate
is less by the transfer, the Lands Tribunal are required to determine the amount
which, on a hypothetical sale, a person would be willing to pay to acquire the lease
held by the deceased subject to the obligation which would fall on the hypothetical
purchaser to make a repayment to the landlord in the event of a disposal within
s 8(3) of the Housing Act 1980 but on the footing that his own hypothetical
acquisition did not itself give rise to such a disposal.

There is, of course, a distinction between s 38, which, like s 7(5) of the 1894 Act,
is to be taken as providing the machinery for estimating value by means of an
hypothesis, on the one hand, and s 22(1) of the 1975 Act, on the other hand, which
is a deeming provision: 'On the death of any person . . . tax shall be charged as if,
immediately before his death, he had made a transfer of value'. I do not know, in
common with the Special Commissioner, whether the impact of those words on the
provisions of s 8(3) of the 1980 Act was intended and understood at the time that the
1980 Act was passed. The effect, in my judgment, is that, for the purposes of
charging capital transfer tax on death, the transfer of value is deemed to have been
made. A transfer of value includes, of course, a transfer by way of gift inter vivos.
Such a gift would be a disposal within s 8(3) of the 1980 Act, which includes an
assignment of a lease, irrespective of whether it is a gratuitous assignment by way of
gift or of assignment for full market value. It is necessary for the purposes of the
charging of this tax, to assume that there has been a disposal which would cause the

relevant percentage of discount to be repayable although in fact no such disposal has occurred. Under s 8(3) the vesting in a person taking under a will or on intestacy is not a disposal falling within the subsection. The principles stated in *Crossman*'s case, which were concerned with the construction of the predecessor of s 38, which deals with valuation, cannot, of course, cause there to be no deemed transfer of value under s 22, but that does not affect the conclusion as to how the lease is to be valued. The same conclusion would be reached in the case of an actual gift inter vivos. The principles in *Crossman*'s case are applicable, in my judgment, to the process of establishing the value of the estate immediately before the death by the application of s 38.

The deemed transfer under s 22 at first caused me to see much force in the arguments which were accepted by the Lands Tribunal and by the Special Commissioner. The open market value of the flat had been determined by the Lands Tribunal and the question of repayment by itself need raise no question of land valuation if it could be resolved by application of the presumption of a transfer triggering the obligation to pay and of the effect at the date of death of the terms of the covenant in the lease. I have, however, reached the conclusion that the primary submission of counsel for the Crown is nevertheless correct. On a transfer of value of the leasehold interest by the deceased, the amount by which the estate would be reduced is the amount of the value of that leasehold interest in the hands of the deceased. In her hands, no obligation had arisen but it would arise if at some point she chose to sell or make a gift of the leasehold interest. Her property in the leasehold interest, subject to the charge securing the obligation to repay, must be valued by applying the rules contained in s 38: it must be taken to be worth that which it might reasonably be expected to fetch if sold in the open market at the date of death. As explained in *Crossman*, the hypothetical buyer must be treated as paying the open market price for an interest which in his hands would be subject to the charge. He would pay such price, below the price which he would pay if the leasehold interest did not contain that charge, as he may be shown by evidence to have been reasonably expected to pay.

I would therefore remit this matter to the Lands Tribunal for further hearing and for determination in accordance with the opinion of this court. I would add that, as proposed by the Crown without opposition from the executor, each side should be at liberty to call further evidence before the Lands Tribunal on the resumed hearing.

NICHOLLS LJ. At first sight the executor's case is attractive: it cannot be right that, for capital transfer tax purposes, the lease should be valued in a sum greater than could have been obtained had the lease been sold at the time of the death. Had the lease been sold, the relevant repayment of discount would have become due and payable. Tax ought not to be payable on a greater amount than the net sum which, in the event of such a sale, would have been received by the deceased's estate. Neither she nor her executor could have obtained more than the net sum.

Unfortunately for the executor, this simple proposition does not accord with the basic scheme of this tax, now known as inheritance tax. For present purposes the scheme can be sufficiently summarised as follows:

(1) Stated in its broadest and simplest form, the underlying scheme of the legislation is that inheritance tax is payable when property is given away. The tax is payable, not (a) in respect of the value of that which is given, but (b) in respect of the amount by which the donor's estate is diminished by reason of the gift. In most cases these two different measures will produce the same result, but not always. One example is where a donor holds a controlling interest in a company and he gives away part of his shareholding, with the result that thereafter neither he nor the donee has a controlling interest. In such a case (a) the value of the shares given may well be substantially less than (b) the extent to which the value of the donor's estate

was diminished by the gift. But tax is payable in respect of (b), not (a). This is the
a effect of s 20 of the Finance Act (the 1975 Act). The 'disposition' which the gift
constitutes is a 'transfer of value' and as such a 'chargeable transfer'. The 'value
transferred by the transfer' is the amount by which 'the value of [the transferor's]
estate immediately after the disposition is less than it would be but for the disposition'
(see s 20(2)). Thus the legislation focuses attention on what the transferor possessed
pre-gift; the tax is payable by reference to what he lost.

b   (2) A like principle is applied in the case of death. There is then a deemed transfer
of value immediately before the death. In short, the deceased is deemed to have
made a transfer of value of the whole of his estate. Tax is chargeable 'as if' he had
made a transfer of value equal to 'the value of his estate immediately before his
death'. That is the basic provision in s 22(1). So, here also, it is necessary to value
that which the deceased possessed. In the case of death, tax is chargeable in respect
c of the whole of that value.

    (3) Thus, the legislation makes it necessary to identify the 'value' of an estate at a
particular time. In short, value means market value: 'the price which the property
might reasonably be expected to fetch if sold in the open market at that time' (see
s 38(1)). This mode of valuation involves a notional sale, of the property in question
at the relevant time. But in prescribing a notional sale, the section is doing no more
d than prescribe the basis on which the valuation shall be made. The notional sale does
not change the subject matter of the valuation. What is being valued is property
belonging to the transferor, and it is being valued as at a time when he still owned it.
The notional sale is designed merely to identify the sum which a purchaser in the
open market might reasonably be expected to pay to be placed, in respect of that
property, in the same position as the transferor. This interpretation of s 38 accords
e with the decision of the House of Lords in *IRC v Crossman* [1937] AC 26 regarding
the comparable valuation provisions in the estate duty legislation (see s 7(5) of the
Finance Act 1894). As Viscount Hailsham LC said (at 42–43), the notional sale is
'merely a statutory direction as to the method by which the value is to be ascertained'.

    These principles have now been reproduced in corresponding provisions in
ss 2, 3, 4 and 160 of the Inheritance Tax Act 1984. In my view, application of these
f principles leads inevitably to the primary conclusion for which the Crown contended
on this appeal. Immediately before her death on 17 January 1984 the deceased
owned a long lease of 44 Speed House. The lease was assignable and transmissible in
the usual way. The only unusual feature was that, in accordance with the 'right to
buy' legislation, a sum diminishing in amount year after year would be payable by
her under the lease and was charged on the lease if, in short, she sold or otherwise
g disposed of the flat before 4 March 1988. This was the asset she possessed when she
died. This is the asset which has to be valued: what would a hypothetical purchaser
in the open market reasonably be expected to pay to acquire *that* asset?

    The lease was a lease of land, and thus this valuation exercise concerns 'the value
of land'. As such, an appeal on this question lies exclusively to the Lands Tribunal,
under para 7(4) of Sch 4 to the 1975 Act.

h   Clearly, in carrying out this valuation exercise it may well be convenient and
sensible for the Lands Tribunal to consider, first, how much the lease would be
likely to have fetched if sold in the market on 17 January 1984 but disregarding the
subsisting discount repayment liability and, second, the amount by which this price
would be likely to be reduced if the notional purchaser who acquired the lease did so
subject to an obligation to make repayments as provided in the lease if thereafter
there were to be a disposal of the lease as defined in the 1980 Act and reproduced in
j clause 3 of the lease. But the exercise remains exclusively 'a question as to the value
of land' even if the route followed in making the valuation involves two steps such as
these.

    For these reasons I agree that an order should be made as proposed by Ralph
Gibson LJ.

SIR DENYS BUCKLEY. I agree with both judgments delivered.

Appeal allowed. No order for costs in this court. Order for costs below set aside and the costs of the first hearing and of the subsequent hearing to be in the discretion of the Lands Tribunal.

Solicitor: *Solicitor of Inland Revenue.*

Siew Ling Choo   Barrister.

Note
Billows v Robinson (Inspector of Taxes)

COURT OF APPEAL, CIVIL DIVISION
PARKER, BALCOMBE, RALPH GIBSON LJJ
31 JANUARY 1991

Emoluments from office or employment – Emoluments – Quantum of emoluments – Benefits in kind received from company of which the taxpayer and his wife were directors – Inspector computing emoluments by reference to taxpayer's living expenses for the year 1972 and using that figure for determining taxpayer's requirements for subsequent years by reference to the cost of living index – Commissioners accepting inspector's method – Whether commissioners' determination supported by evidence.

Notes

For the amount chargeable under Sch E, see Simon's Taxes E4.401.

Appeal

Leonard Kay Billows, the taxpayer, appealed against the decision of Vinelott J ([1990] STC 162) dated 18 December 1989 dismissing an appeal by the taxpayer against the determination of the General Commissioners that the taxpayer's living expenses exceeded his disclosed income and that the shortfall was met by funds improperly diverted from the company, Billows Ltd, of which the taxpayer was a director and shareholder. The facts are set out in the judgment of Parker LJ.

The taxpayer appeared in person.
Alan Moses QC for the Crown.

PARKER LJ. Mr Billows (the taxpayer) appeals in person from the decision of Vinelott J dated 18 December 1989 (see [1990] STC 162) on a case stated by the General Commissioners for the division of Bletchley on 3 May 1988 under s 56 of the Taxes Management Act 1970 (the 1970 Act). By his order the judge affirmed the determination of the commissioners contained in the case stated.

By his notice of appeal the taxpayer seeks an order that Vinelott J's judgment be set aside and that the determination of the commissioners be quashed or remitted. Under s 56 of the 1970 Act an appeal to the High Court from a determination of the commissioners on an appeal lies on points of law only (see s 56(1) and (6)). Section 56(6) reads:

> 'The High Court shall hear and determine any question or questions of law arising on the case, and shall reverse, affirm or amend the determination in respect of which the case has been stated, or shall remit the matter to the Commissioners with the opinion of the Court thereon, or may make such other order in relation to the matter as to the Court may seem fit.'

There is also power under sub-s (7) to send the case back for amendment and, if the High Court does so, the case is then amended. But an application for the case to be sent back for amendment is an application which must be made by separate motion and supported by proper evidence.

This appeal is not concerned with remission of the case. The case has been stated, the judge has ruled on the case and there is an appeal from the judge. The powers of the High Court, and therefore also of this court, are limited to determining whether there is an error of law disclosed in the case and to take appropriate action if it finds that there has been such an error. The judge (see [1990] STC 162 at 173) concluded his judgment with the following words: 'It is sufficient to say that I can discern no error of law on the part of the commissioners capable of being corrected on an appeal under s 56 of the Taxes Management Act 1970.'

The appeal to the commissioners concerned Sch E assessments in respect of the taxpayer for the years from 1972–73 to 1985–86 both inclusive in respect of emoluments and benefits received by him and his wife as directors of his company. The company's appeals against corporation tax assessments were heard at the same time by the commissioners. There was a separate case stated in respect of that matter. The company's appeal to this court was dismissed for want of prosecution.

The essence of the Crown's case was that for the years in question the taxpayer and his wife's required expenditure, which was referred to as 'the computed requirement', exceeded the disclosed income and that the difference between the two had come from cash diverted from the company and not disclosed in their accounts.

The taxpayer says, quite rightly, that there were no figures before the commissioners with regard to required expenditure except for the year 1972–73.

The Crown's case, which the commissioners specifically accepted, was that the figure for 1972–73 should be extrapolated forward in accordance with the published cost of living index, and that is what happened.

The explanation which was put forward by the taxpayer for what might appear to have been a shortfall was that his wife and he lived very modestly and that any shortfall that there might be was made up out of capital, of which he had plenty. He complains to this court saying that there are matters of law which he is entitled to raise. When he was before the commissioners he appeared by his accountant who gave evidence on his behalf. He did not, he tells us, give evidence himself. He says that the commissioners had no evidence available on which they were entitled to act. He did not put before them the figures which would have enabled them to say: 'we need not resort to extrapolation or calculation; we have got the evidence from the taxpayer'. They therefore proceeded on the basis of what they had got.

I can find no error of law in this case at all. There may be complaints, and indeed there are complaints, by the taxpayer that the commissioners should have shown him the draft case and they did not. Whether that be true or not does not arise on this appeal. This appeal is concerned, and concerned only, with seeing if we can determine a question of law or find a question of law to be determined.

Before the hearing of the appeal we had studied the papers in this case and, speaking for myself, and being perfectly aware that the taxpayer had not presented his case possibly as well as he might have done, I searched to see if I could find some question of law and not be bound by what the taxpayer should think were questions of law but which were plainly an attack on the facts as found by the commissioners. Neither in the notice of appeal nor in the documents which have been submitted to us was I able to find any question of law. I still cannot do so and I felt it necessary to stop the taxpayer halfway through his argument because it had become abundantly apparent that he was under a misapprehension as to what were questions of law and what were attacks on questions of fact, and it was not proper that public time should be occupied further in a fruitless exercise. Accordingly I would dismiss this appeal.

BALCOMBE LJ. I agree.

RALPH GIBSON LJ. I also agree.

Appeal dismissed with costs. Application for leave to appeal to the House of Lords refused.

Solicitor: *Solicitor of Inland Revenue.*

Siew Ling Choo   Barrister.

R v Department of Social Security, ex parte Overdrive Credit Card Ltd

QUEEN'S BENCH DIVISION (CROWN OFFICE LIST)
LLOYD LJ AND TUDOR EVANS J
22, 23 JANUARY, 8 FEBRUARY 1991

National insurance – Earnings-related contributions – Computation of employees' earnings – Provision of free petrol to employees for private use – Payment by employer's fuel charge cards – Whether equivalent to payment in cash for purposes of earnings-related contributions – The Social Security (Contributions) Regulations 1979, SI 1979/591, reg 19(1)(d).

The applicants, Overdrive Credit Card Ltd (Overdrive), were one of a number of companies which issued fuel charge cards for use by the employees of their corporate customers. By an agreement (the customer agreement) between Overdrive and an employer, Overdrive agreed to issue as many cards as the employer required. The individual employees or card holders, were 'constituted' the employer's representatives with full authority to use the cards on the employer's behalf. The cards could only be used for the purchase of goods or services from garages appointed by Overdrive. The employer acknowledged that in selling goods to a card holder the garage acted as agent for Overdrive. Under a second agreement (the merchant agreement) between Overdrive and the garage, the garage agreed to accept cards tendered by the card holders. When a card holder used the card to purchase petrol, the price of the petrol purchased (less a discount) was debited by the garage to Overdrive's account and Overdrive claimed the price from the employer. By an aide-memoire issued in April 1990, the Department of Social Security (the DSS) revised the official view concerning the liabilities for national insurance contributions in connection with employers' payment of their employees' petrol expenses. Where an employer provided his employees with petrol purchased with an employer's credit card, the advice and instructions contained in the aide-memoire had the effect of rendering that employer liable for national insurance contributions on the value of all petrol so provided unless the employer proved by documentary evidence that the petrol used by the employee was for business purposes. Overdrive contended (a) that the Social Security Act 1975 and the regulations made thereunder contemplated that earnings would be paid by the employer, and not by a third party, and that since the debt incurred by the card holder was discharged by Overdrive, it could not fall within the description 'earnings' and did not therefore attract liability to contribute, or (b) in the alternative that the payment of an employee's debt by means of a charge card was 'by way of the provision of . . . other facilities' and accordingly was excluded from the employee's earnings by virtue of reg 19(1)(d)[a] of the Social Security (Contributions) Regulations 1979, SI 1979/591. Overdrive applied to the High Court seeking, inter alia, a declaration that payment of an employee's petrol expenses by use of an employer's credit card did not attract liability to national insurance contributions.

Held – (1) There was no difficulty in treating the payment of the debt, incurred by an employee, by a third party as being made on the employer's behalf. Since the ultimate discharge of the card holder's personal liability fell on the employer it made no difference whether it was done directly by the employer or indirectly by a third party on the employer's behalf.

(2) The right approach was to regard the discharge of an employee's debt as the

---

a Regulation 19(1)(*d*), so far as material is set out at p 131 *b*, post equivalent of a payment in cash, and not less so because that payment was made easier by the use of a charge card. The extent to which the payment was made easier *a* (if it could be measured in money terms) was to be disregarded under reg 19(1)(*d*) of the Social Security (Contributions) Regulations 1979, but not the payment itself.

Accordingly, the discharge of the card holder's debt by Overdrive fell within the description 'earnings' for the purposes of the Social Security Act 1975 and the regulations made thereunder. Therefore Overdrive were not entitled to a declaration that payment for an employee's petrol by use of an employer's credit card did not *b* attract liability to national insurance contributions.

Notes

For the calculation of earnings and earnings-related contributions, see 33 Halsbury's Laws (4th edn) para 336. *c*

Cases referred to in judgments

Charge Card Services Ltd, Re [1989] Ch 497, [1988] 3 All ER 702, CA.
Customs and Excise Comrs v Diners Club Ltd [1989] STC 407, [1989] 1 WLR 1196, [1989] 2 All ER 385, CA. *d*
Hartland v Diggines (Inspector of Taxes) [1926] AC 289, 10 TC 247, HL.
Richardson (Inspector of Taxes) v Worrall [1985] STC 693, 58 TC 642.

Application

The applicants, Overdrive Credit Card Ltd, applied for judicial review seeking, *e* inter alia, a declaration that payment of an employee's petrol expenses by use of an employer's credit card did not attract liability to national insurance contributions. The facts are set out in the judgment of Lloyd LJ.

David Goldberg QC and *John Walters* for Overdrive.
Alan Moses QC and *Robert Jay* for the Crown. *f*

Cur adv vult

8 February. The following judgments were delivered.

g

LLOYD LJ. The tactics of the Department of Social Security (the DSS) in this case resemble those of the Russian army in 1812. They have conceded so much ground that the applicants, Overdrive Credit Card Ltd (Overdrive), are now in some difficulty.

The case concerns the incidence and computation of Class 1 contributions under s 4 of the Social Security Act 1975 (the 1975 Act). *h*

Overdrive are one of a number of companies which issue fuel charge cards for use by the employees of their corporate customers. Fuel sales made by use of Overdrive cards are currently running at an annual rate of £135m. There are 135,000 cards in circulation.

The way the system works was described by Scott J in *Richardson (Inspector of Taxes) v Worrall* [1985] STC 693 and by Sir Nicolas Browne-Wilkinson V-C in the *j* Court of Appeal in *Re Charge Card Services Ltd* [1989] Ch 497. I do not repeat what they have said. Their analysis was adopted by the Court of Appeal in the subsequent case of *Customs and Excise Comrs v Diners Club Ltd* [1989] STC 407, [1989] 1 WLR 1196, though that case did not relate specifically to the supply of petrol. This is, so far as is known, the first case in which the courts have had to consider charge cards in the context of the 1975 Act.

The particular question is whether, when an employee obtains free petrol for
a private use by means of a charge card, the value of the petrol is to be taken into
account in arriving at his earnings for the purpose of calculating earnings-related
contributions under s 4 of the 1975 Act. This question turns on the application of
reg 19(1)(d) of the Social Security (Contributions) Regulations 1979, SI 1979/591,
(the 1979 regulations) which provides:

b   'For the purposes of earnings-related contributions, there shall be excluded
        from the computation of a person's earnings . . . any payment in so far as it is . . .
        (d) any payment in kind . . . or by way of the provision of board or lodging or of
        services or other facilities . . .'

The present scheme falls within the general description given by Scott J in
c *Richardson v Worrall*. But since there may be differences between the two cases,
and in particular in the terms of the underlying bilateral agreements, I set out the
main features of the present scheme as briefly as possible.
    There is an agreement, known as the customer agreement, between Overdrive
and the employer under which Overdrive agrees to issue as many cards as the
employer may require. The individual employees, or card holders, are 'constituted'
d the employer's representatives with full authority to use the card on the employer's
behalf. The cards may only be used for the purchase of goods, or services, from
garages (merchants) appointed by Overdrive. The employer acknowledges that in
selling goods to a card holder the garage acts as agent for Overdrive. When the card
covers the provision of services, the garage acts as sub-contractor. The card holder
is obliged to present his card to the garage before taking delivery of the goods or
e services, but this obligation does not apply to fuel. There are then provisions for
payment by the employer of Overdrive's account.
    There is a second agreement, known as the merchant agreement, between
Overdrive and the garage, under which the garage agrees to accept cards tendered
by the card holder. But instead of supplying the petrol direct to the card holder, as
one would expect, the garage first sells the petrol to Overdrive. Property passes as
f soon as the petrol is 'identified'. The garage then acts as Overdrive's agent in selling
the petrol to the card holder. The sale by Overdrive to the card holder is at pump
price. The sale by the garage to Overdrive is at pump price less a discount. The
purpose of these elaborate provisions, or one of the purposes, is that Overdrive
should be the supplier of the petrol for value added tax purposes. Whether it achieves
that, or any other purpose, is not for us to decide.
g   We do not know whether there is a third bilateral agreement in writing between
the employer and the card holder under which the card holder is appointed the
employer's agent for the purchase of petrol. If there is such an agreement, we have
not seen it.
    Any agreement between the card holder and the garage, the so-called forecourt
agreement, would obviously not be in writing. In the old days, before the arrival of
h the self-service station, the contract would have been made orally at the pump
between the driver and the pump attendant. But self-service has made a difference.
In the case of a supermarket, the contract is usually made at the check-out desk. If
the sale does not go ahead for any reason because, for example, the customer does
not have enough money, the goods can always be returned to the shelf. But in the
case of petrol, the goods could hardly be returned to the underground tank, or
j syphoned out into another customer's car. So in the case of a self-service station it
has been decided that the contract is made gallon by gallon, or drop by drop, as the
petrol passes what in ships is called the vessel's permanent hose-pipe connection but
which in cars has a shorter name. We return later in this judgment to the nature and
terms of the forecourt agreement.
    I now turn to consider the origin of these proceedings and the causes of the
applicant's present discontents.

The DSS issue a manual, known as the Green Book, for the guidance of employers. The question of free petrol is dealt with under the heading 'What is or is not included in gross pay'. There is no mention of the sort of charge card with which we are concerned. But there is mention of vouchers, whereby an employer provides his employees with free petrol for private motoring. So long as the vouchers are redeemable for petrol, and not for cash, the value of the petrol need not be included in gross pay. Although, as I have said, charge cards are not mentioned, it appears to have been accepted on all sides that, like vouchers, they did not attract liability for contribution.

The next event was a supplement to the Green Book published during 1989. The supplement contains the first reference to agency cards and company credit cards, but only for business use. According to the supplement, if some of the petrol purchased for business use is used for private motoring, it could be ignored. The supplement might be said, by implication, to exclude agency and company credit cards issued for private use. But there was still no express provision to that effect and the practice continued as before.

It was an aide-memoire issued in April 1990 under the heading 'Paying Employees' Petrol Expenses—NIC Liability' which first caused alarm. On any view the aide-memoire is a slovenly document. Counsel for the Crown did not seek to defend it. Although vouchers continued to be free of liability, charge cards were put firmly on the other side of the fence. Furthermore it was stated that, as this had been made clear in the Green Book in April 1989, (which it had not) employers would be charged contribution retrospectively on all petrol purchased by employees since that date, unless employers could provide documentary evidence to prove the amount of petrol used for business purposes. There is evidence from Mr Barry Burford, corporate purchase director of Thorn EMI that with 10,000 company cars this would be an administrative nightmare. It is not surprising that the aide-memoire caused such concern.

From Overdrive's point of view there were two objections to the aide-memoire. First it draws an unjustifiable distinction between vouchers and charge cards. The administrative nightmare would inevitably lead employers to prefer vouchers to charge cards and thereby affect Overdrive's business. Second the aide-memoire is, they say, quite simply erroneous in point of law. Free petrol for private use is exempt by virtue of reg 19(1)(*d*) because it is either a payment in kind, or else a payment by way of a facility provided by the employer.

At this stage I should quote in terms the relief sought by Overdrive:

> 'Relief sought
>
> (A) An Order that the DSS should forthwith withdraw the Aide-Memoire.
>
> (B) A Declaration that payment of an employee's petrol expenses by use of an employer's credit card or petrol agency card does not attract liability to primary or secondary Class 1 national insurance contributions ("NICs")
>
> or alternatively to (B) above
>
> (C) A Declaration that no distinction is to be drawn in point of liability for NICs between payment of an employee's petrol expenses (a) by use of an employer's credit card or petrol agency card and (b) by issuing to the employee vouchers which cannot be exchanged for cash and (c) by charging such petrol to an employer's garage account.
>
> or alternatively to (B) or (C) above
>
> (D) A Declaration that the treatment for the purposes of NICs of payment of an employee's petrol expenses whether such payment is made by the use of an employer's credit card or petrol agency card or by the issue to the employee of vouchers which cannot be exchanged for cash or by charging such petrol to an employer's garage account depends upon whether or not the employee is liable as principal for the price of the petrol in the first instance and that such treatment is the same whichever method is used, namely that a liability

for NICs is attracted if the employee is so liable as principal and there is no
liability for NICs if the employee is not so liable as principal.'

These proceedings were commenced on 11 June 1990. On 3 September 1990 Mr
Hewitt swore an affidavit in which he accepted for the first time on behalf of the
DSS that there is no valid distinction between vouchers and charge cards.
Accordingly the declaration claimed in para (C) above is now conceded, though not
in the sense for which Overdrive had hoped. There is no longer any discrimination
in favour of vouchers. But, according to the DSS, vouchers and charge cards are
both subject to contribution.

Once it was accepted that the aide-memoire was erroneous, one would have
expected it to be withdrawn forthwith. But this was not done. It was thought better
to await the outcome of these proceedings. In the meantime instructions have
been given that the aide-memoire should not be implemented. Whether it has
been implemented or not, the fact remains that the aide-memoire has not yet been
withdrawn. In those circumstances Overdrive are clearly entitled to the declaration
claimed in para (A), as well as para (C).

That leaves paras (B) and (D). In the course of the hearing before us, counsel for
the Crown, made a further concession. He conceded (or more accurately did not
dispute) that where there has never been any personal liability on the part of the
card holder to pay for the petrol, there is no correlative liability to contribute. Thus
where the card holder tenders his Overdrive card before filling his car with petrol,
and thereby makes clear to the attendant that he is buying as agent for his employer,
and not as principal, and where the contract proceeds on that basis, then the value
of the petrol is not to be included in the employee's earnings. But where, as in the
normal case, the charge card is not tendered until _after_ the contract has been made,
then the position is, he says, different. In such a case the card holder incurs a
personal debt to the garage. The debt is then discharged by the garage accepting in
its place the liability of Overdrive. In _Re Charge Card Services Ltd_ ([1989] Ch 497 at
513), Sir Nicolas Browne-Wilkinson V-C called the arrangement a quasi-novation,
no doubt because the liability accepted by Overdrive is less (by reason of the discount)
than the liability incurred by the card holder.

Counsel for the Crown argues that, wherever the employee's liability is charged in
this way, there is a payment of money's worth to the employee which must be
included in his gross pay for the purposes of calculating national insurance
contributions, unless the card holder can show that the petrol was bought for
business purposes only. The date on which the payment is deemed to have been
made is the date on which the charge card is accepted. In support of his argument,
Counsel for the Crown cited _Hartland v Diggines (Inspector of Taxes)_ [1926] AC 289,
10 TC 247 as applied to this class of case in _Richardson v Worrall_.

Counsel for Overdrive accepts the general principle that the discharge of an
employee's debt represents money's worth in his hands. But he submits that the
principle has no application in the present case for two reasons.

In the first place the discharge of an employee's debt does not fall easily within the
description of 'earnings ... paid to or for the benefit of an earner' (see s 4(2) of the
1975 Act). The 1975 Act, and the regulations made thereunder, contemplate that
earnings will be paid by the employer, and not by a third party. Thus para 13 of
Sch 1 of the 1979 regulations entitles an employer to deduct contributions when
'making any payment of emoluments to the employee', and para 26 obliges him to
pay any contributions not deducted under para 13 'in respect of emoluments paid
by him during that income tax month'. These provisions would not work, so counsel
for Overdrive argues, where the debt is discharged by Overdrive. Moreover, the
employers would not even know the amount of the debt discharged by Overdrive
until they receive an account, which might not be until the next income tax month.
If the discharge of the debt does not fall within the description of 'earnings', then
clearly it cannot give rise to liability to contribute.

I do not find the first reason persuasive. It is true that the card holder's debt, where he incurs a personal liability, is paid by Overdrive. But there is no difficulty *a* in treating that payment as being made on behalf of the employer. Since the ultimate discharge of the card holder's personal liability falls on the employer, it should make no difference whether it is done directly or indirectly.

Counsel for Overdrive's second reason is much more finely balanced. Assuming the discharge of the card holder's liability would otherwise be included in his earnings, nevertheless it is to be disregarded by virtue of reg 19(1)(*d*). At the outset *b* of this part of this argument, counsel submitted that, looking at the reality, what the employee receives is petrol in his tank. This should be regarded as a payment in kind. There should be no difference between petrol from a pump on the employer's own premises, which is admittedly a payment in kind, and petrol from a commercial pump. But there are difficulties here; so much so that, by the close of his case, counsel was content to rely on the alternative argument that the payment was 'by *c* way of the provision of . . . other facilities' (see reg 19(1)(*d*)).

This brings one to the heart of the problem in the present case. Counsel for Overdrive submits that the discharge of an employee's liability by means of a charge card is the clearest possible example of a payment by way of a facility. That is what a charge card is for. It is something which renders easier the performance of the employee's obligation to pay for the petrol, and therefore falls four square within the *d* definition of 'facility' in the Oxford English Dictionary.

Again counsel for the Crown is prepared to yield ground. The fact that an employee does not have to carry cash is, he accepts, a 'facility' in the broadest sense of the word. But he argues that the use of the card to discharge the card holder's debt goes beyond even the broadest sense of the word, and certainly beyond the meaning of the word in the context of 'board or lodging or . . . services or other facilities' (see *e* reg 19(1)(*d*)).

I have found the point, as I say, finely balanced. 'Facility' is a slippery word. One sense in which it is commonly used by bankers, namely, an overdraft facility, is not even mentioned in the dictionary. But in the end I have been persuaded that counsel for the Crown's construction is correct. The right approach is to regard the discharge of an employee's debt as the equivalent of a payment in cash, and not less so because *f* that payment is made easier by the use of a charge card. The extent to which the payment is made easier (if it could be measured in money terms) is to be disregarded under reg 19(1)(*d*). But the payment itself is not.

If that be right, then Overdrive is not entitled to the declaration claimed in para (B). There may be cases where the employee's petrol vouchers will not attract liability to contribute, as where the petrol is used for business purposes, or *g* where he has incurred no personal liability. But as it stands, the declaration is too wide.

Counsel for Overdrive invited us to indicate the sort of circumstances in which the employee would not incur personal liability. Otherwise there may have to be a further application for judicial review when the aide-memoire is reissued. But it is no part of the function of the court to draft the DSS's documents. We sympathise *h* with counsel for Overdrive's reasons for seeking further enlightenment. But I am unwilling to comply with his request. Counsel for the Crown argues that Overdrive have no locus standi to ask for any other relief. Whether it is put on that ground, or whether it is put on the unwillingness of the court to answer hypothetical questions, may not matter.

In summary, Overdrive are entitled to the declarations claimed in paras (A) and *j* (C), but not (B).

As to the declaration claimed in para (D), counsel for the Crown has conceded that there is no liability for national insurance contributions if the employee is not personally liable for the cost of the petrol. To that extent Overdrive are entitled to that declaration as well. But otherwise it does not carry matters any further.

TUDOR EVANS J. I agree.

a

Order accordingly.

Solicitors: *Marriott Harrison Bloom & Norris* (for Overdrive); *Solicitor to the Department of Social Security.*

Rengan Krishnan Esq   Barrister.

Ensign Tankers (Leasing) Ltd v Stokes (Inspector of Taxes)

COURT OF APPEAL, CIVIL DIVISION
SIR NICOLAS BROWNE-WILKINSON V-C, STUART-SMITH AND LEGGATT LJJ
10, 11, 12, 13 DECEMBER 1990, 30 JANUARY 1991

Capital allowances – Expenditure on provision of machinery or plant – Taxpayer company entering into partnerships to produce films – Partnerships appointing sole agents to distribute and exploit films – Transactions entered into by taxpayer company to take advantage of first–year allowances – Whether partnerships trading – Finance Act 1971, s 41(1).

The taxpayer company, Ensign, was a member of a group of companies. Ensign became interested in films when it discovered from a Revenue statement of practice that first–year allowances would be available in respect of capital expenditure on their production. It became a partner in two limited partnerships set up to finance the production and exploitation of two films. The first partnership contributed 25% of the estimated cost of the first film and the second partnership contributed 25·5% of the estimated cost of the second film. The remainder was met by non-recourse loans repayable exclusively out of the receipts of the films. The partnerships thus acquired the entire interest in each venture. The partnerships appointed sole and exclusive agents to distribute and exploit the films on their behalf. For the purposes of s 41(1)[a] of the Finance Act 1971, master prints of films were to be treated as plant when ownership thereof carried with it the right to distribute and exploit the films. Ensign claimed first–year allowances on its percentage of the capital expenditure incurred on the films under s 41(1). The Crown contended, inter alia, that the partnerships did not carry on a trade and that accordingly the expenditure incurred by Ensign did not qualify for relief under s 41(1). Ensign appealed on the grounds that the transactions entered into by the partnerships constituted trading and that the presence of fiscal motives could not affect the nature of those transactions. The Special Commissioners dismissed Ensign's appeal holding that transactions entered into with fiscal motives as their paramount object were not trading transactions and consequently neither partnership could be said to be trading. Ensign appealed. Millett J allowed the appeal holding, inter alia, that the purpose of the transaction had to be determined objectively solely by reference to the nature of the transaction itself, not subjectively by reference to the motives of the parties to the transactions, and that the transactions were commercial transactions entered into by the partnerships with a view of profit even though they were financed by investors who were motivated by the hope of obtaining a fiscal advantage rather than a commercial profit and were structured to obtain the fiscal advantage. Accordingly, on the facts found by the commissioners, the only true and reasonable conclusion was that the partnerships were trading. The Crown appealed to the Court of Appeal.

Held – Whether a transaction was a trading transaction was a question of fact for the commissioners to be determined by an objective analysis of the transaction viewed as a whole. The transaction should be similar in nature to transactions in the commercial world and it had to have a commercial purpose. The ultimate question was 'What was the purpose of the transaction?'. If the transaction was equivocal, the subjective intention of the parties to the transactions would be relevant in determining that question. If the sole objective was to gain a fiscal advantage, then it was not a trading transaction. However, if the paramount objective was fiscal, that

---

a Section 41(1), so far as material, is set out at p 138 *h j*, post

a   was not decisive as it postulated the existence of some other purpose which might be commercial. If so, the commissioners would have to weigh the fiscal elements against the non-fiscal elements to decide whether the transaction was entered into by the taxpayer for essentially commercial purposes but in a fiscally advantageous form or essentially for the purpose of obtaining a fiscal advantage under the guise of a commercial transaction. As the circumstances of the present case were clearly equivocal, the commissioners were entitled to have regard to the motives of the

b   partnerships. Accordingly, the grounds on which Millett J had decided that the commissioners had erred in law and the grounds on which he had based his decision were incorrect, and the commissioners' decision purporting to reach their conclusion as one of law was erroneous. The Crown's appeal would therefore be allowed and the case would be remitted to the commissioners for reconsideration.

c   **Notes**

For first-year allowances, see Simon's Taxes B2.321.
  For the Finance Act 1971, s 41(1), see ibid, Part H1.

d   **Cases referred to in judgments**

Coates (Inspector of Taxes) v Arndale Properties Ltd [1984] STC 637, [1984] 1 WLR 1328, [1985] 1 All ER 15, 59 TC 516, HL.
F A & A B Ltd v Lupton (Inspector of Taxes) [1972] AC 634, [1971] 3 All ER 948, 47 TC 580, HL.
Griffiths (Inspector of Taxes) v Harrison (J P) (Watford) Ltd [1963] AC 1, [1962] 1

e   All ER 909, 40 TC 281, HL.
IRC v Livingstone (1926) 11 TC 538, CS.
Iswera v IRC [1965] 1 WLR 663, PC.
Newton v Comr of Taxation [1958] AC 450, [1958] 2 All ER 759, PC.
Overseas Containers (Finance) Ltd v Stoker (Inspector of Taxes) [1989] STC 364, [1989] 1 WLR 606, CA.

f   *Ramsay (W T) Ltd v IRC* [1981] STC 174, [1982] AC 300, [1981] 1 All ER 865, 54 TC 101, HL.
Reed (Inspector of Taxes) v Nova Securities Ltd [1984] STC 124, [1984] 1 WLR 537, CA; [1985] STC 124, [1985] 1 WLR 193, [1985] 1 All ER 686, 59 TC 516, HL.
Religious Tract and Book Society of Scotland v Forbes (Surveyor of Taxes) (1896) 3 TC 415, CS.

g   *Thomson (Inspector of Taxes) v Gurneville Securities Ltd* [1972] AC 661, [1971] 3 All ER 1071, 47 TC 633, HL.

Cases also cited

Abbey National Building Society v Cann [1991] 1 AC 56, [1990] 1 All ER 1085, HL.

h   *Barclays Bank Ltd v Quistclose Investments Ltd* [1970] AC 567, [1968] 3 All ER 651, HL.
Bishop (Inspector of Taxes) v Finsbury Securities Ltd [1966] 1 WLR 1402, [1966] 3 All ER 105, 43 TC 591, HL.
Californian Copper Syndicate (Limited and Reduced) v Harris (Surveyor of Taxes) (1904) 5 TC 159, CS.

j   *Craven (Inspector of Taxes) v White* [1988] STC 476, [1989] AC 398, [1988] 3 All ER 495, HL.
Furniss (Inspector of Taxes) v Dawson [1984] STC 153, [1984] AC 474, [1984] 1 All ER 530, 55 TC 324, HL.
General Motors Acceptance Corp (United Kingdom) Ltd v IRC [1987] STC 122, 59 TC 651, CA.
IRC v Incorporated Council of Law Reporting (1888) 3 TC 105.

Lord Advocate v Gibb (1905) 5 TC 194, CS.
Oram (Inspector of Taxes) v Johnson [1980] STC 222, [1980] 1 WLR 558, [1980] 2
    All ER 1, 53 TC 319.
Ransom (Inspector of Taxes) v Higgs [1974] STC 539, [1974] 1 WLR 1594, [1974] 3
    All ER 949, 50 TC 1, HL.
Reed (Inspector of Taxes) v Young [1986] STC 285, [1986] 1 WLR 649, 59 TC 196,
    HL.
Royal Agricultural Society of England v Wilson (Inspector of Taxes) (1924) 9 TC 62.
Stokes (Inspector of Taxes) v Costain Property Investment Ltd [1984] STC 204, [1984]
    1 WLR 763, [1984] 1 All ER 849, 57 TC 688, CA.
Yarmouth v France (1887) 19 QBD 647.

Appeal

The Crown appealed against the decision of Millett J (see [1989] STC 705) dated
14 July 1989 allowing an appeal by Ensign Tankers (Leasing) Ltd, the taxpayer
company, from a determination of the Special Commissioners upholding the
Crown's refusal of its claims to first-year allowances pursuant to s 41(1) of the
Finance Act 1971. The grounds of appeal were, inter alia, that on the facts found by
the commissioners the judge ought to have upheld the commissioners' conclusion
that neither of the partnerships set up to finance the production and exploitation of
two films had carried on a trade and that the sole purpose of both partnerships in
entering into the transactions concerning the films was to obtain a fiscal advantage
and not a commercial purpose. The facts are set out in the judgment of Sir Nicolas
Browne-Wilkinson V-C.

Christopher McCall QC and *Launcelot Henderson* for the Crown.
John Gardiner QC and *Roger Thomas* for Ensign.

Cur adv vult

30 January 1991. The following judgments were delivered.

SIR NICOLAS BROWNE-WILKINSON V-C. This is an appeal by the Crown
against the decision of Millett J (see [1989] STC 705), who allowed an appeal by the
taxpayer company, Ensign Tankers (Leasing) Ltd (Ensign), against a decision of
the Special Commissioners. The Special Commissioners held that Ensign was not
entitled to claim initial allowances under s 41(1) of the Finance Act 1971 (the 1971
Act) in respect of two transactions related to two films ('Escape to Victory' and
'Outland').
    Section 41(1) provides as follows:

    ' Subject to the provisions of this Chapter, where —
        (*a*) a person carrying on a trade incurs capital expenditure on the provision
        of machinery or plant for the purposes of the trade, and
        (*b*) in consequence of his incurring the expenditure, the machinery or plant
        belongs to him at some time during the chargeable period related to the
        incurring of the expenditure,
    there shall be made to him for that period an allowance (in this Chapter referred
    to as "a first-year allowance") which shall be of an amount determined in
    accordance with section 42 below.'

At the material time, the master negative of a film constituted plant for the
purposes of this section. The first-year allowance was 100%.

The transactions in question were carried out by two limited partnerships (one
a for each film) in each of which Ensign was a partner. It is common ground that, for
the purposes of s 41, the 'person' referred to in that section is the partnership. The
questions which arise are (a) was the partnership 'a person carrying on a trade', (b)
did the film 'belong' to the partnership, and (c) did the partnership incur expenditure
in the purchase of the film?

If the partnerships qualified for first-year allowances under s 41, under s 155 of
b the Income and Corporation Taxes Act 1970 (the 1970 Act) the partnership is to be
treated for tax purposes as though it were a limited company, but in computing its
tax liability no deduction is to be allowed for capital allowances. Instead, under
s 155(2) of the 1970 Act, each partner is entitled in computing his or its profit to take
into account its share of the partnership capital allowances. Hence, although the
claim to the first-year allowances in this case is rightly made by Ensign (both on its
c own account and in relation to group relief for other companies in the same group)
it is of fundamental importance to appreciate that the relevant questions all depend
not on the actions and intentions of Ensign alone but on the actions and intentions
of the partnership as a body.

The case stated by the Special Commissioners and the judge's judgment are
reported at [1989] STC 705. The judgment is also reported at [1989] 1 WLR 1222.
d Although there are factual differences between the 'Escape to Victory' and the
'Outland' transactions, it is common ground that those differences are immaterial
for present purposes. I will therefore deal exclusively with the 'Escape to Victory'
transaction, the outline facts of which I gratefully adopt, often verbatim, from the
judge's judgment.

e *The facts*

At all material times Ensign was a member of the Thomas Tilling group (the
Tilling group) of companies, which had substantial group profits. Mr Whitfield was
the managing director of Ensign. He was a chartered accountant and a member of
the group's treasury committee. He was also the group's tax controller and was
principally concerned with the financial and fiscal aspects of the group's activities.
f Prior to 1980 Ensign was profitably engaged in the short-term leasing of plant and
machinery and the provision of non-recourse finance in connection with the
purchase and leasing of oil drilling rigs.

In 1979 the Revenue issued a statement (SP 9/79) that first-year allowances were
to be available for expenditure in connection with the making of films.

'Escape to Victory' was a full-length motion picture directed by John Houston
g and starring Michael Caine, to be shot on location in Hungary. It was to be produced
by Lorimar Productions Incorporated (LPI), a Californian company engaged in the
production of films, and to be distributed by Lorimar Distribution International
Incorporated (LDII), an associated company of LPI. By March 1980 LPI had made
all the arrangements necessary for the making of the film. The estimated cost of
producing the film was just under $US 13m. LPI had secured the necessary finance
h which was to be provided by means of a revolving credit from Chemical Bank on
the security (inter alia) of the film. Principal photography began on 26 May 1980.

A Mr Wilde on behalf of his employer, the merchant bank Guinness Mahon &
Co Ltd (Guinness Mahon), had devised a scheme whereby United Kingdom
investors could take advantage of first-year allowances in relation to films. Mr Wilde
had also negotiated with LPI in early 1980 the terms on which his scheme could be
j used for investment in 'Escape to Victory'. The advantages of the scheme to LPI
were that it provided cheaper finance and to investors that it made available to them
first-year allowances in respect of the film. These first-year allowances could be used
as a tax shelter against other profits. Mr Wilde marketed his scheme in the United
Kingdom as a tax deferral scheme, charging a fee of 7% payable to Guinness Mahon.
Mr Wilde brought the scheme to Mr Whitfield, who recommended it to the treasury
committee and the group main board.

The scheme was implemented all on one day, 14 July 1980. The basic document was a partnership agreement made between Victory Film Productions Ltd (Victory *a* Productions) as general partner and five other companies, of which Ensign was one. The other companies were not connected with Ensign but, as I understand the position, were also purchasers of the scheme from Guinness Mahon. That agreement established the Victory Partnership, the objects of which were 'to engage in the production making and/or acquisition exploitation and distribution of full-length cinematographic films and all ancillary rights on a commercial basis and with a view *b* to profit'. The initial capital of the partnership was $3,250,000 (25% of $13m), all of which was contributed by the limited partners. Ensign's contribution was $2,375,000. The partnership was a limited partnership, Victory Productions alone having the conduct and management of the business. Victory Productions was a company beneficially owned by LPI. Its principal director was Mr Wilde, who had devised the scheme. *c*

On the same day, 14 July 1980, and in the course of the same meeting, 16 further documents were entered into between eight different parties. The most important of these were a loan agreement made between LPI as lender and Victory Partnership by its general partner, Victory Productions, as borrower, a production services agreement made between the same parties, and a distribution agreement made between Victory Partnership as producer and LDII as distributor. The effect of the *d* various transactions was as follows:

1. LPI agreed to lend Victory Partnership the additional $9,750,000 (75% of $13m) it needed to meet the budgeted cost of making the film (the production loan) and any further money needed to complete the film in case it ran over budget (the completion loan). Both loans were non-recourse loans, that is to say they were repayable exclusively out of the receipts of the film without recourse to Victory *e* Partnership or its general or limited partners or their other assets.

2. Victory Partnership acquired the uncompleted film for $4,780,951, being the cost of making it to date. LPI agreed to complete the manufacture of the film for and on behalf of Victory Partnership substantially in accordance with the approved budget. Victory Partnership agreed to pay LPI the balance of the approved budget for doing so. Any finance needed in excess of the approved budget would be *f* provided for by LPI in accordance with the terms of the completion loan. LPI assigned to Victory Partnership all its rights in the film, including the ownership of that part of the film which had already been made.

3. Victory Partnership retained the ownership of the master negative, but granted to LDII in perpetuity an exclusive licence to distribute and exploit the film outside the United Kingdom. LDII was to charge distribution fees at what the commissioners *g* accepted were near market rates and to retain the gross receipts until it had recouped its distribution expenses and the shares of profit payable to members of the cast and other participators in the film. Victory Partnership appointed Firrilee Ltd (Firrilee), another LPI company, its sole and exclusive agent to distribute and exploit the film in the United Kingdom.

4. The net receipts of the film were payable to Victory Partnership and were *h* divisible (a) as to 25% to Victory Partnership and as to 75% to LPI in repayment of the production loan until Victory Partnership should have recouped its capital outlay of $3,250,000, described as 'the break even point', at which time LPI would have recovered a sum equal to the production loan of $9,750,000 but without interest; thereafter (b) as to 100% to LPI until it should have recovered further sums equal to interest on the production loan together with the completion loan (if any) *j* with interest; and thereafter (c) as to 25% to Victory Partnership and as to 75% to LDII.

Looking at these arrangements in purely financial (as opposed to legal) terms, Victory Partnership was in effect a sleeping partner with a minority interest. It was putting up 25% of the cost and taking a 25% equity participation. LPI was putting up the remaining 75% of the cost and retaining a 75% participation. In legal terms, however, LPI was not an equity participant. Victory Partnership owned 100% of the film. LPI was making its contribution by way of loan. A loan creditor would normally expect to be repaid before equity participants recovered any part of their capital. However, LPI's advance was recoverable only out of film receipts and was repayable pari passu with Victory Partnership's capital investment.

The approved budget included two sums payable to LPI, a completion fee of $618,000 and a supervisory and overhead fee of $1,120,000. The first was a charge made by LPI to Victory Partnership as the price of LPI making itself liable to provide the necessary further funds to complete the film if it overran budget. This was an important safeguard to Victory Partnership which effectively insulated it from the risk of budgetary overrun. The second was a payment towards the overhead cost of making the film. LPI was carrying out the work and bearing the overheads: hence the fee for so doing. The commissioners accepted evidence that both the completion fee and the overhead provision were normal incidents of film budgets and that the rates charged were not out of the ordinary.

However, although the substance of the transaction in financial terms was that Victory Productions was a 25% equity participant, that was not the way in which it was structured by the documentation. Victory Partnership did not acquire merely a 25% interest in the venture but a 100% interest. Nor, according to the documentation, did Victory Partnership pay only 25% of the cost; that would not have suited the purpose of the partners. Instead Victory Productions acquired from LPI 100% of the film and paid 100% of the total budgeted cost. However, out of the total liability for the cost Victory Productions provided 75% out of loans from LPI, whose associated company, LDII, took a 75% equity participation.

This structure provided Victory Partnership with the element of 'gearing' necessary to achieve the fiscal advantages that the limited partners were seeking and Mr Wilde's scheme was designed to achieve. By borrowing 75% of the capital cost of the film, Victory Partnership was able to spend four times its own capital in the provision of 'plant' and obtained first-year allowances of an amount equal to that expenditure. As receipts from the film came in, the gearing would have a corresponding but deleterious effect for tax purposes. Until the indebtedness to LPI was repaid, Victory Partnership would be taxed on 100% of its receipts, although it had to pay over 75% of such receipts to LPI. But since expenditure on the film necessarily precedes the receipt of income, Mr Whitfield had calculated that the availability of 100% first-year allowances to be set against group profits made the investment financially attractive whether the film was a complete flop (and produced no income at all), recouped the investment in full, or made substantial profits. According to Mr Whitfield's calculations the optimum position between nil receipts for the film and receipts amounting to 300% of the investment was if the receipts amounted to only 50% of the investment.

The way in which the scheme was intended to work was as follows. A partnership acts through the partners or their servants or agents, in this case through the general partner. If a partnership engages in a trading transaction, that is trading by the partnership (ie by all the partners whether active or sleeping). As I have explained, each partner would be entitled under s 155 of the 1970 Act to its share of the first-year allowances. The availability of first-year allowances would create an immediate allowance for each of the partners. In the inevitable absence of any film receipts during the year in which the expenditure was incurred, the whole amount of the first-year allowance would be available to set against group profits for the year 1980. In later years, as receipts from the film came in, such receipts would be taxable on the basis that I have mentioned. The initial fiscal advantage which Mr Whitfield and the scheme sought to achieve (ie first-year allowances on 100% of the cost of the film), like the later fiscal disadvantages which could not be avoided, derived from the 'gearing' effect obtained by the use of borrowed money to acquire assets for which first-year allowances were available in the course of a business where expenditure normally preceded the receipt of income by two or three years.

'Escape to Victory' ran nearly $2m over budget. The commissioners found that
the film was not the financial success for which LPI had hoped. By the end of 1983
Victory Partnership had received from LDII and Firrilee a total of $11,126,134. Of
that amount, Victory Partnership retained 25% ($2,781,533) and paid 75%
($8,344,601) to LPI towards repayment of the production loan. Thus Victory
Partnership suffered a loss of $468,467 or 14·4% of its investment. Although further
income was to be anticipated, the commissioners found that there was no reasonable
prospect of the film making a profit for Victory Partnership or even breaking even.

The financial outcome for LPI is more difficult to quantify. It depends on the
treatment of the completion fee, the budgetary overrun and the overhead charge.
As to this, there is a disagreement between the commissioners and the judge. In my
judgment, the dispute is irrelevant since it is not in question that LPI and its
associates entered into the transactions on a genuine commercial basis.

The commissioners' decision

The commissioners start by setting out the common ground between the parties
and the issues that they treated as before them. They say this ([1989] STC 705 at
744):

> 'It is common ground in these appeals that Ensign's investment in films was
> tax motivated and tax orientated ... Ensign and the [Crown] part company
> however over the extent to which the fiscal motive has invaded the transactions
> entered into by Ensign in relation to the two films 'Escape to Victory' and
> 'Outland'. Mr Thornhill put Ensign's position very succinctly on the penultimate
> day of the hearing, in his reply, when he said that whatever fiscal reasons may
> have prompted Ensign to go into films, once it had done so, it did so on a wholly
> commercial basis. That analysis is rejected by the [Crown], for Mr Ferris
> submits that what was done by Ensign was so moulded by fiscal considerations
> that the whole character of the transactions relating to the two films was
> denatured by their fiscal content to such an extent that they ceased to be
> commercial.'

Having considered the expert evidence that the transactions were of a kind, and
on terms normal in the film business and expressing certain reservations about that
evidence, they continued (at 744–745):

> 'But even if we were to accept that the transactions considered by the expert
> witnesses were entirely normal and usual in the film business we do not agree
> that such evidence must lead us inevitably to the conclusion that the film
> transactions in these appeals were commercial or that Victory Partnership and
> Outland Productions or either of them were in consequence engaged in the
> trade of producing films. In our judgment we must look not only at the
> component parts of the transactions but at their totality and we must come to a
> decision as to whether the two limited partnerships were trading, having
> considered all the evidence adduced before us in these appeals.'

They then quoted from the speech of Lord Donovan in *F A & A B Ltd v Lupton*
(*Inspector of Taxes*) [1972] AC 634, 47 TC 580 and continued:

> 'Bearing this in mind, we proceed to an examination of the evidence, in order
> to come to a conclusion as to whether the limited partnerships in these appeals
> were trading.'

They then found the facts as follows, inter alia: (1) It was never the intention of the
Tilling group that Ensign should be a commercial success but that its primary
purpose was to improve the group's earnings and cash flow by tax deferral.
(2) Guinness Mahon (through Mr Wilde) negotiated the terms of the scheme with
LPI as bankers seeking to offer a tax avoidance scheme to investors. As to the
commercial terms, Guinness Mahon 'took what Lorimar was prepared to give'.

(3) In considering the importance to Ensign of making a commercial profit, they held that Mr Whitfield's calculations demonstrated 'that even the cash flow position of 300% cost recovery is markedly inferior to that obtaining on a complete flop. The best position by far . . . is obtained on 50% cost recovery'. (4) The transaction was aptly described in documents which predated the formation of Victory Partnership by Guinness Mahon as 'a tax deferral scheme' and by Mr Black (a senior executive of the Tilling group) as 'a scheme'. (5) 'Escape to Victory' was originally budgeted at $11·5m, but this budget had increased to $13m. Mr Whitfield was aware that by 21 June 1980 the film was already $20,000 over the budget of $13m, contingency allowance of $1m having been exhausted, and may have been aware that by 5 July it was $0·5m over budget. Yet this caused Ensign no concern. (6) The Tilling group had envisaged that, since the completion of the film was dependent on LPI finance, the possibility of LPI's insolvency would be covered by a bank guarantee, but no such guarantee was ever sought. (7) There were certain features of the documents executed on 14 July which, in their view, 'tend to diminish any faith in their commerciality'. (8) The partnership did little after 14 July 1980. (9) Mr Wilde and Guinness Mahon (as controllers of Victory Productions) did not take very seriously their responsibilities as managing partners, paying little or no regard to cost control of the film. This was inconsistent with 'normal commercial behaviour' even taking into account the non-recourse basis of the loans from LPI. (10) Ensign's motive and objective in entering into the 'Escape to Victory' transaction was to produce for the Tilling group beneficial tax allowances by means of first-year allowances. (11) Ensign had no commercial motive in entering into the transaction: 'it invested in "Escape to Victory". . . for fiscal reasons not caring whether they made a profit or not'. (12) The total uncommerciality of Ensign's approach was demonstrated when Mr Black, in the course of his re-examination, was asked whether the Tilling group would have entered into the transaction 'at any cost', and replied 'yes'.

The commissioners concluded their decision (at 751) as follows:

> 'As we understand the authorities (*Coates (Inspector of Taxes) v Arndale Properties Ltd* [1984] STC 637, [1984] 1 WLR 1328, *Reed (Inspector of Taxes) v Nova Securities Ltd* [1985] STC 124, [1985] 1 WLR 193 and *Lupton*), transactions which are entered into with fiscal motives as their paramount object are not . . . trading transactions . . . In our judgment the well-known principles established in *Lupton* apply to these appeals and we rely in particular on the oft-quoted speeches of Viscount Dilhorne ([1972] AC 634 at 657, 47 TC 580 at 628) and of Lord Simon ([1972] AC 634 at 659–660, 47 TC 580 at 631). In the circumstances, we find that neither Victory Partnership nor Outland Productions was trading.'

The judgment

I will not attempt to summarise the propositions of law which are stated at [1989] STC 705 at 762–764. As will appear, I do not agree with a number of the judge's propositions, but it is easier to demonstrate this by considering how the judge decided the instant case.

He first pointed out (at 764), in my judgment correctly, that the commissioners were wrong in holding that, *as a matter of law*, transactions entered into 'with fiscal motives as their *paramount* object' are not trading transactions. The judge then went on to hold that the commissioners had largely misdirected their inquiries. It was, and is, common ground that the only relevant question is whether Victory Partnership (as opposed to Ensign) entered into the arrangements as commercial transactions. The judge took the view that the commissioners had not directed their findings to this point, but had largely concentrated on the 'motives' of Ensign.

The judge also appears to have held that the commissioners were in error in having regard to motive or intention at all; in ascertaining whether the transaction was commercial, he considered that they should have concentrated on the terms of the deal made between Victory Partnership and LPI. He describes (at 766) the crucial question as being 'whether the transactions entered into by the partnerships were on commercial terms with a view to profit'. He dismissed the commissioners' findings as to Mr Wilde's negotiations as being concerned only with 'Mr Wilde's subjective motivation'.

Having found that the commissioners had misdirected themselves, the judge held that on the primary facts found by the commissioners there was only one possible conclusion in law,viz that they were trading transactions. The steps by which he reached this conclusion are illuminating (see [1989] STC 705 at 767).

First, he held that Ensign had invested in Victory Partnership as a tax deferral scheme; Ensign's investment 'merely provided the finance necessary to enable alleged trading transactions to be entered into'. Since this motivation had not been found by the commissioners to have had any adverse effect on the terms offered by LPI, Ensign's motivation 'can be laid aside as having no further relevance'.

Second, he looked at the matter from LPI's point of view and analysed the deal as an arrangement whereby Victory Partnership put up 25% of the budgeted finance in return for 25% of the profit for a film which LPI was making commercially. If the deal had taken this form, says the judge, Victory Partnership would plainly have been trading.

Third, the judge extrapolated from his second proposition by inserting into the transaction those factors which the second proposition omitted: the insertion, for purely fiscal reasons, of the provision whereby Victory Partnership acquired 100% (instead of 25%) of the film by means of the non-recourse loan of the necessary finance from the vendor, LPI. He held that the transaction as actually carried through also, prima facie, constituted a trading transaction; since LPI was in it for profit, so prima facie must Victory Partnership have been. The fact that the partnership acquired 100% instead of 25% of the film by means of the non-recourse loan repayable out of profits of the film was a different 'legal means of achieving the same financial result' (ie a 25% equity interest). If the taxpayer chooses one legal means of giving effect to the financial result desired, he cannot be taxed as if he had chosen another means of achieving the same result, 'even if his choice is dictated exclusively by fiscal considerations'.

Having first characterised the transaction as a trading transaction, the judge then identified (at 768) the relevant question of law as follows:

> 'Where a partnership enters into a commercial transaction with a view of profit, can it fairly be regarded as carrying on a trade even if (i) it obtained the necessary finance from investors who were primarily motivated by the hope of obtaining a fiscal advantage rather than a commercial profit; and (ii) the transaction itself was deliberately structured in order to secure the fiscal advantage without ceasing to be commercial or jeopardising the prospects of profit?'

He said that the answer to that question was in the affirmative and therefore that the only possible finding was that the transaction was a trading transaction.

Commercial purpose

In the ordinary case, the question whether a transaction is a trading transaction will be answered by looking objectively at what was done in order to see if it is similar to transactions of the same nature in the commercial world and carried out in a similar way (see *IRC v Livingstone* (1926) 11 TC 538 at 542 per Lord Clyde). But it is established that a transaction which has all the features of trade must also have a commercial purpose (see *Lupton*; *Coates (Inspector of Taxes) v Arndale Properties Ltd* [1984] STC 637, [1984] 1 WLR 1328; *Overseas Containers (Finance) Ltd v Stoker (Inspector of Taxes)* [1989] STC 364 at 369, [1989] 1 WLR 606 at 613).

The judge accepted both those propositions of law, but rejected the commissioners' approach primarily on two grounds. First, he held (at 763) that the purpose of the transaction had to be ascertained objectively and solely by reference to the nature of the transactions themselves, not subjectively by reference to the motive or intentions of the party to the transaction. Second, he held (at 762) that in any event the relevant purpose was the purpose, not of Ensign, but of the Victory Partnership.

Subjective intention

The judge rightly held that motive, as such, was irrelevant. In each case the only relevant question is 'what was the purpose or object of the transaction?' But it does not follow that, in deciding what was the purpose of the transaction, the motives or intentions of the parties to that transaction are immaterial. A seller of religious tracts who travels from door to door selling his wares, appears to be conducting an ordinary business of sale and purchase. Yet if his object is to engage the customer in religious discussion so as to spread the gospel that intention is decisive and the selling of the tracts does not constitute trading (see *Religious Tract and Book Society of Scotland v Forbes (Surveyor of Taxes)* (1896) 3 TC 415). A dealer in shares who buys and sells shares is engaging in a transaction which, objectively viewed, would be a share-trading transaction. Yet such a transaction is not trading if the sole object of the purchase or sale is not to make a commercial profit on such purchase but to obtain a fiscal advantage (see *Lupton*; *Coates v Arndale*; *Overseas Containers*).

The judge, in holding that the existence of such a non-trading purpose has to be gathered from the transaction itself objectively viewed, relied on certain remarks made by Lord Denning in *Newton v Comr of Taxation* [1958] AC 450 at 465. But that case was concerned with the interpretation of a taxing statute, not the general law of what constitutes trading. In my judgment, that case provides little assistance. The judge further relied on the fact that in none of the dividend-stripping cases to which he referred had the courts relied on evidence of intention beyond what could be gathered from the transactions themselves and their implementation. But, in my judgment, other authorities show that evidence of the subjective intention of the parties is admissible and relevant.

In *Lupton*, Viscount Dilhorne ([1972] AC 634 at 657, 47 TC 580 at 628) held that, in deciding whether a transaction was a trading transaction, regard must be had to the whole transaction. Lord Donovan ([1972] AC 634 at 658, 47 TC 580 at 629) held that it was wrong to regard as irrelevant the fact that fiscal advantage was in view. Lord Simon ([1972] AC 634 at 660, 47 TC 580 at 631) said:

'... (3) share dealings and other business transactions vary almost infinitely; and to determine whether the transaction is, on the one hand, a share-dealing which is part of the trade of dealing in shares or, on the other, merely a device to secure a fiscal advantage, all the circumstances of the particular case must be considered; (4) a share-dealing which is palpably part of the trade of dealing in shares will not cease to be so merely because there is inherent in it an intention to obtain a fiscal advantage, or even if that intention conditions the form which such share-dealing takes; (5) what is in reality merely a device to secure a fiscal advantage will not become part of the trade of dealing in shares just because it is given the trappings normally associated with a share-dealing within the trade of dealing in shares; (6) if the appearance of the transaction leaves the matter in doubt, an examination of its paramount object will always be relevant and will generally be decisive.'

In my judgment, Lord Simon's proposition (6) plainly shows that the 'paramount object' to which he is referring may be ascertained even though 'the appearance' of the transaction does not demonstrate what the paramount object of the transaction was.

In *Iswera v IRC* [1965] 1 WLR 663 the Privy Council plainly regarded the
subjective intention of the taxpayer (i e to have a house close to her daughter's school)
as being relevant and admissible in determining whether she was trading. In *Reed
(Inspector of Taxes) v Nova Securities Ltd* , the Crown were criticised in the Court of
Appeal ([1984] STC 124, [1984] 1 WLR 537) and the House of Lords ([1985] STC
124, [1985] 1 WLR 193) for failing to require the taxpayers to prove their case since,
if they had been required to do so, the Crown might have elicited in evidence the
taxpayers' intentions in entering into the transactions (see [1984] STC 124 at 138,
[1984] 1 WLR 537 at 554 per Fox LJ, whose decision was affirmed by the House of
Lords, see also [1985] STC 124 at 126, [1985] 1 WLR 193 at 195 per Lord Bridge).

In my judgment, these authorities demonstrate that, at least where the transaction
is equivocal and the purpose may or may not have been commercial, the
commissioners are entitled to look at evidence of the subjective intention or motives
of the relevant party. That is *not* because the legally relevant question is 'with what
motive did the parties enter into the transaction', but because such motive is
evidence, sometimes compelling, on which to decide the legally relevant question,
viz was the *purpose* of the transaction a trading purpose?

In the present case the circumstances were plainly equivocal; quite apart from the
fact that the motive of Ensign (as one of the partners in the Victory Partnership) was
fiscal, the provisions involving the vendor of the film, LPI, lending on a non-
recourse basis 75% of the purchase price, such loan being repaid out of profits of the
film, raises immediate questions as to the true nature of the transaction. Therefore,
in my judgment, the commissioners were fully entitled to have regard to the motives
or intentions of the Victory Partnership in deciding whether the purpose of the
transaction was a commercial one.

The relevance of Ensign's intentions

As I have said, the judge criticised the commissioners for having regard to the
motives or intentions of Ensign since the question was not whether Ensign had been
trading but whether the Victory Partnership was trading. In my judgment, such
criticism is justifiable only to the extent that the commissioners were relying on
Ensign's intentions as such, rather than as evidence of the intentions of Victory
Partnership. Although the commissioners never spelt this out in so many words, in
my judgment it is clear that they were relying on Ensign's intentions only to the
extent that they provided evidence as to the intention of Victory Partnership. The
commissioners were in no doubt as to the correct question they had to ask themselves;
they twice expressed it correctly—'whether the two limited partnerships were
trading having considered all the evidence adduced before us?' They then considered
all the matters in question, including the motives or intentions of Ensign, before
reaching their final conclusion that the Victory Partnership was not trading.

Given that subjective intention was material, the relevant intention must be that
of the Victory Partnership itself as the party which entered into the transactions.
Ensign and the four other enterprises who joined in the scheme were all partners in
the Victory Partnership and their intentions, together with that of the sixth partner
Victory Productions, must together constitute the intentions of the partnership.
The partnership itself did not come into existence until the same day, 14 July, as
that on which the allegedly trading transactions took place. Ensign and the four
other companies had acquired the tax deferral scheme from Guinness Mahon. In
the absence of other evidence as to the intentions of the other sleeping partners, the
commissioners were fully entitled to infer that their intentions were the same as
Ensign's. As to the sixth partner, Victory Productions, its management was
controlled by Guinness Mahon and Mr Wilde and the commissioners formed the
view that they were merely implementing the tax deferral scheme.

Therefore, although the commissioners do not expressly spell out the route
whereby they reached the conclusion, on a fair reading they were finding that the

subjective intention of Victory Partnership in entering into the transactions was not

a commercial.

In my judgment, therefore, the grounds on which the judge decided that the commissioners were wrong in law in reaching their conclusion and the grounds on which he based his own decision that there was only one possible result, viz that these were trading transactions, were incorrect.

b   *Paramount or sole object of fiscal advantage*

It will be remembered that the commissioners expressed their conclusion by holding that, *as a matter of law*, this was not a trading transaction since the *paramount* intention was to obtain a fiscal advantage. In my judgment, this constitutes an error of law (see *Overseas Containers (Finance) Ltd v Stoker (Inspector of Taxes)* [1989] STC 364, [1989] 1 WLR 606). In summary, that case decides: (a) trade involves not

c only the badges of trade but a commercial purpose; (b) the question whether a transaction is a trading transaction is a question of fact for the commissioners, not a question of law; (c) if the commissioners find as a fact that the *sole* object of the transaction was fiscal advantage, that finding can in law only lead to one conclusion, viz that it was not a trading transaction. Since a fiscal advantage was the sole purpose there is no place for there being any commercial purpose; *but* (d) if the commissioners

d find as a fact only that the *paramount* intention was fiscal advantage, as a matter of law that is not decisive since it postulates the existence of some other purpose (albeit not paramount) which may be commercial. In such a case, the commissioners have to weigh the paramount fiscal intention against the non-fiscal elements and decide as a question of fact whether in essence the transaction constitutes trading for commercial purposes.

e Therefore, on its face, the commissioners' decision purporting to reach their conclusion as one of law is erroneous.

The Crown, however, submits that whatever words the commissioners used they were not misdirecting themselves in law but were reaching an overall decision of fact after weighing the various elements. I am unable to accept this. There is substance in the judge's criticism that in the long section of their decision headed

f '*Conclusion*' they are dealing almost exclusively with the subjective intentions of the parties and do not expressly refer to those factors which might point the other way eg the possibility that if the film were a major 'hit' a commercial profit to Victory Partnership would have accrued and the fact that a large sum of money had been invested by the partners in the transaction. Since the decision does not clearly show that the misdirection was only verbal but may have represented a misunderstanding

g as to the basic law, in my judgment, the case must be remitted to the commissioners.

Since the case is far from straightforward, it may be helpful to the commissioners if we give some guidance as to how they should approach this case, especially as there are other points beyond those I have already dealt with which have been dealt with by the judge and have been argued before us.

h   *What is the ultimate question?*

When a transaction contains some element of trade but also a paramount fiscal objective, how should the commissioners approach the question 'was this a trading transaction?' The judge appears to have considered that if there was some element of commercial trading that was enough. Counsel for the taxpayer has argued that

j since there was some possibility of profit and therefore some element of commercial trade, that was decisive.

I reject both those views. First, Lord Simon's proposition (6) in *F A & A B Ltd v Lupton (Inspector of Taxes)* [1972] AC 634 at 660, 47 TC 580 at 631 ('. . . if the appearance of the transaction leaves the matter in doubt, an examination of its paramount object will always be relevant and will generally be decisive') shows that there are cases where, notwithstanding commercial features, the fact that the object

is fiscal is decisive. The mere possibility of profit is not decisive. In *Reed (Inspector of Taxes) v Nova Securities Ltd* the fact that the debts might have realised a profit *a*
was enough to justify a finding by the commissioners that it was a trading transaction. Yet it is manifest that both the Court of Appeal (see [1984] STC 124, [1984] 1 WLR 537) and the House of Lords ([1985] STC 124, [1985] 1 WLR 193) considered that, if there had been a finding that the objective was primarily to obtain a fiscal advantage, the commissioners could properly have found that the transaction was not trading despite the possibility of profit. So, in the present case, the mere fact *b*
that there was a possibility that Victory Partnership might make a truly commercial profit if the film were a great success does not preclude a finding that it was not a trading transaction.

In my judgment, the relevant questions (adapted from propositions (4) and (5) of Lord Simon's speech in *Lupton* (see [1972] AC 634 at 660, 47 TC 580 at 631) are these: was this a transaction which was palpably part of the trade of engaging in film *c*
production? If so, it will not cease to be so because there was an intention to obtain a fiscal advantage, even if that intention conditioned the form of the agreements. Or was it in reality merely a device to secure first-year allowances on 100% of the film? If so, it will not be trading notwithstanding that the documents and terms were normal in commercial transactions of the same kind. If the matter is in doubt, the intentions of the Victory Partnership will be relevant and may be decisive. *d*

I must emphasise that it is the intentions of the Victory Partnership, not those of LPI, which are relevant. Although it is right to take into account the position of a third party, the relevant question is whether the transaction constituted trading *by the partnership*. In relation to the same transaction, one of the parties may be trading but the other not. Where a private individual sells his investments to a share-dealer, he is not trading but the share-dealer is. It is the nature of the transaction viewed *e*
from the position of the taxpayer (or in this case the partnership) that is relevant (see *Lupton* [1972] AC 634 at 654, 47 TC 580 at 626 per Viscount Dilhorne and *Thomson (Inspector of Taxes) v Gurneville Securities Ltd* [1972] AC 661 at 678, 47 TC 633 at 678 per Lord Simon).

It is not legitimate to argue, as did the judge, (a) that if Victory Partnership had bought a 25% equity share in the film, that would have been trading and therefore *f*
(b) since the actual transaction effected merely recast that financial transaction in a different, fiscally advantageous, structure the recast transaction must itself constitute trading. As I understand the commissioners' findings, Victory Partnership would never have entered into a transaction to buy only a 25% equity share; it was an essential ingredient of the scheme devised by Guinness Mahon that 100% of the first-year allowances would be obtained in return for only a 25% investment. The *g*
commissioners must look at the actual transaction entered into, not another transaction that was never under consideration at all.

Finally the judge relied on a dictum of Lord Morris in *Lupton* ([1972] AC 634 at 647, 47 TC 580 at 619–620). In *Lupton* the majority regarded *Griffiths (Inspector of Taxes) v J P Harrison (Watford) Ltd* [1963] AC 1, 40 TC 281 as either being wrongly decided or (per Lord Simon) as establishing such a narrow proposition as to be *h*
irrelevant. The minority, Lord Morris and Lord Guest, had been parties to the *Harrison* decision and regarded it as still being good law. In my judgment, it is not safe to rely on the views of the minority in *Lupton* since they were not taking the same view as the majority. To summarise my views on the law in this case the position, in my judgment, is as follows:

(A) Whether a transaction is to be classified as commercial normally falls to be *j*
determined objectively by reference to the nature of the transaction itself ie is it a transaction of a kind similar to transactions of the same nature in the commercial world and carried out in a similar way.

(B) In addition to the outward badges of trade, in order to be a trading transaction its purpose must be commercial.

(C) The question 'was it trading?' is a question of fact for the commissioners.

a (D) In deciding that question, the commissioners must look at the transaction as a whole including the steps taken for its implementation.

(E) The commissioners must decide whether the transaction was in reality merely a device to secure a fiscal advantage or a genuine trading activity.

(F) The ultimate question always remains 'what was the *purpose* of the transaction?' That question will normally be answered by an objective analysis of the transactions viewed as a whole.

b (G) If the appearance of the matter (as shown by an objective analysis of the transactions) is equivocal, the subjective intention of the taxpayer is relevant in determining the purpose of the transaction and will generally be decisive.

(H) A transaction can be equivocal and therefore evidence of subjective intention relevant even if there was a possibility of the transaction producing a commercial profit (as opposed to a tax benefit) to the taxpayer.

c (I) Although the purpose of the other party or parties to the transactions (being part of the circumstances) is relevant, the question in each case is whether *the taxpayer* was trading. Just because the other party to the transaction in question may have no fiscal object and viewed from his angle the transaction is one by way of trade, it does not follow that the taxpayer as a party to the same transaction is also engaged in trade.

d (J) If the sole purpose of the transaction is to gain a fiscal advantage, in law that cannot amount to trade.

(K) If the transaction has some commercial features but also an element of fiscal advantage, it is for the commissioners to weigh the conflicting elements to decide whether the transaction was entered into by the taxpayer for essentially commercial purposes but in a fiscally advantageous form or essentially for the purpose of e obtaining a fiscal advantage under the guise of a commercial transaction. In the former case, the transaction would constitute trading; in the latter it will not.

For these reasons I would allow the appeal and remit the case to the Special Commissioners to reconsider their decision in the light of our judgments.

That is enough to dispose of the matter in this court but the judge, on the view he took, had to decide three other points.

f
The remaining points
The judge held ([1989] STC 705 at 770–772) that the principle in *W T Ramsay Ltd v IRC* [1981] STC 174, [1982] AC 300 did not enable the creation and existence of the limited partnership to be ignored for tax purposes. The Crown has not appealed against that decision, which, in my judgment, was plainly right. Second, g the judge held (at 769) that the plant 'belonged' to Victory Partnership. The Crown has appealed against that decision. I have heard nothing which makes me think the judge wrong.

Third, the judge held (at 769–770) that, notwithstanding the fact that the purchase of 75% of the plant was financed by the non-recourse loan from LPI, Victory Partnership had 'incurred' the expense of purchasing 100% of the plant. The Crown h has appealed against this decision. Although I think there is much force in the judge's reasoning, I prefer to express no concluded view on this point since it is not necessary for the decision in this court.

STUART-SMITH LJ. I agree.

j **LEGGATT LJ.** I agree with Sir Nicolas Browne-Wilkinson V-C that for the reasons which he has given this appeal should be allowed and the case remitted to the Special Commissioners. I add only one comment of my own.

It seems to me helpful to keep two questions separate: (1) whether the transaction was a trading transaction; and (2) whether in entering into it Victory Partnership was 'carrying on a trade'. The first question naturally comes first, because unless the transaction was a trading transaction, the second question cannot arise. The first question must, if possible, be determined objectively, and the motives of the parties are initially irrelevant. If the true nature of the transaction cannot be determined, its paramount object must be examined. For my part, I should have thought that the ascertainment of the paramount object of the transaction is also an objective process. But it is at this stage, when other features of the case are taken into account, and the paramount object of the transaction may not prove decisive, that the second question falls to be considered. In answering it, evidence of subjective intention should obviously play its part (see *Iswera v IRC* [1965] 1 WLR 663 and *Reed (Inspector of Taxes) v Nova Securities Ltd* [1985] STC 124, [1985] 1 WLR 193). The fact that a person entered into a transaction with a predominantly fiscal intention may assist the commissioners, having weighed that purpose against the other features of the transaction, to determine whether by engaging in it that person can properly be said to have been 'carrying on a trade'. That is the question which the Special Commissioners must answer here.

Appeal allowed with costs in the Court of Appeal. Case remitted to the Special Commissioners to reconsider their decision in the light of the judgments. No order as to costs in the court below. Application for leave to appeal to the House of Lords granted.

Solicitors: *Solicitor of Inland Revenue; F D Macintosh* (for Ensign).

Siew Ling Choo   Barrister.

Gallic Leasing Ltd v Coburn (Inspector of Taxes)

COURT OF APPEAL, CIVIL DIVISION
FOX, BALCOMBE AND STOCKER LJJ
5, 6 DECEMBER 1990, 13 FEBRUARY 1991

Corporation tax – Group relief – Claim – Claim to be made within two years of end of accounting year – Claim made in notice of appeal and accounts – No specified form for claim – Surrendering companies not identified – Inspector rejected claim as not in identifiable format – Whether valid claim made within two-year period – Taxes Management Act 1970, s 42(5) – Income and Corporation Taxes Act 1970, ss 258, 264(1)(c).

By an estimated assessment dated 1 October 1982, the taxpayer company was assessed to corporation tax for the accounting period ended 31 March 1982. On 31 October the taxpayer company appealed against the assessment and applied for postponement of payment of the full amount of tax on the grounds that the 'profits would be covered by group relief'. The postponement was agreed by the inspector on 15 November 1982. On 30 June 1983 the taxpayer company's accountants sent a copy of its accounts for the period to 31 March 1982 setting out the corporation tax payable on the profits and an equivalent amount of group relief. The inspector replied requesting further details of the group relief. Accounts of two of the surrendering companies were submitted in 1983 but they did not indicate the reliefs to be surrendered and there was no further supply of information by the taxpayer company until after 31 March 1984. Although no set form was laid down under s 42(5) of the Taxes Management Act 1970 for making claims for group relief under s 258(1)ᵃ of the Income and Corporation Taxes Act 1970, the inspector rejected the claim on the ground that it was not a formal claim made within the two-year period from the end of the surrendering company's relevant accounting year prescribed by s 264(1)(c)ᵇ of the Income and Corporation Taxes Act 1970. The taxpayer company appealed contending that the notice of appeal and the accounts either individually or collectively constituted a valid claim for group relief within s 264, and that by virtue of s 114 of the Taxes Management Act 1970 lack of form did not invalidate the proceedings. The General Commissioners held that s 42(5) of the Taxes Management Act 1970 required a claim to be in an identifiable form, signed by, or on behalf of the claimant, containing such particulars as were required to make it intelligible: the documents from the taxpayer company merely indicated an intention to make a claim and did not themselves constitute a claim. Accordingly, they determined that the claim was not made within the time limit specified in s 264(1)(c) and dismissed the appeal. Vinelott J, allowing the taxpayer company's appeal, held that in order to make a valid claim, all that was required was for the claimant to make it clear to the inspector that a claim was being made and there was no requirement at the time of making the claim to identify the surrendering companies or the amount of losses to be surrendered by each of them, and that accordingly, the taxpayer company had made a valid claim for group relief within the prescribed two-year period by their notice of appeal and the accounts. The Crown appealed to the Court of Appeal.

Held – In order to constitute a valid claim for group relief under s 258, the claim had to identify the surrendering companies and the amount of losses to be surrendered by each of them. Accordingly, as the notice of appeal and the taxpayer company's accounts did not give any indication as to the identities of the surrendering

---

a　Section 258(1), so far as material, is set out at p 153 *a–b*, post
b　Section 264(1)(c), so far as material, is set out at p 153 *c*, post

companies or of the amount of losses to be surrendered by each of those companies, they could not constitute a valid claim. The taxpayer company had not made a valid claim for group relief within the two-year period specified by s 264(1)(c). The Crown's appeal would therefore be allowed.

Notes

For group relief, claims and adjustments, see Simon's Taxes D2.648.

For the Income and Corporation Taxes Act 1970, ss 258, 264 (now the Income and Corporation Taxes Act 1988, ss 402, 412), see ibid, Part G1.

For the Taxes Management Act 1970, ss 42(5), 114, see ibid, Part G2.

Cases referred to in judgment

IRC v Hood Barrs (1959) 39 TC 683, HL.
Thompson v Goold & Co [1910] AC 409, HL.

Cases also cited

Elliss (Inspector of Taxes) v BP Oil Northern Ireland Refinery Ltd [1985] STC 722; affd [1987] STC 52, 59 TC 474, CA.
Farmer (Inspector of Taxes) v Bankers Trust International Ltd [1990] STC 564.
Procter & Gamble Ltd v Taylerson (Inspector of Taxes) [1988] STC 854; affd [1990] STC 624, CA.
R v Arkwright (1848) 18 Law Journal (NS) 26.

Appeal

The Crown appealed against the decision of Vinelott J (see [1989] STC 354) dated 2 March 1989 allowing an appeal by Gallic Leasing Ltd, the taxpayer company, against a determination of the General Commissioners upholding the Crown's refusal of the taxpayer company's claim for group relief for the accounting period ended 31 March 1982 under s 258 of the Income and Corporation Taxes Act 1970. The grounds of appeal were, inter alia, that the judge had erred in law in holding (i) that the notice of appeal and the accounts constituted a valid claim for group relief within the two-year period specified in s 264(1)(c); and (ii) that there was no requirement to identify the surrendering companies or the amount of losses to be surrendered by each company. The facts are set out in the judgment of the court.

Alan Moses QC and *Launcelot Henderson* for the Crown.
David Goldberg QC for the taxpayer company.

Cur adv vult

13 February 1991. The following judgment of the court was delivered.

FOX LJ. This is an appeal by the Crown from a decision of Vinelott J (see [1989] STC 354) that a valid claim had been made for group relief under s 258 of the Income and Corporation Taxes Act 1970 (the 1970 Act). The claim was made by Gallic Leasing Ltd (the taxpayer company) in respect of its profits for the accounting period ending on 31 March 1982.

Section 258(1) of the 1970 Act provides that relief for trading losses may be surrendered by one company within a group of companies and on the making of a claim by another company in the same group may be allowed to that company by way of relief from corporation tax.

The subsection is in the following terms:

> 'Relief for trading losses and other amounts eligible for relief from corporation tax may in accordance with the following provisions of this Chapter be surrendered by a company (called "the surrendering company") which is a member of a group of companies and, on the making of a claim by another company (called "the claimant company") which is a member of the same group, may be allowed to the claimant company by way of a relief from corporation tax called "group relief".'

The taxpayer company was at all material times a member of a group which included five other companies. During the accounting period to 31 March 1982, each of those companies sustained trading losses which were capable of being surrendered. All the companies had accounting periods to 31 March.

Section 264(1)(c) of the 1970 Act provides that a claim for group relief—

> '... must be made within two years from the end of the surrendering company's accounting period to which the claim relates.'

The issue in the case is whether the taxpayer company made a valid claim before 31 March 1984.

The other material facts relating to the claim are as follows: (1) On 1 October 1982 the inspector of taxes sent to the taxpayer company a notice of assessment to corporation tax for the period to 31 March 1982. On 31 October 1982 an appeal was lodged on behalf of the taxpayer company by its accountants. In the notice of appeal application was made to postpone payment of tax (which was due on 1 January 1983). The notice of appeal (which is a printed form) bore a manuscript note at its foot stating: 'Profits will be covered by group relief'. The postponement was agreed by the inspector on 15 November 1982. (2) On 30 June 1983 the accountants sent a copy of the accounts of the taxpayer company for the period ending 31 March 1982 to the inspector, together with a corporation tax calculation. The profit and loss account showed nothing payable in respect of tax. Note 6 to the accounts under the heading 'Taxation' set out the corporation tax payable at 52% on the profits for the period, and an equivalent amount of group relief. (3) The inspector acknowledged receipt of the accounts and computations on 18 July 1983. He added that he had no inquiries to raise and awaited details of the group relief. (4) The accounts of two of the other companies in the group—Gallic Shipping Ltd and Gallic Management Co Ltd—were sent to the inspector in August 1983 and June 1983 respectively. The accounts do not show that any reliefs were to be surrendered. (5) There was no further correspondence, or supply of information by or on behalf of the taxpayer company, until after 31 March 1984. In particular, no notice of consent by any company in the group to the surrender of any losses was given to the inspector by any of the companies by 31 March 1984.

The issue is whether the notice of appeal or the accounts (or the both together) constituted a 'claim' for any group relief by the taxpayer company.

We should now refer further to the statutory provisions. The statutory references are to the Income and Corporation Taxes Act 1970.

> (a) As we have already indicated, s 258(1) permits trading losses and other amounts eligible for relief to be surrendered by one company within a group and 'on the making of a claim' by another company in the same group may be allowed to the claimant company by way of relief from corporation tax.
> (b) Two or more companies may make claims relating to the same surrendering company and the same accounting period of that surrendering company (see s 258(3)).
> (c) One company is deemed to be a member of the same group as another if it is a 75% subsidiary of that other company, or if both are 75% subsidiaries of a third company (see s 258(5)).

(d) The amount of surrendered relief may be set off against the total profits of the claimant company's corresponding accounting period, subject to certain exclusions (see s 259).

(e) Where the accounting period of the claimant company does not coincide with the accounting period of the surrendering company, the losses available for surrender are reduced by applying a fraction of which the numerator is the period common to the two accounting periods, and the denominator the length of the accounting period of the surrendering company. The profits against which the losses so reduced can be set are reduced by applying a fraction of which the numerator is the period common to the two accounting periods and the denominator the length of the corresponding accounting period of the claimant company (see s 261).

(f) If a company joins or leaves a group during an accounting period, the profits and losses are apportioned on a time basis, and s 261 is then applied (see s 262).

(g) A surrendering company must give consent (see s 264(1)).

Section 42 of the Taxes Management Act 1970 contains general provisions as to relief to be given on the making of a claim. Section 42(5) provides that a claim shall be in such form as the Board may determine. No determination as to the form of a claim for group relief has been made by the Board.

The Crown asserts that no claim for group relief was made by the taxpayer company within the two-year period. On appeal, the General Commissioners for the City of London upheld the Crown's contention. On appeal to the High Court, Vinelott J allowed the appeal.

The first question is: what is the nature of the claim with which the case is concerned? In answering that, it is necessary to bear in mind that the basis of the statutory provisions as to group relief is that each claim to losses of a surrendering company is a separate claim. Although the relief is conveniently referred to as group relief, the group only consists of two companies which must satisfy the 75% shareholding requirements of s 258(5). There may be a number of claims, but the number depends on the number of surrendering companies. In relation to a particular claim, there will be one claimant company and one surrendering company. Accordingly, each claim must be considered separately. This is emphasised by the provisions of s 264(1)(c), which relates each claim to a particular surrendering company. The two-year provision is tied to the surrendering company's accounting period to which the claim relates.

Thus far, therefore, a claim must be a claim to losses or reliefs surrendered by a particular company.

Second, the claim must relate to specific losses or reliefs. That follows from s 258(1), which provides that:

> 'Relief for trading losses and other amounts eligible for relief from corporation tax may ... be surrendered ... and, on the making of a claim by ... (... the "claimant company") ... may be allowed to the claimant company by way of relief from corporation tax ...'

The Crown accepts, as we understand it, that losses may be claimed in any objectively determinable manner—for example, in figures or as proportions of total losses or subject to a limit or by reference to a formula relating to the losses of the surrendering company or the profits of the claimant company for the relevant accounting period.

A claim, it seems to us, must be in such a form that the inspector is able to accept or reject it, wholly or partially, within the provisions of the legislation. A claim which does not identify each surrendering company and the amount surrendered by that company is not a valid claim. Its content is not such that the inspector can determine whether it should be accepted or not. A claim, of course, can be accepted in a different amount from that claimed. There may well be disputes as to questions

on the facts and the law. But to constitute a claim, a sufficiently defined quantification
a of the sums to be surrendered is, it seems to us, a necessary requirement. That does
not mean that it must be immediately quantifiable. It may have to await figures and
calculations not yet available.

In the present case, the documents relied on as constituting the claim are: (i) the
manuscript note on the notice of appeal of 31 October 1982 'Profits will be covered
by group relief'; and (ii) the taxpayer company's accounts to 31 March 1982 (sent to
b the inspector on 30 June 1983) which state, in note 6: 'Corporation Tax at 52% on
profits of the year—£167,000; Group relief—£167,000'.

These statements give no indication of the identity of a surrendering company or
companies, or of the amount to be surrendered by any company. They do not, in
our view, constitute a valid claim.

The contention of the taxpayer company, in effect, is that there is a sufficient
c claim if, within the two-year period, the claimant company notifies the inspector
that it claims group relief on the whole of its profits. All further information to
explain and justify the claim can be supplied outside the two-year period. If that
were right it would, it seems to us, largely deprive the statutory time limit of real
effect. It seems to us improbable that Parliament, having imposed a time limit for
claims, can have intended such a consequence. It can be said that if the inspector
d feels that there is undue delay by a claimant company in providing necessary
information relating to the claim, he can issue a notice of assessment and let the
company appeal. We do not, however, think that it is acceptable in relation to the
present issue. The purpose of the appellate procedure is to resolve disputes, not to
extract information which the taxpayer has failed to give.

Thompson v Goold & Co [1910] AC 409 and *IRC v Hood Barrs* (1959) 39 TC 683,
e do not, in our view, assist the taxpayer company. They are examples of claims based
on existing and ascertainable facts. In the case of a claim in the present form the
claim cannot be resolved until the taxpayer discloses who are the surrendering
companies and what are the amounts to be surrendered. The taxpayer leaves itself
free to disclose those particulars when it thinks fit. On the taxpayer company's case,
the identity of the surrendering company and the amounts to be surrendered need
f not be determined at all at the time of the claim. They can be determined at a future
date outside the two-year period.

In a case such as *Thompson v Goold & Co*, the employer knows of the accident
and knows of the claim. He is in as good a position as anybody to know what is a
reasonable sum to offer. The inspector, in such a case as the present, is not in any
comparable position. He does not know the essential facts required to base a valid
g claim.

Counsel for the taxpayer company referred us to a number of examples which he
said might give rise to difficulty on the Crown's case.

The examples undoubtedly show that it will not always be easy to demonstrate
logically why one claim which does not satisfy the statutory criteria should fail, while
another which does satisfy those criteria should succeed. The short answer is that
h Parliament, having established these criteria, it is for the courts to apply them. But
what the court is applying is an arbitrary time rule. The arbitrary nature of the rule
has the consequence that there are bound to be some hard cases and some cases
which give rise to the logical difficulties which we have mentioned. The problem is
exemplified by facts postulated by Vinelott J in stating his conclusions on the case.
He said ([1989] STC 354 at 363):

j   'I have come to the conclusion after some hesitation that counsel for the
taxpayer company's approach is to be preferred. Counsel for the Crown's
submissions, if well founded, would lead to some very anomalous and I think
unjust results. Suppose for instance that company "A" is a member of a group
which includes companies "B" and "C". Company "A" made a profit in a given
accounting period of £15,000 and claims group relief specifying company "B"

as the company by which the surrender will be made. In the event company "B" refuses to consent or perhaps is unable to consent to the surrender before its accounts are finally determined. The claim is invalid, and company "A" fails to obtain group relief even though company "C" had losses available to be set against company "A's" profit and is willing to surrender them—unless, of course, there is still time for company "A" to make another claim within the two-year period.'

We quite see the force of the judge's point here. There is a hardship (assuming it to be the law that consent cannot be given outside the two-year period). But it is not, we think, really an anomaly. It is simply a hardship arising from a time-limit provision.

We should, however, observe in relation to the question of hardship that the two-year period is a period from the end of the surrendering company's accounting period to which the claim relates (see s 264(1)(*c*)). Since it is tied to the end of the surrendering company's relevant accounting period, Parliament must have regarded the two years as adequate to enable the identity of the surrendering company and the amount surrendered to be decided on. If, as we understand counsel for the taxpayer company to suggest, the period may in some cases be inadequate, that is a matter for amending legislation. Parliament having evidently directed its mind to the matter, we can only give effect to the statutory language.

There are two further matters to which we should refer. First, as regards consent to the claims, there was no issue before the commissioners as to that, and no evidence was directed to it. Accordingly the Crown neither sought nor obtained a finding that any necessary consent was not given during the two-year period. The Crown, contrary to its previous practice, does now seek to say that consent must be given within the two-year period. Since, however, the matter does not, on the view which we have taken, affect the result of this appeal and there are no findings of fact relating to it, we do not think it appropriate to express any views about it.

Second, as regards s 114(1) of the Taxes Management Act 1970, the judge (at 362) held (rightly) that, since he held that there was a valid claim, it was unnecessary for him to decide whether a claim for group relief is a 'proceeding' to which s 114(1) applies. The point was raised again on this appeal. Since, however, the Crown is, in our view, right in contending that a valid 'claim' must identify the surrendering company and the amount of losses to be surrendered, it cannot be said to be in conformity or to accord with the intent and meaning of s 258(1) of the 1970 Act to apply the section so as to validate the claim in this case.

Looking at the whole matter we conclude that the Crown is correct and that there was no valid claim in the present case, and that the appeal accordingly succeeds. We think however, as indeed counsel for the Crown concedes, that the Crown might have been more helpful to taxpayers than it has been. Section 42 of the Taxes Management Act 1970 confers powers on the Crown to settle a form of claim. It has not, in fact, done so, and we think it is in the interests of both sides that taxpayers and their advisers know what information has to be provided in order to make a valid claim. That would reduce disputes and delay.

We allow the appeal.

Appeal allowed with costs. Leave to appeal to the House of Lords refused.

9 May. The Appeal Committee of the House of Lords gave leave to appeal.

Solicitors: *Solicitor of Inland Revenue*; *Cameron Markby Hewitt* (for the taxpayer company).

Siew Ling Choo   Barrister.

Yates (Inspector of Taxes) v G C A International Ltd; G C A International Ltd v Yates (Inspector of Taxes)

CHANCERY DIVISION
SCOTT J
12, 13 FEBRUARY 1991

Double taxation – Relief – Profits of trade – Profits in foreign territory chargeable to local taxes – Profits allocated to services performed in foreign territory and to services performed in the United Kingdom – Whether foreign tax 'corresponds to' United Kingdom income tax or corporation tax – Whether some or all of profits 'arising in' foreign territory – Whether credit allowed for foreign tax against United Kingdom corporation tax – Income and Corporation Taxes Act 1970, s 498(1), (3), (6).

The taxpayer company, GCA, was an English company which carried on business as petroleum and natural gas consultants. In May 1979, GCA entered into a contract with a Venezuelan company, M, requiring GCA to carry out a technical study with a view to the rehabilitation of three oilfields in Venezuela. Under the terms of the contract, GCA was to receive in staged payments a total of $ US 209,300 (£97,345) as remuneration for its services: $161,000 for work performed in the United Kingdom and $48,300 for work performed in Venezuela. Under art 54 of the Ley de Impuesto Sobre La Renta (the Venezuelan tax code), 90% of the gross receipts of GCA was deemed to be its net profits and tax amounting to £22,353 was levied accordingly. That amount was withheld by M from the payments made to GCA. GCA claimed that it was entitled to unilateral double taxation relief by way of credit in respect of that amount against United Kingdom corporation tax pursuant to s 498(1)[a] of the Income and Corporation Taxes Act 1970. The claim was refused on the ground that the tax imposed by art 54 did not satisfy the conditions in s 498(3)[b] and (6)[c] . The Crown contended that the Venezuelan tax did not correspond to United Kingdom income tax or corporation tax on the basis that a tax levied on gross receipts was not a tax on income but was in effect a tax on turnover. Alternatively, it was contended that the amount of credit claimed was excessive, that GCA's United Kingdom tax had to be apportioned in order to determine the amount of tax attributable to the Venezuelan income, and that that amount was substantially lower than £22,353. GCA appealed to a Special Commissioner. The commissioner held that the Venezuelan tax corresponded to United Kingdom income tax or corporation tax pursuant to s 498(6), but that only that part of the remuneration received by GCA for work done in Venezuela (ie $48,300) represented 'income arising in' Venezuela for the purposes of s 498(3). Accordingly, GCA was entitled to unilateral tax relief but only in relation to that part of the remuneration which arose in Venezuela, not the whole amount as contended by GCA. The Crown appealed and GCA cross-appealed.

Held – (1) The intention of art 54, as evidenced from the language used, was to charge net profits to income tax. To that extent, art 54 served the same function as United Kingdom income tax and corporation tax. Accordingly, the tax imposed by art 54 corresponded to United Kingdom income tax or corporation tax pursuant to s 498(3) so that unilateral tax relief was available to GCA. The Crown's appeal would therefore be dismissed.

---

a   Section 498(1), so far as material, is set out at p 166 *b–c*, post
b   Section 498(3), so far as material, is set out at p 166 *c–d*, post
c   Section 498(6), so far as material, is set out at p 166 *f*, post

(2)(a) The question whether all or some part, and if so what part, of the contractual remuneration should be regarded as 'income arising in' Venezuela for the purposes of s 498(3), fell to be determined under English law. (b) On a proper construction of s 498(3), an apportionment of the remuneration was possible, and on the facts, it was also required as a matter of common sense. Accordingly, only that part of the remuneration attributed to services performed in Venezuela should be regarded as income arising in Venezuela and GCA would be entitled to unilateral relief only in relation to that part of the remuneration, not the whole amount. GCA's cross-appeal would therefore be dismissed.

Notes

For overseas taxes to which unilateral relief is applicable, see Simon's Taxes Division F1.149.

For the Income and Corporation Taxes Act 1970, s 498(1), (3), (6) (now the Income and Corporation Taxes Act 1988, s 790(1), (4), (12)), see ibid, Part G1.

Cases referred to in judgment

Comr of Inland Revenue v Hang Seng Bank Ltd [1990] STC 733, [1991] 1 AC 306, PC.
Edwards (Inspector of Taxes) v Bairstow [1956] AC 14, [1955] 3 All ER 48, 36 TC 207, HL.
Firestone Tyre & Rubber Co Ltd v Lewellin (Inspector of Taxes) [1957] 1 WLR 464, [1957] 1 All ER 561, 37 TC 111, HL.
Smidth (F L) & Co v Greenwood (Surveyor of Taxes) [1921] 3 KB 583, CA; *affd* [1922] 1 AC 417, 8 TC 193, HL.

Cases also cited

Erichsen v Last (Surveyor of Taxes) (1881) 4 TC 422, CA.
Harrods (Buenos Aires) Ltd v Taylor-Gooby (Inspector of Taxes) (1963) 41 TC 450, CA.
IRC v Dowdall O'Mahoney & Co Ltd [1952] AC 401, [1952] 1 All ER 531, 33 TC 259, HL.
Maclaine & Co (as agents for Maclaine Watson & Co) v Eccott (Inspector of Taxes) [1926] AC 424, 10 TC 481, HL.

Case stated

1. On 12 October 1987, 8, 9 and 10 June 1988 and 31 January 1989 a Special Commissioner heard the appeal of G C A International Ltd (formerly Gaffney Cline & Associates Ltd) (the company), against the refusal by the inspector of taxes of the company's claim to unilateral relief from corporation tax pursuant to s 498 of the Income and Corporation Taxes Act l970 (the 1970 Act).

2. The question for the commissioner's determination, his findings of fact, the respective contentions of Mr Ian Richards on behalf of the company and of Mr Roger S Waterson on behalf of the inspector together with the commissioner's conclusion in principle were set out in the decision which was issued on 7 July 1988 and a copy of which was annexed as part of the case.

3. No oral evidence was adduced.

[Paragraph 4 listed the documents put in evidence before the commissioner.]

5. The following authorities were cited to the commissioner in addition to those referred to in the decision and in the written summaries of the parties' contentions:

A-G v London CC [1901] AC 26, 4 TC 265.
B S C Footwear Ltd v Ridgway (Inspector of Taxes) [1972] AC 544, 47 TC 495.

Duckering (Inspector of Taxes) v Gollan [1965] 1 WLR 680, 42 TC 333.
Thompson (Inspector of Taxes) v Trust and Loan Co of Canada [1932] 1 KB 517, 16 TC 394.
Whimster and Co v IRC (1925) 12 TC 813.

6. The parties were unable to agree figures following the decision in principle. At an adjourned hearing on 31 January 1989 the commissioner determined the amount of the company's claim in the sum of £571.

7. Both parties immediately after the determination of the appeal declared their dissatisfaction therewith as being erroneous in point of law and on 27 February 1989 required the commissioners to state a case for the opinion of the High Court pursuant to the Taxes Management Act 1970, s 56.

8. The questions of law for the opinion of the court were whether, on the facts as agreed and found, the commissioner had erred in law in holding:

(i) that the tax imposed under the Venezuelan tax law was computed by reference to income and corresponded to United Kingdom income tax or corporation tax;
(ii) that income of the company amounting to $US 48,300 had arisen in Venezuela;
(iii) that the amount of the credit for Venezuelan tax available to the company pursuant to s 505 of the 1970 Act was limited to the corporation tax attributable to the item of income which had arisen in Venezuela, namely $48,300;
(iv) that applying the provisions of s 100 of the Finance Act 1972 and s 498 of the 1970 Act the company's claim should be allowed in the sum of £571.

DECISION

The double taxation convention which has been concluded between the governments of the United Kingdom and Venezuela deals only with income, profits and capital gains arising from undertakings concerned with shipping and air transport. The trade of G C A International Ltd, formerly Gaffney Cline & Associates Ltd, (the company) embraces neither of those activities. Having suffered a deduction at source of Venezuelan tax following its completion of a contract with a Venezuelan concern, the company claimed unilateral relief from corporation tax pursuant to s 498 of the Income and Corporation Taxes Act 1970 (the 1970 Act). That claim was refused by the inspector of taxes on 22 July 1982 and it is against that refusal of its claim which the company now appeals.

There is no dispute as to the primary facts in this appeal. They are the subject of an agreed statement.

The facts

The company is incorporated in England and at all material times it has been resident in the United Kingdom for tax purposes and has carried on a trade subject to corporation tax under Sch D, Case I as petroleum and natural gas consultants. It has a single worldwide trade and at all material times its head office, from which the trade has been conducted, has been situated in the United Kingdom. At the relevant times the company has not maintained a branch in Venezuela nor has it had a permanent representative there.

On 9 May 1979, following the submission of a successful tender, the company concluded a written contract in Caracas with a Venezuelan company, Maraven SA (Maraven). The contract required the company to carry out a technical study with a view to the rehabilitation of three oilfields in Venezuela. The proper law of the contract was English law.

Under the terms of the contract the company was to receive a total of $209,300 (£97,345) as remuneration for its services. Certain of the company's obligations were to be performed in the United Kingdom whilst others were to be performed in Venezuela (see art 3 of the contract). By art 4 of the contract the company was to

receive $161,000 as remuneration for its work and services provided in the United
Kingdom and $48,300 for its work and services provided in Venezuela. It is agreed
that this apportionment of the total consideration in the contract provides a
reasonable allocation of the costs to the company of the provision of the two elements
of the contract.

Article 5 of the contract provided for stage payments to be made to the company
as the work proceeded. Payments were to be made in US dollars into the company's
bank account in the United Kingdom.

Venezuelan tax was withheld by Maraven from payments made to the company
under the terms of the contract. Venezuelan tax was levied in accordance with the
provisions of art 54 of the Ley de Impuesto Sobre La Renta (the Venezuelan tax
code). Maraven applied the tax rates prescribed in art 62 of the Venezuelan tax code
to 90% of £97,345 (£87,610) and withheld a total of £22,353 (in sterling terms) from
the payments. Each payment was accompanied by a tax withholding certificate.

The tax withheld by Maraven was paid to the Venezuelan fiscal authority and it
was calculated, deducted and payable pursuant to art 54 of the Venezuelan tax code.
That article is included in Chapter IV (of Title II) of the Venezuelan tax code which
is headed 'The Presumptive Income'. Article 54 states:

> 'The net profits of the Taxpayers not resident or not domiciled in Venezuela,
> originating from non-commercial professional activities, will be constituted by
> ninety per cent (90%) of the amount of their gross receipts . . .'

The sum of £97,345 (in sterling terms) received by the company for its services
performed under the contract was included in its Sch D, Case I receipts for the
company's accounting period ended 31 December 1979. The total turnover for the
company and its subsidiary for that year, according to its consolidated profit and loss
account, amounted to £839,498, whilst the group profit before tax for the same
accounting period amounted to £25,577.

Article 1 of the Venezuelan tax code is as follows:

> 'The net and available income obtained in cash and/or in kind, by reason of
> economic activities carried out in Venezuela or of property or assets located in
> the Country, shall cause the Tax pursuant to the rules provided for in this Law.'

The word 'income' contained in art 1 of the Venezuelan tax code and the word
'profits' contained in art 54 are both renderings into English of the same Spanish
word 'enriquecimientos' which occurs in the original and which in different contexts
can have either meaning.

The contentions of the parties

Mr Ian Richards made the following submissions on behalf of the company:
(1) The fees received by the company under its contract with Maraven constituted
income for the purposes of: (a) art 54 of the Venezuelan tax code and (b) Sch D in
the 1970 Act. (2) The income arose in Venezuela because: (a) its source was in
Venezuela (see *Archer-Shee v Baker (Inspector of Taxes)* [1927] AC 844, 11 TC 749,
Back (Inspector of Taxes) v Whitlock [1932] 1 KB 747, 16 TC 723 and *IRC v
Whitworth Park Coal Co* [1958] Ch 792, 38 TC 531); (b) it is treated for Venezuelan
tax purposes as arising in Venezuela: this determines its treatment for United
Kingdom tax purposes (see *Courtaulds Investments Ltd v Fleming (Inspector of Taxes)*
[1969] 1 WLR 1683, 46 TC 111 and *Rae (Inspector of Taxes) v Lazard Investment Co
Ltd* [1963] 1 WLR 555, 41 TC 1). (3) The Venezuelan tax code imposes a tax on
income. (4) The Venezuelan tax code corresponds to income tax or corporation tax
in the United Kingdom. The fact that it is computed by reference to a notional
percentage of 90% of gross receipts is not material because: (a) 'correspond' does not
connote identity of form but similarity of substance or function in a differing context
or climate; (b) similar provisions exist in United Kingdom income tax law; and (c)

the high notional percentage of gross receipts is counteracted by a low rate of charge
a on net income (effectively 23% in the present case). (5) Accordingly, the company is
entitled to relief under s 498(3) of the 1970 Act. (6) Section 505 of the 1970 Act falls
to be construed in accordance with s 100(4) and (5) of the Finance Act 1972.
(7) Under s 100(4) of the Finance Act 1972 the company is entitled to relief for
Venezuelan tax in so far as it does not exceed United Kingdom corporation tax
attributable to that income. (8) Under s 100(5) of the Finance Act 1972 the
b company is entitled to allocate any deductions from income to other profits.
(9) Accordingly, the company is entitled to the full amount of the relief claimed.

Mr R Waterson of the Inland Revenue Solicitors' Office made the following
submissions on behalf of the inspector of taxes: (1) The tax imposed by art 54 of the
Venezuelan tax code does not qualify for unilateral double taxation relief by way of
credit against United Kingdom tax under s 498 of the 1970 Act at all because: (a) the
c Venezuelan tax is not computed by reference to income within the meaning of
s 498(3); and (b) the Venezuelan tax does not correspond to corporation tax in the
United Kingdom within the meaning of s 498(6). The tax levied under art 54 is
effectively a tax on gross receipts or a turnover tax and not an income tax. (2) (a)
The income of the company by reference to which the Venezuelan tax of £22,353 is
computed arises in Venezuela within the meaning of s 498(3) of the 1970 Act only to
d the extent that it is generated by work performed in Venezuela. (b) The only possible
alternative is that all trading or professional profits which are properly taxable under
Sch D, Case I necessarily arise in the United Kingdom within the meaning of
s 498(3) of the 1970 Act. (3) By the combined effect of s 505 of the 1970 Act and s 100
of the Finance Act 1972, the amount of any tax credit relief for which a taxpayer
company is eligible under s 498(3) of the 1970 Act is so restricted as not to be
e permitted to exceed the figure produced by applying the rate of corporation tax
payable by the company in its relevant accounting period to the amount as measured
for United Kingdom corporation tax purposes of the income on which the foreign
tax eligible for credit relief is levied. (4) In the alternative, under s 498(3) of the 1970
Act, credit for foreign tax to which the company is entitled is allowable only against
United Kingdom corporation tax computed by reference to the same income by
f reference to which the foreign tax eligible for credit relief is computed.

Conclusions

Section 498(1) of the 1970 Act makes provision for unilateral relief in the absence
of double taxation arrangements by allowing the foreign tax as a credit against
United Kingdom income tax or corporation tax.
g Section 498(3) provides:

> 'Credit for tax paid under the law of the territory outside the United Kingdom
> and computed by reference to income arising in that territory shall be allowed
> against any United Kingdom income tax or corporation tax computed by
> reference to that income (profits from, or remuneration for, personal or
> professional services performed in that territory being deemed for this purpose
h > to be income arising in that territory)...'

Section 498(6) provides, where relevant:

> 'In this section, and in Chapter II below in its application to unilateral relief,
> references to tax payable or paid under the law of a territory outside the United
> Kingdom include only references to taxes which are charged on income and
j > correspond to income tax or corporation tax in the United Kingdom...'

Accordingly, in the first instance two questions arise for my decision:
1. Is the tax imposed under the Venezuelan tax law computed by reference to
income and does it correspond to income tax or corporation tax in the United
Kingdom?

2. Did some or all of the income arising to the company under the terms of its contract with Maraven arise in Venezuela ?

In relation to the first question, on the admissibility of Venezuelan tax, Mr Waterson submits that that tax is not a tax on income but a tax on gross receipts or a turnover tax. He says so for two reasons. First and foremost, he is unable to accept that a tax on 90% of receipts can be anything other than a turnover tax. He conceded that a tax on 50% or even 60% of receipts might be regarded as a tax on income but that even though it was difficult to know precisely where to draw the line between an income tax and a turnover tax, a tax on 90% of receipts fell on the wrong side of the line and could not be regarded as a tax on income. Second, Mr Waterson submits that whereas United Kingdom income tax and corporation tax are computed by reference to income or profits which equate to the balance remaining after allowable deductions have been made from gross receipts, art 54 of the Venezuelan tax code is geared not to profits but to gross receipts.

I am unable to accept Mr Waterson's contention with regard to the admissibility or otherwise of the Venezuelan tax. The agreed translation of the Venezuelan tax code bears the title 'Income Tax Law'. In addition art 1 of the Venezuelan tax code makes it clear that it is net income which is to be taxed in Venezuela. Articles 1 to 4 appear under the headings—'Title I, Fundamental Provisions: Chapter I, The Tax and Its Object'.

Article 2 states:

'Net Income is the increment of the patrimony or net worth resulting after having subtracted from the gross receipts, the costs and deductions allowed by this Law.'

Article 39 appears under the heading 'Title II, The Determination of the Net Income: Chapter III : The Deductions and the Net Income'. That article sets out in detail the deductions permitted under the law from gross receipts in order to arrive at the net income. Although more generous in its terms and although it is set out in a positive rather than a negative form, it appears to correspond to the provisions of s 130 of the 1970 Act.

Article 54 refers expressly and in terms to 'the net profits of the Taxpayers'. Other articles in Chapter IV of Title II of the Venezuelan tax code dealing with 'the presumptive income' specify differing percentages of gross receipts varying from 10% to 90%. Article 57, like art 54, specifies 90% of gross receipts.

Mr Richards contends that similar provisions to those to be found in Chapter IV of title II of the Venezuelan tax code exist in United Kingdom income tax law, notably ss 80 and 81 of the Taxes Management Act 1970, ss 91 and 92 (recently repealed) of the 1970 Act, ss 115–117 of the 1970 Act and s 60 of the Finance Act 1976.

In my judgment the tax imposed by the Venezuelan tax code bears all the hallmarks of a tax computed by reference to income and it also corresponds to United Kingdom income tax or corporation tax I do not believe that the inspector can reject the Venezuelan tax merely because he does not like the figure of 90% of gross receipts which is specified by art 54 to be the net income in this particular case.

It now falls to me to decide whether some or all of the profits arising to the company from its contract with Maraven arose in Venezuela. The contract in question is an unusual document. It provides in art 1 in great detail the services to be rendered by the company to Maraven but nowhere does it state in terms that the company should provide a report to Maraven or give its opinion to Maraven concerning the viability or otherwise of the rehabilitation of the three oilfields which the company is to investigate. Article 4 of the contract provides an apportionment of the company's remuneration without there being any obvious reason why such an apportionment should have been made.

It is common ground that the company has a single worldwide trade and in those circumstances I cannot accept Mr Waterson's alternative contention to the effect that because the company's headquarters' office is in the United Kingdom and it has

a single trade for the purposes of Sch D, Case I the whole of its income from the
contract with Maraven arose in the United Kingdom. It is apparent to me that the
company, having a worldwide trade, must necessarily receive income which arises
in various parts of the world I believe that Mr Waterson does not seriously dispute
that some of the company's income in relation to its contract with Maraven arose in
Venezuela.

On the other hand I cannot accept Mr Richards' contention that the whole of the
income from the Maraven contract arose in Venezuela. The authorities on which he
has sought to place reliance each dealt with investment income, where different
considerations arise. They did not concern trading profits.

I have no difficulty, however, in accepting Mr Richards' contention that the
payment of $48,300 received by the company for work done in Venezuela arose in
that country, I hold accordingly.

Mr Richards goes further, however, and suggests that because under art 4 of the
Venezuelan tax code the whole of the income from the contract with Maraven is
deemed to arise in Venezuela, this should determine its treatment for United
Kingdom tax purposes. Mr Richards submits that the company's contract with
Maraven is a single contract which is not severable. I cannot accept that contention.
The contract itself makes it clear that certain works are to be performed in the
United Kingdom and certain other works are to be performed in Venezuela. Those
services are to be separately remunerated with separate provisions as to stage
payments. The services are to be performed at different times over different periods
and, I infer, by different personnel. Even if the contract itself is not severable, as
Mr Richards submits, its provisions lead one to the natural conclusion that
remuneration for the work performed in the United Kingdom arose in the United
Kingdom.

The fact that the contract was made in Caracas is no longer the single determining
factor (see *Firestone Tyre & Rubber Co Ltd v Lewellin (Inspector of Taxes)* [1957]
1 WLR 464 at 471, 37 TC 111 at 142 per Lord Radcliffe). The proper law of the
Maraven contract was English law, payment was to be made to the company's bank
account in the United Kingdom and the work, for which a specified sum of $161,000
was to be paid, was to be performed in the United Kingdom. In such circumstances
I hold that of the consideration received by the company $48,300 arose in Venezuela
and the balance of $161,000 arose in the United Kingdom.

Having come to the conclusion that the tax imposed under the Venezuelan tax
code is an admissible tax and that the company is entitled to relief pursuant to s 498
of the 1970 Act in relation to that part of its remuneration which arose in Venezuela,
namely $48,300, the question of quantum now arises for determination.

Section 505 of the 1970 Act provides:

'The amount of the credit for foreign tax which, under any arrangements, is to
be allowed against corporation tax in respect of any income shall not exceed the
corporation tax attributable to that income.'

The effect of that section was recently considered by the Court of Appeal in
Collard (Inspector of Taxes) v Mining and Industrial Holdings Ltd [1988] STC 15 at
18, where Nicholls LJ said:

'In thus limiting the amount of credit for foreign tax allowed against
corporation tax in respect of "any income" (viz any particular item of income)
to the corporation tax which is attributable to that income, s 505 requires one
to look at the income of the company item by item . . .'

Accordingly, it is clear that the credit available to the company in relation to the
Venezuelan tax which it has paid is limited to the corporation tax attributable to the
item of income which arose in Venezuela, namely $48,300. The company's claim for
a credit for Venezuelan tax paid on that part of the remuneration for the Maraven
contract which arose in the United Kingdom fails and I hold accordingly.

It is now necessary for me to consider the effect of s 100 of the Finance Act 1972, for that section governs the relief available under s 498 of the 1970 Act subject to the ceiling provided by s 505. Once again Nicholls LJ (at 20) has provided guidance in *Collard v Mining and Industrial Holdings Ltd*:

'On its face the language of s 100(3)–(6) is clear enough and gives rise to no apparent difficulty. Section 100(3) introduces three subsections in accordance with which the s 505 ceiling is to be determined. Section 100(4) provides, in short, that the ceiling, namely, the amount of corporation tax attributable to "the relevant income", shall be treated as equal to the proportion of that income corresponding to the rate of corporation tax payable by the company on its income for the relevant accounting period. Whether this subsection brought about a change in the law from the existing position under s 505 is not of moment in the present case. This general provision is subject, expressly, to sub-ss (5) and (6). Each of those two subsections confers a power on the company. As already noted, s 505 sets a ceiling, on the credit allowable for foreign tax, in relation to each item of a company's income. There are certain types of charges or expenses and other items which may be deducted from or set against profits of more than one description: eg charges on income, such as interest [s 248 of the 1970 Act]. Section 100(5)(*a*) empowers the company to allocate such deductions to such of its profits for the period, and in such amounts, as it thinks fit, and s 100(5)(*b*) spells out the consequence of such an allocation. That is the first exception from the general rule enunciated in s 100(4).'

His Lordship then continued to explore the position in relation to advance corporation tax and provisions of s 100(6), which are not in point in this appeal.

It is clear from *Collard* that s 100(5) authorises the allocation by the company of certain deductions against its profits as it thinks fit. I do not know whether the company has made any such allocations and therefore I can decide this appeal in principle only, leaving the parties to agree the relevant calculations and to apply the appropriate United Kingdom corporation tax rate of 52% to the result in order to produce the figure for credit relief due to the company pursuant to s 498 of the 1970 Act.

Mr Waterson's third and fourth submissions are in the alternative but produce the same result arithmetically. That is not surprising as they are almost the same figures, one of which is the company's trading profit of £40,995. That figure may, for all I know, be capable of amendment pursuant to s 100(5) of the Finance Act 1972, thus producing an entirely different final result to the calculations in question I will, however, consider what the broad effect of s 498(3) of the 1970 Act must be.

In an authority not cited to me namely *Brooke Bond & Co Ltd v Butter (Inspector of Taxes)* (1962) 40 TC 342 at 353, Wilberforce J said in relation to the predecessor of s 498(3):

'So that states the simple and intelligible principle that any tax paid under the law of a foreign territory in respect of income arising in that territory is to be allowed.'

The judge was, however, considering the words of a slightly different provision, for the present form of s 498(3) emerged only in s 36 of the Finance Act 1967, when the words 'computed by reference to' replaced words in para 1 of Part I of Sch 17 to the Income Tax Act 1952 in two separate places. Those changes must be given effect to if possible and therefore I can see no alternative to accepting the principle behind Mr Waterson's fourth contention.

Mr Richards says that such a decision would produce unfair and unlooked-for results, dependent entirely on how a company's accounts are made up and the level of profit as compared with, eg the level of a director's remuneration. My answer to a   that is that I must deal with the facts as they are and not as they might have been had the company's accounts been presented differently. The company has chosen to deal with its profits in a certain way and having done so, must live with the result.

Although Mr Waterson had prepared precise figures to put to me in relation to his contentions, Mr Richards was unable to do so. Nevertheless, I have been assured by the parties that if I give a decision in principle only, it should be possible for them to agree figures. I therefore adjourn the matter generally in the hope that they will

b   be able to do so, to enable me to formally determine the appeal.

Christopher McCall QC for the Crown.
Michael Flesch QC and *Ian Richards* for the company.

c   **SCOTT J.** This is an appeal and cross-appeal by case stated against the decision of Mr T H K Everett, Special Commissioner, given on 29 June 1989. There was no dispute of fact before the Special Commissioner. There was before him, as before me, an agreed statement of facts, and the salient facts are repeated in his case stated. The taxpayer is an English company, GCA International Ltd, formerly Gaffney Cline & Associates Ltd (the company). The company has at all material times

d   carried on business as consultants in the petroleum and natural gas industry. On 9 May 1979 the company entered into a written contract with a Venezuelan company, Maraven SA (Maraven), to 'carry out a comprehensive field rehabilitation investigation' of three oilfields situated in Venezuela 'with a view to the possible rehabilitation of the oil producing capacity of said fields' (see art 1.1). Under art 1.2 the company undertook to make available in Venezuela 'a team of at least three

e   specialists for the purpose of gathering all relevant data'; and under art 1.3 the company undertook 'to incorporate one Maraven staff engineer into the GCA study group' to carry out the work required under art 1.1.

Article 3 provided: '1. GCA shall perform all of its obligations under Article 1.1 and 1.3 hereof in the United Kingdom. 2. GCA shall perform all its obligations under Article 1.2 hereof in Venezuela.'

f   Under art 4 it was provided that Maraven would pay the company $ US 161,000 for its work and services in accordance with art 1.1 and 1.3 and $48,300 for its work and services in accordance with art 1.2. So $161,000 was to be paid for the work and services to be performed in the United Kingdom and $48,300 for the work and services to be performed in Venezuela. Article 4.2 entitled Maraven to withhold a percentage of the company's remuneration to cover the company's potential liability

g   under Venezuelan income tax legislation.

The contract was signed by the parties in Venezuela, but it is agreed that the proper law of the contract was English law. The company duly performed the services required of it under the contract and became entitled to receive in staged payments, as art 5 of the contract provided, the contractual remuneration. The contractual remuneration, expressed in sterling was £97,345.

h   Under art 54 of the Ley de Impuesto Sobre La Renta (the Venezuelan tax code) the amount of the company's income liable to tax was 90% of the gross remuneration under the contract; ie £87,610. So Maraven applied the tax rates prescribed in art 62 of the tax code and withheld (in sterling terms) £22,353 from the payments made to the company pursuant to the contract. Each payment to the company was accompanied by a tax-withholding certificate. It is common ground between the

j   parties that the company was liable to tax under art 54 on the whole of its remuneration under the contract and that Maraven was entitled under the contract to withhold £22,353 (in sterling terms) in respect of that liability.

The company is an English company and is liable to pay corporation tax on the profits or gains from its petroleum and gas consultancy business. Its remuneration under the contract with Maraven had to be brought into account for corporation tax purposes, but that remuneration had already borne Venezuelan tax. So the company claimed unilateral tax relief pursuant to s 498 of the Income and Corporation Taxes Act 1970 (the 1970 Act). The questions for decision in this case are whether unilateral tax relief was available to the company, and, if so, to what extent.

Section 498(1) provides:

> 'To the extent appearing from the following provisions of this section, relief from income tax and corporation tax in respect of income shall be given in respect of tax payable under the law of any territory outside the United Kingdom by allowing the last-mentioned tax as a credit against income tax or corporation tax . . .'

I need not read sub-s (2), but sub-s (3) is important. It provides:

> 'Credit for tax paid under the law of the territory outside the United Kingdom and computed by reference to income arising in that territory shall be allowed against any United Kingdom income tax or corporation tax computed by reference to that income (profits from, or remuneration for, personal or professional services performed in that territory being deemed for this purpose to be income arising in that territory) . . .'

There follow three provisos, none of which applies to the present case.

Under sub-s (3) credit is allowed for foreign tax 'computed by reference to income arising in' the foreign territory. One of the questions in the present case is how much of the remuneration paid under the Maraven contract can be regarded as arising in Venezuela. Counsel for the company contends that the whole of the remuneration should be so regarded. Counsel for the Crown contends that only the $48,300 attributed by the contract to the work to be performed in Venezuela should be so regarded. The Special Commissioner agreed with the Crown on this question.

Section 498(6) provides that—

> '. . . references to tax payable or paid under the law of a territory outside the United Kingdom include only references to taxes which are charged on income and correspond to income tax or corporation tax in the United Kingdom . . .'

This language gives rise to the other question arising in this case. The Crown accepts that the Venezuelan tax was 'charged on income' but contends that the Venezuelan tax does not 'correspond to income tax or corporation tax in the United Kingdom'. The basis of this contention is that a tax levied on 90% of gross receipts is not a tax on profits or gains but is, truly viewed, a tax on turnover. A tax on turnover, it is submitted, does not correspond to United Kingdom income tax or corporation tax. On this question the Special Commissioner did not accept the Crown's argument. He held that the Venezuelan tax did, for the purposes of sub-s (6), correspond to income tax or corporation tax, and that unilateral tax relief under s 498 was therefore available to the company.

Before dealing with these two questions I should refer to a few other relevant statutory provisions. Section 505 of the 1970 Act places an important limit on the amount of credit for foreign tax that can be claimed. It provides: 'The amount of the credit for foreign tax which . . . is to be allowed against corporation tax in respect of any income shall not exceed the corporation tax attributable to that income.' Applying this section, and treating $48,300 as the income in respect of which credit for foreign tax was allowable, the Special Commissioner calculated that the corporation tax attributable to that income was £571. So, in the event, the company was allowed only £571 credit against its corporation tax liability for the relevant year. If the company's argument that the whole of the contractual remuneration was income 'arising in' Venezuela had been accepted, the sum for which credit would have been allowed would have been £2,472. These sums—£571 and £2,472—at stake in this case may seem hardly to justify the expense of these proceedings. But

the Crown desires clarification of the manner in which s 498(3) and (6) should be
a construed and applied and has agreed to bear the costs of the appeal and cross-appeal
in any event.

For convenience I will take first the question arising under sub-s (6): Does the
Venezuelan tax imposed under art 54 of its tax code correspond to United Kingdom
income tax or corporation tax? 'Correspond' is defined in the *Shorter Oxford English
Dictionary* in various ways. The definition found therein that is most relevant to the
b use of the word in s 498(6) is, both counsel agree, as follows: 'to answer to, in
character or function; to be similar to'. So is the art 54 tax similar to, or does it
serve the same function as, United Kingdom income tax or corporation tax? To
answer this question I must consider art 54 in its Venezuelan legislative context.

The tax code of which art 54 forms part has 11 titles and 168 articles. Title I is
entitled 'Fundamental Provisions'. Chapter I of this title is entitled 'The Tax And
c Its Object', and art 1 provides:

> 'The net and available income obtained in cash and/or in kind, by reason of
> economic activities carried out in Venezuela or of property or assets located in
> the Country, shall cause the Tax pursuant to the rules provided for in this Law.'

It is relevant to notice from art 1 that income tax in Venezuela is, so to speak, source-
d based. It is based on property or activity in Venezuela: it is not based on residence
in Venezuela.

Article 2 provides: 'Net Income is the increment of the patrimony or net worth
resulting after having subtracted from the gross receipts, the costs and deductions
allowed by this Law.'

This general description of the income liable to tax corresponds, in my judgment,
e to the basis on which income tax and corporation tax are levied in the United
Kingdom. The detail of the costs and deductions allowed by the law are of course
likely to differ from country to country.

Article 4 of the Venezuelan tax code provides:

> 'An income originates from economic activities carried out in Venezuela, or
> from property located in the Country, whenever any of the causes originating
f > such income shall occur within the National Territory, whether such causes
> shall refer to the exploitation of the soil or of the subsoil, to the formation,
> transfer, change or assignment of the use, possession or enjoyment of personal
> property or real property, tangible or intangible, or to services rendered by
> persons domiciled, resident and/or in transit in Venezuela, as well as the
> remunerations, fees or similar payments by reason of technical assistance, or
g > technical services utilized in the Country.'

Given the breadth of this article it is easy to accept that under Venezuelan law the
whole of the remuneration under the Maraven contract had to be brought into
account for Venezuelan tax purposes.

Title II of the code is entitled 'The Determination of the Net Income'. Chapter I
h of this title is entitled 'The Gross Receipts', and the articles of the chapter deal with
the gross receipts of the taxpayers. Chapter III of the title is entitled 'The Deductions
and the Net Income', and its articles deal with the manner in which the net income
for tax purposes is to be ascertained. Article 39 provides: 'In order to obtain the net
income, there will be deducted from the gross income the items expressed hereunder'.
There follow details of various types of expenses that are allowable as deductions.
j The final sub-paragraph of this article permits deduction of: 'All of the other
expenditures caused and/or paid, as the case may be, incurred in the Country for
the purpose of producing the income.' All of this corresponds to comparable
provisions in the United Kingdom tax code.

Chapter IV of Title II is entitled 'The Presumptive Income' and deals under
arts 48–59 with various types of business activity in respect of which there might be

difficulty in ascertaining the net income of the taxpayers. Thus art 48 applies to agricultural businesses and enables the net income of farmers to be presumed to be 10% of their gross sales. Article 49 deals with 'Taxpayers producing abroad moving picture films and other similar films for the cinemas or television' and provides that their net profits 'shall be constituted by ... 25% ... of the amount of their gross income'.

Under art 50: 'The net profits of the international news agencies, shall be constituted by ... 15% ... of the amount of their gross receipts.' Article 51 relates to 'international transportation agencies'; their net profits are to be taken to be 10% of their gross receipts. Article 52 relates to 'Taxpayers which, shall send merchandise on consignment to Venezuela', and their net profits are to be taken to be 25% of their gross receipts. Article 53 relates to insurance companies; their net profits are 'constituted by ... 30%' of their net premium income. Under art 55, relating to the international transport industry, the specified percentage is 10%.

Article 54 is the article which applies to the company's remuneration under the Maraven contract. It provides as follows: 'The net profits of the Taxpayers not resident or not domiciled in Venezuela, originating from non-commercial professional activities, will be constituted by ... 90% ... of the amount of their gross receipts'. It will be noted that 90% is a good deal higher a percentage than the percentages specified in the other articles to which I have referred. Article 57, however, provides: 'The net profits originating from royalties and other similar participations, obtained by Beneficiaries not domiciled in Venezuela, will be constituted by ... 90% ... of the amount obtained for such reason.' So there, too, is a charge on 90% of the gross income.

The main plank of counsel for the Crown's argument was that art 54 constitutes a tax on turnover and that a tax on turnover does not correspond to United Kingdom income tax or corporation tax. It is true that a tax assessed on a percentage of gross receipts may be subjecting to tax a loss-making business, and to that extent is dissimilar from a tax on profits or gains of a business. But the Crown is not prepared to follow its argument to its logical conclusion. It does not contend that none of the articles in Chapter IV of Title II to which I have referred imposes a tax which corresponds to United Kingdom income tax or corporation tax. It accepts that the articles which charge tax on a relatively low percentage of gross receipts do so correspond. It accepts this because, it is said, the percentage on which tax is charged represents a fair assessment, on a broad brush approach, of what the net income of the trade or business in question might be. But 90%, it is argued, is much too high. 10% of gross receipts cannot possibly cover the expenses of an oil consultancy business such as that which the company carries on. So although some of the Chapter IV articles impose taxes which 'correspond to income tax or corporation tax in the United Kingdom' (see s 498(6) of the 1970 Act), art 54, it is submitted, does not.

The purpose behind art 54 is, in my opinion reasonably apparent from the language and context of the article. The article is dealing with profits of taxpayers 'not resident or not domiciled in Venezuela'; profits, that is to say, of foreign individuals or entities. There are obvious difficulties in obtaining full tax returns from foreign taxpayers. The difficulty is dealt with in art 54 by simply providing for 10% of gross receipts to be deducted in order to produce the taxable income—the 'net profits', to use the expression employed in the article.

It is not self-evident that in the majority of cases to which art 54 might apply the 10% deduction would be a gross underestimate of the level of expenses that would have had to be incurred in order to have earned the gross receipts in question. I certainly accept, having seen the accounts of the company for the relevant financial year, that 10% does represent a gross underestimate of the cost to the company expressed as a percentage of its overall gross receipts, of carrying on its consultancy business. But it is not said that no tax expressed as a charge on a percentage of gross receipts can, for s 498 purposes, correspond to United Kingdom income tax or corporation tax. And it is not, in my judgment, practicable to exclude a particular

tax on the ground that the percentage to be deducted was not high enough to
a represent the likely level of expenses incurred by the foreign taxpayer in earning its
gross receipts. Moreover, there were no facts before the Special Commissioner to
justify a conclusion either that the 10% deduction was unrealistic in relation to the
majority of business activities falling to be taxed under art 54 or that the 10%
deduction was unrealistic in relation to the extra expense incurred by the company,
over and above its normal establishment expenses, in executing the Maraven
b contract.

I have already commented that the Crown does not contend that none of the
Chapter IV articles imposes a tax that corresponds to United Kingdom income tax
or corporation tax. I cannot accept that it is right, in order to decide whether the tax
under a particular article does correspond, to require evidence either from the
Crown or from the taxpayer of some average level of business expenses that might
c be incurred by persons coming within the charge to tax. The intention of each of
these articles, evidenced from the language used therein, is to charge 'net profits'.
That expression is used in each of the Chapter IV articles. To the extent that art 54
and the other articles seek to charge net profits to income tax, they are, in my
judgment, serving the same function as income tax and corporation tax serve in the
United Kingdom in relation to the profits of a business carried on by an individual
d or by a company, as the case may be. That was the conclusion to which the Special
Commissioner came. I agree with it, and would dismiss the Crown's appeal against
that part of his decision.

I now turn to the second question, in respect of which the appellant is the
company. As I have already indicated, the question arises out of the language used
in s 498(3). For convenience I will read again the relevant part of the subsection:

e

'Credit for tax paid under the law of the territory outside the United Kingdom
and computed by reference to income arising in that territory shall be allowed
against any United Kingdom income tax or corporation tax computed by
reference to that income . . .'

f It is common ground that the company has paid tax under the law of Venezuela;
namely, £22,353. It is common ground that that tax was, pursuant to the Venezuelan
tax code, computed by reference to the remuneration arising under the Maraven
contract. The question is how much of that remuneration represented income
arising in Venezuela for the purposes of s 498(3).

The Special Commissioner held that $48,300, the part of the contractual
g remuneration attributed by the contract to the services to be provided in Venezuela,
was income arising in Venezuela for the purposes of s 498(3). But he held that the
$161,000 attributed by the contract to the services to be provided in the United
Kingdom was not income arising in Venezuela. He held that it was income arising
in the United Kingdom.

It is that conclusion that counsel for the company challenges. There are two
h alternative bases on which counsel advances his case. First, he submits that the
statutory language, 'computed by reference to income arising in that territory', is
one composite reference to the manner in which, under Venezuelan law, the
computation takes place. One must look, he says, to see how, under the Venezuelan
tax code, the contractual remuneration was treated. If, under the Venezuelan tax
code, the whole contractual remuneration was regarded as income arising in
j Venezuela, then for the purposes of s 498(3) tax was 'computed by reference to
income arising in' Venezuela. In effect, this approach to the construction of s 498(3)
would defer to Venezuelan law the decision as to the part of the contractual
remuneration that was 'income arising in' Venezuela.

For two reasons I do not feel able to accept this submission. First, a reference to
'income arising in' a particular country is not found only in s 498(3) but also in
s 516(1). Section 516(1) provides:

'For the purposes of the Tax Acts, the amount of any income arising in any
place outside the United Kingdom shall, subject to sub-section (2) below, be
treated as reduced by any sum which has been paid in respect of tax on that
income in the place where the income has arisen . . .'

Counsel for the company's argument that the 'income arising in' the foreign
country should, for s 498(3) purposes, be determined by the law of the foreign
country cannot be applied to the identification of the same income for s 516(1)
purposes. There is no possible context in s 516(1) to permit Venezuelan law to be
imported. It is unacceptable that the expression 'income arising in' in s 498(3) should
have a different meaning from the same expression in s 516(1). The meaning of the
expression in these two sections ought, in my opinion, to be consistent. Accordingly,
in my view, the question of what part of the contractual remuneration was 'income
arising in' Venezuela must be answered by applying English law, not Venezuelan
law.

But, second, the Venezuelan tax code does not, at least expressly, impose tax on
income on the ground that the income arises in Venezuela. It imposes tax
'. . . whenever any of the causes originating such income shall occur within the
National Territory' (see art 4). This is not necessarily the same as imposing tax on
income arising in Venezuela. There may be income arising outside Venezuela but
none the less attributable to an act or event that occurred within Venezuela. For
that reason, too, it does not seem to me satisfactory to seek to answer the question
whether there has been income arising in Venezuela by applying the Venezuelan
tax code. The Venezuelan tax code does not address that question.

In my judgment, therefore, it is English law and English concepts, as to the
identification of the place where income arises, that must be resorted to for the
purpose of answering the question whether all or some part, and if so what part, of
the contractual remuneration under the Maraven contract was 'income arising in'
Venezuela.

That brings me to counsel for the company's second point. He puts this point in
alternative ways, but I think they probably come to the same thing. He invited me
to consider what the approach of English law would be to a mirror case; a case, that
is to say, like the present case but in which every United Kingdom and Venezuelan
element were reversed. In such a case, he submitted, English law would treat the
whole of the remuneration payable under the contract as taxable in the United
Kingdom. This would be so notwithstanding that it would be remuneration of a
foreign company whose connection with the United Kingdom would be no more
than that it had signed a contract in England for the provision of services in relation
to the rehabilitation of, say, some oilfields in Dorset but with the services in
connection therewith to be mainly provided in Caracas. Counsel confidently
submitted that in that case English law would treat the Venezuelan company as
liable to English income tax (not corporation tax) on the whole of its contractual
remuneration.

Counsel for the Crown did not dispute, but did not accept, that that would
necessarily be so. But he submitted that it was posing the wrong question. The
question whether or not, under United Kingdom tax legislation, the hypothetical
Venezuelan company would be liable to tax on the whole of its remuneration from
the hypothetical contract would fall to be decided by an application of s 18 of the
Income and Corporation Taxes Act 1988, which provides under sub-s (1)(a)(iii):

'. . . Tax . . . shall be charged in respect of—(a) the annual profits or gains
arising or accruing . . . (iii) to any person . . . although not resident in the United
Kingdom . . . from any trade, profession or vocation exercised within the United
Kingdom . . .'

Counsel for the company regarded it, I think, as self-evident that in the
hypothetical example he was posing the Venezuelan company was exercising its

a
trade, profession or vocation within the United Kingdom and that the whole of the remuneration would be profits or gains arising therefrom. Whether that is self-evident or not I will not decide, because I agree with counsel for the Crown that counsel for the company's hypothesis raises a different question from that which I must decide. The right question, in my opinion, is what construction should be given to the expression 'income arising in that territory' for the purposes of s 498(3) on the footing that the same construction must be given to the comparable expression

b
in s 516(1). What is the criterion that should be applied? Counsel for the company would ask whether, in a mirror case, the whole of the remuneration would be regarded as taxable in England. I do not agree that that is the right approach.

In a case to which I have been referred dealing with the question whether a foreign company was liable to United Kingdom tax in respect of activities in this country, *Firestone Tyre & Rubber Co Ltd v Lewellin (Inspector of Taxes)* [1957] 1 WLR 464

c
at 471, 37 TC 111 at 142, Lord Radcliffe cited with approval a dictum of Atkin LJ in *F L Smidth & Co v Greenwood (Inspector of Taxes)* [1921] 3 KB 583 at 593, 8 TC 193 at 203–204. Atkin LJ had said this:

d
'The contracts in this case were made abroad. But I am not prepared to hold that this test is decisive. I can imagine cases where the contract of resale is made abroad, and yet the manufacture of the goods, some negotiation of the terms, and complete execution of the contract take place here under such circumstances that the trade was in truth exercised here. I think that the question is, Where do the operations take place from which the profits in substance arise?'

e
That question was posed by Atkin LJ and applied by Lord Radcliffe in cases in which the issue was whether a foreign company had made profits from the exercise in the United Kingdom of a trade, profession or vocation. The issue in the present case is different. It is whether the income arising under the Maraven contract was income arising in a foreign country. But the criterion expressed by Atkin LJ is, in my judgment, apposite. I read it again—'. . . the question is, Where do the operations take place from which the profits in substance arise?'

f
I gain further assistance from a dictum of Lord Bridge in *Comr of Inland Revenue v Hang Seng Bank Ltd* [1990] STC 733, [1991] 1 AC 306. This was a Privy Council case in which Lord Bridge was giving the judgment of the Board. The case concerned the question whether certain profits made by the Hang Seng Bank were profits arising in Hong Kong. The relevant expression in the Hong Kong tax ordinance was 'profits arising in or derived from Hong Kong'. In the Court of Appeal of Hong Kong it had been recognised that there might be profits deriving

g
from, so to speak, a multi-source; that is to say, both from Hong Kong and from some outside source. As to that, the Hong Kong Court of Appeal had held that it was not possible to apportion the profits as between a Hong Kong part, on the one hand, and an expatriate part, on the other hand, but that it was necessary to identify 'a dominant factor or factors which put the profits on one side of the line or the other' (see [1990] STC 733 at 738, [1991] 1 AC 306 at 321). The Court of Appeal, applying

h
that test, then concluded that the balance favoured an off-shore derivation. This approach was criticised by Lord Bridge, and he said this ([1990] STC 733 at 739–740, [1991] 1 AC 306 at 322–323)—

j
'. . . the question whether the gross profit resulting from a particular transaction arose in or derived from one place or another is always in the last analysis a question of fact depending on the nature of the transaction. It is impossible to lay down precise rules of law by which the answer to that question is to be determined. The broad guiding principle, attested by many authorities, is that one looks to see what the taxpayer has done to earn the profit in question. If he has rendered a service or engaged in an activity such as the manufacture of goods, the profit will have arisen or derived from the place where the service was rendered or the profit making activity carried on. But if the profit was

earned by the exploitation of property assets as by letting property, lending money or dealing in commodities or securities by buying and reselling at a profit, the profit will have arisen in or derived from the place where the property was let, the money was lent or the contracts of purchase and sale were effected.'

I pause there to observe that thus far Lord Bridge has, to my mind, expanded on but proposed substantially the same test as that proposed by Atkin LJ in the *F L Smidth & Co* case. But Lord Bridge then went on:

'There may, of course, be cases where the gross profits deriving from an individual transaction will have arisen in or derived from different places. Thus, for example, goods sold outside Hong Kong may have been subject to manufacturing and finishing processes which took place partly in Hong Kong and partly overseas. In such a case the absence of a specific provision for apportionment in the Ordinance would not obviate the necessity to apportion the gross profit on sale as having arisen partly in Hong Kong and partly outside Hong Kong. But the present case was a straightforward one where, in their Lordships' judgment, the decision of the Board of Review was fully justified by the primary facts and betrayed no error of law.'

So in this judgment Lord Bridge is expressing the opinion, when faced with the need to determine whether profits had arisen in Hong Kong or outside Hong Kong, that, notwithstanding that the profits may arise out of one individual transaction, none the less it is possible to regard them as arising partly within the territory and partly outside.

Counsel for the company says, rightly, that the passage to which I have referred in the judgment of Lord Bridge is obiter, and in any event is not strictly binding for the purposes of construction of an English statute. I accept that. None the less it seems to me, if I may with respect say so, to represent a commonsense approach to the meaning and correct application of ordinary words in the English language. What conceptually or from a linguistic point of view is the matter with regarding a contract with an international complexion as producing income which, for the purposes of s 498(3), can be regarded as arising partly in one country and partly in another? There is no authority to which I have been referred—and I take it confidently, therefore, that there is none—which precludes me from regarding an apportionment as possible for s 498(3) purposes, and since common sense, particularly in a case exemplified by the facts of the present, seems to me to require an apportionment, I can see no reason why there should not be an apportionment of the remuneration under the Maraven contract.

If an apportionment is possible on the proper construction of s 498(3), that is an end of the cross-appeal because then the only complaint, if there were one, would be as to the apportionment that the Special Commissioner thought it right to make. He made the obvious apportionment. He apportioned the part of the remuneration that the contract itself had attributed to the services to be performed in Venezuela to Venezuela, and the part of the remuneration that the contract had allocated to the services to be performed in the United Kingdom to the United Kingdom. So if his approach was in law permissible, there would not be any reasonable objection to his conclusion on the facts. If counsel for the company had been right in his construction of sub-s (3)—namely, that it was not permissible to apportion remuneration arising under an individual contract as between two different countries—the choice would then have to be made between the United Kingdom and Venezuela as the country in which the whole of the remuneration arose, notwithstanding that it was attributed by the contract partly to one country and partly to the other. Counsel for the Crown, in that event, thought that I could deal with the choice myself on the basis of inferences to be drawn from the agreed statement of facts. Counsel for the company thought that I would in that event have to remit the case to the Special Commissioner to make the choice.

Whether the constraints of *Edwards (Inspector of Taxes) v Bairstow* [1956] AC 14, 36 TC 207 would oblige me to remit or whether counsel for the Crown is right, I do not think it profitable to pursue. I simply say that if the choice had been mine I would have regarded the United Kingdom as the inevitable choice as between that country and Venezuela if apportionment were not possible. The important services, the art 1.1 services, were directed to be performed in the United Kingdom. But as I have concluded that an apportionment is possible, and as in that event there can be no quarrel with the apportionment arrived at by the Special Commissioner, I do not have to decide whether I can slip the shackles of *Edwards v Bairstow*.

In the event I dismiss the cross-appeal as I have dismissed the appeal.

Appeal and cross-appeal dismissed.

Solicitors: *Solicitor of Inland Revenue*; *Wedlake Saint* (for the company).

Siew Ling Choo   Barrister.

Gordon v Inland Revenue Commissioners; Inland Revenue Commissioners v Gordon

FIRST DIVISION OF THE INNER HOUSE OF THE COURT OF SESSION AS THE COURT OF
EXCHEQUER IN SCOTLAND
THE LORD PRESIDENT (LORD HOPE), LORD COWIE AND LORD MCCLUSKEY
22, 23 JANUARY, 15 FEBRUARY 1991

*Case stated – Procedure – Demand for case stated – Whether demand by successful party
appropriate – Taxes Management Act 1970, s 56(1), (7).*

*Capital gains tax – Disposal of assets – Transfer of business by partnership to company
– Roll-over relief – Whether business transferred as a going concern – Whether business
transferred together with whole of its assets – Capital Gains Tax Act 1979, s 123(1).*

By s 123[a] of the Capital Gains Tax Act 1979 'roll-over relief' was available 'where a
person who is not a company transfers to a company a business as a going concern,
together with the whole assets of the business'. In January 1983 the taxpayer and his
brother became pro indiviso owners of the estate of Inchmarlo (the estate), which
their grandfather farmed at a loss until May 1983, when the taxpayer and his wife
took over. Soon after, his brother having agreed to sell him the other half-share, the
taxpayer decided to sell the estate and buy a smaller farming unit elsewhere. On
29 June the taxpayer and his wife formed, and became directors of, N (an unlimited
company); on 17 July they entered into a partnership agreement to farm the estate;
on 21 July missives were entered into for the sale of the estate to N; next day, the
partnership agreed to transfer its business—stated to be that 'of farming the Estate
as a going concern', together with 'the whole assets of the business', to N as and from
25 July. In August N concluded sales of the bulk of the estate for completion on
28 November. On 8 September the partnership ceased, and next day N began
trading. On 16 September N concluded missives for the purchase of another farm,
with entry also on 28 November. On an appeal by the taxpayer against an assessment
to capital gains tax for 1983–84 in respect of the disposal of the business to N, the
taxpayer contended that the partnership had disposed of 'a farming business', as
distinct from 'the business of farming the Estate'. The Special Commissioner rejected
both that contention, and one by the Crown that because N never had any real right
of property in the estate the partnership had failed to transfer to N 'the whole assets
of the business'; but he dismissed the appeal on the ground that the business of
farming that estate had not been transferred 'as a going concern', because 'its end
was too clearly and too closely in sight'. The taxpayer appealed and the Crown,
dissatisfied with the determination that 'the whole assets of the business' had been
transferred, also demanded and secured the statement of an identical case for the
opinion of the Court of Session.

Held – (1) A successful party, wishing to resist an appeal by way of case stated on a
point of law which commissioners had decided against him, should so inform them
either (a) at the time the appellant declares his dissatisfaction, or (if the point has
been omitted from the draft case) (b) when returning the draft suitably amended—
whereafter he could, if necessary, invoke the procedure mentioned in s 56(7) of the
Taxes Management Act 1970. For such a party to demand a case is unnecessary and
inappropriate.
  Dictum of Harman LJ in *Muir v IRC* (1965) 43 TC 367 at 389 applied.
  (2) There was evidence on which the commissioner could reasonably conclude

---

a   Section 123(1), so far as material, is set out at p 182*j*, post

that the business disposed of by the partnership had specifically been the business of
a   farming the estate; but since (a) the only point of time at which to test whether a
business was being transferred 'as a going concern' was the time of transfer, and
(b) that business had continued uninterruptedly past that point of time, and (c) the
existence of a planned move of the entire assets of a business from one place to
another was not inconsistent with the continuation of its trade, the true and only
reasonable conclusion from the facts found was that N had received that business as
b   a going concern and had the ability to continue with it elsewhere if it thought fit.
Robroyston Brickworks Ltd v IRC [1976] STC 329 applied.

(3) Since the effect of what had been agreed between the partnership and N had
been to put N into the identical position previously enjoyed by the partnership, 'the
whole assets of the business' had been transferred by the partnership to N, without
the need for any conveyance to N of any real right of property in the estate.
c   The taxpayer's appeal must accordingly be allowed and that of the Crown
dismissed.

Notes

For the form of the case stated, see Simon's Taxes A3.707.
d   For the transfer of business to a company, see ibid, Division C3.2.
For the Taxes Management Act 1970, s 56, see ibid, Part G2.
For the Capital Gains Tax Act 1979, s 123, see ibid, Part G3.

Cases referred to in opinions

e   *Customs and Excise Comrs v Dearwood Ltd* [1986] STC 327.
*Electricity Commission (Balmain Electric Light Co Purchase) Act 1950 Reference
     under the* (1957) 57 SR (NSW) 100.
Fitzwilliam (Countess) v IRC [1990] STC 65.
Gallemos Ltd (in receivership) v Barratt Falkirk Ltd 1990 SLT 98, CS.
Gibson v Hunter Home Designs Ltd 1976 SC 23, CS.
f   *Kenmir Ltd v Frizzell* [1968] 1 WLR 329, [1968] 1 All ER 414.
McGregor (Inspector of Taxes) v Adcock [1977] STC 206, [1977] 1 WLR 864, [1977]
     3 All ER 65, 51 TC 692.
Margrie Holdings Ltd v Customs and Excise Comrs [1991] STC 80, CS.
Muir v IRC [1966] 1 WLR 1269, [1966] 3 All ER 38, 43 TC 367, CA.
Ramsay (W T) Ltd v IRC [1981] STC 174, [1982] AC 300, [1981] 1 All ER 865,
g   54 TC 101, HL.
Robroyston Brickworks Ltd v IRC [1976] STC 329, 51 TC 230, CS.

Cases stated
Gordon v Inland Revenue Commissioners

h   I. On 6 and 7 June 1989 one of the Commissioners for the special purposes of the
Income Tax Acts heard an appeal by Mr Adam Alexander Gordon of Heatheryleys
Farms, Glenfarg, Perthshire (the taxpayer) against an assessment to capital gains
tax on the sum of £25,000 for 1983–84.
II. The question for the commissioner's decision was whether in that year the
taxpayer and his wife, trading in partnership as 'A & J Gordon—Inchmarlo Farms',
j   transferred to an unlimited company called Nacert a farming business 'as a going
concern, together with the whole assets of the business' so as to be entitled to 'roll-
over' relief under s 123 of the Capital Gains Tax Act 1979 (the 1979 Act).
III. The commissioner heard evidence from: the taxpayer; Mrs Helen Hogg CA,
a chartered accountant with Arthur Young & Co; Mr E O St John WS, a partner in
Lindsays, solicitors and notaries public of Edinburgh. [The documents placed in
evidence before the commissioner were then listed.]

IV. The commissioner reserved his decision and subsequently issued it in writing, holding: (i) that the business was transferred together with the whole assets of the a business; but (ii) that the business was not transferred as a going concern. In the result the commissioner refused the appeal and continued the proceedings for agreement of the figure for the assessment. A copy of the commissioner's decision, dated 24 October 1989, was attached to and formed part of the case.

V. On 20 November 1989 the commissioner determined the appeal by increasing the assessment to the agreed figure of £306,457.

VI. Both parties thereon declared to the commissioner their dissatisfaction with his determination as being erroneous in point of law and each party within the time allowed required the commissioner to state and sign a case for the opinion of the Court of Session as the Court of Exchequer in Scotland.

VII. The questions of law for the opinion of the court were:

(i) on the taxpayer's appeal, whether, on the facts found, the commissioner c had been entitled to hold as a matter of law that the business had not been transferred as a going concern within the meaning of the 1979 Act; and

(ii) on the appeal by the Inland Revenue Commissioners, whether, on the facts found, the commissioner had been entitled to hold as a matter of law that the business had been transferred with the whole assets of the business. d

DECISION

Mr Adam Alexander Gordon (the taxpayer) appeals against an assessment to capital gains tax for 1983–84 in the sum of £25,000. The assessment relates to a gain realised by the taxpayer and Jennifer Susan Gordon (his wife) from a disposition made to an unlimited company called Nacert (the company): and the issue is e whether roll-over relief can be claimed in respect of that gain under s 123 of the Capital Gains Tax Act 1979 (the 1979 Act).

The conditions for claiming that relief are set out in s 123(1):

'This section shall apply for the purposes of this Act where a person who is not a company transfers to a company a business as a going concern, together f with the whole assets of the business, or together with the whole of those assets other than cash, and the business is so transferred wholly or partly in exchange for shares issued by the company to the person transferring the business.'

The question in this case is whether the taxpayer and his wife transferred to the company a business as a going concern together with the whole assets of the business, or the whole of those assets other than cash. g

The history of the matter starts in January 1983 when, by a disposition made by the trustees of a Bowhill Family Trust, the taxpayer and his brother Douglas Gordon (Douglas) became pro indiviso heritable proprietors of the Inchmarlo Estate at Banchory in Kincardineshire. The estate was then farmed as tenant by their grandfather, Mr A H Bowhill, with the help of the taxpayer as manager. Mr Bowhill, aged 90 or more, wished to give up the farm and it was agreed that his h tenancy should come to an end on 15 May 1983. The landlords (the taxpayer and Douglas) agreed to pay the tenant the value of the silage pit which he had constructed on the estate and to pay, or procure an incoming tenant to pay, to the tenant the market value of his tenant's rights at that date. The total value was assessed by Savills, surveyors, at £63,517·06 (made up of livestock £35,294, manurial values £8,744·73, machinery £8,455, building (silage pit) £6,000, and standing crop j £5,023·33). By a separate agreement made on 18 May 1983 the taxpayer and Douglas agreed to buy from Mr A H Bowhill commercial woodlands at Inchmarlo for £57,000.

Douglas is a stockbroker, with no interest in farming, who lives in London. On 23 June 1983 he agreed to sell to the taxpayer his one-half pro indiviso share in Inchmarlo Estate comprising (a) the subjects conveyed to them by the Bowhill

Trustees in January 1983 and (b) the commercial woodlands which they had jointly contracted to buy from their grandfather. The terms were that Douglas should be relieved of all liability to pay for the commercial woodlands and should receive one-half of the consideration paid in an open market sale by a purchaser of the Inchmarlo Estate (including the woodlands) after deducting £57,000 and the expenses of the sale. If the estate were to be sold in lots that formula would be applied with some adjustments to each sale: and if the whole or any part of it had not been sold by 28 November 1984 the sale price of Douglas's share would be based on market value as determined by Savills.

The taxpayer and his wife had taken over the farming of the estate on the termination of Mr A H Bowhill's tenancy. On 17 July 1983 the taxpayer and his wife entered into partnership on the following terms and conditions set out in a contract of that date:

> '*One.* The business of the Partnership shall be farming and shall be carried on at . . . the Estate of Inchmarlo belonging to Mr Gordon, and at such other place or places as may be agreed, under the firm name "A & J Gordon—Inchmarlo Farms".
> *Two.* The Partnership shall be deemed to have commenced on 15 May 1983 and shall subsist until dissolved in manner aftermentioned.
> *Three.* The initial capital shall be as shown by a Balance Sheet to be drawn up by Messrs Arthur Young McClelland Moores & Company, CA . . . as at 15 May 1983 which shall include the heritable property of the Estate of Inchmarlo as part of the firm's assets. Any further contributions of capital required by the firm will be provided in such proportions as the partners may mutually agree.'

Other conditions related to the keeping of accounts, signing of cheques, dissolution on three months' notice, resolution of differences and so forth. Profits were to be divided as to 95% to the taxpayer and 5% to his wife, with losses shared in the like proportions.

On 22 July 1983 an agreement was signed between the firm known as A & J Gordon—Inchmarlo Farms (the firm), the taxpayer and his wife, as the whole partners thereof and as individuals (together called the transferors) of the one part and Nacert, an unlimited company having a share capital, which was incorporated on 29 June 1983 (the company) of the other part. The agreement recited that the taxpayer and his wife had been carrying on in partnership the business of farming the estate at Inchmarlo and were now desirous of transferring to the company the business as a going concern and stated that it was therefore agreed as follows:

> '1. The Transferors hereby agree to transfer to the Company as and from Twenty fifth July [1983] the said business of farming the Estate of Inchmarlo as a going concern together with the whole assets of the business as shown by a Balance Sheet to be drawn up . . . as at the said date of transfer.
> 2. The company shall acquire the business subject to all debts owing by the Transferors in respect thereof and all other liabilities subsisting at the said Twenty fifth day of July [1983].
> 3. Reference is made in this agreement to the Missives of Sale dated Twenty first July [1983] between the Firm and the Company relative to the heritable property owned by the Firm.
> 4. The company shall issue to the Transferors or their nominees Ninety eight new shares of one pound each in the capital of the Company, credited as fully paid-up, in exchange for the said business agreed to be transferred to the Company.'

The missives of sale referred to in the third paragraph of that agreement were missives whereby on 21 July 1983 the firm had contracted to sell to the company the Inchmarlo Estate (defined as the subjects described in the disposition by the Bowhill Trustees to the taxpayer and Douglas). The price was to be the sum at which the

said subjects were valued in a balance sheet of the firm drawn up at 15 May 1983 and
actual occupation was to be given, subject to tenant's rights, if any, on 25 July 1983 *a*
when the price would become payable with interest at 12% pa until payment.

The taxpayer and his wife continued to farm the Inchmarlo Estate as before after
the sale agreement had been concluded with the company on 22 July 1983. The
firm's only business accounts were made up for the period 15 May to 8 September
1983 and showed a trading loss of £6,414. The firm then ceased to trade.

The company's first accounts were made up for the period 29 June 1983 to *b*
28 November 1983 showing a trading loss of £11,341. In the directors' report with
those accounts, signed by the taxpayer and his wife it was said, under the heading
'Review of the business and future development':

> 'The Company commenced farming on September 9 1983. The income in
> the three months was insufficient to cover expenses.
>
> With effect from November 29 1983 the company sold Inchmarlo Farm and *c*
> invested in Heatheryleys Farm. The latter has been operated since that date in
> partnership with one of the directors, A A Gordon.'

The decision to sell the Inchmarlo Estate had been taken by the taxpayer soon
after he went into occupation, at the end of May or early in June. He knew that his
grandfather had farmed the estate at a loss and, after taking time to make his own *d*
assessment of the position, he quickly came to the conclusion that it would be wise
to sell the estate and buy a smaller, more viable, farming unit. On his instructions
Savills prepared an illustrated brochure offering the estate for sale either as a whole
or in ten specified lots. No sales had been concluded on the open market but
negotiations were in progress when missives of sale were exchanged between the
firm and the company on 21 July 1983. Sales of Inchmarlo House with 75 acres of *e*
land and of the Home Farm with 357 acres, which together made up the bulk of the
estate, were concluded on 10 August and 22 August 1983 respectively, with entry
and vacant possession on 28 November 1983 in each case.

Returning now to the transfer of the farming business from the firm to the
company, I am asked on the taxpayer's side to note that the figures for fixed and
current assets in the firm's closing accounts at 8 September 1983 are precisely *f*
repeated as the opening figures in the company's trading accounts at 9 September
1983. The figures are:

Fixed assets:	Land and Buildings	£660,100
	Implements and Tractors	8,455
Current assets:	Livestock	38,910
	Grain	11,000	*g*
	Forage crops	8,732
	Unexhausted manures	2,261
	Debtors	200

The only difference of substance between the two balance sheets is that the entry
'Partners interests—£379,596' in the firm's accounts is replaced by two items 'Share *h*
capital—£100' and 'Share premium account—£379,496' in the company's accounts.
The figures for fixed assets represent the value of the Inchmarlo Estate and the
farming equipment which the taxpayer had acquired from his grandfather in May
of that year.

To complete the picture I should add that on 16 September 1983 the company
concluded an agreement to purchase Heatheryleys Farm with entry on 28 November. *j*
The movable machinery and the unsold cattle (about 100 animals out of 128 which
had been taken over on 9 September) were moved from Inchmarlo to Heatheryleys
on that date and cattle-raising operations have continued at Heatheryleys on much
the same scale as at Inchmarlo. In addition a flock of sheep was bought from the
previous owner of Heatheryleys, which is situated in sheep-farming country in
Perthshire.

On those facts Mr Penrose QC contends for the taxpayer that the conditions of s 123(1) are satisfied with the result that any gain on the disposal of the business is 'rolled-over' into the computation of gain on a future disposal of the shares in the company. The Crown disputes that proposition on two grounds. It contends, first that no right of property in the Inchmarlo Estate was transferred to the company and the requirement that the business should be transferred with the whole assets of the business is therefore not satisifed; and, second, that the business was not transferred as a going concern.

On the first point Mr McNeill contends for the Crown, on the authority of *Gibson v Hunter Home Designs Ltd* 1976 SC 23, that the missives of sale dated 21 July 1983 gave the company no interest in the heritable estate of Inchmarlo but only a contractual right to require the firm to procure a good title to it. That remained the position right up to the time when dispositions of the several parts of the estate were executed in favour of the ultimate purchasers, with the result, in his submission, that the company did not at any time possess an asset in the form of an interest in the land on which the business was conducted. Indeed Mr McNeill is not prepared to admit that the firm ever had an interest in the whole of the Inchmarlo Estate. The partnership agreement provided in clause 3 that a balance sheet drawn up at 15 May 1983 'shall include the heritable property of the Estate of Inchmarlo as part of the firm's assets' but the taxpayer was the infeft owner of one-half of the estate only and that, says Mr McNeill, was all that he could put into the partnership. As to the other half he had only a contractual right against Douglas.

I approach any question of Scots law with diffidence but I am not convinced that the issue in this case turns on niceties of the law of property. The question whether a business was transferred with the whole of its assets requires a broader approach based on commercial reality. The accounts of the firm and of the company are clearly drawn on the footing that there was a transfer of all the assets of the business, including land and buildings representing the Inchmarlo Estate, and that view is consistent with the documentary evidence. For example, in the deed of disposition conveying the Home Farm to the ultimate purchaser in March 1984 the narrative recites:

'(a) the disposition of the Inchmarlo Estate by the Bowhill Trustees to Adam and Douglas Gordon

(b) the sale by Douglas of his half share to Adam by Missives dated 23 and 27 June 1983

(c) the contract of partnership between Adam and Jennifer Gordon under the terms of which "the beneficial interest in Inchmarlo passed to the said Firm"

(d) the sale of Inchmarlo by the Firm to Nacert by missives dated 21 July 1983

(e) the sale by Nacert of their whole right, title and interest in and to the subjects to Banchory Contactors Ltd [and so on to the ultimate disposition by Inchmarlo Land Co Ltd to Refrigeration (Aberdeen) Ltd].'

I heard evidence from Mr E O St John, WS, who prepared the dispositions of the several lots, that he had deemed it necessary in accordance with good conveyancing practice to refer in the narrative to all heritable and beneficial interests in the land. He had referred to the contract of partnership because he considered that the beneficial interest in the land originally owned by the taxpayer and Douglas had been made over to the partnership. Although a partnership cannot be infeft in Scots law it can have a beneficial interest in land held on its behalf by trustees.

It may be that clause 4 of the partnership agreement was incorrect in stating that the entire heritable property of the estate of Inchmarlo would be part of the firm's assets because at that time the taxpayer was the heritable proprietor of one-half of the estate only. As to the other half he had a personal right against Douglas entitling him to call for a disposition under the missive of 23 June coupled with a right of entry under clause 5 thereof and an obligation to maintain the estate in good repair under clause 9. But it seems to me that from the date of the partnership agreement he necessarily held his proprietary interest in one-half of the Inchmarlo Estate and his contractual rights against Douglas in respect of the other half as agent or trustee for the firm. And the firm was able to transfer those rights, which together carried the right to farm the whole estate, to the company with the other assets of the business. In fact, by missives dated 21 July 1983 the firm undertook to deliver to the company a good and marketable title to the whole estate; and it fulfilled that undertaking in due course as the company sold the estate on in lots.

The proper conclusion on all the evidence is, in my opinion, that the firm acquired a beneficial interest in or rights in respect of the Inchmarlo Estate by the taxpayer's contribution and transferred that interest and those rights to the company. I therefore decide the first point in the taxpayer's favour and hold that the firm's business was transferred with its whole assets to the company in exchange for shares. The fact that the estate and the business were the subject of separate agreements on different dates is not, I think, of any significance.

The transfer of the business took effect on 8–9 September 1983, as appears from the accounts and the directors report of the company; and I next have to consider whether the business was transferred at that date 'as a going concern'. One has first to identify the business; and it is one plank of Mr Penrose's argument on this aspect of the case that the firm's business was simply farming, a business which could be carried on anywhere. There is a distinction between the business of farming and the assets used in that business, as the Crown successfully argued in *McGregor (Inspector of Taxes) v Adcock* [1977] STC 206, [1977] 1 WLR 864. On the facts here the company took over the firm's business and continued it first at Inchmarlo and then, in partnership with the taxpayer, at Heatheryleys.

I cannot accept that argument. *McGregor v Adcock* decided that the sale of 5 out of 35 acres of farm land was not the sale of part of the taxpayer's business for the purpose of another provision in the 1979 Act. That is a wholly different point and I do not find the decision of any assistance in the present context. It may be correct that the firm was established simply for the purpose of farming but the business which it carried on and which it transferred to the company was farming the estate of Inchmarlo. That is specifically stated in the agreement of 22 July 1983 and it is that business which must have been transferred as a going concern if the claim under s 123 is to succeed.

The agreement states that the business is to be transferred as a going concern together with the whole assets of the business but I cannot regard that as conclusive. It indicates only that the document was drafted with the terms of s 123 in mind and I make no criticism of that. But whether the business was a going concern at 8–9 September is a question of fact to be answered in the light of the circumstances then existing: and in the absence of any indication that the term 'going concern' has a technical meaning in this context it can only be construed according to normal usage as part of the English language. It must however, be assumed that the phrase was introduced into the subsection to impose an additional requirement. Transfer of the business does not in itself suffice: it must be transferred as a going concern. It may in the end be a matter of general impression rather than scientific analysis.

The taxpayer had decided to sell the Inchmarlo Estate and move away by the end of May or soon after: and his intentions continued to prevail through the subsequent transactions since his was the guiding mind of the firm and of the company. By 22 July, the date of the agreement between the firm and the company, the estate had been advertised for sale either as a single entity or in lots and negotiations were in progress for sales on the open market. By 8–9 September the company had itself concluded agreements for the sale of the farm and other parts of the estate with entry on 28 November. When it took over the farming business, it could not do so with any sense of continuity or ability to plan for the future. It knew that possession would have to be given up in 11 weeks time and the business would then come to an end. In those circumstances it does not seem to me that, on the ordinary use of language, the firm's business of farming the Inchmarlo Estate could be said to have been tranferred to the company as a going concern. Its end was too clearly and too closely in sight.

The claim to roll-over relief therefore fails and the proceedings are continued for agreement of the figure in which the assessment is to be determined.

Inland Revenue Commissioners v Gordon

The case stated by the Special Commissioner in the case of *Inland Revenue Commissioners v Gordon* was identical to that stated in respect of *Gordon v Inland Revenue Commissioners.*

P S Hodge for the taxpayer.
J E Drummond Young QC and *J W McNeill* for the Crown.

The court made avizandum.

15 February. The following opinions were delivered.

THE LORD PRESIDENT (HOPE). This case concerns an appeal by Adam Alexander Gordon (the taxpayer), who appealed to the Special Commissioners against an assessment to capital gains tax for 1983–84 in the sum of £25,000. In that year the taxpayer and his wife Jennifer, who were trading in partnership as 'A & J Gordon—Inchmarlo Farms', transferred a farming business to Nacert, an unlimited company having a share capital (the company), thus realising a gain which was chargeable to capital gains tax. The issue in the appeal was whether the farming business had been transferred to the company as a going concern, together with the whole assets of the business, so as to entitle the taxpayer to roll-over relief under s 123 of the Capital Gains Tax Act 1979 (the 1979 Act). The Special Commissioner held that the business was transferred together with the whole assets of the business but that it was not transferred as a going concern. So he refused the appeal which he determined by increasing the assessment to an agreed figure of £306,457. Both parties then declared their dissatisfaction with his determination and required him to state a case for the opinion of this court. As a result we now have before us two separate but identical cases, one at the instance of the taxpayer and the other at the instance of the Inland Revenue Commissioners (the Crown). Each case contains the same two questions of law which the Special Commissioner has stated in these terms:

'(i) on [the taxpayer's] appeal, whether, on the facts found, I was entitled to hold as a matter of law that the business was not transferred as a going concern within the meaning of the [1979] Act: and

(ii) on the appeal by the Commissioners of Inland Revenue, whether, on the facts found, I was entitled to hold as a matter of law that the business was transferred with the whole assets of the business.'

I must say something at the outset as to whether it was appropriate for the Special Commissioner to prepare two separate cases in these circumstances. We were informed by counsel that this is the first time that this has been done in an appeal to the Court of Session, and that concern has been expressed by the clerk to the commissioners as to whether two separate cases are really necessary. In my opinion it is not necessary to duplicate effort in this way, and it would have been both sufficient and more appropriate for only one case to be prepared. The fact is that in the present case only one party could claim to be dissatisfied with the determination of the Special Commissioner within the meaning of s 56(1) of the Taxes Management Act 1970 (the 1970 Act). This was the taxpayer, since his claim for roll-over relief under s 123 of the 1979 Act was refused. He was successful on one of the two points

which were argued in the appeal, but his claim to roll-over relief failed because the
Special Commissioner held that the business was not transferred to the company as
a going concern. The Crown could not say that it was dissatisfied with the Special
Commissioner's decision that the claim for relief should be refused, since the result
of this was a determination in its favour. It is clear that it would have had no interest
in maintaining a cross appeal if the taxpayer had decided to acquiesce in the decision
of the Special Commissioner. On the other hand it was entitled to insist that the
court should not dispose of the case on the one point which the taxpayer proposed to
raise without having decided the other point on which the taxpayer was successful
but which, on its argument, provided another ground for refusing the claim for
relief. I think that the position in this case is the same as that described by
Harman LJ in *Muir v IRC* [1966] 1 WLR 1269 at 1281, 43 TC 367 at 389, where he
said:

> 'It was the taxpayer who was dissatisfied with the "determination," that is to
> say, the result of his appeal to the special commissioners, and it was, therefore,
> for him to declare his dissatisfaction and require the commissioners to state a
> case. It was not for the Revenue to do anything of the sort, for it was not
> dissatisfied. It was, in my judgment, nonetheless open to the Revenue to seek
> to uphold the decision in its favour on any ground of law available, including a
> ground decided against it by the special commissioners.'

We were referred to *Countess Fitzwilliam v IRC* [1990] STC 65, in which a similar
point arose. That was a case about capital transfer tax, in which both parties had
required the Special Commissioners to state a case for the opinion of the High Court
under para 10(1) of Sch 4 to the Finance Act 1975. The Special Commissioners did
so by preparing a single stated case which contained separate questions for the
opinion of the court in the appeals by the taxpayers and in the cross-appeals by the
Crown. I am not aware of any previous case where it has been thought necessary to
prepare separate stated cases, and *Fitzwilliam* illustrates that it is unnecessary to do
so even if, as here, both parties have expressed dissatisfaction with the determination
by the commissioners.

The appropriate course was for the Crown to invite the Special Commissioner,
when he came to state the case, to include in it an additional question related to that
other ground so that both points could be put before the court, with the relevant
facts, for its opinion. This invitation could have been made either immediately after
the determination of the appeal following the taxpayer's declaration of his
dissatisfaction with it, or at a later stage while the case was still in draft. If necessary,
since the court has power under s 56(7) to send the case back to the Special
Commissioners for amendment, this power could have been exercised so as to
require him to include an additional question and such additional facts as might be
necessary to enable the court to consider it. I do not wish to insist on undue formality
in these matters, but it must be remembered that all we can do, in terms of s 56(6) of
the 1970 Act, is hear and determine any question of law arising in the case on the
facts found proved by the commissioners. If a question of law is to be raised with us
the necessary findings must be included in the case so that we can consider them and
decide whether, on these facts, the commissioners were entitled as a matter of law to
decide the case as they did.

The relief with which we are concerned in this case is designed to facilitate the
transfer of a business to a company. It is available only where the conditions set out
in s 123(1) of the 1979 Act are satisified. These conditions are described in that
subsection in the following terms:

> 'This section shall apply for the purposes of this Act where a person who is
> not a company transfers to a company a business as a going concern, together
> with the whole assets of the business, or together with the whole of those assets
> other than cash, and the business is so transferred wholly or partly in exchange
> for shares issued by the company to the person transferring the business.'

It is not disputed that what the taxpayer and his wife transferred to the company
on the relevant date was the business which had previously been carried on by them
in partnership. The point at issue is whether they transferred that business as a
going concern, together with the whole assets of the business.

The first question then is whether the farming business which the taxpayer and
his wife had carried on in partnership was transferred to the company as a going
concern. The agreement between the partnership and the company dated 22 July
1983 recited that the taxpayer and his wife had been carrying on in partnership the
business of farming the estate at Inchmarlo and that they were desirous of transferring
to the company that business as a going concern. Clause 1 stated that the transferors
agreed to transfer to the company as and from 25 July 1983 'the said business of
farming the Estate of Inchmarlo as a going concern' together with the whole assets
of the business as shown by a balance sheet to be drawn up as at the date of the
transfers. Clause 2 stated that the company was to acquire the business subject to all
debts owing by the transferors in respect thereof and all other liabilities subsisting at
that date. The farming business was still being carried on by the partnership at the
date of the agreement, and the taxpayer and his wife continued to farm the
Inchmarlo Estate as before until 8 September 1983 when the partnership ceased to
trade. The company commenced trading there on the following day, and the
opening figures in its trading accounts repeated precisely the figures for fixed and
current assets which appear in the closing accounts of the firm. The company
continued to farm at Inchmarlo without interruption until 28 November 1983.
Taken by themselves these facts might suggest that there could only be one answer
to the question whether the business was transferred to the company as a going
concern. But the Special Commissioner held that this was not what had happened
because, when the business was transferred to the company, the company knew that
its possession of the Inchmarlo Estate would have to be given up on 28 November
and, accordingly, that the business could not be regarded as a going concern because
its end was too clearly and too closely in sight.

In order to understand his approach to the matter it is necessary to look in more
detail at the history. This has been described in detail by the Special Commissioner
in his decision and it is not necessary to do more than summarise it in outline. The
Inchmarlo Estate is situated at Banchory in Kincardineshire. The taxpayer and his
brother Douglas Gordon became pro indiviso heritable proprietors of the estate in
January 1983. The estate was then farmed by their grandfather as tenant with the
help of the taxpayer as its manager, but the grandfather was of advanced years and
wished to give up the farm. His tenancy came to an end on 15 May 1983, whereon
the taxpayer and his wife took over the farming of the estate. They entered into
partnership with effect from that date in terms of a contract of partnership dated
17 July 1983. Soon after he took over occupation of the farm, at the end of May or
early June, the taxpayer decided that the estate should be sold. He was aware that
his grandfather had farmed it at a loss and, following his own assessment of the
position, he concluded that it would be wise to sell the estate and buy a smaller, more
viable, farming unit elsewhere. Various steps were then taken in quick succession to
bring this about. The taxpayer's brother lived in London and had no interest in
farming, and he agreed on 23 June 1983 to sell his one-half pro indiviso share to the
taxpayer on terms which enabled him to receive a share of the consideration paid in
an open market sale by a purchaser of the estate provided this was achieved by
28 November 1984, failing which he was to be paid a price based on the market
value of the estate. On 29 June 1983 the company was incorporated as an unlimited
company having a share capital and the taxpayer and his wife became its directors.
On 21 July 1983 missives of sale were entered into between the firm and the company
for the sale of the estate to the company. On the following day, 22 July 1983, an
agreement for the transfer of the business to the company was entered into. In the
meantime negotiations were in progress for the sale of the estate, and on 10 August
and 23 August 1983 sales were concluded by the company of Inchmarlo House with

75 acres of land and of the Home Farm with 357 acres, which together made up the bulk of the estate. Entry and vacant possession was to be given to the purchasers on 28 November 1983 in each case. By 8 September 1983, therefore, when the firm ceased trading and the company was about to take over farming of the estate, it was known that the business of farming there would have to come to an end on 28 November because vacant possession of the estate would have to be given then to the purchasers. On 16 September 1983 the company concluded missives for the purchase of Heatherleys Farm at Glenfarg in Perthshire with entry on 28 November 1983. When that date arrived the movable machinery and the unsold cattle were moved from Inchmarlo to Heatherleys, since cattle-raising operations have continued there on much the same scale as at Inchmarlo.

Against the background of these facts the Special Commissioner approached the matter by asking himself two questions. The first task to which he addressed himself was to identify the business which was transferred to the company. Having done that he then turned to consider whether the business which was transferred to it was a going concern. The issue so far as the identity of the business was concerned was whether the firm's business was simply that of farming, that is to say a business which could be carried on anywhere, or whether it was confined to the business of farming the estate of Inchmarlo. As he approached the matter the answer to the first question was to a large extent decisive of the second one, as to whether the business was transferred as a going concern. If the business was simply farming as contended for by the taxpayer, then plainly it made no difference to the question whether or not it was a going concern that farming operations at Inchmarlo Estate were soon to cease. A business described in these terms could be carried on anywhere wherever there was land to farm, and a move of the business from Inchmarlo to another farm would not involve the ending of one business and the starting-up of another. But if the business was confined to the business of farming the estate of Inchmarlo, then the question arose as to whether it was confined essentially to that one place. On this approach he found it relatively easy to regard the business as being no longer a going concern if its operations there were about to cease. Having decided that what was transferred to the company was the business of farming the estate, he held that, since the company could not have taken it over with any sense of continuity or ability to plan for the future, it was not then a going concern.

Counsel for the taxpayer submitted that the Special Commissioner's decision was erroneous on both of these points. The business with which we were concerned in this case was, he said, simply that of farming with a view to profit. It did not depend for its existence on the occupation of particular land. This could be seen from the terms of the contract of partnership which had envisaged that it could be carried on elsewhere as well as at Inchmarlo. The land which was being farmed for the time being was simply an asset of the business, and this was not to be confused with the commercial activity which was then being carried on. The Special Commissioner had erred because he had treated as conclusive the statement in the recital of the agreement of 22 July 1983 that the business which was being transferred was that of farming the estate at Inchmarlo. That was merely a statement of where the business was being carried on for the time being and it did not follow that it could not be moved elsewhere. As for the question whether it was a going concern, he submitted that the Special Commissioner had erred because he had regard to steps taken by the company after the date of transfer, which he maintained was 25 July 1983 when the company acquired a right under the agreement to take the business from the partnership. It was irrelevant that missives for the sale of the estate were concluded by the company after that date. The only questions for the Special Commissioner were whether the business was still in operation when it was transferred to the company in exchange for shares, and whether the transferor had taken any steps to prevent the transferee from continuing the business in whatever way it wished. Had he confined his attention to these questions he would have had no reason to do otherwise than find in favour of the taxpayer. In reply to these arguments it was

submitted for the Crown that the place at which the business of farming was being
carried on could not be considered in the abstract. It had an overwhelming
importance in the context of a farming business, since this was the principal factor
in what that business could produce. It was significant that the agreement had stated
in terms that it was the business of farming the estate at Inchmarlo which was being
transferred. The Special Commissioner was right to regard the end of that business
as being too clearly and too closely in sight for it to be a going concern. This was the
result of a series of prearranged steps which the taxpayer had been taking all along.
It was not suggested that any of these steps should be disregarded as having no
business purpose other than the avoidance of tax, but we were referred to the speech
of Lord Wilberforce in *W T Ramsay Ltd v IRC* [1981] STC 174 at 179, [1982] AC
300 at 323, where he said: 'There may, indeed should, be considered the context and
scheme of the relevant Act as a whole, and its purpose may, indeed should, be
regarded'. The purpose of s 123 of the 1979 Act was to enable a business to be
incorporated without incurring a charge to capital gains tax, but a strict view of
what was being done was appropriate since the relief was not intended to be used to
facilitate asset stripping. It was important that the business should be transferred to
the company as a going concern together with all its assets if that was not to occur.
It was unrealistic to ignore the fact that the transferor was in a position to control
the activities of the transferee, so the taxpayer's expectations and state of knowledge
about the future of the business were relevant as part of the whole facts and
circumstances of the case. The issue was, at the end of the day, primarily one of fact
for the commissioner to decide, and since his decision was not unreasonable it should
not be disturbed.

I am not persuaded that the conclusion which was reached by the Special
Commissioner, at the outset of his discussion on this point, about the identity of the
business which was being transferred to the company, was unreasonable or that it
was one which he was not entitled to reach on the evidence. I do not understand
him as saying that he regarded the description of the business in the recital as
conclusive, although he plainly did attach importance to the fact that it was
specifically stated there that the business which was being transferred to the company
was the business of farming the estate at Inchmarlo. I agree that this was important,
but it was also consistent with the facts since this was indeed where the business was
being carried on by the firm at the date of the agreement. I am also in no doubt that
he was well-founded in taking the date of the transfer as being 8–9 September 1983.
The roll-over relief does not depend on the date at which the disposal was made,
which, in terms of s 27(1) of the 1979 Act, was the time when the contract was made.
Nor does it depend on the state of the business at the date fixed by the contract for
the transfer if the transfer did not in fact take place on that date. What is in issue is
whether the business was a going concern at the date when it was actually handed
over from one party to the other. It is clear from the facts that this was on
8–9 September when the firm ceased to trade and the company began to carry out
its own farming operations on the estate. The significance of the later date is that by
9 September missives had already been entered into by the company for the sale of
the bulk of the estate with entry to be given to the purchasers on 28 November 1983.

It seems to me, however, that the Special Commissioner attached too little
importance to the fact that the farming business was still in operation when it was
transferred to the company and that the estate continued to be farmed by the
company without interruption after that date. This was due, I think, to a
misunderstanding on his part as to the point of time at which he had to test the
question whether the business was transferred as a going concern. He also overlooked
the possibility that the business might alter its place of operations without loss of
continuity after the date when it was transferred. I shall discuss these points in more
detail in a moment, but I should say at this stage that I do not find the Crown's
contentions about the purpose of s 123 of any particular assistance in this case. It is
clear that the section is intended to enable persons who are carrying on a business

either as individuals or as a partnership to transfer the business to a company without having to pay capital gains tax immediately on the disposal which must then inevitably occur. That company may be one which is controlled by others, or it may be one which the persons have incorporated themselves for the particular purpose of accepting the transfer of the business. It does not seem to me to matter for present purposes which of these alternatives applies, although in this case it is clear that the taxpayer, who had decided to sell the estate and move to a more viable farming unit elsewhere, saw it as being to his advantage to incorporate a company in order to facilitate that move by obtaining the roll-over relief. I do not regard this as being anything other than he was entitled to do, so long as he was able to satisfy the conditions which s 123(1) provides. Mention was made of the risks of asset stripping, but I do not detect anywhere in the agreement or in the facts and circumstances of this case any suggestion that it was the intention of the taxpayer to bring this about. What the firm agreed to do was to transfer to the company the business, together with all its assets, and there is no indication in the facts as described by the Special Commissioner that any of its assets were retained by the firm after the business was transferred. The only point of importance which emerges from this discussion is that one must pay close attention to the language of s 123(1) when applying it to the facts. It is for the taxpayer to conduct the transaction in a manner which brings it within the conditions which have been laid down for the relief by that subsection. The question to which I now turn is whether the Special Commissioner's decision is consistent with this approach.

The phrase with which we are concerned here begins with the word 'transfers'. The word is used in its active sense, and it directs attention to what is transferred to the company on the relevant date by the person who is not a company. The business which he transfers to the company must be transferred to it 'as a going concern'. The word 'as' is linked to the word 'transfers', and this shows that it is the state of the business at the date of the transfer which must be considered. There is no requirement that the business shall answer to the description of being a going concern at any future date or that it shall continue to be a going concern for any period after the date of the transfer, nor is the relief said to be affected by what the transferee company may do with the business once it has been received by it. The words 'going concern' do not in themselves carry any implication about what may happen in the future or about the length of time which the business must remain in that condition once it has been taken over by the transferee. It has been said that:

> 'To describe an undertaking as a "going concern" imports no more than that, at the point of time to which the description applies, its doors are open for business; that it is then active and operating, and perhaps also that it has all the plant etc. which is necessary to keep it in operation, as distinct from its being only an inert aggregation of plant.'

(See *Reference under the Electricity Commission (Balmain Electric Light Co Purchase) Act 1950* (1957) 57 SR (NSW) 100 at 131 per Sugerman J.) We were referred also to *Kenmir Ltd v Frizzell* [1968] 1 WLR 329 at 335 in which Widgery J said: 'In the end the vital consideration is whether the effect of the transaction was to put the transferee in possession of a going concern the activities of which he could carry on without interruption.' That was a case about redundancy payments, the important question being whether the employees were continuously employed after the date of the transfer, but in *Customs and Excise Comrs v Dearwood Ltd* [1986] STC 327, the passage which I have quoted was regarded as relevant also to the question whether there had been a transfer of a business as a going concern in the context of reg 12(1) of the Value Added Tax (Special Provisions) Order 1981. I think that the same test can reasonably be applied here also in order to see whether what has been transferred to the company was a business as a going concern. But the question whether its activities could be carried on without interruption should be directed to the date of the transfer and not to some later date after the business has been transferred.

The Special Commissioner ended his discussion of this point, after summarising
a   the steps which had been taken to sell the estate and to conclude agreements
providing for entry on 28 November, with these words:

> 'In those circumstances it does not seem to me that, on the ordinary use of
> language, the firm's business of farming the Inchmarlo Estate could be said to
> have been transferred to the company as a going concern. Its end was too clearly
b   and too closely in sight.'

I think that this passage reveals a misdirection on his part about the point of time to
which the words 'as a going concern' must be applied. The statement that its end
was too clearly and too closely in sight implies that at the date of the transfer its end
had not yet come. Indeed it is clear on the facts found proved by the commissioner
c   that the business was still active and operating at the date of the transfer and that the
company was able to take it over without interruption on that date. What the Special
Commissioner has done is to substitute a different test from that which is laid down
by the statute, as to the ability of the business to continue as a going concern for
some time in the future after it has been transferred to the company. Looking into
the future on this matter raises inevitably questions of degree. The agreed date of
d   entry in this case was 28 November 1983. But what if it had been fixed for
28 November 1984 or perhaps some date even further into the future in the following
year? Can it really be said that the setting of a time limit to the possession of the
estate was enough to deprive the business of the essential characteristic of its being
active and operating as at the date of the transfer? No doubt a business cannot any
longer be described as a going concern if the transferor has taken steps before the
e   date of the transfer to prevent the transferee company from carrying on the business
without interruption as it wishes after that date. But the agreement to give up
possession of the estate on 28 November 1983 was entered into here not by the
taxpayer or by the firm but by the company, and this was done after the date of the
agreement to transfer the business to the company as a going concern. The decision
was taken therefore by the transferee not by the transferor, and it cannot be said in
f   this case that the transferor did anything to prevent the company from making up
its own mind on the matter and selecting its own date when possession of the estate
was to be given up. I do not overlook the point made by the Special Commissioner
that the guiding hand of the firm and the company throughout was that of the
taxpayer himself, but I do not think that there is anything in s 123 which requires us
to lift the corporate veil in this way and to treat the actings of the company as those
g   of the person by whom the business is transferred.

The Special Commissioner's approach led him into another area which in my
opinion also invalidates his decision on this point. As I have said, I see no reason to
disturb his decision that the identity of the business which was transferred to the
company at the date of the transfer was the business of farming at Inchmarlo Estate.
But he seems to have assumed from this that the business could not continue if it
h   had to give up its possession of the estate. That is the basis for his comment that
when it took over the business on 9 September 1983 the company could not do so
with any sense of continuity or ability to plan for the future. I do not see why this
should be so. I think that counsel for the Crown were right to stress the paramount
importance which must be attached to the land where a farming business is carried
on, but this does not mean that a farming business is incapable of being moved from
j   one piece of land to another without being brought to an end. In this connection
counsel for the taxpayer referred us to *McGregor (Inspector of Taxes) v Adcock*
[1977] STC 206, [1977] 1 WLR 864, in support of his argument that a distinction
must be drawn between a business and its individual assets. He made the point that
the assets of a farming business, including land, could be changed from time to time
without bringing the business itself to an end. But that case did not deal with the
question which arises here, as to the effect of the sale of the entire farm and the

purchase of another farm in its place. As Fox J put it ([1977] STC 206 at 210, [1977] 1 WLR 864 at 867):

a

'It must be a question of fact in each case whether there has been such an interference with the whole complex of activities and assets as can be said to amount to a disposal of the business or a part of the business.'

More directly in point was *Robroyston Brickworks Ltd v IRC* [1976] STC 329, to which counsel for the taxpayer also referred. It was held in that case that although a manufacturing company had closed down its operations and sold its entire stock, plant and machinery, this was all as part of a planned move to somewhere else and it had not discontinued its trade. The question whether a trade has been discontinued is essentially one of fact, but it can at least be seen from that case that a planned move of the entire assets of a business from one place to another is not inconsistent with the continuation of its trade. No doubt the matter will depend on the characteristics of the particular business which is being carried on, but so far as the present case is concerned there are powerful indications that the farming business could be carried on elsewhere if this was thought appropriate. Clause 1 of the contract of partnership states that the business shall be carried on at the estate of Inchmarlo 'and at such other place or places as may be agreed', and the Special Commissioner tells us that, having concluded an agreement to purchase Heatheryleys Farm with entry on 28 November, the movable machinery and the unsold cattle were moved from Inchmarlo to Heatheryleys on that date and cattle raising operations have continued at Heatheryleys on much the same scale as at Inchmarlo. The decision whether to close down the business or to move it elsewhere was one which the partnership could have taken before the date of the transfer, and one which the company could take for itself after that date. Indeed the purchase of Heatheryleys by the company on 16 September 1983 is an indication that the company was making plans for the future with a view to moving the farming business elsewhere once its possession of the estate at Inchmarlo had come to an end. So I do not agree with the conclusion by the Special Commissioner that the end of the business was in sight when it was transferred to the company. In my opinion the true and only reasonable conclusion was that the company received the business from the firm as a going concern and that it had the ability to continue with it without interruption elsewhere or to close it down as it saw fit.

b

c

d

e

f

For these various reasons I consider that the decision of the Special Commissioner on this point was erroneous in point of law, and that the appeal against his determination should be allowed on this point. I would answer the first question in these cases in the negative.

I turn now to the second question, which is whether the Special Commissioner was entitled to hold as a matter of law that the business was transferred with the whole assets of the business. The argument for the Crown was that no right of property in the Inchmarlo Estate was transferred to the company because the missives of sale dated 21 July 1983 conferred on the company no more than a contractual right to require the firm to demand performance of the obligation to convey a good title to the property. No steps were taken to enforce that right, and in the result the company did not at any time possess an asset in the form of a right of property in the land where the farming business was being carried on. This argument was based on the familiar principles described by Lord President Emslie in *Gibson v Hunter Home Designs Ltd* 1976 SC 23 at 27. We were also referred to *Margrie Holdings Ltd v Customs and Excise Comrs* [1991] STC 80, in which it was held that, since a disposition of the land in question in that case had not been delivered to the company, they never had an interest in the land at all, as the law of Scotland understood that expression, but simply a right to demand performance of the contractual obligations to convey the land to them. The Special Commissioner was not impressed by this argument, which seemed to him to be inconsistent with

g

h

j

the commercial reality of what had occurred. His view was that the proper
a conclusion, on all the evidence, was that the firm acquired a beneficial interest in, or
rights in respect of, the estate by the contribution which the taxpayer had made to
its assets, and that it transferred that interest and those rights to the taxpayer. The
result was that the firm's business was transferred with its whole assets to the
company in exchange for shares. It was submitted that his decision on this point did
not give full weight to the meaning of the word 'transfers', which in this case meant
b that a real right in the estate had to be conveyed to the company, and we were
invited to apply the same reasoning as in *Margrie Holdings Ltd* to the facts of this
case.

The starting point for an examination of this argument is the position which was
enjoyed by the partnership. In terms of clause 3 of the contract of partnership the
heritable property of the estate of Inchmarlo was to be included in the balance sheet
c as part of the assets of the firm. By entering into a contract in these terms the
taxpayer agreed that such title and interest as he held in the estate was to become
partnership property, in terms of s 20(1) of the Partnership Act 1890, and was to be
held and applied by him exclusively for the purposes of the partnership. As at the
date of that contract he was the heritable proprietor of a one-half pro indiviso share
in the estate which had been conveyed to him and his brother Douglas Gordon in
d January 1983. He had acquired a personal right to the other one-half pro indiviso
share which his brother had agreed to sell to him by missives dated 23 and 27 June
1983. These two interests, the one being a real right in the subjects as regards his
own one-half pro indiviso share and the other being a personal right to demand from
his brother a disposition of his one-half pro indiviso share, remained vested in the
taxpayer throughout the period from 17 July 1983 when he entered into the contract
e of partnership with his wife until the granting of the dispositions to the ultimate
purchasers. It was not until these dispositions were recorded in the name of the
ultimate purchasers that the taxpayer and his brother were divested of their real
rights of property in the estate. At no time was a title to the heritable estate taken in
the name of trustees for the firm, nor was a disposition delivered to the company so
that it could record a title to the estate in its own name. There is no doubt therefore
f that, if it was essential to confer a real right on the company in order to transfer to it
the whole assets of the business of the partnership, this was not done.

But I do not think that it was necessary in this case for a real right of property in
the estate to be conveyed to the company in order to satisfy the condition that the
whole assets of the business were to be transferred to it. So far as the partnership was
concerned the estate was partnership property because the taxpayer had agreed with
g his wife that the estate was to be included in the balance sheet as part of the assets of
the firm. Section 20(1) of the Partnership Act 1890 provides that all property and
rights and interests in property originally brought into the partnership stock must
be held and applied by the partners exclusively for the purposes of the partnership
and in accordance with the partnership agreement. As I see it therefore the matter
rested entirely on the taxpayer's personal obligation to his wife in terms of the
h partnership agreement. He remained throughout the heritable proprietor of his own
one-half pro indiviso share and he was throughout the only person who had a
personal right to obtain a conveyance of the other one-half pro indiviso share from
his brother.

It was submitted by counsel for the Crown that these rights and interests were
held by the taxpayer in trust for the partnership in terms of s 20(2) of the 1890 Act,
j and that in order to achieve a transfer of its beneficial interest in the estate it was
necessary for the firm to convey a real right in the estate to the company. In any
event it was necessary for its beneficial interest in the estate to be assigned to the
company. The beneficial interest of the partnership was, it was said, to be
equiparated with a real right because it was an interest in a bare trust and was thus
radically different from a personal right which the insolvency of the debtor in that

right could defeat. But there had been a failure to assign the beneficial interest to the company because, at best for the taxpayer, the agreement of 22 July 1983 was no more than an agreement to assign.

I disagree with this analysis because it is plain from the facts as described by the Special Commissioner that no steps were taken at any stage to complete title to the estate in the name of the firm. As J M Halliday, *Conveyancing Law and Practice in Scotland* (1985), Vol I para 2-127 points out, a partnership is thought not to be able to sustain the feudal relationship, so the title to heritable property belonging to a firm is usually taken in the names of partners as trustees for the firm. That was not done, nor were any other steps taken to constitute an irrevocable trust for the firm, which is the context in which the provisions of s 20(2) of the 1890 Act are to be understood. The taxpayer's one-half pro indiviso share remained vested in him alone in his own name and nothing was done to assign to the firm the taxpayer's personal interest under the missives with his brother of 23 and 27 June 1983. As counsel for the Crown pointed out, an effectual assignation must contain words which may be construed as effecting an immediate transference of the right, and the transfer is completed when intimation of the transfer is made to the debtor in the obligation which is being assigned (see *Gallemos Ltd (in receivership) v Barratt Falkirk Ltd* 1990 SLT 98 at 100 per Lord Dunpark). No such steps were taken, and the whole matter rested therefore on the taxpayer's agreement with his wife and the personal right which she acquired under the contract of partnership to insist that the estate was to be included in the balance sheet as part of the assets of the firm.

The effect of the missives of 21 July 1983 and the agreement of the following date, when taken together with the giving of actual occupation of the estate to the company on 8–9 September 1983, was to place the company into an equivalent position to that which the partnership had previously enjoyed. The company did not have a real right to the heritable property, but in that respect it was no different from the partnership which had taken no steps to complete title to the estate. The company did not acquire an interest in the land as a beneficiary under a trust, but it had the benefit of actual occupation of the estate, so it was able to carry on business there just as the partnership had been able to do previously. And it was entitled to demand performance of the firm's contractual obligation to convey a good and marketable title to the whole estate which it could enforce against the firm at any time and which it did enforce when the dispositions were granted to the ultimate purchasers. The effect of the transaction was that the taxpayer was obliged to use his rights and interests in the estate, as heritable proprietor in regard to his one-half pro indiviso share and under his agreement with his brother in regard to the other one-half pro indiviso share, to bring this about. Thus the firm's entire rights as against the taxpayer had been transferred to the company, and the firm was left with no right title or interest in the estate which could thereafter be said to form any part of its property.

I consider that the Special Commissioner was right to hold that the whole assets of the business were transferred to the company. Accordingly, I would answer the second question of law in these cases in the affirmative.

LORD COWIE. I have had the opportunity of reading the opinion of your Lordship in the Chair in relation to these two cases and I concur in the manner in which your Lordship proposes to answer the questions in each of them.

I am bound to say, however, that my initial reaction was that the first question in each case fell to be answered in the affirmative. It seemed to me that the question whether the business which was transferred was 'a going concern' was one of fact for the Special Commissioner to decide, and that, in the light of the evidence before him, it could not be said that his decision was so unreasonable that it could not stand. However, having read your Lordship's opinion I am persuaded that the Special Commissioner misdirected himself, in particular on the proper construction of the

provisions of s 123 of the Capital Gains Tax Act 1979 (the 1979 Act) in so far as they
a lay down the point of time to which the words 'as a going concern' relate.

In these circumstances the question whether the business was 'a going concern',
when it was transferred, is open for us to decide and for the reasons which your
Lordship has given I am satisfied that it was 'a going concern' at the time of transfer.

Accordingly, the first question in each case falls to be answered in the negative
and I would only add that for the reasons which your Lordship has given I have no
b doubt that the second question in each case falls to be answered in the affirmative.
The result is that in my opinion both these cases should be decided in favour of the
taxpayer.

LORD McCLUSKEY. I have had the advantage of reading the opinion of your
Lordship in the Chair and I am in entire agreement with it. I would wish to add
c some observations on the correct approach to the first question.

As your Lordship had indicated, the issue giving rise to the first question in the
stated case involved several subsidiary matters. In particular it was necessary for the
Special Commissioner to identify what business it was that was said to be the subject
of transfer within the meaning of s 123(1). Second, it was necessary to establish the
date when the transfer took place. Third, it was essential to determine whether or
d not that business was transferred 'as a going concern' at the time of transfer. On the
first of these matters, I am content with the approach which your Lordship in the
Chair has taken. Whatever may have been the plans or intentions or wishes of any
of the parties invovled, there was only one business in existence at the material time,
namely the business under the name of 'A & J Gordon-Inchmarlo Farms', a business
which was carrying on farming at the said estate and nowhere else. At any time from
e June to September 1983 that business was the business of farming at Inchmarlo. It
is true that the first term of the partnership document dated 17 July 1983 stated,
inter alia: 'The business . . . shall be carried on at . . . the Estate of Inchmarlo . . . *and
at such other place or places as may be agreed*' (my emphasis), but, as a matter of fact,
the partnership was not carrying on farming at any place other than the estate of
Inchmarlo between 17 July and 8 September 1983. Equally Nacert (the company),
f was not, on 9 September or in the 11 following weeks, carrying on farming at a place
other than at the estate of Inchmarlo. Accordingly, I consider that the Special
Commissioner was right to conclude that the business which was transferred was
'the Firm's business of farming the Inchmarlo Estate'.

Second, for the reasons given by your Lordship, I consider that there can be no
doubt that the date of transfer for the purposes of s 123 was 8–9 September 1983
g when the business ceased to be run by the partnership and commenced being run
by the company.

On the question of whether or not that business was then a 'going concern' I
consider that the Special Commissioner fell into error. It is of interest to note that
he does not hold, and the Crown does not argue, that the business ceased to be a
going concern on any particular date; it was undoubtedly a going concern on 17 July
h 1983. What is found by the Special Commissioner and argued by the Crown is that
by 8–9 September 1983 it would not be right to describe the business as a 'going
concern' because, by then, all parties had in contemplation that the business of
farming the Inchmarlo Estate would come to an end in 11 weeks time. As the Special
Commissioner puts it: 'Its end was too clearly and too closely in sight'. What makes
me doubt the soundness of that approach is the arbitrariness of the 11 weeks. It is
j perfectly conceivable that when the company concluded agreements for the sale of
the farm and other parts of the estate the company might have given entry at
Whitsunday 1984 or even later, in November 1984, a date which was in contemplation
when the taxpayer and his brother reached agreement about the brother's one-half
share in the estate. In those circumstances it might well have made sense, and might
have been the intention of all concerned, to continue the business of farming on the

estate not for 11 but for 37 weeks. Would it then be a proper use of language to say that the end of *that* business was 'too clearly and too closely in sight'? How close is 'too' close? In the course of the debate I suggested that there could well be circumstances in which a person running a business could foresee, and indeed intend, that his business would end at a known date in the future, a date related either to expected trading circumstances or to his own personal circumstances or some other likely event; but it might be envisaged that that event would not end trading until perhaps a year or two, or even more, had elapsed. Thus it would be easy to envisage that the owner of a business decided that the business should come to an end in three years time when he reached retiral age; he might decide to go out of business when the lease of his business premises was due to come to an end; or he might decide to go out of business because the product was likely to fall foul of some EC directive at a known date several years ahead. So it is easy to envisage circumstances in which a person, having decided that his business should be wound up at a certain date in the future, would receive advice from his accountant that he could, none the less, avail himself of the roll-over provisions of s 123. All the steps which were taken in the present case could be taken in such a case, the only difference being that the premises were to remain in the occupation of the business and the company for a period of years rather than weeks. I cannot see why the provisions of s 123 could not be invoked by such a person. This way of looking at the matter serves only to direct attention to what I consider to be the correct moment at which it falls to be determined whether or not the business is a 'going concern'. In my opinion that moment must be the moment when the transfer takes place, in this case midnight on 8 September 1983. The business is 'going' on 8 September and it is still 'going' on 9 September. It is in fact still going in exactly the same shape or form until 28 November 1983. It is not difficult to envisage circumstances in which, whatever the intentions of the company or its controlling mind, the business might have continued in exactly the same way in all material particulars well beyond 28 November 1983. It is conceivable that a receiver might have taken control of the company away from the board and the shareholders and have arrived at the conclusion that he should simply continue with the current business of the company. It is not impossible that a receiver, or indeed the company itself, might have decided that it had been a mistake to part with the Inchmarlo Estate and to decide that, even at the cost of paying a premium, the personal right contained in the missives should be bought back so that the business could continue at Inchmarlo. I consider that there is no real warrant in the statute for holding that the plans and intentions of the transferee company in relation to the future of the business fall to be taken into account so as to rob a business—which is in fact a going concern—of that character for the purposes of s 123. In my opinion, the Special Commissioner has misdirected himself by looking away from the character of the business which was transferred to the intentions of the transferee as to what would happen to the business in the future. I can see no warrant for holding that the business was not a going concern in September simply because the intention of the transferee might then have been that it should cease to be a going concern 11 weeks later, if indeed that was the transferee's intention. But I should also go further and expressly agree with your Lordship in the Chair that the same business continued at Heatheryleys. Accordingly, I consider that the first question should be answered in the negative.

I am entirely content with your Lordship's treatment of the other matters. There is nothing I can usefully add to your Lordship's treatment of them.

In the whole circumstances I agree that the matter should be disposed of as your Lordship in the Chair has proposed.

Appeal allowed and cross-appeal dismissed.

Solicitors: *Lindsays, WS*, Edinburgh (for the taxpayer); *Solicitor of Inland Revenue*.

Rengan Krishnan Esq　Barrister.

Hamann v Finanzamt Hamburg-Eimsbüttel

(Case 51/88)

COURT OF JUSTICE OF THE EUROPEAN COMMUNITIES (SECOND CHAMBER)
JUDGES O'HIGGINS (PRESIDENT), MANCINI AND SCHOCKWEILER
ADVOCATE GENERAL S G JACOBS
14, 21 FEBRUARY, 15 MARCH 1989

Value added tax – European Communities – Place of supply – Forms of transport – Whether ocean-going sailing yachts used by hirers for the sport of sailing forms of transport – EC Council Directive 77/388, arts 9(1), 9(2)(d).

Knutt Hamann, the taxpayer, carried on a yacht-charter business operating from Kiel in the Federal Republic of Germany. The yachts were generally sailed by the charterers for pleasure outside German territorial waters and were therefore outside the German tax jurisdiction, but within the tax jurisdiction of other countries including countries which were not members of the European Communities. In 1981 and 1982, the taxpayer submitted tax returns declaring a turnover net of value added tax. These were accepted, subject to verification, by the local tax office (the finanzamt). In 1983, a tax inspector took the view that the chartering of ocean-going sailing yachts such as those hired out by the taxpayer was a hiring out of a form of transport and consequently fell to be regarded as a taxable service supplied in Germany. The finanzamt upheld the inspector's interpretation and issued revised assessment notices. The taxpayer brought an action before the Finanzgericht Hamburg (the finance court) contending that the hiring out of yachts for sporting purposes for use in water outside the German tax jurisdiction was not liable to value added tax in Germany by virtue of art 9(2)(d)ª of EC Council Directive 77/388 (the Sixth Directive). Under that article, for the hiring-out of tangible movable property, with the exception of all forms of transport, which was exported by the lessor from one member state with a view to its being used in another member state, the place of supply of the service was deemed to be the place of utilisation. The finanzamt considered that the term 'forms of transport' covered anything which might be used to go from one place to another, that the ocean-going sailing yachts were forms of transport and that the hiring out of them was, under art 9(1)ᵇ of the Sixth Directive, subject to value added tax at the place where the lessor had established his business. The Finanzgericht, Hamburg, however considered that the rule governing the hiring out of forms of transport was introduced into the German legislation in order to transpose the Sixth Directive into national law and, taking the view that the dispute involved the interpretation of the Sixth Directive, stayed the proceedings and referred the following question to the Court of Justice of the European Communities for a preliminary ruling: 'Is Article 9(2)(d) of the Sixth Directive to be interpreted as meaning that ocean-going sailing yachts that are used by their hirers for the sport of sailing are to be regarded as "forms of transport" within the meaning of the Directive?'

Held – The place where a service was supplied was in principle deemed to be the place where the supplier had established his business. The term 'forms of transport' ought to be interpreted widely and it covered anything which might be used to go from one place to another. Ocean-going sailing yachts, even if used by hirers for sailing purposes, must be regarded as forms of transport within the meaning of art 9(2)(d) of the Sixth Directive. The hiring out of ocean-going sailing yachts was

---

a   Article 9(2)(d), so far as material, is set out at p 202 *j*, post
b   Article 9(1), so far as material, is set out at p 202 *h*, post

therefore a taxable service deemed to be supplied by the taxpayer within the German
tax jurisdiction.

a

Notes
For the place of supply of forms of transport, see De Voil Value Added Tax, A5.24.
    For EC Council Directive 77/388, arts 9(1), 9(2)(*d*), see ibid, Division E3.

Reference   *b*
By an order of 22 December 1987, the Finanzgericht (the Finance Court) Hamburg
referred to the Court of Justice of the European Communities for a preliminary
ruling under art 177 of the EEC Treaty a question on the interpretation of art 9(2)(*d*)
of EC Council Directive 77/388. The question, which was raised in proceedings
between Knutt Hamann, the taxpayer, and the Finanzamt (Tax Office) Hamburg-
Eimsbüttel (the finanzamt), was whether the hiring out of ocean-going sailing yachts   *c*
for sporting purposes by an undertaking in the Federal Republic of Germany was
subject to value added tax in that state. The taxpayer, the finanzamt, the government
of the Federal Republic of Germany and the Commission of the European
Communities made submissions (in the written procedure) to the court. The
language of the case was German. The facts are set out in the report for the hearing.

d

The Judge Rapporteur (F Schockweiler) presented the following report for the
hearing.

I Facts and written procedure
    1. Article 9(1) of EC Council Directive 77/388 of 17 May 1977 on the harmonisation
of the laws of the member states relating to turnover taxes—common system of value   *e*
added tax: uniform basis of assessment (the Sixth Directive) provides that the place
where a service is supplied is to be deemed to be the place where the supplier has
established his business or has a fixed establishment from which the service is
supplied or, in the absence of such a place of business or fixed establishment, the
place where he has his permanent address or usually resides. However, under
art 9(2)(*d*), in the case of hiring out of movable tangible property, with the exception   *f*
of all forms of transport, which is exported by the lessor from one member state with
a view to its being used in another member state, the place of supply of the service is
to be the place of utilisation.
    2. The Sixth Directive was amended by EC Council Directive 84/386 of 31 July
1984 on the harmonisation of the laws of the member states relating to turnover
taxes, amending EC Council Directive 77/388—application of value added tax to   *g*
the hiring out of movable tangible property (the Tenth Directive). The Tenth
Directive was intended to enter into force by 1 July 1985. The fourth recital in its
preamble states that, as regards the hiring out of forms of transport, art 9(1) should,
for reasons of control, be strictly applied, the place where the supplier has established
his business being treated as the place of supply of such services.
    3. In the course of his business, the plaintiff in the main proceedings, Knut   *h*
Hamann (the taxpayer), hired out (uncrewed) ocean-going sailing yachts in 1980
and 1981—the years to which the dispute relates.
    4. The charterers took possession of the yachts in their home port of Kiel (Federal
Republic of Germany) and generally left German territorial waters to go sailing
mainly in Danish and Swedish waters, but also as far away as Norway and Finland.
They came back just before the expiry of the charter period in order to return the   *j*
yachts, which were thus mainly used outside German tax territory.
    5. In respect of the financial years 1980 and 1981 the taxpayer declared a turnover
net of tax, which was accepted by the Finanzamt (Tax Office) Hamburg-Eimsbüttel
subject to verification in accordance with German tax legislation.
    6. In the course of an inspection in 1983, the inspector took the view that the
offering of ocean-going yachts on charter constituted a hiring out of a means of
transport, which had to be treated as a taxable service provided in Germany.

Accordingly, he calculated the appropriate turnover tax for the financial years 1980
a and 1981. The finanzamt upheld the inspector's interpretation and drew up notices
of revised assessment in respect of 1980 and 1981.

7. The taxpayer brought an action before the Finanzgericht (Finance Court)
Hamburg against the decision of the finanzamt which had rejected his complaints.
He argued that the chartering of ocean-going yachts is not subject to turnover tax,
by virtue of para 1 of the German Umsatzsteuergesetz (Turnover Tax Law) of 1980,
b because he had realised a non-taxable turnover outside German tax territory,
movable tangible property being deemed to be hired out at the place where it is used.
The exception laid down for 'forms of transport' did not operate because ocean-
going yachts were not such means of transport.

8. The finanzamt, on the other hand, considered the ocean-going yachts to be
means of transport for the purposes of German legislation, and concluded that the
c hiring out of such goods was an activity to be taxed at the place where the lessor had
established his place of business—in this case, on German territory.

9. The Finanzgericht Hamburg took the view that the special rule in respect of
the hiring out of means of transport was inserted into the 1980 Umsatzsteuergesetz
in order faithfully to transpose the Sixth Directive into national law.

10. The Finanzgericht Hamburg held that the dispute involved the interpretation
d of the relevant Community legislation, and accordingly, by an order of 22 December
1987, decided pursuant to art 177 of the EEC Treaty to stay the proceedings until
the Court of Justice of the European Communities had given a preliminary ruling
on the following question:

> Is art 9(2)(*d*) of the Sixth Directive to be interpreted as meaning that ocean-
> going sailing yachts that are used by their hirers for the practice of the sport of
e > sailing are to be regarded as 'forms of transport' within the meaning of that
> directive?

11. The order of the Finanzgericht Hamburg was lodged at the court registry on
17 February 1988.

12. In accordance with art 20 of the Protocol on the Statute of the Court of
f Justice, written observations were submitted on 6 May 1988 by the Commission of
the European Communities, represented by Daniel Calleja, a member of its Legal
Department, assisted by Reinhard Wagner, a German judge attached to the
Commission as part of the exchange programme for officials, on 11 and 17 May 1988
by the director of the finanzamt, on 13 May 1988 by the taxpayer, represented by
P Müller-Kemler, Rechtsanwalt, Hanover, and on 16 May 1988 by the government
g of the Federal Republic of Germany, represented by Martin Seidel, Ministerial
Adviser at the Federal Ministry for Economic Affairs, assisted by Jochim Sedemund,
Rechtsanwalt, Cologne.

13. On hearing the report of the Judge Rapporteur and the views of the Advocate
General the court decided to open the oral procedure without any preparatory
inquiry.

h 14. Pursuant to art 95(1) and (2) of the Rules of Procedure, the court, by a decision
of 27 October 1988, assigned the case to the Second Chamber.

II   Written observations submitted to the court

1. The taxpayer, the plaintiff in the main proceedings, points out that the
j interpretation of the term 'forms of transport' is a matter of controversy in the
Federal Republic of Germany. He explains that the most meticulous attempt so far
to define the term has been made by the Finanzgericht Schleswig-Holstein in its
judgment of 29 September 1983. In order to classify objects capable of use as either
sporting means of transport or sports equipment serving as a means of transportation,
the main criteria should, according to the decision of the finanzgericht, be the
inherent qualities and functional purpose which give the equipment its essential
character according to prevailing public opinion and the circumstances of the case.

The finanzgericht accepted that sailing boats do not a priori belong within the category of 'forms of transport'. The transportation of yachtsmen and of their equipment and cargo to any given place is, in principle, merely the factual result and not the purpose, certainly not the main purpose, of sailing. The main purpose in chartering an ocean-going yacht lies in the pursuit of sport and relaxation. The movement of persons and things is merely subsidiary and concomitant, put up with because it would otherwise be impossible to practise sailing at all. On those grounds a sailing boat is, according to the judgment quoted, primarily an item of equipment for sports and leisure and not a means of transport for the purposes of tax legislation.

The taxpayer concedes that the Bundesfinanzhof (Federal Finance Court) took a different view in its judgment of 8 December 1983 in which it ruled that transportation is a consequence of the movement of a conveyance and that transportation by a conveyance (designed for that purpose) occurs even when the reason for sailing is not the pecuniary exploitation of a sea voyage but the pursuit of a sporting activity or other purposes connected with the organisation of leisure. Nevertheless, the taxpayer takes the view that, if all the implications of that judgment were accepted, there would be some absurd results; he cites the example of a hired windsurfer, racing bicycle or racing-car, and also refers to a regulation of the Federal Transport Minister of 7 April 1981 on the commercial hiring out and use of pleasure craft in coastal waters, which expressly takes into account the sporting or relaxation purposes for which pleasure craft are used.

In conclusion, the taxpayer takes the view that, for the purposes of the law on turnover tax, a 'form of transport' can only mean an object whose main function is to transport persons or things from one place to another—that is, to provide a transport service. If, on the other hand, one considers solely whether the object and the persons and things in it or on it move from place to place, one moves further away from the concept of 'form of transport'. The main purpose of using a sailing yacht, in particular an ocean-going yacht, is not to transport persons or things from one place to another but solely to practise sailing. Someone looking for a means of transportation from Kiel to Copenhagen, for example, would certainly not choose a sailing yacht.

Accordingly, the plaintiff in the main proceedings suggests the following answer to the question referred to the court:

> 'Article 9(2)(d) of the Sixth Directive must be interpreted as meaning that ocean-going sailing yachts that are used by their hirers for the practice of the sport of sailing are not to be regarded as "forms of transport" within the meaning of that directive.'

2. The finanzamt, the defendant in the main proceedings, argues that the exemption in the Sixth Directive for means of transport was created for the sake of simplifying taxation so as to avoid insuperable practical problems of demarcation and proof. The desire for simplification underlying those provisions calls for a broad interpretation of the term 'form of transport', so as to apply to any object serving to transport persons or things when the determination of its place of use would involve practical difficulties. In support of its opinion the finanzamt quotes the opinion of the Advisory Committee on Value Added Tax of 22 September 1983. In enumerating 'forms of transport', that opinion included not only boats for sport and pleasure but also bicycles and saddle-horses, which are usually, and almost exclusively, hired out for the purposes of sport, recreation or leisure. The finanzamt observes that the interpretation of 'forms of transport' advocated by the taxpayer overlooks the fact that all transport, regardless of the means used, is not intended merely for locomotion but seeks primarily, and necessarily, the attainment of other aims, with the result that any distinction by reference to the principal and the secondary aim of such locomotion is neither possible or practicable.

3. The government of the Federal Republic of Germany claims that the question referred to the court should receive an affirmative answer. Such an interpretation is

indicated by the generally accepted view of the term 'forms of transport', and also by
a the fundamental purpose of the rule contained in art 9 of the Sixth Directive. Since
the Community legislature has not defined the term at issue, it clearly relied on
consistent linguistic usage and standard administrative practice, which had long
prevailed in the member states. According to that linguistic usage, it is an essential
feature of a means of transport that it should serve to move persons and goods from
place to place, such movement being necessarily the intrinsic, or the main, object of
b the activity. Accordingly, there are two conditions essential to the concept of 'forms
of transport': the means of transport must be immediately suitable for locomotion
and must be used, as intended, for the transportation of persons or objects. According
to the Federal German government, a sailing yacht fulfils both the conditions to be
met by a means of transport, even if it is used solely for the sport of yachting. The
purpose of the transportation is irrelevant. According to the Sixth Directive, the
c hiring out of property is taxed as a supply of services, irrespective of the extent and
manner of its use. The set of rules laid down in art 9 of the Sixth Directive does not
concern the question whether or not the property was actually used, but confines
itself to determining the place of taxation.

That interpretation is borne out by art 15(2) of the Sixth Directive, which
expressly identifies 'pleasure boats' as a means of transport. It is also supported by
d the Advisory Committee on Value Added Tax, which, during its twelfth sitting on
30 June and 1 July 1987, ruled in favour of classifying sports boats and pleasure boats
as means of transport.

4. The Commission submits that, in order to avoid conflicts of jurisdiction in
cases in which a supply of services is liable to be governed by the legal system of
more than one member state, art 9(1), in derogation from the strict principle of
e territoriality, lays down the general rule under which the place where a service is
supplied is deemed to be the place where the supplier has established his business or
has a fixed establishment from which the service is supplied; art 9(2), however,
qualifies that general rule by introducing a number of exceptions in respect of
specific services for which the fictitious identification of the supplier's business
premises as the place of supply would be inappropriate, and with regard to which it
f sets out other determining criteria. According to the Commission, the a contrario
conclusion to be drawn from art 9(2)(*d*) means that the place where a service
consisting in the hiring out of means of transport is supplied is always the supplier's
place of business, by virtue of the principle laid down in art 9(1).

Turning to the question whether the expression 'forms of transport' is applicable
to a sailing boat, the Commission takes the view that such is indeed the case. It
g concedes that the expression 'forms of transport' is not expressly defined in the Sixth
Directive. None the less, it maintains that it is a Community concept which must
be interpreted broadly. Such an interpretation, which may be inferred from the
general term used in the German version of the directive (ausser Beförderungsmitteln), is confirmed by the other language versions, which refer to means of transport
of all kinds. Article 15(2) of the Sixth Directive supports that interpretation; the
h phrase 'or any other means of transport' clearly shows that pleasure boats are means
of transport for the purposes of the Sixth Directive. The Commission states that in
all the language versions the Community legislature chose a broad and general
wording which must be construed in accordance with general usage. By using the
term 'all forms of transport', the Community legislature intended to extend the
provision to a range of conveyances capable of performing the function of
j transportation, and the expression 'all forms of transport' includes sailing craft
suitable for marine navigation beyond national territorial waters, even if used
primarily for the sport of sailing. A sailing boat is therefore always a form of transport
if it is possible to travel from one place to another with it. Such is indeed the case
with ocean-going sailing yachts.

The Commission points out that in 1987 the Advisory Committee on Value Added
Tax decided unanimously in favour of a broad interpretation of the term 'forms of

transport' and that most of the delegations took the view that the term covered
pleasure boats.

The Commission further refers to EC Council Directive 83/182 of 28 March 1983
on tax exemptions within the Community for certain means of transport temporarily
imported into one member state from another, which provides for the grant of an
exemption from turnover tax and any other consumption tax on the importation of
certain means of transport, including pleasure boats. The Commission takes the
view that the term 'pleasure boat' covers the boats concerned in this case.

According to the Commission, that interpretation is also in keeping with the spirit
of the Sixth Directive. The statement of reasons for the Commission's proposal for
the Sixth Directive shows that art 9(1) deems the place where a service is supplied to
be the business premises or permanent address of the supplier essentially for the sake
of simplification and in order to avoid all the difficulties of interpretation which
could arise from the phrase 'place of the use or enjoyment of a service'. On the other
hand, in the case of the hiring out of movable tangible property, with the exception
of forms of transport exported by the lessor from one member state with a view to its
being used in another member state, it is the place of utilisation which is regarded as
the place where the service is supplied. That appeared necessary in order to avoid
distortions in competition which were liable to arise from different rates of value
added tax. Such considerations, however, do not apply to means of transport. If it
were otherwise, there would be problems of monitoring, because the property in
question is, by definition, movable and hence can cross frontiers with ease. The
problem of supervision arises in the case of the pleasure boats at issue here as much
as it does for other means of transport. An interpretation different from the one
proposed by the Commission would give rise to precisely the problems which the
simplifying rules in art 9 of the Sixth Directive were designed to avoid.

Lastly, the Commission points out that in this case the boats are not 'exported by
the lessor from one Member State with a view to [their] being used in another
Member State', as envisaged in art 9(2)(d). Instead, the charterers take possession of
the boats in the home port of Kiel. There cannot therefore be any derogation from
the principle laid down in art 9(1) of the Sixth Directive, even if yachts were not
regarded as means of transport for the purposes of that provision.

In the light of all those considerations, the Commission proposes the following
answer to the question referred to the court:

> 'Article 9(2)(d) of the Sixth Directive is to be interpreted as meaning that
> ocean-going sailing yachts that are used by their hirers for the practice of the
> sport of sailing are to be regarded as "forms of transport" within the meaning of
> that provision of the directive.'

21 February 1989. **The Advocate General (F G Jacobs)** delivered the following
opinion.

My Lords,

1. The plaintiff, Mr Hamann (the taxpayer), owned a yacht-charter business
established in the Federal Republic of Germany and operating from Kiel. It appears
from the order of reference that the yachts were generally sailed by the charterer for
pleasure outside German territorial waters in Danish and Swedish waters—
presumably in the Baltic Sea—and also as far as Norway and Finland. Therefore a
large part of the utilisation of the service supplied—the use of a yacht—took place
outside German tax jurisdiction and within the tax jurisdiction of other countries,
including countries which were not member states of the European Communities.

2. In 1981 and 1982 the taxpayer submitted tax returns declaring a tax-free
turnover of DM75,074 and DM132,943 for the years 1980 and 1981 respectively.
These were accepted by the defendant, the local tax office (the finanzamt), subject
to verification. An inspector examined the taxpayer's books in 1983 and calculated

an increase in value added tax of DM7,703·22 and DM15,103·73 for the years 1980
and 1981 respectively. The increase was based on the fact that the service provided
by the plaintiff was the hiring out of a form of transport not of movable tangible
property. The finanzamt agreed with this assessment (both of tax due and the reason
on which it was based) and claimed the payment of tax accordingly on 7 May 1984.
The taxpayer challenged the claim but the finanzamt rejected the challenge on
20 September 1985.

3. The taxpayer then challenged the latter decision before the Finanzgericht,
Hamburg. That court, by order of 22 December 1987 received at the court registry
on 17 February 1988, referred the following question on the interpretation of EC
Council Directive 77/388 of 17 May 1977 (the Sixth Directive):

'Is Article 9(2) of the Sixth Directive to be interpreted as meaning that ocean-
going sailing yachts, rented out in order to exercise sailing as a sport, are a
"means of transport" within the meaning of that Directive?'

4. The purposes of the Sixth Directive are clear from the preamble: they include
establishing 'a basis of assessment determined in a uniform manner according to
Community rules' (see the second recital) and—with particular relevance to the
present case—to resolve possible conflicts of jurisdiction between member states as
regards the supply of services (see the seventh recital).

5. Article 2 of the Sixth Directive provides, so far as material:

'The following shall be subject to value added tax:

1. the supply of goods or services effected for consideration within the
territory of the country by a taxable person acting as such . . .'

Article 3 governs the territorial application of the Sixth Directive: by art 3(1), the
'territory of the country' is the area of application of the EEC Treaty as stipulated in
respect of each member state in art 227. It has not been suggested that the application
of the Sixth Directive is affected by the fact that the yachts may have been sailed in
part outside the territories of any of the member states.

6. Article 9(1) of the Sixth Directive, giving effect to the seventh recital of the
preamble, provides as follows:

'The place where a service is supplied shall be deemed to be the place where
the supplier has established his business or has a fixed establishment from which
the service is supplied or, in the absence of such a place of business or fixed
establishment, the place where he has his permanent address or usually resides.'

7. Article 9(2) of the Sixth Directive provides certain exceptions to that general
rule. In particular, sub-para (d) states (before amendment):

'. . . in the case of hiring out of movable tangible property, with the exception
of all forms of transport, which is exported by the lessor from one Member State
with a view to its being used in another Member State, the place of supply of
the service shall be the place of utilisation . . .'

The reason for the exception made in the case of the hiring out of movable property
is no doubt to prevent distortion of trade and distortion of competition. To take the
illustration given at the hearing by the agent of the Commission, if there were a
substantial difference in the rate of value added tax on the hiring out of television
sets, between the Federal Republic of Germany and Denmark, then to tax the hiring
in the member state from which the goods were supplied might lead to a substantial
distortion.

8. However, that exception for the hiring out of movable property is expressed to

exclude 'all forms of transport', so that the hiring out of forms of transport (other than for purely internal purposes) falls within the general rule in art 9(1). Thus the *a* chartering of the yachts, if they are forms of transport, is to be deemed to take place where the supplier has established his business.

9. Again, the purpose of the exclusion from the exception of forms of transport is, in the ordinary case, readily apparent, since where such forms of transport as cars, vans, or even bicycles or horses, may be used across national frontiers, it would be wholly impracticable to seek to tax the hiring out of such forms of transport in the *b* 'place of utilisation'.

10. Before addressing the issue whether yachts are to be regarded as forms of transport, I would add that it seems very doubtful whether, even if yachts are to be regarded as not being forms of transport, the present case would fall within the exception in art 9(2)(*d*), which requires that movable property, to come within the exception, should have been exported by the lessor from one member state with a *c* view to its being used in another member state. While that issue has not been addressed by the national court, it seems manifestly not the case that the yachts were exported by the lessor, the taxpayer, with a view to their being used in another member state, and therefore the hiring of the yachts would not fall within the exception even if they were to be regarded as movable property. The reason why the issue has not been addressed by the national court appears to be that the German *d* legislation, the German Law of 1980 on Turnover Tax (Umsatzsteuergesetz), does not contain the requirement set out above; it merely provides, in art 3*a*(2)4, that the hiring out of movable physical objects is carried out where the objects are used ('Die Vermietung beweglicher körperlicher Gegenstände—ausgenommen Beförderungs-mittel—wird dort ausgeführt, wo die Gegenstände genutzt werden').

11. Although it is therefore likely that the reference in this case was not strictly *e* necessary to decide the dispute, it is well established that this court must nevertheless rule on the question referred and I therefore turn to that question. The taxpayer argues, in essence, that yachts sailed for pleasure purposes are not forms of transport since transport is not the main purpose for which they are used. That view is contested by the finanzamt, by the German government and by the Commission, which contend in substance that the term 'forms of transport' must be understood *f* more widely as covering any means of conveyance even if it is not used principally as a means of conveyance.

12. At first sight, it would seem that the expression 'forms of transport' might be interpreted either in the sense contended for by the taxpayer or in the wider sense. On the one hand, it could be contended that the essential criterion of a means of transport is its functional purpose; and that the transportation of yachtsmen, and *g* the contents of the yacht, is merely incidental to the purpose of sailing, which is primarily a recreational activity. On that view, a sailing boat is primarily an item of leisure equipment rather than a means of transport. On the other hand, it could be said that, although the reasons for sailing may be of a purely recreational or sporting character, nevertheless transportation occurs whatever the reasons for which it is undertaken, and that a boat is a form of transport, whatever the purposes for which *h* it is used. Indeed, these two views, it appears, are reflected in the case law of the German courts.

13. However, in my view, there is a clear answer to the question of interpretation as it arises in the context of the Sixth Directive. First, as I have already pointed out, the purpose underlying the provisions points to a broad interpretation of the term. Indeed, because of the practical difficulties in taxing such supplies of services, if a *j* narrower interpretation were adopted, there would be a risk that such supplies of services would escape taxation altogether. Moreover any derogation from the Sixth Directive must be interpreted restrictively, which points here to a broad interpretation of the term in issue. Such an interpretation also finds some support in the language of the provision itself; while in the German version of art 9(2)(*d*) the

term used is 'ausser Beförderungsmitteln', that is 'with the exception of means of
a   transport', other language versions include an additional encompassing adjective; in
English 'all', in French 'tout' and so on, indicating that the term is intended in the
most comprehensive sense.

14. Of no less significance is the fact that, as the Commission has pointed out,
art 15(2) of the Sixth Directive expressly refers to 'pleasure boats and private aircraft
or any other means of transport for private use', thus clearly—although in another
b   context—including pleasure boats, which chartered sailing yachts are, within the
meaning of 'means of transport'. I do not regard the slightly different formulation in
the English version—'means' instead of 'forms'—as significant, and other language
versions use the same words in both places.

15. Later legislation in the same field, which may be used for comparative
purposes, is also of interest. In EC Council Directive 83/182 of 28 March 1983,
c   art 1(1) includes in the scope of the directive (and, by implication, within the
meaning of 'certain means of transport') inter alia 'pleasure boats'. On this occasion,
there is a slight difference of wording in other language texts. Instead of
'Beförderungsmitteln' the German has 'Verkehrsmittel'. The French continues to
use 'moyens de transport'. Once again, however, the linguistic differences are not
significant and it is clear that the concept, as envisaged by the Community legislator,
d   remains the same since the directive itself is designed to fit into the general value
added tax system.

16. Taking these points together I am led to the conclusion that pleasure boats
(including chartered yachts) were intended to be included in the expression 'forms
of transport'.

17. In reaching that conclusion I do not take account of the fact that art 9 of the
e   Sixth Directive was amended by the EC Council Directive 84/386 (the Tenth
Directive), since the Tenth Directive was adopted on 31 July 1984 and was to be
implemented by 1 July 1985 and therefore does not affect this case. The fourth
recital of the preamble to the Tenth Directive makes it clear that the Community
legislator wished to ensure strict application of the general rule in art 9(1):

f   '... as regards the hiring out of forms of transport, Article 9 (1) should, for
reasons of control, be strictly applied, the place where the supplier has
established his business being treated as the place of supply of such services...'

18. Accordingly, in my opinion the answer to be given to the referring court
should be as follows:

g   Ocean-going sailing yachts, hired out for the purpose of sailing, are a 'means
of transport' within the meaning of art 9(2) of the Sixth Directive on the
harmonisation of the laws of the member states relating to turnover taxes.

15 March 1989. **THE COURT OF JUSTICE** delivered the following judgment.

h
1. By an order of 22 December 1987, which was received at the court on
17 February 1988, the Finanzgericht Hamburg referred to the court for a preliminary
ruling under art 177 of the EEC Treaty a question on the interpretation of art 9(2)(*d*)
of EC Council Directive 77/388 of 17 May 1977 (the Sixth Directive).

2. That question was raised in proceedings between Knut Hamann (the taxpayer)
j   and the Finanzamt (Tax Office) Hamburg-Eimsbüttel (the finanzamt) concerning
the question whether the chartering of ocean-going sailing yachts for sporting
purposes by an undertaking established in the Federal Republic of Germany is
subject to value added tax in that state.

3. According to the documents relating to the main proceedings, the taxpayer
owns a yacht-charter business established in the Federal Republic of Germany. The

yachts were chartered for sailing, primarily in Danish and Swedish waters but also as far away as Norway and Finland and were therefore used by the charterers mainly outside German tax jurisdiction.

4. For the 1980 and 1981 financial years, the taxpayer declared a turnover net of tax which was accepted by the finanzamt, subject to verification.

5. During an inspection carried out in 1983 the inspector of taxes considered that the chartering by the taxpayer of ocean-going sailing yachts was a hiring out of a form of transport which should be regarded as a taxable service supplied in Germany; he therefore calculated the value added tax payable for 1980 and 1981. The finanzamt confirmed the inspector's interpretation and issued revised assessment notices for 1980 and 1981.

6. After his objection was rejected, the taxpayer brought an action before the Finanzgericht Hamburg. He argued that the chartering of ocean-going sailing yachts was not subject to value added tax under the German legislation on the ground that the turnover had occurred at the place where the goods hired out were used and therefore outside German tax jurisdiction. The rule laid down in German legislation for the hiring out of forms of transport, whereby such hiring out was deemed to be the place where the lessor pursued his business, was not applicable in this case since ocean-going sailing yachts were not to be regarded as means of transport.

7. The finanzamt, however, considered that ocean-going sailing yachts were forms of transport within the meaning of the German legislation and that the hiring out of such goods was therefore subject to value added tax at the place where the lessor had established his business, that is to say within the territory of the Federal Republic of Germany.

8. The Finanzgericht Hamburg considered that the rule governing the hiring out of forms of transport was introduced into the German legislation in order to transpose the Sixth Directive into national law.

9. Taking the view that the dispute involved the interpretation of the relevant Community rules, the Finanzgericht Hamburg decided, by an order of 22 December 1987, to stay the proceedings pursuant to art 177 of the EEC Treaty until the court had given a preliminary ruling on the following question:

'Is Article 9(2)(*d*) of the Sixth Directive to be interpreted as meaning that ocean-going sailing yachts that are used by their hirers for the practice of the sport of sailing are to be regarded as "forms of transport" within the meaning of that directive?'

10. Reference is made to the report for the hearing for a fuller account of the facts of the case, the law applicable, the course of the procedure and the observations submitted to the court, which are mentioned or discussed hereinafter only in so far as is necessary for the reasoning of the court.

11. It should be noted first of all that art 9(1) of the Sixth Directive provides that:

'The place where a service is supplied shall be deemed to be the place where the supplier has established his business or has a fixed establishment from which the service is supplied or, in the absence of such a place of business or fixed establishment, the place where he has his permanent address or usually resides.'

12. Second, it should be noted that art 9(2) of the Sixth Directive lays down a number of exceptions to this general rule. In particular, art 9(2)(*d*) provides that—

'... in the case of hiring out of movable tangible property, with the exception of all forms of transport, which is exported by the lessor from one Member State with a view to its being used in another Member State, the place of supply of the service shall be the place of utilisation ...'

13. It follows from that provision that all forms of transport are outside the scope of the exception laid down for the hiring out of movable tangible property, which therefore remains subject to the general rule in art 9(1) of the Sixth Directive.

14. In order to answer the question asked by the national court, it is necessary to determine whether ocean-going yachts that are chartered for the practice of the sport of sailing are forms of transport within the meaning of art 9(2)(*d*) of the Sixth Directive.

15. In this connection the taxpayer states that the definition of the term 'forms of transport' depends on the main function of the object in question. The main purpose of the chartering of an ocean-going sailing yacht is not to transport persons and goods from one place to another but to practise the sport of sailing or to sail for pleasure. Consequently, the yachts concerned in the main proceedings are not to be regarded as forms of transport within the meaning of art 9(2)(*d*) of the Sixth Directive.

16. The Commission, however, considers that the term 'forms of transport' must be interpreted widely and that it covers anything which may be used to go from one place to another. According to the Commission, any sailing boat suitable for sailing is therefore a form of transport within the meaning of the Sixth Directive even if it is used primarily for the purposes of sport.

17. The Commission's argument must be accepted. It is clear from the seventh recital in the preamble to the Sixth Directive that one of the aims of the Sixth Directive was to delimit in a rational way the scope of the legislation of member states, in particular as regards the supply of services. Thus the place where a service is supplied is in principle, for the sake of simplification, deemed to be the place where the supplier has established his business. However, according to the aforesaid recital, an exception to this general rule must be made in certain specific cases; thus in the case of the hiring out of movable tangible property, the place of supply of the service is the place in which the goods hired out are used, in order to prevent distortions of competition which may arise from the different rates of value added tax applied by the member states.

18. Those considerations do not apply, however, to the hiring out of forms of transport. Since they may easily cross frontiers, it is difficult, if not impossible, to determine the place of their utilisation. However, in each case a practical criterion must be laid down for value added tax charging. Consequently, for the hiring out of all forms of transport, the Sixth Directive provides that the service should be deemed to be supplied not at the place where the goods hired out are used but, in conformity with the general rule, at the place where the supplier has established his business.

19. In view of the reasons for the exclusion of all forms of transport from the exception laid down in art 9(2)(*d*) of the Sixth Directive and the fact that exceptions to the general rule laid down by the Sixth Directive must be interpreted narrowly, ocean-going sailing yachts, even if used by the hirers for sporting purposes, must thus be regarded as forms of transport within the meaning of the aforesaid provision of the Sixth Directive. Yachts of that kind enable persons and goods to be moved over long distances, so that it is difficult to determine the place where they are used and therefore deeming the place where the service is supplied to be the place where the goods are used entails the risk that no value added tax would be paid on the hiring out of such vessels, contrary to the aim of the Sixth Directive.

20. This interpretation is confirmed by art 15(2) of the Sixth Directive, according to which 'pleasure boats'—the category to which ocean-going sailing yachts belong— are 'means of transport for private use'.

21. The same interpretation was also adopted in EC Council Directive 83/182 of 28 March 1983, art 1(1) of which provides that 'pleasure boats' are within the scope of the directive and are therefore covered by the term 'certain means of transport'.

22. The answer to the question raised by the national court must therefore be that

ocean-going sailing yachts that are used by their hirers for the practice of the sport of sailing are 'forms of transport' within the meaning of art 9(2)(d) of the Sixth Directive.

a

Costs

23. The costs incurred by the government of the Federal Republic of Germany and the Commission of the European Communities, which have submitted observations to the court, are not recoverable. Since these proceedings are, in so far as the parties to the main proceedings are concerned, in the nature of a step in the action pending before the national court, costs are a matter for that court.

b

On those grounds, the court (Second Chamber), in answer to the question submitted to it by the Finanzgericht Hamburg by an order of 22 December 1987, hereby rules:

> Ocean-going sailing yachts that are used by their hirers for the practice of the sport of sailing are 'forms of transport' within the meaning of art 9(2)(d) of the Sixth Directive.

c

Agents: *P Muller-Kemler*, Rechtsanwalt, Hanover (for the taxpayer); *Director of the Finanzamt Hamburg-Eimsbüttel* (for the finanzamt); *M Seidel*, Ministerial Adviser at the Federal Ministry for Economic Affairs, and *J Sedemund*, Rechtsanwalt, Cologne (for the government of the Federal Republic of Germany); *M D Calleja* and *R Wagner* (for the Commission).

d

Rengan Krishnan Esq   Barrister

e

a
Ufficio Distrettuale delle Imposte Dirette di Fiorenzuola d'Arda v Comune di Carpaneto Piacentino
(Case 231/87)

b
Ufficio Provinciale Imposta sul Valore Aggiunto di Piacenza v Comune di Rivergaro and others
(Case 129/88)

c
COURT OF JUSTICE OF THE EUROPEAN COMMUNITIES
JUDGES DUE (PRESIDENT), SIR GORDON SLYNN AND SCHOCKWEILER (PRESIDENTS OF CHAMBERS) MANCINI, JOLIET, O'HIGGINS, MOITINHO DE ALMEIDA, RODRIGUEZ IGLESIAS AND GRÉVISSE
ADVOCATE GENERAL J MISCHO
1 FEBRUARY, 15 MARCH, 17 OCTOBER 1989

d
Value added tax – European Communities – Taxable person – Activities or transactions engaged in as public authorities – Whether provision had direct effect – Obligations of member states when transposing provision into national law – Whether transactions carried out by local authorities 'activities or transactions in which they engage as public authorities' – EC Council Directive 77/388, art 4(5).

e
The returns submitted by the local authority of Carpaneto in respect of direct taxes for 1980, 1982 and 1983 and those concerning value added tax submitted by the local authority of Rivergaro for 1981, 1982, 1983 and 1985 were all the subject of rectified assessments made by the competent Italian authorities on the ground that they did not take account of sums of money or fees received for certain transactions regarded f as commercial activities within the meaning of national legislation. The transactions at issue were the following: concessions in respect of graves, cemetery vaults and chapels, leasing and selling of land in connection with subsidised house-building, the taking-out of public ownership and sale of a piece of roadway, the supply of water, the concession for the operation of a public weighbridge, the sale of wood obtained from the lopping of trees and the sale of fittings for cemetery vaults. Before g the national courts the local authorities concerned, together with 23 other local authorities that intervened in support of the claims of the local authority of Rivergaro, claimed that under art 4(5)[a] of EC Council Directive 77/388 (the Sixth Directive) they were not taxable persons and were therefore entitled not to charge value added tax on the transactions at issue. The questions referred by the national courts to the Court of Justice of the European Communities sought to determine, h inter alia: (a) The essential characteristics of the activities exercised 'as a public authority' referred to in the first sub-paragraph of art 4(5) of the Sixth Directive and the obligations imposed by that provision on the member states. (b) The scope of the expression 'such activities' contained in the second sub-paragraph of art 4(5) and whether the member states were required to incorporate into their tax legislation the criterion in that provision of 'significant distortions of competition' or to fix j quantitative limits for the transposition of the criterion into national law. (c) Whether the third sub-paragraph of art 4(5) required the member states to transpose into their tax legislation the criterion of the non-negligible scale of activities as a condition for treating bodies governed by public law as taxable persons in respect of the activities listed in Annex D to the directive and whether the member states had to

---

a Article 4(5), so far as material, is set out at p 234 *c–e*, post

establish a threshold below which such bodies were to be treated as non-taxable persons. (d) Whether a body governed by public law could rely on art 4(5) for the **a** purpose of opposing the application of a national provision making it subject to value added tax in respect of an activity in which it was engaged as a public authority and which was not listed in Annex D, where treatment of the activity as non-taxable was not liable to give rise to significant distortions of competition.

Held – (1) Activities pursued 'as public authorities' within the first sub-paragraph of **b** art 4(5) of EC Council Directive 77/388 were those engaged in by bodies governed by public law under the special legal regime applicable to them and did not include activities pursued by them under the same legal conditions as those that applied to private traders. It was for each member state to choose the appropriate legislative technique for transposing into national law the rule of treatment as a non-taxable person laid down in that provision.

(2) The second sub-paragraph of art 4(5) required the member states to ensure **c** that bodies subject to public law were treated as taxable persons in respect of activities in which they engaged as public authorities where their treatment as non-taxable persons could lead to significant distortions of competition, but the member states were not obliged to transpose that criterion literally into their national law or to lay down precise quantitative limits for such treatment.

(3) The third sub-paragraph of art 4(5) did not require the member states to **d** transpose into their tax legislation the criterion of the non-negligible scale or activities as a condition for treating the activities listed in Annex D as taxable.

(4) A body governed by public law could rely on art 4(5) for the purpose of opposing the application of a national provision making it subject to value added tax in respect of an activity in which it engaged as a public authority, which was not **e** listed in Annex D and whose treatment as non-taxable was not liable to give rise to significant distortions of competition.

Notes

For the liability of local authorities to value added tax, see De Voil: Value Added **f** Tax A3.11.

For EC Council Directive 77/388, art 4(5), see ibid, Division E3.

Cases cited

Apple and Pear Development Council v Customs and Excise Comrs (Case 102/86) **g** [1988] STC 221, [1988] 2 All ER 922, [1988] ECR 1433, CJEC.

Becker v Finanzamt Münster-Innenstadt (Case 8/81) [1982] ECR 53, CJEC.

Borrie Clarke v Chief Adjudication Officer (Case 384/85) [1987] ECR 2865, CJEC.

EC Commission v Federal Republic of Germany (Case 107/84) [1985] ECR 2655, CJEC.

EC Commission v French Republic (Case 307/84) [1986] ECR 1725, CJEC. **h**

EC Commission v Kingdom of the Netherlands (Case 235/85) [1987] ECR 1471, CJEC.

Giménez Zaera v Instituto Nacional de la Seguridad Social y Tesorería General de la Seguridad Social (Case 126/86) [1987] ECR 3697, CJEC.

Marshall v Southampton and South West Hampshire Area Health Authority (Teaching) (Case 152/84) [1986] QB 401, [1986] 2 All ER 584, [1986] 2 ECR 723, CJEC. **j**

Naturally Yours Cosmetics Ltd v Customs and Excise Comrs (Case 230/87) [1988] STC 879, [1988] ECR 6365, CJEC.

Smanor SA (Case 298/87) [1988] ECR 4489, CJEC.

Staatssecretaris van Financiën v Coöperatieve Aardappelenbewaarplaats G A (Case 154/80) [1981] ECR 445, CJEC.

Staatssecretaris van Financiën v Hong Kong Trade Development Council (Case 89/81)
[1982] ECR 1277, CJEC.

Reference

By orders of 8 May 1987 and 28 April 1988, the Commissione Tributaria di Secondo Grado (Tax Appeals Board), Piacenza and the Commissione Tributaria di Primo Grado (First Instance Tax Board), Piacenza referred to the Court of Justice of the European Communities for a preliminary ruling under art 177 of the EEC Treaty several questions on the interpretation of art 5(4) of EC Council Directive 77/388. The questions were raised in two actions, one between the Ufficio Distrettuale delle Imposte Dirette (District Office for Direct Taxes) di Fiorenzuola d'Arda and the Comune di Carpaneto Piacentino (Case 231/87); and the other between the Ufficio Provinciale Imposta sul Valore Aggiunto (Provincial Value Added Tax Office) di Piacenza and the Comune di Rivergaro, supported by 23 other local authorities, (Case 129/88). By an order of 23 November 1988, the court joined the two cases for the purposes of the oral procedure and the judgment on the ground that they were related. The questions concerned the claims by the local authorities that under art 4(5) they were not taxable persons and were therefore entitled not to charge value added tax on the following transactions: concessions in respect of graves, cemetery vaults and chapels, leasing and selling of land in connection with subsidised house-building, the taking-out of public ownership and sale of a piece of roadway, the supply of water, the concession for the operation of a public weighbridge, the sale of wood obtained from the lopping of trees and the sale of fittings for cemetery vaults. The Italian Republic and the Commission of the European Communities made written submissions to the court in both cases. In Case 231/87, written submissions were made by the Comune di Carpaneto Piacentino. In Case 129/88, the government of the Netherlands, the Comune di Piacenza, the Comune di Rivergaro and 23 other local authorities made written submissions. The language of the case was Italian. The facts are set out in the report for the hearing.

The Judge Rapporteur (G C Rodríguez Iglesias) presented the following report for the hearing.

I Legal background

1 Community law

Article 4 of EC Council Directive 77/388 of 17 May 1977 on the harmonisation of the laws of the member states relating to turnover taxes—common system of value added tax: uniform basis of assessment (the Sixth Directive) defines 'taxable person' in regard to value added tax as any person who independently carries out in any place any economic activity. An exception to that general rule is contained in art 4(5), the interpretation of which is the subject of these cases.

Article 4(5) is worded as follows:

'States, regional and local government authorities and other bodies governed by public law shall not be considered taxable persons in respect of the activities or transactions in which they engage as public authorities, even where they collect dues, fees, contributions or payments in connection with these activities or transactions.

However, when they engage in such activities or transactions, they shall be considered taxable persons in respect of these activities or transactions where treatment as non-taxable persons would lead to significant distortions of competition.

In any case, these bodies shall be considered taxable persons, in relation to the activities listed in Annex D, provided they are not carried out on such a small scale as to be negligible.

Member States may consider activities of these bodies which are exempt under Article 13 or 28 as activities which they engage in as public authorities.'

2 National law

Article 1 of Presidential Decree 633/72 (subsequently amended several times) defines the transactions which are taxable for the purposes of value added tax. That tax applies to the supply of goods or services carried out within the country in the context of the operation of a business or the practice of an art or profession and on imports, regardless of the person who carries them out.

Article 4 of the same decree provides that the expression 'operation of a business' means the carrying-out, by way of a habitual but not necessarily exclusive activity, of the commercial and agricultural activities referred to in arts 2135 and 2195 of the Civil Code, even if those activities are not organised in the form of a business undertaking.

The conditions for the application of those provisions to the state, local authorities and, in general, to public bodies, which, by definition, do not have as their exclusive or principal object the carrying-out of commercial or agricultural activities, are fixed by art 4(4) of the decree, according to which 'the above-mentioned public bodies shall be regarded as taxable persons only in respect of sales of goods and supplies of services carried out in the course of commercial or agricultural activities'.

With regard to local authorities, circular 18/360068 of 22 May 1976 of the Ministry of Finance provides a detailed, although not exhaustive, list of activities fulfilling the conditions for being subject to value added tax, 'in order to dispel any ambiguity which may exist and to arrive at a precise definition of the transactions which fall within the scope of the tax'.

In *Ufficio Distrettuale delle Imposte Dirette di Fiorenzuola d'Arda v Comune di Carpaneto Piacentino* (Case 231/87), the order for reference points out that even for the purposes of direct taxation under art 51 of Presidential Decree 597/73, the legislature has recourse—even in the case of non-commercial bodies—to the concept of commercial activity, with the result that the two sets of rules, cited above, are connected to such an extent that if a given activity is not liable to value added tax, the income arising from it can also not be subject to direct taxation, and vice versa.

II Factual background and main proceedings

Ufficio Distrettuale delle Imposte Dirette di Fiorenzuola d'Arda v Comune di Carpaneto Piacentino (Case 231/87)

In a report of 7 August 1984, the Guardia di Finanza (Customs and Excise Enforcement Service) in Piacenza found that the local authority of Carpaneto Piacentino had not subjected to value added tax certain transactions in consideration of which that local authority had received certain sums of money, contrary to art 4 of Presidential Decree 633/72. The transactions involved were as follows: concessions in respect of graves and vaults, selling concessions of surface rights in, and the sale, with full ownership rights, of land in connection with subsidised home-building, the taking-out of public ownership and sale of a piece of roadway, water supply, the concession for the operation of the public weighbridge, the sale of wood resulting from the lopping of trees and the sale of fittings for cemetery vaults.

The Ufficio Distrettuale delle Imposte Dirette (District Office for Direct Taxes) of Fiorenzuola d'Arda (the district office) adopted the above report and, since it considered that all of the aforesaid activities were of a commercial nature and hence subject to both indirect and direct taxation, it rectified the annual returns submitted by the local authorities for the purposes of direct taxation (corporation tax and local tax) for 1980, 1981, 1982 and 1983.

The local authority brought an action against the district office's decision relying, in particular, on an infringement of art 4(4) of Presidential Decree 633/72 and art 4(5) of the Sixth Directive.

The Commissione Tributaria di Primo Grado (First Instance Tax Board) allowed the application, taking the view that all the above-mentioned transactions, with the exception of water supply, could not be regarded as commercial activities within the meaning of art 4(5) of the Sixth Directive.

The district office appealed against that decision before the Commissione Tributaria di Secondo Grado (Tax Appeals Board) arguing that the question arose out of the classification of the transactions effected by the local authorities. The local authority of Carpaneto, which made itself a party to the proceedings, emphasised the need to make a reference for a preliminary ruling on that point to the Court of Justice of the European Communities.

Ufficio Provinciale Imposta sul Valore Aggiunto di Piacenza v Comune di Rivergaro and others (Case 129/88)

By assessments of 2 and 17 October 1986, the Ufficio Provinciale Imposta sul Valore Aggiunto (Provincial Value Added Tax Office) (the value added tax office), Piacenza, rectified value added tax returns for 1981, 1982, 1983 and 1985 made by the local authority of Rivergaro on the ground that that local authority had failed to include the concession fees obtained in respect of cemetery vaults and chapels and, since it considered that those were commercial activities within the meaning of art 4 of Presidential Decree 633/72 and that cemetery vaults are to be found at point 19 of the list annexed to circular 18/360068 of the Ministry of Finance, took steps to recover the amount due by way of value added tax by imposing the appropriate fines on the local authority.

The local authority of Rivergaro brought an action against those assessments before the Commissione Tributaria de Primo Grado, Piacenza, alleging an infringement of art 4 of Presidential Decree 633/72 and art 4(5) of the Sixth Directive. Twenty-three other local authorities intervened in support of the local authority of Rivergaro.

All the local authorities requested that the Court of Justice of the European Communities be asked to give an interpretation of the relevant provision of the Sixth Directive.

III Preliminary questions

Ufficio Distrettuale delle Imposte Dirette di Fiorenzuola d'Arda v Comune di Carpaneto Piacentino (Case 231/87)

By order of 8 May 1987, the Third Chamber of the Commissione Tributaria di Secondo Grado, Piacenza, decided to stay the proceedings and refer the case to the Court of Justice for a preliminary ruling under art 177 of the EEC Treaty on the questions indicated in the part of the order relating to the issues of law.

Those questions may be formulated as seeking to ascertain:

(1) Whether the principle set out in the first sub-paragraph of art 4(5) of the Sixth Directive, which excludes from the category of activities subject to value added tax so-called 'institutional' activities, is directly applicable in the absence of a specific national provision.

(2) Whether the Community legislature intended to identify by means of the phrase 'activities or transactions in which they engage as public authorities' in the first sub-paragraph of art 4(5) those activities which the public authorities carry out directly and exclusively pursuant to powers vested in them as public authorities, albeit delegated to them.

(3) Whether, the assumption that the institutional activities are carried out exclusively by a public body, the Community legislature, by the use of the

expression 'such activities' in the second sub-paragraph of art 4(5), intended to refer to residual activities relating to public services, governed by Royal Decree 2578 of 15 October 1925.

(4) Whether the second sub-paragraph of art 4(5) must be interpreted as requiring the member states to incorporate in their value added tax legislation the criterion of 'significant distortions of competition' in regard to the taxation of the transactions referred to in the said sub-paragraph.

(5) Whether the third sub-paragraph of art 4(5) of the Sixth Directive, which provides that public bodies are to be considered taxable persons in relation to the activities listed in Annex D, provided that they are not carried out on such a small scale as to be negligible, requires the member states to incorporate in their tax legislation the criterion of 'negligibility'.

Ufficio Provinciale Imposta sul Valore Aggiunto di Piacenza v Comune di Rivergaro (Case 129/88)

By order of 28 April 1988, the Commissione Tributaria di Primo Grado stayed the proceedings and referred the following questions to the court for a preliminary ruling under art 177 of the EEC Treaty:

(1) Are the Community provisions contained in art 4(5) of the Sixth Directive immediately and directly applicable?

(2) In order to make the Italian system of value added tax consistent with the Community provisions was the Italian legislature under an obligation under art 1 of the Sixth Directive—

(a) to lay down the general principle set out in the first sub-paragraph of art 4(5) of the Sixth Directive by stipulating specific criteria for defining the activities engaged in by local authorities 'as public authorities';

(b) to exclude from tax public activities which, although they may be described as commercial activities, are, under the national legislation, in the nature of activities of a public authority;

(c) in any event, not to subject to tax, in compliance with the second sub-paragraph of art 4(5), public activities where they do not lead to significant distortions of competition, and to specify the necessary quantitative limits;

(d) to fix, pursuant to the third sub-paragraph of art 4(5) of the Sixth Directive, a threshold below which the public activities listed in Annex D to the Sixth Directive are not subject to tax?

IV Procedure before the court

The orders for reference were registered at the court registry on 30 July 1987 and 4 May 1988 respectively. Pursuant to art 20 of the Protocol on the Statute of the Court of Justice of the European Communities written observations were submitted as follows.

In both cases, by the Italian Republic, represented by L Ferrari Bravo, Head of the Department for Contentious Diplomatic Affairs, acting as agent, assisted by F Favara, Avvocato dello Stato; by the Commission of the European Communities, represented by E Traversa, a member of its Legal Department.

In *Ufficio Distrettuale delle Imposte Dirette di Fiorenzuola d'Arda v Comune di Carpaneto Piacentino* (Case 231/87), by the local authority of Carpaneto Piacentino, represented by U Pototschnig, F Tesauro, G Tesauro and M Avantaggiati.

In *Ufficio Provinciale Imposta sul Valore Aggiunto di Piacenza v Comune di Rivergaro* (Case 129/88), the government of the Netherlands, represented by H J Heinemann, Secretary General of the Ministry of Foreign Affairs; by the local authority of Piacenza, represented by F Capelli and F Tesauro; by the local authority of Rivergaro and 23 other local authorities, represented by F Tesauro, M Avantaggiati and F Mancini.

By an order of 23 November 1988, the court joined the two cases for the purposes of the oral procedure and the judgment on the ground that they were related.

On hearing the report of the Judge Rapporteur and the views of the Advocate General the court decided to open the oral procedure without any preparatory inquiry.

V Summary of the written observations submitted to the court

By way of introduction, the Italian government points out that the disputes before the Commissione Tributaria di Secondo Grado, Piacenza, in *Ufficio Distrettuale delle Imposte Dirette di Fiorenzuola d'Arda v Comune di Carpaneto Piacentino* (Case 231/87) do not deal with value added tax but with income tax and that since the rules governing each type of tax are independent of each other, the court's interpretation will at very most serve as a mere argument by analogy and will not be, as such, of such a nature as to have a direct influence on the decision of the national court. The questions referred to the court by the national court are not among those to which a reply is necessary for the purpose of the decision to be given by the national court.

1 The question concerning the direct effect of art 4(5) of the Sixth Directive

The Italian government expresses doubts as to the relevance of a reply to the first question. Italian legislation has adopted an essentially subjective approach in implementing the Sixth Directive, regarding businesses as taxable persons for the purposes of value added tax whereas the Community rules are expressed in more objective terms, referring to transactions.

Under those circumstances, the fact that the first sub-paragraph of art 4(5) of the Sixth Directive is or is not directly applicable changes nothing.

The local authority of Carpaneto Piacentino points out that the first sub-paragraph of art 4(5) is a precise and categoric provision from which no derogation is possible. It thus constitutes a rule which is directly applicable and from which persons subject to the Community legal order derive rights which member states are bound to respect.

The local authority of Piacenza compares this case to that decided by the court in its judgment of 19 January 1982, *Becker v Finanzamt Münster-Innenstadt* (Case 8/81) [1982] ECR 53, and from this it concludes that the Italian state cannot claim payment of value added tax from local authorities but, on the contrary, must amend its own internal legislation to take account of the provisions of the Sixth Directive, which are unconditional and are sufficiently precise and which require it to exempt local authorities from value added tax in respect of the transactions at issue.

In the view of the local authority of Rivergaro, art 4(5) lays down provisions which produce direct and immediate effects because they place limits or prohibitions on the member states and are sufficiently clear and precise.

Under the first sub-paragraph, public bodies have a right not to pay taxes and the member states have an obligation not to demand payment of them. The second sub-paragraph permits the member states to tax only activities engaged in by public bodies on the basis of free competition and on condition that not subjecting them to tax would lead to significant distortions of competition; in all other cases, public bodies are entitled not to be subject to the tax. Finally, the third sub-paragraph has the immediate and direct effect of giving public bodies a right not to be subject to the tax in respect of the transactions listed in Annex D which appear to be of negligible importance and imposes a binding obligation on the member states to lay down a quantitative limit distinguishing activities which are negligible from those which are not.

In order to reply to the first question, the Commission assimilates transactions not subject to value added tax, such as those involved in the present case, to exempt transactions. This enables it to rely on the criteria for interpretation concerning the direct effect of the provisions of a directive laid down by the court in the judgment

of *Becker*. Since the first sub-paragraph of art 4(5) determines what services are to
be exempted and those who are to benefit from the exemption, it is sufficiently *a*
precise to be relied on by a party to legal proceedings and applied by a court.

In that regard, the Commission considers that, vis-à-vis the state as a tax collector,
a local authority must be regarded as a mere taxpayer and therefore, as an individual
who is entitled to rely on the provisions of the Sixth Directive.

That conclusion is not invalidated by the fact that the second and third sub-
paragraphs of art 4(5) of the Sixth Directive give member states a discretion as to the *b*
degree of significance of distortions of competition and as to the negligible nature of
the activities in question in deciding whether activities engaged in by local authorities
and other public bodies are to be made subject to value added tax.

In the Commission's view, the relevance of those exceptions to the general rule of
treatment as a non-taxable person are merely potential in nature. The third sub-
paragraph applies only to the activities listed in Annex D to the directive, the second *c*
sub-paragraph is relevant only in cases in which the activity engaged in by the
public body in its capacity as a public authority competes to a significant degree
with an economic activity defined in art 4(2).

Consequently, when assessing whether or not a public body which engages in
activities that are not listed in Annex D to the directive and which compete to an
undeniably insignificant degree with the private sector qualifies as a taxable person, *d*
the Commission considers that the provision contained in the first sub-paragraph of
art 4(5) of the Sixth Directive imposes a clear, precise and unconditional obligation
on member states which may be relied on by an individual before the national courts.

*2 The question concerning the expression 'activities or transactions in which they engage
as public authorities' (see art 4(5), first sub-paragraph)* *e*

The Italian government proposes to reply to that question to the effect that by
'activities or transactions in which they engage as public authorities' the directive is
referring to all non-commercial activities engaged in by public administrations even
if they are not engaged in directly and exclusively.

In its view, the alleged equivalence between activities engaged in in the exercise
of public authority and activities carried out by public authorities in the exercise of *f*
powers vested in them as such cannot be accepted. In modern states many public
administrative activities are carried out otherwise than by an exercise of authority
and without any exercise of powers of the above nature. That does not mean that
the public administration is not acting in such cases as a public authority.

It was for that reason that the Italian legislature, in order to distinguish between
activities constituting an exercise of public authority and those which could not be *g*
regarded as such an exercise used the concept of 'carrying out of commercial or
agriculture activities'. Those activities constitute the operation of a business and a
public body which carries them out will be subject to value added tax. The doubts
which subsist concerning the use of that concept may be resolved by reference to
circular 18/360068 of 22 May 1976 of the Ministry of Finance, which contains an
exhaustive list of the activities having the objective characteristics necessary in order *h*
to be taxable and in respect of which there is therefore a presumption of operation
of a business within the meaning of the Italian value added tax legislation.

According to the Netherlands government, activities of public authorities must
be understood as activities which derive from the fundamental tasks and powers of
the organs of the state. With regard to the Netherlands legal system, the settled case
law of the Hoge Raad is that such activities consist of the implementation of tasks *j*
under a mandate conferred for that purpose by the legislature.

Furthermore, bodies governed by public law are also not taxable persons when
they engage in activities which the public authorities consider desirable by virtue of
the duty of care which they owe to the citizen but which cannot be or are not carried
out by the normal economic system. In that regard, certain extremely costly
activities, certain activities involving special risks for the public or the environment

or which operate at a deficit spring to mind. For that reason, they are not offered by undertakings subject to the normal mechanism of the market.

The local authority of Carpaneto Piacentino argues that the phrase 'activities in which they engage as public authorities' includes, first, activities engaged in by public bodies subject to the rules of public law. Next, it also includes activities which, although subject to rules of private law, are intended to meet essential public needs or have been traditionally reserved to public bodies. The latter activities are covered by the expression 'activities in respect of which they collect ... payments' and may also be engaged in by other persons, since they are subject to value added tax where treatment as non-taxable persons would lead to significant distortions of competition.

National legislation which, like the Italian legislation here in point, sets out the activities engaged in by public administrations which are subject to value added tax without excluding them in cases in which they are engaged in by public bodies in their capacity as public authorities and are subject to a legal regime involving the exercise of public authority, is therefore contrary to the Sixth Directive.

In the view of the local authority of Piacenza, activities of public bodies which could be treated as not subject to value added tax are those in which they engage on a non-contractual basis, in a context in which competition does not operate (or if it does, is not significantly distorted), outside the sectors listed in Annex D to the Sixth Directive. Concessions of cemetery vaults fulfil all of the above-mentioned conditions.

They are the result of a unilateral administrative act and thus lack any contractual basis, because property in the public domain cannot be the subject of legal relations under private law. Consequently, the fees paid by the concessionaries can only be a tax. As a result, such a concession is an act of a public authority and involves the levying of a tax which expresses the power of that authority to make rules having binding force.

It is also clear that that activity is carried on in the absence of competition and that it is not one of the activities set out in Annex D to the Sixth Directive. Consequently, the local authority of Piacenza concludes that concessions of cemetery vaults and chapels should not be subject to value added tax.

The local authority of Rivergaro provides a series of guidelines which could contribute to a definition of activities engaged in as public authorities, namely, the monopolistic nature of the public service, the purpose for which the public body provides the service and the way in which the consideration obtained by the public body is calculated.

Activities engaged in by public bodies under a monopolistic regime or to the exclusion of other persons must be regarded essentially and intrinsically as an exercise of public powers even if they are engaged in the form of the operation of a business. There may also be activities, in the exercise of public powers, which are not engaged in to the exclusion of other persons and such activities can be made subject to the tax only for the purpose of protecting free competition.

With regard to the second factor, a distinction must be drawn between the 'dues, fees, contributions or payments' collected by public bodies in the performance of their public activities and the consideration or price arising under a bilateral relationship governed by private law. Once the consideration obtained in respect of an activity engaged in by a public body is regulated by an exercise of public powers, whether it be a price which is imposed or a political price, fixed on the basis of political criteria having no direct relationship with the market value of the service and not taking account of that market value, it must be concluded that the activity is an exercise of public authority.

Even if such activities are engaged in both by private persons and public bodies, this still does not come within a context in which free competition must be protected, so that recourse must be had to a third factor to verify whether the activities constitute an exercise of public powers, namely the objective which the public body seeks to achieve by assuming and providing a certain public service. In so far as a service is provided by the public body for social purposes, to satisfy the essential needs of individuals, the service is an exercise of public authority in the sense of the Sixth Directive.

The local authority of Rivergaro also criticises the observations submitted by the Commission in *Ufficio Distrettuale delle Imposte Dirette di Fiorenzuola d'Arda v Comune di Carpaneto Piacentino* (Case 231/87). In its view, the Commission has defined activities engaged in as a public authority as those in which the public body is required to engage, those in which the public body engages through unilateral measures or conduct and those in which it engages to the exclusion of any competition from private persons.

However, in the view of the local authority of Rivergaro, the distinction between compulsory activities and those engaged on a voluntary basis makes no sense. Not merely compulsory activities, but also activities in which local authorities may decide to engage in, in the exercise of their political and administrative discretion may be public in nature and for that reason not be subject to the tax. On the other hand, the requirement that activities which are public in nature should be engaged in through unilateral measures or conduct is a formalistic requirement alien to the criteria for the interpretation of fiscal rules which should take account of the economic nature of the taxable activity and not its legal form. Finally, the requirement that activities of a public nature should be pursued to the exclusion of other persons is contradicted by the second sub-paragraph of art 4(5) of the Sixth Directive, which presupposes that the activities referred to in the first sub-paragraph are carried out in competition with private operators.

The Commission takes as its point of departure in interpreting the concept of activities engaged in as public authorities the court's decision in its judgment of 26 March 1987 in *EC Commission v Kingdom of the Netherlands* (Case 233/85) [1987] ECR 1471, and of 1 April 1982 in *Staatssecretaris van Financiën v Hong Kong Trade Development Council* (Case 89/81) [1982] ECR 1277 at 1286. Those two judgments laid down a number of principles for the interpretation of the Sixth Directive which may be applied to this case.

In the first place, the court decided that the Sixth Directive confers on value added tax a very wide scope and all exemptions must therefore be expressly mentioned and set out in detail. In the Commission's view, they must therefore be interpreted restrictively. In the second place, the court accepted that the concept of a taxable person for the purposes of value added tax is a concept of Community law and, as such, must be interpreted and applied in the same way in the entire Community.

On the basis of that case law, the Commission rejects the two criteria proposed as a basis for the definition of the concept of activities engaged in as a public authority. On the one hand, the unacceptable consequence of employing as a criterion the fact that persons subject to private law may engage in the same activity is that a public body in a member state which has an exclusive responsibility for a public duty involving the exercise of public authority must be regarded as subject to value added tax where, in another member state, the same activity could be entirely or partially engaged in by two private undertakings. In the second place, the criterion proposed by the Italian Minister of Finance in circular 18/360068 of 22 May 1976, namely making subject to value added tax services provided in the interest of private persons in return for payment, is also not valid because it does not provide a solution for cases in which the interest of the private person in having the benefit of the service and the public interest in providing it are inextricably linked. In that case, the public interest takes precedence over the private interest and, for that reason, the activities should be regarded as activities engaged in as a public authority and therefore excluded from value added tax.

What the Commission proposes is not to seek a universal and probably wholly elusive criterion defining activities engaged in by public bodies in their capacity as

public authorities, but to have recourse to a series of guidelines capable of providing
a   a solution in each individual case. Those guidelines may be deduced from the letter
and spirit of art 4 of the Sixth Directive and from the general principles governing
the entire system for the application of value added tax. The Commission
distinguishes two types of situation.

In the first place, there are activities which are unquestionably engaged in as a
public authority. Those are the activities which the national court defined as being
b   engaged in by public authorities *jure imperii*. In the Commission's view, to be
regarded as such, the activities must be engaged in directly by the public body,
regardless of whether it is by virtue of powers conferred directly on it by law or
powers delegated to it by another public body. The need for this direct engagement
in the activity in question was recognised by the court in *EC Commission v Kingdom
of the Netherlands* (Case 233/85) [1987] ECR 1471 at 1490.
c   On the other hand, the Commission considers that it is not essential that the
activity should constitute the exercise of exclusive authority by the public body.
The activities of notaries are a good example of activities which, although engaged
in the capacity of a public authority, may be pursued either by public officials or by
members of a liberal profession such as notaries. When they are engaged in by public
officials, such activities are not subject to value added tax, which is not the case if
d   they are engaged in by notaries, as the court pointed out in the judgment in
EC Commission v Kingdom of the Netherlands (Case 233/85) [1987] ECR 1471 at
1490.

Nevertheless, there are other activities engaged in by public bodies which it is not
so simple to classify. They are activities which do not involve the use of coercive
power and which consist, not of formal measures typical of the public authorities,
e   but of the provision of public services such as those referred to by the Commissione
Tributaria di Secondo Grado, Piacenza, in its order of reference and which are set
out in Royal Decree 2578 of 15 October 1925. That decree contains a list of 19
activities among which is to be found the construction of water mains and fountains,
the construction of sewers, the installation and management of pharmacies, burial
services, etc.

f   In order to determine whether the activities concerned are engaged in as a public
authority and therefore excluded from value added tax, the Commission proposes
three tests. The public body must have an *obligation* to engage in the activities but
may engage in them directly or through municipal enterprises. Next, they must be
engaged in through *unilateral* measures or conduct on the part of the public body,
establishing between that body and the public legal relations based on public law.
g   The measures or conduct involved must therefore be the expression of public law
rights or powers. Finally, the activities must be engaged in by the public body in an
exclusive manner, in other words, it must have an absolute monopoly, preventing
private operators from engaging in similar activities to those administered by the
public body (that is the case in Italy in regard to concessions for graves and cemetery
vaults or the collection and transport or solid urban refuse). It is perfectly possible
h   that such activities may be engaged in competition with private operators, as is the
case in the United Kingdom in regard to the provision and management of
cemeteries, but in that case, the activity engaged in by the public body is not
excluded from value added tax because there is of necessity a significant degree of
competition within the meaning of the Sixth Directive.

In its observations in *Ufficio Provinciale Imposta sul Valore Aggiunto di Piacenza
j   v Comune di Rivergaro* (Case 129/88), the Commission provides particulars regarding
the guidelines for determining the nature of the activity engaged in by a public
body.

The Commission bases itself on the judgment of the court of 8 May 1988 in *Apple
and Pear Development Council v Customs and Excise Comrs* (Case 102/86) [1988] STC
221 in which the court decided that the functions exercised by the council did not
constitute the supply of services effected for consideration within the meaning of
art 2(1) of the Sixth Directive and provided certain guidelines on the concept of the

supply of services effected for consideration which is also useful as a source of indications for defining the concept of activities engaged in by public bodies in their capacity as public authorities.

The court decided in *Apple and Pear Development Council* that the concept of the supply of services effected for consideration presupposes the existence of a direct link between the service provided and the consideration received and not merely an indirect and general connection between the amount paid by the citizen to the public body and the service rendered by that body.

The Commission deduces from the court's statement to the effect that no relationship existed between the level of the benefits which individual growers obtained from the services provided by the council and the amount of the mandatory charges which they were obliged to pay that in order for such a link to be regarded as direct, there must be a direct relationship of cause and effect or of economic equivalence, or both, not merely between the service rendered and the consideration received but between the level of the benefits obtained by the individual and the amount of the contribution asked of him. Consequently, when there is no fundamental relationship between the value of the two contributions, that is a significant indication that the service provided by the public body is not effected for consideration.

Finally, the court emphasised that the charges which growers had to pay to the council were imposed by virtue not of contractual but of statutory obligations. That is also the case in regard to dues, fees, contributions or payments within the meaning of art 4(5) of the Sixth Directive, the basis of which is to be found in the laws, regulations or administration provisions governing the activities of the public body and which cannot constitute consideration for or the price of the service provided by the public body but are that part of the expenditure inherent in the provision of services which the legislature had decided to impose unilaterally on the recipient of the services on the basis of fiscal, social or other considerations.

The Commission concludes that the criterion employed by the court in *Apple and Pear Development Council* to define services effected other than for consideration and, therefore, not subject to value added tax, namely, the absence of a connection between the legal obligations to be borne by the two parties to the exchange and the absence of a connection between the economic value of the two obligations, coincides largely with the two positive indicators which the Commission proposed in its observations in *Ufficio Distrettuale delle Imposte Dirette di Fiorenzuola d'Arda v Comune di Carpaneto Piacentino* (Case 231/87) in order to define activities engaged in as a public authority, when it referred to activities of the public administration which do not involve the exercise of coercive powers in the strict sense of the term, that is to say, an *obligation* on the public body to engage in a given activity, *independently* of the revenue which it may thereby obtain, and the pursuit of the activity in question not by means of ordinary contracts but by means of *unilateral measures or conduct* on the part of the public body.

3 The question concerning activities or transactions which, although engaged in as a public authority, must be taxed (see art 4(5), second sub-paragraph)

According to the Italian government, the expression 'such activities or transactions', used in the second sub-paragraph of art 4(5) to refer to the activities in respect of which public bodies are to be regarded as taxable persons, simply means activities or transactions referred to in the preceding sub-paragraph, that is to say, activities or transactions in which public bodies engage as public authorities. In its view, the statement of the Commissione Tributaria di Secondo Grado to the effect that the 'institutional activities' engaged in by a public body are merely those engaged in to the exclusion of other persons cannot be regarded as correct because, in the modern state, institutional activities may be engaged in by a public body under a system not involving public rights. It is therefore possible for distortions of competition to occur if public bodies were not taxable in respect of certain transactions whereas the same transactions would be taxable if they had been carried out by private competitors. The purpose of the second sub-paragraph of art 4(5) of the Sixth Directive is precisely to prevent such distortions from occurring.

According to the Netherlands government, the second sub-paragraph of art 4(5) of the Sixth Directive implies that if the activities defined in the first sub-paragraph are engaged in also by private undertakings, the public bodies engaging in such activities are themselves also subject to value added tax if their treatment as non-taxable persons would lead to significant distortions of competition. The determination of the existence or otherwise of a distortion of competition must be made independently by each member state except in regard to the activities listed in Annex D to the directive. With regard to those activities, it had already been concluded at the time when the directive was drafted that they would be carried on very largely outside the sphere of the public authorities, so that they would always be subject to the tax except if they were on a negligible scale. The question whether the activities referred to in Annex D are negligible must be considered in each individual case.

The local authority of Carpaneto Piacentino interprets this question as seeking to ascertain whether the activities of local authorities governed by Royal Decree 2587 of 15 October 1925, which are not engaged in to the exclusion of others persons, fall within the scope of the Community rule. It replies in the affirmative to the question this formulated in as much as it considers that if such public activities are engaged in in competition with private operators, they will be subject to the tax if exemption therefrom disturbs competition. On the other hand, the local authority of Carpaneto Piacentino considers that where such activities are engaged in to the exclusion of other persons or where their treatment as non-taxable does not disturb competition, it is contrary to Community law to make them subject to value added tax.

The local authority of Rivergaro emphasises first that the concept of activities carried out in the operation of a business or commercial activities and the concept of the exercise of public authority are not two alternative concepts. It is perfectly possible for public authority to be exercised through the medium of a business undertaking. Such activities should not be subject to value added tax under the Sixth Directive.

Furthermore, the Sixth Directive does not merely exclude from the basis of assessment activities governed by public law and producing receipts of a fiscal nature or, in general, of a public nature. It also excludes income governed by private law where the public body obtains it from activities engaged in for public motives and purposes. On the other hand, under the Italian legislation, such commercial activities are subject to tax in as much as they cannot be distinguished from activities engaged in in the operation of a business, which are always subject to the tax, and activities which are not so engaged in and are not so subject.

In particular, circular 18/360068 of 22 May 1976 of the Ministry of Finance includes in the list of activities subject in every case to value added tax not merely the activities which are listed in Annex D to the directive and which, for that reason, are subject to the tax, but also other services that are rendered by public bodies for a consideration and must be regarded, by reason both of the purposes for which they are performed and of the form of consideration received by the local authorities, as the exercise of public authority and, therefore, as excluded from the tax regime. Such a situation is incompatible with the Sixth Directive.

The Commission interprets the expression 'such activities or transactions' in the second sub-paragraph of art 4(5) as being equivalent to 'activities or transactions mentioned above'. However, it does not include in that category all activities engaged in by public bodies as public authorities but only those referred to in the second part of the first sub-paragraph, namely those in respect of which public bodies collect dues, fees, contributions or payments. That is fully in accordance with the principles laid down by the court in *Staatssecretaris van Financiën v Hong Kong Trade Development Council* (Case 89/81) [1982] ECR 1277 at 1286–1287 according to which any person who carries on activities with the object of obtaining payment of consideration and does not carry them on exclusively free of charge is taxable, whether the services are private in nature or a fortiori, where they constitute free services intended for the public.

That conclusion is also the most logical one if regard is had to the purpose of the provision in question. Only activities or transactions in respect of which a public body receives a consideration of whatever kind are capable of competing with similar activities engaged in by private persons.

In any event, in order to determine whether such activities may be regarded as being engaged in as a public authority, reference must be made to the guidelines worked out by the Commission in its reply to the second question.

4 The question concerning the criteria to be used to determine the existence of significant distortions of competition

It follows from the replies given by the Italian government to the first three questions that it considers that the Italian legislature is not required to incorporate in the legislation on value added tax the criterion of 'significant distortions of competition' but, on the contrary, it is entitled to determine a priori the activities which are likely to give rise to such distortions and to make them for that reason subject to value added tax.

The local authority of Carpaneto Piacentino argues that the criterion of significant distortion of competition must be introduced into the national legislation implementing the Sixth Directive, which amounts to saying that where the activities of public authorities are engaged in to the exclusion of other persons and cannot therefore interfere with free competition, they must be excluded from value added tax. It concludes that national legislation such as that in force in Italy which makes subject to the tax public activities engaged in by the public body to the exclusion of other persons is contrary to the Community rules.

According to the local authority of Rivergaro, the Italian legislation is incompatible with the Sixth Directive because it has made subject to the tax all public activities engaged in for consideration without distinguishing between those which are carried on in competition with private contractors and those which are not.

In those circumstances, the public bodies are entitled, even where there are no national provisions defining the concept of significant distortions of competition, to argue vis-à-vis the tax authorities that the activity which the latter are seeking to tax is an activity which failure to tax will not cause major distortions of competition and it is for the courts to judge in each individual case whether the conditions for treatment as non-taxable persons laid down in the second sub-paragraph of art 4(5) have or have not been fulfilled.

The Commission points out that, in accordance with the second sub-paragraph of art 4(5) of the Sixth Directive, member states merely have an obligation to obtain a particular result, namely to tax activities and transactions engaged in by public bodies as public authorities and in respect of which they collect dues, fees, contributions or payments, in so far as treatment as non-taxable persons would lead to significant distortions of competition.

The fact that those results are achieved, either by the literal transposition into national legislation of the general criterion of significant distortion of competition, leaving the problems inherent in the taxation of specific activities or transactions to be resolved in each individual case, or by the drawing-up by the legislature or the tax authorities of lists of activities falling within the scope of the tax on the ground that they lead to significant distortions of competition is of no importance, the choice of the one or the other legislative technique being an expression of the choice of form and methods which member states have under the third paragraph of art 189 of the EEC Treaty in regard to the transposition of directives.

Consequently, the Commission considers that the second sub-paragraph of art 4(5) of the Sixth Directive does not impose an obligation on member states to transpose literally into the national law the criterion concerning significant distortions

of competition. However, they are required to apply that criterion in practice and
a to make a concrete assessment of the situation in regard to competition in order to
avoid distortions occurring by virtue of the fact that public activities are not subject
to value added tax.

5 The question concerning the criterion for determining whether activities are negligible

For the Italian government, the question whether the Italian legislation on value
b added tax must or must not use the criterion of negligible scale laid down in the
third sub-paragraph of art 4(5) to exclude from value added tax the transactions
listed in Annex D to the directive is of very little interest. All that is required is to
state that the negligible scale of an activity must be assessed vis-à-vis the taxable
person and not vis-à-vis each ultimate consumer taken individually.

Since the criterion adopted by the Community rules is to leave a broad discretion
c to the national legislatures, it is possible to draw up selective rules excluding persons
whose tax liability is very small, or non-selective rules making even minimal added
values subject to taxation. However, the result would be the same because in the
second case a larger number of traders would have to be permitted to benefit from
the deduction provided for in art 17 of the Sixth Directive.

The local authority of Carpaneto Piacentino claims that legislatures, such as that
d in Italy, which make the public activities listed in Annex D to the directive subject
to value added tax without excluding those of negligible importance do not comply
with the Community rules laying down an obligation to fix a threshold below which
there is no liability to value added tax.

According to the local authority of Rivergaro, since the Italian legislation regards
as taxable all the activities listed in Annex D to the directive, without taking into
e consideration whether or not they are of negligible importance, public bodies are
entitled to object, when payment of the tax is demanded by the administration, that
the activity in question, although falling within Annex D to the directive, is not
taxable because it is of negligible importance. Having regard to the direct
applicability of the directive, it is for the courts to judge in each case whether the
conditions for treatment as non-taxable persons laid down in the directive have been
f fulfilled.

For its part, the Commission points out that the third sub-paragraph of art 4(5) of
the Sixth Directive grants member states a mere option to exclude from liability to
value added tax the activities engaged in by public bodies which are set out in
Annex D to the directive in so far as the scale of those activities is negligible. Just as
in the case of the previous question, and with even greater force since what is here
g concerned is the exercise of an option and not the implementation of an obligation
to obtain a particular result, the member states are not absolutely required to
incorporate literally into their fiscal legislation the general criterion of negligible
scale so as to exclude from the scope of value added tax one or other of the activities
set out in Annex D to the directive.

There is nothing to prevent the competent national authorities from themselves
h making an assessment as to whether or not any of the activities referred to in
Annex D are of negligible scale and to provide directly in legislative or administrative
texts of a general nature that one or other of those activities is excluded from the
scope of value added tax by virtue of the fact that it is of little practical significance.

15 March 1989. **The Advocate General (J Mischo)** delivered the following
j opinion.

Mr President, members of the court,
1. The returns submitted by the local authority of Carpaneto for the purposes of
the levying of direct taxes for 1980, 1981, 1982 and 1983 and those concerning value
added tax submitted by the local authority of Rivergaro for 1981, 1982, 1983 and
1985 were all the subject of rectified assessments made by the competent Italian

authorities on the ground that they did not take account of sums of money or fees received for certain transactions regarded as commercial activities within the *a* meaning of art 4 of Presidential Decree 633/72.

2. The transactions at issue were the following: concessions of graves, cemetery vaults and chapels, leasing and selling of land in connection with subsidised house-building, the taking-out of public ownership and sale of a piece of roadway, water supply, the concession for the operation of a public weighbridge, the sale of wood obtained from the lopping of trees and the sale of fittings for cemetery vaults.   *b*

3. Before the national courts, both of Piacenza, namely the Commissione Tributaria di Secondo Grado (Tax Appeals Board) in *Ufficio Distrettuale delle Imposte Dirette di Fiorenzuola d'Arda v Comune di Carpaneto Piacentino* (Case 231/87) and the Commissione Tributaria di Primo Grado (First Instance Tax Board) in *Ufficio Provinciale Imposta sul Valore Aggiunto di Piacenza v Comune di Rivergaro* (Case 129/88), the local authorities concerned, as well as 23 other local authorities *c* which intervened in support of the claims of the local authority of Rivergaro, claimed that under art 4(5) of EC Council Directive 77/388 on the harmonisation of the laws of the member states relating to turnover taxes—common system of value added tax: uniform basis of assessment (the Sixth Directive), they were not 'taxable persons' in respect of the transactions at issue and, therefore, were entitled not to charge value added tax on them.   *d*

4. Article 4(5) of the Sixth Directive is drafted in the following terms:

'States, regional and local government authorities and other bodies governed by public law shall not be considered taxable persons in respect of the activities or transactions in which they engage as public authorities, even where they collect dues, fees, contributions or payments in connection with these activities or transactions.   *e*

However, when they engage in such activities or transactions, they shall be considered taxable persons in respect of these activities or transactions where treatment as non-taxable persons would lead to significant distortions of competition.

In any case, these bodies shall be considered taxable persons in relation to the activities listed in Annex D, provided they are not carried out on such a small *f* scale as to be negligible.

Member States may consider activities of these bodies which are exempt under Article 13 or 28 as activities which they engage in as public authorities.'

5. The series of questions referred to this court by the national courts, to be found in the report for the hearing, deal exclusively with the interpretation of that *g* provision and not with its concrete application to the local authorities and to the activities in question in the main proceedings. The questions concern, on the one hand, the problem of the 'direct effect' of art 4(5) (first question in both cases), which is linked to that of the exact scope of the obligation to transpose that provision of the directive into national law (questions 4 and 5 in *Ufficio Distrettuale delle Imposte Dirette di Fiorenzuola d'Arda v Comune di Carpaneto Piacentino* (Case 231/87) and *h* question 2 in *Ufficio Provinciale Imposta sul Valore Aggiunto di Piacenza v Comune di Rivergaro* (Case 129/88)), and, on the other hand, the concept of activities or transactions engaged in 'as public authorities' which are not subject to value added tax (question 2 in Case 231/87), including the question whether such activities or transactions are covered by the second sub-paragraph of the provision at issue (question 3 in Case 231/87).   *j*

6. Before considering those questions in the order in which they were referred to the court, let me go on to point out that the preliminary observation of the Italian government to the effect that the dispute in the main proceedings in *Ufficio Distrettuale delle Imposte Dirette di Fiorenzuola d'Arda v Comune di Carpaneto Piacentino* (Case 231/87) is not concerned with value added tax but with income tax and that, therefore, a decision is not 'necessary' to enable the national court to 'give

judgment' (see the terms of art 177 of the EEC Treaty) cannot be accepted.
a According to established case law of the court, under the system laid down in art 177, it is for the national court to examine, in the light of the facts of the case, whether a preliminary ruling on the part of the Court of Justice of the European Communities is necessary or relevant (see *Smanor SA* (Case 298/87) [1988] ECR 4489 and *Giménez Zaera v Instituto Nacional de la Seguridad Social y Tesorería General de la Seguridad Social* (Case 126/86) [1987] ECR 3697). Moreover, in its order for reference, the
b national court expressly pointed out that the Italian legislation on value added tax and the legislation on direct taxation 'are connected to such an extent that if a given activity is not liable to value added tax, the income arising from it can also not be subject to direct taxation, and vice versa' (see the report for the hearing).

I The 'direct effect' of art 4(5) of the Sixth Directive

c   7. Whereas the first question in *Ufficio Distrettuale delle Imposte Dirette di Fiorenzuola d'Arda v Comune di Carpaneto Piacentino* (Case 231/87) seeks to know whether 'the principle set out in the first sub-paragraph of art 4(5) of the Sixth Directive, which excludes from the category of activities subject to value added tax so-called "institutional" activities, is directly applicable even in the absence of a specific national provision', that referred to the court in *Ufficio Provinciale Imposta*
d *sul Valore Aggiunto di Piacenza v Comune di Rivergaro* (Case 129/88) deals with art 4(5) in its entirety. That approach seems to me to be particularly appropriate in this case since the 'principle' set out in the first sub-paragraph is singularly modified and weakened in the following sub-paragraphs.

   8. It should be noted that art 4(5) is built in 'tiers', so to speak, proceeding by exceptions and counter-exceptions. Moreover, in the second and third sub-
e paragraphs, it employs terms such as 'significant distortions of competition' or 'activities . . . not carried out on such a small scale as to be negligible', which leave a certain discretion to those called on to apply them. It is in fact, in particular, the problem of whether the member states are required merely to insert those criteria into their national legislation or if they must lay down in detail the quantitative limits resulting from them with which questions 4 and 5 in *Ufficio Distrettuale delle*
f *Imposte Dirette di Fiorenzuola d'Arda v Comune di Carpaneto Piacentino* (Case 231/87) and question 2(c) and (d) in *Ufficio Provinciale Imposta sul Valore Aggiunto di Piacenza v Comune di Rivergaro* (Case 129/88) are concerned.

   9. In *Becker v Finanzamt Münster-Innenstadt* (Case 8/81) [1982] ECR 53, the court was called on to rule on the direct effect of a provision of the Sixth Directive, namely art 13B(d)1.
g   10. In its judgment of 19 January 1982 the court in *Becker* (at 71) pointed out that

> '. . . wherever the provisions of a directive appear, as far as their subject-matter is concerned, to be unconditional and sufficiently precise, those provisions may, in the absence of implementing measures adopted within the prescribed period, be relied upon as against any national provision which is incompatible with the directive or in so far as the provisions define rights which
h individuals are able to assert against the State.'

   11. That is valid not merely when the provisions of a directive have not been given effect at the expiry of the period prescribed for its implementation but also where a member state has not correctly implemented a directive (see *Marshall v Southampton and South West Hampshire Area Health Authority (Teaching)* (Case
j 152/84) [1986] QB 401 at 422, and *Borrie Clarke v Chief Adjudication Officer* (Case 384/85) [1987] ECR 2865).

   12. The rule contained in the first sub-paragraph of art 4(5) is, considered in itself, sufficiently precise: the member states must exclude from liability to value added tax activities or transactions engaged in by bodies governed by public law as 'public authorities'.

   13. The fact that the first sub-paragraph does not indicate precisely what those

activities are makes no difference. That concept is part of a provision of Community law the interpretation of which cannot be left to the discretion of each member state.   *a*

14. However, the question is whether, notwithstanding the exceptions which follow, the rule is unconditional. The Commission draws attention to the fact that those exceptions are formulated in such a way as to leave the member states a discretion as to the degree of significance of the distortions of competition and whether or not the activities listed in Annex D are carried out on such a small scale as to be negligible. Like the Commission, I consider that that discretion necessarily   *b* permits the member states to place conditions on or to restrict the scope of the exceptions in the second and third sub-paragraphs and, thereby, the general rule laid down in the first sub-paragraph itself.

15. However, I also share the Commission's opinion, based in particular on the judgment in *Marshall* (Case 152/84) [1986] QB 401, according to which the rule laid down in the first sub-paragraph is unconditional and precise in so far as a given   *c* activity can in no case come within the scope of the exceptions.

16. That is so in regard to an activity which, at the same time, can in no case give rise to distortions of competition because it is reserved by statute exclusively for bodies governed by public law; is not included among the activities listed in Annex D to the directive.

17. In Italy, concessions for graves and cemetery vaults seem to fulfil both of those   *d* conditions. On the other hand, the supply of water, even if it is reserved exclusively for bodies governed by public law, does not fulfil the second condition because it is expressly listed in Annex D.

18. As we shall will see in a moment, an activity reserved exclusively for bodies governed by public law must be regarded as an activity engaged in by them 'as public authorities' within the meaning of the first sub-paragraph of art 4(5).   *e*

19. It may therefore in any event be concluded that art 4(5) may be relied on by a body governed by public law in support of a plea that a specific activity engaged in by it can under no circumstances come within the scope of the exceptions provided for in the second and third sub-paragraphs of art 4(5) and must therefore qualify for the application to it of the rule of treatment as a non-taxable person provided for in the first sub-paragraph.   *f*

20. Is it possible to go a step further and say, as the Commission does, that treatment as a non-taxable person may also be claimed in regard to an activity in respect of which 'competition from the private sector is undoubtedly insignificant'? Let us imagine for example that the law in a member state requires local authorities to organise the removal of domestic refuse but does not prohibit private individuals from providing that service in parallel. May a local authority claim to be treated as   *g* non-taxable for value added tax purposes in respect of that activity on the ground either that, in the country as a whole, very few private individuals have taken advantage of the opportunity available to them or that in its district no private individual is offering such a service and that the distortion of competition which could result from the treatment of that activity as non-taxable is not therefore 'significant' or indeed that it is non-existent in that district?   *h*

21. In that regard, it seems to me first that a member state may, without infringing the directive, provide that, in principle, that activity is subject to value added tax whilst permitting the competent administration to grant derogations in the light of local circumstances. However, what is the situation if the member state has not made any provision for derogating from the rule?

22. I consider that in such a case, a local authority could not plead the absence of   *j* distortions of competition at local level as a basis for seeking a declaration in the courts that the rule adopted by the member state is incompatible with the directive and must be set aside. A member state cannot be obliged to provide for derogations from its legislation in order to take account of special local situations. It has a discretion in that regard.

23. Could a local authority plead the absence of significant distortions of
a competition at the level of the country as a whole? Here again I am of the opinion
that the state has a discretion in deciding the point from which a distortion of
competition fulfils that condition. It might consider that the distortion is sufficiently
significant in certain places to justify making the activity in question subject to value
added tax in the entire country.

24. The criterion of 'significant distortions of competition' is thus not sufficiently
b precise to be relied on by a body governed by public law in opposition to a provision
of national law.

25. It remains for me to consider whether, in respect of one of the activities listed
in Annex D to the directive, a body governed by public law may argue before a
national court that that activity is carried out on such a small scale as to be negligible
and should therefore not be subject to tax.

c 26. There are several ways in which member states may take account of that
criterion. They may include it as such in their national legislation and make the
competent administration responsible for applying it in each individual case. They
may also designate the kinds of activities listed in Annex D which, generally and for
the whole country, are deemed to be carried out on such a small scale as to be
negligible (eg local fairs). Lastly, they may also make a type of activity subject to
d value added tax while providing a *threshold* below which the activity in question is
not so subject (eg the annual turnover of a local authority in respect of water supply).
The criterion of the negligible scale of the activity could therefore lead to different
situations in different local authority areas.

27. However, what is the situation if a member state totally disregards that
provision of the directive, that is to say, if it simultaneously fails to adopt the
e negligible-scale criterion, as such, in its legislation, to exclude from liability to
taxation specifically designated activities which it regards as negligible or to lay
down a threshold in respect of the activities listed in Annex D?

28. I consider that in that case, the member state has not correctly transposed the
directive into its national law because it is beyond dispute that the directive lays
down the principle that the activities listed in Annex D which are carried out on
f such a small scale as to be negligible are not subject to taxation. Perhaps the Council
opened the way to excessive complications by placing that criterion in art 4(5) but
the criterion in question does not constitute an option which the member states are
free to make use of or not. The third sub-paragraph of art 4(5) clearly lays down two
concurrent conditions: bodies governed by public law 'shall be considered taxable
persons in relation to the activities listed in Annex D, *provided* they are not carried
g out on such a small scale as to be negligible'. The word 'provided' means here 'in so
far as'.

29. The *principle* thus established is clear and unconditional. However, it cannot
be determined from the provision itself what is to be understood by 'negligible'. In
the last analysis, the obligation thus imposed on the member states is not sufficiently
precise for it to be relied on by bodies governed by public law before the national
h courts even if the state has been at fault in totally disregarding that component of
art 4(5) when transposing the directive into its national law. If that indeed has been
the case, it is for the Commission, if necessary, to bring an action against the member
state in question for failure to fulfil its obligations.

30. Consequently, I propose that the reply to the first question referred to the
court in both cases should be as follows:

j
> Article 4(5) of the Sixth Directive may be relied on by a body governed by
> public law before the national courts in opposition to the application of a
> national provision making it subject to value added tax in regard to an activity
> which is not listed in Annex D to the directive and the pursuit of which is
> reserved exclusively for bodies governed by public law.

II The concept of activities or transactions engaged in 'as public authorities'

31. In the second question referred to the court in _Ufficio Distrettuale delle Imposte Dirette di Fiorenzuola d'Arda v Comune di Carpaneto Piacentino_ (Case 231/87), the national court asks whether the Community legislature intended 'to identify by means of the phrase "activities or transactions in which they engage as public authorities" in the first sub-paragraph of article 4(5) those activities which the public authorities carry out directly and exclusively pursuant to powers vested in them as public authorities, albeit delegated to them'.

32. I consider that that question must be interpreted as meaning that the national court wishes to know whether the activities in which bodies governed by public law engage directly and exclusively in the exercise of their powers under public law constitute activities engaged in as public authorities, which may in no circumstances give rise to liability to value added tax.

33. I will therefore consider in turn what are the criteria which make it possible to determine the meaning of the expression 'activity engaged in as a public authority' and in which cases such an activity necessarily comes within the scope of the rule of treatment as a non-taxable person for value added tax purposes as laid down in the first sub-paragraph of art 4(5).

A Activities or transactions engaged in as public authorites

34. In its judgment of 26 March 1987 in the 'notaries and bailiffs' case, _EC Commission v Kingdom of the Netherlands_ (Case 235/85) [1987] ECR 1471 at 1490 the court confirmed, referring to its judgment of 11 July 1985, in _EC Commission v Federal Republic of Germany_ (Case 107/84) [1985] ECR 2655, that—

> '. . . bodies governed by public law are not automatically exempted in respect of all the activities in which they engage but only in respect of those which form part of their specific duties as public authorities.'

35. It follows, as a secondary consideration, from that statement of the court that the fact that an activity is engaged in directly by the local authority itself does not of itself lead to the conclusion that it is part of the local authority's specific duties as a public authority. (In my view, activities engaged in through municipal undertakings must, so long as they are pursued in the name and on behalf of the local authority, also be included among the activities 'engaged in directly'.)

36. On the other hand, activities engaged in by a local authority pursuant to 'powers vested in it as a public authority' undoubtedly form part of its specific duty as a public authority. What does that mean?

37. Like the Commission, I would suggest that the court adopt in that regard the definition proposed by the Advocate General (G Mancini) in his opinion in _EC Commission v French Republic_ (Case 307/84) [1986] ECR 1725 at 1732, namely that that concept refers to activities which involve 'acts of will which affect private individuals by requiring their obedience or, in the event of disobedience, by compelling them to comply'.

38. Powers vested in a body as a public authority are exercised in concrete terms by authorisations, licences, permits, concessions, registrations, issue of certified copies, penalties for failure to comply with laws or regulations, etc.

39. Although 'activities engaged pursuant to powers vested [in a body] as a public authority' therefore constitute in all cases 'activities engaged in as public authorities', the latter concept also covers other types of activity. The concepts of 'activities or transactions engaged in as public authorities' and 'activities engaged in pursuant to powers vested [in a body] as a public authority' are not in fact synonymous.

40. That follows clearly from the travaux préparatoires for the Sixth Directive. In its commentary on art 4 in the presentation which it made of its proposal for the

Sixth Directive, the Commission stated that—

'... persons governed by public law must be regarded as taxable persons in so far as they engage in economic activities which may be separated from the concept of public authority, that is to say, activities which could be engaged in by persons governed by private law without damaging the fundamental powers and authority in regard to general administration, justice, or national security and defence of States, provinces, local authorities and other bodies governed by public law.'

41. However, art 4(5), as the Commission proposed it, was different from the version finally adopted. The proposal was worded as follows (see (1973) OJ C80, p 4):

'States, regional and local government authorities, and other bodies governed by public law shall not be considered taxable persons as regards their activities pursued as public authorities.

However, when they engage in the transactions referred to in paragraph 1, they shall be considered taxable persons in respect of such transactions ...'

42. The 'transactions referred to in paragraph 1' were 'transactions pertaining to the occupations specified in paragraph 2', which defined 'the occupations referred to in paragraph 1' in the same terms as the version of art 4(2) now in force, that is to say, as 'all activities of producers, traders and persons supplying services' (see (1973) OJ C80, p 3). The Commission's proposal thus distinguished clearly between activities engaged in as public authorities and economic activities, and it defined the first concept as meaning activities constituting an exercise of powers conferred by public law.

43. It must therefore be concluded that by adopting the version of art 4(5) now in force, the Council deliberately abandoned that clear distinction and gave the concept of 'activities or transactions engaged in as public authorities' a wider meaning, including activities other than merely those falling under the fundamental powers of the public authority in the areas of general administration, justice or national security and defence. The Council thus opted for an intermediate solution between, on the one hand, the extreme position of the Commission, which sought to make all the economic activities of bodies governed by public law liable to value added tax and, on the other hand, EC Council Directive 67/228 of 11 April 1967 on the harmonisation of legislation of the member states concerning turnover taxes—structures and procedures for application of the common system of value added tax (the Second Directive), under which the member states were entitled to exempt bodies governed by public law from value added tax in respect of such activities (see the last two paragraphs of s 2 of Annex A to the Second Directive, which, according to art 20, forms an integral part thereof).

44. It is therefore clear that certain activities of producers, traders and persons supplying services (see art 4(1) and (2) of the Sixth Directive) engaged in by local authorities must be regarded as 'activities engaged in as public authorities'. However, how can such activities be recognised?

45. The various parties to the dispute, the Italian and Netherlands governments and the Commission proposed several criteria for that purpose.

46. The local authority of Rivergaro put forward the criterion of the *purpose to be achieved*. However, at the hearing, the Commission rightly pointed out that in its judgment in the 'notaries and bailiffs' case, *EC Commission v Kingdom of the Netherlands* (Case 235/85) [1987] ECR 1471 at 1487, the court decided that the term economic activities is 'objective in character, in the sense that the activity is considered *per se* and without regard to its purpose or results'. That must also apply to an economic activity engaged in by a public body in its capacity as a public authority. Practically any activity engaged in by a local authority pursues an objective in the public interest, including the supply of water or the provision of a transport network. However, the third sub-paragraph of art 4(5) and Annex D

provide that in respect of such activities, local authorities are taxable persons. On the other hand, among the exemptions provided for in art 13 is to be found a considerable number of activities which may be engaged in also by public bodies (see art 13A(1)(b), (g) and (h)) in the public interest in order to satisfy essential individual or public needs, see art 13A(1)(i). The last sub-paragraph of art 4(5) merely permits the member states to regard such activities as being engaged in as public authorities but does not require them to do so.

47. I am also not convinced that the reference to the judgment of the court of 8 March 1988 in *Apple and Pear Development Council v Customs and Excise Comrs* (Case 102/86) [1988] STC 221, made by the Commission in its written observations in *Ufficio Provinciale Imposta sul Valore Aggiunto di Piacenza v Comune di Rivergaro* (Case 129/88) in support of the criteria which it put forward in *Ufficio Distrettuale delle Imposte Dirette di Fiorenzuola d'Arda v Comune di Carpaneto Piacentino* (Case 231/87) is necessarily relevant to this case.

48. *Apple and Pear Development Council* was concerned with the interpretation of art 2 of the Sixth Directive in order to determine whether the exercise by the Development Council of functions assigned to it by law and the fact that it imposed an annual charge on its members for the purpose of enabling it to meet administrative and other expenses incurred or to be incurred in the exercise of such functions constituted in 'the supply of . . . services effected for consideration', that is to say, transactions which were taxable within the meaning of the article. In these cases, the court is being asked to interpret art 4(5) in order to determine whether a public body is or is not a taxable person in respect of certain activities in which it engages.

49. It is true that in his opinion of 28 October 1987 in *Apple and Pear Development Council*, the Advocate General (Sir Gordon Slynn) ([1988] STC 221 at 232) considered that there was a link between the concepts of taxable transaction and taxable person in the sense that 'for there to be liability to tax there must be both a taxable transaction and a taxable person'. However, he pointed out that they are 'distinct concepts' and, further on, he emphasised their autonomous nature and stated that if, as he concluded (at 235), the transactions in question did not constitute the supply of services for consideration, 'then there is no liability to value added tax even if the person involved in what has been done is a taxable person'.

50. Furthermore, contrary to what appears to be the Commission's view, I do not believe that it was the mandatory, that is to say, not contractual but statutory, nature of the charges in question nor even the fact that the amount thereof did not reflect the economic value of the services provided which was the decisive factor in determining the court's decision. On the one hand, it can be seen from the judgment (see [1988] STC 221 at 238) that it was not because the individual producer was obliged to pay the charge but because he had to pay it 'whether or not a given service of the Council confers a benefit on him' that the court concluded that there was no direct relationship between the service rendered and the consideration received. On the other hand, according to the court's case law (see *Staatssecretaris van Financiën v Coöperatieve Ardappelenbewaarplaats G A* (Case 154/80) [1981] ECR 445), which has once again been confirmed in the judgment of 23 November 1988 in *Naturally Yours Cosmetics Ltd v Customs and Excise Comrs* (Case 230/87) [1988] STC 879 at 894, that consideration 'is a subjective value, since the basis of assessment is the consideration actually received and not a value estimated according to objective criteria'. It was therefore more by virtue of the *absence of the necessary link between the advantages and the consideration therefor* than by virtue of the imbalance between the level of those two items that the court decided in *Apple Pear Development Council* (Case 102/86) [1988] STC 221 at 238 that 'mandatory charges of the kind imposed on the growers in this case do not constitute consideration having a direct link with the benefits accruing to individual growers as a result of the exercise of the Council's functions'. That seems to me to be all the more true because the first argument on which the court based its judgment (at 237–238) was precisely the fact that those

benefits were to the advantage of the entire industry concerned and not necessarily
a to that of each individual grower.

51. Finally, the Commission's argument does not seem to me to be free of all
contradictions because, while seeing an indication that an activity is carried on as a
public authority in the fact that the dues or contributions paid do not constitute
consideration for the service provided 'but are that part of the expenditure inherent
in the provision of services which the legislature has decided to impose unilaterally
b on the recipient of the services on the basis of fiscal, social or other considerations'
(see the report for the hearing), it rightly contested at the hearing the criterion based
on the method of calculating the consideration proposed by the local authority of
Rivergaro, according to which an activity in respect of which a public body obtains
consideration 'regulated by an exercise of public powers, whether it be a price which
is imposed or a political price, fixed on the basis of political criteria having no direct
c relationship with the market value of the service' (see the report for the hearing)
constitutes activity engaged in as a public authority.

52. I would add that if that criterion were to be accepted, a local authority could
never be subject to value added tax for the transport services, swimming pools,
theatres and museums which it brings into being because the price charged to the
user is almost always a 'political price', that is to say, a price which does not
d correspond to the cost of the service provided.

53. For the reasons I have just indicated and for those mentioned when considering
the criterion of the objective to be achieved, I therefore consider that the *method of
fixing* (unilaterally and by an exercise of public authority) *or the calculation of the
consideration* obtained by a public body cannot be regarded as decisive in defining
the activities engaged in 'as public authorities'.

e 54. What is the situation in regard to the *criterion based on the obligation on the
body governed by public law to engage in the activities*, put forward by the Commission?
That institution proposes to regard as activities engaged in as a public authority by
a body governed by public law those which form part of the powers which are
absolutely necessary for the purpose of achieving the public objective for which the
body was set up or those which derive from binding obligations imposed by the legal
f order of the member state.

55. I, too, consider that the activities thus defined or, to adopt the expression used
by the Netherlands government, those which are exercised under a 'mandate
conferred by the legislature', constitute in any event activities engaged in 'as public
authorities' even if they are not reserved exclusively for bodies governed by public
law.

g 56. Once the legislature considers that a given activity is of such importance from
the point of view of the public good that it must in all cases be carried on by local
authorities or other bodies governed by public law, it necessarily becomes an activity
engaged in by those bodies as public authorities.

57. The Commission also referred to activities engaged in by means of unilateral
*acts or conduct which are the expression of rights and powers derogating from the
h generally applicable rules of law* (e g concessions). Here again I share the Commission's
opinion that such activities are engaged in by bodies governed by public law 'as
public authorities'.

58. Finally, it must be considered that any activity—even if it is not mandatory
or not engaged in under public law rights and powers—the exercise of which is
reserved exclusively, by the constitution, by statute or by another provision of
j equivalent force, for local authorities or other bodies governed by public law must
be regarded as being engaged in by them 'as public authorities'. It may properly be
considered that such activities have been reserved for bodies governed by public law
by reason of the specific tasks for which they are responsible or by reason of the
special assurances which they offer in regard to the proper performance of those
activities.

59. I therefore propose that the court should adopt four *alternative* criteria for 'recognising' such an activity, namely: (1) the exercise by a body of powers vested in it as a public authority; (2) the mandatory nature of the activity; (3) the use of rights or powers derogating from the general applicable rules of law; (4) the fact that the activity in question is, by law, a monopoly.

60. However, what the national courts wish to know is whether there are also criteria making it possible to determine with certainty that an activity coming within one of those categories cannot give rise to treatment as a taxable person for the purposes of value added tax.

B *Activities engaged in as a public authority which cannot in any case give rise to its treatment as a taxable person*

61. Let me point out first that art 4(5) of the Sixth Directive lays down a general principle and an exception.

62. The *general principle* is that in respect of activities or transactions engaged in as public authorities, bodies governed by public law are not subject to value added tax.

63. The *exception* is that they are none the less so subject in cases in which their treatment as non-taxable persons would be liable to lead to significant distortions of competition.

64. It is therefore for the member states to determine the activities in support of which significant distortions of competition are to be found if the public bodies which engage in them were not subject to value added tax in respect of them. As a general rule, the problem may thus be resolved only by an assessment made by the member state of each of those activities. Furthermore, that assessment may lead to different results in each member state.

65. However, there is one case in which no distortion of competition can manifest itself, namely that in which the constitution, a statute or a provision of equal force reserves the exercise of the activity in question exclusively to bodies governed by public law.

66. As we have just seen, such activities must in any event also be regarded as being engaged in by bodies governed by public law 'as public authorities'. We thus have a sound criterion for determining the activities in respect of which a body governed by public law can *never* be subject to value added tax. In Italy, concessions for graves or cemetery vaults seem to constitute a typical example in that regard.

67. However, there is also an exception to the criterion of exclusivity. Annex D to the Sixth Directive lists the activities which must in all cases be subject to value added tax (unless they are carried out on such a small scale as to be negligible). However, it may be that in a member state one or other of those activities is reserved exclusively for local authorities. That seems to be the case in Italy in regard to the supply of water. In such a case, the criterion of exclusivity is thus not decisive in determining whether or not there is to be treatment as a taxable person. The third sub-paragraph of art 4(5) thus constitutes a very special provision which sets out, on the one hand, the cases in which the existence of a distortion of competition is, so to speak, presumed, but, on the other, also the cases which give rise to treatment as a taxable person even if there is no likelihood of a distortion of competition. It is fairly clear that art 4(5), by virtue of having been amended during the negotiations, has ceased to have any rigorously logical structure. That also can be seen from the use in the French, Dutch, Greek, and Portuguese versions of the third sub-paragraph of the word 'notamment' (in particular), which makes no sense in a sentence which refers to activities which must 'in any case' give rise to treatment as a taxable person. Since a word corresponding to 'notamment' is not to be found in the Danish, English, German, Italian and Spanish versions, I consider that there is no need to attach much importance to it.

68. It might still be asked whether the activities pursued under powers vested in a body as a public authority must not be regarded, ipso facto, as not subject to tax.

It seems to me that that cannot be the case, even if those activities give rise only very
a rarely to treatment as a taxable person.

69. In the first place, most of those activities are not economic activities and, for
that reason alone, cannot give rise to treatment as a taxable person. They are also
mainly reserved exclusively for bodies governed by public law and in that case the
above-mentioned criterion comes into operation. However, as is shown by
EC Commission v Kingdom of the Netherlands (Case 235/85) [1987] ECR 1471 at
b 1489–1490, the 'notaries and bailiffs' case, it cannot be excluded that certain activities
involving the exercise of powers conferred by public law would be carried out in
parallel by private persons and bodies governed by public law. It could therefore
become necessary to make those bodies subject to value added tax in order to avoid
a significant distortion of competition. The criterion of the exercise of powers
conferred by public law cannot therefore be of itself sufficient.

c 70. With regard to mandatory activities, those which bodies organised under
public law are required by law to carry out, it is also not possible to conclude that
they must necessarily be excluded from value added tax because private enterprise
might enter into competition with the public body (for example, the law might
require local authorities or other regional bodies to organise shipping services
between the mainland and off-shore islands without prohibiting private individuals
d from setting up a competing service).

71. The assessment is more difficult in regard to activities engaged in by means of
unilateral acts or conduct which are the expression of rights or powers derogating
from the generally applicable rules of law. Cases in which the *same* activity may be
engaged in by private individuals, using the means provided by private law, are
probably fairly rare. However, it does not seem to me to be possible to exclude a
e priori the possibility that such cases could exist and that distortions of competition
could therefore occur.

72. Ultimately, it is therefore necessary to conclude that the only criterion which
makes it possible to say with certainty that an activity engaged in by a body governed
by public law cannot be subject to value added tax is the fact that that activity is
reserved exclusively for such bodies. If I have correctly understood the Commission,
f it proposes to use that test concurrently with two others. However, if the criterion
of exclusivity is fulfilled, other criteria are no longer necessary because in that case
there cannot be any distortion of competition.

73. The same is true with regard to the wording of the national court's second
question, with which we are concerned here. That question refers to activities which
are engaged in by public bodies directly, exclusively and pursuant to powers vested
g in them as public authorities.

74. If the national court used the word 'exclusively' to refer to activities reserved
by law for bodies governed by public law (de jure exclusivity and not de facto
exclusivity) the reply to that question must certainly be in the affirmative. However,
I think it is possible to give the national court a broader reply by indicating to it that
it is sufficient that an activity should be reserved exclusively for bodies governed by
h public law, even if that activity is not carried out under powers vested in such bodies
as public authorities, for it not to give rise to treatment as a taxable person.

75. However, as we have already seen, the activities listed in Annex D, which, on
condition that they are not carried out on such a small scale as to be negligible, are
always subject to value added tax, even if one or other of them is reserved exclusively
for bodies governed by public law, must be put into a separate category.

j 76. Consequently, I propose that the court should reply as follows to the second
question referred to it in *Ufficio Distrettuale delle Imposte Dirette di Fiorenzuola
d'Arda v Comune di Carpaneto Piacentino* (Case 231/87):

> The first sub-paragraph of art 4(5) must be interpreted as meaning that the
> member states, regional and local authorities and other bodies governed by
> public law may in no circumstances be regarded as taxable persons in respect of
> activities or transactions in which they have the exclusive right to engage,

except if such activities or transactions are among those listed in Annex D to
the Sixth Directive.

a

*III The third question referred to the court in Ufficio Distrettuale delle Imposte Dirette
di Fiorenzuola d'Arda v Comune di Carpaneto Piacentino (Case 231/87)*

77. That question seeks to ascertain:

'Whether, the assumption that the institutional activities are carried out
exclusively by a public body, the Community legislature, by the use of the
expression "such activities" in the second sub-paragraph of art 4(5), intended to
refer to residual activities relating to public services, governed by Royal Decree
2578 of 15 October 1925.'

b

78. In the context of a reference for a preliminary ruling, the court cannot rule on
the conformity of provisions of national law with Community law. On the other
hand, national courts may be provided with criteria enabling them to determine in
which cases an activity comes within the scope of a given provision of Community
law.

c

79. It follows from the analysis made in regard to the second question that the
expression 'such activities' used in the *second sub-paragraph* refers to activities or
transactions engaged in by bodies governed by public law in their capacity as public
authorities, that is to say, those involving the exercise of powers vested in them as
such, those which are carried out by virtue of a binding obligation imposed by the
legal order of the state and from which they cannot be dispensed or those carried out
by unilateral acts or conduct involving the rights or powers derogating from the
generally applicable rules of law, in so far as such activities are not reserved
exclusively for such bodies. That is how I propose that the court should reply to that
question.

d

e

80. In my view, it goes without saying that the second sub-paragraph of art 4(5)
refers only to activities or transactions in respect of which a public body receives
consideration, of whatever kind, because only 'the supply of goods or services
effected for consideration within the territory of the country' falls within the scope
of value added tax (see art 2 of the Sixth Directive).

f

IV Obligations of member states concerning the method of transposition of the directive

81. Questions 4 and 5 referred to the court by the Commissione Tributaria di
Secondo Grado in *Ufficio Distrettuale delle Imposte Dirette di Fiorenzuola d'Arda v
Comune di Carpaneto Piacentino* (Case 231/87) and the second question referred to
the court by the Commissione Tributaria di Primo Grado in *Ufficio Provinciale
Imposta sul Valore Aggiunto di Piacenza v Comune di Rivergaro* (Case 129/88)
concern the way in which the member states must transpose art 4(5) into their
national law. Essentially, those questions raise the following five problems.

g

82. (a) Were the member states required to lay down the general principle set out
in the first sub-paragraph of art 4(5) by defining the specific criteria for determining
the activities engaged in by local authorities 'as public authorities'?

h

83. Under the third paragraph of art 189 of the EEC Treaty, the member states
are required to adopt the measures necessary to ensure that the result aimed at by a
directive can be achieved. On the other hand, they alone are competent to choose
the form and methods by which that obligation is to be fulfilled.

84. One of the methods for achieving the result aimed at by art 4(5) of the Sixth
Directive might consist in simply incorporating in the national legislation the
principle laid down in the first sub-paragraph of that provision. The member state
is free to add, if it wishes, specific criteria making it possible to determine not merely
which activities are engaged in by bodies governed by public law 'as public
authorities' but above all those which must give rise to treatment as a taxable person
for value added tax purposes.

j

85. A more simple method could therefore be to draw up a list of the activities in

a question. That could be done concurrently with the incorporation of the general
principle or as an alternative to this.

86. (b) Were the member states required to exclude from taxation public activities
which, although they might be regarded as commercial under national legislation,
constitute an exercise of public authority?

87. We have seen that the concept of 'activities or transactions engaged in as
public authorities' acquired, in the measure adopted by the Council, a wider scope
b than that which it had in the Commission's proposal and that it covers both activities
engaged in by public bodies in the exercise of their public powers (jure imperii) and
activities which could be regarded as economic, that is to say, activities as producers,
traders and persons supplying services, according to the definition contained in
art 4(2).

88. It follows from art 4(5) that the member states are also required not to make
c activities regarded as commercial under national legislation subject to value added
tax if those activities fulfil the criteria worked out in reply to the second question
referred to the court in *Ufficio Distrettuale delle Imposte Dirette di Fiorenzuola d'Arda
v Comune di Carpaneto Piacentino* (Case 231/87).

89. (c) Were the member states obliged to incorporate into their tax legislation
the criterion of 'significant distortions of competition' (fourth question in *Ufficio
d Distrettuale delle Imposte Dirette di Fiorenzuola d'Arda v Comune di Carpaneto
Piacentino* (Case 231/87)) or were they required *not* to tax activities engaged in as
public authorities by bodies governed by public law when they do *not* lead to
significant distortions of competition, by laying down the necessary quantitative
limits (question 2(c) in *Ufficio Provinciale Imposta sul Valore Aggiunto di Piacenza v
Comune di Rivergaro* (Case 129/88))?

e 90. As I have already pointed out above, the provision before the court lays down
a principle and provides for an exception. The principle requires the member states
to adopt all appropriate measures for ensuring that activities coming within the
definition contained in the first sub-paragraph of art 4(5) are not subject to value
added tax, unless this is likely to lead to significant distortions of competition.

91. The member states are obviously free to provide for that exception in their
f national legislation but this, of itself, would leave too many uncertainties both for
the competent administrative authority and for the bodies governed by public law
concerned.

92. On the other hand, it is hardly conceivable that the mere establishment of a
quantitative limit, without more, would be of such a nature as to dispel those
uncertainties. Distortion of competition is a concept which does not lend itself to an
g assessment in figures valid for all economic activities likely to be engaged in by
bodies governed by public law. I do not see how the member states could do
otherwise than to draw up either a positive list of activities not subject to value added
tax or a negative list of activities which are so subject (the solution chosen by the
Italian Ministry of Finance) or both. A negative list is composed obviously of
activities deemed to create significant distortions of competition. If it should none
h the less appear that one of the activities included in that list can in no circumstances
give rise to distortion (while none the less being an activity engaged in 'as a public
authority') the member state would have incorrectly fulfilled its obligations under
the directive in that regard.

93. (d) Are the member states required to incorporate into their tax legislation
the criterion of the negligible scale of certain activities (fifth question in *Ufficio
j Distrettuale delle Imposte Dirette di Fiorenzuola d'Arda v Comune di Carpaneto
Piacentino* (Case 231/87)) or are they required to fix a threshold below which the
activities listed in Annex D are not subject to taxation (question 2(d) in *Ufficio
Provinciale Imposta sul Valore Aggiunto di Piacenza v Comune di Rivergaro* (Case
129/88))?

94. As I have already pointed out above in regard to the problem of 'direct effect',
the activities listed in Annex D must be subject to value added tax only in so far as
they are not carried out on such a small scale as to be negligible. The member states

have several possibilities when it comes to implementing that principle. One of them consists of laying down a threshold below which the activity is not subject to taxation.

95. I therefore propose to give the two Italian courts the additional replies set out in paragraphs 4, 5 and 6 of the general conclusion.

Conclusion

For all the foregoing reasons, I propose that the court should reply as follows to the questions referred to it:

(1) Article 4(5) of the Sixth Directive may be relied on by a body governed by public law before the national courts in opposition to the application of a national provision making it subject to value added tax in respect of an activity not appearing in the list contained in Annex D to the Sixth Directive, the exercise of which is reserved exclusively for bodies governed by public law.

(2) The first sub-paragraph of art 4(5) is to be interpreted as meaning that the member states, regions, local authorities and other bodies governed by public law cannot in any circumstances be regarded as taxable persons in respect of activities or transactions which may be engaged in only by them, save where such activities or transactions are listed in Annex D to the Sixth Directive.

(3) The expression 'such activities' used in the second sub-paragraph of art 4(5) refers to activities or transactions engaged in by bodies governed by public law in their capacity as public authorities, that is to say, those which involve the exercise of powers vested in them as such, those engaged in by virtue of an obligation imposed by the legal order of the member state and from which they cannot be dispensed or those engaged in by means of unilateral acts or conduct under rights or powers derogating from the general applicable rules of law, in so far as those activities are not reserved exclusively for such bodies.

(4) The first sub-paragraph of art 4(5) must be interpreted as meaning that the member states are required to adopt the measures which they consider the most appropriate for ensuring that the activities or transactions engaged in by public bodies in their capacity as public authorities are not subject to value added tax in so far as they are not covered by the exceptions laid down in the second and third sub-paragraphs.

(5) The second sub-paragraph of art 4(5) of the Sixth Directive does not impose an obligation on the member states to transpose literally into their national law the criterion of 'significant distortions of competition'. On the other hand, they are required to apply that criterion in practice and to make a concrete assessment of the competitive position in a form and in accordance with methods which they consider the most appropriate, making activities or transactions engaged in by bodies governed by public law in their capacity as public authorities subject to value added tax whenever not to do so would be liable to lead to significant distortions of competition.

(6) The third sub-paragraph of art 4(5) does not require the member states to transpose literally into their national law the criterion concerning the 'negligible' scale of the activities listed in Annex D to the Sixth Directive; *however*, the above-mentioned provision *requires* the member states, using the form and in accordance with the methods which they regard as most appropriate, *not to* make subject to value added tax those of the activities engaged in by bodies governed by public law and referred to in Annex D which are carried out on such a small scale as to be negligible.

17 October 1989. **THE COURT OF JUSTICE** delivered the following judgment.

1. By orders of 8 May 1987 and 28 April 1988, which were received at the court on 20 July 1987 and 4 May 1988, the Commissione Tributaria di Secondo Grado di Piacenza (Tax Appeals Board, Piacenza) and the Commissione Tributaria di Primo Grado di Piacenza (First Instance Tax Board, Piacenza) referred to the court for a

preliminary ruling under art 177 of the EEC Treaty several questions on the
a interpretation of art 4(5) of EC Council Directive 77/388 of 17 May 1977 on the
harmonisation of the laws of the member states relating to turnover taxes—common
system of value added tax: uniform basis of assessment (the Sixth Directive).

2. Those questions arose in two actions, one between the Ufficio Distrettuale delle
Imposte Dirette di Fiorenzuola d'Arda (District Office for Direct Taxes of
Fiorenzuola d'Arda), Piacenza, and the Comune di Carpaneto Piacentino, and the
b other between the Comune di Rivergaro, supported by 23 other local authorities,
and the Ufficio Provinciale Imposta sul Valore Aggiunto (Provincial Value Added
Tax Office), Piacenza, concerning, in particular, the classification for the purposes
of liability to value added tax of the following transactions engaged in by the local
authorities: concessions in respect of graves, cemetery vaults and chapels, and selling
concessions of surface rights in and the sale, with full ownership rights, of land in
c connection with the subsidised building of homes, the taking out of public ownership
and sale of a piece of roadway, water supply, the concession for the operation of the
public weighbridge, the sale of wood resulting from the lopping of trees and the sale
of fittings for cemetery vaults.

3. The national courts decided to refer questions to the Court of Justice for a
preliminary ruling in order to resolve those disputes.

d 4. In *Ufficio Distrettuale delle Imposte Dirette di Fiorenzuola d'Arda v Comune di
Carpaneto Piacentino* (Case 231/87), the national court's questions seek to ascertain:

(1) Whether the principle set out in the first sub-paragraph of art 4(5) of the
Sixth Directive, which excludes from the category of activities subject to value
added tax so-called 'institutional' activities, is directly applicable in the absence
of a specific national provision.

e (2) Whether the Community legislature intended to identify by means of the
phrase 'activities or transactions in which they engage as public authorities' in
the first sub-paragraph of art 4(5) those activities which the public authorities
carry out directly and exclusively pursuant to powers vested in them as public
authorities, albeit delegated to them.

f (3) Whether, on the assumption that the institutional activities are carried
out exclusively by a public body, the Community legislature, by the use of the
expression 'such activities' in the second sub-paragraph of art 4(5), intended to
refer to residual activities relating to public services, governed by Royal Decree
2578 of 15 October 1925.

(4) Whether the second sub-paragraph of art 4(5) must be interpreted as
requiring the member states to incorporate in their value added tax legislation
g the criterion of 'significant distortions of competition' in regard to the taxation
of the transactions referred to in the said sub-paragraph.

(5) Whether the third sub-paragraph of art 4(5) of the Sixth Directive, which
provides that public bodies are to be considered taxable persons in relation to
the activities listed in Annex D, provided that they are not carried out on such
a small scale as to be negligible, requires the member states to incorporate in
h their tax legislation the criterion of 'negligibility'.

5. In *Ufficio Provinciale Imposta sul Valore Aggiunto di Piacenza v Comune di
Rivergaro* (Case 129/88), the national court's questions are as follows:

'(1) Are the Community provisions contained in art 4(5) of the Sixth Directive
j immediately and directly applicable?

(2) In order to make the Italian system of value added tax consistent with the
Community provisions was the Italian legislature under an obligation under
art 1 of the Sixth Directive—

(a) to lay down the general principle set out in the first sub-paragraph of
art 4(5) of the Sixth Directive by stipulating specific criteria for defining the
activities engaged in by local authorities "as public authorities";

(b) to exclude from tax public activities which, although they may be described as commercial activities, are, under the national legislation, in the *a* nature of activities of a public authority;

(c) in any event, not to subject to tax, in compliance with the second sub-paragraph of art 4(5), public activities where they do not lead to significant distortions of competition, and to specify the necessary quantitative limits;

(d) to fix, pursuant to the third sub-paragraph of art 4(5) of the Sixth Directive, a threshold below which the public activities listed in Annex D to *b* the Sixth Directive are not subject to tax?'

6. Reference is made to the report for the hearing for a fuller account of the facts of and legal background to the main proceedings, the course of the proceedings and the observations submitted to the court, which are mentioned or discussed hereinafter only in so far as is necessary for the reasoning of the court.

7. All the questions referred to the court are concerned with the interpretation of *c* art 4(5) of the Sixth Directive, which reads as follows:

'States, regional and local government authorities and other bodies governed by public law shall not be considered taxable persons in respect of the activities or transactions in which they engage as public authorities, even where they collect dues, fees, contributions or payments in connection with these activities *d* or transactions.

However, when they engage in such activities or transactions, they shall be considered taxable persons in respect of these activities or transactions where treatment as non-taxable persons would lead to significant distortions of competition.

In any case, these bodies shall be considered taxable persons in relation to the *e* activities listed in Annex D, provided they are not carried out on such a small scale as to be negligible.

Member States may consider activities of these bodies which are exempt under Article 13 or 28 as activitities which they engage in as public authorities.'

8. The questions raised by the national courts may conveniently be rearranged *f* under four headings concerning the interpretation of the first, second and third sub-paragraphs of art 4(5) and the direct effect of that provision, respectively.

The interpretation of the first sub-paragraph of art 4(5) of the Sixth Directive

9. The first question seeks to determine, on the one hand, what are the essential *g* characteristics of the activities exercised 'as public authorities' referred to in the first sub-paragraph of art 4(5) of the Sixth Directive and, on the other, to clarify the obligations imposed on the member states by that provision.

10. It should be pointed out that it follows from art 2 of the Sixth Directive, which defines the scope of value added tax, that within the territory of the member states only activities of an economic nature are subject thereto. The concept of economic *h* activities is defined in art 4(2) as comprising all activities of producers, traders and persons supplying services.

11. According to art 4(1), 'taxable person' is to mean any person who independently carries out any of those economic activities. It is thus by way of exception to that rule that the first sub-paragraph of art 4(5), of which the first question seeks an interpretation, excludes from the category of taxable persons states, regional and *j* local government authorities and other bodies governed by public law in respect of some of the activities or transactions in which they engage, 'even where they collect dues, fees, contributions or payments in connection with these activities or transactions'.

12. As the court held in its judgments of 11 July 1985 in *EC Commission v Federal Republic of Germany* (Case 107/84) [1985] ECR 2655 at 2667 and 26 March 1987 in

EC Commission v Kingdom of the Netherlands (Case 235/85) [1987] ECR 1471 at
a   1490, it is clear from that provision, when examined in the light of the aims of the
directive, that two conditions must be fulfilled in order for the rule of treatment as a
non-taxable person to apply: the activities must be carried out by a body governed
by public law and they must be carried out by that body acting as a public authority.

13. A definition of the latter condition cannot be based, as has been argued, on
the subject matter or purpose of the activity engaged in by the public body since
b   those factors have been taken into account by other provisions of the directive for
other purposes.

14. The subject matter or purpose of certain economic activities falling within the
scope of value added tax is a decisive factor, on the one hand for the purpose of
limiting the scope of the treatment of bodies subject to public law as non-taxable
persons (see the third sub-paragraph of art 4(5) of and Annex D to the Sixth
c   Directive) and, on the other for that of determining the exemptions referred to in
Title X of the directive. Article 13A(1) of that title of the directive provides, inter
alia, for exemptions in favour of certain activities carried out by bodies governed by
public law or by other bodies regarded as social in nature by the member states
concerned by reason of their activities being in the public interest.

15. An analysis of the first sub-paragraph of art 4(5) in the light of the scheme of
d   the directive shows that it is the way in which the activities are carried out that
determines the scope of the treatment of public bodies as non-taxable persons. In so
far as that provision makes such treatment of bodies governed by public law
conditional on their acting 'as public authorities', it excludes therefrom activities
engaged in by them not as bodies governed by public law but as persons subject to
private law. Consequently, the only criterion making it possible to distinguish with
e   certainty between those two categories of activity is the legal regime applicable
under national law.

16. It follows that the bodies governed by public law referred to in the first sub-
paragraph of art 4(5) of the Sixth Directive engage in activities 'as public authorities'
within the meaning of that provision when they do so under the special legal regime
applicable to them. On the other hand, when they act under the same legal
f   conditions as those that apply to private traders, they cannot be regarded as acting
'as public authorities'. It is for the national court to classify the activity at issue in the
light of that criterion.

17. With regard to the transposition of the rule laid down in the first sub-
paragraph of art 4(5) into national law, it should be pointed out that since the
directive imposes an obligation to achieve a result, it is for each member state in
g   accordance with the third paragraph of art 189 of the EEC Treaty to choose the
appropriate form and methods to attain that result.

18. It follows that although the member states are required to ensure that the
activities or transactions engaged in by bodies governed by public law as public
authorities are not subject to value added tax in so far as they do not come within
one of the exceptions specified in the second and third sub-paragraphs, they may
h   choose for that purpose the legislative technique which they regard as the most
appropriate. Thus they may, for example, merely incorporate into national law the
form of words used in the Sixth Directive or an equivalent expression or they may
draw up a list of activities in respect of which bodies governed by public law are not
to be regarded as taxable persons.

19. The answer to the first question should therefore be that the first sub-
j   paragraph of art 4(5) of the Sixth Directive must be interpreted as meaning that
activities pursued 'as public authorities' within the meaning of that provision are
those engaged in by bodies governed by public law under the special legal regime
applicable to them and do not include activities pursued by them under the same
legal conditions as those that apply to private traders. It is for each member state to
choose the appropriate legislative technique for transposing into national law the
rule of treatment as a non-taxable person laid down in that provision.

The interpretation of the second sub-paragraph of art 4(5) of the Sixth Directive

20. The second question seeks to determine, on the one hand, the scope of the expression 'such activities' in the second sub-paragraph of art 4(5) of the Sixth Directive and, on the other, whether the member states are required to incorporate into their tax legislation the criterion of 'significant distortions of competition', laid down in that provision, or to fix quantitative limits for the transposition of the criterion into national law.

21. It should first be pointed out that it follows from both the wording and structure of art 4(5) of the Sixth Directive that the expression 'these activities or transactions' in the second sub-paragraph corresponds to the activities or transactions referred to in the first sub-paragraph, that is to say, activities or transactions engaged in by bodies governed by public law as public authorities, to the exclusion, as indicated above, of activities engaged in by them as persons subject to private law.

22. It should next be noted that the second sub-paragraph of that provision contains a derogation from the rule of treatment of bodies governed by public law as non-taxable persons in respect of activities or transactions engaged in by them as public authorities where that treatment would lead to significant distortions of competition. Thus, with a view to ensuring the neutrality of the tax, which is the major objective of the Sixth Directive, that provision envisages the situation in which bodies governed by public law engage, under the special legal regime applicable to them, in activities which may also be engaged in, in competition with them, by private individuals under a regime governed by private law or on the basis of administrative concessions.

23. In that situation, the member states are required by the third paragraph of art 189 of the EEC Treaty to ensure that bodies governed by public law are treated as taxable persons where the contrary would lead to significant distortions of competition. On the other hand, they are not obliged to transpose that criterion literally into their national law or to lay down precise quantitative limits for treatment as non-taxable persons.

24. The answer to the second question should therefore be that the second sub-paragraph of art 4(5) of the Sixth Directive must be interpreted as meaning that the member states are required to ensure that bodies governed by public law are treated as taxable persons in respect of activities in which they engage as public authorities where those activities may also be engaged in, in competition with them, by private individuals, in cases in which the treatment of those bodies as non-taxable persons could lead to significant distortions of competition, but they are not obliged to transpose that criterion literally into their national law or to lay down precise quantitative limits for such treatment.

The interpretation of the third sub-paragraph of art 4(5) of the Sixth Directive

25. The third question seeks to determine whether the third sub-paragraph of art 4(5) of the Sixth Directive requires the member states to transpose into their tax legislation the criterion of the non-negligible scale of activities as a condition for treating bodies governed by public law as taxable persons in respect of the activities listed in Annex D to the directive and whether they must lay down for that purpose a threshold below which such bodies are treated as non-taxable persons.

26. It should be noted that by providing that bodies governed by public law are in any case to be regarded as taxable persons in respect of the activities listed in Annex D provided they are not on such a small scale as to be negligible, the provision in question makes the rule that such bodies are not to be regarded as taxable persons subject to a limitation which must be added to those resulting from the condition laid down in the first sub-paragraph, namely that the activities must be engaged in as public authorities, and from the derogation laid down in the second sub-paragraph in cases where treatment as non-taxable persons would lead to significant distortions of competition. The third sub-paragraph of art 4(5) thus seeks to ensure that certain categories of economic activity the importance of which derives from their subject

matter are not subject to value added tax on the ground that they are carried out by
a bodies governed by public law as public authorities.

27. However, the obligation to treat bodies governed by public law as taxable
persons in respect of the activities listed in Annex D to the directive is imposed on
the member states only in so far as the activities in question are not negligible in
scale. Having regard to the structure of the provision in question, it must be
interpreted as meaning that the member states are free to exclude from the scope of
b such compulsory treatment the activities listed in Annex D in so far as they are
carried out on a negligible scale, but are not required to do so. Consequently, they
are also not required to fix a ceiling for treatment as non-taxable persons in respect
of the activities at issue.

28. The answer to the question referred to the court should therefore be that the
third sub-paragraph of art 4(5) of the Sixth Directive must be interpreted as meaning
c that it does not require the member states to transpose into their tax legislation the
criterion of the non-negligible scale of activities as a condition for treating the
activities listed in Annex D as taxable.

The direct effect of art 4(5) of the Sixth Directive

29. The fourth question seeks to ascertain whether a body governed by public law
d may rely on art 4(5) of the Sixth Directive for the purpose of opposing the application
of a national provision making it subject to value added tax in respect of an activity
in which it was engaged as a public authority and which is not listed in Annex D,
where treatment of the activity as non-taxable is not liable to give rise to significant
distortions of competition.

30. As the court has consistently held, (see, in particular, the judgment of
e 19 January 1982 in *Becker v Finanzamt Münster-Innenstadt* (Case 8/81) [1982]
ECR 53), wherever the provisions of a directive appear, as far as their subject matter
is concerned, to be unconditional and sufficiently precise, those provisions may, in
the absence of implementing measures adopted within the prescribed period, be
relied on as against any national provision which is incompatible with the directive
f or in so far as the provisions define rights which individuals are able to assert against
the state.

31. Article 4(5) of the Sixth Directive fulfils those criteria, since the bodies and
activities in regard to which the rule of treatment as non-taxable persons applies are
clearly defined in that provision. Bodies governed by public law, which, in this
context must be assimilated to individuals, are therefore entitled to rely on that rule
in respect of activities engaged in as public authorities but not listed in Annex D to
g the directive.

32. That conclusion is not invalidated by the fact that the second sub-paragraph
of art 4(5) of the Sixth Directive requires activities to be treated as taxable if their
treatment as non-taxable would lead to significant distortions of competition. That
limitation placed on the rule of treatment as non-taxable persons is thus only a
conditional limitation, and whilst it is true that its application involves an assessment
h of economic circumstances, that assessment is not exempt from judicial review.

33. The answer to the fourth question should therefore be that a body governed
by public law may rely on art 4(5) of the Sixth Directive for the purpose of opposing
the application of a national provision making it subject to value added tax in respect
of an activity in which it engages as a public authority, which is not listed in
Annex D and whose treatment as non-taxable is not liable to give rise to significant
j distortions of competition.

Costs

34. The costs incurred by the Italian Republic, the Netherlands government and
the Commission, which have submitted observations to the court, are not recoverable.
Since these proceedings are, in so far as the parties to the main proceedings are

concerned, in the nature of a step in the action pending before the national court, the decision on costs is a matter for that court.

On those grounds, the court in answer to the questions submitted to it by the Commissione Tributaria di Secondo Grado, Piacenza, and the Commissione Tributaria di Primo Grado, Piacenza, by orders of 8 May 1987 and 28 April 1988, respectively, hereby rules:

1. The first sub-paragraph of art 4(5) of the Sixth Directive must be interpreted as meaning that activities pursued 'as public authorities' within the meaning of that provision are those engaged in by bodies governed by public law under the special legal regime applicable to them and do not include activities pursued by them under the same legal conditions as those that apply to private traders. It is for each member state to choose the appropriate legislative technique for transposing into national law the rule of treatment as a non-taxable person laid down in that provision.

2. The second sub-paragraph of art 4(5) of the Sixth Directive must be interpreted as meaning that the member states are required to ensure that bodies subject to public law are treated as taxable persons in respect of activities in which they engage as public authorities where those activities may also be engaged in, in competition with them, by private individuals, in cases in which the treatment of those bodies as non-taxable persons could lead to significant distortions of competition, but they are not obliged to transpose that criterion literally into their national law or to lay down precise quantitative limits for such treatment.

3. The third sub-paragraph of art 4(5) of the Sixth Directive must be interpreted as meaning that it does not require the member states to transpose into their tax legislation the criterion of the non-negligible scale of activities as a condition for treating the activities listed in Annex D as taxable.

4. A body governed by public law may rely on art 4(5) of the Sixth Directive for the purpose of opposing the application of a national provision making it subject to value added tax in respect of an activity in which it engages as a public authority, which is not listed in Annex D and whose treatment as non-taxable is not liable to give rise to significant distortions of competition.

Agents: *L Ferrari Bravo*, Head of the Department for Contentious Diplomatic Affairs, and *F Favara*, Avvocato dello Stato, (for the Italian Republic); *E Traversa*, Legal Adviser (for the Commission); *V Pototschnig, F Tesauro* and *M Avantaggiati* (for the Comune di Carpaneto Piacentino); *H J Heinemann*, Secretary General of the Ministry of Foreign Affairs, (for the Netherlands government); *F Capelli* and *F Tesauro* (for the Comune di Piacenza): *F Tesauro, M Avantaggiati* and *F Mancini* (for the Comune di Rivergaro and 23 other local authorities).

Rengan Krishnan Esq   Barrister.

Genius Holding BV v Staatssecretaris van Financiën
(Case 342/87)

COURT OF JUSTICE OF THE EUROPEAN COMMUNITIES (FIFTH CHAMBER)
JUDGES SIR GORDON SLYNN (PRESIDENT) ZULEEG, JOLIET, MOITINHO DE ALMEIDA AND
RODRIGUEZ IGLESIAS
ADVOCATE GENERAL J MISCHO
15 FEBRUARY, 14 MARCH, 13 DECEMBER 1989

Value added tax – European Communities – Deduction from tax due – Whether right to deduct extends to tax due solely because it is mentioned on an invoice – Circumstances in which right to deduct from value added tax due exists – EC Council Directive 77/388, arts 17(2)(a), 27(1).

The taxpayer company, Genius Holding BV, carried out assembly and machine-tooling work using sub-contractors to fulfil its orders on a regular basis. It received an assessment in respect of the period 1 July to 31 December 1982 on the grounds that, contrary to national legislative provisions in force, it had deducted from the value added tax for which it was liable the value added tax invoiced to the employer, GM, by two sub-contractors, V and M. The taxpayer company appealed against the assessment to the Gerechtshof Amsterdam which confirmed the assessment. On appeal, the Hoge Raad took the view that that deduction was permitted only where the tax mentioned on the invoice was due. Under the Netherlands rules, enacted pursuant to a derogation authorised by the Council under art 27(1)[a] of EC Council Directive 77/388 (the Sixth Directive), the sub-contractor was not liable to pay value added tax in respect of the supplies made to the principal contractor, that tax being due only from the principal contractor on the amount which it invoiced to the employer. It followed that the taxpayer company could not deduct the value added tax on the grounds that it had been invoiced to it by the sub-contractors contrary to the Netherlands rules. Under art 17(2)(a)[b] of the Sixth Directive, the taxable person was to be entitled to deduct from the tax which he was liable to pay value added tax due or paid in respect of goods or services supplied or to be supplied to him by another taxable person. The taxpayer company and the Commission submitted that that provision meant that any tax mentioned on the invoice could be deducted. The Hoge Raad had doubts concerning the compatibility of the rules with the Sixth Directive and stayed the proceedings, referring two questions to the European Court for a preliminary ruling to determine, inter alia, whether the right of deduction provided for in the Sixth Directive extended to tax which was due exclusively because it was mentioned on the invoice.

Held – The right to deduct could only be exercised in respect of taxes actually due, ie the taxes corresponding to a transaction subject to value added tax or paid in so far as they were due. Accordingly, the right to deduct provided for in the Sixth Directive did not apply to tax which was due solely because it was mentioned on the invoice.

Notes

For transactions giving rise to input credit tax, see De Voil: Value Added Tax A13.11.

For EC Council Directive 77/388, arts 17(2)(a), 27(1), see ibid, Division E3.

---

a   Article 27(1), so far as material, is set out at p 248 *g–h*, post
b   Article 17(2)(a), so far as material, is set out at p 250 *c–d*, post

Cases cited

EC Commission v French Republic (Case 50/87) [1988] ECR 4797, CJEC.   *a*
Jeunehomme v Belgian State (Joined Cases 123 and 330/87) [1988] ECR 4517, CJEC.
Rompelman (D A) and Rompelman-Van Deelen (E A) v Minister van Financiën (Case
    268/83) [1985] ECR 655, CJEC.
Schul (Gaston) Douane Expediteur BV v Inspecteur der Invoerrechten en Accijnzen
    (Case 15/81) [1982] ECR 1409, CJEC.
                                                                                         b

Reference

By an order of 28 October 1987 the Hoge Raad der Nederlanden (Supreme Court of
the Netherlands) referred to the Court of Justice of the European Communities for   *c*
a preliminary ruling under art 177 of the EEC Treaty two questions on the
interpretation of several provisions of EC Council Directive 77/388 (the Sixth
Directive). The questions arose in proceedings between Genius Holding BV, the
taxpayer company, and the Staatssecretaris van Financiën (Secretary of State for
Finance). The taxpayer company, the Netherlands government, the government of
the Federal Republic of Germany, the Spanish government and the Commission   *d*
made submissions (in the written procedure) to the court. The language of the case
was Dutch. The facts are set out in the report for the hearing.

The Judge Rapporteur (J C Moitinho de Almeida) presented the following   *e*
report for the hearing.

I Facts and procedure

A The main proceedings

The tax entity Genius Holding BV (called 'Genius BV' at the material time) (the
taxpayer company), carries out assembly and machine-tooling work. It regularly   *f*
uses sub-contractors to fulfil the orders which it obtains.

For the period from 1 July 1982 to 31 December 1982 inclusive, the amount of
turnover tax owed by the taxpayer company was adjusted upward to 79,833
Netherlands guilders, that amount being single rate only, without surcharge. The
notice of adjustment concerned turnover tax invoiced to Genicon Montage BV by
two sub-contractors, Vissers Pijpleiding en Montage BV and Montagebedrijf J van   *g*
Mierlo. The amounts entered on the invoices concerned work which had been
contracted for before 1 July 1982.

Since the inspector of taxes rejected the objection lodged against the adjustment,
the taxpayer company brought an action before the Gerechtshof Amsterdam
(Regional Court of Appeal, Amsterdam). Since that court upheld the inspector's
decision, an appeal was brought before the Hoge Raad der Nederlanden (Supreme   *h*
Court of the Netherlands) which, since it considered that the appeal raised questions
the answers to which required an interpretation of the opening words of art 17(2),
art 17(2)(*a*), art 21(1) and art 22(3) and (8) of EC Council Directive 77/388 of 17 May
1977 on the harmonisation of the laws of the member states relating to turnover
taxes—common system of value added tax: uniform basis of assessment (the Sixth
Directive), stayed the proceedings and referred the following questions to the Court   *j*
of Justice of the European Communities for a preliminary ruling:

'1. Does the right to deduct provided for in the Sixth Directive apply to the
tax which is due solely because it is mentioned on the invoice?
2. If so, does the directive still allow the Member States to exclude—either
entirely or in certain special cases—the right to deduct such tax by laying down
requirements regarding the invoice?'

B Written procedure

1. The Hoge Raad der Nederlanden considers that the decision which it is called on to give depends on the interpretation of the provisions of the Sixth Directive.

The order for reference, made on 28 October 1987, was received at the court registry on 4 November 1987.

2. In accordance with art 20 of the Protocol on the Statute of the Court of Justice, written observations were submitted on 1 February 1988 by the taxpayer company, on 2 February 1988 by the Netherlands government, represented by H J Heinemann, Acting Secretary General of the Ministry of Foreign Affairs, on 5 February 1988 by the Commission of the European Communities, represented by Johannes Fons Buhl, a member of its Legal Department, acting as agent, assisted by M Mees, of the Hague Bar, on 12 February 1988 by the government of the Federal Republic of Germany, represented by Martin Seidel and Hans-Joachim Horn, acting as agents of the government of the Federal Republic of Germany before the court, and on 18 February 1988 by the Spanish government, represented by J Conde de Saro and R Garcia-Valdecasas y Fernandez, acting as agents.

On hearing the report of the Judge Rapporteur and the views of the Advocate General, the court decided to open the oral procedure without any preparatory inquiry.

II The applicable rules

A Community rules

Article 17(2)(*a*) of the Sixth Directive provides that in so far as the goods and services are used for the purposes of his taxable transactions, the taxable person is to be entitled to deduct from the tax which he is liable to pay 'value added tax due or paid in respect of goods or services supplied or to be supplied to him by another taxable person'.

Article 18(1)(*a*) of the Sixth Directive provides that to exercise his right to deduct, the taxable person must hold an invoice, drawn up in accordance with art 22(3).

Article 22(3)(*a*) requires every taxable person to 'issue an invoice, or other document serving as invoice in respect of all goods and services supplied by him to another taxable person, and [is to] keep a copy thereof'.

According to the same article, every taxable person is likewise to issue an invoice in respect of payments on account made to him by another taxable person before the supply of goods or services is effected or completed. The invoice is also to state clearly the price exclusive of tax and the corresponding tax at each rate as well as any exemptions (see sub-para (*b*)). The member states are to determine the criteria for considering whether a document serves as an invoice (see sub-para (*c*)).

Article 22(8) provides that, without prejudice to the provisions adopted by the Council pursuant to art 17(4), member states may impose other obligations which they deem necessary for the correct levying and collection of the tax and for the prevention of fraud.

Article 21(1) provides:

'The following shall be liable to pay value added tax:

1. under the internal system:

(*a*) taxable persons who carry out taxable transactions other than those referred to in Article 9(2)(*e*) and carried out by a taxable person resident abroad. When the taxable transaction is effected by a taxable person resident abroad Member States may adopt arrangements whereby tax is payable by someone other than the taxable person residing abroad. *Inter alia* a tax representative or other person for whom the taxable transaction is carried out may be designated as such other person. The Member States may also provide that someone other than the taxable person shall be held jointly and severally liable for payment of the tax;

(*b*) persons to whom services covered by Article 9(2)(*e*) are supplied and carried out by a taxable person resident abroad. However, Member States may require that the supplier of services shall be held jointly and severally liable for payment of the tax;

(*c*) any person who mentions the value added tax on an invoice or other document serving as invoice.'

B National legislation

On 1 July 1981, the Law of 4 June 1981 known as the Wet Ketenaansprakelijkheid (Liability Transfer Law) (Staatsblad, 370) came into force. That law contains inter alia amendments to the Wet op de Omzetbelasting (Law on Turnover Tax) 1968 (the Law). Article IX of the Liability Transfer Law provides that, for a period of one year after its entry into force, the Law is not to apply to contractors and sub-contractors who had entered into a contract before that date.

Section 1 of Resolution 282-9690 of the Secretary of State for Finance of 25 June 1982 (the resolution) provides that for the time being the Liability Transfer Law is not to be applied at all as far as turnover tax is concerned. In the building, metal construction (immovable constructions only) and shipbuilding industries, so-called transfer rules, to the effect that where sub-contracting takes place the levying of value added tax is transferred from the sub-contractor performing the service to the (principal) contractor receiving it, are to apply to turnover tax. In other words, the (principal) contractor does not pay the value added tax payable in respect of the sub-contracted work to the sub-contractor (who would then have to pay that value added tax to the authorities) but himself declares it as a tax due. On the same declaration the (principal) contractor may deduct that tax under the transfer rules. As a result, no turnover tax is in fact paid downstream from the (principal) contractor in respect of the work carried out. Therefore, the effect of the transfer rules in practice is that value added tax is levied only once on the amount charged by the (principal) contractor to his client. Those rules were incorporated in art 24*b* of the Uitvoeringsbesluit Omzetbelasting (Turnover Tax Implementation Order) 1968 (the Order) as from 1 July 1982.

In s 5 of the resolution, it is stated that no transitional provisions are contained in the Order and that this means that the transfer rules also apply to work done under contracts concluded before 1 July 1982.

In accordance with art 15(1)(*b*) of the Law, the right to make deductions of input tax is excluded if the invoice is not in accordance with the legislative provisions. Among those provisions, reference should be made, on the one hand, to art 35(1)(*g*) of the same Law, according to which only the amount legally due must be mentioned on the invoice and, on the other, to art 24*b*(8) of the Order, which provides that the words 'turnover tax transferred' must appear on invoices in the context of the special rules applicable to undertakings in the building industry and their sub-contractors.

On 22 March 1982, the Netherlands government informed the Commission that it intended to introduce into Netherlands legislation rules derogating from the Sixth Directive and designed to combat certain fraudulent activities on the part of sub-contractors and persons providing labour which exist in the building, structural steelwork and shipbuilding industries. To that end, a request was made for a derogation from the Sixth Directive under art 27(1)–(4). Under that derogation, authorised by the Council, which entered into force on 20 June 1982 (see OJ C197, p 1), the Kingdom of the Netherlands was authorised to adopt the transfer rules mentioned above.

III Written observations submitted to the court

Written observations were submitted to the court by the taxpayer company, the Commission, and the governments of the Netherlands, the Federal Republic of Germany and Spain.

First question

The taxpayer company argues that it is implicit in the system of consumer taxes that the person receiving the services must be able to deduct the turnover tax invoiced to him. If that person, who must himself pay the tax, cannot, in such a case, deduct the amount of tax he has paid to his suppliers, there would be double taxation, contrary to the neutrality of turnover tax in relations between undertakings.

The Commission considers that the first question raised by the national court should be answered in the affirmative. In support of its view it refers to the court's case law according to which the procedure for deduction is the cornerstone of the common system of value added tax (see, in particular, the judgment of 5 May 1982 in *Schul (Gaston) Douane Expediteur BV v Inspecteur der Invoerrechten en Accijnzen* (Case 15/81) [1982] ECR 1409, and of 14 February 1985 in *Rompelman (D A) and Rompelman-Van Deelen (E A) v Minister van Financiën* (Case 268/83) [1985] ECR 655). The right to deduct the amount of tax already paid at an earlier stage is subject solely to the condition that another taxable person has supplied goods and services and has invoiced value added tax for that transaction. There is no requirement that the tax be knowingly paid.

The Netherlands, German and Spanish governments argue that the answer to this question should be in the negative. The right to deduct presupposes that the substantive conditions in art 17(2) of the Sixth Directive and the evidentiary conditions in arts 18(1) and 22(3) thereof have been fulfilled. According to the first of those provisions, the right to deduct is limited to amounts of value added tax whose basis in law is the performance of a taxable transaction. Tax mentioned on an invoice relating to another matter and due under art 21(1)(c) of the Sixth Directive may therefore not be deducted. Moreover, the invoice in question does not fulfil the conditions laid down in art 22(3) of the directive.

Second question

The taxpayer company maintains that art 22(3)(c) of the Sixth Directive permits the member states to lay down criteria in their legislation for determining whether a document may be regarded as serving as an invoice. The member states are not entitled to lay down conditions as to the contents of the invoice such as, in particular, the conditions at issue the effect of which is that the economic risk of the payment of taxes due from third parties is imposed on the principal contractor.

According to the Commission, the Community legislature did not wish to regulate exhaustively the conditions which documents must fulfil in order to be regarded as invoices. The member states may require that a number of additional matters be mentioned in order to ensure that value added tax is correctly applied and that its application is subject to supervision by the tax authorities. However, the matters to be mentioned must not go beyond what is strictly necessary to supervise the implementation of value added tax and must not, by reason of their number or technical nature, make it difficult or impossible in practical terms to exercise the right to deduct. In the Commission's view, the current prohibition in the Netherlands of mentioning on the invoice any amount of tax other than that legally due must not be accompanied by a sanction depriving the customer of his right to deduct the tax unduly invoiced to him.

However, the Commission considers that the Netherlands rules applying to principal contractors in the building industry and their sub-contractors contains a special feature which makes exclusion of the right of deduction permissible if the invoice does not comply with the provisions of art 24*b* of the implementing order and art 35 of the Law.

The Netherlands and Spanish governments maintain that art 22(3) and (8) of the Sixth Directive permits the member states to lay down criteria for determining whether a document may serve as an invoice and to impose such other obligations as they regard as necessary to ensure that the tax is collected correctly and to prevent

fraud. That is true of the obligation laid down in art 35 of the Law, which was
regarded as necessary to avoid fraudulent practices. According to the Netherlands
government, this makes it possible to avoid a situation in which, by mentioning on
an invoice devoid of any legal basis a tax on the added value, a right to deduct could
deliberately be created, that right not being paralysed even if the person who draws
up the invoice has no intention to pay the tax to which he has thus become liable.

Even supposing that it is not permitted to lay down additional requirements for
invoices which limit the right to deduct, measures such as those adopted in the
Netherlands may be based on art 18(1)(d) of the Sixth Directive.

14 March 1989. **The Advocate General (J Mischo)** delivered the following
opinion.

Mr President, members of the court,

1. An adjustment of the taxable amount for the purposes of turnover tax was
imposed on Genius Holding BV, the plaintiff in the main proceedings (called
'Genius BV' at the material time) (the taxpayer company), by the inspector of taxes
for the period from 1 July to 31 December 1982. Later confirmed by a judgment of
28 May of the Gerechtshof Amsterdam (Regional Court of Appeal, Amsterdam),
that decision was adopted on the ground that the taxpayer company wrongly
deducted tax invoiced to it by one of its sub-contractors because the tax in question
had been charged in error and could not therefore be deducted. The taxpayer
company therefore brought an appeal before the Hoge Raad der Nederlanden
(Supreme Court of the Netherlands), which concluded that the appeal raised
questions the answer to which required an interpretation of the opening words of
art 17(2), art 17(2)(a), art 21(1) and art 22(3) and (8) of EC Council Directive 77/388
(the Sixth Directive).

First question

2. The Hoge Raad formulated its first question in the following terms:

'Does the right to deduct provided for in the Sixth Directive apply to the tax
which is *due* solely because it is mentioned on the invoice?' [Emphasis added.]

3. According to art 21(1)(c) of the Sixth Directive 'any person who mentions the
value added tax on an invoice or other document serving as invoice' is liable to pay
value added tax.

4. The German and Spanish governments argue essentially that art 21(1)(c) was
inserted only in order to prevent fraud. Even if any amount appearing on an invoice
had to be paid to the Treasury by the person who drew up the invoice, that amount
would not give rise to a right to deduct unless it corresponded to tax actually due
under the legislation.

5. The German government argues in particular that a deduction made by reason
of undue payment of turnover tax is incompatible with art 17(2)(a). Article 17(2)
reads as follows:

'In so far as the goods and services are used for the purposes of his taxable
transactions, the taxable person shall be entitled to deduct from the tax which
he is liable to pay: (a) value added tax *due* or *paid* in respect of goods or services
supplied or to be supplied to him by another taxable person.' [Emphasis added.]

6. The expression 'tax due' thus refers, according to the German government,
exclusively to the tax which must be paid to the collecting authority on the basis of a
correct application of the legislation and not that due only because it is mentioned
on the invoice.

7. At the hearing, the German government emphasised in particular the changes
a that the Council had made to the proposal for a directive submitted by the
Commission. Article 17(2)(*a*) of that proposal provided that the taxable person was
to be entitled to deduct from the tax which he was liable to pay—'. . . value added
tax invoiced to him . . . in respect of goods or of services supplied to him'. The
Council replaced the expression 'tax invoiced' by 'tax due or paid' and added at the
end the words 'by another taxable person'. By doing so, it wanted to exclude cases in
b which the tax is due solely because it is mentioned on the invoice.

8. There can obviously be no question of my contesting that such was the
Council's intention, or at least, that of some of its members, but the fact remains
that according to art 21 any person who mentions the value added tax on an invoice
is to be *liable to pay* that tax. However, art 17(2)(*a*) refers to tax *due* or paid and I
consider that it is for the court to interpret the directive on the basis of the terms in
c which it is worded and not in accordance with what one or other of the member
states believes to have been the real intention of the Council.

9. The Spanish government argues that according to art 17(1), the right to deduct
arises as soon as the deductible tax becomes chargeable. It concludes that taxes
which are not *chargeable* to the taxable person who passes them on cannot give rise
to deduction. Taxable persons in that situation are liable to pay only the amounts
d due in accordance with the applicable law.

10. Article 21 of the Sixth Directive is entitled 'Persons liable to pay tax to the
authorities' and art 21(1)(*c*) provides that any person who mentions the value added
tax on an invoice is liable to pay it. A taxable person who so mentions it must
therefore be liable to pay it whether or not it is legally due.

11. Moreover, according to art 10(1):

e
'(*a*) "Chargeable event" shall mean the occurrence by virtue of which the
legal conditions necessary for tax to become chargeable are fulfilled.
(*b*) The tax becomes "chargeable" when the tax authority becomes entitled
under the law at a given moment to claim the tax *from the person liable to pay* . . .'
[Emphasis added.]

f   According to art 10(2): 'The chargeable event shall occur and the tax shall become
chargeable when the goods are *delivered* or the services *are performed*.' [Emphasis
added.]

12. Any tax mentioned on an invoice, even if it is not legally due, thus becomes
chargeable once the transaction to which it relates has been carried out.

13. The governments which have submitted written observations also refer to
g art 18(1)(*a*) which provides that to exercise his right to deduct, the taxable person
must hold an invoice, drawn up in accordance with art 22(3). Sub-paragraph (*b*) of
that provision provides that: 'The invoice shall state clearly the price exclusive of
tax and the corresponding tax at each rate as well as any exemptions.'

14. In my opinion, that provision lays down a lex generalis from which the lex
specialis in art 21(1)(*c*) derogates. In principle, every invoice must mention the exact
h amount of tax applicable to the goods or services to which it refers. However, when
that rule is not observed and an amount not legally due, or which is erroneous,
appears on the invoice, the person who drew up the invoice is none the less liable, by
virtue of art 21(1)(*c*), to pay the amount actually mentioned, and that amount may
later be deducted by the taxable person to whom the goods were delivered or for
whom the service was performed.

j   15. The Netherlands government, although it, too, considers that only tax 'in fact
due' may be deducted, adopts a position which is less radical than that of the other
governments by referring to the practice developed in the Netherlands. In
accordance with that practice—

'. . . the tax authorities at first look to the person who improperly mentioned
the tax on the invoice. It is only if that step appears to have no chance of

producing a result that, *under certain conditions, for example, in the absence of good faith on the part of the person who received the invoice*, the tax deducted is later also charged to the latter. That course of conduct is based on the principles of sound administration . . .'

16. The Netherlands government thus indicates to the court the path it ought to follow in order to resolve the problem. Since it is clear from art 21(1)(c) that all tax mentioned on an invoice is due to the authorities, it is logical to claim it in the first place from the person who drew up the invoice. If the amount thus due can be recovered, there is no longer any reason to claim it a second time from the person to whom the goods were delivered or to whom the service was rendered (the second taxable person).

17. If the tax was not automatically paid by the first taxable person or cannot be recovered from him, the following distinction must, to my mind, be drawn: (a) if the second taxable person has also not paid the tax to the supplier, there is a strong presumption of fraudulent collusion and the administration is then fully justified in claiming payment from the second taxable person, thus rendering ineffective the deduction made by him; (b) if, on the other hand, it transpires that the second taxable person has actually paid the amount in question to the first, it should not be possible for the authorities to claim that amount from the second taxable person.

18. To treat, in such a situation, both taxable persons as jointly and severally liable to pay the tax, and to do so in the absence of any provision prescribing such liability, would not be in accordance with the principles of justice and equity. Article 21(1)(a) and (b) permits the member states to impose joint and several liability where the taxable transaction is carried out by a taxable person resident abroad but art 21(1)(c) makes no such provision.

19. Moreover, if recognition of a right to deduct were refused in such a case, the selfsame right could just as well be denied every time the first taxable person failed to pay to the authorities an amount legally due and correctly calculated.

20. Furthermore, if such joint and several liability were to be laid down, it would impose a wholly excessive duty of care on all traders; can it be imagined that all firms could verify whether each amount of value added tax mentioned on the countless invoices which they receive each year from their suppliers is correct?

21. Like the Commission and the taxpayer company, I also consider that it would be contrary to the scheme and purpose of the Sixth Directive to refuse to permit a deduction to be made in the circumstances of this case. The purpose of the value added tax system is to ensure neutrality of taxation so as, in particular, not to distort the conditions of competition. The essential factor is, therefore, to avoid double taxation of the same 'added value'. It follows that the right to deduct must be acquired each time that the tax has to be paid, which is the case if it appears, even incorrectly, on an invoice.

22. Moreover, the court has pointed out in *Rompelman (D A) and Rompelman-Van Deelen (E A) v Minister van Financiën* (Case 268/83) [1985] ECR 655 at 664, para 19 the importance of the above considerations in its case law in holding that—

'. . . the deduction system is meant to relieve the trader entirely of the burden of the VAT *payable or paid* in the course of all his economic activities. The common system of value-added tax therefore ensures that all economic activities, whatever their purpose or results, provided that they are themselves subject to VAT, are taxed in a wholly neutral way.' [Emphasis added.]

23. I think the judgment in *Schul (Gaston) Douane Expediteur BV v Inspecteur der Invoerrechten en Accijnzen* (Case 15/81), [1982] ECR 1409 at 1426, para 10 is even more instructive in as much as it is there stated that—

'. . . value-added tax is chargeable on each transaction only after deduction of the amount of value-added tax borne directly by the cost of the various price components.'

24. It follows that what matters is whether the second taxable person actually paid the value added tax to the first. If so, he may deduct it even if it was incorrectly claimed from him.

25. In its judgment of 21 September 1988 in *EC Commission v French Republic* (Case 50/87) [1988] ECR 4797 at 4817, paras 16, 17, the court was also led to point out that—

> '... in the absence of any provision empowering the Member States to limit the right of deduction granted to taxable persons, that right must be exercised immediately in respect of all the taxes charged on transactions relating to inputs. Such limitations on the right of deduction have an impact on the level of the tax burden and must be applied in a similar manner in all the Member States. Consequently, derogations are permitted only in the cases *expressly provided for* in the directive.' [Emphasis added.]

However, there is no provision in the Sixth Directive providing that an amount due solely because it is mentioned on the invoice does not give rise to a right to deduct.

26. Finally, with regard to the need to prevent fraud, the court stated in the same judgment (see [1988] ECR 4797 at 4818, para 22) that that need cannot justify measures derogating from the directive otherwise than under the procedure which is provided for in art 27.

27. I therefore consider that the objections raised by the governments are not convincing and that the right to deduct provided for in the Sixth Directive extends to tax due solely because it is mentioned on the invoice, except where it is shown that the amount in question was not paid to the taxable person who drew up the invoice.

Second question

28. In the event that the first question is answered in the affirmative, the Hoge Raad also asks the court whether the Sixth Directive allows the member states to exclude—either entirely or in certain cases—the right to deduct such tax by laying down requirements regarding the invoice.

29. It can be seen from art 18(1)(a) that to exercise his right to deduct, the taxable person must hold an invoice drawn up in accordance with art 22(3). According to art 22(3)(b), the invoice is to state clearly the price exclusive of tax and the corresponding tax at each rate as well as any exemptions.

30. In its judgment of 14 July 1988 in *Jeunehomme v Belgian State* (Joined Cases 123 and 330/87) [1988] ECR 4517, the court held that although the Sixth Directive does no more than require an invoice containing certain information, member states may provide for the inclusion of additional information. Article 22(8) provides that—'Member States may impose other obligations which they deem necessary for the correct levying and collection of the tax and for the prevention of fraud.'

31. In the operative part of the judgment in *Jeunehomme*, the court (at 4545) ruled that:

> 'Articles 18(1)(a) and 22(3)(a) and (b) of the Sixth Council Directive (77/388/ EEC) of 17 May 1977 allow Member States to make the exercise of the right to deduction subject to the holding of an invoice which must contain *certain particulars which are necessary* in order to ensure the levying of value-added tax and permit supervision by the tax authorities. Such particulars must not, by reason of their number or technical nature, render the exercise of the right to deduction practically impossible or excessively difficult.' [Emphasis added.]

32. In the main proceedings, it is not, properly speaking, additional information which is in question but the following requirements.

33. According to art 35(1)(g) of the Wet op de Omzetbelasting (Law on Turnover Tax) 1968, the invoice which a trader must issue to another trader in respect of

goods or services he supplies to the other trader must mention clearly 'the amount of the tax due in respect of the goods or services supplied. *A different amount of tax may not be stated*'. [Emphasis added.]

34. Second, art 24*b* of the Uitvoeringsbesluit Omzetbelasting (Turnover Tax Implementation Order) 1968 provides that, where there is sub-contracting, value added tax is charged not to the sub-contractor who performs the service but to the (principal) contractor who purchases it. The sub-contractor should not mention any amount in respect of value added tax on his invoice but should insert in its place the words 'turnover tax transferred'.

35. It follows moreover from the Netherlands legislation that when a principal contractor receives an invoice which infringes one of the provisions summarised above, he is not entitled to deduct the amount incorrectly mentioned on the invoice because it is not drawn up in the prescribed manner, notwithstanding the fact that the person who mentioned that amount on the invoice is also liable to pay it to the authorities.

36. Let me now consider the general rules and the 'transfer' rules.

37. (a) I would like to make the following observations concerning the prohibition of mentioning on an invoice an amount of value added tax other than that legally due.

38. I consider that even if that obligation is not complied with, a member state cannot be permitted to deprive a (principal) contractor of his right to deduct on the basis of an argument of form to the effect that the invoice does not correspond to the provisions of national law on the drawing-up of invoices.

39. In my opinion, the obligation not to mention an amount of value added tax other than that legally due does not constitute one of the 'other obligations' which the member states may impose under art 22(8) for the correct levying and collection of value added tax. On the contrary, it is an obligation which, although not provided for expressly in the directive, is none the less implicit therein.

40. Moreover, the Sixth Directive has already laid down a sanction if that obligation is not fulfilled: any person who mentions (even incorrectly) a tax on an invoice or other document serving as an invoice is liable to pay it.

41. Furthermore, I pointed out in connection with the answer to be given to the first question that the right to deduct applies to tax which is due solely because it is mentioned on the invoice.

42. It is also therefore inconceivable that the member states may derogate from so fundamental a principle of the Sixth Directive as the right to make deductions on the basis of a provision of their national law requiring that an invoice mention the exact amount of value added tax legally due, to the exclusion of any other amount.

43. (b) Let me now turn my attention to the transfer rules. Those rules were brought into effect in the Netherlands only by virtue of a derogation from the Sixth Directive granted by the Council (see (1982) OJ C197, p 1) under art 27.

44. Article 27(1) commences as follows:

'The Council, acting unanimously on a proposal from the Commission, may authorise any Member State to introduce *special measures for derogation* from the provisions of this Directive, in order to simplify the procedure for charging the tax or to prevent certain types of tax evasion or avoidance.' [Emphasis added.]

45. The basic provision of the value added tax transfer rules derogates from one of the fundamental principles of the Sixth Directive, namely the principle that the invoice must state clearly the price exclusive of tax and the corresponding tax at each rate as well as any exemptions. In this case, there is no exemption from but a transfer of value added tax, with the effect that there is undoubtedly a derogation from that principle.

46. However, I consider that rules derogating from the Sixth Directive, authorised by the Council, must necessarily be regarded as a body. The value added tax transfer

rules are intended to prevent certain types of tax evasion. In order for the rules to achieve those objectives, the principal contractor would have to supervise the activities of each of his sub-contractors and accept from them only invoices bearing the words 'value added tax transferred'. The prohibition of deducting tax incorrectly mentioned on such an invoice is intended to make the principal contractor exercise care. The prohibition is therefore an essential element of those special rules. This second derogation from the principles of the Sixth Directive must also therefore be regarded as covered by the Council's authorisation.

Conclusion

47. On the basis of the foregoing considerations, I would propose that the court should answer the Hoge Raad's questions as follows:

    1. The right to make the deduction provided for in the Sixth Directive applies to the tax which is due solely because it is mentioned on the invoice except in cases in which it can be established that the amount in question was not paid to the taxable person who drew up the invoice.

    2. The Sixth Directive does not allow the member states to exclude the right to deduct value added tax by laying down a requirement that the invoice mention the exact amount of value added tax legally due, to the exclusion of any other amount.

The situation is different where a member state has been authorised by the Council under art 27 of the Sixth Directive to apply rules derogating from the directive, and prohibiting the mention of an amount of value added tax on the invoice and excluding the right to deduct if that prohibition is not complied with.

13 December 1989. **THE COURT OF JUSTICE** delivered the following judgment.

    1. By an order of 28 October 1987, which was received at the court on 4 November 1987, the Hoge Raad der Nederlanden (Supreme Court of the Netherlands) referred to the court for a preliminary ruling under art 177 of the EEC Treaty two questions on the interpretation of several provisions of EC Council Directive 77/388 of 17 May 1977 (the Sixth Directive).

    2. Those questions arose in proceedings between the tax entity Genius Holding BV (called 'Genius BV' at the material time) (the taxpayer company), whose premises are in IJmuiden and which carries out assembly and machine-tooling work, and the Staatssecretaris van Financiën (Secretary of State for Finance).

    3. For the period from 1 July 1982 to 31 December 1982 inclusive, the amount of tax owed by the taxpayer company, which uses sub-contractors to fulfil its orders, was adjusted on the ground that, contrary to the legislation in force, it had deducted from the turnover tax due from it value added tax invoiced to Genicon BV by two sub-contractors, Vissers Pijpleiding en Montage BV and Montagebedrijf J van Mierlo.

    4. Since the Inspecteur der Omzetbelasting (Turnover Tax Inspector) rejected the taxpayer company's objection to the above-mentioned adjustment, that company brought an action before the Gerechtshof Amsterdam (Regional Court of Appeal, Amsterdam), which upheld the contested decision.

    5. On appeal, the Hoge Raad considered that according to the rules of Netherlands law deduction was permitted only when the tax mentioned in the invoice was actually due. However, in accordance with the transfer rules applicable in the Netherlands to the activities in question by virtue of an authorisation issued by the Council under art 27 of the Sixth Directive, a sub-contractor was not liable to pay value added tax in respect of services rendered to a principal contractor, the tax being due only from the latter on the amount which he invoiced to the person who had placed the order. It followed that the taxpayer company could not deduct

value added tax on the basis that it was invoiced to the taxpayer company by sub-contractors contrary to the above-mentioned rules.

6. Since it had doubts as to the compatibility of such rules with the Sixth Directive, the Hoge Raad stayed the proceedings and referred the following two questions to the court for a preliminary ruling:

'1. Does the right to deduct provided for in the Sixth Directive apply to the tax which is due solely because it is mentioned on the invoice?

2. If so, does the directive still allow the Member States to exclude—either entirely or in certain special cases—the right to deduct such tax by laying down requirements regarding the invoice?'

7. Reference is made to the report for the hearing for a fuller account of the facts of the case, the course of the procedure and the written observations submitted to the court are mentioned or discussed hereinafter only in so far as is necessary for the reasoning of the court.

8. For the purpose of the answer to be given to the first question, it should be pointed out that according to art 17(2)(a) of the Sixth Directive, the taxable person is to be entitled to deduct from the tax which he is liable to pay—'value added tax due or paid in respect of goods or services supplied or to be supplied to him by another taxable person'.

. 9. The taxpayer company and the Commission maintains that that provision must be interpreted as meaning that any tax mentioned in the invoice may be deducted.

10. They consider that the interpretation to the effect that only taxes corresponding to the supply of goods or services may be deducted is contrary to the purpose of the system of deductions, which is designed to ensure, as the court pointed out in its judgment of 14 February 1985 in *Rompelman (D A) and Rompelman-Van Deelen (E A) v Minister van Financiën* (Case 268/83) [1985] ECR 655, complete neutrality in regard to the fiscal burden borne by all economic activities, regardless of their purpose or results, on condition that those activities are themselves subject to value added tax. Since, under art 21(1)(c) of the Sixth Directive, any person who mentions value added tax on an invoice or other document serving as invoice is liable to pay that tax even if it is not legally due, the exclusion in such cases of the right to deduct implies the taxation of an activity in a manner contrary to the principle of the neutrality of value added tax.

11. Furthermore, that interpretation would lead to traders being required to check whether the value added tax being invoiced is legally due, which requires an assessment of the rate of tax chosen and a knowledge of the exemptions granted. It would therefore be an obstacle to the efficient conduct of commercial relations.

12. In that regard, it should be pointed out, first of all, that in drafting art 17(2)(a), the Council departed both from the wording of art 11(1)(a) of EC Council Directive 67/228 of 11 April 1967 (the Second Directive) and from that of art 17(2)(a) of the Commission's proposal for a Sixth Directive ((1973) OJ C80, p 1), provisions under which the taxable person was entitled to deduct any tax invoiced to him in respect of goods or of services supplied to him.

13. It must be inferred from the changes made to the above-mentioned provisions that the right to deduct may be exercised only in respect of taxes actually due, that is to say, the taxes corresponding to a transaction subject to value added tax or paid in so far as they were due.

14. That interpretation of art 17(2)(a) is confirmed by the other provisions of the Sixth Directive.

15. According to art 18(1)(a), to exercise his right to deduct, the taxable person must hold an invoice, drawn up in accordance with art 22(3), which requires the invoice to state clearly the price exclusive of tax and the corresponding tax at each rate as well as any exemptions. In accordance with that provision, mention of the tax corresponding to the supply of goods and services is an element in the invoice on

which the exercise of the right to deduct depends. It follows that that right cannot
a be exercised in respect of tax which does not correspond to a given transaction,
either because that tax is higher than that legally due or because the transaction in
question is not subject to value added tax.

16. Furthermore, according to art 20(1):

b 'The initial deduction shall be adjusted according to the procedures laid down
by the Member States, in particular: (*a*) where that deduction was higher or
lower than that to which the taxable person was entitled . . .'

It follows from that provision that where the deduction initially carried out does not
correspond to the amount of the tax legally due, it has to be adjusted, even if it
corresponds to the amount of the tax mentioned on the invoice or other document
serving as invoice.

c 17. That interpretation of art 17(2)(*a*) is the one which is best adapted to prevent
tax evasion which would be made easier if any tax invoiced could be deducted.

18. Finally, with regard to the argument put forward by the taxpayer company
and the Commission to the effect that the fact of limiting the exercise of the right to
deduct taxes corresponding to the supply of goods and services calls into question
the neutrality of value added tax, it should be pointed out that, in order to ensure
d the application of that principle, it is for the member states to provide in their
internal legal systems for the possibility of correcting any tax improperly invoiced
where the person who issued the invoice shows that he acted in good faith.

19. The answer to the first question should therefore be that the right to deduct
provided for in the Sixth Directive does not apply to tax which is due solely because
it is mentioned on the invoice.

e 20. Having regard to the answer to the first question, there is no need to answer
the second question referred to the court.

Costs

21. The costs incurred by the Netherlands government, the Spanish government,
the government of the Federal Republic of Germany and the Commission of the
f European Communities, which have submitted observations to the court, are not
recoverable. Since these proceedings are, in so far as the parties to the main
proceedings are concerned, in the nature of a step in the proceedings pending before
the national court, the decision on costs is a matter for that court.

On those grounds, the court (Fifth Chamber) in answer to the questions submitted
to it by the Hoge Raad der Nederlanden hereby rules:

g The right to deduct provided for in the Sixth Directive does not apply to tax
which is due solely because it is mentioned on the invoice.

Agents: *P A Dijkman Dulkes* and *J A F van Haaster* (for the taxpayer company);
H J Heinemann, Acting Secretary General of the Ministry of Foreign Affairs (for the
h Netherlands government); *M Seidel* and *H-J Horn* (for the government of the
Federal Republic of Germany); *J Conde de Saro* and *R Garcia-Valdecasas y
Fernandez* (for the Spanish government); *J F Buhl*, a member of the Legal
Department and *M Mees*, Hague Bar (for the Commission).

Rengan Krishnan Esq   Barrister.

Lord Advocate v Butt and others

OUTER HOUSE OF THE COURT OF SESSION
LORD PROSSER
9, 21 NOVEMBER 1990

Assessment – Estimated assessment – Tax due and payable – Obligation to account – Part payment of tax payable under assessment – Action by Crown to recover the balance with interest – Whether taxpayers under an 'obligation of accounting' in respect of tax payable under assessment – Prescription and Limitation (Scotland) Act 1973, s 6, Sch 1, para 1(a), (f).

The taxpayers had been the partners in a firm. They were assessed to income tax under Sch D in respect of the three years 1979–80 to 1981–82. Each of the assessments was appealed against. The assessment for 1979–80 was confirmed and those for the other two years were determined by agreement under s 54 of the Taxes Management Act 1970. The taxpayers paid part of the tax due under each assessment. On 9 October 1989 the Crown began proceedings to recover the tax outstanding under each assessment with interest. The taxpayers submitted that the obligation on them to settle the outstanding amount had subsisted for a continuous period of five years and that during that time the Crown had neither made a claim in relation to the obligation nor acknowledged its subsistence and accordingly under s 6(1) of the Prescription and Limitation (Scotland) Act 1973 (the 1973 Act) the obligation had been extinguished. The obligations to which s 6 applied were defined in para 1[a] of Sch 1 to the 1973 Act. The taxpayers contended that the obligation which the Crown was attempting to enforce was an 'obligation of accounting' within para 1(f) and that the obligation to pay under the assessments was an element of the single overall obligation of accounting. With regard to the interest claimed, the taxpayers submitted that it was either not due as a result of the prescription of the primary obligation or that, as a result of para 1(a) of Sch 1 which applied the provisions of s 6 to interest, the obligation to pay interest had itself prescribed.

Held – (1) An obligation to account was distinct from an obligation to pay. An obligation of payment under an assessment could not be merged with any obligations prior to the assessment such as the obligation to make a return. The obligation to make a return could be seen as an obligation to account. However, the obligation to pay tax on the basis of an assessment was quite unlinked to any obligation which was even comparable to an accounting. The obligation being enforced in the present action was an obligation to pay which did not fall within para 1(f) of Sch 1 to the 1973 Act and therefore s 6(1) of that Act did not operate to extinguish the obligation.

(2) Paragraph 1(a) of Sch 1 to the 1973 Act applied the provisions of s 6 to interest on the unpaid tax. Accordingly, the obligation to pay interest before 9 October 1984 (being five years before the Crown commenced proceedings to recover the unpaid tax with interest) was extinguished.

A decree de plano for the principal sums and for interest accruing from 9 October 1984 would therefore be granted in favour of the Crown.

Notes

For the time limits on the commencement of proceedings for the recovery of tax or of interest on tax, see Simon's Taxes A3.1406.

---

a Paragraph 1, so far as material, is set out at p 254 *b–d*, post

Cases referred to in opinion

Hutcheson & Co's Administrator v Taylor's Executrix 1931 SC 484, CS.
Lord Advocate v Hepburn 1990 SLT 530, CS.

Application

The pursuers, the Crown, applied to the Outer House of the Court of Session for a decree de plano to recover tax and interest on tax outstanding on three assessments. The defenders, the taxpayers, contended that the obligation on them to settle the outstanding amount due under each assessment had subsisted for a continuous period of five years, during which time the Crown had neither made a claim in relation to the obligation nor acknowledged its subsistence and accordingly under s 6(1) of the Prescription and Limitation (Scotland) Act 1973 (the 1973 Act) the obligation had been extinguished. The facts are set out in the opinion of Lord Prosser.

J W McNeill for the Crown.
Colin J Tyre for the taxpayers.

The court made avizandum.

21 November 1990. The following opinion was delivered.

LORD PROSSER. The pursuer is the Lord Advocate, suing on behalf of the Inland Revenue Commissioners (the Crown). The defenders are the whole former partners of a now dissolved firm (the taxpayers). It is a matter of admission that the taxpayers were assessed to income tax (Sch D) in respect of the three income tax years 1979–80 to 1981–82. Each of the assessments was appealed against, that for 1979–80 being confirmed, and those for the other two years being determined in accordance with the provisions of s 54 of the Taxes Management Act 1970 by certain reductions. Certain payments to account of the tax payable under each of these assessments are acknowledged to have been made and, by its first conclusion, the Crown seeks payment of the balance which is alleged to remain payable in respect of each assessment. By its second conclusion, the Crown seeks a sum in respect of the aggregated interest claimed to be payable by the taxpayers in respect of the balances allegedly due from time to time from the reckonable dates applicable to the assessments in question until 6 July 1989. Interest accruing from that date onwards until payment is sought under the first conclusion. By its third conclusion, the Crown seeks a sum claimed to be due in respect of Class 4 national insurance contributions due under the Social Security Act 1975.

At procedure roll, it was argued on behalf of the taxpayers that any obligation incumbent on them to make payment of the sums first and third concluded for had prescribed and that, so far as the interest sought under the second conclusion was concerned, it was either not due (as a result of the prescription of the primary obligations) or that it itself related to an obligation which had prescribed. On behalf of the Crown, it was contended that there was no relevant defence and that I should grant decree de plano in terms of all three conclusions. It was common ground that the position in relation to the Class 4 contributions would be the same as the position in relation to the Sch D assessments and that accordingly the fate of conclusion 3 would be the same as conclusion 1.

Section 6(1) of the Prescription and Limitation (Scotland) Act 1973 (the 1973 Act) provides that if an obligation to which the section applies has subsisted for a continuous period of five years, without any relevant claim having been made in relation to the obligation, and without the subsistence of the obligation having been relevantly acknowledged, then as from the expiration of that period the obligation shall be extinguished. This provision is the foundation of the argument for the taxpayers, both in relation to the claim for principal sums and in relation to the claim for interest. If the section applies to any of the obligations here in question, it was not suggested on behalf of the Crown that the required period of five years had not expired, or that there had been a relevant claim or relevant acknowledgment interrupting prescription. The sole issue in relation to each obligation is therefore whether it is indeed an obligation to which the section applies.

Section 6(2) provides that Sch 1 to the 1973 Act is to have effect for defining the obligations to which the section applies. Paragraph 1 of that Schedule provides that (subject to para 2) s 6 applies to seven types of obligation, listed as (*a*) to (*g*). Only head (*a*) and head (*f*) are directly relied on by the taxpayers, the former in relation to the claim for interest and the latter in relation to the claims for principal sums. In terms of head (*a*), s 6 applies—

'. . . to any obligation to pay a sum of money due in respect of a particular period—

    (i) by way of interest;

    (ii) by way of an instalment of an annuity;

    (iii) by way of feuduty . . .'

and so on, with a list of various items covering such matters as ground annuals, rent and the like. In terms of head (*f*), s 6 applies 'to any obligation of accounting, other than accounting for trust funds'. In terms of the remaining heads of para 1, s 6 applies (and I summarise) to any obligation based on redress of unjustified enrichment, to any obligation arising from negotiorum gestio, to any obligation arising from liability (whether arising from any enactment or from any rule of law) to make reparation, to any obligation under a bill of exchange or a promissory note, and finally, under head (*g*), to any obligation arising from, or by reason of any breach of, a contract or promise, not being an obligation falling within any other provision of this paragraph. It is also worth noticing that by para 2 of Sch 1 it is provided that notwithstanding anything in the foregoing paragraph, s 6 does not apply inter alia to any obligation to recognise or obtemper a decree of court, or to any obligation specified in Sch 3 as an imprescriptible obligation. Among the obligations so specified in Sch 3 is (at head (*e*) of that Schedule):

'Any obligation of a trustee—

    (i) to produce accounts of the trustee's intromissions with any property of the trust;

    (ii) to make reparation or restitution . . .

    (iii) to make furthcoming to any person entitled thereto, any trust property, or the proceeds of any such property . . .'

This class of imprescriptible obligations is plainly to be looked at alongside the exclusion from para 1(*f*) of Sch 1, of 'accounting for trust funds'.

In relation to the principal sums concluded for, the contention of the taxpayers was that the obligation in question was an obligation of accounting within the meaning of para 1(*f*) of Sch 1 to the 1973 Act. While the question was thus essentially one of interpreting that provision, it was necessary to look to the Taxes Acts in order to obtain a fuller picture of the nature of the obligation in question. It was accepted that the obligations in question were not enforceable by an ordinary action of count reckoning and payment, but that mechanism for enforcement was not definitional of an obligation of accounting, and examination of the Taxes Acts would show that the obligation here in question had indeed the essential or defining characteristics of an obligation of accounting.

It was submitted that the obligation which the Crown was trying to enforce arose from or consisted of three identifiable elements. There was the receipt of income from a trade. There was the charging provision to the effect that the tax shall be charged in respect of that income. And finally there was the making of the assessment (however it might become final). The receipt of income and the charging provisions produced an obligation to account to the Revenue for tax, and the third element, the assessment, was to be regarded as this obligation to account becoming exigible by court action. An analogy could be drawn between this analysis and the structure of an action of count reckoning and payment, in which the obligation to account and the obligation to pay were distinct elements of the single overall obligation of accounting.

In support of this analysis and analogy, counsel drew attention to the provisions of ss 7 and 8 of the Taxes Management Act 1970, contending that the 'return' required of a taxpayer was in effect what would normally be called an 'account' or 'accounting'. Similarly and contrariwise, if one looked at ss 349 and 350 of the Income and Corporation Taxes Act 1988, one found a requirement to deliver an account, which was essentially the same process of submitting information in a form which could be regarded as a return. Reference was also made to s 216 of the Capital Transfer Tax Act 1984 (now the Inheritance Tax Act 1984) (which was said to illustrate the fact that an account could be a return intimating to the Revenue that an event had occurred which was the basis for chargeability), and also to Part III of the Taxes Management Act 1970 itself, showing how one person might have to make a return which was relevant for the liability of others, and that such returns might extend beyond any direct information as to income or indeed money. These provisions in relation to returns and accounts in the Taxes Acts showed that one was within the ordinary general meaning of accounting, and provisions of s 55(9) of the Taxes Management Act 1970, rendering the tax exigible by court action on the expiry of 30 days from assessment merely provided the final element in the obligation of accounting becoming effective.

Counsel for the taxpayers acknowledged that if I were to find in his favour, I would have to distinguish or differ from the decision in *Lord Advocate v Hepburn* 1990 SLT 530. It was, however, apparent that the arguments now advanced had not been advanced, not, at least, in quite the same form, in *Hepburn*, and I should accept these arguments rather than the reasoning of Lord Dervaird in that case. His Lordship had in any event treated 'accounting' as if it had to be equiparated with a right to an action of count reckoning and payment. That was wrong: an accounting was an accounting whether it was enforced by that ordinary action or by other methods. Any other party, having to use an action of count reckoning and payment, would be deprived of his rights by the provisions of para 1(*f*) of Sch 1 to the 1973 Act. By s 24 of that Act, it was expressly provided that the Act binds the Crown. The Crown should not escape the effects of head (*f*) simply because a different form of action applied to the enforcement of its right to an accounting under the Taxes Acts. If the Revenue disposed of a tax dispute by agreement, it was plain that their rights would prescribe under para 1(*g*) of Sch 1. Where the matter was resolved, not by agreement but by the ordinary statutory mechanisms, one would expect prescription to run in the same way.

So far as the claim for interest was concerned, it was submitted that head (*a*)(i) plainly applied. That had been the view of the Lord Ordinary in *Hepburn*. Under that head, there was no word requiring interpretation, as 'accounting' might under head (*f*). The obligation to pay interest was precisely an obligation to pay a sum of money 'due in respect of a particular period'. In the context of interest on tax, that was effectively the terminology of s 89 of the Taxes Management Act 1970, at least as it had existed prior to amendment. The right to interest accrued from day to day. The effect of head (*a*)(i) was that rights to interest for later periods would remain unprescribed while interest attributable to earlier dates would prescribe from day to day with the passage of time. In the present case, interest attributable to all periods prior to 9 October 1984 had prescribed, while interest attributable to periods since then had not prescribed, but would not be due if the argument in relation to principal sums were decided in favour of the taxpayers. I should therefore assoilzie the taxpayers from all three conclusions.

On behalf of the Crown it was submitted that I should refuse the taxpayers' motion and grant decree de plano in favour of the Crown in terms of all three conclusions for payment. Dealing first with the taxpayers' submissions on para 1(*f*) of Sch 1 to the 1973 Act, counsel for the Crown submitted that an obligation to account was not only a familiar type of obligation in itself, but was quite different from an obligation to pay. As regards an obligation to account, the Crown submitted that it was something which emerged only where the obligant had intromitted with estates to which the claimant had a right or in which he was interested. (Reference was made to *Hutcheson & Co's Administrator v Taylor's Executrix* 1931 SC 484.) That was what gave rise to an obligation to account, quite apart from the question of whether an action of count reckoning and payment was the appropriate mode of enforcement. The fact that such an action would also include conclusions for payment (whether on the basis of the count and reckoning, or in the event of failure to account) did not mean that the obligation to pay was one and the same as, or part of the same single obligation as, the obligation to account. On that simple and general basis, and whether or not the obligation to make a return could be seen as an obligation to account, the obligation being enforced in the present action was an obligation to pay, and did not fall within head (*f*).

An illustration of the separateness of these obligations was to be found in Sch 3(*e*) to the 1973 Act. Head (*e*)(i), referring to an obligation to produce accounts, was the only part of that head which was concerned with an obligation of accounting and it was the status of this particular item as an imprescriptable obligation which accounted for the exception, in para 1(*f*) of Sch 1, of 'accounting for trust funds'. The other obligations covered by Sch 3(*e*) were not part of any accounting obligation, were not within the expression 'accounting for trust funds' in head (*f*), and were correspondingly not within the general reference of head (*f*) to an obligation of accounting. Furthcoming or payment was a quite separate matter from accounting.

I am not sure that the reference to Sch 3 throws much light on the matter. On the other hand, I think that as a general proposition the contrast between an obligation to account and an obligation to pay is well founded. I think I would accept that as a matter of ordinary language, a reference to accounting (or failing to account) for funds in one's hands may spill over into the field of paying or failing to pay. But in any reasonably precise reference to legal obligations, the distinction seems to me to be a clear one, and while the looser usage to which I have referred makes it possible to contend that the two obligations are essentially elements of the same obligation, that contention none the less seems to me to be essentially unsound. The structure and procedures of an action of count reckoning and payment seem to me to confirm this. The enforcement of the obligation to account is one thing, and the enforcement of the obligation to pay, although dealt with in the same action, seems to me to be quite separate.

Turning to the taxing statutes, counsel for the Crown submitted that the various stages and mechanisms covered by the statutes demonstrated the general distinction between obligations to account and obligations to pay. The earning of relevant income gave rise to a number of obligations which involved the providing of information or making returns. These had some similarity to an obligation to account, inasmuch as they were procedures which had to be gone through before any question of an obligation to pay could arise. But even the fulfilment of the obligation to make a return did not create an obligation to pay. The creation of the new legal relationship in which there was a right to payment and an obligation to pay was effected not by the submission of a return, but by the quite separate act of assessment. A consideration of Part IV of the Taxes Management Act 1970, and in particular s 29, showed not merely that assessment was something new and separate from the stage when returns were made, but that assessment might indeed have little or no relationship with that prior, information-providing stage. It was wrong to regard the obligations of accounting and payment, in the general situation, as a

single obligation; but it was all the more wrong to attempt to merge an obligation of
a   payment arising from assessment with any obligations prior to assessment such as
the obligation to make a return. it was only at that prior stage that any analogy could
be drawn between the statutory procedures and an accounting, and the obligation
to pay tax on the basis of an assessment was quite unlinked to any obligation which
was even comparable to an accounting.

In my opinion, these contentions are well founded. Moreover, it seems to me that
b   when one considers the taxing provisions in relation to questions of prescription or
time for enforcement, the separateness of the various obligations becomes all the
more evident. The argument advanced on behalf of the taxpayers proceeded on the
basis that the prescriptive period began to run from the date of assessment. It is
implicit in that submission that the relevant obligation of accounting arose at the
time of the assessment. But by that time, the obligation in question had none of the
c   features of an accounting, and was quite simply an obligation to pay. If on the other
hand one tries to regard the whole procedure as a single obligation, beginning with
the obligation to make a return, the prescriptive period (ignoring for the moment
statutory provisions) should be seen as beginning to run as soon as the obligation
emerges in its original form of a duty to make a return. Counsel for the taxpayers
was in my view right in feeling unable to argue that such a prescriptive period might
d   run, even in principle. But in any event, in the context of the Taxes Acts, it is clear
from the provisions of s 34 of the Taxes Management Act 1970 that an assessment
can be raised within the specified six-year period, quite regardless of the position in
relation to returns or any prescription which might notionally apply to that stage of
matters. In my opinion this merely confirms the impossibility of regarding the
obligation to pay on an assessment as integral with the original obligation to make a
e   return, or as being in any sense an obligation of accounting.

Counsel for the Crown advanced a much wider argument in relation to s 6 of the
1973 Act contending that it applied only to private rights, and not to rights which
were either public or statutory in their foundations. I was referred to the background
of the 1973 Act, as revealed by the comments and recommendations of the Scottish
Law Commission. I have not found these useful in interpreting the terms of the
f   statute as it was eventually enacted. It was further contended that apart from heads
(*a*) and (*f*), the obligations dealt with in para 1 of Sch 1 were indeed all matters of
private right, and that on the principle of noscitur a sociis, heads (*a*) and (*f*) likewise
should be seen as limited to situations of private right and obligation. The obligations
dealt with under the other heads would no doubt typically be found in situations
created in the realm of private law, with a basis such as contract or promise such as
g   is mentioned in head (*g*). But I find nothing in their terms to rule out the possibility
that the obligation in question might be created by statute, or might, however
created, arise in the realm of public law. Head (*d*) expressly envisages the possibility
of a liability which might arise under an enactment rather than at common law. In
any event in the absence of any clear indication of limitation under other heads, I do
not consider that it would be right to read a limitation into head (*a*) or head (*f*)
h   which was not evident from its own terms. The simple terms of s 24 of the 1973 Act
make it all the harder, in my opinion, to contend that the Crown is only bound when
its rights derive from contract or the like. In relation to head (*f*), I see no need to
limit its terms so as to exclude either public or statutory relationships, and indeed if
a statute created an obligation of accounting, as it well might, between private
citizens, I can see no reason why that should not be subject to the ordinary
j   prescriptive rules set out in the Schedule. So too, I see nothing in the terms of head
(*a*) which suggest that one is concerned only with private law, or with non-statutory
law. In my view this argument for the Crown is unsound.

In relation to the claim for interest, it was again submitted, on behalf of the
Crown, that the present obligation did not fall within the terms of para 1(*a*) of Sch 1
to the 1973 Act. That provision did not say that s 6 applied to any obligation to pay

a sum of money by way of interest. It had to be 'due in respect of a particular period'. All the other items set out in head (a) related to payments in respect of a particular and identifiable period. It was accepted that interest accruing from day to day did not fit that pattern precisely, but since the requirement that the money must be due in respect of a particular period covered interest under sub-head (i), those words had to be given a meaning in relation to interest, and should be construed as meaning that the obligation must be looked at over the period as a whole, from the reckonable date up until the present. The obligation to pay money due in respect of the period before 9 October 1984 could not be separated from the obligation to pay money by way of interest in respect of the period after that date, so that the earlier obligation could prescribe, while the later did not. More particularly, as I understood the argument, the provision could not be read in such a way as to have a 'rolling' prescription, with the obligation to pay interest in respect of a particular day prescribing, day by day, five years later.

I have some sympathy with these submissions, and am uneasy as to whether the opening words of head (a) were carefully considered in relation to sub-head (i) as well as the other sub-heads. On the other hand, it is plain that claims for interest are indeed intended to be subject to the five-year prescription, and I am not persuaded that the concept of a single period in respect of which all accrued interest is due will normally make sense. The argument perhaps appears more presentable in a case such as the present, where the interest has been aggregated for a specified period. But the aggregation to a particular chosen date does not rest on, or create, any objectively particular period. The period in respect of which interest is due will in fact continue beyond the date to which it happens to have been aggregated. It is, on that view, a constantly extending period, and does not appear to me to fit the words of the statute at all well. I have come to the view that where interest accrues from day to day, the interest in respect of a particular day is to be treated as prescribing when the obligation to pay that interest has subsisted for a continuous period of five years in terms of s 6.

In these circumstances, I am satisfied that the Crown is entitled to decree for the principal sums sued for in the first and third conclusions. I am also satisfied that the Crown is entitled to interest in respect of the period since 9 October 1984, but not in respect of any time before then. By agreement of parties, I put the case out by order in order that figures may be produced to resolve the question of interest in the light of my decision. I shall grant the appropriate decrees and dispose of pleas-in-law at that stage.

Decree de plano for the tax claimed and interest accruing since 9 October 1984 granted.

Solicitors: *Solicitor of Inland Revenue*; *John G Gray & Co, SSC*, Edinburgh (for the taxpayers).

Rengan Krishnan Esq Barrister.

Lawson (Inspector of Taxes) v Johnson Matthey plc

COURT OF APPEAL, CIVIL DIVISION
FOX, McCOWAN AND BELDAM LJJ
13, 14 FEBRUARY, 27 MARCH 1991

Deduction in computing profits – Capital or revenue expenditure – Payment to preserve existing trade – Insolvency of taxpayer company and subsidiary – Purchase of subsidiary by Bank of England subject to injection of £50m into subsidiary by taxpayer company – Whether payment capital or revenue – Whether incurred wholly and exclusively for purposes of trade – Income and Corporation Taxes Act 1970, s 130(a).

The taxpayer company carried on the business of refining and marketing precious metals and JMB, which carried on the business of banking, was one of its subsidiaries. In 1984, JMB experienced financial difficulties. At a board meeting of the taxpayer company it was concluded (i) that JMB was insolvent and could not open its doors for business the following day unless further financing, which the taxpayer company could not afford to supply, was made available; (ii) that the collapse of JMB and the resulting loss of confidence in the taxpayer company would lead to demands by lending institutions for the repayment of metals and moneys owed to them by the taxpayer company which the taxpayer company would be unable to meet and that the taxpayer company would therefore have to cease trading; (iii) that there was no alternative but to wind up JMB; and (iv) that a receiver should be appointed to facilitate the orderly disposal of the taxpayer company's assets. When that decision was communicated to the Bank of England it made a non-negotiable offer to purchase the issued share capital of JMB for £1 provided the taxpayer company injected £50m into JMB (free from any obligation to repay) prior to the sale. The taxpayer company accepted the offer on condition that the Bank provided a stand-by facility of £250m. The agreement was implemented by the opening of business the following day and was subsequently confirmed in a formal agreement. The taxpayer company was assessed to corporation tax for the year 1984–85. The taxpayer company appealed to the General Commissioners claiming that the payment of £50m was an allowable deduction in computing its trading profits. The taxpayer company contended that the payment was an expense of a revenue nature because it was made to preserve its trade from collapse as a result of the collapse of JMB and that it was incurred wholly and exclusively for the purpose of its own trade and was therefore not precluded by s 130(a)ᵃ of the Income and Corporation Taxes Act 1970. The Crown contended that the payment was of a capital nature on three grounds: (i) the payment was made to procure the disposal of a capital asset which were the JMB shares; (ii) the payment was made to free the taxpayer company from a liability of a capital nature relating to JMB's business; and (iii) the payment was not made wholly and exclusively for the purpose of the taxpayer company's trade since its purpose was, inter alia, to rescue JMB and to preserve the business and goodwill of other companies in the group. The commissioners, allowing the appeal, accepted the taxpayer company's contentions and found that the preservation of the taxpayer company was the purpose and result achieved by the payment and that a payment made to preserve an existing trade was a payment of a revenue nature. Vinelott J allowed the Crown's appeal holding that the payment was a payment of a capital nature and that accordingly it would not be allowable as a deduction in computing the taxpayer company's profits. The taxpayer company appealed to the Court of Appeal.

ᵃ Section 130(a), so far as material, provides: '... in computing the amount of the profits or gains to be charged..., no sum shall be deducted in respect of—(a) any ... expenses, not being money wholly and exclusively laid out or expended for the purposes of the trade ...'

Held – There was a single agreement under which the Bank would acquire the JMB
shares for £1 on terms that, prior to the sale, the taxpayer company would inject   *a*
£50m into JMB. Those two elements could not be severed—one being the disposal
of a worthless asset for a nominal consideration and the other a payment made to
preserve the business of the taxpayer company. Accordingly, the payment was a
capital expenditure and the taxpayer company would not be entitled to deduct it as
an allowable expense in computing its profits. The appeal would therefore be
dismissed.   *b*

Notes

For the distinction between capital and revenue expenditure, see Simon's Taxes
B3.1241.
    For the Income and Corporation Taxes Act 1970, s 130(a) (now the Income and   *c*
Corporation Taxes Act 1988, s 74(a)), see ibid, Part G1.

Cases referred to in judgments

Atherton (Inspector of Taxes) v British Insulated and Helsby Cables Ltd [1926] AC
    205, 10 TC 155, HL.   *d*
B P Australia Ltd v Comr of Taxation of the Commonwealth of Australia [1966] AC
    224, [1965] 3 All ER 209, PC.
Comr of Taxes v Nchanga Consolidated Copper Mines [1964] AC 948, [1964] 1 All
    ER 208, PC.
IRC v Carron Co (1967) 45 TC 18, HL.
Mallett (Inspector of Taxes) v Staveley Coal and Iron Co Ltd [1928] 2 KB 405, 13 TC   *e*
    772, CA.
Morgan (Inspector of Taxes) v Tate & Lyle Ltd [1955] AC 21, [1954] 2 All ER 413,
    35 TC 367, HL.
Southern (Inspector of Taxes) v Borax Consolidated Ltd [1941] 1 KB 111, [1940] 4 All
    ER 412, 23 TC 597.
Strick (Inspector of Taxes) v Regent Oil Co Ltd [1966] AC 295, [1965] 3 All ER 174,   *f*
    43 TC 1, HL.
Sun Newspapers Ltd v Federal Comr of Taxation (1938) 61 CLR 337.
Tucker (Inspector of Taxes) v Granada Motorway Services Ltd [1979] STC 393,
    [1979] 1 WLR 683, [1979] 2 All ER 801, 53 TC 92, HL; *affg* [1978] STC 587,
    [1979] 1 WLR 87, [1979] 1 All ER 23, CA; *affg* [1977] STC 353, [1977] 1 WLR
    1411, [1977] 3 All ER 865.   *g*

Cases also cited

Cooke (Inspector of Taxes) v Quick Shoe Repair Service (1949) 30 TC 460.
Usher's Wiltshire Brewery Ltd v Bruce (Surveyor of Taxes) [1915] AC 433, 6 TC 399,
    HL.   *h*

Appeal

Johnson Matthey plc, the taxpayer company, appealed against the decision of
Vinelott J (see [1990] STC 149) dated 15 December 1989 allowing an appeal by the
Crown against a determination of the General Commissioners that a payment of   *j*
£50m by the taxpayer company to one of its subsidiaries was a payment of a revenue
nature made solely to preserve the existing trade of the taxpayer company. The
grounds of appeal were inter alia (i) that the judge had erred in law in holding that
the payment was not of a revenue nature; (ii) that the payment was not made in
consideration of or in return for the disposal of the shares; and (iii) that the judge
had erred in concluding that the two elements could not be severed, one being the

disposal for a nominal sum of a worthless asset and the other a payment to preserve
a the taxpayer company's trade. The facts are set out in the judgment of Fox LJ.

Andrew Park QC and *Thomas Ivory* for the taxpayer company.
Jonathan Parker QC for the Crown.

Cur adv vult

b
27 March. The following judgments were delivered.

FOX LJ. This is an appeal by Johnson Matthey plc (the taxpayer company) from a
decision of Vinelott J (see [1990] STC 149) that a payment of £50m by the taxpayer
company to its subsidiary Johnson Matthey Bankers Ltd (JMB) at the time when
c the shares of JMB were sold to the Bank of England is not an allowable expense in
computing the profits of the taxpayer company's trade for tax purposes.

The facts as found by the General Commissioners were as follows.

The taxpayer company is a United Kingdom quoted company which carries on
business in refining and selling precious metals, particularly platinum. It also
manages a number of subsidiaries in the United Kingdom and abroad. Prior to
d October 1984 one of the taxpayer company's wholly-owned United Kingdom
subsidiaries was JMB, which carried on the business of bankers including the
merchanting of bullion.

In August 1984 JMB got into difficulties on its commercial loan business. Large
advances had been made on what turned out to be inadequate security.

A board meeting of the taxpayer company was held at the Bank of England (the
e Bank) on the night of 30 September–1 October 1984 to deal with the resulting crisis.
At about 12.30 am on 1 October the board reached the following conclusions:

> '(i) that JMB was insolvent and could not open its doors for business later
> that day unless further financing, which [the taxpayer company] could not
> afford to supply, was made available;
> (ii) that the cessation of business by JMB, and resulting damage to confidence
f > in [the taxpayer company], was likely to lead to demands by lending institutions
> for the repayment of metals and moneys owing to them by [the taxpayer
> company] and that [the taxpayer company] would be unable to meet its
> obligations as they fell due in the absence of further financial support, which
> did not seem to be available: [the taxpayer company] would therefore have to
> cease trading;
g > (iii) that there was no alternative to the winding up of JMB and that a liquidator
> should be appointed;
> (iv) that they should however do everything in their power to protect the
> interests of the [taxpayer company's] shareholders and employees and to
> facilitate the orderly disposal of the [taxpayer company's] assets in which
> unsecured creditors would be dealt with on an equitable basis, and that therefore
h > they would ask for the appointment of a receiver for the [taxpayer company];
> (v) that these decisions to ask for a liquidator for JMB and a receiver for the
> taxpayer company should be implemented an hour later at 1.30 am.'

The Bank was told of these decisions at once. The Bank at once made the following
offer, which was not negotiable, to the board of the taxpayer company: (i) the Bank
j would acquire the issued share capital of JMB for the sum of £1; and (ii) prior to
this sale, which would be free of all warranties, the taxpayer company would inject
£50m into JMB.

The Bank also informed the taxpayer company that it was assisting in actively
pursuing the provision of a stand-by facility for the taxpayer company in the event
of the Bank purchasing the JMB shares. Later that night JMB assessed the necessary
facility as £250m.

In consequence of these arrangements, on the advice of its legal and financial advisers the board of the taxpayer company recognised that:

'(i) JMB was insolvent on the advice given by its advisers of the proper level of provision for bad and doubtful debts;
(ii) [the taxpayer company] would be unable to provide sufficient capital for JMB to enable the latter to maintain the prudential ratios appropriate for a recognised bank;
(iii) JMB would be unable to open its doors for business while it remained a subsidiary of [the taxpayer company];
(iv) if the proposal were not acceptable [the taxpayer company] would not be able to meet its obligations if called;
(v) the making of the £50 million loan to JMB and the waiver of repayment of such loan (the form proposed by the Bank for the £50 million repayment) was necessary to retain goodwill and confidence in all the remaining group companies and enable them to stay in business;
(vi) the only practical alternative to the Bank's proposals was to implement their previous decision to ask for the appointment of a receiver for [the taxpayer company] and a liquidator for JMB.'

The board of the taxpayer company resolved conditionally on a stand-by facility of at least £250m being agreed and existing drawings by the taxpayer company of moneys and metals remaining in place, to accept the Bank's proposals for the acquisition by the Bank of the whole of the issued share capital of JMB by the Bank for £1 and for the taxpayer company to make the £50m loan and waiver to JMB.

The commissioners found that the sole purpose for which (or to serve which) the taxpayer company resolved to make the payment of £50m was to enable the taxpayer company to open the doors of its platinum trade on the Monday morning.

The board's decisions were communicated to the Bank and were implemented by the opening of business later that day and confirmed by a formal agreement between the taxpayer company and the Bank on 2 October 1984.

In the taxpayer company's accounts to 31 March 1985 it deducted the £50m as an expense of its platinum trade. The Crown disputed that deduction on two grounds: (i) that it was an expense of a capital nature; and (ii) that it was not paid out wholly and exclusively for the purposes of the trade.

The commissioners stated ([1990] STC 149 at 154):

'We, therefore, find on the evidence and arguments put before us, that the £50 million payment was made to preserve the trade of [the taxpayer company] from collapse, that it did, in fact, preserve the trade from collapse and, as a payment to preserve an existing business, it was of a revenue nature. We further find that [it] was not converted into a payment of a capital nature by the circumstance that it was associated with the disposal of the JMB shares.'

Thus, the commissioners decided both those points in favour of the taxpayer company.

The Crown appealed to the High Court. On the appeal the Crown did not dispute that the moneys were laid out wholly and exclusively for the trade. The Crown did (and does), however, contest the decision that the payment was a revenue expense. The judge accepted the Crown's contention as to that. He said (at 160):

'The purpose of the board of the taxpayer company in agreeing to make that payment was no doubt to preserve the taxpayer company's business. But the means by which that purpose was achieved and indeed in the situation of crisis in the early hours of 1 October the only means by which it could be achieved was to transfer the shares of JMB to the Bank and as part of a single transaction or arrangement to pay £50m to JMB and to release JMB from any obligation to repay it. These two elements cannot be severed, the one being treated as the disposal for a nominal consideration of a worthless but not an onerous asset and the other as a payment made to preserve the business of the taxpayer company.'

Accordingly, the judge concluded that the £50m was a capital payment. From that decision the taxpayer company appeals.

The question arises in determining whether a payment is to be treated as being of an income nature, the court should look at the matter subjectively (what was the purpose of the transaction) or objectively (what did the transaction actually do). The authorities are not conclusive. In *Atherton (Inspector of Taxes) v British Insulated and Helsby Cables Ltd* [1926] AC 205 at 213, 10 TC 155 at 192 Viscount Cave LC said:

'But when an expenditure is made, not only once and for all, but with a view to bringing into existence an asset or an advantage for the enduring benefit of a trade, I think that there is very good reason (in the absence of special circumstances leading to an opposite conclusion) for treating such an expenditure as properly attributable not to revenue but to capital.'

That, as Lord Wilberforce observed in *Tucker (Inspector of Taxes) v Granada Motorway Services Ltd* [1979] STC 393 at 396, [1979] 1 WLR 683 at 686, was regarded as having quasi-statutory force until it was revealed that it might cover an advance more of a revenue character.

In *IRC v Carron Co* (1967) 45 TC 18 at 68, Lord Reid said: 'In a case of this kind what matters is the nature of the advantage for which the money was spent'. And Lord Guest (at 70) said: 'It is legitimate, in my view, to consider what the expenditure was intended to effect'.

On the other hand, Lord Radcliffe giving the advice of the board (Lord Radcliffe, Lord Morris and Lord Upjohn) in *Comr of Taxes v Nchanga Consolidated Copper Mines Ltd* [1964] AC 948 at 958 refers to 'the undesirability of determining the nature of a payment by the motive or object of the payer'.

It seems to me that the court has to consider all the circumstances of the case, one of which is the purpose of the transaction.

In *IRC v Carron Co* (1967) 45 TC 18 at 74 Lord Wilberforce said:

'To make the distinction between capital and revenue, by nature a commercial distinction, it is necessary to go further and to ascertain the nature and purpose of the changes made.'

Although it is necessary to consider all the circumstances, the problem in the end is the true nature of the transaction. Intentions may throw some light on the matter, but cannot relieve the court from analysing in terms of capital and income account the true nature of what the parties actually did.

There are numerous decided cases on the question whether a payment is to be treated as being a capital or revenue account. They vary widely in their facts. The facts in the present case are unusual and derive from very special circumstances. Authorities are accordingly of limited value, but I should refer to some of the cases cited by counsel for the taxpayer company.

Morgan (Inspector of Taxes) v Tate & Lyle Ltd [1955] AC 21, 35 TC 367. The taxpayers were sugar refiners. They claimed to deduct in the computation of their trading profits for tax purposes the expenses incurred in a propaganda campaign designed to show that nationalisation of the sugar refining industry would be harmful to workers, consumers and stockholders alike.

The commissioners found that the primary object of the campaign was to prevent the company losing its business and to preserve its assets intact. The Crown contended that, so far as that was the object of the campaign, the expenditure was not incurred directly for the earning of its profits. The commissioners held that the expenses were incurred wholly and exclusively for the purpose of the company's trade. The House of Lords held that the commissioners were entitled so to find.

Accordingly, the case was concerned with that limited issue of fact.

Southern (Inspector of Taxes) v Borax Consolidated Ltd [1941] 1 KB 111, 23 TC *a*
597. The taxpayer company held all the shares in an American company whose
business fell to be treated for tax purposes as a branch of the company's business.
The company acquired land in America and put the subsidiary company into
possession. The company's title was challenged and the American company incurred
substantial legal costs on litigation. The commissioners found that the legal expenses
were incurred wholly and exclusively by the American company for the purposes of *b*
its trade. On appeal, the High Court upheld that determination.

That again was a limited issue which does not seem to me to throw light on the
present case.

IRC v Carron Co (1967) 45 TC 18. Lord Guest (at 70) cited a statement of Lord
Reid in *Strick (Inspector of Taxes) v Regent Oil Co Ltd* [1966] AC 295 at 313, 43 TC
1 at 29–30— *c*

'. . . the determination of what is capital and what is income must depend
rather on common sense than the strict application of any single legal principle.'

I quite accept that and it seems to me to be an approach of some importance in
the present case. *d*

Counsel for the taxpayer company makes the following submissions: (1) There is
a finding of fact by the commissioners that the £50m was laid out to preserve the
platinum trade of the taxpayer company from collapse. (2) There is no ground for
saying that it was laid out to secure the disposal of a capital asset (the JMB shares).
That is because: (i) the shares were not an onerous asset (as, for example, were the
leases in *Mallett (Inspector of Taxes) v Staveley Coal and Iron Co Ltd* [1928] 2 KB *e*
405, 13 TC 772) but were a worthless asset; and (ii) the taxpayer company did not
need to pay £50m or any other sum apart from some costs, to get rid of the JMB
shares. The taxpayer company could have disposed of them to a shelf company or
could have liquidated JMB. (3) Prior to receiving the Bank's offer the taxpayer
company had, in fact, decided that it would put JMB into liquidation.
(4) Accordingly, it is said, it does not represent the realities of the matter to say either *f*
that the £50m was paid to dispose of the JMB shares or that it achieved a disposition
of the shares. (5) It is not a case of a 'negative consideration or reverse premium'
being paid for the JMB shares. The essence of the transaction was that the taxpayer
company paid £50m to preserve its own trade. The commissioners, it is emphasised,
found that the moneys were wholly and exclusively laid out for the purpose of the
taxpayer company's trade. At the end of it all, the taxpayer company lost its JMB *g*
shares (which were worthless and would be lost anyway) but saved its platinum
trade.

I think it is necessary first of all to be clear as to the position in which the taxpayer
company found itself on the night of Sunday 30 September. It was as follows:
(1) JMB was a wreck. It would not be able to continue trading on Monday morning.
(2) That state of affairs, in relation to a wholly-owned subsidiary, produced in turn *h*
a perilous situation for the taxpayer company because the resulting loss of confidence
in the taxpayer company was likely to produce demands for repayments by its own
customers which it could not meet.

The core of the problem so far as the taxpayer company was concerned was its
close association with the insolvent JMB. The Bank, for its part, was presumably
concerned with the stability of an English banking company. The matter was solved *j*
by the Bank taking over JMB by acquiring all the taxpayer company's shares in
JMB. That secured financial confidence in JMB.

The sale of the JMB shares by the taxpayer company to the Bank was for a
nominal consideration of £1 only. But the Bank was not prepared to take over the
shares unless *prior* to the sale (see the case stated para 3(e) [1990] STC 149 at 151)
the taxpayer company injected £50m into JMB.

The commissioners (at 151) found that the Bank also informed the taxpayer company that it was 'assisting in actively pursuing the provision of a stand-by facility for the taxpayer company'.

Counsel for the taxpayer company says that this was a rescue operation by the Bank. I think that is right. But the description, accurate as it is, does not take one any distance in solving the present dispute. The real question is, what was the nature of the rescue operation? Counsel for the taxpayer company says, in effect, that the £50m was not for, and did not have the effect of, securing the sale of the JMB shares. I do not feel able to accept that. There was a single agreement. The terms of that agreement were simple. The taxpayer company would sell the JMB shares to the Bank for £1. Prior to the sale, the taxpayer company would inject £50m into JMB. The taxpayer company could not be extricated from its predicament unless somebody with adequate resources took over JMB. The Bank was ready to acquire the shares in JMB but only on terms that prior to the sale, the taxpayer company paid JMB £50m. I can only regard that as a transaction in which the Bank acquired the shares in JMB (for a nominal sum) on terms that the taxpayer company provided the £50m to JMB. There was no other way in which the taxpayer company could rid itself of JMB without disaster. No other terms were on offer. The taxpayer company could have got rid of the JMB shares by transferring them to a shelf company or by putting JMB into liquidation, but it would not have solved the taxpayer company's problem simply to detach itself from an insolvent JMB. The solution offered by the Bank was the only way out. JMB had to be rescued, not liquidated or ignored.

It is true that the purpose of the taxpayer company was to preserve its own trade. But that is not determinative of the capital/income issue. Thus, in *Mallett v Staveley Coal and Iron Co Ltd* the payments were made 'for the enduring benefit of the trade' (see [1928] 2 KB 405 at 420, 13 TC 772 at 786 per Sargant LJ) but the expenditure was held to be of a capital nature.

The position then, it seems to me, is as follows: (i) JMB was a capital asset of the taxpayer company; (ii) the taxpayer company disposed of JMB to the Bank; (iii) the only terms on which the Bank was willing to acquire JMB was on payment of the £50m by the taxpayer company to JMB.

The position was, in reality, the same as if the Bank had said 'We will take over JMB if you pay us £50m'. Whichever way it was done, the payment seems to me to be a payment by the taxpayer company to enable it to get rid of a capital asset. That asset was not onerous in the sense that the leases in *Mallett v Staveley Coal and Iron Co Ltd* were onerous, but its continued retention was harmful to the taxpayer company. In my view the common sense of the matter is that the £50m was capital expenditure.

In my opinion Vinelott J was right. I would dismiss the appeal.

McCOWAN LJ. In his skeleton argument counsel for the taxpayer company said: 'Given that JMB was a limited company the JMB shares were not an onerous asset: they were a worthless asset'. In elaboration of this in oral argument, he submitted that the £50m could not be said to have been paid for the divesting by the taxpayer company of the shares in JMB when the taxpayer company could easily have divested itself of any responsibility for the shares by putting JMB into liquidation. To do this, he said, would have cost the taxpayer company virtually nothing. In a revealing phrase, however, he added: 'But that would not have suited it, because of the knock-on effect on its own trade'. That, to my mind, is the clue to the case. Simply letting JMB go into liquidation would have been extremely damaging to the taxpayer company's financial status. It was their association with an insolvent JMB that was onerous to them.

Counsel further argued that the taxpayer company would not have paid £50m just to get rid of the shares in JMB. I agree. But what they did, and what they wanted to do, was to get rid of the shares to a body that would keep JMB solvent and trading. They were not of course being altruistic. Their purpose was, it is true, to preserve their own platinum trade; but that does not, in my judgment, turn the payment into a revenue payment.

One of the cases cited to the court was *Mallett (Inspector of Taxes) v Staveley Coal and Iron Co Ltd* [1928] 2 KB 405 at 420, 13 TC 772 at 786, where Sargant LJ said—

'... the payment was being made for the purpose of putting an end to the existence of a disadvantage or onerous asset for the enduring benefit of the trade.'

Those words, in my judgment, are most apt to describe what happened here. The JMB shares represented 'a disadvantage or onerous asset' and the taxpayer company paid £50m to put an end to the existence of that disadvantage or onerous asset for the enduring benefit of the taxpayer company's trade. I conclude, therefore, that the £50m payment can properly be described as a negative consideration for the shares.

Counsel for the taxpayer company made the further submission, however, that, as seen at the material time, what might save JMB was a rescue operation, not a transfer of the shares; and what in fact saved JMB was that it was the Bank of England that did the rescuing. The answer to that, in my judgment, is that had there been no transfer of the shares there would have been no rescue operation. It was in fact a package deal; and both parts of the package were necessary. On that analysis, it becomes plain that Vinelott J ([1990] STC 149 at 161) was right in concluding:

'These two elements cannot be severed, the one being treated as the disposal for a nominal consideration of a worthless but not an onerous asset and the other as a payment made to preserve the business of the taxpayer company.'

I would dismiss the appeal.

BELDAM LJ. Johnson Matthey plc (the taxpayer company) specialises in the refining of precious metals and the production of chemicals, catalysts and by-products widely used in industry.

It has divided its activities among a number of subsidiary companies. One of the most important, Johnson Matthey Bankers Ltd (JMB), was wholly owned by the taxpayer company. It carried on business as bankers, dealing in gold bullion on the markets of the world and making loans of metal and money to its customers. Established in 1965, it was one of the five members of the London gold fixing, concentrating its business on bullion and foreign exchange dealing, commercial banking and trade finance.

By 1984 JMB's reputation had become so associated and its business and credit so intimately bound up with that of its parent, the taxpayer company, that the fortunes of the taxpayer company were particularly susceptible to any serious decline in the business or standing of its subsidiary. In the consolidated accounts for the year ended 31 March 1984 there was no hint of any such decline. JMB's net assets were put at £102m, and the value of the taxpayer company's interest was shown as £99·7m. By September 1984 there had come to light a very different state of affairs. Liabilities of JMB so far exceeded its assets that it was insolvent. Unless it could be recapitalised or its operations refinanced in some other way it would have to go into liquidation. The deficiency was so great that it was beyond the resources of the taxpayer company to rescue the position. Worse, if JMB was not rescued, the taxpayer company itself would be unable to survive the demands on its funds which loss of confidence would stimulate.

This state of affairs had come to the attention of the Bank of England (the Bank), who were concerned that the failure of JMB would undermine general confidence in the banking system and might lead to disorder in the bullion markets. One solution which had been explored was a proposal by the Bank of Nova Scotia (Nova Scotia) to purchase the issued share capital of JMB and all save two of its subsidiaries

but, according to minutes of a meeting held on 30 September 1984, the board of the
taxpayer company had previously been informed by the Bank that 'it was considered
essential that agreement be reached on proposals for the recapitalisation or disposal
of JMB by midnight on 30th September 1984'.

The board met at 10.00 pm on that day, a Sunday. During the meeting it became
apparent that Nova Scotia would not go ahead and that in the absence of further
finance JMB was insolvent and could not open for business the following day. The
board also recognised that the taxpayer company would be unable to meet its
obligations when they fell due unless it could obtain further resources. With the
object of securing an orderly realisation of the group's assets, it was decided to invite
the trustee of the taxpayer company's debenture stocks to appoint a receiver of the
company. When the Bank was told of this decision it put forward a proposal that:
(a) the Bank would acquire the issued share capital of JMB for £1; and (b) prior to
the sale, the taxpayer company should inject £50m cash into JMB.

As the taxpayer company did not have the resources to provide the £50m, it
accepted an offer from one of its shareholders, Charter Consolidated, to subscribe
for £25m of convertible preference shares and arranged a stand-by facility from
which the remaining £25m could be raised. The board then resolved to accept the
offer of the Bank to acquire the issued share capital of JMB for £1 and to provide
£50m to JMB by way of loan, 'repayment thereof to be waived'.

On 2 October 1984 the taxpayer company agreed to sell to the Bank the whole of
the issued share capital of JMB 'subject to [the taxpayer company] advancing a loan
of £50m to JMB and waiving repayment of the same today' for the sum of £1. The
Bank undertook to use its best endeavours to procure the release of the taxpayer
company and its subsidiaries from any guarantees, indemnities and other liabilities
and obligations assumed by the taxpayer company in favour of third parties in
respect of JMB. Thus, with the backing of the Bank, catastrophe was averted; JMB
was able to open on Monday morning and the assets and business of the taxpayer
company were saved.

In due course the taxpayer company was assessed for corporation tax for the year
of assessment, 1 April 1984 to 31 March 1985, in a sum of £7,500,000. It sought to
set off as a revenue expense the £50m it had paid on the disposal of JMB. The
Crown refused to accept such a deduction, contending that the payment was a
payment of a capital nature. The taxpayer company appealed to the commissioners.
They found that the £50m payment was made to preserve the trade of the taxpayer
company from collapse, that it did in fact do so and, as a payment to preserve an
existing business, it was of a revenue nature. In their view the payment was not
converted into a payment of a capital nature by the circumstance that it was
associated with the disposal of JMB shares. They found that the payment was made
wholly and exclusively for the purposes of the taxpayer company's trade. That
finding was accepted by the Crown, but it appealed by way of case stated to the
High Court against the finding that the payment of £50m was of a revenue nature.
The Crown's appeal was allowed by Vinelott J (see [1990] STC 149). He held that,
although the purpose of the board of the taxpayer company in making the payment
was to preserve the business of the taxpayer company, the means by which it was
achieved was by transferring the shares of JMB to the Bank and as part of a single
transaction or arrangement to pay £50m to JMB and to release JMB from any
obligation to repay it. He said (at 161):

> 'These two elements cannot be severed, the one being treated as the disposal
> for a nominal consideration of a worthless but not an onerous asset and the other
> as a payment made to preserve the business of the taxpayer company.'

In his argument before this court on behalf of the taxpayer company, counsel
relied on the finding of the commissioners that the £50m payment was made to
preserve the trade of the taxpayer company from collapse, that it did in fact preserve
the trade from collapse and, as a payment to preserve an existing business, it was of

a revenue nature and he relied on statements in the judgments in *IRC v Carron Co*
(1967) 45 TC 18 at 68 by Lord Reid:

> 'In a case of this kind what matters is the nature of the advantage for which
> the money was spent. This money was spent to remove antiquated restrictions
> which were preventing profits from being earned. It created no new asset. It
> did not even open new fields of trading which had previously been closed to the
> Company. Its true purpose was to facilitate trading by enabling the Company
> to engage a more competent manager and to borrow money required to finance
> the Company's traditional trading operations under modern conditions.'

And by Lord Guest (at 70):

> 'It is legitimate, in my view, to consider what the expenditure was intended
> to effect and the way in which the advantage was to be used.'

And by Lord Wilberforce (at 74)—

> '. . . it is necessary to go further and to ascertain the nature and the purpose of
> the changes made . . .'

Further counsel for the taxpayer company relied on passages in the judgments in
Morgan (Inspector of Taxes) v Tate & Lyle Ltd [1955] AC 21, 35 TC 367, but the
issue in that appeal was confined to the question whether money expended on a
campaign to resist nationalisation was exclusively laid out for the purposes of the
taxpayer's trade.

I approach the question for decision with the words of Lord Wilberforce in his
judgment in *Tucker (Inspector of Taxes) v Granada Motorway Services Ltd* [1979]
STC 393 at 396, [1979] 1 WLR 683 at 686 very much in mind:

> 'It is common in cases which raise the question whether a payment is to be
> treated as a revenue or as a capital payment for indicia to point diferent ways.
> In the end the courts can do little better than form an opinion which way the
> balance lies. There are a number of tests which have been stated in reported
> cases which it is useful to apply, but we have been warned more than once not
> to seek automatically to apply to one case words or formulae which have been
> found useful in another (see *Comr of Taxes v Nchanga Consolidated Copper
> Mines Ltd* [1964] AC 948). Nevertheless reported cases are the best tools that
> we have, even if they may sometimes be blunt instruments. I think that the key
> to the present case is to be found in those cases which have sought to identify an
> asset. In them it seems reasonably logical to start with the assumption that
> money spent on the acquisition of the asset should be regarded as capital
> expenditure. Extensions from this are, first, to regard money spent on getting
> rid of a disadvantageous asset as capital expenditure and, secondly, to regard
> money spent on improving the asset, or making it more advantageous, as capital
> expenditure. In the latter type of case it will have to be considered whether the
> expenditure has the result stated or whether it should be regarded as expenditure
> on maintenance or upkeep, and some cases may pose difficult problems.'

As an unaccustomed 'traveller in these regions', I have found guidance from the
passages in the judgment of Dixon J in *Sun Newspapers Ltd v Federal Comr of
Taxation* (1938) 61 CLR 337 at 363 quoted by Lord Pearce in *BP Australia Ltd v
Comr of Taxation of the Commonwealth of Australia* [1966] AC 224 at 261:

> 'There are, I think, three matters to be considered, (*a*) the character of the
> advantage sought, and in this its lasting qualities may play a part, (*b*) the manner
> in which it is to be used, relied upon or enjoyed, and in this and under the
> former head recurrence may play its part, and (*c*) the means adopted to obtain
> it; that is, by providing a periodical reward or outlay to cover its use or

enjoyment for periods commensurate with the payment or by making a final
a   provision or payment so as to secure future use or enjoyment.'

And in the same case ((1938) 61 CLR 337 at 362, quoted [1966] AC 224 at 261)—

'... the expenditure is to be considered of a revenue nature if its purpose
brings it within the very wide class of things which in the aggregate form the
constant demand which must be answered out of the returns of a trade or its
b   circulating capital and that actual recurrence of the specific thing need not take
place or be expected as likely.'

With this guidance, I return to the facts of the case. The commissioners' finding
that the payment was made to preserve the trade of the taxpayer company from
collapse, and as such was of a revenue nature, selects from the complex circumstances
with which the directors of the taxpayer company were faced on 30 September 1984
c   only one of the manifest purposes for which the payment of £50m and the disposal
of JMB were made. The payment was made because there was no other means by
which to divest the taxpayer company of the by now disastrous association with
JMB and to avoid the realisation of all the taxpayer company's assets. The meeting
to discuss the crisis was, according to the minutes, to consider various proposals for
the refinancing of the group and the disposal of JMB. The discussions with the Bank
d   were for the recapitalisation or disposal of JMB. It was recognised that the taxpayer
company on its own was unable to provide sufficient capital for JMB to maintain
the appropriate liquidity ratio for a recognised bank. At the same time it was
essential to provide further capital for the taxpayer company and this was done by
the issue of convertible loan stock to Charter Consolidated. Had the taxpayer
company been able to raise sufficient funds, or if the amount required to recapitalise
e   JMB had been no more than £50m, the method which would have been adopted
would no doubt either have been to make a loan to JMB or to recapitalise it in a
similar way to the taxpayer company by an issue of convertible stock. If either of
those courses had been adopted, the payment would unquestionably have been of a
capital nature. Can it make any difference that the liabilities of JMB were so
extensive that the payment of £50m had to be made as an out-and-out payment to
f   persuade the Bank to acquire the capital of JMB? I do not think that it can. One
consequence of the payment was the preservation of their subsidiary JMB as a going
concern with the backing of the resources of the Bank. That, in turn, 'preserved the
existing business' of the taxpayer company. It did so by saving its assets from
realisation, by releasing it from an existing risk of catastrophic liabilities and from
the consequences of being unable itself to recapitalise JMB. Thus merely to
g   characterise the payment by the label 'preservation of an existing business' does not
determine how the payment should be regarded for accounting and revenue
purposes. In short it is merely descriptive and not definitive.

To my mind the payment has to be seen against the background of the search by
the directors for a means of recapitalising JMB. But for the size of sum needed the
taxpayer company would have retained its interest in JMB and in one way or
h   another the sum of £50m would have been reflected in its balance sheet as a long-
term capital asset. It was a lump sum paid to procure an immediate advantage for
the long term; it did not represent an aggregation of day-to-day payments which
would have been incurred in the ordinary way in running the business. Considering
the three matters highlighted by Dixon J in *Sun Newspapers v Federal Comr of
Taxation* against the background to the payment, I have no doubt it was a capital
j   payment for tax purposes. The advantage sought was of a lasting non-recurring
nature. It was to be used once and for all to secure existing assets and to avoid
liabilities which threatened immediate final collapse. The advantage was obtained
by making the payment as a final provision to secure the disposal of a capital asset.
It appears to me to have none of the attributes of a revenue payment and every
appearance of an outlay for capital purposes.

I would dismiss the appeal.

Appeal dismissed with costs. Leave to appeal to the House of Lords refused.

5 June. The Appeal Committee of the House of Lords gave leave to appeal.

Solicitors: *Taylor Joynson Garrett* (for the taxpayer company); *Solicitor of Inland Revenue.*

Siew Ling Choo   Barister.

R v Inland Revenue Commissioners, ex parte Commerzbank AG

QUEEN'S BENCH DIVISION (CROWN OFFICE LIST)
NOLAN LJ, HENRY J
26, 27, 28 FEBRUARY, 12 APRIL 1991

Judicial review – Interest – Repayment supplement – Repayment of overpaid corporation tax to non-resident company – Company claiming repayment supplement – Whether company entitled to repayment supplement – Whether company discriminated against on grounds of nationality under Community law – Taxes Management Act 1970, s 78 – Finance (No 2) Act 1975, s 48 – Income and Corporation Taxes Act 1988, s 788(3).

Commerzbank AG (the bank) was a bank incorporated in the Federal Republic of Germany. Under the Double Taxation Relief (Taxes on Income) (Federal Republic of Germany) Order 1967, SI 1967/25, it was for tax purposes a resident of Germany and not of the United Kingdom. However, at all material times a branch of the bank traded in the United Kingdom. The branch qualified under the double taxation convention as a permanent establishment situated in the United Kingdom. The bank was liable to United Kingdom corporation tax on the profits attributable to the branch. In the course of its banking business, over a number of accounting periods, the bank paid United Kingdom corporation tax in respect of interest received on loans to United States corporations. After protracted litigation (see [1990] STC 285), the bank succeeded in recovering the tax paid under art XV of the double taxation convention between the United Kingdom and the United States as set out in the Double Taxation Relief (Taxes on Income) (The United States of America) Order 1966, SI 1966/1188. The bank sought to obtain repayment supplement in respect of the tax overpaid. This was refused by the Revenue on the basis that eligibility for such repayment supplement depended on the bank being resident in the United Kingdom. The bank applied to the High Court for judicial review. Its contentions were threefold: (i) that by virtue of s 78[a] of the Taxes Management Act 1970, s 48[b] of the Finance (No 2) Act 1975 was equally applicable to the United Kingdom branch of a non-resident company and hence, as a matter of construction of s 48 and s 78, the bank was entitled to the repayment supplement; (ii) that the residence requirement of s 48 was inconsistent with art XX of the UK/FRG double taxation convention, since it resulted in treatment in connection with taxation that was more burdensome than that imposed on United Kingdom nationals; and (iii) that the residence requirement of s 48 was inconsistent with the European Communities Act 1972, ss 2, 3 and the EEC Treaty, leading to interference with its right of establishment (arts 52–58) and discrimination on grounds of nationality (art 7).

Held — (1) No distinction as regards entitlement to repayment supplement could be drawn between non-residents with a United Kingdom branch and those without such a branch, under s 78 of the Taxes Management Act 1970 or otherwise. Section 78 could not therefore avail the bank.

(2) Section 48 of the Finance (No 2) Act 1975 was neither a charging nor a relieving provision and therefore repayment supplement did not fall within the matters, specified in s 788(3)[c] of the Income and Corporation Taxes Act 1988, to which double taxation conventions applied. Article XX of the UK/FRG double taxation convention could not therefore avail the bank.

Accordingly, so far as United Kingdom law was concerned, the application would fail.

---

a   Section 78, so far as material, is set out at p 274 *f–g*, post
b   Section 48, so far as material, is set out at p 274 *b–c*, post
c   Section 788 (3), so far as material, is set out at p 277 *d–e*, post

(3) Under Community law, the bank had the right not to be discriminated against, whether directly or indirectly, on the ground of nationality. The issue to be decided *a* under Community law was whether, in considering if discrimination had occurred in a composite transaction, the court should focus only on the actual incident (ie the claim for interest in the instant case) or look to the whole transaction, namely the overpayment of tax, the circumstances of the recovery of that tax and the claim for interest on it. The decision on this issue was likely to be the determinative factor in this case. The decision was not self-evident; it was a matter of policy and therefore *b* the question was to be referred, suitably formulated, to the Court of Justice of the European Communities.

Notes

For repayment supplement, see Simon's Taxes A3.604.   *c*
    For the application of double taxation conventions in general, see ibid, F1.111.
    For the Taxes Management Act 1970, s 78, see ibid, Part G2.
    For the Finance (No 2) Act 1975, s 48 (now the Income and Corporation Taxes Act 1988, s 825), see ibid, Part G1.
    For the Income and Corporation Taxes Act 1988, s 788(3), see ibid, Part G1.
    For the Double Taxation Relief (Taxes on Income) (Federal Republic of *d* Germany) Order 1967, SI 1967/25, see ibid, Part F4.
    The Double Taxation Relief (Taxes on Income) (The United States of America) Order SR & O 1946/1327, art XV, as substituted by the Double Taxation Relief (Taxes on Income) (The United States of America) Order 1966, SI 1966/1188 is now spent and has been replaced by the Double Taxation Relief (Taxes on Income) (The United States of America) Order 1980, SI 1980/568, art 11, for which, see ibid, *e* Part F4.

Cases referred to in judgment

Biehl v Administration des Contributions du Grand-Duché de Luxembourg (Case C-175/88) [1991] STC 575, [1990] 3 CMLR 143, CJEC.   *f*
EC Commission v French Republic (Case 270/83) [1986] ECR 273, CJEC.
Smidth (F L) & Co v Greenwood (Surveyor of Taxes) [1922] 1 AC 417, 8 TC 193, HL.
Factortame Ltd v Secretary of State for Transport [1990] 2 AC 85, [1989] 2 All ER 692, HL.
Sotgiu v Deutsche Bundespost (Case 152/73) [1974] ECR 153, CJEC.   *g*

Cases also cited

Amministrazione delle Finanze dello Stato v Simmenthal SpA (Case 106/77) [1978] ECR 629, CJEC.
Boussac Saint-Frères SA v Brigitte Gerstenmeier (Case 22/80) [1980] ECR 3427, *h* CJEC.
C I L F I T Srl v Minister of Health (Case 283/81) [1982] ECR 3415, CJEC.
East End Dwellings Co Ltd v Finsbury BC [1952] AC 109, [1951] 2 All ER 587, HL.
Royer (Case 48/75) [1976] ECR 497, CJEC.
R v H M Treasury, ex p Daily Mail and General Trust plc (Case 81/87) [1988] STC 787, [1989] QB 446, [1989] 1 All ER 328, CJEC.   *j*
R v Kensington Income Tax Comrs, ex p Aramayo (1914) 6 TC 613, HL.
Reyners v Belgian State (Case 2/74) [1974] ECR 631, CJEC.
Rijksinstituut voor de Sociale Verzekering der Zelfstandigen v Wolf and NV Microtherm Europe (Joined Cases 154/87 and 155/87) [1988] ECR 3897, CJEC.
Stanton and SA belge d'assurances L'Etoile 1905 v Inasti (Case 143/87) [1988], ECR 3877, CJEC.
Whitney v IRC [1926] AC 37, 10 TC 88, HL.

Application for judicial review

a Commerzbank AG applied for judicial review of the decision of the Board of Inland Revenue (the Crown) refusing to pay repayment supplement in respect of an overpayment of corporation tax, itself the subject of earlier litigation (see *IRC v Commerzbank AG* [1990] STC 285). The grounds of the application and the facts are set out in the opinion of Nolan LJ.

b *Stephen Oliver QC, Gerald Barling QC* and *David Ewart* for the bank.
Alan Moses QC and *Derrick Wyatt* for the Crown.

Cur adv vult

12 April. The following judgment of the court was delivered.

c
NOLAN LJ. In this application for judicial review the applicant (the bank) is a German bank which, in respect of accounting periods from 1973 to 1976, paid to the United Kingdom authorities more tax than was in fact due from it. The overpayments amounted in all to £4,222,234. The bank succeeded in recovering this tax, but not until many years later. The Crown has refused to pay the bank anything by way of, *d* or equivalent to, interest on it for the period that the bank was out of its money. The bank now seeks to recover such an additional payment by this application for judicial review.

The bank was incorporated in the Federal Republic of Germany. Under the provisions of the double taxation agreement between the United Kingdom and Germany (the convention of 26 November 1964 incorporated into United Kingdom *e* law by the Double Taxation Relief (Taxes on Income) (Federal Republic of Germany) Order 1967, SI 1967/25, (the UK/FRG convention)) which in this instance reflect the normal provisions of United Kingdom tax law, the bank is a resident of the Federal Republic of Germany and is not a resident of the United Kingdom for tax purposes.

However, a branch of the bank has traded in the United Kingdom since 1973. *f* That branch provides a full range of banking services and is a recognised bank under the provisions of the Banking Act 1979. The branch qualifies as a permanent establishment situated in the United Kingdom under the UK/FRG convention.

The bank was at all material times within the charge to United Kingdom corporation tax on the profits attributable to the branch, computed in accordance with s 246 of the Income and Corporation Taxes Act 1970 (the 1970 Act) (now re-*g* enacted as s 11 of the Income and Corporation Taxes Act 1988 (the 1988 Act)). It has been recognised throughout by the Crown as carrying on a banking business in the United Kingdom for the purposes of s 54 of the 1970 Act (now s 349 of the 1988 Act).

In the course of its banking business over the years 1973 to 1976, the branch made loans to United States corporations and received interest on those loans. Under the *h* laws of the United States the interest on such loans was liable to tax there, subject to the provisions of the various double taxation conventions. The same interest also fell to be included in the computation of the bank's chargeable profits for the purposes of United Kingdom corporation tax, subject again to the provisions of the double taxation convention between the United Kingdom and the United States (the Double Taxation Relief (Taxes on Income) (The United States of America) Order *j* 1946, SR & O 1946/1327 as amended by the Supplementary Protocol dated 17 March 1966 scheduled to the Double Taxation Relief (Taxes on Income) (The United States of America) Order 1966, SI 1966/1188) (the UK/US convention).

The sums thus received by way of interest in respect of those United States loans were included by the Crown in the assessment of the bank's chargeable profits over the relevant period and United Kingdom corporation tax was paid on them. The total corporation tax paid on such interest received on the United States loans over the relevant period amounted to £4,222,234.

The bank claimed to recover that tax. Its claim was based on art XV of the UK/US convention, which provides that dividends and interest paid by a United States corporation shall be exempt from United Kingdom income tax except where the recipient is a United Kingdom citizen, resident or corporation.

After protracted litigation the matter finally came before Mummery J sitting in the Chancery Division on a case stated pursuant to s 56 of the Taxes Management Act 1970 (see *IRC v Commerzbank AG* [1990] STC 285). He held (at 304) that the bank was exempt from paying United Kingdom tax on the interest paid by the United States corporations by virtue of art XV because the bank was not resident in the United Kingdom within the meaning of that article. Accordingly, on 12 February 1990, he ordered the Crown to repay the disputed tax of £4,222,234 to the bank. The bank now applies to this court for a further payment in respect of interest on that sum.

The statutory right to recover interest or its equivalent on the repayment of corporation tax that has been paid in excess of legal liability is now to be found in s 825(2) of the 1988 Act (at the material time s 48(2) of the Finance (No 2) Act 1975 (the 1975 Act)). This provides that in the circumstances applicable to this case the repayment of overpaid corporation tax 'shall be increased ... by an amount (a "repayment supplement") equal to interest on the amount paid'. But (under sub-s (1)) such increased payments are only made in connection with any accounting period for which the company was resident in the United Kingdom.

That repayment supplement would, in this case, have amounted to £5,199,258. The Crown refused to pay that additional sum to the bank on the basis that eligibility for such payment depended on the bank being resident in the United Kingdom and it was not so resident.

In these proceedings the bank challenges that construction of the 1975 Act and seeks to recover that sum on three bases. First, it submits that, as a matter of construction of s 48 of the 1975 Act and s 78 of the Taxes Management Act 1970, the bank is entitled to the repayment supplement. Second, it submits that the residence requirement in s 48 of the 1975 Act is inconsistent with art XX of the UK/FRG convention. Third, it submits that the residence requirement in s 48 is inconsistent with the European Communities Act 1972 and the EEC Treaty and in particular with arts 5, 7, 52, 53 and 58 thereof.

The first submission is advanced by counsel for the bank on the basis that the reference in s 48 to a company resident in the United Kingdom is equally applicable to the United Kingdom branch of a non-resident company. This follows, he submits, from the language of s 78 of the Taxes Management Act 1970 which, so far as is relevant, provides that—

> '(1) ... a person not resident in the United Kingdom ... shall be assessable and chargeable to income tax in the name of ... any branch or agent, whether the branch or agent has the receipt of the profits or gains or not, in like manner and to the like amount as such non-resident person would be assessed and charged if he were resident in the United Kingdom and in the actual receipt of such profits or gains.'

Accordingly, it is argued, where another provision of the Taxes Acts dealing with assessment and charge imposes an obligation or grants a right relating to a matter connected with assessment and charge, and where that obligation or right is imposed or granted by reference to the taxpayer concerned being resident in the United Kingdom, the provision will apply not only to residents but also to persons treated as such under s 78 of the Taxes Management Act 1970. The process of assessment and charge may very well involve an initial overpayment of tax as it has done in the present case. On proof of the overpayment, the taxpayer, whether resident or a branch of a non-resident company, becomes entitled to a repayment of tax under either s 42(7) or s 55(9)(*b*) Taxes Management Act 1970. In either case the right to a repayment supplement is intimately bound up with the right to repayment of tax.

In the terms of s 48(2) of the 1975 Act, the repayment is to be 'increased' by the amount of the supplement. It follows that the bank is entitled to have s 48 applied as if it were a company resident in the United Kingdom.

Counsel for the bank accepted that a non-resident company which did not have a branch in the United Kingdom might equally become entitled to a repayment of tax, but would be debarred by the plain terms of s 48 from claiming the repayment supplement. The reason for that, said counsel, was quite simply that s 78 of the Taxes Management Act 1970 only applied to non-residents with a United Kingdom branch. It was only these latter non-residents who were assessable and chargeable in the name of the branch 'in like manner and to the like amount as . . . if [they] were resident in the United Kingdom'.

In our judgment, this argument places more weight on the language of s 78 than it will bear. The section must be construed against the background of the fundamental principle that United Kingdom residents are taxable on all of their income, wherever it arises, but non-residents, irrespective of whether or not they have a branch in the United Kingdom, are liable to tax only on their income from United Kingdom sources. In *F L Smidth & Co v Greenwood (Surveyor of Taxes)* [1922] 1 AC 417, 8 TC 193 the House of Lords held that s 31 of the Finance (No 2) Act 1915 (the 1915 Act), the predecessor to s 78 of the Taxes Management Act 1970, did not have the effect of making a non-resident with a United Kingdom branch taxable on profits arising abroad. It was not a charging section. It merely provided machinery for the collection of tax due under the charging provisions. It is true that s 31 of the 1915 Act did not include the phrase 'in like manner and to the like amount', but it has never been suggested, and counsel for the bank did not suggest, that the addition of these words has altered the character of the section. In other words, it is not suggested that s 78 of the Taxes Management Act 1970 has the effect of making a non-resident company with a branch in the United Kingdom liable to tax on its income from overseas sources. The reason why the bank is taxable on interest and dividends from sources in the United States is that such interest and dividends form part of the profits of the banking business which the bank carries on through its United Kingdom branch. It is in respect of the profits of that United Kingdom branch that the bank is assessable and chargeable in the name of the branch in like manner and to the like amount as if it were resident in the United Kingdom.

Granted then that s 78 of the Taxes Management Act 1970 is not intended to and does not alter the burden of tax to be borne by non-resident companies with United Kingdom branches, nor place them in a different category of liability from non-residents without a United Kingdom branch, is it none the less to be interpreted as conferring on them the right to be treated as United Kingdom residents for the purposes of the repayment supplement? In our judgment it is not. Non-resident companies with United Kingdom branches are assimilated to United Kingdom residents only for the purposes of assessment and charge. These purposes do not extend to the repayment supplement. The supplement is not a repayment of tax wrongly assessed and charged. It is an interest payment funded from other Exchequer sources. It is the converse of the interest which is charged against taxpayers on overdue payments of tax. Under s 86 of the Taxes Management Act 1970 such interest is levied equally on non-residents with a United Kingdom branch and those without (and of course, on United Kingdom residents as well). In other words, as regards liability for interest, the Taxes Management Act 1970 does not distinguish, under s 78 or otherwise (save for the machinery of collection), between non-residents with and those without a United Kingdom branch. Equally, in our judgment, no such distinction can be drawn between them as regards entitlement—or rather disentitlement—to the repayment supplement.

We turn to counsel for the bank's second submission based on United Kingdom law. It is that the Crown's denial of repayment supplement to the bank is in breach of art XX of the UK/FRG convention, which reads as follows:

'{*Non-discrimination*}

(1) The nationals of one of the Contracting States shall not be subjected in the other State to any taxation or any requirement connected therewith which is other or more burdensome than the taxation and connected requirements to which nationals of that other State in the same circumstances are or may be subjected.

(2) The term "nationals" means—

(*a*) in relation to the Federal Republic, all Germans within the meaning of Article 116(1) of the Basic Law for the Federal Republic of Germany, and all legal persons, partnerships and associations deriving their status as such from the law in force in the Federal Republic;

(*b*) in relation to the United Kingdom, all British subjects and British protected persons—

(i) residing in the United Kingdom or any territory to which the present Convention is extended under Article XXI or

(ii) deriving their status as such from connexion with the United Kingdom or any territory to which the present Convention is extended under Article XXI,

and all legal persons, partnerships and associations deriving their status as such from the law in force in the United Kingdom or in any territory to which the Convention is extended under Article XXI.

(3) The taxation on a permanent establishment which an enterprise of one of the territories has in the other territory shall not be less favourably levied in that other territory than the taxation levied on enterprises of that other territory carrying on the same activities. This provision shall not be construed as obliging one Contracting State to grant to residents of the territory of the other Contracting State any personal allowances, reliefs and reductions for taxation purposes on account of civil status or family responsibilities which it grants to its own residents.'

Counsel for the bank submits that the bank is required, like a United Kingdom national (or resident), to pay tax on demand but, unlike a United Kingdom national, is denied the repayment supplement on proof that it has made an overpayment. It is thus subjected to a requirement connected with taxation which is more burdensome than that imposed on United Kingdom nationals. Counsel refers in this connection to the Organisation for Economic Co-operation and Development (OECD) commentary on art 24 of the model convention on which art XX of the UK/FRG convention is based (see the Model Double Taxation Convention on Income and on Capital: Report of the OECD Committee on Fiscal Affairs, 1977, Paris). The commentary includes the following passage:

'Subject to the foregoing observation, the words ". . . shall not be subjected . . . to any taxation or any requirement connected therewith which is other or more burdensome . . ." mean that when a tax is imposed on nationals and foreigners in the same circumstances, it must be in the same form as regards both the basis of charge and the method of assessment, its rate must be the same and, finally, the formalities connected with the taxation (return, payment, prescribed times, etc) must not be more onerous for foreigners than for nationals.'

Counsel for the Crown submits that the words 'requirement connected' with taxation cannot be stretched to cover the entitlement to a repayment supplement. He says that they are primarily directed to the amount of tax payable, in respect of which there is no discrimination. He agrees that they are not limited to the amount of tax payable. They would also cover, for example, a requirement that German nationals should pay the tax assessed on them more promptly than United Kingdom nationals. But no such requirement exists and, if it did, it would be a different case.

Further, submits counsel, there was no need for the bank to have made an overpayment of tax in the first place. It could have applied to postpone the payment of tax on the United States interest under s 55(3) of the Taxes Management Act 1970—though it is true that if the bank had done so and had then failed to establish its entitlement to exemption from tax on the United States interest it would have had to pay interest under s 86 of the Taxes Management Act 1970 on the postponed payment of tax.

We are not persuaded by these submissions of counsel. In deciding whether to make an immediate payment or to seek a postponement of a tax bill which he considers to be excessive, the United Kingdom national or resident can balance the prospect of having to pay interest if he fails on the substantive issue against the prospect of receiving a repayment supplement if he succeeds. The prospective repayment supplement will not match the prospective interest liability because interest runs against the taxpayer from the date when the tax was originally due under the assessment, whereas the repayment supplement only begins to run in his favour 12 months after that date, but at least it offers the possibility of some compensation for the initial overpayment. If the German national is entitled to no such compensation, then it seems to us that he is subjected to a more burdensome requirement as regards the payment of tax than is his United Kingdom counterpart.

There are, however, three other grounds on which the Crown contends that the bank cannot rely on art XX of the UK/FRG convention. The first is that, by virtue of the provisions now contained in s 788(3) of the 1988 Act, double tax conventions such as the UK/FRG convention are to have effect in the domestic law 'in so far as they provide' for the matters specified in paras (*a*) to (*d*) of that sub-section. Counsel for the Crown submits that none of these paragraphs covers the repayment supplement. (We would mention in passing that the supplement came into existence long after the provisions now contained in s 788 of the 1988 Act were originally enacted and, for that matter, long after the UK/FRG convention was made.) Counsel for the bank submits that the repayment supplement falls within the terms of para (*b*) which deals with provisions 'for charging the income arising from sources, or chargeable gains accruing on the disposal of assets, in the United Kingdom to persons not resident in the United Kingdom'. We cannot accept counsel for the bank's submission. Section 48 of the 1975 Act is not a charging nor, for that matter, a relieving provision. It merely provides, as we have said, for the addition of what amounts to interest on an overdue repayment of tax. It follows in our judgment that neither art XX nor any other provision of the UK/FRG convention can apply to the repayment supplement.

Second, and in any event, counsel for the Crown submits that the comparison required by art XX(1) is a comparison between German and United Kingdom nationals in the same circumstances. The bank is a German national as defined by art XX(2) because it is a legal person deriving its status as such from the law in force in the Federal Republic of Germany and so its taxation treatment must be compared with that of a company which is a United Kingdom national, that is to say, a company which derives its status as a legal person from the laws in force in the United Kingdom. But the comparison is meaningless because United Kingdom tax law in general, and corporation tax in particular, does not depend on nationality, nor on the law from which a legal person derives its status: it depends on residence. Thus, a company which derived its status from the laws of the United Kingdom, which was resident in the Federal Republic of Germany, and which traded through a branch in the United Kingdom would be treated for tax purposes in precisely the same manner as the bank. Consequently, there is no basis on which the bank can allege discrimination on the ground of nationality.

It is fair to say that counsel for the Crown did not put this argument in the forefront of his case. It leads to the unattractive conclusion that art XX(1) is of no assistance whatever to German companies, partnerships or associations. It is not uncommon, however, for provisions in double tax conventions to operate solely for

the benefit of one party, with no compensating advantage to the other. Article XV
of the UK/US convention, the article by which the bank has established its　a
entitlement to exemption from United Kingdom tax on United States interest, has
a similar effect, though in that case it is the United Kingdom which is the loser.
Accordingly, there is some poetic justice in the comment which counsel for the
Crown makes on this and other aspects of the case to the effect that the bank cannot
have it both ways. The comparative diffidence displayed by counsel for the Crown
over the contrast between nationality and residence in the context of art XX is, we　b
think, also attributable to his acceptance that in the wider context of Community
law the contrast is not always recognised. But, judged by the standards of United
Kingdom law, these submissions of counsel on art XX(1) cannot be faulted and on
this ground too, we hold that the bank is unable to invoke that provision in relation
to the repayment supplement.

Before leaving the UK/FRG convention we should mention that counsel for the　c
bank additionally submitted that, irrespective of nationality and residence, the bank
was entitled to the repayment supplement by virtue of art XX(3) because otherwise
taxation would be 'less favourably levied' on its United Kingdom branch than on a
United Kingdom enterprise carrying on the same activities. Again, however, we
must reject the submission because the repayment supplement, although connected
with the levy of taxation, does not affect the amount of that levy and cannot be　d
brought within the language of s 788(3) of the 1988 Act.

Third, counsel for the Crown relied in relation to art XX on the same broad
argument which he advanced in relation to the EEC Treaty, namely that the bank
can hardly complain of unfair discrimination by reference to its non-resident status
in the matter of the repayment supplement when its right to the repayment itself is
based solely on that very status. That is the subject which we now turn to consider　e
in the context of Community law. So far as United Kingdom domestic law is
concerned we are of the opinion that the bank must fail because neither s 78 of the
Taxes Management Act 1970 nor the UK/FRG convention can avail it.

So far as Community law is concerned, the bank's case is that it is entitled to the
repayment supplement by virtue of ss 2, 3 of the European Communities Act 1972
and, inter alia, arts 5, 7, 52 to 58 of the EEC Treaty.　　　　　　　　　　　　f

It is not in dispute before us that the provisions of Community law relied on have
'direct effect', and therefore create rights for individuals and companies which the
national courts are obliged to protect. To ensure that such protection is effective,
the national court is under a duty, in appropriate cases, to give full effect to the
Community provisions either by 'disapplying' any conflicting national provision (i e
s 48 of the 1975 Act) or by construing such provision 'to be without prejudice to the　g
directly enforceable Community rights of nationals of any member state of the EEC'
(see *Factortame Ltd v Secretary of State for Transport* [1990] 2 AC 85 at 140 per
Lord Bridge). The relief here sought is that: 'Section 48 of [the 1975 Act] is to be
construed and/or have effect in relation to [the bank's] claim for repayment
supplement as if the words "for which the company was resident in the United
Kingdom" were absent' i e as though residence were not a condition precedent for　h
such a payment.

The attack on s 48 of the 1975 Act is therefore necessarily based on the facts
governing the bank's claim: that is to say, the bank having successfully recovered
the corporation tax on the basis that it was not resident in the United Kingdom, it
now complains that the repayment supplement is only available to corporations that
were so resident. This factual basis clearly lays the bank open to the accusation in so　j
contending they are trying to have the best of both fiscal worlds, that of the non-
resident under the provisions of the UK/US convention, and that of the resident
under s 48.

The claim being based on those facts, the court on this occasion is not being asked
to look at the provisions of s 48 of the 1975 Act in any wider perspective.

The bank's case is straightforward. It paid more tax than the law required it to.

Having done so, when it came to recover that tax, it found itself disadvantaged vis-
à-vis companies resident in the United Kingdom as it could only recover the amount
overpaid and not that amount plus supplement.

It complains of this, first as an interference with its right of establishment
(Chapter 2 of the EEC Treaty, arts 52 to 58), and second, as a breach of art 7,
discrimination on grounds of nationality.

Certain matters are common ground between the parties: (1) The articles relied
on have direct effect and have had such effect at all material times. (2) The bank
qualifies for the right of establishment. That right is not limited to one place of
establishment within the Community, but can extend to any number of secondary
establishments such as branches. (3) The right of establishment encompasses a
number of rights which include but are not limited to a right not to be discriminated
against by the host member state on grounds of nationality. Therefore, the general
right of establishment prohibits national legislation which places Community
citizens at a disadvantage when they are seeking to extend their activities beyond
the territory of a single member state and does so even when the legislation in
question contains no element of direct or indirect discrimination on grounds of
nationality. (4) It is no answer to the infringement of such a right that the
disadvantages complained of could be avoided by setting up the subsidiary company
(with residence) instead of a branch (though we note in passing that such a subsidiary,
being a United Kingdom resident, could not, of course, claim the benefit of art XV
of the UK/US convention). (5) The right not to be discriminated against (positively
expressed as the right of equal treatment) is a fundamental principle and
discrimination on grounds of nationality is expressly prohibited by art 7 of the EEC
Treaty. (6) It is no automatic answer to discrimination on the grounds of nationality
that the criterion for different treatment is expressed to be not nationality but
residence— discrimination on grounds of residence can, in appropriate circumstances, be indirect discrimination on grounds of nationality. (7) A disadvantage
suffered by the branch of a foreign company as a result of a difference in treatment
having been identified, it is not necessary to go further and consider the extent of
that disadvantage, as art 52 of the EEC Treaty prohibits all discrimination even if
only of a limited nature.

The Crown's case asserts that far from the bank being discriminated against by
the tax regime it is in fact in a preferential position. It came to be subjected to the
suggested disadvantage only imposed on non-residents (the inability to recover
interest on overpaid tax) because it had enjoyed and made use of an advantage only
available to non-residents, namely the ability to recover the overpaid tax in the first
place. Had the bank been a resident it would have had to have paid the tax and no
question of its recovery would have arisen. So, says the Crown, in this situation the
comparison sought to be made by the bank between a resident and a non-resident
claiming interest on overpaid tax recovered is a comparison too narrowly drawn.
Once the comparison is properly widened to embrace the whole transaction, namely
the circumstances of the claim for overpaid tax as well as the linked claim for interest
on that tax, then as the resident company could never be in a position to reclaim that
tax in those circumstances, so no meaningful comparison with a resident corporation
can be made, and if no comparison can be made, then neither an advantage nor a
disadvantage can be identified.

In these circumstances it seems to us that the issue for the court in deciding
whether the non-resident bank has received the equal treatment that Community
law requires may be simply stated. Should the court when considering a composite
transaction focus only on the actual incident in which the alleged disadvantage is to
be found (the claim for interest in this case)? Or alternatively, should the court look
to the whole transaction, namely the overpayment of tax, the circumstances of the
recovery of that tax and the claim for interest on it?

A comparison with a resident is possible in the first instance and, if such a
comparison is legitimate, the disadvantage to the non-resident is plain. But once the

court's perspective is widened to include the circumstances of the recovery of the tax, no such comparison between treatment of a resident and a non-resident is possible, and so the disadvantage or unequal treatment vanishes, as one is then looking at a transaction which is only open to non-residents, which brings them some benefits, but not all that they would wish for. In our view, the decision on this issue is likely to be the determinative factor in this case.

Article 177 of the EEC Treaty authorises the Court of Justice of the European Communities (the Court of Justice) to give preliminary rulings in some circumstances. It has been common ground before us that those circumstances would include a properly framed question on the issue that we have identified as being likely to be determinative of the Community law point.

The second paragraph of art 177 gives us a discretion, if we consider that a decision on the question is necessary to enable us to give judgment, to request the Court of Justice to give a ruling on such a question. The Crown is opposed to us giving any such ruling at this stage. The bank initially adopted a neutral stance on the question, but modified that neutrality to a position where it favoured such a course if the court thought it would be useful.

We have considered the leading authorities on this matter, and we have decided in the exercise of our discretion to invite a ruling at this stage. We list our reasons for doing so:

1. While a successful appeal against our decision on the points of domestic law would settle this issue without recourse to Community law, we believe that ultimately this application is likely to stand or fall on the Community law issue, and accordingly at some time is likely to be referred to the Court of Justice.

2. It cannot sensibly be contended that the answer to the Community law issue is acte claire or self evident. That the answer to it cannot confidently be arrived at from the decided cases is evidenced by the fact that both parties before us rely on the same cases to justify their diametrically opposed positions on this question (see *Sotgiu v Deutsche Bundespost* (Case 152/73) [1974] ECR 153, *EC Commission v French Republic* (Case 270/83) [1986] ECR 273 and *Biehl v Administration des Contributions du Grand-Duché de Luxembourg* (Case C-175/88) [1991] STC 575, [1990] 3 CMLR 143).

3. The answer to the question is essentially a matter of degree, and therefore a question of policy. The Court of Justice seems to us to be best placed to decide whether the orderly development of the Community will be best served by the domestic court taking a narrow view in its identification of disadvantage, or looking at a broader perspective to see whether the disadvantage is in fact real.

4. The facts here are not in dispute.

In all those circumstances we think it right to refer a suitably formulated question at this stage.

Order accordingly.

Solicitors: *S J Berwin & Co* (for the bank); *Solicitor of Inland Revenue*.

Rengan Krishnan Esq   Barrister.

Guild v Inland Revenue Commissioners

FIRST DIVISION OF THE INNER HOUSE OF THE COURT OF SESSION AS THE COURT OF
EXCHEQUER IN SCOTLAND
THE LORD PRESIDENT (HOPE), LORD MAYFIELD, LORD McCLUSKEY
12, 13 FEBRUARY, 15 MARCH 1991

Capital transfer tax – Exempt transfer – Charity – Whether charitable trust came into existence at date of death – Whether use by sports centre or similar purpose in connection with sport for charitable purposes only – Finance Act 1975, Sch 6, para 10 – Recreational Charities Act 1958, s 1.

David Guild was the executor nominate of the late James Russell (the testator), who died leaving a will directing that the residue of his estate be left '. . . to the Town Council of North Berwick for use in connection with the Sports Centre in North Berwick or some similar purpose in connection with sport'. The town council of North Berwick was no longer in existence at the date of the testator's death and in *Russell's Executor v Balden* 1989 SLT 177, Lord Jauncey had held that the bequest in question had not fallen into intestacy. In due course the executor presented a cy-près scheme to the Inner House of the Court of Session for its approval and an interlocutor granting such approval was pronounced by the court on 14 June 1988. On 8 June 1990 the Revenue issued a notice of determination in respect of capital transfer tax. The notice was issued in relation to the transfer of value which was deemed to have occurred under the Finance Act 1975, s 22(1) on the death of the testator. It stated that such part of that transfer of value as was attributable to the property comprised in the bequest of the residuary estate in the will was not an exempt transfer for the purposes of the Finance Act 1975, Sch 6, para 10*a*, by which transfers of value attributable to property given to charities were exempt from capital transfer tax. The executor appealed under the Finance Act 1975, Sch 4, para 7(3) against the notice of determination.

Held – (1) Paragraph 10(3) of Sch 6 to the Finance Act 1975 did not require that the residue be capable of application for charitable purposes immediately after the death of the testator. Its only requirement was that a trust, under which the residue was held for charitable purposes only, should have come into existence at the date of death. The executor held the residue on trust for the purposes described in the bequest from the date of death to the date the cy-près scheme came into effect.

(2) (Lord McCluskey dissenting): The bequest was intended to provide facilities for recreation or other leisure-time occupation and to be for the public benefit. The facilities of the sports centre in North Berwick were provided in the interests of social welfare and therefore the first part of the bequest, ie the direction that the residue be used in connection with the sports centre in North Berwick, was for charitable purposes by virtue of s 1 of the Recreational Charities Act 1958. However, the second part of the bequest, ie the alternative direction that the residue be used for some similar purpose in connection with sport, was not limited to those features of the sports centre which made it charitable under s 1. The second part allowed the real and substantial possibility of non-charitable use. The bequest as a whole was therefore not 'for charitable purposes only' and accordingly the Crown's refusal of the claim for exemption under para 10 of Sch 6 to the Finance Act 1975 was correct. The appeal would be dismissed.

Notes

For exempt transfers to charity, see Foster: Inheritance Tax D2.15.

a   Paragraph 10 is set out at p 295 *a–b*, post

For the Finance Act 1975, Sch 6, para 10 (now the Inheritance Tax Act 1984, s 23), see ibid, part S.

For the Recreational Charities Act 1958, s 1, see 5 Halsbury's Statutes (4th edn) 805–806.

Cases referred to in opinions
Davidson's Trustees v Arnott 1951 SC 42, CS.
Fogo's Judicial Factor v Fogo's Trustees 1929 SC 546, CS.
Fulton v Fulton and others 1864 2 M 893, CS.
Gibson's Trustees 1933 SC 190, CS.
IRC v Baddeley [1955] AC 572, [1955] All ER 525, 35 TC 661, HL.
IRC v Glasgow Police Athletic Association [1953] AC 380, [1953] 1 All ER 747, 34 TC 76, HL.
IRC v McMullen [1978] 1 WLR 664, [1978] 1 All ER 230; [1979] 1 WLR 130, [1979] 1 All ER 588, CA; [1981] AC 1, [1980] 1 All ER 884, 54 TC 413, HL.
Lindsay's Trustees v Lindsay 1938 SC 44, CS.
Nottage, Re [1895] 2 Ch 649, CA.
Russell's Executor v Balden 1989 SLT 177, CS.
Scottish Flying Club v IRC 1935 SC 817, CS.

Appeal
David James Guild, WS, the executor nominate of the late James Young Russell, appealed under para 7(3) of Sch 4 to the Finance Act 1975 against a notice of determination dated 8 June 1990 made by the Inland Revenue Commissioners. The facts are set out in the opinion of the Lord President.

J E Drummond Young QC and *A J Hamilton* for the executor.
D R A Emslie QC and *J W McNeill* for the Crown.

The court made avizandum.

15 March. The following opinions were delivered.

THE LORD PRESIDENT (HOPE). This is an appeal under para 7(3) of Sch 4 to the Finance Act 1975 (the 1975 Act) (now s 222(3) of the Inheritance Tax Act 1984 (the 1984 Act)) against a notice of determination dated 8 June 1990 which was made by the Inland Revenue Commissioners in respect of a charge to capital transfer tax. The notice was issued in relation to the transfer of value which was deemed to have occurred under s 22(1) of the 1975 Act on the death of the late James Young Russell (the testator) on 11 September 1982. It stated that such part of that transfer of value as was attributable to the property comprised in the bequest of his residuary estate in his will dated 7 April 1971 was not an exempt transfer for the purposes of para 10 of Sch 6 to the 1975 Act. In terms of that paragraph transfers of value which are attributable to property which is given to charities are exempt from capital transfer tax, to the extent of the value transferred by the gift. The point at issue in this case depends on the meaning and effect of para 10(3) of Sch 6 which provides: 'For the purposes of this paragraph property is given to charities if it becomes the property of charities or is held on trust for charitable purposes only'. The application of that provision to the bequest of residue in this case raises two questions on which we listened to a careful and interesting argument. The first is whether, in view of a defect in the bequest which led to delay until it could receive effect, the residue can be said to have been held on trust for charitable purposes as from the date of death of the testator. The second is whether, having regard to the terms of the residue clause, the bequest can be said to have been for charitable purposes only.

The residue clause was in these terms:

a   'And I leave the whole, rest, residue and remainder of my said means and estate to the Town Council of North Berwick for the use in connection with the Sports Centre in North Berwick or some similar purpose in connection with sport and the receipt of the Treasurer for the time being of the Burgh of North Berwick shall be a sufficient receipt and discharge for my Executor.'

   The testator died on 11 September 1982, and the town council of North Berwick was no longer in existence at that date. This was because, as a result of s 1(5) of the

b   Local Government (Scotland) Act 1973 all local government areas existing immediately before 16 May 1975 including small burghs, such as North Berwick, ceased to exist on that date. All property formerly vested in the town council was transferred to and vested in East Lothian District Council or Lothian Regional Council on that date according to the functions for which it was held. The provision of sporting and recreational facilities in North Berwick and the surrounding area

c   became the responsibility of the district council, with the same statutory powers, duties and responsibilities as the town council formerly possessed. Thus the operation and management of the sports centre in North Berwick ceased to be a function of the town council on that date and became a function of the district council, and since there was no longer a treasurer for the time being of the burgh of North Berwick there was no one to give a sufficient receipt and discharge to the executor

d   for the bequest. The testator had made no alteration to his will to take account of these events, and when he died the question arose as to whether the bequest of residue to the town council for these purposes had lapsed. An action of multiplepoinding was raised by the executor in order to resolve these questions, in which claims were lodged by the heirs in intestacy on the one hand and by the executor on the other. The executor's claim was an administrative claim so that he

e   might apply to the court for the approval of a scheme for the future administration of the bequest, and it was supported by East Lothian District Council and by the North Berwick Community Council. In an opinion reported as *Russell's Executor v Balden* 1989 SLT 177 at 179, Lord Jauncey held that the bequest disclosed a general charitable intention and (at 180) that there was nothing in the will to suggest that the testator wished the town council and no other body who might succeed them to

f   administer the bequest. In the result it was held not to have fallen into intestacy, and he ranked and preferred the executor to the fund in medio for the purposes of his administrative claim.

   In due course the executor presented a scheme to the Inner House of the Court of Session for its approval. All that was necessary in this case, since the sports centre continued to exist in North Berwick and there was thus no obvious failure of the

g   essential purpose of the bequest, was to make good the defect in the machinery for its operation which had arisen due to the reorganisation of local government. The appropriate course would have been to do what was done in *Lindsay's Trustees v Lindsay* 1938 SC 44 and appoint persons to take the place of the town council of North Berwick to receive the bequest and carry it into effect. As Lord President Normand pointed out (at 49), the failure of machinery does not have the effect of

h   invalidating the purpose for which it was to have been created, and it is the duty of the court in such circumstances to provide the trust machinery which is required. This case provides an example of the second of the three categories to which Lord President Clyde referred in *Gibson's Trustees* 1933 SC 190 at 199 of the ways in which the court will not allow a charitable bequest or trust to be held void for uncertainty, or fail, if that can possibly be avoided. It is not a case within the third category

j   where, although sufficient powers and machinery have been provided, the charitable endowment itself is incapable of operation owing to changed circumstances with the result that the settlement has to be varied so as to preserve the underlying charitable purpose in accordance with the doctrine of cy-près. Nevertheless, the scheme which was presented to the court, and which was approved by it on 14 June 1988, provided not only for the administrative machinery to be altered by the appointment of

ex officio trustees to administer the bequest, but also for the charitable purposes to
be altered so that the funds were to be used, not 'in connection with the Sports
Centre in North Berwick or some similar purpose in connection with sport' as the
bequest provides, but for a variety of purposes designed to promote or otherwise
benefit sport in and around North Berwick.

The purposes of the scheme, which became operative on the date of the
interlocutor of 14 June 1988, are consistent with Lord Jauncey's view that the
bequest of residue constituted a trust in which a section of the public had an interest,
and in particular that the reference to 'some similar purpose in connection with
sport' meant a purpose related to sport in and around North Berwick (see *Russell's
Executor v Balden* 1989 SLT 177 at 180). But it is now conceded, contrary to what
was said in the grounds of appeal, that the purposes as defined in the scheme do not
constitute a charity for the purposes of the Income Tax Acts. Section 51(1) of the
1975 Act provides that, for the purposes of capital transfer tax, 'charity' and
'charitable' have the same meanings as in the Income Tax Acts. Accordingly, if the
purposes of the bequest had been expressed in the terms which are now set out in
the scheme there would have been no answer to the determination with which we
are concerned in this case. For their part the Crown have departed from their
contention, as set out in their answers to the grounds of appeal, that the bequest as
varied by the scheme took effect on and as from the death of the testator so that it
was to the bequest as varied by the scheme that we were to look to see if there was a
trust for charitable purposes only when the transfer of value took place. In these
circumstances the scheme no longer has a direct bearing on the issues which we have
to decide. Nevertheless, the Crown are able to say that the fact that the residue is
now being held in trust for purposes which are admitted not to be charitable
purposes only shows that the point which they have taken in this case is not a
technical one. And, while it has not been suggested that the scheme can be used in
order to construe the bequest, the fact that it takes the form which it does, as an
expression of the general charitable intention of the testator, gives some credibility
to the Crown's argument that the purposes of the bequest were not for charitable
purposes only and, accordingly, that the transfer of value was not exempt.

The first point to be considered is whether the residue was 'held on trust' within
the meaning of para 10(3) of Sch 6 during the period between the date of death of
the testator and the date when the scheme which was approved by the court became
operative. The executor contended that as from the date of death the residue was
held on trust by the executor, pending the setting up of the machinery which was
necessary to achieve the purposes of the residuary bequest. The executor could not
make over the bequest to anyone until the appointment of the trustees who were to
receive it in terms of the scheme, but he was nevertheless holding it in a fiduciary
capacity as executor for the purposes described in the bequest. This was disputed by
counsel for the Crown, who argued strongly that the executor could not be said to
be holding the bequest for trust purposes since his function was purely administrative
and he had no power to apply the residue for the purposes of the trust. As counsel
observed, to hold otherwise would lead to what he described as the odd result that
the charitable exemption could be claimed for property which never had been, nor
was ever capable of being, applied for charitable purposes only. It was said that no
charity had a vested right in the residue until the scheme became operative, because
nobody had a right to demand payment from the executor until that had been
achieved. In the meantime the executor was holding the residue for what Lord
Cowan described in *Fulton v Fulton and others* 1864 2 M 893 at 900 as 'the purpose
of management'. It was emphasised that the carrying into operation of the scheme
could not validate retrospectively what, on the Crown's approach, was the ineffective
bequest in the will—ineffective, because the residue could not be applied for the
purposes of the bequest.

I think that these arguments were unduly influenced by the peculiar situation
which has arisen in this case where it is contended by the executor that the residue,

while admittedly now being held for purposes which are not charitable purposes
only, was nevertheless being held in trust for charitable purposes only during the
period up to the operative date. It is not unusual for property which is given in trust
for charitable purposes only to be incapable of being applied for those purposes
immediately after the death of the testator. Especially in cases where the trustees of
that trust are not the executors who must administer the estate, there is bound to be
a delay while the executor is fulfilling his functions before he can transfer the
property to the trustees. If this delay, during which the property is not yet capable
of being applied for the trust purposes, were to result in that property not being held
for charitable purposes only it would have the result in many cases that the exemption
which para 10 of Sch 6 provides would not be available. In any event it seems to me
to be irrelevant to consider whether the property is or is not capable of being applied
for charitable purposes for the time being. That is not what para 10(3) of Sch 6
requires in those cases where property which is given to charities is not given to the
charities themselves but is to be held for charitable purposes on trust. It seems to me
that the only requirement is that a trust should have come into existence at the date
of the transfer. If it has, then so long as that trust is for charitable purposes only, the
exemption is available on the ground that, by this means, the property has been
given to charities.

The question then is whether, as from the date of death in this case, the residue
was held in trust for the purposes of the bequest although the funds could not yet be
applied for these purposes because of the defect. The scheme must, of course, be left
out of account in this regard because it was not retrospective. It took effect only
from the date of the court's interlocutor, and then only with respect to the funds
then held by the executor for the purposes of the residuary bequest. But to describe
the bequest as being of no effect, or as giving no vested right to charity for the
purposes which it describes, is I think incorrect. On the contrary, the bequest was
effective in a question with the only competing interest, which was that of the heirs
in intestacy. As Lord Jauncey held in the action of multiplepoinding, it was clearly
intended to benefit a section of the public, so it could be enforced if necessary by
popularis actio against the executor (see *Russell's Executor v Balden* 1989 SLT 177 at
179). Furthermore, it is plain that the executor was under a duty, as from the date
of death, not only to retain the residue against competing claims but to take such
steps as were necessary to bring the bequest into effect. As Lord Cowan put it in
Fulton v Fulton's Trustees 1864 2 M 893 at 900: 'An executor well confirmed stands
in the position of a trustee. It is a judicial trust. He is vested with the estate for the
purpose of management . . . and he cannot give over the estate to others'. In *Fogo's
Judicial Factor v Fogo's Trustees* 1929 SC 546 at 551, Lord Ormidale said that if
there is no provision in the will involving a continuing duty on the part of the
executor and the retention of the whole or part of the estate in his hands, there is no
occasion to call in aid the provisions of the Trusts (Scotland) Acts or, indeed, any
room for their application. Counsel for the Crown relied on this remark, but I think
that what Lord Ormidale had in mind in that passage was the simple case of the
executor whose duty was only to ingather the estate, to pay the deceased's debts and
then to satisfy the legacies. He did not have in mind in that case the complications
which have arisen here where the executor's duties involved holding the estate for a
prolonged period in order to resolve competing claims and cure a defect in the
machinery before the operation of the bequest. In any event, as Lord Cowan pointed
out in *Fulton* (at 900), although an executor may have no need of these provisions,
he is nevertheless a trustee. Section 2 of the Trusts (Scotland) Act 1921 defines the
expression 'trustee' as including any executor nominate. A similar provision is
contained in s 20 of the Succession (Scotland) Act 1964, by which an executor dative
is also a trustee for the purposes of the Trusts (Scotland) Acts. In this case the
executor's functions were far from simple, and I have no difficulty in regarding him
as holding the residue in a fiduciary capacity throughout the period from the
testator's death until the scheme took effect. In my opinion the executor's argument

is sound on this point, and the effect of the gift was that as from the date of death the residue was held on trust for the purposes described in the bequest.

This brings me to the second point, which is whether this was a trust for charitable purposes only, on a proper construction of what the bequest provides. It is not enough that one of its purposes is seen to be charitable, since what the exemption requires is that the property be held on trust for charitable purposes only. This makes it necessary to examine the bequest bearing in mind that what one is looking for here is whether, viewing the matter in a reasonable sense, its predominant or sole object is charitable (see *Scottish Flying Club v IRC* 1935 SC 817 at 822 per Lord Fleming, *IRC v Glasgow Police Athletic Association* [1953] AC 380 at 402, 34 TC 76 at 103 per Lord Reid). The bequest falls naturally into two parts. First, there is the direction that the residue is to be used in connection with the sports centre in North Berwick, and then there is the alternative that it is to be used for some similar purpose in connection with sport. It was accepted that, since we are concerned here with a taxing statute, the words 'charitable purposes' must be interpreted according to English law. It was also agreed that a bequest for the encouragement of a sport or game or for the purposes of recreation and enjoyment cannot be said to be charitable at common law. In *re Nottage* [1895] 2 Ch 649, in which it was held that a gift for the encouragement of a mere sport—in that case the sport of yacht racing—though it might be beneficial to the public, could not be upheld as charitable. In *IRC v Glasgow Police Athletic Association*, it was held that, although the purpose of promoting the efficiency of the police force was a charitable purpose, it had not been established for charitable purposes only, since it also had the purpose of providing for the recreation of its members which was a non-charitable purpose. The whole matter, therefore, turns on the question whether the purposes of this bequest are charitable in terms of s 1 of the Recreational Charities Act 1958 (the 1958 Act).

This is a complicated section which requires some analysis. Section 1(1) provides that it shall be and be deemed always to have been charitable to provide, or assist in the provision of 'facilities for recreation or other leisure-time occupation'. But that innovation on the common law is subject to two qualifications, one of which gives rise to particular difficulty. First, there is a requirement that 'the facilities are provided in the interests of social welfare', and second, there is the proviso that nothing in the section shall be taken to derogate from the principle that a trust or institution to be charitable must be for the public benefit. Subsection (2) provides that the requirement that the facilities are provided in the interests of social welfare is not to be treated as satisfied unless two further conditions are met. These are that:

> '(a) the facilities are provided with the object of improving the conditions of life for the persons for whom the facilities are primarily intended; and
> (b) either—
>
> (i) those persons have need of such facilities as aforesaid by reason of their youth, age, infirmity or disablement, poverty or social and economic circumstances; or
> (ii) the facilities are to be available to the members or female members of the public at large.'

Subsection (3) provides some guidance as to what is meant by 'facilities' in this context. This includes the provision and maintenance of grounds and buildings to be used for purposes of recreation or leisure-time occupation, and extends to the provision of facilities for those purposes by the organising of any activity. Clearly the sports centre in North Berwick is a facility used for the purposes of recreation or leisure-time occupation, and to this extent at least the bequest comes within the scope of sub-s (1). I think that the same view can be taken of the phrase 'some similar purpose in connection with sport' in the alternative branch of the bequest. The description of 'facilities' in sub-s (3) is not exhaustive, so the word may be taken to include anything which is designed to provide the equipment, resources or

opportunity for recreation or other leisure-time occupation, of which sport is an
example. Nor does the proviso to sub-s (1), which preserves the principle that a trust
must be for the public benefit in order to be charitable, give rise to difficulty in this
case. I think that the bequest was clearly intended to be one for the public benefit.
It was to be given to the town council to be administered by them and not by private
individuals, and the purposes which it describes are public purposes which are
designed to benefit at least a section of the public, which, as Lord Jauncey described
it (see *Russell's Executor v Balden* 1989 SLT 177 at 180), was the sporting community
in North Berwick. The points at issue turn, therefore, on the requirement that the
facilities are provided in the interests of social welfare. This requirement must be
satisfied by both branches of the bequest, since in order to obtain exemption the
bequest must be for charitable purposes only. There is no indication in the bequest
that its object was to benefit persons in need of facilities for recreation or other
leisure-time occupation by reason of their youth, age, infirmity or disablement,
poverty or social and economic circumstances (see sub-s (2)(*b*)(i)). In this situation it
seems to me that the questions which must be considered, when one is examining
the bequest, are these: (1) for whom are the facilities comprised in the sports centre
or other 'similar purpose' primarily intended? (2) is the object of providing these
facilities that of improving the conditions of life for those persons? and (3) are these
facilities to be available to the members—no separate point arises in this case about
female members—of the public at large?

According to the admitted facts, the whole of the facilities in the sports centre are,
and were at the date of the testator's death, available to the general public. These
consist of a main sports hall which can be used for various indoor sports and
activities, and a number of other rooms and courts of a more particular character,
together with changing and showering accommodation, a cafeteria and a library.
Although emphasis has been placed on casual use by members of the public, they do
not have unrestricted access to these facilities at all times. They are used from time
to time by a number of local clubs, by local schools and by the Lothian Region
Education Authority who, in addition to use during school terms, run a programme
of activities which are open to members of the public on a random attendance basis.
I think that it can reasonably be said in these circumstances that the facilities are
primarily intended for the public, and that they are available to members of the
public at large within the meaning of sub-s 2(*b*)(ii). That provision does not require
that the facilities must be available exclusively to members of the public at all times,
but in any event I think that those clubs which make use of the facilities can be
regarded as a section of the public for this purpose. Any use of the facilities by
private clubs can be regarded as purely incidental. The important point is that the
sports centre is available for a variety of public uses to be enjoyed by the public in a
variety of ways appropriate to the particular activities which are involved.

The question remains, however, whether the facilities at the sports centre 'are
provided with the object of improving the conditions of life for the persons for whom
the facilities are primarily intended' (see sub-s (2)(*a*)). I have found this to be a
question of some difficulty. We were referred to *IRC v McMullen*, in which it was
held both by Walton J (see [1978] 1 WLR 664, 54 TC 413) and by a majority in the
Court of Appeal (see [1979] 1 WLR 130, 54 TC 413) that a trust known as the
Football Association Youth Trust which had been created to organise, provide or
assist in the organisation and provision of facilities to enable and encourage pupils of
schools and universities in any part of the United Kingdom to play association
football or other games and sports was not a valid charitable trust under s 1 of the
1958 Act. This was because, among other reasons, the trust fund could be used in a
manner which did not satisfy the requirements of sub-s (2)(*a*) of that section. The
decision of the Court of Appeal was reversed in the House of Lords (see [1981] AC 1,
54 TC 413) on grounds which made it unnecessary to consider whether the trust
could qualify as charitable under the 1958 Act. Walton J ([1978] 1 WLR 664 at 675,
54 TC 413 at 423) said that the words 'provided in the interests of social welfare' in

themselves indicate that there is some kind of deprivation, and that the persons for whom the facilities are primarily intended must be to some extent in some way deprived persons. The majority in the Court of Appeal were of a similar opinion. The ideas of need and social deprivation were the basis of this approach. Stamp LJ, with whom Orr LJ agreed, said ([1979] 1 WLR 130 at 137–138, 54 TC 413 at 428) that, while the purchase of a playing field in part of a great town where there were no facilities for fresh air or recreation to be used by the public at large for the playing of games might well qualify, the requirement for the promotion of social welfare could not be satisfied simply by providing funds to encourage persons who had access to one sport to play another. He took the view that to provide sporting facilities for pupils of schools and universities could not reasonably be argued to have as its object improving their conditions of life. But Bridge LJ ([1979] 1 WLR 130 at 143, 54 TC 413 at 433) was of a different opinion. He rejected the idea that the interests of social welfare could only be served in relation to some 'deprived' class. This was on the view that it was not only the deprived who can have their conditions of life improved, and also because he considered that the class of pupils at schools and universities as part of their education were in need of facilities for organised games and sports by reason of either their youth or their social and economic circumstances, or both. The question of need does not arise directly in this case, because we are not concerned here with facilities which are intended primarily for persons of the description in sub-s (2)(*b*)(i). The facilities at the sports centre are primarily intended, as I have said, for use by the public at large in North Berwick. Subsection (2)(*b*)(ii) does not require it to be shown that the public at large have need of the facilities, no doubt on the view that where facilities are available to the members of the public at large there is a sufficient element of public benefit. But even in the context of sub-s (2)(*b*)(ii) the object of providing the facilities must be to improve the conditions of life for those persons. And it is clear from the structure of s 1 as a whole that this is a distinct requirement from that stated in sub-s (1), namely that the facilities are for recreation or other leisure-time occupation. So one must ask oneself how this requirement can be said to be satisfied in the case of the sports centre.

The difficulty for the executor is that we have no obvious basis in the facts available to us to assess in what respect the conditions of life of the members of the public in North Berwick are intended to be improved by the presence there of the sports centre. Counsel for the Crown, Mr McNeill, said that the requirement cannot be satisfied unless some specific object of the kind contemplated by sub-s (2)(*a*) can be identified. He invited us to follow the opinion of the majority in *IRC v McMullen* as to the meaning of the requirement, on the view that Bridge LJ's approach did not do sufficient justice to the word 'improving'. Counsel for the executor submitted that the object of the sports centre was self-evident from the nature of the facilities which were provided there, and that it was clear that this was to improve the conditions of life for both the inhabitants and visitors to the town. With some hesitation I have reached the view that counsel for the executor's submission is to be preferred and that the admitted facts are sufficient for us to be able to say that the requirement is satisfied in the case of the sports centre. The facilities which are provided there are all concerned in one way or another with physical training and exercise. Various kinds of competitive sports and similar activities such as fitness exercises and keep fit and aerobic classes can be carried on in the main sports hall and in the other accommodation which it contains. Recreation or other leisure-time occupation may take various forms, no doubt all pleasurable but not all of them conducive to physical health. As Lord Reid remarked in *IRC v Baddeley* [1955] AC 572 at 596, 35 TC 661 at 704, recreation is a very wide term. But it is the emphasis on fitness and exercise which satisfies me that the object of the sports centre can properly be regarded as that of improving the conditions of life of those members of the public who choose to go there. I respectfully agree with Bridge LJ (see *IRC v McMullen* [1979] 1 WLR 130 at 143, 54 TC 413 at 433) that it is not necessary to find a state of deprivation before the object of improving the conditions of life can be

satisfied. All one need do in order to improve something is to make it in some way
a better than it was before. And we are concerned here with facilities which are
provided for the public benefit. This is important because, as counsel for the Crown
reminded us, sporting facilities as such are not considered to be charitable at common
law. In *IRC v Baddeley* Viscount Simonds said ([1955] AC 572 at 589, 35 TC 661 at
699):

b   'The moral, social and physical well-being of the community or any part of it
    is a laudable object of benevolence and philanthropy, but its ambit is far too
    wide to include only purposes which the law regards as charitable.'

But I think that it is worth noting that in his dissenting speech Lord Reid said
([1955] AC 572 at 596–597, 35 TC 661 at 704) that a charitable purpose such as
c education may well be achieved in part at least by promoting sport or games, and
that while encouragement of a mere sport or game had been held not to be charitable
it was a different matter when the encouragement of sport or games was a means to
achieve a charitable purpose for those who took part in it. As I understand it, the
1958 Act was intended to remove the doubts which had been raised by that case
about the charitable nature of trusts and institutions whose purpose was to provide
d facilities for recreation in the interests of social welfare. So as matters now stand it is
the provision in the interests of social welfare that is the principal criterion as to
whether or not the trust or institution is charitable. It seems to me that where one
finds, as we do in the case of the sports centre, facilities which are to be available to
members of the public at large, and whose object is to promote the physical well-
being of those members of the public who go there in a way which they could not
e achieve for themselves if they remained at home, one has all that is needed to satisfy
this requirement.
But that is not an end of the matter, because there remains the second branch of
the bequest. The exemption in para 10(3) of Sch 6 to the 1975 Act requires that the
property be held on trust for charitable purposes only, and this means that the
executor must show that the use of the funds for 'some similar purpose in connection
f with sport' confines the bequest to purposes which fall within s 1 of the 1958 Act.
Here again it is the requirements of sub-s (2) about provision in the interests of social
welfare which cause the difficulty. It may be that this branch of the bequest is wide
enough to enable the funds to be applied in the provision or to assist in the provision
of facilities which are undoubtedly charitable within the meaning of s 1. But in my
opinion there are no words of restriction or limitation to prevent their being used in
g some other way which falls outside the scope of that section, such as to provide
benefit for private sports clubs or other facilities which are not for persons who have
need of them or are not available for use by members of the public or female
members of the public at large. Counsel for the executor maintained that the word
'similar' was sufficient to achieve this, since the town council would have been in
breach of trust if they were to use the funds for a purpose in connection with sport
h which was not similar to the purposes of the sports centre itself. But I am not satisfied
that the word 'similar' has the effect of limiting this branch of the bequest to those
features of the sports centre which make it charitable under s 1 of the 1958 Act—and
in particular the availability of its facilities to the public at large. A thing can be
similar to something else without being precisely the same, and in any event it is at
least open to argument that the only feature about the sports centre to which the
j town council was required to have regard was that it was in North Berwick. In his
opinion in *Russell's Executor v Balden* 1989 SLT at 180, Lord Jauncey said that he
construed the reference to 'some similar purpose in connection with sport' as
meaning a purpose related to sport in and around North Berwick. It was that
interpretation which led to the scheme which in due course the court approved by
its interlocutor of 14 June 1988 as being in accordance with the general charitable
intention evinced by the testator. It gives a scope to this part of the bequest which
extends it beyond the provision of facilities only in the interests of social welfare,

and plainly to that extent it does not satisfy the requirements of s 1(2) of the 1958 Act. No doubt any non-charitable element which is merely incidental or ancillary to the bequest can be overlooked, but I see here a provision of such width and generality that the possibility of some benefit which is non-charitable is both real and substantial. That is enough to defeat the claim for the exemption, irrespective of any view which may be taken about the use of the bequest in connection with the sports centre.

Accordingly, while I reject the argument for the Crown that the residue was not held on trust while it was in the hands of the executor, I think that they were right to refuse to grant the exemption in this case because the trust, while no doubt a public trust, was not for charitable purposes only. On this view the coming into operation of the scheme made no difference as regards this exemption, since its purposes are admitted to be not of that character. I mention this only because it would be a matter for regret if the benefit of the exemption were to be lost by a variation of the terms of the bequest which went beyond what was strictly necessary to achieve what was required.

On the whole matter, therefore, I invite your Lordships to refuse this appeal and to confirm the determination which has been appealed against.

LORD MAYFIELD. This is an appeal against a notice of determination made by the Inland Revenue Commissioners in respect of a charge to capital transfer tax.

David James Guild, WS is the executor nominate (the executor) of the late James Young Russell (the testator), who resided at the The Croft, Gosford Road, Longniddry conform to confirmation by the sheriff of Lothian and Borders at Haddington dated 18 November 1982. The testator died on 11 September 1982 leaving a will dated 7 April 1971 and registered in the Books of Council and Session on 14 September 1982. By the will the testator appointed the appellant to be his executor. In his will the testator made provision for the payment of a number of pecuniary legacies. Thereafter it directed that the residue of the testator's estate should be held for the following purposes:

> 'And I leave the whole, rest, residue and remainder of my said means and estate to the Town Council of North Berwick for the use in connection with the Sports Centre in North Berwick or some similar purpose in connection with sport and the receipt of the Treasurer for the time being of the Burgh of North Berwick shall be a sufficient receipt and discharge for my Executor.'

At the date of the testator's death North Berwick sports centre consisted of: (1) a main sports hall used for badminton and five-a-side football but marked and equipped for a variety of indoor sports and activities, including basketball, table tennis, judo, bowling and volleyball; (2) a bowling hall; (3) a fitness room; (4) squash courts; (5) a trampoline room designed for use by younger children but also for advanced acrobatic skills; (6) a table tennis room also with two full-sized snooker tables. That room is also used as a crèche for a mothers' group. The centre also contained changing and showering accommodation, a cafeteria and a small library of sports books. The whole of these facilities is available to the general public. It is casually used by members of the public, and the facilities, since the opening of the centre, have been used at certain times by a number of clubs, by local schools and for coaching sessions. The facilities are used during school terms by Lothian Region Education Authorities for squash, badminton and team sports. There is a programme for activities for ladies' keep fit and aerobics on two mornings per week and there is roller skating for children on two afternoons, all of which are open to members of the public on a random attendance basis. The centre houses the Inter Town Sports Festival for a variety of sports with teams from various towns in East Lothian, also the County Sports Festival on an annual basis and certain annual championships such as the East Lothian Badminton Association Championship. There are sessions for physically and mentally handicapped people and there are also free and reduced-

charge facilities for the unemployed and for single parents each morning. The centre
a   also runs a sports scholarship class for young people in East Lothian who show good
potential.

The town council of North Berwick was no longer in existence at the date of the
testator's death and the executor accordingly raised an action of multiplepoinding
in order to determine the succession to the residue of the testator's estate. The
matters in dispute in that action were determined by an interlocutor of Lord Jauncey
b   dated 5 August 1986 by which he ranked and preferred the executor to the fund in
medio for the purposes of an administrative claim in order that he might apply to
the court for approval of a cy-près scheme. The executor presented a petition to the
court for approval of such a scheme and an interlocutor granting such approval was
pronounced by the First Division of the Inner House of the Court of Session on
14 June 1988. There was thus a period of six years between the executor's
c   confirmation and the approval of the scheme. The purposes of the scheme are in
accord with the view of the Lord Ordinary that the bequest constituted a trust in
which the public had an interest and that 'some similar purpose in connection with
sport' meant a purpose related to sport in and around North Berwick (see *Russell's
Executor v Balden* 1989 SLT 177 at 180). On 8 June 1990 the Inland Revenue
Commissioners issued a notice of determination in respect of capital transfer tax in
d   the following terms:

'In relation to the transfer of value in respect of the estate of the late James
Young Russell deemed under section 22(1) of the Finance Act 1975 to have
been made immediately before his death on 11 September 1982. That such part
of the said transfer of value as is attributable to the property comprised in the
bequest of his residuary estate in his will dated 7 April 1971 is not [an] exempt
e   transfer for the purposes of paragraph 10 of Schedule 6 of the Finance Act 1975.'

Section 22(1) of the Finance Act 1975 (the 1975 Act) states:

'(1) On the death of any person after the passing of this Act tax shall be
charged as if, immediately before his death, he had made a transfer of value and
the value transferred by it had been equal to the value of his estate immediately
f   before his death, but subject to the following provisions of this section.'

Paragraph 10 of Sch 6 to the 1975 Act states:

'(1) Subject to the provisions of Part II of this Schedule, transfers of value are
exempt to the extent that the values transferred by them—

g   (a) are attributable to property which is given to charities; and
(b) so far as made on or within one year of the death of the transferor, do not
exceed £250,000 . . .

(3) for the purposes of this paragraph property is given to charities if it becomes
the property of charities or is held on trust for charitable purposes only.'

h   The first matter to be decided in determining the exemption is whether the
residue was held in trust within the meaning of para 10(3). It is clear that, although
the town council of North Berwick had ceased to exist at the date of death and the
executor could not obtain a receipt, the bequest remained intact. In such
circumstances, following *Lindsay's Trustees v Lindsay* 1938 SC 44 and *Gibson's
Trustees* 1933 SC 190, it is open to the court to make good any defect in the
j   machinery. In this case a cy-près scheme was selected to achieve that purpose and
in effect to widen the purposes of the bequest. It did so to the extent that the
executor conceded that the purposes so widened are not for charitable purposes only.

Counsel for the executor submitted that at the date of death the executor held the
residue in trust for charitable purposes only and did so in a fiduciary capacity.
Counsel for the Crown on the other hand maintains that the executor's function was
solely administrative. He had no power to dispose of the residue for the trust
purposes. He held the residue for 'the purpose of management' as stated by Lord

Cowan in *Fulton v Fulton and others* 1864 2 M 893 at 900. In my opinion the residue
was held in trust by the executor in a fiduciary capacity and for charitable purposes
only up to the operative date of the scheme. He submitted, and I agree, that it is not
unusual that there might be a delay before an executor can transfer property to
trustees. It is in my view clear that the executor had a duty to ingather and hold the
residue against competing claims and thereafter to take any necessary steps to give
effect to the bequest. As Lord Cowan stated in *Fulton* (at 900):

> 'An executor well confirmed stands in the position of a trustee. It is a judicial
> trust. He is vested with the estate for the purpose of management . . . he cannot
> give over the estate to others.'

While in many instances an executor may have simple duties such as to ingather the
estate and to satisfy the legacies, in this case the executor had to ingather, hold the
residue, resolve competing claims and remedy a defect in the machinery. In such
circumstances I consider that the executor held the residue in a fiduciary capacity
from the date of death up to the date of the scheme. Accordingly, as the residue was
held in trust at the date of transfer the requirements of para 10(3) have been satisfied.
The exemption is available provided that the trust is for charitable purposes only. I
am thus in complete agreement with your Lordship in the Chair.

The next matter accordingly is whether the property was held on trust for
charitable purposes only. In my view that must depend on a construction of the
bequest and the agreed facts. The purposes expressed in the cy-près scheme have no
application because the residue was held in trust at the date of death not for those
purposes but those set out in the will. It is clear, following *Scottish Flying Club v
IRC* 1935 SC 817 and *IRC v Glasgow Police Athletic Association* [1953] AC 380, 34
TC 76, that the bequest has to be considered closely to determine whether its sole
object is charitable. The matter has to be viewed in a reasonable sense. Purposes
which are incidental but not charitable will not necessarily detract from the overall
charitable object.

It is clear that the English law of charity falls to be regarded for income tax
purposes as part of the law of Scotland. That was so held in *IRC v Glasgow Police
Athletic Association* [1953] AC 380, 34 TC 76. It was not in dispute that a bequest
for the encouragement of sport or for the purposes of recreation was not charitable
at common law. Accordingly the question is whether the bequest is charitable in
terms of s 1 of the Recreational Charities Act 1958 (the 1958 Act). Section 1 states:

> '(1) Subject to the provisions of this Act, it shall be and be deemed always to
> have been charitable to provide, or assist in the provision of, facilities for
> recreation or other leisure-time occupation, if the facilities are provided in the
> interests of social welfare:
>
> Provided that nothing in this section shall be taken to derogate from the
> principle that a trust or institution to be charitable must be for the public
> benefit.
>
> (2) The requirement of the foregoing subsection that the facilities are provided
> in the interest of social welfare shall not be treated as satisfied unless—
>
> (*a*) the facilities are provided for the object of improving the conditions of
> life for the persons for whom the facilities are primarily intended; and
> (*b*) either—
>
> (i) those persons have need of such facilities as aforesaid by reason of their
> youth, age, infirmity or disablement, poverty or social and economic
> circumstances; or
> (ii) the facilities are to be available to the members or female members of
> the public at large.
>
> (3) Subject to the said requirement, subsection (1) of this section applies in
> particular to the provision of facilities at village halls, community centres and

women's institutes, and to the provision and maintenance of grounds and
buildings to be used for purposes of recreation or leisure-time occupation, and
extends to the provision of facilities for those purposes by the organising of any
activity.'

In my opinion the sports centre at North Berwick is a facility used for the purposes
of recreation or leisure time occupation and thus falls under the provisions of
sub-s (1). Plainly, also, the proviso which states that a trust in order to be charitable
must be for the public benefit raises no obstacle. The bequest was clearly for the
public benefit. It was made to the town council to carry out the purposes of the
bequest. Those purposes are public which have the object of benefiting a section of
the public namely those who participate in sport in North Berwick.

Subsection (2) states a requirement that the facilities are provided in the interests
of social welfare. That requirement is not satisfied unless (a) the facilities are
provided 'with the object of improving the conditions of life for the persons for
whom the facilities are primarily intended' and either in sub-s (2)(b)(i) a class of
persons not applicable to the bequest or sub-s (2)(b)(ii) members of the public at
large. I take the view that as sub-s (2)(b)(i) and sub-s (2)(b)(ii) are expressed as 'either'
sub-s (2)(b)(i) or sub-s (2)(b)(ii) and as sub-s (2)(b)(i) has no application in this case
then it is sufficient to satisfy the statute if the facilities are provided with the object
of improving the conditions of life for the persons for whom the facilities are
primarily intended and those facilities are to be available to the members of the
public at large. On the agreed facts I do not have any difficulty in reaching the
conclusion that the facilities are available to the public at large within the meaning
of sub-s (2)(b)(ii). As counsel for the executor pointed out, the provision does not
require that the facilities be exclusively available for members of the public at all
times. As he also pointed out, the clubs that use the centre must be regarded as
members of the public.

In my view, also, the requirement at sub-s (2)(a) namely, whether the facilities
are provided with the object of improving the conditions of life for the person for
whom the facilities are primarily intended, is also satisfied. That is subject to the
overriding requirement that the facilities must be provided in the interest of social
welfare. The interests of social welfare are satisfied because, in my view, the object
of improving the conditions of life are apparent from the terms of the bequest. The
phrase 'improving the conditions of life' is in itself couched in wide terms. It lacks
precision and if given a restricted meaning it would make it difficult for a testator to
make a charitable bequest. Furthermore, as Lord Hailsham LC pointed out in *IRC
v McMullen* [1981] AC 1 at 15, 54 TC 413 at 439, in the context of an educational
trust, regard had to be paid to contemporary circumstances. It is in my view a
contemporary view that recreational facilities such as provided at the sports centre
have as their object the 'improving of the conditions of life'. The facilities are
available to the sporting public at North Berwick and members of the public at
large. I have difficulty in accepting the views of Walton J (*IRC v McMullen* [1978]
1 WLR 664 at 675, 54 TC 413 at 423) that 'provided in the interests of social welfare'
is necessarily connected with deprivation. In that respect I agree with Bridge LJ
(*IRC v McMullen* [1979] 1 WLR 130 at 143, 54 TC 413 at 433) in the Court of
Appeal. I also agree that it is not only the deprived who can have their conditions of
life improved. The bequest will serve to 'assist' (see s 1(1)) in the provision of the
facilities. I am prepared to draw the inference from the agreed facts and the terms
of the bequest that the facilities are provided in the interests of social welfare with
the object of improving the conditions of life. I should add that in sub-s (3) the words
'by the organising of any activity' have the effect of widening the meaning of
facilities.

Counsel for the executor submitted that in the words in the bequest 'or some
similar purpose in connection with sport' considerable importance be attached to
'similar'. He submitted that 'similar' limited the use of the bequest to that which was

in use in connection with the sports centre. In other words that 'similar' limited the
use of the trust to its main purposes. He also maintained that the trustees would
have been in breach of trust if they had applied the fund for a purpose not similar to
the purposes which applied to the sports centre. He also pointed out that the trustees
would be the local authority in place of the now defunct North Berwick town
council. I found the above submissions attractive but not convincing. The question
to be answered, in my view, is whether the bequest, looked at as a whole, is for
charitable purposes only and that the use of the bequest is within the provisions of
s I of the 1958 Act. While the main bequest (preceding 'or some similar purpose in
connection with sport') is for charitable purposes only I am not satisfied that when
the bequest is looked at as a whole it can be held to be for charitable purposes only.
With some hesitation I have come to the conclusion that 'similar' would not have the
result of ensuring that 'or some similar purpose in connection with sport' sufficiently
limited the use of the funds to the charitable purposes relating to the sports centre
within the requirements of the 1958 Act. 'Similar' in my view signifies 'the like'. It
does not obviously mean the same. It would be possible, therefore, to use the funds
in such a way as to be applied for limited purposes outwith the scope of use by the
public at large. It is not clear enough to me that such a use could be limited under
the words of the secondary clause to a purpose which is merely incidental or ancillary
to the principal cause. The requirement is for charitable purposes 'only'. That is a
severe limitation in relation to charitable purposes. Accordingly, I have come to the
conclusion, in agreement with your Lordship in the Chair, that the appeal be
refused.

LORD McCLUSKEY. The appellant (the executor), executor nominate of the late
James Young Russell (the testator), and the respondents, the Inland Revenue
Commissioners (the Crown), agreed that the matters in issue between them should
be resolved by an appeal to this court. What is at issue is whether or not the executor
is entitled to claim exemption in respect of a transfer of value attributable to property
comprised in the bequest by the testator of his residuary estate in his will dated
7 April 1971. The testator died on 11 September 1982. By his will he appointed the
appellant to be his executor. The executor was instructed to pay legacies of sums of
£5,000 or £10,000 to named relatives. The only other provision of the will relating
to the estate was in the following terms:

> 'And I leave the whole, rest, residue and remainder of my said means and
> estate to the Town Council of North Berwick for the use in connection with the
> Sports Centre in North Berwick or some similar purpose in connection with
> sport and the receipt of the Treasurer for the time being of the Burgh of North
> Berwick shall be a sufficient receipt and discharge for my Executor.'

By the date of death, however, the town council of North Berwick was no longer
in existence, having been a victim of the reorganisation of local government in
Scotland which took final effect in May 1975. Your Lordship in the Chair has set
forth the history, on which parties were agreed, as to the raising of an action of
multiplepoinding and the successful application to the court for approval of a
cy-près scheme. I need not repeat it.

Capital transfer tax was created by s 19 of the Finance Act 1975 (the 1975 Act).
Section 19(1) reads: 'A tax, to be known as capital transfer tax, shall be charged on
the value transferred by a chargeable transfer'. Section 20(5) provides: 'A chargeable
transfer is any transfer of value made by an individual after 26th March 1974 other
than an exempt transfer'. Section 22(1) provides inter alia:

> 'On the death of any person after the passing of this Act tax shall be charged
> as if, immediately before his death, he had made a transfer of value and the
> value transferred by it had been equal to the value of his estate immediately
> before his death . . .'

Section 29 provides inter alia: 'Schedule 6 to this Act shall have effect with respect
a to exempt transfers'. Section 51(1) provides inter alia—'. . . "charity" and "charitable"
have the same meanings as in the Income Tax Acts'. Section 360(3) of the Income
and Corporation Taxes Act 1970 provides that—'"charity" means any body of
persons or trust established for charitable purposes only'. Schedule 6 to the 1975 Act
provides, in para 10(1), inter alia '. . . transfers of value are exempt to the extent that
the values transferred by them—(a) are attributable to property which is given to
b charities'. Paragraph 10(3) provides: 'For the purposes of this paragraph property is
given to charities if it becomes the property of charities or is held on trust for
charitable purposes only'.

Your Lordship in the Chair has already summarised the terms of the determination,
dated 8 June 1990. The reasoning which underlay that determination was presented
to us in the form of the submissions for the Crown. It is not in dispute, however,
c that, in so far as there is a burden on either party, it is for the executor, as the
taxpayer, to bring himself within the exemption. In the present instance, questions
of onus do not arise because all the necessary facts are agreed and admitted.

In the remainder of this opinion I refer to the estate forming the subject of the
bequest, and in respect of which partial exemption is claimed, as 'the residue'.

The executor submitted that in determining whether or not the residue qualified
d for exemption from capital transfer tax regard should be had only to the terms of the
clause containing the bequest of the residue, and not to the terms of the cy-près
scheme approved by the court some years later. Second, it was submitted that the
bequest effected by the residue clause was 'charitable' by reason of the effect of the
Recreational Charities Act 1958 (the 1958 Act). Third, it was submitted that the
residue was, at the material time, held for charitable purposes only and, in the
e language of para 10 of Sch 6 to the 1975 Act, was 'property . . . given to charities'.
From these propositions it followed that the transfer of value attributable to the
residue was exempt from the tax, in so far as it did not exceed £250,000, the figure
contained in para 10(1)(*b*) of Sch 6. It was not now to be argued that the purposes
contained in the cy-près scheme fell to be described as charitable purposes 'only'.

Developing these propositions, the executor argued that the effect of the relevant
f provisions in the 1975 Act was that regard had to be had to the point in time specified
in s 22(1) namely 'immediately before his [the testator's] death'. The bequest of the
residue took place at the moment when death occurred and the tax was to be charged
as if that transfer of value had been made immediately before the testator's death.
The effect was that it would be treated as if it had been a transfer of value made inter
vivos at that moment. The tempus inspiciendum was then and no later. The actings
g of the executor in relation to the action of multiplepoinding and, more particularly,
in relation to the application to the court for the approval of the cy-près scheme
were not relevant to the issue. The cy-près scheme was not substitutional for the
bequest in any retrospective sense. It was abundantly plain from the petition to the
court and from the scheme itself that the scheme was not to have retrospective effect
and that it looked to the future. This was the general position in relation in all
h cy-près schemes; they did not have retrospective effect. Turning to the Crown's
answer to the executor's grounds of appeal, attention was directed to the argument
introduced by the sentence there:

> 'Explained and averred that in the circumstances narrated in this Appeal, the
> said bequest of residue in the deceased's Will failed at the outset and never took
> effect.'

j
The argument for the executor was that the bequest did not fail. It was true that the
executor was unable on taking office to do what the will required him to do, namely
to pay the residue over to the treasurer for the time being of the burgh of North
Berwick, because the town council and the treasurer had by then been abolished by
statute. However, it was essential to distinguish between a trust purpose and the
machinery for putting that purpose into effect. If the purpose was clear but the

machinery had failed then the court would supply new machinery. In some instances it might be enough, in exercise of the nobile officium, to appoint persons to receive the funds. In other cases it might be necessary, alternatively or additionally, to set up a scheme in order to give effect as near as may be to the testator's charitable intention, where there was such an intention. This was not a case where there had been a failure of the beneficiary. It would not be disputed that if a legacy was bequeathed to a beneficiary but the beneficiary predeceased the testator then the legacy fell into residue; but here there was no prior or other failure of the beneficiary. Neither the treasurer of the burgh of North Berwick nor the town council was the beneficiary; they were the machinery; they were merely to receive the residue in trust to be expended on the purposes specified in the will. This distinction was clear in *Lindsay's Trustee v Lindsay* 1938 SC 44 and also in the opinion of Lord Jauncey when he dealt with the action of multiplepoinding (see *Russell's Executor v Balden* 1989 SLT 177). The residue was at the material time, namely at the moment of death, given to charity in the sense that then and thereafter it was to be 'held on trust for charitable purposes only'. In order to make a sound analysis of the legal position, it was necessary to ask whether or not, immediately after the testator's death, the executor 'held on trust' and, if he did, whether or not he so held 'for charitable purposes only'. It was not disputed that the executor then held the residue for administrative purposes. But to hold for administrative purposes did not mean that he did not also hold for charitable purposes. Holding for administrative purposes was merely a means to an end. The end was the payment over to the charitable purposes chosen by the testator. Whether one described the executor as an executor or as a trustee did not matter. What mattered was that on taking office he held the residue in a fiduciary capacity. It was not necessary, in terms of the statute, that he should be the person on whom the testator had conferred the function of applying the estate to the intended charitable purposes. If one asked for what purpose or purposes the executor held the estate at the material time the answer had to be found in the residue clause. Turning to that aspect of the matter the submission was that on a correct application of the 1958 Act to the circumstances disclosed in the statement of facts in this case it was plain that the purposes contained in the residue clause were not only 'charitable' but 'charitable only'. Looking at the wording of the bequest contained in the will, it was seen to be divided into two parts. The first part comprised the words, 'for the [sic] use in connection with the sports centre in North Berwick'. The second comprised the words, 'or some similar purpose in connection with sport'. However, in both instances, the intention of the testator could be discovered partly by considering the instruction to pay the entire estate to the town council of North Berwick. There could be no room for doubt that what the testator was doing was to provide, or rather to assist in the provision of, facilities for recreation. It was also clear that the named facilities at the sports centre were provided by the local authority with the object of improving the conditions of life for the persons for whom the facilities were primarily intended, namely persons who went to use the facilities in North Berwick. It was indisputable, indeed it was matter of admission that the facilities in question are and were at the date of death available to the general public; accordingly the conditions of s 1(1) and (2) were met. If the proviso to s 1(1) added a requirement of 'public benefit' that requirement was easily met. There was no difficulty in relation to the second part of the bequest. The critical word therein was 'similar'. Given that the administrator of the residue fund was to be the local authority which provided the existing sports centre it was clear that the concept of 'similar purpose' involved the expenditure by the local authority of the residue on facilities of a character similar to those provided at the sports centre. That meant that the facilities were mainly physical facilities, that they were to be open to the public and that they were to be in North Berwick or its immediate vicinity. Counsel explored the interpretation of s 1 of the 1958 Act under reference to the opinions in *IRC v McMullen* [1981] AC 1, 54 TC 413 as quoted by your Lordship in the Chair, and I need not rehearse that submission in detail. In the

whole circumstances, the correct view was that the residue fell within the terms of
para 10(1) and (3) of Sch 6 to the 1975 Act. In the result the appeal should be allowed
and the determination quashed.

For the Crown, it was pointed out that the submission advanced by the executor
in the present appeal was different to that which he had advanced to Lord Jauncey
in the action of multiplepoinding (see *Russell's Executor v Balden* 1989 SLT 177). It
was not, however, suggested that the petitioner was personally barred by reason of
the fact that he had previously advanced a different submission. But the fact that he
had done so served to demonstrate that the Crown was not relying merely on a
technicality. It also lent some support to the Crown's submission, particularly as
Lord Jauncey had accepted the submission then made by the executor. The real
starting point, in the submission of the Crown, was to ask, 'What is the bequest?'
Having regard to the terms of the 1975 Act, the bequest, before it could qualify for
exemption, must bring about the transfer of the property to the beneficiary. It was
necessary to look for the effective provision. The charging provisions were not
concerned with whether or not there was a transfer in a particular manner when a
person died; on death there must be a transfer to someone. What had to be looked
for was the effective transfer to the ultimate beneficiary. In this instance, that
transfer was not achieved by or under the will directly. The bequest intended by the
will failed not just because the machinery failed; the beneficiaries, ie the town
council, no longer existed when the testator died. The transfer took effect only when
the residue was transferred to cy-près trustees. Not before then was the bequest an
effective bequest to a charity. Looking at the position of the executor between the
date of death and the date of transfer to the cy-près trustees, the true position was
(1) that the executor held not on trust or as a trustee but simply as an executor for
administrative purposes, (2) that he did not hold for charitable purposes but for
purely administrative purposes, and (3) that, in any event, the purposes in the
bequest were not 'charitable purposes only'. Developing these submissions the
Crown argued that the initial bequest failed because it was inoperative or ineffective.
Indeed, to give effect to the executor's present submission would mean that, in this
case, property which had never been applied for charitable purposes, and never
would be, and indeed had only ever been applied for purposes which were admittedly
not wholly charitable, would be entitled to exemption. That was such an
extraordinary result that it showed there was a flaw in the executor's submission.
The true position was that no one had a vested right in the residue before the cy-
près scheme came into operation. During that hiatus, even if the residue could be
said to be 'held', it was not held for the stated purpose of the testator or for any
beneficiary; it was held administratively to be paid over to those who would
ultimately be found entitled to receive it. It was wrong to describe an executor such
as the present executor as holding on trust for charitable purposes when he could
neither apply the estate to any such purposes nor even know, until the court
approved a cy-près scheme, precisely what those purposes were ultimately to be. In
essence, the provisions in para 10 of Sch 6, were concerned with a vested right. In
the normal case it would be correct to speak of the trustees as having a vested right
on the death of a testator. Here, because there were no trustees and no identified
beneficiaries, there was no vesting; no one had the right to apply to the executor for·
disbursement until the cy-près scheme was approved. It was the application of or
the entitlement to the funds that ultimately mattered, and they were not applied to
any charitable purpose before that later date.

Turning to the character of the purposes, it could not be said that those contained
in the provision in the will were charitable purposes only. It was accepted that the
1958 Act was applicable. Indeed, but for the 1958 Act, the position of the executor
would be unstateable. The Crown accepted, at least for the purposes of this case,
that the provision in s 1(2) was definitive of the words 'social welfare' contained in
the conditional clause in s 1(1), namely, 'if the facilities are provided in the interests
of social welfare'; in other words, it was accepted that facilities which were provided

with the object specified in s 1(2)(a) and which also met either of the conditions
specified in s 1(2)(b) would be 'facilities . . . provided in the interests of social welfare'.
It was evident from the facts agreed in this case that the facilities pertaining to the
sports centre were sometimes used by private clubs and the like and accordingly it
could not be said that the residue was to be dedicated to charitable purposes 'only'.
In any event, the words 'or some similar purpose in connection with sport' were so
wide as to raise the clear likelihood that some of the residue funds, and even possibly
all of them, could be dedicated to non-charitable purposes. In fact, that was what
had admittedly happened after the cy-près scheme was approved. Furthermore, the
1958 Act is concerned with 'facilities' and the words 'some similar purpose in
connection with sport' went well beyond that concept. In the whole circumstances
the appeal should be refused.

In my opinion, it is important first to ascertain the point in time at which the
judgment falls to be made as to whether or not the exemption can be claimed. In my
opinion, that time is the date of death. The tax is to be charged, under s 22(1) of the
1975 Act, as if the transfer of value had been made immediately before death. The
actual transfer is made at the moment of death. I can see no reason, within the terms
of the statute, for reading in some provision to the effect that the transfer must be
taken as occurring when the real beneficiary effectively receives the estate. Equally
I see no reason for reading in the notion of vesting in a particular beneficiary when
the statute refers to no such concept. In considering this matter I obtained no
assistance whatsoever from para 15(1) contained in Part II of Sch 6 to the 1975 Act
to which reference was made by the Crown. That sub-paragraph applies to quite
specific situations where the ultimate disposition is postponed and takes effect on the
termination of some intervening interest or period. I cannot spell out of that any
notion that the effective date of transfer in a case such as the present is different from
the date of death. Any transfer of value that took place at the time of death was a
transfer to the executor for the benefit of the ultimate beneficiaries. Paragraph 10 of
Sch 6, does not require that the person who holds the property is a 'trustee' in some
technical sense. What it desiderates is that he holds 'on trust'. It appears to me to be
beyond argument that the executor held the residue on trust at all times until he
disposed of it. And it appears to me to be clear that there was no failure of the
beneficiaries here. The beneficiaries were not to be the town council of North
Berwick or the treasurer for the time being. As Lord Fleming put the matter in
Lindsay's Trustees v Lindsay 1938 SC 44 at 50—

> '. . . this is not a case of a failure of the beneficiary whom the testator intended
> to benefit, but merely a failure on his part to provide the machinery required to
> carry out the bequest. I think it is settled practice that, in the case of a charitable
> bequest, the necessary means or machinery to carry it into effect can be supplied
> by the Court if there is failure of the means or machinery which the testator
> himself intended.'

In *Davidson's Trustees v Arnott* 1951 SC 42 at 61, Lord Patrick dealing with a
submission like that of the Crown in relation to vesting said:

> 'It was not clear to me in what sense the term "vests" was used in this
> argument. If it was intended to mean the vesting of an immediate interest in a
> particular individual or defined class of individuals or in a particular institution,
> it is quite inapplicable as a test whether the Court will devise a cy-près scheme
> where the particular object of a charitable bequest has failed. Thus in the case
> where the particular charitable object has failed in the lifetime of the testator
> there is no vesting of such an interest in anyone. Nevertheless, if there appears
> in the bequest the expression of a general charitable purpose, a cy-près scheme
> will be applied. *Thus also in the case of many bequests for public purposes no
> individual or defined class of individuals or institution can at any time, whether
> before or after the opening of the succession, qualify an enforceable interest in such a
> bequest. Yet such bequests are perfectly good, and may be the objects of cy-près*

*schemes. I instance a bequest to provide and maintain a public park or a library or
the like.'* [My emphasis.]

In that sense, it appears to me to be clear that the intended beneficiaries here were
the persons who would come to the North Berwick area to claim access to and use of
the sports facilities in question. In a non-technical sense they had a 'vested' right
once the testator died and I do not doubt that members of the public who could have
qualified an interest could have sought a court order to prevent the executor, in his
office as executor, from disbursing the residue estate for purposes which were
inconsistent with his duty in terms of the will. I see no reason to read the words 'held
on trust for charitable purposes' as meaning 'held by a person whose function it is, as
trustee, to apply the funds for specified charitable purposes'. Yet that was the effect
of the contention advanced by the Crown. If one asks, in the present case, for what
purposes the executor held the funds after the date of death, it is certainly true that
he held them administratively. But he was holding them administratively only as a
means to an end, the end being that they should be applied ultimately to certain
specified purposes. If these purposes are found to be charitable then it appears to me
that in the ordinary use of language he was holding the funds for charitable purposes.
He certainly was not holding them for any purpose other than the testator's purposes
as specified in the will.

I next turn to the question as to whether or not the purposes could properly be
described as charitable. This matter is governed by the 1958 Act. If the executor
cannot show that the purposes are charitable within the meaning of the 1958 Act he
must fail. I need not repeat the section in full as it has been quoted earlier; but,
reading it short, what s 1(1) provides is that—'... it shall be ... charitable to provide,
or assist in the provision of, facilities for recreation ... if the facilities are provided in
the interests of social welfare'. So far as the sports centre in North Berwick is
concerned it is abundantly plain that it is a facility for recreation. It is equally plain
that in so far as the residue was to be applied 'for the use in connection with the
Sports Centre in North Berwick' the testator was assisting in the provision of
facilities for recreation. In order to discover whether or not the 'interests of social
welfare' requirement is met, one goes to sub-s (2). It appears to me to be plain
beyond a peradventure that facilities of the kind described in the case, which are
provided by a public local authority which derives its income from public funds and
is charged with the welfare of local people, facilities which are available indoors for
all ages and both sexes and for many interests from weightlifting to snooker, from
reading books to drinking coffee, are provided with the object of improving the
conditions of life for the users. The object of such provision must be to encourage
'mens sana in corpore sano', to enable members of the community to meet and enjoy
social intercourse, to enable children to engage in healthy, or at least, harmless
pursuits under adult supervision, to provide supervised and regulated opportunities
for competition. I have difficulty in understanding the contrary view which I
consider to be far too narrow. If there are no such facilities the opportunities of
people and families to mix indoors and enlarge their horizons by recreational
intercourse are restricted. For many teenagers, the true alternative to the sports
centre is the street corner. It is a matter of admission in the case that at the date of
the testator's death the facilities were 'available to the general public'. Accordingly I
have no difficulty in holding that the social welfare requirement is satisfied. The
proviso to s 1(1) does not, in my view, add any requirement; all it does is to save the
principle therein referred to. In any event, even if it were thought to add a
requirement of 'public benefit', then I should have no difficulty with that: the
bequest was clearly intended for the public benefit. In relation to the meaning of the
word 'facilities' I observe that the word is not defined in the 1958 Act. When one
looks, however, at s 1(3) one sees that it includes the words—'... subsection (1) of
this section ... extends to the provision of facilities ... *by the organising of any
activity'*. [My emphasis.] That means that the concept of 'facilities' includes, in

addition to tangible corporal facilities, 'the organising of any activity', because a
person can by organising an activity 'provide facilities'. Thus I do not consider that   *a*
the word 'facilities' in the 1958 Act is restricted to physical facilities or even to such
items as footballs, whistles, billiard cues, nets, jerseys or the like. As used in this
section the concept is, in my opinion, a very wide one indeed.

Finally, I come to consider the term 'or similar purpose in connection with sport'.
In my opinion, the executor is correct in maintaining that the crucial word is the
word 'similar'. The word 'similar' can mean 'like' or 'alike', but equally it can be used   *b*
to mean, 'of the same kind'. (The argument for the executor would have been more
difficult had the adjective been 'other'.) If one looks, as I think we must, at the
testator's intention when he used the words 'for . . . use in connection with the Sports
Centre in North Berwick or some similar purpose in connection with sport . . .' it is
clear that he was thinking of the possibility that part or all of his gift might not be
needed for the express primary purpose of supporting the North Berwick sports   *c*
centre itself. But plainly he could not choose precise alternative facilities for a future
which was unknowable to him. The fact that he selected the local authority as the
trustees to make that choice, if it proved necessary, the choice of an alternative set
of facilities of the same kind, is itself, in my opinion, a most telling circumstance.
But the matter must also be looked at in this way: I have already concluded, as
indeed your Lordships have done, that on a proper construction of the first part of   *d*
the provision (preceding the word 'or') the testator's intention was charitable within
the meaning of the law as at the date both of the death and of the signing of the will.
Thus what the testator was really saying here is:

> 'I leave the residue to be expended by the local authority, as trustees, for the
> charitable purpose which I have specified, failing which, for a similar charitable
> purpose chosen by them.'   *e*

So read, the words 'some similar purpose' mean 'some [charitable] purpose of the
same kind'. The whole phrase following 'or' therefore means 'for charitable purposes
of the same kind in connection with sport in North Berwick'. If the first part of the
provision is charitable then, in my opinion, the 'similar' part must be charitable also.
Why should it be supposed that, if the leading and expressed intention of the testator   *f*
was that his estate should be devoted to charitable purposes, the intention, when he
came to provide for the failure of the expressed and primary charitable purpose,
should be non-charitable? The use of the adjective 'similar', in my opinion, was
intended to impose on the administrators of the residue funds a duty to apply them
in connection with the 'charitable' provision of recreational facilities similar in
character to those provided at and available to the public at the North Berwick   *g*
sports centre. If we need to look at the intention of those who operate the facilities,
namely the elected local authority, I have no difficulty in concluding that their
intention must be that moneys made available to them from such a bequest, if not
needed in connection with the sports centre itself, will be applied in connection with
the development and maintenance of facilities of the same kind situated elsewhere
in North Berwick and serving the same public in the same way. Finally, if it were   *h*
necessary to apply some principle of construction to resolve an ambiguity which
your Lordships have detected in the words under consideration, I should be content
to adopt and apply the principle of Scots and English law to which Lord Hailsham
LC, with the agreement of all their Lordships, referred in *IRC v McMullen* [1981]
AC 1 at 14, 54 TC 413 at 438—

> '. . . in construing trust deeds the intention of which is to set up a charitable   *j*
> trust, and in others too, where it can be claimed that there is an ambiguity, a
> benignant construction should be given if possible.'

I do not consider that the mere fact that private clubs may occasionally gain access
to the facilities prevents the facilities from being regarded as used for charitable
purposes only. Indeed I am not entirely convinced that the 'only' in para 10(3) is of

any great importance here, given the application of the 1958 Act. For if the
construction which I put on the bequest is correct and the whole residue funds were
intended to be devoted to the provision of facilities for recreation deemed charitable
by the 1958 Act, then the effect of s 1 is that the whole providing is 'charitable'. The
use of the adjective 'primarily' in s 1(2)(*a*) and the absence of the adverb 'exclusively'
before the word 'available' in s 1(2)(*b*)(ii) point, in my view, to the possibility, without
the loss of charitable status, of incidentally devoting the provided facilities to uses
other than their principal, charitable uses.

I need not separately set out my reasons for concluding that the history of the
matter subsequent to the date of death is of no relevance in determining the question
before us. My reasons for so thinking should be plain from what I have said earlier
in choosing the tempus inspiciendum.

Although I disagree with your Lordships on the construction and effect of part of
the bequest, I agree entirely with your Lordship in the Chair on all other matters.

In the whole circumstances, however, I consider that the executor should succeed.

Appeal dismissed.

Solicitors: *Guild & Guild*, WS, Edinburgh (for the executor); *Solicitor of Inland
Revenue.*

Rengan Krishnan Esq   Barrister.

Customs and Excise Commissioners v Steptoe   *a*

QUEEN'S BENCH DIVISION (CROWN OFFICE LIST)
KENNEDY J
I MAY 1991

Value added tax – Return – Failure to furnish return and pay tax due – Reasonable   *b*
excuse for delay – Insufficiency of funds – Council unexpectedly slow in paying for work
done by taxpayer – Taxpayer consequently unable to pay by due date – Commissioners
imposing surcharge for late payment – Whether taxpayer having reasonable excuse for
late payment of tax – Finance Act 1985, ss 19(6), 33(2)(a).

c

The taxpayer, an electrical contractor, worked almost exclusively for the London
Borough of Redbridge. During the relevant period the borough was persistently late
in paying invoices, never paying an amount due on an invoice less than six weeks
after it was delivered and usually paying upwards of two months late. As a result the
taxpayer was without funds to pay value added tax due for three prescribed
accounting periods and accordingly failed to render returns and pay value added tax   *d*
by the relevant due dates. The commissioners imposed surcharge assessments in
respect of each of the three periods. The taxpayer contended before a value added
tax tribunal that he had a reasonable excuse for his default under s 19(6)[a] of the
Finance Act 1985 (the 1985 Act). The tribunal held that the council's persistent
delay in paying its invoices could not be regarded as a normal hazard of trade
producing a temporary shortage of funds. The prolonged shortage of funds arising   *e*
from the unexpected and continuing conduct of the council was not precluded by
s 33(2)[b] of the 1985 Act from providing a reasonable excuse for the taxpayer's default.
The tribunal accordingly allowed the taxpayer's appeal against the assessment. The
commissioners appealed.

Held – (1) Where insufficiency of funds was due to unforeseen and inescapable   *f*
misfortune rather than to culpable default, it was not precluded by s 33(2) of the
Finance Act 1985 from providing a reasonable excuse for the purposes of s 19(6) of
that Act.

Customs and Excise Comrs v Salevon Ltd [1989] STC 907 applied.

(2) Section 19(6) required that the commissioners or value added tax tribunal be
satisfied as to the existence of a reasonable excuse for default. Unless their decision   *g*
was perverse it would prevail and in the instant case the tribunal's decision could not
be faulted. Accordingly, the appeal would be dismissed.

Notes   *h*

For the meaning of reasonable excuse, see De Voil: Value Added Tax A18.75.
For the Finance Act 1985, ss 19(6), 33(2), see ibid, Part C1.

Cases referred to in judgment   *j*

Customs and Excise Comrs v Palco Industry Co Ltd [1990] STC 594.
Customs and Excise Comrs v Salevon Ltd [1989] STC 907.

---

a   Section 19(6), so far as material, is set out at p 304 *a*, post
b   Section 33(2), so far as material, is set out at p 304 *b*, post

Cases also cited

a   *Beechill Building Services v Customs and Excise Comrs* (BEL/90/20, unreported).
C & B Car Hire v Customs and Excise Comrs (LON/90/1259, unreported).
Dove Services (Manchester) Ltd v Customs and Excise Comrs (MAN/90/695, unreported).
Fat Sam's American Food & Beverage Co Ltd v Customs and Excise Comrs (LON/90/1408, unreported).
b   *Fleet Car Hirings v Customs and Excise Comrs* (LON/90/1499, unreported).
Mallon Builders Ltd v Customs and Excise Comrs (LON/89/783, unreported).
Wolverhampton Washing Services Ltd v Customs and Excise Comrs (MAN/90/333, unreported).

c   **Appeal**

By notice of appeal, the Commissioners of Customs and Excise (the commissioners) appealed against the decision of a London value added tax tribunal (chairman: Judge Medd QC) released on 9 November 1989 allowing the appeal against three out of four assessments to surcharges made by the commissioners on the taxpayer. The taxpayer, Mr Steptoe, was respondent to the appeal. The facts are set out in
d   the judgment.

Nigel Pleming for the commissioners.
The taxpayer appeared in person.

e   **KENNEDY J.** This is an appeal by the Customs and Excise Commissioners (the commissioners) from the decision of the Value Added Tax Tribunal sitting in London on 30 October 1989, which allowed the taxpayer's appeal against three out of four assessments to surcharges which had been made on him by the commissioners.
The assessments were made because of late payment of value added tax by the taxpayer, Mr Steptoe, in four quarters starting with the quarter ending 30 November
f   1987. The figures are not disputed. For the quarter ended 30 November 1987, the payment was made on 25 January 1988 (about three-and-a-half weeks late). For the quarter ended 29 February 1988, the payment was made on 22 April 1988 (about three-and-a-half weeks late). For the quarter ended 31 May 1988, the payment was made on 2 August 1988 (about four-and-a-half weeks late). For the quarter ended 30 November 1988, the payment was made on 23 January 1989 (just over three
g   weeks late).
The taxpayer was at that time, and still is, in business as an electrical contractor and he had two employees. 95% of his business, so the tribunal found, was for one customer—Redbridge London Borough. At the material time that borough was slow in making payments. It paid at least six weeks after invoice, and usually in excess of two months. There was some improvement after the end of 1988 because
h   there was a joint protest by the contractors who worked for the borough, but the late payment meant that the taxpayer at the material time had insufficient funds to pay the taxes in the first three quarters which I have identified.
So far as the fourth quarter was concerned, his delay was due to what happened in the office of his accountants because the person handling his affairs had a family bereavement as is explained in the letter from the accountants dated 19 January
j   1989.
Before the tribunal the taxpayer contended that in each case he had a reasonable excuse for tax not having been despatched at the proper time.
That brings me to the statutory provisions which are material in this case. Section 19(4) of the Finance Act 1985 (the 1985 Act) establishes the liability of a taxpayer to pay a default surcharge if his tax return is late—and I interpose—after two quarters

in which it has previously been late. That liability is qualified by s 19(6) which provides:

> 'If a person who, apart from this subsection, would be liable to a surcharge under subsection (4) above satisfies the Commissioners or, on appeal, a value added tax tribunal that, in the case of a default which is material to the surcharge ... (*b*) there is a reasonable excuse for the return or tax not having been ... despatched, he shall not be liable to the surcharge ...'

Section 19(6) has to be read in the light of s 33(2) of the 1985 Act which provides:

> 'For the purpose of any provision of this Chapter [and section 19(6) is such a provision] which refers to a reasonable excuse for any conduct,—(*a*) an insufficiency of funds to pay any tax due is not a reasonable excuse ...'

The tribunal found that but for s 33(2) this taxpayer had shown a reasonable excuse. So the two issues which the tribunal had to decide were first of all whether the Redbridge explanation, if I can so describe it, was caught by s 33(2)(*a*). To that the tribunal provided the answer 'No'. Second, the tribunal had to decide whether the accountancy explanation was caught by the provisions of s 33(2)(*b*). To that the tribunal provided the answer 'Yes', and from that part of the tribunal's decision there is before me no appeal.

The two statutory provisions with which I am concerned were considered by Nolan J in *Customs and Excise Comrs v Salevon Ltd* [1989] STC 907 where a dishonest company secretary had drawn cheques totalling £24,000 in order to pay value added tax liability. Subsequently the company was taken over. It was discovered that the tax had not been paid and the paying of it thereafter caused further defaults due to the stress which it imposed on the company's finances. The company appealed against a default surcharge and Nolan J, having considered the statutory provisions to which I have just referred, and in particular s 33(2)(*a*), said (at 911):

> 'Does it necessarily follow that a trader whose explanation for non-payment or late payment was not simply a temporary cash shortage but the fact that the wrongful act of another had deprived him of the means to pay is unable to plead that he has a reasonable excuse? According to counsel for the commissioners, the answer is "Yes". I think it unlikely however that that is a result which Parliament intended to achieve by the enactment of s 33(2)(*a*). To say of such a trader that his excuse for non-payment was insufficiency of funds would appear to me to be an incomplete and misleading description of the situation. As the chairman pointed out, it fails to distinguish between the reason, in the sense of the direct cause for non-payment, and the excuse for non-payment. Looking at the matter more broadly, I think it is worth bearing in mind that the penalties imposed for a delay or deficiency in payment, however slight, are fixed. Neither the commissioners nor the tribunal have any power to mitigate them by reference to the facts of the particular case. In these circumstances the wide discretion conferred on the commissioners and the tribunal by s 19(6) should not, in my view, be regarded as having been cut down by s 33(2) to any greater extent than the language of the latter subsection strictly requires. The commissioners and the members of the tribunal are well qualified to distinguish between the trader who lacks the money to pay his tax by reason of culpable default and the trader who lacks the money by reason of unforeseeable and inescapable misfortune.'

Despite the reservations expressed by Hodgson J in the case of *Customs and Excise Comrs v Palco Industry Co Ltd* [1990] STC 594, I respectfully agree with the approach adopted by Nolan J, and I would simply add one further consideration. Section 19(6) and s 33(2) apply equally to two types of taxpayer—those who, like members of the bar, have to account to the Customs and Excise Commissioners for tax which they have actually received, and those who, like the taxpayer, have to account to the commissioners for tax which they are only entitled to receive. This distinction is referred to by Nolan J (at 911) in the paragraph following those which I have just quoted, but it seems to me that it would be surprising if Parliament intended to permit the commissioners to surcharge taxpayers for failing to account for funds they had not received without even permitting them to argue that they had a reasonable excuse.

If Nolan J's approach be correct, then in every case in which a taxpayer pays late through lack of funds and claims that he has a reasonable excuse his claim will fail unless he can satisfy the commissioners or a value added tax tribunal that his lack of funds is not due to any culpable default, but rather is due to unforseeable and inescapable misfortune. The burden is a heavy one, but if the taxpayer claims to have a reasonable excuse I do not see why the commissioners or the tribunal should be relieved of the burden of hearing what he has to say.

Counsel for the commissioners would like me best of all not to follow the decision in *Salevon* or to say that as soon as the taxpayer says that he has insufficient funds he must be held to fall foul of s 33(2)(*a*). But he submits, in the alternative, that if it is permissible to look further at what is being said nothing less than a wrongful, dishonest or unlawful act of another or some other wholly unforeseeable and inescapable misfortune, such as a flood or a fire, should really be sufficient. He submits that those are the sort of matters which can be put forward to explain the lack of funds, but nothing else should be regarded as being capable of being a reasonable excuse.

Although I see the attraction to the Customs and Excise Commissioners of this court laying down a narrow category of what may be regarded as reasonable excuses, I see no justification in the statute for attempting to do so, and like Nolan J I have sufficient confidence in the good sense of the commissioners and of the tribunal to leave the matter in their hands. After all s 19(6) requires that they be satisfied. It is their view, not the view of the taxpayer, which matters and unless the conclusion at which the commissioners or tribunal arrives is so unreasonable as to be perverse it will prevail. This approach may well mean that different tribunals come to different conclusions on broadly similar facts—as illustrated by the tribunal decisions to which counsel for the commissioners drew my attention. But that is always a possibility where a discretion is conferred.

Counsel for the commissioners said that this appeal has been lodged to assist the commissioners to know what can properly be regarded as amounting to a reasonable excuse. My response is that under the statute, and subject to s 33(2)(*a*), that is a matter for them. Certainly it is not possible, in my judgment, to say that late payment by a customer can never be a reasonable excuse simply because in business that eventuality can be foreseen, but it is very often an eventuality which could and should be provided for so that it does not affect payment of tax on the due date. Everything, as so often, depends on the facts of the case.

In this case Judge Medd QC said:

'The Council's conduct was not wrongful in the same way that the conduct of the secretary in *Salevon* was, but it seems to me that it was conduct of a sort that a small trader was entitled to expect would not happen. [That—I interpose—was a clear finding of fact and a clear finding by that tribunal that there was here an unforseeable misfortune.] It is not something that can be regarded as a normal hazard of trade such as the failure of one customer amongst several to pay a debt, which would produce a temporary shortage of funds and would not amount to a reasonable excuse. If he had brought pressure to bear on the Council he would probably have received no further orders and the bulk of his livelihood would have disappeared. It seems to me, therefore, that this is one of those rare cases where the taxpayer may legitimately put forward as the reason why he should be excused the unexpected and continuing conduct of the person which gave rise to the prolonged shortage of funds.'

Counsel for the commissioners contends that it was at that point, and in that passage which I have just quoted, that the chairman of the tribunal fell into error

because the circumstances which he outlined are not rare, and nearly all those
taxpayers who lack the funds to pay on time can claim some sort of excuse. Maybe, *a*
but for the reasons which I have attempted to outline I cannot fault the approach
adopted by the chairman on this occasion and, accordingly, this appeal must be
dismissed.

Appeal dismissed.
                                                                                   b
Solicitor: *Solicitor for the Customs and Excise.*

                                        Evelyn M C Budd   Barrister.

Jones (Inspector of Taxes) v Lincoln-Lewis and others

CHANCERY DIVISION
HOFFMANN J
15, 16 MAY 1991

Capital gains tax – Non-resident trust – Beneficiaries domiciled and resident in UK – Apportionment of gain between persons having interests in settled property – Apportionment in such manner as is just and reasonable – Date at which persons having interests in settled property should be ascertained – Whether beneficial interests should be ascertained at the date of the termination of the trust – Finance Act 1965, s 42(2).

Mrs Wright (the settlor) made a settlement dated 13 August 1949 for the benefit of three of her grandchildren (the beneficiaries) under which each of them was entitled to a one-third share of the trust fund contingent on his or her survival until 2 July 1973. The settlor and the trustees were domiciled and ordinarily resident in the United Kingdom. In order to avoid liability to capital gains tax on the termination of the trust under s 25(3) of the Finance Act 1965, on 15 February 1973, trustees resident in Guernsey were appointed and the general administration of the trust was thereafter conducted from Guernsey. On 5 June 1973, in return for a payment of £248,647, each beneficiary assigned his/her interest in the settlement to Meadowview Ltd, a company resident in Guernsey. On 6 June 1973, the Guernsey trustees sold the trust investments for a cash sum which (with interest) amounted to £757,170 at the date of the termination of the trust (2 July 1973) when it was paid over to Meadowview Ltd. The sale of the investments by the trustees on 6 June 1973 was a disposal which resulted in chargeable gains accruing to the trustees. However, the trustees were not resident in the United Kingdom and could not therefore be assessed to capital gains tax. The inspector of taxes raised assessments on the beneficiaries in respect of the chargeable gains accruing to the trustees on the sale of the investments on 6 June 1973 under s 42[a] of the Finance Act 1965, taking the view that the chargeable gains on which the trustees would have been liable to tax had they been resident should be apportioned between the beneficiaries. It was common ground that the inspector would have been entitled to apportion the chargeable gains to the beneficiaries if they had had 'interests in the settled property' at the relevant time. The beneficiaries claimed that the relevant time was 2 July 1973, when the only interest in the settled property was vested in Meadowview Ltd which, as a non-resident company, was not liable to tax. That view was accepted by the Special Commissioner. He discharged the assessments determining that the relevant date for apportionment had to be 2 July 1973 because that was the only date on which the beneficial interests could be ascertained and valued and the chargeable gains to be apportioned could be ascertained. The Crown appealed against that determination to the High Court contending: (a) that the beneficial interests subsisting throughout the year of assessment should be taken into account and not just those interests extant at the date of the disposal; and (b) that it was just and reasonable to apportion the gains between the beneficiaries because (i) they had held interests in the settled property up until the date of the assignments (i e between 6 April 1973 and 5 June 1973 of the year of assessment 1973–74), and (ii) the terms of the assignments had given the beneficiaries virtually the whole of the gains.

Held – In cases where the same interest had been held by different beneficiaries at different times during a year of assessment, for the purposes of apportionment of

---

a   Section 42(2), so far as material, is set out at p 315 *c–f*, post

chargeable gains accruing to the trustees amongst the beneficiaries by reference to their interest in settled property under s 42(2), it would not be appropriate to take into account all beneficial interests subsisting throughout the year of assessment. The relevant beneficial interests had to be ascertained at a single moment. Where a settlement had come to an end in a year of assessment, the time for ascertaining whether or not the beneficiaries had interests in settled property was the date at which the settlement came to an end. Accordingly, since the beneficiaries did not have 'interests in the settled property' on 2 July 1973 (the date of the termination of the trust), s 42(2) could not be applied so as to apportion the chargeable gains among the beneficiaries. The Crown's appeal would therefore be dismissed.

Notes

For the liability of beneficiaries under non-resident trusts to capital gains tax, see Simon's Taxes C4.421.

For the Finance Act 1965, s 42(2) (replaced by the Capital Gains Tax Act 1979, s 17(2), now spent), see ibid, Part G3.

Section 17 of the Capital Gains Tax Act 1979 was repealed by the Finance Act 1981, Sch 19, Part VIII with effect in relation to chargeable gains accruing to trustees after 5 April 1981.

Cases referred to in judgment

C H W (Huddersfield) Ltd v IRC [1963] 1 WLR 767, [1963] 2 All ER 952, 41 TC 92, HL.
Leedale (Inspector of Taxes) v Lewis [1982] STC 169, [1982] 2 All ER 644, CA; [1982] STC 835, [1982] 1 WLR 1319, [1982] 3 All ER 808, 56 TC 501, HL.

Cases also cited

Chinn v Collins (Inspector of Taxes) [1981] STC 1, [1981] AC 533, [1981] 1 All ER 189, 54 TC 311, HL.
Fendoch Investment Trust Co v IRC [1945] 2 All ER 140, 27 TC 53, HL.

Case stated

1. On Tuesday 20 June 1989 one of the Commissioners for the Special Purposes of the Income Tax Acts heard the appeals of Mr J D Lincoln-Lewis (executor of Mr C R Pilkington deceased), Mr N C Pilkington and Mr J L Ingman (the taxpayers) against assessments to capital gains tax, each in the sum of £25,000, in respect of the year of assessment 1973–74.

2. The facts were not disputed; the parties provided an agreed statement of facts [annexed at p 313 post]. [The documents placed in evidence before the commissioner were then listed.]

3. At the close of the hearing the commissioner reserved his decision, and gave it in writing on 20 July 1989, allowing the appeals and so determining them by discharging the assessments.

4. The Solicitor of Inland Revenue immediately thereafter declared his dissatisfaction with the determination and subsequently demanded a stated case.

5. The question of law for the opinion of the court was whether on the true construction of s 42 of the Finance Act 1965 (the 1965 Act) and in the events that happened, the commissioner was in error in that he apportioned no part of the 's 20(4) amount' to any of the three grandchildren of the settlor, Mrs Constance Louisa Wright.

DECISION

The event on which the assessments are founded is a disposal on 6 June 1973 by the trustees of a settlement made on 13 August 1949 by Mrs C L Wright (the settlor)

of the investments constituting the trust fund. The settlor made the settlement for
the benefit of (in the events that happened) three grandchildren (the beneficiaries),
the late Mr C R Pilkington, Mr N C Pilkington and Sallie Elizabeth Pilkington,
who in 1973–74 was the wife of Mr J L Ingman. Under the terms of the settlement
the trustees held the trust fund, in the events that happened, on trust for such of the
said three beneficiaries as should be living on 2 July 1973, in equal shares. Thus,
prior to the year of assessment under appeal, it was evident that, if no action were
taken, the effect of s 25(3) of the 1965 Act would be that the trustees would be
deemed to have disposed of the assets constituting the trust fund for a consideration
equal to their market value on 2 July 1973, on which date the trust would terminate.
Prior to 6 April 1973 the trust was 'exported' to the Channel Islands in that trustees
resident in Guernsey were appointed in place of the existing trustees, and the general
administration of the trust was carried on outside the United Kingdom, namely in
Guernsey. Thus a charge to tax under s 25(3) was, as is common ground, avoided.
As it happened the Guernsey trustees disposed of the assets constituting the trust
fund on 6 June 1973; it is common ground that the chargeable gain realised on that
disposal is not directly chargeable to capital gains tax. What is disputed, and is the
subject matter of the appeals, is the extent, if any, to which s 42 of the 1965 Act
operates so as to cause the amount of the trustees' chargeable gain to be apportioned
between the three beneficiaries.

The parties agreed a written statement of facts which is the basis of my decision,
subject to small variations that were agreed during the hearing, namely: (1) The
settlor and the three beneficiaries were at all material times domiciled, resident and
ordinarily resident in the United Kingdom. (2) The general administration of the
trust was on and after 15 February 1973 carried on outside of the United Kingdom.
(3) The disposal by the Guernsey trustees of the assets constituting the trust fund on
6 June 1973 was not part of a prearranged scheme; indeed until a few weeks prior to
this hearing the parties to this appeal were under the impression that what was in
issue was not an actual disposal on 6 June 1973 but a deemed disposal on 2 July 1973,
when the three beneficiaries obtained absolute vested interests in possession and the
trust terminated.

It is common ground that s 42 of the 1965 Act, in particular sub-s (2) applies in
respect of the disposal by the trustees on 6 June 1973. The parties differ as to how
the 'just and reasonable' apportionment should be made. Counsel for the taxpayers
contends that the only just and reasonable apportionment of the chargeable gain
realised by the trustees is to the company Meadowview Ltd which on 5 June 1973
had acquired for a price paid on that day the interests of the three beneficiaries under
the settlement. Mr K O Butterfield, of the Office of the Solicitor of Inland Revenue,
contends that the only just and reasonable apportionment is a division in equal
shares between the three beneficiaries. Both parties agree that the interests of all
other persons are so minimal as to be negligible; that includes those entitled under
the substitutional gift in the settlement, and presumably the trustees entitled under
the charging clause. Generally, if I look at the value of the interests of the person
entitled absolutely as against the trustees on 2 July 1973, when the trust terminated,
and thus almost absolutely entitled on 6 June 1973, namely Meadowview Ltd, no
liability for capital gains tax attaches to the beneficiaries. However, if I take into
account values of interests throughout the year of assessment 1973–74, which means
in effect the period from 6 April 1973 to 2 July 1973, and the fact that the three
beneficiaries sold their beneficial interests for substantial sums of cash, which I take
to reflect part of the chargeable gain likely to be realised by the trustees, then it is
just and reasonable to apportion the gain to the three beneficiaries equally.
Mr Butterfield contends that I arrive at that conclusion simply on the true
construction of s 42, but also by application of the principles enunciated in the
House of Lords in *Furniss (Inspector of Taxes) v Dawson* [1984] STC 153, [1984] AC
474.

The *Furniss v Dawson* point was argued before me as a separate point and I therefore defer consideration of it for the moment. The parties agree that what has to be apportioned is not the amount of the gain on any specific asset, but 'the amount, if any, on which the trustees would have been chargeable to capital gains tax under section 20(4) of [the 1965] Act, if domiciled and either resident or ordinarily resident in the United Kingdom in that year of assessment' (see s 42(2) of the 1965 Act), namely the year 1973–74. Section 20(4) refers to a charge on the total amount of chargeable gains accruing to the person chargeable in the year of assessment after deducting any allowable losses accruing to that person in that year of assessment and to some extent earlier allowable losses also. Clearly there were chargeable gains which accrued to the trustees on 6 June 1973; I am able to decide the point in principle without ascertaining the exact amount of the chargeable gains or any allowable losses.

The question I have to decide was raised, but not decided, in the House of Lords, in *Chinn v Collins (Inspector of Taxes)* [1981] STC 1, [1981] AC 533, and both parties directed my attention to the arguments of counsel and the observations of the Law Lords, particularly those of Lord Roskill ([1981] STC 1 at 13, [1981] AC 533 at 556). I only echo the view of Lord Roskill that 'the question is novel and to my mind difficult', with which I respectfully agree.

Counsel for the taxpayers relied on s 41 of the 1965 Act. He submitted that ss 41, 42 constitute together a 'code' and since it was clear from s 41(2) that the person to whom apportionment is made is the person who is a shareholder 'at the time when the chargeable gain accrues' it follows that the same date applies under s 42. I reject that contention. I find no assistance from s 41 in construing s 42. Alternatively, counsel submitted that the 'section 20(4) amount' in the case of a continuing trust would be ascertainable as at the end of the relevant year of assessment and at no other date; in the case of a trust terminating by reason of s 25(3) during a year of assessment, by reference to the last day of the trust, when the trustees became nominees for the beneficiaries, in present circumstances 2 July 1973. It was not wholly clear to me at first whether counsel chose as the relevant date 6 June, when the trustees disposed of the trust fund, or 2 July, when the trust terminated; but on either date there was (save as to minimal interests) only one beneficiary and thus one candidate for apportionment, namely Meadowview Ltd. Subsequently counsel preferred 2 July. Mr Butterfield pointed out that capital gains tax is an annual tax like income tax, and that the three beneficiaries had in substance pocketed the total value of the assets. They had got the benefit, they should take the burden. At my invitation Mr Butterfield considered a hypothetical case where the roles are reversed; where the original beneficiaries are outside the charge to capital gains tax, and the purchaser of their interests is within the charge, but seeks to avoid the tax by claiming that the only apportionment must be to the beneficiaries. He did not shrink from the conclusion that the apportionment must be not to the purchaser but the vendors, with consequent avoidance of capital gains tax. I also invited Mr Butterfield to consider the case where the beneficiary does not sell, but makes a gift of his interest, prior to the realisation by the trustees of the trust fund assets. He contended that such a case would be materially indistinguishable from the present, and the donor could be chargeable to the capital gains tax, albeit that he had not enjoyed at whatever remove the chargeable gain, because he had caused the gain to be put, by way of gift, where he wanted it put.

Counsel for the taxpayers contended that s 42(2) operated plainly and simply by reference to a relevant date, being the date on which 'the amount, if any, on which the trustees would have been chargeable' is first ascertainable, and that on a plain reading of the section, the 'persons having interests in the settled property' and 'the respective values' should be ascertained at that date. He referred me to *C H W (Huddersfield) Ltd v IRC* [1963] 1 WLR 767, 41 TC 92 as providing guidance in relation to a similar problem.

I start by considering what is the amount that I have to apportion. As appears from *Leedale (Inspector of Taxes) v Lewis* [1982] STC 835, [1982] 1 WLR 1319, it is the entire amount of chargeable gains, after deducting allowable losses, accruing during the period 6 April to 2 July 1973. It may be that allowable losses brought forward from earlier years of assessment have also to be deducted. However that may be, I assume that when the assets were realised on 6 June both gains and losses were made and it is conceivable, though unlikely, that further gains or losses on investment were made between 6 June and 2 July. At all events, I have to concentrate on a figure or 'amount' for which the relevant date is 2 July 1973 and no earlier date. Until 2 July 1973 no 'amount' existed or could be computed. I perceive a similarity with the well-established principles whereby the profits or gains of a trade, for the purposes of income tax, are ascertainable on or after the end of the relevant accounting period.

Capital gains tax is not an annual tax, although it is charged by reference to years of assessments. As appears from s 19(3) of the 1965 Act it is charged 'for the year 1965–66 and for subsequent years of assessment', whereas, as appears from s 9 of that Act, income tax is not effective unless charged in the Finance Act of each year. Nevertheless, capital gains tax is based on years of assessment, although it is worth noting that corporation tax on chargeable gains is chargeable by reference to the accounting period of the relevant corporation, irrespective of any year of assessment. I derive no guidance from considering whether capital gains tax is or is not 'annual'.

I notice that s 42(2) refers to 'any beneficiary under the settlement who is domiciled and either resident or ordinarily resident in the United Kingdom during any year of assessment'; and that is followed by further references to 'that year of assessment'. However, it seems to me that these references do no more than identify beneficiaries who may suffer tax, or may not, the deciding factor being domicile and residence during any part of the relevant year of assessment. It is trite law that residence and ordinary residence are concepts ascertained in case of individuals by reference to years of assessment. No doubt domicile can be ascertained as at a particular date but certainly ordinary residence relates primarily not to a particular date but to a particular year of assessment.

It appears from *Leedale v Lewis* that regard is had not to the market values of interests but, more broadly, to the values of interests under the settlement as between themselves, regard being had to the wishes of the settlor perhaps expressed in a 'letter of intent'. I also consider that the fact that a beneficiary may have voluntarily or for value disposed of his interest prior to the end of a year of assessment for tax avoidance reasons does not differentiate him from a person who disposes of his interest from motives of bounty. Apportionment is not to be made for the purpose of preventing, or of furthering, avoidance of tax.

Construing s 42(2) as it stands, I reach the conclusion that apportionment must be according to the respective values of 'those interests', being the interests in existence on the relevant date, that date being in this case 2 July 1973. On that date the interests may be ascertained and valued, and the amount to be apportioned may be ascertained; no other date or period of time has these necessary qualities. I do not think that the statutory wording directs or facilitates an apportionment over the entire year of assessment, necessarily giving rise to complicated questions, particularly where, as may often happen, commencement and termination of interest and realisations of chargeable gains and allowable losses occur throughout the period. There is a single 'relevant date' for ascertaining the apportionable amount. I prefer the conclusion that the same date is the date for ascertainment and valuation of the interests among which that amount is to be apportioned.

The conclusion I thus arrive at is consistent with the decision of the House of Lords in *C H W (Huddersfield) Ltd v IRC* [1963] 1 WLR 767, 41 TC 92. Generally the approach preferred by Mr Butterfield resembles that adopted by the Court of Appeal ([1962] 1 WLR 1223, 41 TC 92) and rejected by the Lords ([1963] 1 WLR 767, 41 TC 92). That case concerned an apportionment of the income of a company under s 245 of the Income Tax Act 1952 (a process commonly known as 'surtax direction'). The particular wording under consideration was in s 248(1) of that Act which reads as follows:

> 'Where a direction has been given under section 245 of this Act with respect to a company, the apportionment of the actual income from all sources of the company shall be made by the Special Commissioners in accordance with the respective interests of the members.'

As I understand it, although the 'members' included persons who were members at any time, the circumstance that the trading income was not ascertainable until the end of the relevant accounting period necessarily led to the result that apportionment must be restricted to the 'respective interests of the members' ascertained as at the end of the relevant accounting period. I perceive a sufficient similarity between the wording in s 248 of the Income Tax Act 1952 and the words in s 42(2) of the 1965 Act—'. . . so that the chargeable gain is apportioned, as near as may be, according to the respective values of those interests . . .' to justify the conclusion that in the present case the interests are to be ascertained and valued as at 2 July 1973.

Mr Butterfield relied on *Fendoch Investment Trust Co v IRC* (1943) 27 TC 53. That case appears to be distinguishable from the present for the same reasons which, according to the speeches in the House of Lords ([1963] 1 WLR 767 at 782, 784, 792, 41 TC at 120, 121, 128), it was distinguishable from *C H W (Huddersfield) Ltd v IRC*.

To sum up, it seems to me that the apportionment of the amount that has to be determined as at 2 July 1973 must be restricted to interests in existence on that date. I perceive no justification for taking into account all interests existing during the whole lifetime of the settlement, or during the period when the settlement was abroad, or during the period when unrealised gains were maturing, or during the year of assessment in which gains or losses were realised, or for leaving out of account interests acquired by purchase or by gift prior to the relevant date, namely 2 July 1973. I should add that, were I persuaded that an apportionment should be made according to interests existing at any time between 6 April and 2 July 1973, I would not rule out entirely the interest of Meadowview Ltd. Meadowview Ltd acquired the interests of the three beneficiaries on 5 June for a total consideration less than the then market value of the assets in the trust fund. I do not have sufficient materials to enable me to make the necessary apportionment, nor was I asked to make it.

I now turn to the principles in *Furniss v Dawson*, which were further explained by the House of Lords in *Craven (Inspector of Taxes) v White* [1988] STC 476, [1989] AC 398. Mr Butterfield submitted that I should disregard the steps in paras 10(1), (3), (4), (5), (6) and (8) of the statement of facts. I am asked to make the finding of fact that introducing Meadowview Ltd for the carrying-out of the arrangements had no commercial purpose, so that the transactions with which Meadowview Ltd was concerned were steps inserted having no commercial or business purpose apart from the avoidance of a liability to tax. I find that Meadowview Ltd's participation did have a commercial purpose, namely to make a profit by acquiring the beneficial interests prior to realisation of the trust funds. That purpose was not a commercial purpose of the beneficiaries who were vendors. Nevertheless I think it a justifiable gloss on the *Furniss v Dawson* test to restrict the concept of commercial or business purpose to the purpose of the beneficiaries, ignoring the clear commercial purpose of Meadowview Ltd itself. I cannot ignore the 'export' of the settlement. Consequently I have to examine the case of the three beneficiaries under an exported settlement, faced with potential liability under s 42(2), seeking a tax avoidance transaction to avoid that liability. In fact the transaction whereby the three beneficiaries avoided liability was the single transaction of 5 June 1973, set out in paras 10(5) and 10(6) of the statement of facts, whereby the beneficiaries sold and assigned their interests and received the cash price therefor. That was a single-step transaction. The other steps in para 10 were transactions whereby the trustees, or Meadowview Ltd, protected themselves in a commercial manner from the risks attendant on the purchase at a present cash price of an equitable interest in an unrealised investment portfolio. I should add that the step in para 10(7) was not part of a preordained series of transactions. Indeed, none of the steps other than those in paras 10(5) and (6) were preordained as respects the beneficiaries; they were no more than the acts of a prudent purchaser.

It is well established that if the owner of a debt or of shares sells the debt or shares 'cum div', no part of the purchase price is income (apart from specific statutory provision). Perhaps the most extreme example of that law is the decision of the Court of Appeal in *Paget v IRC* [1938] 2 KB 25, 21 TC 677 where the holder of a debt sold not the debt but merely the right to receive interest; the proceeds of sale were capital and not income. The principles in *Furniss v Dawson* do not override the decision in *Paget*. There is no law, generally, to deem the vendor of a tree laden with fruit to have harvested the fruit before sale or to deem the purchaser not to have harvested the fruit.

Mr Butterfield invited me to find that the disposal by the trustees of the trust fund on 6 June should be treated as a disposal taking place the previous day, but it seems to me that inevitably the disposal on 6 June took place on that day and no earlier.

I therefore conclude that no part of the amount, to be ascertained as at 2 July 1973 (or if it be relevant any amount to be ascertained at any other date), is to be apportioned save among those persons who on 2 July 1973 owned interests in the settled funds. I therefore allow the appeal and discharge the assessments.

Statement of facts

1. Mr Christopher Richard Pilkington (Christopher), Mr Nicholas Charles Pilkington (Nicholas) and Mr John L Ingman (Mr Ingman), the former husband of Sallie Elizabeth Pilkington (Sallie) appealed against assessments to capital gains tax each in the sum of £25,000, for the year 1973–74. Christopher died on 13 March 1988 having by his will dated 6 November 1980 appointed Jeremy Lincoln-Lewis as his executor. The executor wishes to pursue the appeal on behalf of Christopher's estate.

2. On 13 August 1949, Mrs Constance Louisa Wright executed a settlement for the benefit of her grandchildren, including Christopher, Nicholas and Sallie. Under the settlement and in the events which occurred, the capital of the trust fund was to vest in Christopher, Nicholas, and Sallie when Sallie, the youngest grandchild, attained the age of twenty-five years. This was due to happen on 2 July 1973.

3. Sallie married Mr Ingman on 27 November 1971. She and Mr Ingman were divorced on 13 September 1977. She was thus married to Mr Ingman throughout the tax year 1973–74.

4. During 1972, the trustees of the settlement were Mr Raymond Francis Pilkington (Mr Pilkington), the father of Christopher, Nicholas and Sallie, and Mr C J B Hatton (Mr Hatton) who was, and still is, the senior partner in a firm of solicitors, Robert Davies & Co. Mr Hatton acted throughout 1972, and until the settlement came to an end in 1973, as the legal adviser to the trustees.

5. Early in 1972 Mr Hatton became conscious that, for the reasons given in para 2, if nothing was done, the trust fund would, by virtue of the provisions of s 25(3) of the Finance Act 1965 (now s 54(1) of the Capital Gains Tax Act 1979), on 2 July 1973 become liable to a substantial charge to capital gains tax. Mr Hatton discussed the matter with Mr Pilkington and they decided that counsel ought to be consulted as to whether and how the charge to tax might be avoided or mitigated. Counsel advised in principle that it might be possible to take advantage of the exemption provided by para 13(1) of Sch 7 to the Finance Act 1965 (now s 58(1) of the Capital Gains Tax Act 1979). The details were left to Mr Hatton.

6. On 6 October 1972, Mr Hatton wrote to Mr Pilkington as follows:

> 'I have it in mind to utilise the services of National Westminster Bank Executor and Trustee Company in Guernsey and they will, subject to their

agreement of course, purchase your children's interests. This will then be notified to the trustees and your children will also release the trustees from any liability to account to them and request them to account to the Bank ... On termination of the trusts, the trustees will transfer the investments to the Bank and the trust will be wound up.'

7. By a deed dated 15 February 1973, Mr Pilkington and Mr Hatton resigned as trustees of the settlement. Mr J W de Putron and Mr J de C Stringer, both of St Peter Port, Guernsey, were appointed in their place.

8. On 3 April 1973, Mr Hatton went to Guernsey to discuss the details of the arrangements with Mr Misselbrook, who was the manager of the National Westminster Bank Trust Co Ltd in Guernsey. Following their discussions, on the same day, Mr Misselbrook wrote to Mr Hatton summarising the main features of the arrangements which it was proposed to carry out.

9. Christopher, Nicholas and Sallie all gave their approval to the carrying-out of the arrangements. They were then implemented.

10. The steps were as follows: (1) A company, Meadowview Ltd (Meadowview) was incorporated in Guernsey as a corporation tax company for the purpose of purchasing the trust interests. Meadowview had no other functions to perform and went into liquidation shortly after the trust interests had vested on 2 July 1973. (2) On 5 June 1973 Mr J W de Putron and Mr J de C Stringer deposited the assets of the trust fund in the St Peter Port, Guernsey branch of the National Westminster Bank. The total value of the assets was £794,000 approximately. (3) Meadowview insured the lives of Christopher and Sallie (the two beneficiaries with children) in the sum of £400,000 each to cover against the risk of them dying before 3 July 1973 and the trust fund not passing to Meadowview. (4) On 5 June 1973, the National Westminster Bank on the security of the assets which had been deposited made a loan of £745,943·46 to Meadowview. (5) By deeds of assignment dated 5 June 1973, Christopher, Nicholas and Sallie each assigned his or her contingent interest under the settlement to Meadowview. (6) On 5 June 1973, Christopher, Nicholas and Sallie each received the sum of £248,647·82 from Meadowview, these sums being credited to their bank accounts at National Westminster Bank, St Peter Port Branch on that day. (7) On 6 June, Mr J W de Putron and Mr J de C Stringer sold the trust fund for cash to the National Westminster Bank's Investment Division. (8) On 2 July 1973, Mr J W de Putron and Mr J de C Stringer paid to Meadowview by cheque the sum of £757,170·06 representing the cash value of the trust fund at that date.

Nicholas Warren for the Crown.
David Milne QC for the taxpayers.

HOFFMANN J. This is an appeal by the Crown from the Special Commissioner, Mr D C Potter QC, who has discharged three assessments to capital gains tax in respect of the year 1973–74. The assessments were made on two beneficiaries and the husband of another beneficiary under a settlement dated 13 August 1949. The settlor was the beneficiaries' grandmother, who was then domiciled and ordinarily resident in the United Kingdom. So were the trustees. Each of the beneficiaries was entitled to an equal one-third share of the trust fund contingent on his or her survival until 2 July 1973, which was the date on which the youngest beneficiary would attain the age of 25. On 15 February 1973 new Guernsey-resident trustees were appointed and the general administration of the trust was thereafter conducted from Guernsey. On 5 June 1973 the three beneficiaries each assigned his or her interest in the settlement to a Guernsey company called Meadowview Ltd in return for a payment of £248,647·82. On 6 June 1973 the Guernsey trustees sold the trust investments for cash sum which with accrued interest until 2 July amounted to £757,170·06. On 2 July 1973 the settlement duly came to an end and the trustees paid the cash to Meadowview Ltd.

The sale of the investments by the trustees on 6 June 1973 was a disposal as a result of which chargeable gains accrued to the trustees. But being non-resident, they could not be assessed to capital gains tax. Instead, the inspector assessed the beneficiaries by apportioning to them the chargeable gains on which the trustees would, if resident, have been liable to tax. He did so under s 42(2) of the Finance Act 1965 (the 1965 Act), and it is common ground that he was entitled to do so if the beneficiaries had 'interests in the settled property' at the relevant time. The issue in this appeal is what the relevant time was. The beneficiaries say that it was the date on which the settlement came to an end. On this date the only person having an interest in the settled property was Meadowview Ltd, which was happily non-resident and not liable to tax. The Special Commissioner accepted this view and discharged the assessments. The Crown says that the relevant time is any time within the relevant year of assessment. The beneficiaries undoubtedly had interests until the date of the assignments and the terms of the assignments gave them the benefit of virtually the whole of the gains. Therefore it was just and reasonable to apportion the gains between them.

Section 42(2) reads as follows:

> 'Any beneficiary under the settlement who is domiciled and either resident or ordinarily resident in the United Kingdom during any year of assessment shall be treated for the purposes of this Part of this Act as if an apportioned part of the amount, if any, on which the trustees would have been chargeable to capital gains tax under section 20(4) of this Act, if domiciled and either resident or ordinarily resident in the United Kingdom in that year of assessment, had been chargeable gains accruing to the beneficiary in that year of assessment; and for the purposes of this section any such amount shall be apportioned in such manner as is just and reasonable between persons having interests in the settled property, whether the interest be a life interest or an interest in reversion, and so that the chargeable gain is apportioned, as near as may be, according to the respective values of those interests, disregarding in the case of a defeasible interest the possibility of defeasance.'

As Lord Fraser pointed out in *Leedale (Inspector of Taxes) v Lewis* ([1982] STC 835 at 839–840, [1982] 1 WLR 1319 at 1324–1325), the sub-section is in two parts separated by a semicolon and the provision for apportionment between persons having interests in the settled property in the second part must, logically and chronologically, come before an apportionment between persons having interests at the relevant time, whenever that may be. That apportionment having been made, those of the beneficiaries who were domiciled and either resident or ordinarily resident in the United Kingdom during the year of assessment are treated as if the gains apportioned to them had been their own chargeable gains. This is in accordance with the general principle by which liability to capital gains tax depends on residence or ordinary residence in the United Kingdom during any part of the year of assessment. It means that a wholly non-resident beneficiary will not be taxed on his apportioned share, but one who has been resident or ordinarily resident during any part of the year of assessment will. The function of the first part is to define a sub-set of the persons who fall within the apportionment provisions of the second part. Therefore the reference to being 'resident or ordinarily resident in the United Kingdom during any year of assessment' in the first part does not help to decide what is the relevant time for determining the wider class between whom an apportionment must be made under the second part.

Despite the reference in the second part of s 42(2) to the apportionment of 'the chargeable gain', it is clear that what is being apportioned is the amount on which the trustees would have been chargeable under s 20(4), namely the total amount of chargeable gains accruing in the year of assessment after deducting any allowable losses. It is not an apportionment of any particular gains which may have accrued from time to time. The only time at which the amount to be apportioned can be ascertained in accordance with s 20(4) is the end of the year of assessment or, in the case of trustees being assessed on settled property, the date on which the settlement comes to an end. Counsel for the taxpayers said that it was therefore logical to ascertain the beneficiaries for the purposes of apportionment on the same date. He drew an analogy with *C H W (Huddersfield) Ltd v IRC* [1963] 1 WLR 767, 41 TC 92 in which the House of Lords held that an apportionment of undistributed income for surtax purposes could be made only among those persons who were shareholders at the end of the accounting period during which the income arose. It was only on that date that one could ascertain the income (in the income tax sense) which should have been distributed.

I do not think that this analogy is very compelling, because the purpose of the surtax apportionment powers considered in *C H W (Huddersfield) Ltd v IRC* was to penalise the members of a company which failed to ensure that a reasonable part of its income was distributed. The only people who could fail to distribute were those who had the power to do so, namely those who continued to be members after the end of the accounting year. The purpose of s 42 is rather different, namely to ensure so far as possible that a United Kingdom settlor cannot relieve United Kingdom resident beneficiaries of the burden of capital gains tax on the settlement assets simply by appointing non-resident trustees. This suggests that the object is, in the language of Fox LJ in *Leedale v Lewis* ([1982] STC 169 at 177), 'to secure, so far as possible, that the tax burden falls on the [United Kingdom resident] persons who, in truth, are likely to be the main beneficiaries of the settlement'. Such persons need not have beneficial interests at the end of the year of assessment or the earlier termination of the settlement.

Counsel for the Crown gave the illustration of a settlement with non-resident trustees and two resident beneficiaries, each entitled to a half-share contingent on attaining the age of twenty-five. In the course of a year of assessment, one of them turns twenty-five and receives his share. At the end of the year, the other beneficiary is the only person with an interest in the fund. Nevertheless, on the argument of counsel for the taxpayers he is required to be apportioned the whole of the chargeable gains which accrued to the trustees during the year of assessment. Similar examples of injustice are easy to construct and in *Leedale v Lewis* ([1982] STC 169 at 175) the Court of Appeal produced some more. Their common theme is that the apportionment provisions may result in liability to pay capital gains tax being visited on a person who in reality had very little interest in the fund, or an interest the same as or less than that of another United Kingdom resident who escapes liability.

I am always tempted to construe legislation in accordance with what appears to have been the general intention of Parliament, and I confess that my mind has wavered during the argument in this case. But the problem is that the way the legislation was drafted has made it impossible to produce any consistent and sensible scheme. The anomalies to which I have referred are impossible to avoid unless the inquiry as to the beneficial interests covers the whole past and future life of the settlement. Counsel for the Crown accepted that even on his construction of s 42(2), no apportionment could have been made to the beneficiaries if they had stirred themselves quickly enough to execute the assignment to Meadowview Ltd before 6 April 1973. That would have been sufficient to prevent them from having beneficial interests during the relevant year of assessment. But the delay until 5 June 1973 made very little difference to the economic effect of the transaction. In either event, the beneficiaries would have taken virtually the whole of the gains and left Meadowview Ltd with no more than was necessary to pay the fees of its advisers. Section 42(3)(a) is perhaps some indication that the legislature contemplated an inquiry into the remoter past, but counsel for the Crown rightly felt that attempts to integrate this provision with s 42(2) raised as many difficulties as they solved. There is a further difficulty in cases such as the present in which the same interest has been held by different beneficiaries at different times during whatever is the relevant period. As between successive beneficiaries, a just and reasonable apportionment

can hardly avoid inquiry as to the terms on which the interest was assigned from the
a one to the other. It seems to me very unlikely that Parliament intended to burden
the Revenue with an obligation either to examine the whole history of the settlement
or the transactions between beneficiaries. Counsel for the Crown did not suggest the
contrary. But the problem of succession to the same interests can be avoided only if
the relevant beneficiaries are ascertained at a single moment (compare Lord Reid in
C H W (Huddersfeld) Ltd v IRC [1963] 1 WLR 767 at 782, 41 TC 92 at 120).

b   Once one rejects, as I have done, the reference to the year of assessment in the first
part of s 42(2) as an indication that Parliament also intended the class of candidates
for apportionment to be decided by reference to beneficial interests held during that
same year, there can in my judgment be no logical stopping place between looking
at the moment when the gains become ascertainable under s 20(4) and looking back
over the entire life of the settlement. To draw the line at the commencement of the
c relevant year of assessment is, for the reasons I have given, quite arbitrary. No
construction which I put on s 42 would enable it to do justice in all cases. It is not
surprising that in 1981 Parliament decided to scrap it (see ss 80–84 of the Finance
Act 1981). But the view favoured of the Special Commissioner has at least the
advantage of simplicity and a certain schematic consistency. In my judgment it is
the correct interpretation and the appeal must be dismissed.

d
Appeal dismissed with costs.

Solicitors: *Solicitor of Inland Revenue*; *Robert Davies & Co,* Warrington (for the
taxpayers).

Rengan Krishnan Esq   Barrister.

J Sainsbury plc v O'Connor (Inspector of Taxes)

COURT OF APPEAL, CIVIL DIVISION
LLOYD, NOURSE, RALPH GIBSON LJJ
1, 2, 3, 22 MAY 1991

Corporation tax – Group relief – Subsidiary – Joint venture company set up by claimant company and GB – Claimant company holding 75% of issued share capital and GB holding remaining 25% – Option agreement granting call and put options to GB and claimant company respectively over 5% of joint venture company's shares – Whether joint venture company 75% subsidiary of claimant company – Income and Corporation Taxes Act 1970, s 258 – Finance Act 1973, s 28, Sch 12, para 5.

In 1979 Sainsburys and a Belgian company (GB) entered into an agreement (the joint venture agreement) to establish Homebase as a joint venture. Sainsburys held 75% of the issued share capital of Homebase and GB held the remaining 25%. By a further agreement (the option agreement) of the same date, Sainsburys granted to GB an option to purchase (the put option), and GB granted to Sainsburys an option to require GB to purchase (the call option) 5% of the issued share capital of Homebase. The options were not exercisable before the fifth anniversary of the incorporation of Homebase. Neither option was exercised and by a deed dated 9 August 1985 the rights of both parties under the option agreement were formally terminated. Sainsburys claimed group relief under s 258ᵃ of the Income and Corporation Taxes Act 1970 in respect of trading losses incurred by Homebase for the years 1980–81 to 1984–85. Those claims were refused by the Crown and Sainsburys appealed to a Special Commissioner. The commissioner dismissed the appeal, holding that although Sainsburys was the 'beneficial owner' of the whole of its 75% shareholding in Homebase as required by s 258, the put and call options under the option agreement were 'arrangements' within para 5(3)ᵇ of Sch 12 to the Finance Act 1973 and accordingly Sainsburys had not satisfied the additional requirements of s 28(2)ᶜ of the Finance Act 1973 to qualify for the relief. Millett J allowed Sainsburys' appeal holding that options under the option agreement were not 'arrangements' within para 5(3) of Sch 12, and, accordingly, that Sainsburys had satisfied the additional requirements of s 28(2) to qualify for the relief. The Crown appealed.

Held – (1) Where the legal owner of shares was bereft of all the rights which would normally attach to those shares so that his ownership was nothing more than a legal shell then he was not the beneficial owner of the shares. However, in respect of its shares in Homebase, Sainsburys had retained almost all of the rights which normally attach to shares in a joint venture company and even the option agreement had not deprived Sainsburys of all rights in relation to the 5% of the share capital in Homebase pending the exercise of the call option by GB. Sainsburys' ownership had therefore been more than a mere legal shell. Accordingly, Sainsburys was the beneficial owner of not less than 75% of the shares in Homebase as required by s 258 of the Income and Corporation Taxes Act 1970.

Wood Preservation Ltd v Prior (Inspector of Taxes) (1968) 45 TC 112 distinguished.

(2) Paragraph 5 of Sch 12 to the Finance Act 1973 applied only where an arrangement existed which could affect the rights carried by the shares in question, whether in the same or some future accounting period. The option agreement was not such an arrangement, since the rights carried by the shares which were the

---

a   Section 258, so far as material, is set out at p 320 *g–h*, post
b   Paragraph 5(3), so far as material, is set out at p 323 *a–c*, post
c   Section 28(2), so far as material, is set out at p 321 *a–c*, post

subject of the option agreement would have been precisely the same, whether before
a or after the exercise of the option. The option agreement was an arrangement which
could affect ownership of the shares but it could not affect the rights attaching to the
shares. Accordingly, the option agreement was not an 'arrangement' within the
meaning of para 5(3) and Sainsburys had not failed to satisfy the additional
requirements for group relief under s 28(2) of the 1973 Act.

The appeal would therefore be dismissed.

b
Notes

For companies eligible for group relief, see Simon's Taxes D2.642.

For the Income and Corporation Taxes Act 1970, s 258(1) (now the Income and
Corporation Taxes Act 1988, s 402(1)) and the Finance Act 1973, s 28(2) and Sch 12,
para 5 (now the Income and Corporation Taxes Act 1988, s 413(7) and Sch 18, para
c 5), see ibid, Part G1.

Cases referred to in judgment

Andrea Ursula, The [1973] QB 265, [1971] 1 All ER 821.
Ayerst (Inspector of Taxes) v C & K (Construction) Ltd [1975] STC 345, [1976] AC
d   167, [1975] 2 All ER 537, 50 TC 651, HL.
Brooklands Selangor Holdings Ltd v IRC [1970] 1 WLR 429, [1970] 2 All ER 76.
English Sewing Cotton Co Ltd v IRC [1947] 1 All ER 679, CA.
Congreso del Partido, I [1978] QB 500, [1978] 1 All ER 1169; *affd* [1981] 1 All ER
1092, CA; *rvsd* [1983] 1 AC 244, [1981] 2 All ER 1064, HL.
Lysaght v Edwards (1876) 2 Ch D 499.
e *Parway Estates Ltd v IRC* (1957) 45 TC 135, CA.
Rodwell Securities Ltd v IRC [1968] 1 All ER 257.
Wood Preservation Ltd v Prior (Inspector of Taxes) [1968] 2 All ER 849; [1969] 1
WLR 1077, [1969] 1 All ER 364, 45 TC 112, CA.

Cases also cited
f
Bank voor Handel en Scheepvaart NV v Administrator of Hungarian Property
[1954] AC 584, [1954] 1 All ER 969, 35 TC 311, HL.
Griffith v Pelton [1958] Ch 205, [1957] 3 All ER 75, CA.
Holmleigh (Holdings) Ltd v IRC (1958) 46 TC 435.
Leigh Spinners Ltd v IRC (1956) 46 TC 425.
g *Spiro v Glencrown Properties Ltd* [1991] 2 WLR 931, [1991] 1 All ER 600.

Appeal

The Crown appealed against the decision of Millett J dated 6 June 1990 (see [1990]
STC 516) allowing an appeal by J Sainsbury plc (Sainsburys) against a determination
h by a Special Commissioner that Sainsburys was not entitled to group relief under
s 258 of the Income and Corporation Taxes Act 1970 because it had not satisfied the
additional requirements of s 28(2) of the Finance Act 1973. The facts are set out in
the judgment of Lloyd LJ.

Andrew Park QC and *Launcelot Henderson* for the Crown.
Peter Whiteman QC and *Brian Green* for Sainsburys.
j
Cur adv vult

22 May. The following judgments were delivered.

LLOYD LJ. The question in this case is whether the taxpayer, J Sainsbury plc
(Sainsburys), can claim group relief under s 258 of the Income and Corporation

Taxes Act 1970 (the 1970 Act) in respect of trading losses of its subsidiary Homebase
Ltd (Homebase) during the period 12 January 1981 to 9 August 1985.

In October 1978 Sainsburys entered into negotiations with a Belgian company
GB-INNO-BM (GB) for setting up a joint venture company in the United
Kingdom. The purpose was to develop a chain of home-improvement stores, with
or without associated garden centres. The initial intention was that the shares should
be held in the proportion 70% Sainsburys: 30% GB. But in August 1979 it was
realised (it is perhaps surprising that it was not realised before) that Sainsburys
would not be able to take advantage of the group relief provisions unless the new
company were a 75% subsidiary. So the solution which the parties reached was as
follows. By a principal agreement dated 4 October 1979 (the joint venture
agreement), Sainsburys agreed to subscribe 75% of the share capital in the joint
company, and GB 25%. By a separate option agreement of the same date, Sainsburys
granted GB an option to purchase 5% of the share capital (the call option), and GB
granted Sainsburys an option to require GB to purchase 5% of the share capital (the
put option). These options were not to be exercised within five years of the
incorporation of the new company. In the event, neither option was exercised, and
the option agreement was cancelled by deed dated 9 August 1985. It is not suggested
that the agreements were a sham.

Two questions arise. The first is whether Sainsburys was 'the beneficial owner' of
the whole of its 75% holding, for the purpose of s 258 of the 1970 Act, notwithstanding
GB's option to purchase 5% of the share capital after five years. The second question
is whether, if Sainsburys would otherwise have been entitled to claim the benefit of
group relief, the option agreement was an 'arrangement' within the meaning of para
5(3) of Sch 12 to the Finance Act 1973 (the 1973 Act). If so, Sainsburys would lose
the benefit of group relief, by virtue of s 28 of the 1973 Act. The Special
Commissioner answered the first question in favour of Sainsburys, and the second
question in favour of the Crown. On appeal, by way of case stated (see [1990] STC
516), Millett J answered both questions in favour of the taxpayer.

I find myself in complete agreement with the judge, not only with his conclusion,
but also (subject to one minor point) with his reasons; so much so, that I would be
content simply to adopt his judgment as my own. But, as there is always the
possibility of this case going higher, I must spell out my own reasons for dismissing
the appeal.

Statutory framework

I start by setting out for convenience the statutory provisions relevant to both
questions. I start with the 1970 Act.

Section 258 provides:

> '(1) Relief for trading losses ... may in accordance with the following
> provisions of this Chapter be surrendered by a company (called "the surrendering
> company") which is a member of a group of companies and, on the making of a
> claim by another company (called "the claimant company") which is a member
> of the same group, may be allowed to the claimant company by way of a relief
> from corporation tax called "group relief" ...
>
> (5) For the purpose of this section ... (*a*) two companies shall be deemed to be
> members of a group of companies if one is the 75 per cent. subsidiary of the
> other or both are 75 per cent. subsidiaries of a third company ...'

Section 532 provides:

> '(1) For the purposes of the Tax Acts a body corporate shall be deemed to
> be— ... (*b*) a "75 per cent. subsidiary" of another body corporate if and so long
> as not less than 75 per cent. of its ordinary share capital is owned directly or
> indirectly by that other body corporate ...

(3) In this section references to ownership shall be construed as references to beneficial ownership.'

Sections 28 and 29 of the 1973 Act are 'anti avoidance' provisions. Section 28(2) provides:

'Notwithstanding that at any time a company (in this subsection referred to as "the subsidiary company") is a 75 per cent. subsidiary . . . within the meaning of section 532 of the Taxes Act, of another company (in this subsection referred to as "the parent company") it shall not be treated at that time as such a subsidiary for the purposes of the enactments relating to group relief unless, additionally, at that time—

(*a*) the parent company is beneficially entitled to not less than 75 per cent. . . . of any profits available for distribution to equity holders of the subsidiary company; and

(*b*) the parent company would be beneficially entitled to not less than 75 per cent. . . . of any assets of the subsidiary company available for distribution to its equity holders on a winding up.'

Thus the broad effect of s 28 is that it is not enough for group relief that the parent company is beneficial owner of 75% of the ordinary share capital of its subsidiary; it must also be beneficially entitled to 75% of the dividends, and 75% of the assets on winding up. Section 28(5) gives effect to Part 1 of Sch 12 to the 1973 Act.

Section 29 applies to an arrangement whereby a company may cease to be a member of one group, and becomes a member of another group. Where such an arrangement is in existence, the company is treated as not being a member of the first group.

Schedule 12 is simple in concept, but complicated in detail. I shall refer to the relevant companies as parent and subsidiary, and for the sake of clarity I shall omit all reference to assets on a winding up. The provisions relevant to the entitlement to dividends are as follows:

'1.—(1) For the purposes of section 28 of this Act and this Schedule, an equity holder of a company is any person who—(*a*) holds ordinary shares in the company . . .

2.—(1) Subject to the following provisions of this Part of this Schedule, for the purposes of section 28 of this Act, the percentage to which one company is beneficially entitled of any profits available for distribution to the equity holders of another company means the percentage to which the first company would be so entitled in the relevant accounting period on a distribution in money to those equity holders of—

(*a*) an amount of profits equal to the total profits of the other company which arise in that accounting period (whether or not any of those profits are in fact distributed), or

(*b*) if there are no profits of the other company in that accounting period, profits of £100,

and in the following provisions of this Part of this Schedule, that distribution is referred to as "the profit distribution" . . .

4.—(1) This paragraph applies if any of the equity holders—(*a*) to whom the profit distribution is made . . . holds, as such an equity holder, any shares or securities which carry rights in respect of dividend or interest . . . which are wholly or partly limited by reference to a specified amount or amounts (whether the limitation takes the form of the capital by reference to which a distribution is calculated or operates by reference to an amount of profits or assets or otherwise).

(2) Where this paragraph applies there shall be determined—(*a*) the percentage of profits to which, on the profit distribution, the first company referred to in paragraph 2(1) above would be entitled ... if, to the extent that they are limited as mentioned in sub-paragraph (1) above, the rights of every equity holder falling within that sub-paragraph (including the first company concerned if it is such an equity holder) had been waived.

(3) If, on the profit distribution, the percentage of profits determined as mentioned in sub-paragraph (2)(*a*) above is less than the percentage of profits determined under paragraph 2(1) above without regard to that sub-paragraph, the lesser percentage shall be taken for the purposes of section 28 of this Act to be the percentage of profits to which, on the profit distribution, the first company referred to in paragraph 2(1) above would be entitled as mentioned in that paragraph.'

Thus if there is a class of shares carrying limited rights, such rights are deemed to be waived to the extent that they are so limited. If, as a result, the parent company's dividend, as a percentage of the whole, is less than it would have been without the waiver, the lesser percentage is taken for the purpose of s 28.

Paragraph 5 provides:

'(1) This paragraph applies if, at any time in the relevant accounting period, any of the equity holders—(*a*) to whom the profit distribution is made ... holds, as such an equity holder, any shares ... which carry rights in respect of dividend or interest ... which are of such a nature (as, for example, if any shares will cease to carry a right to a dividend at a future time) that if the profit distribution ... were to take place in a different accounting period the percentage to which, in accordance with the preceding provisions of this Part of this Schedule, that equity holder would be entitled of profits on the profit distribution ... would be different from the percentage determined in the relevant accounting period.

(2) Where this paragraph applies, there shall be determined—(*a*) the percentage of profits to which, on the profit distribution, the first company referred to in paragraph 2(1) above would be entitled ... if the rights of the equity holders in the relevant accounting period were the same as they would be in the different accounting period referred to in sub-paragraph (1) above.'

I will return to para 5(3) in a moment.

Paragraph 5(4) provides:

'Sub-paragraphs (3) ... of paragraph 4 above shall apply for the purposes of this paragraph as they apply for the purposes of that paragraph and, accordingly, references therein to sub-paragraphs (2)(*a*) ... of that paragraph shall be construed as references to sub-paragraphs 2(*a*) ... of this paragraph.'

Thus if there is a class of shares carrying rights which may vary in the future, and if as a result, the parent company's dividend as a percentage of the whole will become less than it is in the current accounting period, the lesser percentage is taken for the purpose of s 28.

Paragraphs 4 and 5 are, as the judge said (at 534), the operative paragraphs.

'Paragraph 4 introduces the requirement that the taxpayer should be entitled to not less than 75% of the dividends or distributions on a winding up no matter how large the dividend or distribution, and para 5 the requirement that the taxpayer should be similarly entitled no matter when the dividend or the distribution on a winding up should occur.'

Paragraph 5(5) provides that if there is a class of shares to which both paras 4 and 5 apply, then one applies each paragraph separately, and takes the *lowest* percentage for the purpose of s 28.

I now return to para 5(3) on which the second question turns. It provides:

'If in the relevant accounting period an equity holder holds, as such, any shares or securities in respect of which arrangements exist by virtue of which, in that or any subsequent accounting period, the equity holder's entitlement to profits on the profit distribution or to assets on the notional winding-up could be different as compared with his entitlement if effect were not given to the arrangements, then for the purposes of this paragraph—

(a) it shall be assumed that effect would be given to those arrangements in a later accounting period, and

(b) those shares or securities shall be treated as though any variation in the equity holder's entitlement to profits or assets resulting from giving effect to the arrangements were the result of the operation of such rights attaching to the shares or securities as are referred to in sub-paragraph (1) above.'

Sainsburys argues that para 5(3) applies, and applies only, where an arrangement exists which could affect the rights carried by the shares in question, whether in the same or some future accounting period. The option agreement was not such an arrangement, since the rights carried by the shares which are the subject of the option agreement would have been precisely the same, whether before or after the exercise of the option. The Crown argues that you look at the taxpayer's overall entitlement to dividend. If an arrangement exists which would reduce the taxpayer's overall entitlement in the future, then you assume that the arrangement has been implemented for the purpose of s 28. The option agreement was such an arrangement, since, if the call option had been exercised, it would have reduced Sainsburys' entitlement from 75% of the dividend to 70%.

For reasons which I will explain later, I have no doubt that Sainsburys' argument is to be preferred. But first I must deal with the question whether, apart altogether from para 5(3), Sainsburys should be regarded as 'the beneficial owner' of 75% of the share capital.

Beneficial ownership

As Lord Diplock pointed out in *Ayerst (Inspector of Taxes) v C & K (Construction) Ltd* [1975] STC 345 at 349, [1976] AC 167 at 177, the concept of beneficial ownership owes its origin to the Court of Chancery.

'The archetype is the trust. The "legal ownership" of the trust property is in the trustee, but he holds it not for his own benefit but for the benefit of the cestui que trustent or beneficiaries. On the creation of a trust in the strict sense as it was developed by equity the full ownership in the trust property was split into two constituent elements, which became vested in different persons: the "legal ownership" in the trustee, and what came to be called the "beneficial ownership" in the cestui que trust.'

The term 'beneficial ownership' is therefore very well established. It is first found in a taxing statute, so far as I have been able to ascertain, in s 55 of the Finance Act 1927, where it appears in connection with relief from stamp duty on transfers. But in property legislation the term was already familiar to Parliament from s 7 of the Conveyancing Act 1881. Indeed, it had appeared even earlier in s 1 of the Larceny Act 1868, and again in the cross-heading to s 58 of the Merchant Shipping Act 1894. But nowhere did Parliament see fit to define beneficial ownership. No doubt this was because it was already a term of art, well known and understood among lawyers.

Counsel for the Crown argued the contrary. He submitted that the term should be given its ordinary meaning, whatever that might be. But that approach finds no support in Lord Diplock's speech in *Ayerst (Inspector of Taxes) v C & K (Construction) Ltd*. In that case the House of Lords were concerned with s 17 of the Finance Act 1954. Lord Diplock held ([1975] STC 345 at 348, [1976] AC 167 at 176) that the expression should be given the meaning 'which would have been ascribed to it in 1954 as a term of legal art'.

In *Parway Estates Ltd v IRC* (1957) 45 TC 135 there was an unconditional contract for the sale of the share capital of a wholly-owned subsidiary. Upjohn J held (at 141) that, since the contract was one in respect of which the court would have granted a degree of specific performance, equitable ownership passed to the purchasers at the date of the contract. However, at the end of his judgment he said (at 142):

> 'It seems to me, therefore, that, even taking the most technical view of the whole matter, it is not right to describe the vendors at the date of the transfer as the equitable owner. However, I rest my judgment in the main on this: that when you look at the words "beneficial owner" in s. 42 of the Finance Act 1930, those words must in my judgment be construed in what has been described in connection with another Statute as "its ordinary or popular sense": see *English Sewing Cotton Co. Ltd. v. Commissioners of Inland Revenue* (1946) 62 TLR 608, at page 610. I do not further refer to that case, for it was dealing with a different Statute. But when one looks at the facts of this case, and asks oneself was the Appellant Company in its popular or ordinary sense the beneficial owner of the shares on 28th February 1956, there can only be one answer to that question: it was not; it was bound by contract to transfer them to another the very next day.'

This paragraph lends substance to counsel for the Crown's argument. But the Court of Appeal expressly repudiated Upjohn J's concluding observations. Jenkins LJ (see (1957) 45 TC 135 at 148) said:

> 'I need only add that I find myself in complete agreement with the learned Judge, who reached the same conclusion as I have done; that is, with one qualification ... [Jenkins LJ then quoted from Upjohn J's judgment and referred to *English Sewing Cotton Co Ltd v IRC* [1947] 1 All ER 679.] ... Speaking for myself, I find it difficult as at present advised to derive any assistance from consideration of what the ordinary person would understand by the words "beneficial owner" in their ordinary sense. I am open to conviction, but *prima facie* it seems to me difficult to ascribe any different meaning to those words from their legal meaning, and that little assistance can be derived from speculation as to what an ordinary person would take them to mean in their popular sense. For my part, I prefer to found myself on the ground that there is nothing in this agreement to take the case of the general rule, under which there is no doubt that the equitable interest in the shares became vested in the purchaser when the agreement of 12th January 1956 was signed.'

What then was the 'legal' meaning of which Jenkins LJ spoke? The answer must surely be clear. Jenkins LJ was assimilating beneficial ownership with equitable ownership. Since the courts would have granted a decree of specific performance of the contract of sale, 'the well-established general principle' applied, and the shares became in equity the property of the purchaser. He said (at 146) '... one is coming near to saying that the vendors have become trustees of the shares for the purchaser on the strength of the purchaser's right to call for specific performance'; 'near to saying' because the vendors were not trustees in the full sense, but in the qualified sense in which that word is frequently used, where the property has passed in equity under a specifically enforceable contract (see, for example, Megarry and Wade, *The Law of Real Property* (5th edn, 1984) p 602 and the cases there cited). Jenkins LJ concluded his judgement (at 148) as follows:

> 'The point is not one which admits of any great elaboration, but I cannot see any reason here for excluding the general rule, and if the general rule applies so

a   that Mr. Peck, the purchaser, becomes by virtue of the agreement the owner in equity of the shares in question, then, in my view, it necessarily follows that at the date of the two transfers the Appellant Company, Parway Estates Ltd., was not the beneficial owner of the share capital of Parr (Builders) Ltd. No doubt the Appellant Company was the legal owner and the registered proprietor, but the equitable or beneficial interest in the shares had vested in the purchaser.'

b   So Jenkins LJ was, as I say, treating the equitable and beneficial ownership as being one and the same thing.

Similarly, in *Rodwell Securities Ltd v IRC* [1968] 1 All ER 257 it was argued that 'beneficial owner' is not a term of art, but is an expression which falls to be construed liberally, so as to include anybody who has complete control over the disposition of the shares in question. Pennycuick J rejected the argument. He held (at 261) that

c   the words have a clear, though undefined, legal meaning, following the judgment of Jenkins LJ in the *Parway* case, which I have already quoted.

Finally it is worth referring to a decision of Robert Goff J in a completely different field, namely s 3(4) of the Administration of Justice Act 1956, now s 21 of the Supreme Court Act 1981. Section 3(4) is concerned with the Admiralty jurisdiction in rem. It provides for the jurisdiction to be invoked against—

d

'... (a) that ship, if at the time when the action is brought it is beneficially owned as respects all the shares therein by that person; or
(b) any other ship which, at the time when the action is brought, is beneficially owned as aforesaid.'

In *The Andrea Ursula* [1973] QB 265 Brandon J held (at 272) that the expression

e   'beneficially owned' should be given a broad meaning so as to cover the case of a ship, which, though not legally or equitably owned by a person, was nevertheless in that person's full possession and control, such as a charterer by demise. In *I Congreso del Partido* [1978] QB 500 Robert Goff J declined to follow Brandon J's decision. He held (at 538) that 'beneficially owned' referred only to equitable ownership, whether or not accompanied by legal ownership, and did not include possession and control.

f   He said (at 539):

'A demise charterer has, within limits defined by contract, the beneficial use of the ship; he does not, however, have the beneficial ownership as respects all the shares in the ship.'

g   So there is good authority for the view that 'the beneficial owner' of shares, when that term is used in a statute in contrast to the registered holder, means the equitable owner; neither more nor less. By equitable owner is meant, inter alia, the purchaser under a specifically enforceable contract. Applying that test in the present case, GB was not the equitable owner of 5% of the shares which were the subject of the option agreement, since it could not claim specific performance until it had exercised its

h   option under the agreement, and it could not exercise its option under the agreement until five years after the incorporation of Homebase, namely, 12 November 1984. Indeed, counsel for the Crown did not even argue that equitable ownership had passed to GB.

Does it follow that equitable ownership remained in Sainsburys? In my view it does. For, as Lord Greene pointed out in the *English Sewing Cotton Co* case [1947] 1

i   All ER 679 at 681, it is difficult, at any rate in the case of a contract, to see how the equitable ownership could have become severed from the legal ownership unless it had passed to somebody else. There are, of course, special circumstances in which a person or company may be deprived of the beneficial ownership of his assets, even though it is not yet possible to identify his successors in title. The best known example would be property held by a trustee in bankruptcy, or the property of a company in liquidation (see *Ayerst v C & K (Construction) Ltd*). Another example would be the estate of a deceased person in course of administration, or assets vested in a custodian of enemy property. In such cases it is right to regard the equitable or beneficial ownership as being in suspense. But in all these cases the legal owner is deprived of his beneficial ownership by operation of law as a consequence of supervening events. I would be reluctant to extend the same concept to the case of an ordinary commercial transaction inter partes. So if beneficial ownership means the same as equitable ownership for the purpose of the Taxes Acts and if, as counsel for the Crown concedes, the equitable ownership in the shares has not yet passed to GB, I would be disposed to hold that Sainsburys never ceased to be the beneficial owner of those shares.

But there remains one authority on which counsel for the Crown relies strongly, which I have not yet mentioned, namely, *Wood Preservation Ltd v Prior (Inspector of Taxes)* [1969] 1 WLR 1077, 45 TC 112. In that case there was a contract for the sale of a subsidiary company. The subsidiary was the United Kingdom distributing agent for a German manufacturer. It was a condition of the contract of sale that the vendors would obtain a letter from the German company within one month of the contract assuring the purchasers that the agency agreement would not be terminated. The vendors then assigned their business to the subsidiary, which later claimed to deduct the trading losses of the business from its own profits for tax purposes. At the date of the assignment the letter from the German company had not been obtained. Subsequently the purchasers obtained a satisfactory assurance from the German manufacturers direct. So they wrote to the vendors 'withdrawing' the condition. 'In these circumstances' they said, 'the contract between the two companies has now become unconditional'. The question was whether the vendors remained beneficial owners of the shares until the condition was withdrawn, in which case the trading losses would have been deductible, or whether they ceased to be beneficial owners when the contract was made, in which case they would not.

In a lengthy judgment Goff J held that the vendors had ceased to be beneficial owners at the date of the contract. After referring to *Parway Estates Ltd* he concluded ([1969] 1 WLR 1077 at 1094, 45 TC 112 at 130):

> 'It appears to me to follow quite clearly from that authority that ordinarily where the mutual obligation of sale and purchase is subject to a condition precedent the property does not pass so long as the condition remains unperformed, but in the present case I have to consider whether it makes any difference that this was a condition, as I find, solely for the benefit of the purchaser and which he could, therefore, waive. In a sense, therefore, he had a contract of which he could obtain specific performance by, at any time, waiving the condition, but on the other hand he had expressly provided that he would buy the shares subject to the condition of the letter which he needed being produced to him. Mr. Monroe says, "Well, he could have waived, and if he did waive it the property would then pass to him," but unless and until he waived it, it would not. That, I think is not an entirely easy matter to decide, but on the whole I have come to the conclusion that as the matter of waiving the condition rested entirely with the purchaser, he could at any time require specific performance of the contract, and therefore, to use the words of Jenkins L.J. in the *Parway* case "one is coming near to saying that the vendors have become trustees of the shares for the purchaser on the strength of the purchaser's right to call for specific performance". On the whole, therefore, I have come to the conclusion that under this contract the beneficial interest had sufficiently passed to the purchaser and that the conclusion of the Special Commissioners was right.'

It will be seen that Goff J approached the case much as I have approached the present case, by asking whether the purchasers could have called for specific performance.

But in the Court of Appeal things took a different turn. Instead of asking whether a the purchasers could obtain specific performance by waiving the condition in their favour, the Court of Appeal analysed the nature and extent of the rights retained by the vendors, pending the waiver. In a short judgment Lord Donovan ([1969] 1 WLR 1077 at 1095–1096, 45 TC 112 at 132) summarised the argument for the Crown as follows:

b 'The position (they say) even before this condition was waived was this: First, Silexine could not have disposed of the shares to anybody else: had it tried to do so it could have been restrained by injunction. Second, it could not declare or pay any bonus or dividend on its shares: it had specifically precluded itself from doing so. Third, it would have been bound at any time actually to transfer the shares if British Ratin waived the condition in question—which in law at any rate it could have done at any time after the contract was signed. The shares (in a word) were like a tree which the owner could not sell and could not cut down

c and of which he could enjoy none of the fruit . . . But if one finds, as here, that the company which made the losses, though still the legal owner of the shares, is bereft of the rights of selling or disposing or enjoying the fruits of these shares, then, bearing in mind the purposes of section 17, I have in the end concluded that it would be a misuse of language to say that it still remained the beneficial owner of these shares. I am not deciding this case in the least upon merits; but

d it is difficult to think that the legislature intended the benefit it was conferring to be enjoyed in these circumstances . . . It would be rash indeed to attempt an exhaustive definition, and I do not do it. I merely say that the facts in the present case do not, in my opinion, satisfy any reasonable interpretation, involving, as they do, that on March 25, 1960, by the contract of sale of the shares, which was accepted shortly afterwards, Silexine ceased to be able to

e appropriate to itself any of the benefits of ownership. This does not necessarily involve the consequence that British Ratin became the beneficial owner while the condition remained operative. It is possible for property to lack any beneficial owner for a time, for example property which is still being administered by an executor which will go eventually to the residuary legatee.'

f Harman LJ said ([1969] 1 WLR 1077 at 1097, 45 TC 112 at 133):

'After accepting this offer Silexine was not able to deal with the property in any way at all, as has already been pointed out by my Lord. Therefore it seems to me to be a contradiction in terms to talk about beneficial ownership in Silexine. There was no benefit at all in their ownership: it was a mere legal shell

g . . . They were tied hand and foot. Therefore, merely to say: "Oh well, this is a conditional contract and in the ordinary way a conditional contract does not pass beneficial ownership until the condition is satisfied," does not seem to me to apply to this case at all, and I think that the judge was right, though perhaps not quite for the reasons which he gave in his judgment.'

h Widgery LJ clearly felt some difficulty, as indeed had Lord Donovan. Since his judgment is very short, I will quote his judgment in full ([1969] 1 WLR 1077 at 1097, 45 TC 112 at 133–134):

'I have found it very difficult to accept Mr. Goulding's proposition that on a contract of sale of this kind the beneficial ownership can leave the vendor without simultaneously arriving in the purchaser. I appreciate that there are

j many other circumstances in which there may be no identifiable beneficial owner of property, but I would have thought that where an unquestioned beneficial owner enters into a contract of sale he should be regarded as remaining beneficial owner until that interest has passed to the purchaser. If that were the right test in this case, I would have thought, contrary to the view of the judge below, that as the beneficial ownership had not reached British Ratin it remained at the material time in the original owners. But I have been persuaded

that, having regard to the problem which is posed to this court, as Lord
Donovan has pointed out, one must not look so much at whether beneficial
ownership has reached the purchaser: one must examine the situation of the
vendor and ask whether the legal ownership, which unquestionably remained
in him, retained the attributes of beneficial ownership for the purposes of the
section. In the end, I have reached the same conclusion as that expressed by my
Lords on that point and accordingly I also would dismiss this appeal.'

Counsel for the Crown relies on *Wood Preservation Ltd v Prior* for two purposes:
first, to show that beneficial ownership is not synonymous with equitable ownership,
and second, to show that property may lack a beneficial owner even in a commercial
context.

Wood Preservation Ltd v Prior was considered by Pennycuick J in *Brooklands
Selangor Holdings Ltd v IRC* [1970] 1 WLR 429. On the facts of the latter case, the
contract had become unconditional, so that on any view equitable ownership of the
stock in question had passed to the transferees. But Pennycuick J said (at 450):

> 'I would only add this, that considerable difficulties arise in this connection if
> one seeks to equate the expression "beneficial owner" with the expression
> "equitable owner" in the technical sense in which that term is used in equity
> law ... I do not think, however, that equitable ownership is to be thus equated
> for this purpose with beneficial ownership although, no doubt, in many
> instances they may come to the same thing.'

Although *Brooklands Selangor Holdings Ltd v IRC* supports counsel for the
Crown's argument that equitable and beneficial ownership are not the same concept,
the observations of Pennycuick J were necessarily influenced by the decision in
Wood Preservation Ltd v Prior.

It goes without saying that we are bound by the ratio decidendi of *Wood
Preservation Ltd v Prior* whatever it may be. It follows, I think, that we cannot
decide the first question on the straightforward ground which I would otherwise
favour, that beneficial ownership and equitable ownership are one and the same
thing, and that since Sainsburys retained the equitable as well as the legal title to
75% of the share capital throughout the period in question, it should be regarded as
beneficial owner of the 5%. Instead we must look into the nature and extent of the
rights retained by Sainsburys in relation to the 5%. If Sainsburys was bereft of all
rights which would normally attach to that parcel of shares, so that its ownership
was, in the words of Harman LJ, nothing more than a legal shell, then we would be
bound to hold that Sainsburys was not the beneficial owner of the shares, even
though the rights which would normally attach to the shares had not yet passed to
GB. Counsel for the Crown submitted that that was precisely the position here.

Counsel for the Crown relies on three factors to establish his argument on the
facts. In the first place, Sainsburys had no right to dispose of its shares prior to
12 November 1984, without GB's consent. Secondly, Sainsburys had no expectation
of any dividend on its shares, prior to 12 November 1984, since the payment of a
dividend was in the joint control of Sainsburys and GB, by virtue of clauses 6.4 and
11(vi) of the joint venture agreement. GB would have been most unlikely to agree to
the payment of any dividend while the call option remained outstanding. Thirdly,
the price at which GB was entitled to purchase the shares under the call option was
the aggregate amount paid up on the shares plus interest at 1% over base lending
rate, less the amount of any dividend paid on the shares meanwhile. So if the call
option had been exercised, Sainsburys would have been deprived of any increase in
the value of the shares. Such increase in value would have accrued to GB, not to
Sainsburys, as would any fall in value, should Sainsburys have exercised the put
option.

As to these three factors, the first two, as counsel for the Crown accepted, apply

not only to the 5%, but also to the remaining 70%. It could not possibly be argued
a that Sainsburys was not, by virtue of these factors, the beneficial owner of 70%.
Then does the third factor make all the difference? Counsel submits that the
cumulative effect of the three factors was such as to deprive Sainsburys of all fruits
of ownership. I do not agree. The question is not whether Sainsburys required the
consent of GB before a dividend could be paid, or whether a payment of dividend
was likely or not (it was clearly contemplated as a possibility). The question is rather
b whether Sainsburys would have received the dividend if it had been paid. The
answer is in the affirmative. The fact that the amount of any dividend would have
been deducted from the option price (whether under the call option or the put
option) does not mean that Sainsburys was not beneficially entitled to the dividends
in the meantime. So I am not persuaded that Sainsburys' rights in relation to the
shares were no more than 'a mere legal shell'. That being so, the ground on which
c the Court of Appeal held that the vendors in *Wood Preservation Ltd v Prior* were
not the beneficial owners of the shares in question does not apply.

But counsel for the Crown's argument does not stop there. Assuming Sainsburys
was not entirely bereft of all the fruits of ownership, as in *Wood Preservation Ltd v
Prior*, counsel invites us to form what he called a 'balanced judgment' as to whether
Sainsburys' ownership of the shares was or was not beneficial. But I would not for
d my part be willing to extend the decision in *Wood Preservation Ltd v Prior* beyond
what was actually decided. How, otherwise, could one ever draw the line? Where
legal ownership is a mere shell, as it was in *Wood Preservation Ltd v Prior*, it is
relatively easy to draw the inference, as a matter of construction, that Parliament
cannot have intended to confer the advantages of group relief. But it is much more
difficult to draw such an inference where, as in the present case, Sainsburys retained
e almost all the rights which normally attach to shares in a joint venture company;
and even the option agreement did not, for the reasons already mentioned, deprive
Sainsburys of all rights in relation to the 5%, pending the exercise of the call option
by GB. So I would not accept counsel's further argument. Like the Special
Commissioner and the judge, and for substantially the same reasons, I would answer
the first question in favour of Sainsburys.

f
Schedule 12 to the Finance Act 1973

I have already anticipated my answer to the second question. Once the legislative
purpose underlying s 28 and Part 1 of Sch 12 is understood (and I confess that the
meaning does not exactly leap to the eye) the answer is clear enough. Millett J held
(see [1990] STC 516 at 535) that the option agreement was not an arrangement in
g respect of any particular shares held by Sainsburys, since Sainsburys could in theory
buy in shares from a third party to satisfy the call option. I have some difficulty with
that line of reasoning. I much prefer the alternative line of reasoning, that the whole
of para 5 of Sch 12 is concerned with shares of a certain description, namely, shares
carrying special rights whereby they may, for example, cease to carry the right to
any dividend in the future. If that is the right view, then para 5(3) is concerned
h solely with arrangements whereby shares, or a class of shares, may be brought within
that description. An arrangement affecting the ownership of shares is a very different
sort of arrangement, and quite outside the ambit of para 5.

The judge went on to hold (at 536) that, for para 5 to operate, the 'equity holder'
must be the holder of the shares throughout the material time, that is to say, he must
be the holder of the shares in the future accounting period to which the arrangement
relates, as well as the holder in the current accounting period. The judge may well
j be right about that. But it is sufficient for present purposes that, for para 5 to operate,
the arrangement must be one which affects the rights attaching to the shares. The
option agreement was an arrangement which could affect ownership of the shares.
But it could not affect the rights attaching to the shares. The fact that those rights
would have accrued to the benefit of GB, and not Sainsburys, if the call option had
been exercised, is wholly beside the point. The paragraph is not concerned with a

reduction in the overall right to dividend, but with the reduction in the right to dividend attaching to particular shares. That seems to me to be the plain meaning *a* of the words. It is said that this meaning would emasculate para 5(3). It is sufficient to say that I do not agree.

I say nothing about the third reason given by the judge (at 537) for holding that the option agreement is not caught by s 28 or Sch 12.

For the reasons given I would answer the second question in favour of the taxpayer, as well as the first. It follows that I would dismiss the appeal. *b*

NOURSE LJ. I agree.

The first question is whether, within the meaning of s 532(3) of the Income and Corporation Taxes Act 1970, the 'beneficial ownership' in the 5% of the shares in Homebase Ltd, which were subject to the unexercised put and call options in favour *c* of GB, was vested in J Sainsbury plc (Sainsburys) or not. The broad purpose of s 532(3), which was not, in its application to group relief, modified by the restrictions introduced by the Finance Act 1973, is that in deciding the extent to which one company is owned by another you look not at the legal ownership of the shares but at their beneficial ownership. The only distinction made is between legal and beneficial ownership and there is nothing to suggest that the latter expression is to *d* have some special meaning.

There is no difficulty in ascertaining the legal ownership of shares, which is invariably vested in the registered holder. Equally, it ought not to be difficult to ascertain their beneficial ownership, albeit that it may arise in a variety of ways, for example under a declaration of trust or by operation of law. I therefore approach the construction of s 532(3), a provision having general application for the purposes of *e* the Taxes Acts, in the expectation that the extent to which one company is beneficially owned by another was not intended to depend on fine distinctions between different cases.

Although I might not, with Lord Diplock, have gone so far as to think that the expression 'beneficial ownership' is a term of art, it is certainly one which has for several centuries had a very well-recognised meaning amongst property lawyers. *f* And there can be no doubt that, in enacting a provision such as s 532(3), Parliament must have intended to adopt that meaning. It means ownership for your own benefit as opposed to ownership as trustee for another. It exists either where there is no division of legal and beneficial ownership or where legal ownership is vested in one person and the beneficial ownership or, which is the same thing, the equitable interest in the property in another. Thus, to take the simplest case of divided *g* ownership to which s 532(3) can apply, if company A is the registered holder of shares in company B as nominee, ie as a bare trustee, for company C, the beneficial ownership of the shares or the equitable interest in them is vested in company C.

Another case to which s 532(3) can apply is where company A enters into an unconditional contract to sell shares in company B to company C. Shares in company B not being readily obtainable in the market, such a contract is specifically *h* enforceable at the suit of company C. By parity with contracts for the sale of land, it has long been held that the right to specific performance gives company C the equitable interest in the shares, company A becoming a qualified trustee in the sense that it must preserve the shares for company C while remaining entitled to any dividends accruing before completion.

In that state of affairs in which of the two companies is the beneficial ownership of *j* the shares vested pending completion of the contract? It cannot be doubted that it is vested in company C. In other words, in this instance at any rate, no distinction is to be drawn between the beneficial ownership and the equitable interest. As appears from the passages in their judgments in *Parway Estates Ltd v IRC* (1957) 45 TC 135 to which Lloyd LJ has referred, that is an assumption which has in the past been made by judges as eminent in this field as Lord Jenkins and Lord Upjohn. In the

same company I would cite the observations of Sir George Jessel MR in relation to a
a contract for the sale of land in *Lysaght v Edwards* (1876) 2 Ch D 499 at 506:

> 'It appears to me that the effect of a contract for sale has been settled for more
> than two centuries; certainly it was completely settled before the time of Lord
> *Hardwicke*, who speaks of the settled doctrine of the Court as to it. What is that
> doctrine? It is that the moment you have a valid contract for sale the vendor
> becomes in equity a trustee for the purchaser of the estate sold, and the beneficial
b > ownership passes to the purchaser . . .'

So far, therefore, I see no reason to doubt that Parliament intended, in the
application of s 532(3) to specifically enforceable contracts for the sale of shares, that
there should be no difference between the beneficial ownership of the shares and the
equitable interest in them. Nor, in the absence of authority to the contrary, would I
c be able to grasp the concept of the beneficial ownership being suspended somewhere
between the vendor and the purchaser. I would think that it must be vested in the
one or in the other and, if it has not passed to the purchaser, that it must remain in
the vendor. That is not in any way to cast doubt on the well-known examples of a
suspension of beneficial ownership to which Lloyd LJ has referred. They are far
removed from contracts for the sale of land or of shares.

d   Then take the previous example, but suppose that the contract is subject to a
condition precedent. Until the condition is satisfied the equitable interest in the
shares will not pass to company C. It will remain in company A. What ground is
there for thinking that the beneficial ownership of the shares will not also remain in
company A? In order to answer that question we must look to *Wood Preservation
Ltd v Prior (Inspector of Taxes)* [1969] 1 WLR 1077, 45 TC 112. That is a difficult
e decision. Goff J at first instance did not distinguish between the beneficial ownership
of the shares and the equitable interest in them. In my view he was right not to make
that distinction. However, he thought that, because the purchaser could obtain
specific performance of the contract by waiving the condition precedent at any time,
'the beneficial interest had sufficiently passed to the purchaser'. I respectfully think
that that was an error on the part of the judge. Unless and until the condition was
f either waived or satisfied there could be no right to specific performance and no
passing of the equitable interest.

It seems that Goff J's error was perceived by this court who, in the process of
correcting it, gave a decision whose effect was to draw a distinction between the
beneficial ownership of the shares and the equitable interest in them. Their approach
was bound, as the present case demonstrates, to lead to fine distinctions between
g different cases in the application of s 532(3). Shortly stated, their view was that
Parliament could not have intended that the concept of beneficial ownership should
apply to the 'mere legal shell' of ownership which the vendor there retained. Lord
Donovan, at any rate, was prepared to accept that this view might involve a
suspension of beneficial ownership. It is to be noted that they did not refer, as Goff J
had done, to *Parway Estates Ltd v IRC*. Lord Donovan said that he did not discuss
h the authorities which had been cited because none of them covered beneficial
ownership within the meaning of that expression in s 17 of the Finance Act 1954.
That was certainly correct so far as *Parway Estates Ltd v IRC* was concerned,
because that was a stamp duty decision under s 42 of the Finance Act 1930. However, the conditions for the operation of s 42 were of the same character as the
conditions for the operation of s 17. I am not at all sure on what ground *Parway
Estates Ltd v IRC* could have been distinguished.
j   The decision of this court in *Wood Preservation Ltd v Prior* is binding on us for
what it decided. I would be unwilling to apply it to any case where the vendor
retained more than a mere legal shell of ownership. The grantor of an option which
has not been exercised retains much more than that. For the reasons given by Lloyd
LJ and by Millett J at first instance, I agree that, within the meaning of s 532(3), the
beneficial ownership in the 5% of the shares was vested in Sainsburys.

In regard to the second question I do not wish to add anything to the reasoning of Lloyd LJ and of Millett J. In my opinion the 'arrangements' referred to in para 5(3) *a* of Sch 12 to the Finance Act 1973 were simply not intended to include a transaction of the kind effected by the option agreement in this case.

I too would dismiss this appeal.

RALPH GIBSON LJ. I agree with both judgments.

Appeal dismissed with costs. Leave to appeal to the House of Lords refused.

Solicitors: *Solicitor of Inland Revenue; Denton Hall Burgin & Warrens* (for Sainsburys).

Rengan Krishnan Esq   Barrister.

Cronin (trading as Cronin Driving School) v Customs and Excise Commissioners

QUEEN'S BENCH DIVISION (CROWN OFFICE LIST)
BROOKE J
8, 22 MAY 1991

Value added tax – Supply of goods or services – Supply – Driving school – Supply of driving tuition under franchise agreement with driving school franchisor by franchisee driving instructors – Whether instructors supplying services to franchisor who then supplied tuition services to the general public – Whether alternatively franchisor supplying back-up services to instructors who supplied tuition directly to the public.

The franchisor, Mr Cronin, carried on the business of Cronin Driving School. The driving instructors at the school operated under a franchise agreement and were treated as self-employed for tax and national insurance purposes. Under the franchise agreement, Mr Cronin provided back-up services such as facilities for the screening of video lessons, stationery, appointment cards and handouts all headed 'Cronin Driving School', a central inquiry point and booking service and advertisement of Cronin Driving School in the Yellow Pages. He also supplied the instructors with cars bearing the logo of Cronin Driving School, and was responsible for having the cars taxed and insured, and for repair and maintenance costs. The instructors were not bound by any timetable and were free to advertise in their own names, to have their own names and numbers printed on their cars and to book pupils directly. Most of those pupils who booked centrally requested a specific instructor, but under the franchise agreement the few who did not were distributed equally between instructors. Meetings were held at Mr Cronin's address from time to time to agree a standard tuition fee. A franchise fee which was geared to the standard tuition fee was payable to Mr Cronin by each instructor in respect of each lesson given (except for lessons given on Sundays or late evenings). Instructors were allowed to charge pupils at a rate higher than the standard fee without paying an increased franchise fee if they had to travel unusual distances to and from the point of pick up. The Commissioners of Customs and Excise decided that, as supplier of driving tuition to the public, Mr Cronin was liable to account for value added tax in respect of the tuition fees charged to members of the public by the instructors. Mr Cronin appealed to a value added tax tribunal under s 40(1) of the Value Added Tax Act 1983. The tribunal dismissed the appeal, holding that the driving instructors were self-employed but that the driving tuition was supplied to the public by Mr Cronin, the instructors not being in business on their own account. Mr Cronin appealed to the High Court, contending that the tribunal had erred in law in finding that the driving tuition was supplied by him and in failing to hold that driving tuition was supplied directly to the public by the self-employed franchisee instructors.

Held – The tribunal had not misdirected itself as to the law but had correctly addressed the question whether the driving school business was supplying services to the public via the agency of four self-employed instructors. The tribunal's finding that the instructors were self-employed was not inconsistent with its finding that they were 'not really [in] business on their own account'. There were no grounds for interfering with the tribunal's decision and the appeal would accordingly be dismissed.

Notes

For the meaning of supply, see De Voil: Value Added Tax A5.02.   *a*

Cases referred to in judgment

Bank voor Handel en Scheepvaart NV v Slatford [1953] 1 QB 248, [1952] 2 All ER 956, CA.
Edwards (Inspector of Taxes) v Bairstow [1956] AC 14, [1955] 3 All ER 48, 36 TC *b* 207, HL.
Montreal v Montreal Locomotive Works and A-G for Canada [1947] 1 DLR 161, PC.
Market Investigations Ltd v Minister of Social Security [1969] 2 QB 173, [1968] 3 All ER 732.
New Way School of Motoring Ltd v Customs and Excise Comrs (1979) VATTR 57.
O'Kelly v Trusthouse Forte plc [1984] QB 90, [1983] 3 All ER 456, CA.   *c*
Potter v Customs and Excise Comrs [1985] STC 45, CA.
United States of America v Silk (1946) 331 US 704.

Cases also cited

Customs and Excise Comrs v Paget [1989] STC 773.   *d*
BSM (1257) Ltd v Secretary of State for Social Services [1978] ICR 894.

Appeal

Mr Cronin appealed against a decision of a London value added tax tribunal released on 29 May 1990 dismissing the appeal against the decision of the Commissioners of *e* Customs and Excise that Mr Cronin as supplier of tuition to the public was liable to account for value added tax on tuition fees charged by franchisee driving instructors.

Michael Sherry for Mr Cronin.
Alison Foster for the commissioners.   *f*

Cur adv vult

22 May. The following judgment was delivered.

    g

BROOKE J. In this matter Mr John Cronin, trading as Cronin Driving School, is appealing to the High Court on a point of law pursuant to the Tribunal and Inquiries (Value Added Tax Tribunals) Order 1972, SI 1972/1210, from a decision of the London value added tax tribunal given on 29 May 1990. By that decision the tribunal chairman, Mr Neil Elles, dismissed Mr Cronin's appeal under s 40(1) of the Value Added Tax Act 1983 (the 1983 Act) from a decision of the Commissioners of *h* Customs and Excise that as a driving school franchisor he was liable to account for value added tax in respect of the fees charged to members of the public by franchisee instructors on the basis that he supplied services of driving tuition to the public through the medium of those instructors. The grounds on which Mr Cronin seeks an order that that decision be reversed are that the tribunal erred in law in holding that the driving tuition was supplied by Mr Cronin and in failing to hold that it was *j* supplied by the franchisee instructors.

An unusual feature of this case is that the tribunal held that the franchisee instructors were carrying on business in a self-employed capacity on their own account and were not in a master–servant relationship with Mr Cronin. Although the commissioners disputed this issue before the tribunal they did not contest the tribunal's decision before me. Accordingly the sole issue with which I was concerned

was the question whether, in doing the work which the franchisee instructors did,
they were supplying their services to Mr Cronin, who in turn was supplying the
services of a driving school to members of the public who sought driving lessons, or
whether Mr Cronin was simply involved in supplying back-up services to franchisee
instructors who were supplying their services as driving instructors to the public
direct.

The tribunal heard evidence from Mr Cronin and from Mr Grindley, who was
one of four driving instructors who had signed identical franchise agreements with
Mr Cronin.

It will be convenient to set out the tribunal's findings of fact by considering a
number of different aspects of the relationships between Mr Cronin, the four
instructors and the driving school pupils in turn.

For all practical purposes Mr Cronin supplied the capital, in the sense of supplying
a headquarters at which training lessons by video were available for the pupils of all
four instructors and from which stationery, appointment cards and training
handouts, all of which bore the heading of 'Cronin Driving School', were issued to
each instructor, and from which advertisements advertising the driving school were
inserted in the Yellow Pages. Mr Cronin also supplied each instructor with a car
which he might use not only for giving driving instruction to his pupils but also for
his own private purposes. Mr Cronin was responsible for having the cars taxed and
insured and for all their running repairs: he was also responsible for paying for
maintenance services after each 6,000 miles. All that the instructor was bound to do
was to keep the car clean and in good condition and to pay the cost of all petrol and
oil.

All the motor cars bore the 'logo' of the Cronin Driving School. However, each
instructor was permitted, if he wished, to have his own name and telephone number
painted on the car which was issued to him.

In addition to the advertisements which Mr Cronin placed in the Yellow Pages,
each instructor was entitled to advertise in his own name. Mr Grindley, for example,
did so in the local Thomson's Directory and also on postcards in shop windows, and
his evidence that most of his work came from these advertisements and from personal
recommendations was accepted by the tribunal. Mr Cronin, for his part, was unable
to say how much business was generated from the advertisements he placed in the
Yellow Pages.

Mr Cronin was obliged under his agreements with the instructors to maintain an
inquiry point and booking service in respect of inquiries from prospective new
pupils who wished to take driving lessons with Cronin Driving School. The tribunal
appears to have accepted his evidence that 95% of the pupils who approached him
asked for a specific instructor. The remaining 5% were distributed between the
instructors equally in accordance with a provision which obliged him to give each
instructor an equitable proportion of such unallocated pupils. The tribunal also
found as a fact that many pupils booked direct with an instructor without going
through the central booking service.

Under the franchise agreements, each instructor was bound to pay Mr Cronin
what was described as a franchise fee of a determined amount in respect of each
lesson he gave and for which he was paid by a pupil whom he instructed. They
rendered him an account each week which showed the number of lessons they had
given and the lesson fees they had received. The franchise fee was said to be geared
to the current lesson fees and the then current cost of the lesson fees was set out in
the agreements. It was clearly envisaged in the agreements that instructors would
be at liberty to charge pupils at a higher rate than the current lesson fee if they had
to travel unusual distances to and from the point of pick up. In such cases, however,
it was agreed that the franchise fee would remain unaltered. The agreements
provided that in the event of any general revision of the lesson fee the amount of the
franchise fee would be subject to renegotiation between Mr Cronin and the
instructors.

At the time of the hearing before the tribunal the current lesson fee was £13·00 and the current franchise fee was £5·40. Each instructor, therefore, retained £7·60 *a* out of the total fee which he was paid. The tribunal found as a fact that meetings were held from time to time at Mr Cronin's address when he and the instructors might reach agreement about increases which should be made to the standard lesson fee. If it was increased the franchise fee would also be renegotiated. Although Mr Grindley, who was described by the tribunal as being a man of an independent character who gave robust evidence, sought to persuade the tribunal that instructors *b* were at liberty to charge pupils what they wished, the tribunal rejected his evidence. It held that this freedom was more apparent than real and that instructors in practice conformed to the basic lesson fee which was agreed at these meetings. The only exception to this related to small marginal increases, no doubt connected with unusual travelling distances to and from an individual pupil's home.

It was within this agreed framework that each instructor would negotiate his *c* lesson fee with each individual pupil, who would already have been told the standard lesson fee if he had rung up the central inquiry point and booking service. The tribunal appears to have found that Mr Grindley sometimes gave free lessons. In such a case, however, he would still account to Mr Cronin for the franchise fee. It also found that when instructors gave lessons on Sundays or late in the evening, they were not expected to account to Mr Cronin for those lessons: in Mr Cronin's words, *d* this had always been done to keep them happy. The tribunal also received unchallenged evidence, which it apparently accepted, from Mr Grindley that he regarded his pupils as having a personal relationship with him and that if he left the Cronin Driving School and went elsewhere his pupils would follow him.

The tribunal found that Mr Cronin accepted the instructors' weekly returns on trust without checking their figures and that none of them were required to give any *e* particular number of lessons; if they gave no lessons they received no fees, and they were not bound by a timetable of any kind. The instructors were all treated for income tax and national insurance purposes as self-employed persons.

In order to determine whether a master–servant relationship existed between Mr Cronin and the four instructors, the tribunal applied the test suggested by Lord Wright in *Montreal v Montreal Locomotive Works and A-G for Canada* [1947] *f* 1 DLR 161 which had been applied in the past by value added tax tribunals in this type of case, most notably in *New Way School of Motoring Ltd v Customs and Excise Comrs* (1979) VATTR 57 at 65–66. In the *Montreal* case Lord Wright said (at 169):

'In earlier cases a single test, such as the presence or absence of control, was often relied on to determine whether the case was one of master and servant, mostly in order to decide issues of tortious liability on the part of the master or *g* superior. In the more complex conditions of modern industry, more complicated tests have often to be applied. It has been suggested that a fourfold test would in some cases be more appropriate, a complex involving (1) control; (2) ownership of the tools; (3) chance of profit; (4) risk of loss. Control in itself is not always conclusive. Thus the master of a chartered vessel is generally the employee of the shipowner though the charterer can direct the employment of *h* the vessel. Again the law often limits the employer's right to interfere with the employee's conduct, as also do trade union regulations. In many cases the question can only be settled by examining the whole of the various elements which constitute the relationship between the parties. In this way it is in some cases possible to decide the issue by raising as the crucial question whose business is it, or in other words by asking whether the party is carrying on the *j* business, in the sense of carrying it on for himself or on his own behalf and not merely for a superior.'

In applying this fourfold test the tribunal found that the degree of control was apparently light, the 'tools of the trade' were owned and insured by Mr Cronin; that because there was no real freedom in negotiating the lesson fee there was no chance

of the instructors making a profit on their own account; and conversely that the
instructors faced no real risk of loss. It balanced all these matters against each other
and concluded that they were independent contractors and not in a master–servant
relationship with Mr Cronin. As I have already said, there is no challenge to that
part of the decision.

The judgment of the tribunal then continued:

> 'That does not, however, conclude the matter in favour of [Mr Cronin]
> because the point still remains to be decided whether the Instructors were really
> in business on their own account or were providing the services of tuition on
> behalf of [Mr Cronin].'

The tribunal then considered the factual evidence which I have already summarised,
and concluded in these terms:

> 'The facts show that the Instructors were independent in the sense that they
> could give as many lessons as they wished and they were bound by no tight time
> schedule. Their independent standing was emphasised by the robust nature of
> Mr Grindley's evidence and his independent character. On the other hand the
> Instructors were using cars owned by [Mr Cronin] and bearing the logo of
> "J. Cronin's Driving School" [sic], although their names and telephone numbers
> were also permitted to be shown on the cars. Much has been made by
> Mr Grindley of the freedom of Instructors to charge what they wished, but I
> find that this freedom was more apparent than real, in that Instructors
> conformed to the basic fee which was agreed by consensus of all the Instructors.
> It is also apparent that the Instructors depended on [Mr Cronin] for
> documentation and also on the meetings for tuition in the evenings where
> videos were shown. Having carefully considered the evidence before me and
> the submissions of both parties I reach the conclusion that the driving tuition
> was supplied by [Mr Cronin] and that the Instructors were not really [in]
> business on their own account.'

Before I consider the attack which was made on these findings I must first say
something about the relevant background of value added tax law and the parameters
within which the High Court is permitted to interfere with a finding by a value
added tax tribunal in a case like this.

By s 2(1) of the 1983 Act, tax is to be 'charged on any supply of goods or services
made in the United Kingdom, where it is a taxable supply made by a taxable person
in the course or furtherance of any business carried on by him'. By s 3(2)(*a*) '"supply"
. . . includes all forms of supply', and by s 3(2)(*b*) 'anything which is not a supply of
goods but is done for a consideration . . . is a supply of services'. By para 1 of Sch 1 to
the 1983 Act, a person who makes taxable supplies is liable to be registered if the
value of his taxable supplies exceeds certain limits, and if the commissioners consider
an unregistered person to be registrable and place his name on the register he is
entitled to appeal to a tribunal against registration pursuant to s 40(1)(*a*) of the 1983
Act.

It is for this reason that the tribunal in my judgment correctly identified the issue
it had to decide in these terms:

> 'The question for the decision of this tribunal is who provided the services,
> and in particular whether the driving tuition was provided by [Mr Cronin] or
> whether it was provided by each individual Instructor.'

This is in my judgment only a different way of posing the critical issue from the
words I adopted towards the start of this judgment—

> '. . . the sole issue with which I was concerned was the question whether, in
> doing the work which the franchisee instructors did, they were supplying their
> services to Mr Cronin, who in turn was supplying the services of a driving

school to members of the public who sought driving lessons, or whether
Mr Cronin was simply involved in supplying back-up services to franchisee   *a*
instructors who were supplying their services as driving instructors to the public
direct.'

Because there was an unchallenged finding of fact that not only Mr Cronin but
also the four instructors were self-employed people carrying on business on their
own account, the only issue the tribunal had to decide was whether the instructors   *b*
were supplying their services upwards to Mr Cronin, who deployed their services in
the driving school services he supplied to the public, or whether they were, as I have
said, supplying services to the public direct.

A comparable issue arose in *Potter v Customs and Excise Comrs* [1985] STC 45, a
case involving the relationship between tupperware salesmen and wholesale
distributors of tupperware. In that case the Court of Appeal held that the value   *c*
added tax tribunal had asked itself the right question when it said (at 50):

> 'I take the view that the question for my determination is "whether the
> [taxpayers] expressly or impliedly agreed with their dealers that their dealers
> should represent them or act on their behalf in selling and supplying tupperware
> to guests at the parties, and their dealers similarly agreed with the [taxpayers]
> to represent them or so to act".'   *d*

Robert Goff LJ put the issue very simply in these terms (at 53):

> 'The question which the chairman of the tribunal (Lord Grantchester QC)
> had to determine was whether the relationship between distributors and dealers
> of tupperware was that of principal and agent, under which the dealers acted as
> agents for the distributors in selling tupperware to customers; or whether the   *e*
> relationship between them was that of vendor and purchaser, under which the
> dealers bought the tupperware from the distributors and then themselves sold
> it to the customers as principals.'

As to this court's power to interfere with the decision of a value added tax tribunal in this class of case, the position has been helpfully set out by Sir John   *f*
Donaldson MR in *O'Kelly v Trusthouse Forte plc* [1984] QB 90, in a passage with
which Fox LJ (at 119–121) agreed in different language.

Sir John Donaldson MR said (at 122–123):

> 'The judgment of the appeal tribunal in this case suggests that there is a
> difference of judicial view as to whether the question "Is a contract a contract of
> employment or a contract for services?" is a mixed question of fact and law or a   *g*
> question of law, but I do rather doubt whether the triple categorisation of issues
> as "fact", "law" and "mixed fact and law" is very helpful in the context of the
> jurisdiction of the appeal tribunal. The appeal tribunal is a court with a statutory
> jurisdiction. So far as is material, that jurisdiction is limited to hearing appeals
> on questions of law arising from any decision of, or arising in any proceedings
> before, an industrial tribunal: section 136(1) of the Employment Protection   *h*
> (Consolidation) Act 1978. If it is to vary or reverse a decision of an industrial
> tribunal it has to be satisfied that the tribunal has erred on a question of law.
> Whilst it may be convenient for some purposes to refer to questions of "pure"
> law as contrasted with "mixed" questions of fact and law, the fact is that the
> appeal tribunal has no jurisdiction to consider any question of mixed fact and
> law until it has purified or distilled the mixture and extracted a question of pure   *j*
> law. The purification methods are well known. In the last analysis all courts
> have to direct themselves as to the law and then apply those directions in finding
> the facts (in relation to admissibility and relevance) and to the facts as so found.
> When reviewing such a decision, the only problem is to divine the direction on
> law which the lower court gave to itself. Sometimes it will have been expressed
> in its reasons, but more often it has to be inferred. This is the point of temptation
> for the appellate court. It may well have a shrewd suspicion, or gut reaction,

that it would have reached a different decision, but it must never forget that
this may be because it thinks that it would have found or weighed the facts
differently. Unpalatable though it may be on occasion, it must loyally accept
the conclusions of fact with which it is presented and, accepting those
conclusions, it must be satisfied that there *must* have been a misdirection on a
question of law before it can intervene. Unless the direction on law has been
expressed, it can only be so satisfied if, in its opinion, no reasonable tribunal,
properly directing itself on the relevant questions of law, could have reached
the conclusion under appeal. This is a heavy burden on an appellant. I would
have thought that all this was trite law, but if it is not, it is set out with the
greatest possible clarity in *Edwards v Bairstow* [1956] AC 14.'

The principal ground on which the tribunal's decision was attacked was that after
making the finding as to self-employed status the tribunal went on to say:

'That does not, however, conclude the matter in favour of [Mr Cronin]
because the point still remains to be decided whether the Instructors were really
in business on their own account or were providing the services of tuition on
behalf of [Mr Cronin].'

It was submitted that this passage suggested a confusion of thought because in the
previous sentence the tribunal had held that the instructors were independent
contractors which, it was said, was equivalent to finding that they were really in
business on their own account, and that this finding effectively concluded the whole
dispute in favour of Mr Cronin. My attention was drawn not only to the final
sentence in the passage in Lord Wright's judgment in the *Montreal* case to which I
have already referred, but also to a passage in the judgment of Cooke J in *Market
Investigations Ltd v Minister of Social Security* [1969] 2 QB 173 at 184:

'The observations of Lord Wright [in the *Montreal* case], of Denning LJ [in
Bank voor Handel en Scheepvaart NV v Slatford [1953] 1 QB 248] and of the
judges of the Supreme Court [in *United States of America v Silk* (1946) 331 US
704] suggest that the fundamental test to be applied is this: "Is the person who
has engaged himself to perform these services performing them as a person in
business on his own account?" If the answer to that question is "yes", then the
contract is a contract for services. If the answer is "no", then the contract is a
contract of service.'

I am not, however, satisfied that the tribunal did fall into error in the way that is
suggested. The use of the words 'whether the Instructors were really in business on
their own account' might suggest that it did, but words used by tribunals should not
be pored over with meticulous care by lawyers as if they were the language of a
statute. That the tribunal was asking itself the right questions is in my judgment
quite clear from two passages:

(1) 'The question for the decision of this tribunal is who provided the services,
and in particular whether the driving tuition was provided by [Mr Cronin] or
whether it was provided by each individual Instructor.'
(2) 'It was contended by Mr Ferrington [who appeared for Mr Cronin] on
the other hand that the Instructors were in business on their own account and
did not give their tuition on behalf of or as agent for [Mr Cronin].'

These passages make it quite clear in my judgment that the tribunal was correctly
addressing the question whether there was one driving school business, Mr Cronin's,
supplying services to the public through the agency of the four self-employed
instructors or four such businesses, each deriving back-up help, as a true franchisee
often does from its franchisor, from Mr Cronin, and that this is the issue which the
tribunal chairman was addressing when he concluded:

'Having carefully considered the evidence before me and the submissions of
both parties I reach the conclusion that the driving tuition was supplied by

[Mr Cronin] and that the Instructors were not really [in] business on their own
account.'

In these circumstances I do not find this conclusion inconsistent with the finding
that the four instructors were self-employed. As I suggested in argument, the
position seems to me to be comparable to that in which self-employed barristers
provide their services for a fee as tutors to the Inns of Court School of Law. To the
extent that they do so they are supplying their services upwards to the school who
deploys their services in the teaching it provides to its students, but they are none
the less still self-employed barristers carrying on business on their own account.

In fact, if the position was different and these four instructors were really all
supplying services direct to the public as different independent emanations of the
Cronin Driving School then the fee fixing arrangements which are described in the
tribunal's decision would appear to constitute a registrable agreement under
restrictive trade practices legislation and would be void in the absence of registration.

Counsel for Mr Cronin suggested a number of factors which pointed to a
conclusion that the instructors were supplying driving school services direct to the
public and not as agents for Mr Cronin, viz that they were allowed to insert Yellow
Pages advertisements in their own name, that they could give as many lessons as
they wished, that they were bound by no tight time schedule, that they were allowed
to show their own names and telephone numbers on the cars, that they were free to
set their own fee and that in fact they agreed the basic fee together. On the other
hand, counsel for the commissioners pointed to 12 matters which supported the
tribunal's finding, viz that Mr Cronin provided the car, that he taxed and insured
it, that he had it serviced and maintained and paid for all spare parts, that he
provided a replacement car, that he paid for all car repairs, that he guaranteed each
instructor a fair share of all 'unallocated' bookings, that the school's name was on the
stationery, that the film-shows were on Mr Cronin's premises, that the school had
an absolute discretion as to advertising, that the school's name (not necessarily
exclusively) was on each car, that the instructors were not free to charge any fee they
chose nor had they any real freedom to negotiate and that the instructors depended
on Mr Cronin for documentation.

This recital of the arguments tending in each direction shows very clearly that a
decision in a case like this may not be an easy one, and that on deceptively similar-
looking factors different tribunals may come to different decisions. Parliament has,
however, entrusted the decision-making to the tribunal. Provided that it has not
misdirected itself as to the law to apply, the High Court could only interfere if it was
satisfied that in its opinion no reasonable tribunal could have reached the decision of
fact under appeal. I can see no such ground for interfering with the careful decision
of the tribunal in the present case.

Finally, counsel for Mr Cronin made some interesting submissions about the
essential nature of franchise agreements and suggested that the tribunal had been
confused because of the perception, through the licensed use of the franchisor's
name, that there was a single business whereas in reality there were more than one,
all bearing the same name. He submitted rather unconvincingly that one normal
feature of a franchise agreement, that the franchisee takes an independent commercial
risk, may be of limited significance when the arrangement involves the provision of
a professional service.

While I accept that the tribunal may have placed rather more weight on the use
of the common name than it might have done if it had had the benefit of counsel's
arguments, I can see no grounds for interfering with its decision on this account.
The decision of fact was one for the tribunal and, although if I had been the decision-
maker I might have placed more weight on some facts and less on others, I must not
usurp the function bestowed by Parliament on the tribunal as the fact-finding body.

For all these reasons the appeal must be dismissed. I would add, by way of
addendum, that those who are engaged in the business of drafting so-called franchise

agreements in these circumstances as a means of avoiding fiscal liabilities would do well, on the evidence in this case, to consider the effect of restrictive trade practices legislation on the arrangements they create.

Appeal dismissed with costs. Leave to appeal to the Court of Appeal refused.

Solicitors: *Collyer-Bristow* for Mr Cronin; *Solicitor for the Customs and Excise.*

Rengan Krishnan Esq   Barrister.

Kirkham v Williams (Inspector of Taxes)

COURT OF APPEAL, CIVIL DIVISION
LLOYD, NOURSE AND RALPH GIBSON LJJ
24, 25 APRIL, 24 MAY 1991

Profits – Capital or income receipts – Land – Disposal – Taxpayer acquiring site to be used as office and for storage of his demolition and plant hire equipment – Development of land – Erection of dwelling house on site – Sale of site and purchase of new premises to carry on his business – Income and Corporation Taxes Act 1970, s 109.

The taxpayer worked on his own account as a general dealer, demolition contractor and hirer of plant. In May 1977 he purchased a ten-acre site including a mill. In October 1977, after he had acquired the site, he applied for planning permission to erect an agricultural worker's dwelling. That application was refused. Planning permission was granted in 1980 for the erection of a dwelling house, which the taxpayer built himself. He sold the whole site and house in October 1982 and moved to a farm. The commissioners found that the taxpayer did not terminate his business as a general dealer and demolition contractor when he moved to his new premises. The gain on the sale was assessed under Sch D, Case I for the year 1982–83 as a trading profit within s 109[a] of the Income and Corporation Taxes Act 1970. The taxpayer claimed that the site was a capital asset of his business and that the gain realised on its sale was chargeable to capital gains tax and therefore capable of being rolled over and set against the purchase price of his new premises. The General Commissioners found that the site was acquired principally to provide office accommodation and storage space for his demolition and plant hire business. The commissioners further found that the taxpayer did not intend to use the whole of the land for office and storage space nor to live there. He did intend, however, to carry on limited farming activities on the land. The commissioners held that the purchase, development and resale of the site was an adventure in the nature of trade and confirmed the assessment under Sch D, Case I. Vinelott J dismissed the taxpayer's appeal, holding that there was ample foundation for the conclusion that the taxpayer, in order to acquire a site for his demolition and plant hire business, had embarked on a transaction which had all the characteristics of trading and that therefore the commissioners' conclusions were consistent with their findings of fact. The taxpayer appealed on the grounds, inter alia: (a) that in the case stated by the commissioners there was no finding of fact nor could such a finding be properly inferred that at the time of the acquisition of the site the taxpayer had intended to develop the site for the purposes of resale at a profit; (b) that therefore the commissioners' conclusion that the subsequent purchase, development and sale of the site by the taxpayer was an adventure in the nature of trade was inconsistent with their findings of fact, in particular with their finding that the site was acquired principally to provide office accommodation and storage space.

Held – (Ralph Gibson LJ dissenting). The true and only reasonable conclusion from the facts found was that the site had been acquired by the taxpayer as a capital asset and it was not therefore open to the commissioners to determine that the purchase, development and sale of the site by the taxpayer was an adventure in the nature of trade.

Per Nourse LJ. The taxpayer's acquisition of the site viewed on its own was an equivocal transaction as one could not determine whether the property was acquired as trading stock or as a capital asset. Therefore account had to be taken of its purpose. The commissioners' express finding as to the principal purpose characterised the

---

a   Section 109, so far as material, provides: 'Tax under Schedule D shall be charged under ... Case I ... in respect of any trade carried on in the United Kingdom or elsewhere ...'

transaction as the acquisition of a capital asset. It could properly be inferred from the commissioners' primary findings of fact that the subsidiary purpose had been the development and sale of the site. However, this subsidiary purpose was severely circumscribed and its implementation indefinite in point of time. Accordingly, it was not open to the commissioners, having made a finding which characterised the transaction as an acquisition of a capital asset, to deny it that character by reason of an intention thus circumscribed and indefinite.

Per Lloyd LJ. The commissioners had not made an express finding that the taxpayer's subsidiary purpose in acquiring the site was a trading purpose. Accordingly, it was not open to the court to draw an inference that the commissioners might have found that the taxpayer's subsidiary purpose was a trading purpose in order to support the commissioners' conclusion. The commissioners' only other finding in relation to the taxpayer's purposes in acquiring the site was that he intended to carry on limited farming. The taxpayer's acquisition of the site was therefore not an equivocal transaction since neither of the two purposes found by the commissioners was a trading purpose. It was clear that they must have held that the gain on the sale of the site was assessable as a trading profit because of a subsequent change of intention on the part of the taxpayer. However, there was no evidence to support the view that such a change had occurred, and the commissioners had therefore erred in law.

Accordingly, the appeal would be allowed and the assessments would be discharged.

Notes

For trading transaction or capital realisation, see Simon's Taxes B3.231.

For what constitutes trading in land, see ibid, B3.616–618.

For the Income and Corporation Taxes Act 1970, ss 109, 488 (now the Income and Corporation Taxes Act 1988, ss 18, 776), see ibid, Part G1.

Cases referred to in judgments

Cunliffe v Goodman [1950] 2 KB 237, [1950] 1 All ER 720, CA.
Edwards (Inspector of Taxes) v Bairstow [1956] AC 14, [1955] 3 All ER 48, 36 TC 207, HL.
Ensign Tankers (Leasing) Ltd v Stokes (Inspector of Taxes) [1989] STC 705, [1989] 1 WLR 1222; [1991] STC 136, [1991] 1 WLR 341, CA.
Iswera v IRC [1965] 1 WLR 663, PC.
Overseas Containers (Finance) Ltd v Stoker (Inspector of Taxes) [1989] STC 364, [1989] 1 WLR 606, CA.
Royal Choral Society v IRC [1943] 2 All ER 101, 25 TC 263.
Sharkey (Inspector of Taxes) v Wernher [1956] AC 58, [1955] 3 All ER 493, 36 TC 275, HL.
Simmons (as liquidator of Lionel Simmons Properties Ltd) v IRC [1980] STC 350, [1980] 1 WLR 1196, [1980] 2 All ER 798, 53 TC 461, HL.
Taylor v Good (Inspector of Taxes) [1973] STC 383, [1973] 1 WLR 1249, [1973] 2 All ER 785; *rvsd* [1974] STC 148, [1974] 1 WLR 556, [1974] 1 All ER 1137, 49 TC 277, CA.

Cases also cited

Bromilow & Edwards Ltd v IRC [1969] 1 WLR 1180, [1969] 3 All ER 536; [1970] 1 WLR 128, [1970] 1 All ER 174, 46 TC 128, CA.
Cooksey and Bibbey v Rednall (Inspector of Taxes) (1949) 30 TC 514.
Golder (Inspector of Taxes) v Great Boulder Proprietary Gold Mines Ltd (1952) 33 TC 75.

Appeal

William Brian Kirkham, the taxpayer, appealed against the decision of Vinelott J
dated 13 February 1989 (see [1989] STC 333) upholding the General Commissioners'
determination that the purchase, development and sale of a plot of land by the
taxpayer was an adventure in the nature of trade and the gain realised was assessable
under Sch D, Case 1 as a trading profit. The facts are set out in the judgment of
Nourse LJ.

Giles Goodfellow for the taxpayer.
Launcelot Henderson for the Crown.

Cur adv vult

24 May. The following judgments were delivered.

NOURSE LJ (giving the first judgment at the invitation of Lloyd LJ). The question
here is whether it was open to the General Commissioners for the division of
Macclesfield to decide that the purchase, development and sale of a piece of land
was an adventure in the nature of trade giving rise to a charge for income tax under
Sch D, Case I. On an appeal by the taxpayer to the High Court by way of case stated
Vinelott J held that it was. The taxpayer now brings a further appeal to this court.
In both courts he has contended that the true and only reasonable conclusion from
the facts found by the commissioners is that the transaction was not an adventure in
the nature of trade.

The facts are fully stated or referred to in the judgment of Vinelott J (see [1989]
STC 333), where the case stated is also set out in full. I will restate the facts so far as
the arguments advanced on this appeal make it necessary to do so.

From June 1974 to November 1982 the taxpayer, Mr William Brian Kirkham,
worked on his own account as a general dealer and demolition contractor doing a
limited amount of farming as well. His work included plant hire, sub-contract work,
levelling, draining and ditching. During that period he and his family lived at Purdy
House, 81 Rudyard Road, Biddulph Moor, Stoke-on-Trent.

The facts on which the outcome of this appeal mainly depend are stated in
para 5(ii), (iii) and (iv) of the case stated (see [1989] STC 333 at 335). I will restate
them in the commissioners' own words, although I have rearranged the sentences in
para 5(iii) so that they conform with what both sides agree is their chronological
sequence:

'(ii) ... Whilst living at Purdy House [the taxpayer] experienced difficulties
with the Local Authority over the storage of demolition materials at his Mother's
address at Fairview, Biddulph Moor, Staffordshire. (iii) An opportunity
presented itself to [the taxpayer] to carry out demolition works at Havannah
Mills, Congleton, Cheshire, for a Mr Radivan. The Contract involved the
demolition of one of the two Mills which were on site, together with five
Cottages and some outbuildings. After the Contract had been concluded the
owner of Havannah Mills offered to sell [the taxpayer] what was left, which by
that time comprised of one remaining Mill and ten acres of adjoining land. The
site was acquired principally to provide office and storage space for [the
taxpayer's] demolition and Plant Hire business. Havannah Mills was purchased
in [the taxpayer's] sole name for the sum of £17,000 by a Conveyance dated 9th
May 1978. Of the purchase price £8,000 was left outstanding under a private
Mortgage with the Vendor Mr Radivan. Subsequently [the taxpayer] used the
site for the storage of materials for use in connection with his business. He used
part of the Mill as his office. He grew a few crops on the land and bought a few
calves for fattening up for re-sale; but the level of his farming activities in this
regard were very limited to the extent that they were never recorded in his

a

books of Account. The site continued to be used in these various ways until its sale in October 1982. (iv) Subsequently in or about October 1978 [the taxpayer] applied for Planning Permission for the erection of an Agricultural workers dwelling at Havannah Mills. That application was refused. A further Application was submitted to the Local Planning Authority and Outline Planning Permission was granted on 22nd August 1980 for the erection of an Industrial/Agricultural Dwellinghouse for [the taxpayer] at The Old Mill,

b

Havannah Lane, Eaton . . .'

Before the judge an additional fact was agreed, namely that the contract to purchase Havannah Mills was entered into by the taxpayer in the summer of 1977 at the latest. It is also agreed that the reference in para 5(iv) to October 1978 as being the month when the taxpayer first made an application for planning permission is

c

an error for October 1977. It is therefore agreed that the taxpayer entered into the contract before making any application for planning permission.

Following the grant of outline planning permission on 22 August 1980 the taxpayer instructed a local builder to draw up plans for the construction of a dwelling house on the property and thereafter, with some assistance from his brother-in-law and over a period of about nine months, he erected a dwelling house on the property.

d

In para 5(vii) of the case stated we find this: 'It was never [the taxpayer's] intention at any time to purchase Havannah Mills as a residence for himself and his family.'

In about November 1980, before he erected the dwelling house at Havannah Mills, the taxpayer first became interested in another property, Sandy Lane Farm, Giants Wood Lane, Hulme Walfield, Congleton, Cheshire. On 6 October 1982 Havannah Mills was sold by the taxpayer for £110,000, realising a net profit of

e

£90,971. Completion of the sale took place on 29 October 1982. On 3 June 1982 contracts had been exchanged for the purchase of Sandy Lane Farm in the joint names of the taxpayer and his wife at a price of £176,000. Completion of the purchase took place on 9 November 1982. In the same month the taxpayer and his family moved into Sandy Lane Farm as their home. Purdy House was sold in September 1983 for £13,000. The commissioners found that the taxpayer did not

f

entirely cease in business as a general dealer and demolition contractor when he moved into Sandy Lane Farm, but that thereafter he increased his interest in business as a farmer.

In due course the inspector of taxes assessed the taxpayer to income tax for the year 1982–83 under Sch D, Case I on a sum of £91,000, being the approximate amount of the net profit on the sale of Havannah Mills. The business of the taxpayer

g

not having included dealings in land, the assessment can only be supported if the purchase, development and sale of Havannah Mills was an adventure in the nature of trade, for which purpose it must, inter alia, have been acquired as trading stock, that is to say with the intention of disposing of it at a profit. The taxpayer has throughout contended that Havannah Mills was acquired not as trading stock but as a capital asset of his business, on whose disposal at a profit capital gains tax was

h

chargeable, subject to roll over relief allowable by virtue of his purchase of Sandy Lane Farm. It is not appropriate to determine the taxpayer's liability for capital gains tax unless and until he succeeds in defeating the claim for income tax, and no such determination has been made. Before the commissioners the Crown raised an alternative claim for income tax under Sch D, Case VI pursuant to s 488 of the Income and Corporation Taxes Act 1970, which relates to artificial transactions in

j

land. That claim was rejected by the commissioners and there has been no attempt to revive it.

The commissioners expressed their decision (at 336) as follows:

'We the Commissioners, having carefully considered all the evidence put before us were of the opinion that the Profits of £90,971 arising on the sale of Havannah Mills were assessable under Case I of Schedule D.'

In other words, it must be assumed that they were of the opinion, inter alia, that Havannah Mills was acquired as trading stock and not as a capital asset of the taxpayer's business. The commissioners gave no reasons for their decision. In that state of affairs the taxpayer, in order to succeed on an appeal to the court, must show that the facts which they found are such that no person acting judicially and properly instructed as to the relevant law could come to the same conclusion or, if you prefer, that the true and only reasonable conclusion from the facts found contradicts the decision (see *Edwards (Inspector of Taxes) v Bairstow* [1956] AC 14 at 36, 36 TC 207 at 229 per Lord Radcliffe).

The convenient course is for me to start with the facts found by the commissioners, including inferences which they could properly draw from the primary facts found. It cannot be doubted that their most significant finding was that 'the site' was acquired principally to provide office and storage space for the taxpayer's demolition and plant hire business, being one which followed their earlier finding that the taxpayer had experienced difficulties with the local authority over the storage of demolition materials at his mother's address. The first question which arises out of this finding is what did the commissioners mean by 'the site'? Although the case stated, especially perhaps in para 5(iii), is not artistically drawn, I am in no doubt that in referring to the site, they intended throughout to refer to the whole of the site, that being the area of land whose purchase, development and sale had given rise to the assessment.

And so the commissioners found that the taxpayer's principal purpose in acquiring the site as a whole was the provision of office and storage space for his business. I see no reason why that purpose should have had any the less substance because there was a probability, even a certainty, that at any given time large areas of the site could not and would not be used as office or storage space. But the finding of a principal purpose presupposes the co-existence with it of one or more subsidiary purposes, as to which the commissioners have not enlightened us. What might those purposes have been? One possibility was agricultural use of the whole or some part or parts of the land available for such use; another was development and sale of some part or parts of the site; a third was development and sale of the whole of the site.

Notwithstanding counsel for the taxpayer's arguments to the contrary, I am in no doubt that it was open to the commissioners to infer from the primary facts found that the taxpayer's subsidiary purpose in acquiring the site was development and sale either of some part or parts of it or of the whole. It necessarily follows from their determination that they inferred that the purpose extended to the whole, an inference which was entirely consistent with the taxpayer's subsequent actions. That is a point of some importance. But simply to say that the taxpayer's subsidiary purpose in acquiring the site was development and sale of it as a whole does not go far enough to enable us to answer the question raised by this appeal. In order to define the limits of the inference which the commissioners could properly draw, we must look more closely at the other primary facts as found or agreed.

The taxpayer entered into the contract to purchase Havannah Mills before making any application for planning permission. He could not have developed the site without permission and at the date of the contract he did not know whether he would be able to obtain it or not. Moreover, if the principal purpose of the acquisition was the provision of office and storage space for his business, he must have intended to retain the site for the immediate future, perhaps for longer, and certainly not to dispose of it unless and until he had made such provision elsewhere. This view of the matter is rather confirmed by his erection of the dwelling house at Havannah Mills *after* he first became interested in Sandy Lane Farm. None of this, I may add, is inconsistent with the commissioners' finding that it was never the taxpayer's intention at any time to purchase Havannah Mills as a residence for himself and his family, a finding on which counsel for the Crown naturally relied.

Viewing the primary facts found by the commissioners and the inferences which they could properly draw from them in the light least favourable to the taxpayer, I

would state the position thus. The taxpayer acquired Havannah Mills in order to
a provide the office and storage space which he needed for his business as a result of
the difficulties he had had with the local authority over storage at his mother's
address. He also intended to develop and sell the site as a whole if he could obtain
planning permission to do so and if and when he had been able to provide himself
with suitable office and storage space elsewhere, an event which would not occur in
the immediate future and might not occur for some time.

b Was that state of facts a sufficient basis in law for the conclusion that Havannah
Mills was acquired as trading stock and not as a capital asset of the taxpayer's
business? In order that that question may be answered, an examination of some of
the authorities is necessary.

It was established by the decision of this court in *Taylor v Good (Inspector of
Taxes)* [1974] STC 148, [1974] 1 WLR 556 that where a taxpayer, not being a dealer
c in land, acquires a property, enhances its value and disposes of it at a profit, there is
no adventure in the nature of trade unless he had the intention of so disposing of it
at the time of its acquisition. In *Simmons v IRC* [1980] STC 350 at 352, [1980] 1
WLR 1196 at 1199, in a passage which both sides accept as a correct statement of
the law, Lord Wilberforce said:

d 'Trading requires an intention to trade; normally the question to be asked is
whether this intention existed at the time of the acquisition of the asset. Was it
acquired with the intention of disposing of it at a profit, or was it acquired as a
permanent investment? Often it is necessary to ask further questions: a
permanent investment may be sold in order to acquire another investment
thought to be more satisfactory; but that does not involve an operation of trade,
whether the first investment is sold at a profit or at a loss. Intentions may be
e changed. What was first an investment may be put into the trading stock, and,
I suppose, vice versa. If findings of this kind are to be made precision is
required, since a shift of an asset from one category to another will involve
changes in the company's accounts, and, possibly, a liability to tax (cf *Sharkey
(Inspector of Taxes) v Wernher* [1956] AC 58, 36 TC 275). What I think is not
f possible is for an asset to be both trading stock and permanent investment at
the same time, nor for it to possess an indeterminate status, neither trading
stock nor permanent asset. It must be one or the other, even though, and this
seems to me legitimate and intelligible, the company, in whatever character it
acquires the asset, may reserve an intention to change its character. To do so
would, in fact, amount to little more than making explicit what is necessarily
implicit in all commercial operations, namely that situations are open to review.'
g

In the present case the Crown has never suggested that there was any change in
the character of the asset between its acquisition in 1977 and its disposal in 1982.
Counsel submitted that Havannah Mills was acquired as trading stock, for which
purpose he accepted that the date of acquisition was the date of the contract and not
h the date of its completion. In an argument which at no point sought to discount the
difficulties with which the commissioners' finding as to the taxpayer's principal
purpose had confronted him, he nevertheless submitted that the property was
acquired with a sufficient intention to dispose of it at a profit to give it the character
of trading stock. In regard to dual purpose cases generally, he placed special reliance
on the decisions of the Privy Council in *Iswera v IRC* [1965] 1 WLR 663 and of this
j court in *Ensign Tankers (Leasing) Ltd v Stokes (Inspector of Taxes)* [1991] STC 136,
[1991] 1 WLR 341.

In *Iswera v IRC* the taxpayer, in order to finance the acquisition of two lots on a
building site in Colombo for a house of her own, had to buy the whole of the site and
sell off nine of the other ten lots to sub-purchasers, each of whom took a direct
conveyance from the vendor. The sub-sales having been effected on terms favourable
to the taxpayer, she only had to find Rs 15,275 in order to acquire two lots worth

Rs 87,040. She was assessed to income tax on the difference of Rs 71,765, on the footing that the whole transaction was an adventure in the nature of trade.

The Board of Review in Ceylon, the equivalent of the Special or General Commissioners in England, confirmed the assessment on the ground that the taxpayer's dominant motivation in the transaction had been to sell the property in lots so as to make a profit on the transaction and obtain two lots for herself below the market value. The Privy Council, affirming the judgment of the Supreme Court of Ceylon, held that the decision of the Board of Review could not be interfered with. In delivering the judgment of the Board (see [1965] 1 WLR 663 at 668), Lord Reid said:

> 'Before their Lordships, counsel for the appellant came near to submitting that, if it is a purpose of the taxpayer to acquire something for his own use and enjoyment, that is sufficient to show that the steps which he takes in order to acquire it cannot be an adventure in the nature of trade. In their Lordships' judgment that is going much too far. If, in order to get what he wants, the taxpayer has to embark on an adventure which has all the characteristics of trading, his purpose or object alone cannot prevail over what he in fact does. But if his acts are equivocal his purpose or object may be a very material factor when weighing the total effect of all the circumstances. In the present case not only has it been held that the appellant's dominant motive was to make a profit, but her actions are suggestive of trading as regards the greater part of the site which she bought. She had to and did make arrangements for its subdivision and immediate sale to the nine sub-purchasers before she could carry out her contract with the vendor of the site.'

In *Ensign Tankers (Leasing) Ltd v Stokes* the taxpayer company, having become a partner in two limited partnerships set up to finance the production and exploitation of two films, claimed that it was 'a person carrying on a trade' which had incurred capital expenditure on the provision of plant for the purposes of the trade, so as to entitle it to first-year allowances under s 41(1) of the Finance Act 1971. The Special Commissioners rejected the claim, holding that the partnerships were entered into with fiscal motives as their paramount object and could not therefore have been trading transactions. An appeal by the company was allowed by Millett J, who held (see [1989] STC 705 at 762–763, [1989] 1 WLR 1222 at 1232–1233) that the purpose of the transactions had to be determined objectively solely by reference to their nature, not subjectively by reference to the motives of the parties. On an appeal by the Crown to this court (see [1991] STC 136, [1991] 1 WLR 341) it was held that if a transaction was equivocal in nature the subjective intention of the parties was relevant; on the other hand, a paramount fiscal purpose was not decisive because it postulated the existence of some other purpose which might be commercial. The case was accordingly remitted to the commissioners for reconsideration.

The leading judgment in this court was delivered by Sir Nicolas Browne-Wilkinson V-C. Having considered a number of earlier decisions, including *Iswera v IRC*, he said ([1991] STC 136 at 146, [1991] 1 WLR 341 at 353–354):

> 'In my judgment, these authorities demonstrate that, at least where the transaction is equivocal and the purpose may or may not have been commercial, the commissioners are entitled to look at evidence of the subjective intention or motives of the relevant party. That is *not* because the legally relevant question is "with what motive did the parties enter into the transaction", but because such motive is evidence, sometimes compelling, on which to decide the legally relevant question, viz was the *purpose* of the transaction a trading purpose?'

He said ([1991] STC 136 at 147, [1991] 1 WLR 341 at 355):

> 'It will be remembered that the commissioners expressed their conclusion by holding that, *as a matter of law*, this was not a trading transaction since the

paramount intention was to obtain a fiscal advantage. In my judgment, this
constitutes an error of law (see *Overseas Containers (Finance) Ltd v Stoker
(Inspector of Taxes)* [1989] STC 364, [1989] 1 WLR 606). In summary, that
case decides: (a) trade involves not only the badges of trade but a commercial
purpose; (b) the question whether a transaction is a trading transaction is a
question of fact for the commissioners, not a question of law; (c) if the
commissioners find as a fact that the *sole* object of the transaction was fiscal
advantage, that finding can in law only lead to one conclusion, viz that it was
not a trading transaction. Since a fiscal advantage was the sole purpose there is
no place for there being any commercial purpose; *but* (d) if the commissioners
find as a fact only that the *paramount* intention was fiscal advantage, as a matter
of law that is not decisive since it postulates the existence of some other purpose
(albeit not paramount) which may be commercial. In such a case, the
commissioners have to weigh the paramount fiscal intention against the non-
fiscal elements and decide as a question of fact whether in essence the transaction
constitutes trading for commercial purposes.'

These two authorities show that the first question to be answered is whether the
transaction is equivocal or unequivocal. If it has all the characteristics of trading,
that is to say, if it is unequivocal, then, in the words of Lord Reid in *Iswera v IRC*
[1965] 1 WLR 663 at 668, the taxpayer's—

'. . . purpose or object alone cannot prevail over what he in fact does. But if
his acts are equivocal his purpose or object may be a very material factor when
weighing the total effect of all the circumstances.'

Similarly, if an equivocal transaction is entered into for two different purposes, both
must be taken into account when weighing the total effect of all the circumstances.
In the words of Sir Nicolas Browne-Wilkinson V-C in *Ensign Tankers (Leasing) Ltd
v Stokes (Inspector of Taxes)* [1991] STC 136 at 147, [1991] 1 WLR 341 at 355:

'In such a case, the commissioners have to weigh the paramount fiscal
intention against the non-fiscal elements and decide as a question of fact
whether in essence the transaction constitutes trading for commercial purposes.'

The taxpayer's acquisition of Havannah Mills was an equivocal transaction. If
viewed on its own, it does not tell you whether the property acquired was trading
stock or a capital asset of the taxpayer's business. It might have been either. So
account must be taken of the two purposes which the commissioners have attributed
to the taxpayer, in the one case by express finding and in the other by presumed
inference. At this point counsel for the Crown, relying on the judgment of
Sir Nicolas Browne-Wilkinson V-C in *Ensign Tankers (Leasing) Ltd v Stokes*,
submits that, just as it was there held to be open to the commissioners to find that a
paramount fiscal purpose did not prevent the activities of the partnerships from
being trading transactions, so it was open to the commissioners here to find that the
taxpayer's principal purpose of providing office and storage space for his business
did not prevent the acquisition of Havannah Mills from being an acquisition of
trading stock. That submission, although superficially persuasive, is one which on
reflection I feel bound to reject.

It is important to bear in mind that the activities of the partnerships in *Ensign
Tankers (Leasing) Ltd v Stokes* were continuing transactions, whose fiscal and
commercial purposes, if both there were, would necessarily have been implemented
concurrently. In such a case, it is easy to understand that the commissioners, looking
at the two purposes, the nature of the activities and all the circumstances of the case,
might reasonably conclude, despite the paramount fiscal purpose, that there had
been trading for commercial purposes. But here we have a different state of affairs.

I have already expressed my view, in the light least favourable to the taxpayer, of
the primary facts found by the commissioners and the inferences which they could

properly draw from them. From that it is clear that the taxpayer's subsidiary purpose
of developing and selling Havannah Mills could not have been implemented *a*
concurrently with his principal purpose of providing office and storage space for his
business. To begin with, there was no certainty that he would be able to obtain
planning permission. True, if he had obtained it straightaway, he could no doubt
have got on with part at least of the development. But he would not have been able
to sell the site unless and until he had been able to provide himself with suitable
office and storage space elsewhere, an event which might not have occurred for some *b*
time.

And so the taxpayer's 'purpose' or 'object' or 'intention' in regard to the
development and sale of the property was severely circumscribed, its implementation
indefinite in point of time. The question is whether it was capable of amounting in
law to an intention sufficient to give the property the character of trading stock. If it
was, it was open to the commissioners to come to the conclusion to which they came. *c*
If it was not, their determination cannot stand. It is not an easy question. In the end
I have formed a clear opinion that it must be answered in the negative. It was not
open to the commissioners, having made a finding which was apt to characterise the
transaction as an acquisition of a capital asset, to deny it that character by reason of
an intention thus circumscribed and indefinite. In my judgment no body of
commissioners acting judicially and properly instructed as to the relevant law could *d*
have come to the conclusion that the property was acquired as trading stock. On
that view of the matter the assessment must be discharged and it becomes
unnecessary to consider an alternative argument which was advanced by counsel for
the taxpayer both here and in the court below.

On one view of the case it is unfortunate that the commissioners did not make a
finding as to the taxpayer's subsidiary purpose in the acquisition of Havannah Mills. *e*
The absence of such a finding, coupled with the bare determination of liability to
income tax under Sch D, Case I, has forced us, under the principles of *Edwards v
Bairstow* as I understand them, to attribute to the commissioners a process of
thought which I suspect is not only artificial but contrary to what they in fact
thought. The other view is that the commissioners did not make a finding as to the
taxpayer's subsidiary purpose because they thought that such a purpose was *f*
irrelevant; and that they thought that it was irrelevant because they did not realise
that there could not have been an adventure in the nature of trade if the taxpayer
did not, at the time of its acquisition, have the intention of disposing of the property
at a profit. Indeed, if they had realised that and had thought that the taxpayer had a
subsidiary, but nevertheless decisive, purpose of development and sale, it is almost
inconceivable that they would not have made a finding to that effect. It may be of *g*
real significance that the authorities to which the commissioners were referred did
not include either *Taylor v Good* or *Simmons v IRC*.

Accordingly, while I have sought to apply the principles of *Edwards v Bairstow* in
their full rigour, I am gratified to find that their application leads to the same result
as that which would have followed if the commissioners had stated their process of
thought in the form which I suspect that it actually took. *h*

Vinelott J ([1989] STC 333 at 341) thought that the question which must have
presented itself to the commissioners was what use the taxpayer intended to make of
the parts of the property which he did not need for office and storage space. He said
(at 342):

> 'He intended to use part of the land to provide storage for his demolition and *j*
> plant hire business and part of the mill as an office. But it is, I think, plain in
> these circumstances that he would only require a very small part of the land for
> that purpose. The commissioners must I think have taken the view that he
> intended to develop the land not so required using the materials to hand for the
> construction of a house and to improve and landscape the surrounding area
> with a view to selling it at a profit. That is what he in fact did. As I have pointed

out the first application for planning consent (for the erection of a dwelling
which the commissioners found he never intended to occupy himself) was made
before the contract for the purchase of the Havannah Mills site had been
completed.'

I respectfully think that that was an incomplete, and therefore an incorrect,
approach. Although, as I have said, if the taxpayer had obtained planning permission
straightaway, he could no doubt have got on with part at least of the development,
there was no certainty that he would obtain it. Moreover, the judge did not consider
the inevitable consequence of the commissioners' finding as to the taxpayer's
principal purpose in the acquisition. Whatever the position in regard to the
development might have been, he could not sell the property unless and until he had
been able to provide himself with suitable office and storage space elsewhere.

I would allow this appeal.

RALPH GIBSON LJ. The facts on which the appeal turns have been restated by
Nourse LJ in the words of the commissioners in rearranged sequence. The taxpayer
entered into the contract for the acquisition of the site before making any application
for planning permission for any development. He acquired the site—and by that
word I understand the commissioners to have been referring to the whole of the
site—'principally to provide office and storage space for [his] demolition and plant
hire business'. If that was the only effective or relevant purpose which he had, then
the acquisition was not for the purpose of trade; the site was never trading stock; it
was never suggested that the taxpayer changed his intention after acquisition so that
the site became trading stock at a later date; and on that basis there was no adventure
in the nature of trade.

The commissioners, however, having heard evidence from the taxpayer and his
accountant, concluded that, notwithstanding the fact that the site was acquired
principally to provide office and storage space for the business, the profits arising on
the sale of the site were assessable under Sch D, Case I. So to conclude, the
commissioners must have held that the purchase, development and sale of the site
was an adventure in the nature of trade.

It was submitted for the taxpayer that such an inference was not open to the
commissioners on the ground that the true and only reasonable conclusion from the
facts found was that the site was acquired as a capital asset. It was pointed out by
counsel for the taxpayer that the commissioners did not expressly direct themselves
as to the importance of the intentions of the taxpayer at the time of acquisition of
the site. Particular reliance was placed on the facts that the taxpayer needed premises
for storage of his demolition material because of difficulties over the use of his
mother's home for that purpose; on the express finding of the taxpayer's principal
purpose in acquiring the site; on his subsequent use of the site for storage and of part
of the mill as his office; and on his continued use of the site in various ways, including
agricultural work, until the sale in October 1982. I was unconvinced by these
submissions. The commissioners are not required to set out all the relevant principles
of law. It seems clear to me that it was open to the commissioners to hold by inference
on the facts found by them, that, at the time of the acquisition of the site, the
taxpayer had the intention of developing and/or of selling part, or parts, or the whole
of the site as an adventure in the nature of trade, although such an intention must
have been a subsidiary purpose or intention because, as they expressly found, the
site was acquired principally to provide office and storage space for the business.
I see no reason whatever why a general dealer and demolition contractor, who is in
immediate need of premises for storage and office space for his demolition and plant
hire business, should not decide to acquire a site for that purpose which is also seen
to be suitable for and intended for development and resale in parts or as a whole.
The implementation of a subsidiary purpose to develop and sell would necessarily
take some time unless an opportunity to dispose of the site in its then condition

should present itself on terms which the taxpayer might decide should be accepted. The making of such an inference was assisted by the fact that the site was much *a* larger than was required for storage and office use and that it was obviously suitable for development, at least in part, in that all the buildings on it had been demolished or were intended to be demolished.

I have been troubled over the technicality and, indeed, unreality of much of the discussion conducted in this case on the issue of intention to trade. Before we get to any question as to the nature and quality of any such intention, and as to its *b* sufficiency for the purposes of the conclusion reached by the commissioners, the existence or non-existence of an intention, present at the date of acquisition, on the part of the taxpayer to develop and sell the site by way of trade is decisive of this appeal. The commissioners could have put that issue out of contention by stating whether or not they did infer the existence of such a subsidiary purpose. Why must the court deal with the issue by examination of what inference may be regarded as *c* reasonably possible when the commissioners could have answered the question expressly? It has occurred to me that, since the suggested inference is an essential part of the Crown's case, it might not be unreasonable for the law to require that, if the inference is not expressly stated to have been drawn, the Crown should be held to be unable to argue that it be implied. The appeal, however, as I understood the submissions, was not argued on that ground. It was rightly acknowledged by counsel *d* for the taxpayer, as I understood his submissions, and as I understand the law, that it was open to either side to have asked for further findings of fact to be added to the case stated; and that, as it seems to me, would include a request to the commissioners to state expressly whether or not they had found by inference an intention of any sort on the part of the taxpayer at the date of acquisition of the site with reference to development and sale of part or parts or the whole of it and, if yes, what that *e* intention was. Neither side made any such request. Having chosen not to ask for an express finding, it seems to me that both sides must be held to the established rules by which the court considers an appeal from the commissioners by case stated (see *Edwards (Inspector of Taxes) v Bairstow* [1956] AC 14, 36 TC 207).

If I am right so far, and the commissioners are to be treated as having inferred the existence of a subsidiary intention on the part of the taxpayer held by him at the *f* date of acquisition to develop and sell the site, the remaining question is whether that subsidiary intention, on the whole of the facts found, must be held to have been so contingent and uncertain of fulfilment, both as to means and as to date, that it is not a sufficient basis in law for the conclusion that the site was acquired as trading stock and not as a capital asset of the taxpayer's business. Nourse LJ has concluded, for the reasons set out in his judgment, that it was not open to the commissioners to *g* conclude that the site was acquired otherwise than as a capital asset, and he has stated the relevant principles of law to be derived from the authorities. I have, with diffidence and after much hesitation, reached a different conclusion on my understanding of the facts found.

It seems to me that the commissioners must have concluded that there was a single adventure in the nature of trade, commencing with the acquisition of the site, and *h* that the taxpayer intended to and did use the site in implementation of his principal purpose of providing office and storage space, pending the development and sale of the site. That conclusion seems to me to have been fairly open to them on the facts which they found.

I assume that the transaction is to be regarded as equivocal in the sense of the phrase used by Lord Reid in *Iswera v IRC* [1965] 1 WLR 663 at 668. I understand *j* that sense to be that, on analysing objectively what the taxpayer did at the time of the acquisition and in subsequent dealing with the land, his acts are consistent with the land having been acquired as a capital asset which was subsequently sold to best advantage, and also consistent with the site having been acquired as a trading asset which was subsequently applied to that purpose. On that assumption the taxpayer's purpose or purposes at the time of acquisition may be a 'very material factor when weighing the total effect of all the circumstances' (see *Iswera v IRC* [1965] 1 WLR 663 at 668 per Lord Reid).

It was argued that the subsidiary purpose of development and sale must be regarded as having been, from the outset, in some way uncertain of fulfilment both as to means and as to date. The taxpayer had no planning permission. He did not know what sort of permission he would get, or when he would get it; and he did not know when an opportunity of sale, whether of part or of the whole, would present itself at a price which would make such sale or sales sufficiently attractive. In addition, the implementing of the principal purpose of providing office and storage space for his demolition and plant hire business would mean that some restriction on the marketing of the site, even when the planning position was clarified, would be imposed by the need for alternative space for office and storage purposes.

I acknowledge the force of these points but I am unable to accept that they cast any doubt on the propriety of the conclusions which the commissioners reached. Nothing suggests that the taxpayer's requirements for office space for his demolition and plant hire business were elaborate or that, if the benefit of an advantageous sale of the site was thought to be worth it, they could not be met by some temporary arrangements, even in his home. We may surely attribute to the commissioners knowledge that sale of a site for development, in part or as a whole, could normally be arranged on terms that would give the taxpayer such time to make alternative arrangements to deal with his demolition and plant hire equipment as he judged to be necessary. I see nothing surprising or inconsistent with the primary facts found in the attribution to the taxpayer of an intention to use parts of the site for the principal purpose of office and storage space for his business until the site should be sold in parts or as a whole. Land taken into stock for development and sale can, in my view, sensibly be used before sale for the principal purpose described. The process of marketing land for sale, including the making of plans for development and the waiting for the right buyer or buyers to appear, would be implemented while the principal and immediate purpose of providing accommodation for the business is put into effect. The commissioners were, in my judgment, entitled to hold that the whole site was acquired by the taxpayer as trading stock.

For my part, therefore, I would uphold the order of the judge although not by precisely the same process of reasoning.

LLOYD LJ. At the outset of this appeal, I had every inclination to uphold the decision of the General Commissioners. We cannot disturb that decision unless it is erroneous in law. Vinelott J, with his great experience in this field, has shown a way whereby, without any error of law, and consistently with the principles in *Edwards (Inspector of Taxes) v Bairstow* [1956] AC 14, 36 TC 207, the commissioners may have progressed from their findings of fact to their conclusion. So my instinctive reaction was to dismiss the appeal. But as the hearing proceeded, I have been persuaded to change my mind.

Before one comes to apply the principles in *Edwards v Bairstow*, one must first be clear what it is that, on a fair reading of the case, the commissioners have actually decided. The crucial finding is, of course, the finding in para 5(iii) that the site was acquired principally to provide office and storage space. As I read Vinelott J's judgment, he held (see [1989] STC 333 at 341) that that finding (which I shall refer to as the primary finding) relates only to part of the site, and not to the whole site. This is certainly how the finding is understood by the taxpayer in the grounds of appeal, and also by the Crown in counsel's skeleton argument. Had the judge held otherwise, then, as he says himself, he would have found difficulty in reconciling that finding with the commissioners' conclusion.

I have had the advantage of reading Nourse LJ's judgment in advance. Though I feel greater doubt than he does, I agree with him that the better construction of para 5(iii) of the case is that the commissioners were throughout intending to refer to the whole site, that is to say the whole of the land, the purchase, development and sale of which has given rise to the assessment. So I respectfully part company from the judge at his very first step.

On the basis that the primary finding relates only to the area required for office and storage space (the first area) and not the adjoining land (the second area) it was easy enough for counsel for the Crown to argue in his skeleton argument that the second area at any rate was acquired as trading stock, and that such a finding is implicit, not only in the express findings in the case, but also in the correspondence to which the judge referred. But if, as I think, the primary finding relates to the whole site, then that argument does not get off the ground.

Before us, the argument took a different turn. A principal purpose, says counsel for the Crown, implies a subsidiary purpose. If, contrary to the view expressed in his skeleton argument, the principal purpose was to acquire the whole site for storage and office space, then it was open to the commissioners to find that the subsidiary purpose was to acquire the whole site as trading stock. That is, he says, the correct inference, to be drawn from the case as a whole; in other words this was a dual purpose transaction.

Counsel for the Crown summarised the correct approach of the court in dual purpose transactions in the following four propositions: (1) If, on objective analysis, the transaction has all the characteristics of trading, that analysis must prevail over the subjective intention of the taxpayer. (2) If, on objective analysis, the transaction is equivocal, the subjective intention of the taxpayer is relevant in weighing-up the circumstances, and concluding whether it is a trading transaction or not. (3) If, in an equivocal case, the taxpayer's sole objective is non-commercial, then that is conclusive against the transaction being a trading transaction. (4) In all other cases, including cases where the taxpayer's principal or paramount objective is non-commercial, it is a question of fact for the commissioners to determine what the overall nature of the transaction is.

I would be content to accept these propositions as accurate, although the expression 'non-commercial' may need some refinement. On the assumption that this is a dual purpose transaction, it seems to come within counsel for the Crown's fourth proposition, in which case it would be difficult for us to hold, consistently with *Edwards v Bairstow*, that the commissioners must have erred in law. But was it a dual purpose transaction?

Nourse LJ has held, accepting counsel for the Crown's argument, that it was open to the commissioners to infer from the primary facts found that the taxpayer's subsidiary purpose in acquiring the site was development and sale of the whole or some part of the site. Viewing the primary facts and the inferences which the commissioners could properly draw from them in the light least favourable to the taxpayer he has held that the taxpayer had two purposes in mind, namely, (1) providing himself with storage and office space and (2) developing and selling the site as a whole. But the second purpose could not be implemented concurrently with the first purpose, unlike the position in *Iswera v IRC* [1965] 1 WLR 663 at 668, where, as Lord Reid pointed out, the sub-division and *immediate* sale of the bulk of the land was an essential part of the taxpayer's plan. In the present case, by contrast, the second purpose was severely circumscribed, and its implementation indefinite in point of time. The taxpayer could not develop or sell the site until he had obtained planning permission, and found an alternative site for office space and storage. Nourse LJ has held that such an intention is insufficient in law to give the property acquired by the taxpayer the character of trading stock.

I accept at once that an intention can be so vague and indefinite as not to amount to an intention in law, as where the taxpayer has not 'moved out of the zone of contemplation—out of the sphere of the tentative, the provisional and the exploratory—into the valley of decision' (see *Cunliffe v Goodman* [1950] 2 KB 237 at 254 per Asquith LJ). If this was the nature of the intention in the present case, it was not a dual purpose transaction at all.

But if there was here an intention to trade at all, I doubt whether the hurdles

which the taxpayer still had to surmount were such as to relegate that intention from
the valley of decision to the zone of contemplation. I would hesitate before holding
that there cannot in law be an intention to acquire land as trading stock merely
because the carrying out of that intention is conditional.

So I go back to the starting point. Is this a dual purpose transaction at all? I agree
with Nourse LJ that it was open to the commissioners to find that the subsidiary
purpose in acquiring the site as a whole was a trading purpose. But is this consistent
with what they have in fact found? The most conspicuous feature of the case is the
absence of any finding as to the subsidiary purpose. It is, I think, inconceivable that
if the commissioners had intended to find that the subsidiary purpose at the time of
acquisition was a trading purpose, they would not have made an express finding to
that effect, bearing in mind (i) their express finding as to the principal purpose,
(ii) their conclusion. If that is so, it is not open for us to draw an inference that the
commissioners *may* have found that the subsidiary purpose was a trading purpose,
in order to support their conclusion. There is no room for any such inference on a
fair reading of the case.

What then was the subsidiary purpose which the commissioners had in mind?
One is tempted to think that the subsidiary purpose must have been a purpose of
substantial significance, and must have been relevant in some way to the
commissioners' conclusion. But why should it? Having read, and reread, para 5 of
the case stated, I am now convinced that the only subsidiary purpose which the
commissioners can have had in mind was the farming purpose. It is true that the
commissioners find that the level of farming was very limited. But the limited nature
of the purpose is irrelevant. It is common ground that a principal purpose implies a
subsidiary purpose. But it does not exclude a *very* subsidiary purpose.

So on a fair reading of the case, I would hold that this is not a dual purpose case at
all, since neither of the two purposes found (or implied) by the commissioners is a
trading purpose. Looking at it another way, the case comes within counsel for the
Crown's third proposition, rather than his fourth.

There remains the question how, on a fair reading of the case, the commissioners
can have reached their conclusion if they were *not* intending to find that the
subsidiary purpose on acquisition was a trading purpose. The answer is clear. They
must have held that the taxpayer was assessable because of a subsequent change of
intention or, in the words of Lord Wilberforce in *Simmons v IRC* [1980] STC 350 at
352, [1980] 1 WLR 1196 at 1199, because of 'a shift of an asset from one category to
another'. There would have been nothing wrong in the commissioners so finding if
there had been any evidence to support such a finding, or if it had been part of the
case for the Crown. But it was not. So if, as I think, this is the explanation of the
commissioners' conclusion, they have regrettably fallen into an error, not of fact,
but of law.

I am conscious that I may have attributed to the commissioners a meaning which
they did not intend. If so, I can only express my regret. But I console myself with
the observations of du Parcq LJ in *Royal Choral Society v IRC* (1942) 25 TC 263 at
277:

> 'But in the case of Magistrates or Commissioners or Arbitrators who have to
> state a Case, it is necessary that they should shew to the superior Court precisely
> what facts they have found. Nobody has been there to direct them as to the law.
> They may have gone wrong about the law. We can only tell whether they have
> gone wrong about the law by knowing what the facts are; and it is their province
> to tell us what the facts are. If they do that and then state their conclusion, it is
> possible for this Court to see whether they have accurately applied the law, or
> whether they have erred in point of law.'

If I have wrongly attributed to the commissioners an error of law, it is because the
facts found are incomplete.

For the reasons I have given, I am satisfied that the commissioners have erred in law. Their conclusion is inconsistent with their primary finding of fact. The case is covered by *Simmons v IRC*. Like Nourse LJ, though for somewhat different reasons, *a* I would allow this appeal and discharge the assessment.

I have two concluding observations.

In the first place, I do not accept, as counsel for the taxpayer argued, that the judge can be criticised for looking at the correspondence, which was expressly incorporated in and accompanied the case, in order to elucidate the commissioners' findings. *b*

In the second place I found it intensely unsatisfactory that we should have had to spend so much time wracking our brains as to what the commissioners may or must have found. It was open to the parties to seek to obtain from the commissioners the findings of fact they wanted. It is, as I understand it, open to the court to remit a case of its own motion, in order to elucidate the facts, if it is necessary in the interests of justice so to do, just as it is open to the court to remit an award for further findings *c* of fact under s 22 of the Arbitration Act 1950. Unfortunately that was not practicable in the present case, since one of the commissioners had died, and another has retired, or is at any rate too ill to resume the hearing. The comparison with arbitration, which du Parcq LJ drew in the *Royal Choral Society* case, and long experience of the old special case procedure of which I have been reminded during the hearing of the current appeal, has brought home to me how greatly superior is the new *d* procedure for hearing appeals on questions of law under s 1 of the Arbitration Act 1979. It may be that a similar procedure could be introduced with benefit into the hearing of tax appeals.

Appeal allowed with costs. Leave to appeal to the House of Lords refused.

e

Solicitors: *Poole Alcock & Co,* Sandbach (for the taxpayer); *Solicitor of Inland Revenue.*

Rengan Krishnan Esq   Barrister.

a

Note
Inland Revenue Commissioners v West

COURT OF APPEAL, CIVIL DIVISION
MUSTILL, BALCOMBE AND BINGHAM LJJ

b   21 MAY 1991

*Appeal – Settlement by agreement – Agreement – Accountant agreeing settlement on
taxpayer's behalf – Whether accountant had authority to enter into agreement with
inspector on taxpayer's behalf – Whether inspector had acted reasonably in accepting
that accountant had authority to act on taxpayer's behalf – Whether leave ought to be*
c *granted to the taxpayer to defend the action – Taxes Management Act 1970, s 54(1), (5) –
RSC Ord 14, r 3(1).*

Notes

For settlement of appeals by agreement, see Simon's Taxes A3.515.
d   For the Taxes Management Act 1970, s 54(1), (5), see ibid, Part G2.

Case referred to in judgments

Miles v Bull [1969] 1 QB 258, [1968] 3 All ER 632.

e   ### Appeal

Mr West, the taxpayer, appealed against an order of Drake J, dated 31 January
1990, granting the Crown leave to enter summary judgment against the taxpayer,
under RSC Ord 14, r 1(1) on the grounds that the taxpayer had no defence to the
Crown's claim for payment of unpaid income tax, surtax and interest thereon. The
f   Crown's claim which formed part of a statement of claim included in a writ of
summons issued in February 1983 related to assessments to income tax for the year
1972–73 and surtax for the years 1971–72 and 1972–73 which had been determined
under s 54 of the Taxes Management Act 1970 by an agreement entered into by an
inspector of taxes with Mr Mitchell, an accountant said to be acting on behalf of the
taxpayer. The taxpayer appealed against the Ord 14 judgment and sought leave to
g   defend the action contending (a) that Mr Joseph was his accountant and that Mr
Mitchell had no authority to enter into an agreement with the inspector on his
behalf; (b) that he had made it clear to the inspector that Mr Joseph was his
accountant and representative and that therefore the inspector had not acted
reasonably nor in good faith in taking Mr Mitchell as authorised to act on his behalf;
and (c) that under RSC Ord 14 r 3(1) there ought to be a trial because there were
h   circumstances which required to be closely investigated. The facts are set out in the
judgment of Bingham LJ.

The taxpayer appeared in person.
Launcelot Henderson for the Crown.

j

BINGHAM LJ (giving the first judgment at the invitation of Mustill LJ). This is an
appeal by Mr West (the taxpayer), who is the defendant in this action, against a
judgment given by Drake J on 31 January 1990 when he dismissed an appeal by the
taxpayer against an order of summary judgment under RSC Ord 14 made in the
Crown's favour by Master Grant on 8 May 1989. The plaintiffs in the action are the
Crown and the claim that is made is for unpaid income tax, surtax and interest.

The writ was issued as long ago as February 1983 and it is an unfortunate fact that the matters to which this appeal relates are of very considerable antiquity. The claims in the reamended writ fall into three groups. First of all there is a claim for unpaid income tax in respect of a number of years (1969–70, 1971–72, 1972–73 and 1973–74) together with interest. Second, there is a claim for unpaid surtax for the years 1971–72 and 1972–73, again with interest, and then third, there is a claim for unpaid interest. All of these assessments were the subject of appeal by the taxpayer and all, save three, were determined by the General Commissioners in July 1980 and the effect of that determination by the General Commissioners is to render the assessments for all practical purposes absolute.

There were three which in the event were not determined by the General Commissioners and which the Crown claims to have been settled by an agreement made by the Revenue with an accountant, said to have been acting for the taxpayer, under s 54 of the Taxes Management Act 1970 (the 1970 Act). Those agreements relate to income tax for the year 1972–73 and surtax for the years 1971–72 and 1972–73, although it is right to add that so far as this appeal is concerned there is no issue raised as to the s 54 agreement relied on in respect of the surtax assessments.

It is not I think necessary to refer in detail to s 54 of the 1970 Act which has been before the court on a number of occasions. It suffices for present purposes to say that an agreement between the Revenue and a taxpayer, for the settlement of an appeal by the taxpayer against an assessment pending before the General Commissioners, has the same effect as a decision by the General Commissioners on the appeal in like terms. That is subject only to this: that by virtue of s 54(2) the taxpayer may by notice in writing withdraw from such an agreement if he does so within 30 days. It is also right, given the issue in this appeal, to make reference to s 54(5) which provides:

'The references in this section to an agreement being come to with an appellant and the giving of notice or notification to or by an appellant include references to an agreement being come to with, and the giving of notice or notification to or by, a person acting on behalf of the appellant in relation to the appeal.'

I stress that reference because the issue in this case concerns the authority of an accountant alleged by the Crown to have been acting on behalf of the taxpayer or to have been understood by them to have been so acting.

It is not I think necessary to go into the chronology of this matter in great detail. Income tax assessments for the years in question were posted to the taxpayer on dates between November 1969 and October 1973, the material assessment for income tax for the year 1972–73 being sent in August 1972. On later dates there were assessments to surtax, the latest of those being as late as March 1978.

The important part of the chronology for present purposes begins on 6 November 1979 when, in a document signed by the taxpayer and addressed to the inspector of taxes for the Piccadilly district, authority was conferred by the taxpayer on Mitchell & Co, Chartered Accountants, of 12 New Burlington Street, London W1, to receive notices of assessment to income tax and other forms of tax. The form also goes on to withdraw any earlier requests that copies of notices of assessment should be sent to any other agent and says, 'I wish this authority to be applied to all my income or gains currently subject to assessment.'

That notice was followed by communications between the inspector in post at the time and Mr Mitchell of Mitchell & Co acting, or apparently acting, on behalf of the taxpayer. Our attention has been drawn to a letter dated 21 December 1979 when the inspector refers to discussions between himself and Mr Mitchell and says:

'After the protracted correspondence I shall now expect to receive [the taxpayer's] written agreement to the figures yet to be agreed, together with any information which is necessary within the next month, and also his completed

1978–79 and 1979–80 tax return forms. In the absence of [the taxpayer's] written agreement by the end of January, I intend, as I mentioned, to prepare for all open appeals to be listed for hearing before the General Commissioners at an early date with a view to seeking their determination of the amounts of the assessments.'

It is plain from that letter that the inspector was of the opinion that it was time that the taxpayer's tax affairs were brought to some finality, but the taxpayer himself draws attention to the fact that the inspector was not relying on Mr Mitchell but was apparently calling for the taxpayer's written agreement.

There were further letters following that one, in particular a letter in which the inspector wrote to Mr Mitchell on 14 February 1980 referring to various tax matters, calling for various documents and expressing his renewed intention that all outstanding matters should be finalised in the very near future.

There was a further letter of 11 March 1980 in which the inspector writes again to Mr Mitchell, referring to a telephone call and also referring to a request, apparently made by Mr Mitchell, to spread some of the fees received over more than one year, and the inspector observes:

'As I mentioned in our telephone conversation your client's assessable profits are computed on the cash basis rather than the statutory earnings basis in accordance with his request and undertaking . . . a copy of which I enclose. I cannot agree that the basis should be changed retrospectively and certainly not for one or two years only.'

At first blush, therefore, these appear to be the sort of letters that are exchanged between an inspector and an accountant acting for a taxpayer relating to tax liabilities and the taxpayer's obligations to make payment.

On 9 July 1980 there were appeals against the assessments made for three years, 1969–70, 1971–72, 1973–74, and those were determined by the General Commissioners sitting in Westminster. This event is drawn to our attention because both Mr Mitchell and another accountant named Mr Joseph attended that hearing. We have a note of the hearing and it appears from that, according in any event to the General Commissioners' understanding, that the accountants acting for the taxpayer were Mitchell & Co, although there is a subsidiary reference to Mr Joseph and it is apparent that both Mr Mitchell and Mr Joseph attended. Following that, notices were issued calling for payment.

Then one comes to an important event which was a meeting of 4 August 1980. We have a note of that meeting bearing the inspector's signature and dated 7 August 1980, just three days after the meeting. It is headed, 'Note of interview of 4th August 1980' and the inspector notes as being present: Mr West as taxpayer, Mr Mitchell as accountant, Mr Josephs (his name was I think 'Joseph' not 'Josephs') described as Mr Mitchell's associate, and the inspector himself. It is a long note and I shall not go through it all. It suffices to say that although there is one reference to production of a document by Mr Joseph, and although a great deal of the document is taken up with recording observations and representations made by the taxpayer himself, the document gives a very clear impression that so far as the taxpayer's professional advisers were concerned, the running was made by Mr Mitchell. Thus, in the first paragraph we find him requesting a short adjournment of the 1979–80 appeals; in the third paragraph we find him producing a letter; in the last paragraph he made a statement as to what the capital statement included; and then one comes to an important part of the note written in the first person by the tax inspector in these terms:

'After some discussion in order to settle the case I offered without prejudice to suggest to the Commissioners that they determined the 1970–71 assessment at nil on the basis of no profit or loss and the 1972–73 assessment at a profit of £13,000 although I did not agree that there was conclusive evidence of the

correct assessable profits. [The taxpayer] maintained that his income in the
latter year had not exceeded £10,000. I pointed out that this was not in
accordance with the evidence I had seen, such as it was, and that I had no
further time for discussion and was prepared to leave the decision to the
Commissioners. Mitchell asked whether I would agree to spread the £13,000,
£3,000 to 1970–71 and £10,000 to 1972–73. I replied that he had attempted to
persuade me that there was no assessable profit for 1970–71. I could not be
expected to agree now to excessive assessment. I suggested that as I had no
more time available they should go away and discuss my offer among themselves.'

The note ends with this record by the inspector:

'Mitchell agreed that they should discuss my offer for 1970–71 and 1972–73
and he would contact me during the afternoon.'

It is important to put this meeting in context. The context is that the appeals
before the General Commissioners were listed for hearing three days later, on
7 August, and it is plain from the inspector's note that he either wanted an agreement
before that date or he wanted the appeals to go ahead; but one infers that he was not
content that the matter should remain in limbo.

There was a further letter, undoubtedly written by Mr Mitchell on behalf of
Mitchell & Co, undated but stamped within the Revenue on receipt 7 August 1980.
The letter reads:

'I apologise for this late communication to you but I have endeavoured to
contact you without avail. I am pleased to inform you that [the taxpayer] has
agreed to accept your offer of agreement to 1970/71 at nil and 1972/73 at
£13,000. In view of this, we are assuming our attendance of the appeal meeting
is unnecessary.'

The inspector replied to that letter on 9 August 1980:

'With reference to your letter which I received on 7 August 1980, I note that
[the taxpayer] is in agreement with the offer which I made when we met on
4 August. The appeals are therefore determined under Sec. 54 Taxes
Management Act 1970 in the following figures . . .'

and the offer made is repeated and set out. I should add that no attendance took
place, certainly on behalf of the taxpayer, or so far as we know by the inspector, at
the hearing before the commissioners on 7 August.

Following that exchange of correspondence, a correspondence between Mr
Mitchell and officers of the Revenue continued. In letters of 12 August and
18 August surtax assessments were settled by agreement and by letters of
15 September and 19 September further surtax assessments were settled by
agreement and, as I say, there is no challenge to those agreements.

There was a letter of 10 April 1981, again written by Mr Mitchell on the writing
paper of his firm, to the enforcement office of the Revenue setting out in some detail
facts relating to the taxpayer's tax position and plainly retailing instructions which
Mr Mitchell had received from the taxpayer. That letter enclosed a cheque for £500
and was followed by two letters of 8 May 1981 and 11 June 1981 again from Mr
Mitchell enclosing further cheques for £500 in each case.

On 4 September 1982 a further notification was given to the Revenue by the
taxpayer on a document in the same form as I have already mentioned, asking that
in future notices and assessments should be sent to Bernard Joseph & Co, Chartered
Accountants, 223 Finchley Road, and that was forwarded to the inspector with a
covering letter from Bernard Joseph & Co saying:

'We refer to our recent telephone conversation when we explained that we
are now dealing with the above, which was formerly dealt with by our associated
firm Mitchell & Co . . .'

'the above' being the taxpayer.

The next relevant development was the issue of the writ in February 1983.

a
The issue which has been succinctly and accurately defined by the taxpayer in the course of his helpful argument is what authority the Revenue could reasonably have understood Mitchell & Co to have had in all the circumstances and whether the Revenue did accept in good faith that Mitchell & Co had authority to act on his behalf. The Crown contends—and we have the benefit of a most helpful and able skeleton argument from counsel for the Crown, although we have not heard oral

b
argument from him—that on its face the correspondence that I have referred to shows a clear case of agreement made by an authorised professional accountant on behalf of the taxpayer.

The taxpayer, however, contends that Mitchell & Co never had actual authority to act on his behalf and never had apparent authority either and he says that he remained entirely unaware of the alleged agreement made in the letters of 7 and

c
9 August 1980 until the writ was served on him. In support of that contention the taxpayer relies on his own affidavits, particularly the first one, and the affidavit of Mr Joseph, his accountant. The Crown has endeavoured, I think accurately, to extract from those affidavits the points that are made and they are really, I think, fourfold. The first is that Mr Joseph and not Mr Mitchell was the taxpayer's accountant and that it was for somewhat mysterious private reasons that Mr Joseph

d
engaged Mitchell & Co to act as his nominee, there being apparently some reason why he did not wish overtly to appear to be the taxpayer's professional adviser. It was described by Mr Joseph as 'a domestic arrangement between Mr Mitchell and myself in the conduct of [the taxpayer's] affairs'. Second, and this should be acknowledged, both the taxpayer and Mr Joseph deny that Mr Mitchell was ever authorised to reach any agreement on the taxpayer's behalf. Furthermore, third,

e
they disclaim any contemporary knowledge of the agreement relied on as constituting an agreement under s 54 of the 1970 Act, and the taxpayer says last that at the meeting with the inspector on 4 August 1980 which he and Mr Joseph and Mr Mitchell attended, it was made quite plain to the inspector that the taxpayer's accountant was Mr Joseph and not Mr Mitchell. And he deposes that 'it was sufficiently conveyed to the inspector that he (meaning Mr Joseph) was and had

f
been my accountant, and that Mitchell & Co were a nominee firm for Mr Joseph'. That is confirmed to some extent at least by Mr Joseph in his affidavit.

The Crown submits that little weight should be attached to the evidence of the taxpayer and Mr Joseph as to what took place at the meeting of 4 August. It makes the obvious point that the inspector made a detailed note of the meeting at a time when he can have had no axe to grind, since he could scarcely have been expected

g
to foresee the present dispute, and that on the other hand there is nothing more than the taxpayer's and Mr Joseph's uncorroborated account of what happened many years ago. Accordingly, the Crown submits that this court should decline to accept the statements made as to Mr Mitchell's lack of actual authority.

Speaking for myself, I must confess to very serious scepticism as to whether Mr Mitchell lacked authority to act as he did, since on the face of it it would seem an

h
astonishing thing for an experienced professional accountant to write letters quite clearly claiming to have authority which he entirely lacked. It is, however, unnecessary to reach a final opinion on that matter because the Crown relies on an alternative argument to the effect that whether or not Mr Mitchell actually had authority, he was certainly, so it says, 'held out' to the inspector as having authority and the inspector acted on that basis.

j
In support of that submission it relies on a number of the matters I have already mentioned: the sending of the notification, dated 6 November 1979; the exchanges between Mr Mitchell and the inspector between December 1979 and March 1980; the attendance of Mr Mitchell before the General Commissioners on the taxpayer's behalf on 9 July 1980; the meeting of 4 August 1980 as recorded by the inspector; the letters written by Mr Mitchell on behalf of, or apparently on behalf of, the taxpayer following that meeting; the correspondence with the surtax authorities in

August to September 1980; the letter that I have referred to in April 1981, enclosing the first of the £500 cheques, and the two later letters enclosing further cheques; and, last, the terms in which Bernard Joseph & Co wrote indicating that they were now dealing with the taxpayer's affairs which had formerly been dealt with by their associate firm. From all that material the Crown submits that it is plain that Mr Mitchell was being held out by the taxpayer to the Revenue as having authority to act on his behalf and that the Revenue did so act in good faith, accepting that Mr Mitchell had the authority which he appeared to have.

In argument before us today, the taxpayer has made a number of points with reference to the authorities, which he has clearly grasped the effect of, and he has presented his argument in a very moderate and attractive way. He has urged that this is an extremely old case with a number of strange features; in particular, he has drawn our attention to the fact that the Revenue were at one stage asking for documents relating to events 13 years before, being documents they already had. Because of the delay which has characterised almost every step of the case, the taxpayer urges that it is a case to be approached with great caution and in which every circumstance should be very carefully examined. He has urged that in all the circumstances it would be quite wrong to shut him out and has drawn our attention to the need which he says presses on him to obtain discovery, in order that he can establish his defence and show that Mr Mitchell had no actual or apparent authority. He has drawn our attention to para 14/3–4/9 in Volume 1 of *The Supreme Court Practice 1991*, and has relied on the principle in *Miles v Bull* [1969] 1 QB 258 to suggest that this is a case in which there ought, in all the circumstances, to be a trial. So he relies on both the familiar limbs of RSC Ord 14, both to say that he discloses a defence and also to say that the circumstances are such that there should in all the circumstances be a trial, and having defeated the Crown's claim, as he hopes, based on the agreement under s 54 of the 1970 Act, he then hopes to be able to go back before the General Commissioners and show that he is not in truth liable for the tax claimed at all since these were not revenue transactions but capital transactions which gave rise, if anything, to liability for capital gains tax and not income tax.

Those are submissions that we have heard with care and we have had the opportunity of studying the documents and of reading helpful skeleton arguments not only on behalf of the Crown, which I have already referred to, but a helpful skeleton argument placed before us on behalf of the taxpayer also.

As I have indicated, on the subject of express authority I have some scepticism as to the assertion that Mr Mitchell had none, but would not, for my part, shut the taxpayer out altogether on that ground. When it comes to apparent authority, however, I have no such hesitation. The material appears to me to be quite overwhelming that Mitchell & Co and Mr Mitchell were, over a longish period, held out by the taxpayer as having authority to act on his behalf and the correspondence that one has seen is precisely the sort of correspondence that one finds in the course of a long negotiation between a taxpayer's professional adviser and a Revenue inspector. Despite all the points made on the taxpayer's behalf, both in his skeleton argument and by him personally, I am entirely unpersuaded that there is a shadow of a defence in this case or that there is any other reason why the case ought to be tried.

I should perhaps just mention in closing one matter which the taxpayer has drawn to our attention and that is a point raised on the detailed language of RSC Ord 14. The taxpayer submits that, because the inspector swore his affidavit verifying the statement of claim before it was reamended, there was a technical failure to verify the reamended statement of claim on the basis of which judgment was given against him. It is not a hopeful point from the taxpayer's point of view because if the reamended statement of claim were ignored the claim against him would be larger than in fact it is, each amendment having reduced the figures in his favour. But in any event it is a point that was not raised before the Master or the judge, nor was it

raised in the notice of appeal, and had it been raised, I have no doubt that the
a   Crown, if they had thought there was any merit in the point, would have taken steps
to cure this purely technical defect. I do not therefore, for my part, see any force in
that particular argument even if it is open to the taxpayer to raise it.

In all the circumstances I conclude that both the Master and the judge reached a
conclusion which was abundantly justified and I would dismiss the appeal.

b   **BALCOMBE LJ.** I agree.

MUSTILL LJ. I also agree. In my opinion nothing would be gained by allowing the
taxpayer to maintain an action for the purpose of establishing a defence which, in
my judgment, would be bound to fail.

c   *Appeal dismissed with costs.*

Solicitor: *Solicitor of Inland Revenue.*

Rengan Krishnan Esq   Barrister.

Woolwich Equitable Building Society v Inland Revenue Commissioners

COURT OF APPEAL, CIVIL DIVISION
GLIDEWELL, RALPH GIBSON AND BUTLER-SLOSS LJJ
18, 19, 20, 21, 22 MARCH, 22 MAY 1991

Building Societies – Interest and dividends – Transitional charge on payment of interest and dividends in 1985–86 – Payment of tax pursuant to demand under regulations subsequently declared ultra vires – Whether payments recoverable – Whether interest payable on payments recovered – Supreme Court Act 1981, s 35A.

The Woolwich Equitable Building Society (Woolwich) paid to the Revenue, in response to a demand by the latter, the sum of £56,998,211 in three instalments under the Income Tax (Building Societies) Regulations 1986, SI 1986/482 (the 1986 regulations) and Sch 20 to the Finance Act 1972. Woolwich had challenged the validity of the 1986 regulations from the time they were in draft, and made the payments expressly without prejudice to any right of recovery which might arise as a result of legal proceedings. The payments were made because refusal to pay might result, inter alia, in damage to Woolwich's reputation and liabilities to interest which would not be deductible for tax purposes. Nolan J held, in a decision given on 31 July 1987 (reversed by the Court of Appeal, but later affirmed by the House of Lords (see [1990] STC 682)), that the 1986 regulations were ultra vires and void in so far as they purported to provide for the imposition of tax on dividends and interest paid by building societies prior to 6 April 1986. In anticipation of that decision, Woolwich had issued a writ on 15 July 1987 initiating an action for money had and received, seeking to recover the payments together with interest under s 35A[a] of the Supreme Court Act 1981 on the grounds that the Revenue's demand was made without lawful authority. Following the decision on 31 July 1987 but before the hearing of the action for repayment, negotiations took place between the parties which resulted in the repayment to Woolwich of the sum of £56,998,211 with interest from 31 July 1987, but not from any earlier date. The substantial issue in the hearing was therefore whether or not Woolwich was entitled to interest on the three instalments running from the dates on which they were respectively paid to 31 July 1987. Nolan J held (see [1989] STC 111) that the capital payments were not recoverable under a general restitutionary principle, but under an implied agreement with the Revenue that the sums would be repaid if Woolwich's contentions as to the invalidity of the 1986 regulations proved to be correct. He held that the right to repayment arose only at the moment of the decision as to the invalidity of the regulations and therefore refused the claim to interest from the time the payments were made. Woolwich appealed to the Court of Appeal, contending that (i) under the law of restitution a subject who made a payment in response to an unlawful demand for tax immediately acquired a prima facie right to be repaid the amount so paid; or alternatively (ii) Woolwich paid under duress and thus had immediate right to claim repayment. The Crown contended that (i) there was no such general principle as that suggested by Woolwich; (ii) the facts of the case did not come within the established principles of restitution of sums paid under duress; (iii) the Revenue were under no obligation to make any repayment and did so only as a matter of grace; or alternatively (iv) Nolan J was correct and interest was due only from 31 July 1987.

---

a   Section 35A, so far as material, is set out at p 368 *h–j*, post

Held – (Ralph Gibson LJ dissenting) Where a subject made a payment in response
a to an unlawful demand for tax or any like demand, he immediately acquired a right
in law to recover the amount so paid under a general restitutionary principle unless
the payment had been made voluntarily to close a transaction or had been made
under a mistake of law. Neither limitation applied in this case and accordingly under
s 35A of the Supreme Court Act 1981 interest was payable from the date the
payments were made. The appeal would therefore be allowed.

b   *Slater v Mayor and Corp of Burnley* (1888) 59 LT 636, *William Whiteley Ltd v
The King* (1910) 101 LT 741 and *Twyford v Manchester Corp* [1946] Ch 236
distinguished.

Notes

c For payment of tax by building societies, see Simon's Taxes D4.721.

Cases referred to in judgments

A-G v Wilts United Dairies Ltd (1921) 37 TLR 884, CA; (1922) 127 LT 822, HL.
Air Canada v British Columbia (1989) 59 DLR (4th) 161.
d *Amministrazione delle Finanze dello Stato v San Giorgio SpA* (Case 199/82) [1983]
     ECR 3595, CJEC.
Atchison, Topeka & Santa Fe Railway Co v O'Connor (1911) 223 US 280.
Atlee v Backhouse (1838) 3 M & W 633 at 650.
Auckland Harbour Board v R [1924] AC 318, PC.
B & S Contracts and Design Ltd v Victor Green Publications Ltd [1984] ICR 419,
     CA.
e *Barton v Armstrong* [1976] AC 104, [1975] 2 All ER 465, PC.
Bilbie v Lumley (1802) 2 East 469.
Blackpool and Fleetwood Tramroad Co v Bispham with Norbreck UDC [1910] 1 KB
     592.
Bourgoin SA v Ministry of Agriculture, Fisheries and Food [1986] QB 716, [1985] 3
f   All ER 585.
BP Exploration Co (Libya) Ltd v Hunt (No 2) [1983] 2 AC 352, [1982] 1 All ER 925,
     HL.
Brocklebank Ltd v R [1924] 1 KB 647.
Brown v M'Kinally (1795) 1 Esp 279.
Browning v Morris (1778) 2 Cowp 790.
Buckingham v Francis [1986] 2 All ER 738.
g *Campbell v Hall* (1774) 1 Cowp 204.
Chase Manhattan Bank NA v Israel-British Bank (London) Ltd [1981] Ch 105,
     [1979] 3 All ER 1025.
Dew v Parsons (1819) 2 B & Ald 562.
DPP for Northern Ireland v Lynch [1975] AC 653, [1975] 1 All ER 913, HL.
h *Fairbanks v Snow* (1887) 13 NE Reporter 596.
Fibrosa Spolka Akcyjna v Fairbairn Lawson Combe Barbour Ltd [1943] AC 32,
     [1942] 2 All ER 122, HL.
Glasgow Corp v Lord Advocate 1959 SC 203, CS.
Great Western Railway Co v Sutton (1869) LR 4 HL 226, HL.
Hamlet v Richardson (1833) 9 Bing 644.
j *Harse v Pearl Life Assurance Co* [1904] 1 KB 558.
Hooper v Mayor and Corp of Exeter (1887) 56 LJQB 457.
Hydro Electric Commission of Township of Nepean v Ontario Hydro (1982) 132 DLR
     (3d) 193.
IRC v National Federation of Self-Employed and Small Businesses Ltd [1981] STC
     260, [1982] AC 617, [1981] 2 All ER 93, HL.

IRC v Nuttall [1990] STC 194, [1990] 1 WLR 631, CA.

Irving v Wilson (1791) 4 Term Rep 485.

James, ex p (1874) LR 9 Ch App 609.

Kelly v R (1902) 27 VLR 522.

Kiriri Cotton Co Ltd v Dewani [1960] AC 192, [1960] 1 All ER 177, PC.

Maskell v Horner [1915] 3 KB 106, CA.

Mason v New South Wales (1959) 102 CLR 108.

Maxwell v Griswold (1850) 10 How 242.

Morgan v Palmer (1824) 2 B & C 729.

Moses v McFerlan (1760) 2 Burr 1005.

Muschinski v Dodds (1986) 62 ALR 429.

National Pari-Mutuel Association Ltd v R (1930) 47 TLR 110, CA.

O'Sullivan v Management Agency and Music Ltd [1985] QB 428, [1985] 3 All ER 351, CA.

Paal Wilson & Co A/S v Partenreederei Hannah Blumenthal [1983] 1 AC 854, [1983] 1 All ER 34, HL.

President of India v La Pintada Cia Navegacion SA [1983] 1 Lloyd's Rep 37, QBD; *rvsd* [1985] 1 AC 104, [1984] 2 All ER 773, HL.

Preston v IRC [1985] STC 282, [1985] AC 835, [1985] 2 All ER 327, HL.

R v IRC, ex p MFK Underwriting Agencies Ltd [1989] STC 873, [1990] 1 WLR 1545.

R v IRC, ex p Woolwich Equitable Building Society [1987] STC 654; *rvsd* [1989] STC 463, CA; *affd* [1990] STC 682, [1990] 1 WLR 1400, HL.

R v Chief Constable of the Merseyside Police, ex p Calveley [1986] QB 424, [1986] 1 All ER 257.

R v Tower Hamlets London BC, ex p Chetnik Developments Ltd [1988] AC 858, [1988] 1 All ER 961, HL.

Rogers v Ingham (1876) 3 Ch D 351.

Robertson v Frank Bros Co (1889) 132 US 17.

Sargood Bros v The Commonwealth (1910) 11 CLR 258.

Sebel Products Ltd v Customs and Excise Comrs [1949] Ch 409, [1949] 1 All ER 729.

Sharp Bros and Knight v Chant [1917] 1 KB 771, CA.

Sharpe, re [1980] 1 WLR 219.

Slater v Mayor and Corp of Burnley (1888) 59 LT 636.

Simmonds, ex p (1885) 16 QBD 308.

Somes v British Empire Shipping Co (1860) 8 HLC 338, HL.

South of Scotland Electricity Board v British Oxygen Co Ltd [1959] 1 WLR 587, [1959] 2 All ER 225, HL.

Steele v Williams (1853) 8 Ex 625.

The Queens of the River Steamship Co Ltd v The Conservators of the River Thames (1899) 15 TLR 474.

Twyford v Manchester Corp [1946] Ch 236, [1946] 1 All ER 621.

Tyler, re [1907] 1 KB 865.

Universe Tankships Inc of Monrovia v International Transport Workers' Federation [1983] 1 AC 366, [1982] 2 All ER 67, HL.

William Whiteley Ltd v The King (1910) 101 LT 741.

Cases also cited

Cordell v Second Clanfield Properties Ltd [1969] 2 Ch 9, [1968] 3 All ER 746.

Eadie v Township of Brantford (1967) 63 DLR (2d) 561.

IRC v Aken [1990] STC 497, [1990] 1 WLR 1374, CA.

Neste Oy v Lloyd's Bank plc [1983] 2 Lloyd's Rep 658.

Newdigate v Davy (1693) 1 Ld Raym 742.

Pao On v Lau Yiu [1980] AC 614, [1979] 3 All ER 65, PC.

Wallersteiner v Moir (No 2) [1975] QB 373, [1975] 1 All ER 849, CA.

Western United Investment Co Ltd v IRC [1958] Ch 392.

Appeal

a Woolwich Equitable Building Society (Woolwich) made payments to the Revenue pursuant to demands made under the Income Tax (Building Societies) Regulations 1986. On 31 July 1987 Nolan J held that the regulations were ultra vires and void in so far as they purported to provide for the imposition of tax on dividends and interest paid by building societies prior to 6 April 1986. The payments were repaid to Woolwich with interest from 31 July 1987. Woolwich, in an action for money had
b and received, sought to recover interest from the date the payments were made. Nolan J held in a decision given on 12 July 1989 that Woolwich was entitled under an implied agreement to repayment of the tax paid but that the payments were not a debt for the purposes of s 35A of the Supreme Court Act 1981, and accordingly interest was not payable from the dates the payments were made. Woolwich appealed to the Court of Appeal. The facts are set out in the judgment of Ralph
c Gibson LJ.

John Gardiner QC, Nicholas Underhill and *Jonathan Peacock* for Woolwich.
Anthony Grabiner QC and *Alan Moses QC* for the Crown.

d
Cur adv vult

22 May 1991. The following judgments were delivered.

e **GLIDEWELL LJ.** In his judgment, Ralph Gibson LJ explains the judicial review proceedings which resulted in the relevant parts of the Income Tax (Building Societies) Regulations 1986, SI 1986/482 (the 1986 regulations) being declared ultra vires and therefore void in so far as they purported to require the payment by building societies of tax on dividends and interest paid by such societies for the period immediately preceding 6 April 1986. He also summarises the circumstances
f in which Woolwich paid the total sum of £56,998,211 to the Revenue, including the relevant correspondence before and at the time of payment, and the history of this action. I gratefully adopt what Ralph Gibson LJ says.

I therefore need only summarise briefly certain of the facts referred to by Nolan J (see [1989] STC 111) and Ralph Gibson LJ in their judgments, which are in my view necessary for the determination of this appeal. They are: (i) From the start,
g Woolwich challenged the validity of the 1986 regulations, even when they were in draft. (ii) The form on which Woolwich was required to make a return for the period ending 31 May 1986 and for subsequent quarterly periods, and the accompanying notes for guidance, made it clear that when each form was returned to the Revenue it had to be accompanied by payment of the amount calculated in accordance with the form. There was also in the notes a reminder that interest was chargeable on tax
h paid late, which was not an allowable deduction for tax purposes. (iii) All three payments made by Woolwich were made without prejudice to its contention that the 1986 regulations were ultra vires. (iv) At the same time as it made the first payment on 16 June 1986—to be precise on the following day—Woolwich applied for leave to move for judicial review of the validity of the 1986 regulations. (v) Nolan J summarised the factors which induced Woolwich to make the three
j payments in the following terms ([1989] STC 111 at 116):

'First and foremost, the requirements of the Regulations as amplified in communications from the Revenue amounted on their face to lawful demands from the Crown. Woolwich would have expected any refusal of payment to lead to collection proceedings which would have been gravely embarrassing for Woolwich, the more so as it would have been the only building society refusing to pay. Any publicity suggesting that Woolwich might be in difficulty in meeting its financial obligations, or that alone amongst building societies it was pursuing a policy of confrontation with the Crown, might have damaging effects far outweighing Woolwich's prospects of success on the issue of principle. Second, Woolwich feared that if it failed in its legal arguments it might incur penalties. Third, the three payments to which I have referred formed parts of larger quarterly payments, the other parts of which were agreed to have been correctly charged. At the time when the payments were made, it had not been possible to identify the amounts in dispute. Fourth, Woolwich was not, of course, to know at the time of the payments that it would succeed in the judicial review proceedings. Had Woolwich failed in those proceedings, it would have faced a bill for interest, which would not have been deductible for tax purposes, in an amount far exceeding the net return which Woolwich could have obtained from investing the money withheld.'

The judge found (at 116) in relation to these reasons:

'It seems to me, judging from the language of para 4(1) of Sch 20 to the Finance Act 1972, that Woolwich could reasonably have anticipated at least the raising of an assessment under para 4(3), and possibly the issue of a writ pursuant to s 68 of the Taxes Management Act 1970 with the result in either case of highly undesirable publicity for Woolwich if it had withheld the very large sums claimed by the Revenue to be due ... The substantial point made by Woolwich in the first of its reasons for making the payment lies in the damage to its reputation which it feared from failing to meet an ostensibly lawful claim for tax, and the importance of this factor is something on which the judgment of Woolwich is entitled to respect. Again, although the risk of penalty proceedings must have seemed remote, there being no question of negligence, let alone fraud, on the part of Woolwich, and although Mr Green and Mr Bousher say that in practice there was no risk of penalty proceedings at all, I can understand that the prospect of being even technically in breach of a penal provision if it failed in the judicial review proceedings is one which would weigh with Woolwich. And there can be no dispute about the significance of the interest factor. Subject to the outcome of the present case, the scales in this respect were tilted heavily in favour of the Revenue. I accept that, as a practical matter, Woolwich had little choice but to make the three payments.'

Nolan J gave his decision in the judicial review proceedings on 31 July 1987 (see [1987] STC 654). He declared the 1986 regulations ultra vires and void. Before that date, the writ in the present action claiming repayment of the capital sum with interest had been issued. Although the Crown appealed against Nolan J's decision, by agreement pending the hearing of the appeal it made repayment of the capital sum, leaving the issue as to whether the interest was payable to be decided later.

Woolwich's claim therefore is to interest on the capital sum, calculated from the various dates on which it paid the three sums which make up the total to the date of Nolan J's judgment in the judicial review proceedings. The claim is made under s 35A of the Supreme Court Act 1981 which, so far as is relevant, provides:

'(1) ... in proceedings ... before the High Court for the recovery of a debt ... there may be included in any sum for which judgment is given simple interest, at such rate as the court thinks fit or as rules of court may provide, on all or any part of the debt ... in respect of which judgment is given, or payment is made before judgment, for all or any part of the period between the date when the cause of action arose and—(a) in the case of any sum paid before judgment, the date of the payment ...'

It follows that in order to succeed in its claims to interest, Woolwich must show: (i) that the Revenue were under a legal obligation to repay the capital sum, and thus owed Woolwich a debt; and (ii) that Woolwich had a right to be repaid, so that its cause of action arose, at the dates on which it made the three payments which together totalled £56,998,211.

The case argued for Woolwich before Nolan J and in this court can be summarised as follows: (i) The primary submission of counsel for Woolwich is that a subject who makes a payment in response to an unlawful demand for tax, or any like demand, ie a demand for which there is no basis in law, immediately acquires a prima facie right to be repaid the amount so paid. This is a distinct head of the law of restitution. (ii) Alternatively, Woolwich made payment under duress, and thus had an immediate right to claim repayment.

The response of counsel for the Crown, before this court as before Nolan J, is: (i) There is no such general principle as that suggested by Woolwich. (ii) The facts of this case do not come within the established principles of restitution of sums paid under duress. (iii) Thus the Revenue were under no obligation to make any repayment, and did so only as a matter of grace. (iv) Alternatively, Nolan J was correct to find an implied agreement that the Revenue would hold the moneys paid by Woolwich as a deposit on account of tax which might be held to have been due at the dates of payment. The judge held that on this basis Woolwich only became entitled to reclaim the money once the risk that the tax might be due was set at nought and thus interest only began to run from that date, ie the date of Nolan J's judgment in the judicial review proceedings (see [1989] STC 111 at 120).

The principal issue is therefore is there such a general principle of law as that for which Woolwich contends? If so, what, if any, are the limitations on the operation of that principle? This issue, which is obviously of considerable importance, has been much discussed by distinguished academic commentators, but has not been directly the subject of any modern decided case.

I think it right to draw a distinction between cases in which a plaintiff claims restitution, ie repayment from a defendant who is a private citizen or body or who, although acting on behalf of a public body, had received the payment in the course of a commercial transaction between them, and cases in which the defendant is an instrument or officer of central or local government, exercising a power to require payment of a tax, customs duty, licence fee or other similar impost. Cases in the first category are clearly part of ordinary private law. Cases in the second category, however, seem to me properly to fall in the sphere of what is now called public law. The main distinguishing feature between the two types of case is that in the public law cases there is no question of the defendant having given, offered, or purported to give any consideration for the payment by the plaintiff. The payment is required under what purports to be a statutory power entitling the defendant to claim such a payment, sometimes in return for a licence, in other cases simply as part of a general power to levy a tax or customs duty.

The argument which counsel for Woolwich advances in support of his primary proposition that, since the Revenue were not empowered to demand or receive the payments of tax under the invalid 1986 regulations, it was repayable immediately to Woolwich when paid, is based in part on general principle, and in part on previous decided cases. I will examine each in turn.

General principles

Counsel for Woolwich starts by reminding us of the words of art 4 of the Bill of Rights (1688):

> 'That levying money for or to the use of the Crowne by [pretence] of prerogative without grant of Parlyament for longer time or in other manner than the same is or shall be granted is illegal.'

As to the general principles of the law of restitution, in a well-known passage in his judgment in *Moses v Macferlan* (1760) 2 Burr 1005 at 1012, Lord Mansfield CJ described the basis of the action for money had and received, ie for restitution:

> 'It lies for money paid by mistake; or upon a consideration which happens to fail; or for money got through imposition (express, or implied); or extortion; or

oppression; or an undue advantage taken of the plaintiff's situation, contrary to laws made for the protection of persons under those circumstances. In one word, the gist of this kind of action is that the defendant, upon the circumstances of the case, is obliged by the ties of natural justice and equity to refund the money.'

In his speech in the House of Lords in *Fibrosa Spolka Akcyjna v Fairbairn Lawson Combe Barbour Ltd* [1943] AC 32 at 61, Lord Wright said at the beginning of his speech:

'The claim was for money paid for a consideration which had failed. It is clear that any civilized system of law is bound to provide remedies for cases of what has been called unjust enrichment or unjust benefit, that is to prevent a man from retaining the money of or some benefit derived from another which it is against conscience that he should keep. Such remedies in English law are generically different from remedies in contract or in tort, and are now recognized to fall within a third category of common law which has been called quasi-contract or restitution.'

On the following page Lord Wright quoted the passage from the judgment of Lord Mansfield CJ which I have set out above.

Clearly in the circumstances of the present case there was no question of consideration for the payment by Woolwich to the Revenue. The question is, to use Lord Mansfield CJ's phraseology, was the Revenue's demand for the tax an implied imposition, or did the Revenue take an undue advantage of Woolwich? Is it obliged by the ties of natural justice and equity to refund the money?

Decided cases

There have been decisions in what is now recognised as the field of public law in which a plaintiff who has paid to an officer of government or of some other public body a sum which he was under no legal obligation to pay has successfully claimed repayment of that sum. The decisions are by no means unanimous, nor indeed sometimes clear, as to the principle under which such repayment was ordered by the court. In some of the cases it is said that the right to recover arose because the unjustified demand for payment was made by the officer under 'colour of his office'. This archaic phrase is at best vague and at worst almost meaningless at the present day. Certainly of itself I find it unhelpful.

However, in his judgment in the decision of the High Court of Australia in *Mason v New South Wales* (1959) 102 CLR 108 at 140, Windeyer J gave a most helpful definition of one category of the cases with which we are concerned:

'Yet, although all forms of extortion will ground an action for money had and received, all forms of extortion by officials are not properly described as being by colour of office. Extortion by colour of office occurs when a public officer demands and is paid money he is not entitled to, or more than he is entitled to, for the performance of his public duty. Examples of such exactions are overtolls paid to the keepers of toll-bridges and turnpikes, excessive fees demanded by sheriffs, pound-keepers, &c. The parties were not on an equal footing; and generally the payer paid the sum demanded in ignorance that it was not due.'

Some of the textbook writers have referred to cases in this category as 'withholding cases'. Whatever description is applied to them, there have been over the past two centuries a number of decisions of the courts in which the plaintiffs have succeeded in recovering the money they had paid in circumstances which fell within Windeyer J's definition. These cases include:

Irving v Wilson (1791) 4 Term Rep 485. The plaintiff's goods were unlawfully seized by a Revenue officer, who refused to return the goods without payment of a fee. The plaintiff paid, and recovered the goods. He then sued to recover the payment and succeeded.

Morgan v Palmer (1824) 2 B & C 729. The mayor of a borough improperly charged a fee for renewing a publican's licence. The fee was recoverable.

Maskell v Horner [1915] 3 KB 106, a decision of the Court of Appeal. For many years the plaintiff had carried on business in a market. The market owner each year demanded a toll from the plaintiff under threat of seizure of his goods if he refused to pay. On the first occasion the plaintiff objected and the market owner did seize the goods. The plaintiff thereon paid the toll in order to secure the release of the goods. In later years the plaintiff paid under protest.

After 12 years it was held in other proceedings that the defendant had no right or power to demand the toll, which was therefore unlawful. The plaintiff brought an action to recover the amounts he had paid. This court held that he was entitled to recover the amount of tolls he had paid except those which were barred by the Statute of Limitations, ie he was entitled to recover for the preceding six years.

In his judgment, Lord Reading CJ said (at 118):

> 'Upon the second head of claim the plaintiff asserts that he paid the money not voluntarily but under the pressure of actual or threatened seizure of his goods, and that he is therefore entitled to recover it as money had and received. If the facts proved support this assertion the plaintiff would, in my opinion, be entitled to succeed in this action. If a person with knowledge of the facts pays money, which he is not in law bound to pay, and in circumstances implying that he is paying voluntarily to close the transaction, he cannot recover it. Such a payment is in law like a gift, and the transaction cannot be reopened. If a person pays money, which he is not bound to pay, under the compulsion of urgent and pressing necessity or of seizure, actual or threatened, of his goods he can recover it as money had and received. The money is paid not under duress in the strict sense of the term, as that implies duress of person, but under the pressure of seizure or detention of goods which is analogous to that of duress. Payment under such pressure establishes that the payment is not made voluntarily to close the transaction . . . the payment is made for the purpose of averting a threatened evil and is made not with the intention of giving up a right but under immediate necessity and with the intention of preserving the right to dispute the legality of the demand.'

Later, his Lordship said (at 121–122):

> 'There is no doubt that if a person pays in an action or under threat of action the money cannot be recovered by him, as the payment is made to avoid the litigation to determine the right to the money claimed. Such payment is not made to keep alive the right to recover it, inasmuch as the opportunity is thus afforded of contesting the demand, and payment in such circumstances is a payment to close the transaction and not to keep it open. Even if the money is paid in the action accompanied by a declaration that it is paid without prejudice to the payer's right to recover it, the payment is a voluntary payment, and the transaction is closed. (See *Brown v M'Kinally* (1795) 1 Esp 279.) It is argued that as unpaid tolls can be recovered by distress levied upon the goods of the person who fails to pay, the seizure is to be regarded like the issue of a writ, and therefore that a payment of tolls on seizure must be treated as a voluntary payment. I cannot agree with this contention. When goods are seized, the owner can only relieve them from seizure by payment. He has no opportunity of contesting the right to demand tolls from him except by allowing the seizure and detention of his goods to continue, or by making payment to protect them.'

Buckley LJ quoted (at 124) a dictum of Parke B (see *Atlee v Backhouse* (1838) 3
M & W 633 at 650):

> 'If my goods have been wrongfully detained, and I pay money simply to
> obtain them again, that being paid under a species of duress or constraint, may
> be recovered back . . .'

Buckley LJ then commented:

> 'The same is true, I think, when payment is made not to release goods seized
> but to intercept a threat to seize them. When the defendant demanded payment
> of the plaintiff, the latter, if he refused payment, exposed himself to the seizure
> and sale, rightfully or wrongfully, of his goods. When he made payment to
> escape such seizure and sale, the payment was, I think, within Parke B.'s words,
> not a voluntary payment. Further, if there be added to the above facts the
> further fact that the party making the payment protests that the money is being
> wrongfully taken from him, a further factor is added which goes to show that
> the payment was not voluntary.'

Pickford LJ gave judgment to the same effect.

A-G v Wilts United Dairies Ltd (1921) 37 TLR 884 was another decision of this
court. Under wartime legislation, the defendant company, who were milk
wholesalers, applied for a licence entitling them to purchase milk outside the area
where they were based. The food controller required them to pay 2d per gallon for
the grant of the licence. The defendants agreed to the payment and the licence was
granted. The defendants then refused to make any payment. The Attorney General
claimed from them the amount due under the agreement. This court held that the
imposition of the charge was not within the statutory powers of the food controller,
and thus could not be justified. The defendants therefore could not be required to
make payment despite their agreement. Atkin LJ, in a judgment agreeing with
Bankes and Scrutton LJJ, said (at 887):

> 'It makes no difference that the obligation to pay the money is expressed in
> the form of an agreement. It was illegal for the Food Controller to require such
> an agreement as a condition of any licence. It was illegal for him to enter into
> such an agreement. The agreement itself is not enforceable against the other
> contracting party; and if he had paid under it he could, having paid under
> protest, recover back the sums paid, as money had and received to his use.'

The decision of this court was upheld in the House of Lords (see (1922) 127 LT 822).

The same result followed in another decision of this court, *Brocklebank Ltd v R*
[1925] 1 KB 52, which expressly followed the decision in *A-G v Wilts United Dairies
Ltd*. That was a case, also under wartime legislation, in which the shipping controller
had required an unlawful payment as a condition of a licence to the plaintiffs to sell
one of their ships to a foreign firm.

Counsel for Woolwich makes the point that, although both *A-G v Wilts United
Dairies Ltd* and *Brocklebank Ltd v R* were cases within Windeyer J's definition,
nevertheless the passage which I have quoted from Atkin LJ's judgment is of wider
application. To this counsel for the Crown answers that if that be so, Atkin LJ's
observation in the circumstances was not part of his reasoning in the decision itself.

In a number of other cases the present parties dispute whether or not the facts of
the case were withholding cases, ie within Windeyer J's definition. These cases
include:

Dew v Parsons (1819) 2 B & Ald 562 in which the sheriff charged an attorney's
clerk for issuing warrants for a sum greater than the amount he was authorised to
charge. It was held that the attorney was entitled to reclaim the balance. The
defendant's plea that the payment was made under a mistake of law failed.

Counsel for Woolwich points out correctly that in none of the three judgments is
there any suggestion that the basis of the entitlement to payment was that the

attorney's clerk paid under compulsion. Indeed the reasoning in the second
a judgment, that of Holroyd J (at 566), is in the following terms:

> 'If the defendant has paid more money than the sheriff is allowed by law to
> demand as his fee, the sheriff cannot retain that surplus, and must (if required
> so to do) return it to the defendant.'

Counsel for Woolwich therefore argues that this case is one which does not fall
b within Windeyer J's definition.

In *Steele v Williams* (1853) 8 Ex 625, the defendant, a parish clerk, was entitled to
charge fees for making certified copies of extracts from the parish registers. The
plaintiff, an attorney's clerk, wished to examine the registers and to make his own
extracts, which would not be certified by the defendant. Nevertheless the defendant
said that the charge would be the same whether the plaintiff made the extracts
c himself or was given certificates. After the plaintiff had made the extracts he desired,
the defendant demanded a charge from him which the plaintiff paid. The attorney
then sought to recover it and succeeded.

In his judgment Parke B said (at 630):

> 'I think that, upon the true construction of the evidence, the payment in this
d > case was not voluntary, because, in effect, the defendant told the plaintiff's
> clerk, that if he did not pay for certificates when he wanted to make extracts, he
> should not be permitted to search.'

Later, the judge said (at 631):

> 'Therefore, in the first place, I think that there is evidence that this payment
e > was not voluntary, but necessary for the exercise of a legal right; and further, I
> by no means pledge myself to say that the defendant would not have been guilty
> of extortion in insisting upon it, even without that species of duress, viz. the
> refusal to allow the party to exercise his legal right, but colore officii. *Dew v
> Parsons* certainly goes to that extent. But it is not necessary to decide this case
> on that ground.'

f Platt B agreed. Martin B said (at 632–633):

> 'As to whether the payment was voluntary, that has in truth nothing to do
> with the case. It is the duty of a person to whom an Act of Parliament gives
> fees, to receive what is allowed, and nothing more. This is more like the case of
> money paid without consideration—to call it a voluntary payment is an abuse
g > of language. If a person who was occupied a considerable time in a search gave
> an additional fee to the parish clerk, saying, "I wish to make you some
> compensation for your time," that would be a voluntary payment. But where a
> party says, "I charge you such a sum by virtue of an Act of Parliament," it
> matters not whether the money is paid before or after the service rendered; if
> he is not entitled to claim it, the money may be recovered back.'

h Martin B was thus not basing his judgment on facts which fall within Windeyer J's
definition, though it seems that the other two judges probably were.

Another case in this category was *The Queens of the River Steamship Co Ltd v
The Conservators of the River Thames* (1899) 15 TLR 474. That decision is not
binding on us, and for my part I do not think it adds anything to what is contained
j in the decisions to which I have already referred.

We were referred also by counsel for Woolwich to two cases on which he strongly
relies in which the plaintiff recovered payments he had made in circumstances
which undoubtedly do not fall within Wendeyer J's definition. The first was
Campbell v Hall (1774) 1 Cowp 204, another decision of Lord Mansfield CJ. The
customs collector, without any lawful authority, imposed on the export of sugar
from the island of Grenada a customs duty. The plaintiff paid and then brought

action to recover back the amount he had paid. He was held entitled to recover. Lord Mansfield CJ's reasoning was contained in one short passage (at 205) in his judgment:

> 'The action is an action for money had and received; and it is brought upon this ground; namely that the money was paid to the defendant without any consideration; the duty, for which, and in respect of which he received it, not having been imposed by lawful or sufficient authority to warrant the same.'

The second case is the decision of the Divisional Court in *Hooper v Mayor and Corp of Exeter* (1887) 56 LJQB 457. The corporation had power under a private act to charge dues for the landing of stone, but there was an exception that dues were not payable on limestone intended to be burned into lime. The plaintiff, who landed considerable quantities of limestone to burn into lime, was unaware of this exception. On discovering it, he reclaimed the dues he had paid on stone to be burned into lime. The corporation refused but he succeeded in his claim. *Morgan v Palmer* (1824) 2 B & C 729 was cited during the course of the argument. In his judgment Lord Coleridge CJ said ((1887) 56 LJQB 457 at 458):

> 'From the case cited in the course of argument it is shewn that the principle has been laid down that, where one exacts money from another and it turns out that although acquiesced in for years such exaction is illegal, the money may be recovered as money had and received, since such payment could not be considered as voluntary so as to preclude its recovery. I am of the opinion that that principle should be adopted here, and that accordingly the plaintiff is entitled to recover his money on the ground that he has paid it involuntarily.'

Smith J agreed and referred also to the decision in *Steele v Williams* (1853) 8 Ex 625.

The proposition set out by Lord Coleridge CJ undoubtedly is much wider than that relating merely to the cases which fall within Windeyer J's definition, and thus supports the argument of counsel for Woolwich.

We were on the other hand referred to a number of cases which tend to suggest that there is no such general principle as that submitted on behalf of Woolwich. The first is *Slater v Mayor and Corp of Burnley* (1888) 59 LT 636. The corporation demanded and the plaintiff paid water rates for some houses based on the gross value of the properties. The corporation were only empowered to charge rates based on the net value. The plaintiff claimed back the balance. He succeeded in the County Court but failed on appeal to the Divisional Court. *Steele v Williams* and *Hooper v Mayor and Corp of Exeter* were referred to in the argument but not in either of the judgments. The defence which succeeded was that the payment was voluntary. It is set out most clearly in the judgment of Wills J ((1888) 59 LT 636 at 639):

> 'In my opinion, the payment in this case was a voluntary payment. The respondent gave way and paid. It seems to me in these circumstances that it is idle to say that there is anything like duress—there was nothing in the nature of a threat used; it is simply the ordinary case of a person raising a contention when a demand is made upon him. This is not sufficient to constitute duress, so as to prevent a payment being a voluntary one. It seems to me, therefore, in this case that the contention of the appellants on this ground is well founded, and that on this ground the appeal must succeed.'

A case on which counsel for the Crown much relies is the decision of Walton J in *William Whiteley Ltd v The King* (1910) 101 LT 741. The employers of 'male servants' were required to take out licences for such employees, for which fees were payable to the Revenue. Whiteley employed a number of men to prepare and serve meals to their shop assistants. The Revenue claimed that these men were 'male servants', but Whiteley consistently disputed this. Nevertheless, for six years under protest Whiteley paid the fees claimed by the Revenue. In the seventh year it refused

to pay. The Revenue took proceedings to recover the fees for the seventh year, but
a Whiteley was held to be correct in its contention that the employees were not 'male
servants' within the proper interpretation of the relevant regulations. Whiteley then
sought to recover the moneys it had paid during the past six years, but was held not
entitled to do so. Walton J held that it was not entitled to recover because it had paid
voluntarily, not under compulsion. He held, correctly in my view, that the facts did
not show anything in the nature of duress or a demand for payment colore officii
b within Windeyer J's definition. Therefore he decided that since Whiteley had not
taken the stop in earlier years of refusing to make payment and arguing the matter
in court, it must be taken to have paid voluntarily.

In *National Pari-Mutuel Association Ltd v R* (1930) 47 TLR 110 the company,
without objection, paid betting duty to operate a totalisator. Later another company,
on identical facts, brought proceedings in which it was held not liable to pay the
c duty. The plaintiff company now brought an action for repayment of the duty it
had paid. It failed in this court, on the ground that the payment had been made as a
result of a mistake of law made by the company, and thus on general principle the
amount paid could not be recovered. Scrutton LJ, in a judgment with which Greer
and Romer LJJ agreed, said (at 111):

d   'What was the mistake which the appellants had made in this case? They
knew all the facts, their own rules, and what they were doing with the totalisator.
They had considered the Finance Act, 1926, and they had come to the
conclusion that they were liable to pay the betting tax ... The question of,
liability was one of law. It was a question of the construction of the Act of
Parliament. The Act of 1926 provided for a tax on every bet made with a
bookmaker, and a bookmaker was defined as a person receiving and negotiating
e   bets. The appellant company carried on business of that class ... The company
thought that they were liable to pay the tax. After they had paid it, the House
of Lords, in the case already referred to, decided that a company doing similar
business were not liable to the tax. Mr Justice Branson held that the mistake
was one of law, and that the company could not recover. That decision was
right ...'

f In *Twyford v Manchester Corp* [1946] Ch 236 the corporation sought to charge
fees to a monumental mason for permission to work on memorials in the cemetery.
The plaintiff paid fees under protest. After some time he brought an action claiming
that the corporation was not entitled to make the charges. It was held that the
charges had been levied improperly, but nevertheless the plaintiff was not entitled
g to recover them.

In his judgment Romer J referred to *William Whiteley Ltd v The King* (1910) 101
LT 741 and *Slater v Mayor and Corp of Burnley* (1888) 59 LT 636. He said (see
[1946] Ch 236 at 241) of the former case that Walton J—

'... treated the case as one of payment under a mistake of law. I should myself
have doubted whether it was a true case of money paid under a mistake of law,
h   because William Whiteley, Ld., on their view of the law, were not liable to pay
it and, indeed, said so. Even so, however, I respectfully agree with the rest of
Walton J.'s judgment, particularly with his statement that a general rule applies,
namely, the rule that, if money is paid voluntarily, without compulsion,
extortion, or undue influence, without fraud by the person to whom it is paid
and with full knowledge of all the facts, it cannot be recovered, although paid
j   without consideration, or in discharge of a claim which was not due or which
might have been successfully resisted. In my judgment that covers the present
case in which, having regard to the evidence, the principle of duress colore
officii cannot prevail.'

In *Sebel Products Ltd v Customs and Excise Comrs* [1949] Ch 409, Sebel Products
claimed a declaration that one of the articles it manufactured was not liable to

purchase tax within the Finance Act 1947. The action was heard on 2 July 1948, when Vaisey J granted a declaration in favour of the plaintiffs. Two months before that the plaintiffs paid the Customs and Excise the amount of purchase tax which would have been owing if their claim had failed. They now took out a summons for an account of the purchase tax which they had paid and for repayment of the amount due.

The Customs and Excise, basing themselves on *William Whiteley* and *National Pari-Mutuel*, argued that the money had been paid voluntarily and was thus irrecoverable.

Vaisey J found that Sebel Products were entitled to recover the money paid on the ground that when they made payment to the Customs and Excise, it was the intention of both parties, and thus there was an implied agreement, that if Sebel Products succeeded in their action for a declaration the money would be repaid. This of course is the basis on which Nolan J had found for Woolwich in the present case.

However, in the course of his judgment Vaisey J said (at 413):

> 'By the Crown Proceedings Act 1947, the defendants are placed in the same position as the ordinary subjects of the Crown (see s. 21) and I see no reason why they should not in appropriate cases refuse to refund money paid to them voluntarily under a mistake of law, as the Revenue Authorities were held to be entitled to do in the case of *William Whiteley Ltd v The King* (1910) 101 LT 741 and *National Pari-Mutuel Association Ltd v R* (1930) 47 TLR 110. At the same time I cannot help feeling that the defence is one which ought to be used with great discretion, and that for two reasons. First, because the defendants being an emanation of the Crown, which is the source and fountain of justice, are in my opinion bound to maintain the highest standards of probity and fair dealing, comparable to those which the courts, which derive their authority from the same source and fountain, impose on the officers under their control: see *In re Tyler* [1907] 1 KB 865. Secondly, because the taxpayer, who is too often tempted to evade his liability and to keep in his own pocket money which he ought to have paid to the Revenue, will find too ready an excuse in the plea that the Revenue Authorities will, if they can, keep in their coffers, if they can get it there, money which the taxpayer was under no obligation to pay to them, and they had no right to demand. Although such an excuse would have no validity in either a court of law or in the forum of the taxpayer's own conscience, I think that, in the public interest, grounds for proffering it should, so far as possible, be avoided.'

These last observations of Vaisey J find an echo in the speech of Lord Bridge in *R v Tower Hamlets London BC, ex p Chetnik Developments Ltd* [1988] AC 858, to which counsel for Woolwich refers as guidance on the general approach which taxing or rating authorities, and thus the courts, should adopt.

Chetnik Developments constructed two warehouse units under a consent granted under the London Building Acts. The consent was subject to a condition that the buildings should not be occupied until the consent of the Tower Hamlets London Borough Council had been obtained to the proposed user. Chetnik could not say what the proposed user would be until it had obtained a tenant for each of the warehouses. This, for some time, it failed to do. The council served a completion notice on Chetnik under para 8 of Sch 1 to the General Rate Act 1967 (the 1967 Act). Chetnik did not appeal against the notice. Accordingly from 16 November 1976 it was required to pay rates on the warehouses, although unoccupied, as if it was the occupier. Chetnik duly paid rates until 31 March 1979, on which date the first warehouse was eventually let and occupied. The second warehouse remained unoccupied until November 1980.

It was only after 31 March 1979 that Chetnik appreciated that para 2 of Sch 1 to the 1967 Act provides that no rates shall be payable on an unoccupied hereditament *a* under that Schedule for any period during which the owner is prohibited by law from occupying the hereditament or allowing it to be occupied. Chetnik therefore declined to pay any further rates on the second warehouse. It argued that until it had obtained consent to the proposed user of the warehouse, it was prohibited by law from allowing it to be occupied. This contention was upheld in proceedings brought by the London Borough Council in the Magistrates' Court, and the council did not appeal. Chetnik then sought to reclaim the amount of rates it had paid on

b both warehouses for the period from November 1976 to 31 March 1979.

The claim was made under s 9 of the 1967 Act which provides so far as is material—

'. . . where it is shown to the satisfaction of a rating authority that any amount paid in respect of rates, and not recoverable apart from this section, could properly be refunded on the ground that . . . (*e*) the person who made a payment in respect of rates was not liable to make that payment, the rating authority

c may refund that amount or a part thereof.'

It was conceded that this gave the council a discretion to decide whether to repay the amount of rates which Chetnik had not been liable to pay. The council decided not to make any repayment. Chetnik applied for judicial review of that decision. It failed at first instance, but succeeded on appeal to the Court of Appeal, and the

d council's appeal to the House of Lords was dismissed.

The case was of course one in which the power to repay was contained in the statute. Nevertheless the issue before the court was whether the reasons which the council gave for exercising its discretion not to repay were proper and valid reasons, or whether they did not justify the exercise of the discretion to refuse repayment. Although the decision is of course direct authority in relation to the Rating Act 1967,

e in his speech with which the remainder of their Lordships all agreed, Lord Bridge based his decision on general principles. Counsel for Woolwich submits, and I agree, that his Lordship's observations apply as much to an authority exercising a power to levy taxes as they do to a rating authority.

Lord Bridge said (at 873–874):

f 'In general terms it is, of course, obvious that the section authorises the refund of rates overpaid. But, to articulate the apparent principle underlying the section more precisely it is surely envisaged in each of the five cases where the section authorises refunds of amounts paid in respect of rates which would otherwise be irrecoverable that the ratepayer who has paid rates in compliance with a demand note which he might have successfully resisted may appropriately

g be relieved of the consequences of his oversight.'

Lord Bridge then shortly described the five situations in which under s 9 a rating authority may decide to make a repayment. He said (at 874–875):

'The common feature of all the five cases is an error or oversight on the part of the ratepayer. Only in the case of paragraph (*b*) is it necessary to predicate

h any error on the part of the rating authority, which may in any event have been no more than a clerical error. In none of the other cases is the rating authority likely to have been aware of the ratepayer's error which occasioned the overpayment. To these considerations must be added the important qualification that section 9(2)(*b*) precludes any refund of overpaid rates when the underlying error affected current general practice, so that either ratepayers

j generally or all ratepayers in the class affected by the error are in the same position. In each case, except paragraph (*a*), where the obstacle to recovery is the conclusive evidential effect of an unchallenged entry in the valuation list, the amount paid would be irrecoverable apart from the section because paid under a mistake of law. In each case because of his mistake the individual ratepayer has borne more than his proper share of the rate burden. In each case the section envisages that the amount overpaid in a past year may be refunded in a future year. The rule that money paid under a mistake of law is irrecoverable is said to stem from the principle that there must be an end to litigation. But there is an instructive line of authority showing circumstances in which the court will not permit the rule to be invoked. In *Ex parte James* (1874) L.R. 9 Ch. App. 609, a judgment creditor had levied execution in satisfaction of a judgment debt against a debtor subsequently adjudicated bankrupt. The judgment creditor later paid over the proceeds of the execution to the trustee in bankruptcy mistakenly believing that he was legally obliged to do so. The trustee in bankruptcy claimed to retain this sum for the benefit of the general body of unsatisfied creditors on the ground that it had been paid under a mistake of law. Rejecting this claim, James L.J. said, at 614: "I am of the opinion that a trustee in bankruptcy is an officer of the court. He has inquisitorial powers given him by the court, and the court regards him as its officer, and he is to hold money in his hands upon trust for its equitable distribution among the creditors. The court, then, finding that he has in his hands money which in equity belongs to someone else, ought to set an example to the world by paying it to the person really entitled to it. In my opinion, the Court of Bankruptcy ought to be as honest as other people." *Ex parte Simmonds* (1885) 16 Q.B.D. 308 was another case of a trustee in bankruptcy claiming to retain money paid to him under a mistake of law. Lord Esher M.R. said, at 312: "When I find that a proposition has been laid down by a Court of Equity or by the Court of Bankruptcy which strikes me as a good, a righteous, and a wholesome one, I eagerly desire to adopt it. Such a proposition was laid down by James L.J. in *Ex parte James*, L.R. 9 Ch. App. 609. A rule has been adopted by courts of law for the purpose of putting an end to litigation, that, if one litigant party has obtained money from the other erroneously, under a mistake of law, the party who has paid it cannot afterwards recover it. But the court has never intimated that it is a high-minded thing to keep money obtained in this way; the court allows the party who has obtained it to do a shabby thing in order to avoid a greater evil, in order that is, to put an end to litigation. But James, L.J., laid it down in *Ex parte James* that, although the court will not prevent a litigant party from acting in this way, it will not act so itself, and it will not allow its own officer to act so. It will direct its officer to do that which any high-minded man would do, viz., not to take advantage of the mistake of law."'

Later Lord Bridge said (at 876–877):

> 'So it emerges from these authorities that the retention of moneys known to have been paid under a mistake at law, although it is a course permitted to an ordinary litigant, is not regarded by the courts as a "high-minded thing" to do, but rather as a "shabby thing" or a "dirty trick" and hence is a course which the court will not allow one of its own officers, such as a trustee in bankruptcy, to take.'

He said a little later (at 877):

> 'I in no way dissent from this reasoning [ie that of the Court of Appeal], but I should myself have been content to derive the same conclusion from the broader consideration that Parliament must have intended rating authorities to act in the same high principled way expected by the court of its own officers and not to retain rates paid under a mistake of law, or in paragraph (a) upon an erroneous valuation, unless there were, as Parliament must have contemplated there might be in some cases, special circumstances in which a particular overpayment was made such as to justify retention of the whole or part of the amount overpaid.'

There have, of course, been cases in other common law jurisdictions both of the payment of taxes later held to be invalid or unconstitutional and of fees or other duties demanded under some threat or duress. I wish to refer to three such cases.

The first is *Sargood Bros v The Commonwealth* (1910) 11 CLR 258, a decision of
the High Court of Australia. Customs duty was demanded and paid under a change
in legislation which was proposed and announced but which at the relevant time
had not yet come into force. It was held that the amount paid was recoverable as not
having been paid voluntarily. O'Connor J said (at 276):

> 'The first ground is taken that the payment was voluntary. In one sense it
> was. It was in fact made without protest and in the ordinary course of Customs
> business. But it was paid with the knowledge on both sides that Customs control
> over goods imported may be exercised in support of illegal as well as of legal
> demands of duty. The principle of law applicable in such cases is well recognized.
> Where an officer of Government in the exercise of his office obtains payment of
> moneys as and for a charge which the law enables him to demand and enforce,
> such moneys may be recovered back from him if it should afterwards turn out
> that they were not legally payable even though no protest was made or question
> raised at the time of payment. Payments thus demanded *colore officii* are
> regarded by the law as being made under duress. The principle laid down in
> *Morgan v Palmer* (1824) 2 B. & C., 729, *Steele v Williams* (1853) 8 Ex., 625 and
> adopted in *Hooper v Exeter Corporation* (1887) 56 L.J.Q.B., 457 clearly
> establishes that proposition.'

It will be seen that in this passage O'Connor J was using the expression colore
officii in a much wider sense than that used by Windeyer J and was enunciating a
principle which effectively was the same as that for which Woolwich is contending
in the present case.

A year later, in *Atchison, Topeka & Santa Fe Railway Co v O'Connor* (1911) 223
US 280, a decision of the US Circuit Court for the District of Colorado, the plaintiff
was held entitled to recover money paid as tax under a law which was later held
unconstitutional, and which he had paid under threat of distress and under protest.
Holmes J said (at 285–286):

> 'It is reasonable that a man who denies the legality of a tax should have a clear
> and certain remedy. The rule being established that apart from special
> circumstances he cannot interfere by injunction with the State's collection of its
> revenues, an action at law to recover back what he has paid is the alternative
> left. Of course we are speaking of those cases where the State is not put to an
> action if the citizen refuses to pay. In these latter he can interpose his objections
> by way of defence, but when, as is common, the State has a more summary
> remedy, such as distress, and the party indicates by protest that he is yielding
> to what he cannot prevent, courts sometimes perhaps have been a little too slow
> to recognize the implied duress under which such payment is made. But even
> if the State is driven to an action, if at the same time the citizen is put at a
> serious disadvantage in the assertion of his legal, in this case of his constitutional,
> rights, by defence in the suit, justice may require that he should be at liberty to
> avoid those disadvantages by paying promptly and bringing suit on his side. He
> is entitled to assert his supposed right on reasonably equal terms.'

Holmes J then referred to disadvantages which the taxpayer would suffer under the
relevant statute if he did not pay, and continued:

> 'As appears from the decision below, the plaintiff could have had no certainty
> of ultimate success, and we are of opinion that it was not called upon to take the
> risk of having its contracts disputed and its business injured and of finding the
> tax more or less nearly doubled in case it finally had to pay. In other words, we
> are of opinion that the payment was made under duress.'

It follows that this decision also was made on facts very similar to those of the
present case, and on a principle similar to that for which Woolwich is arguing.

The third case is one to which I have already referred, the decision of the High
Court of Australia in *Mason v New South Wales* (1959) 102 CLR 108. The plaintiffs

were carriers of goods by road based in the State of Victoria. Under New South Wales legislation, they required a licence to entitle them to carry goods in their vehicles into that state. The New South Wales authorities demanded the payment of a fee for the issue of the licence. The plaintiffs paid under protest. There was some tenuous evidence that the plaintiffs believed that if they did not pay the fee and nevertheless ran their vehicles into New South Wales they might be seized. After some years it was decided in another case that the requirement of the licence fee was unconstitutional. The plaintiffs brought action to recover the fees they had paid and were held by a majority entitled to succeed. Windeyer J, who gave the last judgment, said (at 140):

> 'Extortion by colour of office occurs when a public officer demands and is paid money he is not entitled to, or more than he is entitled to, for the performance of his public duty.'

Both he and Menzies J held that on the facts the money had been demanded by the state officials bona fides, under the law as they understood it to be, and thus not within his restricted definition. Windeyer J said (at 142–143):

> '[The plaintiffs] must . . . establish that there was, in a legal sense, compulsion by something actually done or threatened, something beyond the implication of duress arising from a demand by persons in authority, which suffices in a true *colore officii* case. Further the plaintiffs must establish that they actually paid because of this compulsion, and not voluntarily despite it. "Voluntary payment" has a special meaning here. Clearly it does not import a payment by way of gift. And equally clearly it means more than payment willingly, in the sense of without reluctance . . . In my view a payment may be said to be voluntary, in this context and for present purposes, when the payer makes it deliberately with a knowledge of all relevant facts, and either being indifferent to whether or not he be liable in law, or knowing, or having reason to think, himself not liable, yet intending finally to close the transaction . . . It seems plain that a man compelled by pressure *colore officii* or any other form of duress may yet say "well I have really no option but to pay, nevertheless I will not dispute the matter further. I will pay to put an end to the question".'

Dixon CJ and Kitto J went rather further. The former said (at 117):

> 'I have not been able completely to reconcile myself to the view that if the weight of a *de facto* governmental authority manifested in a money demand is not resisted although it is incompatible with s. 92 the money belongs to the Crown unless the payment was the outcome of the actual threatened or apprehended withholding of something to which the payer was entitled or the actual threatened or apprehended impeding of him in the exercise of some right or liberty. But English authority seems now to say that moneys paid to the Crown as and for taxes cannot be recovered from the Crown upon its turning out that the moneys were not exigible notwithstanding that they were demanded by the Crown, unless the circumstances were such that they would be recoverable as between subject and subject, *exempli gratia* as involuntary payments or payments made under a mistake of fact. See *William Whiteley Ltd. v. The King* (1910) 101 L.T. 741; *National Pari-Mutuel Association Ltd. v. The King* (1930) 47 TLR 110, and *Sebel Products Ltd. v Commissioners of Customs and Excise* (1949) Ch. 409 . . .'

However, he held that the plaintiffs were entitled to recover because of the implied threat to seize the plaintiffs' vehicles if they did not pay.

Kitto J said (at 125):

> 'The general principle to be considered is that which *Pollock* called "the common principle . . . that if a man chooses to give away his money, or to take

his chance whether he is giving it away or not, he cannot afterwards change his mind; but it is open to him to show . . . that he really had no choice": *Principles of Contract*, 13th ed. (1950), p. 481. The defendant says that the plaintiffs had ample choice. They might defy the State of New South Wales, entering its territory and using its roads in their inter-State journeys without regard to its statute, pinning their faith to s. 92 as a guarantee that they would emerge scatheless from the enterprise. But when *Pollock* referred to a choice he was using the language of practical affairs. He meant a free choice, uninfluenced by compulsion of any sort. *Hodges* J. expressed the conception in *Kelly v The King* (1902) 27 V.L.R. 522: "The expression 'voluntary payment' does not mean a payment which the petitioner or any other person wishes to make. In the case of many persons such payments never are voluntary in that sense. A 'voluntary payment' means at most a payment made to get rid of a liability (*scil.* asserted by the payee though not sustainable in law), made with a free exercise of the will, where no advantage is taken of the position of the person or the situation of his property." (1902) 27 V.L.R., at p. 532. An actual or threatened seizure or detention of the payer's property has often been the feature relied upon as showing that there really was no choice. But other circumstances may show it also.'

Kitto J then referred to two other earlier decisions of the US Supreme Court, *Maxwell v Griswold* (1850) 10 How 242 and *Robertson v Frank Bros Co* (1889) 132 US 17, and quoted (at 126) the judgment in the latter case as follows:

'When such duress [moral duress not justified by law] is exerted under circumstances sufficient to influence the apprehensions and conduct of a prudent business man, payment of money wrongfully induced thereby ought not to be regarded as voluntary. But the circumstances of the case are always to be taken into consideration. When the duress has been exerted by one clothed with official authority, or exercising a public employment, less evidence of compulsion or pressure is required,—as where an officer exacts illegal fees, or a common carrier excessive charges. But the principle is applicable in all cases according to the nature and exigency of each.'

Kitto J continued:

'These observations, accurately reflecting, as I believe they do, the common law of England, seem to me to have special force in the case of a payment made to a government in order to obviate adverse consequences which a statute invalidly purports to provide as the alternative.'

The judge concluded (at 129):

'I do not myself feel justified in attaching much weight to the tenuous evidence upon which we were invited to find that the plaintiffs made their payments because of apprehensions induced by words or conduct of State officials that vehicles would or might be seized and detained under s. 47. My judgment rests upon the view that the plaintiffs had quite enough compulsion upon them from the terms of the Act itself, apart altogether from anything that might have been said or done by officers of government. Under that compulsion they parted with their money . . . it was still their money that they parted with, and there is nothing to account for their parting with it except the pressure they were under. In my opinion they are entitled by law to have it back.'

It seems that the reasoning of Menzies and Windeyer JJ in that case would not entitle Woolwich to succeed on the facts of the present case, but the principle enunciated by Kitto J would support Woolwich's propositions as probably would have Dixon CJ.

I should also refer to a decision of the Court of Session, in which the issues canvassed were similar, but not identical, to those before us. In *Glasgow Corp v Lord Advocate* 1959 SC 203, the corporation sued the Customs and Excise Commissioners for a declarator that purchase tax was not chargeable on stationery manufactured in its own printing department, and for repayment of purchase tax paid for the years 1951 to 1957. The First Division of the Inner House of the Court of Session concluded that stationery manufactured for the purposes of carrying out the corporation's public services was not chargeable to purchase tax, that the corporation had paid tax in the past as a result of a mistake made by it as to the proper interpretation of s 18(1) of the Finance Act 1946, and that moneys paid under a mistake as to the proper interpretation of a statute were irrecoverable. In their judgments both Lord Wheatley, the Lord Ordinary, and the Lord President specifically referred with approval to the conclusion of this court to the same effect in *National Pari-Mutuel*.

The judgment of Nolan J

Nolan J's judgment in this action is reported at [1989] STC 111. The reasons which led the judge to his eventual conclusion are to be found in various places in his judgment. He quoted (see [1989] STC 111 at 114) a passage from a work by Professor Birks, his *Introduction to the Law of Restitution* (1985) p 295, to the following effect:

> 'Where the challenge is made after payment, the effect of a declaration that the demand was unlawful is sometimes to induce repayment on an *ex gratia* basis. The crucial question is, however, whether there is ever restitution as a matter of right. The dominant modern view appears to be that the citizen who pays an *ultra vires* demand must establish the same facts against the public authority as would entitle him to restitution from a private individual. This is assumed to mean that he must in practice show that he paid under a mistake of fact or under duress, or that he made a contract for repayment in the event that it should turn out that the money was not payable. On the other side of the line, those who pay by mistake of law, or even under no mistake at all but simply because they despair of making their view prevail against the position taken by the bureaucratic machine, must on this view be said to have no hope whatever of obtaining restitution.'

Nolan J said ([1989] STC 111 at 117):

> 'Now that [the payments made by Woolwich to the Revenue] have been shown not to have been lawfully claimed, were they immediately recoverable? The first ground on which Woolwich contends for an affirmative answer to this question is, as I have mentioned, that the payments were immediately recoverable by virtue of a general restitutionary principle which may be invoked by a subject who has paid money in response to a tax demand made by the Crown without lawful authority. Money thus paid is recoverable, says Woolwich, even in the absence of duress or of a mistake of fact. It is, I think, necessarily implicit in this contention that, contrary to what Professor Birks described as the dominant modern view in the passage which I have cited above, different considerations apply to claims by the subject against the Crown or public authority from those which apply as between subject and subject. Woolwich relies in this connection on the doubt expressed obiter as to the correctness of this view by Dixon CJ in *Mason v New South Wales* (1959) 102 CLR 108 at 116. For my part, however, I cannot find any positive support in the decided cases for the application of a general restitutionary principle, operating in the absence of mistake of fact or duress, on claims by the subject against the Crown or public authorities. What the decided cases do show, to my mind, is a realistic though limited acknowledgment that the ability of the Crown or a public authority to apply duress to the subject may be very much greater than that of another subject.'

The judge then referred to cases where money has been exacted from the subject
a under colour of office, quoting the definition of that concept in the judgment of
Windeyer J in *Mason*'s case. Nolan J commented: 'The principle thus defined,
clearly does not apply to the present case.' I respectfully agree, and indeed counsel
for Woolwich concedes that this is correct.

The judge then contrasted the situations in *Mason*'s case and *William Whiteley*,
and said ([1989] STC 111 at 118):

b   'Counsel for the Crown submits that, so far as the presence or absence of
         duress is concerned, the present case falls on the *William Whiteley* rather than
         the *Mason* side of the line. I agree. The potential cost to Woolwich of refusing
         to pay in terms of damage to reputation and interest liabilities may have been
         commercially unacceptable but I cannot regard it as involving duress on the
         part of the Revenue. The position might be different if Woolwich had paid
c   under threat of the Revenue taking distress proceedings without a court order
         under s 61 of the Taxes Management Act 1970, but as I have said there is no
         evidence that such drastic and highly unusual proceedings were either
         threatened by the Revenue or anticipated by Woolwich, still less that Woolwich
         had a reasonable apprehension of being put out of business by them.'

d   The judge then went on to consider whether Woolwich had a right to recover the
capital sum under any other head, and concluded that it was so entitled under an
implied agreement with the Revenue which arose when it made the payments, ie
that if its contentions about the invalidity of the 1986 regulations proved to be
correct, the moneys would be repaid, but that the right to repayment would only
arise at the moment when the decision as to the invalidity of the 1986 regulations
e was made. It was for this reason that Nolan J refused the claim by Woolwich to be
awarded interest.

Summary of arguments

What then are the arguments in favour of there being a general restitutionary
principle, ie a principle of law that, if a government body or officer makes a demand
f for the payment of a tax or duty which he has no legal power to require, and payment
is made in response to the demand, there is a presumption of law that the payer has
an immediate right to recover the payment? There is no doubt that such a
presumption arises in the withholding cases, ie where there has been an actual or
threatened seizure of the plaintiff's goods, or the withholding of a service he wishes
to receive, as a sanction for the plaintiff complying with the demand made by the
g official. This concept, though it may not strictly amount to duress in the sense in
which that word is understood in private law, nevertheless clearly bears a relationship
to duress.

The argument for Woolwich in the present case is that it is illogical and unjust
that the presumption should only arise in such circumstances. I summarise the
arguments in favour of the wider presumption as follows: (i) The Bill of Rights
h (1688), ie that where there is no parliamentary authority for the imposition of a tax
or duty, the taxing authority never was entitled to any money paid on an invalid
demand, and thus must be obliged to repay. (ii) The taxing officer or body has
powers conferred by statute to enforce his demand over and above the private
citizen's right to bring an action at law. In addition, in some situations, of which this
is one, the statutory provisions may put the taxpayer at a disadvantage if he does not
j make a payment which in the end it proves he was obliged to make as against his
position if he does make a payment which he was not obliged to make. I refer here
to what Nolan J called 'the interest factor'. (iii) Such a general restitutionary principle
must have underlain, though it was not expressly articulated, the decisions in
Campbell v Hall (1774) 1 Cowp 204 (which expressly relied on the Bill of Rights
ground); *Dew v Parsons* (1819) 2 B & Ald 562; the judgment of Martin B and that of
Parke B, possibly obiter, in *Steele v Williams* (1853) 8 Ex 625; and *Hooper v Mayor*

and Corp of Exeter (1887) 56 LJQB 457. (iv) It accords also with the general approach
of the House of Lords in *R v Tower Hamlets London BC, ex p Chetnik Developments*
Ltd [1988] AC 858. (v) It also accords with the judgments in Australia and America
of O'Connor J in *Sargood Bros v The Commonwealth* (1910) 11 CLR 258, Holmes J
in *Atchison Topeka and Santa Fe Railway Co v O'Connor* (1911) 223 US 280 and
Dixon CJ and Kitto J in *Mason v New South Wales* (1959) 102 CLR 108. (vi) Not
least, the principle is based on a general standard of fairness in the relations and
dealings between officers and organs of government who require the payment of a
tax or customs duty, and the taxpayer.

I am persuaded by these arguments. I am clearly of the view that there should, in
the interests both of justice and good government, be such a general restitutionary
principle as that for which Woolwich contends. The authorities I have quoted
support the view that such a principle is part of the common law, though it is not
always by any means articulated clearly in those decisions. I have therefore
considered whether there are any authorities, binding on this court, which would
compel us to adopt the contrary view.

Limitations on the principle

Before I do so, however, I must refer to two concepts which are established by the
decided cases, and which are relevant to the question. The first is, to use the words
of Lord Reading CJ in *Maskell v Horner* [1915] 3 KB 106 at 118, in a passage which
I have already quoted more extensively:

> 'If a person with knowledge of the facts pays money, which he is not in law
> bound to pay, and in circumstances implying that he is paying it voluntarily to
> close the transaction, he cannot recover it. Such a payment is in law like a gift,
> and the transaction cannot be reopened.'

Later in his judgment Lord Reading CJ referred (at 121) to the analogous principle:

> 'There is no doubt that if a person pays in an action or under threat of action
> the money cannot be recovered by him, as the payment is made to avoid the
> litigation to determine the right to the money claimed.'

I also revert to a short passage from the judgment of Windeyer J in *Mason v New*
South Wales (1959) 102 CLR 108 at 143, where he said:

> 'In my view, a payment may be said to be voluntary, in this context and for
> present purposes, when the payer makes it deliberately with a knowledge of all
> relevant facts, and either being indifferent to whether or not he be liable in law,
> or knowing, or having reason to think, himself not liable, yet intending finally
> to close the transaction.'

The second concept is that of mistake of law. It is frequently said that a person
who makes a payment under mistake of fact has a right to recover it, while a person
who makes a payment under a mistake of law has not. The subject is discussed by
Lord Goff and Professor Jones in *The Law of Restitution* (3rd edn, 1986) p 117
onwards. They argue that confusion arises from the misunderstanding of a judgment
of Lord Ellenborough in *Bilbie v Lumley* (1802) 2 East 469. The authors suggest that
the true rationale of that decision was that a payment made in settlement of an
honest claim is irrecoverable. They comment (at p 119):

> 'In our view the principle in *Bilbie v. Lumley* should only preclude recovery
> of money which was paid in settlement of an honest claim. Any other payment
> made under a mistake of law should be recoverable if it would have been
> recoverable had the mistake been one of fact.'

They are also of the view that many of the English cases which appear to be based
on a mistake of law are, when properly analysed, based on the principle of settlement
of a claim.

In *National Pari-Mutuel*, a decision of this court to which I have already referred,
it is clear that the issue argued in the court below and in the Court of Appeal was
whether the mistake which the company had made when it made payment of betting
duty was one of fact or of law. No reference was made to any of the earlier cases on a
different line, such as *Hooper v Mayor and Corp of Exeter* (1887) 56 LJQB 457.
Branson J, and this court, held unanimously that the mistake was of law, and thus
that the company could not recover. Although the case was no doubt one in which
it could equally have been argued by the Revenue that the company had paid to
close the transaction, it is short but clear authority for the proposition that a payment
under a mistake as to the interpretation of the statute is not thereafter recoverable.

However, our attention was also drawn to a passage in the judgment of Lord
Denning, giving the decision of the Judicial Committee of the Privy Council in
Kiriri Cotton Co Ltd v Dewani [1960] AC 192 at 204:

> 'Nor is it correct to say that money paid under a mistake of law can never be
> recovered back. The true proposition is that money paid under a mistake of
> law, by itself and without more, cannot be recovered back. James L.J. pointed
> that out in *Rogers v Ingham* (1876) 3 Ch.D. 351, 355. If there is something more
> in addition to a mistake of law—if there is something in the defendant's conduct
> which shows that, of the two of them, he is the one primarily responsible for the
> mistake—then it may be recovered back. Thus, if as between the two of them
> the duty of observing the law is placed on the shoulders of the one rather than
> the other—it being imposed on him specially for the protection of the other—
> then they are not in pari delicto and the money can be recovered back; see
> *Browning v Morris* (1778) 2 Cowp. 790, 792, by Lord Mansfield. Likewise, if
> the responsibility for the mistake lies more on the one than the other—because
> he has misled the other when he ought to know better—then again they are not
> in pari delicto and the money can be recovered back; see *Harse v Pearl Life
> Assurance Co.* [1904] 1 K.B. 558, 564, by Romer L.J.'

I come back therefore to consider the cases on which counsel for the Crown relies
for his submission that there is no general restitutionary principle in English law.
Neither *Slater v Mayor and Corp of Burnley* (1888) 59 LT 636 nor *William Whiteley*
are binding on us, and for my part I am inclined to think that they were both
wrongly decided. Nevertheless they have been referred to and relied on in a number
of later decisions, and for that reason we should not lightly set them aside. On one
view, both decisions were based, not on a denial of any general principle, but on one
or more of the possible limitations to that principle to which I have just referred. In
Slater v Mayor and Corp of Burnley both judges in the Divisional Court decided
that the payment was made voluntarily and thus could not be recovered. Wills J
based his judgment on the principle that a payment made to close the transaction
may not be recovered. He said (at 639):

> 'The respondent gave way and paid. It seems to me in these circumstances
> that it is idle to say that there is anything like duress—there was nothing in the
> nature of a threat used; it is simply the ordinary case of a person raising a
> contention when a demand is made upon him. This is not sufficient to constitute
> duress, so as to prevent a payment being a voluntary one.'

In *William Whiteley* Walton J based his decision on two principles, first that the
payment had been made by the company under a mistake of law and thus could not
be recovered, and second, on the principle that the company had paid to close the
transaction. As to the first of those matters, I do not myself think that the reported
facts of the case justify Walton J's conclusion, with all respect to him. In my view
therefore if these two decisions were correct, they should be held to be so only
because they were based on the 'close the transaction' principle.

As I have already said, the decision of this court in *National Pari-Mutuel* is
binding on us and was undoubtedly decided on the basis that money paid under a

mistake of law as to the proper interpretation of a statute, is irrecoverable. Subject to what I say below, the general restitutionary principle must therefore be subject to that limitation.

In *Twyford v Manchester Corp* [1946] Ch 236 at 241, Romer J expressed the view, with which I have just said I agree, that in *William Whiteley* it seems that the payment by the company had not been made under a mistake of law. However, Romer J agreed with the remainder of Walton J's judgment. This case also must therefore be considered as a 'close the transaction' case. If it was not decided on this principle, again I believe it to have been wrongly decided.

Finally in *Sebel Products*, Vaisey J was bound by the decision in *National Pari-Mutuel* to hold that a payment under a mistake of law as to the proper interpretation of a statute was irrecoverable. It is clear to me from the passage in his judgment (see [1949] Ch 409 at 413) I have already quoted that if he had not held himself so bound, he would have found for *Sebel Products* on a general principle of restitution, rather than on the applied agreement which he found was the basis on which he was able to give judgment in its favour.

It follows in my view that none of these authorities, even the decision of this court which is binding on us, impels us to the view that there is no general restitutionary principle. What they appear to show is that there are limitations on the application of such a principle, both in cases where it can properly be said that the payment was made in order to close the transaction, and in cases where the payment was made as a result of the payer being mistaken as to the proper interpretation of the relevant statute. It is arguable that it is illogical that a general restitutionary principle should be subject to these limitations. However, in the light of the authorities to which I have referred, it is not in my view open to us in this court to accept this argument. We are bound by this court's previous decisions in *Maskell v Homer* and *National Pari-Mutuel*.

I therefore conclude that there is such a general principle as that for which Woolwich contends, but, at least in cases where the matter in issue is the interpretation of the statute, that principle is subject to the two limitations to which I have just referred, ie that the payment may not be recoverable if it was made to close the transaction or under a mistake of law. Whether these limitations apply in a situation where what is in issue is not the proper interpretation of the statute, but an ultra vires regulation, I doubt. But in the circumstances of this case I do not find it necessary to consider that matter further.

I have considered whether there may not be one further limitation to the general principle of restitution. This, however, is a matter which has not been argued before us, and I therefore wish to do no more than refer to it without expressing any concluded view. In a case such as the present where a demand is made for payment of tax and the taxpayer wishes to contend that the regulation under which the tax is claimed is ultra vires and therefore invalid, he brings his proceedings as Woolwich did by way of judicial review. It is, however, a normal principle of administrative law that the judicial review jurisdiction will not be exercised where there is an alternative remedy by way of appeal, save in exceptional circumstances (see the decision of this court in *R v Chief Constable of the Merseyside Police ex p Calveley* [1986] QB 424, and cases there cited).

If a claim is made for tax and the dispute is as to whether the particular provision of the statute has been properly interpreted, or even more basically whether the amount assessed is too great, then the taxpayer will normally have a statutory right of appeal. If for instance a person charged to income tax appealed to the commissioners under s 55 of the Taxes Management Act 1970, and the commissioners concluded in the event that he had overpaid tax, then s 55(9)(*b*) requires that 'any tax overpaid shall be repaid'.

It may be that the courts would decide that where there was a clear avenue of appeal laid down by statute, that was the course which should be taken and that a remedy by way of judicial review was not available even if the result was that the

taxpayer was repaid the capital overpayment without any interest. As I say, however,
a this possible limitation has not been discussed before us, and I do not wish to express
any concluded view about it.

Conclusion
I have considered the limitations on a general restitutionary principle in cases of
payment made to close the transaction or under a mistake of law, and the possible
b further limitation where there is an alternative remedy available. However, in my
view on the facts of this case none of these limitations applies. Woolwich made it
quite clear from the start that it was not making payment to close the transaction; it
paid without prejudice to the argument in the judicial review proceedings that the
1986 regulations were invalid. Since Woolwich correctly asserted that invalidity
from the start, it cannot be suggested that it made any payment under a mistake of
c law. The suggestion of an alternative statutory remedy has not been canvassed.
I would therefore hold that when Woolwich made the various payments under
the ultra vires 1986 regulations, it immediately acquired a right in law to recover the
amount of those payments. It follows that it was entitled also to be paid interest on
those amounts, at an appropriate rate, from the date of payment to the date of Nolan
J's judgment in the judicial review proceedings.
d I would therefore allow the appeal. It follows in my view that Woolwich is entitled
to judgment for the appropriate amount of interest, and it remains to be considered
how that amount should be assessed.

RALPH GIBSON LJ. Woolwich Equitable Building Society (Woolwich) appeals
against the decision of Nolan J of 12 July 1988 (see [1989] STC 111) whereby he
e dismissed the claim of Woolwich against the Inland Revenue Commissioners (the
Revenue). The claim was for interest on sums of money, totalling £56,998,211,
which Woolwich had paid to the Revenue in respect of claims to tax, which claims
were unlawful because based on regulations which were ultra vires and void. No
issue arose as to recovery of the capital sum of £56,998,211 because that had been
repaid. The amount claimed for interest, which would require to be assessed by the
f court if not agreed, is put by Woolwich at about £7·8m.
The appeal raises issues of great public importance and, in particular, the
relationship of the constitutional principle, namely that there can be no taxation
without the authority of Parliament, to the rules of law governing recovery from the
Crown of money paid in respect of an unlawful demand for tax.

g *The judicial review proceedings*
(i) Woolwich obtained in earlier proceedings a declaration that the relevant
regulations were void. The course of those proceedings, which provide the
background to the present dispute, can be summarised briefly because a full account
is available in the reported decisions of Nolan J on 31 July 1987 [1987] STC 654; of
the Court of Appeal of 12 April 1989 [1989] STC 463; and of the House of Lords of
h 25 October 1990 [1990] STC 682, [1990] 1 WLR 1400.
(ii) Between 1894 and 1985 the tax position of building societies, so far as
concerned accounting for tax deducted by a society on interest paid or credited to
its members, was regulated by extra-statutory arrangements made between
individual building societies and the Revenue. By s 23 of the Finance Act 1951,
those arrangements received parliamentary recognition—later s 343 of the Income
j and Corporation Taxes Act 1970 (the 1970 Act). The effect of such an arrangement
was that a building society was required to account to the Revenue for a lump sum
representing the tax on the interest paid to its members.
(iii) For the year 1985–86 the lump sum paid by Woolwich, whose accounts were
made up to 30 September in each year, only took into account payments to members
down to 30 September 1985; the interest paid during the period 1 October 1985 to
5 April 1986 (interest for the omitted period) was not taken into account.

(iv) In 1986, under powers contained in s 343(1A) of the 1970 Act (now s 476 of the Income and Corporation Taxes Act 1988 (the 1988 Act)) the Board of Inland Revenue made regulations imposing a new system whereby building societies from 1986–87 onwards were required to account in respect of interest payments made to members on a quarterly basis in respect of interest paid in the quarter concerned. The Income Tax (Building Societies) Regulations 1986, SI 1986/482, (the 1986 regulations) contained transitional provisions which purported to require building societies to account in respect of interest payments made to members after the end of the last accounting period but before 1 March 1986.

(v) Section 343(1A) of the 1970 Act was amended by section 47(1) of the Finance Act 1986, which provided that section 343(1A) 'shall have effect and be deemed always to have had effect' as providing that the sums in respect of which the Board was empowered to make regulations requiring building societies to account included '. . . sums paid or credited before the beginning of [1986–87] but not previously brought into account under [s 343(1) or s 343(1A)]'.

(vi) Woolwich challenged the validity of the 1986 regulations and applied by judicial review for a declaration that the 1986 regulations were void. On 31 July 1987 Nolan J (see [1987] STC 654) granted the application and declared that, to the extent that the 1986 regulations purported to impose a liability on Woolwich in 1986–87 and 1987–88 in respect of interest for the omitted period, they were ultra vires and void.

(vii) On appeal to this court, the Revenue contended that interest for the omitted period consisted of sums paid or credited before the beginning of 1986–87 but not previously brought into account under s 343(1), within the meaning of s 343(1A) as amended, and that therefore the 1986 regulations could not be ultra vires in imposing liability in respect of that interest. It was conceded by the Revenue that reg 11(4) was ultra vires. Regulation 11(4) provided that—

'. . . the sum payable to the Board to which paragraph (3) refers is the sum of the reduced rate amount arrived at by reference to a rate of 25·25 per cent and the basic rate amount arrived at by reference to a rate of 30 per cent.'

The invalidity of that provision was accepted because it purported to charge the sum so brought into account at a reduced rate of 25·25% and a basic rate of 30% which were the rates appropriate to the tax year 1985–86; but s 343(1A) provided that the sum for which the society was to be liable in respect of the interest brought into account was to be an amount representing income tax calculated at the rates 'determined for the year of assessment concerned'. It was, however, contended for the Revenue that that partial invalidity did not invalidate the rest of reg 11.

(viii) This court allowed the appeal of the Revenue (see [1989] STC 463). It was held that reg 11 did not have the effect of charging to tax the income of a period of more than one year; and reg 11 did not involve any element of double taxation. The fact that, as had been conceded, reg 11(4) was invalid did not render the whole of the 1986 regulations invalid.

(ix) On appeal to the House of Lords the order of Nolan J was, on 25 October 1990, restored (see [1990] STC 682, [1990] 1 WLR 1400). Their Lordships upheld the reasoning of the Court of Appeal so far as concerned their holding that Parliament had conferred power on the Revenue to make regulations requiring the taxation in the year 1986–87 and subsequent years of assessment of sums paid or credited in the omitted periods; but they held that the admitted invalidity of reg 11(4) infected the whole of that regulation and, therefore, reg 11 and reg 3, so far as it related to the period after February and before 6 April 1986, were declared to be invalid.

The payment of the money

The judicial review proceedings were commenced by notice of application on 17 June 1986. The first relevant payment, of an amount of £42,426,421, was made on 16 June 1986 in the following circumstances. Woolwich had disputed the validity

of the 1986 regulations when they were in draft and before they were made on
a 13 March 1986. The 1986 regulations came into force on 6 April 1986. Regulation 3
provided that each building society 'shall pay' to the Revenue on the specified
quarterly dates the appropriate amount of tax in respect of dividends and interest
paid by it to its members. By letter of 11 April to Woolwich, Mr Brunsden, the
district inspector, referred to the 'need to agree the income tax due for the
"transitional" period 1 October 1985 to 28 February 1986, splitting figures between
b basic rate and composite rate in the usual way' and asked for Woolwich's 'computation
on the same basis as that used in previous years for the annual assessment'. That was
followed by a letter of 17 April 1986 in which Mr Fletcher, the collector of taxes,
sent to Woolwich the return form CT61(Z), with which Woolwich was required to
make its returns at the end of each of the stated return periods, together with the
payment, calculated in accordance with the form, within 14 days of the end of each
c period. With the form were sent printed notes for guidance which included a
statement that 'your returns have to be made to the collector of taxes and this form
provides you with space for both types of return'. The form itself contained the
reminder that 'interest is chargeable on tax paid late—it is not an allowable deduction
for tax purposes'.

By letter of 12 June 1986, Woolwich returned to the Revenue the form CT61(Z)
d for the period 1 March to 31 May 1986. The form showed the 'net tax due on
payments' as £42,426,421 due on 14 June. The letter noted that, on transfer by
automated payment of that sum on 16 June to the account of the Revenue, no
interest would be charged in respect of the two days between 14 and 16 June. The
letter concluded:

e   'You should be aware that we are presently seeking leave to commence legal
proceedings in connection with the regulations and accordingly this payment is
made without prejudice to any right to recover any payments made pursuant to
the regulations which may arise as a result of legal proceedings, or as a result of
any future extinguishment or reduction of any liability under the said
regulations or otherwise.'

f On 15 September 1986 Woolwich paid £2,856,821 and on 16 March 1987
£11,714,969. It is common ground that the second and third payments were made
on the same 'without prejudice' basis and it is not necessary to consider the terms of
any further letter.

The statutory background
g   The 1986 regulations were directed at the tax liabilities of building societies. The
provisions contained in the regulations and the demands and requirements sent by
the Revenue to Woolwich in reliance on the validity of the regulations inevitably
made it clear to the responsible managers of Woolwich that the Revenue possessed
and would, if necessary and when appropriate, use the powers of enforcement which
the Revenue have under the provisions of the Taxes Acts. That statutory
h background, which is said by Woolwich to justify a finding that the payments were
made under duress, was as follows. Regulation 7 provided that Sch 20 to the Finance
Act 1972, with certain modifications, should have effect for the collection of the tax
under the 1986 regulations and that interest should be chargeable on overdue
payments. Paragraph 4(1) of Sch 20 provides that income tax, in respect of any
payment which is required to be included in a return under the Schedule, 'shall be
j due' at the time when the return is made and 'shall be payable' without the making
of any assessment. An assessment may, however, be made under para 4(3) of Sch 20
if the taxpayer fails to include in his return a payment which in the inspector's
opinion ought to have been included. The issue of liability will then be resolved by
way of an appeal against the assessment. If the appeal fails, then interest runs in
favour of the Revenue from the time when the tax should have been paid. If it turns
out that the taxpayer has paid more tax than was due, then the payment becomes

repayable on the determination of the appeal but without interest (see para 10(4) of
Sch 20). It is not expressly provided that there shall be no interest but it is common
ground that that is the effect of the absence of any express provision for the payment
of interest. A power of distress on goods and chattels in the case of failure to pay a
sum charged is provided by s 61 of the Taxes Management Act 1970; and, by ss 66
and 68, tax may be recovered from the person charged as a debt due to the Crown
by action in the County Court or the High Court. Under s 98 of the same Act a
penalty not exceeding £50 may be imposed on a taxpayer who fails to make a return
which has been required of him, and provision is made for greater penalties if the
failure is fraudulent or negligent.

The proceedings to recover the money and interest

Woolwich issued its writ on 15 July 1987 between the conclusion of the hearing
before Nolan J and the giving by him of his reserved judgment on 31 July 1987 (see
[1987] STC 654). The claim asserted that, since the payments were made pursuant
to demands based on void regulations, the demands were unlawful; the payments
had been made under protest; and, therefore, the Revenue were liable to repay the
capital sums with interest pursuant to s 35A of the Supreme Court Act 1981 (the
1981 Act).

After the giving of judgment by Nolan J on 31 July 1987, Woolwich and the
Revenue agreed, after discussions, for the repayment of the capital sums with
interest from the date of the judgment. It has always been the contention of the
Revenue that the payments were voluntary; and that Woolwich, although it may
have had a confident expectation that the Revenue would return the capital as an ex
gratia payment if Woolwich succeeded in the judicial review proceedings, had in
law no right to recover the capital sums save under any contract for repayment
which could be implied from the circumstances in which the payments were made.

The defence of the Revenue set out those contentions, and alleged that, if
Woolwich had any entitlement in law to repayment, the Revenue would contend—

'. . . that the payments were made pursuant to an implied agreement between
the Woolwich and the Revenue whereby it was agreed that the Revenue would
hold the sums pending the outcome of proceedings to determine the validity of
the regulations. Any entitlement to repayment arose on the date of judgment of
Nolan J and interest ran from that date.'

At the hearing of the recovery proceedings before Nolan J, in response to
submissions for the Revenue that the statement of claim disclosed no cause of action,
the claim of Woolwich was amended so as to allege that the payments were made in
discharge of unlawful claims to tax and that, therefore, since the payments were
thus made without consideration, the capital was repayable by the Revenue as
money had and received to the use of Woolwich. Further, it was alleged that the
payments were, in the circumstances, made under compulsion and were recoverable
on that ground.

Since the capital sums had been repaid with interest from 31 July 1987, the only
issue before Nolan J was whether Woolwich could make good a claim to be paid
interest for the periods of time that the Revenue had held the capital between the
dates of payment and 31 July 1987. That depended on proof that Woolwich had a
cause of action to recover the capital independent of any contract arising by
implication on the circumstances of payment. Woolwich did not then allege that
any such agreement could be held to have contained a term providing for such
interest.

The judgment of Nolan J

It was common ground before Nolan J, as it has been in this court, that if
Woolwich had a valid claim against the Revenue, based on ordinary principles of
restitution, by reason of the invalidity of the regulations, or because the circumstances

in which the payments were made are in law the equivalent of duress, then the sums
repayable were debts within the meaning of s 35A of the 1981 Act (see *BP Exploration
Co (Libya) Ltd v Hunt (No 2)* [1983] 2 AC 352); and that, therefore, interest would
be recoverable at such rate and for such period as the court might think fit. There
were placed before Nolan J the relevant authorities and the comments on those
authorities made in textbooks of learned authors and in articles in the journals of
academic lawyers. His conclusions are set out fully in the report of his judgment at
[1989] STC 111. In brief summary he held: (i) He was greatly attracted by the
argument advanced for Woolwich since it was clear that the capital would never
have been received by the Revenue but for the ultra vires regulations made by them.
In effect the Revenue had, in times of inflation, received a large interest-free loan
from Woolwich. (ii) Nevertheless, it was clear that the courts had not extended the
general principle of restitution to those who have submitted to unauthorised
demands for tax. On the contrary, the general rule has been that the maker of the
payment has no right to recover the principal sum paid let alone to recover interest
on it. (iii) After stating the statutory context in which the purported claims by the
Revenue had been made under the void regulations, and after reference to the letters
and documents passing between the parties, Nolan J held that four factors had
induced Woolwich to make the payments, namely: (a) The requirements of the 1986
regulations, as stated in communications from the Revenue, amounted to apparently
lawful demands from the Crown. Refusal of payments could be expected to lead to
enforcement proceedings and to result in publicity, possibly suggesting that
Woolwich might be in difficulty in meeting its financial obligations, or that it alone
among building societies was pursuing a policy of confrontation with the Crown,
and such publicity might have damaging effects outweighing the prospects of success
in the judicial review proceedings. (b) Woolwich feared that, if it failed in the judicial
review proceedings, it might incur penalties. (c) The payments made formed part
of larger quarterly payments of which the remainder was correctly charged and, at
the time of payment, the amount in dispute was not precisely identified. (d) The
prospects of success in the judicial review proceedings were uncertain. If Woolwich
had failed, sums due for interest on the unpaid demands, which would not have
been deductible for tax purposes, would have far exceeded the net return which
Woolwich could have obtained by investing the £56,998,211. The overall cost to
Woolwich in interest, if it had refused to pay and had failed in the judicial review
proceedings, was estimated at £4m. He concluded that 'as a practical matter . . .
Woolwich had little choice but to make the three payments'. (iv) No positive support
could be found in the decided cases for the application of a general restitutionary
principle, in the absence of mistake of fact or duress, on claims by the subject against
the Crown or public authorities. (v) The principles applied in cases where money
has been exacted from the subject colore officii are confined to cases where 'a public
officer demands and is paid money he is not entitled to, or more than he is entitled
to, for the performance of his public duty' (see *Mason v New South Wales* (1959) 102
CLR 108 at 140 per Windeyer J) and were thus not applicable in this case. (vi) The
analogous and broader principle of duress is not applicable where there is no threat
to the person of the subject or to his goods (see *Mason*'s case) and where the sanction
involves only the threat of legal proceedings (see *William Whiteley Ltd v The King*
(1910) 101 LT 741). (vii) The decision of Walton J in *William Whiteley* has been
consistently followed and this case falls within the principles stated in that case.
(viii) The potential cost to Woolwich of refusing to pay, whether in terms of damage
to reputation or of interest liabilities, may have been commercially unacceptable but
did not amount to duress by the Revenue. (ix) There had, however, been a right at
law in Woolwich to recover the capital on the principle stated by Vaisey J in *Sebel
Products Ltd v Customs and Excise Comrs* [1949] Ch 409 at 412–413, namely on an
implied contract for the repayment of the capital by the Revenue in the event of
Woolwich succeeding in the judicial review proceedings. There was, however, no
basis in law for implying an agreement to pay interest.

The appeal to this court

The contentions and argument of Woolwich on appeal have been substantially a the same as they were before Nolan J save for one further point. Woolwich has submitted that, if the only ground of recovery of the capital available to Woolwich was in contract arising by implication on the facts, that contract should be held to include a term that the Revenue would pay interest on the capital sums from the dates of payment. No objection was taken by the Revenue to the raising of that point in this court. The Revenue's notice under RSC Ord 59 r 6(1)(b) maintained that, if b there was no implied agreement for repayment of the capital, no right to repayment ever arose; alternatively, it was said that once the dispute was resolved in favour of Woolwich in the judicial review proceedings, it became unconscionable for the Revenue to retain the money and that it was open to the court to impose on the defendants a constructive trust in respect of that money.

It is to be noted that the Revenue did not there contend that, if Woolwich should c show that the circumstances in which the demands for tax and payments on account of tax were made gave rise to a right to recover the capital sums with interest, nevertheless the making of the implied agreement for repayment of capital without interest should be held to have compromised or brought that right to an end. Counsel for the Crown submitted that such a result might well be effected by an agreement in similar circumstances, but did not argue that the court should so find on the facts d of this case.

The submissions for Woolwich

(i) Counsel for Woolwich has contended that the relevant authorities are inconsistent and confused and that there is no authority binding on this court which prevents this court from giving effect to the claim of Woolwich as properly based on e well-established principles (see *Fibrosa Spolka Akcyjna v Fairbairn Lawson Combe Barbour Ltd* [1943] AC 32 at 61–64 per Lord Wright and *Kiriri Cotton Co Ltd v Dewani* [1960] AC 192 at 204–205).

(ii) The claim was advanced on two grounds. The first was that, on principle, he who makes a payment in response to an unlawful demand of taxation, or other like demand from the Crown, acquires a prima facie right to recover the money forthwith f as money had and received. This should be held to be a distinct head of recovery independent of mistake or duress. It could be limited in this case to circumstances where the demand is based on an ultra vires regulation.

(iii) The law should, as a matter of policy, encourage by its rules the sort of responsible conduct shown by Woolwich in this case, namely to pay under protest and to seek at once the ruling of the court. The law should not permit the Revenue g to enjoy the right to behave with less than the highest standard of conduct (see *Sebel Products* [1949] Ch 409 at 412–413 per Vaisey J and *R v Tower Hamlets London BC, ex p Chetnik Developments Ltd* [1988] AC 858 at 876–877 per Lord Bridge). Further, to deny the prima facie right of recovery would be to depart from the constitutional principle, contained in the Bill of Rights (1688), against taxation unauthorised by Parliament (see *A-G v Wilts United Dairies Ltd* (1921) 37 TLR 884 at 886–887 per h Atkin LJ). Reference was also made to art 13 of the European Convention for the Protection of Human Rights and Fundamental Freedoms for the proposition that there should be an effective remedy for the violation of a substantive right (see *Amministrazione delle Finanze dello Stato v San Giorgio SpA* (Case 199/82) [1983] ECR 3595).

(iv) It was acknowledged for Woolwich that such a right may, in particular j circumstances, be defeated by defences arising on the facts, eg that the payer voluntarily submitted to the unlawful demand in full knowledge of the position and intending to close the transaction. Proof of such intention would depend not on subjective uncommunicated intention but on that which the recipient would reasonably understand from what was said and done.

(v) The second basis of claim was duress or practical compulsion which should be

held to be proved on the findings of the judge that Woolwich had 'little choice but to
a   make the three payments' (see [1989] STC 111 at 116).

(vi) To have to resort to implied agreement, as the basis for holding that the
Revenue had not on the facts been free in law to retain the capital sums paid by
Woolwich, was to apply a fiction and to revert to the discredited 'implied contract'
analysis of restitutionary rights (see Goff and Jones *The Law of Restitution* (3rd edn,
1986) pp 5–12). There was on the facts no agreement according to ordinary principles
b   of contract law. To hold, as Nolan J did (see [1989] STC 111 at 119), that—

> '... generally ... whenever money is paid to the Revenue pending the
> outcome of a dispute which, to the knowledge of both parties will determine
> whether or not the Revenue are entitled to the money, an agreement for the
> repayment of the money if and when the dispute is resolved in the taxpayer's
> favour must inevitably be implied unless the statute itself produces that result,
c   > as it does, for example, in cases falling within para 10(4) of Sch 20 to the Finance
> Act 1972.'

is to create a cause of action under a 'contract' imposed by law as contrasted with an
agreement made by the parties.

(vii) If, however, it is to be held that there was an implied contract, there should
d   be implied a term for the payment of interest by the Revenue from the date of
receipt of the sums paid.

(viii) Woolwich never argued that this was a 'mistake' case. If, however, the case
should be categorised as one of mistake, then it was submitted that the sums paid
were recoverable notwithstanding that the mistake was one of law. The rule
excluding recovery for mistake of law should be abrogated as wrong (see *Air Canada
e   v British Columbia* (1989) 59 DLR (4th) 161 and *Hydro Electric Commission of
Township of Nepean v Ontario Hydro* (1982) 132 DLR (3d) 193). In the alternative,
the case was said to be within established exceptions to the rule (see *Kiriri Cotton*).

The submissions for the Revenue
f   The Revenue have claimed no special right or immunity. Their case has been that
the law applicable to the claims of Woolwich is the same as that applicable in disputes
between private individuals. In summary, the case put forward by counsel for the
Crown was as follows:

(i) The law allows no general right of restitution. Since there was no duress, and
no unlawful demand colore officii, the payments were made voluntarily; ie in law
g   there was no right to recover them save under any implied contractual promise.

(ii) Counsel for the Crown relied on the *William Whiteley* case as authority,
strikingly similar on its facts, which has been consistently followed and never
doubted; he referred, for support, to: *Twyford v Manchester Corp* [1946] Ch 236;
Mason v New South Wales (1959) 102 CLR 108; *Sharp Bros and Knight v Chant*
[1917] 1 KB 771; *Slater v Mayor and Corp of Burnley* (1888) 59 LT 636; *National
h   Pari-Mutuel Association Ltd v R* (1930) 47 TLR 110; and Goff and Jones *The Law
of Restitution* (3rd edn, 1986) pp 120–122, 218.

(iii) The colore officii line of authority is, said counsel for the Crown, clearly
distinguishable. The Revenue, as Nolan J held (see [1989] STC 111 at 117), did not
demand money in return for the performance of a public duty.

(iv) The only implied threat which supported the claims to tax under the void
j   regulations was that of legal process. It is well established in law, he submitted, that
payments made 'under compulsion of legal process' are not to be held to be
recoverable as involuntary payments (see *Brown v M'Kinally* (1795) 1 Esp 279;
Hamlet v Richardson (1833) 9 Bing 644; *Maskell v Horner* [1915] 3 KB 106 at 121–
122; *William Whiteley*; and *Goff and Jones* p 207).

(v) On examination of the statutory provisions enacted by Parliament for the
recovery of sums overpaid in respect of claims to tax, it appeared that, when recovery

is ordered after successful appeal, interest is not generally allowed. Parliament should be taken to have made provisions for recovery on the assumption that the common law gives no right of action to recover money overpaid in respect of tax in the absence of ordinary grounds of claim such as mistake of fact or duress.

(vi) The implied contract was properly found by Nolan J to have been made. There was no fiction and it was implied on the facts and not imposed by law. No term for payment of interest could properly be implied on the facts (see *President of India v La Pintada Cia Navegacion SA* [1985] 1 AC 104).

(vii) This court was invited to resist any temptation to make new law in this field and in particular to resist the beguiling submission that the Revenue, by the making of ultra vires regulations, had been unjustly enriched to the extent of the interest on the payments made by Woolwich. Woolwich was, in effect, in the same position as any other taxpayer who has demonstrated that the Revenue have taken his money without lawful authority. The fact that, in this case, the relevant regulations were made in good faith but without statutory authority should not secure to Woolwich the lost interest which would not be recoverable under the statutory provisions in a case where, for example, the Revenue had in good faith misconstrued the regulation lawfully made. The statutory provisions relating to tax are considered frequently by Parliament and the making of new law, most particularly in the field of taxation, should be left to the legislature.

The Revenue and ex gratia repayment of money

If there is no right of recovery of a payment, made in response to a bona fide but unlawful demand of tax, then, if the circumstances do not give rise to a claim based on duress or mistake of fact or to an implied promise by the Revenue to repay the money, the only hope of recovery by the payer must rest on the ability and willingness of the Revenue to repay either as a matter of grace or by the exercise of a discretion to make repayment. The court asked for assistance from counsel as to the nature and origin of such a right of payment by the Revenue because, if money is received which the Revenue are at law entitled to retain, whence comes the right to pay it back? In *Auckland Harbour Board v R* [1924] AC 318, cited by *Goff and Jones* p 134, Viscount Haldane said (at 326)—

> '... it has been a principle of the British Constitution now for more than two centuries ... that no money can be taken out of the consolidated Fund into which the Revenues of the State have been paid, excepting under a distinct authorization from Parliament itself. The days are long gone by in which the Crown, or its servants, apart from Parliament, could give such an authorization or ratify an improper payment. Any payment out of the consolidated fund made without Parliamentary authority is simply illegal and ultra vires, and may be recovered by the Government if it can, as here, be traced.'

The Revenue submitted that they have a general right outside statute to agree and settle disputed assessments and claims and, as part of their duty of care and management of the recovery of taxes imposed by Parliament, a discretion to make ex gratia payments (see *IRC v National Federation of Self-Employed and Small Businesses Ltd* [1981] STC 260, [1982] AC 617; *Preston v IRC* [1985] STC 282, [1985] AC 835; *R v IRC, ex p MFK Underwriting Agencies Ltd* [1989] STC 873, [1990] 1 WLR 1545; and *IRC v Nuttall* [1990] STC 194, [1990] 1 WLR 631). It was acknowledged that, on ordinary principles, the decisions of the commissioners are open to judicial review but, it was said, in restricted circumstances only, because of the rule that, if there is an alternative remedy provided by Parliament, relief by judicial review is not available. The Revenue did not seek to set out any principles by reference to which there might be assessed the reasonableness of any refusal to repay money received in respect of an unlawful demand to tax. That was not surprising because, as we understand it, there are waiting for resolution possible claims by other building societies by which tax was paid under the ultra vires

regulations without, it may be, such protestations as might justify a finding of an
a implied promise to repay.

The question of the reasonableness of the exercise of the discretion to make or to
refuse payment under a statutory provision, namely under s 9(1) of the General Rate
Act 1967 (the 1967 Act), was considered in *ex p Chetnik*. That section provides:

b
'(1) Without prejudice to sections 7(4)(*b*) and 18(4) of this Act, but subject to
subsection (2) of this section, where it is shown to the satisfaction of a rating
authority that any amount paid in respect of rates, and not recoverable apart
from this section, could properly be refunded on the ground that ... (*e*) the
person who made a payment in respect of rates was not liable to make that
payment, the rating authority may refund that amount or a part thereof.'

Lord Bridge (see [1988] AC 858 at 874) referred to the rule that money paid under a
c mistake of law is irrecoverable and noted that it was said to stem from the principle
that there must be an end to litigation. There was, however, an instructive line of
authority showing circumstances in which the court will not permit the rule to be
invoked. After reference to *ex p James* (1874) 9 Ch App 609, to *ex p Simmons* (1885)
16 QBD 308, to *Re Tyler* [1907] 1 KB 865 and to *Blackpool and Fleetwood Tramroad
Co v Bispham with Norbreck UDC* [1910] 1 KB 592, Lord Bridge continued (at
d 876–877):

'So it emerges from these authorities that the retention of moneys known to
have been paid under a mistake at law, although it is a course permitted to an
ordinary litigant, is not regarded by the courts as a "high-minded thing" to
do ... and hence is a course which the court will not allow one of its own officers,
such as a trustee in bankruptcy, to take.'

e
Therefore, the conclusion that the purpose of s 9 of the 1967 Act was to enable rating
authorities to give redress and to remedy the injustice that would otherwise ordinarily
arise, if they were to retain sums to which they had no right, in cases where persons
had paid rates which they were not liable to pay, could properly be derived (per
Lord Bridge at 877)—

f
'... from the broader consideration that Parliament must have intended
rating authorities to act in the same high principled way expected by the court
of its own officers and not to retain rates paid under a mistake of law, or ...
upon an erroneous valuation, unless there were, as Parliament must have
contemplated there might be in some cases, special circumstances in which a
particular overpayment was made such as to justify retention of the whole or
g part of the amount overpaid.'

For my part, although we have not heard full argument on the point because
neither side has had occasion to dispute it, and although it is not necessary in this
case to reach any detailed conclusions on it, it seems clear to me that the Revenue
must be held to have in law the capacity to make such an ex gratia payment. By that
h I mean a repayment of money, which has been paid to the Revenue in respect of an
ultra vires claim to tax and which, because of the circumstances of payment, was in
law a voluntary payment to recover which the payer has no cause of action. Such a
power of repayment is, I think, a necessary part of the power of the management of
the recovery of taxes. A decision by the Revenue whether or not to repay such a
voluntary payment must be made, as it seems to me, in the exercise of the discretion
j which the Revenue has been left by Parliament to use in the care and management
of the recovery of taxes imposed by Parliament, and would be prima facie reviewable
by the court. In the absence of such delay or other circumstances which could justify
a decision not to repay, a refusal to repay could, of course, be held by the court to be
unreasonable and therefore unlawful. No doubt, difficult questions could arise as to
the nature of the circumstances which could be regarded as justifying a decision not
to repay, such as, for example, a contention that the tax was in substance intended
by Parliament to be exacted and that the lack of vires for the particular demand had

resulted from no more than a technical failure in drafting the rule or regulation. The principles stated by Lord Bridge with reference to the discretion under s 9 of the *a* 1967 Act appear to me to be generally applicable to the exercise of the non-statutory discretion which the Revenue, rightly as I think, claim to have. In the absence of statutory guidelines the relevant principles will have to be further developed as cases arise.

The relevance in this case of the existence and nature of the power to make such ex gratia repayments, as it seems to me, is that it is part of the whole structure of the *b* existing rules of law relating to the repayment by the Crown of money paid in respect of an unlawful claim to tax. To the extent that the citizen is thus effectively protected against the misfortune of paying tax which is not lawfully due, the need for any extension of the existing law of restitution is reduced. There is, of course, no reason to suppose that the Revenue would, in any event, refuse to refund money which it would be unreasonable for the Crown to retain but there is a large and *c* important difference between a right to claim restitution at law and the mere ability to ask that money paid be returned in the exercise of executive discretion even if the exercise of that discretion is subject to judicial review. Retention may be reasonable from the point of view of the Revenue and public interest but appear both unfair and unprincipled to the person who has paid.

d

The implied contract

Before considering the two main submissions for Woolwich it is convenient to consider the issue of implied contract. It was argued for Woolwich that Nolan J was wrong to find an implied contract for repayment on the facts of this case; and wrong to hold ([1989] STC 111 at 119) that, generally—

e

'... whenever money is paid to the Revenue pending the outcome of a dispute which, to the knowledge of both parties will determine whether or not the Revenue are entitled to the money, an agreement for the repayment of the money if and when the dispute is resolved in the taxpayer's favour must inevitably be implied unless the statute itself produces that result ...'

The force of this point, if it is right, would be that the taxpayer who pays, as did *f* Woolwich, would be in greater need of protection by means of right of recovery contended for by Woolwich. For my part, I do not accept the submissions made for Woolwich on the implied contract point.

The point is, I think, of greater complication than importance. Nolan J (see [1989] STC 111 at 119) cited and applied the judgment of Vaisey J in *Sebel Products* [1949] Ch 409 at 412. The cited passage begins— *g*

'... I ask myself first with what intention the plaintiffs paid the money, and, secondly, with what intention the defendants received it? If the intention was the same on both sides, the result, in my judgment, was that an agreement was made between the parties by implication.'

As stated, that, I think, cannot be right. Contracts cannot be made merely by *h* uncommunicated subjective intentions. Thus, in *Paal Wilson & Co A/S v Partenreederei Hannah Blumenthal* [1983] 1 AC 854, Lord Diplock said (at 915):

'To create a contract by exchange of promises between two parties where the promise of each party constitutes the consideration for the promise of the other, what is necessary is that the intention of each *as it has been communicated to and* *j* *understood by the other* (even though that which has been communicated does not represent the actual state of mind of the communicator) should coincide. That is what English lawyers mean when they resort to the latin phrase consensus ad idem and the words that I have italicised are essential to the concept of consensus ad idem, the lack of which prevents the formation of a binding contract in English law.'

Nevertheless, in *Sebel Products* Vaisey J, as the above passage in his judgment
shows, based his finding of implied contract on the inferences which a reasonable
person, knowing what was said and done, would draw from those facts. Counsel for
Woolwich argued that there was no evidence here of offer or acceptance, that the
terms of any agreement were wholly uncertain, and that the officers of the parties to
the contract, who are said to have made it, can have had no authority to do so. I
accept that the question of authority was barely considered in the evidence and not
mentioned in the judgment. The reason is clear. Neither party had raised the
implied contract as a basis of relief. The Revenue had pleaded that—

> '... if ... the Woolwich ... is entitled as a matter of law to repayment of the
> said sums, the Revenue will contend that the said payments were made pursuant
> to an implied agreement ... whereby it was agreed that the Revenue would
> hold the said sums pending the outcome of proceedings to determine the
> validity of the regulation. In pursuance of that agreement, entitlement to a
> repayment arose on the date of the ... declaration and interest runs from that
> date.'

There was no reply disputing authority. In his affidavit, Mr Mason, on behalf of
Woolwich, did not contend that those concerned on either side lacked authority or
ostensible authority to make the implied agreement which the Revenue had alleged.
Mr Mason said in his affidavit of 1 December 1987:

> 'I did not intend by my correspondence with the Revenue ... to enter into
> any agreement or contract with regard to the sums paid or to be paid. Had that
> been the [Woolwich's] intention, we would not have sought to achieve it by
> means of a covering letter accompanying our return, without prior discussion,
> and immediately preceeding payment. Nor, in my opinion, would either
> Mr Fletcher or myself have been the appropriate individuals to commit our
> respective employers to an agreement. Nor to the best of my knowledge did
> anyone else at the Woolwich or in the Revenue seek such an agreement.'

The substance of the implied agreement as alleged was no more than that, if
Woolwich succeeded in its contention, the money would be repaid. No other terms
were alleged or found. There was, in my view, nothing uncertain about the terms of
the promise by the Revenue. On the part of Woolwich, the consideration for the
promise was the act of payment. The agreement was said to have arisen on the
undisputed actions of the parties which were of stark simplicity, namely the express
reservation by Woolwich that the payment should not prejudice its right of recovery
and the receipt and retention of the money in apparent acceptance of that term.
Both sides obviously intended the agreed term to control the legal relationships
between the parties. I think the judge was plainly right in his conclusion that the
Revenue had agreed to refund the money.

It is convenient to deal at this point with the issue whether Woolwich could found
a claim to interest on the money, for the time between payment and repayment, on
a term to be implied into the implied agreement. The argument of counsel for
Woolwich was that a term providing for compound interest at commercial rates
should be implied, if this court should uphold the finding of this 'fictitious' or 'judge
made' agreement. It was, he said, inconceivable that Woolwich should have agreed
to pay over to the Crown £56m for an indeterminate period on the basis that no
interest should be paid on principal eventually found to be repayable. The answer
of counsel for the Crown was that on the ordinary principles by which terms are to
be implied into contracts no such term could be implied since it was not necessary to
give business efficacy to the agreement made and it was impossible to assert that, if
asked, the Revenue would at once have acknowledged that an obligation to pay
interest from the date of receipt had been assumed by the Revenue. In addition,
counsel for the Crown relied on the decision of their Lordships in *La Pintada*.

For my part, although, for the reasons given, I accept the finding of Nolan J that
there was a real agreement properly implied on the facts, I reject without hesitation
this submission for an implied term to pay interest. Express reference was made by
Woolwich at the time to interest payable by Woolwich. None was made by either
side to payment of interest by the Revenue. I agree that it is impossible to imply
such a term for the reasons put forward by counsel for the Crown.

I do not think that much, if any, assistance is to be derived from the reasoning of
their Lordships in *La Pintada*, which was not concerned with the implication of a
term for the payment of interest but with the power of the court or of an arbitrator
to ward interest in the absence of any promise to pay it. The contention for
Woolwich that it is inconceivable that Woolwich should have agreed to pay over
£56m on the basis that no interest should be paid seems to me to be acceptable but
entirely irrelevant. The implied agreement, as I have explained earlier in this
judgment, was not at any stage relied on by the Revenue as excluding any right to
interest which Woolwich might have under a cause of action prior to and
independent of the agreement. It is not suggested that Woolwich impliedly agreed
to forgo interest; it is only asserted by the Revenue that, in impliedly agreeing to
repay the capital sum if the court should hold the claim to have been ultra vires, they
did not promise to pay interest on that sum from the date of payment. Such belief as
Woolwich has had that it is entitled to interest from the date of payment has clearly,
in my view, rested on a belief in some right at law to recover the money with interest
and not on any apparent promise by the Revenue.

As to Nolan J's general observation, to the effect that in similar circumstances a
promise of repayment must inevitably be implied, I see no reason to disapprove or
to qualify it. It was, I think, no more than recognition of the fact that, if the Revenue
receive money on the express stipulation that it is paid, by a payer who asserts the
illegality of the demand, without prejudice to the payer's right of recovery if the
payer's contention is upheld, the Revenue will, in the absence of some circumstances
justifying a different answer, be held to have promised to repay it when and if the
payer's contention is upheld. The fact that such a promise may properly be held to
have been impliedly made, does not mean that the payer is thereby deprived of any
other cause of action to recover the money, which he may have independently of
that promise.

In summary, therefore, the recognised principles of law provide for the payer of
money in respect of an ultra vires tax demand more protection than the argument
for Woolwich acknowledged. When the payment is made under mistake of law, the
payer would have at least such protection as is given by the reviewable power of the
Revenue to repay; where the payment is made without mistake on the part of the
payer but with express reservation of the right of recovery, a contractual obligation
to repay would normally arise. It should, I think, be emphasised that the payer could
stipulate for the payment by the Revenue of interest from the date of payment if he
should succeed on the issue of law. The Revenue could lawfully, as I understand the
law, and no submission was made to the contrary, agree to pay such interest. The
Revenue, however, would also be free to refuse to agree to pay interest in those
circumstances. Parliament, as it seems to me, has expressly approved a scheme,
where the legislation is applicable, whereby if a payer does not pay pending
determination of his liability, he must pay interest on the unpaid sums if they are
found to be due and that such interest is not chargeable to profits. There is, in other
words, and not surprisingly, no provision for the remission of interest during
resolution of a dispute, whether bona fide or not. When it paid, Woolwich assessed
the position as being such that, having regard to the position with reference to
interest, it had no real option but to pay, and Nolan J in substance accepted that. It
was, in my view, intended by Parliament that proceedings to dispute liability to tax
should be to that extent at the risk of the taxpayer at least in the sorts of cases covered
by specific legislation. There is, therefore, nothing which the court can regard as
inherently unjust in the fact that Woolwich would have risked the payment of

unchargeable interest if it had refused to pay and had thereafter lost on the issue of
liability.

a

Examination of the submissions made for Woolwich
Constructive trust

It is necessary first to mention one matter which was introduced into the case but
not, in this court, relied on by either side. Woolwich did not rely on constructive
trust before Nolan J. The Revenue, however, raised before Nolan J and in their
b respondents' notice in this court the contention that, if there was no implied
agreement by the Revenue for the repayment of the capital it might be held that,
once the dispute over the legality of the demand was resolved in favour of Woolwich
by the court, it became unconscionable for the Revenue to retain the money and a
constructive trust for repayment might be imposed by the court. The force of the
point was, presumably, to show that, in the absence of the right contended for by
c Woolwich, and where no agreement for repayment could be implied, the law could
afford protection to the taxpayer greater than that provided by the power to review
a decision not to exercise the discretion to repay. This point of constructive trust
was not developed by counsel for the Crown before us. The written summary of
argument for Woolwich gave notice that Woolwich would, if necessary, submit that
the Revenue held the capital sums on constructive trust arising as at the date when
d payment was made (see *Chase Manhattan Bank NA v Israel-British Bank (London)*
Ltd [1981] Ch 105; *Re Sharpe* [1980] 1 WLR 219; and *Muschinski v Dodds* (1986) 62
ALR 429). Therefore, it was submitted, compound interest at commercial rates was
due as a matter of equity from the date of payment (see *President of India v La
Pintada Cia Navegacion SA* [1983] 1 Lloyd's Rep 37; *O'Sullivan v Management
Agency and Music Ltd* [1985] QB 428; *Buckingham v Francis* [1986] 2 All ER 738).
e In argument, however, counsel for Woolwich did not develop the submission save
to say, in answer to a question from Butler-Sloss LJ, that the principle of constructive
trust supported the position of Woolwich.

In my judgment, Woolwich cannot in this case recover on the ground of
constructive trust the interest which it claims. If the primary submission for
Woolwich succeeds, no question of trust arises. If that submission fails, then, in my
f judgment again, no question of trust arises. The Revenue, having received the
money without (if I am right) having used duress to obtain it, were entitled to retain
it subject to the lawful exercise of the discretion to repay and subject to any obligation
arising from the terms on which or from the circumstances in which the payment
was made. That obligation was, in my judgment, rightly held by the judge to be
contractual. If the Revenue received money, voluntarily paid, on terms that the
g money be repaid in the event that the payer succeeded on the issue as to lawfulness
of the demand, but without any implied promise to pay interest between receipt and
repayment, it cannot, in my judgment, be held to be unconscionable for the Revenue
not to pay interest for that period.

The claim based on duress

h I will take first the alternative submission of counsel for Woolwich, to the effect
that Woolwich is entitled to succeed on the ground of duress or 'practical compulsion'.
I take it first because it seemed to me to be necessary, before dealing with the
primary submission, to determine whether Woolwich is to be held in law to have
made the payments under duress. If it is to be so held, then the cause of action to
recover the money arose, in my judgment, on the making of the payments and not
j at the time when the illegality of the demand was demonstrated by the first decision
of Nolan J and it would not be strictly necessary to decide whether the payments
would have been recoverable in the absence of duress. Further, I reached the
conclusion without hesitation that this duress submission could not succeed.
Examination of the primary submission must therefore proceed, as I see this case,
on the basis that the appeal of Woolwich must fail if the primary submission does
not succeed.

Counsel for Woolwich submitted that the concept of duress should be held to
extend, beyond threats of physical injury or imprisonment or detention of goods, to *a*
include all circumstances where the actor is to be held to have been illegitimately
deprived of his right of voluntary action (see *Universe Tankships Inc of Monrovia v
International Transport Workers' Federation* [1983] 1 AC 366; *Barton v Armstrong*
[1976] AC 104; *DPP for Northern Ireland v Lynch* [1975] AC 653; and *B & S
Contracts and Design Ltd v Victor Green Publications Ltd* [1984] ICR 419). Since, as
Nolan J found, Woolwich had 'little choice but to make the three payments' and *b*
since the consequences of non-payment were perceived by Woolwich to be
'commercially unacceptable', Woolwich, it was said, had been subjected to duress
because 'subjected to an improper motive for action' in the phrase used by Holmes J
in *Fairbanks v Snow* (1887) 13 NE Reporter 596 at 598 and cited in *Barton v
Armstrong* [1976] AC 104 at 121, or because subjected to 'pressure . . . which the law
does not regard as legitimate' (see *Universe Tankships Inc of Monrovia v International* *c*
Transport Workers' Federation [1983] 1 AC 366 at 384 per Lord Diplock). Counsel
for Woolwich acknowledged that the duress submission, although theoretically
distinct, could be regarded as overlapping with his primary submission which, itself,
might be regarded as justified by a presumption of duress.

I have found it impossible to accept the alternative submission for Woolwich
based on duress because nothing done or communicated by the Revenue, whether *d*
expressly or impliedly, could, in my judgment, properly be held to be the exerting
of pressure which the law regards as illegitimate. The claim to tax was made by the
Revenue in good faith. It was the duty of the Revenue, therefore, to advance the
claim and to obtain the decision of the court on it if it was disputed. The Revenue
did nothing more. There was nothing which in the law applicable to private citizens
could be regarded as duress or unlawful coercion. I see no good reason to treat the *e*
threat of legal proceedings by the Revenue as the equivalent of duress in order to
create a right to repayment against the Revenue where the bona fide threat of legal
proceedings is made in respect of an ultra vires demand. If the right to repayment
exists as contended for, it must rest, in my judgment, on the ultra vires nature of the
demand although, of course, the burden of such a demand made by the Revenue is
relevant to the question whether that right should be held to exist. *f*

If I am right on this part of this case, Woolwich must be held to have chosen to
pay the ultra vires demands for the reasons which it gave; it decided that it was
better for it to pay and to exercise such rights to recovery as the law might provide.
Such payment would not prevent Woolwich from recovering the payments, under
the right of recovery asserted upon the primary submission, if that right exists. If
payment in respect of an ultra vires demand to tax creates a cause of action to recover *g*
the money paid, it would be for the Revenue to prove some ground in law which
would justify retention and none has been alleged.

The primary submission

The primary submission put forward by counsel for Woolwich invites the court
to revive what is said to be an old rule, once recognised, which was thereafter lost to *h*
view, namely, a right of recovery independent of mistake or duress and based simply
on the ultra vires nature of the demand to tax. It is first necessary to consider what
must be the nature and extent of such a right, if the submission were accepted, and
the consequences, as they would be likely to be, of holding that such a right exists.
In particular, consideration of these matters will show how far such a general right
to recovery of money paid in respect of an ultra vires tax demand could be established *j*
by decision of this court having regard to authority.

(i) It is first to be noted that the right contended for is concerned with cases where
the claim to tax is made in good faith without any actionable misrepresentation or
duress. Any claim based on misfeasance in public office (see *Bourgoin SA v Ministry
of Agriculture, Fisheries and Food* [1986] QB 716) or in respect of a payment induced
by actionable misrepresentation would be covered by separate and recognised rules.

(ii) Woolwich, in this case, proceeded on the basis that a necessary preliminary to the civil action for restitution of the sums paid was the obtaining of a declaration in judicial review proceedings that the demand was unlawful and that separate subsequent proceedings for restitution were necessary because the court had no power in the judicial review proceedings to order payment of a liquidated sum. By s 31(4) of the 1981 Act there is provision for the award of damages but, unlike the provision in Scotland, there is no express reference to an order for restitution. No submissions were addressed to the court on these points by counsel for the Crown. The importance of a requirement, in these circumstances, for the initial proceedings by judicial review is that the time limit imposed by RSC Ord 53 r 4, subject to the power of extension of time, would provide some protection to the Revenue against delayed claims, which would otherwise be limited only by the six year period of limitation of action. When, however, a demand for tax has been held in proceedings by one payer to be unlawful, because the basis of the charge to tax is ultra vires, it is not clear why there would be any bar, other than under the statute of limitations, in subsequent proceedings by other payers who have paid in respect of demands based on the same ultra vires provision.

(iii) It has been submitted that the right contended for by Woolwich can be in this case, and may generally be, limited to a case where there is no basis whatever in law for any such charge as was sought to be made. Counsel for Woolwich described the point by comparing it to a claim to tax windows when there is no statutory authority for a window tax. For my part, I do not see how the right, if it exists in law, can properly be limited to such 'window tax' cases. In principle, payment in respect of any demand which is bad in law, is payment of tax exacted without the authority of Parliament and it should matter not whether the demand is bad because based on a bona fide but mistaken construction of a valid provision or on a bona fide belief that an invalid provision has been lawfully enacted. If the right exists, I do not see how it could, consistently with principle, be limited in the way suggested.

(iv) Next, in this case Woolwich asserts that there was no mistake; Woolwich believed the demand to be ultra vires—asserted that it was—and then made the payments without prejudice to the right to recover. But if the right of recovery asserted by Woolwich is based on the established principles of justice to which counsel for Woolwich has referred (Lord Wright in *Fibrosa* and Lord Denning in *Kiriri Cotton*) I am unable to see why (apart from the existence of any authority which prevents such a course) that right should not be equally available to the person who has paid under mistake of law. Most people who receive a tax demand are likely to suppose that the basis in law is valid and concentrate upon the factual basis. The essential justice of their position is no different, by reference to those established principles of justice, from that of the vigilant payer who believes the demand to be invalid in law but calculates that his position as to interest will be protected better by paying than by withholding payment while he puts his belief to the test. The rule of mistake of law, as I understand it, is not that a mistake of law bars recovery if a right of recovery exists independently of the mistake; the rule is that, if the only ground of claim is mistake and the mistake is a mistake of law, the law gives no right of recovery.

(v) So far as concerns payment under mistake of law, there is authority binding on this court, namely *National Pari-Mutuel Association Ltd v R* (1930) 47 TLR 110. There a claim to recover tax paid in circumstances where in law the money was not payable was rejected by this court. The case was argued for the claimant on the basis that the payment was made under mistake of fact. No argument was advanced to the effect that there could be recovery if the mistake was rightly held to be a mistake of law. Glidewell LJ has cited the passage from the judgment of Scrutton LJ (see (1930) 47 TLR 110 at 111) in which the ground of decision is set out. The mistake was, as he has pointed out, a mistake as to the construction of a valid statutory provision. Counsel for Woolwich submitted that it is therefore to be distinguished from a case where the statutory provision is ultra vires. For my part, I do not think that such a distinction could be properly made. As I have said, there is, in my judgment, no relevant difference between honest misconstruction of a statutory provision and honest assertion of the validity of an invalid statutory provision. The point was not argued in *National Pari-Mutuel* on the constitutional ground put forward in this case but the decision there was that there is no general right to recover money paid as tax which was not due in law. It follows that, if the primary submission is accepted, the general right of recovery would arise in cases of ultra vires demands and in cases of demands based on misconstruction where there has been payment, but not under mistake of law, and, in cases of ultra vires demands even if payment is made under mistake of law if the court were able to distinguish the *National Pari-Mutuel* case on the ground put forward. This seems to me to be an unsatisfactory description of a general right of recovery and suggests that no such general right exists.

(vi) If the general right of recovery contended for by Woolwich is held to exist in our law it is likely to extend to a considerable number of cases. The number would depend, of course, on whether it is limited to cases of ultra vires demands or extends also to demands based on misconstruction of statutory provisions. Counsel for Woolwich submitted that the concept of 'paying to close the transaction' would be available, when appropriate, to the Revenue particularly in cases of mistake of law by the payer because in such cases the payer will not do what Woolwich did in this case, namely protest at the illegality of the demand, stipulate that the payment should be without prejudice to recovery, and take immediate steps to establish the illegality by proceedings at law. Counsel for Woolwich submitted that, when a taxpayer has paid 'so as to close the transaction', he has accepted that the money has gone with no right of recovery and, thereby, he has waived any right to restitution. For my part, I am uncertain as to the efficacy of a defence of 'payment to close the transaction' and as to the principles by which it would be held to be or not to be established. The question whether a payment is made voluntarily to close a transaction seems to me to be apt to an inquiry whether the payer was acting under duress by, for example, a threat to seize his goods or was paying to settle an honest claim. If, on the other hand, the law gives the right of action to recover money paid as tax based simply on the illegality of the demand, as contended for by Woolwich, it is not clear to me why, short of contract or estoppel, that right of recovery should be lost because, when he paid, the taxpayer appeared to be paying to close the transaction. When a payment is made in the belief that there is a valid basis in law for the claim which is made, I cannot see on what basis the payer could be taken to have paid to close the transaction so as to be taken to have waived his right of recovery. Nor can I see that the repetition over time of such payments would by itself amount to waiver. For such a waiver, it would be essential, I think, to prove that the payer knew of the point as to the legality of the demand and nevertheless made the payment with the apparent intention of not seeking to recover it. I would add that it is not clear to me how an intention not to seek recovery would be demonstrated.

(vii) Next, in this case, Woolwich protested about the terms of the regulation before any payment was made; payment was made without prejudice to the right to recover the money and proceedings to establish the invalidity of the claims were at once commenced. Little difficulty for the management of the Revenue would arise, in my view, from the existence of a right of recovery arising on payment in such circumstances. The right asserted, however, goes far beyond such limits. It could, to the extent explained above, arise in the case both of ultra vires demands and of demands based on misconstruction, and subject to the point mentioned above with reference to the requirement of preliminary proceedings for a declaration under Ord 53, the proceedings could be commenced within six years of payment. No doubt, in some circumstances, as counsel for Woolwich submitted, having regard to any knowledge of and reference to the possible invalidity of the demand on the part of the payer, payment might be held to be irrecoverable because 'paid voluntarily to

close the transaction', but potentially, as it seems to me, the right could be asserted
by a large number of payers. It is true that, if grave difficulties should be anticipated
for the Revenue, Parliament might agree to enact retrospective legislation since
there is, in our law, no bar to such legislation, but the trouble and expense arising
from such proceedings if not prevented by legislation has been in the past, and
should in my judgment still be, regarded as a relevant consideration when the court
is asked to extend the law.

Thus, in *Glasgow Corp v Lord Advocate* 1959 SC 203, the corporation claimed to
recover sums paid for purchase tax which were not lawfully due. It was argued in
that case that on constitutional grounds, since the Crown could not levy tax without
the authority of Parliament, it should not be permitted to retain it if collected
without such authority, notwithstanding any supposed rule against recovery of
money paid under mistake of law. Lord Wheatley, the Lord Ordinary, refused to
allow recovery on that ground. His decision was upheld by the Inner House of the
Court of Session. Lord President Clyde, in a judgment with which Lord Carmont
and Lord Russell on this point agreed, said (at 230):

> 'This brings me to the second main issue in the case, namely, the question of
> repayment of the tax in so far as it was wrongly charged and paid. Repayment
> was sought to be justified on two separate grounds. The first was a broad
> constitutional point. It was said that the Commissioners of Customs and Excise
> had no authority from Parliament, nor from anyone else, to impose these
> charges now found to be illegal; that no one could be forced to pay a single
> shilling of tax which was not legally due, and that therefore the Corporation
> were entitled to recover what now turns out to have been unwarrantably
> charged upon them. But although the premises are unexceptionable, the
> conclusion does not follow from them, and no authority of any kind was quoted
> to us to justify the conclusion. The case of the *Attorney-General v Wilts United
> Dairies, Limited* is not in point in this connexion. If the conclusion did follow
> from the premises, I should have expected the point frequently to have arisen
> before now. Indeed, the elaborate statutory provisions in various Finance Acts
> regarding the precise circumstances in which income tax already paid may be
> reclaimed would have been quite unnecessary if the conclusion sought to be
> drawn by the Corporation were sound. It may well be that the payment thought
> erroneously to be due at the time should never have been made. But it does not
> therefore follow that, when the error is established, the money must
> automatically be paid back by the taxing authority. For a repayment in such
> circumstances has wider repercussions, and affects far more interests than those
> of the one taxpayer. It would, in my opinion, introduce an element of quite
> unwarrantable uncertainty into the relations between the taxpayers and the
> Exchequer if there could be a wholesale opening up of transactions between
> them whenever any Court put a new interpretation upon an existing statutory
> provision imposing a tax. Yet this is necessarily involved in the argument for
> repayment upon this constitutional ground.'

That case is not, of course, binding on this court but it is, in my view, of persuasive
authority. At this point, I have referred to it only in justification of reference to the
possibly damaging effect of accepting the primary case for Woolwich.

(viii) The right contended for would, if I have understood the nature and extent
of it correctly, in the case of payment of tax in respect of an ultra vires demand, be
effective in widely differing circumstances and (subject to the decision in *National
Pari-Mutuel* being distinguished on the grounds that it is limited to cases of
misconstruction of a valid provision) would set aside in this context two generally
accepted principles, namely that a payment made under mistake of law is not
recoverable and that a payment made in the absence of any mistake of fact and
under no compulsion other than the threat of legal proceedings, is not recoverable.

The attractiveness of the primary submission

Our law has long recognised a rule that, subject to exceptions, money paid under a
a mistake of law is irrecoverable. It has also long been a principle of our law that, if a
defendant is under an obligation from the ties of natural justice to refund money
which he has received, the law implies a debt which the payer may recover (see the
speech of Lord Wright in the *Fibrosa* case (see [1943] AC 32 at 62), quoting Lord
Mansfield CJ in *Moses v Macferlan* (1760) 2 Burr 1005 which Nolan J cited in his
judgment (see [1989] STC 111 at 113)). There is, clearly, much to be said in favour b
of the contention that money paid in respect of an ultra vires tax demand should
prima facie be recoverable on that ground alone. Nolan J described the submission
as attractive and I agree with him. The argument advanced for Woolwich based on
constitutional principle seems to me to have much force and to deserve to be given
effect unless there is some reason to be found in the authorities to prevent that
course. Since the Bill of Rights (1688) forbids 'levying money for or to the use of the c
Crowne ... without grant of Parlyament ...' (see *A-G v Wilts United Dairies Ltd*
(1921) 37 TLR 884 at 886 per Scrutton LJ) money obtained by an ultra vires demand
for tax should be recoverable, even though the only form of compulsion has been the
implied threat of recovery by legal proceedings, unless there is some reason to deny
the right.

Our law, however, has not in all respects developed rules which can be regarded d
as fully in accordance with what 'an ideal system of justice would ensure' (see *La
Pintada* [1985] AC 104 at 129 per Lord Brandon). Sometimes the reasons for the
apparent deficiency in a rule are to be found in a wider view of the public interest
than that required by the private economic interest of individual citizens. A blunt-
edged rule may fail to distinguish as carefully between the circumstances of one
person and another as payers would wish, but the general good is not always e
advanced by the extended refinement of rules. Such refinement may well produce
an ever increasing number of justiciable issues which will require to be resolved
largely at public expense. In short, the theoretical attractiveness of the primary
submission does not mean that this court is necessarily able to accept it.

Conclusion f

I do not think that the right answer to this case is to be found by examination of
the precise words used by various judges in a large number of different cases. The
basic principles of our law clearly favour, I think, the primary submission. There
are dicta which support it. The limitations upon the rule of recovery, for which
limitations the Revenue contend, seem to me to be necessarily based, particularly
where the limitation is applied so as to protect the Revenue as contrasted with the g
private citizen, on policy grounds.

If in this court we were free, as we are not, to approach this matter as a law reform
exercise, I would start with a preference in favour of the law being based on a prima
facie right of recovery, such as contended for by Woolwich, but as in any law reform
exercise, that preference would have to be tested by consideration of the answers
given on consultation by those capable from experience of discerning the difficulties h
which might be caused by following that preference. We have received the help
(similar in effect to the response on consultation, but necessarily incomplete) of
being referred to a number of learned articles and text books, and to the decisions of
courts in other jurisdictions, where various possible improvements in the law have
been considered together with possible forms of protection for the Revenue and
other recipients of money if the improvements should be made. I wish to express my j
gratitude for the assistance and instruction I have obtained from those sources.

Our task, however, is narrower. We cannot mould and limit a cause of action as
we might wish to see it defined by legislation. If the principles of the common law
and of the Bill of Rights, properly understood, create the right of recovery for which
Woolwich contends, then we must so find and the Revenue must look for protection
to Parliament. If our law has developed the limitations on recovery which the

Revenue say are to be found in the authorities, then we should, in my view, only set
a aside those authorities if we are convinced that they are wrong either because of
defects in the reasoning on which they are based or because they cannot stand in the
light of decisions in the House of Lords. It is also relevant, in my view, to the
question whether long-accepted authority should be reversed, to consider how far
Parliament itself has apparently accepted the law as set out in that authority,
whether expressly or impliedly, in legislation enacted in the relevant context.

b The main cases concerned with claims to recover money exacted on ultra vires
demands of public officials or authorities began in the eighteenth century. There
was, then, little direct taxation by central government and most of the cases were
concerned with the exaction of fees or tolls or duties by public officials whether for
performance of a duty or for release of goods. Those cases, accordingly, tend to
justify any order for recovery by reference to the circumstances of those cases,
c namely a demand for payment of money not lawfully due for performance of a
public duty or for release of goods to seize which there was no lawful right. Even so,
as counsel for Woolwich has pointed out, there are examples to be found of reliance
being placed more upon the unlawfulness of the demand than on the coercion
exercised by the threat, express or implied, to withhold performance of the duty or
the goods.

d Thus, in *Irving v Wilson* (1791) 4 Term Rep 485, a revenue officer seized goods as
forfeited which were not liable to seizure, and then took money from the owner for
the release of the goods. The owner was held entitled to recover the money in an
action for money had and received by Lord Kenyon CJ, Ashhurst and Grose JJ.
Lord Kenyon said that, since the taking of the money could not be justified, the
payment was not voluntary. Ashhurst J described the payment as 'by coercion'.
e Grose J held that the money could be recovered because it had been taken for
delivery up of the goods.

In *Morgan v Palmer* (1824) 2 B & C 729, Abbott CJ, Bayley, Holroyd, Littledale
JJ, the plaintiff was a publican. In order to obtain a renewal of his liquor licence he
was required by the mayor of Yarmouth, who had the power to grant and renew
licences, to pay a sum of money. The conduct of the mayor was illegal. He had no
f right to any payment as a condition for granting or renewing a licence. The plaintiff
was held entitled to recover the money paid. Abbott CJ said (at 734–735):

> 'It has been well argued that the payment having been voluntary, it cannot
> be recovered back in an action for money had and received. I agree that such a
> consequence would have followed had the parties been on equal terms. But if
> one party has the power of saying to the other, "That which you require shall
g > not be done except upon the conditions which I choose to impose", no person
> can contend that they stand upon any thing like an equal footing. Such was the
> situation of the parties to this action.'

Bailey J agreed on that aspect of the case with Abbott CJ. Holroyd J merely held
that the payment was not voluntary. Littledale J agreed, saying (at 739) that—
h
> '... the plaintiff was merely passive, and submitted to pay the sum claimed,
> as he could not otherwise procure his licence.'

In *Steele v Williams* (1853) 8 Ex 625, the plaintiff, a lawyer, applied to the
defendant, a parish clerk, for liberty to search the register book for burials and
baptisms. He did not want certificates but only to make extracts. He was told by the
j defendant that the charge would be the same whether he made extracts or had
certificates. He was charged £4 7s 6d for 25 extracts. The court (Parke, Platt and
Martin BB) held that the charge for extracts was illegal and that, since the payment
was not voluntary, it could be recovered. Parke B said (at 630):

> '... upon the true construction of the evidence, the payment in this case was
> not voluntary, because, in effect, the defendant told the plaintiff's clerk, that if

he did not pay for certificates when he wanted to make extracts, he should not
be permitted to search.'

He continued that 'this payment was not voluntary, but necessary for the exercise
of a legal right'. Platt B agreed with Parke B. The decision of Martin B was on wider
ground (at 632):

> 'As to whether the payment was voluntary, that has in truth nothing to do
> with the case. It is the duty of a person to whom an Act of Parliament gives
> fees, to receive what is allowed, and nothing more. This is more like the case of
> money paid without consideration—to call it a voluntary payment is an abuse
> of language.'

Hooper v Mayor and Corp of Exeter (1887) 56 LJQB 457 (Lord Coleridge CJ and
Smith J) belongs in this category of decisions but goes further. Counsel for the
Crown has submitted that it was wrongly decided unless it can be seen as a mistake
of fact case. The defendants were empowered by statute to charge dues 'upon the
landing . . . of stone'. There was an exception in favour of limestone landed for the
purpose of being burned into lime. The statute also contained a power of distress in
a case of non-payment. The plaintiff was unaware that he was entitled to the benefit
of the exception and paid the dues demanded. He then claimed the return of the
moneys previously paid. The report is brief and unsatisfactory. The plaintiff cited
Morgan v Palmer (1824) 2 B & C 729 but was stopped by the court. For the
defendants it was submitted that the payments were voluntary. The court reversed
the county court judge and held that the plaintiff was entitled to recover what he
had paid. By reference, it would appear, to *Morgan v Palmer*, Lord Coleridge CJ
held (at 458) that—

> '. . . where one exacts money from another and it turns out that although
> acquiesced in for years such exaction is illegal, the money may be recovered as
> money had and received, since such payment could not be considered as
> voluntary so as to preclude its recovery.'

Smith J was of the same opinion.

It was in the 1880s that, in the contention of Woolwich, the courts began to go
wrong in deciding the cases on which the Revenue relies.

About one month after the Divisional Court decided *Hooper v Mayor and Corp
of Exeter*, the case of *Slater v Mayor and Corp of Burnley* (1888) 59 LT 636 was also
decided by the Divisional Court, Cave and Wills JJ. The plaintiff there claimed to
recover an overcharge which he had paid in respect of water rates. There was no
statutory power to distrain for the water rates but the defendant had the power to
cut off the water supply on non-payment. There had been, however, no cutting off
of the water, nor any threat to do so, nor legal proceedings for recovery of the rates.
The County Court judge held the payments to have been not voluntary and therefore
recoverable, because of the powers which were available to the defendants. The
Divisional Court reversed that decision. Reference was made by counsel for the
plaintiff to *Hooper v Mayor and Corp of Exeter* and to *Steele v Williams* (1853) 8 Ex
625. It was treated as common ground in argument that the plaintiff could have
waited for the six year period of limitation before applying for recovery. (There was
then no question of the requirement for proceedings by judicial review within the
time limited for such proceedings under Ord 53.) The reasons for the decision of the
Divisional Court were that the payment was not shown to have been involuntary
merely by reason of the existence of the power to stop the water; so to hold would be
very far reaching and no payment of rent to a landlord would be a voluntary
payment. Nothing was said to distinguish the case from *Hooper v Mayor and Corp
of Exeter* or from *Steele v Williams*. Counsel for the Crown has contended that the
court must be taken to have regarded those two cases as distinguishable because they
were within the principle of the colore officii cases, where money is unlawfully
demanded and received in return for the performance of a public office. Although it

is not, in my view, possible to fit *Hooper v Mayor and Corp of Exeter* into the
category so limited, I think counsel for the Crown is correct in his submission as to
how the Divisional Court must be taken to have regarded those two cases.

More than 20 years later came the case of *William Whiteley Ltd v The King* (1910)
101 LT 741, a decision of Walton J. This case was concerned with tax demanded by
the Revenue on behalf of the Crown. Waiters employed by Whiteley were said to be
'male servants' within the meaning of a statutory taxing provision and duties were
claimed. Whiteley disputed its liability. It was informed that, if the duties were not
paid, it would incur penalties. Whiteley paid. Later, the duties were paid under
protest. Some six years after the dispute first arose, in proceedings by the Revenue
to recover penalties, it was held that, on the true construction of the provision, the
duties were not payable but the claim by Whiteley to recover duties previously paid
was rejected. Again, *Steele v Williams* (1853) 8 Ex 625, and *Morgan v Palmer* (1824)
2 B & C 729 and *Hooper v Mayor and Corp of Exeter* (1887) 56 LJQB 457 were cited
and the submission was advanced in precisely the terms now put forward for
Woolwich, namely that when money is paid under an illegal demand colore officii
the payment can never be voluntary. Walton J referred to the general rule that if
money is voluntarily paid under a mistake of law then it cannot be recovered back.
As to the question whether the payments were voluntary, he held that they were
because there had been no duress or compulsion beyond the threat of proceedings
for penalties. Then he continued (at 745):

> 'But it was suggested that the case came within that class of cases in which
> money has been held to be recoverable back if it has been paid in discharge of a
> demand illegally made under colour of an office. Those cases . . . seem to me all
> to come within that class of cases to which I have just referred, which is
> described in Leek on Contracts (5th edit., p. 61) in these words: "Money
> extorted by a person for doing what he is legally bound to do without payment,
> or for a duty which he fails to perform, may be recovered back." In all those
> cases in order to have that done which the person making the payment was
> entitled to have done without a payment, he had to make the payment, and
> someone who was bound to do something which the person paying the money
> desired to have done, refused to do his duty unless he was paid the money. If in
> those circumstances money is paid, then it can be recovered back. There is
> there an element of duress.'

Next, 36 years later in *Twyford v Manchester Corp* [1946] Ch 236, Romer J
followed and applied the decision in *William Whiteley*. For the proposition that fees
unlawfully charged for permission to recut and regild monumental stones in a
cemetery, were recoverable, the plaintiff cited only *Somes v British Empire Shipping
Co* (1860) 8 HLC 338 and relied on the fact that the fees had been paid under protest.
Romer J differed from Walton J in refusing to regard the *William Whiteley* case as a
case of mistake of law but continued (at 241):

> 'Even so, however, I respectfully agree with the rest of Walton J.'s judgment,
> particularly with his statement that a general rule applies, namely, the rule that,
> if money is paid voluntarily, without compulsion, extortion, or undue influence,
> without fraud by the person to whom it is paid and with full knowledge of all
> the facts, it cannot be recovered, although paid without consideration, or in
> discharge of a claim which was not due or which might have been successfully
> resisted.'

My first impression was that Romer J was right to regard *William Whiteley* as not
having been a case of mistake of law. I am now not sure. I do not think that the point
is of great importance and it is, I think, no more than an issue as to the use of words.
Payment under mistake of law is not, and, I think, has never been itself a ground for
relief; frequently it is used to describe a payment made under mistake where there
was no mistake of fact and hence no ground of recovery. Nor, as I have said above,
does mistake of law, by itself, bar recovery if there is a recognised basis of claim, for

example duress or actionable misrepresentation inducing the mistaken belief. Accordingly, if payment is made under mistake, in the sense that it would not have been made but for a mistaken belief which induces the payment, then if it is not a mistake of fact it is probably capable of being categorised as a mistake of law. The fact that the point of law has been perceived does not by itself prevent there having been an effective mistake of law by reference to the prospects of success in legal proceedings to settle the point. Mistake of law could be categorised in such a way as to exclude mistake of law if the point has been perceived. This matter is not, in my view, of importance. The question whether a right of recovery exists, or does not exist, in the case of payment of an ultra vires demand should not depend, if the decision can be made on basic principles of justice, on whether the point of law on which refusal to pay could be justified was or was not perceived at the time of payment.

Those three cases, *Slater v Mayor and Corp of Burnley* (1888) 59 LT 636 in the Divisional Court and *William Whiteley* and *Twyford v Manchester Corp* at first instance, have not hitherto been doubted or commented on adversely in any decision in this country. Counsel for Woolwich relied on *A-G v Wilts United Dairies Ltd* (1921) 37 TLR 884 as providing support for his primary submission and therefore as casting doubt on the three decisions on which the Revenue case is based. The *A-G v Wilts United Dairies Ltd* case contains no matter of decision on the recovery of payments made because there had been no payments. In that case the food controller sought to impose, by means of an agreement to that effect, a charge of 2d per gallon on purchases of milk as a condition of the grant of a licence to buy milk. Bailhache J gave judgment for the Crown for the sum claimed under the agreement. The question before the Court of Appeal was whether the Food Controller had legal authority to impose that condition and it was held that he had not. The contract was therefore illegal and unenforceable. Atkin LJ in a passage much relied on by counsel for Woolwich said (at 887):

'It makes no difference that the obligation to pay the money is expressed in the form of an agreement. It was illegal for the Food Controller to require such an agreement as a condition of any licence. It was illegal for him to enter into such an agreement. The agreement itself is not enforceable against the other contracting party; and if he had paid under it he could, having paid under protest, recover back the sums paid, as money had and received to his use.'

Atkin LJ did not explain, and it was not necessary in that case to explain, on what ground in law, after payment under protest, recovery could have been claimed.

In *Mason v New South Wales* (1959) 102 CLR 108 the colore officii cases in England were considered by the High Court of Australia. Counsel for the Crown cited the case as persuasive authority in support of the submission of the Revenue. The plaintiffs in that case sued the defendant state for money had and received being fees paid for permits to carry goods for payment issued under a state statute of 1931. The requirement of payment was held to be ultra vires. It was argued for the plaintiffs that the right to recover rested on a general principle such as that now contended for by Woolwich, namely that payments in respect of an official demand for payment, which was illegal, gave rise to a right of recovery. In addition, it was argued that the plaintiffs had paid under compulsion because (a) the defendants had been withholding plaintiffs' common law right to use the highway except on payment; (b) the parties were in an unequal situation; (c) the plaintiffs were threatened with ruinous legal proceedings and had no practical choice but to pay; or (d) they were threatened with seizure of their vehicle. Dixon CJ, after reference to the English cases which seemed 'to say that moneys paid to the Crown as and for taxes cannot be recovered . . . unless the circumstances were such that they would be recoverable as between subject and subject . . .' (see (1959) 102 CLR 108 at 117) said that 'However this may be, the plaintiffs must I think recover' because they had paid 'only because they apprehended on reasonable grounds that without the permit . . .

the State . . . would or might stop the motor vehicle . . .' (see (1959) 102 CLR 108 at
a 116). Dixon CJ clearly had doubts whether the possible grounds of recovery were so
limited but found it unnecessary to resolve those doubts. Kitto J accepted, in effect,
the primary submission now made for Woolwich. The majority view, however, was
expressed by Menzies J and Windeyer J with whom Fullagar J and Taylor J agreed.
Menzies J held that the charges were unlawfully exacted by a threat to force the
plaintiffs' vehicles off the road and recovery was justified on the principles stated in
b such cases as *Morgan v Palmer* (1824) 2 B & C 729, *Steele v Williams* (1853) 8 Ex 625,
and *Hooper v Mayor and Corp of Exeter* (1887) 56 LJQB 457. *William Whiteley* was
distinguished because in that case, there was no compulsion beyond the threat of
legal proceedings.

Windeyer J held that it could not be said that any official had extorted or even
demanded money by colour of his office. The plaintiffs could not succeed simply
c because of the superior position of the defendant. In his view the plaintiffs were
required to go further and establish that there was, in a legal sense, compulsion by
something actually done or threatened, something beyond the implication of duress
arising from a demand by person in authority, which suffices in a true colore officii
case. It was not sufficient for the plaintiffs merely to point to the provisions of the
statute. They were required to show that the Crown by its servants was exercising
d or threatening to exercise power under the statute in such a way as to constitute
compulsion in law. A threat of proceedings for a mere pecuniary penalty did not
make a payment made thereafter involuntary because the payer might have defended
the proceedings and relied on the unlawfulness of the demand (see *William Whiteley*).
In the end Windeyer J held that the evidence did enable the plaintiffs to bring
themselves within the principles stated by him.

e   Although the reasons given by Menzies and Windeyer JJ are not the same they
clearly agreed in holding that the claim to recovery could not be based simply on the
ultra vires nature of the original demand.

In my judgment, the principles applied in the colore officii cases decided in this
country, and of which some have been examined above, are accurately summarised
by Windeyer J in *Mason*'s case (1959) 102 CLR 108 at 140 in the passage cited by
f Nolan J in his judgment, namely that they should be confined to cases where 'a
public officer demands and is paid money he is not entitled to, or more than he is
entitled to, for the performance of his public duty'. Those cases do not establish a
principle from which the primary case for Woolwich can be derived. If it is to
succeed, that primary case must be based in the first place on the basic principle
stated by Lord Wright in *Fibrosa* in 1943 (see [1943] AC 32 at 61) and must
g demonstrate that the limitations imposed by the *William Whiteley* case were wrong
when devised or must be held to be wrong in the light of later authority such as the
decision of the House of Lords in *ex p Chetnick*.

For my part, I am unable to accept that the grounds of decision in *Slater v Mayor
and Corp of Burnley* (1888) 59 LT 636, in *William Whiteley*, and in *Twyford* were
wrong in refusing to recognise any general right of recovery of money paid in respect
h of an unlawful claim to tax. I acknowledge that the law could have been developed
in accordance with the wider basis of decision in *Hooper v Mayor and Corp of Exeter*
(1887) 56 LJQB 457, but it was not and the decision that no general right of recovery
exists, based simply on the unlawfulness of the demand, was clearly based on the
court's assessment of the requirements of the policy of the law. That view has stood
without effective challenge for 100 years.

j   It is also clear, in my judgment, that when Parliament has accepted the need for
additional protection for the taxpayer, specific statutory provision has been enacted
for repayment of money wrongly paid as tax, such as s 9 of the 1967 Act and s 33 of
the Taxes Management Act 1970 (the 1970 Act), on the assumption that there is in
law no such general right of recovery as that now asserted by the Woolwich. Thus,
in s 33 of the 1970 Act, in the case of an excessive assessment by reason of error or
mistake in a return, the board may give by repayment such relief as is reasonable

and just provided that 'no relief shall be given under this section in respect of an error or mistake as to the basis on which the liability of the claimant ought to have been computed where the return was in fact made on the basis or in accordance with the practice generally prevailing at the time when the return was made'. That provision would, of course, have no application to a case such as this but, if the primary case made for Woolwich is right, I am, as I have said, unable to see how the alleged right could be limited to cases where the basis of purported charge is non-existent in law, and, if it is not so limited, there could be concurrent remedies available in some cases to the taxpayer to one of which the limitations posed by Parliament would not be applicable. It might be said that, where Parliament has created a specific remedy, the taxpayer must be limited to that remedy in cases to which it applies but, to employ such reasoning, it would be necessary to attribute to Parliament an intention to disapply any relevant common law remedy which was already recognised or which might thereafter be held to exist, and I find it difficult to see clear justification for so doing.

One other persuasive authority, which in my view supports the Revenue case, should be mentioned. It was not separately relied on by counsel for the Crown but was discussed in the essay by Professor Birks to which we were referred in argument ('Restitution from the Executive' in *Essays on Restitution* (Ed Finn, 1990) pp 164–205). I refer to the decision of the Court of Session in *Glasgow Corp v Lord Advocate* 1959 SC 203. It is clear from that decision that, when the rule against recovery of money paid in respect of an unlawful tax demand, in the absence of duress, was expressly challenged on the constitutional ground put forward here by Woolwich, the argument was rejected by the Court of Session at least so far as concerns a claim based on misconstruction as contrasted with a claim based on an ultra vires decision. In other words, the Court of Session rejected the argument which was not advanced in *National Pari-Mutuel*. Lord Wheatley, in a passage which, in reverse, seems to me to apply precisely to our consideration of this decision of the Court of Session, said (at 220):

> '[It is] said that it would be most unfortunate, particularly in regard to exactions of tax, if the law of Scotland and England were to differ on the question of the right of recovery of tax paid but not due as a result of an error in law, and while I agree that it would be unfortunate, that in itself is no reason for equiparating the law of Scotland to the law of England if the principles of the law of Scotland do not justify such a course. On the other hand, if the matter is open it is always proper to consider the persuasiveness of the English opinions in matters touching the laws of both countries without being bound by them.'

I find the decision persuasive because, although it was concerned with misconstruction and not an invalid provision, the present argument based on basic principles of justice was raised, argued and rejected. So far as concerns the force of the basic principles, there is, in my judgment, no sustainable distinction between cases of misconstruction and cases of ultra vires demand.

I come now to consideration of the later cases which, it was submitted, require or justify the overruling of *William Whiteley* and its attendant cases. The main cases relied on were *A-G v Wilts United Dairies Ltd, ex p Chetnick*, and *South of Scotland Electricity Board v British Oxygen Co Ltd* [1959] 1 WLR 587, supported by the Canadian case of *Air Canada v British Columbia* (1989) 59 DLR (4th) 161 in the Supreme Court of Canada.

Reference has already been made to the passages in the judgments in *A-G v Wilts United Dairies Ltd*. That case was not concerned with the recovery of payments made but with an attempt by the Crown through the form of an action on a contract to enforce a claim to tax not authorised by Parliament. It provides, in my view, no significant support for the primary case of Woolwich.

The *South of Scotland Electricity Board* case was concerned with a claim by British Oxygen to recover from an electricity board alleged overpayments exacted in breach of s 37(8) of the Electricity Act 1947 which forbade 'any undue

discrimination against any person' in the fixing of tariffs. It was held by the House
a of Lords that there was nothing in law to prevent the recovery of sums which could
be proved to have been overcharged.

Viscount Kilmuir LC said (at 596)—

> '... the first governing principle is that a tariff which imposes a charge upon
> the respondents involving their being unduly discriminated against is contrary
> *b* to section 37(8) of the Electricity Act, 1947. The respondents were charged
> more than is warranted by the statute. Then it is clear that, until a court so
> declares, the respondents have no alternative but to continue to pay the charges
> demanded of them. In principle the appellants should not be permitted to
> retain payments for which they have no warrant to charge.'

Lord Tucker (at 615) agreed with the reasons given by Viscount Kilmuir LC. Lord
c Merriman said (at 606):

> 'As regards the claim for the repayment of moneys overpaid ... it is sufficient
> to say that in *Maskell v Horner* [1915] 3 KB 106, 119, Lord Reading C.J.,
> referring ... in particular to the advice given by Willes J. in *Great Western
> Railway Co v Sutton* (1869) L.R. 4 H.L. 226, 249—where that learned judge said
> *d* that he had "always understood that when a man pays more than he is bound to
> do by law for the performance of a duty which the law says is owed to him for
> nothing, or for less than he has paid, there is a compulsion or concussion in
> respect of which he is entitled to recover the excess by condictio indebiti, or
> action for money had and received"—said that "such claims made in this form
> of action are treated as matters of ordinary practice and beyond discussion."'

e Lord Reid said (at 609)—

> '... I think there is nothing in law to prevent recovery of any sums which can
> be proved to have been overcharged. The only reason advanced for the contrary
> view was that overcharges made by railway companies were said to be
> irrecoverable if they were due to the company having given an undue preference
> *f* to another consumer. It is therefore necessary to look at the railway legislation
> and the authorities under it. [The report says "unnecessary"—that must be an
> error in the report.] The Railways Clauses Acts of 1845, and certain other
> private Acts, contained an equality clause which made it illegal for a company
> to charge one customer more than they charged another under similar
> circumstances, and it is quite clear that a person who proved breach of an
> *g* equality clause could recover from the company any overcharge which he had
> paid, i.e., the difference between what he had paid and what he would have
> paid if the company had charged him as the equality clause required (*Great
> Western Railway Co. v Sutton* (1869) L.R. 4 H.L. 226), and recovery was not
> prevented by the fact that when he paid the charge demanded he knew that he
> was being overcharged.'

h
Later Lord Reid said:

> 'If there were clear and binding authority under the railway legislation that
> overcharges resulting from undue preference or prejudice could not be
> recovered, I might be inclined to hold that the same rule should apply here, but
> there is not.'

j
It is to be noted that the decision in the *South of Scotland Electricity Board* case
was dated 16 April 1959 on appeal from the Court of Session. The decision in
Glasgow Corp v Lord Advocate was dated 20 March 1959. Neither case at any stage
appears to have been cited in the other. The references set out above to the speeches
of their lordships are sufficient to demonstrate that they did not consider the question
whether the law applied in *William Whiteley* was right or wrong. The passage in the
speech of Lord Reid cited above shows the case was argued for the Electricity Board

on the basis that the issue of recovery of overpayments was to be decided on the construction of the particular statute and cases decided on the railway legislation. The comments of Viscount Kilmuir LC and of Lord Merriman show that the case was seen by them as similar to the colore officii cases in that the users of electricity had no choice but to pay the price demanded if they were to obtain the electricity and were thus in the position of the plaintiff in *Maskell v Horner* which was, in effect, a duress case. The plaintiff was there held to have paid to avoid seizure of his goods. There is, in my judgment, nothing in the reasoning of their Lordships which requires this court to overrule *William Whiteley*.

Ex p Chetnick has been considered above in this judgment. The ratepayer had paid, through mistake of law, some £51,000 as rates which were not payable. The question was whether, in refusing to repay the money under the power given by s 9 of the 1967 Act, the council had misdirected itself or acted unreasonably. The argument was directed to the proper construction of the statutory provisions by which the discretion to make repayment was conferred. No doubt was cast on the proposition that, without the statutory power, the council would have been unable to repay the money paid to it under a mistake of law. Cases such as *William Whiteley* were not mentioned. The rule of our law which provides no recovery for money paid under mistake of law, even when the money is paid to a public authority such as a council receiving rates, was not doubted although it was noted by Lord Goff as a rule much criticised and especially by comparative lawyers ([1988] AC 858 at 882). The decision, of course, provides support, which in my view is not required, for the basic principle of our law stated by Lord Wright in the *Fibrosa* case, namely that a man should not retain the money of or some benefit derived from another which it is against conscience that he should keep (see [1943] AC 32 at 61); but the decision was not directed at, nor does it in my view cast doubt on, the validity of the limitation of the principle long established by *William Whiteley* and the other cases.

In the end, and after much hesitation, I have reached the conclusion that this appeal should be dismissed. In summary, my reasons for reaching that conclusion, which are more fully set out above in this judgment, are as follows:

(i) The rules applied in *Slater v Mayor and Corp of Burnley* (1888) 59 LT 636, *William Whiteley* and *Twyford v Manchester Corp* were based on the rule which denies recovery of voluntary payments, and the principle that the threat of bona fide legal proceedings is not in law duress, coupled with the principle that those rules apply to claims against the state as they apply to claims against a private citizen or corporation. The mistake of law rule was seen as part of the relevant system of rules although, as explained above, the correctness of the application of the rule in the *William Whiteley* case is arguable.

(ii) The mistake of law rule can be criticised but has long been part of our law. It is a central part of the law of restitution. Legislation which apparently assumes the validity of the rule has been passed, and Parliament has, apparently, been content not to abolish it. It was treated, without question, as part of our law with reference to a public body with taxing powers in *ex p Chetnick*. If the primary submission is right, the mistake of law rule would be set aside in cases of ultra vires demand if *National Pari-Mutuel* is distinguished, but would be applicable in cases of mere misconstruction by reason of the decision in *National Pari-Mutuel*. I am not persuaded by a submission which, if right, disturbs the long established mistake of law rule in one class of case, that of ultra vires demand, but cannot be applied in another class of case, that of misconstruction of a valid provision, although there is no satisfactory distinction in principle between the two classes.

(iii) The rules in *Slater v Mayor and Corp of Burnley*, *William Whiteley* and *Twyford v Manchester Corp* have stood unquestioned in our courts for 100 years. A large number of claims, by taxpayer or the Revenue, must have been settled or not pursued or not defended on the assumption that the rules are good law. If this court should overrule those cases and accept the primary submission for Woolwich, the law must be regarded as always having provided for that cause of action; we cannot

provide for it to exist only from the date of our decision or attach limitations on the
a advancing of other existing or past claims. Such claims could be advanced or revived
on the basis that the cause of action has always existed, subject to any effective
defences or answers based on limitation, compromise or estoppel.

(iv) The reasoning on which the rules in those cases were based rests substantially
on an assessment of the policy consequences of recognising the existence of the cause
of action contended for. In my judgment, the policy consequences could, with no
b less convincing reasoning, have been assessed differently; and if the cause of action
contended for had been recognised long ago, it would rapidly have been assimilated
into the law with such special legislative provisions as would have been judged to be
necessary. That, however, does not in my judgment justify the upheaval and
potential consequences which would be likely to follow from overruling at this date
Slater v Mayor and Corp of Burnley, William Whiteley and *Twyford v Manchester*
c *Corp.*

(v) The argument based on legality, constitutional propriety and simple fairness
was as clear and compelling in 1888 when *Slater v Mayor and Corp of Burnley* was
decided or in 1959 when the Court of Session decided *Glasgow Corp v Lord Advocate*
and the High Court of Australia decided *Mason*'s case as it is today. There are,
however, respectable reasons of public interest and in the convenience of public
d administration for retaining the rules as they are. The nature of the consequences of
overruling the long-standing authorities is such that, in my judgment, that course
should be left to legislation.

BUTLER-SLOSS LJ. Woolwich Equitable Building Society (Woolwich) paid the
Inland Revenue Commissioners (the Revenue) nearly £57m in response to an
e income tax demand formulated under provisions of regulations found by the House
of Lords to be ultra vires. (See *R v IRC, ex p Woolwich Equitable Building Society*
[1990] STC 682, [1990] 1 WLR 1400.) The Revenue repaid the £57m but have
refused to pay interest claimed by Woolwich of approximately £7m. I gratefully
adopt the summary of the facts set out in the judgment of Ralph Gibson LJ which I
have had an opportunity of reading in draft. In order to decide whether, and if so,
f on what basis Woolwich is entitled to claim interest on the money paid to the
Revenue in response to an unlawful demand, it is necessary to consider first the
bases on which the payments were made by Woolwich and the repayment made by
the Revenue. If a cause of action arose at the dates of payment of the tax, interest
would be payable, but if the right to repayment arose at the date of judgment or did
not arise at all, no interest would be payable. Woolwich makes two main submissions:
g (1) the primary submission, that as a matter of principle a subject who makes a
payment in response to an unlawful demand for tax (or other like demand) from the
Crown, thereby acquires a prima facie right to its repayment forthwith as money
had and received; (2) in the alternative, there is a right to restitution on the basis of
duress or practical compulsion. In either case, the cause of action would arise at the
date of payment and interest would be payable on a claim for the recovery of a debt
h within the meaning of s 35A of the Supreme Court Act 1981.

If both submissions fail, Woolwich contends that the implied agreement as found
by the judge (see [1989] STC 111) included repayment of the sum from the dates of
payment and not the date of judgment and consequently interest would be payable.

The Revenue contend that there is no general principle of restitution, that the
payment by Woolwich was made voluntarily and not under duress and was repaid
j by the Revenue either: (1) by virtue of the implied agreement found by the judge,
which did not include the payment of interest; or (2) alternatively it was an ex gratia
payment made in accordance with their general powers under the Taxes
Management Act 1970, to settle disputed claims and make compromises with
taxpayers in pursuance of their duties to collect taxes (see *IRC v Nuttall* [1990] STC
194, [1990] 1 WLR 631). There was no question of the Revenue not repaying the
£57m to Woolwich.

The primary submission

This is the general principle of restitution of moneys had and received through unjust enrichment. I start, as Nolan J did, with the speech of Lord Wright in *Fibrosa Spolka Akcyjna v Fairbairn Lawson Combe Barbour Ltd* [1943] AC 32 at 61:

'It is clear that any civilized system of law is bound to provide remedies for cases of what has been called unjust enrichment or unjust benefit, that is to prevent a man from retaining the money of or some benefit derived from another which it is against conscience that he should keep. Such remedies in English law are generically different from remedies in contract or in tort, and are now recognized to fall within a third category of the common law which has been called quasi-contract or restitution.'

Historically, these claims were brought in the Court of King's Bench in the action of indebitatus assumpsit and during the eighteenth century, actions for money had and received had increased in number and variety. Lord Wright in his speech in *Fibrosa* said (at 62–63):

'Lord Mansfield C.J., in a familiar passage in *Moses v Macferlan* (1760) 2 Burr. 1005, 1012, sought to rationalize the action for money had and received, and illustrated it by some typical instances. "It lies," he said, "for money paid by mistake; or upon a consideration which happens to fail; or for money got through imposition (express, or implied;) or extortion; or oppression; or an undue advantage taken of the plaintiff's situation, contrary to laws made for the protection of persons under those circumstances. In one word, the gist of this kind of action is, that the defendant, upon the circumstances of the case, is obliged by the ties of natural justice and equity to refund the money." Lord Mansfield prefaced this pronouncement by observations which are to be noted. "If the defendant be under an obligation from the ties of natural justice, to refund; the law implies a debt and gives this action [sc. indebitatus assumpsit] founded in the equity of the plaintiff's case, as it were, upon a contract ('quasi ex contractu' as the Roman law expresses it)." Lord Mansfield does not say that the law implies a promise. The law implies a debt or obligation which is a different thing. In fact, he denies that there is a contract; the obligation is as efficacious as if it were upon a contract. The obligation is a creation of the law, just as much as an obligation in tort. The obligation belongs to a third class, distinct from either contract or tort, though it resembles contract rather than tort. This statement of Lord Mansfield has been the basis of the modern law of quasi-contract, notwithstanding the criticisms which have been launched against it. Like all large generalizations, it has needed and received qualifications in practice. There is, for instance, the qualification that an action for money had and received does not lie for money paid under an erroneous judgment or for moneys paid under an illegal or excessive distress. The law has provided other remedies as being more convenient. The standard of what is against conscience in this context has become more or less canalized or defined, but in substance the juristic concept remains as Lord Mansfield left it.'

The question is whether there is a general right to repayment of moneys unlawfully demanded subject to certain defences which may be raised, or whether a specific right arises in certain narrow categories and there is no redress for those outside those categories. Lord Goff and Professor Jones in *The Law of Restitution* (3rd edn, 1986) said at p 15 of the introduction:

'In our view the case law is now sufficiently mature for the courts to recognise a generalised right to restitution.'

But the learned editors then point out that this is not a recognition of palm-tree justice. The law of restitution has its own highly-developed and reasonably systematic complex of rules.

The judge found (see [1989] STC 111 at 114):

a
    'It is plain, however, from the decided cases that the courts have not extended the general principle of restitution to those who have submitted to unauthorised demands for tax. On the contrary, the general rule has been that the maker of the payment has no right to recover the principal sum paid, let alone to receive interest on it.'

b
    That conclusion is challenged by counsel for Woolwich and from the many decision cited to us he has sought to extract the general proposition contained within his primary submission. Counsel for the Revenue has sought to limit restitution to specific categories also derived from the cases cited.

    I respectfully agree with Glidewell LJ, whose judgment I have had an opportunity of reading in draft, that a distinction should be drawn between public and private
c
law. In the category of public law, someone with actual or ostensible authority to require payment in respect of tax, duty, licence fee or other payment on behalf of central or local government makes the demand for payment by a private individual or company or other organisation. In respect of such a demand no question of consideration arises. If demanded unlawfully, however, is it, to use Lord Mansfield's phrase, money obtained by imposition, express or implied, which the authority is
d
obliged by the ties of natural justice and equity to repay to the payer? Lord Mansfield applied the general obligation to repay by the ties of natural justice and equity, to demands imposed by the Crown in *Campbell v Hall* (1774) 1 Cowp 204. This was an action by a plantation owner in the island of Grenada against the collector of duty unlawfully imposed on the export of sugar from the island after its capture by the British from the French. He paid the duty and claimed it back. Lord Mansfield said
e
(at 205):

    'The action is an action for money had and received; and it is brought upon this ground; namely, that the money was paid to the defendant without any consideration; the duty, for which, and in respect of which he received it, not having been imposed by lawful or sufficient authority to warrant the same.'

f
    The plantation owner was held entitled to recover the duty paid.

    There is one group of cases described as 'colore officii' or 'withholding cases' where the private citizen has successfully recovered money demanded under claim of authority. The narrow definition of this group was expressed by Windeyer J in *Mason v New South Wales* (1959) 102 CLR 108 at 140, to be:

g
    'Extortion by colour of office occurs when a public officer demands and is paid money he is not entitled to, or more than he is entitled to, for the performance of his public duty. Examples of such exactions are overtolls paid to the keepers of toll-bridges and turnpikes, excessive fees demanded by sheriffs, pound-keepers, &c. The parties were not on an equal footing; and generally the payer paid the sum demanded in ignorance that it was not due.'

h
    Examples of this group where the plaintiff succeeded include *Irving v Wilson* (1791) 4 Term Rep 485; *Morgan v Palmer* (1824) 2 B & C 729; *Maskell v Horner* [1915] 3 KB 106.

    Nolan J held, in my view correctly, that the present case could not fall within the definition of colore officii cases.

    There are, however, other decisions which do not come within Windeyer J's
j
definition but are wider in ambit. They include *Campbell v Hall* (1774) 1 Cowp 204; *Dew v Parsons* (1819) 2 B & Ald 562; *Steele v Williams* (1853) 8 Ex 625 and *Hooper v Mayor and Corp of Exeter* (1887) 56 LJQB 457. I have already referred briefly to the facts in *Campbell v Hall*. In *Hooper v Mayor and Corp of Exeter*, a decision of the Divisional Court, the corporation of Exeter was entitled to charge dues on all stone landed at Exeter docks. There was an exception that dues were not payable on limestone to be burned into lime. The plaintiff landed considerable quantities of

limestone over many years in ignorance of this exemption and on becoming aware
of it, reclaimed the dues already paid from the corporation. He succeeded in his
claim. In his judgment Lord Coleridge CJ referred to *Morgan v Palmer* (1824) 2
B & C 729 and said (at 458):

> 'From the case cited in the course of argument it is shewn that the principle
> has been laid down that, where one exacts money from another and it turns out
> that although acquiesced in for years such exaction is illegal, the money may be
> recovered as money had and received, since such payment could not be
> considered as voluntary so as to preclude its recovery. I am of [the] opinion that
> that principle should be adopted here, and that accordingly the plaintiff is
> entitled to recover his money on the ground that he has paid it involuntarily.'

Those observations of Lord Coleridge supported by Smith J are much wider than
the definition of colore officii cases and both *Campbell v Hall* and *Hooper v Mayor
and Corp of Exeter* in my view support the primary submission of Woolwich.

Support for the principle of repayment of tax unlawfully demanded is also to be
found in the decision of the House of Lords in *R v Tower Hamlets London BC, ex p
Chetnik Developments Ltd* [1988] AC 858. The facts related to repayment of rates
which the applicant was not liable to pay but the principles enunciated by Lord
Bridge in his speech are of more general application. He said (at 876–877):

> 'So it emerges from these authorities that the retention of monies known to
> have been paid under a mistake at law, although it is a course permitted to an
> ordinary litigant, is not regarded by the courts as a "high-minded" thing to do,
> but rather as a "shabby thing" or a "dirty trick" and hence is a course which the
> court will not allow one of its own officers, such as a trustee in bankruptcy, to
> take.'

Later he said—

> '. . . I should myself have been content to derive the same conclusion from the
> broader consideration that Parliament must have intended rating authorities to
> act in the same high principled way expected by the court of its own officers
> and not to retain rates paid under a mistake of law, or in paragraph (*a*) upon an
> erroneous valuation, unless there were, as Parliament must have contemplated
> there might be in some cases, special circumstances in which a particular
> overpayment was made such as to justify retention of the whole or part of the
> amount overpaid.'

There are two categories of cases in which it is clear from decisions binding on
this court that a plaintiff cannot succeed. The first is where he has paid voluntarily
in order to close the transaction. In *Maskell v Horner* [1915] 3 KB 106 at 118 Lord
Reading CJ said:

> 'If a person with knowledge of the facts pays money, which he is not in law
> bound to pay, and in circumstances implying that he is paying it voluntarily to
> close the transaction, he cannot recover it. Such a payment is in law like a gift,
> and the transaction cannot be reopened.'

The second is a payment under a mistake of law (subject to the observations of Lord
Bridge in *ex p Chetnick*).

The Revenue relied on a number of decisions to demonstrate that there is no
general principle of restitution. In *Slater v Mayor and Corp of Burnley* (1888) 59
LT 636, Wills J in the Divisional Court did not refer to *Hooper v Mayor and Corp
of Exeter* (1887) 56 LJQB 457 which had been cited in argument and held that the
overpayment of water rates by the plaintiff was a voluntary transaction and not paid
under duress. In *William Whiteley Ltd v The King* (1910) 101 LT 741, a decision of
Walton J much relied on by the Revenue, Whiteley paid fees under protest to the
Revenue in respect of male employees for six years. It refused to pay the fees for the

seventh year and was held to be correct in its interpretation of the relevant
a regulations. Walton J held that the payments were voluntary and not under
compulsion and had been paid under mistake of law. In *National Pari-Mutuel
Association Ltd v R* (1930) 47 TLR 110 the company without making any objection
paid betting duty on the operation of a totalisator, but after another company was
held not liable to pay the duty sought the repayment of the duty it had paid. This
court held that the question of liability was one of law and the construction of an Act
b of Parliament and the company had made a mistake of law in respect of which it
could not recover. In *Twyford v Manchester Corp* [1946] Ch 236 the corporation
unlawfully levied fees on a monumental mason working on memorials in the
cemetery, which he paid under protest. He brought an action to recover the fees
and Romer J held that the payments were not made under duress or colore officii
and were therefore voluntary.
c   This question has also been considered in the United States and Australia. Holmes J,
sitting in the US Circuit Court for the District of Colorado in *Atchison, Topeka &
Santa Fe Railway Co v O'Connor* (1911) 223 US 280, found for the taxpayer who
had paid under a law later found to be unconstitutional, in circumstances very
similar to those of the present case and on grounds supporting the argument
advanced by Woolwich. In two decisions, *Sargood Bros v The Commonwealth* (1910)
d 11 CLR 258 and *Mason's* case, the first relating to custom duty unlawfully demanded
and the second to the payment of a fee for a licence for a road haulier which was also
held later to have been demanded unlawfully, the High Court of Australia found
that the money should be repaid. In *Sargood Bros v Commonwealth*, O'Connor J, in
coming to that conclusion, set out principles which support the contentions of
Woolwich. In *Mason's* case the majority of the court held the money repayable on
e the narrow ground of duress. However, Kitto J clearly and Dixon CJ by implication
enunciated wider principles which support the primary submission of Woolwich.
    Both in principle and from decided cases, I consider that there is a general
principle of repayment of tax unlawfully demanded. The decisions to the contrary
can be distinguished as coming within the well-established categories of a voluntary
payment to close the transaction or a mistake of law. The decisions in *William
f Whiteley, Slater v Mayor and Corp of Burnley* (1888) 59 LT 636 and *Twyford v
Manchester Corp* have stood for many years but I am inclined to the view that they
were wrongly decided.
    We were urged not to extend the law and to leave it to Parliament to deal with
any injustice which may arise. But significantly, Parliament in the legislative
structure which governs taxation has provided for repayment of tax which has been
g overpaid under regulations which are intra vires. No structure is in place to deal
with the demand for and payment of tax which has been unlawfully demanded
under legislation found to be ultra vires. To deal with that eventuality the courts are
thrown back on the common law and precedent. Although there is no decision on
facts which are entirely similar, I do not see an enunciation of the general principle
of restitution subject to limitations as an extension of the law but rather as a
h redefining of long-established principles, enshrined in the Bill of Rights, established
and acted on in many decisions both in this jurisdiction and in the United States and
Australia. It accords also with the general standards of fair dealings between the
taxpayer and the emanations of government where the individual is likely to be at a
disadvantage.
    In the present case, the judge found that although the Revenue would not have
j instituted collection proceedings pending the judicial review proceedings, nonetheless (see [1989] STC 111 at 116):

> 'Subject to the outcome of the present case, the scales in this respect were
> tilted heavily in favour of the Revenue. I accept that, as a practical matter,
> Woolwich had little choice but to make the three payments.'

I agree with the judge that the demand from the Revenue did not amount to duress.

But it was clearly not a voluntary payment made to close the transaction, nor was there any mistake of law. The money was paid throughout under protest and proceedings were immediately instituted to establish that the regulations were ultra vires. In my judgment, for the reasons I have set out above, I consider the judge was wrong to find there was no general principle of restitution and to limit categories of relief to mistake of fact or duress.

Had it been necessary to consider the alternative argument of the implied agreement, I agree with the judge that an agreement could well be implied in these circumstances that the money was to be repaid to Woolwich. I do not consider, however, that into that agreement could be inferred a term to pay interest. Equally, I do not consider that the repayment by the Revenue was ex gratia. But, having come to the conclusion that the primary submission of Woolwich is correct, it is not necessary further to explore the alternative arguments.

I would allow the appeal.

Appeal allowed with costs. Leave for appeal to House of Lords granted.

Solicitors: *Solicitor of Inland Revenue ; Clifford Chance* (for Woolwich).

Rengan Krishnan Esq   Barrister.

a # McMenamin (Inspector of Taxes) v Diggles

CHANCERY DIVISION AT MANCHESTER
SCOTT J
6, 7 JUNE 1991

b *Emoluments from office or employment – Office – Head clerk of chambers, previously under contract of employment, entering into new contractual arrangements with members of chambers to provide full clerking service – Whether head clerk holding an 'office' – Income and Corporation Taxes Act 1970, s 181.*

The taxpayer, Mr Diggles, was at all material times the senior clerk of a leading set
c of barristers' chambers in Manchester. It was common ground that for a considerable number of years until 7 October 1985 he was senior clerk under a contract of employment and was assessable to tax under Sch E as an employee. On 7 October 1985 new contractual arrangements were brought into effect between the taxpayer and each member of the chambers. Under those arrangements, the taxpayer, in return for a specified percentage of the gross income of each member, agreed to
d provide at his own cost and expense a full clerking service for each member. The agreement held it open to the taxpayer either to act as head clerk himself or to provide some other suitably qualified or experienced person to act as one. In the event, throughout the relevant period he acted as head clerk himself and the services which he supplied in discharging his contractual obligation to provide full clerking services included all the traditional services provided by head clerks to barristers'
e chambers. The taxpayer appealed to the Special Commissioners against assessments to income tax under Sch E for the years 1985–86, 1986–87 and 1987–88. The questions before the commissioners were (1) whether for the three years the taxpayer was an employee and hence assessable under Sch E and (2) whether the assessments under Sch E could be upheld on the alternative ground that during the relevant years he was the holder of an 'office' within the meaning of that word in s 181[a] of the
f Income and Corporation Taxes Act (the 1970 Act). The Special Commissioners concluded that the taxpayer was not an employee and also that he was not an office holder for the purposes of s 181. On appeal, the Crown accepted that the taxpayer was not an employee but contended that the taxpayer was an office-holder for the purposes of s 181.

g **Held** – The Special Commissioners had not misdirected themselves in law and it was open to them on the evidence to conclude that the taxpayer was not the holder of an office for the purposes of s 181 of the Income and Corporation Taxes Act 1970. The appeal would accordingly be dismissed.

Notes
h For the meaning of office, see Simon's Taxes E4.201.
     For the Income and Corporation Taxes Act 1970, s 181 (now the Income and Corporation Taxes Act 1988, s 19), see ibid, Part G1.

Cases referred to in judgment
j *Edwards (Inspector of Taxes) v Clinch* [1979] STC 148, [1979] 1 WLR 338, [1979] 1
     All ER 648; [1980] STC 438, [1981] Ch 1, [1980] 3 All ER 278, CA; [1981] STC
     617, [1982] AC 845, [1981] 3 All ER 543, 56 TC 367, HL.
     Edwards (Inspector of Taxes) v Bairstow [1956] AC 14, [1955] 3 All ER 48, HL.
     Great Western Railway Co v Bater (Surveyor of Taxes) [1920] 3 KB 266, 8 TC 231.

---

a   Section 181, so far as material, is set out at p 428 *d–e*, post

Case stated

1. On 21, 22, 23 and 26 February 1990, two of the Commissioners for the special *a* purposes of the Income Tax Acts, heard appeals by Stephen John Diggles (the taxpayer) against assessments to income tax under Sch E, each in the sum of £35,000, for 1985–86, 1986–87 and 1987–88.

2. Shortly stated the question for the commissioners' decision was whether, in those years, the taxpayer's remuneration as a barristers' clerk was properly taxable under Sch E as emoluments from an office or employment.   *b*

3. The commissioners heard oral evidence from the taxpayer; Mr B Maddocks, barrister; and Mr F Taylor, an inspector of taxes (retired).

[The agreed documents which were put in evidence were then listed.]

4. In addition to the cases referred to in the commissioners' decision they were referred to the following.

> *Ellis (Inspector of Taxes) v Lucas* [1967] Ch 858, 43 TC 276.   *c*
> *Fall (Inspector of Taxes) v Hitchen* [1973] STC 66, [1973] 1 WLR 286.
> *Hill v Beckett* [1915] 1 KB 578.
> *IRC v Brander & Cruickshank* [1971] 1 WLR 212, 46 TC 574.
> *McMillan v Guest (Inspector of Taxes)* [1942] AC 561, 24 TC 190.
> *Magraw v Havers* (1978) Case no 29915/77/A: Industrial Tribunal.
> *Mitchell and Edon v Ross* [1962] AC 814, 40 TC 11.   *d*
> *Nethermere (St Neots) Ltd v Gardiner* [1984] ICR 612.
> *O'Kelly v Trusthouse Forte plc* [1984] 1 QB 90.
> *Robinson v Hill* [1910] 1 KB 94.
> *Sidey v Phillips (Inspector of Taxes)* [1987] STC 87.
> *Walls v Sinnett (Inspector of Taxes)* [1987] STC 236.   *e*

The tribunal's decision in *Magraw v Havers* contained a list (a) of the duties undertaken by the senior clerk and (b) of his powers and responsibilities, which the taxpayer considered to be broadly applicable to his case.

5. The commissioners reserved their decision and gave it in writing on 29 March 1990, allowing the appeals and discharging the assessments. A copy of the decision, which sets out the facts, the contentions of the parties and the reasons for their *f* conclusion, was annexed to and formed part of the case.

6. The inspector immediately after the determination of the appeal declared to the commissioners his dissatisfaction therewith as being erroneous in point of law and on 20 April 1990 required them to state a case for the opinion of the High Court pursuant to the Taxes Management Act 1970, s 56.

7. The question of law for the opinion of the court was whether the commissioners *g* had erred in law in holding that the taxpayer performed the duties of a barristers' clerk as an independent contractor and not as the holder of an office nor as an employee during the years in question.

DECISION

The appellant, Mr Diggles (the taxpayer), appeals against assessments to income *h* tax under Sch E for 1985–86, 1986–87 and 1987–88.

The taxpayer is the senior clerk to the barristers' chambers known as St James's Chambers, 68 Quay Street, Manchester and the question for decision is whether he is properly assessed under Sch E on emoluments from an office or employment or whether, as he contends, the assessment should be made under Sch D on the profits of a trade, profession or vocation. The following facts are agreed: *j*

1. This set of chambers has been in existence for over 70 years originally at 3 St James's Square, Manchester and from 1984 at their present address where they adopted the name 'St James's Chambers'. The head of chambers then was Mr L J Porter, who retired in March 1987 and was succeeded by Mr B C Maddocks. The original premises were held under successive tenancies at full market rents. The present building was purchased by four members as trustees for the members in 62

shares held in varying proportions, the arrangement being that new members
a purchase the shares of retiring members.

2. The taxpayer became a junior clerk to the chambers in January 1964 at the age
of 17. The senior clerk then was Mr R C Randall. At that time there were some nine
members. The senior clerk was rewarded in the traditional manner by the clerk's fee
collected from the solicitor client along with the fee in guineas payable to the
barrister. Thus a fee note for a conference would be £2 7s being two guineas for the
b barrister and five shillings for the clerk. He did not receive the shilling in the guinea
(a practice in some chambers), but some junior members paid an additional sum of
10s or £1 per week to the clerk.

3. This system was abolished with decimalisation in 1971, following which the
senior clerk was paid a commission at an agreed percentage of all fees collected.

4. The taxpayer became senior clerk on 20 April 1970 when Mr Randall retired.
c There were then ten members of the chambers. His initial commission was 5% of
gross fees earned by the members. It was increased to 5½% in January 1972 and then
to 6½% in February 1974.

5. On 28 April 1970 the then head of chambers, Mr R J Hardy, gave the taxpayer
a written statement of his terms of employment under s 4 of the Contracts of
Employment Act 1963. That statement set out the basis of his remuneration, his
d normal hours of working, his holiday entitlement, and his right to payment during
sickness or incapacity through injury. It provided that the employment could be
terminated by three months' notice on either side. The statement was signed by Mr
Hardy on behalf of himself and the other members of the chambers.

6. Between August 1978 and October 1985 the taxpayer paid a contribution
towards chambers expenses calculated as a percentage of his commission in the same
e way as the members.

7. Down to 7 October 1985 the taxpayer was treated as an employee for the
purposes of income tax and national insurance and value added tax, paying income
tax under Sch E by way of assessment, following the practice then and now generally
applied by the Revenue to barristers' senior clerks.

8. Immediately before that date there were two junior clerks to the chambers,
f Miss Paula Magnall (now Mrs Garlick), who was first employed in the year 1980
and Miss Susan Barnes (now Mrs Bamberger), who was first employed in the year
1981. They were both paid salaries by the chambers which deducted tax under the
PAYE system.

9. On 7 October 1985 an agreement was signed between the taxpayer and the 20
barristers who were then members of the chambers whereby, as a separate contract
g between each of the barristers of the one part and the taxpayer of the other part, the
taxpayer agreed to provide at his own cost and expense for each barrister a 'Full
Clerking Service' in return for 8·3% of the barrister's gross earnings (defined to
include remuneration from a part-time legal appointment as well as professional
fees).

10. The expression 'Full Clerking Services' was stated to include:

h
> '(a) The provision of the services of a full-time Head Clerk of not less than 10
> years experience in that capacity being either Mr Diggles or some other Clerk
> with that qualification.
> (b) The provision of a Junior Clerk or Junior Clerks and other ancillary staff
> (but not including any typists) whose services may be reasonably necessary to
> enable the Head Clerk to render efficiently the Full Clerking Services.'

j
And to enable the head clerk and other staff supplied by the taxpayer to render the
full clerking services efficiently they were to be provided with an adequate clerk's
room and facilities at the chambers.

11. The taxpayer was to render an account of the barrister's gross earnings for the
preceding month on the first day of every month and the barrister was to pay the
sum due to the taxpayer within seven days of the delivery of the account.

12. The agreement was to continue until determined by either party on 12 months' written notice, or 6 months in the case of a barrister who was retiring from practice: and it would terminate forthwith if a barrister obtained a full-time judicial appointment. After termination the taxpayer would do his best to collect outstanding fees and he would be entitled to his commission on them.

13. As from 7 October 1985 the taxpayer was registered for value added tax and made his quarterly value added tax returns as a person in business on his own account, making taxable supplies of services, on which he charged and collected value added tax.

14. As from the same date and in accordance with the agreement, the taxpayer engaged Miss Magnall and Miss Barnes as junior clerks and he also engaged an assistant Mr Liam Mooney and occasional casual helpers. Miss Magnall (Mrs Garlick) left in June 1989 to have a child and was paid statutory maternity pay by the taxpayer who engaged a new junior clerk Miss Helen Berkley with effect from 29 March 1989. Written statements of terms required by the Employment Protection (Consolidation) Act 1978 (as amended) were signed by the taxpayer as employer in respect of Miss Magnall, Miss Barnes, Mr Mooney and Miss Berkley.

15. The work of the junior clerks covers the full range of the senior clerk's responsibilities and is allocated to them by the taxpayer as required. But in general the negotiation of fees on privately paid work is carried out by the senior clerk personally.

16. At all material times, the *Code of Professional Conduct for the Bar of England and Wales* (3rd edn, 1985) (the code of conduct) required that a barrister might not practice unless he were a member of (or temporarily permitted the use of) professional chambers and that he must have the services of the clerk of chambers. The rules also provide that a partnership is not permissible between practising barristers, but they may agree to share expenses.

17. The expenses of chambers (apart from rates apportioned according to occupation) are apportioned between the members rateably according to income. Subject to that sharing of expenses, each member is in practice on his own account and in competition with other barristers including other members of chambers. He may, and not infrequently does, appear in court against another member and advises and acts for a client against the client of another member.

18. At all material times the taxpayer's name was exhibited on the exterior of the St James's Chambers beside the description 'clerk' and the words 'Clerk S J Diggles' appeared at the foot of the list of barristers at the St James's Chambers in entries for Waterlow's *Solicitors' and Barristers' Directory and Diary*.

19. The taxpayer was at all material times a qualified member of the Barristers' Clerks' Association.

We heard oral evidence of the taxpayer and of Mr Maddocks from which we find that the proposal to give the taxpayer self-employed status came from the head of the chambers. Changes in the national insurance regulations in 1984 had substantially increased the employer's class 1 contribution in respect of a well-paid employee by removing the top limit of salary at which contributions had previously ceased. Even before that the position of the senior clerk had been seen as somewhat hybrid, capable of being treated as employment or as self-employment. Mr Porter in particular had thought it unsatisfactory that the senior clerk should be paid on a commission basis for providing his services as clerk while the chambers paid the junior staff to assist him. Mr Porter and Mr Maddocks decided that it would be better to make him responsible for providing all clerking services on a self-employed basis. But they preferred to keep the typists in their employment since typing services were rendered directly to the members of chambers.

The taxpayer was at first reluctant to make the change because he would lose the security of employment, including the right to a redundancy payment if things went wrong, and he would assume the responsibilities of an employer towards the junior clerks. But he realised that self-employed status would have some advantages. He a would have 12 months' notice of termination; he could take his holiday when he chose; and he would be free to take on staff as he wished without consulting anyone. The right to put in a substitute as head clerk might also be useful if he were sick or, later on, if he should want to ease up as he approached retirement. On reflection he was content to accept the change. So far as he knew the option of keeping his employed status was not available to him.

b The term 'full clerking services' was not defined in the new agreement because it was thought that all concerned would know what it meant and any attempt to define it was likely to do more harm than good. The taxpayer has continued to manage the chambers as before and does his best to further the practice of each member. But since his personal stake in maintaining the chambers' income is now higher he would feel more independent if he had to answer criticism from members (which in fact he has not) about matters such as the distribution of work. He now manages the c clerking arrangements entirely on his own without consultation. In 1988, for example, he took on and paid some temporary staff to assist in putting the chambers' records on to a computer.

d The taxpayer submits a monthly account of clerking fees, plus value added tax, to each member of chambers and this should be paid within seven days. For one reason or another, however, he may be owed at any one time something between £3,000 and £6,000 by a member of chambers. Since he has to meet all the expenses of employing staff out of his fees, as well as meeting some chambers' expenses for which he is entitled to be reimbursed, he may run into cash flow problems which he did not experience before October 1985. He estimates that he needs to hold about £15,000 of his own money available to fund his financial obligations under the agreement.

e The attention of each witness was directed in cross-examination to passages in the code of conduct as in force from 1985 onwards. Each acknowledged that the work of everyone in chambers, including clerks and typists, may involve matters for which the head of chambers has responsibility under the code of conduct. He must, for example, take all reasonable steps to ensure that the chambers are administered competently and efficiently and in a manner which is fair and equitable for all f members and pupils: and to ensure that the clerks and other staff carry out their duties in a correct and efficient manner. The code of conduct also places obligations on each individual barrister, not to allow touting on his behalf, for example, nor to communicate confidential information entrusted to him by his lay client: and he is made responsible for the actions of his clerks. The Barristers' Clerks' Association issues its own code of conduct but its contents were not in evidence.

g The taxpayer's remuneration was fixed at 8·3% of gross earnings under the agreement on the basis of figures prepared by Thornton Baker, Chartered Accountants. The object was to remunerate him at much the same level as before, bearing in mind that in future he would have to pay the junior clerks but would not be contributing to the general chambers expenses.

The first question which arises on those facts is whether the taxpayer's h remuneration came from an employment, or perhaps from a number of employments which would lead to the same result for tax purposes.

We were referred, as is usual in cases of this kind, to a number of authorities in which the distinction has had to be drawn between a contract for services and a contract of service. In some of them the question has arisen in relation to a series of short engagements, as in *Market Investigations Ltd v Minister of Social Security* j [1969] 2 QB 173 (where part-time interviewers were held to be employed under contracts of service) and in *W F & R K Swan (Hellenic) Ltd v Secretary of State for Social Services* (18 January 1983, unreported) (where tour managers were held to be engaged under contracts for services). And there is the case of *Davies (Inspector of Taxes) v Braithwaite* [1931] 2 KB 628, 18 TC 198 in which a series of acting engagements constituted the exercise of a profession. That is not the situation in the present case, since the taxpayer has been clerk to the same chambers for a number of years but counsel for the taxpayer claims some support nevertheless from cases such as *Braithwaite*. In general, he says, a number of separate contracts indicates *a* professional activity rather than employment: and he points out that the taxpayer had a separate contract with each member of the chambers, about 20 in all.

Closer to the facts of this case are *Massey v Crown Life Insurance Co* [1978] 1 WLR 676, in which the branch manager of an insurance company entered into a new agreement designed to give him self-employed status while continuing to perform the same duties as before, and *Ready Mixed Concrete (South East) Ltd v Minister of* *b* *Pensions and National Insurance* [1968] 2 QB 497, in which persons previously employed by the company in a different capacity were invited to become owner-drivers and deliver concrete on the company's behalf as independent contractors. In both of those cases the facts were found to justify the conclusion that the legal relationship accorded with the parties' declared intention. In *Ferguson v John Dawson & Partners (Contractors) Ltd* [1976] 1 WLR 1213 on the other hand the *c* true legal relationship was held to be that of employer and employee although the plaintiff had specifically been taken on as a labour-only sub-contractor.

In the search for guiding principles one usually starts from the judgment of MacKenna J in *Ready Mixed Concrete* ([1968] 2 QB 497 at 515):

> 'A contract of service exists if these three conditions are fulfilled. (i) The *d* servant agrees that, in consideration of a wage or other remuneration, he will provide his own work and skill in the performance of some service for his master. (ii) He agrees, expressly or impliedly, that in the performance of that service he will be subject to the other's control in a sufficient degree to make that other master. (iii) The other provisions of the contract are consistent with its being a contract of service.' *e*

His Lordship emphasised in relation to his first condition the servant's obligation to provide his own work and skill, for he added:

> 'Freedom to do a job either by one's own hands or by another's is inconsistent with a contract of service, though a limited or occasional power of delegation may not be . . .' *f*

In the *Swan (Hellenic)* case McCullough J went through a check list, first compiled by Waterhouse J in *Addison v London Philharmonic Orchestra Ltd* [1981] ICR 261 at 271, of ten, or possibly eleven, aspects of the relationship between parties which, in the light of the authorities, may prove to be of significance in resolving questions of this kind. He found none of them decisive and concluded in the end that the only *g* factor of major significance was the intention of the parties as deduced from the terms which they agreed as to tax and national insurance. We do not propose to run through the whole of the check list but we shall refer to some items from it as we consider the rival arguments.

Counsel for the taxpayer, applying the control test which, although no longer regarded as decisive, remains a relevant factor, says that the taxpayer was not under *h* the control necessary for an employment. He had wide discretion as to the way in which he provided clerking services, with no fixed hours of work and no obligation to obey orders. He had to avoid breaches of the code of conduct because he was supplying services to barristers who were bound by that code of conduct but that does not mean that he was controlled in the sense required for a contract of service. Applying another test from the check list, counsel for the taxpayer submits that the *j* taxpayer was carrying on business on his own account and not for a master or masters. By his efforts he could increase the fees coming into the chambers, and thereby increase his income, and he had a financial stake in the provision of clerking services. He had to bear the cost of hiring junior clerks and he had £15,000 of his own money committed to the business. He intended to provide services, not

necessarily his own, as an independent contractor and that is precisely what he did.
a Admittedly the chambers provided the premises and equipment for him and his
employees to use but that is not a significant factor since his function was to provide
management services only.

Mr Cotton, for the Crown, contends that the agreement of 7 October 1985 effected
no change in the taxpayer's status. He has remained an employee, albeit now serving
20 masters under separate contracts of employment. The relationship between a
b barrister and his senior clerk involves a degree of control by the barrister which
necessarily makes the clerk an employee because the clerk's duties have to be
performed in such a way as to comply with the code of conduct and the barrister is
responsible for his actions. The same is true of the junior clerks and if the senior
clerk engages them he must do so as agent for the chambers. All the conditions set
out in *Ready Mixed Concrete* are satisfied. As to (1), the provision of personal
c services, the taxpayer does not have unlimited power to delegate his functions. He
can put in another head clerk but the agreement puts some obligations on him
personally.

If one asks whether the taxpayer is in business on his own account the answer
must be no, in the Crown's submission. He provides no equipment and only some
of the junior staff who assist him, assuming for the moment that the clerks are his
d servants. His ability to increase his profits by his own efforts is limited because he
has to provide clerking services within the established framework of the chambers.
By attracting work to the chambers he can increase his remuneration but that was
equally so before October 1985 and it is true of any employee remunerated on a
commission basis. Applying another test from the check list, taken from the
judgment of Denning LJ in the *Bank voor Handel en Scheepvaart NV v Slatford*
e [1953] 1 QB 248 at 295, 35 TC 311 at 334, he is inescapably 'part and parcel' of the
chambers' organisation and in its service. The parties may have intended to change
his status but they could not effectively do so. Even if the agreement had stated in
terms that the taxpayer should provide clerking services as an independent
contractor, which it did not, it would not have been conclusive because the parties
may misdescribe their relationship, as in *Ferguson v John Dawson & Partners*
f *(Contractors) Ltd.*

There is some force in the Crown's contentions and they were cogently presented,
but we have come to the conclusion that they should not succeed. The 'part and
parcel' test, though possibly decisive in some cases, is not always so. McCullough J
found it unhelpful in *Swan (Hellenic)*. The decisive factors here are, in our opinion,
the intention of the parties to change the status of the senior clerk and the terms of
g the agreement of 7 October 1985 which was designed to give effect to that intention.
The agreement was drawn in broad terms, with little provision for matters of detail,
but it covered the main features, that the taxpayer should provide full clerking
services for each barrister at his own cost, that he could render those services through
a suitably qualified head clerk other than himself if he chose and that he was to
employ the junior clerks whom he needed to assist him. Those features point to a
h contract for services rather than a contract of service and the existence of 20 separate
contracts does, we think, point to the same conclusion, even though not conclusively.

The Crown's argument says, in effect, that the relationship between a barrister
and his clerk can be conducted only on a master and servant basis; but we are not
convinced that that is right. The barrister's responsibility for the actions of his clerks
under the code of conduct is a matter between himself and the Bar Council which
j does not dictate the terms on which the clerks (senior and junior) are engaged. His
remedy, if the code of conduct is breached, is surely to dismiss an employed clerk or
terminate the contract of an independent contractor. Nor does it seem to us that the
obligations imposed on the taxpayer by the agreement are necessarily those of an
employed person, requiring him to render personal services under the control of a
master.

We accept that the solution to the question does not lie simply in the minds of the parties. As McCullough J said in *Swan (Hellenic)*—   *a*

> 'I have to determine the nature of the obligations of the parties to one another. This depends on the terms which they expressly agreed and on such further terms as are to be implied. One asks: what was their intention? This does not mean what was the relationship they wanted to create, nor what was the relationship they thought they had created. The only relevant intention is that which is to be inferred from the agreed terms.'   *b*

But in this case we find that the agreed terms reflected the parties' intention to put the senior clerk onto a self-employed footing and we are satisfied on the evidence that those agreed terms were given practical effect. We conclude that the taxpayer has not been in the employment of the chambers nor of any member of those chambers since 7 October 1985. And we move on to consider whether he held an   *c* 'office' within the meaning of that term in s 181 of the Income and Corporation Taxes Act 1970.

In *Edwards (Inspector of Taxes) v Clinch* [1981] STC 617, [1982] AC 845 the House of Lords reconsidered Rowlatt J's definition of an office in *Great Western Railway Co v Bater (Surveyor of Taxes)* [1920] 3 KB 266 at 274, 8 TC 231 at 235 as something—   *d*

> '... which was a subsisting, permanent, substantive position, which had an existence independent of the person who filled it, and which went on and was filled in succession by successive holders ...'

and gave it broad approval, although the wording is not to be treated as sacrosanct and it is not to be applied too rigidly. Lord Wilberforce said ([1981] STC 617 at 619,   *e* [1982] AC 845 at 861):

> 'For myself I would accept that a rigid requirement of permanance is no longer appropriate, nor is vouched by any decided case and continuity need not be regarded as an absolute qualification. But still, ... the word must involve a degree of continuance (not necessarily continuity) and of independent existence: *f* it must connote a post to which a person can be appointed, which he can vacate and to which a successor can be appointed.'

Counsel for the taxpayer submits, in reliance on a passage from the judgment of Buckley LJ in the same case ([1980] STC 438 at 441, [1981] Ch 1 at 6), that to satisfy the requirement of an independent existence an office must owe its existence to 'some constituent instrument, whether it be a charter, statute, declaration of trust,   *g* contract (other than a contract of personal service) or instrument of some other kind'. While we think it probable that most offices will be created by some such instrument (and the list is an extensive one) we do not find sufficient authority for that statement to add it as a necessary requirement of an office in all cases.

Counsel for the taxpayer also submits that an office must contain a 'public' element: an office-holder must be a person to some extent in the public domain,   *h* although he concedes that the degree of publicity required is incapable of precise definition. This element was stated most clearly by Lord Bridge ([1981] STC 617 at 635, [1982] AC 845 at 881) in his dissenting speech in *Clinch* where he relied on a dictionary definition of 'office' as: 'A position or place to which certain duties are attached, esp. one of a more or less public character ...' but the majority of their Lordships found dictionary definitions unhelpful. Again it seems to us that this may   *j* be a relevant factor, since an office will more often than not contain some public element, but the authorities do not establish that it is an essential requirement, or at any rate not one that can be usefully quantified.

The Crown contends in this case that the taxpayer holds an office, or possibly a number of separate offices, as clerk to the St James's Chambers, a recognised post to

which someone else would be appointed if he were to retire or die. If a constituent
a instrument is required, which Mr Cotton does not admit, it is the code of conduct
which, at the relevant time, required every barrister to have the services of a clerk.
In so far as a public element is required it is present since the clerk to chambers had
a public function in the provision of legal services to those members of the public
who need them.

The speeches in *Edwards v Clinch* have to be read in their context. Mr Clinch's
b appointment to conduct an inquiry for the Secretary of State for the Environment
had its origin in statute and required him to perform duties of an obviously public
nature. The question was whether it had the necessary elements of permanence and
continuity in the sense that it could be vacated and filled by someone else: and the
House of Lords held that it did not. As Lord Lowry put it ([1981] STC 617 at 627,
[1982] AC 845 at 870):

c
'To be in a position of authority is not necessarily to hold an office, and when
you appoint somebody to *do* something you do not thereby appoint him to *be*
something (in other words to hold an office), unless the Act or other relevant
instrument says so.'

In other cases the area of debate will be different. There must, for example, be
d many positions in commercial organisations which will have to be filled by others
when the present holders leave: and in some of those cases the name of the holder
may be displayed for the information of the public. But not all such persons could
be said to hold offices for the purposes of Sch E: they are simply employees appointed
to perform duties of a managerial or supervisory nature. A hotel manager is an
example of that sort of post. In the end it comes down, we think, to a matter of
e impression in each case: and reviewing all the relevant circumstances of this case we
conclude that the taxpayer did not hold an office, nor a number of offices. The
strongest features in the Crown's case are that, at the time, barristers were required
to have the services of a clerk and that the taxpayer's name appears as clerk both at
the entrance to the chambers and in various professional publications, but those
features of the case are not sufficient for the success of their argument. The taxpayer's
f function has been at all times to perform the duties of senior clerk to the members of
the chambers. Those are important duties but we find it impossible to say that when
he took them on he was appointed to a post which can be classed as an office for the
purposes of Sch E.

The right conclusion is, in our judgment, that he has peformed those duties as an
employed person before 7 October 1985 and as an independent contractor, providing
g clerking services under contract, since that date.

The appeal succeeds and the Sch E assessments for the three years under appeal
are discharged.

Launcelot Henderson for the Crown.
Stephen Oliver QC and *Timothy Lyons* for the taxpayer.

h
SCOTT J. This is an appeal by the Crown against the determination by the Special
Commissioners of appeals by the taxpayer against assessments to income tax under
Sch E for the years 1985–86, 1986–87 and 1987–88.

The taxpayer, Mr Diggles, is and was at all matterial times the senior clerk of a
leading set of barristers' chambers in Manchester known as St James's Chambers.
j   The first main question before the Special Commissioners was whether for the
three years of assessment I have mentioned the taxpayer was employed and hence
amenable to assessments under Sch E or was self-employed, in which case he would
have been amenable to being assessed for tax under Sch D. The second question was
whether the assessments under Sch E could be upheld, even though on a true view
of the relevant facts the taxpayer was self-employed, on the ground that during the

relevant years of assessment he was the holder of an 'office' within the meaning of that word in the relevant provision in the Income and Corporation Taxes Act 1970 *a* (the 1970 Act).

In the event, the Special Commissioners concluded, first, that the taxpayer was self-employed and, second, that as 'a matter of impression' the taxpayer was not the holder of an office for the purposes of the relevant statutory provision.

The Crown appealed by case stated against the decision of the Special Commissioners. The grounds of appeal were, first, that the Special Commissioners *b* were wrong in finding in favour of self-employment rather than employment. That part of the appeal is no longer pursued. It is accepted by the Crown that the conclusions of fact made by the Special Commissioners in regard to that issue are such as to prevent the success of the appeal. But the appeal has continued on the second point, namely, whether during the relevant period the taxpayer was the holder of an 'office'. The office the Crown has in mind is the office of senior clerk to *c* the chambers.

It is accepted by counsel for the Crown, that the appeal can succeed only if one of two possible bases is established. The Crown must establish either that the Special Commissioners misdirected themselves in law or that they reached a conclusion that no tribunal properly directed could have reached.

I should start by referring to s 181 of the 1970 Act which contains the relevant *d* charging provision. In sub-s (1), under the heading 'Schedule E', it is provided as follows:

> '1. Tax under this Schedule shall be charged in respect of any office or employment on emoluments therefrom which fall under one, or more than one, of the following Cases—Case I: where the person holding the office or employment is resident and ordinarily resident in the United Kingdom . . .' *e*

I need not read anything further.

In my opinion, the question whether a particular occupation followed by the taxpayer during the relevant taxing period constitutes an 'office' for the purpose of this statutory provision involves an issue of mixed fact and law. It involves law to the extent that the meaning to be given to the word 'office' is a matter of construction, *f* and it involves fact because the nature and incidents of the occupation in question are essentially matters of fact. The determination of the issue requires the application of the facts, as found, to the proper legal meaning of the word 'office'.

The most recent case relevant to the matters argued before me is *Edwards (Inspector of Taxes) v Clinch* [1981] STC 617, [1982] AC 845. In that case, Lord Wilberforce referred to the manner in which the resolution of the question whether *g* or not there was the holding of an office for tax purposes ought to be approached ([1981] STC 617 at 620, [1982] AC 845 at 861):

> 'It is necessary to appraise the characteristics of the taxpayer's "appointment". There is in this task an element of common sense evaluation of fact: a task which is committed in the first place to the General Commissioners. Their *h* finding was for the taxpayer, and though this is far from sacrosanct, indeed I think that they applied the Rowlatt definition [see *Great Western Railway Co v Bater (Surveyor of Taxes)* [1920] 3 KB 266 at 274, 8 TC 231 at 235] too literally, nevertheless it is not in my opinion, wholly to be disregarded. They described it as "merely a transient, indeterminate, once-only execution of a task for which [the taxpayer] was peculiarly qualified" ([1979] STC 148 at 150), adding an *j* analogy which I do not find appropriate.'

The primary facts as found by the Special Commissioners were not the subject of any substantial dispute. The taxpayer had been the senior clerk at St James's Chambers for a considerable number of years before the tax years to which I have referred. Up until 7 October 1985 it is common ground that he was senior clerk of

the chambers under a contract of employment. It is also common ground that up to
a that date he was properly amenable to being assessed to tax under Sch E as an
employed person.

But on 7 October 1985 new contractual arrangements were brought into effect
between the taxpayer and each of the members of the chambers. There was a written
agreement of that date signed by each member of the chambers and by the taxpayer.
The recitals to the agreement included the following—

b   '. . . whereas in this Agreement the expression "Full Clerking Services" shall
include: (a) The provision of the services of a full-time Head Clerk of not less
than 10 years experience in that capacity being either [the taxpayer] or some
other Clerk with that qualification. (b) The provision of a Junior Clerk or Junior
Clerks and other ancillary staff (but not including any typists) whose services
may be reasonably necessary to enable the Head Clerk to render efficiently the
c   Full Clerking Services.'

Then followed the operative part of the agreement—

'. . . it is agreed as a separate contract between each of the Barristers of the one
part and [the taxpayer] of the other part that [the taxpayer] will at his own cost
and expense provide for each of the Barristers a Full Clerking Service at the
d   Chambers upon the terms and conditions set out in the second Schedule hereto.'

The terms set out in the second schedule included provision for a specified
percentage of gross earnings to be paid by each barrister to the taxpayer, and
imposed the obligation on the taxpayer to account to each barrister for the gross
earnings of that barrister during the preceding calendar month and to show the
e amount owed by the barrister to him under the remuneration provision to which I
have just referred.

One paragraph in the second schedule provided as follows:

'The Head Clerk and other staff supplied by [the taxpayer] shall be provided
with an adequate Clerk's Room and facilities at the Chambers to enable them to
carry on the Full Clerking Services efficiently.'
f

As a matter of construction of the agreement, it seems reasonably clear to me that
the agreement held it open to the taxpayer in rendering the 'Full Clerking Services'
to each of the barristers with whom he had contracted, either himself to act as head
clerk or to provide some other suitably qualified or experienced person to do so.

After 7 October 1985 the occupation by the taxpayer of the position of head clerk
g was not a necessary consequence of the contractual provisions of the agreement. He
could, consistently with those provisions, have nominated some other individual as
head clerk while none the less remaining entitled to receive the emoluments due to
him under the agreement. In the event, throughout the relevant period he acted,
and I believe still acts, as head clerk. He has been described as head clerk in various
publications and reference books. The services which the taxpayer has supplied in
h discharging his contractual obligation to provide 'Full Clerking Services' have
included all the traditional services provided by head clerks to barristers' chambers.

There is one additional matter of fact on which great reliance was placed by the
Crown and to which I must refer. The barristers' profession is, to a degree, controlled
by self-regulation. The Bar Council issues a code of conduct approved by the
profession itself. The code of conduct in force during the relevant period—the three
j years I have mentioned—included a rule in the following terms:

'26. A barrister who is a member of professional chambers must: (a) have his
name exhibited at the chambers; (b) have the right to make such use of the
chambers, and of its administration and facilities, as his practice requires;
(c) have the services of the clerk of the chambers. (See the *Code of Professional
Conduct for the Bar of England and Wales* (3rd edn, 1985).)'

It is implicit in that rule that every chambers is expected to have a clerk; otherwise, barristers could not comply with rule 26(c). It was thus argued by counsel for the Crown that the structure of the profession of barrister envisaged that each barrister should have the services of a person occupying the office of clerk of chambers, and in a sense that is so. But it does not follow that a clerk in barristers' chambers holds an 'office' within the meaning of that expression in s 181 of the 1970 Act.

In *Edwards v Clinch* Lord Wilberforce dealt with the meaning of the word 'office' ([1981] STC 617 at 619–620, [1982] AC 845 at 861):

> 'It would seem to me that the legislature, by continuing to use the word ["office"] in the taxing words of Sch E without any corrective definition, showed a general intention to adopt the judicial interpretation of it which, though uncritically, has been consistent and continuous. For myself I would accept that a rigid requirement of permanence is no longer appropriate, nor is vouched by any decided case and continuity need not be regarded as an absolute qualification. But still, if any meaning is to be given to "office" in this legislation, as distinguished from "employment" or "profession" or "trade" or "vocation" (these are the various words used in order to tax people on their earnings), the word must involve a degree of continuance (not necessarily continuity) and of independent existence: it must connote a post to which a person can be appointed, which he can vacate and to which a successor can be appointed. This is the concept which was accepted by all three of the members of the Court of Appeal, who all desired, in my opinion rightly, to combine some degree of consistency with what had become accepted notions in the law of income tax, with practical common sense requirements, and without "treating as authoritative decisions which were reached for reasons which may no longer be appropriate" (see [1980] STC 438 at 441, [1981] Ch 1 at 5 per Buckley LJ). Thus Buckley LJ accepted that to constitute an office a post need not be capable of permanent or prolonged or indefinite existence, a development of the law with which I agree.'

In argument before me counsel for the Crown and counsel for the taxpayer have referred to various features which an 'office' might be expected to have. Counsel for the taxpayer referred to the circumstance that, in general, one would expect an office to be associated with some constituent instrument (as he called it) creating and defining the office in question. Counsel for the Crown for his part accepted that many, perhaps most, offices caught by Sch E would be offices associated with constituent instruments of the sort referred to by counsel for the taxpayer. But counsel for the Crown said, and counsel for the taxpayer agreed, that a constituent instrument was not an essential requirement. It was no more than a feature usually associated with a Sch E 'office'. It was also suggested that an 'office' should have some degree of public relevance. If that is right, a wholly private occupation would never be an office for the purpose of Sch E. Many posts or occupations which are, beyond argument, offices do involve a public element. But I think it is accepted that it would be possible to have an office for the purpose of Sch E which was not associated with any public element.

Another feature of possible importance is the manner in which the individual came to hold the alleged office. Appointment to many offices is made in a formal manner, e g by letters patent, or under the sign manual. Some appointments are made by formal documents referring to the post to be filled and defining it. Formality of appointment is a feature which may be associated with most offices falling within Sch E. But again it probably would be going too far to say that without some formal appointment there could not be an 'office' falling within Sch E.

Counsel for the Crown referred to the well-known remark about an elephant being a beast easy to recognise but difficult to define. An 'office', he suggested, might

be in the same state. I think that approach is one that the Special Commissioners
a may have adopted. In the case stated they referred to *Edwards v Clinch* and a dictum
of Lord Lowry ([1981] STC 617 at 627, [1982] AC 845 at 870):

> 'To be in a position of authority is not necessarily to hold an office, and when
> you appoint somebody to *do* something you do not thereby appoint him to *be*
> something (in other words to hold an office), unless the Act or other relevant
b > instrument says so.'

Another way of putting the same point would be that an office is something more
than a job description. That this sort of consideration was in the minds of the Special
Commissioners may be seen from their remarks in the case stated:

> 'The taxpayer's function has been at all times to perform the duties of senior
c > clerk to the members of the chambers. Those are important duties but we find
> it impossible to say that when he took them on he was appointed to a post which
> can be classed as an office for the purposes of Sch E.'

The bulk of the case stated deals with the main question argued before the Special
Commissioners, namely, whether the taxpayer was employed under a contract of
d employment or was self-employed. The text dealing with the point regarding an
'office' forms a relatively short part of the case stated. It is no criticism of the Special
Commissioners, but it is a fair comment, that they dealt fairly cursorily with that
part of the argument. However, they referred to the leading cases. They cited the
tests which the dicta in those cases suggest should be applied in order to decide
whether an individual is the holder of an 'office'.
e   It is difficult for counsel for the Crown to point to any misdirection of law. If there
was no misdirection of law, the only remaining attack on the Special Commissioners'
conclusion is that the primary facts which they found did not permit the conclusion
that the taxpayer was not the holder of an 'office' for the purpose of Sch E. But if the
various indicia of an 'office' to which reference was made in argument and to which
reference had been made in the cases are adopted and if the taxpayer's duties under
f the 7 October 1985 agreement are weighed against those indicia, it becomes very
difficult to apply an *Edwards (Inspector of Taxes) v Bairstow* [1956] AC 14, 36 TC
207 criticism to the Special Commissioners' conclusion. There is no obvious
constituent instrument in the present case. The best that counsel for the Crown can
do is point to rule 26(c) of the code of conduct. But that code is not precise as to the
manner in which barristers' chambers are to be administered. Provided that the
g arrangements made result in the efficient running of chambers, I do not believe that
a disciplinary case for breach of the code could be made against a barrister on the
ground that there was no person specifically appointed as clerk of chambers.
    The taxpayer's duties as clerk of St James's Chambers were in no sense public
duties. His assumption of the role of senior clerk was not under any formal
appointment. He was not so appointed by the written agreement of 7 October 1985
h itself. His assumption of the role of senior clerk was the result of his own decision to
fill that role. That was the means most convenient to him for the discharge of the
contractual obligations he owed the individual barristers under the agreement. I
find it very difficult to regard the position filled by the taxpayer as a consequence of
his decision thus to discharge his contractual obligations as an 'office'. I, like counsel
for the Crown, can picture an elephant but if I try to picture a Sch E 'office' I do not
j bring to mind a barristers' senior clerkship. I think that the taxpayer's senior
clerkship was more of a job description than the holding of a Sch E 'office'.
    In my judgment, whether or not it is possible for barristers' chambers to arrange
their affairs so as to constitute their senior clerk the holder of an 'office'—and it may
be possible—the Special Commissioners' conclusion in the present case that that had
not happened was one which it was open to them on the evidence before them to

come to. I do not think their decision is vulnerable to attack on *Edwards v Bairstow* lines. Accordingly, I dismiss the appeal.

There is a minor point which is not the subject of dispute between the parties. The Special Commissioners discharged the assessment for 1985–86 notwithstanding it was common ground that until 7 October 1985 the taxpayer had been working under a contract of employment and therefore up to that date was amenable to being taxed under Sch E. To that extent, therefore, the discharge of the assessment cannot be maintained and some appropriate order must be made.

Appeal dismissed with costs.

Solicitors: *Solicitor of Inland Revenue*; *Bullock Worthington & Jackson*, Manchester (for the taxpayer).

Rengan Krishnan Esq   Barrister.

Moodie v Inland Revenue Commissioners and another and related appeal

COURT OF APPEAL, CIVIL DIVISION

BALCOMBE, McCOWAN LJJ AND SIR CHRISTOPHER SLADE

12, 13, 14 MARCH, 30 APRIL 1991

Annual payment – Tax avoidance scheme – Sale of 'annuities' by surtax payers to charitable companies in return for capital – Capital sums invested by payers in promissory notes or gilt-edged securities and payments met out of proceeds of notes or securities – Whether 'annuity or other annual payment' – Whether payments in reality repayments of capital – Whether payments out of profits or gains already taxed – Whether court bound by House of Lords' decision in earlier case – Income and Corporation Taxes Act 1970, s 52(1).

The taxpayers (M and S) participated in tax avoidance schemes similar to that which was upheld by the House of Lords in *IRC v Plummer* [1979] STC 793. In the first appeal, the scheme (Mark I) operated as follows: HOVAS (a charitable company incorporated for the purposes of the scheme) purchased a five-year annuity from M in consideration of a capital sum. M agreed to make five annual payments to HOVAS net of standard rate income tax. HOVAS would recover from the Revenue the tax deducted from the annuity payments and M would deduct the grossed-up amount of those payments from his total income. Using the consideration money received from HOVAS, M would buy promissory notes and deposit them with HOVAS as security. The annual payments would be met by repayment of the appropriate number of promissory notes year by year. M would pay the difference between the cost of the promissory notes and the consideration money from his own resources. M would also provide additional security in the form of short-dated gilt-edged securities or acceptable equities which would be released to him as the annual payments were made. M would retain any income derived from this security and in the event of his death during the term of the scheme, the outstanding promissory notes and the additional security would be released to his estate. HOVAS would insure against that event. M appealed to the Special Commissioners against assessments to surtax for the years 1970–71 to 1972–73 and to income tax for the years 1973–74 to 1976–77 claiming that each payment made by him to HOVAS under the scheme was deductible in computing his total income for the purposes of surtax or higher rate tax because it was an 'annuity or other annual payment' within s 52(1)[a] of the Income and Corporation Taxes Act 1970. The commissioners, in dismissing M's appeal, took the view that the argument in *Plummer* (where the scheme had been held to have commercial reality) had proceeded on different lines and that they were not therefore precluded from applying the principle formulated in the later case of *W T Ramsay Ltd v IRC* [1981] STC 174. Accordingly, the commissioners held that the scheme was a fiscal nullity under the *Ramsay* principle since (i) the payments were not annuities in the sense contemplated by the legislation; (ii) the scheme was one that was preordained possessing all the characteristics set out by the House of Lords in the *Ramsay* case; and (iii) the scheme was self-cancelling in that the movement of money was entirely circular, and that it was irrelevant that M had been unaware of the details of the scheme. That determination was upheld

---

a Section 52(1), so far as material, provides: 'Where any annuity or other annual payment charged with tax under Case III of Schedule D ... is payable wholly out of profits or gains brought into charge to income tax— ... the person liable to make the payment ... shall be entitled on making the payment to deduct and retain out of it a sum representing the amount of income tax thereon ...'

in the High Court (see [1990] STC 475). Hoffmann J sanctioned the approach taken
by the commissioners and distinguished the House of Lords' decision in *Plummer* on
the grounds: (i) that a decision of the House of Lords was authority only for the
question it actually decided; (ii) that *Plummer* decided only that payments were not
deprived of the character of being an annuity simply because they had been paid out
of the capital sum which the taxpayer had received for the annuity; and (iii) that
Plummer could not be authority for the proposition that the *Ramsay* principle did
not apply to the scheme in the instant case when the House of Lords had never
directed its mind to whether or not it did.

In the second appeal, the taxpayer, S, participated in a tax avoidance scheme
called Mark II. The issues involved, the contentions of the parties, the determination
of the commissioners and the judgment of the High Court were the same as those in
the first appeal.

The taxpayers appealed to the Court of Appeal contending, inter alia, that the
judge had erred in law in holding (a) that the decision of the House of Lords in
Plummer had not compelled him to reverse the commissioners' determinations; and
(b) that the payments made by the taxpayers under the scheme were not deductible
in computing their respective total incomes for income tax purposes.

Held – The court was bound by *Plummer* to hold that the payments made by the
taxpayer under the scheme in that case did have the character of an 'annuity or other
annual payment' within s 52(1) of the Income and Corporation Taxes Act 1970. The
facts in the instant case were indistinguishable from *Plummer* and accordingly, the
court was bound to hold that the annuity payments made by the taxpayers pursuant
to the schemes had the character of an 'annuity or other annual payment' within
s 52(1) and were therefore deductible in computing their respective total incomes
for income tax purposes. The appeals would therefore be allowed and the cases
would be remitted to the Special Commissioners for their further findings in the
light of the court's decision.

IRC v Plummer [1979] STC 793 applied.

Notes

For the construction of composite transactions, see Simon's Taxes A1.316.

For annuities or other annual payments in general, see Simon's Taxes A3.408.

For the Income and Corporation Taxes Act 1970, s 52 (now the Income and
Corporation Taxes Act 1988, s 348), see ibid, Part G1.

Cases referred to judgments

A-G v Parsons [1955] Ch 664, [1955] 2 All ER 466, CA.
Chinn v Collins (Inspector of Taxes) [1981] STC 1, [1981] AC 533, [1981] 1 All ER
189, 54 TC 311, HL.
Craven (Inspector of Taxes) v White [1988] STC 476, [1989] AC 398, [1988] 3 All ER
495, HL.
Duke v Reliance Systems Ltd [1988] QB 108, [1987] 2 All ER 858, CA.
Furniss (Inspector of Taxes) v Dawson [1984] STC 153, [1984] AC 474, [1984] 1 All
ER 530, 55 TC 324, HL.
IRC v Burmah Oil Co Ltd [1982] STC 30, 54 TC 200, HL.
IRC v Duke of Westminster [1936] AC 1, 19 TC 490, HL.
IRC v Plummer [1977] STC 440, [1977] 1 WLR 1227, [1977] 3 All ER 1009; [1978]
STC 517, [1979] Ch 63, [1978] 3 All ER 513, CA; [1979] STC 793, [1980] AC 896,
[1979] 3 All ER 775, 54 TC 1, HL.
Jones (Inspector of Taxes) v South-West Lancashire Coal Owners' Association [1927]
AC 827, 11 TC 790, HL.

Morelle Ltd v Wakeling [1955] 2 QB 379, [1955] 1 All ER 708, CA.
Morelle Ltd v Waterworth [1955] 1 QB 1, [1954] 2 All ER 673, CA.
Ramsay (W T) Ltd v IRC [1981] STC 174, [1982] AC 300, [1981] 1 All ER 865, 54
TC 101, HL.
Roberts v Cleveland Health Authority sub nom *Garland v British Rail Engineering
Ltd* [1979] 1 WLR 754, [1979] 2 All ER 1163, CA.

Cases also cited

Cairns v MacDiarmid (*Inspector of Taxes*) [1983] STC 178, 56 TC 566, CA.
Customs and Excise Comrs v Faith Construction Ltd [1989] STC 539, [1990] 1 QB
905, [1989] 2 All ER 938, CA.
Rank Xerox Ltd v Lane (*Inspector of Taxes*) [1979] STC 740, [1981] AC 629, [1979]
3 All ER 657, 53 TC 185, HL.
Rhokana Corp v IRC [1938] AC 380, 21 TC 552, HL.

Appeal

Mr Moodie and Mr Sotnick, the taxpayers, appealed against a decision of
Hoffmann J given on 4 May 1990 (see [1990] STC 475) upholding a determination
by the Special Commissioners that payments made by the taxpayers under a tax
avoidance scheme which had previously been upheld by a decision of the House of
Lords (see *IRC v Plummer* [1979] STC 793) did not have the character of an 'annuity
or other annual payment' within s 52(1) of the Income and Corporation Taxes Act
1970 and were therefore not deductible in computing the respective total incomes of
the taxpayers for income tax purposes. The Crown, by a respondent's notice, sought
to distinguish *Plummer* on the facts. The facts are set out in the judgment of
Balcombe LJ.

Andrew Thornhill QC and *Kevin Prosser* for the taxpayers.
Jonathan Parker QC and *Peter Cranfield* for the Crown.

Cur adv vult

30 April. The following judgments were delivered.

BALCOMBE LJ. These two appeals, by taxpayers from orders made by Hoffmann J
on 4 May 1990 (see [1990] STC 475), raise the question whether a tax avoidance
scheme, which was accepted as effective for its purpose by the House of Lords in
IRC v Plummer [1979] STC 793, [1980] AC 896, has been rendered ineffective by
the subsequent decision of the House of Lords in *W T Ramsay Ltd v IRC* [1981]
STC 174, [1982] AC 300. The Special Commissioners so held and their decision was
affirmed by Hoffman J by the orders under appeal.

The first appellant, Mr Moodie, heard of the scheme, known as the Cardale
Capital Income Plan, from his bank. The scheme subsequently went through several
editions, but the version with which Mr Moodie was concerned was Mark I and, as
the Special Commissioners found, was in its essential features identical to that which
was considered in *Plummer*. Those essential features may be summarised as follows:
(a) By an annuity agreement made on 8 March 1971 with Home and Overseas
Voluntary Aid Services Ltd (HOVAS), a company with charitable status, in
consideration of the sum of £59,400 paid by HOVAS, Mr Moodie agreed to pay to
HOVAS for five years, or during the remainder of his life if shorter, an annuity at
such rate as should after deduction of income tax at the standard rate equal £12,000.

(b) HOVAS paid this consideration by overdrawing on its account with Slater Walker Ltd (SWL). (c) The consideration was paid into Mr Moodie's account with SWL. (d) Mr Moodie used the consideration money (plus £600) to purchase from Old Change Court (Investments) Ltd (OCC), another company in the Slater Walker group, ten promissory notes to the total value of £60,000. By a collateral agreement between Mr Moodie and OCC, these promissory notes carried interest at the rate of 6·5% p a (less tax); no interest was to be paid before 1 April 1973 or after 1 April 1975. (e) The promissory notes were then deposited with HOVAS, together with 3,764 British Investment Trust shares and 3,600 Scottish United Investors shares belonging to Mr Moodie, as security for the payment of the annual sums due under the annuity agreement. The dividends on these shares were to be paid to Mr Moodie. (f) The annual sums of £12,000 payable by Mr Moodie to HOVAS under the annuity agreement were paid by standing order by Mr Moodie on his account with SWL. The overdraft so created was immediately liquidated by HOVAS releasing promissory notes to the value of £12,000, and OCC paying the amount of these promissory notes to SWL for the credit of Mr Moodie. (g) The possibility of Mr Moodie dying during the period of the annuity agreement was covered by an insurance policy taken out at the inception of the scheme. (h) Mr Moodie signed certificates of deduction of income tax (forms R185) to be sent to HOVAS with each annual payment under the annuity agreement. The intention was that HOVAS, as a charity, should then claim repayment of this tax.

These were the essential features of the Mark I scheme undertaken by Mr Moodie (although there were many other matters of detail which it is unnecessary to mention) and, as the Special Commissioners rejected the Crown's contention that the arrangements made pursuant to the scheme were a sham and held that they had reality and substance, the Crown now accepts that the scheme was effective to give rise to the legal relationships and consequences which it purported to create. Nevertheless, there are a number of other matters which should be mentioned since they are directly material to the Crown's 'fiscal nullity' argument: (1) The only cash or 'real money' in the system was the sum of £3,693 paid by Mr Moodie to SWL to set the scheme in motion. That sum was made up of £20 'overdraft interest'; £103 stamp duty; £2,970 initial fee payable to S Cardale & Co Ltd, the promoters of the scheme; and £600 insurance premium. (2) All other steps in the scheme were effected by bookkeeping entries in the participants' accounts with SWL. The Special Commissioners found that at each stage of the scheme, i e the payment of the initial consideration for the annuity by HOVAS to Mr Moodie with the purchase by him of the promissory notes, and then the subsequent annual payments of the annuity and the encashment of the promissory notes, the money represented by these bookkeeping entries went round in a complete circle, albeit with the introduction of other Slater Walker companies into the circle.

So, as Hoffmann J said ([1990] STC 475 at 495) in his judgment:

> 'The scheme was thus self-cancelling at two levels. First, the aggregate of payments cancelled each other out over the five-year period of the annuity ... But second and more importantly, the scheme was self-cancelling at the level of each annual payment. The capital sum which Mr Moodie was supposed to receive in exchange for the annuity was only released to him by instalments equal to and simultaneous with the annuity instalments.'

The second appellant, Mr Sotnick, entered into the Mark II version of the scheme. In his case the annuity agreement was made on 16 February 1972, the annuity was for £9,000 p a, the consideration for the annuity was the sum of £37,700 and the charitable company was the Deprived Children's Aid Fund Ltd (DCAF), but these are matters of detail. The Mark II scheme differed from the Mark I scheme in the following respects: (a) Mr Sotnick paid the first annuity payment of £9,000 out of his own resources. (b) DCAF borrowed the £37,700 from within the Slater Walker group, and paid it into a new account opened for Mr Sotnick at the National

Westminster Bank, into which account Mr Sotnick paid a sum of £1,900 plus £25
a bank charges. (c) The total sum of £39,600 (representing 110% of the amount of the
four annuity payments yet to be made) was applied in the purchase of 3% Savings
Bonds 1965/75 (the gilts). (d) The gilts were then deposited with DCAF as security
for the four remaining annuity payments. (e) DCAF in turn deposited the gilts with
the Slater Walker group as security for the repayment of its loan. (f) As each annuity
date came round, the sum of £9,000 was paid to DCAF by standing order on
b Mr Sotnick's bank account and the money so used was replaced by the release and
sale of the requisite amount of the gilts. (g) Mr Sotnick received interest year by year
on the amount of the gilts remaining unsold.

In this case also the Special Commissioners rejected the Crown's contention that
the annuity agreement was a sham. Nevertheless they made a number of findings
pertinent to the Crown's 'fiscal nullity' argument which I need not set out in detail;
c the judge summarised the effect of the Mark II scheme by saying that it 'retained its
self-cancelling character both at the overall and at the annual levels'.

In the implementation of both schemes certain minor variations of detail occurred.
Thus in Mr Moodie's case he waived his right to receive the accrued interest on the
promissory notes. In Mr Sotnick's case the gilts were sold before the scheme had
worked itself out and were replaced as security by promissory notes to the value of
d the outstanding annuity payments; Mr Sotnick received £3,362·71 from the
proceeds of sale of the gilts. Nevertheless these variations of detail are irrelevant to
the issues on this appeal.

In each case before the Special Commissioners the question was whether, in
computing his total income for tax purposes in the years under appeal, the taxpayer
was entitled to deduct the annuity payments under the schemes. Mr Moodie's
e appeals against assessments to income tax and surtax which did not allow for the
deduction of the annuity payments were heard shortly before similar appeals by
Mr Sotnick. In each case the Special Commissioners, relying on their understanding
of the principles expounded by the House of Lords in *Ramsay*, held that the appeals
failed. In *Moodie* ([1990] STC 475 at 484–485) they said:

f
'Our task, as we see it, is not simply to compare this case with the case stated
in *Plummer* but to review the facts established by the very full evidence which
was put before us and to consider whether they come within the principles of
fiscal nullity as those principles are now understood in the light of the decided
cases from *Ramsay* to *Furniss (Inspector of Taxes) v Dawson* [1984] STC 153,
[1984] AC 474 ... The question remains, whether Mr Moodie made payments
of an annuity in the sense contemplated by the legislation ... The annuities
g
contemplated by the Taxes Acts are, in our opinion, those by which a taxpayer's
financial resources are in reality diminished. Since we are satisfied that
Mr Moodie's resources were not in fact, nor were intended to be, diminished
by the payments provided for in the annuity agreement the agreement was
ineffective to create a charge on Mr Moodie's income for tax purposes.'

h In *Sotnick* (at 494) they said:

'Looking at the preplanned series of operations as a whole in accordance with
the *Ramsay* principle we can find no commercial reality in it. Payment of the
second and subsequent annuities was effected by a series of circular, progressively
self-cancelling, arrangements which resulted in a sum of money provided by
j
the Slater Walker group being returned to it by instalments. Payment of
interest on the amount outstanding to Mr Sotnick helped to create the illusion
of commerciality, but it was in reality only a part of the scheme and was, no
doubt, taken into account in calculating the terms on which he was able to
participate in the scheme. Viewed as a whole, the transaction had no place in
the real world. Although clothed with the appearance of greater reality than the
Mark I scheme it was none the less, on closer examination, so artificial and

devoid of any purpose other than a fiscal purpose that it must, in our opinion, be treated as a fiscal nullity . . . There remains for consideration the decision in *Plummer* on which counsel for Mr Sotnick sought to rely, contending that, although preceding *Ramsay* in time, it had been decided on the same approach. We do not accept that contention. The argument in *Plummer* proceeded on different lines and the decision is not, in our opinion, authority on the application of the *Ramsay* principle which had not then emerged. Nor has the law stood still since *Ramsay*. In *Furniss (Inspector of Taxes) v Dawson* ([1984] STC 153 at 156, [1984] AC 474 at 513) Lord Scarman said: "The law will develop from case to case" and he cited Lord Wilberforce's reference ([1981] STC 174 at 181, [1982] AC 300 at 324) to "the emerging principle" of the law in *Ramsay*. It would not in our opinion be right to approach the issues before us by comparing the evidence in this case with the facts found in *Plummer*. We have to assess the effectiveness of the Mark II scheme under the law as it now stands; and we must apply the *Ramsay* principle as it has emerged through the cases. On that principle, for the reasons given above, we conclude that the annuity agreement was a fiscal nullity, ineffective to create a charge on Mr Sotnick's income for tax purposes.'

The judge agreed with the Special Commissioners.

Before us the argument proceeded under two main heads: (1) Are we bound by the decision of the House of Lords in *Plummer* to hold that the taxpayers' payments under the annuity agreements were annual payments within s 52 of the Income and Corporation Taxes Act 1970 (the 1970 Act)? (2) If we are not so bound, were the annuity payments not annual payments for fiscal purposes as a result of the application of the *Ramsay* principle?

The binding effect of Plummer

As already mentioned, the scheme considered in *Plummer* was the Mark I version, identical in all essential features to that with which Mr Moodie was concerned. As Lord Wilberforce said ([1979] STC 793 at 797, [1980] AC 896 at 908): 'In the courts the plan has been subjected to a four-way attack'.

Those four ways were the following: (i) The annuity payments were in reality payments of capital, being a repayment to HOVAS of the capital sum which it had paid to the taxpayer at the inception of the scheme. This argument was rejected on the grounds that, once it was accepted that the transactions were not a sham, the court could not disregard their legal structure. (ii) The annuity payments were not made wholly out of profits or gains brought into charge to income tax as required by s 52(1)(c) of the 1970 Act. This argument was rejected on the grounds that the actual source out of which the payments were made was irrelevant provided that (as was the case) the taxpayer had taxed income of an amount sufficient to cover the annual payments. (iii) Under s 434(1) of the 1970 Act, the annuity payments were not made for valuable and sufficient consideration. This argument was summarily rejected at all levels above that of the Special Commissioners. (iv) The scheme was a 'settlement' under s 457 of the 1970 Act, the annuity payments were income arising under a settlement and that accordingly the annuity payments were to be treated for the purposes of surtax as the income of the taxpayer. This argument was rejected on the grounds that the scheme lacked the necessary element of 'bounty' to constitute a settlement within the meaning of s 457. As Lord Wilberforce said ([1979] STC 793 at 801, [1980] AC 896 at 913):

'My Lords, there cannot be any doubt that in this case no element of bounty existed. The Special Commissioners indeed said that they regarded the transaction as a bona fide commercial transaction without any element of bounty. The taxpayer therefore succeeds on this point.'

The reference to the finding of the Special Commissioners is to para 9(3)(c) of the stated case ([1977] STC 440 at 447) where, in a passage dealing with the arguments based on ss 434 and 457 of the 1970 Act, they said:

'We regard it as a fair description of the transaction to say that it was a bona
fide commercial transaction without any element of bounty notwithstanding
that the benefits from it were largely to be derived from the tax advantages
which the parties expected would accrue to them.'

None of their Lordships in *Plummer* dealt expressly with a 'fiscal nullity' argument.
Nevertheless, such an argument was foreshadowed by the Crown's printed case in
the House of Lords. It also appears to have been made in oral argument by counsel
for the Crown, although by no means in the forefront of their case (see the argument
of counsel as reported in [1980] AC 896 at 900, 904, 54 TC 1 at 32, 36). Nevertheless,
for the reasons given below, it is irrelevant whether the 'fiscal nullity' argument was
presented to the House of Lords in *Plummer*.

For my part I have to confess that I do not find it easy to reconcile the decision in
Plummer with the subsequent decision in *Ramsay*. Nevertheless that is not a difficulty
which appears to have troubled the House of Lords in subsequent cases. In *Ramsay*
itself Lord Wilberforce considered *Plummer* in the following passage ([1981] STC
174 at 181, [1982] AC 300 at 324):

'*IRC v Plummer*. This was a prearranged scheme, claimed by the Revenue to
be "circular", in the sense that its aim and effect was to pass a capital sum round
through various hands back to its starting point. There was a finding by the
Special Commissioners that the transaction was a bona fide commercial
transaction, but in this House their Lordships agreed that it was legitimate to
have regard to all the arrangements as a whole. The majority upheld the
taxpayer's case on the ground that there was a commercial reality in them: as I
described them they amounted to "a covenant, for a capital sum, to make annual
payments, coupled with security arrangements for the payments" and I
attempted to analyse the nature of the bargain with its advantages and risks to
either side. The case is no authority that the court may not in other cases and
with different findings of fact reach a conclusion that, viewed as a whole, a
composite transaction may produce an effect which brings it within a fiscal
provision.'

Of the other Law Lords in *Ramsay* only Lord Fraser mentions *Plummer* and then
only in passing ([1981] STC 174 at 190, [1982] AC 300 at 337) as authority for the
proposition that the court is entitled and bound to consider a tax-saving scheme as a
whole.

In *IRC v Burmah Oil Co Ltd* [1982] STC 30 the House of Lords accepted that
Ramsay marked a significant change in the approach adopted by the House to tax
avoidance schemes. As Lord Diplock said (at 32):

'It would be disingenuous to suggest, and dangerous on the part of those who
advise on elaborate tax avoidance schemes to assume, that *Ramsay*'s case did
not mark a significant change in the approach adopted by this House in its
judicial role to a preordained series of transactions (whether or not they include
the achievement of a legitimate commercial end) into which there are inserted
steps that have no commercial purpose apart from the avoidance of a liability to
tax which in the absence of those particular steps would have been payable.
The difference is in approach. It does not necessitate the overruling of any
earlier decisions of this House . . .'

In *Burmah Oil* there was a certain ambiguity in the approach to *Plummer*.
Immediately before the passage cited, Lord Diplock (at 32) had mentioned the fact
that the decision of the Court of Session, whence had come the appeal to the House
of Lords, was—

'. . . being reversed on a ground [the *Ramsay* principle] that was never argued
before them and at the time of the hearing, which was after . . . [*Plummer*] . . .
but before *Ramsay*'s case had been determined by this House, may well have
not been open to the Court of Session.'

That certainly suggests that Lord Diplock considered that *Plummer* may well be inconsistent with *Ramsay*. Nevertheless he went on to say, as quoted, that *Ramsay* a did not necessitate the overruling of any earlier decisions of the House, which clearly included *Plummer*. Lord Fraser ([1982] STC 30 at 38) referred to *Plummer* only in the context of what he had said about it in *Ramsay*, although he appears to have misinterpreted a passage from his speech in *Ramsay* [1981] STC 174 at 190, [1982] AC 300 at 337, where he was clearly referring to the schemes under consideration in *Ramsay*, as being a reference to the schemes in *Plummer* and *Chinn v Collins* [1981] b STC 1, [1981] AC 533. Nevertheless there is nothing in Lord Fraser's speech to suggest that he considered that *Plummer* was inconsistent with *Ramsay*. None of the other Law Lords mentioned either *Plummer* or *Ramsay*.

Craven (Inspector of Taxes) v White [1988] STC 476, [1989] AC 398, decided after the decisions of the Special Commissioners in *Moodie* and *Sotnick*, contains some helpful guidance on the jurisprudential basis of the *Ramsay* principle. Lord Oliver, c with whose speech both Lord Keith and Lord Jauncey expressly concurred, made it clear that the principle was one of statutory construction. He said in reference to *Ramsay* ([1988] STC 476 at 498–499, [1989] AC 398 at 504):

> 'Nor did it decide that the court is entitled, because of the subject's motive in entering into a genuine transaction, to attribute to it a legal effect which it did not have. Both Lord Wilberforce and Lord Fraser emphasise the continued d validity and application of the principle of *IRC v Duke of Westminster* [1936] AC 1, 19 TC 490, a principle which Lord Wilberforce described as a "cardinal principle". What it did decide was that that cardinal principle does not, where it is plain that a particular transaction is but one step in a connected series of interdependent steps designed to produce a single composite overall result, compel the court to regard it as otherwise than what it is, that is to say, merely e a part of the composite whole. In the ultimate analysis, most, if not all, revenue cases depend on a point of statutory construction, the question in each case being whether a particular transaction or a particular combination of circumstances does or does not fall within a particular formula prescribed by the taxing statute as one which attracts fiscal liability. As part of that process it f is, of course, necessary for the courts to identify that which is the relevant transaction or combination before construing and applying to it the statutory formula. Reduced to its simplest terms that is all that *Ramsay* did.'

Later he said ([1988] STC 476 at 500, [1989] AC 398 at 505):

> 'What the case does demonstrate, as it seems to me, is that the underlying problem is simply one of the construction of the relevant statute and an analysis g of the transaction or transactions which are claimed to give rise to the liability or the tax exemption ... Every case has to be determined on its own facts and every series of transactions has to be examined and analysed to determine whether in truth, it constitutes a single composite and integrated whole entitling the court, in construing the statute, to ignore the legal effect of individual steps because they are not and never were contemplated as other than part of a single h whole.'

In the course of his speech in *Craven v White* Lord Oliver referred to *Plummer* with apparent approval. He said ([1988] STC 476 at 500, [1989] AC 398 at 505):

> 'But it does not follow that because the court, when confronted with a number j of factually separate but sequential steps, is not compelled, in the face of the facts, to treat them as if each of them had been effected in isolation, all sequential steps must invariably be treated as integrated, interdependent and without individual legal effect. Indeed, *IRC v Plummer* [1979] STC 793, [1980] AC 896 was a case in which, although the transactions effected were integrated as part of a preconceived scheme which was commercially marketed and had no other

conceivable purpose than that of saving tax, the construction of the statute
compelled the acceptance of a fiscal result which accorded very ill with the true
"substance" of the transactions taken as a whole.'

In summary, therefore, notwithstanding my own reservations, the House of
Lords has at no time said that *Plummer* is inconsistent with *Ramsay* and is no longer
good law; on the contrary, in *Ramsay* itself and in subsequent decisions *Plummer*
has more than once been referred to with apparent approval.

In *Moodie* the Special Commissioners relied on the final sentence of Lord
Wilberforce's comments on *Plummer* in *Ramsay* ([1981] STC 174 at 181, [1982] AC
300 at 324) as entitling them to review the Mark I scheme in the light of the *Ramsay*
principle. On that approach they said that they could not 'describe the annuity
agreement as a commercial transaction in any relevant sense of that term', and that
'the proper description of the annuity agreement is simply "a device to secure a fiscal
advantage"'. In *Sotnick* they went further and held that *Plummer* was no longer
authority, on the application of the *Ramsay* principle which had not then emerged.

Hoffmann J adopted a different approach to the argument that *Plummer* was
binding on him. He said ([1990] STC 475 at 496):

'But even a decision of the House of Lords is authority only for the question
it actually decides. In *Plummer* the argument for the Crown was, first, that
payments were not an annuity because they were of a capital nature and,
second, that they had not been paid "wholly out of profits or gains" as s 52 [of
the 1970 Act] requires (see the argument of Mr Dillon QC ([1979] STC 793 at
807, [1980] AC 896 at 900). Both arguments were rejected. The argument for
the payments being capital was simply that they had been paid out of the capital
sum which the taxpayer had received for the annuity. In my judgment *Plummer*
decides only that the payments are not on that account deprived of the character
of being an "annuity or other annual payment". Although it is clear from the
dissenting speech of Viscount Dilhorne that the self-cancelling nature of the
scheme was appreciated by the House, no argument was based on the *Ramsay*
principle, which had not yet "emerged". *Plummer* cannot be authority for the
proposition that the *Ramsay* principle does not apply to this scheme when the
House never directed its mind to whether it did or not.'

There are two decisions of this court which make it clear that a decision can have
binding effect as a precedent notwithstanding that some point may not have been
argued. In *Morelle Ltd v Waterworth* [1955] 1 QB 1 and *Morelle Ltd v Wakeling*
[1955] 2 QB 379, both in the Court of Appeal, it had been held that a short unexpired
residue of a term of years in land was within the scope of the Mortmain and
Charitable Uses Act 1888; that an assignment of the lease to a foreign company
meant that the leasehold interest was automatically and immediately forfeited so as
to vest in the Crown; and that the Crown thereby became subject to all the liabilities
under the lease. In *A-G v Parsons* [1955] 1 Ch 664, the Crown sought in a similar
case to contend that it was not liable on the covenants in the lease since—(1) a
damnosa hereditas might always be disclaimed; and (2) it was not liable on the
covenants until entry into possession. This court held that, although those arguments
were not raised in the *Morelle* cases, whatever might be the general validity of the
arguments, they were incompatible in their present application with the decision in
those cases and that accordingly the Crown was liable on the covenants in the lease.
In the more recent case in this court of *Duke v Reliance Systems Ltd* [1988] QB 108,
it was sought to distinguish an earlier decision of this court in *Roberts v Cleveland
Health Authority* [1979] 1 WLR 754 on the grounds that the court did not have
brought to its attention a relevant EC Council directive. It was held that the fact
that the previous decision of this court might have been different if it had been
referred to the directive was not enough to establish that the decision had been made

per incuriam and accordingly this court was bound by that decision unless and until it was overruled by the House of Lords.

Accordingly, the House of Lords decision in *Plummer* is binding on us as a matter of precedent and establishes that, on the facts of that case, the annual payments made by the taxpayer under the scheme did have the character of an 'annuity or other annual payment' within s 52 of the 1970 Act. The judge was wrong in holding that *Plummer* was not a binding precedent because the 'fiscal nullity' argument was not mentioned in the speeches in that case. Counsel for the Crown did not seek to contend that the judge was right in his reasons for declining to follow *Plummer*. Counsel accepted that we are bound to apply the ratio decidendi of *Plummer* to the facts of these two appeals unless either—(i) the House of Lords had overruled itself; or (ii) there was a reasonable legal distinction between the current facts and those considered in *Plummer*, ie that *Plummer* is distinguishable on the facts. He further conceded before us that the House of Lords had not overruled *Plummer*, though he reserved the right to argue elsewhere that *Plummer* had been, or should be, overruled.

So the issue before us finally came down to the comparatively narrow one—is *Plummer* distinguishable on the facts? We gave leave to the Crown to put in a respondent's notice so as to raise this issue.

Counsel for the Crown submitted that the main distinction between the facts of *Plummer* and those of the present appeals was the finding by the Special Commissioners in *Plummer* quoted above that the transaction was a 'bona fide commercial transaction', whereas in each of the instant appeals there was an express finding to the contrary. In *Moodie* ([1990] STC 475 at 484) the Special Commissioners said—'. . . we cannot describe the annuity agreement as a commercial transaction in any relevant sense of that term'; in *Sotnick* ([1990] STC 475 at 494) they said of the scheme—'. . .we can find no commercial reality in it'. However, in my judgment counsel for the taxpayers had the answer to that submission when he said that the finding of a 'bona fide commercial transaction' in *Plummer* related only to the argument under s 457 of the 1970 Act and was there used in the context of 'a bona fide commercial transaction without any element of bounty', the latter part of the phrase being the more significant. It is clear that all their Lordships in *Plummer* were fully alive to the fact that the sole reason for the Mark I scheme was to avoid tax; indeed Lord Fraser said ([1979] STC 793 at 813, [1980] AC 896 at 928):

> 'The Crown contended that the definition [of settlement] in s 454(3) [of the 1970 Act] applied to all transactions that did not have a bona fide commercial reason, and that it applied to the present transaction, the sole reason for which was to avoid tax.'

If we were to hold that the finding about commercial reality in the present appeals constituted a relevant distinction between the facts of these cases and those in *Plummer*, it would be just such a fine distinction as was deprecated by Viscount Cave LC in *Jones (Inspector of Taxes) v South-West Lancashire Coal Owners' Association* [1927] AC 827 at 830, 11 TC 790 at 837:

> 'My Lords, when a question of law has been clearly decided by this House, it is undesirable that the decision should be weakened or frittered away by fine distinctions . . .'

If *Plummer* cannot stand in the light of *Ramsay*, it is for the House of Lords to say so; it is not for lower courts to try to distinguish *Plummer* out of existence.

The other distinctions of fact which counsel for the Crown sought to draw between the present cases and *Plummer* were even finer than that relating to 'commercial reality' and I do not find it necessary to consider them in detail. Although *Plummer* was only concerned with the Mark I version of the scheme, counsel did not seek to argue that the differences between that and the Mark II version as used by Mr Sotnick were relevant for the purposes of distinguishing Mr Sotnick's case from

Plummer; indeed he sought to rely on the finding as to the total circularity of the
a   movement of funds in *Moodie*, which was not the case in *Sotnick*, and as to which
there was no express finding in *Plummer*, as one of the grounds for distinguishing
Moodie from *Plummer*.

In my judgment, therefore, *Plummer* is indistinguishable and we are bound by it
to hold that the annuity payments made by Mr Moodie and Mr Sotnick pursuant to
their respective schemes were annual payments within s 52 of the 1970 Act .

b   In this court that decision is conclusive of this appeal and it is unnecessary to
consider the second main head of argument, namely if we were not bound, would
the annuity payments not be treated as annual payments for fiscal purposes on the
application of the *Ramsay* principle? That question was fully argued before us, but
the only purpose of our considering it (other than deference to the careful arguments
presented to us) would be an attempt to assist the House of Lords should the case go
c   further. But that attempt would involve a consideration of the *Ramsay* principle,
and in particular the extent of that principle if *Plummer* is not to be overruled. In
my judgment, unless and until the House of Lords explains how *Plummer* and
Ramsay are reconcilable, in order to answer the second question this court would
have to speculate as to the extent of the *Ramsay* principle in the light of *Plummer*, if
not overruled. I cannot see that we could offer any useful help to the House of Lords
d   by embarking on so speculative an exercise.

I would allow these appeals and remit these two cases to the Special Commissioners
for their further findings in the light of this decision.

SIR CHRISTOPHER SLADE. For the reasons given in the judgment of
e   Balcombe LJ, with which I entirely agree, I agree that the decision of the House of
Lords in *IRC v Plummer* [1979] STC 793, [1980] AC 896 is still binding on this
court, and (however difficult it may be to reconcile with subsequent decisions of the
House of Lords beginning with *W T Ramsay v IRC* [1981] STC 174, [1982] AC
300) is indistinguishable from the two cases before us on its material facts. It
accordingly obliges us to allow these appeals.

f   Hoffmann J was of course right in saying ([1990] STC 475 at 496) that 'even a
decision of the House of Lords is authority only for the question it actually decides'.
In my judgment, however, with all respect to him, he was not right in saying that
the decision of the House of Lords in *Plummer* decided 'only' [sic] that the payments
there in question were not deprived of the character of being an 'annuity or other
annual payment' merely because they had been paid out of the capital sum which
g   the taxpayer had received for the annuity. The *Plummer* decision went further than
that. It decided that on the facts of that case the payments in question *did* have the
character of an 'annuity or other annual payment' within s 52 of the Income and
Corporation Taxes Act 1970 (the 1970 Act); otherwise the decision would necessarily
have been in favour of the Crown.

That was a fundamental feature of the decision. The fact that their Lordships in
h   *Plummer* heard no argument based on the *Ramsay* principle, and did not direct their
minds to that principle, renders the *Plummer* decision no less binding on this court.

Counsel for the Crown has not attempted to submit that the House of Lords has
overruled *Plummer* by any subsequent decision. The references to that case in the
subsequent decisions in *Ramsay* itself, *IRC v Burmah Oil Co Ltd* [1982] STC 30 and
Craven v White [1988] STC 476, [1989] AC 398 suggest quite the contrary. Indeed,
j   in *Craven (Inspector of Taxes) v White* ([1988] STC 476 at 500, [1989] AC 398 at 505)
Lord Oliver accepted that the construction of the statute in *Plummer* 'compelled' the
acceptance of the fiscal result in favour of the taxpayer, even though this result
'accorded very ill with the true "substance" of the transactions taken as a whole'.

In these circumstances, counsel for the Crown had to found his argument in
support of the judge's decision on the point raised in the respondent's notice, namely
that—

'... there is a reasonable legal distinction between the said case [*Plummer*] and the case herein, in that the findings of fact made by the said Commissioners herein are materially distinguishable from the findings of fact on which their Lordships based their decision in *Plummer*.'

For the reasons given by Balcombe LJ, I do not think they are materially distinguishable. I would merely mention one point. Counsel laid some stress, as did the judge, on the circularity of the schemes which in the case of *Moodie* was total. No express finding as to the circularity was made by the commissioners in *Plummer*, though in all the essentials the scheme there under consideration was the same as the *Moodie* scheme. It is, however, apparent from Lord Wilberforce's speech in *Ramsay* [1981] STC 174 at 181, [1982] AC 300 at 324 that the scheme in *Plummer* had, in his words, been 'claimed by the Revenue to be "circular", in the sense that its aim and effect was to pass a capital sum round through various hands back to its starting point'. The same point is reflected in the printed case on the appeal in *Plummer*. Their Lordships must clearly have had the point in mind.

On the hypothesis that we regarded the *Plummer* decision as concluding these appeals in this court, we were invited to proceed to express our opinion as to the legal position which would arise if, contrary to our view, *Plummer* were distinguishable from the cases before us on its facts and thus did not bind us. In the light of *Craven v White* it is common ground that on this hypothesis the issue would ultimately be one of construction of the relevant statutory provisions. On the same hypothesis, the Crown's submission in essence was that the *Ramsay* principle would entitle and oblige this court to hold that, on the facts of the present cases, the alleged payment of the covenanted sums did not, on the true construction of s 52 of the 1970 Act, have the character of an 'annuity or other annual payment', on the grounds that there were no 'payments' within the meaning of such provisions, just as on the facts of *Ramsay*, there was no 'loss' within the relevant statutory provision. Viewing the schemes before us as a whole, as authority obliges us to do, it seems to me (without any reference to the *Plummer* decision) that the arguments in favour of saying that there were 'payments' under the schemes in the statutory sense would be rather stronger than were the arguments in *Ramsay* in favour of the contention that there was a 'loss' in the statutory sense. Presumably it was an equivalent line of thought which led the House of Lords apparently to regard the *Ramsay*, *Burmah* and *Craven* decisions as reconcilable with *Plummer* (or vice versa). I do not, however, think it would serve any useful purpose to embark on this further hypothetical exercise without the benefit of a fuller explanation and understanding of the reasons why their Lordships took this view.

As things are, the principle of stare decisis in my judgment leaves this court with no alternative but to allow these appeals.

McCOWAN LJ. I agree.

Appeals allowed. Cases to be remitted to the Special Commissioners for further findings in the light of the court's decision. Leave to appeal to the House of Lords granted on the conditions that the order for costs in favour of the taxpayers in the Court of Appeal and below would not be disturbed and that the Crown would not apply for an order for costs before their Lordships.

Solicitors: *Berwin Leighton* (for the taxpayers); *Solicitor of Inland Revenue*.

Rengan Krishnan Esq   Barrister.

Collins v Addies (Inspector of Taxes);
Greenfield v Bains (Inspector of Taxes)

CHANCERY DIVISION
MILLETT J
12 JUNE 1991

Close company – Loans or advances to participators in close company – Substitution by another participator as debtor instead of taxpayers – Whether close company 'released' the taxpayers from liability to repay loan – Whether the grossed-up amount of the loan should be included in the computation of the taxpayers' respective total incomes for higher rate tax purposes – Income and Corporation Taxes Act 1970, s 287.

C and G, the taxpayers, were directors of and shareholders in an unlimited close company. As at 11 November 1980 they were indebted to the company on current accounts in the sum of £79,000. On 11 November 1980, the taxpayers, together with other shareholder members of their families, agreed by written contract to sell for £200,000 all their shares in the company to B, a fellow director of and shareholder in the company. Pursuant to the contract, the taxpayers, B and the company executed a deed of novation whereby the company released the taxpayers from liability on their current accounts up to a limit of £68,000 and B was substituted for them as debtor to the company. The taxpayers paid £11,000 to B's solicitors (being the sum outstanding on the current accounts) and B subsequently repaid £79,000 to the company to clear the debt. It was common ground that prior to 11 November 1980 the taxpayers' current accounts constituted loans to participators under s 286 of the Income and Corporation Taxes Act 1970 (the 1970 Act). The taxpayers were assessed to income tax for the year 1980–81 on the grounds that by substituting B for the taxpayers as debtor, the company had 'released' the taxpayers from their obligation to repay the loan under s 287[a] of the 1970 Act and that therefore the grossed-up amount of the debt should be included in the computation of the taxpayers' respective total incomes for higher rate tax purposes. A Special Commissioner dismissed the taxpayers' appeals on the grounds: (a) that 'release' in s 287 should bear its plain and ordinary meaning; and (b) that the correct approach was to ascertain whether the company had released the taxpayers from their obligation to repay and not to ascertain whether the company had suffered any depletion of its assets as a result of the release. Accordingly, the commissioner held that the company had released the taxpayers from their obligation to repay the loan and that the grossed-up amount of the debt should be included in the computation of the taxpayers' respective total incomes. The taxpayers appealed to the High Court contending (a) that the novation did not constitute a 'release' because in the context of s 287 a release ought to be confined to one which was either wholly voluntary or made for less than adequate consideration; and (b) that the company had not released the taxpayers from their obligation, rather that the taxpayers had satisfied the obligation since (i) there had been no depletion of the company's assets following the discharge of the taxpayers' liability and (ii) the taxpayers had furnished full consideration in the form of B's promise under seal to repay the debt.

Held – (a) 'Release' in s 287 should bear its plain and ordinary meaning. If Parliament had intended to qualify the application of that term 'released' under s 287 it would have done so expressly. It was therefore not permissible to read into that section the

---

a Section 287, so far as material, is set out at p 450 *b c*, post

qualification that a release ought to be confined to one which was either wholly voluntary or made for less than adequate consideration.

(b) The correct approach was not to ascertain whether the company's assets had been depleted but to ascertain whether the taxpayers had been released from their legal obligation to repay the loan. Where the obligation was extinguished by payment or satisfaction then no charge to tax would arise. However, where the obligation was extinguished by release a charge to income tax would arise under s 287(1)(a). In the instant case, B's promise under seal to repay the loan did not extinguish the taxpayers' obligation by payment or by satisfaction. The effect of the novation had been to release the taxpayers from their obligation to repay the loan and to replace it with a fresh obligation undertaken by B.

Accordingly, the company had released the taxpayers from the obligation to repay the loan within s 287 and the grossed-up amount of the debt fell to be included in the computation of the taxpayers' respective total incomes for higher rate tax purposes. The appeals would therefore be dismissed.

Notes

For loans by close companies generally, see Simon's Taxes Division D3.4.

For liability to tax on the release by a close company of a loan to a participator, see ibid, D3.407.

For the Income and Corporation Taxes Act 1970, s 287 (now the Income and Corporation Taxes Act 1988, s 421) see ibid, Part G1.

Case referred to in judgment

IRC v Plummer [1979] STC 793, [1980] AC 896, [1979] 3 All ER 775, 54 TC 1, HL.

Case also cited

British Mexican Petroleum Co Ltd v Jackson (Inspector of Taxes) (1931) 16 TC 570, HL.

Cases stated

Collins v Addies (Inspector of Taxes)

1. On 6 February 1990 a Special Commissioner heard the appeal of Mr Jack Collins (the taxpayer) against an assessment to income tax for 1980–81 made pursuant to s 287 of the Income and Corporation Taxes Act 1970 (the 1970 Act).

2. The commissioner heard the taxpayer's appeal together with a connected appeal by Mr Anthony Michael Jon Greenfield and issued a single decision in relation to both appeals. The facts and the questions of law were common to both appeals.

3. The question for the commissioner's determination, his findings of fact, the respective contentions of counsel for the taxpayer and Mr E Ali on behalf of the inspector and the commissioner's conclusions were set out in the written decision which was issued on 13 February 1990 and a copy of which was annexed as part of this case.

4. No oral evidence was adduced.

5. The evidence consisted of a statement of agreed facts together with a copy of an agreement dated 11 November 1980.

6. By his decision the commissioner dismissed the taxpayer's appeal and determined the assessment in accordance with figures agreed between the parties.

7. The taxpayer immediately after the determination of the appeal declared to the commissioners his dissatisfaction therewith as being erroneous in point of law

and on 21 February 1990 required them to state a case for the opinion of the High Court pursuant to the Taxes Management Act 1970, s 56.

8. The question of law for the opinion of the court was whether the commissioner had erred in construing the effect of s 287(1) of the 1970 Act in its context and in relation to the facts of this appeal.

DECISION

Mr J Collins and Mr A M J Greenfield (the taxpayers) each appeal against assessments to income tax for 1980–81 made pursuant to s 287 of the Income and Corporation Taxes Act 1970 (the 1970 Act).

There is no dispute as to the facts which are the subject of an agreed statement, accompanied by an agreed copy of an agreement dated 11 November 1980 and to which the taxpayers were parties with others.

For the purposes of these appeals the relevant part of s 287 of the 1970 Act is as follows:

'(1) Subject to the following provisions of this section where a company is assessed or liable to be assessed under section 286 above in respect of a loan or advance and *releases* or writes off the whole or part of the debt in respect of it, then,—(a) for the purpose of computing the total income of the person to whom the loan or advance was made a sum equal to the amount so *released* or written off shall be treated as income received by him after deduction of income tax from a corresponding gross amount . . . [emphasis added]'

I have emphasised the words 'releases' and 'released' where they occur in s 287 as the point at issue in these appeals is the precise meaning of those words in their context. Counsel for the taxpayers, submits that in the context of s 287 a release should be confined to one which is either wholly voluntary or made for less than adequate consideration. Mr E Ali, of the Inland Revenue Solicitor's Office, appearing for the inspectors of taxes, submits that there is no justification for such a qualification for the meaning of the word 'release' which should bear its plain and ordinary meaning.

The relevant facts are as follows:

1. As at 11 November 1980 the taxpayers were directors of and shareholders in Brent & Collins (the company), an unlimited close company. They were indebted to the company on current accounts as follows:

Mr J Collins	£27,115
Mr A M J Greenfield	£41,063
Total	£68,178

On later quantification the taxpayers' indebtedness to the company as at 11 November 1980 proved to be £79,000 in total.

2. On 11 November 1980 the taxpayers, together with other shareholder members of their respective families agreed by the terms of a written contract (the contract) to sell all their shares to a fellow director, Mr S Brent, for the sum of £200,000 and on the other terms contained in the contract.

3. Pursuant to clause 6 of the contract Mr Brent was obliged on completion to deliver to his vendors a duly executed counterpart of a deed completed in the form of the draft deed appearing in the fifth schedule to the contract. Such a counterpart was so delivered and a deed in that form (the deed) was completed on 11 November 1980.

4. Under the terms of the deed the company released the taxpayers from liability on their current accounts up to a limit of £68,000 on the condition that Mr Brent should be substituted for the taxpayers as debtor to the company. As the taxpayers' current accounts were found to total £79,000, they paid a total of £11,000 to Mr Brent's solicitors in full and final repayment of their current account liabilities. Mr Brent subsequently procured repayment of the balance of the current accounts.

5. It is common ground that the taxpayers' current accounts constituted loans to participators as at 11 November 1980, within the provisions of s 286 of the 1970 Act, the release (within the meaning of s 287 of the 1970 Act) of which loans would give rise, pursuant to s 287, to the receipt of income by the participators to whom the loans were made for the year of assessment 1980–81.

6. On 10 February 1986 an assessment pursuant to s 286 of the 1970 Act was raised on the company for its accounting period ending 31 May 1981, by reference to the sum of £68,000. The company has paid the tax so charged.

7. The taxpayers' capital gains tax assessments for 1980–81 were determined by agreement pursuant to s 54 of the Taxes Management Act 1970 on the basis that the £68,000 forming part of their current accounts with the company, the burden of which was assumed by Mr Brent on 11 November 1980, did not form part of the consideration received by the taxpayers on the disposal of their shares in the company.

Clauses 2 and 3 of the deed are as follows:

'2. In consideration of the covenant by [Mr Brent] hereinafter contained the Company hereby releases and discharges [the taxpayers] from all liability to repay to the Company the Current Accounts (insofar as the same does not exceed £68,000) and from all actions claims proceedings and demands in respect thereof (up to the said sum of £68,000).

3. In consideration of such release and discharge [Mr Brent] hereby covenants with the Company that he will henceforth assume liability for and pay and discharge the Current Accounts due and owing to the Company by [the taxpayers] (insofar as the same does not exceed £68,000) and the Company hereby accepts [Mr Brent] as debtor up to the said sum of £68,000 in place of [the taxpayers].'

No evidence was led as to the taxpayers' motives in structuring the terms of the contract and I do not know whether the consideration of £200,000 paid by Mr Brent for the shares owned by the Collins and Greenfield families took account of the state of the taxpayers' current accounts with the company. Mr Brent paid £6·66 for each of the 30,000 shares which he purchased despite the fact that 6,000 of those shares were ordinary voting shares whilst the remaining 24,000 shares were 'A' ordinary non-voting shares. It is, however, an agreed fact that, in relation to the taxpayers' capital gains tax assessments, they have agreed with the Revenue that the £68,000 which forms the subject of the provisions of the deed did not form part of the consideration received by them on their disposal of their shares in the company.

Although the capital gains tax assessments on the taxpayers are entirely separate from the assessments which form the subject of these appeals, the taxpayers are not entitled to blow hot and cold and therefore I infer that in practice, as a result of the terms of the contract and the terms of the deed, the taxpayers received £6·66 for each of their shares in the company and in addition between them received a total of £68,000 by reason of Mr Brent's assumption of their liability in respect of that sum of money towards the company.

It is common ground in these appeals that a novation of the contract of indebtedness to the company took place under the terms of the deed. The taxpayers' liability to the company came to an end and in its place the company accepted Mr Brent as its debtor in relation to the sum of £68,000. The question for my decision is therefore, did that novation of the taxpayers' contract with the company amount to a release by the company for the purposes of s 287 of the 1970 Act?

The actual words of the deed could not be plainer: '... the Company hereby releases and discharges [the taxpayers] from all liability to repay to the company [the sum of £68,000] ...' Counsel for the taxpayers, however, submits that that is not the end of the matter and that although it is not necessary to insert an additional word or words into s 287, the meaning of the word 'releases' must be qualified to import into it the inference that any such release must be either wholly voluntary or

gratuitous or made for less than adequate consideration. He points to the use of
similar words in s 136 of the 1970 Act and s 66 of the Finance Act 1976. I do not find
such comparisons helpful, however, as s 287 is an anti-avoidance and penal section,
unlike either s 136 of the 1970 Act or s 66 of the Finance Act 1976.

Counsel also places reliance on *IRC v Plummer* [1979] STC 793, [1980] AC 896
where the word settlement received a restricted interpretation.

I do not gain much assistance from this authority. In *Plummer*, the meaning of
the word settlement was in question, but that expression was given an extended
meaning by s 454(3) of the 1970 Act, where settlement is defined as '. . . any
disposition, trust, covenant, agreement or arrangement', and 'settlor', in relation to
a settlement, means '. . . any person by whom the settlement was made'. No such
extended definition of the word 'release' is imported into the Taxes Acts in relation
to these appeals and therefore (in the absence of any technical meaning) I am obliged
by the rules of interpretation to give the expression in question its ordinary meaning.
Such ordinary meaning, even in its present context, does not import the qualification
contended for by counsel for the taxpayer.

It is also the contention of counsel for the taxpayer that one must look to see
whether anything has left the company. That contention is denied by Mr Ali for the
inspector who submits that one must look only at what has reached the taxpayer. In
that context it is helpful to look at the words of s 287 of the 1970 Act and to note that
there is reference to '. . . a sum equal to the amount so released or written off'. It is
common ground that releasing and writing off are different operations for a company.
A release is a final and conclusive act if completed according to law whereas the act
of writing off by a company may not be. A debt which is written off may yet be
recovered by a company if it discovers that the debtor's circumstances have changed
so that it is no longer unable to repay the creditor company. A release is generally a
transaction involving more than one person, whereas by its very nature an act of
writing off by a company is unilateral. It does not seem to me that one's attention is
necessarily directed to the sum of money which leaves the company. The taxpayers
received £68,000 from the company by way of loan which the company released
subsequently. In my view the facts of this case fall clearly within the ambit of s 287
of the 1970 Act. Although counsel has argued his clients' case in a most persuasive
manner, I cannot accept his contentions.

In my judgment on the facts in these appeals the company released for the
purposes of s 287 of the 1970 Act a total of £68,000 to the taxpayers by virtue of
clause 2 of the deed.

I dismiss the appeals and I determine the assessments in the figures which have
been agreed between the parties as follows: (1) In relation to the assessment on
Mr A M J Greenfield the sum of £58,664 is to be included in his total income for the
year 1980–81. (2) In relation to the assessment on Mr Jack Collins, the sum of
£38,735 is to be included in his total income for the year 1980–81.

Greenfield v Bains (Inspector of Taxes)

The case stated by the Special Commissioner in the case of *Greenfield v Bains*
(Inspector of Taxes) was identical to that stated in respect of *Collins v Addies*
(Inspector of Taxes).

Andrew Thornhill QC for the taxpayers.
Launcelot Henderson for the Crown.

MILLETT J. These are two appeals from decisions of the Special Commissioner on
6 February 1990 against assessments to income tax for 1980–81 on two taxpayers,
Mr Jack Collins and Mr Anthony Greenfield (the taxpayers). The cases are identical
except for the figures and it is convenient to treat them as a single case, as did the

Special Commissioner. The facts are straightforward and are not in dispute. The assessment was made under s 287 of the Income and Corporation Taxes Act 1970 *a* (the 1970 Act). The taxpayers submitted that on the facts of the case the section did not apply. The Special Commissioner dismissed the taxpayers' appeals and they appeal to me.

Section 287 applies only where the company in question is a close company within the meaning of the 1970 Act and where the loan is made to a participator or his associate. Section 287 reads as follows: *b*

> '(1) Subject to the following provisions of this section where a company is assessed or liable to be assessed under section 286 above in respect of a loan or advance and releases or writes off the whole or part of the debt in respect of it, then,—(a) for the purpose of computing the total income of the person to whom the loan or advance was made a sum equal to the amount so released or written *c* off shall be treated as income received by him after deduction of income tax from a corresponding gross amount . . .'

On 11 November 1980 the taxpayers were directors and shareholders of a company called Brent & Collins (the company), an unlimited close company. Each of them was indebted to the company on current account: Mr Collins in the sum of £27,115 *d* and Mr Greenfield in the sum of £41,063. The total shown was a little over £68,000. On later quantification it appeared that the actual amount of the taxpayers' indebtedness to the company at that date was £79,000.

On 11 November 1980 the taxpayers together with other shareholder members of their respective families agreed to sell all their shares to a fellow director, Mr Brent, for the sum of £200,000 on the terms contained in the contract. Under clause 6 of *e* that contract Mr Brent was obliged on completion to execute and deliver to the vendors a duly executed counterpart of a deed in the form of a draft which appeared in the fifth schedule to the contract. Such counterpart was so delivered and a deed in that form was duly executed on 11 November 1980.

Under the terms of the deed the company released the taxpayers from liability on their respective current accounts up to a limit of £68,000 in consideration of the *f* substitution of Mr Brent for the taxpayers as debtor to the company in that amount. The difference between £68,000 and £79,000 was paid by the taxpayers to Mr Brent's solicitors in full and final payment of their current account liabilities, and that sum was paid to the company. In due course, Mr Brent procured repayment of the balance of the current accounts.

It is common ground between the parties that the taxpayers' current accounts *g* constituted loans to participators at 11 November 1980 within the provisions of s 286 of the 1970 Act and that if what occurred on 11 November constituted a release within the meaning of s 287 the assessment was rightly made.

The Special Commissioner may have been influenced by the fact that the taxpayers' capital gains tax assessments for 1980–1981 were determined on the basis that the £68,000 forming part of their current accounts with the company—the *h* burden of which was assumed by Mr Brent—did not form part of the consideration received by the taxpayers on the disposal of their shares in the company. As a matter of law, it plainly did form part of the consideration received by the taxpayers on the disposal of their shares in the company, but the likelihood is that it was left out of account in pursuance of s 31 of the Capital Gains Tax Act 1979 under which there should be excluded from the consideration any sum subject to income tax. Therefore, *j* at that stage the Revenue were assuming, rightly or wrongly, that the £68,000 was taxable in the taxpayers' hands under s 287(1). The question is whether what occurred was a release.

First, I propose to read the actual terms of the relevant paragraphs in the fifth schedule to the contract and then turn to the statutory context in which s 287(1) is set. The fifth schedule recites, inter alia:

'D. The vendors are indebted to the Company on Current Accounts . . . and are desirous of being released and discharged from liability to repay the said Current Accounts (up to a maximum of £68,000) to the Company.

E. The Company has agreed so to release and discharge the Vendors on the terms that the Purchaser should be substituted as debtor to the Company in respect of the said Current Accounts up to a maximum of £68,000 and the Purchaser has agreed to be so substituted.'

I refer to the operative clauses:

'2. In consideration of the covenant by [Mr Brent] hereinafter contained the Company hereby releases and discharges [the taxpayers] from all liability to repay to the Company the Current Accounts (insofar as the same does not exceed £68,000) and from all actions claims proceedings and demands in respect thereof (up to the said sum of £68,000).

3. In consideration of such release and discharge [Mr Brent] hereby covenants with the Company that he will henceforth assume liability for and pay and discharge the Current Accounts due and owing to the Company by [the taxpayers] (insofar as the same does not exceed £68,000) and the Company hereby accepts [Mr Brent] as debtor up to the said sum of £68,000 in place of [the taxpayers].'

The taxpayers then covenant with the company and Mr Brent to repay to the company forthwith on demand the difference between £68,000 and the full amount of the indebtedness of the taxpayers to the company.

It is not in dispute before me that as a matter of law what took place was a novation under which Mr Brent was substituted as debtor in respect of £68,000, part of the liability of the taxpayers to repay the company.

Sections 286 and 287, which are linked by the opening words of s 287(1), apply in relation to close companies and are concerned with the fiscal consequences of loans by such companies to participators.

If one looks at the definition of 'taxable distributions' in earlier sections of the 1970 Act one is taken back to s 233 where 'distribution' is defined. This has general application and applies to both close and non-close companies. Not surprisingly, 'distribution' includes 'dividend'. Under sub-s (2)(b) it is provided that 'distribution' means—

'. . . any other distribution out of assets of the company (whether in cash or otherwise) in respect of shares in the company, except so much of the distribution, if any, as represents a repayment of capital on the shares or is, when it is made, equal in amount or value to any new consideration received by the company for the distribution.'

There is a definition of 'new consideration' in s 234(3).

Section 233(3) provides:

'Where on a transfer of assets or liabilities by a company to its members or to a company by its members, the amount or value of the benefit received by a member (taken according to its market value) exceeds the amount or value (so taken) of any new consideration given by him, the company shall be treated as making a distribution to him of an amount equal to the difference.'

It is common ground that the effect of those sections is that a loan by a company to a member is not a distribution because the obligation to repay is treated as 'new consideration' which excludes it from being a distribution within the meaning of s 233(3).

When one comes to consider close companies, s 286 deals with the fiscal consequences to the company of a loan to a participator or associate of a participator. In short, it provides that if a close company makes a loan or advance to a participator, or associate of a participator, it is assessable to a sum equal to the amount of advanced corporation tax which would have been chargeable to the company if the loan or advance had been a distribution.

Section 286(5) provides:

'Where, after a company has been assessed to tax under this section in respect of any loan or advance, the loan or advance or any part of it is repaid to the company, relief shall be given from that tax, or a proportionate part of it, by discharge or repayment.'

Accordingly, if a close company makes a loan to a participator or associate that is not treated as a distribution because of the obligation to repay; but the company will be assessed to advanced corporation tax in an amount equal to the tax which it would have paid had it been treated as a distribution. If eventually the loan is repaid the advanced corporation tax becomes repayable to the company.

Section 286(2) extends the application of the section to a case where a participator or associate incurs a debt to the company. That is to be treated as if it were a loan by the company in an amount equal to the debt. I say that because it is not clear in this case how these current accounts arose. However, it is common ground between the parties that the taxpayers were participators in a close company and their current accounts represented loans to participators within the meaning of s 286.

I have already read s 287(1) which applies only where the company is assessed, or liable to be assessed, under s 286, as was the case here. It provides that the participator shall be assessed to income tax in respect of the loan or advance if it is released or written off. He is taxable at the higher rate of tax on the grossed up amount of the loan which is released or written off.

The question before me comes down to this: did the transaction on 11 November 1980 constituting a novation of the two loans, by which Mr Brent's obligation to repay was substituted for that of the taxpayer, amount to a release of part of the debt in the sum of £68,000 previously due from the taxpayers?

Before the Special Commissioner only one argument was raised. Before me the argument has ranged a little more widely. The taxpayers' main argument is that a novation of this kind is simply not a release of the kind contemplated by the section.

Counsel for the taxpayers submitted that while it was true as a matter of technical analysis that a novation amounted to the release of a debt due from the original debtor and its replacement by a debt due from a new debtor, this was not enough to bring the transaction within the meaning of the word 'releases' in s 287(1). He submitted that the meaning of the word 'releases' must be qualified by importing the requirement that any such release must be wholly voluntary or gratuitous or made for less than full consideration. He pointed to the fact that the word 'releases' went with 'writes off' and while the writing off of a debt did not affect the legal relationship of the parties, it constituted for all practical purposes a release of the debt in the sense that the debtor would be unlikely to be pursued by the company for repayment of the debt, and the writing off of a debt would invariably be voluntary or gratuitous. He submitted that the word 'releases' should be similarly construed.

I do not find that argument of much help. The mere fact that the writing off of a debt is almost certainly gratuitous does not mean that the release of a debt must mean a gratuitous release. In my judgment, it is not permissible to import any such qualification into the word 'releases'. To adopt the language of Lord Wilberforce in *IRC v Plummer* [1979] STC 793 at 800, [1980] AC 896 at 911, that would be legislation not interpretation. If Parliament had intended the word to mean 'releases otherwise than for full value' it could and must have said so. Nor am I impressed by counsel for the taxpayers' submission that ss 286 and 287 are concerned with the depletion of the assets of the company. If the company claims full value for the release of the loan its assets are unaffected and, it is submitted, the section should have no application. But in my judgment s 286 is focused on the company's position and s 287 on that of the participator. The question under s 287 is not whether the *a*   company's assets are or are not depleted but whether the legal obligation of the participator has been released.

In my judgment, the true analysis of s 287 is that it is linked for this purpose with s 233 which exempts the original loan from being a distribution and thus being taxable in the participator's hands only because it is made for full consideration consisting of the obligation to repay. As long as that obligation to repay subsists the exemption from tax likewise subsists. If the obligation to repay should come to an *b*   end by payment of the debt then clearly there should be no tax charge; the distribution would be nullified by the repayment. If on the other hand it should come to an end by release so that the obligation is terminated without repayment, a balancing charge or payment of the deferred charge on the distribution should be raised. That is the essential relationship between s 287(1) and the other provisions relating to participators in close companies and distributions to them.

c   Counsel for the taxpayers relied, inter alia, on s 136 of the 1970 Act as pointing in the direction which he favoured, but I find no assistance in that provision. It raises the same point in a different context and, if anything, suggests that a release for full value ought to give rise to a taxable charge. Whether or not that be so under s 136, the question remains as to the meaning of the word 'releases' in s 287.

The second argument raised very briefly before me by counsel for the taxpayer *d*   (perhaps almost by the way) was that s 287(1) required the release of the debt, not of the debtor. The wording of the contract is phrased so as to release the taxpayers from their obligation to repay their current accounts and to substitute the obligation of Mr Brent to pay, thus seemingly keeping the debt alive but substituting a different debtor. While that is true, the subject matter of the release is the debt or legal obligation of the taxpayer. A novation discharges the legal obligation of the original *e*   obligee and replaces it by a new obligation of a new obligee. It does not merely substitute a new debtor for the old in respect of the same debt or liability because as a matter of law it is not possible for a debtor to assign a legal liability. It is for that reason that the transaction has to take the form of a novation. As a matter of law, that undoubtedly constitutes a release of the old debt and its replacement by an entirely new debt owed by Mr Brent.

f   But that is not the end of the case because the next argument of counsel for the taxpayers is that the word 'releases' must mean the discharge of the debt otherwise than by payment or satisfaction. If a creditor accepts payment from a third party in satisfaction of the debtor's liability that would clearly constitute the repayment of the debt, not the release of the debt. The debt is discharged by payment and not release. Again, if a creditor accepts something of equal value, whether from the *g*   debtor or a third party, that would equally constitute a discharge of the debt; it would be discharged by satisfaction rather than repayment, but not by release. Again, that would not give rise to a charge to tax. Payment in kind from the debtor himself or payment by a third party on behalf of the debtor would bring the liability to an end by repayment or satisfaction and not release. The Crown rightly accepts both contentions.

h   Counsel for the taxpayers submits that in the present case all that happened was that the company accepted Mr Brent's obligation in satisfaction of the taxpayers' indebtedness. That, he submitted, amounted to the discharge of the taxpayers' indebtedness not by release but by accord and satisfaction. Indeed, as he points out, accord and satisfaction have been judicially defined as meaning the purchase of a release. Thus the word 'releases' is perfectly capable of extending to an accord and *j*   satisfaction. Yet it would be absurd to regard s 287(1) as biting in either of the cases postulated where there was payment in kind or by a third party.

Accordingly, counsel for the taxpayers submits that where a debt is discharged by the acceptance of a promise to repay it made by a third party, the debt is not released within the meaning of the section but is to be treated as discharged by satisfaction. It is not in dispute in the present case that Mr Brent ultimately repaid the debt so that his covenant was as good as that of the taxpayers.

In support of his argument counsel for the taxpayers points to a curiosity in s 286(5) which deals with repayment to the company of advanced corporation tax on the repayment of the loan. In the present case counsel points out that if the novation is treated as a repayment or satisfaction and not a release of the taxpayers' indebtedness to the company, the advanced corporation tax ought to have been notionally repaid by the Revenue under s 286(5) and immediately reassessed and repaid by the company to the Revenue, because Mr Brent was also a participator and his accepting the indebtedness to the company would bring him within s 286 by virtue of sub-s (2)(*a*) thereof. When Mr Brent in due course repaid the indebtedness the advanced corporation tax would again be repaid to the company and all would work as it should. But it was pointed out that if the Crown was correct in the present case and the novation were treated as a release, the advanced corporation tax, if any, originally paid by the company when the loan to the taxpayers was made would not be repayable. It is clear that the two sections treat the phrases 'repaid to the company' and '[release] . . . of the debt' as mutually exclusive. Indeed, in s 286(7)(*b*) the words 'releases' and 'satisfies' are used in contradistinction to each other. Therefore, if the Crown is right, on the taxpayers' debt being released there would be no repayment of the advanced corporation tax previously paid by the company but there would (or should) be a new assessment to corporation tax on the assumption of the liability by Mr Brent, with the result that it would appear that one amount of advanced corporation tax too many would be payable by the company. That may be a defect in the drafting of sub-s (5).

Although it has perplexed me for some time, I have come to the conclusion that such a consideration ought not to deflect me from what I perceive to be the true construction of s 287. In my judgment, ss 286 and 287 draw a clear distinction between the release or writing off of the debt on the one hand and its repayment or satisfaction on the other. While payment by a third party on behalf of the debtor, or payment in kind by the debtor himself or by a third party, accepted in full discharge of the debt may well constitute repayment or satisfaction and not a release for the purpose of these sections, I do not consider that the substitution of a fresh promise to pay by a third party can be similarly treated. A promise to pay by a new debtor constitutes valuable consideration and may properly be accepted by the company in substitution of the debt of the original obligee, but as a matter of ordinary usage it would not be regarded as payment. In my judgment there is a clear distinction to be drawn between a novation which involves the release of one debt and the substitution of another, and all other forms of payment or satisfaction under which the debt is treated as repaid with no outstanding obligation on any party in respect of the debt or any similar sum.

Counsel for the taxpayers, in reply, instanced the mere rescheduling of a debt as amounting to a release of the old debt and the acceptance of a new debt on new terms, and submitted that it would be absurd to treat such a case as falling within s 287(1). I doubt that a mere rescheduling agreement would be so construed, at least if it were competently drafted; the mere fact that incompetent drafting could expose the debtor to an unintended charge to tax cannot be material to the true construction of the section.

Accordingly, for the reasons I have expressed I come to the same conclusion as the Special Commissioner that the novation was a release within the meaning of s 287(1), and I dismiss the taxpayers' appeals.

Appeals dismissed with costs.

Solicitors: *Franks Charlesly & Co* (for the taxpayers); *Solicitor of Inland Revenue.*

Rengan Krishnan Esq   Barrister.

a

O'Rourke (Inspector of Taxes) v Binks

CHANCERY DIVISION
VINELOTT J
14, 17 JUNE 1991

b   *Capital gains tax – Computation of chargeable gains – Capital distribution by company
– Merger agreement – Transaction involving capital distribution amounting to 15·28%
of the value of the shares transferred – Taxpayer's allowable expenditure less than
amount distributed – Whether taxpayer entitled to elect to reduce the amount distributed
by the entire allowable expenditure irrespective of whether amount distributed small –
Whether capital distribution amounting to 15·28% was 'small' – Capital Gains Tax Act*
c   *1979, s 72(2), (4).*

The taxpayer held 560,500 ordinary shares in C Ltd. The total sum deductible in
computing a gain accruing on a disposal of all those shares (the entire allowable
expenditure) was £214,602. Pursuant to a merger agreement between C Ltd and
R plc, the taxpayer exchanged his shares in C Ltd for a total consideration of
d   £1,583,491 comprising (a) 840,750 ordinary shares in R plc having a market value of
£1,336,792; and (b) 75,328 shares in LASMO Ltd having a market value of £246,699.
C Ltd had owned the shares in LASMO Ltd transferred to the taxpayer and under
s 72(1) of the Capital Gains Tax Act 1979 (the 1979 Act) the distribution of the shares
in LASMO Ltd (the capital distribution) was treated as the disposal of an interest in
part of the shares in C Ltd. It was common ground therefore that the transaction as
e   a whole constituted a part disposal. In calculating the taxpayer's liability to capital
gains tax for the year 1982–83, the inspector of taxes apportioned the taxpayer's
entire allowable expenditure to reflect the proportion of the total consideration
represented by the capital distribution in accordance with the apportionment
provisions to be applied to a part disposal contained in s 35 of the 1979 Act. The
apportioned allowable expenditure so calculated amounted to £33,435. The taxpayer
f   appealed to a Special Commissioner against the assessment on the grounds (a) that
the entire allowable expenditure (£214,602) was less than the capital distribution
(£246,699), and that he should therefore be entitled to elect to reduce the amount
distributed by the entire allowable expenditure under s 72(4)[a] of the 1979 Act, and
(b) that the capital distribution, which amounted to 15·28% of the total consideration,
was 'small, as compared with the value of the shares in respect of which it was
g   distributed', within the meaning of s 72(2)[b] of the 1979 Act. The Special
Commissioner upheld the first contention which was sufficient to determine the
appeal in the taxpayer's favour. However, he further held that the capital distribution
was not small for the purposes of s 72(2) of the 1979 Act. The Crown appealed to the
High Court contending, inter alia, (i) that on the true construction of s 72 of the
1979 Act, the taxpayer was entitled to elect to reduce the amount distributed by the
h   entire allowable expenditure under s 72(4) of the 1979 Act only where the capital
distribution was small, (ii) that the capital distribution (£246,699) was not small as
compared with the value of the shares in respect of which it was distributed (ie the
total consideration of £1,583,491), and (iii) accordingly, that the taxpayer's entire
allowable expenditure ought to be apportioned in accordance with the apportionment
provisions to be applied to a part disposal.

j   **Held** – (1) The words of s 72(4) of the Capital Gains Tax Act 1979 were clear and
unambiguous. There were therefore no grounds for the court to interpret that
section so as to restrict its application to situations where the capital distribution was

---

a   Section 72(4), so far as material, is set out at p 461 *g–j*, post
b   Section 72(2), so far as material, is set out at p 461 *e–g*, post

small. The taxpayer was therefore entitled to elect to reduce the amount distributed by the entire allowable expenditure under s 72(4).   *a*

(2) It was not possible to stipulate a categoric percentage which would be applicable in every case to determine whether or not a capital distribution was comparatively small for the purposes of s 72(2) of the Capital Gains Tax Act 1979. That question would have to be determined on the facts of each case. In the instant case the amount distributed had not been small.

Accordingly, the Crown's appeal would be dismissed.   *b*

Notes

For the computation of chargeable gains on a capital distribution, see Simon's Taxes C2.425–428.

For the Capital Gains Tax Act 1979, s 72(2), (4), see ibid, Part G3.   *c*

Cases referred to in judgment

Ayrshire Employers Mutual Insurance Association Ltd v IRC 1946 SC (HL) 1, 27 TC 331, HL.   *d*
Carver v Duncan (Inspector of Taxes) [1985] STC 356, [1985] AC 1082, [1985] 2 All ER 645, 59 TC 125, HL.
IRC v Joiner [1975] STC 657, [1975] WLR 1701, [1975] 3 All ER 1050, 50 TC 449, HL.
Luke v IRC [1963] AC 557, [1963] 1 All ER 665, 40 TC 630, HL.
Stock v Frank Jones (Tipton) Ltd [1978] 1 WLR 231, [1978] 1 All ER 948, HL.   *e*
Sutherland Publishing Co Ltd v Caxton Publishing Co Ltd [1938] Ch 174, [1937] 4 All ER 405, CA.

Cases also cited   *f*

Bank of England v Vagliano Bros [1891] AC 107, HL.
Farrell v Alexander [1976] 3 WLR 145, [1976] 2 All ER 721, HL.
Johnson v Moreton [1980] AC 37, [1978] 3 All ER 37, HL.
Mangin v IRC [1971] AC 739, [1971] 1 All ER 179, PC.
R v Curran [1976] 1 WLR 87, [1976] 1 All ER 162, HL.
R v West Yorkshire Coroner, ex p Smith [1983] QB 335, [1982] 3 All ER 1098, CA.   *g*

Case stated

1. On 23 April 1990 a Special Commissioner heard the appeal of Mr Edward Binks (the taxpayer) against an assessment to capital gains tax for the fiscal year   *h*
1982–83 in the sum of £224,046.

2. The dispute between the parties related to the calculation of one element in the computation of the taxpayer's chargeable capital gains for that year. Two questions of law arose for decision on the application of s 72 of the Capital Gains Tax Act 1979 (the 1979 Act) to the agreed facts of the case, namely: (i) whether an election may be made under s 72(4) in a case where the relevant capital distribution was not 'small'   *j*
within the meaning of s 72(2); and if not (ii) whether a capital distribution representing 15·58% of the value of the shares in respect of which it has been made was 'small' within the meaning of s 72(2).

3. There was no oral evidence. The Special Commissioner had before him a statement of facts agreed between the parties. [The documents placed in evidence before the commissioner were then listed.]

a   4. The facts of the case, the contentions of the parties and the reasons for the decisions on the points in issue are set out in the decision, which was issued in writing on 14 May 1990. As will be seen therefrom, the first question was decided in the affirmative which sufficed to conclude the matter in the taxpayer's favour in principle. The second question was answered in the negative.

  5. Shortly after the hearing the parties indicated that, in the event of the appeal being successful the assessment should be reduced to £25,901. That figure was *b*   accordingly adopted in the formal determination of the appeal.

  6. Immediately after receiving the decision the inspector of taxes declared to the commissioners his dissatisfaction therewith as being erroneous in point of law and on 25 May 1990 required them to state a case for the opinion of the High Court pursuant to the Taxes Management Act 1970, s 56.

  7. The question of law for the opinion of the court was whether the commissioner *c*   had erred in the answers which he had given to the two questions set out in para 2.

DECISION

  The taxpayer appeals against an assessment to capital gains tax for the year *d*   1982–83 in the figure of £224,046. The figure includes certain gains as to which no dispute arises, but the greatest element by far—£212,361—is in respect of the gain which accrued to the taxpayer on 25 May 1982 when Redlands plc (Redlands) acquired all the shares in Cawoods Holdings Ltd (Cawoods). The issue between the parties is as to the computation of that gain. (The assessment also includes a much smaller sum in respect of the gain which accrued on the same occasion to the taxpayer's wife but no separate issue arises there.)

e   Redlands provides materials for the construction industry. Cawoods' principal business lies in the same field but it had also developed interests in the fuel industry. In particular, prior to May 1982, it held by way of investment a substantial number of shares in London & Scottish Marine Oil Co Ltd (LASMO).

  In April 1982 Redlands made an offer for all the issued share capital of Cawoods. *f*   Under the terms of that offer, which was accepted, the ordinary shareholders in Cawoods became entitled, by way of exchange for every 200 existing Cawoods shares held by them, to 300 new shares in Redlands together with a certain number of LASMO shares then held by Cawoods. As I understand it the latter part of the consideration for the transfer of Cawoods shares brought about a distribution of the majority of Cawoods' LASMO holding.

  Immediately before the merger, the taxpayer held (as beneficial owner) 560,500 *g*   ordinary shares in Cawoods. The allowable expenditure—that is, the sum deductible in computing any gain accruing on a disposal of those shares—was £214,602.

  On or about 25 May 1982, in accordance with the merger terms, the taxpayer exchanged those shares for: (i) 840,750 ordinary shares in Redlands, having a market value at that time of £1,336,792; and (ii) 75,328 LASMO shares, having a market value at that time of £246,699.

h   It is common ground that by reason of the statutory provisions relating to company reconstructions and amalgamations, the taxpayer's transfer of his Cawoods shares did not constitute a disposal of them so far as the consideration consisted of shares in Redlands (they being a 'new holding' as defined in s 77 of the 1979 Act). It is, however, also common ground that the transaction gave rise to a chargeable part disposal (a disposal of an interest in the Cawoods shares) by reason of the distribution *j*   of LASMO shares in addition. Section 72(1) of the 1979 Act provides:

> 'Where a person receives or becomes entitled to receive in respect of shares in a company any capital distribution from the company (other than a new holding as defined in section 77 below) he shall be treated as if he had in consideration of that capital distribution disposed of an interest in the shares.'

The inspector's computation of the chargeable gain is accordingly as follows:

Consideration received (LASMO share value)   £246,699   *a*
Appropriate fraction of the allowable expenditure, viz:

$$\frac{£246,699}{£246,699+£1,336,792} \times £214,602 = \qquad (£33,435)$$

Unadjusted gain	£213,264
Indexation allowance	(£903) *b*
Chargeable gain:	£212,361

Section 72 contains further provisions. I shall pass over sub-ss (2) and (3) for the moment, and proceed to sub-s (4):   *c*

'Where the allowable expenditure is less than the amount distributed (or is nil)—

   (*a*) subsections (2) and (3) above shall not apply, and
   (*b*) if the recipient so elects (and there is any allowable expenditure)—

     (i) the amount distributed shall be reduced by the amount of the allowable   *d*
     expenditure, and
     (ii) none of that expenditure shall be allowable as a deduction in computing
     a gain accruing on the occasion of the capital distribution, or on any
     subsequent occasion.

In this subsection "allowable expenditure" means the expenditure which immediately before the occasion of the capital distribution was attributable to   *e* the shares under paragraphs (*a*) and (*b*) of section 32(1) above.'

In the present case the allowable expenditure (£214,602) is less than the amount distributed (£246,699) and on 22 May 1984 the taxpayer made an election under sub-s (4). On that basis, the computation would become:

Amount distributed (sub-s (4)(*b*)(i))	*f*
(£246,699 − 214,602)	£32,097
Fraction of allowable expenditure (sub-s (4)(*b*)(ii))	(NIL)
Unadjusted gain	£32,097
Indexation allowance	(£5,794)
Chargeable gain:	£26,303 *g*

(I will just mention that the parties are no longer in dispute over the admissibility of the indexation allowance in these circumstances.)

The inspector challenges the taxpayer's entitlement to make an election under sub-s (4). The challenge is founded on the terms of sub-s (2) (with which sub-s (3) is   *h* associated), together with the reference to those subsections in sub-s (4)(*a*). Those two subsections read as follows:

'(2) If the inspector is satisfied that the amount distributed is small, as compared with the value of the shares in respect of which it is distributed, and so directs—   *j*

   (*a*) the occasion of the capital distribution shall not be treated for the purposes
of this Act as a disposal of the asset, and
   (*b*) the amount distributed shall be deducted from any expenditure allowable
under this Act as a deduction in computing a gain or loss on the disposal of
the shares by the person receiving or becoming entitled to receive the
distribution of capital.

a
(3) A person who is dissatisfied with the refusal of the inspector to give a direction under this section may appeal to the Commissioners having jurisdiction on an appeal against an assessment to tax in respect of a gain accruing on the disposal.'

In a nutshell, the inspector's contentions are, first, that the capital distribution (the value of the LASMO shares received) was not 'small' as compared with the total value of the taxpayer's holding in Cawoods (it amounted to some 15·58% of that
b value); and, second, that on the true construction of s 72 an election under sub-s (4) is available only in cases where (but for that subsection) it would be open to the inspector to make a direction under sub-s (2).

On the first point, Miss Lawunmi of the Inland Revenue Solicitor's Office had little to add to the Revenue's published practice of treating 5% or less as 'small'
c within the meaning of sub-s (2) and of other parallel provisions in the 1979 Act. She accepted that the inexactness of the phrase allowed some latitude but submitted that 15·58% could not properly be regarded as 'small' in the required sense.

The principal question, however, is whether the 'smallness' condition, expressed in sub-s (2), also affects sub-s (4). The Crown's contention is that an affirmative answer is required by what Miss Lawunmi called 'the logic of the section'. The
d argument, as I understand it, runs as follows. Subsection (1) having provided that certain consideration should be treated as consideration for a part disposal, sub-s (2) sets up an alternative special regime in cases where the amount involved is comparatively small. Examination of sub-s (2), however, discloses an evident defect; the second of the two stated consequences of a direction does not comfortably fit a case where the amount distributed cannot be fully deducted from the allowable
e expenditure, because of the inadequacy of the latter. None the less, the first consequence (no part disposal) would apply, with the result that so much of the distribution as exceeded the allowable expenditure would escape taxation, not only immediately but, it seems, permanently. Subsection (4) was simply designed to avoid that result. (I may add that in the light of sub-s (4)(*a*), sub-s (2) cannot be construed as a provision applying only to cases where the allowable expenditure
f exceeds the amount distributed. If sub-s (2) were subject to such an implicit condition, there would have been no need, in sub-s (4), to mention sub-s (2) and its associated sub-s (3) at all.) The logical pattern of the section provides the link between sub-ss (2) and (4), and hence the requirement that for sub-s (4), as for sub-s (2), the amount distributed must be 'small'.

Miss Lawunmi submitted further that there is ambiguity in sub-s (4)(*a*). While
g her primary argument was that on a true reading of s 72, sub-s (4) operated as a sort of gloss on sub-s (2), she acknowledged that sub-s (4)(*a*) can be read as requiring sub-ss (2) and (3) to be totally disregarded where the opening condition of sub-s (4) is satisfied. That ambiguity entitles me, she contended, to look at the statutory antecedents (para 3(2) of Sch 7 to the Finance Act 1965 for s 72(2), and para 9 of Sch 10 to the Finance Act 1966 for s 72(4)). I am bound to say that if I am entitled to
h look at those earlier provisions—and particularly the latter—the argument that sub-s (4) should be read with sub-s (2) is materially reinforced.

Finally, Miss Lawunmi produced some figures which demonstrated that the taxpayer's construction of sub-s (4) was capable of producing some startling results. But it is clear that such results arise not so much from the 'smallness' question (though that plays a part) as from the proximity of the allowable expenditure to the
j amount of the distribution. The Crown accepts, as I understand it, that if, in relation to shares worth £500,000, there is a distribution of £25,000, the immediately chargeable gain will be only £1 if the allowable expenditure was £24,999.

Counsel for the taxpayer submitted that s 72, and s 72(4) in particular, was wholly unambiguous and that the facts fell four-square within sub-s (4). That subsection says nothing about 'smallness', as it could so easily have done if that condition had been intended. The sub-s (4) election was accordingly available.

Alternatively, or additionally, counsel for the taxpayer submitted that the distribution in the present case was in fact 'small, as compared with' the value of the taxpayer's Cawoods holding. As a matter of ordinary English, he said, if one thing is smaller than another, it is 'small, as compared with' that other. I may say at once that I do not accept that proposition, baldly stated: 99p is not, in my view, 'small, compared with' £1. But I need not pursue that because counsel accepted that in the present context at least there must be a fair margin of difference in magnitude between the two things otherwise nearly all cases would fall within sub-s (2) (or sub-s (4) if necessary). So counsel suggested that anything up to 50% could be regarded as relevantly 'small': and that 15·58% was accordingly clearly so. Anyone would accept that David was 'small, as compared with' Goliath: but one is not required to picture a difference between their sizes involving a factor of 20.

I have come to the conclusion that this appeal should succeed on the construction of s 72(4) of the 1979 Act. I entirely accept that that subsection exists to make good a deficiency in sub-s (2); but it cannot, in my view, be regarded as if it were merely a more appropriate substitute for the second consequence under sub-s (2). Each of the subsections (if operated) materially affects what would otherwise be done under sub-s (1), but they work in totally different ways. Subsection (2) negates the existence of a part disposal, and makes provision for future computations. Subsection (4), by contrast, retains the part disposal concept and makes provision (primarily) for the immediate computation. I see no logical connection between sub-ss (2) and (4).

Nor do I see any ambiguity in the words 'subsections (2) and (3) above shall not apply'. Of course, their appearance in sub-s (4) necessarily implies that a case satisfying that subsection's basic condition may also satisfy the 'smallness' condition in sub-s (2), but that alone is quite enough to justify the disapplication. The two regimes cannot stand together. The words of disapplication are plain and on modern authority I should have regard to them only, notwithstanding that the 1979 Act is a consolidation. Indeed, it seems to me that the 'ambiguity' detected by the Crown arises only from its coming to the 1979 Act with a preconceived notion of what it was supposed to mean, derived from its knowledge of its antecedents. That does not suffice.

I am not greatly moved by the figures which may result from adopting this view. As I have already noted, the more extreme results depend not so much on the relationship between current share values and the amount of the distribution as on the relationship between the latter and historic cost. Indeed, I might add that if the Crown's view (including its view as to what is 'small') were correct, sub-s (4) would rarely be applicable (since the allowable expenditure has to be even smaller). The vice in the taxpayer's argument, as seen by the Crown, seems to be that it enables premature advantage to be taken of the cost of the whole asset in computing a gain on a notional disposal of part. But except to the extent that the distribution does exceed the allowable expenditure, no real gain has at that stage actually been realised.

That leaves it strictly unnecessary for me to address the alternative question: is 15·58% relatively 'small' but I should do so in case the matter goes further. Section 72 is not the only provision to employ this unsatisfactory formula (see s 21 and (originally) s 107 of the 1979 Act). (Thankfully, it has been replaced in the latter by a fixed percentage.) I regard it as especially unsatisfactory because the exercise of a taxpayer's option hangs on it, and unless and until it is quantified through a process of litigation (involving, perhaps, a number of 'ranging' shots), the taxpayer has little practical choice but to accept whatever the Revenue says. At any rate, that appears to have been what has happened during the last 25 years.

I recognise the force of the argument of counsel for the taxpayer on this question and I would ordinarily find it compelling. But at the end of the day the contexts in which the 'smallness' provision appears (including in particular s 72(2)) lead me to the view that the Crown is right, and that 'small' here means something of the order of 5%.

The provisions appear as exceptions to the operation of normal computational
rules and I can perceive no basis of principle for their existence. I conclude that they
exist for administrative convenience: and I would infer from that that they are
minor in character. In the case of s 72(2), that view is rather reinforced by the fact
that the election is primarily in the hands of the inspector (though the effect of
sub-s (3) is that it is also exercisable by the taxpayer), and also by the fact that the
taxpayer cannot appeal against the inspector's direction.

Indeed, speaking generally, administrative convenience appears to be the sole
justification for resorting to the loosely-worded formula.

Needless to say, I will not attempt a definition of 'small' in this context—especially
as Parliament apparently does not want the concept to be defined. But I am satisfied
that 15·58% is not 'small'.

The parties have, I understand, agreed that if the appeal succeeds, the assessment
should be reduced to £25,901. I allow the appeal and determine accordingly.

Launcelot Henderson for the Crown.
G R A Argles for the taxpayer.

VINELOTT J. This is an appeal from one of the Special Commissioners. It raises a
short but difficult question as to the true construction of s 72 of the Capital Gains
Tax Act 1979 (the 1979 Act).

I will start by reading the first four subsections of that section in full.

'(1) Where a person receives or becomes entitled to receive in respect of
shares in a company any capital distribution from the company (other than a
new holding as defined in section 77 below) he shall be treated as if he had in
consideration of that capital distribution disposed of an interest in the shares.

(2) If the inspector is satisfied that the amount distributed is small, as compared
with the value of the shares in respect of which it is distributed, and so directs—

(*a*) the occasion of the capital distribution shall not be treated for the purposes
of this Act as a disposal of the asset, and

(*b*) the amount distributed shall be deducted from any expenditure allowable
under this Act as a deduction in computing a gain or loss on the disposal of
the shares by the person receiving or becoming entitled to receive the
distribution of capital.

(3) A person who is dissatisfied with the refusal of the inspector to give a
direction under this section may appeal to the Commissioners having jurisdiction
on an appeal against an assessment to tax in respect of a gain accruing on the
disposal.

(4) Where the allowable expenditure is less than the amount distributed (or is
nil)—

(*a*) subsections (2) and (3) above shall not apply, and

(*b*) if the recipient so elects (and there is any allowable expenditure)—

(i) the amount distributed shall be reduced by the amount of the allowable
expenditure, and

(ii) none of that expenditure shall be allowable as a deduction in computing
a gain accruing on the occasion of the capital distribution, or on any
subsequent occasion.

In this subsection "allowable expenditure" means the expenditure which
immediately before the occasion of the capital distribution was attributable to
the shares under paragraphs (*a*) and (*b*) of section 32(1) above.'

Paragraphs (*a*) and (*b*) of s 32(1) set out the way in which the consideration for the
acquisition of an asset and the amount of allowable expenditure for the asset are to
be ascertained.

Section 72(5) then defines the 'amount distributed' as the amount or value of the capital distribution, and 'capital distribution' as any distribution which in the hands of the recipient is not an income distribution.

The purpose of s 72 is clearly to bring into charge to capital gains tax all distributions by a company which are not brought into charge to income or corporation tax by the Income and Corporation Taxes Act 1988. Under s 72(1) the recipient of the distribution is to be treated as if he had made a part disposal of his shares.

The facts are shortly as follows: the taxpayer, Mr Binks, was a substantial shareholder in a company called Cawoods Holdings Ltd (Cawoods). Cawoods held shares in London and Scottish Marine Oil Co (LASMO), as an investment. In May 1982 Cawoods was acquired by Redlands plc. Redlands had an option to acquire Cawoods' LASMO shares and under the terms for the acquisition of the Cawoods shares it exercised that option; the Cawoods shares were then acquired in exchange for shares of Redlands and LASMO. It was accepted by the inspector that by virtue of the provisions of Chapter II of the 1979 Act (dealing with the reorganisation of share capital) the transfer of the shares of LASMO to the shareholders of Cawoods was to be treated as a distribution by Cawoods. There was of course no disposal of shares of Cawoods to the extent to which shares of Redlands were substituted for them. The taxpayer was accordingly assessed to capital gains tax on the footing he had made a part disposal of his shares, and that the gain fell to be ascertained in accordance with s 72(1).

The aggregate of the value of the Redlands shares (the new holding) and of the amount of the capital distribution was £1,583,491, and of that total £246,699 represented the value of the LASMO shares. The taxpayer's expenditure on the Cawoods shares, allowable as a deduction in calculating the gain on a disposal of all the Cawoods shares was £214,602. The proportion of the expenditure attributable to the LASMO shares was thus 246,699 over 1,583,491, and the amount of the allowable expenditure so attributable was £33,435. That yields a chargeable gain of £213,264, from which must be deducted a modest indexation allowance.

The taxpayer had made or has purported to make an election under s 72(4)(*b*). If sub-s (4) applies, then under sub-s (4)(*b*)(i) the amount of the capital distribution is reduced to £32,097 (246,699 less 214,602). That is the chargeable gain but again an indexation allowance must be deducted. The base cost of the shares of Redlands is reduced to nil.

The case for the taxpayer is put on two grounds. First, it is submitted that sub-s (4) is free-standing—that is that it applies in any case where there is a capital distribution and the allowable expenditure on the shares in respect of which the distribution is made is less than the amount of the distribution or is nil. Subsection (4) does not apply (as the Crown contends) only where the amount of the capital distribution is small compared with the value of the shares in respect of which it is made. It is submitted in the alternative that the £246,699 was small compared with the value of the Cawoods shares—£1,583,491; the proportion is in fact 15·58%.

The Special Commissioner accepted the first of these two submissions but he held that if sub-s (4) were to be restricted in the way suggested by the Crown, the taxpayer could not succeed on his second ground; the capital distribution was not 'comparatively small'.

As a matter of first impression, on a first reading of s 72, it is natural to read sub-s (4) as one of a group of subsections dealing only with cases where the amount of a capital distribution is comparatively small, that is where the expense of a full capital gains tax computation on the footing of a part disposal would be disproportionate to the amount of the capital distribution.

There are three reasons. First, s 72(2) taken in isolation is patently incomplete. It deals with the case where a comparatively small capital distribution is less than the expenditure allowable as a deduction in computing a gain or loss on the shares in respect of which the capital distribution was made. It does not deal with the case where the capital distribution is equal to or greater than the allowable expenditure. It is natural to read sub-s (4) as filling that gap.

Second, if s 72(4) is read as free-standing, that is as applying in any case where the capital distribution is equal to or greater than the allowable expenditure, it has precisely the opposite effect to that which the informed reader would expect. That can be illustrated by the following example. Suppose a taxpayer purchased shares for £500; there is no other allowable expenditure. He receives a capital distribution of £499 and the residual value of the shares after the capital distribution is £1,001. Subsection (4) does not apply because the capital distribution is less than the allowable expenditure. Under s 72(1), together with the part disposal provisions in s 35, the proportion of the allowable expenditure attributable to the part disposal is 499 over (499 plus 1,001), and the amount of the deduction attributable to the part disposal is that fraction of £500—say £167. The gain is then £499 less £167, that is £332. If the amount had been larger, say £501, the chargeable gain would have been only £1.

Third, if sub-s (4) is read as free-standing, it is out of line with other provisions in the 1979 Act which deal with part disposals, or deemed part disposals, where the amount received by the taxpayer is comparatively small.

Section 20(1) provides that subject, so far as material, to s 21 there is a notional disposal when a capital sum is derived from an asset but no asset is acquired by the person paying that sum; in particular where compensation is paid for the loss of or damage to the asset, or a sum is received under an insurance policy, or for the forfeiture or surrender or non-exercise of rights, or for the use or exploitation of the asset. Section 21 provides that if the recipient so claims, receipt of a capital sum within s 20(1) derived from an asset which is not lost or destroyed is not to be treated as a disposal if, amongst other things—'. . . (c) (subject to subsection (2) below), the amount of the capital sum is small, as compared with the value of the asset'. The sum which apart from s 21(1) would have been brought into account as consideration for the part disposal of the asset is then to be deducted from any expenditure allowable as a deduction in computing a gain on the subsequent disposal of the asset.

So far, s 21 reflects s 72(2).

Section 21(2) then provides that if the allowable expenditure is less than the consideration for the notional part disposal or is nil, s 21(1)(c) is not to apply; instead if the recipient so elects and if there is any allowable expenditure, the consideration for the part disposal is reduced by the amount of the allowable expenditure, and '. . . none of that expenditure shall be allowable as a deduction in computing a gain accruing on the occasion of the disposal or any subsequent occasion'.

The part of s 21(2) which I have cited mirrors s 72(4)(b)(ii) and it is followed by precisely the same definition of allowable expenditure.

Section 107 as originally framed applied where there is a transfer of part of a holding of land and where, amongst other things—'. . . (a) the amount or value of the consideration for the transfer is small, as compared with the market value of the holding as it subsisted immediately before the transfer'. Section 107(1) was amended by s 60 of the Finance Act 1986 by the substitution of 'does not exceed one-fifth of' for 'is small, as compared with'.

Section 107(2) then provides that if the transferor so claims, the transfer is not to be treated as a part disposal but the sums which, if it had been so treated, would have been brought into account as consideration for that part disposal are to be deducted from any allowable expenditure in computing a gain on any subsequent disposal of the holding.

Section 107(3) originally excepted cases where the consideration for the transfer exceeded £10,000, or in the same year of assessment the transferor made other disposals and the aggregate amount of all disposals exceeded £10,000. Section 63 of the Finance Act 1984 substituted £20,000 for £10,000.

Section 108 deals in similar terms with the transfer of part of a holding to an authority exercising compulsory powers save that the exception of cases where the consideration exceeds £10,000 (or, with respect to disposals after 5 April 1983, £20,000) does not apply. Both sections are then restricted by s 109 which provides that the provisions of ss 107(2) and 108(2) are to have effect subject to s 109. Section 109(2) starts by providing: 'Where the allowable expenditure is less than the consideration for the part disposal (or is nil)—(a) the said provisions shall not apply . . .'; the following para (b) is in precisely the same terms as para (b) of s 72(4), and there follows a similar definition of allowable expenditure.

The difficulty which confronts the Crown is that s 72(4) cannot be made to fit the pattern which it is said emerges clearly from ss 107, 108 and 109 (though less clearly if at all from s 21) unless it is substantially rewritten. If sub-s (4) is read as impliedly limited by the opening words of sub-s (2): 'If the inspector is satisfied that the amount distributed is small, as compared with the value of the shares in respect of which it is distributed, and so directs . . .', the effect is to give the inspector a discretion which is not subject to an appeal to the commissioners; it could only be controlled by an application for judicial review. That would largely nullify the right given to the taxpayer by para (b) to elect for the gain to be ascertained in accordance with sub-s (4).

Counsel for the Crown, did not seek to persuade me that that is a permissible construction. He submitted that effect could be given to the presumed intention of the legislature if the opening words of sub-s (4) and para (a) are modified to read:

'Where *in a case to which subsections (2) and (3) above would otherwise apply* the allowable expenditure is less than the amount distributed (or is nil)—(a) subsections (2) and (3) above shall not apply *save for the purpose of ascertaining whether or not the amount distributed is small*) . . .'

I have emphasised the words added. That would preserve the taxpayer's right under sub-s (3) to appeal to the commissioners against the inspector's refusal to direct that the amount of the capital distributed is to be treated as comparatively small. But it involves substantially rewriting sub-s (4).

The alternative construction advanced by counsel for the Crown is to treat sub-s (4) as impliedly prefaced by the words: 'If the amount of the distribution is small as compared with the value of the shares in respect of which it is distributed'. Then if an assessment were made by the inspector under s 72(1) it would be open to the taxpayer in an appeal to claim that the amount of the distribution was comparatively small and that he was entitled to make an election under sub-s (4) to have the gain calculated in accordance with that subsection. That requires the implication of a condition which is not there and cannot be derived by implication from sub-s (2) as reflecting the contingency set out in the opening words of that subsection.

I find myself compelled to the conclusion that although sub-s (4) construed as free-standing leads to conclusions which are so anomalous as to justify the description of absurd and which cannot have been present to the minds of the draftsman or legislature, to give effect to the presumed intention would, in the words of Lord Diplock in *Carver v Duncan (Inspector of Taxes)* [1985] STC 356 at 362, [1985] AC 1082 at 1118, involve 'so great a distortion of the actual words the draftsman chose to use and Parliament to approve as to fall beyond the bounds of what it is permissible to achieve by any process of judicial construction'.

I was referred by counsel for the Crown to a passage in the speech of Lord Scarman in *Stock v Frank Jones (Tipton) Ltd* [1978] 1 WLR 231 at 239, where Lord Scarman said:

'If the words used by Parliament are plain, there is no room for the "anomalies" test, unless the consequences are so absurd that, without going outside the statute, one can see that Parliament must have made a drafting mistake. If words "have been inadvertently used," it is legitimate for the court to substitute what is apt to avoid the intention of the legislature being defeated: *per*

MacKinnon LJ in *Sutherland Publishing Co Ltd v Caxton Publishing Co Ltd*
a   [1938] Ch 174, 201. This is an acceptable exception to the general rule that
plain language excludes a consideration of anomalies, i.e. mischievous or absurd
consequences. If a study of the statute as a whole leads inexorably to the
conclusion that Parliament has erred in its choice of words, e.g. used "and"
when "or" was clearly intended, the courts can, and must, eliminate the error
by interpretation. But mere "manifest absurdity" is not enough: it must be an
b   error (of commission or omission) which in its context defeats the intention of
the Act.'

However, it is implicit in this observation that the mischievous and absurd
consequences can be eliminated by interpretation. That limitation is made explicit
in the speech of Lord Simon (at 236):

c   'But it is essential to bear in mind what the court is doing. It is not declaring
"Parliament has said X: but it obviously meant Y; so we will take Y as the effect
of the statute." Nor is it declaring "Parliament has said X, having situation A in
mind: but if Parliament had had our own forensic situation, B, in mind, the
legislative objective indicates that it would have said Y; so we will take Y as the
effect of the statute as regards B." What the court is declaring is "Parliament
d   has used words which are capable of meaning either X or Y: although X may
be the primary, natural and ordinary meaning of the words, the purpose of the
provision shows that the secondary sense, Y, should be given to the words." So
too when X produces injustice, absurdity, anomaly or contradiction.'

To the same effect is the well-known passage in the speech of Lord Reid in *Luke
e   v IRC* [1963] AC 557 at 577, 40 TC 630 at 646:

        'How, then, are we to resolve the difficulty? To apply the words literally is to
defeat the obvious intention of the legislation and to produce a wholly
unreasonable result. To achieve the obvious intention and produce a reasonable
result we must do some violence to the words. This is not a new problem,
though our standard of drafting is such that it rarely emerges. The general
f   principle is well settled. *It is only where the words are absolutely incapable of a
construction which will accord with the apparent intention of the provision* and will
avoid a wholly unreasonable result, that the words of the enactment must
prevail.' [My emphasis.]

Counsel for the Crown submitted that the anomalies to which sub-s (4), construed
g   in the sense contended for by the taxpayer, gives rise, are so striking that sub-s (4)
can fairly be described as ambiguous in the wide sense of that word, explained by
Lord Diplock in *IRC v Joiner* [1975] STC 657 at 665–666, [1975] 1 WLR 1701 at
1710. He submitted that in these circumstances it is permissible to look at the
legislation re-enacted in this 1979 Act (which is a consolidating Act) to ascertain the
true intention of the legislation. I think the answer to that submission is that the
h   pre-consolidated legislation cannot be looked at save where the consolidating Act is
capable of more than one interpretation. If the consolidating Act is only susceptible
to one interpretation, there is no room for any presumption that it was not intended
to alter the pre-existing law.

I should, however, add that the earlier legislation would not in my judgment assist
the Crown's case if it could be referred to. Section 72(1), (2) and (3) reproduces with
j   immaterial modifications, provisions to be found in para 3 of Sch 7 to the Finance
Act 1965 (the 1965 Act); ss 20 and 21(1) of the 1979 Act have their origin in para
13(1) of Sch 6 to the 1965 Act; and s 108 has its origin in para 4 of Sch 10 to the
Finance Act 1966 (the 1966 Act). Paragraph 9 of Sch 10 provided that the provisions
of sub-paras (b) and (c) of para 13(1) of Sch 6 to the 1965 Act, para 3(2) of Sch 7 to
the 1965 Act and para 4 of Sch 10 to the 1966 Act 'shall have effect subject to the
provisions of this paragraph'. Paragraph 9(2) then provides that—'None of these

provisions shall apply if immediately before the part disposal' either the allowable expenditure was nil or the consideration for the part disposal exceeded that *a* expenditure, but that the taxpayer might then elect that the consideration should be dealt with in the manner now set out in para (*b*) of s 72(4). The exclusion of the whole of para 3(2) of Sch 7 to the 1965 Act, which corresponds to s 72(2), gives rise to the difficulty which arises in this case—that is, whether para 9(2) of Sch 10 to the 1966 Act by excluding para 3(2) of Sch 7 to the 1965 Act removed the limitation to comparatively small gains or only the power of the inspector to direct that the *b* amount of the capital distribution should be treated as comparatively small (and by implication the taxpayer's right of appeal under para 3(3) of Sch 7) or should be construed in accordance with the Crown's preferred construction of s 72(4). Thus the antecedent legislation offers no clear guide to the interpretation of s 72(4).

In my judgment, therefore, this appeal fails. The case is, I think, one where although the court may be satisfied that the result is not one which the draftsman *c* intended and the legislature approved, effect cannot be given to the apparent intention by any process of interpretation. In the words of Lord Macmillan in *Ayrshire Employers Mutual Insurance Association Ltd v IRC* (1944) 27 TC 331 at 347: 'The Legislature has plainly missed fire'.

I should, however, add that I agree with the commissioner also that the capital distribution in this case was not comparatively small. What is comparatively small *d* must be judged in the light of the evident purpose of s 72(2), that is to avoid the delay and expense of a full computation on the basis of a part disposal under s 72(1) in cases where the delay and expense would be out of proportion to the amount of the capital distribution as compared with the remaining value of the shares in respect of which the distribution was made. No percentage figure can be specified which would be applicable in all cases; each case must depend on its particular facts. *e*

Appeal dismissed with costs.

Solicitors: *Solicitor of Inland Revenue ; Simpson Curtis*, Leeds (for the taxpayer).

Rengan Krishnan Esq   Barrister. *f*

Beautiland Co Ltd v Commissioner of Inland Revenue

PRIVY COUNCIL
LORD KEITH OF KINKEL, LORD TEMPLEMAN, LORD OLIVER OF AYLMERTON, LORD
JAUNCEY OF TULLICHETTLE, SIR ROBERT MEGARRY
13, 14, 15 MAY, 19 JUNE 1991

*Hong Kong – Profits tax – Capital or income receipts – Shares – Whether acquisition
and disposal of shares carried out by way of trade – Whether acquisition and disposal of
shares one-off adventure in the nature of trade – Inland Revenue Ordinance (Hong
Kong) Cap 112, s 14.*

The taxpayer company, Beautiland Co Ltd, was the vehicle of a joint venture
agreement between two Hong Kong companies, Cheung Kong (Holdings) Ltd
(Cheung Kong) and Wheelock Marden & Co Ltd (Wheelock Marden) acting
through its subsidiary, Cranmore Land Co Ltd (Cranmore). The first approach
regarding the venture was made in March 1979 and during that month agreement
in principle was reached for the joint development of certain landed properties
owned wholly or partly by Cheung Kong and Wheelock Marden or their subsidiaries.
Among the assets offered by Cheung Kong was a 30% shareholding in Rostock
Enterprises Ltd (Rostock) which owned 52·36% of the shares of a company which
owned valuable land at Tin Shui Wai. In May 1979 an outside party approached
Cheung Kong offering to purchase Rostock's interest in the land at Tin Shui Wai
but the offer was not accepted. The joint venture agreement was executed on 8 June
1979. The agreement provided that Cranmore and Cheung Kong would each hold
50% of the shares in the taxpayer company and that they would sell or cause to be
sold to the taxpayer company or its subsidiaries certain 'Properties' (including the
30% holding in Rostock) set out in the schedules to the agreement. Included in the
agreement was a clause headed 'Development Policy' which provided, inter alia,
that all land owned by the taxpayer company or its subsidiaries should be developed
to the best and fullest extent permitted by the relevant authorities. On the same day
as the joint venture agreement was executed, Cranmore confirmed in writing to
Cheung Kong that the managing director of the taxpayer company had full authority
and power to negotiate and agree on behalf of the taxpayer company the sale of
either the interest held by Rostock in the land at Tin Shui Wai or the shares in
Rostock to be acquired by the taxpayer company. The taxpayer company resolved
to purchase the areas of land and shares (the 'Property') set out in the schedules to
the agreement and, on 28 June 1979, contract notes for the purchase and sale of the
30% shareholding in Rostock at a price of approximately $60m were executed. In
August 1979 an approach was made to Cheung Kong by Commotra Co Ltd
(Commotra) with a view to acquiring an interest in the land at Tin Shui Wai. The
result was that on 6 November the taxpayer company joined with other shareholders
in Rostock in an agreement for the sale to Commotra of 25% out of its 30% holding
of Rostock shares at an agreed price of $103·75m. The commissioner made an
assessment to profits tax for the year 1980–81 charging, inter alia, the gain made on
the sale of the Rostock shares and a gain made on the disposal to Cheung Kong of
shares in another company, Hoi Tuen Investment Co Ltd (Hoi Tuen). The taxpayer
company appealed to the Board of Review against the assessment so far as it related
to those gains. The Board of Review allowed the appeal in relation to the shares in
Hoi Tuen, holding that these were acquired as a long-term investment and were
never part of the taxpayer company's stock in trade, but dismissed the appeal in
relation to the sale of the Rostock shares, holding that it was either carried out by

way of trade or was an adventure in the nature of trade. On appeal to the High
Court, the relevant question of law was whether it was open to the Board of Review
to hold that the Rostock shares were acquired and disposed of by way of trade or
adventure in the nature of trade. The High Court decided that question in the
negative and allowed the taxpayer company's appeal. The Court of Appeal reversed
the decision of the High Court and the taxpayer company appealed to the Privy
Council.

Held – (1) A proper construction of the operative parts of the agreement bore out
the fact that the intended purpose of the parties was the turning into account of land
by development or sale or both, whether such land was to be owned directly by the
taxpayer company or by subsidiaries or associates of the taxpayer company. There
was nothing in the agreement which indicated that the parties had in contemplation
trading in the shares of subsidiary or associated companies. If there was no such
contemplation there could be no question of a separate contemplation of trading in
land via shares. There was no material before the Board of Review on which it could
properly find that the Rostock shares were acquired and disposed of by way and in
the course of a general trade in shares.

(2) The Rostock shares were acquired by the taxpayer company on exactly the
same basis as the shares in the other companies acquired under the joint venture
agreement, ie not as trading stock but as part of the capital structure of the taxpayer
company. The only true and reasonable conclusion on a consideration of the whole
facts and circumstances of the case was that the acquisition and disposal by the
taxpayer company of the Rostock shares was not an adventure in the nature of trade.

Accordingly, the appeal would be allowed.

Notes
For the distinction between trading stock and capital assets, see Simon's Taxes
Division B3.2.

Appeal
The taxpayer company, Beautiland Co Ltd, appealed against the decision of the
Court of Appeal of Hong Kong (Power JA, Macdougall JA and Hooper J) of
4 September 1990 reversing the decision of Barnet J in the High Court of
9 November 1989 allowing the taxpayer company's appeal from the decision of the
Board of Review of 3 June 1989 whereby it dismissed an appeal by the taxpayer
company against an assessment to profits tax on the sale of shares for 1980–81. The
facts are set out in the judgment of the Board.

John Gardiner QC and *Jonathan Peacock* for the taxpayer company.
Peter Feenstra, Senior Assistant Crown Solicitor, and *Anthony Wu*, Senior Crown
Counsel, for the commissioner.

19 June 1991. The following judgment of the Board was delivered.

LORD KEITH OF KINKEL. The proceedings with which this appeal is concerned
arose out of a joint venture agreement entered into on 8 June 1979 between two
important Hong Kong companies, Cheung Kong (Holdings) Ltd (Cheung Kong)
and Wheelock Marden & Co Ltd (Wheelock Marden), acting through its subsidiary
company Cranmore Land Co Ltd (Cranmore). The first approach for this venture
was made by Cheung Kong on 12 March 1979. In the course of an exchange of
letters during that month, agreement in principle was reached for the joint
development of certain landed properties owned by subsidiaries of Wheelock
Marden together with certain other such properties owned wholly or partially by
subsidiaries of Cheung Kong. The development was to be carried out through the
vehicle of a company called Beautiland Co Ltd (the taxpayer company), which was
incorporated on 27 March 1979 and is the appellant in this appeal. Among the assets
offered by Cheung Kong was 30% of the issued share capital of a company called

Rostock Enterprises Ltd (Rostock) which owned 52·36% of the shares of Luen Tak
Co, which itself owned valuable land at Tin Shui Wai in the New Territories.

On 19 April 1979 Cheung Kong sent to Wheelock Marden a draft of the proposed
agreement for the joint venture. In May 1979 an outside party approached Cheung
Kong offering to purchase Rostock's interest in the land at Tin Shui Wai. This offer
was not accepted. The draft joint venture agreement was subjected to various
alterations, and in its final form was executed by Cranmore and Cheung Kong on
8 June 1979. It was provided that each of Cranmore and Cheung Kong should hold
50% of the shares in the taxpayer company. Clause 1 of the agreement defined 'the
Properties' as meaning:

> 'All the assets and shares and proportions thereof referred to in Schedules I
> and II of this Agreement and which are to be acquired from the sellers by [the
> taxpayer company].' \

It further defined 'the Seller' as:

> 'Any party which is to sell to [the taxpayer company] the property owned by
> it or the shares in any of its related companies as set out in the relevant Schedules
> hereto.'

Clause 7.1 provided:

> '[The taxpayer company] or its subsidiaries shall purchase from the Sellers,
> and Cranmore and Cheung Kong shall sell or otherwise cause the Sellers to sell
> to [the taxpayer company] or its subsidiaries the Properties at the prices and
> upon the terms of payment and conditions as are respectively set out in Schedule
> I and Schedule II hereto and subject to the provisions of this Agreement.'

Schedule I set out the Properties (in the sense of assets and shares) to be put into the
venture by Wheelock Marden. These comprised ten areas of land each owned by a
separate subsidiary and a 100% holding of shares in another subsidiary. Schedule II
set out the Properties to be put in by Cheung Kong. These consisted entirely of
shareholdings in nine different subsidiaries, ranging from a 10% to a 100% holding,
and including the 30% shareholding in Rostock. The schedules also set out the price
to be paid by the taxpayer company for each area of land and each shareholding to
be acquired by it, the price to be paid for the Rostock holding being $60,124,688·17,
and provided for the prices to be paid as to 5% on signing of the agreement, 5%
within 12 months of signing and 90% within 48 months of signing.

Clause 10 of the agreement (in which, as elsewhere, the taxpayer company is
called 'the Company') is headed 'Development Policy'. It provided:

> '10.1. All the land owned by the Company and/or by the subsidiary companies
> of the Company shall be developed by erecting thereon New Buildings at such
> time and in such manner as the Managing Director shall decide: Provided that
> the building plans, specifications and the budgetted costs for each New Building
> shall be subject to the approval of the Board of Directors.
>
> 10.2. Notwithstanding Clause 10.1. hereof, the existing buildings on any land
> owned by the Company or the subsidiary companies of the Company may be
> turned to account otherwise than by the Development thereof if the Board of
> Directors shall so resolve.
>
> 10.3. The rights of exchange for land under Letters of Exchange and the
> right (legal or equitable) to any land held by the subsidiary companies of the
> Company shall be utilized or otherwise turned to account at such time and in
> such manner as the Managing Director shall, subject to the approval from time
> to time of the Board of Directors, decide.
>
> 10.4. Any land to be developed by the Company or the subsidiary companies
> of the Company shall be developed as expeditiously as possible and to the best
> and fullest extent as shall for the time being be permitted by the relevant
> Government authorities.

10.5. Each of the parties hereto shall use its best endeavours to procure the
board of directors of such of its related companies, of which issued share capitals
less than 50% have been sold to the Company, to have the land and the existing
buildings thereon owned by such related companies, or the right to exchange
for land held by such related companies, to be developed or otherwise turned to
account as the Board of Directors shall decide.'

On the same day as the joint venture agreement was executed, namely 8 June
1979, Cranmore sent to Cheung Kong a letter containing the following passage:

'We refer to the Joint Venture Agreement of even date and made between
ourselves, [Cranmore], of the one part and yourselves, [Cheung Kong], of the
other part for the formation of a consortium in [the taxpayer company] of
which your Mr. Li Ka Shing is to be the Managing Director as provided in the
said Joint Venture Agreement. We hereby confirm our agreement that your
Mr. Li Ka Shing shall have the full authority and power for and on behalf of
[the taxpayer company]: (1) To negotiate and agree with prospective purchaser
or purchasers, at such prices and on such terms and conditions as would in his
absolute opinion generate a reasonable profit, for the sale or disposal of either
the interest held by [Rostock] of and in the pieces of land registered in the
District Office Yuen Long respectively as Subsection land The Remaining
Portion of Section B of Lot No. 165 in Demarcation District No. 126 or the
shares in [Rostock] to be acquired by [the taxpayer company].'

By board resolution dated 27 June 1979 the taxpayer company resolved to purchase
the areas of land and the shares set out in the schedules to the joint venture
agreement, including the 30% shareholding in Rostock. On 28 June 1979 contract
notes for the purchase and sale of that shareholding were executed. In August 1979
approaches were made to Cheung Kong by Commotra Co Ltd (Commotra) with a
view to acquiring an interest in the land at Tin Shui Wai. Commotra was a different
party from the one who had made the offer in May 1979. The result of the approaches
was that on 21 August 1979 Cheung Kong offered to sell to Commotra 81% of the
shares in Rostock, including 25% out of the 30% acquired by the taxpayer company,
at a total price of $336,150,000 of which the taxpayer company's share was
$103,750,000. On 6 November 1979 the taxpayer company joined with other
shareholders in Rostock in an agreement for the sale to Commotra of, inter alia, 25%
out of its 30% holding at the agreed price of $103,750,000. The taxpayer company
thus made a gain. The exact amount does not appear anywhere in the record.

The Commissioner of Inland Revenue, the respondent in this appeal (the
commissioner), made an assessment to profits tax on the taxpayer company for the
year 1980–81 charging, inter alia, the gain so made by it. The taxpayer company
appealed to the Board of Review against the assessment so far as relating to the gain
on the Rostock shareholding, and also to a gain made on the disposal to Cheung
Kong on 20 October 1979 of shares in a company called Hoi Tuen Investment Co
Ltd (Hoi Tuen). By a decision dated 3 June 1989 the Board of Review dismissed the
appeal in so far as relating to the assessment in respect of the Rostock share
transaction, holding that it was either carried out by way of trade or was an adventure
in the nature of trade, but allowed the appeal as regards the Hoi Tuen share
transaction, holding that these shares were acquired by the taxpayer company as a
long-term investment and were never part of its stock in trade. At the taxpayer
company's request the Board of Review stated a case for the opinion of the High
Court. The case contained a number of questions of law, but it will be sufficient to
mention only the first of these, which is in these terms:

'Whether, as a matter of law, and on the facts found by the Board, it was
open to the Board of Review to hold that the Rostock shares were acquired and
disposed of by way of trade or adventure in the nature of trade.'

On 9 November 1989 Barnett J delivered judgment whereby he answered this
a question in the negative and allowed the taxpayer company's appeal. On appeal by
the commissioner the Court of Appeal (Power JA, Macdougall JA and Hooper J) on
4 September 1990 reversed the decision of Barnett J. The taxpayer now appeals to
Her Majesty in Council.

Section 14 of the Hong Kong Inland Revenue Ordinance (the Ordinance) imposes
for each year of assessment a charge for profits tax on every person carrying on 'a
b trade, profession or business in Hong Kong' in respect of his assessable profits arising
in or derived from Hong Kong 'from such trade, profession or business'. Section 2(1)
of the Ordinance defines 'trade' as including 'every trade and manufacture, and
every adventure and concern in the nature of trade'. This does not differ materially
from the United Kingdom definition 'every trade, manufacture, adventure or
concern in the nature of trade', which has given rise to a great many cases each
c turning largely on its own facts and circumstances. In the present case the first
matter for consideration is whether or not the joint venture agreement contains any
indication of an intention to carry on a general trade in the shares of the land-
owning companies which were to be acquired by the taxpayer company. In this
connection the Board of Review said in the course of its decision:

d   'We find nothing in the bargain which excluded from the parties'
contemplation the sale of shares owned by the joint venture company. We find
that the parties' general intent to enter into a long-term venture for developing
and/or turning landed properties to profitable account made allowance for
profit-taking sales before development, the phrase "development and/or sale of
the properties described in the Schedules" being perfectly consistent with this
e   general intention. We also find such profit-taking sales were intended to form
part of the venture and that the intention was sufficiently broad to encompass
trading in shares or trading in land *via* shares in relation to specific assets
owned.'

The phrase to which the Board of Review here refers comes from the first recital to
f the agreement, which is in these terms:

'The parties hereto are desirous of participating in the development and/or
sale of the properties described in the Schedules hereto.'

g The schedules are headed by the names of various companies, and against the words
'Location of Property' and 'Description' they describe under each name the landed
properties owned by the company in question. In some instances the taxpayer
company was to acquire shares in the company, and in others the landed properties
owned by the company. The words 'properties described in the Schedules' in their
natural meaning refer to the landed properties so described and are not apt to
h embrace shares in companies. Shares are not normally referred to as properties and
although shares are mentioned in the schedules, against the words 'Percentage of
shares to be acquired', they can hardly be regarded as described there. It is true that
in the definition clause 'the Properties' (with a large 'P') is defined as including 'assets
and shares', being those 'referred to' (not 'described') in the schedules. But the
context of the reference to 'the properties' (with a small 'p') in the recital makes it
j clear that the definition of 'the Properties' is not imported. When attention is turned
to the operative parts of the agreement, a proper construction of these bears out that
what was in the contemplation of the parties, and their intended purpose, was the
turning to account of land by development or sale or both, whether such land was to
be owned directly by the taxpayer company or would be owned by subsidiary or
associated companies of the taxpayer company. This is particularly apparent from

clause 10, dealing with development policy, which has been quoted above. The
taxpayer company was to own certain landed properties as its stock in trade and the   *a*
subsidiary and associated companies were to own other landed properties as their
stock in trade.

Their Lordships are unable to find anything in the agreement which indicates
that the parties had in contemplation trading in the shares of subsidiary or associated
companies. In so far as the Board of Review found such a contemplation to exist,
their Lordships consider that the Board of Review misinterpreted the agreement. If   *b*
there was no contemplation of trading in the shares of subsidiary or associated
companies there can be no question of a separate contemplation of trading in land
via shares, a concept which their Lordships in any event find difficult to understand.
The Board of Review placed some weight on the terms of clause 7.1 of the first draft
agreement, which contained a provision for accelerated payment to either of the
parties of the price of any land or shares in a related company acquired by the   *c*
taxpayer company from that party in the event, inter alia, of the taxpayer company
having by sale disposed of such land or shares before the due dates for payment of
instalments of the purchase price set out in the schedules. This provision was,
however, omitted from the agreement as finally executed, which tends to suggest, if
anything, that the sale of the shares in the related companies which were to be
acquired by the taxpayer company was not at the end of the day in the general   *d*
contemplation of the parties.

The actual activities of the taxpayer company after acquiring the agreed assets do
not present any characteristics of a general trade in shares. The land to be acquired
from Wheelock Marden, apart from two parcels, TWIL No 2 and TWIL No 16,
was acquired through wholly-owned subsidiaries of the taxpayer company. The
taxpayer company sold TWIL No 2 and TWIL No 16 in December 1980 and   *e*
accepted an assessment to profits tax on the resulting gain. On 25 October 1979 the
taxpayer company sold back to Cheung Kong the 100% shareholding in Hoi Tuen
which it had acquired from Cheung Kong under the joint venture agreement. This
resulted in a gain to the taxpayer company of $80,000,000, and the commissioner
assessed the taxpayer company to profits tax in respect of this gain. As already
mentioned the Board of Review heard an appeal by the taxpayer company against   *f*
this assessment along with the Rostock appeal and allowed it, holding that the Hoi
Tuen shares were acquired by the taxpayer as a long-term investment and never
formed part of its stock in trade. The Board of Review decision sets out certain
acquisitions and disposals by the taxpayer of shares in certain companies between
September 1979 and February 1986, but the Board of Review nowhere suggests that
any of these were trading transactions. The acquisition and disposal of the Rostock   *g*
shares, if it was a trading transaction, was unique.

The conclusion is that there was no material before the Board of Review on which
it could properly find that the Rostock shares were acquired and disposed of by the
taxpayer company by way and in the course of a general trade in shares. It remains
to consider whether it could properly be regarded as a one-off adventure in the
nature of trade. The broad purpose of the joint venture agreement was to bring   *h*
about the profitable development of land. The taxpayer company was to become
owner of a number of parcels of land as stock in trade, and it was also to become the
holding company for a number of subsidiary or related companies which themselves
would own land as stock in trade. In the result the taxpayer company came to own
only two parcels of land, TWIL No 2 and TWIL No 16, and all the other parcels
were owned by subsidiary or related companies. In general, the shares in these   *j*
companies held by the taxpayer company constituted its capital structure, and the
question is whether the Rostock shares were exceptional in respect that they were
acquired not as part of that capital structure but as trading stock. The Board of
Review held that the latter was the position. Its principal reason for so holding was
that when the taxpayer company acquired the Rostock shares on 28 June 1979 it did
not have any intention to hold the shares for long-term investment, because the

shares were marketable items and there would be legal and other problems in the
a way of either developing the land at Tin Shui Wai or selling Rostock's shares in
Luen Tak Co, which owned that land. The Board of Review was much influenced
by the circumstances that in May 1979 there had been an approach to Cheung Kong
with a view to the purchase for $300,000,000 of Rostock's interest in Tin Shui Wai,
and that on 8 June 1979 Mr Li Ka Shing had been authorised to negotiate for the
sale either of that interest or of the Rostock shares to be acquired by the taxpayer
b company.

In their Lordships' opinion these circumstances are quite insufficient to support
the Board of Review's conclusion. The Rostock shares were originally put forward
by Cheung Kong for the joint venture on exactly the same basis as the shares in the
other eight companies which they were offering. Cheung Kong refused an offer for
Rostock's interest in the land at Tin Shui Wai in May 1979. The offer by Commotra
c in August 1979 was a better one. In June 1979 there was undoubtedly the prospect
of further and better offers, but that prospect gives no grounds whatever for inferring
an intention on the part of the parties to the joint venture that the Rostock shares
should be acquired by the taxpayer company not as part of its capital structure but
as trading stock. The true view is that the appearance of a fortuitous offer at a very
good price caused the taxpayer company to decide to sell part of its capital structure.
d No doubt the difficulties which would confront the development of the land at Tin
Shui Wai contributed to that decision, but the presence of those difficulties is no
ground for inferring that the Rostock shares were not originally acquired as part of
the capital structure of the taxpayer company. The contrary conclusion to that
reached by the Board of Review is the only true and reasonable one on a consideration
of the whole facts and circumstances of the case. The acquisition and disposal by the
e taxpayer company of the Rostock shares was not an adventure in the nature of trade.

For these reasons their Lordships will humbly advise Her Majesty that the appeal
should be allowed and the order of Barnett J restored. The commissioner must pay
the taxpayer's costs here and before the Court of Appeal.

Appeal allowed with costs.

f
Solicitors: *Charles Russell* (for the taxpayer company); *Macfarlanes* for the
commissioner).

Rengan Krishnan Esq   Barrister.

Lloyds Bank Export Finance Ltd v   a
Commissioner of Inland Revenue

PRIVY COUNCIL
LORD KEITH OF KINKEL, LORD TEMPLEMAN, LORD JAUNCEY OF TULLICHETTLE, SIR
ROBERT MEGARRY AND SIR DAVID CROOM-JOHNSON
20, 21 MAY, 19 JUNE 1991   b

*New Zealand – Assessment – Assessment out of time – Making of an assessment –
Additional assessment to tax after expiry of time limit – Whether original assessments
made – Whether when process of determining assessable income results in a nil or negative
figure an 'assessment made' – Income Tax Act 1976 (New Zealand), ss 19, 25.*
c

The taxpayers submitted returns for the years of assessment for 1976 and 1977
showing small profits. However, because of substantial losses in prior years which
they were entitled to carry forward and set off, the commissioner made determinations
to the effect that no tax was payable by them in the two years in question. Some five
years after the last of the two determinations the commissioner sought to assess the d
taxpayers to tax in respect of the two years 1976 and 1977. The taxpayers challenged
the assessments on the ground, inter alia, that under s 25[a] of the New Zealand
Income Tax Act 1976 (the 1976 Act) the four-year time limit within which the
commissioner was entitled to increase the assessments already made had expired and
that therefore the commissioner was time-barred from making further assessments.
Tompkins J upheld the taxpayers' appeal. The Court of Appeal allowed the e
commissioner's appeal against that decision holding (a) that an 'assessment' under
s 19[b] of the 1976 Act was made only when the process of determining the assessable
income resulted in a taxable income of a positive amount; (b) that where no positive
figure of taxable income was produced by the process no assessment had been made;
(c) that the determinations made by the commissioner that no tax was payable by
the taxpayers for 1976 and 1977 had not constituted assessments; and (d) that s 25 f
did not therefore apply to time-bar the commissioner from making fresh assessments
for 1976 and 1977. The taxpayers appealed to the Privy Council contending, inter
alia: (a) that when the process of determining the assessable income was complete an
assessment had been made irrespective of whether the amount on which tax was
payable produced by that process resulted in a positive figure, a nil figure or a
negative figure; (b) that the commissioner's determinations that no tax was payable g
for 1976 and 1977 had constituted assessments; and (c) that therefore the
commissioner was time-barred from increasing the assessments already made under
s 25 of the 1976 Act.

Held – The expression 'make assessments' in s 19 of the 1976 Act meant the process
by which the commissioner carried out his statutory obligation to ascertain the h
amount on which tax was payable and the amount of tax. When the process of
determining the assessable income was complete an assessment had been made
irrespective of whether the amount on which tax was payable, produced by that
process, was a positive, a nil or a negative figure. The commissioner's determinations
that no tax was payable by the taxpayers for 1976 and 1977 had therefore constituted
the making of 'assessments' for the purposes of s 19 and accordingly, s 25 applied to j
time-bar the commissioner from increasing the assessments already made. The
appeal would therefore be allowed.

---

a   Section 25, so far as material, is set out at p 476 *e g*, post
b   Section 19, so far as material, is set out at p 476 *b c*, post

Notes

a For the making of assessments generally, see Simon's Taxes Division A3.2.
   For the assessing procedure, see ibid, A3.202.

Cases referred to in judgment

Batagol v Comr of Taxation of the Commonwealth of Australia (1963) 109 CLR 243.
b *Comr of Inland Revenue v V H Farnsworth Ltd* [1984] 1 NZLR 428.

Appeal

The taxpayers appealed against the decision of the Court of Appeal of New Zealand
(Cooke P, Richardson and Hardie Boys JJ) of 3 April 1990 (see [1990] 2 NZLR 154)
c allowing an appeal by the Commissioner of Inland Revenue against the decision of
Tomkins J of 31 May 1988 (see (1988) 11 TRNZ 733): (i) that determinations made
by the commissioner that no tax was payable by the taxpayers for the years 1976 and
1977 constituted assessments for the purposes of s 19 of the New Zealand Income
Tax Act 1976; and (ii) that because the four-year time limit within which the
commissioner was entitled to increase those assessments had expired, the commis-
d sioner was time-barred from making further assessments under s 25 of the 1976 Act.
The facts are set out in the judgment of the Board.

Sydney Kentridge QC and *David Simcock* (New Zealand Bar) for the taxpayers.
Peter Jenkin QC and *Grant Pearson* (both of the New Zealand Bar) for the
   commissioner.

e 19 June 1991. The following judgment of the Board was delivered.

LORD JAUNCEY OF TULLICHETTLE. This appeal involves the construction
of certain sections of the New Zealand Land and Income Tax Act 1954 (the 1954
Act) which was consolidated in the Income Tax Act 1976 (the 1976 Act). Before
looking in detail at the relevant sections it may be convenient to summarise the
f circumstances giving rise to the appeal. The fiscal year in New Zealand runs from
and to 31 March, so that the year ending 31 March 1980 would be described as the
1980 year. The appellants, Lloyds Bank Export Finance Ltd (the taxpayers),
submitted the necessary returns for the years 1976 and 1977 showing small profits.
However, because of substantial losses in prior years which they were entitled to
carry forward and set off, the respondent (the commissioner) made determinations
g to the effect that no tax was payable by them in the two years in question. Some five
years after the last of the two determinations the commissioner sought to assess the
taxpayers to tax in respect of the above two years. The taxpayers challenged the
assessments on the ground, inter alia, that they were statute-barred by reason of the
provisions of s 24 of the 1954 Act. Tompkins J upheld the taxpayers' objection to the
assessments (see (1988) 11 TRNZ 733) but the Court of Appeal quashed the orders
h made in the High Court and declared that the commissioner was not barred by s 25
of the 1976 Act (the re-enactment of s 24 of the 1954 Act) from making the
assessments (see [1990] 2 NZLR 154). The judgment of the Court of Appeal which
was delivered by Richardson J found it convenient to refer to the provisions of the
1976 Act rather than to the corresponding provisions of the 1954 Act and their
Lordships are content to do likewise.

j   It is now necessary to examine the relevant provisions of the 1976 Act in detail.
Section 9, which imposes the duty on a taxpayer to make annual returns, is in the
following terms:

   'Subject to this Act or any regulations under this Act, every taxpayer shall for
   the purposes of the assessment and levy of income tax furnish to the
   Commissioner in each year a return or returns in the prescribed form or forms

setting forth a complete statement of all the assessable and non-assessable income derived by him during the preceding year, together with such other particulars as may be prescribed.'

'Assessable income' is defined by s 2 of the 1976 Act as 'income of any kind which is not exempted from income tax otherwise than by way of a special exemption expressly authorised as such by this Act'. In calculating assessable income, expenditure or loss incurred in the production of that income may be taken into account (see s 104).

Section 19 of the 1976 Act which imposes the duty on the commissioner to make assessments is in the following terms:

'From the returns made as aforesaid and from any other information in his possession the Commissioner shall in and for every year, and from time to time and at any time thereafter as may be necessary, make assessments in respect of every taxpayer of the amount on which tax is payable and of the amount of that tax.'

Section 23 deals with amendment of assessments in the following manner:

'(1) The Commissioner may from time to time and at any time make all such alterations in or additions to an assessment as he thinks necessary in order to ensure the correctness thereof, notwithstanding that tax already assessed may have been paid.

(2) If any such alteration or addition has the effect of imposing any fresh liability or increasing any existing liability, notice thereof shall be given by the Commissioner to the taxpayer affected.'

Section 25 which is relied on by the taxpayers provides:

'(1) When any person has made returns and has been assessed for income tax for any year, it shall not be lawful for the Commissioner to alter the assessment so as to increase the amount thereof after the expiration of 4 years from the end of the year in which the assessment was made.

(2) Notwithstanding subsection (1) of this section, in any case where, in the opinion of the Commissioner, the returns so made are fraudulent or wilfully misleading or omit all mention of income which is of a particular nature or was derived from a particular source, and in respect of which a return is required to be made, it shall be lawful for the Commissioner to alter the assessment (being an assessment made on or after the 1st day of April 1958) at any time so as to increase the amount thereof.'

Section 29 requires the commissioner to give notice to the taxpayer after an assessment has been made and is in the following terms:

'(1) As soon as conveniently may be after an assessment is made the Commissioner shall cause notice of the assessment to be given to the taxpayer: Provided that where—

(a) The taxpayer has, in his return to which the assessment relates, calculated the amount on which tax is payable or the amount of the tax; or

(b) The assessment has been made on default by the taxpayer in furnishing any return for the year to which the assessment relates; or

(c) The Commissioner causes a separate statement in relation to the assessment to be given to the taxpayer setting forth the amount on which tax is payable and the amount of the tax,—

it shall not be necessary to set forth in the notice of the assessment any particulars other than particulars as to the amount of tax to be paid by the taxpayer or the amount of tax to be refunded, as the case may require.

(2) The omission to give any such notice shall not invalidate the assessment or in any manner affect the operation thereof.'

The issue between the parties is whether the determinations, to use a neutral word, by the commissioner for the years 1976 and 1977 that no tax was payable by the taxpayers constituted assessments for the purposes of s 25(1). If they did, the commissioner accepts that the later assessments were out of time and therefore ineffective. If they did not, the later assessments were not time-barred. The determinations in question took the following form:

(1) By what appears to be a printed form of letter the District Commissioner on 5 April 1977 wrote to the taxpayers as follows:

'Dear

Your 1976 return of income has been checked. There is no refund, or further tax to pay.

Yours faithfully ...'

Accompanying that letter was a document headed 'Income Tax Assessment Notice 1976', with a line drawn through the words. The document included the following entries:

	$
'Assessable Income as returned	14,227·00
Loss b'fwd	973,237·38
Losses to be c'fwd	959,010·38
Balance of Tax	NIL'

(2) On 6 March 1978 the District Commissioner sent to the taxpayers an undated letter relating to the 1977 return in terms identical to that which he had sent on 5 April 1977, save that the second sentence began with the words, 'On the basis of the return furnished'. Accompanying that letter was another document, dated 6 March 1978 and headed 'Income Tax Assessment Notice 1977', with two lines drawn through the first three words. This document contained figures of assessable income, loss brought forward, loss available to be carried forward and a nil balance of tax.

Counsel for the taxpayers submitted that the word 'assessment' meant the process of determining the income of a taxpayer, if any, of determining the allowable deductions or rebates and ascertaining thereby the balance of income, if any, on which tax is payable. This process might show up a positive figure, a nil figure or a negative figure, but in each case an assessment had been made. Counsel for the commissioner on the other hand adopted the reasoning of the Court of Appeal in arguing that an assessment only took place when the foregoing process threw up taxable income which is defined by s 2 of the 1976 Act as meaning 'the residue of assessable income after deducting the amount of all special exemptions to which the taxpayer is entitled'. If no figure of taxable income was produced by the process no assessment had taken place. Counsel for the commissioner also relied on the terms of three further sections to which their Lordships will refer later.

Section 9 requires a taxpayer to make a return even though he may well know that he will be required to pay no tax. The return required is of assessable income but such income is capable of producing nil taxable income by the deduction therefrom of special exemptions. Section 19 imposes on the commissioner the duty to make assessments in respect of every taxpayer of the amount on which tax is payable. This involves, inter alia, calculating the assessable income. If, as counsel for the commissioner contended, the process of assessment has not taken place until some taxable income has been ascertained, it means that the commissioner will not know until he has completed the whole exercise of examining the returns and relevant documents whether he has been making an assessment or not, even though he has in that process calculated the assessable income. If he has not been making an assessment what has he been doing and what is the statutory warrant therefor? Counsel for the commissioner's contention also produces the somewhat curious result that a determination by the commissioner that $5 tax is payable is an assessment which cannot be increased after the period specified in s 25(1) has run, whereas a determination that there is no taxable income or that there is a loss can be revised at any time without limit.

Some support for counsel for the taxpayer's argument is to be found in s 23(2) which, in the context of amendment of assessments, uses the words 'imposing any fresh liability or increasing any existing liability'. The reference to fresh liability suggests that the section contemplated an alteration which imposed liability to tax where none existed before. Further support for the argument is to be found in s 29(1) which clearly contemplates that a notice of assessment given after an assessment has been made shall in certain circumstances contain a statement of the amount of tax to be refunded. In this situation the assessment would necessarily have produced the result that not only was no tax payable by the taxpayer but that tax was repayable to him by the commissioner. If an assessment is made in such a situation it is difficult to see why it is not also made when no tax is payable without a refund.

Counsel for the commissioner, however, argued that the consideration of three sections of the 1976 Act, namely s 188(1), s 38(2) and (3) and s 21, showed that the taxpayers' argument was wrong. Section 188(1) and (2) is in the following terms:

'(1) For the purposes of this section any loss incurred by a taxpayer shall be ascertained in accordance with the provisions of this Act for the calculation of assessable income.

(2) Any taxpayer who satisfies the Commissioner that he has, in any income year, incurred a loss shall, subject to this section, be entitled to claim that the loss be carried forward and deducted from or set off against the assessable income derived in the first income year after the income year in which the loss was incurred, so far as that income extends, and, so far as it cannot then be deducted or set off, be deducted from or set off against the assessable income derived in the next income year, and so on.'

It was as a result of the application of s 188(2) that the prior losses incurred by the taxpayers resulted in nil determinations in the years 1976 and 1977. Counsel for the commissioner argued that the distinction between assessable income and taxable income was crucial to s 188(1). If s 188 had intended that a loss could be a subject of an assessment, the set off in sub-s (2) would have been against taxable and not assessable income. Their Lordships consider that this argument is unsound and that in any event the terms of s 188 cannot assist in the proper construction of ss 19 and 25. It is purely fortuitous that the new determinations in this appeal arose as a result of the application of s 188; they could equally well have arisen because the taxpayers had made a loss in the year of assessment or because their assessable income had been exactly reduced to nil by the special exemptions.

Counsel for the commissioner next argued that s 38 contemplated that there could only be a year of assessment in relation to a taxpayer when he had taxable income. Section 38 so far as relevant for this argument is in the following terms—

'... (2) Subject to this Act, income tax shall be payable by every person on all income derived by him during the year for which the tax is payable.

(3) The year in which income is so derived is in this Act referred to as the income year, and the year for which income tax is payable is in this Act referred to as the year of assessment.'

If income tax was not payable by a taxpayer for a particular year then that year could not be a year of assessment and therefore no assessment had been made on it. Their Lordships reject this argument. Section 9 requires the taxpayer to make a return of

all income, assessable or not, derived during the *preceding* year (emphasis added),
and s 38(3) draws a distinction between the years in which income is derived and
assessed. Income is derived in one year which is the income year and the tax is
assessed in another year, probably the following, which is the year of assessment. If
in s 38(2) the words 'during the year' etc are read with 'shall be payable' rather than
with 'income derived' the whole thing falls into place and the subsections cannot
bear the construction which counsel for the commissioner seeks to place on them.
There can still be a year of assessment although the relevant income year produces
no income on which tax is payable.

Finally, counsel for the commissioner referred to s 21 which provides, inter alia,
that 'if any person makes default in furnishing any return' the commissioner—

> '... may make an assessment of the amount on which in his judgment tax
> ought to be levied and of the amount of that tax, and that person shall be liable
> to pay the tax so assessed, save in so far as he establishes on objection that the
> assessment is excessive or that he is not chargeable with tax.'

Counsel submitted that the final eight words of the section showed that if a person
had a nil tax liability no assessment should be made on it. Their Lordships do not so
construe these words. They appear to have been intended to cover a situation where
a person was not a taxpayer at all within the definition in s 2 at the relevant time, e g
because he had by then ceased to be an agent or trustee or had never been such, and
not to cover the situation where an admitted taxpayer has a nil taxable income.

Reference was also made to the Australian case of *Batagol v Comr of Taxation of
the Commonwealth of Australia* (1963) 109 CLR 243 where there was a similar issue
as to whether an assessment was time-barred. However, the wording of the statute
under consideration was significantly different and their Lordships agree with
Tompkins J that it is not of assistance in this case.

Their Lordships have no doubt that the arguments for the taxpayers are to be
preferred and that the commissioner's statutory duties under s 19 in relation to a
taxpayer's return extend not only to the production of a result which produces
taxable income but also to results which produce a nil return or a loss. Any other
construction would produce the anomalies and illogicalities already referred to.
Whichever of these three results the commissioner arrives at he has made an
assessment for the purposes of s 19 and hence s 25. It is to be noted that the latter
section uses the words 'assessed for income tax' that is to say 'for the purposes of
income tax' rather than 'to income tax'. Their Lordships cannot do better than quote
the following passage from the judgment of Tompkins J:

> 'In my opinion the expression "make assessments" in the context of s 17,
> means the process by which the Commissioner carries out his statutory
> obligation to ascertain the amount on which tax is payable and the amount of
> tax. I find nothing in the section, nor in the statutory scheme to justify a
> conclusion that the Commissioner only makes an assessment where he
> determines that there is tax payable. A conclusion that there is no amount on
> which tax is payable and that as a consequence there is no tax payable involves
> making an assessment from the returns and other information in his possession
> just as much as if the result of the assessment were to find that there was an
> amount on which tax was payable and consequently there was tax payable.'
> [The reference is to s 17 of the 1954 Act which was later replaced by s 19 of the
> 1976 Act.]

In reaching this conclusion their Lordships are fortified by two further
considerations. In the first place the purpose of s 25(1) is to achieve finality and to
enable the taxpayer and the commissioner to close the books and dispose of their
papers after the stipulated period. The exercise required to be carried out by the
commissioner in terms of s 19 is capable of producing three different results namely:
(1) that the taxpayer has taxable income; (2) that he has no taxable income;

and (3) that he has a loss which he may carry forward in terms of s 188. To accept the argument of counsel for the commissioner and the reasoning of the Court of Appeal would mean that only in the first instance would finality be achieved whereas in the other two the commissioner could reopen his determination at any time in the future. A result which would appear to be 'contrary to the spirit of section 25', to quote the words of Cooke J in *Comr of Inland Revenue v V H Farnsworth Ltd* [1984] 1 NZLR 428 at 430.

In the second place the provisions of Part III of the 1976 Act headed 'Objections to Assessments' envisage that such objections will be dealt with by the Taxation Review Authority, a body particularly experienced in taxation matters. It would be entirely logical that the legislature should have intended that all matters involving determinations by the commissioner consequent on receipt of a taxpayer's return as to tax payable or not payable should be dealt with by that body. Such a result would follow from the conclusions which their Lordships have reached. If on the other hand counsel for the commissioner's argument were correct it would mean that the determinations by the commissioner resulting in a nil payment of tax or in a loss could only be challenged by a taxpayer in the ordinary courts by judicial review or some other legal process. This would appear to defeat substantially the purpose of Part III.

It only remains to refer to one further matter to which the Court of Appeal had some regard namely the amendment to s 19 occasioned by s 20 of the Income Tax Amendment Act 1980. The amendment of s 19 required the commissioner to make determinations of losses and provided that such determinations were to be treated as assessments. This amendment, it was said, reflected the common understanding in income tax practice that a letter confirming the assessment of the amount of a loss to be carried forward under s 188 was not an assessment. It is noteworthy that the amendment does not deal with a situation where there is no loss but simply no taxable income. Had the construction of the relevant section of the 1976 Act been in dubio it might have been appropriate to turn to the amendments for assistance. However, as their Lordships are of the opinion that the construction and intention of those sections are clear, it follows that the construction cannot be affected by the later amending Act.

Their Lordships will therefore humbly advise Her Majesty that this appeal should be allowed, the order of the Court of Appeal set aside and the order of Tompkins J restored. The commissioner must pay the taxpayers' costs in the Court of Appeal and before their Lordships' Board.

Appeal allowed with costs.

Solicitors: *Linklaters & Paines* (for the taxpayers); *Allen & Overy* (for the commissioner).

Rengan Krishnan Esq   Barrister.

Andrews v King (Inspector of Taxes)

CHANCERY DIVISION
SIR NICOLAS BROWNE-WILKINSON V-C
26, 28 JUNE 1991

Emoluments from office or employment – Employment – Meaning – Contract of service or contract for services – Whether taxpayer self-employed gangmaster or employee – Whether taxpayer liable to deduct tax from the earnings of his fellow workers under PAYE system – Income and Corporation Taxes Act 1970, s 109 – Income Tax (Employments) Regulations 1973, SI 1973/334, reg 29.

The taxpayer was engaged by S Ltd, a firm of potato merchants, on various days between 1 March 1985 and 13 March 1987, in connection with potato picking and/or potato grading. During this period he worked only for S Ltd. S Ltd would contact the taxpayer to inform him how many men were required—six men (if picking) or four men (if grading). The taxpayer would accordingly select and contact three or five men, but none of them was obliged to accept the work he offered them. The taxpayer drove the other workers to the site in his own van but the cost of the petrol was shared between the taxpayer and the other workers. S Ltd supplied the machinery and equipment for the work. The price for the work was agreed from time to time between S Ltd and the taxpayer and the other workers. There was no holiday pay nor was any payment made if the work was prevented as a result of adverse weather conditions. These terms applied to the taxpayer and the other workers alike. S Ltd decided the time, place and nature of the work carried out by the taxpayer and the other workers and occasionally their work would be supervised by an employee of S Ltd. The various functions of the jobs were carried out by the taxpayer and the other workers in rotation. S Ltd paid the taxpayer in cash. After making allowances for each person's petrol contribution, the taxpayer divided the balance of the payment equally between himself and the other workers. S Ltd never supplied the taxpayer with any written statement of the amount of the earnings and did not give any indication that any tax had been deducted or national insurance paid. The taxpayer had not kept any records of the payments he had received. An inspector of taxes took the view that the taxpayer was a self-employed gangmaster and raised assessments to income tax under Sch D, Case I on the taxpayer for the years 1984–85, 1985–86 and 1986–87 and corresponding Class IV national insurance contributions on his profits as a gangmaster. The inspector also made determinations under reg 29[a] of the Income Tax (Employments) Regulations 1973, SI 1973/334, (the 1973 regulations) on the grounds that the taxpayer had paid emoluments to the other workers from which he should have deducted tax under the PAYE system. The General Commissioners found that the taxpayer was a self-employed gangmaster, that the various men in his gang were employees and that the payments made by the taxpayer to the men were payments of emoluments and on those grounds upheld the assessments under Sch D, Case I and the determinations under reg 29 of the 1973 regulations. The taxpayer appealed to the High Court contending that on the facts found the true and only reasonable conclusion open to the commissioners was that the taxpayer was not a self-employed gangmaster and that he was not the employer of the other workers for the purposes of the 1973 regulations.

Held – (1) The fundamental test to be applied in determining whether services were performed under a contract for services or under a contract of service was the test of whether the person performing the services was in business on his own account. The

---

a   Section 54(1), so far as material, is set out at p 493 *c d*, post

General Commissioners had failed to apply that test. On the facts, by reference to the relevant legal principles, it was not open to the commissioners to conclude that the taxpayer was in business on his own account. Accordingly, the taxpayer was not a self-employed gangmaster.

(2)(a) Applying reg 3(1) of the 1973 regulations (to which the commissioners had not been referred), the taxpayer and the other workers worked under 'the general control and management' of S Ltd. Accordingly, S Ltd was 'the principal employer' and as such was deemed to be the employer for the purpose of the 1973 regulations. Regulation 29 would therefore permit a determination to be served on S Ltd but not on the taxpayer. It was not open to the commissioners to hold that because the taxpayer paid emoluments to the other workers, he was to be treated as their employer for the purposes of the 1973 regulations.

(b) Alternatively, the conclusion that the taxpayer was in fact the employer of the other workers was a conclusion of mixed fact and law which could not be reached on a proper application of the referable law.

Accordingly the appeal would be allowed and the assessment under Sch D and the determination under reg 29 would be discharged.

Notes

For the distinction between employment and self-employment, see Simon's Taxes E4.202–203.

For an outline of the PAYE system, see ibid, E4.902.

For the Income and Corporation Taxes Act 1970, s 109 (now the Income and Corporation Taxes Act 1988, s 18), see ibid, Part G1.

For the Income Tax (Employments) Regulations 1973, SI 1973/334, reg 29, see ibid, Division H2.

Cases referred to in judgment

Edwards (Inspector of Taxes) v Bairstow [1956] AC 14, [1955] 3 All ER 48, 36 TC 207, HL.

Lee Ting Sang v Chung Chi-Keung [1990] 2 AC 374, PC.

Market Investigations Ltd v Minister of Social Security [1969] 2 QB 173, [1968] 3 All ER 732, CA.

Nethermere (St Neots) Ltd v Gardiner [1984] ICR 612, CA.

O'Kelly v Trusthouse Forte plc [1984] 1 QB 90, [1983] 3 All ER 456, CA.

Case also cited

Fall (Inspector of Taxes) v Hitchen [1973] STC 66, [1973] 1 WLR 286, [1973] 1 All ER 368, 49 TC 433.

Case stated

1. At meetings of the Commissioners for the general purposes of the income tax for the division of Spalding in the county of Lincolnshire held on 10 June 1988 and 29 September 1988, Robert Leslie Andrews (the taxpayer) appealed against the following assessments to income tax.

Year of assessment	Sch D, Case 1	Amount	Class IV NIC
1984–85	Gangmaster	£13,500	£13,500
1985–86	Gangmaster	£14,250	£14,250
1986–87	Gangmaster	£15,000	£15,000

a   Determinations under reg 29 of the Income Tax (Employments) Regulations 1973, SI 1973/334

1985–86	£10,683
1986–87	£11,250

2. Shortly stated, the questions for the commissioners' determination were:

b   (i) whether the assessments on the profits as a gangmaster were correctly made under Sch D, Case I or whether, as the taxpayer contended, those profits should have been assessed under Sch E.

(ii) whether the determinations under reg 29 were correctly made or whether as the taxpayer contended the other men working in his gang were fellow employees or self-employed workers.

c   (iii) the quantum of the assessments and determinations under appeal.

3. The taxpayer was represented by his solicitor Mr P G Frost of Peter Frost and Co, 1 London Road, Spalding, Lincolnshire. The respondent (the inspector) was represented by James William Main (an inspector of taxes). The only evidence was given orally by the taxpayer.

4. On the basis of the oral evidence given by the taxpayer the commissioners

d   found the following facts: (a) The taxpayer, who was born in 1955, was engaged by J W Stanberry Ltd (Stanberrys), potato merchants of Moulton Chapel near Spalding, on diverse days between on or about 1 March 1985 to on or about 13 March 1987 in connection with potato picking and/or potato grading. During this period the taxpayer worked only for Stanberrys. (b) Arrangements were made between the taxpayer and Stanberrys each day usually on the telephone after 6 pm

e   in respect of the following day's work; Stanberrys informed the taxpayer as to whether they required a gang at all and if so whether of six men (if picking) or four men (if grading) for the following day. The taxpayer selected and contacted the men necessary, supplied their transport and arranged for them (together with himself) to be on site for the necessary work for 7·00 am or 7·30 am the following morning. If only four men were required then the taxpayer would arrange for three other persons

f   to report for work. If six men were required, the taxpayer would select two additional men from whoever might be available. None of the other men were obliged to accept the work offered by the taxpayer. (c) Transport was in the taxpayer's van and the men transported and the taxpayer shared the cost of petrol. The taxpayer and the other men used to club together for the petrol money. (d) The machinery and equipment for the work was supplied by Stanberrys or by their contractor or agent.

g   A Mr Gray, an employee/contractor of Stanberrys, was responsible for the machinery. (e) The price for the work was agreed from time to time between Stanberrys and the taxpayer and the men accompanying the taxpayer at either an hourly rate or a price per tonne depending on the nature of the work that was being done. (f) There was no holiday pay nor was there any payment made if the work was washed out. These terms applied to the taxpayer and the other men alike. (g) Mr

h   Stanberry, the managing director of Stanberrys, or Mr Gray decided the time place and nature of the work carried out by the taxpayer and the other men: they (Mr Stanberry or Mr Gray) would decide which farm and what type of potato would be picked. From time to time Mr Gray would supervise the work of the taxpayer and the other men. The taxpayer and these men would carry out the various functions required by the jobs in rotation. (h) All payments made by Stanberrys for the work

j   were made in cash to the taxpayer who signed for the money at the end of the week's work (usually on a Friday). After making allowances for each person's petrol contribution, the balance of the payment was divided between the taxpayer and the other workers equally. (i) Stanberrys never supplied the taxpayer with any written statement as to the amount of the earnings and did not give any indication that any tax had been deducted or national insurance paid. (j) The taxpayer had previously been in an employment situation with another party and had then received a wage slip showing tax deducted and national insurance paid. (k) The taxpayer did not keep any records of the payments he received. (l) The taxpayer was not prepared to reveal to the inspector or to the commissioners the names and addresses of the other men engaged in the work.

5. The commissioners were referred to the following authorities:

Fall (Inspector of Taxes) v Hitchen [1973] STC 66, [1973] 1 WLR 286.

Ferguson v John Dawson & Partners (Contractors) Ltd [1976] 1 WLR 1213.

Massey v Crown Life Insurance Co [1978] 1 WLR 676.

6. It was contended on behalf of the taxpayer that the taxpayer was an employee of Stanberrys and not self-employed. After reference to the cases and authorities referred to in para 5 above, the taxpayer maintained that Stanberrys, by their employee/contractor, Mr Gray, gave instructions and supervised the work and disciplined the men; that the taxpayer received the same payment as all the men, save for petrol money; that the taxpayer believed that tax and national insurance was being deducted; that tools and equipment were provided by Stanberrys; that the hours and times of work were specified by Stanberrys and that work was paid for by the hour or as piece work at the end of each week; that nothing was said or agreed about dismissal; accordingly, having regard to the above that the taxpayer was an employee.

7. It was contended on behalf of the inspector: (i) that the taxpayer was part of the gangmaster system prevailing in Lincolnshire and East Anglia. The gangmaster was the person who was the contact for and was in control of the supply of labour and received the payment; some gangs were large and some small; (ii) that, having regard to the oral evidence of the taxpayer and in particular the facts that the taxpayer having received his instructions from Stanberrys thereafter arranged everything including who would be in the gang and their transport, received payment for the gang, was not provided with a payslip or a P60 and had refused to give the names and addresses of the other men with whom he worked, the taxpayer was a self-employed person and not a casual farm employee. Accordingly, the Sch D assessments should be upheld; (iii) that it followed from the fact that the taxpayer was a gangmaster, and from the control which admittedly he exercised over the affairs of his gang, that for tax purposes the members of his gang were his employees, and the payment they received were subject to tax under Sch E; (iv) that the taxpayer had admitted in his oral evidence that he was the person who made the payments of wages to the various men in his gang. In reg 2 of the Income Tax (Employments) Regulations 1973, SI 1973/334, (the 1973 regulations) an employer meant 'any person paying emoluments'. Again taking all the evidence into account the taxpayer was the employer of the men in his gang and accordingly the reg 29 determinations should be upheld.

8. The commissioners held (i) that the assessments under Sch D, Case I had been correctly made and that the taxpayer should not have been assessed under Sch E on the grounds that the taxpayer was a self-employed gangmaster and was not employed by Stanberrys; and (ii) that the determinations under reg 29 of the 1973 regulations had been correctly made on the grounds that the taxpayer was a gangmaster who made payments of emoluments to the various men in his gang who the commissioners found to be employees and the taxpayer was therefore the employer of the men in his gang.

9. Accordingly following the commissioners' determination in para 8 above they determined the assessments and determinations in the following amounts as agreed between the parties:

Year of assessment	Sch D, Case I	Class IV NIC
1984–85	£1,108	£1,108
1985–86	£2,528	£2,528
1986–87	£3,365	£3,365

Determinations

a   under reg 29

1985–86	£9,454
1986–87	£12,290

10. The taxpayer immediately on the determination of the appeal, declared to the commissioners his dissatisfaction therewith as being erroneous in point of law and in *b* due course required them to state a case for the opinion of the High Court pursuant to the Taxes Management Act 1970, s 56.

11. The question of law for the opinion of the court was whether on the basis of the facts found by the commissioners, at para 4 above, their determination, as set out at para 8 above, was erroneous in a point of law.

c   *Giles Goodfellow* for the taxpayer.
   Launcelot Henderson for the Crown.

SIR NICOLAS BROWNE-WILKINSON V-C. This is an appeal by way of case stated from a decision of the Commissioners for the general purposes of the income tax for the division of Spalding in Lincolnshire. First, the commissioners upheld *d* assessments made by the Revenue against Mr Andrews, the taxpayer, under Sch D, Case I as a gangmaster in respect of the years 1984–85, 1985–86 and 1986–87. Second, the commissioners upheld determinations made by the Revenue under reg 29 of the Income Tax (Employments) Regulations 1973, SI 1973/334, (the 1973 regulations) that the taxpayer was accountable in respect of payments made to members of the potato-picking gang organised by him by way of PAYE deduction in respect of the *e* years 1985–86 and 1986–87. The taxpayer appeals against both decisions on the grounds: first, that he was not a self-employed gangmaster assessable under Sch D; second, that he was not the employer of the other members of the potato-picking gang and therefore there was no power to make a determination against him under reg 29.

I will take the facts from the case stated. The taxpayer was engaged by J W *f* Stanberry Ltd (Stanberrys), potato merchants near Spalding, on a number of days between 1 March 1985 and 13 March 1987 in connection with potato picking and/or grading. During that period the taxpayer worked only for Stanberrys.

Each day arrangements were made between the taxpayer and Stanberrys (usually on the telephone after 6.00 pm) in respect of the following day's work. Stanberrys told the taxpayer whether or not they required a gang at all and if so whether of six *g* men (if engaged in picking) or four men (if engaged in grading). The taxpayer selected and contacted the necessary men, supplied their transport and arranged for them (together with himself) to be on site for work the following morning at 7·00 am or 7·30 am. If only four men were required the taxpayer arranged for three other persons to report for work; if six men were required the taxpayer would select two additional men from those available. None of the other men selected was obliged to *h* accept the work offered by the taxpayer.

Transport to the place of work was in a van belonging to the taxpayer. The taxpayer and the other members of the gang transported shared the cost of petrol. All of the machinery and equipment for the work done was supplied by Stanberrys or their contractors. Mr Gray, an employee of Stanberrys, was responsible for the machinery.

j The price for the work done for Stanberrys was agreed from time to time between Stanberrys on the one hand and the taxpayer and the men in the gang on the other hand at either an hourly rate or a price per tonne depending on the nature of the work done.

Neither the taxpayer nor the members of the gang were entitled to holiday pay or to any payment if the work was washed out.

Mr Stanberry, the managing director, or Mr Gray decided the time, place and nature of the work to be carried out by the taxpayer and the other members of the gang. Mr Stanberry or Mr Gray would decide which farm and what type of potato would be picked. From time to time, Mr Gray would supervise the work of the taxpayer and the other men. The taxpayer and the other members of the gang would carry out the various functions connected with potato picking in rotation, that is to say, none of them had any fixed job.

All payments made by Stanberrys for the work were made in cash to the taxpayer who signed for the money at the end of the week's work (usually on Friday). After making allowance for the personal contribution of each member of the gang to the cost of petrol, the balance of the payment received from Stanberrys was immediately divided between the taxpayer and the other members of the gang in equal shares. Stanberrys never provided the taxpayer with any written statement as to the amount of earnings and did not give any indication that any tax had been deducted or national insurance paid. The taxpayer had previously been in employment and had received a wage slip showing tax deducted and national insurance paid. The taxpayer himself did not keep any records of the payments he received from Stanberrys, and he was not prepared to reveal to the inspector or commissioners the names and addresses of the other men involved in the gang.

The taxpayer contended before the commissioners that he was an employee of Stanberrys and therefore should not have been assessed as a self-employed gangmaster under Sch D. He further contended that the other members of the gang were not employed by him but by Stanberrys.

The commissioners reached their conclusions in para 8 of the case stated:

'We, the Commissioners, who heard the Appeal, held that (i) the assessments under Case I of Schedule D of the Income and Corporation Taxes Act 1970 were correctly made and that [the taxpayer] should not have been assessed under Schedule E on the grounds that [the taxpayer] was a self-employed Gangmaster and was not employed by Stanberrys; (ii) the determinations under Regulation 29 . . . were correctly made on the grounds that [the taxpayer] [was] a Gangmaster who made payments of emoluments to the various men in his gang, who we found to be employees, and [the taxpayer] was therefore the employer of the men in his gang.'

I have no doubt that on the primary facts found by the commissioners I would have reached a different conclusion on each of those issues. But an appeal to the High Court against the commissioners' decision lies only on a point of law. Therefore, the commissioners' decision must stand unless it is shown that they misdirected themselves in law or that their decision was such that no tribunal properly directing itself in law could have reached that result (see *Edwards (Inspector of Taxes) v Bairstow* [1956] AC 14, 36 TC 207).

It is further established by the authorities that the question whether or not the contract between the parties is a contract of employment is a mixed question of fact and law. Unless it was impossible in law for the commissioners to reach the conclusion that the taxpayer was not employed by Stanberrys, or was the employer of the other members of the gang, the commissioners' decision must stand (see *O'Kelly v Trusthouse Forte plc* [1984] 1 QB 90; *Nethermere (St Neots) Ltd v Gardiner* [1984] ICR 612; and *Lee Ting Sang v Chung Chi-Keung* [1990] 2 AC 374).

On that basis, I consider first the assessments made against the taxpayer under Sch D on the footing that he was a self-employed gangmaster. Where a person provides services for another there is no single satisfactory test on the basis of which one can decide whether those services are provided by that person as an independent contractor under a contract for services as opposed to an employee under a contract of employment.

In the *Lee Ting Sang* case Lord Griffiths, giving the opinion of the Privy Council, indicated (at 382) that the approach to the question whether or not there was a

contract of employment had never been put better than by Cooke J in *Market*
a *Investigations Ltd v Minister of Social Security* [1969] 2 QB 173 at 184–185—

> '. . . the fundamental test to be applied is this: "Is the person who has engaged
> himself to perform these services performing them as a person in business on
> his own account?" If the answer to that question is "yes," then the contract is a
> contract for services. If the answer is "no," then the contract is a contract of
> service. No exhaustive list has been compiled and perhaps no exhaustive list
b> can be compiled of the considerations which are relevant in determining that
> question, nor can strict rules be laid down as to the relative weight which the
> various considerations should carry in particular cases. The most that can be
> said is that control will no doubt always have to be considered, although it can
> no longer be regarded as the sole determining factor; and that factors which
> may be of importance are such matters as whether the man performing the
c> services provides his own equipment, whether he hires his own helpers, what
> degree of financial risk he takes, what degree of responsibility for investment
> and management he has, and whether and how far he has an opportunity of
> profiting from sound management in the performance of his task.'

It does not appear from the case stated that the commissioners had the benefit of
d much relevant guidance as to the approach to the question whether or not a
particular contract constituted a contract of employment or a contract for services.
The basic question is whether it can be said that the taxpayer was in business on his
own account. That is not a question which the commissioners put to themselves,
nor is there any consideration of the various factors which Cooke J indicated might
be relevant.

e   Beyond the selection of the members of the gang the taxpayer had no rights of
control. Where and when the work was to be done were matters for Stanberrys. The
work of the whole gang including the taxpayer was supervised by Stanberrys. There
is no indication that the taxpayer had any powers of control over the members of the
gang. The evidence was that he was subject to the control of Stanberrys.

Turning to the question whether the taxpayer provided equipment for carrying
f out the work, it is clear that he did not. The only equipment he provided was a van
which was not used to do the work but to get to the place of work. Even in relation
to the van, the direct cost of getting there in the form of petrol was not paid by him
alone but was shared by the other members of the gang.

As to the question whether or not he hired his own helpers, he certainly selected
them but he did not himself pay them any wages. He did not engage men, pay them
g and then provide a gang en bloc to Stanberrys in return for a fixed charge. Having
selected his gang, they all went together to the place of work selected by Stanberrys
and the total sum paid for the work by Stanberrys was a sum which all the members
of the gang had agreed, not the taxpayer by himself. The net proceeds, after
deduction of petrol money, were divided equally between them. In my judgment, it
is impossible to call that 'hiring helpers'.

h   As to the question whether or not the taxpayer was running any financial risk, I
can see none beyond the risk run by many casual labourers in agriculture that if
there is no work because of weather conditions there is no payment.

There was no question of investment or management as far as the taxpayer was
concerned. There was no question of his profiting from sound management since he
took the same reward as all the other members of the gang. He had no extra
j remuneration reflecting in any way the quality of his management in the selection
and production of the gang at the work place.

Looking at those elements and standing back and considering the case as a whole,
one asks the basic question: Was the taxpayer in business on his own account? I
cannot see that he was carrying on any business. One is prompted to ask: What
business could he be said to be carrying on? The essence of business is that it is
carried on with a view to profit. But his position as gangmaster, if that be the right

description, produced no profit as such. All he got out of his activities was the same return as the other members of the gang he brought along, all of whom shared the fruits of their joint labours and the expenses of getting to work. True it is that he made the arrangements with Stanberrys and received the payment but only for equal division among the gang. In the absence of some profit to him arising from his activities as selector of the gang I cannot see that he any more than other members of the gang can be described as being in business on his own account.

For those reasons, I am satisfied that the commissioners for want of the right principles having been placed before them reached a conclusion that was simply not open to them as a matter of law. The conclusion that the taxpayer was in business on his own account and taxable under Sch D is incapable of being upheld consistently with any of the factors which in law are relevant to the determination of that mixed question of fact and law. I therefore allow the appeal against the assessments under Sch D.

I turn to the determination served on the taxpayer under reg 29 of the 1973 regulations. Regulation 29(1) provides as follows:

'Where it appears to the Inspector that there may be tax payable under Regulation 26 which has not been paid to the Collector nor certified by him in pursuance of Regulation 27, 27A, 30 or 32, the Inspector may determine to the best of his judgment the amount of such tax and shall serve notice of such determination on the employer.'

It is to be noted that a determination under reg 29 can be served only on somebody answering the description 'the employer'.

Under the PAYE system the employer has to pay wages to his employees under deduction of tax and account to the Revenue for the net tax which he has deducted. Regulation 2 contains the following definition of 'employer': '"employer" means any person paying emoluments'. The Crown relied on reg 2 before the commissioners. Against that background I turn again to read para 8 of the commissioners' reasons—

'... (ii) the determinations ... were correctly made on the grounds that [the taxpayer] [was] a Gangmaster who made payments of emoluments to the various men in his gang, who we found to be employees, and [the taxpayer] was therefore the employer of the men in his gang.'

That finding is rather obscure. Although the commissioners find that the other members of the gang were employees, they do not expressly find whether they were the employees of Stanberrys or the employees of the taxpayer. One view of that sentence is that they are seeking to apply reg 2. While considering that the other members of the gang were in ordinary terms the employees of Stanberrys, by reason of the fact that the taxpayer received the payment from Stanberrys and then divided it among all the members of the gang he had made payments of emoluments to members of the gang and therefore under reg 2 was to be treated as 'the employer'. The other view is that they were finding that the members of the gang were in the ordinary sense and ordinary law employed by the taxpayer.

I tend to the view that the commissioners were seeking to apply reg 2. If that was their approach, the Crown now concedes solely for the purposes of this case that the commissioners' decision was erroneous in point of law. The commissioners were not referred to reg 3(1) which provides as follows:

'Where an employee works under the general control and management of a person who is not his immediate employer, that person (referred to in this and the next following Regulation as "the principal employer") shall be deemed to be the employer for the purpose of these Regulations, and the immediate employer shall furnish the principal employer with such particulars of the employee's emoluments as may be necessary to enable the principal employer to comply with the provisions of these Regulations.'

Applying that regulation to the present case, the gang including the taxpayer
worked under the general control and management of Stanberrys. They were

a therefore 'the principal employer' within the meaning of reg 3. As a result, reg 3
requires Stanberrys to be treated for all the purposes of the regulations as 'the
employer'. It is accepted that that provision overrides what is otherwise the definition
of 'employer' in reg 2. It follows that when one comes to reg 29 providing for a
determination to be served on 'the employer' the provision operates so as to permit a

b determination to be served on Stanberrys but not the taxpayer.

If contrary to my tentative view the commissioners were holding in para 8(ii) of
the case that the members of the gang were in fact the employees of the taxpayer
and not the employees of Stanberrys, in my judgment that was a conclusion of mixed
fact and law which was incapable of being reached by the proper application of the
referable law.

c I can see no feature of the case which could suggest that the taxpayer employed
the members of the gang apart from the fact that he selected those members who
were to work on any given day. The taxpayer did not pay the members of the gang
wages; they shared the take equally. He did not pay their expenses. They shared the
costs of petrol. He did not control where, when or how they worked; Stanberrys did.
He worked alongside them and interchanged jobs with him. There is no indication

d on the findings that he had any authority or power over them as to the way in which
they carried out their work. I can see no features indicating that the taxpayer was
the employer of the other members of the gang. Accordingly, I can see no virtue in
remitting the matter to the commissioners for the elucidation of what they meant in
para 8(ii). Whatever they meant by those words, the conclusion they reached was an
impossible one in law.

e In my view, the determination under reg 29 was invalid. I will therefore allow the
appeal and quash the assessment under Sch D and the determination under reg 29.

Appeal allowed with costs.

Solicitors: *Peter Frost & Co,* Spalding (for the taxpayer); *Solicitor of Inland Revenue.*

f
Rengan Krishnan Esq   Barrister.

Swires (Inspector of Taxes) v Renton   *a*

CHANCERY DIVISION
HOFFMANN J
20 JUNE 1991

Capital gains tax – Settlement – Discretionary power to appoint capital – Whether **b**
exercise of power created new settlement or grafted new trusts onto old settlement –
Whether appointment amounted to a deemed disposal – Capital Gains Tax Act 1979,
s 54(1).

On 21 January 1954, Jack Meek (the settlor), made a settlement (the 1954 settlement)
which, during an appointed period, comprised (i) a discretionary trust of income in   **c**
favour of his wife, his daughter (Isabelle) and her husband and two sons; and (ii) a
discretionary power empowering the trustees 'to pay or apply any part or parts of . . .
the trust fund . . . freed and released from the trusts affecting the same' to or for the
benefit of any member of the class of beneficiaries. On 16 June 1981 (within the
appointed period) the trustees of the settlement (Michael Renton (the trustee) and
Isabelle) pursuant to the discretionary power vested in them executed a deed of   **d**
appointment which was stated to be 'supplemental' to the settlement. The deed
divided the trust fund into two parts by reference to a schedule of assets irrevocably
appointing (a) one part to Isabelle absolutely, and (b) the other part (the appointed
fund) on trust to pay the income to Isabelle for life, with power to the trustees,
during Isabelle's life, 'to pay transfer or apply the whole or any parts of the capital of
the appointed fund to or for Isabelle's benefit freed and discharged from the trusts   **e**
affecting the same under the [1954] Settlement and this deed', with remainder as to
both capital and income, for Isabelle's sons, in equal shares, absolutely. It was
accepted by the trustees that the first appointment to Isabelle absolutely gave rise to
a deemed disposal of that part of the trust fund under s 54(1)*a* of the Capital Gains
Tax Act 1979 and capital gains tax was assessed and paid accordingly. However, the
inspector of taxes took the view that the second appointment had also amounted to   **f**
a deemed disposal and he raised a further assessment to capital gains tax on the
grounds that a new and separate settlement of the appointed fund had been created
and the trustees, as trustees of the new settlement, had become absolutely entitled
to the appointed fund against themselves as the trustees of the 1954 settlement within
the meaning of s 54(1). The trustee appealed to a Special Commissioner, contending
that the exercise by the trustees (himself and Isabelle) of the power of appointment   **g**
had not created a new settlement of the appointed fund but had merely grafted new
trusts onto the 1954 settlement. The Special Commissioner allowed the trustee's
appeal and discharged the assessment on the grounds (i) that there was sufficient
evidence both in the documents and in the way in which the trustees had exercised
the power of appointment to support the conclusion that the trustees had not
intended to take the appointed fund out of the 1954 settlement and resettle it; (ii)   **h**
that the trustees had not become absolutely entitled to the appointed fund as against
themselves as trustees of the 1954 settlement; and (iii) that therefore there had been
no deemed disposal of the appointed fund under s 54(1). The Crown appealed.

Held – Where, in the original settlement, the trust power was expressed in terms   .
wide enough to permit the creation of a new settlement of the trust assets, the   **j**
question as to whether a new settlement had been created when the trust power was
exercised depended on whether the trustees, in exercising the power, had intended
to create a new settlement of the trust assets. In the instant case the language of the

---

a   Section 54(1), so far as material, is set out at p 493 *c d*, post

a   deed of appointment clearly demonstrated that the trustees, in exercising the trust
power contained in the 1954 settlement, had not intended to create a new settlement
of the appointed fund but rather, had intended to subject the appointed fund to new
trusts grafted onto the 1954 settlement. Accordingly, the trustees had not become
absolutely entitled to the appointed fund as against themselves as trustees of the 1954
settlement and there had been no deemed disposal of the appointed fund under
s 54(1). The Crown's appeal would therefore be dismissed.

b

Notes

For the liability to capital gains tax when a person becomes absolutely entitled to
settled property as against the trustee, see Simon's Taxes C4.208.
   For the Capital Gains Tax Act 1979, s 54(1), see ibid, Part G3.

c

Case referred to in judgment

Bond (Inspector of Taxes) v Pickford [1982] STC 403; [1983] STC 517, 57 TC 301,
   CA.
Hart (Inspector of Taxes) v Briscoe, Hoare Trustees v Gardner (Inspector of Taxes)
d   [1978] STC 89, [1979] Ch 1, 10, [1978] 1 All ER 791, 52 TC 53.
Pilkington v IRC [1964] AC 612, [1962] 3 All ER 622, 40 TC 416, HL.
Roome v Edwards (Inspector of Taxes) [1981] STC 96, [1982] AC 279, [1981] 1 All
   ER 736, 54 TC 359, HL.

Case also cited
e
Ewart v Taylor (Inspector of Taxes) [1983] STC 721, 57 TC 401.

Case stated

   1. At a hearing before a Commissioner for the special purposes of the Income Tax
f   Acts, held on 12 and 13 July 1989, Mr M P Renton (the trustee) appealed against
the following assessment to capital gains tax:

Year of assessment	Amount of assessment
1981–82	£116,799

[Paragraph 2 listed the agreed documents admitted before the commissioner.]
g   3. Shortly stated, the question in dispute between the parties was whether the
execution, by the trustees of the settlement dated 21 January 1954 (the 1954
settlement), of a deed of appointment dated 16 June 1981, in pursuance of a
discretionary power given to them under the terms of the 1954 settlement, had given
rise to a deemed disposal of the appointed assets within the meaning of s 54(1) of the
Capital Gains Tax Act 1979 (the 1979 Act).
h   4. No witnesses were called by either party and the facts were agreed.
   5. The following cases were referred to:
Bond (Inspector of Taxes) v Pickford [1982] STC 403; [1983] STC 517.
Ewart v Taylor (Inspector of Taxes) [1983] STC 721.
Hart (Inspector of Taxes) v Briscoe [1978] STC 89, [1979] Ch 1.
Roome v Edwards (Inspector of Taxes) [1981] STC 96, [1982] AC 279.
j   6. It was contended by the trustee that, in the light of the authorities referred to
above and on a proper construction of s 54(1) of the 1979 Act, the exercise by the
trustees of the power of appointment contained in the 1954 settlement did not create
a new settlement of the appointed fund and that, therefore, it did not amount to a
deemed disposal of the appointed fund within the meaning of s 54(1), with the result
that no capital gains tax was chargeable and the appeal should be allowed, and the
assessment should be discharged.

7. It was contended on behalf of the Crown that the exercise by the trustees of the power of appointment contained in the 1954 settlement did create a new and *a* separate settlement of the appointed fund and that the appointment resulted in a deemed disposal of the appointed fund within the meaning of s 54(1) of the 1979 Act, and the assessment should be confirmed.

8. The commissioner who heard the appeal took time to consider his decision and gave it in writing. It was issued on 9 August 1989, and was attached to the case as an annexe and formed part of the case. In the decision the commissioner set out the *b* facts and the contentions of the parties and the reasons for his decision.

9. Immediately after the determination of the appeal the Crown, by letter dated 10 August 1989, expressed its dissatisfaction therewith as being erroneous in point of law, and in due course required the commissioner to state a case for the opinion of the High Court pursuant to the Taxes Management Act 1970, s 56.

10. The question of law for the opinion of the court was whether the commissioner's *c* decision as set out in the decision was correct.

DECISION

This appeal is brought by Mr Renton (the trustee) in his capacity as a trustee of the Jack Meek settlement against an assessment to capital gains tax in the sum of *d* £116,799. The assessment, which was a further assessment, relates to the year of assessment 1981–82 and was issued on 5 May 1987.

The facts are not in dispute and are conveniently set out in an agreed statement of facts. I may summarise them shortly as follows. On 21 January 1954, Jack Meek (the settlor) made a settlement (the 1954 settlement) in which he transferred to trustees a trust fund to be held on trust during an appointed period. The 1954 settlement *e* provided that, subject to a discretionary power to appoint capital, the trustees were to pay, divide or apply the income of the trust fund in their absolute discretion to or between or for the maintenance, support or benefit of any one or more to the exclusion of the other or others of a class consisting of the settlor's wife, Sophie Meek, his daughter, Isabelle Rubin, his daughter's husband, Harold Rubin, and the two sons of Isabelle and Harold Rubin, Anthony and Mark. *f*

The settlor died on 5 November 1959, Sophie Meek, his widow (the mother of Isabelle) died on 14 February 1974, Harold Rubin (Isabelle's husband) died on 14 October 1976. The only living members of the class are therefore Isabelle and her two sons, Anthony and Mark.

On 16 June 1981, the trustees of the 1954 settlement (then being the trustee and Isabelle) executed a deed of appointment in exercise of the discretionary power to *g* appoint capital.

The power was contained in clause 3 of the 1954 settlement which, by then, empowered the trustees at their absolute discretion to pay or apply any part or parts of the capital of the trust fund to or for the benefit of all or any one or more to the exclusion of the other or others of the specified class freed and released from the trusts concerning the same. *h*

The effect of the exercise of the power of appointment was to designate part of the assets of the trust fund, set out in a schedule to the deed of appointment (which in fact consisted of a number of houses in Knutsford and Hale Barns in Cheshire) as the appointed fund and to make two irrevocable appointments. (1) Of the trust fund and the income thereof less the assets comprised in the appointed fund (which consisted of various shares and securities) to Isabelle absolutely. (2) Of the appointed *j* fund on trust to pay the income to Isabelle during her life with power at any time during her life to pay, transfer or apply the whole or any part or parts of the capital of the appointed fund to or for Isabelle's benefit freed and discharged from the trusts affecting the same under the settlement or under the deed of appointment. Subject to that trust and to every exercise of that power the appointed fund was to be held in trust as to both capital and income for Mark and Anthony in equal shares absolutely.

It is accepted by the trustees that the appointment of the trust fund, less the appointed fund, to Isabelle absolutely gave rise to a deemed disposal of that part of the trust fund within the meaning of s 54(1) of the 1979 Act, with the result that capital gains tax became payable in respect of the gain shown up by that disposal. The trustees were assessed on 16 May 1983 in the sum of £35,655 in respect of that gain and the tax has been paid.

The assessment against which this appeal is brought was made on the basis that the appointment of the appointed funds on the basis I have described also gave rise to a deemed disposal within the meaning of s 54(1) of the 1979 Act, with the same consequence that capital gains tax is payable on the gain shown up by this disposal. It is the trustee's case that no such disposal should be deemed to have taken place and that, therefore, the assessment should be discharged as no capital gains tax is payable.

Section 54(1) of the 1979 Act is in these terms:

'On the occasion when a person becomes absolutely entitled to any settled property as against the trustee all the assets forming part of the settled property to which he becomes so entitled shall be deemed to have been disposed of by the trustee, and immediately reacquired by him in his capacity as a trustee within section 46(1) above, [ie, as a bare trustee] for a consideration equal to their market value.'

It follows from this provision that it is only if the trustees of the appointed fund became, as a result of the appointment, absolutely entitled to the assets comprised in the appointed fund as against the trustees of the settlement that there can be a deemed disposal within the meaning of the section.

Even though the trustees of the 1954 settlement remain, as a result of the 1981 appointment, trustees of the appointed fund, it is possible for the trustees of the appointed fund to be absolutely entitled to the assets comprised in that fund as against the trustees of the settlement. This can happen if, but only if, the effect of the deed of appointment was to create a second settlement subject to the trusts of which the appointed fund was held. I do not need to explain this aspect of the law more fully as it was accepted by the parties and may be extracted from the judgments in the various cases cited to me (see, however, *Bond (Inspector of Taxes) v Pickford* [1983] STC 517 at 521 per Slade LJ).

The only question, therefore, that I have to decide is whether, when the trustees of the 1954 settlement executed the deed of appointment in 1981, a new and separate settlement within the meaning of s 54(1) came into existence. If it did it is accepted by the trustee that there was a deemed disposal, but if it did not then the Crown accepts that there was no deemed disposal.

When Nourse J was faced in *Bond (Inspector of Taxes) v Pickford* [1982] STC 403 with the same question of whether the exercise of a power over settled property gave rise to a deemed disposal for capital gains tax purposes he started his judgment (see [1982] STC 403 at 409–410) with these words:

'The present state of the law can be summarised as follows. In *Hart (Inspector of Taxes) v Briscoe* and *Hoare Trustees v Gardner (Inspector of Taxes)* [1978] STC 89, [1979] Ch 1, 10 Brightman J held that a deemed disposal does take place where the trustees of a settlement, pursuant to a power of advancement, either transfer assets to the trustees of another ad hoc settlement or execute a deed declaring a series of trusts of the advanced assets so as to take them out of the head settlement and subject them to new trusts. The grounds of those decision were, first, that the head settlement and the ad hoc settlement, in relation to the advanced assets, constitute two settlements for capital gains tax purposes and, secondly, that the trustees of the ad hoc settlement or declaration of trust (whether they be the same as the trustees of the head settlement or others) became absolutely entitled to the advanced assets as against the trustees of the head settlement for the purposes of s 25(3) [of the Finance Act 1965, now s 54(1) of the Capital Gains Tax Act 1979] notwithstanding that they have no beneficial interest in these assets. More recently, in *Roome v Edwards (Inspector of Taxes)* [1981] STC 96, [1982] AC 279 the House of Lords, agreeing on this point with Brightman J at first instance ([1979] STC 546), held, shortly stated, that the exercise of a joint special power of appointment under a marriage settlement in conventional form coupled with the assignment of the life interest in possession so as to procure that the appointed funds should be held on trusts which were not exhaustive did not result in that fund becoming subject to the trusts of a separate settlement for capital gains tax purposes. Both *Hart v Briscoe* and *Roome v Edwards* contain valuable and authoritative observations which must guide me to a decision in the present case . . .'

I have the added advantage that in *Bond v Pickford* both at first instance (see [1982] STC 403) and in the Court of Appeal (see [1983] STC 517) there are to be found further valuable and authoritative observations which shed further light to guide me.

In *Bond v Pickford* the trustees of a settlement executed deeds of allocation as a result of which certain of the trust assets were thereafter to be held on the trusts set out in those deeds. These trusts were exhaustive of the beneficial interests in the allocated funds. The administrative powers of the settlement were to continue to apply and the trustees of the settlement were to be the trustees of the allocated funds. It was held that a separate settlement of the allocated funds had not come into existence. The factor in that case which seems to have weighed most heavily with the judges was the nature of the power under which the deeds of allocation were executed.

Slade LJ said ([1983] STC 517 at 522–523)—

'. . . I feel no doubt that as a matter of trust law trustees, who are given a discretionary power to direct which of the beneficiaries shall take the trust property and for what interests, do *not* have the power thereby to remove assets from the original settlement, by subjecting them to the trusts of a separate settlement, unless the instrument which gave them the power expressly or by necessary implication authorises them so to do.'

Oliver LJ (at 529) spoke in the same vein.

The earlier cases I have mentioned are, it seems to me, particularly helpful in indicating how one should approach the problem. Brightman J in *Hart (Inspector of Taxes) v Briscoe* [1978] STC 89 at 105, [1979] Ch 1 at 8 said:

'In my judgment, the question whether a disposition which exercises a fiduciary power is to be viewed as a separate settlement, or as part of a single fiduciary arrangement headed by the disposition which created the power, must be answered in the context of the circumstances of the particular case.'

Lord Wilberforce in *Roome v Edwards (Inspector of Taxes)* [1981] STC 96 at 100, [1982] AC 279 at 293 expressed the same thought rather more fully.

'Since "settlement" and "trusts" are legal terms, which are also used by business men or laymen in a business or practical sense, I think that the question whether a particular set of facts amounts to a settlement should be approached by asking what a person, with knowledge of the legal context of the word under established doctrine and applying this knowledge in a practical and common-sense manner to the facts under examination, would conclude.'

Both Brightman J and Lord Wilberforce gave examples of hypothetical cases which seemed to them likely to fall either side of the dividing line. Lord Wilberforce also pointed to a number of indicia which may be helpful to show whether a settlement separate from another settlement exists, but pointed out, too, that those indicia though helpful were not decisive.

In the light of this guidance it seems to me, therefore, that what I must do in the present case is place myself in the position of a person of the sort that Lord Wilberforce envisaged and ask myself how such a person would answer the question when he was presented with the facts of the present case.

The detailed facts are set out in the agreed statement of facts which I have already summarised and the precise terms of the 1954 settlement and of the deed of appointment of 16 June 1981 are to be found in the two documents themselves.

From those documents it can be seen that the power under which the deed of appointment was executed is contained in clause 3 of the 1954 settlement. It is in these terms (omitting words that are not relevant to this appeal).

'It shall be lawful for the trustees at any time or times during the appointed period ... at their absolute discretion to pay or apply any part or parts of the Capital of the trust fund to or for the benefit of all or any one or more to the exclusion of the others or others of the specified class freed and released from the trusts concerning the same ...'

That is a power which it seems to me created a special power of appointment and would authorise the trustees, if at their discretion it seemed appropriate to do so, to take part, or all, of the assets of the trust fund out of the 1954 settlement and resettle them under trusts of a different settlement.

Turning to the deed of appointment, the first recital states that the deed is 'supplemental' to the 1954 settlement which, said counsel for the trustee, suggested that the trustees intended that it should form part of the 1954 settlement rather than set up a new settlement. The second recital indicates that the trustees are the same as the trustees of the 1954 settlement. Both counsel for the trustee and Mr McDonagh, who appeared for the Crown, claimed that this provision was a pointer in favour of the view for which they were contending.

Clause 3 of the deed appoints the assets comprised in the part of the trust fund that was not specified as the appointed fund to Isabelle absolutely. Isabelle therefore became absolutely entitled to that part of the trust fund as against the trustees with the consequence that there was a deemed disposal of so much of the trust fund, and, as I have said, capital gains tax has been paid in respect of that gain.

Clause 4 of the deed requires the trustees to hold the appointed fund and its income on trust:

'(a) to pay the income to Isabelle during her life and before the expiration of the appointed period.

(b) the trustees shall have power at any time or times during Isabelle's life and before the expiration of the appointed period to pay, transfer or apply the whole or any parts of the capital of the appointed fund to or for Isabelle's benefit freed and discharged from the trusts affecting the same under the Settlement and this deed and subject as aforesaid and to every exercise of the foregoing power.

(c) Subject thereto the trustees shall hold the appointed fund in trust as to both capital and income for the sons of Isabelle Mark Rubin and Anthony Rubin ... in equal shares absolutely.'

Clause 5 provided that at the expiration of the appointed period the appointed fund was to be held in trust as to both capital and income for Mark and Anthony in equal shares absolutely.

It is, I think, clear from clauses 3, 4 and 5 that the trusts affecting the trust fund after the deed of appointment were 'exhaustive, that is to say, that there is neither any part of the original trusts still subsisting nor any possible room in the future for their revival' (see *Bond v Pickford* [1983] STC 517 at 529 per Oliver LJ).

The Crown argued that this being the case, and the appointment being made under a power in the 1954 settlement which entitled them to take the assets out of the 1954 settlement, the position was very similar to the position envisaged by Lord

Wilberforce in *Roome v Edwards* [1981] STC 96 at 100, [1982] AC 279 at 293 where he was dealing with the second of the two 'fairly typical' cases he put forward. He said:

> 'On the other hand, there may be a power to appoint and appropriate a part or portion of the trust property to beneficiaries and to settle it for their benefit. If such a power is exercised, the natural conclusion might be that a separate settlement was created, all the more so if a complete new set of trusts were declared as to the appropriated property, and if it could be said that the trusts of the original settlement ceased to apply to it.'

Counsel for the trustee countered this by pointing to the fact that Lord Wilberforce did not say that the conclusion would be that a separate settlement was created but only that the conclusion *might* be to that effect. He pointed out that the words in clause 4(b) 'freed and discharged from the trusts affecting the same under the Settlement and this deed' indicated that the trustees considered that the 1954 settlement together with the deed was the source of the trusts affecting the appointed fund.

He also relied on clause 7 of the deed of appointment which provided that while the trusts created by the deed lasted—

> '...the administrative and other powers and provisions declared and contained in clauses 7–10 inclusive of the [1954] Settlement shall continue to apply to the appointed fund so far (but so far only) as the same are consistent with the beneficial provisions hereinbefore appointed.'

This indicated, counsel argued, that the deed expressed to be supplemental to the 1954 settlement was to be administered in accordance with the administrative power and provisions of the 1954 settlement, which pointed strongly to the conclusion that no new settlement was intended to be created.

Mr McDonagh in reply to this said that clause 7 could equally well be interpreted as intending to incorporate by reference into a new settlement the administrative provisions of the 1954 settlement. To complete the description of the deed it remains only to mention clause 6 of the deed which entitled the trustees of the deed to disregard the provisions of the Apportionment Act so far as they think fit. Mr McDonagh argued that this gave to the trustees of the deed of appointment new powers, not given to the trustees of the 1954 settlement, which pointed towards the creation of a separate settlement.

To sum up it seems to me that Lord Wilberforce's informed observer would in this case be looking at a situation in which trustees of a settlement were given by the terms of the settlement a special power of appointment which entitled them to remove some or all of the assets of the settlement out of the settlement. This power was one of the type that Slade LJ described in *Bond v Pickford* [1983] STC 517 at 525 as being in the 'wider form'. The trustees deliberately exercised this power in such a manner as to cause the trusts which affected the assets under the settlement to be wholly replaced by a new set of trusts. In that situation Slade LJ said that the conclusion would probably be irresistible that both the purpose and the effect of the transaction was to create a wholly new settlement. But it is, I think, implicit in what he then said that one would have to draw the inference from those facts that the purpose, as well as the effect, of the transaction was to create a new settlement.

It is clear from the speech of Lord Wilberforce in *Roome v Edwards* [1981] STC 96 at 101–102, [1982] AC 279 at 294–295 and from Slade LJ's comment on it in *Bond v Pickford* [1983] STC 517 at 524 that the intention of the parties, viewed objectively from the provisions of the documents in question, is a relevant consideration. I must therefore ask myself whether the informed observer looking at the matter in the practical and commonsense manner indicated by Lord Wilberforce would consider

that the parties themselves at the time of the execution of the deed of appointment
intended to create a new settlement of the appointed fund or intended only to alter
the trusts on which it was originally held and to retain it in the 1954 settlement.

In this connection it seems to me desirable that I should bear in mind what was
said by Oliver LJ in *Bond v Pickford* [1983] STC 517 at 528–529:

> 'Where property which is held on trust becomes subject to trusts other than
> those to which it was originally subject in the hands of the trustees, it is no doubt
> a convenient way of testing whether there has been a disposal of the settled
> property for the purposes of capital gains tax to ask whether a new or separate
> settlement has been created. The question is not, however, one which is easily
> answered and in seeking to answer it, it is important to bear always in mind the
> words of the statute. Section 25(3) of the Finance Act 1965 creates a deemed
> disposition only if the occasion is one "when a person becomes absolutely
> entitled to any settled property as against the trustee" ... Inevitably, however,
> difficult questions arise where there is no actual transfer; where the trustees
> remain the same, but where an event occurs as a result of which the trust
> property falls to be held by them on trusts other than those to which it was
> subject immediately before the event but which are themselves envisaged by
> the original disposition constituting the trust. Inevitably each case is going to
> depend on its particular facts and the weight to be given to the various indicia
> mentioned by Lord Wilberforce ...'

I have referred to this passage because it makes clear the perhaps obvious fact that
the presence in the 1954 settlement of the power to appoint indicates that the settlor
envisaged the possibility that, depending on the happening of events then still in the
future, his trustees might in the exercise of their fiduciary duties deem it desirable
to alter the trusts on which the assets of the trust fund were held. The passage also
emphasises that what has to be decided is whether or not the trustees of the deed
became absolutely entitled to the assets in question as against the trustees of the
settlement. These two facts are both matters that, it seems to me, Lord Wilberforce's
informed layman would have in mind when considering objectively what the
trustees' purpose was when they were exercising the power. The fact that the power
was drawn in the wider form seems to me to show that the settlor intended that the
trustees should have as free a hand as possible when the time came at which they
considered it right to appoint. They could if they wished take the assets of the trust
fund out of the 1954 settlement and create a new settlement, but they did not have
to achieve their purpose this way. They could, if they considered it desirable,
appoint in such a way as to keep the assets in the 1954 settlement and alter the trusts
on which they were held. If, without indicating in any other way which course they
intended to take, they altered the trusts so that the trust fund was thereafter held on
entirely different trusts to those which had formally bound it and were exhaustive,
then, as Slade LJ indicated, the conclusion that the trustees' purpose was to set up a
new settlement would probably be irresistible. But if there is evidence in the
documents themselves and evidence of the way they exercised the power which
shows that their purpose in doing what they did was not to create a new settlement
of the relevant assets, but to keep the assets in the original settlement and subject
them to different trusts, then, in my opinion, the contrary view may cease to be
irresistible.

I have not found this aspect of the case easy but have formed the opinion that
there is evidence both in the documents and in the way that the trustees exercised
the power of appointment in clause 3 of the 1954 settlement which would cause the
informed layman viewing the position in a practical and commonsense manner to
reach the conclusion that the trustees did not intend to take the appointed fund out
of the 1954 settlement and resettle it in a different settlement.

The statement in the recital that the deed is to be supplemental to the 1954 settlement does not seem to me to be easily interpreted as indicating that the deed is *a* intended to set up a new settlement. If there were no other internal indications of the trustees' purpose this fact might not be conclusive but, it seems to me, its tendency is to support the trustee's case. The words in clause 4(b) of the deed 'freed and discharged from the trusts affecting the same under the Settlement and this deed' point even more strongly in my view to the same conclusion. Clause 7 of the deed which provides that the administrative and other powers and provisions in *b* clauses 7–10 of the settlement are to continue to apply to the appointed fund does not seem to me to point very strongly either way. If the trustees' purpose was to create a new trust it would, by reference, indicate what the administrative powers and provisions of the new settlement were to be, but equally if the purpose was to retain the appointed fund in the 1954 settlement it would make clear that the administrative powers and provisions of the 1954 settlement were to continue *c* unaltered after the power of appointment had been exercised.

Mr McDonagh set much store in clause 6 of the deed as an indication that the trustees' purpose was to create a new settlement. Counsel for the trustee said that the primary importance of this provision was in relation to the separation of the fund appointed by clause 3 to Isabelle absolutely and this, it seems to me, detracts from the weight that might otherwise be given to it as a pointer in favour of the Crown's *d* contention.

The distinction between the provisions of clause 3 and of clause 4 which shows how the power to appoint capital was exercised is also, it seems to me, significant as an indication of what the trustees' intention was at the time that the power was exercised. By clause 3 the assets of the trust fund, less the assets of the appointed fund, were appointed to Isabelle absolutely and so, clearly, she became absolutely *e* entitled to those assets as against the trustees. Under clause 4 she was only given a life interest in the assets of the appointed fund, but the life interest could, by the exercise of the power in clause 4(b), later be enlarged into an absolute interest. This I consider points to the intention of the trustees being that neither she nor the trustees themselves should become absolutely entitled as against the trustees of the 1954 settlement until, at least, that power was exercised. That is consistent with an *f* intention not to create a new settlement. An intention to create a new settlement would, on the other hand, seem to be inconsistent with that purpose.

Finally, the informed layman would, as Lord Wilberforce made clear, be alive to the established doctrine of trust law that the trusts declared by a document exercising a special power of appointment are to be read into the original settlement. As Lord Wilberforce said in *Roome v Edwards* [1981] STC 96 at 100, [1982] AC 279 at 293:   *g*

> 'If such a power is exercised, whether or not separate trustees are appointed, I do not think that it would be natural for such a person as I have presupposed to say that a separate settlement had been created, still less so if it were found that provisions of the original settlement continued to apply to the appointed fund . . .'   *h*

I do not see why it should not be true that the sort of person presupposed by Lord Wilberforce would consider prima facie that no new settlement had been created even if what had been done by the trustees was done in exercise of what Slade LJ called a wider power, rather than under a narrower power. It may be that it would be less difficult, if the evidence was present, to dislodge such a prima facie view, but *j* in the absence of such evidence it seems to me that that, too, is a factor to be brought into consideration.

For these reasons I have reached the conclusion that on the execution of the deed of appointment on 16 June 1981, the trustees as trustees of the deed did not become absolutely entitled to the assets of the appointed fund as against themselves as

trustees of the 1954 settlement and that therefore there was no deemed disposal of
those assets within the meaning of s 54(1) of the 1979 Act.

The appeal, therefore, succeeds and the further assessment for the year 1981–82
must be discharged.

Launcelot Henderson for the Crown.
Leolin Price QC and *David Ritchie* for the trustee.

HOFFMANN J. The issue in this appeal from the Special Commissioner is whether
the exercise of a power of appointment under a settlement has resulted in a deemed
disposal under s 54(1) of the Capital Gains Tax Act 1979 (the 1979 Act). The
settlement was made on 21 January 1954 by Mr Jack Meek (the settlor) and its
relevant provisions may be summarised as follows. First, for a period defined by a
royal lives clause there was a discretionary trust of income in favour of a class
consisting of the settlor's wife, his daughter Isabelle, her husband and her two sons
Mark and Anthony. Second, during the period of the income trust the trustees had
power under clause 3 to pay or apply capital to or for the benefit of any member of
the class 'freed and released from the trusts concerning the same'. Third, there was
an ultimate trust of capital for members of the class living at the expiry of the income
trust. Fourth, the settlement contained various administrative powers.

The power to apply capital was exercised by a deed of appointment dated 16 June
1981 which was expressed to be supplemental to the settlement. It divided the trust
fund into two parts by reference to a schedule of assets. One part was declared to be
held on trust for Isabelle absolutely. The other part (called the appointed fund) was
to be held to pay the income to Isabelle during her life or for the remainder of the
income trust period, whichever was the shorter, with power to pay or apply capital
to or for her benefit 'freed and discharged from the trusts affecting the same under
the Settlement and this deed'. Subject to the income trust, the capital was to be held
for Mark and Anthony in equal shares absolutely. The remaining clauses of the
appointment gave the trustees power to disregard the Apportionment Act and
declared that the administrative provisions of the settlement were to continue to
apply to the appointed fund as far as they were consistent with the other provisions
of the deed.

Section 54(1) of the 1979 Act provides that a disposal of assets comprised in a
settlement shall be deemed to have taken place when any person has become
absolutely entitled to those assets against the trustees. There is no dispute that by
virtue of the appointment there was such a deemed disposal of the assets to which
Isabelle became absolutely entitled. The issue in this appeal is whether there was
also a deemed disposal of the appointed fund. This remained vested in the trustees.
But the 1979 Act treats the trustees of settled property as a single continuing body of
persons distinct from the actual persons who may from time to time be the trustees.
It is conceptually possible for persons acting in their capacity as trustees of a new
settlement to become absolutely entitled to assets against themselves as trustees of
the old settlement. Therefore, the appeal turns on the question whether the assets
remain subject to the trusts of the settlement as varied by the appointment or
whether the effect of the appointment was to subject them to the trusts of a new
settlement.

The decision of the House of Lords in *Roome v Edwards (Inspector of Taxes)*
[1981] STC 96 at 100, [1982] AC 279 at 293, as expressed in the speech of Lord
Wilberforce, shows that the question must be answered according to the view which
would be taken of the transaction by a person with knowledge of trusts who uses
language in a practical and commonsense way. Which description would be
considered more appropriate: that new trusts had been grafted onto the old
settlement or that a new settlement had been created?

The more recent decision of the Court of Appeal in 1983 in *Bond (Inspector of Taxes) v Pickford* [1983] STC 517 shows that a critical element in deciding how to *a* describe the transaction may be the scope of the power which has been exercised. If that power allows the trustees to define or vary the beneficial interest but not remove the assets from the settlement or delegate their powers and discretions it is difficult to imagine any appointment within the scope of the power which could be construed as the creation of a new settlement. On the other hand, the power may be expressed in terms wide enough to permit the creation of a new settlement, and the question *b* will then be whether this is what the trustees have chosen to do.

The cases show there is no single litmus test for deciding that question. The paradigm case of the creation of a new settlement would involve the segregation of particular assets, the appointment of new trustees, the creation of fresh trusts which exhaust the beneficial interest in the assets and administrative powers which make further reference to the original settlement redundant (see *Hart (Inspector of Taxes)* *c* *v Briscoe* [1978] STC 89 at 105, [1979] Ch 1 at 8 per Brightman J). The absence of one or more of those features is not necessarily inconsistent with a resettlement. It seems to me that the question is one of construction of the settlement using the approach recommended by Lord Wilberforce and looking at the documents in the light of the surrounding circumstances. Putting the same thing another way, it is a matter of endeavouring to ascertain the intention of the parties. The Special *d* Commissioner decided that various indications in the deed of appointment led to the conclusion that it declared new beneficial trusts without creating a new settlement in respect of the appointed fund.

Before me counsel for the Crown took what might be called a preliminary point. He said that whatever might be the indications in the deed of appointment as to the intentions of the trustees, the power which they purported to exercise did not permit *e* them to make an appointment otherwise than by way of outright payment or the creation of a new settlement. Just as in *Bond v Pickford* the power in question did not allow the trustees to remove assets from the settlement, so this power did not allow them to do anything else. For that submission counsel relied on the words 'freed and released from the trusts concerning the same' in clause 3 of the settlement. There can be no doubt that that clause empowered the trustees to make an *f* appointment which would remove assets from the settlement altogether. An outright appointment of capital to a beneficiary would obviously have that effect. A further indication is to be found in the proviso that the power should not be exercised during the life of the settlor so as to reduce the capital of the trust fund 'remaining subject to the trusts of the settlement' below £50.

But was that the only way in which the power could be exercised? Such a *g* construction would mean that an appointment which expressly purported only to vary the beneficial capital trust in some relatively minor respect would have to be held ultra vires or else somewhat artificially construed as the creation of a new settlement with all the provisions of the old one together with the variation.

In the absence of clearer language I am reluctant to construe the clause in this all-or-nothing way. It seems to me that 'freed and released from the trusts concerning *h* the same' can easily mean that the assets are to be released from any trust inconsistent with the appointment. There is no reason why such an appointment should necessarily involve the discharge of the assets from all the trust powers and provisions of the settlement.

Counsel for the Crown drew attention to the fact that clause 3 was expressed in language very similar to that of the statutory power of advancement in s 32 of the *j* Trustee Act 1925. That was the provision which the House of Lords in *Pilkington v IRC* [1964] AC 612, 40 TC 416 held could be used to create a fresh settlement for the benefit of an object of the power. But counsel said that one could also infer from the speech of Viscount Radcliffe (see [1964] AC 612 at 630, 40 TC 416 at 434) that he thought any use of the statutory power otherwise than by way of absolute payment would inevitably involve the creation of a new settlement.

However, in my judgment Viscount Radcliffe was dealing with an express
proposal to create a fresh settlement and did not address the question whether this
was the only way in which the power could be used to achieve the same result. In
my view, clause 3 gave the trustees a choice. They could have disposed of the
appointed funds to themselves as trustees of the new settlement or declared that it
was to be subject to new trusts within the existing settlement. The difference goes
entirely to the method adopted and not to the substantial result achieved, which in
either case was precisely the same.

In *Bond v Pickford* [1983] STC 517 at 525 Slade LJ said that where trustees had
what he called a power in the wider form, that is, a power which enabled the trustees
to take assets out of the settlement altogether, and they exercised it—

'... in such manner as to cause the trusts which currently affect the relevant
assets to be wholly replaced by a new set of trusts, the conclusion will probably
be irresistible that both the purpose and the effect of the transaction is to create
an entirely new settlement.'

Counsel for the Crown said that such a conclusion could be drawn in this case
because the appointed fund had been made subject to a wholly new set of trusts
which exhausted the beneficial interest. However, I rather think that in referring to
a new set of trusts Slade LJ had in mind the whole of the trust powers and provisions
of the settlement including the administrative powers, much the same as Brightman J
said in the passage in *Hart v Briscoe* [1978] STC 89 at 105, [1979] Ch 1 at 9 to which
I have already referred.

In this case the question whether the administrative powers were intended to
survive is part of the question of construction which has to be decided. Furthermore,
although Slade LJ said that such a conclusion would probably be irresistible he
emphasised elsewhere in his judgment that the purpose and effect of the transaction
must be gathered from the whole of the documents and the surrounding
circumstances. Nevertheless, I accept, as Nourse J did in *Bond v Pickford* [1982]
STC 403, that the creation of trusts under a power in the wider form which exhaust
the beneficial interest is a powerful indication of an intention to create a new
settlement.

It seems to me the question here is whether that inference is rebutted by the
language of the deed of appointment. Both sides have drawn attention to various
features of the deed which they say favour their construction. For example, the deed
is expressed to be supplemental to the settlement. That is said to be an indication
that the settlement is intended to survive. In my view, that phraseology carries little,
if any, weight because on any view resort to the settlement would have been
necessary partly in order to ascertain that the trustees had power to make the
appointment and partly because the appointment uses by way of shorthand various
definitions contained in the settlement. On the other side, it is said that the creation
of a power to disregard the Apportionment Act indicates an intention to make a new
settlement. Again, that seems to me to be entirely neutral. There is no reason why
an additional power should not be conferred by the exercise of the power under
clause 3 without having to recast the entire settlement.

In my judgment, there are only two provisions in the deed of appointment which
really matter. First, clause 7 provides that:

'During the subsistence of the foregoing trusts or any of them the
administrative and other powers and provisions declared and contained in
clauses 7–10 inclusive in the Settlement shall continue to apply to the Appointed
Fund so far (but so far only) as the same are consistent with the beneficial
provisions hereinbefore appointed.'

The more natural effect of the words 'shall continue to apply' is to connote the
continuation of the settlement, but standing by itself that clause would not necessarily
have been sufficient. The words are also capable of meaning that the administrative

clauses in question are to be incorporated by reference in the new settlement. In *Bond v Pickford* [1982] STC 403 at 414, Nourse J would have been willing to construe similar words as words of incorporation by reference if the power in question had been in the wider form.

But clause 7 does not stand by itself. The other counter-indication is clause 4(b) which gives the trustees power to appoint capital from the appointed fund to Isabelle during her lifetime 'freed and discharged from the trusts affecting the same under the Settlement and this deed'. The words 'under the Settlement' clearly indicate that the trustees contemplated that there would be provisions of the settlement continuing to be applicable to the appointed fund. That language can be given meaning and effect if clause 7 is construed as words which continue the application of the administrative powers and with them the old settlement.

Counsel for the Crown, while accepting that in a well-drawn settlement these words would carry the implication which I have given them, submitted that the deed of appointment was in a number of respects clearly an inartistically drafted document and that the reference to the trusts of the settlement in clause 4(b) could be treated as surplus words which had merely been put in for greater caution in case, contrary to the actual intentions of the trustees, some part of the settlement could be held to survive. He pointed to various other provisions in the deed which clearly are redundant, for example, clause 4(b) also says that the appointment of capital shall be 'subject as aforesaid and to every exercise of the foregoing power', words which are plainly unnecessary. In addition, the appointment goes on in clause 5 to create an ultimate trust for Mark and Anthony of the capital on the termination of the former income trust when on any view an exactly similar trust would have taken effect under the previous clauses.

However, it does not seem to me to be a permissible method of construction to say that words which are capable of being given an intelligible effect should be rejected as surplusage because the draughtsman has shown a penchant for surplusage in other parts of his document. In my judgment, the reference to the trusts of the settlement in clause 4(b) should be taken at face value and, if so taken, it shows a sufficient intention on the part of the trustees to create new trusts under the old settlement rather than to set up a new one.

The Special Commissioner gave a number of other reasons for coming to his conclusion with which I must not necessarily be taken as agreeing, but I share his view that in the end the question is not an easy one. Like many questions of construction, it is somewhat finely balanced but in the end my conclusion is the same as his and the appeal must be dismissed.

Appeal dismissed with costs.

Solicitors: *Solicitor of Inland Revenue*; *Nabarro Nathanson* (for the trustee).

Rengan Krishnan Esq   Barrister.

Colonial Life Insurance Co (Trinidad) Ltd v Board of Inland Revenue

PRIVY COUNCIL
LORD KEITH OF KINKEL, LORD BRANDON OF OAKBROOK, LORD TEMPLEMAN, LORD OLIVER OF AYLMERTON, SIR ROBERT MEGARRY
4 JUNE, 1 JULY 1991

Trinidad and Tobago – Corporation tax – Approved annuity business – 'Profits of approved annuity business' exempt from corporation tax – Whether profit on investment of moneys paid as consideration for provision of pensions for employees of contributing companies was 'profits of approved annuity business' – Corporation Tax Act (Trinidad and Tobago), Sch 4, para 3(4).

The taxpayer company, Colonial Life Insurance Co (Trinidad) Ltd, carried on a 'deposit administration business' in which it received moneys from the trustees of approved pension schemes as consideration for the provision of the benefits prescribed by the schemes. Under the trust deed of an approved pension scheme, the trustees were empowered to contract out the duty of providing pensions and other benefits under a 'deposit administration contract', and in fact did so by entering into such a contract with the taxpayer. The taxpayer company agreed to administer a 'deposit administration fund' for the benefit of members of the scheme, purchasing benefits in accordance with the rules of the plan at the direction of the trustees. The trustees agreed to pay to the taxpayer company such deposits as were required for the funding of the benefits. The credits to the deposit administration fund comprised the deposits and interest at an agreed rate allocated to the fund by the taxpayer; the charges on the fund comprised the cost of purchase of the benefits provided and administrative charges. The taxpayer company further agreed, inter alia, to keep account of the fund and to furnish an annual statement, to keep records of prospective accrued benefits and contributions and to provide when necessary an estimate of any additional deposit required to fund benefits.

In the relevant year, the income generated by the deposit administration fund was $893,540. There were expenses of $71,024 and $681,315 was credited to the fund as allocated interest. A balance of $141,201 remained, representing the profit for the year on the deposit administration business. In December 1977 the taxpayer company was assessed to corporation tax in respect of this profit. The taxpayer company appealed against the assessment to the Tax Appeal Board, which allowed the appeal, holding that the profits concerned were profits from the carrying on of approved annuity business and were exempt from corporation tax pursuant to para 3(4)[a] of Sch 4 to the Corporation Tax Act of Trinidad and Tobago. The Board of Inland Revenue's appeal to the Court of Appeal was allowed on the ground that the taxpayer company's business under the deposit administration contracts was not limited to the purchase of annuities. The taxpayer company appealed to the Privy Council.

Held – The true nature of the deposit administration contract was as a single agreement for the carrying out by the taxpayer company of its obligations under the trust deed. The fact that it contained accounting provisions for the establishment of a separate fund could not alter its essential nature as a contract for the provision of annuities and it was impossible to regard the profits generated from it as other than profits of 'approved annuity business'.

Accordingly, the appeal would be allowed.

---

a   Paragraph 3(4), so far as material, is set out at p 504 *j*, post

Appeal

The taxpayer company appealed against the decision of the Court of Appeal of
Trinidad and Tobago (des Iles, McMillan and Davis JJA) of 28 July 1989 allowing
an appeal by the Commissioner of Inland Revenue against the decision of the Tax
Appeal Board of 9 November 1984 that profits assessed to corporation tax were
profits from the carrying on of approved annuity business and were exempt from
corporation tax pursuant to para 3(4) of Sch 4 to the Corporation Tax Act of
Trinidad and Tobago.

David Goy QC, Philip Baker for the taxpayer company.
Christopher McCall QC, Myrna Robinson-Walters, Senior State Counsel (Trinidad
and Tobago bar), for the board.

1 July 1991. The following judgment of the Board was delivered.

LORD OLIVER OF AYLMERTON. This appeal from the Court of Appeal of
Trinidad and Tobago (des Iles, McMillan and Davis JJA), although involving a
consideration of some lengthy and somewhat ill-drafted documents, raises what is,
in the end, a very short point, that is to say whether income received by Colonial
Life Insurance Co (Trinidad) Ltd (the taxpayer company) during the year 1971
from the investment of moneys paid to it as the consideration for the provision of
pensions for employees of a number of contributing companies is exempt from
corporation tax as 'profits of approved annuity business' pursuant to the provisions
of para 3(4) to Sch 4 to the Corporation Tax Act of Trinidad and Tobago.

In December 1977 the taxpayer company was assessed to tax in respect of, inter
alia, the income concerned. On 29 December 1978 it appealed against the assessment
to the Tax Appeal Board which on 9 November 1984 allowed the appeal and referred
the assessment back to the respondent, the Board of Inland Revenue (the board), for
reassessment on the basis that the income concerned was exempt from tax. At the
request of the board a case was stated for the opinion of the Court of Appeal and on
28 July 1989 that court allowed the appeal with costs and confirmed the assessment.
From that decision the taxpayer company now appeals to their Lordships' Board.

In the year to which the assessment relates the relevant legislation was contained
in Part II of the Finance Act 1966, as amended, but it was subsequently published
separately in the Corporation Tax Act (Ch 75:02) (the Act) and since, both in the
Tax Appeal Board and in the Court of Appeal, the arguments were addressed by
reference to the provisions of that Act, it will be convenient if their Lordships adopt
the same course. Corporation tax is imposed by s 3 of the Act on the annual profits
of 'any company' but special provision is made (in s 14) for, inter alia, insurance
companies (including life insurance companies) to which there are applied the
provisions of Sch 4. The rate of tax payable under s 3 is specified in Sch 1 which
prescribes a rate of 45% except in the case of profits of the long-term insurance
business of an assurance company not transferred to the shareholders' account,
where the rate is 15%. Paragraphs 2 and 3 of Sch 4 contain provisions for various
aspects of the business of assurance companies carrying on 'long-term insurance
business' to be treated as separate classes of business and for the deduction of
expenses (regulated by para 3) to be calculated separately in the computation of the
profits arising from each class. 'Long-term insurance business' is defined (in para 5)
as meaning, inter alia, 'general annuity business' and 'approved annuity business'.
The critical provision for the purposes of this appeal is that contained in para 3(4) of
Sch 4 which provides that 'the profits of approved annuity business shall not be
chargeable to tax except to the extent that such profits are distributed to shareholders'.
The Act itself contains no definition of 'approved annuity business' but para 5(2)

applies Sch 1 to the Insurance Act 1966 where the expression is defined as including
'any annuity business undertaken for the purpose of establishing and conducting a
deferred annuity or approved fund or scheme under section 16 and an approved
deferred annuity plan under sections 16A to 16E of the Income Tax Ordinance'. It
is unnecessary for present purposes to refer to those sections of the Income Tax
Ordinance (which do not refer to an approved plan which is not a deferred annuity
plan) because the board concedes that the definition is merely an inclusive one and
that if (which is disputed) the income with which this appeal is concerned can
properly be described as a profit arising from 'annuity business' that annuity business
is in fact 'approved annuity business'.

The aspect of the taxpayer company's business which has given rise to this appeal
is that which is described, perhaps rather ineptly, as 'deposit administration business',
an expression which, as will be seen, embraces the receipt of moneys from the
trustees of approved pension schemes as the consideration for the provision by the
taxpayer company of the pension and other benefits prescribed by the schemes.
Broadly the board's contention, which succeeded in the Court of Appeal, was and is
that the taxpayer company was in fact carrying on two severable businesses, that is
to say, a business of receiving and managing deposits, which was not an annuity
business at all and from which the profit in question arose, and a separate business
of providing annuities whose connection with the deposit business was simply that
it was provided for in the same contract and was paid for out of the deposited funds.

In order to appreciate the basis for this submission, it is necessary to consider, at
least in outline, the pattern of the pension schemes which underlie the deposit
administration business. It is agreed that these are represented by the specimen
scheme referred to both by the Tax Appeal Board and by the Court of Appeal,
namely that relating to the Orange Grove National Co Ltd. The company pension
scheme takes the familiar form of a trust deed and rules approved by the Revenue.
In the particular case the trustee was the Bank of Nova Scotia Trust Co Ltd and the
deed recites that by agreement between the company and the trustees the pensions
provided by the rules have been secured by means of a deposit administration
contract. Clause 2 establishes a staff pension fund plan and incorporates the rules
which are contained in the schedule, and clause 3 provides for the payment by the
company to the trustees of the contributions payable or to be deducted under the
rules. Clause 3(ii) imposes on the trustees the obligation of providing the benefits of
the scheme but at the same time empowers them to delegate that responsibility. It is
in the following terms:

> 'The Trustees shall out of the Fund pay or provide for the payment of all such
> benefits to Members or to their designated beneficiaries as shall be payable in
> accordance with the Rules, provided that the Trustees shall be deemed to have
> provided such benefits by entering into a Deposit Administration Contract or
> any other contract under which the benefits required by the Rules are provided.'

The only other provision of the deed which requires mention is the investment
clause (clause 9) which confers an absolute unrestricted power of investment but also
includes expressly a power to invest in deposit administration contracts.

The rules also follow a familiar pattern, providing for employees of the company
to become members of the scheme, for contributions by members and by the
company to be paid to the trustees, and for pensions to be payable on retirement at
the rate of one-sixtieth of average annual salary over the past five years of employment
multiplied by the appropriate number of years of pensionable service. There are
provisions for early retirement, for lump sum payments on death before retirement
and for deferred pensions for employees leaving the company's service before
retirement.

As already mentioned, the trust deed recites that the trustees have already
exercised their power to delegate by entering into a deposit administration contract

and it is on the terms of that contract that the argument for the board relies. It is
dated 24 January 1972, is made between the taxpayer company and the trustees, and   *a*
takes the rather curious form of a short single-page agreement whose detailed
provisions are contained in a separate annex. By its terms the taxpayer company
agrees as follows:

> 'TO ADMINISTER A DEPOSIT ADMINISTRATION FUND for the
> benefit of certain Employees of the ORANGE GROVE NATIONAL   *b*
> COMPANY LIMITED (Hereinafter called the Employer) who are included
> under this Deposit Administration Contract (hereinafter called the Contract)
> and who continue to be included hereunder until retirement date or prior
> death, and to pay to the person or persons entitled the Pensions and other
> Benefits to be determined in accordance with the Provisions hereof. The
> effective date of this Contract shall be the 1st day of March, 1970. This Contract   *c*
> is issued in consideration of the payment of Deposits by the said Trustees to the
> [taxpayer company] as provided for in the Provision 4 hereof. The provisions
> appearing on the subsequent pages hereof form part of this Contract as fully as
> if recited at length over the signatures hereto affixed.'

The provisions commence with a number of definitions of which the following
are material for present purposes: *d*

> '1.1—"Plan" shall mean the Pension Plan for the Employees of Orange Grove
> National Company Limited, as constituted by the Trust Deed and Rules dated
> the 2nd day of December, 1970, together with those amendments thereto that
> are both delivered to and accepted by the [taxpayer company] ...
> 1.3—"Member" shall mean any employee who upon fulfilling the eligibility
> requirements of the Plan, becomes a Member of the Plan.   *e*
> 1.4—"Registered Member" shall mean any person who is a member or former
> Member of the Plan for whom or for whose beneficiary the [taxpayer company]
> is directed by the trustees to purchase Benefits under this Contract in accordance
> with the terms of the Plan.
> 1.5—"Pension" except where specifically otherwise provided, shall mean an   *f*
> annual amount payable in monthly instalments in advance, to which a
> Registered Member or his beneficiary is entitled under this Contract.
> 1.6—"Deposits" shall mean any amounts of money which shall be paid to the
> [taxpayer company] by the Trustees from time to time under this Contract.
> 1.7—"Fund" shall mean the fund established in accordance with Provisions 4
> and 5 wherein Deposits are invested with the general funds of the [taxpayer
> company].'   *g*

Clause 2.2 provides that pensions as determined by the plan may not be provided for
a registered member except through the provisions of the contract. Provision 3 sets
out the administrative responsibilities of the trustees and the company respectively.
In summary, the company is to keep an account of the fund and furnish an annual
statement of the balance up to the last day of February of the previous year of   *h*
'Deposits' made during the year, interest allocated to the fund, 'deductions made to
purchase Pensions and to meet Administration Charges', and any other financial
transactions affecting the fund; it is to prepare and print members' rule books and
literature for distribution to members; it is to keep records of prospective accrued
benefits and contributions, to deliver to the trustees an annual statement for each
member showing his prospective retirement and accrued death benefits, to provide   *j*
when necessary an estimate of any additional deposit required to fund benefits, to
maintain a record of beneficiaries, to calculate death, retirement or termination of
service benefits of members, to provide a quinquennial actuarial report and valuation
and to submit to the Internal Revenue Department such material as may be required.

The following provisions are important and must be recited verbatim:

'PROVISION 4 – <u>DEPOSITS</u>.

4.1—Subject to the provisions of Provision 8 hereof the Trustees shall make and [the taxpayer company] shall accept Deposits to the Fund required for the funding of the Pensions and other Benefits payable under the Plan being the contributions to be made by the Employer and the Members under the Rules.

PROVISION 5 – <u>THE FUND</u>

5.1—The [taxpayer company] shall establish a Fund wherein the balance at any time shall be the excess of the amounts credited to the Fund in accordance with this Provision over the amounts charged by [the taxpayer company].

5.2—Credits to the Fund shall consist of:—(a) The Deposits referred to in Provision 4.1. (b) Interest shall be credited on the 31st day of December in each year and shall be calculated on the minimum monthly balance during each month. The rate of interest to be credited shall during the first five (5) years of the Fund be not less than $6\frac{1}{4}\%$ per annum and during the next ten (10) years shall not be less than 5% and thereafter shall be at such rate as the [taxpayer company] shall from time to time determine.

5.3—Charges against the Fund shall consist of:—(a) Purchase payments in accordance with Provision 7.1 for the purchase of Benefits. (b) The Administration Charges which the [taxpayer company] shall be entitled to make for administering the Fund as set out in the Schedule to this Contract. Such charges shall include all fees for Actuarial services performed by or on behalf of the [taxpayer company]. (c) Expenses incurred by the [taxpayer company] in connection with the printing of Members' Rules Books and other printing expenses incidental thereto.'

Their Lordships note in parenthesis that the reference in 5.3(a) to provision 7.1 is clearly a misprint for provision 6.1.

'PROVISION 6 – <u>RETIREMENT BENEFIT PURCHASES</u>

6.1—(a) <u>Normal Retirement Benefit</u> – At the direction of the Trustees [the taxpayer company] shall, by a deduction of the required purchase payment from the Fund, purchase the immediate normal retirement Benefit or any deferred annuity on termination of service with respect to any Member who qualified for such Benefit or annuity as determined by the Trustees in accordance with the Plan . . .'

Provision 7 relates to payment of the benefits and contains little of significance for present purposes save that provision 7.3 refers to the making of 'annuity pension or other payments' and provision 7.4 provides that the liability of the company with respect to any member shall be determined 'on the basis of the deposits actually received by [the taxpayer company] on such Member's behalf in accordance with the terms of this Contract'. Provision 8.1 provides for the contingency of suspension or discontinuance of deposits, in which event the contract continues with respect to any balance remaining in the fund until the fund is exhausted. Finally, provision 8.2 enables the trustees, on discontinuing deposits, to direct the taxpayer company to transfer 95% of the accumulated balance of the fund to another depository or to the trustees but subject to a right of retention for a period of ten years during which, if required, the taxpayer company will be liable to provide benefits due under the plan to the extent to which the accumulated balance is able to meet them.

An analysis of the true nature of these provisions discloses at once the inappropriateness of some of the terms used. For instance it is clear that the term 'deposit' is not used in the conventional sense of the deposit with a banker where the depositor is entitled to withdraw sums deposited, either with or without notice, and to receive interest in the meantime. There are, it is true, provisions such as 8.2 which

enable the trustees to achieve a return of the unapplied balance of the fund if it is
decided to terminate the arrangement for the future, but the essence of the   *a*
transaction is that the pension contributions are paid over to the taxpayer company
outright as the consideration for providing to members of the pension plan with the
appropriate annuities. Similarly, although the word 'purchase' is used in provision 6,
the contract does not in fact contemplate a purchase in any normally accepted sense
of the word, for the taxpayer company cannot utilise its own moneys to purchase
from itself.   *b*

   Realistically, the trust deed and the rules and the deposit administration contract
have to be read together as a single scheme. Under the trust deed the trustees assume
the obligation of providing the pension benefits prescribed by the rules and that
obligation is discharged by the taxpayer company in consideration of the receipt, as
part of its funds, of the employers' and employees' contributions. The fund
established under provision 5 and consisting of the contributions and guaranteed   *c*
interest is necessary accounting machinery not only for the taxpayer company's own
internal purposes but also to enable it to provide the trustees with the necessary
valuations for it to be determined whether additional deposits may be required and
to ascertain the extent of the taxpayer company's liability in the event of the scheme
being discontinued. It does not, however, represent a trust fund in which either the
trustees or the members of the scheme can claim any proprietary interest. In essence, *d*
the contract is simply one for the purchase by the trustees from the taxpayer
company of annuity benefits for the members and for the provision by the taxpayer
company of all the administrative services required for implementing the pension
scheme.

   The way in which the income received by the taxpayer company from deposits
under the contract was dealt with in the relevant year was as follows. The global   *e*
investment income earned during the year was apportioned amongst classes of
business in the ratio of the average of the opening and closing balances of the various
funds attributable to those classes. The deposit administration contract scheme
represented a ratio of 22·09% of the global assets to which was attributed net income
of $893,540, from which there fell to be provided a sum of $681,315 guaranteed
interest and a sum of $71,024 as the scheme's proportionate share of expenses of   *f*
earning the income. There thus remained a balance of $141,201 representing the
profit for the year on the deposit administration business and it was on this sum that
the corporation tax which is the subject matter of this appeal was assessed. It is not
in dispute that the sum in question was never distributed to the shareholders of the
taxpayer company but was retained as part of the fund and in fact was utilised in
fulfilment of the taxpayer company's obligations under the contract in subsequent   *g*
years.

   The salient facts as found by the Tax Appeal Board were as follows:

   '(1) The pension plan under which benefits were to be provided was one that
   had been approved by the Board of Inland Revenue under the Ordinance;
   (2) Under the deed, the trustees were empowered to contract out the duty of   *h*
   providing pensions under a deposit administration contract and had in fact so
   done;
   (3) The members of the plan were included in the deposit administration
   contract and the [taxpayer company] was responsible for providing pensions
   directly to them;
   (4) The benefits due under the pension plan were a charge on the fund;   *j*
   (5) Under the deposit administration contract, the [taxpayer company] was
   more than a mere depositary for the management of investments, as it was also
   obligated to provide pension benefits.'

The fourth finding was strictly inaccurate, in that what is charged on the fund is in
fact the capital value at retirement of the benefits due, but this is immaterial. On

these findings the Tax Appeal Board concluded:

> 'In the light of the above, we hold that the earnings of the [taxpayer company]
> under the deposit administration contract are profits from the carrying on of
> approved annuity business, and that pursuant to section 3(4) [of Sch 4] are
> exempt from corporation tax to the extent that they have not been distributed
> to shareholders.'

In the Court of Appeal the leading judgment was delivered by des Iles JA. It was
his view, with which the other two members of the court concurred, that what was
of essential importance was the purpose for which the profits of the deposit
administration business might be applied. He accepted that if the contract provided
for the immediate purchase of deferred annuities on receipt of the contributions, the
profits might then have been exempt from tax, but held that because the profits over
and above the guaranteed rate of interest were available to the taxpayer company as
part of its general funds they were not profits of annuity business and so were taxable
even though not distributed to shareholders. The ratio of the decision is contained
in the following passage from his judgment:

> 'In my view, even though both operations are contained in the Contract, they
> nevertheless remain separate and distinct transactions and whilst the [taxpayer
> company] is obligated to provide the Trustees with the "total of the contributions
> payable or to be deducted in accordance with the Rules", the monies from
> which the [taxpayer company] pays these contributions belong entirely to the
> [taxpayer company], albeit derived from the Deposit Administration business,
> and not part of the Approved Annuity business, and was thus available as part
> of the [taxpayer company's] general funds to do with as it pleased . . . I would
> hold that the transaction of business under the Contract was in the nature of
> commercial trading and not limited to the purchase of annuities.'

There is clearly some confusion here which is perhaps understandable having
regard to the unusual way in which the relevant documents have been drafted. The
phrase 'the total of the contributions payable or to be deducted in accordance with
the Rules' comes from the trust deed, not the deposit administration contract, and
refers to the employers' and employees' contributions payable by the employer to
the trustees. What the taxpayer company was obliged to provide was not the
contributions but the pension annuities provided for in the rules. Nor does the board
now seek to uphold the court's reasoning that because profits earned from investment
of contributions over and above the guaranteed interest payments are available to
the taxpayer company as part of its general funds they cannot constitute profits
exempt from tax under para 3(4) of Sch 4. That paragraph is concerned only with
the business from which the profits arise and not with their disposition in the hands
of the recipient so long as they are not distributed to shareholders. Nevertheless the
board submits that the Court of Appeal's decision that the contract constituted two
separate transactions, only one of which was 'approved annuity business', ought to
be upheld. What is said is that the true analysis of the contract is that up to the point
at which, in relation to each retiring employee, the taxpayer company receives the
instructions of the trustees to 'purchase' the appropriate pension annuity, by debiting
the fund with the market value of such annuity at that time, it is engaged simply in
the carrying on of a business of taking deposits on behalf of the trustees just as if the
contribution had been deposited with the bank or other deposit-taking company.
On this analysis, the approved annuity business did not commence until the effecting
of the notional 'purchase' of each separate annuity and constituted a separate and
independent business.

Their Lordships find themselves unable to accept this as a realistic view of the
true nature of the contract. The contract is a single agreement for the carrying out
by the taxpayer company on behalf of the trustees of their obligations under the
trust deed to provide pension annuities for the members of the scheme in accordance

with the rules, and the fact that it contains accounting provisions for the
establishment of a separate fund to cover such provision and for maintaining the
actuarial solvency of the fund so established cannot alter the essential nature of the
contract as one for the provision of annuities. The sole purpose of the fund is to
provide annuities and it is, in their Lordships' opinion, impossible to regard the
profits and losses generated or sustained from it, whether they take the form of a
surplus or deficit of investment income, surplus of administration fees over costs or
an excess of the 'purchase' price of annuities over the actual cost of provision, as
other than profits of 'annuity business'. The trust deed having provided expressly
for the benefits to be secured by a deposit administration contract and the pension
plan thus constituted having been approved by the Revenue there can, as is
conceded, be no room for argument that the business is other than 'approved annuity
business'.

The Lordships accordingly allow the appeal and restore the decision of the Tax
Appeal Board. The board must pay the taxpayer company's costs before the Tax
Appeal Board, the Court of Appeal and their Lordships' Board.

Appeal allowed with costs.

Solicitors: *Osmond Gaunt & Rose* (for the taxpayer company); *Charles Russell* (for
the board).

Rengan Krishnan Esq   Barrister.

New Zealand Stock Exchange and another v Commissioner of Inland Revenue

PRIVY COUNCIL
LORD KEITH OF KINKEL, LORD BRANDON OF OAKBROOK, LORD TEMPLEMAN, LORD OLIVER OF AYLMERTON, SIR ROBERT MEGARRY
10, 11 JUNE, 1 JULY 1991

New Zealand – Information – Power of Commissioner of Inland Revenue to require information – Whether commissioner had power to require information from stockbrokers and banks in respect of unidentified taxpayers – Inland Revenue Department Act 1974 (New Zealand), s 17.

The New Zealand Commissioner of Inland Revenue issued notices under s 17[a] of the Inland Revenue Department Act 1974 requiring some members of the New Zealand Stock Exchange to produce a list of their largest clients with details of purchases and sales of shares; similarly, he required some banks, including the National Bank of New Zealand Ltd (the bank) to produce names and details of customers who had bought and sold or obtained the fruits of commercial bills. He required the information in order to determine whether any taxable income from trading or dealing in shares or commercial bills had been generated and to discover the relevant taxpayers. The Stock Exchange and the bank obtained a declaration against the commissioner and, when the Court of Appeal quashed the order, appealed to the Privy Council seeking to imply into s 17 a limitation whereby the commissioner would be able to require information only in respect of a named taxpayer whose tax affairs were under investigation. The applicants contended that the commissioner was seeking information which was confidential and that he had exceeded or abused the powers conferred on him by s 17(1) by making demands on sharebrokers and bankers which were onerous and expensive to obey.

Held – (1) There was no distinction between the secrecy and confidentiality which attached to an identified taxpayer and that which attached to a non-identified taxpayer; confidentiality had to be broken if the commissioner was to obtain the information to enable him to carry out his statutory function of assessing and collecting tax.

(2) Section 17 required information to be produced which the commissioner considered 'necessary or relevant'. In the instant case the particulars sought did not go substantially beyond that which was required for the purpose of enabling the commissioner to carry out his statutory functions, and they could not be properly described as unduly oppressive or burdensome. There was no doubt that sharebrokers and bankers had or ought to have had the information that the commissioner requested. The commissioner had not exceeded or abused his powers and the court was not entitled to intervene.

Accordingly the commissioner was entitled to require information concerning a class of unidentified possible taxpayers and the appeal would be dismissed.

Clinch v IRC [1973] STC 155 followed.

Notes

For powers to require information, see Simon's Taxes E1.766.

---

a   Section 17, so far as material, is set out at p 513 *d e*, post

Cases referred to in judgment

Associated Provincial Picture Houses Ltd v Wednesbury Corp [1948] 1 KB 223, [1947] **a**
2 All ER 680, CA.
Bullivant v A-G for Victoria [1901] AC 196, HL.
Canadian Bank of Commerce v A-G of Canada (1962) 35 DLR (2d) 49.
Clinch v IRC [1973] STC 155, [1974] QB 76, [1973] 1 All ER 977, 49 TC 52.
Comr of Inland Revenue v West-Walker [1954] NZLR 191.
Federal Comr of Taxation v Australia and New Zealand Banking Group Ltd (1979) **b**
143 CLR 499.
R v McKinlay Transport Ltd (1990) 68 DLR (4th) 568.
Richardson (James) & Sons Ltd v Minister of National Revenue (1984) 9 DLR (4th) 1.

Appeal
c

The applicants, the New Zealand Stock Exchange and the National Bank of New
Zealand Ltd, appealed against the decision of the Court of Appeal of New Zealand
(Richardson, Somers, Casey, Bisson and Hardie Boys JJ) of 26 July 1990 (see [1990]
3 NZLR 333), quashing a declaration against the New Zealand Commissioner of
Inland Revenue who had issued notices requiring certain information under s 17 of **d**
the Inland Revenue Department Act 1974.

G P Barton QC, R A Dobson and *R J Cullen,* all of the New Zealand Bar, for the
applicants.
J J McGrath QC, Solicitor General, *G D Pearson* and *Angela Satterthwaite,* all of **e**
the New Zealand Bar, for the commissioner.

1 July 1991. The following judgment of the Board was delivered.

LORD TEMPLEMAN. By s 9 of the Income Tax Act 1976 of New Zealand, as **f**
amended, (the 1976 Act) a taxpayer, defined by s 2 as a person chargeable with
income tax, shall for the purposes of the assessment and levy of income tax furnish
to the respondent commissioner in each year a return or returns in the prescribed
form or forms setting forth a complete statement of all the assessable income derived
by him during the preceding year together with such other particulars as may be
prescribed. **g**
Assessable income is defined by s 2 of the 1976 Act as income of any kind which is
not exempted from income tax.
By s 19 of the 1976 Act:

'(1) From the returns made ... and from any other information in his
possession the Commissioner shall in and for every year, and from time to time **h**
and at any time thereafter as may be necessary, make assessments in respect of
every taxpayer of the amount on which tax is payable and of the amount of that
tax.'

By s 21:

'If any person makes default in furnishing any return, or if the Commissioner **j**
is not satisfied with the return made by any person, or if the Commissioner has
reason to suppose that any person, although he has not made a return, is a
taxpayer, he may make an assessment of the amount on which in his judgment
tax ought to be levied and of the amount of that tax, and that person shall be
liable to pay the tax so assessed, save in so far as he establishes on objection that
the assessment is excessive or that he is not chargeable with tax.'

By s 27, except in proceedings on objection to an assessment under the 1976 Act:

a

> 'No assessment made by the Commissioner shall be disputed in any Court or in any proceedings ... and ... every such assessment and all the particulars thereof shall be conclusively deemed and taken to be correct, and the liability of the person so assessed shall be determined accordingly.'

By s 34:

b

> '(3) Where, in relation to a person being a taxpayer and to any assessment the tax assessed in which has become due and payable, any amount of deferrable tax is unpaid and any amount of tax that is not deferrable tax is unpaid, each such amount of unpaid tax may be recovered by the Commissioner as a separate debt arising from a separate cause of action.'

c By ss 38 and 39 income tax shall be payable by every person on all income derived by him during the year for which the tax is payable and shall be assessed and levied on the taxable income of every taxpayer at such rate or rates as may be fixed from time to time.

Thus income tax at a stipulated rate is levied for the benefit of the community on the assessable income of every taxpayer and it is the duty of the commissioner to see that such income is assessed to tax and that the tax is paid.

d By accident or design, a taxpayer may default in his obligation to furnish a return or to disclose all his assessable income. In order to discharge his duty of assessing and recovering tax on all taxable income the commissioner must discover the names of taxpayers and the respective sources and amounts of their assessable income. By s 17(1) of the Inland Revenue Department Act 1974 (the 1974 Act):

e

> 'Every person ... shall, when required by the Commissioner ... furnish in writing any information and produce for inspection any books and documents which the Commissioner ... considers necessary or relevant for any purpose relating to the administration or enforcement of any of the Inland Revenue Acts.'

By s 2 and Sch 1 of the 1974 Act, the Inland Revenue Acts mentioned in s 17(1)
f include the 1976 Act.

If a person trades or deals in shares or commercial bills, profits thereby generated may constitute taxable income. In order to determine whether taxable income had been generated and to discover the relevant taxpayers, the commissioner required information which would disclose to the commissioner names of taxpayers who had bought and sold shares or bills and which would disclose sufficient detail to enable
g the commissioner to assess those taxpayers in respect of assessable income generated by dealings in shares and commercial bills. Under s 17 of the 1974 Act the commissioner therefore required some members of the Stock Exchange to produce a list of their largest clients and details of their purchase and sale of shares. The commissioner also required the National Bank of New Zealand and some other banks to produce the names and details of bank customers who had bought and sold
h or obtained the fruits of commercial bills.

In these proceedings the applicants, the New Zealand Stock Exchange (acting in the interests of its members) and the National Bank of New Zealand Ltd (acting in the interests of banks generally), sought and obtained from Jeffries J a declaration against the commissioner. As it emerged, the real issue was whether under s 17 of the 1974 Act the commissioner had any power to require information except in
j respect of a named individual whose tax affairs were under investigation. The Court of Appeal (Richardson, Somers, Casey, Bisson and Hardie Boys JJ) quashed the order of Jeffries J. The applicants now appeal to Her Majesty in Council.

Their Lordships would be content to adopt the comprehensive judgment of the Court of Appeal which was delivered by Richardson J but, in deference to the full and careful argument advanced before the Board by counsel for the applicants, they will deal fully with the arguments put forward.

As Richardson J pointed out, s 17 is expressed in the widest terms. The applicants
seek to imply in s 17 a limitation whereby the commissioner may only require *a*
information—'... where the Commissioner has a specified taxpayer in mind in
respect of whom there is a serious question in mind as to the tax liability of that
taxpayer.' It is impossible to insert that limitation as a matter of statutory
construction. The limitation could only be inserted as a matter of policy by a process
of judicial legislation on the grounds that Parliament could not have intended to
confer on the commissioner a power so wide as not to be subject to such a limitation. *b*

Two reasons are suggested for the insertion of the proposed limitation, first, that
the commissioner is seeking information which is confidential and, second, that the
commissioner is imposing on sharebrokers and bankers an onerous burden of
research and report.

If the commissioner, exercising his undoubted powers under s 17(1) of the 1974
Act, requires the bankers of a specified taxpayer under investigation to produce *c*
information about that taxpayer's activities, then the confidentiality which attaches
to the relationship between banker and customer must be broken. The whole
rationale of taxation would break down and the whole burden of taxation would fall
only on diligent and honest taxpayers if the commissioner had no power to obtain
confidential information about taxpayers who may be negligent or dishonest. In
recognition of the fact that confidential information cannot be concealed from the *d*
commissioner, the 1974 Act imposes stringent restrictions on the commissioner.
Section 13 requires every officer of the Revenue to maintain and aid in maintaining
the secrecy of all matters relating to the 1976 Act and other taxing statutes and
requires every officer of the Department of Inland Revenue to make a statutory
declaration of fidelity and secrecy. There are other provisions which are designed to
secure and do secure the secrecy of information obtained by the commissioner about *e*
the affairs of every taxpayer. There is no distinction between the secrecy and
confidentiality which attach to an identified taxpayer and a non-identified taxpayer.
Confidentiality must be broken if the commissioner is to obtain the information to
enable him to carry out his statutory functions of assessing and collecting tax. Every
taxpayer is protected by the secrecy obligation imposed on the commissioner. If the
applicants' argument is correct, confidentiality does not assist the taxpayer who *f*
makes an honest return of his income or the dishonest taxpayer who is under
investigation by the commissioner but assists the dishonest taxpayer who conceals
both his identity and his liability to tax from the commissioner.

The applicants relied on the decision of the Court of Appeal in *Comr of Inland
Revenue v West-Walker* [1954] NZLR 191. In that case the commissioner sought
information about a taxpayer from his solicitor and the court held that the solicitor *g*
was entitled to withhold information to which the common law legal professional
privilege attached. The commissioner was entitled to ask but the solicitor was
entitled to decline to answer without the consent of his client. In the present case
the applicants deny the right of the commissioner to ask for the required information.
Under the common law, but not under other systems of law, legal professional
privilege forms a defence to a claim for information because as Fair J, citing *h*
Lord Halsbury in *Bullivant v A-G for Victoria* [1901] AC 196 at 200–201, said in the
West-Walker case ([1954] NZLR 191 at 204)—

> '... *for the perfect administration of justice,* and for the protection of the
> confidence which exists between a solicitor and his client, it has been established
> *as a principle of public policy* that those confidential communications shall not *j*
> be subject to production.' [Emphasis added by Fair J.]

The court in *West-Walker* held that, in the absence of any express provision in the
Income Tax Acts abrogating the principle of legal professional privilege, that
principle excused the solicitor from supplying privileged information to the
commissioner. That case is of no assistance in the present case where it is manifest

and is conceded that the principle of confidentiality was abrogated by s 17 of the
a 1974 Act.

The applicants referred to Australian authorities. None of those authorities dealt
directly with the present point at issue and all concerned statutory provisions in
forms different to that of the New Zealand Act. In *Federal Comr of Taxation v
Australia and New Zealand Banking Group Ltd* (1979) 143 CLR 499, the High Court
of Australia dealt with the power conferred by s 264(1) of the Income Tax Assessment
b Act 1936 on the commissioner to require any person to attend and give evidence—

'... concerning his or any other person's income or assessment, and may
require him to produce all books, documents and other papers whatever in his
custody or under his control relating thereto.'

Mason J said (at 536):
c

'It is the function of the Commissioner to ascertain the taxpayer's taxable
income. To ascertain this he may need to make wide-ranging inquiries, and to
make them long before any issue of fact arises between him and the taxpayer.
Such an issue will in general, if not always, only arise after the process of
assessment has been completed. It is to the process of investigation before
d   assessment that s. 264 is principally, if not exclusively, directed.'

The applicants also relied on the Canadian case of *James Richardson & Sons Ltd
v Minister of National Revenue* (1984) 9 DLR (4th) 1. In that case Wilson J, giving
the judgment of the Supreme Court of Canada, held that a general power conferred
on the Minister of National Revenue by s 231 of the taxing statute to require from
any person any information for any purposes related to the administration or
e enforcement of the Act only enabled the Minister to require information concerning
a specified taxpayer. But in that case s 221 of the Act expressly authorised the
making of regulations 'requiring any class of persons to make information returns
respecting any class of information required in connection with assessments under
this Act'. The court held that the express power in s 221, a power which had not
been exercised, limited the general power conferred by s 231. If the Minister wished
f to seek information regarding a class of persons then he must obtain a regulation
under s 221. Wilson J also relied on the earlier Canadian decision of *Canadian Bank
of Commerce v A-G of Canada* (1962) 35 DLR (2d) 49 but in that case the Minister
asked for information concerning a particular alleged taxpayer. That case is of no
assistance in deciding whether in the present case the commissioner is entitled to
information concerning a class of possible taxpayers.
g   Counsel for the applicants sought to pray in aid the New Zealand Bill of Rights
Act 1990, which affirmed, inter alia, in s 21 that:

'Everyone has the right to be secure against unreasonable search or seizure,
whether of the person, property, or correspondence or otherwise.'

h   Their Lordships are content to assume that in the present case the commissioner
is seeking to search the property or correspondence of taxpayers. Having regard to
the secrecy provisions of the 1974 Act and to the fact that in the interests of the
community the commissioner is charged with ensuring that the assessable income of
every taxpayer is assessed and the tax paid, the 'search' involved in the application
of s 17 of the 1974 Act cannot be said to be unreasonable. A similar conclusion was
j reached by the Supreme Court of Canada in *R v McKinlay Transport Ltd* (1990) 68
DLR (4th) 568 under the Canadian Charter of Rights and Freedoms. In that case
there was an elaborate consideration (at 580) of 'different expectations of privacy in
different contexts' but their Lordships are content simply to decide that the exercise
of the powers conferred on the commissioner by s 17 of the 1974 Act is not, for the
purposes of s 21 of the New Zealand Bill of Rights Act 1990, 'unreasonable'.

The applicants also contended that in the present case the commissioner had exceeded or abused the powers conferred on him by s 17 of the 1974 Act by making *a* demands on sharebrokers and bankers which were onerous and expensive to obey. In the case of sharebrokers they were asked to supply lists of their largest clients together with details of their share dealings through the sharebroker. Bankers were asked to identify investors with them in commercial bills and to give details of each investment, cost and realisation. One sharebroker complained that he was asked for information over a 12-month period and that he only had information over an 11- *b* month period because of a merger which had taken place. There is no doubt that sharebrokers and bankers have or ought to have the information which the commissioner has requested. The commissioner has demonstrated that he is prepared to modify his requirements to meet any particular genuine difficulty.

In *Clinch v IRC* [1973] STC 155, [1974] QB 76 the British Commissioners of Inland Revenue sought information which was described by the recipient as a *c* 'fishing' or 'snooping' exercise. Similar complaints were made in the present case. In *Clinch v IRC* ([1973] STC 155 at 163, [1974] QB 76 at 87) Ackner J was unmoved by this emotive language but had no doubt that if the particulars sought went substantially beyond that which was required for the purposes of enabling the commissioners to carry out their statutory functions ([1973] STC 155 at 167, [1974] QB 76 at 92)— *d*

> '... so that they could be properly described as unduly oppressive or burdensome... a court would be entitled to intervene... One of the vital functions of the courts is to protect the individual from any abuse of power by the executive, a function which nowadays grows more and more important as governmental interference increases.'
e

Of course in New Zealand every sharebroker or banker will understandably resent the receipt of a notice from the commissioner requiring information about the clients of the sharebroker or the banker. Every sharebroker or banker will resent the time and expense incurred in complying with the notice. But the commissioner must carry out his functions of ensuring that assessable income is assessed and that the relevant tax is paid. Section 17 of the 1974 Act requires information to be *f* produced which the commissioner 'considers necessary or relevant'. There is nothing in the point that the commissioner wisely did not require every sharebroker and every banker to disclose information about all his clients and customers.

The court can only interfere if satisfied that in making a particular requirement the commissioner exceeded or abused his powers (see *Associated Provincial Picture Houses Ltd v Wednesbury Corp* [1948] 1 KB 223 and *Clinch v IRC* [1973] STC 155, *g* [1974] QB 76). In the present case the Court of Appeal decided that as a matter of principle and construction the commissioner was entitled to require information concerning a class of unidentified possible taxpayers. The court declined to speculate on the circumstance which might lead to interference by way of judicial review. Their Lordships agree with the Court of Appeal and find nothing in the evidence adduced in the present case which could justify judicial review. *h*

Their Lordships will humbly advise Her Majesty that this appeal ought to be dismissed. The applicants must pay the costs of the commissioner before the Board.

Appeal dismissed with costs.

Solicitors: *Simmons & Simmons* (for the applicants); *Allen & Overy* (for the *j* commissioner).

Rengan Krishnan Esq   Barrister.

Alongi v Inland Revenue Commissioners

FIRST DIVISION OF THE INNER HOUSE OF THE COURT OF SESSION AS THE COURT OF
EXCHEQUER IN SCOTLAND
THE LORD PRESIDENT (HOPE), LORD MAYFIELD, LORD McCLUSKEY
21 MAY, 12 JUNE 1991

*Trade – Adventure in the nature of trade – Meaning of 'trade' – Taxpayer receiving or
entitled to receive profits arising from trade – Taxpayer proprietor of restaurant
business – Whether profits of business accrued to taxpayer – Income and Corporation
Taxes Act 1970, s 108.*

The taxpayer was the proprietor of a restaurant business. He appealed to the General
Commissioners against an assessment to income tax under Sch D, Case I on the
profits of the restaurant, contending that although he had assisted in the carrying on
of the business he had divested himself of the right to receive its profits. The
commissioners dismissed the appeal, holding that the business had been owned and
controlled by the taxpayer and that its profits had accrued to him. On appeal to the
Court of Session the taxpayer submitted: (i) that his activities in facilitating the
running of the business had not amounted to the carrying on of a trade by him;
(ii) that the profits of the business had not accrued to him; and (iii) that he was
therefore not assessable to income tax on the profits of the restaurant business.

Held – In order to satisfy the court that the assessments should be discharged the
taxpayer had to establish that the profits of the restaurant business had not accrued
to him. There was no evidence to show that the taxpayer had agreed to divest
himself of the profits in favour of anyone else and therefore the commissioners had
reached the only true and reasonable conclusion which had been open to them. The
taxpayer's appeal would accordingly be dismissed.

Notes

For the definition of trade, see Simon's Taxes, B3.201.
    For the Income and Corporation Taxes Act 1970, s 108 (now the Income and
Corporation Taxes Act 1988, s 18), see ibid, Part G1.

Cases referred to in opinion

Nasim v Customs and Excise Comrs [1987] STC 387.
Ransom (Inspector of Taxes) v Higgs [1974] STC 539, [1974] 1 WLR 1594, [1974]
    3 All ER 949, 50 TC 1, HL.
Spedding v Sabine (Inspector of Taxes) (1954) 35 TC 239.

Case stated

    1. At meetings of the Commissioners for the general purposes of the income tax
for the division of Midlothian held on 6, 20 and 28 May 1987, and 25 May 1988,
Cavaliere Victor A D Alongi (the taxpayer), 22 Elm Row, Edinburgh, appealed
against assessments to income tax under Sch D, Case I for the years 1981–82, 1982–
83, 1983–84, 1984–85 and 1985–86 in the sum of £20,000 for each year in respect of
profits arising from the business known as the Caprice Restaurant, situated at 325–
331 Leith Walk, Edinburgh, hereinafter referred to as the Caprice.
    2. The taxpayer was represented by Mr R Crawford of Jeffrey Crawford & Co,
C A, Edinburgh. The Crown was represented by Mr S M Duffus, inspector of
taxes, Edinburgh 8 District.

3. Shortly stated, the question for decision was whether the taxpayer was the proprietor of the business at the Caprice, and as a result whether assessable profits arising therefrom were assessable on him for the five years 1981–82 to 1985–86 inclusive.

4. There was lodged with the commissioners a statement of agreed facts which had been agreed between the parties.

[The documents which were put in evidence were then listed.]

5. Evidence was given under oath by the taxpayer on his own behalf. In addition, evidence was heard under oath on the facts in dispute from Antonio Gaetano Alongi (Tony), the brother of the taxpayer, and Mrs Anna Alongi (Anna), the wife of the said Tony. Further evidence was given by Mr D Paton, a bookkeeper who had dealt with the preparation of records and books, PAYE income tax matters and value added tax returns for the Caprice as well as for other business establishments of the taxpayer.

6. Evidence was given under oath on behalf of the Crown by Mr J Bald, inspector of taxes, Edinburgh 4 District (previously of Edinburgh 8 District), and Mr J Barbour, collector of taxes, Edinburgh audit.

7. As a result of the evidence adduced before the commissioners the following facts were admitted or proved: (a) The business known as the Caprice Restaurant, 325–331 Leith Walk, Edinburgh, was, prior to 1982, owned by Tony. Tony was sequestrated in 1982 and the business was advertised for sale. An offer by the taxpayer to buy the business, including the business premises, was accepted and the premises were disponed to the taxpayer on 2 July 1982 for the sum of £195,000, with entry given from 1 April 1982. The taxpayer borrowed the sum of £161,733 from the Royal Bank of Scotland (the bank) in order to finance the purchase. A standard security was granted by the taxpayer in favour of the bank as security for the loan. (b) Three bank accounts for the business were opened with the bank in Musselburgh in the names of the taxpayer and his wife, Lady Alongi. One account was a business account, the second was a loan account, and the third was for value added tax. Tony, the taxpayer and Lady Alongi were authorised signatories to the business account and the taxpayer alone was the signatory to the loan account. Only one signature was required to operate the business account and in practice cheques on this account were signed only by Tony. The loan account represented the moneys borrowed from the bank to finance the transaction. The sum of £1,000 was paid into that account each week. The sum was paid out of an account into which the business receipts of the restaurant were paid and was paid by a standing order which had been authorised by the taxpayer. That sum was regarded by the parties as rent but was payable at that rate on the understanding that when the loan account (including interest charges) was reduced to nil the taxpayer would reconvey the Caprice to Tony for a nominal sum. Tony subsequently fell behind in these payments. After about a year the payments fell to £700 per week, then £500 a week and later ceased altogether. (c) The taxpayer owned several other businesses and maintained a number of accounts with the same branch of the bank in Musselburgh. Money was regularly transferred by standing order from the Caprice business account to one of these other accounts. (d) From 1 April 1982 the books of the business were maintained by Mr D Paton who was also employed by the taxpayer to maintain the books of the taxpayer's other businesses. (e) The business books and records for the Caprice were in due course furnished by the taxpayer to D S Brown & Co, Chartered Accountants, who prepared accounts for the accounting years ended 30 November 1983 and 30 November 1984. These accounts were approved and signed by the taxpayer and thereafter submitted to the taxpayer's inspector of taxes. (f) Value added tax registration was in the name of the Caprice Restaurant, a partnership. The partnership was nominally one of which the taxpayer and his wife were the partners but all value added tax returns were prepared, signed and submitted by Mr Paton under Tony's instructions. All payments of value added tax were made by Tony. (g) During 1983 and 1984 the Revenue carried out a PAYE audit of the business. Mr Barbour, collector of taxes, Edinburgh audit, on two occasions in

September 1983 met Mr Paton and a Mr Alongi, whom he assumed to be the
taxpayer. On 1 September 1984 an offer in settlement was made in respect of PAYE
emoluments and penalties. Although the offer bore to be from the taxpayer and to
have been signed by him, the signature was not in fact his but had been adhibited
by Paton, as Paton admitted in evidence. (h) Tony and his wife, Anna, were
employed by the taxpayer throughout the period from 1 April 1982 until 19 March
1987 and did not carry on business as restaurateurs there on their own account. The
taxpayer, as proprietor, remained throughout in overall control of the business.
(i) On 3 and 4 December 1985 a formal lease of the business premises was entered
into between the taxpayer on the one part, and Tony's wife, Anna, and his son, Mr
Richard Alongi (Richard), on the other. The lease was signed by Anna and Richard
on Tony's instructions. The lease bore to run for the period from 19 August 1982
until 18 August 1989. Inter alia it provided that the taxpayer would be entitled to
supervise the day to day running of the business, and that he would have authority
to employ and dismiss staff, to inspect the books of the business and generally to do
everything which he deemed necessary to ensure that the business was run to his
satisfaction. The lease further provided that if the taxpayer was not so satisfied he
would be entitled instantly to determine the lease. No rent was ever paid under the
lease. (j) The taxpayer sold the restaurant premises to Anna on 19 March 1987.

8. It was contended on behalf of the taxpayer that any assessable profits from the
Caprice were assessable on the taxpayer's brother Tony, or alternatively on the wife
of the said Tony, namely Anna, or alternatively on the said Tony, Anna and
Richard, the son of the said Tony.

The contentions were founded on the following matters: (1) The lease should have
been accepted by the commissioners as a genuine transaction having regard to the
rent payable by Tony to the taxpayer. (2) The commissioners had previously
determined an assessment on Tony for the years 1972 to 1975 as trader at the Caprice
and this was never appealed. (3) Tony's statements to the Revenue at all times
showed that he regarded himself as the party deriving profit from the Caprice.
(4) The taxpayer never at any time met the Revenue PAYE audit examiner dealing
with the PAYE. (5) Entries in the PAYE records for the Caprice as employees did
not necessarily preclude Tony, Anna and Richard from being the parties deriving
the profits of the business at the Caprice.

9. It was contended on behalf of the Crown: (i) that the taxpayer was the sole
proprietor of the Caprice throughout the period from 1 April 1982 until 5 April
1986, and was chargeable to income tax on the entire profits arising therefrom
during that period; (ii) that the assessments under appeal should be determined as
follows:

1981–82	Case I profits	£722
	Stock relief	513
	Capital allowances	209
1982–83	Case I profits	£51,997
	Capital allowances	33,441
1983–84	Case I profits	£43,021
	Stock relief	293
1984–85	Case I profits	£51,997
1985–86	Case I profits	£26,147

10. The commissioners were referred to the following cases:

Haythornthwaite and Sons Ltd v Kelly (Inspector of Taxes) (1927) 11 TC 657.
Mann v Nash (Inspector of Taxes) [1932] 1 KB 752, 16 TC 523.
Nasim v Customs and Excise Comrs [1987] STC 387.
Paddington Burial Board v IRC (1884) 2 TC 46.
Southern (Inspector of Taxes) v A B [1933] 1 KB 713, 18 TC 59.
Spedding v Sabine (Inspector of Taxes) (1954) 35 TC 239.

11. At the conclusion of the hearing the commissioners gave their decision as follows. The taxpayer was the proprietor of the business known as the Caprice. Accordingly the assessments under appeal for the relevant years were determined in the following figures:

1981–82	Profit	£722
	Less stock relief	513
	Capital allowances	209
1982–83	Profit	£51,997
	Less capital allowances	33,441
1983–84	Profit	£43,021
	Less Stock relief	293
1984–85	Profit	£51,997
1985–86	Profit	£26,147

The commissioners did not accept as credible the evidence given on behalf of the taxpayer. On the basis of the facts as proved or admitted they found that on the balance of probabilities the Caprice was owned and controlled by the taxpayer and that the business profits therefrom accrued to the taxpayer. The commissioners discounted the purported lease on the basis that it was not a genuine transaction entered into for business purposes, but was simply a device by the taxpayer to obtain a tax advantage.

12. Immediately after the determination of the appeal, dissatisfaction therewith as being erroneous in point of law was expressed on behalf of the taxpayer and in due course the commissioners were required to state a case for the opinion of the Court of Session as the Court of Exchequer in Scotland, pursuant to s 56 of the Taxes Management Act 1970.

13. The questions of law for the opinion of the court were (1) whether on the facts found the commissioners were entitled to determine the assessments as set out in para 11 above, and (2) whether there was evidence to support finding 7(h).

A C Hamilton QC for the taxpayer.
G N H Emslie QC and *R A Smith* for the Crown.

The court made avizandum.

12 June. The following opinion was delivered.

THE LORD PRESIDENT (HOPE). This is an appeal by the taxpayer against a decision of the General Commissioners that he was assessable for income tax on the profits of the business known as the Caprice, Leith Walk, Edinburgh. The assessments which were before the commissioners were for the years 1981–82 to 1985–86. They were assessments made under Sch D, Case I by which, in terms of s 108 of the Income and Corporation Taxes Act 1970 (now s 18 of the Income and Corporation Taxes Act 1988), income tax was to be charged in respect of 'the annual profits or gains arising or accruing ... (ii) to any person residing in the United Kingdom from any trade, profession or vocation, whether carried on in the United Kingdom or elsewhere'. The commissioners held that the taxpayer was the proprietor of the business, that the business was owned and controlled by him and that the business profits therefrom accrued to the taxpayer.

The taxpayer contends that their determination of the assessments was erroneous in point of law, on the ground that the decision was not justified by the evidence and that it was one which no person acting judicially and properly instructed could have reached. No distinction was made between the various assessments under appeal. There was no dispute that a trade was being carried on in the premises or that there

were profits and gains which were assessable to income tax. Nor was it disputed that
the onus of proof was on the taxpayer to establish sufficient facts and circumstances
to displace the assessments on the ground that the profits or gains of the business did
not accrue to him. The challenge was directed to a single point which, in the last
analysis, was plainly a question of fact, and to the conclusions which the
commissioners were entitled to draw from a statement of agreed facts which was
placed before them and from the evidence.

The business in question was carried on at a restaurant known as the Caprice in
Leith Walk, Edinburgh. Prior to 1982 it had been owned by the taxpayer's brother,
Mr Antonio G Alongi, who is referred to in the case stated as Tony. Tony was
sequestrated in 1982, following which the business was advertised for sale and
ultimately sold to the taxpayer. Much of the evidence was taken up with the actings
of the taxpayer and his wife, Lady Alongi, on the one hand and Tony and his wife,
Mrs Anna M Alongi (Anna), and their son, Mr Richard A Alongi (Richard), on the
other. There was also a bookkeeper named Mr D Paton, who operated the wages
records of the business and gave certain advice to Tony and Anna as to the sums
which they could draw from the business following its sale to the taxpayer.

The commissioners saw the principal question for their decision as being whether
the taxpayer was the proprietor of the business for the years to which the assessments
relate. Counsel for the taxpayer criticised this approach because, he said, the
question of proprietorship was ambiguous. He submitted that it did not necessarily
follow that the proprietor of a business was the person to whom its profits or gains
arose or accrued. The important question was what, if anything, the taxpayer
actually did in regard to the trade which was being carried on in the premises. The
fact that he assisted or facilitated the carrying-on of that trade or business, or
procured things to be done by others in that regard, would not necessarily result in
his activities amounting to the carrying-on of a trade by him. Reference was made
to *Ransom (Inspector of Taxes) v Higgs* [1974] STC 539 at 550, [1974] 1 WLR 1594
at 1606, where Lord Morris of Borth-y-Gest said that in considering whether a
person carried on a trade it was essential to discover and to examine what exactly it
was that the person did. So, said counsel for the taxpayer, if the taxpayer took no
active part in the business and did not employ others, whether as his servants or
agents to carry it on on his own behalf, he could not properly be said to be carrying
on the trade at all and was not assessable to income tax on its profits or gains. It was
against this background that he attacked finding (h) in para 7 of the case stated
which is in these terms:

'Tony and his wife, Mrs Anna M Alongi, were employed by the [taxpayer]
throughout the period from 1st April 1982 until 19th March 1987 and did not
carry on business as Restaurateurs there on their own account. The [taxpayer],
as proprietor, remained throughout in overall control of the business.'

This critical finding was, he said, not justified by the evidence and, in its absence,
there was insufficient material in the facts to entitle the commissioners to hold that
the taxpayer was the person to whom the profits or gains of the business arose. He
submitted that it was quite unnecessary for the taxpayer to prove who it was who
was actually in receipt of the profits or gains of the business. The only question was
whether the commissioners were entitled on the facts found proved by them to
arrive at the decision which they had reached that that person was the taxpayer.
Underlying this approach was an acceptance that the commissioners' decision that
the taxpayer was the proprietor of the business was in itself not open to criticism.
Indeed it seems to us that their decision on this point could scarcely have been
otherwise. In the statement of agreed facts they were told that the restaurant
premises and business were purchased by the taxpayer in his own name from Tony
with entry on 29 April 1982. Finding (a) in para 7 of the case stated records that an
offer by the taxpayer to buy the business including the business premises was
accepted and that the premises were disponed to the taxpayer on 2 July 1982 with

entry given as from 1 April in that year. And missives were produced dated
5 February and 16, 17 and 19 March 1987 which showed that the taxpayer agreed to
sell the premises and the licensed restaurant business carried on there, together with
the goodwill thereof and the furniture, furnishings, fixtures, equipment and
contents, to Tony's wife Anna with entry on 14 August 1987. It is plain that the
commissioners were entitled to hold on the basis of these facts that the taxpayer was
the proprietor of both the business premises and the business which was being
carried on there between these dates.

Now, as counsel for the Crown pointed out, this conclusion provides a convenient
and important starting point for an examination of the question which is principally
at issue in this case. This is because prima facie the proprietor of a business is the
person who is entitled to the profits or gains which arise or accrue from it. The
profits or gains of a business do not, as it were, emerge into a vacuum. They arise or
accrue to the person who is entitled to receive them. The person to whom one would
naturally look as the recipient of the profits or gains is the proprietor of the business,
because with ownership normally goes the right to control or direct what goes on. In
the simple case therefore, where there is no other candidate as the recipient, the
concept of proprietorship involves no ambiguity because there is no one else to
whom the profits or gains can accrue. It is not inconceivable that an agreement may
exist by which the right to receive the profits or gains is given by the proprietor to
someone else. But if that situation exists the proprietor can reasonably be expected
to know about it and to be able to produce evidence to show who the recipient is and
by what right the profits and gains arise or accrue to him. We agree with counsel for
the Crown that, if the proprietor is setting out to show that he is not that person, he
cannot convincingly do this unless he sets out also to show who the person is to
whom the profits arise or accrue. It is a significant weakness in the taxpayer's
argument in this appeal that, although it was contended to the commissioners that
any profits from the business were assessable on his brother Tony or Tony's wife,
Anna, or on Tony, Anna and their son, Richard, the commissioners have not found
any facts proved to establish any of these alternatives. While it may not strictly
speaking have been necessary for the taxpayer to establish who else was entitled to
the profits or gains if it was not him himself, his failure to demonstrate who this was
makes it very difficult for us now to hold that the commissioners were not entitled to
decide that the profits of the business accrued to the taxpayer.

The taxpayer's argument was directed especially to finding (h) as not being
justified by the evidence, but in our opinion that challenge was not successful and
for this reason the commissioners' decision cannot be said to be one which they were
not entitled to reach. The statement of agreed facts records that Tony sold the
Caprice to the taxpayer as a direct result of his sequestration, and it is clear that for
at least part of the relevant period Tony was an undischarged bankrupt. It seems
unlikely, to say the least, that after having gone to the trouble of selling the business
to the taxpayer in these difficult circumstances, Tony would run the risk of exposing
the profits or gains of the business to the claims of his creditors by retaining the
entitlement to their receipt. The logical step for him to take was to ensure that the
profits or gains accrued to someone else, for the time being at least, and that the
goodwill of the business was preserved, and to derive such income as he properly
could from the business in the character of an employee. That indeed is what the
documents produced to the commissioners seem to indicate was done. The statement
of agreed facts records that Mr Paton, the bookkeeper, advised Tony and Anna to
draw such sums from the business as were below the PAYE threshold to avoid
PAYE and national insurance contributions. This was hardly the advice one would
expect to be given to someone who was entitled to receive the profits or gains of the
business and who was assessable to income tax on these profits and gains under
Sch D. The commissioners were entitled to conclude from this agreed fact that both
Tony and Anna were being treated as employees of the business, and that it was

understood that they would be liable to deduction of income tax under the PAYE
a scheme if their wages and other emoluments assessable to income tax under Sch E
exceeded the appropriate rate per week. The PAYE return forms and deduction
cards which were produced in evidence appear to confirm this approach, because
Tony and his son Richard were both included among the employees for whom
deductions working sheets were prepared and end of year returns P14 were
completed in their names.

b Counsel for the taxpayer submitted that the commissioners ought not to have had
regard to the documents indicating that Tony and Richard were treated as employees
because there were no findings to suggest that the taxpayer had any concern with
them or that he was privy to or agreed to what was done. He contended that the
facts showed that the taxpayer played no active part in the business at all and that
the arrangements described in the statement of agreed facts were arrangements
c which were entered into between Tony and Anna and the bookkeeper and not with
him. But this submission falls well short of what is necessary to satisfy us that the
conclusion reached by the commissioners was one which they were not entitled to
reach on the evidence. Although the taxpayer was not proved to have been involved
directly in the various bookkeeping exercises such as the preparation of the PAYE
records, the commissioners had before them business accounts which had been
d approved and signed by him. These had been prepared by accountants on the basis
of business books and records furnished to them by the taxpayer and the accounts
were thereafter submitted to the taxpayer's inspector of taxes. They had before them
principal accounts for the two years ended 30 November 1983 and 30 November
1984, each of which contained a certificate in the name of the taxpayer and signed
by him stating that he approved the accounts and confirming that he had made
e available all relevant records and information for the purposes of preparing them
and authorising his accountants to forward them to the Revenue. The commissioners
were entitled to conclude from these certificates that the taxpayer accepted
responsibility for the accuracy of all the entries in these accounts including the
figures stated in them for wages, and furthermore that all the various books and
records of the business were subject to his control. It should be noted that in para 11
f of the case stated it is stated that the commissioners did not accept as credible the
evidence given on behalf of the taxpayer. Accordingly they are not to be criticised
if, having been told that the taxpayer was unaware of the PAYE records, they
disbelieved him, or, when faced with the contention that these records did not
necessarily preclude Tony, Anna and Richard from being the parties who were
entitled to the profits of the business, they decided to reject it as being inconsistent
g with the documents which were before them.

It is not necessary in these circumstances to go over every detail which was
canvassed before us in argument. Counsel for the taxpayer said that the financial
arrangements as shown by the bank accounts pointed positively away from the
taxpayer as the person who was entitled to receive the profits of the business. He
referred us to the bank statements in the taxpayer's name which showed among
h other things that sums of £1,000 were being transferred each week from the business
account which was in the name of the taxpayer and his wife to another account in
their names designated as the Caprice Restaurant, Leith Walk Loan Account.
Finding (b) of para 7 of the case stated tells us that these sums were regarded by the
parties as rent. They might also have been seen as payments of a loan. But what is of
greater significance is that these sums were being transferred from one account to
j another both of which were in the name of the taxpayer and his wife. Furthermore
the accounts which were signed by the taxpayer did not include in the list of
overheads or trading expenses any corresponding item in the name of rent or
anything else to indicate that these transfers were a charge against the profits of the
business. The way in which these accounts were prepared is entirely consistent with
these amounts having been drawn out of profits which belonged to the taxpayer.

There is no documentary evidence to show that any money was going to Tony or any members of his family during the relevant period in any way other than as wages.

Counsel for the taxpayer sought to illustrate the point that the proprietor of a business could divest himself of the right to run the business from day to day and receive the profits by reference to *Nasim v Customs and Excise Comrs* [1987] STC 387. In that case, Simon Brown J was satisfied that the value added tax tribunal had erred in law, and that on the clear and undisputed primary facts there was only one reasonable and proper conclusion available to them which was that the taxpayer had wholly divested herself of the business so that it had become solely and exclusively the business of another. But far from supporting counsel's argument, that case demonstrates the weakness of the taxpayer's position in this appeal. In that case the evidence consisted of a series of written agreements between the taxpayer and a former employee which provided expressly that, after paying certain agreed amounts, all takings and profits were to belong to the former employee, together with evidence that these agreements were in practice implemented. Here, there is a complete absence of any such evidence to show that the taxpayer, having purchased the premises and the business, agreed to divest himself of the profits of the business in favour of anyone else. What evidence there was, taken together with the statement of agreed facts, serves only to confirm the decision which the commissioners reached as being the only reasonable conclusion which was open to them in the circumstances. They decided that the taxpayer was assessable to tax on the profits of the business on the footing that he was the proprietor of the business. This was, as Harman J said in *Spedding v Sabine (Inspector of Taxes)* (1954) 35 TC 239 at 242, a very natural inference for them to draw, and we are quite unable to say that it was a conclusion which was not open to them on the facts of this case.

For these reasons this appeal must be refused. We shall answer the questions of law in the case in the affirmative and affirm the determination by the commissioners of the assessments under appeal.

Appeal dismissed.

Solicitors: *A & W M Urquhart*, Edinburgh (for the taxpayer); *Solicitor of Inland Revenue*.

Rengan Krishnan Esq   Barrister.

Juman v Board of Inland Revenue

PRIVY COUNCIL
LORD TEMPLEMAN, LORD OLIVER OF AYLMERTON, LORD GOFF OF CHIEVELEY, SIR
MICHAEL KERR AND SIR CHRISTOPHER SLADE
3, 22 JULY 1991

Assessment – Estimated assessment – Burden of proof – Appeal against assessment – Comparison of taxpayer's declared income and estimated expenditure – Failure of taxpayer to account for apparent excess of expenditure over income – Burden of proof that failure to disclose income was not due to fraud or gross neglect – Income Tax Ordinance (Trinidad and Tobago), s 39.

The taxpayer was the director of a number of limited companies. For the tax year 1971 he submitted an income tax return which showed taxable income of only $5,000; the return was accepted and tax was assessed and paid accordingly. In 1977 the Board of Inland Revenue (the Revenue) undertook a tax audit of his income for the years 1971 to 1975. Both the taxpayer and his accountant failed to provide the information requested by the Revenue, and the Revenue therefore sought to compute the taxpayer's chargeable income by comparing his declared income for each year with his expenditure for the same period. For the year 1971 the comparison showed that the taxpayer's expenditure exceeded his declared receipts by over $250,000. In the absence of a satisfactory explanation for the discrepancy, further assessments to income tax and unemployment levy for 1971 were made on the taxpayer and he was also assessed to additional tax (under s 39(4) of the Income Tax Ordinance of Trinidad and Tobago) for gross neglect. On appeal, the Tax Appeal Board held that the further assessments had been excessive and that there was no evidence of gross neglect such as to justify the additional assessment under s 39(4). The Court of Appeal held inter alia that the burden of disproving the correctness of the assessments to income tax and unemployment levy and of the additional assessment under s 39(4) was on the taxpayer. The court allowed the Revenue's appeal, recalculating the amount of the taxpayer's chargeable income and reimposing additional tax under s 39(4). The taxpayer appealed to the Privy Council, contending, inter alia, that the Court of Appeal had misdirected itself as regards the burden of proof.

Held – The burden of disproving the correctness of the assessments to income tax and unemployment levy and of the additional assessment under s 39(4) lay with the taxpayer. That burden had not been discharged and the conclusions of the Court of Appeal were unassailable. The appeal would accordingly be dismissed.

Notes

For assessments to the best of an inspector's judgment, see Simon's Taxes A3.206.

Appeal

The taxpayer, Alim Khan Juman, appealed against the decision of the Court of Appeal of Trinidad and Tobago (Kelsick CJ, Warner and Persaud JJA) allowing an appeal by the Board of Inland Revenue from the decision of the Tax Appeal Board whereby it allowed in part an appeal by the taxpayer against additional assessments to income tax, unemployment levy and additional tax under s 39(4) of the Income Tax Ordinance of Trinidad and Tobago. The facts are set out in the judgment of the Board.

Sudeesh Shivarattan for the taxpayer.

Christopher McCall QC and *Myrna Robinson-Walters* (Senior State Counsel of the   a
Trinidad and Tobago bar) for the Revenue.

22 July. The following judgment of the Board was delivered.

LORD OLIVER OF AYLMERTON. Section 39 of the Income Tax Ordinance of
Trinidad and Tobago (the Ordinance) (now re-enacted as s 83 of the Income Tax   b
Act (the Act)) provides for the making of assessments to tax to the best of the
judgment of the Board of Inland Revenue (the Revenue) in cases where a taxpayer
either makes a return of income which is not accepted or fails to make a return. It
also (by sub-s (4)) empowers the Revenue to charge additional tax, not exceeding
the amount of tax chargeable on the excess where the taxpayer has been assessed to
a sum in excess of the chargeable income disclosed in his return, if the taxpayer fails   c
to prove that the omission or incorrectness of the return did not amount to fraud,
covin, art or contrivance or gross or wilful neglect.

Under ss 53 and 68A of the Ordinance (ss 97 and 117 of the Act) the Revenue is
empowered, for the purpose of carrying out its duties, to seek information from any
person (other than one in a confidential relationship) and to inspect a taxpayer's
records relating to his income. Section 45(1) of the Ordinance (now s 89 of the Act)   d
provides that where it appears to the Revenue that any person liable to tax has not
been assessed, or has been assessed at a less amount than that which ought to have
been charged, the Revenue may, within the year of income or within six years after
the expiration thereof, assess such person at such amount or additional amount as
according to its judgment ought to have been charged. Finally, s 43E(2) of the
Ordinance (now s 8(2) of the Tax Appeal Board Act) provides that in appeals against   e
assessments the onus of proving that the assessment or other decision complained of
is excessive or wrong lies on the taxpayer.

Alim Khan Juman (the taxpayer) is the director of a number of limited companies
including Juman's Garment Factory Ltd (the company). For the tax year 1971 he
submitted an income tax return disclosing a chargeable income of only $5,007. That
return was accepted and he was assessed to tax in a sum of $711. It appears that   f
during the ensuing years the Revenue had or thought that it had reason to doubt
whether the returns made by the taxpayer fully disclosed his chargeable income and
on 14 April 1977 he was told that a tax audit of his income for the years 1971 to 1975
was to be undertaken, for which purpose he was requested to produce the relevant
accounting books and records. That audit made little progress for a number of
reasons, in particular because it was said that a fire at the company's premises in   g
April 1975 had destroyed virtually all the accounting books and records of the
taxpayer, the company and the other companies in which the taxpayer was
interested, and because the taxpayer was abroad for long periods during the audit.

Finally, in November 1977 the Revenue required the taxpayer's accountant to
provide a statement of the taxpayer's net worth as at 1 January 1971 and 31 December
of each year from 1971 to 1976 inclusive. These were never supplied and the   h
Revenue proceeded to compute the taxpayer's chargeable income as best it could by
the method known as 'source and application of funds'. As their Lordships
understand it, this involves the computation on the one hand of all the funds received
by the taxpayer during the year and on the other of his expenditure during the same
period. If this computation demonstrates an excess of expenditure (application) over
receipts (source), the taxpayer, who alone knows the true facts, can properly be   j
called on to explain the source of the excess and if he either cannot or will not do so
the inference is virtually irresistible that the balance represents undisclosed income
chargeable to tax. In the result the taxpayer's chargeable income for the year 1971
was adjusted by the Revenue from the return figure of $5,007 to a sum of $590,655
in respect of which it was proposed to assess additional tax of some $294,615. Further
correspondence ensued and on 20 December 1977 notices of additional assessments

to income tax, unemployment levy and additional tax under s 39(4) were issued.

a   The adjusted chargeable income for the year computed by the Revenue was $256,484 on which there was assessed income tax of $128,242, unemployment levy of $12,324 and additional tax under s 39(4) of $127,530.

The Revenue having refused to amend this assessment on objection from the taxpayer's accountants, the taxpayer appealed to the Tax Appeal Board on 15 January 1979. The Revenue's case was that an examination of the taxpayer's bank

b   accounts and such other records as had been produced disclosed that the taxpayer's expenditure for the year 1971 exceeded his total funds by a sum of $250,848 which, in default of credible information from the taxpayer, the Revenue accordingly treated as unreported income.

The Tax Appeal Board conducted a careful investigation of the figures contended for by the accountant who conducted the audit and by the taxpayer's accountant

c   and concluded that there was properly attributable to the taxpayer as 'sources of funds' during the year a sum of $492,846 (which included a sum of $60,000 described as a loan from the company). Under the heading 'application of funds', however, the taxpayer's expenditure amounted to $547,409 so that there was an excess of $54,562 in the taxpayer's expenditure over the amount of his receipts which, unless satisfactorily explained (as to which the burden lay on the taxpayer), was properly

d   to be treated as undisclosed income. To that there fell to be added two items of interest on bank deposits (amounting to $956) which it was common ground ought to have been but which had not been disclosed. The taxpayer having failed to discharge the burden of proof resting on him, there was thus a sum of $55,519 representing additional chargeable income for the year. Accordingly, to the extent that the Revenue's assessment was based on a figure in excess of that sum, the appeal

e   was allowed and the matter was remitted to the Revenue for assessment of that sum as chargeable income for the year. The Tax Appeal Board, however, found that there was no evidence of gross neglect such as to justify a charge to additional tax under s 39(4) and allowed in full the taxpayer's appeal against the additional tax assessed under this sub-section.

From this decision the Revenue appealed to the Court of Appeal. That court

f   (Kelsick CJ and Warner and Persaud JJA) allowed the appeal to the extent of (a) increasing the figure of the taxpayer's chargeable income to a sum of $115,519 and remitting the matter to the Revenue for income tax and unemployment levy to be assessed on that figure, and (b) imposing additional tax under s 39(4) on unreported income of $25,256 (being half the amount of the taxpayer's additional chargeable income as found by the Tax Appeal Board after deduction of the sum of

g $5,007 which had been disclosed in the taxpayer's return for the year 1971). In fact, in both increasing the figure of the taxpayer's chargeable income to a sum of $115,519 and calculating the additional tax imposed by reference to a sum of $50,512, the Court of Appeal wrongly assumed that the figure of $55,519 representing the additional chargeable income as found by the Tax Appeal Board included the $5,007 which had been returned by the taxpayer for the year in question. The Revenue

h   does not now seek to challenge the figures resulting from this incorrect assumption (which operated in favour of the taxpayer) and accordingly does not seek any amendment of the sums $115,519 and $25,256 which appear in the order of the Court of Appeal.

As regards the increase in the amount of the chargeable income, the court held that the Tax Appeal Board had clearly misdirected itself in its computations by

j   rightly including the sum of $60,000 loaned by the company to the taxpayer as a source of funds but wrongly failing to take into account as an application of funds the fact that that sum had in fact been expended by the taxpayer in reduction of his overdraft with his bankers. That sum, accordingly, fell to be added to the amount of the chargeable income of the taxpayer for the year. As regards the additional tax, the court held that the Tax Appeal Board had misdirected itself in point of law in concluding, on the ground that there was 'no evidence of gross neglect that would

justify' the imposition, that no additional tax was payable. This reversed the burden
of proof which was cast by s 39(4) on the taxpayer and the Tax Appeal Board had
already found that '[the taxpayer] could offer no satisfactory explanation to account
for a discrepancy thrown up under the source and application method'. The court
accordingly determined that additional tax was properly assessed under s 39(4) on
the amount of unreported income determined by the Tax Appeal Board (subject to
the adjustment already mentioned) but further determined that additional tax
should not be assessed on the further chargeable income of $60,000. The Revenue
does not seek to challenge that determination.

It is from this decision that the taxpayer appeals to their Lordships' Board. The
first submission made on behalf of the taxpayer is that the Court of Appeal
misdirected itself as to the application of the burden of proof as contemplated by
s 43E(2) of the Ordinance, in as much as Warner JA stated that 'the burden rests
with the taxpayer, on his objection, to his assessment before the Revenue, on his
appeal before the Tax Appeal Board and on the appeal by case stated before the
Court of Appeal'. So far as their Lordships have been able to follow the relevance of
this submission in the context of this appeal, it appears to be this, that the taxpayer
contends that although initially the burden rested on him of disproving the
correctness of an assessment, nevertheless once he had identified on oath a particular
receipt as derived from a non-taxable source, the evidential burden shifted to the
Revenue to show that that sum represented taxable income. In the context of a
comparison of source and application, however, this is irrelevant. What is relevant
is simply whether the amount applied exceeds the amount received and whether the
taxpayer satisfactorily accounts for the discrepancy. In any event, having regard to
the express terms of the section, their Lordships are entirely unable to see any
inaccuracy in the statement of the position by Warner JA and find no substance in
this submission.

It is then submitted that the court misdirected itself in increasing the amount of
the taxpayer's chargeable income by the sum of $60,000. Their Lordships need say
no more than that they find the court's reasoning as regards this sum and its
conclusions unassailable. On the taxpayer's own documents it was clear that the sum
of $60,000, whether treated as capital or income, had been applied in reduction of
the taxpayer's overdraft and there could be no justification for including it on one
side of the account in order to boost the amount received whilst omitting it from the
application side of the account so as to reduce the excess. Either it was a self-
cancelling entry which should not have figured in the account at all or it had to be
brought in both on the source and the application sides for the purpose of calculating
the excess.

Their Lordships equally find no substance in the taxpayer's final submission that
the court misdirected itself in finding, as regards the additional tax, that the Tax
Appeal Board had wrongly reversed the burden of proof. The provisions of s 39(4)
are quite unequivocal and quite clearly place on the taxpayer the burden of
demonstrating positively that his omission to disclose was not due to any of the
circumstances enumerated in that section. The Tax Appeal Board's approach was,
therefore, quite clearly erroneous. Even if, as Warner JA was prepared to assume,
the Tax Appeal Board had correctly appreciated that the burden lay on the taxpayer
and had intended, by their judgment, to express themselves as satisfied that the
burden had been discharged, there was not in fact any material before them from
which such a finding could be substantiated.

In their Lordships' opinion this appeal involves no possible point of principle. It
lacks both merit and substance and must be dismissed with costs.

Appeal dismissed with costs.

Solicitors: *Minet Pering* (for the taxpayer); *Charles Russell* (for the Revenue).

Rengan Krishnan Esq   Barrister.

Bergandi v Directeur Général des Impôts
(Case 252/86)

COURT OF JUSTICE OF THE EUROPEAN COMMUNITIES

JUDGES LORD MACKENZIE STUART (PRESIDENT), BOSCO, RODRIGUEZ IGLESIAS (PRESI-
DENTS OF CHAMBERS), KOOPMANS, EVERLING, GALMOT, KAKOURIS, JOLIET AND
SCHOCKWEILER

ADVOCATE GENERAL G F MANCINI

9 JULY, 15 DECEMBER 1987, 3 MARCH 1988

*Value added tax – European Communities – Classification of turnover tax – State tax
charged annually on the operation of automatic games machines installed in public places
at fixed rates determined by machine's characteristics – Subsequent imposition of value
added tax on operation of such machines – Whether state tax could be characterised as a
tax on turnover – Whether member state prohibited from maintaining the imposition of
state tax from the date at which value added tax was first introduced – EC Council
Directive 77/388, art 33.*

*Value added tax – European Communities – Internal taxation on the products of other
member states in excess of that imposed on similar domestic products – State tax charged
annually on the operation of automatic games machines installed in public places at fixed
rates determined by machine's characteristics – Subsequent imposition of value added tax
on operation of such machines – Highest rate of state tax imposed on operation of
machines of predominantly foreign manufacture – Graduation of state tax to achieve
legitimate social purposes – Whether state tax directly or indirectly discriminatory or
protective – EEC Treaty, art 95.*

*Value added tax – European Communities – Free movement of goods – State tax charged
annually on the operation of automatic games machines installed in public places at fixed
rates determined by machine's characteristics – Subsequent imposition of value added tax
on operation of such machines – Overlapping of the imposition of state tax and value
added tax causing reduction in imports of Community manufacture – Whether barrier
to free movement of goods – Whether barrier of a fiscal nature – EEC Treaty, art 30.*

In France state tax was charged annually on the operating receipts from automatic
games machines installed in public places at a fixed rate (per machine) which varied
according to the characteristics of the machines. The taxpayer, an operator of
automatic games machines, applied to the Directeur des Services Fiscaux, La
Manche, for a reduction in the assessment to state tax made on him for 1985 on the
grounds that as from 1 July 1985 the operation of automatic games machines had
become subject to value added tax. That application was refused and in response the
taxpayer appealed to the Tribunal de Grande Instance (the Regional Court),
Coutances, contending: (a) that state tax constituted a tax on turnover and that as
from the date at which value added tax was imposed art 33[a] of EC Council Directive
77/388 (the Sixth Directive) prohibited a member state from maintaining any tax
which could be characterised as a turnover tax; (b) that because the highest rate of
state tax was chargeable on the operating receipts from machines of predominantly
foreign manufacture, the imposition of state tax contravened art 95[b] of the EEC
Treaty; and (c) that the overlapping of the imposition of both state tax and value
added tax caused a reduction in the imports of Community manufacture which
restricted the free movement of goods contravening art 30[c] of the EEC Treaty. The

---

a Article 33, so far as material, is set out at p 542 g, post
b Article 95, so far as material, is set out at p 550 g–h, post

Tribunal de Grande Instance took the view that the dispute involved the
interpretation of certain provisions of Community law, stayed the proceedings and   *a*
referred, inter alia, the following questions to the Court of Justice for a preliminary
ruling: (a) whether state tax could be characterised as a turnover tax within the
meaning of art 33 of the Sixth Directive; (b) whether a tax, which was introduced in
the pursuance of legitimate social purposes, was incompatible with art 95 of the EEC
Treaty in that the operating receipts from machines of predominantly foreign
manufacture came within the most heavily taxed category and the operating receipts   *b*
from machines of predominantly domestic manufacture came within the most
favourable tax category; and (c) whether art 30 of the EEC Treaty could be
interpreted as applying to a barrier to the free movement of goods which was of a
fiscal nature.

Held – (1) The basis for an assessment to state tax was that the taxpayer had placed   *c*
an automatic games machine at the disposal of the public; no account was taken of
the revenue which could be generated thereby. The state tax had not therefore
levied a charge on the movement of goods and services nor on commercial
transactions in a way comparable to value added tax and could not be characterised
as a turnover tax. Accordingly, art 33 of the Sixth Directive did not operate so as to
prohibit the French authorities from maintaining the imposition of state tax as from   *d*
the date at which value added tax was imposed.

 *Rousseau Wilmot SA v Caisse de Compensation de l'Organisation Autonome
Nationale de l'Industrie et du Commerce (Organic)* (Case 295/84) [1985] ECR 3759
applied.

 (2) A tax would be incompatible with art 95 of the EEC Treaty if, despite making
no formal distinction as to the origin of the products taxed, it had been adjusted so   *e*
that the majority of imported products came within the most heavily taxed category
whereas the majority of domestic products came within the most favourable tax
category. Community law did not, however, prohibit a member state from imposing
such a tax if it was introduced to serve legitimate economic or social purposes. State
tax was graduated not to procure a fiscal advantage for machines of domestic
manufacture to the detriment of competing machines of foreign manufacture but to   *f*
achieve legitimate social objectives and was not therefore incompatible with art 95.

 EC Commission v Denmark (Case 171/78) [1980] ECR 447 considered; *Hansen (H)
Jun & O C Balle GmbH and Co v Hauptzollamt Flensburg* (Case 148/77) [1978] ECR
1787 applied.

 (3) Article 30 of the EEC Treaty covered all barriers to the free movement of
goods which were not already specifically covered by other provisions of the EEC   *g*
Treaty. The overlapping of the imposition of both state tax and value added tax was
a barrier of a fiscal nature whose compatibility with the EEC Treaty could only be
assessed by reference to art 95.

Notes
                                    h

For the maintenance and introduction of taxes by member states from the date at
which value added tax was first imposed, see De Voil: Value Added Tax A1.05.

 For the requirement that member states avoid indirect protection of domestic
products by means of turnover taxation, see ibid, A1.03.

 For EC Council Directive 77/388, art 33, see ibid, Division E3.

 For the EEC Treaty, art 95, see ibid, Division E1.

 For the EEC Treaty, art 30, see 50 Halsbury's Statutes 276.   *j*

---

c Article 30, so far as material, provides: 'Quantitative restrictions on imports and all measures
having equivalent effect shall, without prejudice to the following provisions, be prohibited
between Member States.'

Reference

a By judgment of 18 September 1986 the Tribunal de Grande Instance, Coutances, referred to the Court of Justice of the European Communities for a preliminary ruling under art 177 of the EEC Treaty six questions on the interpretation of art 33 of EC Council Directive 77/388 (the Sixth Directive) and arts 95 and 30 of the EEC Treaty. The questions were raised in proceedings brought by Gabriel Bergandi (the taxpayer), an operator of automatic games machines, against the Director General

b of Taxes, La Manche, in respect of the collection of state tax on automatic games machines operated by the taxpayer for 1985. The taxpayer, the government of the French Republic, the government of the Federal Republic of Germany and the Commission of the European Communities made submissions (in the written procedure) to the court. The language of the case was French. The facts are set out

c in the report for the hearing.

Cases cited

d *EC Commission v Denmark* (Case 171/78) [1980] ECR 447, CJEC.
EC Commission v French Republic (Case 168/78) [1980] ECR 347, CJEC.
EC Commission v French Republic (Case 287/83) (1984, unreported), CJEC.
EC Commission v French Republic (Case 18/84) [1985] ECR 1339, CJEC.
EC Commission v Italian Republic (Case 169/78) [1980] ECR 385, CJEC.
Feldain v Directeur des Services Fiscaux (Case 433/85) [1987] ECR 3521, CJEC.
Hansen (H) Jun & O C Balle GmbH and Co v Hauptzollamt Flensburg (Case 148/77) [1978] ECR 1787, CJEC.

e *Iannelli e Volpi SpA v Paolo Meroni* (Case 74/76) [1977] ECR 557, CJEC.
Kerrutt v Finanzamt Mönchengladbach-Mitte (Case 73/85) [1986] ECR 2219, CJEC.
Rousseau Wilmot SA v Caisse de Compensation de l'Organisation Autonome Nationale de l'Industrie et du Commerce (Organic) (Case 295/84) [1985] ECR 3759, CJEC.
Schul (Gaston) Douane Expediteur BV v Inspecteur der Invoerrechten en Accijnzen (Case 15/81) [1982] ECR 1409, CJEC.

f *Staatssecretaris van Financiën v Hong Kong Trade Development Council* (Case 89/81) [1982] ECR 1277, CJEC.
Transports Lesage & Cie v Hauptzollamt Freiburg (Case 20/70) [1970] ECR 861, CJEC.

The Judge Rapporteur (F A Schockweiler) presented the following report for the
g hearing.

I Facts and procedure
 1. Article 2 of EC Council Directive 77/388 of 17 May 1977 on the harmonisation of the laws of the member states relating to turnover taxes—common system of value added tax: uniform basis of assessment (the Sixth Directive) provides that the supply
h of goods and services for consideration within the territory of the country by a taxable person acting as such is to be subject to value added tax.
 Article 13B(*f*) of the Sixth Directive provides that the member states shall, under conditions which they are to lay down for the purpose of ensuring the correct and straightforward application of the exemptions and of preventing any possible evasion, avoidance or abuse, exempt betting, lotteries and other forms of gambling,
j subject to conditions and limitations laid down by each member state.
 According to art 33, the provisions of the Sixth Directive are not to prevent a member state from maintaining or introducing taxes on insurance contracts, taxes on betting and gambling, excise duties, stamp duties and, more generally, any taxes, duties or charges which cannot be characterised as turnover taxes.
 2. On 23 December 1983, the Commission brought an action against the French

Republic for failure to fulfil its obligations (see *EC Commission v French Republic*
(Case 287/83) (1984, unreported)) on the ground that the maintenance of a general
exemption from value added tax for operating receipts from all automatic machines
subject to entertainments tax was incompatible with art 13B(*f*) of the Sixth
Directive. By art 16 of the Loi de Finances (the Finance Law) for 1985 (Law
no 84-1208 of 29 December 1984, see le Journal Officiel de la République Française
(JORF), p 4060), France imposed value added tax on operating receipts from
automatic machines and *EC Commission v French Republic* (Case 287/83) was
removed from the register by order of the court of 16 January 1985 (see (1985)
OJ C45, p 7).

3. In addition to value added tax, which has been levied since 1 July 1985,
automatic games machines are subject to two specific taxes in France, namely
entertainments tax, the amount of which varies according to the size of the
population of the municipality concerned, and a tax known as the state tax.

The state tax on automatic machines is the subject to art 564 *septies* and art 564
octies of the Code Général des Impôts (General Tax Code (the CGI)).

Article 564 *septies* introduced a tax on automatic machines installed in public
places which provide visual or aural entertainment, a game or an amusement, at an
annual rate per machine: of 500 FF for the machines designated in the fourth and
fifth paragraphs of art 1560-II of the CGI (small non-electric games of skill in which
the only automatic devices, of a purely mechanical nature, consist of dispensers of
balls and score recorders, and automatic games consisting solely of small-scale
vehicles or models of animals in or on which children sit), and for automatic sound-
reproduction devices; of 1,500 FF for machines other than those mentioned above,
or 1,000 FF if they were first put into service more than three years earlier.
Automatic machines brought into service in the second half of a year are taxed at
half-rate. The charge of 5,000 FF for machines that operate solely on the basis of
chance and, in particular give prizes of entertainment tokens or more games free of
charge was repealed by Law no 83-628 of 12 July 1983 (see JORF, p 2154), which
prohibits in particular the importation, manufacture, possession, installation and
operation of machines of that type.

Under art 564 *octies*, the tax is payable by the operator of the machine when
making the annual return in respect of machines in operation, and must be paid
within six months of the making of that return and no later than 31 December of the
relevant year.

Article 35I of the Finance Law for 1987 (see Law no 86-1317 of 30 December
1986, JORF 1986, p 15820) repealed art 564 *septies* and *octies* of the CGI.

4. On 2 July 1985, the Centre des Impôts (the tax office) at Saint-Lô addressed to
Mr Bergandi (the taxpayer), a trader and automatic games machines operator, a
claim for the payment of 111,000 FF for the annual tax on automatic machines for
1985, which in this case related to machines brought into service on 1 January 1985,
even though the operation of those machines became subject to value added tax as
from 1 July 1985.

5. The Director of Fiscal Services of La Manche, by decision of 31 December
1985, rejected an application for reduction of the tax demand by half in respect of
the second half of 1985 and Mr Bergandi brought an action against him on 28
February 1986 before the Tribunal de Grande Instance (the Regional Court),
Coutances, the competent court for matters concerning taxes classified as indirect
taxes and charges treated as such, seeking an order that the tax authorities should
grant him an exemption in the principal sum of 38,000 FF and in respect of the
penalties relating thereto, and should reimburse to him the sums already paid.

6. Considering that the dispute involved the interpretation of certain provisions
of Community law, the Tribunal de Grande Instance, Coutances, decided to stay
the proceedings until the Court of Justice of the European Communities had given
a ruling under art 177 of the EEC Treaty on the following questions:

'1. Must Article 33 of [the Sixth Directive] be interpreted as prohibiting Member States from continuing to levy turnover taxes on the supply of goods or the provision of services once such activities become liable to VAT?

2. Must the concept of turnover taxes or any taxes, duties or charges which may be characterized as turnover taxes referred to in Article 33 of [the Sixth Directive] be interpreted as applying to taxes levied on operating receipts, regardless of whether tax is charged on the basis of actual revenue or on an approximate basis where it is difficult to arrive at an exact determination of actual revenue?

3. More particularly, does the concept of turnover taxes or any taxes, duties or charges which may be characterized as turnover taxes referred to in Article 33 of [the Sixth Directive] include an annual, flat-rate fiscal charge levied on all automatic machines installed in public places and providing visual or aural entertainment, a game or an amusement, introduced for the purpose of replacing a tax on the turnover of the operator on the machine and which is broadly adjusted to take account of the profitability of each type of machine and, indirectly, of the operator's receipts?

4. If the replies to Questions 1 and 3 are in the affirmative, does the prohibition of the cumulative levying of VAT and other turnover taxes on the same revenue or turnover mean that where VAT is applied for the first time at the beginning of the second half of a year and the turnover taxes levied in addition to VAT must be paid in a single instalment at the beginning of the calendar year (unless deferred payment has been permitted), one half of the sums due in respect of the taxes in the nature of turnover taxes for the year in which VAT was first applied must, in consequence of the introduction of VAT, be reimbursed or not demanded?

5. Must Article 95 of the EEC Treaty be interpreted as prohibiting the levying on operating receipts of tax at a rate three times higher on products that are principally of foreign origin than on similar products that are principally of domestic manufacture? Must that discrimination be regarded as even more serious when the operating receipts concerned are liable both to VAT and to indirect taxation of another kind?

6. Must Article 30 of the EEC treaty be interpreted as meaning that it is an infringement thereof to make revenue from the operation of certain products liable to VAT pursuant to Community legislation without abolishing existing taxes on such revenue even though certain of the products operated are no longer manufactured in the Member State levying the various taxes concerned and where, in any event, the cumulative levying of such taxes may result in a reduction in imports of such products from the rest of the Community?'

7. The judgment of the Tribunal de Grande Instance, Coutances, was received at the court registry on 1 October 1986.

8. Pursuant to art 20 of the Protocol on the Statute of the Court of Justice, written observations were submitted on 23 December 1986 by the Commission of the European Communities, represented by its legal adviser, Johannes Fons Bühl, on 24 December 1986 by the government of the Federal Republic of Germany, represented by Martin Seidel, Ministerialrat in the Federal Ministry of the Economy, on 30 December by the government of the French Republic, represented by Régis Gouttes, Assistant Director of Legal Affairs in the Ministry of Foreign Affairs, and on 2 January 1987 by Gabriel Bergandi (the taxpayer), the plaintiff in the main proceedings, represented by Robert Collin and Richard Milchior, of the Paris Bar.

9. On hearing the report of the Judge Rapporteur and the views of the Advocate General, the court decided to open the oral procedure without any preparatory inquiry.

II Written observations submitted to the court

1. Gabriel Bergandi (the taxpayer), after explaining that the machines in question are small, purely mechanical games of skill, automatic devices in the form of small-scale vehicles in which children sit, automatic sound-reproduction devices and electric games of skill, and after describing the background to the introduction of the contested legislation, states that the questions submitted to the court raise three legal problems: the lawfulness, in the light of the interpretation of art 33 of the Sixth Directive, of the overlapping of value added tax and other taxes; the interpretation of art 95 of the EEC treaty; and the interpretation of art 30 of the EEC Treaty.

(A) As regards the problem of overlapping, he points out that EC Council Directive 67/227 of 11 April 1967 on the harmonisation of legislation of member states concerning turnover taxes (the First Directive) introduced a harmonised system of turnover taxes designed to ensure that economic operators in the Community bear fiscal charges calculated on equal bases with a view to the unity of the Common Market and to avoiding discrimination. The principle that there should be no overlapping as between taxes in the nature of turnover taxes and value added tax is of fundamental importance and requires a definition of turnover tax which applies throughout the Community.

(i) The prohibition of overlapping laid down in art 33 of the Sixth Directive is unconditional and sufficiently precise to be applied directly by the national courts. Article 33 allows overlapping between value added tax and other taxes except where the other taxes, duties or charges can be characterised as turnover taxes.

The taxpayer therefore proposes that the answer to the first question should be that:

> 'Article 33 of [the Sixth Directive] does not prohibit the imposition upon supplies of goods or the provision of services of taxes, duties and charges other than VAT, in so far as VAT was introduced subject to the condition that such other levies should not be taxes, duties or charges which can be characterized as turnover taxes.
>
> More particularly, taxes on insurance contracts, taxes on betting and gambling, excise duties and stamp duties, provided that they cannot be characterized as turnover taxes within the meaning of Article 33 of [the Sixth Directive], may be charged on the supply of goods or the provision of services in addition to VAT.'

(ii) The applicability of the prohibition of overlapping depends on the definition of the concept contained in art 33 of charges which cannot be characterised as turnover taxes.

That concept undoubtedly has a Community meaning. A member state cannot, by virtue of the features of its tax system or the term used to describe a tax, remove a tax from the scope of that prohibition. The very wording of art 33 expressly refers to all taxes and charges which can be characterised as turnover taxes. Moreover, value added tax is a tax whose characteristics are harmonised at Community level and part of value added tax revenue is paid into the Community budget. It may be inferred from the judgment of the court of 8 July 1986 in *Kerrutt v Finanzamt Mönchengladbach-Mitte* (Case 73/85) [1986] ECR 2219 on the classification of a German duty as a stamp duty within the meaning of art 33 that each of the terms used in that provision must be taken to have a Community definition.

A comparision of the terms 'betting' and 'lotteries' appearing in art 13B(f) and the term 'betting and gambling' in art 33 shows that the latter term cannot refer to games of skill for the entertainment of children and adults. Likewise, the state tax on juke-boxes is not a tax on betting and gambling.

In order to define taxes which can be characterised as turnover taxes, it is necessary to recall the fundamental distinction between income tax, tax on capital and taxes on consumption, including indirect taxes and taxes on turnover. Indirect taxes may be defined as real taxes levied on a product or service, without any distinction being made as to the identity of the person legally or actually required to pay the tax, the

a   rate of which will, in most cases, be specific and proportional to the quantity of the taxable thing. Turnover taxes are synthetic taxes, charged ad valorem, which may be indirectly personalised and of which the basis of assessment is an economic and accounting factor, namely the turnover. Turnover taxes, which may be collected at the various stages of sale or provision of services, are intended to be levied on turnover in such a manner that they are proportional to business output and catch a

b   proportion of the gross proceeds of the economic activities concerned. The evaluation of the taxable thing, namely turnover, may be carried out on a real basis, as in the case of value added tax, by an index-related method, using apparent, tangible and invariable factors, or on a flat-rate basis. The classification advocated here essentially coincides with that of the French administration, which distinguishes between the category of special taxes, including certain customs duties and indirect taxes properly

c   so called, and the category of ad valorem taxes, being essentially taxes on turnover. It has the advantage over that of the French administration that it does not include among indirect taxes certain taxes collected on an ad valorem basis.

In its judgment of 27 November 1985 in *Rousseau Wilmot SA v Caisse de Compensation de l'Organisation Autonome Nationale de l'Industrie et du Commerce (Organic)* (Case 295/84) [1985] ECR 3759 at 3768, the court held that art 33, seen in

d   the context of the process of harmonisation of turnover taxes and the adoption of a common value added tax system, is designed to prevent that common system from being compromised by fiscal measures of a member state taxing the movement of . goods and services in a manner comparable to the way in which value added tax is levied. It cannot be inferred from that judgment that art 33 prohibits only the overlapping with value added tax of taxes which display exactly the same

e   characteristics as value added tax or that only a proportional and deductible tax, like value added tax, can be characterised as a turnover tax. Turnover taxes may be imposed on a turnover evaluated in different ways and not always be deductible, in so far as a flat-rate system, for example, may be operated. The essential feature which those taxes have in common with value added tax relates to their impact, whether direct or indirect, on the consumer.

f   The state tax levied on automatic machines is payable by the operator and is connected with the use of the machine and the duration of such use; it is possible to transfer the tax paid in respect of a machine withdrawn from use to a new machine brought into service and the tax is adjusted according to the type of machine or its age, in other words according to its yield, and all these facts prove that it is the use, and therefore the output of the machine, which is subject to the tax.

g   The second and third questions could therefore be answered as follows:

> 'The concept of turnover taxes or taxes which may be characterized as turnover taxes contained in Article 33 of [the Sixth Directive] must be interpreted as applying to taxes levied on operating receipts regardless of whether tax is charged on the basis of actual revenue or on an approximate basis where it is difficult to arrive at an exact determination of actual revenue.

h   > The foregoing might apply, for example, to a tax, fixed annually, paid by the operator and adjusted according to criteria enabling account to be taken of the profitability of the different kinds of machines whose operation is subject to the tax and thus indirectly fixed according to different criteria relating to the receipts obtained by the operator.'

j   (iii) The prohibition of overlapping became immediately applicable when value added tax came into force and the portion of the tax relating to the part of the year in which value added tax was levied should be reimbursed or set off by way of relief. The following answer should be given to the fourth question:

> 'Where VAT is levied for the first time in mid-year and not as from 1 January, the prohibition of the overlapping of VAT with other taxes related to turnover

laid down in Article 33 of [the Sixth Directive] takes effect upon the introduction of VAT.

From that time and regardless of the date and procedures for the payment of the other taxes which can be characterized as turnover taxes collected previously, the Member State must, in consequence of the introduction of VAT, reimburse or not demand payment of the sums relating to the part of the year during which VAT was first applied.'

(B) The problem of application of art 95 of the EEC Treaty should be examined in the light of the fact that certain products, namely American billiards and table football machines, are for the most part manufactured in France, whereas pinball, electronic billiards and video games are all imported.

The court has always adopted wide definition of similarity, taking as its criterion not strict identity but rather analogy and comparability in use. All the machines concerned, with the exception of juke-boxes, fall within the same common customs tariff heading and are specifically intended for recreation and entertainment purposes. Even if it were not conceded that they are similar, it would have to be acknowledged that those products are in a competitive relationship, even though it might be partial, indirect or potential.

An analysis of the categories covered by art 564 *septies* of the CGI shows that the operation of products of foreign origin is taxed at a rate three times higher than that applied to national products which are similar to or compete with them.

Since the dispute with which the main proceedings is concerned does not relate directly to the entertainments tax, it is unnecessary to consider the question whether discrimination is made worse by the overlapping of the contested tax with value added tax and another charge. It is for the national court to consider whether the overlapping of several taxes, even if only one is discriminatory, may, for economic reasons, aggravate discrimination.

It is therefore proposed that the fifth question should be answered as follows:

'Article 95 of the EEC Treaty must be interpreted as prohibiting the imposition of a tax which is *de facto* based on operating receipts at a higher rate on products that are principally or entirely of foreign origin than on similar or competing products that are principally of domestic manufacture.

The overlapping of a discriminatory tax within the meaning of Article 95 of the [EEC] Treaty and another tax, even if the latter is not discriminatory, may nevertheless have the effect of aggravating the consequences of such discrimination.'

(C) With respect to the free movement of goods, the court recognised in its judgment of 8 May 1985 in *EC Commission v French Republic* (Case 18/84) [1985] ECR 1339 that a fiscal measure may also fall within the scope of art 30. Separate pieces of tax legislation each clearly constitute a set of rules within the meaning of the case law concerning art 30. Even if it were possible that each piece of legislation considered separately did not hinder Community trade, their combined effect might be different. The statistics for imports of automatic machines show that the overlapping of taxes has the effect of reducing imports of Community origin.

The taxpayer therefore proposes that the following answer should be given to the sixth question:

'Article 30 of the EEC Treaty must be interpreted as meaning that it is an infringement thereof to make certain products liable to VAT without abolishing the existing taxes charged on the operating receipts from products which are subject to VAT, so that the free movement of goods of Community origin is thus hindered, and that is the case even if the overlapping of taxes may in itself be lawful under the other Community provisions.

Regard must also be had to the fact that certain of the products which are affected by that hindrance are not manufactured in the territory of the Member

State responsible for the overlapping of taxes whereas national products are
manufactured within that territory which in the consumer's eyes compete with
the imported products.'

2. The government of the French Republic observes that in its judgment of
27 November 1985 in *Rousseau Wilmot SA v Caisse de Compensation de l'Organisation
Autonome Nationale de l'Industrie et du Commerce (Organic)* (Case 295/84) [1985]
ECR 3759 the court held that the prohibition of overlapping of taxes contained in
art 33 was intended to ensure that the functioning of the common value added tax
system was not compromised by fiscal measures applied by a member state to the
movement of goods and services which had an effect on commercial transactions
comparable to that of value added tax. However, that provision does not prevent
the member states from maintaining taxes based on the activities of undertakings
which do not relate directly to the price of goods or services. The tax on automatic
machines is unrelated to their purchase price and is not intended to represent a levy
of any kind, real or flat-rate, on turnover. The tax becomes due when the annual
return is made in respect of the machine regardless of whether the machine is
actually in service.

It should therefore be stated in reply to the first three questions that:

'The application of Article 33 of [the Sixth Directive] does not prevent the
levying by a Member State of a tax such as that introduced by Article 564 *septies*
of [the CGI], in so far as the latter is not a tax on turnover.'

In view of that answer, the fourth question becomes devoid of purpose. In any
event, the flat-rate nature of the tax precludes any partial reimbursement. On the
other hand, the tax ceases to be payable in respect of machines brought into service
after value added tax began to be levied.

The existence of several rates is accounted for by the differing uses of the machines:
a reduced rate for machines designed for children, a higher rate for machines of
which the installation is prohibited and a medium rate in other cases. It is apparent
from the parliamentary debates prior to the inclusion of art 564 *septies* in the CGI
that operating turnover was not taken into account and that the profitability of the
machines was no more than a secondary concern. There is no discrimination against
machines manufactured in other member states: the rate of 500 FF applies equally
to machines produced in France and to imported machines; the rate of 5,000 FF
applied to machines which have been prohibited in the meantime; the rate of
1,500 FF applies to machines intended for a different group of users. The possibility
of that rate being reduced for machines put into service more than three years
previously is explained by the need to ensure a certain availability of entertainment
facilities in small municipalities.

The following answer should therefore be given to the fifth question: 'The said
tax is not contrary to Article 95 of the EEC Treaty.'

As regards the problem of the free movement of goods, the court has recognised
that the scope of art 30, however wide it may be, does not extend to the barriers
covered by other provisions of the EEC Treaty, such as those of a fiscal nature or
those having equivalent effect referred to in arts 9–16 and art 95 of the EEC Treaty.

It may therefore be stated in reply to the sixth question that: 'The said tax is not
contrary to Article 30 of the EEC Treaty.'

3. The government of the Federal Republic of Germany points out in the first
place that it does not make any difference whether the interpretation of art 33 is
focused on the concept of turnover tax or on that of a tax which can be characterised
as a turnover tax. The latter concept may be wider in scope as far as its description
is concerned but not as regards its purpose or nature. Neither of those concepts has
so far been defined in general terms in Community law and it is not necessary for
the court to give an exhaustive definition in the present case. It is sufficient to say
that turnover taxes are characterised, inter alia, by their general scope, which covers
more than a few categories of goods and services, whereas Community value added

tax, which art 33 of the Sixth Directive protects against competing taxes, is a general tax on consumption.

(a) The first question mentions 'taxes on turnover', whereas art 33 of the Sixth Directive refers to 'turnover taxes'. Not every tax which, in one way or another, relates to turnover, has the character of a turnover tax. For example, art 33 classifies taxes on insurance contracts as taxes which cannot be characterised as turnover taxes, although that tax is levied on turnover and comes within the scope of the common system of value added tax.

The answer to be given to the first question should be that:

'Article 33 prohibits the levying of a charge which can be characterized as a turnover tax. However, it does not prohibit the levying of every charge which is related, in one way or another, to turnover.'

(b) The second question relates, in the French original, to 'taxe sur le chiffre d'affaires' or 'taxe ayant le caractère de taxe sur le chiffre d'affaires'. Turnover tax covers supplies of goods and the provision of services for consideration by a taxable person and imports of goods. The remuneration received in respect thereof does not constitute the subject matter of the tax but merely the basis of assessment for it; however, that remuneration will often be in the nature of operating receipts.

The answer to be given to the second question should therefore be:

'Taxes levied on operating receipts cannot be characterized as turnover taxes. It is not, however, contrary to the character of a tax based on turnover for the remuneration on the basis of which the tax is assessed to be constituted by an undertaking's operating receipts.'

(c) The legislature's intention to replace a turnover tax is not relevant to classification of the new tax in the light of art 33. All that is relevant is that the tax should objectively be in the nature of a tax on turnover, which is not the case as regards the contested state tax, which does not fulfil the criterion of generality.

The third question should therefore be answered in the negative.

In view of the answer given to the third question, it is unnecessary to answer the fourth question.

4. The Commission examines in turn the questions relating to art 33 of the Sixth Directive and those relating to arts 95 and 30 of the EEC Treaty.

(a) The purpose of tax harmonisation is to avoid distortions of competition which might hinder the free movement of goods or access to the provision of services within the Community. The turnover taxes referred to in art 33 of the Sixth Directive are taxes levied on goods and services, whether they are cumulative multi-stage taxes or taxes levied at only one stage in the production and marketing chain. According to the purpose of art 33, as stated by the court in its judgment of 27 November 1985 in *Rousseau Wilmot SA v Caisse de Compensation de l'Organisation Autonome Nationale de l'Industrie et du Commerce (Organic)* (Case 295/84) [1985] ECR 3759 at 3767, the decisive criterion for the classification of a tax on turnover within the meaning of the Community directives is whether the chargeable event is the sale of goods or provision of a service, in other words whether the taxable thing is the price of the transaction, and it is not necessary for there to be a formal shifting of the tax in the value added tax sense. In the above-mentioned judgment the court conceded that an annual tax based on turnover, whose purpose was to maintain a social fund, did not constitute a turnover tax. In the present case the chargeable event is not the sale of goods or provision of a service. The two taxes in question are based on the operation of machines and the annual amounts charged thereon are calculated according to rates based on the probable financial yield of the machine, as determined by the place where it is operated, and the quality or novelty of the machine. The taxes are levied on a final use meeting certain needs which the legislature did not intend to encourage, in the same way as excise duties. In *Rousseau Wilmot* the court,

aligning itself with the Commission in that regard, acknowledged that if a tax is to
a be permitted under art 33 of the Sixth Directive, it must not be levied on transactions
which are subject to value added tax or upset the normal functioning of the common
system. The purpose of a tax is of no importance, provided that the policies pursued
by the taxation are legitimate and compatible with Community law and that the tax
is not used to promote national production, thus creating a distortion of competition
jeopardising the free movement of goods or services.

b   It is therefore appropriate to give the following answers to the first three questions:

'An annual tax, periodical charge or other form of levy collected on the basis
of the probable annual yield of a machine is compatible with Article 33 of the
Sixth Directive, in so far as it does not have the effect of impeding the free
movement of goods or hindering access to the provision of services within the
c   Community.
The concept of "taxes, duties or charges which cannot be classified as turnover
taxes" contained in Article 33 of the Sixth Directive must be interpreted as
including a tax calculated on the basis of probable annual or periodic yield, but
not levied on the price of transactions in such a manner that the tax is passed on
in the price of the goods or service.
d   Provided that the policies pursued by a tax levied on automatic entertainment
machines operated in public places are lawful and compatible with Community
law, the fact that the foreseeable periodic yield is the basis of the tax does not
automatically mean that the tax is incompatible with the prohibition of taxes
on turnover laid down in Article 33 of the Sixth Directive.'

Since the answers to the first and third question are in the negative, the fourth
e question becomes devoid of purpose.
(b) As regards art 95 of the EEC Treaty, it should be noted that the French
legislation is not concerned with the machines as such but with the operation of
them. The only way of showing that the tax is a tax on automatic machines which
may be caught by art 95 is to prove that the machine is in fact taxed as the physical
equipment by means of which the service is provided. At the present stage of tax
f harmonisation, the member states are free to pursue national policies by means of
differing tax rates, provided that those policies are lawful and compatible with
Community law and that the benefit of the reduced rates is extended to similar or
competing products, as is the case of the tax at issue here.
The answer to the fifth question should therefore be that:

'Under Article 95 of [the EEC Treaty], a Member State remains free, at the
g   present stage of tax harmonization, to pursue national policies by means of
differing rates of tax, provided that those policies are lawful and that the benefit
of the reduced rates is extended to similar or competing imported products.'

(c) Article 30 of the EEC Treaty, which has direct effect, covers all measures
which impede imports. As the court has stated, the barriers of a fiscal nature and of
h equivalent effect referred to in arts 9–12 and art 95 of the EEC Treaty do not fall
within the prohibition laid down in art 30.
The following answer should therefore be given to the sixth question: 'Article 30
of the EEC Treaty is not applicable to the present case.'

j 15 December 1987. **The Advocate General (G F Mancini)** delivered the following
opinion.

Mr President, members of the court,
1. In connection with a dispute as to whether a tax on the operation of automatic
entertainment machines can be classified as a turnover tax, the Tribunal de Grande

Instance (the Regional Court), Coutances, has asked this court to interpret art 33 of
EC Council Directive 77/338 (the Sixth Directive) and arts 95 and 30 of the EEC   *a*
Treaty.

It is appropriate to point out that the French courts have pending before them
innumerable cases (several hundred according to some sources) on the same question.
At least three Regional Courts—Argentan, Verdun and Nîmes—have submitted to
the court questions similar or even identical to those with which we are concerned
today; two courts—Tarbes and Foix—appear to have submitted questions, but they   *b*
have not yet reached the registry here; and we know that sixteen—Avranches,
Rennes, Thionville, Poitiers, Quimper, Laval, Metz, Agen, Bernay, Clermont-
Ferrand, Charlesville-Mézières, Toulouse, Limoges, Saint Malo, Vesoul and
Chartres—have stayed proceedings before them until this court has given its
judgment on the matter.

Five courts, on the other hand, have already resolved the problem, but of those   *c*
only one—the Tribunal de Grande Instance, Cusset, by judgment of 21 May 1987—
has classified the tax at issue as a turnover tax. The other courts have decided that it
is not a turnover tax, albeit on the basis of different reasoning, namely: Montbeliard
on 23 July 1986, because a tax described as an indirect tax by the Code Général des
Impôts (the CGI) does not constitute a tax on turnover; Sens on 3 July 1986, because
the provisions of a directive cannot be relied on by private individuals to support an   *d*
action in a tax matter (that being the well-known position of the Conseil d'Etat,
expressed in judgment no 51,811 of 1 July 1985, RJF 10/85, p 1286); Auch on
26 November 1986, because the definition of a tax as a turnover tax is a matter of
domestic rather than Community law; and Nevers on 27 November 1987, because
the charge in question is annual whereas the plaintiff had asked for relief in respect
of a period of six months.   *e*

In France therefore the question referred to the court is highly problematical and
the judgment resolving it is awaited with great expectation.

2. On 2 July 1985 the Centre des Impôts (the tax office), Saint-Lô, sent to Gabriel
Bergandi (the taxpayer), a trader and operator of automatic entertainment machines,
a tax assessment for 111,000 FF in respect of the annual tax on those machines.
Pointing out that they had been subject to value added tax since 1 July 1985, the   *f*
taxpayer applied for relief from the portion of the tax relating to the second half of
1985; and when his application was rejected (on 31 December 1985) he instituted
proceedings against the Directeur des Services Fiscaux du Département de La
Manche before the Tribunal de Grande Instance, Coutances, which has jurisdiction
in matters relating to taxes classified as turnover and similar taxes. At the same time
he requested that the tax authorities should be ordered to grant him relief in respect   *g*
of a principal sum of 38,000 FF and exemption from penalties and should be ordered
to reimburse to him the amounts already paid; in that regard, he submitted that the
levying of the state tax on the games machines for the period from 1 July to
31 December was contrary to art 33 of the Sixth Directive and arts 95 and 30 of the
EEC Treaty.

By judgment of 18 September 1986 the national court stayed the proceedings   *h*
before it and referred the following questions to the court for a preliminary ruling
under art 177:

'(1) Must Article 33 of [the Sixth Directive) be interpreted as prohibiting
Member States from continuing to levy turnover taxes on the supply of goods
or the provision of services once such activities become liable to VAT?

(2) Must the concept of turnover taxes or any taxes, duties or charges which   *j*
may be characterized as turnover taxes referred to in Article 33 of [the Sixth
Directive] be interpreted as applying to taxes levied on operating receipts,
regardless of whether tax is charged on the basis of actual revenue or on an
approximate basis where it is difficult to arrive at an exact determination of
actual revenue?

(3) More particularly, does the concept of turnover taxes or any taxes, duties or charges which may be characterized as turnover taxes referred to in Article 33 of [the Sixth Directive] include an annual, flat-rate fiscal charge levied on all automatic machines installed in public places and providing visual or aural entertainment, a game or an amusement, introduced for the purpose of replacing a tax on the turnover of the operator on the machine and which is broadly adjusted to take account of the profitability of each type of machine and, indirectly, of the operator's receipts?

(4) If the replies to Questions 1 and 3 are in the affirmative, does the prohibition of the cumulative levying of VAT and other turnover taxes on the same revenue or turnover mean that where VAT is applied for the first time at the beginning of the second half of a year and the turnover taxes levied in addition to VAT must be paid in a single instalment at the beginning of the calendar year (unless deferred payment has been permitted), one half of the sums due in respect of the taxes in the nature of turnover taxes for the year in which VAT was first applied must, in consequence of the introduction of VAT, be reimbursed or not demanded?

(5) Must Article 95 of the EEC Treaty be interpreted as prohibiting the levying on operating receipts of tax at a rate three times higher on products that are principally of foreign origin than on similar products that are principally of domestic manufacture? Must that discrimination be regarded as even more serious when the operating receipts concerned are liable both to VAT and to indirect taxation of another kind?

(6) Must Article 30 of the EEC Treaty be interpreted as meaning that it is an infringement thereof to make revenue from the operation of certain products liable to VAT pursuant to Community legislation without abolishing existing taxes on such revenue even though certain of the products operated are no longer manufactured in the Member State levying the various taxes concerned and where, in any event, the cumulative levying of such taxes may result in a reduction in imports of such products from the rest of the Community?

3. At the material time, automatic entertainment machines were subject to entertainment tax, value added tax and the so-called 'state tax'. The first is not relevant here. The second, which came into force on 1 July 1985, was introduced by art 16 of the Finance Law for 1985 (Law no 84-1208, JORF 1984, p 4060). That provision repealed art 261-E-3 of the CGI which exempted from value added tax receipts from the operation of all automatic machines subject to entertainment tax; and an incentive for its adoption was provided by the action under art 169 of the EEC Treaty which the Commission—considering that that exemption was incompatible with art 13B(*f*) of the Sixth Directive—brought against the French Republic on 23 December 1983 (that case, *EC Commission v French Republic* (Case 287/83) was removed from the register by order of 16 January 1985, (see (1985) OJ C45 p 7).

Finally, there is the state tax. It was introduced by art 33 of the Finance Law for 1982 (Law no 81-1160, JORF 1981, p 3539) on the ground that automatic games machines 'ne supportent actuellement aucun impôt sur le chiffre d'affaires' (see JORF Débats, Ass. Nat. 1981, p 3056). According to the government bill, the tax was to be a fixed annual sum of 1,500 FF on each machine; but an amendment passed at the sitting on 27 September 1981 set different amounts for different types of machine. The Minister for the Budget, Laurent Fabius, considered the resultant system satisfactory. It distinguished 'entre les appareils qui ont une très faible rentabilité, et pour lesquels le taux de prélèvement sera bas, les appareils intermédiaires qui seront soumis à un double taux, un taux moyen pour les communes urbaines et un taux assez faible pour les appareils mis en service depuis plus de trois ans qu'on trouve souvent dans les petits cafés des communes rurales, . . . et, enfin, les appareils qualifiés de jackpot, concernant les jeux d'argent et de hasard dont la taxation . . . peut être supérieure'. In other words, concluded the minister, the amendment took account 'des exigences des finances publiques, de rendement *a* des appareils et de la distinction entre les communes rurales et urbaines par le biais de l'ancienneté des appareils' (see JORF, Débats, Sénat 1981, p 3253).

In particular, art 33 of the Finance Law for 1982 introduced art 564 *septies* and art 564 *octies*. The first provides that the tax is to apply to automatic entertainment machines providing visual or aural entertainment, a game or an amusement, installed in public places. It is an annual tax and the amount differs according to the *b* type of machine. More particularly: (1) The tax is 500 FF on: (a) machines offering games of skill with devices, consisting of dispensers of balls and score recorders, which are purely mechanical (table football machines); (b) small-scale vehicles or animals on which children can sit; and (c) coin-operated record-players (juke-boxes). (2) A tax of 5,000 FF is payable on machines on which games of chance are played, even where a player requires skill in order to win, and which give prizes of *c* game tokens or a number of free matches (slot machines, pin-ball, Roll-a-top, 'Astoria', 'Rotamint' and so on). However, the manufacture, possession, installation and operation of such machines were prohibited by the Law of 12 July 1983 (Law no 83-628, see JORF 1983, p 2154). (3) All other machines (such as video games, the various types of billiards, mini-bowling, and so on) are subject to a tax of 1,500 FF, which is reduced to 1,000 FF if the machines were brought into service more than *d* three years earlier. It is also provided that machines put into service during the second half of the year are liable to tax at half-rate.

Pursuant to art 564 *octies*, the tax becomes due from the person operating the machine at the time of the annual return indicating that it has been brought into service. The payment must be made within the six months following the return and no later than 31 December in the year to which the return relates. The tax is *e* collected according to the rules, under the conditions and subject to the safeguards and penalties laid down for indirect taxes.

Finally, I would mention that, after the period during which the dispute arose, arts 564 *septies* and 564 *octies* were repealed by art 351 of the Finance Law for 1987 (Law no 86-1317, see JORF 1986, p 15820). In the report annexed to the government bill, it is stated that the tax was introduced 'dans l'attente de l'application de la taxe *f* sur la valeur ajoutée' and that, once the latter tax had come into force 'il convient de revenir au droit commun en supprimant la taxe d'Etat'.

4. Let us first examine the questions concerning the interpretation of art 33 of the Sixth Directive. The wording of the provision is well known:

> 'Without prejudice to other Community provisions, the provisions of this Directive shall not prevent a Member State from maintaining or introducing *g* taxes on insurance contracts, taxes on betting and gambling, excise duties, stamp duties and, more generally, any taxes, duties or charges which cannot be characterised as turnover taxes.'

Among the parties to the proceedings before this court, the Commission of the European Communities, the French government and the German government have *h* taken the view that collection of the contested tax is compatible with art 33. Let me say straight away that the opinion—inter alia, expressed on behalf of the Community executive by Lord Cockfield in the reply which he gave to written question no 2054/84 submitted by the MEP, Mr Vernier (see (1986) OJ C277, p 1)—is not in my view convincing. On the other hand, I find the arguments put forward by the taxpayer in support of the opposing view persuasive. *j*

But let us take things in their proper order, directing our attention first to the nature of the tax. In that regard it is appropriate to note that, with the exception of the German government, the parties before this court have referred to the judgment of 27 November 1985 in *Rousseau Wilmot SA v Caisse de Compensation de l'Organisation Autonome Nationale de l'Industrie et du Commerce (Organic)*

(Case 295/84) [1985] ECR 3759 and, in particular, para 16 thereof. It states (at 3769)
a   that art 33 of the Sixth Directive—

'... seeks to prevent the functioning of the common system of value added
tax from being compromised by fiscal measures of a Member State levied on
the movement of goods and services and charged on commercial transactions
in a way comparable to value added tax.'

b   The provision does not therefore preclude the retention or introduction by member
states of 'charges which are not fiscal but have been introduced specifically in order
to finance social funds and which are based on the activity of undertakings without
directly affecting the price of the goods or services'.

According to the Commission and the French government, this passage contains
the criteria for identification of the features of a charge which indicate that it is a tax
c   on turnover. In the first place, it is necessary to analyse the impact of the charge, for
which the chargeable event is the transfer of goods or the provision of a service, on
the final price. That impact must be direct even though it is not essential, unlike the
case of value added tax, that the person bearing it should be the purchaser or the
recipient of the service. The second requirement is that the turnover obtained from
the use of the goods or the provision of the service must be subjected to a charge on
d   a real or flat-rate basis. To those criteria the Commission adds a third: there must be
a relationship between the subjection of goods or services to the charge and the
movement thereof within the Community.

The government of the Federal Republic of Germany, however, relies on art 33
of the Sixth Directive and takes the view that it is inappropriate to seek an
'exhaustive' definition of taxes which can be characterised as turnover taxes since
e   they may *appear* to be different by reason of the name given to them without in fact
being different as far as their purpose or nature is concerned. Turnover taxes and
Community value added tax are characterised by the fact that they cover all possible
categories of products and for that very reason are general taxes on consumption.
The fact that a tax is stated to relate to turnover is not therefore sufficient reason to
characterise it as a turnover tax. The latter relates both to imports of goods and to
f   transfers of goods and the provision of services for consideration by a taxable person;
on the contrary, often displaying the features of proceeds from business, the
consideration received by the transferor or provider of services does not constitute
the target of the tax but is merely the basis of assessment for it.

The Commission also observes that, for the purpose of classifying a tax, the aim
pursued is all-important; and similarly the German government states that the
g   legislature's intention to introduce a charge replacing the tax on turnover is of no
importance as far as art 33 is concerned, the essential point being that the tax should
display the requisite objective features. It follows—concludes the Commission—
that, as regards the tax with which the questions referred by Tribunal de Grande
Instance, Coutances are concerned, the chargeable event is not the transfer of goods
or the provision of a service but, on the contrary, is closely related to the basis of
h   assessment. The tax is in fact levied on the use of a machine and does not vary
according to the location where the machine is installed; quite apart from that fact,
since it cannot be deducted as Community value added tax under art 17 of the Sixth
Directive, it is not in the nature of a turnover tax.

For its part, the French government notes that the tax at issue is unrelated to the
purchase price of the machines; moreover, it is not intended to represent a deduction
j   from receipts but rather, as is apparent from the fact that it becomes due when the
annual return is made in respect of the machine, it relates to the installation of the
machine. The annual nature of the tax also makes it utterly impossible for the
administration to grant relief in respect of half-years. The French government adds
that the tax at issue clearly cannot be regarded as being in the nature of a turnover
tax if only because the taxpayer brought his action before an ordinary court; as is

well known, such courts have jurisdiction only for proceedings concerning indirect
taxes.

    In the opinion of the German government, finally, the tax cannot be characterised
as a turnover tax because it does not satisfy the requirement of generality.

    5. Personally, contrary to the view expressed by the German government, I
consider that the answer to the questions submitted by the Tribunal de Grande
Instance, Coutances, depends on the definition of a tax which can be characterised
as a turnover tax within the meaning of art 33 of the Sixth Directive. Moreover, the
German government itself, who in any event regards any endeavour in that direction
as superfluous, succeeds only in identifying the tax under review here by reference
to Community value added tax.

    I would point out in the first place that the concept of a tax which can be
characterised as a turnover tax is a Community concept. That follows ineluctably
from the wording of art 33 of the Sixth Directive and the purposes of the system of
which that article forms part. As the legislature made clear, the prohibition of
overlapping does not apply to 'any taxes, duties or charges' which cannot be
characterised as turnover taxes; and it is clear that the very plurality of the terms
used—namely 'taxes', 'duties' and 'charges'—renders impossible any classification
which is dependent on the names used or criteria adopted at national level. The
reason for this is clear and is to be found, as I have pointed out, in the objectives of
the system: value added tax is a tax whose characteristics have been harmonised at
Community level and a percentage of the revenue accruing from it goes towards
financing the Community.

    But that is not all. If no Community definition of the tax were accepted, the
member states would be able to evade the prohibition of overlapping laid down in
art 33 of the Sixth Directive by recourse to criteria and concepts peculiar to their
own national systems of taxation or by choosing one name rather than another (for
example by avoiding the term 'turnover tax'). However, the fact that that situation
exists is to be inferred even from the case law of this court. In its judgment of 8 July
1986 in *Kerrutt v Finanzamt Mönchengladbach-Mitte* (Case 73/85) [1986] ECR 2219,
the court ruled that a tax on transfer and transactions such as the German
'Grunderwerbsteuer' is not caught by that prohibition, and thereby, it seems to me,
the court recognised by implication the existence of a Community concept defining
a charge which can be characterised as a turnover tax.

    The conclusion thus reached provides support for the arguments to the effect that
the tax at issue here is not such a tax, which rely on the fact that it is described in
France as an 'indirect tax' or in the fact that the matter was brought before an
ordinary court (when it is well known that disputes concerning turnover taxes are a
matter for the administrative courts). With respect to the latter point, moreover,
the taxpayer informed us at the hearing that he merely took the advice given to him
by the French tax authorities. At the foot of the document in which the Directeur
des Services Fiscaux de la Manche rejected his complaint it is in fact stated that 'si
vous souhaitez contester ce rejet, vous pouvez dans les deux mois assigner le
Directeur des services fiscaux devant le Tribunal de Grande Instance de Coutances'.

    6. I too am of the opinion that the proper basis for the concept of a charge which
can be characterised as a turnover tax is to be found in the *Rousseau Wilmot*
judgment, notwithstanding that it concerns a charge which, unlike the one at issue
here, was not of a fiscal character. As the taxpayer points out, in para 16 of that
decision (see [1985] ECR 3759 at 3768–3769) the court lays down two criteria which
are relevant to the definition of that concept, but it did not give details in general
and abstract terms. It placed emphasis above all on the 'common system of value
added tax', identifying in art 33 the will to prevent its being compromised by
national fiscal measures; it then stressed that, to meet that requirement, national
measures must neither be levied on the movement of goods and services nor be
charged on commercial transactions 'in a way comparable' to value added tax.

    A first comment: the use of the word 'comparable' seems to me to imply that the

features of a tax which can be characterised as a turnover tax and those of value
a added tax do not necessarily have to coincide completely. Comparability does not
mean identicality. In the same way, the court's reference to the 'common system of
value added tax' does not relate exclusively to the definition of value added tax in
art 2 of EC Council Directive 67/227 of 11 April 1967 on the harmonisation of
legislation of member states concerning turnover taxes (the First Directive). The
terms used by the court refer rather to the system as a whole which, if not entirely
b uniform, is at least 'common' (cf the opinion of the Advocate General (Mrs Rosèz)
in *Schul (Gaston) Douane Expediteur BV v Inspecteur der Invoerrechten en Accijnzen*
(Case 15/81) [1982] ECR 1437 at 1441). The characteristics which a turnover tax
must have can be inferred from the rules laid down on value added tax in the Sixth
Directive, particularly as regards the chargeable event, the method of assessment of
the tax and its impact on the consumer.
c   Let us consider the chargeable event first. As will be recalled, the Commission
and the French government have expressed the view that there is a close relationship
between that event and the basis of assessment, in so far as the tax at issue here is
payable in respect of the availability for use of the machines and is unrelated to their
turnover. For my part, I consider that: (a) the Sixth Directive indicates an intention
to distinguish between the two factors by the very fact that they are dealt with in
d separate provisions (see arts 10 and 11); (b) art 10 allows for the possibility of
derogations, whilst stating that the tax becomes chargeable when the goods are
delivered or the service is performed; and (c) art 10(3) provides that, as regards
imported goods, the chargeable event occurs 'when [the] goods enter the territory of
the country'. Thus, in the case of value added tax—which is *par excellence* a turnover
tax—no direct and individual relationship between the chargeable event and the
e basis of assessment appears to be identifiable.
Nor can it be said—although the German government does so—that the Sixth
Directive endows value added tax with the feature of generality. Certainly, generality
is a particular feature which distinguishes that tax from the other types of indirect
taxation (cf my opinion in *Rousseau Wilmot* [1985] ECR 3759 at 3761–3762). But
particular does not mean exclusive; so much so that as a result of the options and
f exemptions provided for by that directive the tax does not apply to all economic
transactions.
Let us now examine the argument developed with particular vigour by the French
government that the contested charge is not proportional to receipts and for that
very reason is not intended to apply a real or flat-rate deduction to the turnover
achieved by the machines. That argument contains an element of truth. Value
g added tax is in fact calculated as a rule on the basis of the turnover declared and on
the separate transactions represented by transfers of goods or the provision of
services. But it is also true that there are important exceptions to that rule, as in the
case, for example, of the flat-rate system involving the possibility of exemptions and
non-deduction available for small undertakings, farmers and travel agencies (see
arts 24–26 of the Sixth Directive). It follows that, if the basis of assessment does not
h take account of the totality of the turnover declared, the tax, although created on a
flat-rate basis, remains ad valorem.
An even clearer result is arrived at if the impact of the tax is considered. It will be
remembered that in the *Rousseau Wilmot* judgment the court stated (see [1985] ECR
3759 at 3769) that the tax can be characterised as a turnover tax only if commercial
transactions are affected in a way comparable to that of value added tax. But, as the
j Commission itself concedes, the ways in which value added tax is passed on to the
final consumer of the goods or the recipient of the service differ considerably. The
transfer is sometimes direct (as where the amount of the tax is separate from the
price of the goods or service) and sometimes indirect (where, on the contrary, the
tax forms part of the price) and at least in one case (that of the flat-rate system)
entirely non-existent. As is obvious, the same principles apply to taxes which can be
characterised as turnover taxes.

Finally, a few words concerning the criterion—postulated only by the Commission—whereby there must be a relationship between the subjection of goods or services to the tax and their movement within the Community. As the taxpayer points out, that view relies on interpreting art 33 as prohibiting overlapping only where the tax affects trade between member states and not also where its effects are felt within one country. But that reading is unduly reductive; no one can in fact fail to see that it is incompatible with a system such as the value added tax system which requires equality of conditions of competition 'whether at national or Community level' (see the third recital in the preamble to the First Directive).

It is clear from a review of the rules that: (a) the tax is paid by the operator and not by the possessor of the machine; it is not therefore a tax on ownership or possession like for example the road tax for motor vehicles; and (b) the amount varies according to the type of machine, takes account of the period for which it has been in use and takes obsolescence into consideration. Machines intended for the entertainment of children bear a lesser burden than those providing recreation for adults; moreover, a reduction of one-half is available for machines brought into service in the second half of the year and, in the case of machines brought into service more than three years earlier, the tax is reduced by one-third. As the Commission itself conceded, we are dealing with the taxation of an activity according to its profitability or receipts. The latter—as is proved by the graduation of the tax—is calculated on a flat-rate, and therefore approximate, basis but, as we have just seen, it is also based on apparent, specific and almost unvarying factors. There is, in short, no doubt that the operators include the tax in the price charged and hence pass it on to the user of the service.

The result to which this analysis leads seems to me to be clear: the contested tax—which is charged on operating receipts, however the tax basis is defined (that is to say according to the actual proceeds or, if they are not ascertainable, on a flat-rate basis)—is in the nature of a tax on turnover and cannot therefore coexist with value added tax. Furthermore, that conclusion is corroborated by the travaux preparatoires for the Finance Law for 1982. They make it clear that the legislature was moved by two intentions: on the one hand to overcome the difficulties of applying value added tax in an area in which the Commission was taking action to secure the removal of the general tax created by art 261-E of the CGI; and, on the other, to subject the receipts of machines to a tax whose amount reflected their presumed profitability.

With regard to the first purpose, in addition to the statement of Mr Fabius quoted earlier, reference may be made to the observations of Christian Pierret, the Rapporteur General of the Finance Committee of the National Assembly, to the effect that—

'. . . le contrôle de la recette est très difficile et je ne m'étendrai pas sur les pratiques abusives auxquelles la perception de cette recette sous forme de pièces de monnaie donne parfois lieu. L'assujettissement à la TVA serait donc impossible dans la mesure où la recette declarée ne correspondrait pas forcément à la réalité. Le Gouvernement ne pouvait donc s'orienter que vers une taxe forfaitaire' (see JORF Débats, Ass. Nat. 4 November 1981, p 3058).

The second purpose is highlighted by the remarks of the Deputé Charles Josselin. He expressed pleasure at the 'modulation de la taxe par type d'appareils, car on tient compte ainsi des revenus plus ou moins importants qu'ils procurent' and he considered 'que l'on ait pris en consideration l'âge des appareils et que l'on ait retenu le principe de son paiement semestriel . . . car cela permettra d'eviter que les appareils qui fonctionnent seulement une partie de l'année—je pense notamment à la periode estivale—soient frappés d'une taxe annuelle' (see JORF Débats, Ass. Nat. 17 December 1981, p 5063, and see also remarks by the member of the Senate, Francis Palmero, JORF Débats, Senat 27 November, p 3252).

7. I have already said that the classification of a charge as one which can be characterised as a turnover tax gives rise, pursuant to art 33 of the Sixth Directive,

to the prohibition of overlapping with value added tax, that is to say with a burden
a which is itself also levied on the receipts obtained from use of the machine. On that
point the French government maintains that the prohibition should not operate
where the tax is annual and the law does not allow the grant of relief for periods of
less than one year in the year in which value added tax was first applied.

That view, which was subscribed to in the judgment of the Tribunal de Grande
Instance, Nevers, mentioned earlier, is without foundation. Article 33 satisfies the
b conditions consistently laid down by the court for the provisions of a directive to be
recognised as having direct effect. It follows that, once a member state imposes value
added tax on an activity already covered by a charge like the one at issue here, the
prohibition against overlapping may be relied on to prevent the collection of the
latter charge and the tax authorities are obliged to reimburse or not require payment
of the sums in respect of that part of the year during which value added tax was
c applied for the first time.

8. The solution which I have proposed renders devoid of purpose the questions as
to the compatibility of the contested tax with arts 95 and 30 of the EEC Treaty; I
need not therefore give details of and examine all the arguments which have been
expounded in that connection. For the sake of completeness I shall merely make the
following observations: (a) as regards art 95, the tax is not levied on goods but on the
d profitability of the service provided and, in the absence of proof of the non-existence
of nationally manufactured automatic machines, it is impossible to identify
discriminatory intent against the machines manufactured in other member states;
and (b) as regards art 30, according to the decisions of this court, obstacles of a fiscal
nature to imports are not covered by that provision and in any event do not provide
grounds for applying it in conjunction with art 95 (see the judgments of 22 March
e 1977 in *Iannelli e Volpi SpA v Paolo Meroni* (Case 74/76) [1977] ECR 557 and of
7 May 1985 in *EC Commission v French Republic* (Case 18/84) [1985] ECR 1339).

9. For all the reasons which I have given, I propose that the court should give the
following answer to the questions submitted to it by the Tribunal de Grande
Instance, Coutances, by judgment of 18 December 1986 in the proceedings between
the taxpayer and the Directeur des Services Fiscaux du Département de la Manche:

f   The concept of a charge which can be characterised as a turnover tax, within
the meaning of art 33 of the Sixth Directive, is to be interpreted as including a
tax which is determined annually, is due from the operator of an automatic
entertainment machine, and is paid on the basis of criteria which take account,
even though on a flat-rate basis, of the presumed profitability of the machine.

Article 33 of the Sixth Directive prohibits the imposition on transfers of goods
g or the provision of services of any charges, duties or taxes which can be
characterised as turnover taxes as from the time at which value added tax is
applied for the first time, regardless of the detailed arrangements laid down for
the payment of the tax.

h 3 March 1988. **THE COURT OF JUSTICE** delivered the following judgment.

1. By a judgment of 18 September 1986, which was received at the court on
1 October 1986, the Tribunal de Grande Instance (the Regional Court), Coutances,
referred to the court for a preliminary ruling under art 177 of the EEC Treaty six
questions on the interpretation of art 33 of EC Council Directive 77/338 (the Sixth
j Directive) and arts 95 and 30 of the EEC Treaty.

2. Those questions were raised in proceedings brought by Gabriel Bergandi (the
taxpayer), an operator of automatic games machines, against the Director General
of Taxes, La Manche, regarding collection of the annual tax on automatic machines
operated by the taxpayer for 1985.

3. It appears from the order for reference that at the material time automatic
machines installed in public places and providing visual or aural entertainment, a

game or an amusement were subject in France to a tax known as the state tax at an annual rate, according to the category of machine, of 500 FF or 1,500 FF, the latter rate being reduced to 1,000 FF for machines first brought into service more than three years earlier. The tax became due when the annual return was made in respect of machines in use and was to be paid within six months thereafter but no later than 31 December of the relevant year. Since the operation of such machines became subject to value added tax as from 1 July 1985, the taxpayer brought proceedings against the Director of Fiscal Services of La Manche seeking a reduction in the amount of tax assessed as due from him for that year.

4. Considering that the dispute involved the interpretation of certain provisions of Community law, the Tribunal de Grande Instance, Coutances, stayed the proceedings and referred the following six questions to the Court of Justice for a preliminary ruling:

'1. Must Article 33 of [the Sixth Directive] be interpreted as prohibiting Member States from continuing to levy turnover taxes on the supply of goods or the provision of services once such activities become liable to VAT?

2. Must the concept of turnover taxes or any taxes, duties or charges which may be characterized as turnover taxes referred to in Article 33 of [the Sixth Directive] be interpreted as applying to taxes levied on operating receipts, regardless of whether tax is charged on the basis of actual revenue or on an approximate basis where it is difficult to arrive at an exact determination of actual revenue?

3. More particularly, does the concept of turnover taxes or any taxes, duties or charges which may be characterized as turnover taxes referred to in Article 33 of [the Sixth Directive] include an annual, flat-rate fiscal charge levied on all automatic machines installed in public places and providing visual or aural entertainment, a game or an amusement, introduced for the purpose of replacing a tax on the turnover of the operator on the machine and which is broadly adjusted to take account of the profitability of each type of machine and, indirectly, of the operator's receipts?

4. If the replies to Questions 1 and 3 are in the affirmative, does the prohibition of the cumulative levying of VAT and other turnover taxes on the same revenue or turnover mean that where VAT is applied for the first time at the beginning of the second half of a year and the turnover taxes levied in addition to VAT must be paid in a single instalment at the beginning of the calendar year (unless deferred payment has been permitted), one half of the sums due in respect of the taxes in the nature of turnover taxes for the year in which VAT was first applied must, in consequence of the introduction of VAT, be reimbursed or not demanded?

5. Must Article 95 of the EEC Treaty be interpreted as prohibiting the levying on operating receipts of tax at a rate three times higher on products that are principally of foreign origin than on similar products that are principally of domestic manufacture? Must that discrimination be regarded as even more serious when the operating receipts concerned are liable both to VAT and to indirect taxation of another kind?

6. Must Article 30 of the EEC Treaty be interpreted as meaning that it is an infringement thereof to make revenue from the operation of certain products liable to VAT pursuant to Community legislation without abolishing existing taxes on such revenue even though certain of the products operated are no longer manufactured in the Member State levying the various taxes concerned and where, in any event, the cumulative levying of such taxes may result in a reduction in imports of such products from the rest of the Community?'

5. Reference is made to the report for the hearing for a fuller account of the facts of the case, the course of the procedure and the observations submitted under art 20

of the Protocol on the Statute of the Court of Justice, which are mentioned or
a discussed hereinafter only in so far as is necessary for the reasoning of the court.

6. In order to answer the first question, it is necessary to consider art 33 of the
Sixth Directive in the light of the objectives pursued by the introduction of a
common system of value added tax.

7. According to the preamble to the EC Council Directive 67/227 (the First
Directive), the purpose of harmonisation of the legislation concerning turnover
b taxes is to establish a common market within which there is healthy competition and
whose characteristics are similar to those of a domestic market by eliminating tax
differences liable to distort competition and hinder trade.

8. A common system of value added tax was introduced by EC Council Directive
67/228 of 11 April 1967 on the harmonisation of legislation of member states
concerning turnover taxes—structure and procedures for application of the common
c system of value added tax (the Second Directive) and by the Sixth Directive. That
system was to contribute to that objective by introducing, on a basis common to all
the member states, a general tax on consumption levied on the supply of goods, the
provision of services, and imports in proportion to their price, regardless of the
number of transactions taking place as far as the final consumer, the tax being
imposed only on the value added at each stage and being definitively borne by the
d final consumer.

9. To achieve equality of tax conditions for a given transaction regardless of the
member state in which it takes place, the common system of value added tax was
intended, according to the preamble to the Second Directive, to replace the turnover
taxes in force in the member states.

10. Accordingly, art 33 of the Sixth Directive permits a member state to maintain
e or introduce taxes, duties or charges only if they cannot be characterised as turnover
taxes.

11. Consequently, it must be stated in reply to the first question that art 33 of the
Sixth Directive must be interpreted as meaning that as from the introduction of the
common system of value added tax the member states are no longer entitled to
impose on the supply of goods, the provision of services or imports liable to value
f added tax, taxes, duties or charges which can be characterised as turnover taxes.

12. In its second and third questions, the national court asks essentially whether
the concept of a tax which can be characterised as a turnover tax within the meaning
of art 33 of the Sixth Directive must be interpreted as including a tax levied annually
on automatic games machines installed in public places at a fixed rate determined
according to the category of the machine.

g 13. Although it is not for the court, in the present proceedings, to examine the
characteristics of a national law in the light of Community law (see the judgment of
20 October 1970 in *Transports Lesage & Cie v Hauptzollamt Freiburg* (Case 20/70)
[1970] ECR 861), it is nevertheless competent to interpret the concept of tax which
can be characterised as a turnover tax in order to enable the national court to apply
it correctly to the tax at issue. In fact, it is a Community concept in so far as it is
h relied on with a view to the attainment of the objective pursued by art 33, which is
to ensure that the common system of value added tax is fully effective.

14. In order to decide whether a tax can be characterised as a turnover tax it is
necessary in particular to determine, as the court stated in its judgment of
27 November 1985 in *Rousseau Wilmot SA v Caisse de Compensation de l'Organisation
Autonome Nationale de l'Industrie et du Commerce (Organic)* (Case 295/84) [1985]
j ECR 3759, whether it has the effect of compromising the functioning of the common
system of value added tax by levying a charge on the movement of goods and services
and on commercial transactions in a way comparable to value added tax.

15. As the court emphasised in its judgment of 1 April 1982 in *Staatssecretaris van
Financiën v Hong Kong Trade Development Council* (Case 89/81) [1982] ECR 1277 at
1285–1286, the principle of the common system of value added tax consists,

according to the first paragraph of art 2 of the First Directive, in the application to goods and services of a general tax on consumption exactly proportional to the price of the goods and services, whatever the number of transactions which take place in the production and distribution process before the final stage at which tax is charged.

16. Therefore, a tax which is levied solely on the basis that an article is placed at the disposal of the public, regardless of whether it is actually used, and which is not related to the revenue arising therefrom does not display the characteristics of a general tax on consumption levied on the price charged for the provision of services. That is so in particular where the tax is payable even if the article in question is made available to the public free of charge.

17. Although a fixed-rate tax may, in certain circumstances, be regarded as a flat-rate tax on receipts, it may only be so regarded if, on the one hand, the rate was fixed on the basis of an objective evaluation of the foreseeable receipts by reference to the number of occasions on which a service was likely to be provided and to the price charged for the service, and, on the other, it is established that the tax may be passed on in the price for the service so that it will finally be borne by the consumer.

18. The imposition of rates which differ according to the category of the articles is likewise not of itself sufficient to endow the tax with the character of a flat-rate levy on anticipated receipts where the tax is justified by other lawful considerations of an objective nature.

19. The fact that, after the introduction of the tax, the machines whose use was most heavily taxed were the subject of a general prohibition of manufacture and possession shows that considerations of a social character, reflecting a desire to discourage the use of certain types of machine, prompted the adoption of several different rates for the tax.

20. Consequently, it must be stated in reply to the second and third questions that a charge which, although providing for different amounts according to the characteristics of the taxed article, is assessed exclusively on the basis of the placing thereof at the disposal of the public, without in fact taking account of the revenue which could be generated thereby, may not be regarded as a charge which can be characterised as a turnover tax.

21. In view of the answer given to the second and third questions, the fourth question is devoid of purpose.

22. The fifth question submitted by the national court raises two points: the first is whether art 95 of the EEC Treaty applies only to levies on imported products or whether it may also cover taxes on the use of the products and, if so, the second point arising is whether a member state is prohibited by art 95 of the EEC Treaty from imposing on the placing at the disposal of the public of automatic games machines that are principally of foreign origin a tax three times higher than that imposed on machines that are principally of domestic manufacture.

23. Article 95 expressly prohibits the imposition on the products of other member states of 'any internal taxation of any kind in excess of that imposed directly or indirectly on similar domestic products', or of 'any internal taxation of such a nature as to afford indirect protection to other products'.

24. As the court held in its judgments of 27 February 1980, *EC Commission v French Republic* (Case 168/78) [1980] ECR 347, *EC Commission v Italian Republic* (Case 169/78) [1980] ECR 385 and *EC Commission v Denmark* (Case 171/78) [1980] ECR 447, within the system of the EEC Treaty, art 95 supplements the provisions on the abolition of customs duties and charges having equivalent effect. Its aim is to ensure free movement of goods between the member states in normal conditions of competition by the elimination of all forms of protection which may result from the application of internal taxation that discriminates against products from other member states. Thus art 95 must guarantee the complete neutrality of internal taxation as regards competition between domestic products and imported products.

25. The court stated in the same judgments that art 95 must be interpreted widely so as to cover all taxation procedures which, directly or indirectly, conflict with the

principle of equality of treatment of domestic products and imported products; the
a prohibition contained in that article must therefore apply whenever a fiscal levy is
likely to discourage imports of goods originating in other member states to the
benefit of domestic production.

26. If such a situation can arise in the case of taxation levied directly on imported
products, the possibility cannot be ruled out that it may also arise in the case of
internal taxation imposed on the use of imported products where those products are
b essentially intended for such use and are imported solely for that purpose.

27. It must therefore be stated in reply to the first part of the fifth question that
art 95 of the EEC Treaty also applies to internal taxation which is imposed on the
use of imported products where those products are essentially intended for such use
and have been imported solely for that purpose.

28. As regards the tax categories established by French law, it must be borne in
c mind that the court stated in its judgment of 27 February 1980 in *EC Commission v
Denmark* (Case 171/78) [1980] ECR 447 at 448 with respect to alcoholic products
that a national system of taxation, despite making no formal distinction according
to the origin of the products, undeniably contains discriminatory or protective
characteristics if it has been adjusted so that the bulk of domestic production comes
within the most favourable tax category whereas almost all imported products come
d within the most heavily taxed category. The court also emphasised that the
characteristics of such a system are not altered by the fact that a very small proportion
of imported products benefits from the most favourable rate of tax whilst a certain
proportion of domestic production comes within the same tax category as the
imported products.

29. However, in its judgment of 10 October 1978 in *Hansen (H) Jun & O C Balle
e GmbH and Co v Hauptzollamt Flensburg* (Case 148/77) [1978] ECR 1787 at 1806 the
court also stated that at the present stage of its development and in the absence of
any unification or harmonisation of the relevant provisions, Community law does
not prohibit member states from establishing a system of taxation differentiated
according to various categories of products provided that the tax benefits granted
serve legitimate economic or social purposes.

f 30. A legitimate social purpose of that kind may, as the French government states
in its observations, consist in the desire to encourage the use, by certain people and
in certain places, of particular categories of machines and to discourage the use of
other categories.

31. As regards the progressive nature of the taxation as between the categories of
products thus established, the court has held, most recently in its judgment of
g 17 September 1987 in *Feldain v Directeur des Services Fiscaux* (Case 433/85) [1987]
ECR 3521 at 3540, that as Community law stands at present, the member states are
in principle at liberty to subject products to a system of taxation which increases
progressively in amount according to an objective criterion, provided that the system
is free from any discriminatory or protective effect.

32. It must therefore be stated in answer to the second part of the fifth question
h that a system of taxation graduated according to the various categories of automatic
games machines, which is intended to achieve legitimate social objectives and which
procures no fiscal advantage for domestic products to the detriment of similar or
competing imported products, is not incompatible with art 95.

33. As regards the sixth question, it need merely be borne in mind that art 30 of
the EEC Treaty covers in general all barriers to imports which are not already
j specifically covered by other provisions of the EEC Treaty. Since the barriers
referred to in the questions submitted to the court are of a fiscal nature, their
compatibility with the EEC Treaty must be assessed only by reference to art 95 of
the EEC Treaty.

34. Consequently, it must be stated in reply to the sixth question that art 30 of the
EEC Treaty does not apply to the taxation of products originating in other member
states the compatibility of which with the EEC Treaty falls under art 95 thereof.

Costs

35. The costs incurred by the government of the French Republic, the government   *a*
of the Federal Republic of Germany and the Commission of the European
Communities, which have submitted observations to the court, are not recoverable.
Since these proceedings are, in so far as the parties to the main proceedings are
concerned, in the nature of a step in the action pending before the national court,
the decision on costs is a matter for that court.

On those grounds, the court, in answer to the questions submitted to it by the   *b*
Tribunal de Grande Instance, Coutances, by judgment of 18 September 1986,
hereby rules:

> 1. Article 33 of the Sixth Directive must be interpreted as meaning that as
> from the introduction of the common system of value added tax the member
> states are no longer entitled to impose on the supply of goods, the provision of
> services or imports liable to value added tax, taxes, duties or charges which can   *c*
> be characterised as turnover taxes.
>
> 2. A charge which, although providing for different amounts according to
> the characteristics of the taxed article, is assessed exclusively on the basis of the
> placing thereof at the disposal of the public, without in fact taking account of
> the revenue which could be generated thereby, may not be regarded as a charge
> which can be characterised as a turnover tax.   *d*
>
> 3. Article 95 of the EEC Treaty also applies to internal taxation which is
> imposed on the use of imported products where those products are essentially
> intended for such use and have been imported solely for that purpose.
>
> 4. A system of taxation graduated according to the various categories of
> automatic games machines, which is intended to achieve legitimate social
> objectives and which procures no fiscal advantage for domestic products to the   *e*
> detriment of similar or competing imported products, is not incompatible with
> art 95.
>
> 5. Article 30 of the EEC Treaty does not apply to the taxation of products
> originating in other member states the compatibility of which with the EEC
> Treaty falls under art 95 thereof.
>
> *f*

Agents: *Robert Collin* and *Richard Milchior*, of the Paris Bar (for the taxpayer);
Régis Gouttes and *Bernard Botte* (for the French government); *M Seidel* (for the
government of the Federal Republic of Germany); *J F Bühl* (for the Commission).

Rengan Krishnan Esq   Barrister.

a

Ministère Public and Ministre des Finances du Royaume de Belgique v Ledoux
(Case 127/86)

b COURT OF JUSTICE OF THE EUROPEAN COMMUNITIES (FOURTH CHAMBER)
JUDGES RODRIGUEZ IGLESIAS (PRESIDENT OF THE CHAMBER), KOOPMANS AND KAKOURIS
ADVOCATE GENERAL J MISCHO
10 DECEMBER 1987, 9 FEBRUARY, 6 JULY 1988

Value added tax – European Communities – Exemption from value added tax on temporary importation of goods – Frontier worker – Motor vehicle provided by
c *employer established in member state where value added tax paid – Motor vehicle used for business and leisure purposes – Worker resident in another member state – Whether second member state entitled to levy value added tax – EC Council Directive 77/388, art 14(1).*

Mr Ledoux, the taxpayer, was employed by a company established in France but
d was resident in Belgium. A motor vehicle registered in the name of his employer had been placed at his disposal for both business and leisure purposes. The vehicle had been acquired on the French market and value added tax had been paid in France. Value added tax had not been paid in Belgium, and in February 1982, the taxpayer was stopped as he crossed the frontier in the vehicle away from his normal route between home and workplace, and charged with having unlawfully imported the
e vehicle into Belgium. He was subsequently prosecuted before the Tribunal Correctionel (Criminal Court) in Neufchâteau, and was acquitted when the court found that his case was not covered by specific rules. The Minister of Finance of the Kingdom of Belgium brought an appeal against that judgment. The Cour d'Appel (Court of Appeal), Liège, decided that the dispute raised a problem concerning the interpretation of Community law, and referred to the Court of Justice the question
f whether Community rules concerning taxation, and in particular the rules concerning value added tax, permitted the Belgian state to levy value added tax in the circumstances of the instant case, taking account of the fact that the vehicle remained the property of the French employer and that the importation into Belgium was only temporary and of a provisional nature.

g **Held** – In implementing the exemption from value added tax in cases of temporary importation provided for under art 14(1)[a] of EC Council Directive 77/388 (the Sixth Directive), a member state had to observe the fundamental objectives of the harmonisation of value added tax, in particular the encouragement of free movement of persons and goods and the prevention of double taxation. Where the importer was not the owner of the vehicle but had imported it temporarily in the course of the
h duties of his employment, the rule that a member state was entitled to require as a condition for exemption from value added tax on a temporarily imported item that the importer should not reside in its territory did not apply. Private use which was ancillary to the business use of the vehicle and was provided for in the contract of employment formed part of the worker's remuneration, and therefore had to be subject to the same conditions as the business use. If it were not, the worker would
j be placed at a disadvantage compared to colleagues residing in the country of the employer and his right to free movement within the Community would thereby be restricted.

 ˙ A member state was accordingly prevented by the Sixth Directive from levying value added tax on a motor vehicle which was owned by an employer established in

---

a Article 14(1), so far as material, is set out at p 558 *j*, post

another member state where value added tax had been paid and which was used by
a frontier worker residing in the first member state for the performance of his duties
and secondarily for leisure purposes.   *a*

    Abbink (Case 134/83) [1984] ECR 4097 and *Carciati* (Case 823/79) [1980] ECR
2773 distinguished.

Notes   *b*

For exemptions from value added tax in cases of temporary importation, see De
Voil: Value Added Tax A7.35.
    For EC Council Directive 77/388, art 14, see ibid, Division E3.

Cases cited   *c*

Abbink (Case 134/83) [1984] ECR 4097, CJEC.
Carciati (Case 823/79) [1980] ECR 2773, CJEC.
Ministère Public and Ministry of Finance v Profant (Case 249/84) [1985] ECR 3237,
    CJEC.
Schul (Gaston) Douane Expediteur BV v Inspecteur der Invoerrechten en Accijnzen   *d*
    (Case 15/81) [1982] ECR 1409, CJEC.
Staatssecretaris van Financiën v Schul (Gaston) Douane-Expediteur BV (Case 47/84)
    [1985] ECR 1491, CJEC.

Reference   *e*

By an order of 12 March 1986, the Cour d'Appel (Court of Appeal), Liège, referred
a question raised in proceedings between the Minister of Finance of the Kingdom
of Belgium and Yves Ledoux, the taxpayer, to the Court of Justice of the European
Communities for a preliminary ruling under art 177 of the EEC Treaty. The Danish
government and the Commission of the European Communities made submissions   *f*
(in the written procedure) to the court. The language of the case was French. The
facts are set out in the report for the hearing.

The Judge Rapporteur (C N Kakouris) presented the following report for the
hearing.   *g*

I Facts and procedure
    1. As can be seen from the order for reference and the file in the case, Mr Ledoux
(the taxpayer), the defendant in the main proceedings, a technician, domiciled and
residing in Belgium and employed since 1982 by a company established in France,
used a motor vehicle acquired on the French market registered in the name of that   *h*
company in France and placed at his disposal by his employer to visit customers, to
travel between his workplace in France and his residence in Belgium and for leisure
purposes.
    Since value added tax had not been paid in Belgium, the taxpayer was stopped on
22 February 1983 as he crossed the frontier with the vehicle away from the normal
route from his home to his workplace. He was subsequently prosecuted before the   *j*
Tribunal Correctionnel (Criminal Court), Neufchâteau, which acquitted him after
finding that his case was not covered by specific rules. The Minister of Finance of
the Kingdom of Belgium brought an appeal against that judgment.
    The Cour d'Appel (Court of Appeal), Liège, decided that the dispute raised a
problem concerning the interpretation of Community law.
    Therefore, by judgment of 12 March 1986, received at the court registry on
26 May 1986, the Cour d'Appel, Liège, stayed the proceedings and referred the

following question to the court for a preliminary ruling under art 177 of the EEC
a Treaty:

> 'Do the Community rules concerning taxation, and in particular the rules
> concerning value added tax, permit the Belgian State, under the Law of 3 July
> 1969 establishing the Value Added Tax Code and the decrees implementing
> that Law and in accordance with the interpretation of its provisions by the
b > Minister of Finance of the Kingdom of Belgium, in proceedings brought
> against [the taxpayer], residing at 32 Rue Leroy, Marcinelle, to levy value
> added tax on a motor vehicle which is owned by a company incorporated under
> French law with its registered office in France and is subject to value added tax
> in France, where the tax has been paid, in so far as the vehicle is used by an
> employee of the company, who is resident in Belgium, for the performance of
c > his duties under his contract of employment and for leisure purposes, taking
> account of the fact that the vehicle remains the property of the French employer
> and that the importation into Belgium is only temporary and of a provisional
> nature?'

2. The written procedure followed the normal course. Pursuant to art 20 of the
Protocol on the Statute of the Court of Justice, written observations were submitted
d by the Danish government, represented by L Mikaelsen, Legal Adviser, and the
Commission of the European Communities, represented by H Etienne, Principal
Legal Adviser, acting as agent.

On hearing the report of the Judge Rapporteur and the views of the Advocate
General, the court (Fourth Chamber) decided to open the oral procedure without
any preparatory inquiry.

e

II *Written observations submitted to the court*

1. The Danish government observes that the Community rules applicable are
those contained in EC Council Directive 83/182 of 28 March 1983 on tax exemptions
within the Community for certain means of transport temporarily imported into
one member state from another (Directive 83/182).

f According to the Danish government, it can be seen from art 3(*a*)(*aa*) and
art 4(1)(*a*)(*aa*) read together with art 1 of Directive 83/182 that the condition on
which a vehicle may be imported into a member state without being liable to value
added tax is that the person importing the vehicle should have his normal residence
in a member state other than the member state of temporary importation.

With regard to the residence criterion, the Danish government refers to the
g second sub-paragraph of art 7(1) of Directive 83/182 which provides that a person
whose occupational ties are in a different place from his personal ties is to be regarded
as being resident in the place of his personal ties.

Finally, the Danish government emphasises that, as provided by arts 3 and 4(1)(*b*)
of Directive 83/182, the vehicle may not be disposed of, hired out or lent in the
member state of temporary importation.

h The Danish government concludes that where those conditions for temporary
tax-free importation are not fulfilled, the member state of importation may require
payment of value added tax on the vehicle concerned.

The Danish government emphasises that that interpretation has already been
confirmed by the judgments in a series of similar cases (see *Carciati* (Case 823/79)
[1980] ECR 2773 and *Abbink* (Case 134/83) [1984] ECR 4097) in which the court
j decided that Community law is not infringed by national provisions imposing
criminal sanctions on persons residing in a member state who use motor vehicles
temporarily imported under those circumstances. According to the Danish
government, if a member state is entitled in this case to bring a criminal prosecution,
it is all the more entitled to require payment of value added tax.

The Danish government thus proposes that the reply to the question referred to
the court should be that Community law does not prevent the Belgian state from
requiring payment of value added tax in this case on the vehicle concerned.

2. The Commission considers that, in any event, the temporary uses which are required to be permitted and the conditions for the exercise of the right to temporary use as laid down in Directive 83/182 do not meet the requirements of a single market and it intends to make new proposals on that subject shortly.

It considers that the temporary uses provided for by the Community legislature in Directive 83/182, which does not permit the use of the vehicle by persons resident in the country of temporary importation, are, however, the minimum to which citizens are entitled and do not prevent the member states from going further, in accordance with art 9(1) of Directive 83/182, which provides that 'Member States may maintain and/or introduce more liberal arrangements than those provided for in this Directive'. It observes in that regard that Belgium has maintained temporary rules for persons residing near frontiers who use, for the journey from their home to their work, a vehicle placed at their disposal by an employer established in another member state (see the circular of the Belgian Customs and Excise Department of 1 May 1984).

The Commission observes that the application by the member states of their national rules for temporary importation, in accordance with art 14 of EC Council Directive 77/388 of 17 May 1977 on the harmonisation of the laws of the member states relating to turnover taxes—common system of value added tax: uniform basis of assessment (the Sixth Directive) for the purpose of ensuring the correct and straightforward application of the temporary importation system and of preventing any possible evasion, avoidance or abuse must, on the one hand, take account of the applicable Community law and of the degree of liberalisation already achieved and, on the other, consist of measures which comply with the principle of proportionality in regard to the objective to be achieved.

With regard, first of all, to compliance with Community law, in particular the right of free movement, the Commission emphasises that the use by an employee of an undertaking of a motor vehicle belonging to that undertaking for the journey from his place of work to his home and for leisure purposes constitutes part of that employee's remuneration. Consequently, prohibiting the use of the vehicle in such circumstances under the rules of the country of residence has the effect, in that country, of denying the employee the benefit of that part of his remuneration and thereby removing the equality of remuneration existing in the country of employment between residents and non-residents which is required by art 48 of the EEC Treaty and art 7 of EC Council Regulation 1612/68 on freedom of movement for workers within the Community. The Commission also considers that when the member states apply their legislation on temporary importation for the legitimate purpose of preventing tax evasion, avoidance or abuse, they must, in compliance with art 5 of the EEC Treaty, ensure fulfilment of the obligations arising therefrom, abstain from any measure which jeopardises the attainment of the objectives of the EEC Treaty, such as the exercise of the right of free movement, and last, not render ineffective Community action in regard to employment in regions in which there is structural unemployment, where, as in this case, the exercise of workers' rights to free movement, by the conclusion of contracts of employment across frontiers, contributes to reducing unemployment.

With regard to the fact that the measures adopted by member states under art 14 of the Sixth Directive must be proportional to the objectives which those measures are designed to achieve, the Commission emphasises that, according to the court's previous decisions (see *Carciati* and *Abbink*), the temporary uses prohibited by national legislation may be punished by criminal and administrative sanctions, on condition that the national measures concerned are not excessive.

According to the Commission, the discretion left to the member states in that regard must be used in a way which complies with the principle of proportionality by taking into account, in the light of the general purpose of the common system of value added tax and the specific requirements of art 14 of the Sixth Directive, first

the importance of the public interest to be protected and second the degree to which
a the measures adopted by the member states could hinder the exercise of rights
flowing from the EEC Treaty. It emphasises that in this case, the limitation in the
public interest by national legislation of the right to make temporary use of a vehicle,
that is to say, the requirement to pay value added tax on importation, must be put
into effect without infringing the prohibition of double taxation in that regard, as
the court indicated in its judgment in *Abbink*. Consequently, the application of that
b rule prohibiting double taxation in regard to value added tax in cases in which, as in
the main proceedings, the rate of value added tax in the country in which the vehicle
is registered is higher than the rate applied in the country of residence (33·33% in
France, as against 25% in Belgium, with the possibility of a deduction of 50% if the
vehicle is used for private and business purposes) should, according to the
Commission, lead to the conclusion that no value added tax may be demanded in
c the country of residence. In that case, in so far as there has been no tax evasion, no
fine for non-payment, at least of value added tax, may be imposed by the member
state of temporary importation.

The same is true in regard to the sanctions, such as the confiscation of the vehicle
or the payment of its value, to which the defendant is liable in the main proceedings,
which the Commission regards as disproportionate by reason of the absence or
d insignificance of the public interest to be protected, since there has been no evasion
of tax.

According to the Commission, where there is a conflict of laws concerning the
place in which the vehicle is registered, as is the case in the main proceedings, such
measures may be adopted by the member states only after consultations between the
national administrations concerned have been held in order to take, by mutual
e agreement, the decisions necessary to resolve the difficulties to which the practical
application of the Community directives has given rise, as is provided for in art 10(2)
of Directive 83/182.

On the basis of the foregoing considerations, the Commission proposes that the
reply to the question referred to the court by the Cour d'Appel, Liège, should be as
follows:

f   'In so far as under the Community law applicable at the material time no
value added tax was payable on the definitive importation of the vehicle, the
temporary use of the vehicle in the circumstances of the case did not entail
evasion of value added tax and does not justify a fine on that basis. A penalty
such as the confiscation of the vehicle or, in the alternative, payment of its
value, infringes the principle of proportionality. Any fine intended to ensure
g   compliance with national rules concerning the determination of the place in
which vehicles must be registered or to protect other tax revenue must be
applied in such a way as to take account of the circumstances proper to conflicts
of laws the source of which is the exercise of rights under the Treaty which
Member States have an obligation not to hinder.'

h 9 February 1988. **The Advocate General (J Mischo)** delivered the following
opinion.

Mr President, members of the court,

1. Mr Ledoux (the taxpayer), the defendant in the main proceedings, was charged
with having unlawfully imported into Belgium, the country in which he resides, a
j motor vehicle registered in France and belonging to the French company which
employs him, on the basis that on 22 February 1983 he used the vehicle away from
the route he took when travelling to work, that is to say, he used it for private
purposes. It can be seen from the file that the vehicle was placed at the disposal of
the accused under the terms of his contract of employment and he was entitled to
use it both for his work and for leisure purposes.

2. It appears that at the material time there was a practice in Belgium, which has been subsequently officially authorised by a circular of the Belgian Customs and Excise Department of 1 May 1984, permitting frontier workers normally resident in Belgium to use a vehicle placed at their disposal by an employer established in another member state on the Belgian part of the journey from their homes to their foreign workplace. However, that practice did not cover the secondary use of such a vehicle for private purposes.

3. The question which the Cour d'Appel (Court of Appeal), Liège, before which the dispute in the main proceedings was brought after the Tribunal Correctionnel (Criminal Court), Neufchâteau, had acquitted the taxpayer, has referred to the court seeks essentially to know whether the Community rules, in particular those dealing with value added tax, permit a member state to require payment of the value added tax due on importation where a resident uses, for the performance of his duties under his contract of employment and for leisure purposes, a vehicle placed at his disposal by his employer, who is established in another member state in which value added tax has been paid, the vehicle remaining the property of the employer and the importation into the user's country of residence being merely temporary.

4. The particular Community rules applicable at the material time were those in EC Council Directive 77/388 of 17 May 1977 (the Sixth Directive).

5. Since then, EC Council Directive 83/182 of 28 March 1983 on tax exemptions within the Community for certain means of transport temporarily imported into one member state from another (Directive 83/182) was adopted and came into effect on 1 January 1984. Obviously, I can refer to that text only incidentally and can use it only as a source of interest in the reasoning which must be constructed on the basis of the law applicable at the material time. Furthermore, Directive 83/182 does not provide for tax exemption in regard to temporary importations of the kind at issue here. However, on 4 February 1987, the Commission submitted a proposal to the Council for an amendment to Directive 83/182, inserting in it a provision covering that situation.

6. Article 2(2) of the Sixth Directive provides as follows: 'The following shall be subject to value added tax . . . the importation of goods.'

7. Article 10(3) provides that as regards imported goods—'. . . the chargeable event shall occur and the tax shall become chargeable at the time when goods enter the territory of the country . . .' (see sub-para 1), except where goods are placed under arrangements for temporary admission (see sub-para 4).

8. Unlike what occurs in regard to the 'supply of goods' within the country, which requires 'the transfer of the right to dispose of tangible property as owner' (see art 5(1)), it is therefore in principle the mere physical fact of importation, that is to say the entry of the goods into the country, which gives rise to value added tax liability. Whether the person importing the goods is the owner or the user thereof is irrelevant. Under art 21(2) the person liable to pay tax on importation is 'the person or persons designated or accepted as being liable by the Member States into which the goods are imported'.

9. However, those who drafted the Sixth Directive manifestly regarded the mere physical fact of importation as too rigid because in art 14, they provided for exemptions from value added tax on importation. In particular, art 14(1) provides that:

'Without prejudice to other Community provisions, Member States shall exempt the following under conditions which they shall lay down for the purpose of ensuring the correct and straightforward application of such exemption and of preventing any possible evasion, avoidance or abuse . . . (c) importation of goods declared to be under temporary importation arrange-

ments, which thereby qualify for exemption from customs duties, or which
would so qualify if they were imported from a third country . . .'

10. Article 14(2) adds that until the entry into force of Community tax rules
clarifying the scope of the exemptions and the detailed rules for their implementation—

'. . . Member States may:
—maintain their national provisions in force on matters related to the above
provisions,
—adapt their national provisions to minimise distortion of competition and in
particular the non-imposition or double imposition of value added tax within
the Community,
—use whatever administrative procedures they consider most appropriate to
achieve exemption.'

11. The court was called on to interpret those provisions on three occasions, in its
judgments in *Carciati* (Case 823/79) [1980] ECR 2773, *Abbink* (Case 134/83) [1984]
ECR 4097 and *Ministère Public and Ministry of Finance v Profant* (Case 249/84)
[1985] ECR 3237.

12. *Carciati* was concerned with a situation very different from that of the
taxpayer inasmuch as the vehicle was not re-exported every day to the member state
in which was situated the undertaking which owned it but seems to have been used
semi-permanently in the country of residence of the user.

13. In *Abbink*, too, a return journey was not made every day. Furthermore, in
both of those cases the court considered the problem in the light only of the principles
of the EEC Treaty concerning the free movement of goods, as was required by the
terms of the questions referred to it.

14. In its judgment in *Profant*, the most recent case on the subject, the court
considered the problem of exemptions in a wider context.

15. After noting that according to art 14 of the Sixth Directive, the national
provisions in question were to be maintained in force 'on matters related to' the
exemptions provided for by the Community rules and were to be adapted to
minimise cases of double imposition of value added tax within the Community, the
court added that those requirements had in turn to be viewed in the light of one of
the objectives of the harmonisation of value added tax which is, as stated in one of
the recitals in the preamble to the Sixth Directive, to make further progress in the
effective removal of restrictions on the movement of persons and goods and the
integration of national economies.

16. The court concluded ([1985] ECR 3237 at 3258 at paras 25–26) that those
considerations showed that—

'. . . the authorities of the Member States do not enjoy a complete discretion
in implementing the exemptions under Article 14 of the Sixth Council
Directive, for they have to observe the fundamental objectives of the
harmonization of value-added tax such as, in particular, to facilitate the free
movement of persons and goods and to prevent cases of double taxation. It
follows that in applying their national provisions on exemptions from value-
added tax to motor vehicles used by students from another Member State the
tax authorities of a Member State are required to apply the concept of temporary
importation in such a way as to avoid derogating, by taxing their vehicles twice,
from the freedom of nationals of Member States to pursue their studies in the
Member State of their choice.'

The court concluded that in such a case, the rules of Community law preclude the
levying by a member state of value added tax on importation.

17. I consider that the reasoning used in *Profant* may be transposed to the problem

before the court in this case. It is true that Mr Profant, unlike the taxpayer, Mr Ledoux, did not have his principal residence in the country of importation. It is also true that the court expressly added that the result would have been otherwise if the person in question, who had got married in the interim, and his wife 'settled in the host Member State in such a way as to manifest their intention of not returning to the Member State of origin'. In such a situation, the importation would no longer be temporary but would become definitive.

18. However, it can be argued that in this case the fact that the car is imported into the taxpayer's country of residence does not prevent the importation from being temporary since the car continues to be the property of the employer established in the neighbouring country, is regularly re-exported to that country and will return there definitively not later than on the termination of the taxpayer's contract of employment.

19. Since the importation of the goods, regardless of who imports them, constitutes the chargeable event in regard to value added tax, its temporary nature should, of itself, be sufficient to justify the exemption.

20. If a market 'resembling a real internal market' (see the fourth recital in the preamble to the Sixth Directive) is to be achieved, double taxation is in fact quite inconceivable in such a situation. Nevertheless, double taxation subsists in principle even in cases (such as this one) where in practice, in accordance with the judgments in *Schul (Gaston) Douane Expediteur BV v Inspecteur der Invoerrechten en Accijnzen* (Case 15/81) [1982] ECR 1409 and *Staatssecretaris van Financiën v Schul (Gaston) Douane-Expediteur BV* (Case 47/84) [1985] ECR 1491, no value added tax may be collected in the importing country because the rate of value added tax applicable there is lower than that applicable in the exporting country.

21. On the other hand, there is no double taxation and an exemption in the country of temporary importation would not be justified if value added tax had not been paid in the exporting country or if it had been reimbursed.

22. It is therefore quite correct for both Directive 83/182 (see the last recital in the preamble and art 4(1)(c)) and EC Council Directive 85/362 of 16 July 1985 on the harmonisation of the laws of the member states relating to turnover taxes— exemption from value added tax on the temporary importation of goods other than means of transport (the Seventeenth Directive) (see art 10(c)) to make the exemption subject to an express condition that the goods have been liable to value added tax in the exporting member state and have not benefited, by virtue of their exportation, from any exemption from value added tax.

23. On the other hand, it must be established that the vehicle was actually placed at the disposal of the worker by his employer, that is to say, that this is not a case of fraud such as false registration of a vehicle in a neighbouring country whereas it in fact belongs to the user. However, proof of the ownership of the vehicle by the employer may be established by fairly simple administrative techniques.

24. Furthermore, I regard it as revealing that for temporary imports of goods other than means of transport, art 10(d) of the Seventeenth Directive requires that the goods in question should '*belong* to a person established outside the territory of the Member State of importation' [emphasis added].

25. It should also be noted that Directive 83/182 did not deal with all imaginable and possible cases of temporary importation of motor vehicles and certainly does not constitute the final stage of development in that matter. To prove my point, I would refer to art 9(1) of Directive 83/182 which permits the member states to maintain and/or introduce more liberal arrangements than those provided for in Directive 83/182 and to the Commission's proposal for supplementary provisions to which I referred at the beginning.

26. There is thus no imperative reason *inherent in the requirements of the common system of value added tax* to make the grant of exemptions for the temporary importation of motor vehicles subject in this sort of situation to a condition that the

a *user* has his normal residence in a member state other than that into which the vehicle is being imported.

27. In the second place, it should be borne in mind that the exemptions provided for in art 14 of the Sixth Directive should be granted by the member states 'without prejudice to other Community provisions' while continuing to respect the fundamental aim of promoting *free movement of persons.*

b 28. Let me draw attention to the third and fourth recitals in the preamble to EC Council Regulation 1612/68 on freedom of movement for workers within the Community which state expressly that—

'... freedom of movement constitutes a fundamental right of workers and their families ... [which] ... must be enjoyed without discrimination by permanent, seasonal and *frontier* workers and by those who pursue their activities for the purpose of providing services. [Emphasis added.]'

c

The fifth recital in the preamble adds that—

'... the right of freedom of movement, in order that it may be exercised, by objective standards, in freedom and dignity, requires that equality of treatment shall be ensured in fact and in law in respect of all matters relating to the actual pursuit of activities as employed persons ... and also that *obstacles to the mobility*
d *of workers shall be eliminated.* [Emphasis added.]'

29. Furthermore, under art 5 of the EEC Treaty, the member states have a general obligation to take all appropriate measures to ensure fulfilment of the obligations arising out of the EEC Treaty or resulting from action taken by the institutions of the Community, to facilitate the achievement of the Community's
e tasks and to abstain from any measure which could jeopardise the attainment of the objectives of the Treaty.

30. A member state infringes that general obligation to co-operate if, by adopting a national measure, it contributes to the maintenance or introduction of an obstacle to free movement of workers who, although residing on its territory, exercise their activities in another member state.

f 31. That is what a member state does if, by charging value added tax twice, it obliges a frontier worker in practice to give up certain advantages granted to him by his employer solely on the ground that the worker has his residence on that state's territory. The worker is thus placed at a disadvantage in regard to working conditions compared to his colleagues residing in the country in which their employer is established and having the benefit of the same advantage in kind. The attraction of
g employment in a member state other than that in which he has his residence is thereby diminished, which directly affects the exercise of his right to freedom of movement within the Community.

32. The same reasoning holds good when the employer also permits the vehicle to be used for private purposes. It may be considered in that case that that is part of the remuneration, in the broadest sense, paid to the worker. Furthermore, such an
h advantage in kind may well, in certain cases, be compensated for by a salary slightly lower than would be paid to workers who did not enjoy it.

33. The Commission correctly emphasises that—

'... part of the remuneration paid to a worker residing in another Member State would in fact be rendered useless by the legislation of the country of residence, whereas in regard to the country of employment there is complete
j equality of remuneration between residents and non-residents, as is required by Article 48 of the Treaty and provided for in detail by Article 7 of Regulation No. 1612/68 on free movement of workers within the Community.'

34. It is interesting to note in this context that all those who benefit under art 4 of Directive 83/182 from an exemption for the use in the course of their work of a

vehicle of which they are the proprietor do not lose that exemption if, at the end of their day's work, they use the vehicle for private purposes (for example, to go to a restaurant or to the beach). I therefore consider that there is no real reason to deny a worker in the position of the taxpayer the right to use the vehicle placed at his disposal by his employer under the terms of his contract of employment for private purposes.

35. As the court has already seen, the Belgian authorities were perfectly well aware of the problem of the use by a frontier worker of a vehicle placed at his disposal by his employer to travel from his home to his place of work because they first tolerated, then officially permitted that use on a trial basis with effect from 1 May 1984. Furthermore, the circular of 1 May 1984 issued by the Belgian customs authorities has the merit of dealing also with the case in which several workers are driven back to the country in which they live in a staff transport vehicle which remains overnight in that country.

36. For the reasons set out above, I consider that those rules should have been introduced on a definitive basis and not merely on a trial basis (with the possibility of withdrawing them without notice, see the circular of the Belgian Customs and Excise Department of 1 May 1984, p 7) and that it should not have been possible to withdraw the benefit of those exemptions if the vehicle was used secondarily for private purposes.

37. For all of those reasons, I propose that the court should reply as follows to the question referred to it by the Cour d'Appel, Liège:

> The rules of Community law, in particular those dealing with value added tax, prevent a member state from collecting value added tax on the temporary importation of a motor vehicle belonging to an employer established in another member state in which value added tax has been paid when the vehicle is used by an employee residing in the first member state under the terms of his contract of employment and for leisure purposes.

6 July 1988. **THE COURT OF JUSTICE** delivered the following judgment.

1. By a judgment of 12 March 1986, which was received at the court on 26 May 1986, the Cour d'Appel (Court of Appeal), Liège, referred to the court for a preliminary ruling under art 177 of the EEC Treaty a question on the interpretation of the Community rules on value added tax in order to be able to determine the consistency with those rules of the Belgian legislation on value added tax.

2. The question arose in the context of criminal proceedings brought by the Ministère Public and the Ministry of Finance of the Kingdom of Belgium against Yves Ledoux (the taxpayer), a frontier worker residing in Belgium and employed by a company established in France. That company had provided him with a car, belonging to it and registered in France, on which value added tax had been paid. Under his contract of employment, the taxpayer used that car for the performance of his duties under the contract and for leisure purposes.

3. The Belgian customs and excise authorities have long tolerated the use by a frontier worker resident in Belgium of a vehicle placed at his disposal by his employer, established in another member state, for the purpose of travelling from his place of work to his home in Belgium. That practice was approved by a circular of the Belgian Customs and Excise Department of 1 May 1984. However, the circular in question covers only the use of the car for the purpose of travelling to work, to the exclusion of all other use for private purposes.

4. Questioned on 22 February 1983 as he crossed the frontier at a point other than that which he used to go to work, the taxpayer was charged with having unlawfully imported a motor vehicle, which is punishable by either the confiscation of the vehicle or payment of its value.

a
5. Having decided that the taxpayer's case was not covered by specific rules, the Tribunal Correctionnel (Criminal Court), Neufchâteau, acquitted him. The Minister of Finance lodged an appeal before the Cour d'Appel, Liège, against that decision and in order to resolve that dispute the latter court stayed the proceedings and referred the following question to the Court of Justice:

b
'Do the Community rules concerning taxation, and in particular the rules concerning value added tax, permit the Belgian State, under the Law of 3 July 1969 establishing the Value Added Tax Code and the decrees implementing that Law and in accordance with the interpretation of its provisions by the Minister of Finance of the Kingdom of Belgium, in proceedings brought against [the taxpayer], residing at 32 Rue Leroy, Marcinelle, to levy value added tax on a motor vehicle which is owned by a company incorporated under French law with its registered office in France and is subject to value added tax
c
in France, where the tax has been paid, in so far as the vehicle is used by an employee of the company, who is resident in Belgium, for the performance of his duties under his contract of employment and for leisure purposes, taking account of the fact that the vehicle remains the property of the French employer and that the importation into Belgium is only temporary and of a provisional nature?'

d
6. Reference is made to the report for the hearing for a fuller account of the facts in the main proceedings, the Community and national provisions at issue, the course of the procedure and the observations submitted to the court, which are mentioned or discussed hereinafter only in so far as is necessary for the reasoning of the court.

7. It must be pointed out that when the facts at issue in the main proceedings took
e
place, EC Council Directive 83/182 of 28 March 1983 on tax exemptions within the Community for certain means of transport temporarily imported into one member state from another (Directive 83/182) had not yet been adopted. Consequently, the applicable Community rules were contained in EC Council Directive 77/388 of 17 May 1977 on the harmonisation of the laws of the member states relating to turnover taxes—common system of value added tax: uniform basis of assessment
f
(the Sixth Directive).

8. The question put by the national court seeks to determine whether the Sixth Directive prevents a member state from levying value added tax when a motor vehicle belonging to an employer established in another member state, in which value added tax has been paid, is used by a frontier worker residing in the first member state for the performance of his duties under his contract of employment
g
and for leisure purposes.

9. Article 14(1) of the Sixth Directive provides that, without prejudice to other Community provisions, member states are to exempt under conditions which they are to lay down for the purpose of ensuring the correct and straightforward application of the exemptions provided for and of preventing any possible evasion, avoidance or abuse, inter alia the importation of goods declared to be under
h
temporary importation arrangements. Article 14(2) provides for the subsequent laying down of Community tax rules clarifying the scope of the exemptions referred to in para 1 and detailed rules for their implementation. Until the entry into force of those rules, the member states may maintain their national provisions in force on matters related to the provisions of the Sixth Directive or adapt them in order to minimise, in particular, double imposition of value added tax within the Community.

j
10. In the light of those provisions, the conditions required by the legislation of the member states for granting exemption from value added tax for vehicles imported under temporary arrangements must take account, on the one hand, of the objectives of harmonisation of the rules relating to value added tax which are, as is indicated in the recitals in the preamble to the Sixth Directive, the abolition of the imposition of tax on imports and the remission of tax on exports, further progress in

the effective removal of restrictions on the movement of persons and goods and the integration of national economies and, on the other hand, the objective of preventing *a* evasion, avoidance or abuse in cases of temporary importation.

11. It should be pointed out in that regard, as the court decided in its judgment of 3 October 1985, *Ministère Public and Ministry of Finance v Profant* (Case 249/84) [1985] ECR 3237, that the authorities of the member states do not enjoy a complete discretion in implementing the exemptions for imports under art 14 of the Sixth Directive, for they must observe the fundamental objectives of the harmonisation of *b* value added tax, such as, in particular, the encouragement of free movement of persons and goods and the prevention of double taxation. It follows that art 14 of the Sixth Directive must be interpreted in the light of all of the fundamental rules of the Community.

12. In the light of those considerations, a member state would infringe the general obligation to co-operate imposed on the member states by art 5 of the EEC Treaty *c* if it contributed, through a national measure, to the maintenance or introduction of an obstacle to the free movement of workers who, although residing on its territory, pursue their occupations in another member state.

13. In order to consider whether such might be the case in the circumstances set out in the question referred to the court, the case of the use for business purposes of a motor vehicle by a frontier worker residing in the member state of importation *d* must first be considered.

14. It should be observed in that regard that when the member states lay down the conditions for exemption from value added tax in cases of temporary importation provided for under art 14(1)(c) of the Sixth Directive, they must respect the aim of the exemption for temporary imports.

15. The mere fact that the vehicle has been imported into the country of residence *e* of the user does not cause such importation to cease to be temporary where the vehicle has been placed at the disposal of the frontier worker by his employer for the duration of his contract of employment, belongs to the employer who is established in a neighbouring member state in which value added tax has been paid, is regularly re-exported to that member state and will definitively return there not later than on the termination of the contract of employment with the frontier worker, and where, *f* on the other hand, there is no indication of tax evasion, abuse or avoidance.

16. It is true that the court, in its judgments of 9 October 1980, *Carciati* (Case 823/79) [1980] ECR 2773) and of 11 December 1984, *Abbink* (Case 134/83) [1984] ECR 4097), decided that in granting an exemption from value added tax in respect of the temporary importation of a motor vehicle, the importing member state is entitled to require, as a condition of the exemption, that the importer should not *g* reside on its territory. That rule is justified by the fact that it is generally the resident of the member state of importation who, being usually also the owner of the vehicle, imports it permanently for his personal use. However, that justification does not apply when a frontier resident of a member state, without being the owner of the vehicle, actually imports it temporarily in the course of his employment.

17. It now remains to consider cases in which the contract of employment of a *h* frontier worker permits him to use the temporarily imported motor vehicle not only for the purposes of his employment, but also for private purposes.

18. It should be observed in that regard that private use, being ancillary to business use and provided for in the contract of employment and thus forming from an economic point of view part of the worker's remuneration, must be subject to the same conditions as business use. If it were not, frontier workers would be effectively *j* prevented from benefiting from certain advantages granted to them by their employers merely because they resided in the member state into which the vehicle was temporarily imported. Such workers would thereby be placed at a disadvantage in regard to working conditions compared to their colleagues residing in the country of their employer, which would have a direct effect on the exercise of their right to free movement within the Community.

a

19. It is for the national court to decide in each case whether a use which is not strictly a business use is ancillary to the business use, on the basis of all the relevant factors in each case.

20. The reply to the question referred to the court by the Cour d'Appel, Liège, must therefore be that the Sixth Directive prevents a member state from levying value added tax on a motor vehicle which is owned by an employer established in another member state where value added tax has been paid, and which is used by a

b

frontier worker residing in the first member state for the performance of his duties under his contract of employment and, secondarily, for leisure purposes.

Costs

21. The costs incurred by the Belgian government, the Danish government and the Commission of the European Communities, which have submitted observations

c

to the court, are not recoverable. As these proceedings are, in so far as the parties to the main proceedings are concerned, a step in the proceedings pending before the national court, the decision as to costs is a matter for that court.

On those grounds, the court (Fourth Chamber), in answer to the question referred to it by the Cour d'Appel, Liège, by judgment of 12 March 1986, hereby rules:

d

The Sixth Directive prevents a member state from levying value added tax on a motor vehicle which is owned by an employer established in another member state where value added tax has been paid, and which is used by a frontier worker residing in the first member state for the performance of his duties under his contract of employment and, secondarily, for leisure purposes.

e

Agents: *J Herbiet* and *Mr Neckebroeck* (for the Minister of Finance of the Kingdom of Belgium); *L Mikaelson*, Legal Adviser (for the Danish government); *H Etienne*, Principal Legal Adviser (for the Commission).

Rengan Krishnan Esq   Barrister.

Note   a
R v Inspector of Taxes and another, ex parte Kelly

COURT OF APPEAL, CIVIL DIVISION
DILLON, McCOWAN AND NOLAN LJJ   b
19 JULY 1991

*Relief – Interest – Loan for purchase or improvement of land – Mortgage interest relief
at source – Taxpayer taking up remortgage with second building society – Part of loan
used to redeem first mortgage and balance used for living expenses – Whether taxpayer
entitled to mortgage interest relief at source – Income and Corporation Taxes Act 1988,*   c
s 370(2)(b).

Notes

For mortgage interest relief at source in general, see Simon's Taxes A3.430.   d
For the Income and Corporation Taxes Act 1988, s 370, see ibid, Part G1.

Appeal

Wilfrid Kelly (the applicant) appealed against the decision of Vinelott J dated 30
November 1990 (see [1991] STC 38) dismissing his application for judicial review of   e
the decision of the inspector of taxes to deny him interest relief on a remortgage
under the mortgage interest relief at source scheme. The facts are set out in the
judgment of Dillon LJ.

The applicant appeared in person.
Launcelot Henderson for the Crown.   f

DILLON LJ. This is an appeal by Mr Kelly (the applicant), who has appeared in
person, against a decision of Vinelott J of 30 November 1990 (see [1991] STC 38)
when he was sitting as an additional judge of the Queen's Bench Division and
dismissed an application by the applicant for judicial review in respect of certain   g
decisions of the Revenue as a result of which the applicant's wife has so far not been
accorded mortgage interest relief at source (MIRAS) in respect of part of the interest
payable to the Leeds & Holbeck Building Society (the Leeds & Holbeck). The
circumstances of the appeal indicate matters which I find very unhappy.

The position is that in 1988 the applicant and his wife purchased a property, 44
Church Meadow, Platt Bridge, Wigan as their home in joint names with the   h
assistance of a mortgage loan of £45,300 from the Nationwide Anglia Building
Society (the Nationwide). It was never in dispute that the loan was for house
purchase and that the interest on it was entitled to tax relief under the MIRAS
scheme up to the permitted limit of a £30,000 advance.

In 1989 the applicant and his wife carried out certain arrangements which were
completed on 6 November 1989. Part one of the arrangement was that the applicant's   j
interest in the property was transferred to his wife so that the property stood in her
sole name. Part two of the arrangement was that a further advance was raised on the
property. That brought in a different building society, the Leeds & Holbeck, which
provided a total amount of £52,419, which was applied as to £45,300 in paying off
the Nationwide mortgage and as to the balance in payment to the applicant's wife as
an advance for her own purposes.

a
The applicant, on behalf of his wife, sent to the inspector of taxes at Leigh, Lancashire, a form—MIRAS 3—signed by his wife which is dated 14 October 1989 and was presumably therefore signed in anticipation of completion of the new mortgage. That form is headed 'Inland Revenue – Relief for payment of loan interest', and then it says:

b
'If you think that you are entitled to tax relief on your loan interest, please read the notes on the back, give the details asked for below, send the top copy of this form to your Tax Office [and] keep the borrower's copy to refer to in future.'

The notes on the back say, under the heading 'Notes on Mortgage Interest Relief At Source (MIRAS)':

c
'1. You may be able to claim tax relief on the interest you pay on a loan you have taken out to buy your only or main residence. This includes a house, flat, maisonette and in certain circumstances a caravan or houseboat.
2. . . .
3. Where the loan is only partly used for buying a property (within Note 1 or 2 above) or for replacing a loan so used, show against "Amount of loan (or share of loan) on which you claim relief" only that part of the loan. The Tax Office

d
will give you tax relief on the interest relating to that part of the loan which is allowable.'

Then under 6:

e
'If you are entitled to tax relief on your interest payments, the relief will be given either by a reduction in the amount of interest you pay to your lender under MIRAS (if you are liable at higher rates of tax, relief for tax above the basic rate will be given in your PAYE code or tax assessment), or by the Tax Office through your PAYE code or in your tax assessment. The Tax Office will let you know the method appropriate to your interest.'

f
The first part of the form, which was filled in by the applicant for his wife's benefit and is signed by his wife, sets out the tax office reference, and it is addressed to the inspector of taxes, Leigh. It gives the applicant's wife's name and address, ticks the box that shows that she is self-employed, and gives details of the new loan giving the name and address of the Leeds & Holbeck, the address of the property, 44 Church Meadow, and the amount of the total loan, £52,419. The date of first payment due was not given. The purpose of the loan was said to be 'mortgage', which from one

g
point of view is correct, but was not perhaps what was intended. There is then in the printed form a question: 'Amount of loan (or share of loan) on which you claim relief (exclude any amount not used for house purchase or for replacing such an amount in a previous loan)'. That (probably because he did not understand it) the applicant left blank, and so the form was sent off not in itself giving the information which the inspector would need.

h
We were told by counsel for the Crown that although designated MIRAS 3 (1988), that form is in truth merely a general application for relief from tax for payment of loan interest not in any way limited to MIRAS applications, and that it does not automatically follow because, he submits, it cannot automatically follow that a part of a loan can qualify for MIRAS under that application. In other words, the 'Amount of loan . . . on which you claim relief (exclude any amount not used for

j
house purchase or for replacing such an amount in a previous loan)' will, if answered, necessarily have the effect according to the way the statute is drawn of excluding any relief granted from the MIRAS system.

The difference between the two will for many taxpayers be non-existent, but it applies where the payer of the interest does not have sufficient taxable income to frank the tax relief on the loan interest if the loan interest has to be paid gross and the tax is only recoverable by being set against other interest. If the payer of the interest has sufficient other income for the tax on the loan interest, in so far as the loan is attributable to house purchase and does not exceed £30,000, then that can be a achieved by a PAYE adjustment or in the tax assessment of a self-employed person. But unless MIRAS applies the interest payer is left exposed. There is also at the present time no doubt a risk that an interest payer who at the outset has other income and so is not greatly affected whether MIRAS is applied or not may be made redundant and so lose his other source of income.

Any taxpayer or borrower who fills in MIRAS 3 would, as it seems to me, naturally b jump to the conclusion that MIRAS would be applied to as much of the interest as was attributable to the amount, up to £30,000, of the loan used for house purchase or for replacing such an amount in a previous loan. That is the impression he would get from the form and its notes, including the heading with the notes on the back.

The applicant filled in a further form in November (it is wrongly dated) which his wife signed, but again, though he was able to put in that the first payment was due c on 6 November 1989, he failed to answer the question: 'Amount of loan . . . on which you claim relief (exclude any amount not used for house purchase or for replacing such an amount in a previous loan)'. He did, however, supply the Revenue with information as to the amount which replaced the Nationwide loan, namely, as I have already said, £45,300, when he sent a form MIRAS 5 in respect of that to the Revenue in January 1990. He endeavoured to pursue his claim for MIRAS relief d through all available channels without, as it seems, getting any clear appreciation of what the difficulties were.

There was a letter from the Revenue of 13 February 1990 which is from the Inland Revenue Regional Controller for Greater Manchester at Stockport. There it is set out that the writer and assistant group controller understood the position to be that the Nationwide mortgage stood at approximately £45,300 at the time of redemption, e and the new mortgage was in the increased sum, which I have mentioned. The letter then states:

> 'Because the amounts of the two mortgages are different, it follows that the Leeds and Holbeck loan is not wholly a replacement of a qualifying loan for MIRAS purposes. In fact the Leeds and Holbeck mortgage is what is called a f "mixed-loan" being partly for a qualifying purpose and partly for something else. As such your latest mortgage cannot be included in the MIRAS scheme. It is, therefore, appropriate to grant you and your wife any tax relief due on interest paid through your PAYE codings. How this may be best achieved is a matter for Leigh Tax District.'

Then, however, there was a further letter from Somerset House of 8 March 1990. g That was more constructive. It came from the Savings and Investment Division of the Revenue at Somerset House in response to a letter which the applicant had sent to the Chancellor of the Exchequer. The letter set out:

> 'The general position is that tax relief on mortgage interest payments is allowable on a loan (or part of a loan) which is applied to the purchase of the h borrower's only or main residence. Prior to the introduction of the MIRAS (mortgage interest relief at source) scheme in April 1983 any relief due was allowed through a PAYE coding adjustment or set-off against the borrower's overall income. Under the MIRAS scheme, provided the loan is taken out with a MIRAS qualifying lender and provided the loan is *wholly* applied to the purchase (or improvement, if the loan was made before April 1988) of the main j residence, the borrower obtains relief by deducting a sum equivalent to basic rate tax from the interest payments made. But a loan which is for a mixed purpose—partly qualifying and partly non-qualifying—cannot come within the MIRAS arrangements. This is the statutory position. Where a loan remains outside MIRAS, any relief due will be given, as previously, against the

borrower's *overall tax liability*. However, when a person has insufficient income
to use all their tax allowances for particular years then any outstanding relief is
foregone. This . . . remains the position for loans outside the MIRAS scheme.'

The letter then sets out that the original loan from the Nationwide came within the
MIRAS scheme, but that the increase of the borrowing for private use when the
borrowing was moved to the Leeds & Holbeck was partly for a non-qualifying
purpose and so the loan did not qualify under the MIRAS provisions. But relief
could be given appropriately against other income, although as the applicant's wife
did not at present have any tax liability no relief could be given. The letter then
goes on:

'What I can suggest, however, is that you ask your building society to
restructure your wife's borrowing so that it is divided into two separate loans,
one covering the house purchase element and the other covering the non-
qualifying expenditure. If this is achieved—and these are essentially matters to
be settled between borrower and lender—it should enable her thereafter to
receive MIRAS on the house purchase loan.'

That is, of course, a wholly artificial situation because everybody knows that the
total advance of £52,419 represented an advance of £45,300 for paying off the
Nationwide loan which came within the MIRAS scheme and an advance of the
balance for a non-qualifying purpose. Counsel for the Crown accepted in argument
that if the mortgage had recited that the mortgage advance of the £52,419
represented two loans or two loans making up one overall loan, that would have been
sufficient to attract the MIRAS relief on £30,000 of the £45,300. But as it did not
fully recite the underlying transaction, the applicant was told to ask the building
society to restructure his wife's borrowings so that it was divided into two separate
loans.

I will come in a moment to what happened as a result of that. The applicant
comments: 'If there is no entitlement to MIRAS, how come it can be achieved?'
The answer seems to be: 'It can be achieved if the right wording is used in the loan
document, and instead of talking of one loan for two purposes the talk is of two loans
for two separate purposes constituting one advance.' So there is magic in words. The
sums advanced would, of course, have gone in different directions in that the money
to pay off the Nationwide would have gone to their solicitors while the excess would
have gone to the applicant's wife herself.

If one turns to the provisions of the Income and Corporation Taxes Act 1988 (the
1988 Act) which deal with the relief, one finds first a group of sections beginning at
s 353 headed 'Relief for payments of interest (excluding MIRAS)', and the details
are given of the relief available outside MIRAS on loans for house purchase up to
the prescribed limit, now £30,000.

We then come to the MIRAS relief which starts at s 369. In relation to the general
relief under the previous sections there has been express provision in s 367(4) that:

'Where part only of a debt fulfills the conditions required under sections 354
to 364 for interest on the debt to be eligible for relief under section 353, such
proportion of the interest shall be treated as eligible for relief under that section
as is equal to the portion of the debt fulfilling those conditions at the time of the
application of the money in question.'

When we come to MIRAS, however, s 369, which is headed 'Mortgage interest
payable under deduction of tax', states:

'If a person who is a qualifying borrower makes a payment of relevant loan
interest to which this section applies, he shall be entitled, on making the
payment, to deduct and retain out of it a sum equal to income tax thereon at
the basic rate for the year of assessment in which the payment becomes due.'

What is in question therefore is a payment by a qualifying borrower of relevant loan interest. 'Relevant loan interest' is defined in s 370(1) as being 'interest which is paid and payable in the United Kingdom to a qualifying lender and to which subsection (2) or (3) below applies'. It is not in doubt in the present case that the applicant's wife was a qualifying borrower and the Leeds & Holbeck a qualifying lender. Section 370(3) does not apply because it is concerned with loans enforced at a much earlier date and in respect of which option notices applied.

So one turns to sub-s (2) and that sets out three conditions:

'. . . this subsection applies to interest if . . .
(a) it is interest falling within section 354(1) or 365; and
(b) . . . the whole of the interest either would be eligible for relief under section 353 or would be taken into account in a computation of profits or gains or losses for the purposes of Case I, II or VI of Schedule D for any year of assessment . . .'

and then (c) which does not matter. But that must mean that the whole of the interest paid to the qualifying lender would be eligible for relief under s 353. That cannot be so in relation to the whole of the interest payable to the Leeds & Holbeck on their advance for £52,419 because only £45,300 of that was applied for a qualifying purpose. Therefore, that wording in s 370(2)(b) leads to the position that where there is a non-qualifying purpose for part of an advance as well as a qualifying purpose the arrangement with the building society must be structured or restructured so that the advance for the qualifying purpose can be regarded as a separate loan. I find that highly artificial but the inescapable conclusion from the wording of s 370(2)(b).

If the substance of the transaction is looked at it is plain that it can be said that there were two advances made by the Leeds & Holbeck in the total which I have mentioned, but it has been dealt with throughout (and that becomes more apparent as we go further on in the history) by the building society as one loan.

There is a further qualification in s 374(1) of the 1988 Act. That provides that s 369, which I have mentioned, 'does not apply to any relevant loan interest unless [certain further conditions are satisfied]'. One is put as (a) that the borrower has given notice, in effect, self-certifying that the interest is relevant loan interest. The applicant and his wife cannot satisfy that in respect of the whole or any part of the interest payable to the Leeds & Holbeck because of s 370(2)(b).

The next step is (b) which has to be satisfied in the alternative—'. . . the Board have given notice to the lender and the borrower that the interest may be paid under deduction of tax'. The form in which that notice is given is a Revenue form designated as MIRAS 4. It is not a form signed by the lender or the borrower at all. It sets out under the heading 'Tax relief for payments of loan interest' the lender's name and address, the address of the mortgaged property, the name of the borrower and so forth. It then sets out:

'From the information I hold, the interest on the above loan qualifies for tax relief. I give notice that the interest is relevant loan interest from the start of the loan or exceptionally from the following later date . . .'

and there is a reference to a note 5 suggesting that if there has been a change of circumstances the date may be later than the start of the loan. Then it is stated: 'This is the date from which the borrower is entitled to relief under the MIRAS arrangements.'

Section 374(2) provides that:

'Where notice has been given as mentioned in paragraph (a) or (b) of subsection (1) . . . section 369 applies to any relevant loan interest to which the notice relates and which becomes due on or after the relevant date, as defined by subsection (3) below.'

There is then the statutory definition of 'relevant date'. In the case of a notice of self-
a certification by the borrower under para (*a*) of sub-s (1), the date is the date the
notice is given by him. In the case within para (*b*) where the Board have given a
form MIRAS 4, there is a formula which is remarkably difficult either to comprehend
or to reconcile with what appears on the printed form MIRAS 4. It is a date specified
in the notice as being 'the relevant date (which may be earlier than the date so
specified as the date from which the interest may be paid under deduction of tax)'. I
b am left baffled by that, but unfortunately for the applicant in the present case he still
awaits MIRAS 4 which he has to obtain before s 369 applies because until it is
obtained s 374(1) is not satisfied.

What happened was that the applicant wrote to the building society in, it would
seem, June 1990, making certain payments, and there was a letter back from the
building society in effect setting out the difficulties it felt about severing the total
c advance so that one part would be subject to MIRAS relief and the other part would
not, and suggesting that it was administratively impossible to do that retrospectively
before 6 April 1990. The applicant says that he sent a letter on 2 August 1990 to the
Revenue enclosing a MIRAS 5 and a duly completed MIRAS 3. But at the hearing
before Vinelott J (see [1991] STC 38) the Revenue said that they had no trace of
such a document ever having been received. The applicant was asking for MIRAS
d 4.

In the course of the hearing before Vinelott J various assurances were given to
take steps which would resolve matters in the future. But it does not seem that
anything has been effectively done; in particular the Revenue were, it seems, going
to get in touch directly with the building society.

However, matters do not seem to have progressed very far. There is a letter we
e have been supplied with from the Leeds & Holbeck to the applicant's wife of 2 May
1991 in which the writer on behalf of the building society says:

'I have . . . received correspondence from the Inland Revenue indicating that
it is acceptable for us to include your account into the MIRAS scheme provided
tax relief is only given on the qualifying portion of the loan. I have today written
f to the Inland Revenue for a MIRAS 4 form which is their official instruction to
allow tax relief on your mortgage and I will advise you as soon as that form has
been received. In the meantime, in order for me to ascertain exactly what
proportion of the loan will qualify for tax relief, please complete the enclosed
split MIRAS declaration form and return the form to me at your earliest
convenience in the enclosed prepaid envelope.'

g That seems to have been a MIRAS 3 form. Whether that was MIRAS 3 or not, the
applicant's wife apparently, according to the copy letter, sent it back to the Leeds &
Holbeck on 7 May and asked for the 'soonest effective date of MIRAS inclusion of
the mortgage and the new payment requested'.

The building society wrote again to the applicant's wife on 10 June. The writer
says:
h
'Thank you for returning the split MIRAS declaration form to me and I
confirm that tax relief will be allowed on £30,000 of the loan which is the total
amount of tax relief which can be allowed on any mortgage. I have today
received a letter from HM Inspector of Taxes at Leigh which has asked me to
confirm certain details which they require in order to issue the MIRAS 4 form
j which is now the only requirement necessary in order for us to split the account
into non-qualifying and qualifying portions. I have written and confirmed the
details they require and look forward to receiving a MIRAS 4 form from them
in the near future. In their letter, they have stated that they have not received a
MIRAS 3 form from you although I note from our file that a MIRAS 3 has
been sent to yourself with previous correspondence and also when the loan
advance was given.'

It appears that the building society, as that letter of 10 June 1991 indicates, had indeed written to the Revenue in response to the Revenue's requirements of the building society. That was a letter to the Revenue from the building society also of 10 June 1991, but we were told today that in the view of the Revenue the letter of 10 June 1991 did not satisfy the Revenue requirements.

The position apparently remains as between the building society and the Revenue as it was at the time this matter was before Vinelott J and indeed as it has been for many months before that, possibly as far back as the letter from Somerset House of 8 March 1990, that the Revenue will not issue MIRAS 4 so that the MIRAS relief will be available on £30,000 until the building society has split the loan into qualifying and non-qualifying components; but the building society feels that it cannot split the loan so that the interest on one part will be payable under the MIRAS scheme until it has received MIRAS 4 authorising it to do so. That dispute remains unresolved and apparently incapable of being resolved at the level at which it is being handled, though one would have thought that it was a remarkably simple matter which could have been resolved months and months ago; but in the meantime the applicant's wife does not get MIRAS relief.

However, for present purposes we are concerned with whether there has been error of law on the part of the Revenue because that alone is the subject of judicial review. I have to say that I take the view that the construction of the 1988 Act put forward by the Revenue is correct, and that it is necessary that the sum in respect of which MIRAS relief is granted should have been or should be designated as a separate loan. That should not have presented any difficulty, but it has not so far happened. Until it does happen, whether before or after the issue of MIRAS 4, the relief is not available. Therefore there is no basis on which this court, were it minded to differ from Vinelott J, could grant judicial review.

The applicant has raised certain side issues such as whether he might by way of judicial review have a claim for damages and whether he had a right of appeal against a notice changing his wife's tax coding. But whether he has or has not an appeal against any particular decision does not assist unless there are grounds for the appeal succeeding, and whether he can claim damages likewise does not assist unless he has valid grounds for judicial review.

In the upshot I cannot see any grounds in law for granting judicial review, and I am unable to interpret what information we have about the loan made by the Leeds & Holbeck to the applicant's wife as being from its inception two loans rather than one loan for two purposes.

Therefore while deploring that an administrative impasse has come about which one would have thought could have been very speedily resolved by common sense and contact at the appropriate level, as Vinelott J no doubt expected, I see no alternative but to dismiss this appeal.

McCOWAN LJ. The essential fact here, in my judgment, is that there was one loan made by the building society to the applicant's wife, Mrs Kelly. Faced with that fact, the Revenue, it seems to me, had no option but to refuse to allow interest to be paid under the MIRAS scheme, for the simple reason that the loan was taken by the applicant and his wife for mixed purposes—one part being for a qualifying purpose and the other part for a non-qualifying purpose.

However, in a letter dated 8 March 1990 the Revenue pointed out to the applicant a method by which his problem could be overcome, namely by the building society dividing the single loan into two separate loans, one covering the house purchase element and the other the non-qualifying expenditure. The applicant asked the building society to do this, and he got a reply dated 10 July 1990, including this paragraph:

> 'The society would not normally be prepared to amend an account to this basis if it was originally completed on a gross basis but in cases where the

a application of gross interest may cause hardship to our borrowers, we would be prepared to include the account in the MIRAS Scheme on the split basis, if specifically directed to do so by the Inland Revenue.'

While the applicant then wrote to the Revenue asking them to issue a MIRAS 4, it does appear that unfortunately he did not send them a copy of the building society's letter; certainly the Revenue never received it. As Vinelott J accepted (see b [1991] STC 38 at 40), the Revenue were unaware of the difficulties raised by the building society, or that the building society was expecting the Revenue to do anything further.

The learned judge then records what counsel for the Crown told him. It was this:

c '. . . Counsel for the Crown was able to tell me, on instructions, that the Revenue are prepared to do everything within their power to assist the applicant and are prepared themselves to take the responsibility of writing to the building society and to explain the situation that has been reached and to state that if the building society will now split the mortgage in the way that the applicant requires, they will issue the MIRAS Form 4 which will enable the loan interest on the first £30,000 to be paid under deduction of tax.'

d This, we have been told, the Revenue duly did, but they have been met by a brick wall because the building society has been unwilling to split the loan until it receives the MIRAS 4. The Revenue, in my judgment, are obliged under the statute to take the stance that the split must come first. Why the building society takes its position is not clear to me.

e I have the utmost sympathy for the applicant and his wife. They appear to be in an unhappy dilemma not of their own making. I can only express the hope that mediation by the appropriate ombudsman or ombudsmen between the Revenue and the building society can bring forth a solution of the problem which does justice to them.

However, the applicant has sought judicial review against the Revenue, and I am unable to find any error in law on the part of the Revenue which would entitle the applicant to the relief claimed.

f Accordingly, I too would dismiss the appeal.

NOLAN LJ. I agree. By virtue of s 354(1) of the Income and Corporation Taxes Act 1988 (the 1988 Act), the prerequisite both for ordinary tax relief and for the benefit of mortgage interest relief at source (MIRAS) is that the interest in question should g be interest on a loan applied either in purchasing improving or developing land or in paying off another loan applied in that manner.

In the case of normal tax relief, s 367(4) of the 1988 Act provides for the situation where only part of a loan has been so applied. In the case of the MIRAS scheme, the benefit is available only where the whole of the interest has been paid on a loan so applied (see s 370(2)(b)).

h Why this distinction has been drawn counsel for the Crown was unable to explain, but there it is; and the Revenue of course are bound by it. That is the reason why the applicant, Mr Kelly, has not received the benefit of MIRAS. His loan was raised for a purpose in addition to that of repaying the original loan from the Nationwide Anglia Building Society which was itself a qualifying loan.

The problem has been bedevilled by the form MIRAS 3, which for the reasons j explained by Dillon LJ confuses the issue by indicating erroneously that each of the types of loan to which the form applies, whether MIRAS or non-MIRAS, can be split between the qualifying and the non-qualifying elements. Small wonder that the applicant has had difficulty in achieving the conditions for tax relief.

So far as judicial review is concerned, for the reasons which have been given, he has no case. The Revenue have acted perfectly correctly and indeed in the only way open to them in law. So far as the practical aspects of the matter are concerned, it is

plain that the Revenue have taken steps both before and since the judgment of
Vinelott J to help the applicant to obtain the relief for which in substance he should   *a*
be able to qualify.

The building society is not represented before us and therefore it would be wrong
to say where the responsibility lies for the long delay which has elapsed in sorting
out the problem. One can only hope that the problem will now be addressed and
that some means will be found whereby the applicant and his wife will be
recompensed for the unnecessary expense to which they have been put.   *b*

I too would dismiss this appeal.

Appeal dismissed ; no order as to costs. Leave to appeal to the House of Lords refused.

*9 December. The Appeal Committee of the House of Lords (Lord Bridge of Harwich,
Lord Griffiths and Lord Jauncey of Tullichettle) refused leave to appeal.*

Solicitor: *Solicitor of Inland Revenue.*

Rengan Krishnan Esq   Barrister.

a # Biehl v Administration des Contributions du Grand-Duché de Luxembourg
(Case C-175/88)

COURT OF JUSTICE OF THE EUROPEAN COMMUNITIES (FIFTH CHAMBER)
b JUDGES SIR GORDON SLYNN (PRESIDENT OF THE CHAMBER), ZULEEG (PRESIDENT OF CHAMBER), JOLIET, MOITINHO DE ALMEIDA AND GREVISSE
ADVOCATE GENERAL M DARMON
8 NOVEMBER 1989, 24 JANUARY, 8 MAY 1990

Emoluments from office or employment – European Communities – Freedom of
c *movement – Principle of non-discrimination – Taxpayer resident and employed in member state for part of tax year – Employer's deduction of tax from salary exceeded total liability for tax year – Whether member state entitled to retain excess tax deducted – EEC Treaty, art 48 – Loi sur l'Impôt sur le Revenu, art 154(6).*

Klaus Biehl, the taxpayer, was a German national who was resident and employed
d in the Grand Duchy of Luxembourg from 15 November 1973 to 31 October 1983. On 1 November 1983, he moved to the Federal Republic of Germany and was employed there from that date. The taxpayer's Luxembourg employer had deducted income tax from his salary and it emerged from his final assessment for the 1983 tax year that the amount deducted in the period from 1 January to 31 October 1983 exceeded the taxpayer's total tax liability for the year. The taxpayer asked the
e Administration des Contributions (Tax Department) du Grand-Duché de Luxembourg to repay the overdeduction of tax. The request was refused on the ground that art 154(6)[a] of the Loi sur l'Impôt sur le Revenu (Income Tax Law) provided that overdeductions of tax from the salaries of taxpayers who left Luxembourg during the year were not repayable. The taxpayer's complaint against that decision was also rejected on the same basis by the Directeur des Contributions (Director of
f Taxation). The taxpayer challenged the decision before the Conseil d'Etat du Luxembourg (State Council of Luxembourg), contending that art 154(6) introduced covert discrimination between taxpayers, because the article applied mainly to taxpayers who were not Luxembourg nationals. The national court stayed the proceedings and referred to the Court of Justice the question whether art 7 or art 48[b] of the EEC Treaty or any other provision of Community law precluded a member
g state from providing in its tax legislation that sums deducted by way of tax from the salaries and wages of employed persons who were nationals of a member state and resident taxpayers for only part of a tax year because they took up residence in the country or left it during the course of the tax year were not repayable.

Held – The rule regarding equality of treatment forbade not only overt discrimination
h by reason of nationality but also covert discrimination which led to the same result by the application of other criteria of differentiation. There was a risk that provisions such as art 154(6) of the Loi sur l'Impôt sur le Revenu would work particularly against taxpayers who were nationals of other member states. Accordingly, the answer to the question referred to the court was that under art 48(2) of the EEC Treaty a member state was precluded from providing in its tax legislation that sums
j deducted by way of tax from the salaries and wages of employed persons, who were nationals of a member state and were resident taxpayers for only part of the year

---

a   Article 154(6), so far as material, is set out at p 582 *f*, post
b   Article 48, so far as material, provides: 'Such freedom of movement shall entail the abolition of any discrimination based on nationality between workers of the Member States as regards employment, remuneration and other conditions of work and employment.'

because they had taken up residence in the country or had left it during the course of the tax year, were to remain the property of the Treasury and not repayable. *Sotgiu v Deutsche Bundespost* (Case 152/73) [1974] ECR 153 applied.

Notes

For the treatment of overdeductions of tax, see Simon's Taxes, E4.974.
For the EEC Treaty, art 48, see 50 Halsbury's Statutes (4th edn) 283.

Cases cited

EC Commission v French Republic (Case 167/73) [1974] ECR 359, CJEC.
EC Commission v Hellenic Republic (Case 305/87) [1989] ECR 1461, CJEC.
EC Commission v Italian Republic (Case 168/85) [1986] ECR 2945, CJEC.
Sotgiu v Deutsche Bundespost (Case 152/73) [1974] ECR 153, CJEC.
Van Duyn v Home Office (Case 41/74) [1974] ECR 1337, CJEC.

Reference

By an order of 21 June 1988, the Conseil d'Etat du Luxembourg referred to the Court of Justice of the European Communities for a preliminary ruling under art 177 of the EEC Treaty a question on the interpretation of arts 7 and 48 of the EEC Treaty. The question was raised in proceedings between Klaus Biehl, the taxpayer, and the Administration des Contributions (Tax Department) du Grand-Duché de Luxembourg. The Administration des Contributions and the Commission of the European Communities made submissions (in the written procedure) to the court. The language of the case was French. The facts are set out in the report for the hearing.

The Judge Rapporteur (R Joliet) presented the following report for the hearing.

I Facts and procedure

Klaus Biehl (the taxpayer) is a German national who resided in the Grand Duchy of Luxembourg from 15 November 1973 to 31 October 1983 during which time he was employed by a Luxembourg undertaking.

On 1 November 1983 he transferred his residence to the Federal Republic of Germany and has been employed there since that date.

For the period from 1 January 1983 to 31 October 1983 the taxpayer's Luxembourg employer deducted Lfr 972,272 from his salary by way of income tax.

The taxpayer's final tax assessment for the 1983 year of assessment showed that he was liable to the Luxembourg tax authorities for income tax of Lfr 797,258 and solidarity tax of Lfr 65,773, amounting to a total of Lfr 863,031.

The taxpayer requested the Administration des Contributions (Tax Department) du Grand-Duché de Luxembourg to refund to him the deductions made by his former employer in so far as they exceeded his net liability to tax in the year of assessment in question.

On 13 July 1984 the Bureau d'Imposition (Tax Office), Luxembourg refused that request on the basis of art 154(6) of the Loi sur l'Impôt sur le Revenu (Income Tax Law) (Mémorial A no 79, of 6 December 1967). Article 154(6) provides that:

'Amounts duly deducted from capital income shall become the property of the Treasury and are not repayable. The same shall apply to the deduction of tax from the salaries and wages of taxpayers resident during only part of the year because they take up residence in the country or leave it during the course of the year.'

On 20 February 1985 the Directeur des Contributions (Director of Taxation) rejected, on the same ground, the complaint which the taxpayer lodged against the decision of the Bureau d'Imposition.

The taxpayer challenged the decision of the Directeur des Contributions before
a the Conseil d'Etat du Luxembourg (State Council of Luxembourg). In his view,
art 154(6) did not discriminate directly between taxpayers on grounds of nationality.
However, it did constitute a covert form of discrimination prohibited by Community
law since it applied mainly to taxpayers who were not Luxembourg nationals.
Article 154(6) therefore infringed art 7 of the EEC Treaty.

The Administration des Contributions replied to that argument by stating that a
b difference in the treatment afforded to two distinct categories of taxpayers was not
discrimination prohibited under Community law if it was objectively justified. Such
objective justification did in fact exist. Article 154(6) of the Loi sur l'Impôt sur le
Revenu prevented taxpayers who took up residence abroad from obtaining an
unjustified advantage in comparison with taxpayers who remained resident in the
Grand Duchy of Luxembourg.

c The Counseil d'Etat du Luxembourg took the view that the dispute raised a
question concerning the interpretation of arts 7 and 48 of the EEC Treaty and by a
judgment of 21 June 1988 it stayed the proceedings and referred the following
question to the Court of Justice for a preliminary ruling under art 177 of the EEC
Treaty:

d 'Does Article 7 of the EEC Treaty or any other provision of Community law,
in particular Article 48 of the said Treaty guaranteeing freedom of movement
for workers, preclude a Member State from providing in its tax legislation that
sums deducted by way of tax from the salaries and wages of employed persons
who are nationals of a Member State and resident taxpayers for only part of the
year because they take up residence in the country or leave it during the course
e of the tax year are to remain the property of the Treasury and are not repayable?'

The judgment of the Conseil d'Etat du Luxembourg was received at the court
registry on 29 June 1988.

In accordance with art 20 of the Protocol on the Statute of the Court of Justice of
the European Communities, written observations were submitted on 14 September
f 1988 by the Administration des Contributions du Grand-Duché de Luxembourg,
represented by Jacques Loesch, Avocat-Avoué, Luxembourg, and, on 15 September
1988, by the Commission of the European Communities, represented by its Legal
Adviser, Jean-Claude Seché, acting as agent.

On hearing the report of the Judge Rapporteur and the views of the Advocate
General, the court decided to open the oral procedure without any preparatory
inquiry.

g By a decision of 6 July 1989 the court assigned the case to the Fifth Chamber
pursuant to art 95(1) and (2) of its Rule of Procedure.

II Written observations submitted to the court

The Administration des Contributions du Grand-Duché de Luxembourg
h contends that a legislative provision such as art 154(6) of the Loi sur l'Impôt sur le
Revenu is compatible with Community law.

In its view, art 7 of the EEC Treaty is not applicable because the rules governing
the collection of income tax do not fall within the scope of the EEC Treaty. Member
states are therefore free to decide whether or not overdeductions of tax must be
refunded.

j Article 7(2) of EC Council Regulation 1612/68 on freedom of movement for
workers within the Community (Regulation 1612/68) does not prohibit the denial of
a tax advantage to nationals of another member state if that advantage is denied,
under the same conditions, to the nationals of the member state in question. It
provides only that a worker who is a national of a member state is to enjoy, in the
territory of another member state, 'the same social and tax advantages as national
workers'.

The Administration des Contributions contends, moreover, that a tax
disadvantage linked to the exercise of the right of freedom of movement can
constitute an obstacle prohibited under art 48(1) of the EEC Treaty only if the
disadvantage is applied in a discriminatory manner, which is not the case in this
instance.

Finally, art 48(2) of the EEC Treaty does not rule out different treatment for two
distinct categories of taxpayers, namely, resident taxpayers and taxpayers who have
exercised their right to freedom of movement.

Taxpayers who are resident have their entire income for the year of assessment
concentrated in a single state. For them, the rate of tax depends on their total
income. Fairness thus dictates that any overdeduction of tax should be refunded to
them.

On the other hand, taxpayers who have exercised their right to freedom of
movement spread their income among a number of states. That gives them an
advantage over resident taxpayers. The advantage derives from the fact that the
Luxembourg tax authorities do not take into consideration income arising abroad
when they determine the rate of tax payable on income arising in Luxembourg.
Conversely, however, there is no repayment of overdeductions.

In conclusion, the Administration des Contributions proposes that the Court of
Justice should give the following reply to the Conseil d'Etat:

> 'No provision of Community law precludes a Member State from providing
> in its tax legislation that sums deducted by way of tax from the salaries and
> wages of employed persons who are nationals of a Member State and resident
> taxpayers during only part of the year because they take up residence in the
> country or leave it during the course of the tax year are not repayable.'

The Commission points out, first of all, that the principle of equal treatment is
applicable in the field of taxation. As far as employed persons are concerned that
principle is embodied in art 7(2) of Regulation 1612/68, which provides that they are
to enjoy 'the same social and tax advantages as national workers'.

The Commission points out, secondly, that a national provision like art 154(6) of
the Loi sur l'Impôt sur le Revenu introduces indirect or covert discrimination which
is prohibited by Community law. Non-resident employed persons, including
nationals of the other member states, can obtain a refund of tax overpaid only under
strict conditions, whereas employed persons who are residents are always entitled to
demand such a refund.

In conclusion, the Commission proposes that the reply to the question should be
that:

> 'Article 7(2) of Regulation No. 1612/68 of the Council of 15 October 1968
> must be interpreted as meaning that the term "tax advantage" referred to
> therein precludes sums deducted by way of tax, under the legislation of a
> Member State, from the salaries and wages of employed persons who are
> nationals of another Member State and are resident taxpayers during only part
> of the year because they take up residence in the country or leave it during the
> course of the tax year, remaining the property of the Treasury and not being
> repayable.'

24 January 1990. **The Advocate General (M Darmon)** delivered the following
opinion.

The question referred to the court by the Counseil d'Etat du Luxembourg (State
Council of Luxembourg) for a preliminary ruling relates in essence to the
compatibility with Community law of the following tax provision. The refund of
overpayments of income tax is refused if the taxpayer has not resided in the Grand
Duchy of Luxembourg for the whole of the tax year in question. Mr Biehl (the
taxpayer), a German national who left Luxembourg on 1 November 1983, was
consequently refused repayment of amounts of tax in excess of what he should have
paid under the scales in force.

First, it should be pointed out that the principle of equal treatment as between
national workers and workers who are nationals of other member states, as laid down
by art 48(2) of the EEC Treaty and EC Council Regulation 1612/68 (Regulation
1612/68), requires equal treatment with regard to taxation. On the one hand the
EEC Treaty itself, in providing for the abolition of all discrimination as regards
employment, remuneration and other conditions of work and employment, requires
this prohibition to be applied to taxation also. Otherwise the principle of equal
treatment with regard to remuneration could be infringed by virtue of discriminatory
tax provisions. On the other hand, art 7 of Regulation 1612/68, which concerns
equal treatment with regard to tax advantages, is a specific expression of the general
principle of non-discrimination in tax matters.

Second, it should be observed that the rule which is the subject of the action before
the court making the reference does not involve a criterion based on nationality: it is
formally applicable to Luxembourg nationals and Community nationals without
differentiation. However, this does not entirely rule out the existence of potential
discrimination which is indirect or concealed. According to the court's case law:

> 'The rules regarding equality of treatment, both in [the EEC Treaty] and in
> Article 7 of [Regulation 1612/68], forbid not only overt discrimination by reason
> of nationality but also all covert forms of discrimination which, by the
> application of other criteria of differentiation, lead in fact to the same result.
> This interpretation, which is necessary to ensure the effective working of one of
> the fundamental principles of the Community, is explicitly recognized by the
> fifth recital of the preamble to [Regulation 1612/68] which requires that equality
> of treatment of workers shall be ensured "in fact and in law". It may therefore
> be that criteria such as place of origin or residence of a worker may, according
> to circumstances, be tantamount, as regards their practical effect, to discrimi-
> nation on the grounds of nationality, such as is prohibited by [the EEC Treaty]
> and [Regulation 1612/68].' (See *Sotgiu v Deutsche Bundespost* (Case 152/73)
> [1974] ECR 153 at 164.)

Therefore it is necessary to establish, first, whether the legislation which is the
subject of the proceedings before the court making the reference, although it applies
without distinction, leads in fact to different treatment for Luxembourg nationals
and those of other member states of the Community.

On this point it is sufficient to state that use of the criterion of permanent residence
in Luxembourg would have the consequence of depriving mainly non-nationals of
the Grand Duchy of the refund in question. It is in fact primarily non-nationals
who leave the country during the year or take up residence there.

However, is the contested rule likely to infringe the principle of equal treatment?
Not every difference in treatment is necessarily equivalent to an infringement of the
principle of non-discrimination. I am thinking here of the circumstances of the
court's *Sotgiu* judgment in which employees of the Bundespost residing outside the
territory of the Federal Republic of Germany received a separation allowance lower
than that received by those residing in German territory. In this connection the
court (at 165) observed that—

> '... it is not possible to state that there is discrimination contrary to [the EEC
> Treaty] and [Regulation 1612/68] if it is apparent from a comparison between
> the two schemes of allowances taken as a whole that those workers who retain
> their residence abroad are not placed at a disadvantage by comparison with
> those whose residence is established within the territory of the State concerned.'

The court found that, for employees residing in the Federal Republic of Germany,
payment of the allowance was temporary and was connected with the obligation to
transfer their residence to the place of work, whereas there was no such limit or
obligation for workers residing abroad.

So far as the present case is concerned, it is important to note that a specific comparison of situations may show that a situation characterised by different *a* treatment does not amount to prohibited discrimination if, in fact, the national concerned is not placed at a disadvantage in relation to nationals of the host member state.

Therefore difference is not necessarily discrimination. It is this principle on which the Luxembourg government relies in arguing that the provision in question aims to reintroduce a progressive increase clause into the tax of the taxpayer concerned, *b* who would otherwise benefit, by dispersing his income among several states, from his changes of residence which alter the principles of taxation. In other words, what happens to someone who leaves Luxembourg in the course of the year or who takes up residence there is, in the final analysis, justified because if he had remained in Luxembourg his income would have been subject to a higher rate of tax.

I am by no means persuaded that this argument is likely to dispose of any objection *c* concerning infringement of the principle of equal treatment to the provision in question.

Quite obviously, it is for the member states alone to lay down rules on income tax: in the present state of Community law, the sphere of direct taxation is outside the ambit of the EEC Treaty. In this connection the objectives of the Luxembourg legislature are not, as such, subject to comparison with the principles of Community *d* law. However, member states must also observe the limits Community law marks out. Even if there is no question about the aims of the national legislature in seeking to include the equivalent of a progressive increase clause, the manifestly discriminatory nature of the rule in question appears in all cases where the individual concerned has not received income in the year in question in the member state of origin or destination. *e*

For instance, let us say, in October a Luxembourg firm dismisses its staff, who cannot find new jobs immediately. Therefore employees who are nationals of other member states return to their country of origin, where they do not find work until the end of the year in question. The Luxembourg nationals remaining in the Grand Duchy do not find jobs in that year either. In such a case, where the income received is exactly the same, the former are deprived of a refund which the latter will obtain. *f* Likewise, a Community national who takes up residence in Luxembourg at the end of February and obtains work immediately will be refused a refund if the question arises, whereas his colleague who is recruited on the same day but has been a 'resident unemployed' since 1 January, will be refunded any overpayment. Consequently a migrant will, under certain circumstances, be penalised on arrival or on departure. In my opinion, this manifest disadvantage is sufficient to render the provision in *g* question incompatible with the principle of equal treatment.

Therefore this provision infringes the principle of non-discrimination with regard to the situation of Community nationals taking up residence in the Grand Duchy or leaving it.

However, the situation of all Community nationals, including those of Luxembourg, wishing to exercise their right to seek or take up a job in another member *h* state may also reveal an infringement of the basic principle of the freedom of movement of persons as laid down by art 48(1) of the EEC Treaty.

In this case, the exercise of that right will automatically deprive them of the right to a refund of the overpaid tax merely by virtue of using the freedom granted by Community law.

As I have already said, the member states alone have power, as matters stand, to *j* determine the rules applying to income tax. However, as I have also pointed out, they cannot encroach on the freedoms guaranteed by Community law to all the nationals of member states. The non-repayment of overpaid tax will amount to an obstacle which is in any event unjustified for someone who leaves Luxembourg to seek a job in another member state where, for example, he does not succeed in finding employment. The same applies to someone who, in the course of the year,

a arrives in Luxembourg to take up a job which he has not succeeded in finding in another member state. In these cases there is no fear of evasion of the progressive increase in income tax, but the provision in question automatically deprives a worker exercising his freedom of movement, which was confirmed as having direct effect by the court's judgment in *Van Duyn v Home Office* (Case 41/74) [1974] ECR 1337, of a refund of overpaid tax. If necessary, therefore, the member states should use means other than withdrawing the right to a refund of overpaid tax to attain the
b fiscal objectives at which they aim.

Accordingly, I consider that the provision in question is likely to disregard the fundamental principle of freedom of movement of individuals and that of equal treatment which it entails.

I wish to make two final observations.

First, at the hearing the Luxembourg government referred to the opportunity
c offered by a non-contentious appeal procedure for rectifying any discrimination arising from the provision in question.

Even on the assumption that such procedure results in every case in allowing individuals to obtain a refund of excess tax, it cannot always remedy the insecurity created by the tax provision in question. (Cf *EC Commission v French Republic* (Case 167/73) [1974] ECR 359.) It will suffice to mention the court's settled case law to the
d effect that—

> '... mere administrative practices [and a non-contentious appeal is clearly within this category] which by their nature are alterable at will by the authorities and are not given the appropriate publicity, cannot be regarded as constituting the proper fulfilment of obligations under the Treaty.' (See *EC Commission v*
e *Italian Republic* (Case 168/85) [1986] ECR 2945 at 2961.)

Therefore the existence of a non-contentious appeal, to which neither the question before the court nor the judgment of the Conseil d'Etat refers, is unlikely to render compatible with the requirements of the freedom of movement of workers a provision which has the consequence of disregarding the fundamental principle of
f non-discrimination and of constituting an obstacle to the exercise by many private individuals of their basic rights under Community law.

Second, the court making the reference mentioned the possibility of assessing the provision in question in the light of art 7 of the EEC Treaty. On this point I would remind the court of its judgment of 30 May 1989 in *EC Commission v Hellenic Republic* (Case 305/87) [1989] ECR 1461 at 1476–1477 in which the court stated:
g

> 'In that regard, it should be pointed out first that the general prohibition of discrimination on grounds of nationality laid down in Article 7 of [the EEC Treaty] has been implemented, in regard to their several domains, by Articles 48, 52 and 59 of [the EEC Treaty]. Consequently, any rules incompatible with those provisions are also incompatible with Article 7 ... [Therefore] Article 7
h of [the EEC Treaty] applies independently only to situations governed by Community law in regard to which [the EEC Treaty] lay down no specific prohibition of discrimination.'

And the court did not find a specific failure to comply with art 7 as the Commission did not refer to situations other than those covered by arts 48, 52 and 59 of the EEC
j Treaty. Pursuant to this principle, it appears that the non-repayment of tax deductions from the salaries and wages of employed persons, who alone are referred to by the question of the Counseil d'Etat du Luxembourg and the provision which it has to assess, contravenes art 48 of the EEC Treaty and Regulation 1612/68 implementing it, and therefore it is unnecessary to find a specific infringement of art 7 in so far as no reference is made to situations other than those of employed persons who are within the ambit of the national provision in question.

Consequently I propose that the court should rule as follows:

Article 48(1) and (2) of the EEC Treaty and Regulation 1612/68 prohibit a
member state from providing in its tax legislation that sums deducted by way
of tax from the salaries and wages of employed persons who are nationals of a
member state and are resident taxpayers during part of the year only because
they take up residence in a member state or leave it during the tax year are to
remain the property of the Treasury and cannot be refunded.

8 May 1990. **THE COURT OF JUSTICE** delivered the following judgment.

1. By a judgment of 21 June 1988, which was received at the court on 29 June
1988, the Conseil d'Etat du Luxembourg (State Council of Luxembourg) referred
to the court for a preliminary ruling under art 177 of the EEC Treaty a question on
the interpretation of arts 7 and 48 of the Treaty.

2. That question arose in proceedings between Mr Biehl (the taxpayer) and the
Administration des Contributions du Grand-Duché de Luxembourg concerning
the repayment of an overdeduction of income tax.

3. The taxpayer is a German national who was resident in the Grand Duchy of
Luxembourg from 15 November 1973 to 31 October 1983. During that period, he
pursued an activity as an employed person in Luxembourg. On 1 November 1983,
he moved to the Federal Republic of Germany where he now works.

4. For the period from 1 January 1983 to 31 October 1983 the taxpayer's
Luxembourg employer deducted sums by way of income tax from the taxpayer's
salary. It emerged from the taxpayer's final tax assessment for the year of assessment
1983 that the amount deducted by his Luxembourg employer exceeded the total
amount of his liability to tax.

5. The taxpayer asked the Administration des Contributions du Grand-Duché
de Luxembourg to repay the overdeduction of income tax. The Bureau d'Imposition
(Tax Office), Luxembourg refused that request on the basis of art 154(6) of the Loi
sur l'Impôt sur le Revenu (Income Tax Law) (Mémorial A no 79, of 6 December
1967). The taxpayer lodged a complaint against the decision of the Bureau
d'Imposition, which was rejected on the same basis by the Directeur des Contributions
(Director of Taxation).

6. Article 154(6) of the Loi sur l'Impôt sur le Revenu provides that:

'Amounts duly deducted from capital income shall become the property of
the Treasury and are not repayable. The same shall apply to the deduction of
tax from the salaries and wages of taxpayers resident during only part of the
year because they take up residence in the country or leave it during the course
of the year.'

7. The taxpayer challenged the decision of the Directeur des Contributions before
the Conseil d'Etat du Luxembourg. He claimed that art 154(6) of the Loi sur l'Impôt
sur le Revenu introduced covert discrimination between taxpayers, prohibited by
Community law, because the article applied mainly to taxpayers who were not
Luxembourg nationals.

8. The response of the Administration des Contributions to that argument was
that a difference in treatment between two distinct categories of taxpayers did not
constitute discrimination prohibited by Community law if it was justified by
objective reasons. Such reasons did indeed exist in the case at issue. Article 154(6) of
the Loi sur l'Impôt sur le Revenu sought to prevent taxpayers who took up residence
abroad from obtaining, in certain cases, an unjustified advantage over taxpayers
who remained resident in Luxembourg.

9. In those circumstances, the national court stayed the proceedings and referred
the following question to the court:

'Does Article 7 of the EEC Treaty or any other provision of Community law,
in particular Article 48 of the said Treaty guaranteeing freedom of movement

for workers, preclude a Member State from providing in its tax legislation that sums deducted by way of tax from the salaries and wages of employed persons who are nationals of a Member State and resident taxpayers for only part of the year because they take up residence in the country or leave it during the course of the tax year are to remain the property of the Treasury and are not repayable?'

10. Reference is made to the report for the hearing for a fuller account of the facts, the relevant provisions and the observations submitted to the court, which are referred to or mentioned hereinafter only in so far as is necessary for the reasoning of the court.

11. Under art 48(2) of the EEC Treaty, freedom of movement for workers entails the abolition of all discrimination based on nationality between workers of the member states, particularly with regard to remuneration.

12. The principle of equal treatment with regard to remuneration would be rendered ineffective if it could be undermined by discriminatory national provisions on income tax. For that reason the Council laid down, in art 7 of EC Council Regulation 1612/68 on freedom of movement for workers within the Community, that workers who are nationals of a member state are to enjoy, in the territory of another member state, the same tax advantages as national workers.

13. According to the case law of the court, the rules regarding equality of treatment forbid not only overt discrimination by reason of nationality but also all covert forms of discrimination which, by the application of other criteria of differentiation, lead to the same result (see *Sotgiu v Deutsche Bundespost* (Case 152/73) [1974] ECR 153 at 164, para 11).

14. Even though the criterion of permanent residence in the national territory referred to in connection with obtaining any repayment of an overdeduction of tax applies irrespective of the nationality of the taxpayer concerned, there is a risk that it will work in particular against taxpayers who are nationals of other member states. It is often such persons who will in the course of the year leave the country or take up residence there.

15. In order to justify the national rule at issue in the main proceedings, the Administration des Contributions claimed that the purpose was to protect the system of progressive taxation. It pointed out that a taxpayer who took up residence or who left Luxembourg in the course of the year (hereinafter referred to as a temporarily resident taxpayer) spread his income, and consequently his tax liability, among at least two states, namely Luxembourg and the member state he left or in which he took up residence. That distorted the system of taxation. If a temporarily resident taxpayer were to obtain a refund of an overdeduction of tax he would, because he received income in two member states in succession, be taxed at a more favourable rate than that applied to the income of a resident taxpayer who, with the same annual income, must declare to the Luxembourg authorities all his income, whether or not it originated in Luxembourg.

16. That justification cannot be accepted. A national provision such as the one at issue is liable to infringe the principle of equal treatment in various situations. That is so in particular where no income arises during the year of assessment to the temporarily resident taxpayer in the country he has left or in which he has taken up residence. In such a situation, that taxpayer is treated less favourably than a resident taxpayer because he will lose the right to repayment of the overdeduction of tax which a resident taxpayer always enjoys.

17. At the hearing, the Administration des Contributions also observed that there exists in Luxembourg law a non-contentious procedure allowing temporarily resident taxpayers to obtain repayment of an overdeduction of tax by adducing the unfair consequences which the application of art 154(6) of the Loi sur l'Impôt sur le Revenu entailed for them.

18. Even if taxpayers are entitled to commence non-contentious proceedings to have their situation reviewed, the Luxembourg government has not cited any provision imposing an obligation on the Administration des Contributions to remedy

in every case the discriminatory consequences arising from the application of the
national provision at issue.

19. The reply to the national court must therefore be that art 48(2) of the EEC
Treaty precludes a member state from providing in its tax legislation that sums
deducted by way of tax from the salaries and wages of employed persons who are
nationals of a member state and are resident taxpayers for only part of the year
because they take up residence in the country or leave it during the course of the tax
year are to remain the property of the Treasury and are not repayable.

Costs

20. The costs incurred by the Commission of the European Communities, which
has submitted observations to the court, are not recoverable. Since these proceedings
are, in so far as the parties to the main proceedings are concerned, in the nature of a
step in the action pending before the national court, the decision on costs is a matter
for that court.

On those grounds, the court (Fifth Chamber) in answer to the question referred
to it by the Conseil d'Etat du Luxembourg, by a judgment of 21 June 1988, hereby
rules:

> Article 48(2) of the EEC Treaty precludes a member state from providing in
> its tax legislation that sums deducted by way of tax from the salaries and wages
> of employed persons who are nationals of a member state and are resident
> taxpayers for only part of the year because they take up residence in the country
> or leave it during the course of the tax year are to remain the property of the
> Treasury and are not repayable.

Agents: *Mr Rogalla*, Rechtanswalt, Münster (for the taxpayer); *J Loesch*, Luxembourg Bar (for the Administration des Contributions du Grand-Duché de
Luxembourg); *J-C Seché*, Legal Adviser (for the Commission).

Rengan Krishnan Esq   Barrister.

Note
Farmer (Inspector of Taxes) v Bankers Trust International Ltd

COURT OF APPEAL, CIVIL DIVISION
NEILL, RUSSELL, BUTLER-SLOSS LJJ
24 JULY 1991

Corporation tax – Group relief – Claim – Application to adduce fresh evidence – Document discovered after High Court decision that taxpayer company not entitled to change subsequently the basis of claim for group relief – Whether document relevant to taxpayer company's appeal – Whether document admissible as evidence – RSC Ord 59, r 10.

Notes

For claims to group relief, see Simon's Taxes D2.648.

Cases referred to in judgment

Ladd v Marshall [1954] 1 WLR 1489, [1954] 3 All ER 745, CA.
Pattison (Inspector of Taxes) v Marine Midland Ltd [1984] STC 10, [1984] AC 362, 57 TC 219, HL.

Case also cited

Prenn v Simmonds [1971] 1 WLR 1381, [1971] 3 All ER 237, HL.

Application

Bankers Trust International Ltd (BTI) applied to the Court of Appeal for leave to adduce further evidence in connection with its appeal against the decision of Harman J of 22 June 1990 (see [1990] STC 564) allowing the Crown's appeal against the determination of a Special Commissioner that BTI was entitled to decide how its claims to group relief were to be applied. The evidence consisted of a document discovered after the Crown's appeal to the High Court had been allowed. BTI sought an order either: (a) that the document be admitted as evidence under RSC Ord 59, r 10; or (b) that the case be remitted to the commissioners to determine whether the document should be admitted as evidence. The facts are set out in the judgment of Russell LJ.

Harvey McGregor QC and *Philip Baker* for BTI.
Alan Moses QC and *Launcelot Henderson* for the Crown.

RUSSELL LJ (delivering the first judgment at the invitation of Neill LJ). Bankers Trust International Ltd (BTI) is the parent company of a group of companies which at all material times included Bankers Trust Holding (UK) Ltd (BTH), Rodocanachi Leasing Ltd (RL) and Ocean Bulkers (UK) Ltd (Bulkers). Section 258(1) of the Income and Corporation Taxes Act 1970 (the 1970 Act) provides as follows:

> 'Relief for trading losses and other amounts eligible for relief from corporation tax may in accordance with the following provisions of this Chapter be surrendered by a company (called "the surrendering company") which is a member of a group of companies and, on the making of a claim by another

company (called "the claimant company") which is a member of the same group, may be allowed to the claimant company by way of a relief from corporation tax called "group relief".'   a

Section 264(1) of the 1970 Act provides:

'A claim for group relief—

(a) need not be for the full amount available,
(b) shall require the consent of the surrendering company notified to the   b
inspector in such form as the Board may require, and
(c) must be made within two years from the end of the surrendering company's accounting period to which the claim relates.'

On 22 December 1975 BTI made a claim for group relief in respect of the year ending 31 December 1973. That claim was in the following terms: c

'In accordance with the provisions of Section 264 Taxes Act 1970 notice is hereby given on behalf of the company of its claim to the losses surrendered by the following companies in respect of the year ended 31st December 1973:

[BTH]   £66,190·00
[RL]   £563,413·00   d

The above figures are provisional, subject only to agreement of the final computations for the year ended 31st December 1973.'

At that time the profits of BTI had not been computed or agreed, and indeed there was not agreement for a considerable time in relation to those profits thereafter.

On 25 February 1976 a second claim was made on the inspector of taxes by a letter   e
of that date. It related to losses sustained by Bulkers for the accounting period up to 28 February 1974, so that the letter of claim was made within three or four days of the effluxion of the limitation period laid down in s 264 of the 1970 Act. The letter of 25 February 1976 read as follows:

'A Group Relief Agreement was entered into between a fellow subsidiary of [BTI, RL and Bulkers] on 5 March 1973. Under this agreement, [Bulkers] can   f
require [RL] to claim, or procure any of its fellow subsidiaries to claim, group relief in respect of its losses for its accounting periods ending 31 December 1973 et seq. In the tax computations for the year ended 31 December 1973, the taxable profits of [BTI] are covered by group relief from [RL] and [BTH] and therefore no further group relief is apparently required in respect of this period. Nevertheless, in view of the time limit for lodging a claim to group relief we   g
have been requested to notify you of a possible claim to losses from [Bulkers] relating to its accounting period ended 28th February 1974. As you will appreciate, in asking us to notify you of this provisional claim, our clients merely wish to protect the interests of [Bulkers] under their group relief agreement with [RL]. We shall therefore be grateful if you would treat this letter as a provisional claim to group relief from [Bulkers] in respect of its   h
accounting period ended 28 February 1974.'

It is the proper construction of that letter which is at the heart of this case. The inspector of taxes ultimately acknowledged that a claim within that letter had been validly made, but he declined to accept it as a claim taking the place of the claims that had been made in 1975 in respect of the losses incurred by RL and BTH. He   j
took the view that the Bulkers' claim could not replace the earlier claims. The earlier claim could not be withdrawn, and the Bulkers' claim could only serve to top up the earlier claims to the extent of the profits of BTI and would therefore rank behind the earlier claims.

In May 1988 a Special Commissioner upheld submissions made by BTI that it was in fact entitled to choose how it allocated the profits and losses of the company

within the group for the purposes of group relief. The Special Commissioner was
invited to state a case, and this he did.

The appeal by way of case stated came before Harman J, who gave judgment on
the appeal on 22 June 1990. His judgment is now reported (see [1990] STC 564).
Harman J allowed the Crown's appeal, and he held that on a proper construction of
the letter dated 25 February 1976 the views of the inspector of taxes prevailed. The
judge said (at 572):

> 'The letter of 25 February appears to contain a paragraph by way of
> information or recital, referring to the group relief agreement and explaining
> that there are powers under it to require claims to be made; and in the second
> paragraph it says, firstly, that the taxable profits of BTI are covered and then
> goes on "therefore no further group relief is apparently required", plainly
> stressing that on the figures presently available no further group relief is to be
> needed or could be claimed but reserving by the word "apparently" the position
> that since BTI's profits were not settled (and indeed were not I think settled
> until something like ten years later, in 1986 or thereabouts, as a result of the
> vagaries of the case of *Pattison (Inspector of Taxes) v Marine Midland Ltd* [1984]
> STC 10, [1984] AC 362, which was litigated as we all know up to the House of
> Lords) there might be a very substantial period of delay and very different
> figures for the profits might prove to be the correct figures. The result is that
> the phrase is used in this letter that "no further group relief is *apparently*
> required", referring to the fact that the position was not finally established,
> either as to the profits of BTI or I think as to the precise losses of RL at that
> time. The letter then goes on to refer to the time limit, the two-year period that
> I have mentioned, and notifies "a possible claim to losses". It was that phrase, "a
> possible claim to losses", which was pressed on the commissioner as showing
> that it was not in fact a claim but a notification that there might be a claim, a
> proposition which counsel for the Crown has deliberately not pursued in this
> court. It goes on to say, as I have read, that the purpose of notifying the
> provisional claim was only to protect the interests of Bulkers. Accepting that
> that is a valid claim, the question is: what is it a claim for? Is it a claim for group
> relief on losses of Bulkers if it becomes necessary to use such a claim in addition
> to the claims recited as already made and which appeared at that time to be
> adequate to cover BTI's profits, or is it a claim to have such group relief in
> respect of Bulkers against the profits of BTI regardless of the position as to the
> group relief already claimed about two months earlier in respect of the losses of
> RL and BTH? Counsel for the Crown's submission is that the claim has to be
> made in terms which are comprehensible and understandable, but this claim is
> made in terms which are comprehensible and understandable and that when
> one looks at it clearly it is plain that this is adding an additional and back-up or
> top-up claim to the claims already made.'

Later the judge continued (at 573):

> 'What in fact happened later was that BTI put in a computation which
> showed that, far from using the claims in the order in which they were specified
> in the two letters, specifically in the letter of 25 February but initially in the
> other letter, they sought to utilise £550,000-odd of Bulkers' losses and no part
> of RL's losses at all. That, said counsel for the Crown, is not a claim which had
> ever been advanced, and, since one must make a claim and a claim was made,
> one cannot now go back and make (as it were) a different claim; one cannot
> abandon, jettison or disclaim part of the claim you have made and substitute a
> new, different and other claim than that which has already been set out. If that
> were so, said counsel, the inspector would get no benefit whatever from the
> specific time limit of two years imposed by Parliament, and it is impossible for
> anyone to know what claims are being made within the two years if the taxpayer

can later go back and change the claims already made. It seems to me that on that first point counsel's argument is plainly correct and that his construction of the letter is correct, and with all respect to counsel for BTI I do not believe that he had any consistent argument which would validly establish a different construction for the letter of 25 February 1976.'

The judgment of Harman J is currently under appeal, and this court is not concerned with its merits. But there is a summons before this court to adduce fresh evidence in the form of a file note emanating from the accountants, Price Waterhouse, of a meeting held on 17 February 1976 at the offices of BTI. Counsel for BTI has this morning produced for the inspection by this court a copy of the file note which it is sought to introduce—and of course it is sought to be introduced under the well-known principles set out in *Ladd v Marshall* [1954] 1 WLR 1489. In particular it is said that if it is introduced in evidence it will probably have an important influence on the result of the case.

In my view there are insuperable difficulties in the way of this summons succeeding. The first question which has to be asked is whether the file note, if introduced, is relevant. Can it be used as an aid to the construction of the letter dated 25 February 1976? It is a file note compiled unilaterally by or on behalf of the claimants but not in any sense communicated to the Revenue, and of course no representative of the Revenue was present at the meeting which is related in the file note.

No authority was cited to this court to support the proposition that the file note can be used as an aid to the construction of the letter. Counsel for BTI submits that the letter was in some way ambiguous and that the intention of the writer can properly be resolved by the introduction of this file note as an indication of what was in the mind of the writer of the letter. Alternatively, it is suggested that in some way the file note itself forms part and parcel of the claim which was submitted to the inspector.

I have to say that these are startling propositions, unsupported by authority, and, with all respect to counsel for BTI, in my view plainly wrong. In my judgment this file note cannot, in the circumstances of this case, be used as an aid to the construction of the letter dated 25 February 1976, and on that ground alone I would dismiss this summons. But there are other difficulties in the background which have not been argued. There are problems involving the suggested right of the Court of Appeal to receive additional evidence of this kind and make findings of fact. I have grave reservations about that aspect of the case, but express no concluded view about it because it did not form the subject matter of argument.

For those reasons, and really the principal reason I have indicated, namely that this document if introduced into the case would not be admissible evidence along the lines suggested by counsel for BTI, I would for my part dismiss this summons.

BUTLER-SLOSS LJ. For the reasons given in the judgment of Russell LJ I agree that this summons should be dismissed.

NEILL LJ. I also agree.

Application dismissed with costs.

Solicitors: *Slaughter and May* (for BTI); *Solicitor of Inland Revenue.*

Rengan Krishnan Esq   Barrister.

Weissgerber v Finanzamt Neustadt an der Weinstraße
(Case 207/87)

COURT OF JUSTICE OF THE EUROPEAN COMMUNITIES (SIXTH CHAMBER)
JUDGES DUE (PRESIDENT OF THE CHAMBER), RODRIGUEZ IGLESIAS, KOOPMANS, BAHLMANN AND O'HIGGINS
ADVOCATE GENERAL C O LENZ
3 MAY, 14 JUNE, 14 JULY 1988

Value added tax – European Communities – Directives – Direct effect – Member state failing to implement EC directive – Whether credit negotiator entitled to rely on unimplemented article exempting the granting, negotiation and management of credit from value added tax – Whether exemption available if tax passed on covertly to person receiving services – Meaning of covert passing on – EC Council Directive 77/388, art 13B(d)(1).

Article 13B(d)(1)[a] of EC Council Directive 77/388 (the Sixth Directive) provided that 'the granting and the negotiation of credit and the management of credit by the person granting it' should be exempt from value added tax. The Sixth Directive was to have come into force by 1 January 1978, but that time limit was, on 30 June 1978, extended to 1 January 1979. However, the Federal Republic of Germany did not implement the Sixth Directive until 1 January 1980. In its judgment of 19 January 1982 in *Becker v Finanzamt Münster-Innenstadt* (Case 8/81) [1982] ECR 53, the court held that as from 1 January 1979 a credit negotiator could rely on art 13B(d)(1) if he had not passed on the tax to persons following him in the chain of supply. Later, in *Kloppenburg v Finanzamt Leer* (Case 70/83) [1984] ECR 1075, the court reached the same conclusion as regards transactions carried out between 1 January and 30 June 1978. The taxpayer, Gerd Weissgerber, was an insurance agent and finance negotiator who had received commissions during 1978 and 1979 from a German bank in return for introducing and vouching for the solvency of clients seeking credit. The commissions relating to 1978 and 1979 were assessed as taxable turnover in accordance with the taxpayer's tax returns for those years, completed during 1980. However, when the taxpayer became aware of the judgments in *Becker* and *Kloppenburg*, he requested that his assessments to value added tax for the first half of 1978 and for 1979 be amended. The German tax authorities upheld the original assessments on the ground that value added tax had been passed on covertly. The taxpayer brought two joined actions against the notices charging value added tax for 1978 and 1979. The Finanzgericht (Finance Court) Rheinland-Pfalz referred the following questions to the Court of Justice: (1) whether art 13B(d)(1) of the Sixth Directive could be relied on in the absence of the implementation of that directive by a credit negotiator if he did not pass value added tax on to the persons receiving his services; (2) if question (1) was answered in the affirmative, whether value added tax was payable if the passing on of the tax was 'covert', or only if it was 'overt'; and (3) whether it was sufficient for there to have been covert passing on of tax that the credit negotiator, in agreeing his commission, expected that out of it, he would have to pay turnover tax.

Held – The rule that a credit negotiator seeking exemption from value added tax could rely on art 13B(d)(1) of the Sixth Directive before its implementation was subject to the condition that he refrained from passing on value added tax to persons

---

[a] Article 13B(d)(1), so far as material, is set out at p 594 *e*, post

following him in the chain of supply. The purpose of this condition was to prevent a claim for exemption made a posteriori by a credit negotiator from having an adverse effect on a recipient of his services who had already deducted the tax in question as input tax. Such a consequence could arise only if the recipient was subject to value added tax and the credit negotiator had passed on the tax in accordance with the formalities prescribed by the Sixth Directive so as to entitle the recipient of his services to deduct the input tax.

Accordingly, the answer to the question referred to the court was that in the absence of implementation of the Sixth Directive, a credit negotiator could rely on the tax exemption provision contained in art 13B(*d*)(1) of the directive in respect of transactions carried out between 1 January 1978 and 30 June 1978 and as from 1 January 1979, if he did not pass value added tax on to the person receiving his services so as to entitle that person to deduct the input tax.

Notes

For the binding nature of EC Council Directives, see De Voil: Value Added Tax A2.55.

For EC Council Directive 77/388, art 13B(*d*)(1), see ibid, Division E3.

Cases cited

Amministrazione delle Finanze dello Stato v SpA San Giorgio (Case 199/82) [1983] ECR 3595, CJEC.

Becker v Finanzamt Münster-Innenstadt (Case 8/81) [1982] ECR 53, CJEC.

EC Commission v Italian Republic (Case 104/86) [1988] ECR 1799, CJEC.

Grendel (R A) GmbH v Finanzamt für Körperschaften in Hamburg (Case 255/81) [1982] ECR 2301, CJEC.

Just (Hans) I/S v Danish Ministry for Fiscal Affairs (Case 68/79) [1980] ECR 501, CJEC.

Kloppenburg v Finanzamt Leer (Case 70/83) [1984] ECR 1075, CJEC.

Les Fils de Jules Bianco SA and J Girard Fils SA v Directeur Général des douanes et droits indirects (Joined Cases 331/85, 376/85, 378/85) [1988] ECR 1099, CJEC.

Schul (Gaston) Douane Expediteur BV v Inspecteur der Invoerrechten en Accijnzen (Case 15/81) [1982] ECR 1409, CJEC.

Reference

By an order of 15 June 1987 the Finanzgericht Rheinland-Pfalz referred to the Court of Justice of the European Communities for a preliminary ruling under art 177 of the EEC Treaty three questions on the interpretation of art 13B(*d*)(1) of EC Council Directive 77/388 (the Sixth Directive). The questions arose in proceedings between Gerd Weissgerber, the taxpayer, and the Finanzamt Neustadt an der Weinstraße. The Finanzamt and the Commission made submissions (in the written procedure) to the court. The language of the case was German. The facts are set out in the report for the hearing.

The Judge Rapporteur (O Due) presented the following report for the hearing.

I Facts and procedure before the national court

1. The plaintiff in the main proceedings, G Weissgerber (the taxpayer), is an insurance agent and finance negotiator. In 1978 and 1979 he introduced clients who were seeking credit to three German banks: the Vereinsbank in Heidelberg, the CC Bank and the AK Bank. To the Vereinsbank and the CC Bank, the taxpayer vouched for the solvency of the clients whom he introduced.

2. In return for the introductions the banks paid commission, part of which was
a paid to the taxpayer and part of which was paid by the Vereinsbank and the CC
Bank into a blocked account, in case the debts guaranteed were not paid. The credit
statements sent to the taxpayer by the banks did not make any mention of value
added tax.

3. From March 1979, the Vereinsbank, which paid most of the commission,
reduced the commission paid. The taxpayer claims that the bank reduced the
b commission in anticipation of the exemption from value added tax in favour of
transactions consisting of the negotiation of credit. The defendant in the main
action, the Finanzamt Neustadt an der Weinstraße (the Finanzamt), contends that
the reduction was intended to cover loans which were not repaid by the taxpayer's
clients.

4. In determining the basis of assessment for value added tax for 1978 and 1979,
c the German tax authorities included in the taxable transactions the commissions
referred to above, in accordance with the taxpayer's returns.

5. Article 13B(*d*)(1) of EC Council Directive 77/388 of 17 May 1977 on the
harmonisation of the laws of the member states relating to turnover taxes—common
system of value added tax: uniform basis of assessment (the Sixth Directive) provides
for an exemption from value added tax in respect of 'the granting and the negotiation
d of credit and the management of credit by the person granting it'.

6. Article 1 of the Sixth Directive provides that it is to enter into force by
1 January 1978 at the latest. That time limit was extended to 1 January 1979 by art 1
of EC Council Directive 78/583 of 26 June 1978 on the harmonisation of the laws of
the member states relating to turnover taxes (the Ninth Directive).

7. The Sixth Directive was not implemented by the Federal Republic of Germany
e until 1 January 1980, by the Law of 26 November 1979 (Bundesgesetzblatt I p 1953).

8. In its judgments of 19 January 1982 in *Becker v Finanzamt Münster-Innenstadt*
(Case 8/81) [1982] ECR 53 and 10 June 1982 in *Grendel (R A) GmbH v Finanzamt
für Körperschaften in Hamburg* (Case 255/81) [1982] ECR 2301, the court ruled that
as from 1 January 1979 it was possible for the provision concerning the exemption
from value added tax to be relied on by a credit negotiator where he has refrained
f from passing that tax on to persons following him in the chain of supply. In its
judgment of 22 February 1984 in *Kloppenburg v Finanzamt Leer* (Case 70/83) [1984]
ECR 1075, the court reached the same conclusion in relation to transactions carried
out between 1 January and 30 June 1978, the date on which the Ninth Directive was
notified.

9. Following the first two judgments of the court, the Federal Minister of Finance
g stated in a circular dated 27 June 1983 (Bundessteuerblatt I p 348) that credit
negotiators were exempt from value added tax on their commission for the 1979
calendar year if they relied on the Sixth Directive in so far as they had not overtly or
covertly passed on the value added tax payable to their clients.

10. The taxpayer requested that his assessment to value added tax for the first half
of 1978 and for 1979 be amended as regards his credit negotiation transactions. The
h German tax authorities refused those requests but, as a result of an objection lodged
by the taxpayer, granted him, on 11 July 1983, exemption from value added tax for
1979, subject to verification.

11. The verification report of 16 October 1984 concluded that value added tax
had been passed on covertly, and on 9 April 1985 the German authorities reinstated
the original assessment for 1979. After a fresh objection had been rejected, the
j taxpayer brought two actions, which were joined, against the notices charging value
added tax for 1978 and 1979 respectively.

12. In the main action the Finanzamt stressed, inter alia, the fact that in spite of
the circular of 27 June 1983 the Bundesfinanzhof had in several judgments refused
credit negotiators the right to rely on the exemption provided for by the Sixth
Directive.

13. By an order of 15 June 1987, which was lodged at the court registry on 7 July 1987, the Finanzgericht (Finance Court) Rheinland-Pfalz stayed the proceedings and referred to the court the following questions:

'1. In relation to transactions carried out between 1 January 1978 and 30 June 1978 and transactions carried out in 1979, may the provision contained in Article 13B(d)(1) of [the Sixth Directive] concerning the exemption from turnover tax of transactions consisting of the negotiation of credit be relied upon, in the absence of the implementation of that directive, by a credit negotiator if he did not pass that tax on to the persons receiving his services?

2. If Question 1 is answered in the affirmative, must the credit negotiator pay turnover tax if he "covertly" passed on the tax, or only if he "overtly" passed it on?

3. If turnover tax is also payable where the tax is passed on covertly, is it sufficient, for there to have been a covert passing on of turnover tax, that the credit negotiator, in agreeing his commission, expected that out of it he would have to pay turnover tax?'

14. Pursuant to art 20 of the Protocol on the Statute of the Court of Justice, written observations were submitted by the defendant in the main proceedings, represented by Hans Langenbucher, Leitender Regierungsdirektor of the Finanzamt, and by the Commission, represented by Føns Buhl and Götz zur Hausen, acting as agents.

15. On hearing the report of the Judge Rapporteur and the views of the Advocate General, the court decided to assign the case to the Sixth Chamber pursuant to art 95 of the Rules of Procedure and to open the oral procedure without any preparatory inquiry.

II Written observations

The first question

1. Before the court the Finanzamt states that it is withdrawing the argument based on the judgments of the Bundesfinanzhof. The circular issued by the Federal Finance Ministry on 27 June 1983, which is binding on the Finanzamt by virtue of instructions from the central tax administration for the Land Rheinland-Pfalz, accepts that the judgments of the Court of Justice must be applied. On that basis the value added tax paid for 1978 and 1979 has been refunded to credit negotiators in respect of whom it had been established that they had not passed on value added tax to the persons following them in the chain of supply. However, it was necessary to ensure that a taxable person did not obtain an advantage over his co-contractor by being reimbursed value added tax which he had passed on in the price.

2. The Commission refers to the previous judgments of the court on the application of art 13B(d)(1) of the Sixth Directive. The German Government had assured the Commission that the inconsistent judgments of the Bundesfinanzhof had not affected the application of the circular of 27 June 1983 and that the circular was also applicable to the period from 1 January to 30 June 1978.

The second question

3. The Finanzamt stresses that value added tax is an indirect tax covered by arts 98 and 99 of the EEC Treaty, as was also the old German turnover tax, which was accepted as being passed on to the client but which until 31 December 1967 was collected under a system which prohibited the tax from being mentioned on an invoice.

4. The judgment of the court of 5 May 1982 in *Schul (Gaston) Douane Expediteur BV v Inspecteur der Invoerrechten en Accijnzen* (Case 15/81) [1982] ECR 1409 also implies that the value added tax already included in the price of a purchase not

subject to value added tax may be passed on covertly. That is in fact the case of the

a   'residual part' of the value added tax which, according to the judgment, is to be taken into account for purposes of imposing value added tax on the importation of products imported by a private person.

5. Equally, the restriction which the court, by requiring that value added tax not be passed on, has imposed in its judgments on the exemption of credit negotiators from value added tax cannot apply exclusively to cases in which value added tax is

b   passed on overtly, since in such cases it is clear that there can be no exemption.

6. Banks, which are themselves exempt from value added tax and therefore not entitled to deduct value added tax paid, would have no reason to make overt reference to value added tax on the credit statements which they send to credit negotiators. In view of the uncertainty prevailing in the periods in question, it would have been logical for the taxpayer at least to express a reservation as regards value

c   added tax by means of an appropriate clause. The taxpayer himself acknowledged in his tax returns for 1978 and 1979 that his transactions were subject to value added tax.

7. Therefore the Finanzamt considers that the failure to pass on the tax could be proved only by a reduction in commissions as compared with previous years equal to the amount of value added tax, or in the absence of such reduction by documents

d   establishing an equivalent increase in profit or costs. The Finanzamt stresses that there was no change in the taxpayer's commissions between the two halves of 1978 and that it was not alleged that profit or costs had changed. The reduction in commission in March 1979 was not the result of any considerations connected with value added tax but was owing to the fact that the credit negotiated by the taxpayer had given rise to a high rate of default and loss.

e   8. The Commission stresses that, according to art 22(3)(*a*) and (*b*) of the Sixth Directive, an invoice or other document serving as invoice must state the amount of value added tax. That documentary evidence is one of the requirements for the exercise of the right to deduct value added tax.

9. The Commission considers that the only way of determining whether or not value added tax has been passed on is by means of a fiscal control, albeit carried out

f   on the basis of simple rules: the credit negotiator must have invoiced value added tax to his clients, paid the amount to the tax authorities and entered it in his tax declarations. The clients must have deducted value added tax in accordance with the pro rata rule.

10. Last, the Commission points out that, according to the judgments of the court (see the judgments of 27 February 1980 in *Just (Hans) I/S v Danish Ministry for*

g   *Fiscal Affairs* (Case 68/79) [1980] ECR 501, and of 9 November 1983 in *Amministrazione delle Finanze dello Stato v SpA San Giorgio* (Case 199/82) [1983] ECR 3595), it is a matter for each national legal system to determine the conditions on which taxpayers may obtain the repayment of amounts unduly levied. Rules to prevent unjust enrichment must not, however, make it impossible in practice to exercise the right to repayment.

h

The third question

11. The Finanzamt considers that this question involves speculation which, in the light of the consideration of the second question, is not justified in fact. The unanswerable question whether the credit negotiator subjectively expected to have to pay value added tax is irrelevant.

j   12. The Commission refers to the objective requirements listed in its examination of the second question: the invoice, the declaration and deduction of value added tax. If those requirements are not satisfied, it could logically be concluded that the taxpayer did not pass on the tax. In the Commission's view, the results of the control which was carried out by the tax authorities do not appear sufficiently clear to give an accurate answer to this question.

III Suggested replies to the preliminary questions

1. The Finanzamt proposes that the following replies should be given:

　　1. Yes.

　　2. The passing on of tax can also be covert.

　　3. The third question is devoid of purpose in this case.

2. The Commission proposes that the questions should be answered as follows:

　　1. It is possible for the provision concerning the exemption from turn-over tax of transactions consisting of the negotiation of credit contained in art 13B(*d*)(1) of the Sixth Directive to be relied on by a credit negotiator, where he refrained from passing that tax on to persons following him in the chain of supply, both in relation to transactions carried out in 1979 and in relation to transactions carried out between 1 January 1978 and 30 June 1978.

　　2. In order to pass on the tax, a person supplying services must first draw up an invoice or accounting document stating the amount of the tax; second, he must include that tax in his tax returns in such a way as to pay it to the state and; third, the recipient of the service must be able to deduct the tax paid to the supplier on the basis of the invoice.

14 June 1988. **The Advocate General (C O Lenz)** delivered the following opinion.

Mr President, members of the court,

A Facts

1. The case which occupies us today concerns once again the interpretation of EC Council Directive 77/388 (the Sixth Directive) which has been the subject of many decisions of the court.

2. The provision which concerns us in this case is art 13B(*d*)(1) of the Sixth Directive which provides that member states shall exempt from tax 'the granting and the negotiation of credit and the management of credit by the person granting it'. Article 1 provides that the member states are to ensure that the necessary harmonisation provisions should enter into force by 1 January 1978 at the latest. EC Council Directive 78/583 (the Ninth Directive) extended that time limit, inter alia, for the Federal Republic of Germany until 1 January 1979.

3. In fact, as is known from other cases, it was not until the adoption of the Law of 26 November 1979, which had effect from 1 January 1980, that the Sixth Directive was implemented in the Federal Republic of Germany, so that credit negotiators were exempt from tax only from 1 January 1980 (which was not provided for in the Turnover Tax Law in the version adopted on 16 November 1973).

4. In its judgment of 19 January 1982 in *Becker v Finanzamt Münster-Innenstadt* (Case 8/81) [1982] ECR 53, the court held in response to a question for a preliminary ruling from the Finanzgericht Münster that as from 1 January 1979 a credit negotiator could rely on art 13B(*d*)(1) of the Sixth Directive if he had not passed the tax on to the persons following him in the chain of supply. That was confirmed once again in the judgment of 10 June 1982 in *Grendel (R A) GmbH v Finanzamt für Körperschaften in Hamburg* (Case 255/81) [1982] ECR 2301 in response to a question from the Finanzgericht Hamburg.

5. Referring to the fact that the Ninth Directive was not retroactive, the court held in its judgment of 22 February 1984 in *Kloppenburg v Finanzamt Leer* (Case 70/83) [1984] ECR 1075 that, in the absence of the implementation of the Sixth Directive, a credit negotiator could rely on art 13B(*d*)(1) thereof in relation to transactions carried out between 1 January and 30 June 1978 if he had not passed the tax on to the persons following him in the chain of supply.

6. The taxpayer acts, inter alia, as credit negotiator and receives commissions from the banks for which he acts; the credit notes he receives in respect of the commissions do not mention turnover tax separately. The commissions related to

1978 and 1979 were, according to his tax returns made in June and December 1980,
a included in his taxable turnover.

7. When the taxpayer became aware of the decisions of the court mentioned above, he requested an appropriate amendment of his tax assessment.

8. When his request, made in April 1982, for an amendment of the assessment for the year 1979 was rejected, court proceedings ensued. These were settled at first because, by a notice of amendment of 11 July 1983, the Finanzverwaltung exempted
b from tax the taxpayer's turnover in respect of credit negotiation.

9. Further court proceedings ensued, however, after a review of the case which was undertaken in order to determine whether turnover tax had been passed on covertly and which found that to be the case, and following an amendment of the tax notice in April 1985 requiring commission from credit negotiation to be taxed once again.

c 10. Further court proceedings were commenced in relation to the tax assessment for 1978 after the taxpayer's application in December 1984 for an amendment of the tax assessment was rejected in March 1985.

11. So far the taxpayer has not paid any value added tax on the turnover in question. In the court proceedings, which were joined, the taxpayer based his view that he should have been exempt from value added tax on the aforementioned
d decisions of this court. He also argued that only an *overt* passing on of tax gave rise to tax liability and denied that the tax had been passed on covertly.

12. The defendant Finanzverwaltung at first took the view that the taxpayer could not be exempt from tax in 1978 and 1979 because there was no provision for exemption in German turnover tax law at that time; it thus followed the case law of the Bundesfinanzhof and argued that no regard was to be had to the exemption
e provisions contained in the Sixth Directive before they were implemented in national law. In addition, the finance administration relies on a letter from the Bundesminister der Finanzen (Federal Finance Minister) of 27 June 1983 relating to the issue in the main proceedings. According to that letter, *covert* passing on is passing on within the meaning of the case law of this court; as proof that there has been no such passing on, it must be shown that undertakings which were engaged
f in credit negotiation in 1978 have correspondingly reduced their commission in 1979 (in the case of commissions due in 1979 as in 1978 it therefore had to be assumed that passing on had occurred because in the second half of 1978 turnover tax was due on credit negotiations in any case).

13. In view of those arguments the national court believed it could identify points of Community law regarding, first, the direct applicability of the directive and,
g second, the questions whether covert passing on gives rise to tax liability under the case law of the court and when covert passing on must be assumed to have occurred. Accordingly, by order of 15 June 1987, it stayed the proceedings and referred the following questions to the court for a preliminary ruling pursuant to art 177 of the EEC Treaty:

h '1. In relation to transactions carried out between 1 January 1978 and 30 June 1978 and transactions carried out in 1979, may the provision contained in Article 13B(*d*)(1) of [the Sixth Directive] concerning the exemption from turnover tax of transactions consisting of the negotiation of credit be relied upon, in the absence of the implementation of that directive, by a credit negotiator if he did not pass that tax on to the persons receiving his services?

j 2. If Question 1 is answered in the affirmative, must the credit negotiator pay turnover tax if he "covertly" passed on the tax, or only if he "overtly" passed it on?

3. If turnover tax is also payable where the tax is passed on covertly, is it sufficient, for there to have been a covert passing on of turnover tax, that the credit negotiator, in agreeing his commission, expected that out of it he would have to pay turnover tax?'

B Opinion
In view of all we have heard and read, my opinion is as follows.

The first question
14. As I have already explained, this question arose from the case law of the Bundesfinanzhof cited by the finance administration. The Bundesfinanzhof, not wishing to follow the interpretation of the Sixth Directive given by this court, ruled that it was not possible to rely on the exemption provision contained in art 13 before the directive was transposed into national law. Consequently, the Finanzgericht (Finance Court) considered that the first question had not been settled.

15. In its observations on the reference for a preliminary ruling, the finance administration explained to the court that it no longer relied on the view of the Bundesfinanzhof. This was clearly because the judgments of the Bundesfinanzhof were quashed by the Bundesverfassungsgericht (Federal Constitutional Court) in April and November 1987.

16. According to those decisions of the Bundesverfassungsgericht and because no new points of view which could lead to any different assessment have emerged, reference may now simply be made to the case law on the Sixth Directive. Without further argument the first question from the Finanzgericht Rheinland-Pfalz may be answered to the effect that, in the absence of the implementation of the Sixth Directive, a credit negotiator may rely, in respect of transactions carried out between 1 January 1978 and 30 June 1978 and transactions carried out in 1979, on the provision contained in art 13B(*d*)(1) of that directive concerning the exemption from turnover tax of transactions consisting of the negotiation of credit, if he did not pass that tax on to the persons receiving his services.

The second question
17. This question seeks clarification of the phrase 'where he had refrained from *passing* that tax on to persons following him in the chain of supply [emphasis added]' appearing in the judgments in *Becker, Grendel* and *Kloppenburg*, and, more precisely, of the point whether only *overt* or also *covert* passing on is to be taken into account.

18. We have been told that to some extent the Finanzgerichte (Finance Courts) refuse to look at covert passing on because the view recommended by the Federal Finance Ministry is regarded as impractical. According to the letter from the Federal Finance Minister of 27 June 1983 (the principles of which, according to an order of the Oberste Finanzbehörden (principal revenue authorities) of the Bund and the Länder of April 1984, are also to apply to the first half of 1978), covert passing on may indeed be taken into account. Covert passing on may be assumed to exist if it is not shown that, in the case of undertakings which engaged in taxable credit negotiations in 1978, the commission was reduced in 1979 by the amount of tax due in respect of 1978 or if, in relation to 1978 in which tax exemption was possible only in respect of the first six months, it is not shown that in the first half of 1978 the amount of commission due was less than in the second half.

19. (a) As far as this problem is concerned, it may be said at once that the judgment in *Schul (Gaston) Douane Expediteur BV v Inspecteur der Invoerrechten en Accijnzen* (Case 15/81) [1982] ECR 1409, cited in the letter from the Federal Finance Ministry and in the observations of the Finance Administration, does not help to resolve it.

20. As the court will be aware, that judgment related to the question whether on the importation of goods sold in the country of export by a person not liable to tax, the full value added tax chargeable in the country of importation might be levied or whether art 95 of the EEC Treaty (which prohibits imported goods from being subject to greater charges than domestic goods) required that regard should be had to the value added tax paid abroad and not subject to refund. If this means that imported goods could still be burdened with some of the value added tax charged in the country of exportation and that the value added tax due on importation must

therefore be reduced by the residual amount of value added tax paid in the country
a of exportation (which is still contained in the value of the goods at the time of their
importation), it may well be inferred that covert passing on of value added tax is
relevant for the purposes of art 95 (in so far as the sale of goods by persons not liable
to tax is concerned). However, this does not help to resolve the quite different
problem of the passing on of value added tax in connection with a contract for
services by someone who, on his own admission, is liable to tax, and does not explain
b what effect it should have where reliance is placed on the exemption from tax
contained in the Sixth Directive which was not implemented in good time.

21. (b) If regard is had only to the clause 'where he had refrained from passing
that tax on to persons following him in the chain of supply' contained in the operative
part of the judgments in *Becker, Grendel* and *Kloppenburg*, it might seem that the
court had made unjustified enrichment part of Community law. This point has been
c addressed in other judgments in which the court had to rule on the problem of the
refund of national charges levied contrary to Community law with regard to the
nature of certain rights of the member states, which, as is well known, are very
relevant here.

22. The judgment in *Just (Hans) I/S v Danish Ministry for Fiscal Affairs* (Case
68/79) [1980] ECR 501 concerned the Danish legal system, according to which such
d refunds are made under the law on unjustified enrichment and account is taken of
the fact that charges are incorporated in the price of goods and may be passed on
down the line of trade. The court stated (at 523, para 26) that the protection of rights
guaranteed in the matter by Community law did not require an order for the
recovery of charges improperly made to be granted in conditions which would
involve the unjust enrichment of those entitled. There was nothing therefore, from
e the point of view of Community law, to prevent national courts from taking account
in accordance with their national law of the fact that it had been possible for charges
unduly levied to be incorporated in the prices of the undertaking liable for the
charge and to be passed on to the purchasers.

23. A similar conclusion was reached in the judgment in *Amministrazione delle
Finanze dello Stato v SpA San Giorgio* (Case 199/82) [1983] ECR 3595. That case
f concerned Italian law which likewise does not allow charges levied unlawfully to be
refunded if this would lead to unjust enrichment of those entitled. The court also
stated (at 3612, para 13) that there was nothing in Community law to prevent courts
from taking account, under their national law, of the fact that the unduly levied
charges had been incorporated in the price of the goods and thus passed on to
purchasers. Thus national legislative provisions which prevented the reimbursement
of taxes levied in breach of Community law could not be regarded as contrary to
g Community law where it was established that the person required to pay such
charges had actually passed them on to other persons.

24. An examination of the grounds of the judgments in *Becker, Grendel* and
Kloppenburg (in particular the judgment in *Becker*) clearly shows, however, that the
reservation now requiring interpretation is not to be understood in the sense of the
h observations made in the judgments in *Just* and *San Giorgio*; it in no way means the
generalisation of a legal concept known to several legal systems and its incorporation
into tax law (so that it is unnecessary to consider any possible objections to such
generalisation and incorporation). The reservation arose from considerations relating
solely to tax law and based on the scheme of the Sixth Directive as a reaction to the
objections which were made at the time by the defendant finance administration
i and the German government to the possibility that the tax exemption provision in
art 13 of the Sixth Directive might be relied on.

25. It will be recalled that in the discussion of the question whether individuals
might derive rights from the Sixth Directive it was objected that this possibility
could not be accepted (because directives cannot impose *obligations* on individuals
directly) in so far as the legal position of other individuals was affected; if, however,
the exemption provision were relied on a posteriori, persons receiving the services
of the credit negotiator would be affected in that way because their deductions of

input tax would be affected. It seems to me that this question was dealt with in the judgment in *Becker* (Case 8/81) [1982] ECR 53 at 75, para 44, where it was stated a
that by availing themselves of exemption, persons entitled thereto necessarily waived the right to claim a deduction in respect of input and, having been exempted from the tax, they were unable to pass on any charge whatsoever to the persons following them in the chain of supply, with the result that the *rights of third parties* could not be affected. Paragraph 46 (at 76) of the judgment is also relevant; there it is stated
that the Finanzamt's objection that exemptions claimed a posteriori under the b
directive by taxpayers would cause disruption was not relevant to the case of a taxpayer who had claimed the benefit of the exemptions when he submitted his tax return and who had consequently refrained from invoicing the tax to the recipients of his services, with the result that *third parties* were not affected.

26. From that it may be inferred that, where it is a question of passing on of the tax, *overt* passing on was meant since deductions of input tax are possible by persons c
receiving the supplies only if the tax is shown separately in the invoice (to which express reference is made in para 46). The Commission also takes the view that the reservation should be understood only in that sense. In this regard it cites the requirements of clarity and the need to adhere strictly to the system introduced by the Sixth Directive and in particular to art 22 thereof (which provides that the invoice must state clearly the price exclusive of tax and the corresponding tax at d
each rate).

27. One could be tempted to go a step further and, again from considerations of revenue law (which admittedly do not appear in the judgment in *Becker*), arrive at a definition of passing on which also includes so-called *covert* passing on. It is not difficult to think of such considerations and they are clearly apparent in the decision of the defendant Finanzamt. e

28. The main underlying premise of those considerations is the assumption that a right may be exercised only if the aim thereby pursued may actually be achieved, which means that the exercise of the right is correspondingly limited. It would also have to be assumed that the aim of the tax exemption laid down in art 13 of the Sixth Directive was to relieve not the taxable person but the end consumer who normally bears the burden of value added tax. That aim can no longer be achieved where the f
tax exemption is claimed a posteriori, that is to say where the amount of tax (liability for which was presumed when the tax return was lodged) has in the meantime already been passed on to the person receiving the supply and further passed on by him to his credit customer and there is no practical possibility of recovery. However, given that consideration and the fact that normally there is no overt passing on to the end consumer or to persons following in the chain of supply who, like banks, g
cannot claim any deductions of input tax, one might well accept that it would be logical to include covert passing on in a proper interpretation of the reservation expressed in the case law, for only in that way would it be ensured that the exemption provision in the Sixth Directive is not relied on where the aim of exemption can no longer be achieved.

29. However, the question arises whether that interpretation is in accord with the h
intention of the Community legislature as expressed in the directive. The reason for the tax exemption in the directive was stated to be that a common list of exemptions should be drawn up so that the Community's own resources might be collected in a uniform manner in all the member states (see the eleventh recital of the preamble to the Sixth Directive). The exempting provision itself is worded as follows:

'TITLE X: EXEMPTIONS j

Article 13
Exemptions within the territory of the country

...B. *Other exemptions*
Without prejudice to other Community provisions, Member States shall exempt

a   the following under conditions which they shall lay down for the purpose of ensuring the correct and straightforward application of the exemptions and of preventing any possible evasion, avoidance or abuse ... (*d*) the following transactions: 1. The granting and the negotiation of credit ...'

30. It seems to me that the legislature's intention, expressed in that provision, to exempt the negotiation of credit from turnover tax is best achieved if such turnover is not subject to tax. Although that sounds self-evident, it needs to be said in a case *b*   which is precisely concerned with avoiding that result. Thus, if on principle the result of applying the directive can only be tax exemption, any exception must be justified on the basis of either the law or other general principles of law.

31. The conditions mentioned in art 13B of the Sixth Directive could be regarded as justification. The first objective of those 'conditions' is to ensure 'the correct and straightforward application of the exemptions' (see *Becker* (Case 8/81) [1982] ECR *c*   53 at 73, para 33). That objective is certainly best achieved by exempting from tax turnover with 'covert passing on', for any other arrangement leads to complications as this very case shows.

32. The other objects of the 'conditions' mentioned in art 13, namely the prevention of tax evasion and avoidance (see *Becker* (Case 8/81) [1982] ECR 53 at 73, para 34), can be disregarded here, for they hardly apply to the present case.

d   33. The only question which could arise is whether the extension of tax liability to turnover with 'covert passing on' is necessary for the purpose of 'preventing any possible ... abuse'. Here it will be necessary to consider in particular the argument that the objective of the tax exemption, namely to make credit cheaper, cannot be achieved by the retroactive grant of tax exemption. In considering that question, it will not be possible to ignore the fact that it was not the taxpayer but the defaulting *e*   member state which by its late implementation of the Sixth Directive prevented the desired effect from taking place on the intended date (see *Becker* (Case 8/81) [1982] ECR 53 at 76, para 47).

34. It would hardly be conceivable for a member state to be able to levy tax on non-taxable turnover simply because it had itself prevented the desired result from taking place at the right time and an advantage not intended at the outset thus *f*   accrued to the taxpayer. If that argument were accepted, it would allow a member state to profit from its own wrongdoing and to frustrate the effect of Community law, namely the exemption from tax of the turnover concerned. From the standpoint of Community law, this cannot be tolerated.

35. This result is perhaps not entirely satisfactory because the credit negotiator receives an advantage which was originally not intended, but it seems more *g*   acceptable than allowing the member state to profit from its own wrongdoing.

36. I therefore come to the conclusion that a credit negotiator may rely on the directive at least if he has not expressly passed on the turnover tax to the persons to whom he supplies his services. So-called covert passing on does not therefore give rise to tax liability.

h   *The third question*

37. The purpose of this question is to establish whether turnover tax is passed on covertly simply if, on agreeing his negotiation commission, the credit negotiator expected to have to pay turnover tax out of it. It is thus based on the assumption that, under the legal situation prevailing at the time when the commission was agreed (according to which turnover tax was due also on the negotiation of credit), *j*   turnover tax was always passed on in the ensuing period.

38. If the view put forward above is accepted, then this question does not call for an answer, for in the case of 'covert passing on' no tax is payable during the relevant period so that it no longer depends on what the credit negotiator 'expected' when he agreed the negotiation commission.

39. If, however, the argument I have rejected is accepted, namely that reliance

on the directive is not possible where there has been 'covert passing on', then, without attempting to develop a proper and comprehensive theory of passing on, *a* the question may be answered by referring to the court's case law on national law governing refunds and on the question of the exclusion of a refund if an improperly levied charge has been passed on.

40. The governing principle is to be found in the judgment in *San Giorgio* (Case 199/82) [1983] ECR 3595 at 3613, para 14 in which the Court of Justice ruled that the court which has to rule on the refund must be *free* to decide whether or not *b* the burden of the charge has been passed on to other persons, which no doubt means that all the circumstances of the particular case have to be considered (there was a similar ruling in the judgment in *Les Fils de Jules Bianco SA and J Girard Fils SA v Directeur Général des douanes et droits indirects* (Joined Cases 331/85, 376/85, 378/85) [1988] ECR 1099.

41. It must also be recalled that in its judgment in *Just* the court had already *c* stressed that the exercise of a right under Community law, which the national courts are required to protect, should not be made practically impossible. Accordingly, as was made clear in the judgments in *San Giorgio, Bianco* and *EC Commission v Italian Republic* (Case 104/86) [1988] ECR 1799 with regard to the question of the passing on of improperly paid charges, rules of evidence which make it practically impossible or excessively difficult to recover charges levied in breach of Community law are not *d* permissible.

42. The court also made it clear that it was not lawful to presume that indirect taxes had been passed on, that presumption placing the burden of proof on the taxpayer to show that there had been no passing on, nor acceptable to limit the forms of proof (see the judgments in *Bianco* and in *EC Commission v Italian Republic*).

43. Accordingly, it may be said that the third question cannot simply be answered *e* in the affirmative, and that therefore it is not permissible to proceed on the basis of the presumption contained in the question precisely because the question of actual passing on depends on the existence of a real possibility of passing on, which may have changed with the market situation since the agreement on the commission was concluded. It must also be noted that the rigid rule contained in the Federal Finance Minister's circular of 27 June 1983 appears unacceptable, for .he defendant *f* Finanzamt itself observed in its observations that the fact that the amount of commission was not altered may have been due to increased costs or a desire for increased profits.

44. However, in considering all the circumstances of the case, some importance must be attached to the fact that the taxpayer himself assumed when making his tax returns that his credit negotiation transactions were taxable (because at the time *g* there was no case law on the question whether the Sixth Directive could be relied on where it had not been implemented in national law). Moreover, the fact that a taxpayer will normally attempt to pass on to the next persons in the chain of supply value added tax, which, according to the provisions applicable, is intended to be borne by the end consumer, should also be given some weight.

45. Thus, to my mind, everything that is to be said about the third question of *h* the Finanzgericht from the point of view of Community law has been said.

C Conclusion

To sum up, I therefore propose that the questions submitted by the Finanzgericht Rheinland-Pfalz should be answered as follows.

46. In the absence of implementation of the Sixth Directive, a credit negotiator *j* may rely on the provision contained in art 13B(*d*)(1) of that directive, exempting from turnover tax transactions consisting of the negotiation of credit, in respect of transactions carried out between 1 January 1978 and 30 June 1978 as well as in respect of transactions carried out in 1979, if he did not expressly pass on the turnover tax to the persons to whom he supplied his services.

14 July 1988. **THE COURT OF JUSTICE** delivered the following judgment.

a

1. By order of 15 June 1987, which was received at the court on 7 July 1987, the Finanzgericht (Finance Court) Rheinland-Pfalz referred to the court for a preliminary ruling under art 177 of the EEC Treaty three questions on the interpretation of art 13B(d)(1) of EC Council Directive 77/388 of 17 May 1977 (the Sixth Directive) in order to enable it to determine whether that provision may be *b* relied on by credit negotiators in respect of transactions carried out between 1 January and 30 June 1978 and as from 1 January 1979, and if it may, under what conditions.

2. It should be recalled that, under art 1 of the Sixth Directive, the member states were to adopt by 1 January 1978 at the latest the laws, regulations and administrative provisions necessary in order to bring their value added tax systems into line with *c* the requirements of the directive. A number of member states, including the Federal Republic of Germany, were unable to make the necessary adjustments within the prescribed period and therefore, on 26 June 1978, the Council adopted EC Council Directive 78/583 (the Ninth Directive) which was addressed to those member states and authorised them to implement the Sixth Directive by 1 January 1979 at the latest. The Ninth Directive was notified to its addressees on 30 June 1978.

d 3. It was not until the adoption of the Law of 26 November 1979 and with effect from 1 January 1980 that the Federal Republic of Germany implemented the Sixth Directive and in particular the exemption provided for in art 13B(d)(1) in respect of the negotiation of credit.

4. It should further be recalled that in its judgment of 19 January 1982 in *Becker v Finanzamt Münster-Innenstadt* (Case 8/81) [1982] ECR 53 and its judgment of *e* 10 June 1982 in *Grendel (R A) GmbH v Finanzamt für Körperschaften in Hamburg* (Case 255/81) [1982] ECR 2301 the court ruled that as from 1 January 1979 it was possible for the provision concerning the exemption from turnover tax of transactions consisting of the negotiation of credit to be relied on, in the absence of the implementation of the Sixth Directive, by a credit negotiator where he had refrained from passing that tax on to persons following him in the chain of supply. In its *f* judgment of 22 February 1984 in *Kloppenburg v Finanzamt Leer* (Case 70/83) [1984] ECR 1075 the court reached the same conclusion as regards transactions carried out between 1 January and 30 June 1978, the date of the notification of the Ninth Directive.

5. It appears from the documents before the court that the plaintiff in the main proceedings, Gerd Weissgerber (the taxpayer), is an insurance agent and finance *g* negotiator. In 1978 and 1979 he introduced clients who were seeking credit to three German banks. For that activity the banks remunerated him by means of commissions paid into his bank accounts. The credit notes which the banks sent to the taxpayer did not show any amount of value added tax. In the value added tax assessment for 1978 and 1979, the German tax authorities included in the taxable transactions the commissions referred to above, in accordance with the taxpayer's *h* tax returns.

6. In the appeal proceedings which he brought before the Finanzgericht Rheinland-Pfalz against the Finanzamt Neustadt an der Weinstraße (the Finanzamt), the taxpayer relies on the judgments of the court cited above, whilst the Finanzamt contends in particular that the value added tax was passed on, albeit covertly.

j 7. In order to resolve the issue, the Finanzgericht stayed the proceedings and submitted the following questions to the court:

'1. In relation to transactions carried out between 1 January 1978 and 30 June 1978 and transactions carried out in 1979, may the provision contained in Article 13B(d)(1) of [the Sixth Directive] concerning the exemption from turnover tax of transactions consisting of the negotiation of credit be relied

upon, in the absence of the implementation of that directive, by a credit
negotiator if he did not pass that tax on to the persons receiving his services?   *a*
    2. If Question 1 is answered in the affirmative, must the credit negotiator pay
turnover tax if he "covertly" passed on the tax, or only if he "overtly" passed it
on?
    3. If turnover tax is also payable where the tax is passed on covertly, is it
sufficient, for there to have been a covert passing on of turnover tax, that the
credit negotiator, in agreeing his commission, expected that out of it he would   *b*
have to pay turnover tax?'

    8. Reference is made to the report for the hearing for a fuller account of the facts
of the case and the course of the procedure and the observations submitted to the
court, which are mentioned or discussed hereinafter only in so far as is necessary for
the reasoning of the court.   *c*
    9. As regards the first question, it is sufficient to state that the documents in the
case do not contain any new factor in relation to the judgments of the court referred
to in the opinion of the Advocate General and that those judgments must therefore
be confirmed.
    10. The second and third questions essentially seek a fuller explanation of the
condition laid down in those judgments for exemption from tax, namely that the   *d*
trader should have 'refrained from passing the tax on to persons following him in the
chain of supply'. These two questions should therefore be considered together.
    11. In order to provide such a fuller explanation, it is necessary to examine that
condition, which appears in the operative parts of the judgments, in the light of the
grounds of the judgments in order to put it in its context. Since the condition was
first mentioned in the judgment of 19 January 1982 in *Becker*, reference should be *e*
made to that judgment.
    12. An examination of the grounds of the judgment in *Becker* shows that in that
case, in order to demonstrate that the exemption provided for by the directive may
not be relied on by individuals, the German tax authorities, supported by the
government of the Federal Republic of Germany, had put forward a number of
arguments based on the particular features of the tax system concerned, namely the *f*
chain of taxation typical of value added tax on account of the right of deduction.
The tax authorities had emphasised in particular the disruption which could be
caused by the fact that an exemption might be claimed a posteriori, to the detriment
of taxpayers in a business relationship with the person exempted from the tax.
    13. In response to those misgivings the court pointed out that the scheme of the
directive was such that on the one hand, by availing themselves of an exemption   *g*
persons entitled thereto necessarily waived the right to claim a deduction in respect
of inputs and on the other hand, having been exempted from the tax, they were
unable to pass on any charge whatsoever to the person following them in the chain
of supply, with the result that the rights of third parties in principle could not be
affected.
    14. In particular, as regards the disruption caused by exemptions claimed   *h*
a posteriori by taxpayers under the directive, the court observed that that objection
was not relevant to the case of a taxpayer who had claimed the benefit of the
exemption when he submitted his tax return and who had consequently refrained
from invoicing the tax to the recipients of his services, with the result that third
parties were not affected.
    15. It must therefore be stated that the purpose of the condition laid down in the *j*
judgments of the court cited by the Advocate General, viewed in the light of the
grounds of the judgment in *Becker*, is to prevent a claim for the exemption provided
for by the Sixth Directive made a posteriori by a trader from having adverse effects
on other traders who have already deducted the amounts of value added tax in
question as input tax. Such a consequence could arise only if the trader claiming

exemption has passed on the tax in accordance with the formalities prescribed by
a the Sixth Directive in that regard and if the recipient of the services is himself
subject to value added tax.

16. It follows from the foregoing that the answer to the questions asked by the
national court should be that in the absence of implementation of the Sixth Directive,
a credit negotiator may rely on the tax exemption provision contained in art 13B(*d*)(1)
of the directive in respect of transactions carried out between 1 January 1978 and
b 30 June 1978 and as from 1 January 1979 if he did not pass that tax on to the person
receiving his services so as to entitle that person to deduct the input tax.

Costs

17. The costs incurred by the Commission of the European Communities, which
has submitted observations to the court, are not recoverable. Since these proceedings
c are, in so far as the parties to the main proceedings are concerned, in the nature of a
step in the proceedings pending before the national court, the decision on costs is a
matter for that court.

On those grounds, the court (Sixth Chamber), in answer to the questions
submitted to it by the Finanzgericht Rheinland-Pfalz by order of 15 June 1987,
hereby rules:

d
In the absence of implementation of the Sixth Directive, a credit negotiator
may rely on the tax exemption provision contained in art 13B(*d*)(1) of the
directive in respect of transactions carried out between 1 January 1978 and
30 June 1978 and as from 1 January 1979 if he did not pass that tax on to the
person receiving his services so as to entitle that person to deduct the input tax.

e
Agents: *K Widmann*, Ministerialrat in the Ministry of Finance (for the Finanzamt);
G zur Hausen (for the Commission).

Rengan Krishnan Esq   Barrister.

H Krantz GmbH & Co v Ontvanger der Directe Belastingen and Netherlands State (Case C-69/88)

COURT OF JUSTICE OF THE EUROPEAN COMMUNITIES (SECOND CHAMBER)
JUDGES SCHOCKWEILER (PRESIDENT OF THE CHAMBER), MANCINI AND O'HIGGINS
ADVOCATE GENERAL M DARMON
7 NOVEMBER, 12 DECEMBER 1989, 7 MARCH 1990

Imports – European Communities – Freedom of movement of goods – Quantitative restrictions on imports – Provision of national law empowering tax authorities to seize goods at taxpayer's premises – Machines belonging to national of another member state amongst property seized by tax authorities – Whether provision to be regarded as a measure having equivalent effect to quantitative restrictions on imports – EEC Treaty, art 30.

K, a German company, sold some machines under a hire-purchase contract to Z, a company established in the Netherlands. The contract contained a reservation of title clause. Z installed the machines in the factory of its subsidiary VT, another company established in the Netherlands. Following the insolvency of both Z and VT, the Ontvanger der Directe Belastingen, in order to recover outstanding direct taxes, seized all the movable property found on the premises of VT. Amongst the items seized were the machines sold by K to Z. Z had not paid all the hire-purchase instalments to K and therefore the machines remained the property of K. K's challenge against the seizure before the Directeur van de Directe Belastingen was dismissed. By agreement with the Ontvanger der Directe Belastingen, K subsequently obtained the machines from the liquidators on payment of 200,000 Netherlands guilders. K applied to the Arrondissementsrechtbank, Maastricht, for a declaration that the seizure was unlawful and for an order that the sum of 200,000 guilders be repaid on the grounds that the Netherlands legislation was incompatible with art 30[a] of the EEC Treaty. The Arrondissementsrechtbank, taking the view that the case involved the interpretation of Community law, stayed the proceedings and referred two questions to the Court of Justice for a preliminary ruling to determine, inter alia, whether the Netherlands legislation was to be regarded as a measure having an effect equivalent to quantitative restrictions on imports and therefore incompatible with art 30 of the EEC Treaty in that it allowed the tax authorities to seize goods (other than stocks) on the premises of a taxpayer even if the goods were the property of a supplier in another member state.

Held – All measures capable of hindering, directly or indirectly, actually or potentially, intra-Community trade were to be regarded as measures having an effect equivalent to quantitative restrictions and therefore incompatible with art 30 of the EEC Treaty. However, the provision of the Netherlands national law which allowed the tax authorities to seize goods on the premises of a taxpayer applied without distinction to both domestic goods and imported goods and did not seek to control trade with other member states. Furthermore, the possibility that nationals of other member states would hesitate to sell goods on instalment terms to purchasers in the Netherlands because such goods would be liable to seizure by the collector of taxes if the purchasers failed to discharge their Netherlands tax debts was too uncertain and indirect to warrant the conclusion that a national provision authorising

---

a Article 30, so far as material, provides: 'Quantitative restrictions on imports and all measures having equivalent effect shall . . . be prohibited between Member States.'

such seizure was liable to hinder trade between member states. Accordingly, art 30
a of the EEC Treaty did not prohibit national legislation which authorised the tax
authorities to seize goods (other than stocks) which were found on the premises of a
taxpayer even if those goods were the property of a supplier established in another
member state.

Notes
b
For the EEC Treaty, art 30, see 50 Halsbury's Statutes 276.

Cases cited

Blesgen v State of Belgium (Case 75/81) [1982] ECR 1211, CJEC.
c *Cinéthèque SA and others v Fédération nationale des cinémas français* (Joined cases
60/84 and 61/84) [1985] ECR 2618, CJEC.
Direction générale des impôts and Procureur de la République v Forest (Case 148/85)
[1986] ECR 3449, CJEC.
Oebel (Case 155/80) [1981] ECR 1993, CJEC.
Procureur du Roi v Dassonville (Case 8/74) [1974] ECR 837, CJEC.
d *Rewe-Zentral AG v Bundesmonopolverwaltung für Branntwein* (Case 120/78) [1979]
ECR 649, CJEC.
Torfaen BC v B & Q plc (Case 145/88) [1990] 2 QB 19, [1990] 1 All ER 129, [1989]
ECR 3851, CJEC.

Reference
e
By a judgment dated 3 March 1988 the Arrondissementsrechtbank, Maastricht,
referred to the court for a preliminary ruling under art 177 of the EEC Treaty two
questions on the interpretation of arts 30 and 36 of the EEC Treaty. The questions
arose in proceeding between H Krantz GmbH & Co (Krantz GmbH) on the one
hand, and the Ontvanger der Directe Belastingen and the Netherlands State on the
f other, concerning the Ontvanger der Directe Belastingen's decision to seize machines
belonging to Krantz GmbH by reason of the tax debt of Krantz GmbH's customer
pursuant to a provision of the Netherlands national law. The government of the
Kingdom of the Netherlands and the Commission of the European Communities
made submissions (in the written procedure) to the court. The language of the case
was Dutch. The facts are set out in the report for the hearing.

g **The Judge Rapporteur (G F Mancini)** presented the following report for the
hearing.

I Facts

A Legal background
h   1. In the Netherlands, art 16 of the Law of 22 May 1845 (Wet op de Invordering
van's Rijks Directe Belastingen (Law on the collection of the state's direct taxes))
(the Invorderingswet) allows the tax authorities to seize movable property intended
to furnish or equip immovable property when the movable property is on the
premises of a taxpayer who owes outstanding taxes.

j *B Background to the main proceedings*
    2. The plaintiff in the main proceedings, H Krantz GmbH & Co (Krantz GmbH),
whose registered office is in Aachen, Federal Republic of Germany, concluded with
J J Krantz & Zoon NV, Leiden, Netherlands (Krantz & Zoon), a hire-purchase
contract for the supply of machines. The contract contained a reservation of title
clause. Krantz & Zoon installed those machines in the factory of its subsidiary,
Vaalser Textielfabriek BV, in Vaals. In 1978 those two companies were declared

bankrupt. At the time Krantz & Zoon still owed Krantz GmbH about 550,000 DM on the sale price of the machines.

3. In order to collect from Vaalser Textielfabriek BV a tax debt of 1,448,949·69 Netherlands guilders the Ontvanger der Directe Belastingen (Collector of Direct Taxes), Kerkrade (the tax collector), the first defendant in the main proceedings, seized all the movable property in the debtor's factory. Amongst the goods seized were the machines which Krantz GmbH had sold on hire purchase to Krantz & Zoon.

4. Krantz GmbH challenged that seizure before the Directeur van de Directe Belastingen (Director of Direct Taxation) under art 16(1) of the Invorderingswet. That challenge was dismissed. By agreement with the tax collector Krantz GmbH subsequently obtained the machines from the liquidators on payment of about 200,000 guilders. Krantz GmbH now asks the Arrondissementsrechtbank (District Court) to rule that the seizure was unlawful and to order the defendant or defendants in the main proceedings to repay the 200,000 guilders.

5. Before the Arrondissementsrechtbank Krantz GmbH submits that art 16 of the Invorderingswet is incompatible with art 30 of the EEC Treaty, or at least with its object and scope, since art 16 restricts the free movement of goods, services and capital within the Community. The Court of Justice of the European Communities has held that any trade legislation of the member states capable of restricting intra-Community trade, directly or indirectly, actually or potentially, constitutes a measure having equivalent effect within the meaning of art 30 of the EEC Treaty. The tax authorities' right to seize the movable property furnishing a debtor's premises is prejudicial to trade in goods between the Netherlands and the other member states. If the powers of the Netherlands tax authorities were generally known in the other member states sales to the Netherlands requiring financing would fall significantly.

6. The Arrondissementsrechtbank, Maastricht, took the view that the case raised a problem of Community law; in a judgment of 3 March 1988 it therefore stayed the proceedings and requested the Court of Justice, under art 177 of the EEC Treaty, to give a preliminary ruling on the following questions:

'1. Is Article 16 of [the Invorderingswet] to be regarded as a measure having equivalent effect to a quantitative restriction on imports within the meaning of Article 30 of the EEC Treaty where the Netherlands tax authorities seize goods on the premises of a taxpayer even if those goods are from and are the property of a supplier in another Member State?

2. If so, is the application of the aforesaid Article 16 none the less justified under Article 36 of the EEC Treaty on the basis of one of the grounds referred to in Article 36?'

II Procedure

7. The judgment making the reference was received at the court registry on 7 March 1988.

8. By order of 13 July 1988 the court suspended the procedure for a preliminary ruling pending the hearing of an appeal by the national court. The judgment of the Arrondissementsrechtbank, Maastricht, was upheld on appeal. By order of 26 April 1989 the Court of Justice ordered the resumption of its procedure.

9. In accordance with art 20 of the Protocol on the Statute of the Court of Justice written observations were submitted by the government of the Kingdom of the Netherlands, represented by the Ministry of Foreign Affairs, and by the Commission of the European Communities, represented by René Barents, a member of its Legal Department.

10. On hearing the report of the Judge Rapporteur and the views of the Advocate General the court decided to open the oral procedure without any preparatory inquiry.

11. By a decision of 7 June 1989 the court decided pursuant to art 95(1) and (2) of
a   the Rules of Procedure to assign the case to the Second Chamber.

III Summary of the written observations submitted to the court

12. The government of the Kingdom of the Netherlands, the defendant in the
main proceedings, explains as a preliminary matter the law on tax collection and the
law of seizure under the Invorderingswet.
b   It takes the view that in practice art 16(3) of the Invorderingswet allows the tax
collector to obtain satisfaction from the movable property furnishing the taxpayer's
premises. The concepts of premises (bodem) and furnishing (stoffering) have very
wide meanings but, pursuant to a national administrative notice, do not cover stocks
of raw materials, auxiliary materials and finished products. That document also
states guidelines, favourable to third parties, which the Directeur der Rijks-
c   belastingen (Director of National Taxation) observes as a matter of policy in ruling
on challenges made by third parties who assert rights over movable property seized
to satisfy a tax debt.
The government of the Kingdom of the Netherlands takes the view that the tax
authority's preferential right takes precedence over the security of Krantz GmbH,
the seller on hire purchase. From the legal point of view the right of seizure at issue
d   is an infringement of the property rights of a third party. The government adds that
the debtor's property is the creditors' joint security up to the amount of the sums
owed to them but that in almost every member state preferential rights and secured
interests derogate from that rule.
13. The government of the Kingdom of the Netherlands goes on to state that the
right of seizure provided for by art 16 of the Invorderingswet is not trade legislation
e   within the meaning of the judgment of 11 July 1974 in *Procureur du Roi v Dassonville*
(Case 8/74) [1974] ECR 837 but a right to ensure collection of taxes. That implies
that the right of seizure is not a measure having equivalent effect to a quantitative
restriction on imports.
The tax authorities' right of seizure does not relate to imports of products into the
Netherlands and its purpose is not to regulate trade between member states. The
f   right of seizure is applicable without distinction to all movable property on the
taxpayer's premises, irrespective of the origin of those goods or the place where the
holder of the security is established.
Nor is the right of seizure an obstacle to sales of products consigned for sale in the
Netherlands by suppliers established in another member state, because the tax
authorities' right of seizure is not applicable to stock.
g   If the court does take the view that the right of seizure constitutes a barrier to
trade between member states, the Netherlands government considers that that
barrier is a result of the existence of disparities between the rules on preferential
rights and security in the member states. Maintenance of the preferential right is
justified by imperatives linked to the effectiveness of the tax legislation. It is not
discriminatory and does not go beyond what is necessary to achieve the intended
h   goal, that is to say the protection of the tax authorities' right to collect taxes.
14. The government of the Kingdom of the Netherlands proposes that the first
question submitted by the national court should be answered as follows:

'Article 16 of [the Invorderingswet] is not to be regarded as a quantitative
restriction on imports within the meaning of Article 30 of the EEC Treaty
where the Netherlands tax authorities seize goods on the premises of a taxpayer
j   even if those goods are from and are the property of a supplier established in
another Member State.'

15. With regard to the second question submitted by the Arrondissementsrechtbank, the government of the Kingdom of the Netherlands takes the view that
it is not necessary to give a reply but adds that the right of seizure may be justified
for reasons of public policy within the meaning of art 36 of the EEC Treaty.

16. The Commission of the European Communities observes that the tax authorities' right of seizure at issue cannot be regarded as a direct restriction on trade *a* between member states since art 16 of the Invorderingswet does not specifically relate to trade. Nor is it an indirect restriction, since the tax authorities' power of seizure is not linked to other phases of the economic process which are capable of affecting trade between member states.

From a practical point of view there is no actual barrier because the seizure is a contingent event which always takes place after the goods have been imported into *b* the Netherlands.

Furthermore, the tax authorities' right of seizure does not potentially impede trade between member states because importation, sale and use of goods which may be seized are not affected and the importer is free to implement his commercial decisions.

17. The Commission suggests that the following answer should be given to the *c* first question submitted by the national court:

'A power which the tax authorities have to seize goods which can have no demonstrable effect on importation is not a measure having equivalent effect within the meaning of Article 30 of the EEC Treaty.'

18. Having regard to that answer, the Commission takes the view that the answer *d* to the second question is otiose.

12 December 1989. **The Advocate General (M Darmon)** delivered the following opinion.

Mr President, members of the court, *e*
1. By judgment of 3 March 1988 the Arrondissementsrechtbank (District Court), Maastricht, requested this court to give a preliminary ruling on two questions regarding the interpretation of arts 30 and 36 of the EEC Treaty. The questions arose in the context of a dispute between H Krantz GmbH & Co (Krantz GmbH), established in the Federal Republic of Germany, and the Ontvanger der Directe Belastingen (Collector of Direct Taxes), Kerkrade (the tax collector) together with *f* the Kingdom of the Netherlands. Krantz GmbH sold some machines on hire-purchase terms to J J Krantz & Zoon NV (Krantz & Zoon), a company established in the Netherlands. Krantz & Zoon installed the machines in the factory of its subsidiary, Vaalser Textielfabriek BV, in Vaals. Following the insolvency of both Krantz & Zoon and its subsidiary, the tax collector seized all the movable property found on the premises of Vaalser Textielfabriek BV, in order to recover the direct *g* taxes which it owed. The movable property in question included the machines on which Krantz & Zoon had not finished paying the instalments to Krantz GmbH and which therefore remained the property of that company.

2. When its request for the return of the machines was rejected by the tax collector by virtue of the Netherlands Law on the collection of direct taxes, Krantz GmbH was able to obtain possession of the machines only on payment of a sum of 200,000 *h* Netherlands guilders. Seeking to have the seizure of the machines declared illegal and to obtain a refund of the 200,000 guilders, Krantz GmbH commenced proceedings before the Arrondissementsrechtbank, Maastricht, claiming before that court, inter alia, that the Netherlands Law on the collection of direct taxes was incompatible with the principle of the free movement of goods.

3. The national legislation cited in the questions of the national court is the Law *j* of 22 May 1845 on the collection of the state's direct taxes (Wet op de Invordering van's Rijks Directe Belastingen) (the Invorderingswet), in particular art 16. That article governs the pursuit of claims by 'third parties who consider themselves entitled, wholly or in part, to movable property seized by reason of a tax debt' (see the first paragraph of art 16). The third paragraph of art 16 calls for particular attention, inasmuch as it lays down the principle that 'third parties may not bring

an action against seizure on account of a tax debt—except in respect of land tax—if
a   the fruit harvested, or due to be harvested, or movable property intended for
furnishing or equipping a house or farm or for cultivating or working land are on
the debtor's premises at the time of seizure'. The interpretation placed on that
paragraph in the Netherlands extends its restrictions on the claims of third parties
to cover the movable property used for the running of an undertaking, but not to
stocks of raw materials, auxiliary materials or finished products found on the
b   premises.

4. Inasmuch as the Netherlands legislation divests suppliers who are nationals of
another member state of the right to reclaim their property seized by the tax
authorities along with the other goods of its debtors, the court is requested to rule on
whether that legislation is to be regarded as a measure having equivalent effect to a
quantitative restriction on imports within the meaning of art 30 of the EEC Treaty
c   and, if so, whether its application is justified under art 36.

5. As was observed above, in the course of the main proceedings Krantz GmbH
submitted that there was, in the circumstances of the case, a measure having
equivalent effect and stated that the rights of seizure held by the Netherlands tax
authorities was 'prejudicial to trade in goods in the Netherlands' and that a general
awareness of those rights outside the Netherlands would lead to a considerable
d   decline in sales on instalment terms from the other member states.

6. For their part, the Netherlands government and the Commission have argued
in the proceedings before the court that provisions of the kind contained in the
Invorderingswet did not fall within the ambit of the prohibition on measures having
equivalent effect. The Commission contends that the national measure in question
has no bearing on imports, thereby endorsing the view expressed in the main
e   proceedings by the Netherlands government.

7. The provisions of the Invorderingswet on the tax authorities' right of seizure is
not designed to regulate trade with other member states. The Invorderingswet,
which applies without distinction to domestic and imported goods furnishing the
place of residence of the tax debtor, with the exception of stocks, belongs to what
one might call the general legislative framework of business activities. It is distinct
f   from legislative provisions relating directly and exclusively to the conditions for the
production or marketing of certain products or types of product, whose effects on
imports must be assessed, as far as the prohibition under art 30 is concerned, by
reference to the guidelines laid down by this court in its judgment in *Rewe-Zentral
AG v Bundesmonopolverwaltung für Branntwein* (Case 120/78) [1979] ECR 649 of
20 February 1979. The court's recent judgment of 23 November 1989 in the case of
g   *Torfaen BC v B & Q plc* (Case C-145/88) [1990] 2 QB 19, [1989] ECR 3851 seems
to demonstrate that where provisions forming part of the above-mentioned
legislative framework have effects on imports, their compatibility with art 30 is
subject to somewhat different legal criteria.

8. The point at issue in the *Torfaen* case was whether the prohibition in the
United Kingdom on the Sunday opening of retail premises constituted a measure
h   having equivalent effect to a restriction on imports. The court referred to its
judgment of 11 July 1985 in *Cinéthèque SA and others v Fédération nationale des
cinémas français* (Joined cases 60/84 and 61/84) [1985] ECR 2618 and concluded that
the compatibility of the prohibitory provisions with the principle of the free
movement of goods was determined by two conditions: first, that the provisions in
question should serve a justifiable purpose under Community law and, second, that
j   their effects on imports should not go beyond what is necessary for the attainment of
the aim in view—a matter for the appraisal of the national court.

9. On the first point the court, drawing parallels with the judgment of 14 July
1981 in *Oebel* (Case 155/80) [1981] ECR 1993, took the view that national rules
governing the opening hours of retail premises—

'... reflect certain political and economic choices in so far as their purpose is
to ensure that working and non-working hours are so arranged as to accord

with national or regional socio-cultural characteristics, and that, in the present state of Community law, is a matter for the Member States.' (See *Torfaen BC v B & Q plc* (Case 145/88) [1990] 2 QB 19 at 53, [1989] ECR 3851 at 3889.)   *a*

Accordingly, those national rules had to be regarded as consistent with the objectives of public interest pursued by the EEC Treaty. On the second point the court held that the issue whether the restrictive effects exerted by specific national rules on the free movement of goods actually remained within the limit of its intrinsic effects was *b* a question of fact to be determined by the national court.

10. Should the court, in answering the questions submitted by the Arrondissementsrechtbank, adopt a similar approach? If so, the court must consider whether the aim pursued by the Invorderingswet, namely to ensure that action to recover taxes is effective, is in keeping with the broad objectives of the EEC Treaty and, if necessary, inform the national court that it is responsible for ascertaining whether *c* or not the effects on imports of that Law do go beyond what is necessary to ensure the effectiveness of such action. I should note right away that the court can hardly take the view that by regulating the tax authorities' right of seizure in such a way as to ensure the effective recovery of direct taxes, Netherlands legislation is not pursuing an aim consistent with the general objectives of the EEC Treaty. Decisions on such matters remain within the powers of the member states. In that hypothesis *d* the Netherlands court would have the task of determining whether or not the effects on imports were excessive for the attainment of an objective which was in itself legitimate.

11. However, I do not propose that the court should contend with any such problems. It seems to me that a situation such as the one described by the national court does not even lend itself to an approach of the kind adopted in the *Torfaen* *e* judgment. In my opinion it is only where there are perceptible effects on imports that there are grounds for inquiring whether the provisions giving rise to those effects reflect a legitimate objective or whether the effects are disproportionate. On the other hand, such a procedure does not appear to me to be relevant if no perceptible effect on imports can be attributed to legislation. I am very doubtful whether there are any effects on imports due to the application of provisions on the *f* seizure of property such as those at issue here. There is therefore no cause in the present case to make compatibility with art 30 dependent on the extent to which imports are affected; rather, there are grounds for concluding that the compatibility of the national measure with art 30 is shown quite simply by the *absence* of any bearing on imports.

12. I propose to explain briefly my reasons for believing that the Invorderingswet *g* has no bearing on imports. This Law, which applies to movables furnishing the place of residence of a person owing direct taxes irrespective of whether they originate in the Netherlands or elsewhere in the Community, does not cover stocks of raw materials, auxiliary materials, or finished products. Its scope is thus strikingly limited. Moreover, the Invorderingswet has no effect on the volume of demand from buyers on instalment terms. The only possible effect concerns the offering of *h* goods on instalment terms by sellers, who might hesitate to enter into a contract with a buyer subject to Netherlands direct taxation. I should emphasise the merely hypothetical character of any 'reluctance' on the sellers' part, inasmuch as such reluctance could only relate to the materialisation of an uncertain event—indeed, an event uncertain on two counts, since the risk of seizure of goods sold on instalment terms to a Netherlands buyer does not arise unless (i) that buyer also turns out to be *j* a defaulting debtor of direct taxes, and (ii) the competent national authorities decide to resolve the situation by the seizure of property. Lastly, it may be added that in facing that risk (if any) all sellers are on the same footing, whether they are Netherlands nationals or from another member state.

13. In the light of those considerations I find it difficult, to say the least, to describe the Invorderingswet as a measure restricting imports on the basis of the argument—the *only* argument which can be made in this respect—that non-Dutch sellers *might*

hesitate to sell goods on instalment terms to Netherlands nationals when those goods
a *might* be seized *if* the buyers should happen to default on payments to the Netherlands
tax authorities. Such a concatenation of contingencies clearly cannot be treated as a
restriction on imports. Application of the Invorderingswet, in the circumstances
described in the judgment of the Arrondissementsrechtbank, does not disclose any
connection with trade between the Netherlands and the other member states. It is a
national measure having no bearing on imports. That conclusion might perhaps
b have required reconsideration if the Invorderingswet had also applied to stocks,
since the possibility of effects on trade arising out of a greater degree of 'reluctance'
could not then have been ruled out. Such, however, is not the case.

14. I must also make some remarks prompted by the comparison of the present
case with the circumstances which gave rise to the court's judgments of 31 March
1982 in *Blesgen v State of Belgium* (Case 75/81) [1982] ECR 1211 and of 25 November
c 1986 in *Direction générale des impôts and Procureur de la République v Forest*
(Case 148/85) [1986] ECR 3449. In the first judgment the court ruled ([1982] ECR
1211 at 1229) that legislation prohibiting the consumption, with or without charge,
in all places open to the public of spirits whose alcoholic strength exceeded 22° had
'in fact no connection with the importation of the products' and for that reason was
not 'of such a nature as to impede trade between Member States'.
d In the second judgment the court held ([1986] ECR 3449 at 3475) that French
legislation establishing quotas for the milling of wheat 'in fact has no effect on wheat
imports' and was 'not likely to impede trade between Member States'.

In both those cases the national measures at issue, although considered to have no
bearing on imports, were nevertheless of such a nature that their abolition might
have enabled imports to increase. Thus, since according to the case law of the court
e it is possible, in certain circumstances, to regard legislation as having no bearing on
imports when that legislation is in fact not totally without effects in that regard, the
same must be true a fortiori of measures whose restrictive effect, whether actual or
potential, is simply undetectable.

15. Admittedly, the status of the *Blesgen* and *Forest* judgments within the court's
case law on measures having equivalent effect is perhaps rather peculiar. It was to
f that peculiarity that the Advocate General (W Van Gerven) was alluding in his
opinion in the *Torfaen* case when he noted that '[the] factual context of those
judgments was quite specific' and when he referred to the 'empirical judgment' (see
Torfaen BC v B & Q plc (Case 145/88) [1990] 2 QB 19 at 35, [1989] ECR 3851 at
3868) which the court had exercised. Perhaps, in the light of the wording used in the
Cinéthèque and *Torfaen* judgments, the court would today have used slightly different
g terms with which to justify its conviction that measures similar to those considered
in the *Blesgen* and *Forest* judgments are compatible with art 30. However, I also
believe that if ever a national measure deserved to be regarded as having no bearing
on imports, it has to be the one which the national court has referred to this court.

16. The very broad definition of a 'measure having equivalent effect' formulated
in the *Dassonville* judgment has since 1974 served as a constant point of reference for
h subsequent judgments on the subject. The inherent breadth of that definition and
the court's concern, apparent in its judgments, not to reduce its scope fully explain
why businessmen have attempted to have a wide variety of measures treated as
measures having equivalent effect to quantitative restrictions on imports, where
such an effect—however indirect and tenuous—cannot be altogether ruled out. The
court's judgment in *Torfaen*, based on the *Cinéthèque* judgment, provides some
j clarification to the effect that restrictive effects on imports, if inherent in legislation
pursuing goals permitted by the EEC Treaty, cannot, unless they are disproportionate, cause a measure to be regarded as a measure having equivalent effect to
quantitative restrictions. Thus a 'lower limit' for a measure having an equivalent
effect to quantitative restrictions on imports is becoming discernible. The present
case falls short of the lower limit, or the 'lower limit to the lower limit', since the
alleged effects on imports of the Invorderingswet cannot be substantiated in the first
place.

17. In the absence of any perceptible *effect* on imports, there can be no measure having equivalent *effect*. I therefore take the view that the first question submitted for a preliminary ruling must be answered in the negative, from which it follows that it is not necessary to answer the second question.

18. In conclusion, I propose that the court should rule as follows:

Legislation of a member state on the collection of direct taxes which authorises the seizure of property, whether domestic or imported, furnishing the debtor's place of residence, but excluding stocks of raw materials, auxiliary materials or finished products, without the right on the part of suppliers from another member state who own property sold on hire-purchase terms to reclaim it, does not fall under the prohibition contained in art 30 of the EEC Treaty.

7 March 1990. **THE COURT OF JUSTICE** delivered the following judgment.

1. By judgment dated 3 March 1988, which was received at the court on 7 March 1988, the Arrondissementsrechtbank (District Court), Maastricht referred to the court for a preliminary ruling under art 177 of the EEC Treaty two questions on the interpretation of arts 30 and 36 of the EEC Treaty.

2. Those questions arose in proceedings between H Krantz GmbH & Co (Krantz GmbH), of Aachen, Federal Republic of Germany, on the one hand, and the Ontvanger der Directe Belastingen (Collector of Direct Taxes) (the tax collector) and the Netherlands State, on the other, concerning the tax collector's decision to seize machines belonging to Krantz GmbH, pursuant to art 16 of the Netherlands Law of 22 May 1845 on the collection of direct taxes (Wet op de Invordering van's Rijks Directe Belastingen) (the Invorderingswet). The machines had been sold by Krantz GmbH on instalment terms, with reservation of title, to J J Krantz & Zoon NV (Krantz & Zoon), whose registered office is at Leiden, Netherlands, and had been installed on the premises of its subsidiary company, Vaalser Textielfabriek BV, at Vaals.

3. Krantz & Zoon and its subsidiary were declared insolvent. In order to recover a tax debt owed by Vaalser Textielfabriek BV the tax collector, acting under art 16 of the Invorderingswet, seized all the movable property found on the premises of that company.

4. In proceedings before the various courts seised of the matter, Krantz GmbH claimed that art 16 of the Invorderingswet was incompatible with the object and scope of art 30 of the EEC Treaty on the ground that, if the powers of the tax collector were generally known, sales on instalment terms to the Netherlands would decline.

5. The Arrondissementsrechtbank, Maastricht, took the view that the dispute raised problems regarding the interpretation of Community law. Accordingly, it stayed the proceedings and referred the following questions to the Court of Justice:

'1. Is Article 16 of [the Invorderingswet] to be regarded as a measure having equivalent effect to a quantitative restriction on imports within the meaning of Article 30 of the EEC Treaty where the Netherlands tax authorities seize goods on the premises of a taxpayer even if those goods are from and are the property of a supplier in another Member State?

2. If so, is the application of the aforesaid Article 16 none the less justified under Article 36 of the EEC Treaty on the basis of one of the grounds referred to in Article 36?'

6. Reference is made to the report for the hearing for a fuller account of the legal background, the facts of the case, the course of the procedure and the written observations submitted to the court which are mentioned or discussed hereinafter only in so far as is necessary for the reasoning of the court.

7. It must first be pointed out that it is not for the court, under art 177 of the EEC Treaty, to rule on the compatibility with the EEC Treaty of provisions of national

law. It does, however, have jurisdiction to provide the national court with all such
a matters relating to the interpretation of Community law as may enable that court to
decide the issue of compatibility in the case before it.

8. The questions submitted by the Arrondissementsrechtbank, Maastricht, must
therefore be construed as seeking to establish whether art 30 is to be interpreted as
prohibiting national legislation which authorises the tax collector to seize goods,
other than stocks, which are found on the premises of a taxpayer even if those goods
b are from and are the property of a supplier established in another member state,
and, if so, whether that legislation is justified under art 36 of the EEC Treaty.

First question

9. As the court has consistently held, initially in the judgment of 11 July 1974 in
Procureur du Roi v Dassonville (Case 8/74) [1974] ECR 837, all measures capable of
c hindering, directly or indirectly, actually or potentially, intra-Community trade are
to be regarded as measures having an effect equivalent to quantitative restrictions.

10. It must, however, be observed that the national provision referred to by the
national court applies without distinction to both domestic and imported goods, and
does not seek to control trade with other member states.

11. Furthermore, the possibility that nationals of other member states would
d hesitate to sell goods on instalment terms to purchasers in the member state
concerned because such goods would be liable to seizure by the collector of taxes if
the purchasers failed to discharge their Netherlands tax debts is too uncertain and
indirect to warrant the conclusion that a national provision authorising such seizure
is liable to hinder trade between member states.

12. Accordingly, the answer to the first question must be that art 30 of the EEC
e Treaty, properly interpreted, does not prohibit national legislation which authorises
the tax collector to seize goods, other than stocks, which are found on the premises
of a taxpayer even if those goods are from, and are the property of, a supplier
established in another member state.

Second question

f 13. In the light of the answer given to the first question, it is unnecessary to rule
on the second question referred to the court.

Costs

14. The costs incurred by the Netherlands government and by the Commission
of the European Communities, which have submitted observations to the court, are
g not recoverable. Since these proceedings are, in so far as the parties to the main
proceedings are concerned, in the nature of a step in the action pending before the
national court, the decision on costs is a matter for that court.

On those grounds, the court (Second Chamber), in answer to the questions
referred to it by the Arrondissementsrechtbank, Maastricht, by judgment of 3 March
h 1988, hereby rules as follows:

> Article 30 of the EEC Treaty, properly interpreted, does not prohibit national
> legislation which authorises the collector of direct taxes to seize goods, other
> than stocks, which are found on the premises of a taxpayer even if those goods
> are from, and are the property of, a supplier established in another member
> state.

j
Agents: *J E F F M Duynstee* (for Krantz GmbH); *M A Fierstra* and *E F Jacobs*,
Secretary General at the Netherlands Ministry for Foreign Affairs (for the
Netherlands government); *René Barents*, a member of the Legal Department (for
the Commission).

Rengan Krishnan Esq   Barrister.

ORO Amsterdam Beheer BV and Concerto BV v Inspecteur der Omzetbelasting
(Case C-165/88)

COURT OF JUSTICE OF THE EUROPEAN COMMUNITIES
JUDGES DUE (PRESIDENT), KAKOURIS (PRESIDENT OF CHAMBER), KOOPMANS, JOLIET,
MOITINHO DE ALMEIDA, RODRIGUEZ IGLESIAS AND GREVISSE
ADVOCATE GENERAL G TESAURO
12 JULY, 24 OCTOBER, 5 DECEMBER 1989

Value added tax – European Communities – Input tax – Deductibility of input tax – Supply of secondhand goods – Residual tax incorporated in the value of secondhand goods – Whether taxable purchaser entitled to deduction of input tax paid on secondhand goods acquired from non-taxable vendor – EC Council Directive 77/388, art 32.

The tax entity ORO Amsterdam Beheer BV and Concerto BV (the taxpayer companies) traded in new and secondhand records, music cassettes and compact discs. For the month of December 1986 they made sales totalling 256,698 Netherlands guilders of which 250,915 guilders was subject to value added tax at 20%. Having deducted input value added tax the taxpayer companies paid 37,608 guilders to the tax authorities. The taxpayer companies, in proceedings before the Gerechtshof, Amsterdam, claimed a repayment of 6,251 guilders on the grounds that they should be allowed to deduct from the value added tax payable in respect of sales for December 1986, the amount of value added tax that was still contained in the price of the goods they had purchased secondhand. The Gerechtshof found that no provision of Netherlands value added tax law permitted a deduction of input tax paid on secondhand goods purchased by a taxable person from a non-taxable person but stayed the proceedings and requested that the Court of Justice give a preliminary ruling, inter alia, on the following question: 'Is it in conformity with Community law, and in particular with the provisions of [the EEC Treaty] and of [the Sixth Directive], to have charged . . . turnover tax at the full rate on the supply of second-hand goods without taking any account whatsoever of the fact that those goods were bought from individuals, in view of the fact that in [art 32[a] of] the Sixth Directive the Council of the European Communities committed itself to . . . the adoption before 31 December 1977 of a Community taxation system applicable to trade in second-hand goods but has so far taken no action in that regard?'

Held – The Community system of value added tax was the result of a gradual harmonisation of the laws of the member states relating to turnover taxes. That harmonisation was designed in particular to preclude double taxation, so that the deduction of input tax at each stage was an integral part of the system of value added tax. However, harmonisation was still only partial and, as was clear from art 32 of the Sixth Directive, there was no provision in the common system of value added tax for determining and laying down detailed rules for applying a common system of taxation enabling double taxation to be avoided in trade in secondhand goods. Accordingly, Community law did not preclude national legislation which, for the purpose of calculating the value added tax payable on the turnover arising from the sale of secondhand goods, did not allow account to be taken of the tax still contained in the price of goods which had been purchased from non-taxable individuals with a view to their resale.

---

a Article 32, so far as material, is set out at p 624 *a*, post

Notes

a   For used goods schemes, see De Voil: Value Added Tax A14.31.
For EC Council Directive 77/388, art 32, see ibid, Division E3.

Cases cited

EC Commission v Ireland (Case 17/84) [1985] ECR 2375, CJEC.
b   *EC Commission v Kingdom of the Netherlands* (Case 16/84) [1985] ECR 2355, CJEC.
EC Commission v United Kingdom (Case 804/79) [1981] ECR 1045.
Kühne v Finanzamt München III (Case 50/88) [1990] STC 749 [1989] ECR 1925, CJEC.
Ministère Public and Ministry of Finance v Profant (Case 249/84) [1985] ECR 3237, CJEC.
c   *Pluimveeslachterij Midden-Nederland BV and Pluimveeslachterij C van Miert BV* (Joined cases 47/83 and 48/83) [1984] ECR 1721, CJEC.
R v Tymen (Case 269/80) [1981] ECR 3079, CJEC.
Schul (Gaston) Douane Expediteur BV v Inspecteur der Invoerrechten en Accijnzen (Case 15/81) [1982] ECR 1409, CJEC.
Staatssecretaris van Financiën v Schul (Gaston) Douane-Expediteur BV (Case 47/84)
d   [1985] ECR 1491, CJEC.

Reference

By an order of 24 May 1988, the Gerechtshof (Regional Court of Appeal), Amsterdam, referred to the Court of Justice for a preliminary ruling under art 177
e   of the EEC Treaty two questions on the interpretation of the provisions of the EEC Treaty and of EC Council Directive 77/388 in order to determine the compatibility with Community law of Netherlands tax legislation in so far as it did not provide special rules for the application of the system of value added tax to trade in secondhand goods which had been purchased from non-taxable individuals with a view to their resale.

f

The Judge Rapporteur (F Grévisse) presented the following report for the hearing.

I Summary of the facts
     A. ORO Amsterdam Beheer BV and Concerto BV (the taxpayer companies) are retail traders in new and secondhand gramophone records, music cassettes and
g   compact discs. In December 1986 their sales of new and secondhand goods amounted to 256,698 Netherlands guilders net of tax. Of that amount, 250,915 guilders is subject to turnover tax at the rate of 20%.
     During that period, the taxpayer companies purchased secondhand goods for resale at a total cost of 37,509 guilders. In their value added tax declaration for December 1986, they applied a rate of 20% to the sum of 250,915 guilders, thus
h   obtaining a gross amount of tax of 50,183 guilders, from which they deducted the turnover tax which they had paid as input tax. However, the tax entity ORO Amsterdam Beheer BV and Concerto BV challenged the value added tax paid (37,608 guilders) in proceedings before the Gerechtshof (Regional Court of Appeal), Amsterdam, claiming the repayment of 6,251 guilders on the ground that the value added tax still contained in the price of secondhand goods acquired for resale should
j   be deducted from the value added tax payable on the sales transactions. The taxpayer companies claimed that for this purpose an amount equal to 20/120ths of the total amount of its purchases of secondhand goods should be deducted.
     B. The Gerechtshof, Amsterdam, found that there was no provision of national tax legislation permitting the total or partial deduction of the value added tax borne by goods purchased secondhand. It also stated that EC Council Directive 77/388 of 17 May 1977 on the harmonisation of the laws of the member states relating to

turnover taxes—common system of value added tax: uniform basis of assessment (the Sixth Directive) did not itself permit such deduction either, but the Commission had on the basis of art 32 of the Sixth Directive drafted proposals for the adoption of a special system of turnover tax applicable to secondhand goods, which have not yet been accepted. However, in view of the distortion of competition which might be caused by the absence of special rules for secondhand goods and the judgments of the court, and in particular its judgments of 10 July 1985 in *EC Commission v Kingdom of the Netherlands* (Case 16/84) [1985] ECR 2355 and in *EC Commission v Ireland* (Case 17/84) [1985] ECR 2375), the Gerechtshof considered it necessary to request of the Court of Justice a preliminary ruling on the following two questions:

'1. Is it in conformity with Community law, and in particular with the provisions of [the EEC Treaty] and of [the Sixth Directive], for a Member State to have charged, in December 1986, turnover tax at the full rate on the supply of second-hand goods without taking any account whatsoever of the fact that those goods were bought from individuals, in view of the fact that in the Sixth Directive the Council of the European Communities committed itself to, and gave notice of, the adoption before 31 December 1977 of a Community taxation system applicable to trade in second-hand goods but has so far taken no action in that regard?

2. If the first question is answered in the negative, how is account to be taken, in the determination of the turnover tax payable on the supply of second-hand goods, of the fact that the goods were bought from individuals?'

The order of the Gerechtshof, Amsterdam, was lodged at the court on 13 June 1988.

In accordance with art 20 of the Protocol on the Statute of the Court of Justice, written observations were submitted by the Commission of the European Communities, represented by J F Buhl, its Legal Adviser and B J Drijber, a member of its Legal Department, acting as agents, by the government of the Netherlands, represented by E F Jacobs, acting as agent, and by the tax entity ORO Amsterdam Beheer BV and Concerto BV, represented by G Molenaar, acting as agent.

On hearing the report of the Judge Rapporteur and the views of the Advocate General, the court decided to open the oral procedure without any preparatory inquiry.

II Summary of the written observations submitted to the court

A. The taxpayer companies and the Commission of the European Communities consider that it is contrary to the provisions of the Sixth Directive to take no account of the value added tax already levied on goods purchased secondhand.

(1) The taxpayer companies claim that the fact that secondhand goods are charged to value added tax twice is contrary to the provisions of the Sixth Directive. They consider that this conclusion may be drawn both from the two judgments of the court delivered on 10 July 1985 in *EC Commission v Kingdom of the Netherlands* (Case 16/84) and *EC Commission v Ireland* (Case 17/84) and from the judgment of 21 May 1985 in *Staatssecretaris van Financiën v Schul (Gaston) Douane-Expediteur BV* (Case 47/84) [1985] ECR 1491.

The taxpayer companies also claim that the deduction resulting from their proposal to deduct 20/120ths from the amount of the purchases of secondhand goods is not too high and if the scheme provided for in the Commission's proposal for a directive were applied the deduction would be even higher.

(2) The Commission states first that the Netherlands legislation on turnover tax only provides for special rules for secondhand goods in two exceptional cases: first, in the case of the supply of movable property involving the exchange of property of the same type certain exemptions are provided and, second, works of art, antiques and other similar goods are subject to a reduced rate.

In its two judgments of 5 May 1982 in *Schul (Gaston) Douane Expediteur BV v*
a *Inspecteur der Invoerrechten en Accijnzen* (Case 15/81) [1982] ECR 1409, and of
21 May 1985 in *Staatssecretaris van Financiën v Schul (Gaston) Douane-Expediteur*
(Case 47/84) [1985] ECR 1491, the court held that it was contrary to art 95 of the
EEC Treaty to impose value added tax on the importation from another member
state of goods supplied by a private person where value added tax was not charged
on the supply by a private person of similar goods within the importing member
b state, in so far as the residual part of the value added tax paid in the exporting
member state was not taken into consideration. The question is therefore whether
the same principles must apply as far as trade within a state is concerned.

In this regard the Commission states that EC Council Directive 67/227 of 11 April
1967 on the harmonisation of legislation of member states concerning turnover taxes
(the First Directive) and EC Council Directive 67/228 of 11 April 1967 on the
c harmonisation of legislation of member states concerning turnover taxes—structure
and procedures for application of the common system of value added tax (the Second
Directive), which lay down the main principles for the common system of value
added tax, had made no provision for a scheme for secondhand goods. Article 26 of
the Proposal for a sixth Council Directive (see (1973) OJ C80, p 1) defined a special
scheme for value added tax on secondhand goods. This system did not, however,
d obtain the Council's agreement. On 11 January 1978 a Proposal for a seventh Council
Directive was submitted (see (1978) OJ C26, p 2 and (1979) OJ C136, p 8). This
proposal, which provided for a special scheme for secondhand goods, was withdrawn
in November 1987 and a new proposal for a directive in this field is at present being
prepared and is 'at an advanced stage'.

The Commission therefore considers that the Council has failed to act and it is
e necessary to decide what the duties of the states are in view of such failure to act.

In this regard it states first that it is clear from the judgments of the court that, in
the event of a failure to act, there can be no objection to the maintenance or
introduction by states of national measures designed to achieve the objectives of the
Community rules.

Second, it states that the fundamental characteristic of the system of value added
f tax, as was stated in the judgment in *EC Commission v Kingdom of the Netherlands*
(Case 16/84) is that it precludes any double taxation. As the court stated in that
judgment, this is the only method which will permit the elimination of distortions
between ordinary commercial channels and other channels.

Consequently, any rules resulting in double taxation should be regarded as
incompatible with the objectives of the value added tax system. The present situation
g in the Netherlands leads to double taxation on secondhand goods. The Commission
therefore considers that it is necessary to follow the judgments of the court and that
the national measures must be designed to achieve Community objectives in co-
operation with the Commission, as the court held in its judgment of 3 October 1985
in *Ministère Public and Ministry of Finance v Profant* (Case 249/84) [1985] ECR
3237. It is true that art 32 of the Sixth Directive contains a 'standstill' clause, but the
h Commission considers that in the light of the development of Community law the
states are obliged to act in view of the Council's failure to act. Therefore, the
Commission proposes that the reply to the first question should be:

> 'The imposition on supplies of second-hand goods within a Member State of
> turnover tax likely to result in the double taxation of those goods is incompatible
> with the fundamental principles laid down in the Council Directives introducing
j > a common system of value added tax.'

The Commission has doubts about the method to be adopted in order to avoid
such double taxation. It states that it cannot lay down this method, since the power
to do so belongs to the Council, but it considers that it is for the member states to
ensure through national measures that their system of taxation does not result in
double taxation, whilst ensuring that the rules adopted do not constitute an obstacle
to the harmonisation of legislation throughout the Community.

618 Simon's Tax Cases [1991] STC

B. The Netherlands government considers that, as its stands at present, the Netherlands legislation is compatible with Community law. After stating the general rules of the system of value added tax, the Netherlands government states that there is indeed a problem where goods purchased from an individual re-enter the commercial circuit. There is then tax cumulation and a different tax system is applied according to the sales channel. In the Netherlands legislation there are no general rules on secondhand goods but some account is nevertheless taken of the special problems which arise since there are, first, special rules governing the case in which movable goods are sold in exchange for goods of the same kind and, second, there are exemptions for the supply of goods which are used solely for exempt services and reduced rates for works of art, antiques and the like.

The Netherlands government states, however, that the standstill provided for in art 32 of the Sixth Directive prohibits the member states from amending or extending special provisions for secondhand goods. This provision is designed to preclude further disparities between the legislation of the member states. At the same time, national tax provisions must comply with the other provisions of the EEC Treaty, such as art 95 on internal taxation, as was decided by the court in its judgments in *EC Commission v Kingdom of the Netherlands* (Case 16/84) and *EC Commission v Ireland* (Case 17/84). But this case is different since it does not concern the importation of secondhand goods and art 32 of the Sixth Directive does not imply that, after the period which it prescribes, the member states are entitled or required to introduce a special system of taxation for secondhand goods.

As regards the reply to be given to the second question, the Netherlands government considers that, if the court should decide that the states are required to prevent tax cumulation on secondhand goods, the 'tax-on-tax' system, which is more consistent with the general scheme of the value added tax system, should be adopted. Second, any system applying to secondhand goods should enable the states to adopt additional provisions in order to ensure fair taxation and to prevent fraud.

III Replies to the questions asked by the court

In reply to the court's request that it explain the system of value added tax applicable to secondhand goods in the various member states, first, where such goods are purchased with a view to their resale within a state and, second, where they are imported from another member state, once again with a view to their resale—in each case both where the vendor is a taxable person and where he is not—the Commission provided the court with a detailed account of the state of the law in the various member states.

24 October 1989. **The Advocate General (G Tesauro)** delivered the following opinion.

Mr President, members of the court,

1. These questions for a preliminary ruling are the result of the incomplete state of the harmonisation of tax legislation within the Community. Although EC Council Directive 67/277 (the First Directive), EC Council Directive 67/228 (the Second Directive) and EC Council Directive 77/388 (the Sixth Directive) introduced the bases and general principles for a harmonised system of value added tax, the express provision of temporary derogations and the existence of sectors which have not been fully harmonised mean that the court is required to resolve discrepancies arising out of the conflict between the requirement that the general principles must be observed and the lack of any common rules to govern significant parts of the system.

The case with which I am dealing today is a typical example. Whereas it is a fundamental principle of the common system of value added tax—consistently referred to in the judgments of the court—that there should be no tax cumulation, the absence of common rules on the taxation of secondhand goods means that this

principle is not observed in a case such as that pending before the national court.
a Consequently, it is necessary to assess whether or not the failure to observe the principle that double taxation must be eliminated is compatible with Community law.

2. Let me examine briefly the facts of the case pending before the national court, the Gerechtshof (Regional Court of Appeal), Amsterdam, between the plaintiffs, ORO Amsterdam Beheer BV and Concerto BV (the taxpayer companies), and the
b Inspecteur der Omzetbelasting (Inspector of Turnover Taxes), the defendant.

After duly paying to the Netherlands tax authorities the difference between the amount of value added tax resulting from the sale of new and secondhand goods and the amount of turnover tax paid as input tax, the taxpayer companies claimed the repayment of a certain amount in respect of the value added tax still contained in the price of secondhand goods purchased with a view to their resale. The Netherlands
c tax authorities refused that request.

The national court, finding that there was no provision of national law which permitted the total or partial deduction of the value added tax which was still contained in the price of secondhand goods and that the resulting legal situation raised a problem of the interpretation of Community law, and in particular art 32 of the Sixth Directive, referred to the court the following questions for a preliminary
d ruling:

'1. Is it in conformity with Community law, and in particular with the provisions of [the EEC Treaty] and of [the Sixth Directive], for a Member State to have charged, in December 1986, turnover tax at the full rate on the supply of second-hand goods without taking any account whatsoever of the fact that those goods were bought from individuals, in view of the fact that in the
e Sixth Directive the Council of the European Communities committed itself to, and gave notice of, the adoption before 31 December 1977 of a Community taxation system applicable to trade in second-hand goods but has so far taken no action in that regard?

2. If the first question is answered in the negative, how is account to be taken, in the determination of the turnover tax payable on the supply of second-hand
f goods, of the fact that the goods were bought from individuals?'

3. The arguments of the parties are set out in the report for the hearing and did not substantially change at the hearing. There is therefore no need for me to recall them.

4. I would state at the outset that it is clear both from the written observations
g and the argument at the hearing that in this case the parties are agreed as to the analysis of the tax position. It is common ground that, by not permitting the total or partial deduction of the value added tax contained in the price of secondhand goods sold by a private individuals to a taxable person on the subsequent sale of those goods by the taxable person, Netherlands legislation gives rise to double taxation (tax cumulation).

h Article 32 provides as follows:

'The Council, acting unanimously on a proposal from the Commission, shall adopt before 31 December 1977 a Community taxation system to be applied to used goods, works of art, antiques and collectors' items.

Until this Community system becomes applicable, Member States applying a special system to these items at the time this Directive comes into force may
j retain that system.'

As I shall show, the central issue is whether such double taxation can be justified on the basis of art 32 of the Sixth Directive or whether the member states should have made up for the Council's failure to act by introducing in their tax legislation provisions to avoid tax cumulation.

5. The first question submitted by the national court requires an examination of art 32 of the Sixth Directive in order to ascertain whether, in view of the Council's failure to act by not adopting before 31 December 1977 a Community taxation system to be applied to secondhand goods, the member states may retain the special system which they applied before the entry into force of the Sixth Directive.

6. In this regard the government of the Netherlands claimed that art 32 should be interpreted as *prohibiting* the modification of special systems which existed prior to the entry into force of the Sixth Directive until the Council has adopted a Community system.

That view is rejected by the Commission and by the taxpayer companies.

7. It seems to me clear that the Netherlands government's interpretation of the second paragraph of art 32 cannot be accepted. I do not see how it can be thought that a provision authorising the member states to continue to apply a special system can change so radically as to *prohibit* them from amending such a system. Apart from any doubt as to the interpretation of the text, I need only state that the court itself, in its judgment of 10 July 1985 in *EC Commission v Kingdom of the Netherlands* (Case 16/84) [1985] ECR 2355 at 2374, replying on an incidental point to the Commission, which was then arguing—curiously enough—that art 32 'prohibits any amendment of existing national systems', stated that 'that cannot apply to adjustments whose sole objective is to ensure that a national system entirely conforms to that article'.

8. Consequently, I do not feel able to accept the view put forward by the Netherlands government. The standstill provided for in the second paragraph of art 32 must in my view be interpreted in such a way that member states wishing to introduce into their legislation a taxation system for secondhand goods to avoid double taxation are entitled to amend the special taxation system for secondhand goods which existed prior to the entry into force of the Sixth Directive. By so doing, they would not infringe the second paragraph of art 32. The argument of a technical nature that amendment of existing legislation would make harmonisation throughout the Community more difficult does not seem to me to be convincing; the aim in view must, of course, even if the means are different in each member state, be to attain an objective in accordance with the general principles of the system of value added tax, and in particular the principle that double taxation must be eliminated.

9. It is clear that this first conclusion does not resolve the problem submitted by the national court. It is apparent both from the terms of the first question and from the observations submitted to the court by the taxpayer companies and the Commission that the true question is not whether a member state has the *power* to amend its taxation system but rather whether it is *obliged*, in the light of the Council's failure to act, to adopt national measures to avoid double taxation.

10. In this regard I have to state that at first sight it does seem strange that, in spite of the express provision in the first paragraph of art 32, the Council has not yet, thirteen years after the prescribed date, adopted a Community taxation system in a sector as important as that of secondhand goods.

11. However, I do not consider that this situation can impose an *obligation* on the member states to adopt national measures to make up for the Council's failure to act.

12. First, I agree with the Netherlands government that the ratio decidendi of the judgment of the court of 5 May 1982 in *Schul (Gaston) Douane Expediteur v Inspecteur de Invoerrechten en Accijnzen* (Case 15/81) [1982] ECR 1409, does not apply in this case. That case related to the infringement of a specific provision of the EEC Treaty, namely art 95, which is not applicable in this case.

In strictly legal terms, the Council's failure consists in its not having satisfied an obligation to lay down rules within a prescribed period which it *imposed on itself* and which was not prescribed by any specific provision of the EEC Treaty. Applying the theory of the hierarchy of norms, one could even be tempted to argue that the Council has not infringed any higher-ranking norm and has merely failed by its own a inaction to comply with a procedural rule which it imposed on itself and in which the peremptory nature of the time-limit remains entirely open.

To claim that such a failure to comply with a time-limit which is clearly procedural must impose an obligation on all the member states to introduce into their own national law rules having the same effects as those which the Council should have adopted but has not adopted is in practice tantamount to denying that the Council has a discretionary power in the field of tax harmonisation.

b I therefore do not consider that the failure to comply with the prescribed time-limit imposes an obligation on member states to 'anticipate' a Community decision which the Council for reasons of its own has been unable to adopt.

13. I would add that the terms of art 32 do not themselves seem to me to support the Commission's argument. If the legislature had intended that the authorisation given to member states to continue to apply a special system should be limited in
c time solely to the period up to 31 December 1977, it would not have chosen to use in the second paragraph the words 'until this Community system becomes applicable'. It would have been simpler and more straightforward to use the expression 'until 31 December 1977'.

In this regard I would point out that this is the interpretation put forward by the Advocate General (M Darmon) in his opinion in *EC Commission v Kingdom of the*
d *Netherlands* (Case 16/84) [1985] ECR 2355. With reference to art 32, he stated (at 2357) as follows: 'That provision allows, on a transitional basis *pending complete harmonization in the sphere of VAT*, derogation from the common system established by the Sixth Directive . . .' (emphasis added).

14. I do not think that this conclusion may be challenged, as the Commission seeks to do, on the basis of the judgment of the court of 28 March 1984 in
e *Pluimveeslachterij Midden-Nederland BV and Pluimveeslachterij C van Miert BV* (Joined cases 47/83 and 48/83) [1984] ECR 1721 and the judgment of 5 May 1981 in *EC Commission v United Kingdom* (Case 804/79) [1981] ECR 1045. According to the Commission it is clear from those judgments that in principle, where the Council has failed to act, there can be no objection to a member state's retaining or introducing, pursuant to the duty to co-operate imposed by art 5 of the EEC Treaty,
f national measures designed to attain the objectives to be achieved by Community rules.

15. The Commission's argument does not bear critical examination. It is clear that the ratio decidendi of the aforesaid judgments is totally different from that put forward by the Commission. The tenor of the judgments does not raise the slightest doubt: they merely recognise that the member states have a *power*, where the
g Council has failed to act, to 'retain or introduce' national rules. There is an enormous difference between recognising that there is a *power* and alleging the existence of an *obligation*, which not even the court's reference to the fulfilment of an obligation to co-operate under art 5 of the EEC Treaty can bridge. The argument based on art 5, which reappears in the aforesaid judgment in *EC Commission v United Kingdom* (Case 804/79) performs a function that is wholly different from the one which the
h Commission seeks to attribute to it. In other words, the court did not state that, because there is an obligation to co-operate under art 5, the member states are *bound* to remedy the failure on the part of the Community legislature. Instead it had recourse to the argument based on art 5 with a view to limiting the power of member states to legislate in a sector governed by a common organisation of the market. It clearly states, in its judgment in *Pluimveeslachterij Midden-Nederland BV and*
j *Pluimveeslachterij C van Miert BV* (Joined cases 47/83 and 48/83) [1984] ECR 1721 at 1738 as follows: 'However, . . . such measures must not be regarded as involving the exercise of the Member State's own powers'.

Lastly, it is clear from the remainder of the judgment (see [1984] ECR 1721 at 1739) that it is always a matter of a 'power' ('provisions adopted or maintained by Member States in the circumstances described above are permissible') and not of an obligation imposed on member states. Finally I would state, so far as is necessary, that it is clear from the opinion of the Advocate General (Mrs Rozès) that we are concerned here with a 'substitutive' power of the member states (see in particular [1984] ECR 1721 at 1745) and not an obligation to adopt legislation in place of the Council in the event of its failure to act. That would, moreover, raise another problem which I would prefer merely to mention without considering it in detail, as to the purpose of the action for failure to act under art 175 of the EEC Treaty if it were accepted that the Council's inaction gave rise to an obligation to act on the part of the member states.

16. For the sake of completeness I would mention, even though the Commission has not used such an argument, that an obligation on the part of the member states in the event of the Council's failure to act cannot be inferred either from the fact that the Commission has repeatedly submitted proposals for directives in order to implement the first paragraph of art 32. In its judgment of 16 December 1981 in *R v Tymen* (Case 269/80) [1981] ECR 3079 at 3092, the court clearly stated that:

> 'It is to be remarked in this connection that a proposal submitted by the Commission to the Council with a view to taking concerted Community action cannot be considered as constituting in itself approval of a unilateral national measure, even of one having the same content, which is adopted in a sphere coming within the powers of the Community. To accept the reasoning of the British Government would amount to recognizing the lawfulness of national measures adopted in a sphere within which the powers of the Community apply solely by reason of the existence of a Community proposal which is identical in principle. That would not only be contrary to legal certainty but would lead to a distortion of the division of powers between the Community and the Member States and would thus adversely affect the essential balances established by the Treaty.'

17. Since the first question has been answered in the negative, it is unnecessary to reply to the second question.

18. In conclusion, I proposed that the court should rule, in reply to the question submitted by the national court, that in the present state of Community law the fact that a member state imposes turnover tax on the sale of secondhand goods without providing for any reduction and without taking account of the fact that these goods were purchased from private persons is not incompatible with the Sixth Directive and in particular with art 32 thereof.

5 December 1989. **THE COURT OF JUSTICE** delivered the following judgment.

1. By order of 24 May 1988, which was received at the court on 13 June 1988, the Gerechtshof (Regional Court of Appeal), Amsterdam, referred to the court for a preliminary ruling under art 177 of the EEC Treaty two questions on the interpretation of the provisions of the EEC Treaty and of EC Council Directive 77/388 (the Sixth Directive) in order to enable it to assess the compatibility with Community law of Netherlands tax legislation is so far as the latter does not provide special rules for the application of the system of value added tax to trade in secondhand goods which have been purchased from individuals with a view to their resale.

2. The questions were raised in the course of proceedings between two companies, ORO Amsterdam Beheer BV and Concerto BV (the taxpayer companies), and the Netherlands tax authorities concerning the value added tax payable on transactions carried out in December 1986.

3. It appears from the documents before the court that in December 1986 the taxpayer companies, which run a business retailing new and secondhand gramophone records, music cassettes and compact discs, made sales totalling 256,698 guilders net of tax, of which 250,915 guilders was subject to value added tax at the rate of 20%.

After deducting the input tax, the taxpayer companies paid the tax authorities value added tax amounting to 37,608 guilders.

4. On 5 March 1987, however, the taxpayer companies lodged an appeal with the Gerechtshof, Amsterdam, seeking the reimbursement of 6,251 guilders of the tax paid, on the ground that they should be allowed to deduct from the tax payable in respect of sales for December 1986 the amount of value added tax that was still contained in the price of secondhand articles purchased by them from individuals. Calculating this amount at a flat rate of 20/120ths of the total sum of their purchases of secondhand goods in December 1986, which was 37,509 guilders, the taxpayer companies claimed reimbursement of 6,251 guilders.

5. The Gerechtshof, Amsterdam, found that no provision of Netherlands tax legislation allowed the deduction of input tax paid on secondhand goods purchased by a taxable person from a non-taxable person. It noted that it was clear from the value added tax directives and the judgments of the court that one of the fundamental characteristics of the value added tax system was that at each marketing stage the input tax paid on goods was deductible from the tax payable and it therefore stayed the proceedings and referred to the court the following two questions:

'1. Is it in conformity with Community law, and in particular with the provisions of [the EEC Treaty] and of [the Sixth Directive], for a Member State to have charged, in December 1986, turnover tax at the full rate on the supply of second-hand goods without taking any account whatsoever of the fact that those goods were bought from individuals, in view of the fact that in the Sixth Directive the Council of the European Communities committed itself to, and gave notice of, the adoption before 31 December 1977 of a Community taxation system applicable to trade in second-hand goods but has so far taken no action in that regard?

2. If the first question is answered in the negative, how is account to be taken, in the determination of the turnover tax payable on the supply of second-hand goods, of the fact that the goods were bought from individuals?'

6. Reference is made to the report for the hearing for a fuller account of the facts of the case, the relevant Community rules, the course of the procedure and the observations submitted to the court, which are mentioned or discussed hereinafter only in so far as is necessary for the reasoning of the court.

7. By its first question, the Gerechtshof, Amsterdam, seeks to ascertain essentially whether Community law and, in particular the Sixth Directive, preclude national tax legislation which, for the purpose of calculating the value added tax payable on the turnover arising from the sale of secondhand goods, does not allow account to be taken of the tax still contained in the price of goods which have been purchased from non-taxable individuals with a view to their resale.

8. As it stands at present, Community law has no special value added tax rules for secondhand goods. In its Proposal for a sixth Council Directive, submitted to the Council on 29 June 1973 (see (1973) OJ C80, p 1), the Commission had provided, in art 26, for a 'special scheme for second-hand goods', which were defined in para (1) (see (1973) OJ C80, p 17) as follows:

'"Second-hand goods" means used moveable property which can be re-used as it is or after repair, excluding original works of art created by the hand of the artist, antiques, collectors' items, and stamps and coins being collectors' items.'

9. This 'special scheme' provided that, where secondhand goods were acquired from a non-taxable person by a taxable person with a view to their resale, the latter could take account of the value added tax borne by the goods in question and laid down detailed rules for the calculation of the deduction to which the taxable person acquiring the goods was thus entitled.

10. Since no decision could be reached on the basis of the Commission's proposals, the Council adopted a transitional measure in the form of art 32 of the Sixth Directive, which provides as follows:

'The Council, acting unanimously on a proposal from the Commission, shall adopt before 31 December 1977 a Community taxation system to be applied to *a* used goods, works of art, antiques and collectors' items.

Until this Community system becomes applicable, Member States applying a special system to these items at the time this Directive comes into force may retain that system.'

11. On 11 January 1978, the Commission submitted to the Council, pursuant to *b* the first paragraph of that provision, a Proposal for a seventh Council Directive laying down the 'common system of value added tax to be applied to works of art, collectors' items, antiques and used goods' (see (1978) OJ C26, p 2), which was subsequently amended (amendments submitted to the Council on 16 May 1979, see (1979) OJ C136, p 8). Since the Council was unable to reach a decision, this proposal was withdrawn by the Commission in November 1987. A fresh proposal was *c* submitted to the Council on 11 January 1989 (see (1989) OJ C76, p 10) but has not yet been adopted.

12. The taxpayer companies and the Commission contend first that it is clear from the judgments of the court of 5 May 1982 in *Schul (Gaston) Douane Expediteur BV v Inspecteur der Invoerrechten en Accijnzen* (Case 15/81) [1982] ECR 1409 and of 21 May 1985 in *Staatssecretaris van Financiën v Schul (Gaston) Douane-Expediteur* *d* *BV* (Case 47/84) [1985] ECR 1491) that there is a general principle prohibiting double taxation, so that national measures designed to avoid it, in particular in the case of secondhand goods, are valid (see the judgments of 10 July 1985 in *EC Commission v Kingdom of the Netherlands* (Case 16/84) [1985] ECR 2355, and in *EC Commission v Ireland* (Case 17/84) [1985] ECR 2375).

13. The second contention is that if the Council fails to act the member states are *e* entitled, in accordance with the judgments of 5 May 1981 in *EC Commission v United Kingdom* (Case 804/79) [1981] ECR 1045 and of 28 March 1984 in *Pluimveeslachterij Midden-Nederland BV and Pluimveeslachterij C van Miert BV* (Joined cases 47/83 and 48/83) [1984] ECR 1721, to maintain or adopt measures designed to achieve the Community objectives. Although the Council has exclusive *f* power to adopt tax harmonisation measures, the member states themselves are, in their view, obliged, in view of the Council's failure, to take action with regard to the rules on the taxation of secondhand goods in order to ensure that the fundamental principle prohibiting double taxation is observed. That obligation to act is made necessary by the development of Community law in the field of value added tax.

14. The Netherlands government, however, observes that art 32 of the Sixth Directive contains a 'standstill' clause which prohibits the member states from *g* amending or extending the existing special provisions for secondhand goods, in order to prevent additional disparities in national legislation. There is nothing in art 32 to suggest that the member states are obliged to act in order to introduce a special scheme for secondhand goods.

15. Before replying to the question whether the member states are entitled or *h* obliged to act as a result of the Council's failure to lay down a Community system of taxation to be applied to used goods, as provided for in the first paragraph of art 32 of the Sixth Directive, it is necessary to point out that the court has held that if the Council fails to adopt measures falling within the exclusive competence of the European Communities, there can be no fundamental objection in certain cases to member states' maintaining or introducing, pursuant to the duty to co-operate imposed on them by art 5 of the EEC Treaty, national measures designed to achieve *j* Community objectives. However, no general principle requiring the member states to act in the place of the Council whenever it fails to adopt measures falling within its province can be inferred from those judgments.

16. The essential point, however, is that under the system to which the national court refers, if an individual sells goods to a taxable trader, no value added tax is

a
charged on that supply, but on their resale by the taxable person an amount of value added tax proportionate to the resale price is payable and the taxable person may not deduct the value added tax already borne by the goods.

17. The question is thus whether the fact that national legislation does not provide for a special scheme of value added tax for secondhand goods whereby such double taxation may be avoided is contrary to the EEC Treaty and to the Sixth Directive. The question also arises where national legislation contains provisions which,
b because they relate to special arrangements for taxing certain transactions in secondhand goods, are fragmentary and cannot be regarded as a complete system of value added tax rules applicable to used goods. A comprehensive and positive reply to that question cannot be given on the basis of the judgments of the court alone.

18. First, it should be noted that, although in its judgments of 5 May 1982 and 21 May 1985 in the two *Schul* cases, to which reference is made by the taxpayer
c companies and by the Commission, the court held that the imposition of value added tax on the importation of goods supplied by a private person from another member state, where no value added tax was levied on a transaction of the same type within the territory of the state of importation, was incompatible with Community law, those rulings were not based on a general principle prohibiting tax cumulation but on art 95 of the EEC Treaty, which prohibits internal taxation which discriminates
d against imported goods.

19. For the purposes of the application of art 6(2)(a) of the Sixth Directive, which provides that the private use by the taxable person or by his staff of goods forming part of the assets of his business, where the value added tax on such goods is deductible, is to be taxed as a supply of services, the court has indeed ruled that such a charge to tax was precluded in the case of goods which were purchased second-
e hand and which did not therefore give rise to a right of deduction (see the judgment of 27 June 1989 in *Kühne v Finanzamt München III* (Case 50/88) [1990] STC 749, [1989] ECR 1925).

20. However, that ruling is based on the actual terms of art 6(2)(a), the aim of which is to prevent a situation wherein goods belonging to a business might eventually be used free of value added tax through private use and which therefore
f requires the use of those goods to be taxed only if the value added tax paid on the acquisition of the goods is deductible.

21. On the whole the Community system of value added tax is the result of a gradual harmonisation of national legislation pursuant to arts 99 and 100 of the EEC Treaty. The court has consistently held that this harmonisation, as brought about by successive directives and in particular by the Sixth Directive, is still only partial.

g 22. The harmonisation is designed in particular to preclude double taxation, so that the deduction of input tax at each stage of taxation is an integral part of the system of value added tax.

23. That objective has not yet been achieved, however, as is clear from art 32 of the Sixth Directive, and nowhere in the common system of value added tax, as it stands at present, are to be found the necessary bases for determining and laying
h down detailed rules for applying a common system of taxation enabling double taxation to be avoided in trade in secondhand goods.

24. Until the Community legislature has taken action, it is therefore necessary to continue to apply art 32 of the Sixth Directive, which merely authorises member states that apply a special system of value added tax to secondhand goods to retain that system but does not impose on them any obligation to introduce such a system
j if none exists.

25. The answer to the first question should therefore be that Community law and the Community rules governing value added tax do not, as they now stand, preclude national legislation which, for the purpose of calculating the value added tax payable on the turnover arising from the sale of secondhand goods, does not allow account to be taken of the tax still contained in the price of goods which have been purchased from non-taxable individuals with a view to their resale.

26. In the light of the reply to the first question, it is unnecessary to reply to the second question asked by the Gerechtshof, Amsterdam.　　　　　　　*a*

Costs

27. The costs incurred by the Netherlands government and the Commission of the European Communities, which have submitted observations to the court, are not recoverable. Since these proceedings are, in so far as the parties to the main action are concerned, in the nature of a step in the action pending before the national *b* court, the decision on costs is a matter for that court.

On those grounds, the court, in answer to the questions referred to it by the Gerechtshof, Amsterdam, by order of 24 May 1988, hereby rules:

> Community law and the Community rules governing value added tax do not, as they now stand, preclude national legislation which, for the purpose of calculating the value added tax payable on the turnover arising from the sale of *c* secondhand goods, does not allow account to be taken of the tax still contained in the price of goods which have been purchased from non-taxable individuals with a view to their resale.

Agents: *W Molenaar* and *G Molenaar* (for the taxpayer companies) *E F Jacobs* and *M A Fiersta* (for the government of the Netherlands); *J F Buhl* and *B J Drijber* (for *d* the Commission).

Rengan Krishnan Esq　　Barrister.

a # Staatssecretaris van Financiën v Shipping and Forwarding Enterprise Safe BV
(Case C-320/88)

COURT OF JUSTICE OF THE EUROPEAN COMMUNITIES (SIXTH CHAMBER)
b JUDGES KAKOURIS (PRESIDENT OF THE CHAMBER), KOOPMANS, MANCINI, O'HIGGINS
AND DIEZ DE VELASCO
ADVOCATE GENERAL W VAN GERVEN
12 OCTOBER, 9 NOVEMBER 1989, 8 FEBRUARY 1990

Value added tax – European Communities – Supply of goods or services – Supply –
c *Meaning – Whether supply of goods where legal ownership only transferred – Conditions*
under which transfer of economic ownership supply of goods – EC Directive 77/388,
art 5(1).

The Netherlands tax entity Shipping and Forwarding Enterprise Safe BV (Safe)
d sold the rights to a detached house with land to Kats Bouwgroep NV (Kats) for
2,250,000 Netherlands guilders. The contract of sale, dated 19 June 1979, included
the following provisions: Safe undertook to transfer to Kats an unconditional right
to the property; any changes in value of the property and all profits and outgoings
were for the benefit or at the expense of Kats; Kats acquired the right to dispose of
the property; Safe undertook to transfer legal title to the property when required by
e Kats, granting Kats an irrevocable power of attorney to execute the transfer. In
1980, Kats had the house demolished and the property converted to building land.
In 1982, before legal ownership was transferred, Kats went bankrupt. In 1983, the
trustees in bankruptcy of Kats sold all Kats's rights in respect of the property to
Abreka BV (Abreka), and at the same time, Safe transferred legal ownership of the
property to Abreka.
f   Following the transfer of legal ownership to Abreka, Safe received a retrospective
assessment to value added tax on the payment of 2,250,000 guilders in 1979. The
assessment was issued on the ground that that payment should be regarded as
payment in advance for a supply of a building site in 1983, when the legal transfer of
the property took place. Under the Wet op de Omzetbelasting 1968 (Netherlands
Law on Turnover Tax), the supply of a building previously used was exempt from
g value added tax, whereas the supply of a site prepared for building was subject to
value added tax.
       The assessment was annulled by the Gerechtshof (Court of Appeal), but on appeal
by the Staatssecretaris van Financiën (Finance Secretary), the Hoge Raad (Supreme
Court) requested that the Court of Justice give a preliminary ruling on the following
questions: (1) whether art 5(1) of EC Council Directive 77/388 (the Sixth Directive)
h had to be interpreted as meaning that a supply of goods took place only where legal
ownership of the property was transferred; and (2) whether a supply of goods also
took place where their legal owner entered into an agreement with another party
such as that in the instant case.

j   **Held** – (1) It was clear both from the wording of art 5(1) of the Sixth Directive and
from the directive's objective of the establishment of a uniform definition of taxable
transactions that 'supply of goods' did not refer to legal transfers of ownership under
procedures prescribed by applicable national laws, but to any transfers to a party
which had the effect of giving that party the power to dispose of property as if he
were its owner. Accordingly, the answer to the first question was that 'supply of
goods' in art 5(1) had to be interpreted as meaning the transfer of the right to dispose

of tangible property as owner, even if there was no transfer of legal ownership of the property.

a

(2) The second question concerned specific conditions in an individual case. Under art 177 of the EEC Treaty, the national courts had to apply the rules of Community law as interpreted by the Court of Justice to individual cases. Accordingly, the answer to the second question was that it was for the national courts to determine in each individual case, on the basis of the facts of the case, whether there was a transfer of the right to dispose of the property as owner within the meaning of art 5(1) of the Sixth Directive.

b

Notes

For the meaning of supply, see De Voil: Value Added Tax A5.02.
For EC Council Directive 77/388, art 5(1), see ibid, Division E3.

c

Case cited

Verbond van Nederlandse Ondernemingen v Inspecteur der Invoerrechten en Accijnzen (Case 51/76) [1977] ECR 113, CJEC.

d

Reference

By an order of 19 October 1988, the Hoge Raad der Nederlanden (Supreme Court of the Netherlands) referred a question raised in proceedings between the Netherlands Staatssecretaris van Financiën (Finance Secretary) and the tax entity Shipping and Forwarding Enterprise Safe BV to the Court of Justice of the European Communities for a preliminary ruling under art 177 of the EEC Treaty. The Netherlands government and the Commission of the European Communities made submissions (in the written procedure) to the court. The language of the case was Dutch. The facts are set out in the report for the hearing.

e

The Judge Rapporteur (G F Mancini) presented the following report for the hearing.

f

I Facts of the case

A National and Community legislation

1. The Wet op de Omzetbelasting 1968 (Netherlands Law on Turnover Tax) (the Law) provides that the concept of the supply of property (whether movable or immovable) covers, inter alia: the transfer of ownership of the property pursuant to a contract (see art 3(1)(*a*)); and the transfer (overdracht en overgang) of property under which that property leaves the business assets of an undertaking (see art 3(1)(*e*)). According to art 3(3) of the Law:

g

> 'Where agreements are entered into by more than one person entailing the obligation to supply the same item of property, and that item of property is then delivered directly by the first person to the final recipient, the item is considered to have been supplied by each of those persons.'

h

2. The basic rule for the taxing of transfers of immovable property is that the supply of pre-existing immovable property is exempted but that the supply of new immovable property is subject to the tax. Thus, by virtue of art 11 of the Law, the supply of a building previously used or of land which is not built on, and the registration and assignment of rights in rem over immovable property are exempted from value added tax, whereas the supply of a site prepared for building, the supply of immovable property within two years of its original occupation, and the handing-over of certain works of construction are subject to value added tax.

j

The Law was amended in 1979. The amendments were designed to bring the
a Netherlands legislation on turnover tax into line with EC Council Directive 77/388
of 17 May 1977 on the harmonisation of the laws of the member states relating to
turnover taxes—common system of value added tax: uniform basis of assessment
(the Sixth Directive).

3. Under art 5(1) of the Sixth Directive: '"Supply of goods" shall mean the transfer
of the right to dispose of tangible property as owner.'

b
B Background to the main proceedings

4. By a notarial act of 19 June 1979, entitled 'Economic transfer', a taxable entity
known as Shipping and Forwarding Enterprise Safe BV (SAFE Rekencentrum BV)
(Safe), whose registered office is at Hillegom, Netherlands, sold to Kats Bouwgroep
NV (Kats), whose registered office is at Leeuwarden, Netherlands, immovable
c property consisting of a detached house with outbuildings for 2,250,000 Netherlands
guilders. The contract of sale between Safe and Kats included the following
conditions:

'1. The vendor undertakes to transfer to the purchaser a right of ownership
which (subject to the creation of one or more mortgages in the property at the
request of the purchaser or the registration of mortgages on its behalf)
d
(a) is unconditional and not subject to revocation, repurchase, rescission or
annulment in any way;
(b) is not encumbered by mortgage, attachment or other rights *in rem*;
(c) is not encumbered by the registration of mortgages or attachment orders,
etc. . . .

e
5. The purchaser is entitled to all profits and liable for all outgoings in respect
of the property with effect from today.

6. With effect from today the property is entirely at the risk of the purchaser.

7. The purchaser is liable for all notarial costs in respect of this agreement of
purchase and sale and of the legal and actual transfer of the property; the
purchaser is also liable for any transfer tax payable on the legal transfer of the
f property . . .

D. Inasmuch as the legal transfer of the property is to take place as soon as the
purchaser so wishes, but in any event not later than 31 December 1982, the
vendor and the purchaser further agree that:

1. The vendor undertakes to transfer the property to the purchaser on the
g latter's demand.

2. The legal transfer of the property shall take place under the conditions
and at the time or times determined by the purchaser, having regard to what is
agreed by the present act.

3. With effect from today the purchaser shall have the use of the property for
its own benefit and at its own risk. With effect from today, and subject to
h observance of what is agreed in this act between the vendor and the purchaser
the purchaser is entitled to engage in any and all (legal) dealings with regard to
the property. With effect from today, the vendor shall refrain from any (legal)
dealings with regard to the property, save on request of the purchaser.

E. The party of the first part (Safe) hereby grants the purchaser (Kats) an
j irrevocable power of attorney, with right of substitution, for or on behalf of the
vendor:

1. To transfer the property, as referred to above in Part D.

2. To execute a mortgage over the property or such part thereof as the
purchaser may wish, even for the benefit of the purchaser itself, in such amounts
as the purchaser may wish and under such conditions as it may see fit.

3. In general, to comply with the obligations undertaken by the vendor
towards the purchaser.

The above-mentioned power of attorney is granted exclusively in the interest
of the purchaser and constitutes an integral part of this agreement of purchase
and sale, which would not have been entered into without that power of attorney
and if it were not irrevocable; the power of attorney shall have effect as against
third parties, so that its revocation shall have no legal effect whatsoever.'

5. In 1980 Kats had the house and outbuildings demolished, and it prepared the
site for development. On 11 August 1983 the trustees in bankruptcy of Kats entered
into a notarial contract with Abreka BV of Amsterdam, under which they assigned
to Abreka for the sum of 425,000 guilders, plus the turnover tax of 76,500 guilders
due on the transaction, all the rights which Kats had acquired under the 1979
agreement with Safe entitled 'Economic Conveyance'. In accordance with its
undertakings, Safe transferred legal ownership of the immovable property to Abreka
direct, on 11 August 1983.

6. Safe incurred a retrospective assessment for value added tax for the year 1979.
According to the inspector of finances, the notice of retrospective assessment
concerns the supply, within the meaning of art 3(3) of the Law, from Safe to Kats
on 11 August 1983, when the legal transfer of the property took place. The inspector
maintains that the payment of 2,250,000 guilders in 1979 was merely payment in
advance.

Safe lodged an administrative appeal with the inspector of finances against the
notice of retrospective assessment, but the inspector rejected the appeal. Safe
brought an action against the rejection before the Gerechtshof (Court of Appeal),
The Hague, which annulled the inspector's decision and the notice of retrospective
assessment. The Staatssecretaris van Financiën (Finance Secretary) lodged an
appeal in cassation against that judgment.

C Questions submitted for a preliminary ruling

7. The Hoge Raad der Nederlanden (Supreme Court of the Netherlands) took
the view that the dispute raised questions as to the interpretation of a provision of
Community law and accordingly, by judgment of 19 October 1988, stayed the
proceedings and requested the Court of Justice under art 177 of the EEC Treaty to
give a preliminary ruling on the following questions:

'1. Must Article 5(1) of the Sixth Directive be interpreted as meaning that a
supply of goods takes place only where legal ownership of the property is
transferred?

2. If not, does a supply of goods also take place where their legal owner: has
entered into an agreement with another party under which any changes in the
value of the property and all profits or outgoings are for the benefit or at the
expense of that other party; has agreed to transfer legal ownership of the
property to the other party at any future time; has agreed to grant the other
party an irrevocable power of attorney to carry out any transactions necessary
to execute that transfer of legal ownership; has, pursuant to that agreement,
actually placed the property at the disposal of the other party?'

8. The Hoge Raad is of the opinion that, if art 5(1) of the Sixth Directive relates
to certain forms of transfer of immovable property other than the transfer of legal
ownership, it follows that, in view of the concordance in meaning between the term
'supply' used in the Law and the same term as it appears in the Sixth Directive,
art 3(1) of the Law also covers those other forms of transfer. The Hoge Raad adds
that, pursuant to the first paragraph of art 671 of the Netherlands Burgerlijk
Wetboek (Civil Code), the legal ownership of immovable property is tranferred by
entry of the act in question in the relevant official registers; until such entry has been
made, the legal ownership of immovable property remains vested in the person who

was the owner until then, even if he has transferred economic ownership to another

a person.

Consequently, the Hoge Raad takes the view that the question is whether only the transfer of the legal ownership of property may be described as a 'supply of goods' within the meaning of art 5(1) of the Sixth Directive, or whether such a supply can be said to have taken place in all cases or in some cases where only the economic ownership of the property is transferred.

b

II Procedure

9. The judgment making the reference was lodged at the court registry on 3 November 1988.

10. In accordance with art 20 of the Protocol on the Statute of the Court of Justice, written observations were submitted by: the government of the Kingdom

c of the Netherlands, represented by the Ministry for Foreign Affairs; the Commission of the European Communities, represented by J Fons Buhl, Legal Adviser and B Jan Drijber, a member of its Legal Department, acting as agents.

11. On hearing the report of the Judge Rapporteur and the views of the Advocate General the court decided to open the oral procedure without any preparatory inquiry.

d 12. By decision of 7 July 1989 the court, pursuant to art 95(1) and (2) of the Rules of Procedure, assigned the case to the Sixth Chamber.

III Summary of the written observations submitted to the court

A First question

e 13. The Netherlands government notes that the term 'supply of goods' under art 5(1) of the Sixth Directive is not further defined therein. It is therefore natural that member states should refer to their own civil law to determine the scope of the term. The conveyance of the legal ownership of tangible property, as defined under the civil law of the member state concerned, must be described as the 'supply of goods'. By virtue of the first paragraph of art 671 of the Civil Code, legal ownership

f of immovable property is not transferred until the relevant deed has been entered in the official registers. Nevertheless, that civil law approach does not in itself signify that the answer to the first question submitted by the Hoge Raad must be in the affirmative. The Netherlands government maintains that account must be taken of the aim of the Sixth Directive, namely to ensure the neutrality of the Community system of turnover taxes. Accordingly, transactions which from an economic

g viewpoint are to be equated with the transfer of legal ownership should be classified under the heading 'supply of goods'. The principle applies to an act whereby the de facto power of disposal over property is transferred to a third party who thereby secures all the economic interests connected with the property. In such a case that third party holds the property as if he were the owner of it.

14. Such an interpretation of the term 'supply of goods' is borne out by the other

h provisions of art 5 of the Sixth Directive, under which transactions whereby the third party is vested with a less extensive power of disposal than would be the case with the transfer of economic ownership are regarded as a 'supply of goods'. The Netherlands government concludes that art 5(1) of the Sixth Directive covers the transfer of the economic as well as the legal ownership of property.

15. Where the parties agree to transfer the legal and economic ownership at the

j same time, it is the legal ownership which constitutes the 'supply of goods'. The transfer of economic ownership has no significance in itself for the purposes of the levy of value added tax. If the parties agree on the transfer of economic ownership alone, that transfer constitutes the 'supply of goods'. The subsequent transfer of legal ownership has no implications for the application of value added tax.

16. Lastly, the Netherlands government observes that the wording of art 5(1) of the Sixth Directive, and in particular the phrase 'dispose of tangible property *as*

owner [emphasis added]', suggests that art 5 also refers to transfers of economic ownership.

17. In conclusion, the Netherlands government proposes that the court should give a negative answer to the first question referred to it.

18. The Commission also proposes that the first question be answered in the negative.

19. The Commission puts forward the same textual argument as was submitted by the Netherlands government.

20. According to the Commission a Community definition should be given to terms used in directives, in order to ensure the uniform application of the harmonised system of turnover tax. For that reason, 'supply of goods' cannot be defined by reference to the manner in which the transfer of legal ownership is regulated by the national provisions of the member states.

21. The Commission further submits that the framers of the value added tax directives opted for an economic conception of the term 'supply of goods', so as to include any transaction which for commercial purposes may be treated as equivalent to a transfer of legal ownership. 'Supply of goods' is not confined to the acquisition of the power to dispose of property as the legal owner.

22. The Commission proposes that the court should give the following answer to the Hoge Raad's first question: 'Article 5(1) of the Sixth Directive is not confined to the transfer of the legal ownership of goods.'

B Second question

23. The Netherlands government takes the view that a transfer of economic ownership as defined in the second question may constitute a supply for the purposes of art 5(1) of the Sixth Directive. Nevertheless, the fact that the holder of the legal title has undertaken to transfer it at a future date supports the view that, in this case, the transfer of the legal ownership prevails.

24. The question which of the two transfers is to be regarded as the 'supply' for the purpose of art 5(1) of the Sixth Directive must be resolved on a case-by-case basis, having regard to the situation when the economic ownership is transferred. If the interval between that transfer and the transfer of legal ownership is long or of indeterminate duration, it will be the transfer of economic ownership that constitutes the 'supply of goods'.

25. The government of the Netherlands concludes that the second question must be answered in the negative because in the circumstances of the case before the national court it is the transfer of the legal, rather than the economic ownership which is decisive.

26. The Commission takes the view that the transfer of economic ownership falls within the concept of the 'supply of goods'. Such a transfer covers the right to dispose of the property, which includes the power to manage, alter or mortgage the property and the assumption of the risk of any change in value.

27. The Commission contends that a broad interpretation of the term 'supply of goods' is corroborated by the fact that art 5(3) and (4) of the Sixth Directive treat a number of legally distinct but economically similar transactions as a 'supply of goods'. Considerations of neutrality demand that transactions equivalent to the supply of goods be subject to value added tax in the same way as the transfer of legal ownership.

28. The Commission maintains that this broad conception of the term 'supply of goods' is not affected if, on the transfer of economic ownership, the parties make arrangements for the transfer of the legal ownership of the property. For reasons of legal certainty it is justifiable that the liability to tax of a transfer of economic ownership should not be dependent on arbitrary factors such as the content of the agreement or the manner in which the relevant legal system regulates the transfer of legal ownership.

29. The Commission concludes that it is for the national courts to consider, in the
a light of the specific features of any given agreement, whether the right to dispose of
property as owner has been transferred.

30. It proposes that the court should give the following answer to the Hoge Raad's
second question:

'It is for the national courts to determine in each case on the basis of the facts
before them, whether the transferee has obtained the right to dispose of the
b property as the owner.'

9 November 1989. **The Advocate General (W Van Gerven)** delivered the
following opinion.

Mr President, members of the court,
c   1. The Hoge Raad der Nederlanden (Supreme Court of the Netherlands) has
referred to the court for a preliminary ruling on two questions on the interpretation
of art 5(1) of EC Council Directive 77/388 (the Sixth Directive). Article 5(1) provides
as follows: '"Supply of goods" shall mean the transfer of the right to dispose of
tangible property as owner.'

d   *Summary of the facts in the main proceedings*
2. The questions were raised in an action arising from dealings in real property in
which three undertakings were involved: Shipping and Forwarding Enterprise Safe
BV (Safe), Kats Bouwgroep NV (Kats) and Abreka BV (Abreka). By a notarial act
of 19 June 1979 entitled 'Economic transfer', Safe sold to Kats the rights to a detached
house with land attached for a purchase price of 2,250,000 Netherlands guilders,
e excluding value added tax.

The important provisions of that agreement seem to me to be the following: Safe
undertakes to transfer to Kats an unconditional right of ownership; as from the date
of the agreement Kats is entitled to all profits and liable for all outgoings in respect
of the property; as from the date of the agreement the property is entirely at the risk
of Kats; Safe undertakes to transfer legal ownership of the property as soon as Kats
f so wishes and by 31 December 1982 at the latest; as from the date of the agreement
Kats has the use of the property for its own benefit and at its own risk; from that
date Kats is also entitled to engage in all (legal) dealings with regard to the property;
for its part Safe undertakes to refrain from any (legal) dealings with regard to the
property; Safe grants Kats an irrevocable power of attorney to execute the transfer
of legal ownership.

g   3. In 1980 the house was demolished on the orders of Kats and the property was
turned into building land. In 1982, before legal ownership was transferred, Kats
went bankrupt. By a notarial act dated 11 August 1983, the trustees in bankruptcy
of Kats sold to Abreka all Kats's rights in respect of the property. The purchase price
was 425,000 guilders, plus turnover tax of 76,500 guilders on the transaction. At the
same time legal ownership of the property was transferred by Safe to Abreka.
h   4. In 1984 the Inspecteur der Invoerrechten en Accijnzen (Inspector of Customs
and Excise), Leiden, imposed on Safe a retroactive assessment to turnover tax of
343,125 guilders on the ground that the payment of 2,250,000 guilders by Kats to
Safe in 1979 should be regarded as payment in advance for a supply liable to value
added tax. Safe appealed against that assessment. The Gerechtshof (Court of
Appeal), The Hague, annulled the retroactive assessment. The Staatssecretaris van
j Financiën (Finance Secretary) appealed against that judgment. In the course of that
appeal the Hoge Raad requested the court to give a ruling on the following questions:

'1 Must Article 5(1) of the Sixth Directive be interpreted as meaning that a
supply of goods takes place only where legal ownership of the property is
transferred?

2. If not, does a supply of goods also take place where their legal owner: has entered into an agreement with another party under which any changes in the value of the property and all profits or outgoings are for the benefit or at the expense of that other party; has agreed to transfer legal ownership of the property to the other party at any future time; has agreed to grant the other party an irrevocable power of attorney to carry out any transactions necessary to execute that transfer of legal ownership; has, pursuant to that agreement, actually placed the property at the disposal of the other party?'

5. So that the preliminary questions may be properly understood, it seems to me to be useful to give a brief explanation of the concept of 'economic ownership' under Netherlands law, to outline the framework in which this concept is applied according to Netherlands practice and to summarise the judgments of Netherlands courts on the consequences which the concept may have as regards the application of the Netherlands Wet op de Omzetbelasting 1968 (Law on Turnover Tax) (the Law).

The Netherlands legislation, case law and practice

6. 'Economic ownership' is a concept which has been developed by Netherlands courts in judgments in tax cases. In a judgment of 19 October 1955 (see *Beslissingen Nederlandse Belastingsrechtspraak 1955*, p 377), the Hoge Raad expressly mentioned the term for the first time:

'The fact that a person is the owner of and as such objectively entitled to property does not prevent another person from being entitled to the economic benefit thereof, while such benefit—which might be called the economic ownership—may form part of the other person's assets.'

In the many commentaries on this and subsequent judgments, many definitions of the concept of 'economic ownership' may be found. They all stress that the benefit accrues to a person other than the owner as defined in civil law, which essentially presupposes two characteristics: any changes in the value of the property and all profits and outgoings are for the benefit of or at the expense of the other person; and the other person also has effective power to dispose of the property.

7. In the case of movable property the transfer of 'economic ownership' normally coincides with the transfer of ownership under civil law, at least under Netherlands law (unlike French law, for example, where for special cases the principle of consensus applies), at the time of the supply. For immovable property the situation is different. Under art 671 of the Netherlands Burgerlijk Wetboek (Civil Code), the transfer of legal ownership of immovable property does not take place, so far as the parties and third parties are concerned, until the notarial act of transfer has been entered in the appropriate registers. The transfer of 'economic ownership' of immovable property takes place, when it is separate from the transfer of 'legal ownership', at the moment when the property is actually placed at the disposal of the other party.

8. In the Netherlands, in the immovable property sector in particular, the transfer of economic ownership—the legality of which has been recognised by the Hoge Raad, as stated above—has been found to be a device for saving *transfer* tax. Article 2 of the Wet op Belastingen van Rechtsverkeer (Law of Taxation of Legal Transactions) provides in particular that transfer tax is imposed on the acquisition of immovable property situated within the Netherlands. The courts have consistently held that the term 'acquisition' means the transfer of ownership under civil law. If immovable property which is not exempt from transfer tax is purchased with the intention of selling it on to a third party, it is under those circumstances in the interests of the parties to transfer solely economic ownership to the original purchaser and to ensure that legal ownership may be transferred directly from the original seller to the final purchaser. Transfer tax is then payable only once.

9. In practice the circumstances are usually more complicated. Thus on the
a transfer of immovable property, account must be taken of the interaction between
transfer tax and *turnover* tax. Although it cannot be 'consumed', immovable property
does not by its nature fall outside the scope of turnover tax but does pose particular
problems. In this regard the Netherlands legislation is based on the premise that
overlapping of the two taxes should be avoided as far as possible. Thus art 15 of the
Wet op Belastingen van Rechtsverker which governs transfer tax provides that the
b supply of immovable property subject to turnover tax is in principle exempt from
transfer tax.

Account must also be taken of the fact that the nature of the immovable property
frequently changes during the transfer process and this may have important
technical consequences for tax purposes, as is apparent in the present case in which
a house was converted into a building plot. According to the rule governing
c exemption contained in art 11 of the Law, the transfer of an 'old' dwelling is in
principle exempt from turnover tax (but is therefore not exempt from transfer tax).
The transfer of building land, on the other hand, is subject to turnover tax (but not
to transfer tax).

10. The concept of supply, as defined in art 3 of the Law, is the main issue in this
case. Supply covers, inter alia: '1. (*a*) The transfer of ownership of property pursuant
d to an agreement; . . . (*e*) the transfer of property under which that property leaves
the business assets of an undertaking . . .'

In his opinion in the case pending before the Hoge Raad, Advocate General Van
Soest stated that art 3(1)(*e*) was inserted in the legislation in 1954 in order to fill a
'lacuna' which existed at the time, but not in order to cover the transfer of economic
ownership. From this history of the legislation and from the general scheme of the
e article it has up to now been concluded by the courts that (exactly as in the case of
transfer tax) the transfer of ownership under civil law referred to in art 3(1)(*a*) must
be taken as the basis for interpreting the concept of supply, whereas the function of
art 3(1)(*e*) is merely supplementary. In their judgments the courts have inferred
from that that no turnover tax should be charged until the supply of legal ownership,
unless it is clear from the circumstances in which the agreement was concluded or
f from subsequent factors that the supply of legal ownership will not (or will no longer)
take place or will take place considerably later, in which case it is necessary to fall
back on the supply of economic ownership. The observations which the Netherlands
government has submitted to the court in this case are essentially in line with these
judgments.

11. Safe, however, takes a different view and one which was accepted by the
g Gerechtshof, The Hague. It argues basically that the term 'supply' defined in the
national legislation must be interpreted in accordance with the term 'supply' as
defined in art 5(1) of the Sixth Directive. Article 3(1)(*e*) of the Law would best
correspond to this Community concept of supply. Therefore the provision must be
regarded as having an independent and not merely a supplementary function.

If this view is accepted it will lead, in circumstances such as those in the main
h proceedings, to a tax charge favourable to Safe. The transfer of economic ownership
of what was at that time an old dwelling is and would then remain exempt from
taxation, regardless of the time at which legal ownership of the property was later
transferred and irrespective of the fact that at that later date it was taxable. As
regards the general scheme of the legislation, however, that point of view has the
consequence that art 3(1)(*e*) of the Law must be regarded as the fundamental
j provision as regards the concept of supply, whilst other provisions such as art 3(1)(*a*)
are, in cases where economic and legal ownership are transferred separately,
superfluous or at least subsidiary. The adoption of Safe's position might therefore
compel the Netherlands legislature to review the general scheme of the Law and
possibly even the relationship between turnover tax and transfer tax. The questions
asked by the Hoge Raad must in my opinion be seen in this light.

The first question

12. By the first question the Hoge Raad wishes to ascertain whether the only supply covered by art 5(1) of the Sixth Directive is one by which legal ownership of property is transferred.

There is no dispute between the parties as to the answer to this question. The Netherlands government, Safe and the Commission consider that the question must be answered in the negative. I share that view, for the following reasons.

13. The first reason is to be found in the text of art 5(1) of the Sixth Directive. It states that the supply of goods means 'the transfer of the right to dispose of tangible property as owner'. This provision places the emphasis on the transfer of the *right* of disposal, which must enable the transferee to be able to dispose of the goods 'as owner'. This phrase in my opinion means that the transferee does not have to be the formal legal owner but need only obtain a right of disposal provided that he thereby acquires a position which is de facto analogous to that of the formal legal owner.

14. The second reason for which the question should be answered in the negative is that the terms used in the value added tax directives must be defined at Community level unless the directives themselves leave it to the member states to determine the definition of a term (see the judgment of 1 February 1977 in *Verbond van Nederlandse Ondernemingen v Inspecteur der Invoerrechten en Accijnzen* (Case 51/76) [1977] ECR 113 at 124–125, paras 10–11). This ensures a uniform application of the common system of turnover tax. For that reason the expression 'supply of goods' cannot be regarded as meaning 'formal supply in the civil law sense of legal ownership of goods'. The latter expression is not defined in the value added tax directives so that in order to supplement it reference would have to be made to the—to my knowledge—very different ways in which transfer, supply and enforceability of legal, as opposed to economic, ownership are defined in the member states.

The second question

15. The second question submitted by the Hoge Raad is more difficult; whereas the first question asks whether transfers other than transfers of formal legal ownership are covered by the Community concept of supply, the question at issue here is *which* other transfers are covered. The Hoge Raad wishes to know in particular whether there is such a transfer if the parties conclude an agreement the content of which may be summarised as follows: (a) Under the agreement any changes in the value of the property and all profits or any outgoings are for the benefit of or at the expense of the party other than the legal owner; he, moreover, acquires the right to dispose of the property. (b) The legal owner undertakes to transfer legal ownership of the property to the other party at a later date; he grants the other party an irrevocable power of attorney to execute transactions which will transfer legal ownership.

In my opinion the clauses in (a) must be distinguished from those in (b). The former are the same criteria as those on the basis of which the Hoge Raad defines the term 'economic ownership'. The latter are means of transferring legal ownership.

16. Personally I am reluctant to state in general, particularly in terms borrowed from the legal order of one member state, that once the criteria referred to in (a) are satisfied, a supply within the meaning of art 5(1) of the Sixth Directive has taken place. As I have already pointed out, the Community legislature, in defining the Community concept of supply, placed emphasis on a right of disposal which is analogous to that of the formal legal owner. I agree with the Commission that the national court must assess on the basis of the particular facts of each case whether the other party acquires the right to dispose of the property 'as owner'. It seems to me at least that he does if the right of ownership retained by the original seller is so diminished that it is reduced to mere legal title.

17. It remains to consider the effect of the clauses in (b). Here it is essentially a question of determining whether, in assessing in each case whether there is a right of disposal within the meaning of art 5(1) of the Sixth Directive, it makes any

difference if the parties to an agreement for the immediate transfer of 'economic
a ownership' alone have decided on the method by which legal ownership will
subsequently be transferred.

The Netherlands government answers this question in the affirmative. As I have
already outlined, it takes the view that art 5(1) of the Sixth Directive presupposes
the transfer of legal ownership. It therefore considers that if the parties to an
agreement on the transfer of economic ownership of property agree that legal
b ownership shall be transferred at a later stage, this later transfer of ownership must
be regarded as a supply for purposes of the Sixth Directive. It acknowledges,
however, that the transfer of economic ownership may be decisive, especially if no
date is specified for the transfer of legal ownership or if the latter transfer takes place
some considerable time after economic ownership is transferred.

18. I agree with the Commission that no support for this view can be found in the
c Community legislation. Where, in the light of the particular circumstances, a
transfer of economic ownership of property must be regarded as transfer of 'the right
to dispose of tangible property as owner', there is in my view a supply within the
meaning of art 5(1) of the Sixth Directive. That is not altered by any agreement
between the parties concerning the subsequent transfer of legal ownership. If it
were, the precondition for taxation contained in art 5(1) would be defined in such a
d way as to depend on specific agreements between the parties, which would be
contrary to legal certainty and would jeopardise the uniform application of the
conditions governing taxation laid down by the Community.

Conclusion
19. In conclusion I propose that the court should answer the preliminary questions
e as follows:

1. Supply within the meaning of art 5(1) of the Sixth Directive does not cover
solely the transfer of legal ownership of property.

2. Supply within the meaning of that provision covers any transfer of the
right to dispose of property by which a party acquires a position which is de
facto analogous to that of the formal legal owner. It is for the national court to
f assess on the basis of the particular circumstances of the case whether such a
right of disposal is transferred. In that regard it makes no difference that the
parties to an agreement by which such a right to dispose of property is
transferred have reached an agreement as to the subsequent transfer of legal
ownership.

g
8 February 1990. **THE COURT OF JUSTICE** delivered the following judgment.

1. By judgment of 19 October 1988, which was received at the court on
3 November 1988, the Hoge Raad der Nederlanden (Supreme Court of the
Netherlands) referred to the court for a preliminary ruling under art 177 of the EEC
h Treaty questions on the interpretation of art 5(1) of EC Council Directive 77/388
(the Sixth Directive).

2. The questions were raised in proceedings between the Netherlands Staatssecretaris van Financiën (Finance Secretary) and the tax entity Shipping and
Forwarding Enterprise Safe BV (SAFE Rekencentrum BV) (Safe). The proceedings
concern a notice of retroactive assessment by which the tax inspector assessed Safe
j to turnover tax on the supply by Safe to Kats Bouwgroep NV (Kats) of immovable
property comprising a detached house and outbuildings (the immovable property).

3. It is apparent from the documents before the court that, under a notarial act
between Safe and Kats dated 19 June 1979, Safe agreed to transfer to Kats for
payment of 2,250,000 Netherlands guilders an unconditional right to the immovable
property, free of mortgages and other rights in rem. According to the act, any
changes in the value of the property and all profits and outgoings were for the benefit

or at the expense of Kats, which acquired the power to dispose of the property. In addition, Safe undertook to transfer title to the immovable property when required by Kats, and in any event no later than 31 December 1982. For that purpose Safe granted Kats an irrevocable power of attorney to execute the transfer of legal ownership of the immovable property. On 11 August 1983 the trustees in bankruptcy of Kats concluded a notarial act with a third party by which they sold to the third party, for 425,000 guilders, Kats's rights in the immovable property under the notarial act of 19 June 1979. On the same date Safe transferred legal ownership of the immovable property to the third party.

4. Safe appealed against the notice of assessment to the tax inspector and subsequently to the Gerechtshof (Court of Appeal), The Hague. The Staatssecretaris van Financiën then brought proceedings before the Hoge Raad der Nederlanden, which decided to stay the proceedings and refer the following questions to the court for a preliminary ruling:

'1. Must Article 5(1) of the Sixth Directive be interpreted as meaning that a supply of goods takes place only where legal ownership of the property is transferred?

2. If not, does a supply of goods also take place where their legal owner: has entered into an agreement with another party under which any changes in the value of the property and all profits or outgoings are for the benefit or at the expense of that other party; has agreed to transfer legal ownership of the property to the other party at any future time; has agreed to grant the other party an irrevocable power of attorney to carry out any transactions necessary to execute that transfer of legal ownership; has, pursuant to that agreement, actually placed the property at the disposal of the other party?'

5. Reference is made to the report for the hearing for a fuller account of the facts of the case, the course of the procedure and the observations submitted to the court, which are mentioned or discussed hereinafter only in so far as is necessary for the reasoning of the court.

The first question

6. It should be noted that art 5(1) of the Sixth Directive provides as follows: '"Supply of goods" shall mean the transfer of the right to dispose of tangible property as owner.'

7. It is clear from the wording of this provision that 'supply of goods' does not refer to the transfer of ownership in accordance with the procedures prescribed by the applicable national law but covers any transfer of tangible property by one party which empowers the other party actually to dispose of it as if he were the owner of the property.

8. This view is in accordance with the purpose of the Sixth Directive, which is designed, inter alia, to base the common system of value added tax on a uniform definition of taxable transactions. This objective might be jeopardised if the preconditions for a supply of goods—which is one of the three taxable transactions—varied from one member state to another, as do the conditions governing the transfer of ownership under civil law.

9. Consequently, the answer to the first question must be that 'supply of goods' in art 5(1) of the Sixth Directive must be interpreted as meaning the transfer of the right to dispose of tangible property as owner, even if there is no transfer of legal ownership of the property.

The second question

10. It is clear from the documents before the court that the national court sought to establish in particular whether the transfer of 'economic ownership', a concept which has been developed in Netherlands tax law, could be deemed to be a supply

of goods within the meaning of art 5 of the Sixth Directive, and it defined the four
a elements which constituted a transfer of economic ownership in the case before it.

11. By referring in the second question to the four elements thus defined, the
national court is in reality asking the court to apply art 5(1) of the Sixth Directive to
the contract at issue in the main proceedings. Under the division of functions
provided for by art 177 of the EEC Treaty, however, it is for the national court to
apply the rules of Community law, as interpreted by the court, to an individual case.
b No such application is possible without a comprehensive appraisal of the facts of the
case.

12. This is illustrated, moreover, by the specific conditions mentioned in the
second question, since they refer, on the one hand, to an agreement to transfer
ownership under civil law, which does not necessarily seem to entail the transfer of
actual power as indicated by art 5(1) of the Sixth Directive, and, on the other, the
c actual placing of the property at the disposal of the other party, which would
normally point towards a finding that actual power has been transferred.

13. The answer to the second question must therefore be that it is for the national
court to determine in each individual case, on the basis of the facts of the case,
whether there is a transfer of the right to dispose of the property as owner within the
meaning of art 5(1) of the Sixth Directive.

d

Costs

14. The costs incurred by the government of the Netherlands and by the
Commission of the European Communities, which have submitted observations to
the court, are not recoverable. Since these proceedings are, in so far as the parties to
the main proceedings are concerned, in the nature of a step in the action pending
e before the national court, the decision on costs is a matter for that court.

On those grounds, the court (Sixth Chamber), in answer to the questions
submitted to it by the Hoge Raad der Nederlanden, by judgment of 19 October
1988, hereby rules:

    1. 'Supply of goods' in art 5(1) of the Sixth Directive must be interpreted as
f   meaning the transfer of the right to dispose of tangible property as owner, even
    if there is no transfer of legal ownership of the property.

    2. It is for the national court to determine in each individual case, on the
    basis of the facts of the case, whether there is a transfer of the right to dispose of
    the property as owner within the meaning of art 5(1) of the Sixth Directive.

Agents: *B R Bot*, Secretary General in the Ministry for Foreign Affairs (for the
g government of the Kingdom of the Netherlands); *J F Buhl*, Legal Adviser, and *B J
Drijber* (for the Commission).

Rengan Krishnan Esq   Barrister.

Staatssecretaris van Financiën v Velker International Oil Co Ltd NV

(Case C-185/89)

COURT OF JUSTICE OF THE EUROPEAN COMMUNITIES (FIFTH CHAMBER)
JUDGES SIR GORDON SLYNN (PRESIDENT OF THE CHAMBER), ZULEEG (PRESIDENT OF CHAMBER), JOLIET, MOITINHO DE ALMEIDA AND GREVISSE
ADVOCATE GENERAL C O LENZ
8 MARCH, 2 MAY, 26 JUNE 1990

Value added tax – European Communities – Supply of goods or services – Exemption relating to the supply of goods for the fuelling of vessels – Whether supply must coincide with fuelling – Whether exemption can extend to supplies at an earlier commercial stage – EC Council Directive 77/388, art 15.

In 1983, the taxpayer company (Velker) sold two consignments of bunker oil which it had acquired from two different suppliers. The consignments were delivered by Velker's suppliers directly to tanks rented by the purchaser and were subsequently loaded into sea-going vessels. Both of Velker's suppliers had applied a zero rate of value added tax to their sales of bunker oil to Velker, and Velker in turn applied a zero rate to its sales. The Netherlands tax authorities considered that the supplies of oil made by Velker did not qualify for exemption from value added tax and issued an additional assessment notice for 1983. The Gerechtshof (Court of Appeal) annulled the assessment on the ground that the oil supplied by Velker was for the fuelling and provisioning of sea-going vessels and that such supplies were exempt from value added tax under the Netherlands Law on Turnover Tax. On appeal, the Hoge Raad (Supreme Court) held that since the Netherlands legislature had intended in its Law on Turnover Tax to implement art 15(4)*ᵃ* of EC Council Directive 77/388 (the Sixth Directive), the term 'for the fuelling and provisioning of vessels' which appeared in the Netherlands legislation had to be given a meaning identical to that of the same term in art 15(4). The court accordingly stayed the proceedings and referred to the Court of Justice of the European Communities the following questions: (1) whether art 15(4) had to be construed as meaning that only supplies which coincided with fuelling and provisioning could be regarded as supplies of goods for the fuelling and provisioning of vessels defined in that provision; and (2) if question (1) was answered in the negative, whether under art 15(4) the supply of goods for fuelling or provisioning included only the supply of goods to an undertaking which would later use them for fuelling or provisioning vessels, or included also the supply of goods in a previous transaction to an undertaking which in turn supplied them to another undertaking which actually used them for fuelling or provisioning.

Held – (1) The provisions of the Sixth Directive which granted exemptions from tax, in particular those which granted exceptions to the rule that transactions taking place 'within the territory of the country' were subject to tax, had to be interpreted strictly. Supplies 'of goods for the fuelling and provisioning of vessels' were exempted from tax because they were equated in art 15 with exports. Accordingly, art 15(4) was to be interpreted strictly so that the exemption it lay down applied only to the supply of goods to a vessel operator who would use those goods for refuelling and provisioning and could not be extended to the supply of those goods effected at a previous stage in the commercial chain.

---

a Article 15, so far as material, is set out at p 653 *g–j*, post

(2) Under art 5(1) of the Sixth Directive, the 'supply of goods' meant 'the transfer
a   of the right to dispose of tangible property as owner' and accordingly there was
nothing either in the words 'the supply of goods for the fuelling and provisioning of
vessels' or in their context which justified the construction of art 15(4) such that
storage of goods following delivery and before actual fuelling and provisioning would
cause exemption to be lost.

Accordingly art 15(4) of the Sixth Directive had to be construed to the effect that
b   only supplies to a vessel operator of goods to be used by that operator for fuelling and
provisioning were to be regarded as supplies of goods for the fuelling and provisioning
of vessels, but there was no requirement that the goods should be actually loaded on
board the vessels at the time of their supply to the operator.

c   **Notes**

For exemptions of exports and like transactions from value added tax, see De Voil:
Value Added Tax Division A12.
For EC Council Directive 77/388, art 15, see ibid, Division E3.

d   **Cases cited**

EC Commission v Federal Republic of Germany (Case 107/84) [1985] ECR 2655,
CJEC.
EC Commission v Ireland (Case 415/85) [1988] ECR 3097, CJEC.
EC Commission v United Kingdom (Case 416/85) [1988] ECR 3127, CJEC.
Leesportefeuille 'Intiem' CV v Staatssecretaris van Financiën (Case 165/86) [1988]
e   ECR 1471, CJEC.
Stichting Uitvoering Financiële Acties v Staatssecretaris van Financiën (Case 348/87)
[1989] ECR 1737, CJEC.

Reference

f   By a judgment of 24 May 1989 the Hoge Raad der Nederlanden (Supreme Court of
the Netherlands) referred to the Court of Justice of the European Communities for
a preliminary ruling under art 177 of the EEC Treaty two questions concerning the
interpretation of art 15 of EC Council Directive 77/388 (the Sixth Directive). The
questions were raised in the course of proceedings between the Staatssecretaris van
Financiën and Velker International Oil Co Ltd NV (Velker) following the raising
g   of an additional assessment to value added tax on Velker on the grounds that supplies
of oil made by Velker did not qualify for exemption from value added tax. The
governments of the Federal Republic of Germany, the Kingdom of the Netherlands,
the Portuguese Republic and the United Kingdom and the Commission of the
European Communities made submissions (in the written procedure) to the court.
The language of the case was Dutch. The facts are set out in the report for the
h   hearing

The Judge Rapporteur (F Grévisse) presented the following report for the hearing.

I Community law applicable
Article 15 of EC Council Directive 77/388 of 17 May 1977 on the harmonisation
j   of the laws of the member states relating to turnover taxes—common system of value
added tax: uniform basis of assessment (the Sixth Directive) provides:

'Without prejudice to other Community provisions Member States shall
exempt the following under conditions which they shall lay down for the
purpose of ensuring the correct and straightforward application of such
exemptions and of preventing any evasion, avoidance or abuse:

1. the supply of goods dispatched or transported to a destination outside the territory of the country as defined in Article 3 by or on behalf of the vendor;

2. the supply of goods dispatched or transported to a destination outside the territory of the country as defined in Article 3 by or on behalf of a purchaser not established within the territory of the country, with the exception of goods transported by the purchaser himself for the equipping, fuelling and provisioning of pleasure boats and private aircraft or any other means of transport for private use . . .

4. the supply of goods for the fuelling and provisioning of vessels:

(a) used for navigation on the high seas and carrying passengers for reward or used for the purpose of commercial, industrial or fishing activities;

(b) used for rescue or assistance at sea, or for inshore fishing, with the exception, for the latter, of ships' provisions;

(c) of war, as defined in subheading 89.01 A of the Common Customs Tariff, leaving the country and bound for foreign ports or anchorages.

The Member States may, however, restrict the scope of this exemption until the implementation of Community tax rules in this field . . .'

In addition, art 16(2) of the Sixth Directive provides that:

'Subject to the consultation provided for in Article 29, Member States may opt to exempt imports for and supplies of goods to a taxable person intending to export them as they are or after processing, as well as supplies of services linked with his export business, up to a maximum equal to the value of his exports during the preceding 12 months.'

Article 29 of the Sixth Directive provides for the setting up of an advisory committee on value added tax consisting of representatives of the member states and of the Commission.

II Facts and procedure

1. In November 1983, Velker International Oil Co Ltd NV, Rotterdam (Velker), a company incorporated under Antilles law, sold to Forsythe International BV, The Hague (Forsythe), two consignments of bunker oil which it had previously acquired from Handelmaatschappij Verhoeven BV, Rotterdam (Verhoeven). Verhoeven had itself bought the first consignment of oil from Olie Verwerking Amsterdam BV (OVA). The two consignments were supplied to Forsythe directly, the first by OVA on 5 November 1983 and the second by Verhoeven on 11 November 1983. Forsythe stored the consignments of oil in tanks rented from a storage firm and they were then loaded on to sea-going vessels engaged in economic activities other than inshore fishing; the first consignment was loaded on 6, 7 and 8 November 1983 and the second on 17 and 18 November 1983.

2. Such transactions, known as A-B-C transactions, are governed by art 3(3) of the Wet op de Omzetbelasting (Law on Turnover Tax) (the Law). Pursuant to that provision, where there is a chain of several persons undertaking to supply the same goods and in reality physical delivery takes place directly from the first person in the chain to the last, each person in the chain is deemed to have supplied the goods and thus to have effected a taxable transaction.

3. In this case each of the parties to the transactions applied a zero value added tax rate, in reliance on the combined provisions of art 9(2)(b) of the Law and the first sub-paragraph of heading 4(a) of Table II annexed to the Law, which allow the supply of goods for the fuelling and provisioning of sea-going vessels engaged in economic activities other than inshore fishing to be zero-rated.

4. However, the Netherlands tax authorities considered that tax exemption was
a not justified in this case and issued an additional value added tax assessment notice
on Velker for 1983.

5. Velker brought proceedings before the Gerechtshof (Court of Appeal), The
Hague, which, in a judgment of 19 November 1986, annulled the assessment notice,
taking the view that the oil supplied by Velker was for the fuelling and provisioning
of sea-going vessels within the meaning of the provisions cited above.

b The Staatssecretaris van Financiën (State Secretary for Finance) appealed to the
Hoge Raad der Nederlanden (Supreme Court of the Netherlands). He maintained
that only the supply of goods coinciding with the fuelling and provisioning of vessels
and followed by the exportation of those goods could be considered to be a supply of
goods for the fuelling and provisioning of vessels.

6. In its judgment of 24 May 1989, the Hoge Raad explained that the relevant
provisions of the Law in the version applicable resulted from a Law of 28 December
c 1978 adopted to implement the Sixth Directive. It pointed out that it was the
intention of the Netherlands legislature to implement the final paragraph of art 15(4)
of the Sixth Directive and consequently the term 'for . . . fuelling and provisioning'
which appears in the national legislation must be understood in the same way as the
term which appears in the Sixth Directive.

d 7. Hence, by judgment of 24 May 1989, the Hoge Raad der Nederlanden decided
to suspend proceedings and refer the following questions to the court for a
preliminary ruling:

e '1. Must Article 15(4) of the Sixth Directive be construed as meaning that
only supplies which coincide with fuelling and provisioning can be regarded as
supplies of goods for the fuelling and provisioning of the vessels defined in that
provision?

2. If that provision of the Sixth Directive does not have a meaning which is
as restrictive as that defined in Question 1, must the following also be regarded
as supplies within the meaning of that provision: only the supply of goods to an
undertaking which will later use them for fuelling and provisioning vessels, or
f also goods supplied in a previous transaction, that is to say, to an undertaking
which does not itself use the goods for fuelling and provisioning vessels but
supplies them to another undertaking which does use them for that purpose?'

g The judgment of the Hoge Raad der Nederlanden was registered at the court on
29 May 1989.

8. In accordance with art 20 of the Protocol on the Statute of the Court of Justice
of the European Communities, written observations were submitted by the Federal
Republic of Germany, represented by Ernst Röder, Regierungsdirektor at the
Federal Ministry of Economic Affairs, by the government of the Kingdom of the
Netherlands, represented by B R Bot, Secretary-General of the Ministry of Foreign
h Affairs, by the government of the Portuguese Republic, represented by L Fernandes,
Director of the European Communities Directorate-General, and A Correia,
Assistant Director-General of the Value Added Tax Administration Department,
by the government of the United Kingdom represented by J A Gensmantel,
Treasury Solicitor, and by the Commission of the European Communities,
represented by J F Bühl, Legal Adviser, and B J Drijber, a member of the
j Commission's Legal Department, acting as agents.

9. On hearing the report of the Judge Rapporteur and the views of the Advocate
General the court decided to open the oral procedure without any preparatory
inquiry.

10. By decision of 17 January 1990 the court assigned the case to the Fifth
Chamber.

III Summary of the written observations submitted to the court

1. The government of the Federal Republic of Germany states that the exemption provided for in art 15(4) of the Sixth Directive does not apply solely to supplies made directly to maritime shipping companies. It also applies to supplies made at previous stages in the commercial chain if the condition laid down for the exemption, namely that the supply is for the fuelling and provisioning of vessels, is clearly satisfied at the time of the supply.

That interpretation is said to be supported by the wording of the material provisions in some language versions. Furthermore those provisions would have been drawn up differently if the exemption were intended only to apply to a limited range of purchasers.

According to the German government, the exemption of transactions preceding the supply to maritime shipping companies is not subject to consultation with the advisory committee on value added tax set up by art 29 of the Sixth Directive. Pursuant to art 16(2) of the directive such prior consultation is necessary only where states wish to exempt supplies preceding an export transaction. Article 15(4) does not relate to exports but to 'like transactions' and art 16(2) does not therefore apply.

The government of the Federal Republic of Germany adds that it must also be inferred from the sense and purpose of art 15(4) that transactions preceding supply to maritime shipping companies must be exempted. Article 15(4), like art 15(5) and (8), is intended to simplify administration, not to confer a substantive tax benefit, since if there were no exemption maritime shipping companies could obtain reimbursement of the tax they had paid. That same objective of simplification is said to warrant exemption being extended to transactions taking place at previous stages in the commercial chain, since the undertakings carrying out such transactions are in any event entitled to deduct tax paid at previous stages. Thus the exemption applied at previous stages pursuant to art 15(4) would bring with it as few real benefits as exemption applied at the final stage in the commercial chain.

The government of the Federal Republic of Germany emphasises that the material provisions of the Sixth Directive have been transposed into German law in accordance with the above interpretation.

Finally it concludes that if the answer to the first question is in accordance with the foregoing, there is no need to reply to the second question.

2. The Netherlands government points out that pursuant to art 17(3)(b) of the Sixth Directive the exemption provided for in art 15 is accompanied by retention of the right to a deduction or refund of the turnover tax invoiced at preceding stages by other undertakings.

Article 15(1) concerns export transactions, that is to say, the supply of goods by a trader who undertakes their export himself. Article 15(2) and art 15(4) relate to transactions treated as exports constituted by the supply of goods exported by the purchaser or on his behalf.

In the case of exports under art 15(1), and in like transactions under art 15(2), the exemption applies exclusively to supplies which directly precede the actual export of the goods; according to the Netherlands government it is necessary that when they are supplied, the goods are actually 'to be exported'. That interpretation is said to follow from the actual wording of the two paragraphs and to be confirmed by art 16(2) which allows member states to exempt supplies of goods to a taxable person intending to export them.

According to the Netherlands government, the provisions of art 15(4) must be interpreted in the same way. Exemption may thus only be granted for supplies which coincide with the fuelling and provisioning of vessels. The exemption does not apply either where the goods are supplied to a taxable person who does not use them himself for fuelling and provisioning or when they are used for fuelling and provisioning only at some date after their delivery.

That conclusion is, moreover, in accordance with the general principle whereby

turnover tax must be levied on any taxable transaction effected by a taxable person
a and exemptions are to be construed strictly.

The Netherlands government therefore considers that the first question referred
to the court calls for an answer in the affirmative, thus dispensing with the need to
answer the second question.

3. The Portuguese government begins by pointing out that, in contrast to simple
exemption, where the state loses only the benefit of tax at subsequent stages,
b complete exemption or zero-rating allows the deduction of all tax paid at preceding
stages, thus 'purging' the goods of any tax. As is confirmed by the first paragraph of
art 15 of the Sixth Directive, that is the reason why member states must set up
rigorous and well-defined systems to prevent fraud and diversion.

Article 15(4) should thus be interpreted in the light of those principles and,
equally, account should be taken of the objective pursued by the Community
c legislature.

According to the Portuguese government, the term 'the supply of goods for the
fuelling and provisioning of vessels', is capable of bearing several meanings in a
literal sense because it could refer to supplies coinciding with fuelling and
provisioning, to supplies made with a view to the later fuelling and provisioning of
vessels, or to supplies taking place at a previous marketing stage relating to goods
d capable of subsequently being used for fuelling or provisioning.

In order to decide what the term really means, recourse must be had to a
teleological construction and the structure of the system must be considered.

By treating the fuelling and provisioning of vessels as exports, the legislature
intended to benefit merchant navy and fishing activities while at the same time
attempting to obviate any evasion, avoidance or abuse. That treatment, which
e allows for exemption from value added tax, is thought to be warranted because fuel,
for instance, must be used by the sea-bound vessel. If the fuel is put into storage
previously, exemption cannot operate unless all of it is for fuelling and provisioning
to the exclusion of any other end, for example sale or transfer to other undertakings.
Therefore only the supply of goods for the fuelling and provisioning of vessels
coinciding with that operation may be exempted.

f   The same conclusion must be drawn from an examination of the structure of the
system. Since the extension of the application of zero-rating to marketing stages
preceding export transactions is made subject to the procedure laid down in art 16(2)
of the Sixth Directive, a fortiori the same holds true for its extension to marketing
stages preceding 'like transactions'. The Netherlands government has not, however,
availed itself of the possibility provided by that procedure.

g   The Portuguese government therefore considers that the reply to the national
court should be that the provisions of the Sixth Directive at issue must be interpreted
'as meaning that only supplies that coincide with fuelling and provisioning can be
regarded as supplies of goods for the fuelling and provisioning of the vessels described
in those provisions, to the exclusion of supplies of goods for storage and, a fortiori,
sales of the same goods to undertakings other than the undertaking using them'.

h   4. The United Kingdom government points out that the object of art 15(4) is to
relieve from value added tax the export of goods supplied to ships as provisions or
fuel. That object is achieved with the minimum of physical control if the final
delivery in the supply chain (that is to say, the supply to the departing ship) is
relieved of value added tax, and all earlier supplies are taxed as domestic supplies.
The normal value added tax input tax mechanism allows each intermediate supply
j   to be relieved of value added tax. That approach requires no retrospective adjusting
action to be taken where the final export intention is frustrated or intermediate
diversions occur.

Thus, in the view of the United Kingdom, only the final supply in the course of
actual shipment of goods as provisions or fuel is entitled to relief from value added
tax. Member states are not required to allow relief in respect of transactions where

the supplier or recipient of goods asserts an intention that those goods will at some point in the future be shipped as provisions or fuel either by the recipient or a third party.

Such an interpretation is said to accord with the opening words of art 15 of the Sixth Directive, which require member states to 'exempt the following under conditions which they shall lay down for the purpose of ensuring the correct and straightforward application of such exemptions and of preventing any evasion, avoidance or abuse'. Therefore supplies are only relieved of tax where it is certain that the conditions of relief are met at the time of supply. In the case of goods for the fuelling or provisioning of vessels, relief must be limited to the final supply of those goods to vessels and cannot be allowed in respect of earlier supplies of the goods, even where there is a stated intention that the goods are for eventual supply to the vessels.

The United Kingdom government adds that if a different interpretation of art 15(4) were adopted by the court, the last sentence of art 15(4) should be borne in mind, inasmuch as it allows states to restrict the scope of that exemption until the implementation of Community tax rules in that field, and such rules have not yet come about.

Furthermore, if the supply of goods prior to final supply for export were relieved of value added tax, a system of physical checks and controls on the goods would have to be set up to ensure that they were not diverted to the domestic market without having borne value added tax. Such a system would hinder the free movement of goods in domestic markets. Conversely, the restriction of relief to the final supply only of goods as provisions and fuel, as implemented by the United Kingdom legislation, makes control and checking procedures easier and reduces the risk of goods being diverted to the domestic market.

Finally the United Kingdom government emphasises that a negative reply to the first question would have serious implications for other headings of art 15 of the Sixth Directive, and for goods other than fuel. Tax-free diversion to domestic use could have a severe effect on, and lead to complaints by, legitimate traders. In addition, the ability to buy tax free could create trade distortions and affect the cash-flow of both buyer and seller.

According to the United Kingdom government, the first question should therefore be answered in the affirmative, thus dispensing with the need to reply to the second question.

5. The Commission of the European Communities considers that the interpretation of art 15 of the Sixth Directive is closely bound up with interpretation of the term 'supply of goods' which appears in art 5(1). Supply is there defined as 'the transfer of the right to dispose of tangible property as owner'. That Community definition should be given a broad interpretation. In this case the particular circumstances in which the transactions between Verhoeven, Velker and Forsythe took place should not mean that the sale by Velker to Forsythe of consignments of fuel was not subject to value added tax, since Velker had the legal right to dispose of the fuel which had been transferred to it by Verhoeven as owner and it could have disposed of the fuel by reselling it to a final consumer who could not take advantage of the exemption provided for in art 15(4) of the Sixth Directive. Moreover the fact that a taxable person is entitled to dispose of goods as owner is not necessarily linked to physical possession of the goods as is confirmed by the court's judgment of 8 March 1988 in *Leesportefeuille 'Intiem' CV v Staatssecretaris van Financiën* (Case 165/86) [1988] ECR 1471.

The Commission then addresses the concept of value added tax exemption for export transactions. In its view, the common system of value added tax is based on the principle of taxing each stage in the economic cycle of a transaction and includes the right to deduct tax paid on inputs. If it were necessary to make a distinction according to whether supplies had been effected by a subsidiary of company A to company B and then from the latter to the final consumer, or directly from company

A to company C, that would create such administrative complications that it
a suggests that the value added tax system should not be derogated from solely because
the latter situation has arisen.

The Commission points out that the last paragraph of art 15(4) of the Sixth
Directive allows member states to limit the scope of the exemption in respect of
supplies of goods for the fuelling and provisioning of vessels. A broad interpretation
of that exemption would thus run counter to the wording of those provisions. The
b court has, on several occasions, refused to allow chain exemptions in favour of
taxable persons other than the person effecting the final supply giving rise to
exemption (see the judgments of 11 July 1985 in *EC Commission v Federal Republic
of Germany* (Case 107/84) [1985] ECR 2655, and of 15 June 1989 in *Stichting
Uitvoering Financiële Acties v Staatssecretaris van Financiën* (Case 348/87) [1989]
ECR 1737). The same interpretation of the provisions of the value added tax system
c governing entitlement to exemption with reimbursement of tax paid at a preceding
stage is also in accordance with the principles set out by the court in its judgments of
21 June 1988 in *EC Commission v Ireland* (Case 415/85) [1988] ECR 3097 and *EC
Commission v United Kingdom* (Case 416/85) [1988] ECR 3127. If the same principles
are applied to a situation where a value added tax exemption comes into operation
in respect of a transaction constituting an export which, as such, is subject to the
d provisions of art 15 of the Sixth Directive, this necessarily results in only the final
transaction leading to the export of those goods fulfilling the conditions required for
application of the exemption with reimbursement of taxes paid at a preceding stage.

Finally, the Commission suggests that the reply to the first question should be
that 'the provisions of the first paragraph of Article 15 and Article 15(4) of the Sixth
Directive must be interpreted as meaning that only the final supply giving rise to
e fuelling and provisioning may be regarded as a supply of goods for the fuelling and
provisioning of vessels'. In view of that reply, there is no need to reply to the second
question.

2 May 1990. **The Advocate General (C O Lenz)** delivered the following opinion.

f Mr President, members of the court,

A Facts

1. In the case on which I give my opinion today the court has been asked by the
Hoge Raad der Nederlanden (Supreme Court of the Netherlands) to interpret
art 15(4)(*a*) of EC Council Directive 77/388 (the Sixth Directive), that is to say the
provision under which member states exempt from the tax 'the supply of goods for
g the fuelling and provisioning of vessels' of a certain kind.

2. An interpretation was considered necessary in connection with the supply by
Velker International Oil Co Ltd NV (Velker), the respondent in the main
proceedings, of two consignments of bunker oil to Forsythe International BV, The
Hague (Forsythe), on which Velker did not invoice value added tax. It is important
h to be aware of the particular circumstances surrounding the deliveries, which were
that: one consignment originated from Olie Verwerking Amsterdam BV (OVA),
was sold by the latter to Handelmaatschappij Verhoeven BV, Rotterdam
(Verhoeven), resold by Verhoeven to Velker and delivered direct by OVA to
Forsythe; the other consignment was bought by Velker from Verhoeven and also
delivered direct to Forsythe; and both consignments were placed in storage tanks
j rented by Forsythe from a storage company and from there, on instructions from
Forsythe, which did not operate any vessels itself, delivered to departing sea-going
vessels.

3. The value added tax inspector responsible regarded the application of zero-
rating by Velker, that is to say the non-invoicing of value added tax, as unjustified.
In his view 'fuelling and provisioning of vessels' within the meaning of the
Netherlands Law of 28 December 1978 can only mean a delivery which coincides

with the fuelling and provisioning of a vessel, that is to say a delivery *on board* the
vessel followed directly by export. That is also the view taken by the Staatssecretaris
van Financiën (State Secretary for Finance), the appellant in the main proceedings.
He considers also that art 15(4)(*a*) of the Sixth Directive, transposed by the Law of
28 December 1978 into Netherlands law, does not cover supplies to anyone who
merely states that the goods are for the fuelling and provisioning of vessels; that is
too far removed from actual fuelling and provisioning and does not prevent a change
in intended use before the goods are loaded on board. The Staatssecretaris points
out in addition that extension of the exemption to supplies preceding actual fuelling
and provisioning requires prior consultation with the advisory committee pursuant
to art 16(2) of the Sixth Directive, and the Netherlands had not so consulted.

4. Because the rule in art 15(4) of the Sixth Directive had apparently been
transposed unaltered into Netherlands law, when faced with the dispute described
above the national court came to the conclusion that it was appropriate to suspend
proceedings and ask the Court of Justice to clarify art 15(4)(*a*) of the Sixth Directive;
to be more precise, it sought clarification whether that provision covers only supplies
which coincide with fuelling and provisioning (thus shipped on board sea-going
vessels) or whether it should be construed more broadly, and if so whether it applies
only to the supply of goods to an undertaking which subsequently uses them for the
fuelling and provisioning of vessels, or also to supplies effected at a preceding stage.

5. As I see it, the *following observations* may be made.

B Observations

6. (1) Before I address the specific issue, I think I should make *two preliminary
remarks*, prompted by arguments put forward in the course of the proceedings.

7. (a) The Commission submitted written observations concerning, inter alia,
the term 'supply of goods' within the meaning of art 5 of the Sixth Directive. The
point arose in connection with the fact that the bunker oil in question was delivered
by OVA and Verhoeven direct to Forsythe and was apparently mixed with other oil
in the storage tanks Forsythe rented. Because the goods were not brought
immediately into Velker's possession, there might be some doubt whether it was in
a position to dispose of the goods as owner and therefore whether this did actually
constitute a supply within the meaning of the Sixth Directive.

8. I consider that for the purposes of answering the questions referred to the court
we can dispense with an examination of the arguments put forward in that
connection. The national court did not raise questions on the point and that must
be taken to mean that the court did not regard it as causing any difficulties (probably
because it reached the same conclusion as that submitted to us by the Commission).

9. (b) I also think that in dealing with these questions we can ignore the fact that
in the storage tanks rented by Forsythe the oil in question was apparently not stored
separately so as to enable its intended use to be established at any time.

10. On that point the judgment referring questions to the court specifically stated
that that issue—which had apparently not been put forward previously—could not
be raised in the proceedings before the Hoge Raad. The Hoge Raad is obliged to
ignore the point and there is therefore no call for us to examine it further in
connection with our task of construing the Sixth Directive.

11. (2) As far as the *problem actually referred to the court* is concerned, it is
apparent that not only the parties to the main proceedings but also those who took
part in the procedure before the court have different views. On one side there is the
view represented by the Netherlands, Portuguese and United Kingdom governments, that is to say those who suggest that the court reply to the first question in
the affirmative and that there is only a supply for fuelling and provisioning if delivery
is effected on to the vessel. The Commission's position comes close to that view,
advocating in any event a narrow construction of art 15(4) whereby only supplies to
a vessel operator are covered (which would not rule out interim storage before
loading on board).

12. On the other side there is the view taken by the government of the Federal
a Republic of Germany, according to which art 15 should be given a broad
interpretation, as suggested in the second question referred to the court. According
to that interpretation, art 15(4)(a) would also cover supplies at previous stages in the
commercial chain as long as the intended use (fuelling and provisioning of sea-going
vessels) is clearly established. Although of course it could not be inferred from the
observations made during the proceedings, that latter solution would appear to
b correspond to the practice in certain other member states (Denmark, Greece, Italy
and France). (There is, however, a restriction in France, if I understand correctly,
in that only the final supply prior to supply to the vessel operator qualifies.)

13. (a) If, with regard to this set of facts, we turn to existing *case law* to see
whether there are any indications of a solution to the problem raised, it soon becomes
apparent that the few judgments that are relevant have nothing decisive to say on
c the issue.

14. (aa) It is certainly worth noting that in the judgment in *Stichting Uitvoering
Financiële Acties v Staatssecretaris van Financiën* (Case 348/87) [1989] ECR 1737 at
1753, it was stressed that the formulas used in defining tax *exemptions* are to be
construed *strictly*. It should not, however, be overlooked that in that case
art 13A(1)(f) (services supplied by groups of persons *to their members*) clearly did
d apply on the facts. The beneficiaries of the service were thus designated precisely
and transactions effected at an earlier economic stage (namely the supply of services
by one foundation to another, neither of the foundations being a member of the
other) could not therefore be included.

15. (bb) *EC Commission v Federal Republic of Germany* (Case 107/84) [1985] ECR
2655, which turned on art 13A(1)(a) of the Sixth Directive (concerning the supply
e of services by the public postal services), was similar. Although the court, which
found in favour of a strict interpretation, stressed that that provision did not include
services supplied by other undertakings on behalf of the postal services (and that it
was not therefore possible to extend it to operations carried out to the same end but
by other services), it should not be forgotten that that was simply as a result of the
fact that in the provision the body entitled to exemption was referred to explicitly.

f 16. (cc) On the other hand it is rather interesting that in the judgment in *EC
Commission v Ireland* (Case 415/85) [1988] ECR 3097 (and similarly in *EC Commission
v United Kingdom* (Case 416/85) [1988] ECR 3127) in connection with tax exemption
for social reasons for the benefit of the final consumer pursuant to art 17 of EC
Council Directive 67/228, no restrictive interpretation was considered warranted
but rather the provision of goods or services at a preceding stage was also to be
g considered for exemption if it was sufficiently close to the consumer to be of
advantage to him.

17. (b) It must also be admitted (not least in consequence of the last-cited
judgment) that the *wording* of the provision before us—as the German government
has rightly pointed out—by no means suggests that a narrow construction is
mandatory.

h 18. That is apparent from the English version ('supply of goods for the fuelling
and provisioning of vessels') and the German version ('Lieferung von Gegenständen
zur Versorgung von Schiffen'), neither of which implies that the fuelling and
provisioning must be immediate. The Dutch, Italian, French and Portuguese
versions are even clearer, focusing on the intended purpose ('levering van goederen,
bestemd voor de bevoorrading van de nafolgende schepen'; 'cessioni di beni destinati
j al refornimento e al vettovagliamento di navi'; 'livraisons des biens destinés
à l'avitaillement des bateaux'; 'entragas de bens destinados ao abastecimento de
bacos').

19. If one compares the provisions of the Sixth Directive which refer specifically
to the *recipient* of services and goods (such as, for instance, art 13A(1)(f) and (l):
services supplied by groups of persons and bodies to their members; art 15(11):
supplies of gold to central banks; art 15(12): goods supplied to approved bodies),

then it can hardly be unreasonable to assume that supplies effected prior to the actual fuelling and provisioning of vessels should also be covered by art 15(4) as long as they are shown to be for that purpose.

20. It should in addition be acknowledged that (as the German government also pointed out) from the point of view of the apparent *purpose* of the exemption provision (which is not the bestowing of financial advantages, but manifestly administrative simplification) there is an argument for subsuming transactions preceding direct fuelling and provisioning under art 15(4), because undertakings which are engaged therein are in any case relieved of any tax burden by way of deduction. It does not seem unreasonable to spare them from tax procedures from the outset if the final recipient does not have to pay tax.

21. (c) In my opinion it is moreover clear that *two arguments which have been put forward by the advocates of a narrow interpretation* are not very effective in corroborating that point of view.

22. (aa) One of these is the reference to the fact that in a final sub-paragraph in the provision in question it is stated that the member states may '*restrict* the scope of this exemption until the implementation of Community tax rules in this field' [emphasis added]. In my view that does not necessarily suggest that a narrow construction is required at all; rather, it supports the opposite point of view, that is to say that if the introduction of a possibility of restricting its scope was thought to be warranted it must be assumed that the provision itself should be understood in a broad sense.

23. Of course—and this is anticipating another argument put forward in the proceedings—that does not necessarily mean that the final sub-paragraph lends clear support for a *very* broad interpretation of art 15(4) in the sense of the second question referred to the court, thus bearing out the German government's particular viewpoint (as we know, it considered that the final sub-paragraph would be devoid of meaning if the provision were construed narrowly). For even if it must be assumed that art 15(4) only covers supplies to vessel operators, one can easily imagine possible restrictions, for instance with regard to the goods which might be considered for exemption or to the effect that only supplies effected directly on board (excluding previous storage) would be considered. The final sub-paragraph of art 15(4) makes as much sense if it is given a narrow construction as when it is interpreted as the German government suggests.

24. (bb) Secondly, there is the reference to art 16(2) (by virtue of which, subject to the consultation with the advisory committee provided for in art 29, member states may opt to exempt, inter alia, supplies of goods to a taxable person intending to export them).

25. It surely cannot be said of that provision that it is superfluous if art 15(4) is given a broad interpretation.

26. As it is worded, it certainly does not appear to lend itself easily to operations such as those described in art 15(4), but rather—as the German government has rightly pointed out—to be principally designed to cover export operations as such (see the headings to arts 15 and 16). For those, however, it applies in every case, that is to say it is also relevant if the operation of fuelling and provisioning vessels which is treated as an export were to be understood in a broad sense and in consequence application of art 16(2) was excluded.

27. (d) Finally, although—as I believe—when all is said and done there is no alternative but to uphold the view of those who argue for a *narrow interpretation* of art 15(4) of the Sixth Directive, the following considerations are of relevance:

28. (aa) It is certainly significant that the Sixth Directive is made subject to the principle that *every business transaction* within the territory of a country is liable to tax. It follows that—where provision is made for exemptions—an application of an exemption that extends to several economic stages appears justifiable only on very imperative grounds. It is, however, doubtful whether the idea adduced by the German government of administrative simplification suffices (that is to say, the

avoidance of tax computations, tax payment and deduction of inputs by traders
a who, since they are not the final consumer, are not ultimately subject to a tax
burden). It is also quite clear that the interpretation advocated by the German
government—and I shall return to this point—could also involve burdening the
administration, albeit in a different way.

29. (bb) Furthermore, it is significant—and this remark relates to the structure
of art 15 as a whole—that (as must be inferred from the heading to art 15) supplies
b for the fuelling and provisioning of vessels are treated as *like transactions* because it
is to be expected that consumption will take place abroad. If, however, with regard
to the export transactions as such covered in the first numbered paragraphs of art 15,
adherence to a strict criterion is required (*dispatch to a destination outside* the
Community), it must be regarded as only proper and in accordance with the system
to apply to like transactions a similarly strict standard and to stress the importance
c of a close connection between supply and fuelling and provisioning.

30. (cc) One further consideration relating to art 16(2) of the Sixth Directive
cannot be completely disregarded. If—as can be said to be the case—as regards
export transactions an extension of the exemption to persons who only *intend* to
export is only possible after consultation with the advisory committee, it would not
appear logical in the case of like transactions within the meaning of art 15(4) to reach
d the same result (extension to previous input stages in the commercial chain) by
means of a broad interpretation of the term 'the supply of goods for the fuelling and
provisioning of vessels'. Even though it must be admitted that art 16(2) is not directly
designed to cover like transactions, it is much more appropriate to use the provision
by analogy in order to obtain exemption for transactions preceding actual supply for
the fuelling and provisioning of vessels.

e 31. (dd) In my opinion in interpreting art 15(4) weight should also be attached to
the reference in the first paragraph to the need to ensure the correct and
straightforward application of the exemptions and to prevent any evasion or abuse.

32. What strikes one immediately is that it is hard to reconcile that reference with
a systematically generous application of art 15(4) which includes supplies prior to
the actual supply for fuelling and provisioning. It appears possible, if the provision
f is applied in that way, that is to say if the intention of the previous suppliers is
focused on, that that intention might later be changed and the goods supplied reach
the domestic market. In that way distortions of competition could arise and if such
facts subsequently came to light ex post facto correction of the tax treatment would
be necessary (which can hardly be regarded as administrative simplification). If such
irregularities are to be excluded from the outset, however, specific monitoring
g measures are necessary, which (quite apart from the fact that they could amount to
obstacles to trade) do not exactly represent administrative simplification either.

33. The arguments put forward on that point by the German government's
representative at the hearing do not really provide grounds for reaching any other
conclusion. No regard can be had to the fact that the practice of the German
government (the use of computers for checking purposes, inter alia, apparently plays
h a role) might easily become generalised. It must be said, however, that it appears
inconceivable that the relevant part of the first paragraph of art 15 should be seen as
granting a degree of flexibility to the member states according to the administrative
means at their disposal. It must be more correct to assume that the case for exemption
before us is governed by the formula used in art 15(4) and that must in principle be
understood in a uniform Community way. Derogations are only possible pursuant
j to the final sub-paragraph of art 15(4) mentioned previously. To permit derogations
on the basis of the introductory paragraph of art 15 would, on the other hand, be
contrary to the structure of the system and constitute a misinterpretation of the
meaning of its wording, which is also to be found in other provisions in the Sixth
Directive.

34. (e) Accordingly, although a broad interpretation of art 15(4), as advocated by
the German government, cannot be accepted as correct (and, if need be, the same

result can be obtained by applying art 16(2) by analogy), it seems to me on the other hand that it is also clear that there are no imperative reasons for sanctioning the very narrow construction advocated by the governments of the Netherlands, the United Kingdom and Portugal, to the effect that there is supply for the fuelling and provisioning of vessels only when the goods are loaded directly onto the vessel. There is nothing in the wording of the provision to support that (the Commission proposal mentioned by the Netherlands government which has not yet been adopted by the Council is clearly irrelevant). Against that view, reference may be made to the term 'supply' (according to art 5 it is the basis of the right to dispose of property as an owner); that definition surely suggests that the giving of the power of disposal to the person who uses the goods for the fuelling and provisioning of ships, that is to say, to the operator of the vessel, is determinant, and that does not rule out interim storage before the goods are loaded onto the vessel.

35. It should perhaps be added that any misgivings with regard to the risk of abuse (which is seen as the critical factor by the proponents of a very narrow interpretation) can be taken into account by way of recourse to the final sub-paragraph of art 15(4), that is to say that member states who regard it imperative to subject the application of art 15(4) to very strict requirements are quite at liberty to provide for a restriction on the exemption in reliance on that final sub-paragraph.

C Conclusion

36. (3) In view of the foregoing I suggest that the court reply to the questions put by the Hoge Raad as follows:

> Article 15(4) of the Sixth Directive should be interpreted as meaning that the supply of goods to an undertaking which uses the goods subsequently to fuel and provision vessels is to be regarded as the supply of goods for the fuelling and provisioning of the vessels described in the provision. It is not necessary for the supply to coincide with fuelling and provisioning, that is to say, for delivery to be made directly on to the vessel.

26 June 1990. **THE COURT OF JUSTICE** delivered the following judgment.

1. By judgment of 24 May 1989, which was received at the court on 29 May 1989, the Hoge Raad der Nederlanden (Supreme Court of the Netherlands) referred to the court for a preliminary ruling under art 177 of the EEC Treaty two questions concerning the interpretation of art 15 of EC Council Directive 77/388 (the Sixth Directive).

2. The questions were raised in the course of proceedings between the Staatssecretaris van Financiën (State Secretary for Finance) and Velker International Oil Co Ltd NV, Rotterdam (Velker), following an additional assessment in respect of value added tax issued on Velker.

3. The documents in the case show that Velker sold to Forsythe International BV, The Hague (Forsythe), two consignments of bunker oil, the invoices for which were dated 14 November 1983 and 16 November 1983.

4. The consignments of oil had been acquired by Velker from Handelmaatschappij Verhoeven BV, Rotterdam (Verhoeven), which had itself bought one of the consignments from Olie Verwerking Amsterdam BV (OVA).

5. On Forsythe's instructions, the two consignments were delivered, by OVA on 5 November 1983 and by Verhoeven on 11 November 1983, to tanks rented by Forsythe from a company called De Nieuwe Matex, and then loaded on to sea-going vessels on 6, 7 and 8 November 1983 and 17 and 18 November 1983.

6. The invoice raised by OVA on Verhoeven did not include any value added tax. The invoices raised by Verhoeven on Velker were marked 'VAT-O rate'. In turn Velker applied a zero value added tax rate to the two sales invoiced to Forsythe.

7. The Netherlands tax authorities considered that the supplies of oil made by Velker to Forsythe did not qualify for value added tax exemption and issued an additional value added tax assessment notice for 1983 on Velker.

8. The case came before the Gerechtshof (Court of Appeal), The Hague, which annulled the assessment notice, taking the view that the oil supplied by Velker was for the fuelling and provisioning of sea-going vessels and that such supply ought to be exempt from value added tax by virtue of the combined provisions of the first sub-paragraph and para (*b*) of art 9(2) of the Wet op de Omzetbelasting (Law on Turnover Tax) (the Law) and the first sub-paragraph of heading 4(*a*) of Table II annexed to the Law.

9. The Staatssecretaris van Financiën (State Secretary for Finance) appealed to the Hoge Raad against that judgment of the Gerechtshof. He maintained that only the supply of goods coinciding with the fuelling and provisioning of vessels and followed by exportation of those goods could be considered to be a supply of goods for the fuelling and provisioning of vessels within the meaning of the provisions of the Law.

10. In its judgment of 24 May 1989 referring questions to the court, the Hoge Raad explained that when it adopted the Law, the Netherlands legislature had intended to implement the provisions of art 15(4) of the Sixth Directive and that consequently the term 'for the fuelling and provisioning of vessels' which appears in the Law must be given a meaning identical to that of the same term which appears in the Sixth Directive.

11. Consequently, the Hoge Raad decided to suspend the proceedings and refer the following questions to the court for a preliminary ruling:

'1. Must Article 15(4) of the Sixth Directive be construed as meaning that only supplies which coincide with fuelling and provisioning can be regarded as supplies of goods for the fuelling and provisioning of the vessels defined in that provision?

2. If that provision of the Sixth Directive does not have a meaning which is as restrictive as that defined in Question 1, must the following also be regarded as supplies within the meaning of that provision: only the supply of goods to an undertaking which will later use them for fuelling and provisioning vessels, or also goods supplied in a previous transaction, that is to say, to an undertaking which does not itself use the goods for fuelling and provisioning vessels but supplies them to another undertaking which does use them for that purpose?'

12. Reference is made to the report for the hearing for a fuller account of the facts of the main proceedings, the course of the procedure and the written observations submitted to the court, which are mentioned or discussed hereinafter only in so far as is necessary for the reasoning of the court.

13. Under the terms of art 15 of the Sixth Directive:

'Without prejudice to other Community provisions Member States shall exempt the following under conditions which they shall lay down for the purpose of ensuring the correct and straightforward application of such exemptions and of preventing any evasion, avoidance or abuse: 1. the supply of goods dispatched or transported to a destination outside the territory of the country as defined in Article 3 by or on behalf of the vendor; . . . 4. the supply of goods for the fuelling and provisioning of vessels: (*a*) used for navigation on the high seas and carrying passengers for reward or used for the purpose of commercial, industrial or fishing activities . . .'

14. For the purpose of interpreting the provisions of the Sixth Directive at issue, the national court's second question should be examined first.

15. In that question the national court is asking whether the exemption laid down by those provisions applies solely to the supply of goods to a vessel operator who is going to use those goods for fuelling and provisioning or whether it also extends to

supplies effected at previous stages in the commercial chain on condition that the goods are ultimately used for the fuelling and provisioning of vessels.

16. The term 'supply of goods for the fuelling and provisioning of vessels' is capable of bearing several literal meanings. It could refer to the supply of goods which the recipient will use for the fuelling and provisioning of his vessels or the supply, at whatever stage it takes place, of goods which will subsequently be used for that purpose.

17. In order to interpret the term recourse must therefore be had to the context in which it occurs, bearing in mind the purpose and structure of the Sixth Directive.

18. As the court has stated on many occasions (for example, in the judgment of 15 June 1989 in *Stichting Uitvoering Financiële Acties v Staatssecretaris van Financiën* (Case 348/87) [1989] ECR 1737), the Sixth Directive confers a very wide scope on value added tax comprising all economic activities of producers, traders and persons supplying services.

19. The provisions in the Sixth Directive which grant exemption from tax must be interpreted strictly since they constitute exceptions to the general principle that turnover tax is levied on all goods or services supplied for consideration by a taxable person.

20. A strict interpretation is required in particular when the provisions in issue constitute exceptions to the rule that transactions taking place 'within the territory of the country' are subject to the tax.

21. With regard to art 15(4), it should be noted that the operations of fuelling and provisioning vessels mentioned therein are exempted because they are equated with exports.

22. Just as, in the case of export transactions, the mandatory exemption provided for in art 15(1) applies exclusively to the final supply of goods exported by the seller or on his behalf, likewise the exemption laid down in art 15(4) applies only to the supply of goods to a vessel operator who will use those goods for fuelling and provisioning and cannot therefore be extended to the supply of those goods effected at a previous stage in the commercial chain.

23. In its observations before the court the German government submitted, however, that such an interpretation of the provisions in question would be contrary to their purpose. According to the German government, the exemption at issue is designed to allow administrative simplification, not to grant a fiscal benefit. In view of that objective, the exemption should, in its view, be extended to all commercial stages.

24. That argument cannot be accepted. The extension of the exemption to stages prior to the final supply of the goods to the vessel operator would require member states to set up systems of supervision and control in order to satisfy themselves as to the ultimate use of the goods supplied free of tax. Far from bringing about administrative simplification, such systems would amount to constraints on the member states and the traders concerned which it would be impossible to reconcile with the 'correct and straightforward application of such exemptions' prescribed in the first paragraph of art 15 of the Sixth Directive.

25. In view of the reply that must be given to the second question, it remains for the court to examine the Hoge Raad's first question, which is whether, in order to qualify for exemption, the goods should be actually loaded on board the vessel at the time of their supply to the vessel operator.

26. Under art 5(1) of the Sixth Directive, by 'supply of goods' is meant 'the transfer of the right to dispose of tangible property as owner'.

27. In view of that definition, it needs merely to be said that nothing in the wording of the relevant provisions of art 15(4), nor the context in which they appear, nor the objective which they pursue, justifies a construction of those provisions to the effect that storage of the goods after delivery and before the actual fuelling and provisioning operation causes the benefit of the exemption to be lost.

28. It is true, as the United Kingdom government pointed out in its observations
a before the court, that such a construction would ensure that traders did not
subsequently use the goods supplied free of tax for purposes other than the fuelling
and provisioning of vessels.

29. However, that ground alone cannot justify such a construction given that, by
virtue of the first paragraph of art 15 of the Sixth Directive, it is in any event for the
member states to lay down conditions for exemption suitable for 'preventing any
b evasion, avoidance or abuse'.

30. The reply to the questions referred to the court by the Hoge Raad der
Nederlanden must therefore be that art 15(4) of the Sixth Directive must be
construed to the effect that only supplies to a vessel operator of goods to be used by
that operator for fuelling and provisioning are to be regarded as supplies of goods for
the fuelling and provisioning of vessels, but there is no requirement that the goods
c should be actually loaded on board the vessels at the time of their supply to the
operator.

Costs

31. The costs incurred by the governments of the Federal Republic of Germany,
the Kingdom of the Netherlands, the Portuguese Republic and the United Kingdom
d and the Commission of the European Communities, which have submitted
observations to the court, are not recoverable. As these proceedings are, in so far as
the parties to the main action are concerned, in the nature of a step in the proceedings
before the national court, the decision on costs is a matter for that court.

On those grounds, the court (Fifth Chamber), in answer to the questions referred
to it by the Hoge Raad der Nederlanden by judgment of 24 May 1989, hereby rules:

e   Article 15(4) of the Sixth Directive must be construed to the effect that only
supplies to a vessel operator of goods to be used by that operator for fuelling and
provisioning are to be regarded as supplies of goods for the fuelling and
provisioning of vessels, but there is no requirement that the goods should be
actually loaded on board the vessels at the time of their supply to the operator.

f   Agents: *E Röder,* Regierungsdirektor at the Federal Ministry of Economic Affairs
(for the government of the Federal Republic of Germany); *B R Bot,* Secretary-
General of the Ministry of Foreign Affairs and *J W De Zwaan* (for the government
of the Kingdom of the Netherlands); *L Fernandes,* Director of the European
Communities Directorate-General and *A Correia,* Assistant Director-General of
the Value Added Tax Administration (for the government of the Portuguese
g Republic); *J A Gensmantel,* Treasury Solicitor (for the government of the United
Kingdom); *J F Bühl,* Legal Adviser and *B J Drijber* (for the Commission); *C G
Verheij* (for Velker).

Rengan Krishnan Esq   Barrister.

Note

Neely v Ward (Inspector of Taxes)

CHANCERY DIVISION
SIR DONALD NICHOLLS V-C
3 OCTOBER 1991

Capital gains tax – Computation of chargeable gains – Disposal of asset – Allowable loss – Taxpayer selling cottage – Difference between gain arising from the sale and the replacement value of the cottage – Whether difference allowable loss – Theft of assets from cottage – Whether difference between capital sum received by way of compensation for loss of assets and replacement value of assets an allowable loss – Capital Gains Tax Act 1979, ss 20(1)(a), 128(3).

Notes

For the computation of gains and losses, see Simon's Taxes Division C2.1.
For capital sums derived from assets where no asset is acquired, see ibid, C1.404.
For the Capital Gains Tax Act 1979, ss 20(1)(a), 128(3), see ibid, Part G3.

Case stated

1. At meetings of the Commissioners for the general purposes of the income tax for the division of Wellingborough, Northamptonshire, held at 1 High Street, Wellingborough on 28 June 1988 and 6 September 1988, Hugh Bertram Neely (the taxpayer) of Wood House, Tingrith, Bletchley, Milton Keynes appealed against an assessment to capital gains tax for 1981–82 in the sum of £3,174, based on a chargeable gain of £6,174.

2. Shortly stated the questions for the commissioners' determination were whether the taxpayer was entitled to deduct as allowable losses: (i) the difference between the consideration which he received on the disposal of a cottage at Wales and its value at the date of the hearing; (ii) the difference between the cost and the replacement value of certain items of jewellery and antiques stolen from the taxpayer's cottage in 1979.

3. At the first hearing on 28 June 1988 it was accepted by both parties and by the commissioners that the gain on the sale of the cottage was £6,174. The appeal was then adjourned to 6 September to deal with the contested question as to deductibility of losses set out in para 2 above. The taxpayer appeared before the commissioners in person. The respondent inspector of taxes was represented by (on 28 June) Mr K Hughes, inspector of taxes, and (on 6 September) by Mr D Hayes, inspector of taxes.

4. The only document produced and admitted in evidence was a schedule of items stolen from the taxpayer's cottage in 1979.

5. From the oral and documentary evidence adduced before the commissioners, they found the following facts: (i) it was accepted by both parties that the chargeable gain on the sale of the cottage in 1981–82 was £6,174; (ii) the cottage was burgled in 1979 and the items listed in the schedule were stolen; (iii) the items stolen in 1979 were all items of tangible movable property whose value did not exceed £2,000 each.

6. The commissioners heard other evidence from the taxpayer as follows: In 1972 the taxpayer had founded a company, Savident Ltd (the company), of which he and his wife were two of the four directors. Unknown to the taxpayer and his wife trading accounts and profit and loss accounts for the years 1975 and 1976 were

audited, and submitted to and approved at a general meeting of the company on
a 10 September 1976. The taxpayer stated that the accounts were deficient in that:
(a) no directors' salaries were shown and the Revenue subsequently stated that such
had been paid; (b) no stock valuation had been done; (c) vouchers and most of the
company's stock were held by the taxpayer at his home and had not been inspected
for the purpose of accounts; (d) the auditors had entered a caveat in the audited
accounts that of the 1975 figures for purchases totalling £80,000 invoices for a total
b value of £44,000 were untraceable; (e) the company's books were held by Hawkes
who also knew nothing about the accounts. Nevertheless, without the knowledge of
the taxpayer and his wife (who held 70% of the share capital of the company between
them) the accounts had been submitted to and accepted by the Revenue. Loans of
£7,000 from the taxpayer were not shown in the accounts; the company had made
£12,000 losses. Most of his assets were secured by the bank and his creditors. The
c taxpayer had only one disposable asset, the cottage in Wales. He had sold that for
£7,150 in order to save his business. The sale price, he stated, was less than the
Revenue owed him at the time. The taxpayer wanted to know why the Revenue
had not investigated the propriety of the purchases totalling £44,000. The taxpayer
alleged that there was fraud abroad in the Revenue. The taxpayer wished to set off
such losses against his income from other sources such as trust fund income and
d share and stock dividends, but his claim floundered against the company accounts
which he stated were manifestly fraudulent. The taxpayer in protest had refused to
account to the Revenue for PAYE deducted from employees' salaries of his present
business and his debt totalled some £82,000. The value at the date of the hearings of
his cottage in Wales was £160,000 and the Revenue, who had forced him to sell it,
could either pay him £160,000 or give him the cottage back.
e   The commissioners made no findings of fact on this evidence as they did not
consider it to be relevant to the question before them.
     7. It was contended by the taxpayer: (a) that there should be deducted from the
gain on the sale of the cottage an amount equal to the replacement value thereof,
namely £160,000 so that an allowable loss of that amount arose; (b) that the insurance
compensation paid due to the theft of the items of jewellery and antiques from the
f cottage in 1979 did not arise from a disposal within the Capital Gains Tax Act 1979
(the 1979 Act) but was merely compensation for a theft; (c) that an allowable loss
arose on the difference between the cost and the replacement values of those items
of jewellery and antiques.
     8. It was contended on behalf of the inspector of taxes: (a) there had been a
disposal of the cottage in Wales giving rise to a capital gain; (b) there was no basis in
g fact or in law for the taxpayer's contention that he was entitled to an assumed capital
loss of some £160,000 (less £6,174) arising out of the sale of his cottage in Wales in
1979; (c) there was no provision in the 1979 Act which would permit the difference
between the replacement value and the purchase cost of the stolen assets to be
allowed as a capital loss; (d) the taxpayer's contention that reimbursement in respect
of the loss from an insurance company was not a disposal for capital gains tax
h purposes was incorrect. The loss of assets and the receipt of a capital sum from an
insurance company constituted a disposal and the capital sum was the disposal
proceeds. Applying ss 20 and 32 of the 1979 Act in relation to the taxpayer's case,
there was a disposal of the assets set out in the schedule and a gain to be computed
by reference to the insurance proceeds less the cost of the assets. But by virtue of
s 128(1) of the 1979 Act a gain accruing on the disposal of an asset which was tangible
j movable property should not be a chargeable gain if the consideration for the
disposal of that asset had not exceeded a certain limit. For the year in question,
1981–82, the limit was £2,000. For the purpose of applying these provisions, each
asset had to be considered separately. As far as any gains that might have arisen by
virtue of s 20, they would fall to be excluded as no sum exceeding £2,000 was
received for any of the assets. Similarly, if in any instance the insurance proceeds
had been less than the cost (which was the only way that an allowable loss could

accrue), no allowable loss would accrue by virtue of s 128(3) of the 1979 Act because
each item of loss would fall to be considered separately, and had to be restricted by *a*
reference to an amount over £2,000. As none of the losses of jewellery and antiques
in this case exceeded £2,000, no allowable loss was involved.

9. The commissioners determined the appeal on 6 September 1988 as follows:
(i) there was no basis in fact or in law on which the taxpayer's contention that he was
entitled to claim a capital loss on the sale of the cottage could be upheld; (ii) as no
item of jewellery or antique listed in the schedule involved a loss exceeding £2,000, *b*
no allowable loss arose on their disposal; (iii) the chargeable gain for 1981–82 had
been correctly assessed at £6,174.

10. Immediately after the determination of the appeal the taxpayer expressed his
dissatisfaction therewith as being erroneous in point of law and by a letter dated
25 September 1988 required the commissioners to state a case pursuant to s 56 of the
Taxes Management Act 1970.   *c*

11. The question of law for the opinion of the High Court was whether on the
facts found there was evidence on which the commissioners could properly arrive at
their decision in so far as it was a question of fact and whether on the facts as found
their decision was correct in law.

The taxpayer appeared in person.   *d*
Launcelot Henderson for the Crown.

SIR DONALD NICHOLLS V-C. This is an appeal by way of case stated from a
decision of the General Commissioners for Wellingborough, Northamptonshire,
given on 6 September 1988. The taxpayer, Mr Hugh Bertram Neely, unsuccessfully
appealed to the commissioners against an assessment to capital gains tax for the year *e*
1981–82 in an amount of £3,174. That was based on a chargeable gain of £6,174.
The taxpayer was dissatisfied with the decision of the commissioners and has
appealed to this court. He has conducted his appeal in person and, although he
plainly feels very strongly on certain points, he has done so with moderation and
helpfulness.

Some years ago (and all the events to which this appeal relates are now rather stale) *f*
the taxpayer owned a cottage in Wales. He sold this at the end of the 1970s, or
thereabouts. The parties were agreed before the commissioners that a chargeable
gain arose in respect of that sale for the year 1981–82, and that the amount of the
chargeable gain was £6,174.

Before the commissioners, the taxpayer sought to diminish or set off the tax
liability flowing from that chargeable gain in essentially two particular ways. First, *g*
he claimed that there should be deducted from the gain on the sale of the cottage an
amount equal to the replacement value of the cottage, namely, £160,000, so that, as
he contended, an allowable loss of that amount arose. The commissioners held that
there was no basis in fact or in law on which that contention of an entitlement to
claim a capital loss on the sale of the cottage could be upheld. In so far as that
contention is still alive before me (and I am not quite clear whether it is or it is not), *h*
I need say only that I agree with the commissioners' views.

The second particular matter relied on by the taxpayer before the commissioners
arose out of the theft of some jewellery and antiques from the cottage in 1979. Those
items were insured, and some two years after the theft the insurance company made
some payments to the taxpayer. It seems, as not infrequently happens, that the
insurance money was far from sufficient to enable the taxpayer to replace the items *j*
he had lost. He claims that an allowable loss thereupon arose. That claim also was
rejected by the commissioners.

In short, the position regarding that claim is this. The effect of s 20(1)(a) of the
Capital Gains Tax Act 1979 (the 1979 Act) is that capital sums received by way of
compensation for any loss of assets fall to be regarded as an occasion of the disposal
of the asset. In this case the items in question were tangible movable property.

Section 128(1) of the 1979 Act provides that the gain accruing on the disposal of such
a an asset is not a chargeable gain if the consideration for the disposal does not exceed
£2,000. Section 128(3) provides that this does not affect the amount of an allowable
loss accruing on the disposal of an asset—

'. . . but for the purposes of computing under this Act the amount of a loss
accruing on the disposal of tangible movable property the consideration for the
disposal shall, if less than £2,000, be deemed to be £2,000 and the losses which
b are allowable losses shall be restricted accordingly.'

The effect of the latter provision is that there can be no question of an allowable
loss in respect of a disposal of tangible movable property, unless the acquisition cost
exceeds £2,000. For that purpose each item of jewellery and each antique piece of
furniture , or whatever, falls to be considered separately.
c   The taxpayer told me that he acquired all these items by way of inheritance.
Accordingly, in the ordinary course what one would be concerned to ascertain would
be the market value of those assets at the time of their acquisition by the taxpayer.
      As to that, the position is that there was no evidence before the commissioners
that any of the items had a market value in excess of £2,000 at the time the taxpayer
acquired them. The taxpayer has said to me that he could have adduced evidence
d showing that some items were indeed worth in excess of that amount had he
appreciated that such evidence was called for. He has told me that only today has he
understood for the first time that such evidence was needed. On that I have to say
that the position is this. I am hearing an appeal from a decision of the General
Commissioners. I am concerned to adjudicate whether the commissioners came to a
correct decision in law on the basis of the facts presented to them and as set out by
e them in the case stated. I do not think there is any question of my being able, at this
stage, to go into matters of fact such as the taxpayer has now raised on questions not
ventilated before the General Commissioners. The taxpayer had a proper
opportunity of presenting his factual case to that body. The consequence of this, in
the events which have happened, is that there can be no question of an allowable loss
in respect of the items which, unhappily, were stolen from the taxpayer's cottage.
f   Underlying this matter, however, is a much more general grievance by the
taxpayer. He has told me that he was unable to fill in his tax returns for certain years
in the 1970s and, in consequence, he did not claim certain personal allowances or
certain tax losses to which he was entitled. He says he did not fill in his tax returns
and make those claims because he was not able accurately to state the amount of the
salary that he knew he had received. He knew he had been paid a salary, but did not
g know precisely how much it was. Had he been able to fill in his tax returns and make
those claims his financial position would not have been such that, as happened in the
event, he was compelled to sell his cottage. So he says there ought to be no question
of any assessment in respect of the sale of the cottage because, so he says, that was
the fault of the Revenue. He further says that the accounts that were produced in
respect of a certain company were false and they were known by the Revenue to be
h false.
      The taxpayer clearly feels very strongly on these matters. The position before the
commissioners was that these matters were ventilated. In the case stated the
commissioners recorded the substance of the taxpayer's contentions but made no
findings of fact because, as they said, they did not consider those matters to be
relevant to the question before them. So that is the first difficulty confronting the
j taxpayer when he seeks to raise these matters on this appeal: there are no facts
concerning these issues set out in the case stated. Thus the taxpayer lacks the basis
necessary for him to seek to advance any arguments on these issues.
      Quite apart from that difficulty however, I have to say that, on what the taxpayer
has told me, I do not at present understand how he seeks to say that any difficulties
he had in quantifying the amount of his salary, and hence filling in his tax returns,
can fairly be laid at the door of the Inland Revenue Commissioners. Whoever may

have been responsible for his difficulties, if there were any as he puts to me, at the moment I am unable to perceive how those difficulties can be said to have been the fault of the inspector. As the matter has been presented today, I have to say that I think the taxpayer has allowed his grievance against others to overflow against the Revenue without, on the material put to me, any good reason. Be that as it may, for the reasons I have sought to give, this appeal will have to be dismissed.

Appeal dismissed with costs.

Solicitor: *Solicitor of Inland Revenue.*

Rengan Krishnan Esq   Barrister.

Smith (Inspector of Taxes) v Abbott and related appeals

CHANCERY DIVISION
WARNER J
8, 9, 10, 18 OCTOBER 1991

Emoluments from office or employment – Deduction from emoluments – Expenses necessarily incurred in performance of duties of office or employment – Newspaper allowance – Whether cost of newspapers purchased by journalists wholly, exclusively and necessarily incurred in the performance of their duties – Income and Corporation Taxes Act 1970, s 189.

The taxpayers, five journalists, were employed by Associated Newspapers Ltd. Four of them worked for the *Daily Mail.* They were Mr Abbott (news layout journalist); Mr Holt (staff photographer); Mr Scovell (sports reporter); and Mr Shuttleworth (assistant chief sub-editor). The fifth taxpayer, Mr Woodhouse (picture editor), worked for the *Mail on Sunday.* The taxpayers each received a newspaper allowance as reimbursement towards expenses incurred by them in purchasing newspapers and periodicals. On appeal to the General Commissioners against assessments to income tax under Sch E for the years 1980–81 to 1985–86 the taxpayers claimed that the newspaper allowance was deductible under s 189[a] of the Income and Corporation Taxes Act 1970 on the grounds: (a) that it was a condition of their employment that they purchase and read newspapers and periodicals; and (b) that it was an integral part of their duties to do so. In the cases of Mr Holt, Mr Scovell, Mr Shuttleworth and Mr Woodhouse (the four taxpayers) the commissioners found that reading newspapers and periodicals was a necessary part of the duties of their employment and not merely required to qualify them or maintain their qualifications to do their duties. There was no such finding in Mr Abbott's case. Nevertheless, the commissioners allowed all five appeals holding that the expenditure in question had been incurred wholly, exclusively and necessarily in the performance of the taxpayers' duties and that the allowance was therefore deductible under s 189. The Crown appealed to the High Court contending: (a) that the taxpayers read newspapers and periodicals to keep themselves qualified for the purposes of their duties and that the reading was not undertaken 'in the performance of' their duties; (b) that the findings by the commissioners were insufficient to justify the conclusion that the expenditure was 'necessarily' incurred ie that the taxpayers' duties could not be performed without incurring such expenditure; and (c) that, because the expenditure was at least in part incurred in preparation for the duties, it could not be said to have been 'wholly and exclusively' so incurred.

Held – (1) In the cases of the four taxpayers, the commissioners' findings that the reading of the newspapers and periodicals was a necessary part of the performance of the duties of their employment, read with their other findings as to the duties of the taxpayers, were fairly capable of leading to the conclusion that the expenditure had been incurred wholly, exclusively and necessarily in the performance of the taxpayers' duties. The allowance was therefore deductible under s 189 and the Crown's appeals in the cases of the four taxpayers would be dismissed.

(2) In the case of Mr Abbott there was no finding that his reading of newspapers and periodicals was a necessary part of the performance of the duties of his employment. Accordingly, the true and only reasonable conclusion from the facts found by the commissioners was that the expenditure on newspapers and periodicals

---

a   Section 189, so far as material, is set out at p 674 *f–g*, post

had been incurred by Mr Abbott in order to keep himself qualified to perform the
duties of his employment. Therefore the expenditure in question was not incurred   *a*
by Mr Abbott wholly, exclusively and necessarily in the performance of his duties.
The Crown's appeal in Mr Abbott's case would therefore be allowed.

Dicta of Lord Radcliffe in *Edwards (Inspector of Taxes) v Bairstow* (1955) 36 TC
207 at 227 applied.

Notes   *b*

For expenses generally, see Simon's Taxes Division E4.7.

For expenses incurred in maintaining or improving the capacity to carry out
duties, see ibid, E4.717.

For the Income and Corporation Taxes Act 1970, s 189 (now the Income and
Corporation Taxes Act 1988, s 198) see ibid, Part G1.   *c*

Cases referred to in judgment

Blackwell (Inspector of Taxes) v Mills (1945) 26 TC 468.
Brown v Bullock (Inspector of Taxes) [1961] 1 WLR 53, [1961] 1 All ER 206; [1961]
    1 WLR 1095, [1961] 3 All ER 129, 40 TC 1, CA.   *d*
Edwards (Inspector of Taxes) v Bairstow [1956] AC 1, [1955] 3 All ER 48, 36 TC 207,
    HL.
Humbles (Inspector of Taxes) v Brooks (1962) 40 TC 500.
Lomax (Inspector of Taxes) v Newton [1953] 1 WLR 1123, [1953] 2 All ER 801, 34
    TC 558.
Ricketts v Colquhoun (Inspector of Taxes) [1924] 2 KB 347; [1925] 1 KB 725, CA;   *e*
    [1926] AC 1, 10 TC 118, HL.
Simpson (Inspector of Taxes) v Tate [1925] 2 KB 214, 9 TC 314.
Taylor v Provan (Inspector of Taxes) [1972] 1 WLR 1459, [1972] 3 All ER 930;
    [1973] STC 170, [1973] Ch 388, [1973] 2 All ER 65, CA; [1974] STC 168, [1975]
    AC 194, [1974] 1 All ER 1201, 49 TC 579, HL.

                                                                                    f

Cases also cited

Bentleys, Stokes & Lowless v Beeson (Inspector of Taxes) [1951] 2 All ER 667; [1952]
    2 All ER 82, 33 TC 491, CA.
Elwood (Inspector of Taxes) v Utitz (1964) 42 TC 482, CA (NI).
McKie (Inspector of Taxes) v Warner [1961] 1 WLR 1230, [1961] 3 All ER 348, 40   *g*
    TC 65.
Nolder (Inspector of Taxes) v Walters (1930) 15 TC 380.
Pook (Inspector of Taxes) v Owen [1967] 1 WLR 679, [1967] 2 All ER 579; [1969] 1
    Ch 535, [1968] 1 All ER 261, CA; [1970] AC 244, [1969] 2 All ER 1, 45 TC 571,
    HL.

                                                                                    h

Cases stated

Smith (Inspector of Taxes) v Abbott

1. At a meeting of the Commissioners for the general purposes of the income tax
for the City of London division held on 20, 21, 28, 29 and 30 June 1989, Mr Patrick   *j*
John Abbott (the taxpayer) appealed against assessments to income tax under Sch E,
Case I for the years 1980–81 to 1985–86 inclusive in respect of his emoluments as a
journalist of the *Daily Mail*.

2. The question for the commissioners' decision was whether there should be
deducted as expenses under s 189 of the Income and Corporation Taxes Act 1970
(the 1970 Act) so much of the cost of newspapers and periodicals purchased by him

as was reimbursed to him by his employer, Associated Newspapers Ltd, for the
relevant years.

3. The commissioners who heard the appeals gave their decision of principle in
writing on 1 December 1989. A copy of that decision was annexed thereto and
formed part of the case.

4. (1) The witnesses were referred to in para 3 of the decision and a transcript of
the oral evidence was made available to the commissioners. [Sub-paragraph (2) then
listed the documents admitted or proved before the commissioners.]

5. The findings of fact on the evidence adduced and the contentions of the parties
were set out in the commissioners' decision. The cases cited were also referred to
apart from *Humbles (Inspector of Taxes) v Brooks* (1962) 40 TC 500 which, although
taken into account in the commissioners' decision, was omitted in error therefrom.

6. On 14 May 1990, in accordance with the amounts agreed between the parties
based on the commissioners' decision, the commissioners determined the appeals by
amending the assessments to the following amounts:

Year	Assessment	Deductible expenses	Amount determined
	£	£	£
1980–81	18,092	627	17,465
1981–82	20,692	694	19,998
1982–83	16,761	778	15,983
1983–84	18,109	790	17,319
1984–85	19,180	790	18,390
1985–86	20,756	750	20,006

7. Immediately after the commissioners' determination the Solicitor of Inland
Revenue expressed dissatisfaction therewith as being erroneous in point of law and
required them to state a case for the opinion of the High Court pursuant to s 56 of
the Taxes Management Act 1970.

8. The question of law for the opinion of the court was whether the commissioners
had erred in law in concluding on the facts found by them that the expenditure
incurred was deductible from the taxpayer's emoluments under s 189 of the 1970
Act.

DECISION

1. We have before us appeals against assessments under Sch E, Case I for the
years 1980–81 to 1985–86 inclusive on the taxpayer in respect of his emoluments as a
journalist of the *Daily Mail*, his employer being Associated Newspapers Ltd.

2. (a) The question for our decision is whether there should be deducted as
expenses under s 189 of the 1970 Act so much of the cost of newspapers and
periodicals which he purchased as was reimbursed to him by his employer for the
following years of assessment:

Year of assessment	Amount
	£
1980–81	587
1981–82	654
1982–83	733
1983–84	760
1984–85	760
1985–86	720

(b) It was agreed by both parties: (i) that the amount of the reimbursement is
correctly included in the assessment as an assessable emolument; (ii) that amounts
were expended on the newspapers and periodicals at least equal to the sums
reimbursed and that the expenses claimed as a deduction are of the reimbursed
amounts only.

3. In addition to documentary evidence, we have been given oral evidence by the taxpayer and Mr G P Burden, the deputy managing editor of the *Daily Mail*. Mr Burden as deputy managing editor of the *Daily Mail* was responsible for all aspects of management of the paper including employee contracts. He had begun his working life as a reporter in the 1960s and had held various editorial posts on the *Daily Mail*. He was deputy news editor in 1987 when he was promoted to his present post.

The taxpayer was represented by Mr P G Whiteman QC and Miss Simmons of counsel, the inspector of taxes by Mr A G Moses of counsel.

4. For the taxpayer it was contended as follows: (a) The taxpayer was required by his employers to purchase and read newspapers and periodicals. (b) The purchase and reading of them was an incident of his duties and was a condition of his employment. (c) The reading was not preparation for, or to qualify him to carry out, his duties but was an integral part of those duties. (d) No part of the expenditure was incurred for private purposes. (e) The expenditure was necessarily incurred in the performance of the duties. (f) The amount of the newspaper allowance was within the meaning of s 189(1) wholly, exclusively and necessarily expended in the performance of the duties. (g) The appeals should be allowed.

5. For the Crown it was contended as follows: (a) Section 189 requires the taxpayer to prove: (i) that he, as an employee, was necessarily obliged to incur the expenditure in the course of his duties; (ii) that the expenditure was incurred in the actual performance of those duties; and (iii) that the expenditure was wholly and exclusively incurred in the actual performance of the duties. (b) The commissioners had to determine objectively whether the duties of the employment required the expenditure to be made, irrespective of the personal choice or identity of the office holder. (c) The fact that the employers required the employee to incur the expenditure was not enough. (d) For the expenditure to be allowable it must be established that no one could do the taxpayer's job without incurring it. (e) The expenditure must be incurred in the actual performance of the duties; that does not mean expenditure incurred before or after their performance or expenditure incurred in order to enable the taxpayer to perform those duties. (f) Expenditure was not incurred in the performance of duties if it was incurred: (i) to make a person fit to do his duty; or (ii) to qualify or keep a person qualified and prepared for his duties. (g) Expenditure had to be incurred wholly and exclusively in the performance of the duties so that expenditure which provided material which might actually be used from time to time was not so incurred. (h) The expenditure was not deductible because: (i) it derived from the fact that the taxpayer was not required and did not choose to get into the office before his shift and did not choose to stay at the office after the shift; and (ii) it was not incurred wholly and exclusively in the actual performance of his duties because it was for the purposes of keeping abreast of current affairs as presented in newspapers and periodicals or at least in part was incurred to keep up to date, ready and prepared to perform the actual tasks of the day.

6. We were referred to the following cases:

Bentleys, Stokes & Lowless v Beeson (Inspector of Taxes) (1951) 33 TC 491.
Brown v Bullock (Inspector of Taxes) [1961] 1 WLR 1095, 40 TC 1.
Donnelly (Inspector of Taxes) v Williamson [1982] STC 88.
Elwood (Inspector of Taxes) v Utitz (1964) 42 TC 482.
Lomax (Inspector of Taxes) v Newton [1953] 1 WLR 1123, 34 TC 558.
McKie (Inspector of Taxes) v Warner [1961] 1 WLR 1230, 40 TC 65.
Nolder (Inspector of Taxes) v Walters (1930) 15 TC 380.
Pook (Inspector of Taxes) v Owen [1970] AC 244, 45 TC 571.
Ricketts v Colquhoun (Inspector of Taxes) [1926] AC 1, 10 TC 118.
Simpson (Inspector of Taxes) v Tate [1925] 2 KB 214, 9 TC 514.
Taylor v Provan (Inspector of Taxes) [1974] STC 168, [1975] AC 194.

7. We find the following facts:

a   (a) The taxpayer during the years of assessment was employed as news layout journalist for the *Daily Mail*. His duties involved attendance at the *Daily Mail* offices four days a week. If he was on early shift, he worked from 3.00 p m to midnight, if on late shift from 5.30 p m to 2.30 a m.

(b) His duties were to create a page or series of pages with news stories and pictures relative to one another and to the advertisements in such a way as to be **b** attractive and make people want to read it. He organised illustration with types, graphs or drawings. He had to work out measures for headlines for sub-editors to write, the lengths of stories and the sizes of pictures. The creation and preparation of page layouts were designed for the use of sub-editors in order to get the stories sorted out. Everything for a particular page had to be carefully measured for the space available and the taxpayer was directly responsible to the night editor or his **c** deputy and was responsible for the last production stage before the page was published.

(c) The taxpayer needed to read newspapers and periodicals in order to keep himself informed of current news and how other papers were dealing with it so that he would know what pictures to place in relation to a story. He had to have this information so that when he went to the office he did not have to be primed. As a **d** result, when he was given a series of pictures, he would know from his reading which were appropriate to a given story. The relative information had to be known by him before he started work in the office. The pictures had to suit the stories and it was no use printing pictures which had already appeared in other newspapers.

With these objects in view he purchased all the daily and Sunday newspapers. In addition he purchased the *New Statesman, Newsweek, Time, Campaign, UK Press* **e** *Gazette, Kent Messenger, TV Times* and *Radio Times*.

(d) The taxpayer collected the newspapers from the local newsagent. He initially spent about an hour at home scanning them, mainly in relation to the news pages and features pages, with special reference to their graphic presentation. The periodicals were read at other times to serve as a source of news and viewpoints in relation to the news.

f   His reading was especially directed to graphic designs and presentation in order to assist him with ideas for layout in the *Daily Mail*. On holidays he read whatever newspapers were available.

(e) It was necessary for him to do this reading and provide his own reading material otherwise than when he was performing his office duties because: (i) he had to be already equipped with the news and ideas as soon as he started his layout and **g** checking work in the office; one, two or even three pages would be waiting for him on his arrival at the office; (ii) his duties in the office gave him no time for such reading after he arrived and the job involved his working throughout the shift period without a break; (iii) the cuttings library available at the *Daily Mail* offices was not equipped to provide those daily reading facilities; and (iv) newspaper reading outside office hours was regarded by his employer and the taxpayer as an essential part of his **h** duties.

8. (a) We conclude that the reading of the newspapers and periodicals outside the *Daily Mail* offices was in the performance of the duties of the employment, notwithstanding that this was done at home and outside the hours of attendance at the *Daily Mail* offices, and the money expended on them was in each case expended wholly, exclusively and necessarily in the performance of the taxpayer's duties.

j   (b) We find also that the taxpayer spent not less than the sums referred to in para 2 above on newspapers and periodicals, that he purchased them with the sole object of reading the relative material in the performance of the duties of his employment and that there was no private purpose in the purchase.

(c) We hold that the sums expended on newspapers and periodicals by the taxpayer as indicated in para 2 above were sums expended wholly, exclusively and necessarily in the performance of the duties of his employment and are therefore expenses admissible as deductions from his emoluments within s 189(1) of the 1970 Act.

9. We adjourn the hearing to enable the parties to agree and advise us of the amounts assessable in accordance with our decision of principle so that we may determine the appeals accordingly.

Smith (Inspector of Taxes) v Holt

1. At a meeting of the Commissioners for the general purposes of the income tax for the City of London division held on 20, 21, 28, 29 and 30 June 1989, Mr Kevin Peter Holt (the taxpayer) appealed against assessments to income tax under Sch E, Case I for the years 1981–82 to 1985–86 inclusive in respect of his emoluments as a journalist of the *Daily Mail*.

[Paragraphs 2, 3, 4 and 5 were identical to paras 2, 3, 4 and 5 of the case stated in *Smith (Inspector of Taxes) v Abbott*.]

6. On 14 May 1990, in accordance with the amounts agreed between the parties based on the commissioners' decision, the commissioners determined the appeals by amending the Sch E assessments to the following amounts:

Year	Assessment	Deductible expenses	Amount determined
	£	£	£
1981–82	13,498	684	12,814
1982–83	15,320	763	14,557
1983–84	16,805	790	16,015
1984–85	17,416	790	16,626
1985–86	19,240	750	18,490

[Paragraphs 7 and 8 were identical to paras 7 and 8 of the case stated in *Smith (Inspector of Taxes) v Abbott*.]

DECISION

[Paragraphs 1, 2, 3, 4 and 5(a)–(g) were identical to paras 1, 2, 3, 4 and 5(a)–(g) of the decision in *Smith (Inspector of Taxes) v Abbott*.]

5. (h) [For the Crown it was contended, inter alia, that:] The expenditure was not deductible because: (i) if the taxpayer did not incur it he could still do his job, though less well, relying on the picture desk of his newspaper and going out on assignments which were sent to him; and (ii) it was not incurred wholly and exclusively in the actual performance of his duties because it was for the purposes of keeping abreast of current affairs as presented in newspapers and periodicals or at least in part was incurred to keep up to date, ready and prepared to perform the actual tasks of the day.

[Paragraph 6 was identical to para 6 of the decision in *Smith (Inspector of Taxes) v Abbott*.]

7. We find the following facts:

(a) The taxpayer during the years of assessment was employed as a staff photographer for the *Daily Mail*, located in the north of England. He worked at home, at the office or on assignment from Sunday to Friday, there being occasionally an assignment at weekends. He was in telephone contact with the London and Manchester picture desks from home in the morning at between 8.00 am and 9.30 am and in the evening at any time. This involved discussions about how assignments were proceeding or forthcoming assignments. He was on call effectively for 24 hours a day.

(b) The duties of the employment were to provide ideas for photographs as well as taking them. He would telephone or be telephoned to discuss ideas gleaned from reading the newspapers and accept the assignment he was to pursue. He would go

and do the work, return to the office to develop the film, print it and give the pictures
a to the picture editor. There was no set time for going home.

(c) The taxpayer needed to read newspapers to obtain ideas for stories and
photographs and to check that any idea he had was not already dealt with by another
newspaper, whether local or national. We were shown a number of examples in
which such material had resulted in pictures taken by him. Furthermore, he needed
to know the latest news so that he was always ready for discussion of matters raised
b by the picture editor.

(d)(i) With these objects in view, he purchased the *Daily Express*, the *Daily
Mirror*, the *Daily Telegraph*, the *Daily Mail*, the *Star*, the *Liverpool Daily Post*, the
Liverpool Echo, the *Manchester Evening News*, the *Warrington Guardian*, the *Mail
on Sunday* and the *Sunday Times*, and occasionally the *Sun*, the *Sunday Telegraph*
and the *Observer*. In addition, he bought the *Catholic Pictorial*, the *Herald* and the
c *Universe*. (ii) The newspapers were delivered to his house and he read them from
between 7.00 a m and 8.00 a m for three-quarters of an hour to an hour. He scanned
them at first and then read the items that interested him in more detail. He made
notes and also took cuttings for filing and for future use. When he left home early he
bought newspapers in the course of his journey. It was his practice to buy the local
newspapers of the town in which he was carrying on an assignment and read them
d before leaving the town to see whether there was anything of interest to the *Daily
Mail*. He did not read newspapers when he was on holiday although he did so on his
days off.

(e) We accept the evidence of Mr Burden and the taxpayer that the reading of
this material was a necessary part of the duties of a staff photographer as described
above and was not merely required to qualify, or maintain the qualifications of, the
e taxpayer to do the work.

(f) It was necessary for him to do this reading and provide his own reading
material otherwise than when he was in the office or on an assignment because: (i) he
had to be equipped with the news and ideas as soon as he started discussions for
assignments or the assignments themselves; (ii) his duties in the office or on
assignment gave him no time for such reading; (iii) there were no adequate provisions
f at the local offices for such reading; and (iv) newspaper reading was regarded by his
employer and by the taxpayer as an essential part of his duties.

8. (a) We conclude that the reading of newspapers and periodicals was in the
performance of the duties of the employment and the money expended on them was
in each case expended wholly, exclusively and necessarily in the performance of the
taxpayer's duties.

g (b) We find also that the taxpayer spent not less than the sums referred to in
para 2 above on newspapers and periodicals, that he purchased them with the sole
object of reading the relative material in the performance of the duties of his
employment and there was no private purpose in the purchase.

(c) We hold that the sums expended on newspapers and periodicals by the
taxpayer as indicated in para 2 above were sums expended wholly, exclusively and
h necessarily in the performance of the duties of his employment and are therefore
expenses admissible as deductions from his emoluments within s 189(1) of the 1970
Act.

[Paragraph 9 was identical to para 9 of the decision in *Smith (Inspector of Taxes) v
Abbott*.]

j   *Smith (Inspector of Taxes) v Scovell*

1. At a meeting of the Commissioners for the general purposes of the income tax
for the City of London division held on 20, 21, 28, 29 and 30 June 1989, Mr Brian
Souter Scovell (the taxpayer) appealed against assessments to income tax under
Sch E, Case I for the years 1980–81 to 1985–86 inclusive in respect of his emoluments
as a journalist of the *Daily Mail*.

[Paragraphs 2, 3, 4 and 5 were identical to paras 2, 3, 4 and 5 of the case stated in *Smith (Inspector of Taxes) v Abbott.*]

6. On 14 May 1990, in accordance with the amounts agreed between the parties based on the commissioners' decision, the commissioners determined the appeals by amending the assessments to the following amounts:

Year	Assessment	Deductible expenses	Amount determined
	£	£	£
1980–81	14,490	617	13,873
1981–82	16,265	684	15,581
1982–83	18,433	763	17,670
1983–84	19,520	790	18,730
1984–85	20,550	790	19,760
1985–86	22,165	750	21,415

[Paragraphs 7 and 8 were identical to paras 7 and 8 of the case stated in *Smith (Inspector of Taxes) v Abbott.*]

DECISION

[Paragraphs 1, 2, 3, 4 and 5(a)–(g) were identical to paras 1, 2, 3, 4 and 5(a)–(g) of the decision in *Smith (Inspector of Taxes) v Abbott.*]

5. (h) [For the Crown it was contended, inter alia, that:] The expenditure was not deductible because: (i) it derived from the fact that the taxpayer was not required and did not choose to get into the office earlier or stay later but chose to work partly at home for convenience; and (ii) it was not incurred wholly and exclusively in the actual performance of his duties because it was for the purposes of keeping abreast of current affairs as presented in newspapers and periodicals or at least in part was incurred to keep up to date, ready and prepared to perform the actual tasks of the day.

[Paragraph 6 was identical to para 6 of the decision in *Smith (Inspector of Taxes) v Abbott.*]

7. We find the following facts:

(a) The taxpayer during the years of assessment was a sports reporter for the *Daily Mail* specialising in cricket and football. He did not work set hours, working at home, in the office or on location. He used the telephone at home to call or be called from the *Daily Mail* offices to discuss his work or to make reports, and to ring people in sport. Occasionally he worked outside the United Kingdom on tour with an English cricket or football team.

(b) He reported football and cricket matches but most of his time was spent writing about events in the sports world rather than reporting what was happening in the field. He developed and explored the information which he acquired from reading other newspapers and followed up ideas obtained from them to provide stories to report for the *Daily Mail*. He reported to the sports editor at 10.00 a m on an average morning and was expected to know what had been going on as reported in other newspapers.

(c) The taxpayer had the *Daily Mail*, the *Daily Express*, the *Daily Mirror* and the *Times* delivered to his house and he bought the rest of the dailies at the railway station or wherever he was. He also bought an *Evening Standard* on the way home. He had delivered to his home the *Mail on Sunday*, the *Sunday Times*, the *Sunday Telegraph*, the *Observer*, the *Sunday Express*, the *People*, the *Sunday Mirror* and the *News of the World*. When away from home, he purchased the same newspapers which were also delivered to his home. He regularly bought the *Cricketer*, *Wisden Cricket Monthly*, *Shoot*, *Cricketer*, *World Soccer*, *Match Weekly*, *Spectator*, *New Statesman*, *Private Eye*, *Newsweek*, *Time*, *UK Press Gazette* together with other periodicals and foreign newspapers which he considered to be relevant to his sports reporting.

(d) We accept the evidence of Mr Burden and the taxpayer that the reading of
a this material was inherent in the process of fact and idea-finding involved in sports
reporting as described above and was not merely required to qualify, or maintain
the qualifications of, the taxpayer to do the work.

(e) During an average week the taxpayer spent from one to four hours a day
reading newspapers and periodicals and on Sundays a maximum of four hours. On
days he attended the office he read at home from 8.00 a m to 9.00 a m and then spent
b 30 minutes on the train continuing his reading. On Sundays, he read the sports
pages of newspapers for one-and-a-half hours from 8.00 a m. When abroad, he
bought the available English newspapers but continued to have them delivered at
home to be skimmed by him on his return.

(f) It was necessary for him to do this work outside the office because: (i) he had
to be equipped with the news as soon as he started consultations with the sports
c editor; (ii) his duties both inside and outside the office gave him no time to read the
newspapers; (iii) the cuttings library at the *Daily Mail* offices was not equipped to
provide these daily reading facilities; and (iv) newspaper reading outside office hours
was regarded by his employer and by the taxpayer as an essential part of his duties.

8. (a) We conclude that the reading of the newspapers and periodicals outside the
Daily Mail was in the performance of the duties of the employment, notwithstanding
d that this was done at home and outside the hours of attendance at those offices, and
the money expended on them was in each case expended wholly, exclusively and
necessarily in the performance of the taxpayer's duties.

(b) We find also that the taxpayer spent not less than the sums referred to in
para 2 above on newspapers and periodicals, that he purchased them with the sole
object of reading the relative material in the performance of the duties of his
e employment and that there was no private purpose in the purchase.

(c) We hold that the sums expended on newspapers and periodicals by the
taxpayer as indicated in para 2 above were sums expended wholly, exclusively and
necessarily in the performance of the duties of his employment and are therefore
expenses admissible as deductions from his emoluments within s 189(1) of the 1970
Act.

f [Paragraph 9 was identical to para 9 of the decision in *Smith (Inspector of Taxes) v
Abbott*.]

Smith (Inspector of Taxes) v Shuttleworth

1. At a meeting of the Commissioners for the general purposes of the income tax
g for the City of London division held on 20, 21, 28, 29 and 30 June 1989, Mr Terence
Reginald Shuttleworth (the taxpayer) appealed against assessments to income tax
under Sch E, Case I for the years 1980–81 to 1985–86 inclusive in respect of his
emoluments as a journalist of the *Daily Mail*.

[Paragraphs 2, 3, 4 and 5 were identical to paras 2, 3, 4 and 5 of the case stated in
Smith (Inspector of Taxes) v Abbott.]

h 6. On 14 May 1990, in accordance with the amounts agreed between the parties
based on the commissioners' decision, the commissioners determined the appeals by
amending the Sch E assessments to the following amounts:

Year	Assessment	Deductible expenses	Amount determined
	£	£	£
1980–81	18,688	617	18,071
1981–82	19,867	684	19,183
1982–83	22,697	763	21,934
1983–84	25,640	790	24,850
1984–85	27,641	790	26,851
1985–86	26,791	750	26,041

[Paragraphs 7 and 8 were identical to paras 7 and 8 of the case stated in *Smith* (*Inspector of Taxes*) *v Abbott*.]

a

DECISION

[Paragraphs 1, 2, 3, 4 and 5(a)–(g) were identical to paras 1, 2, 3, 4 and 5(a)–(g) of the decision in *Smith* (*Inspector of Taxes*) *v Abbott*.]

5. (h) [For the Crown it was contended, inter alia, that:] The expenditure was not deductible because: (i) it derived from the fact that the taxpayer was not required b and did not choose to get into the office earlier than 2.00 p m and did not choose to stay at the office all day and night; and (ii) it was not incurred wholly and exclusively in the actual performance of his duties because it was for the purposes of keeping abreast of current affairs as presented in newspapers and periodicals or at least in part was incurred to keep up to date, ready and prepared to perform the actual tasks of the day.

c

[Paragraph 6 was identical to para 6 of the decision in *Smith* (*Inspector of Taxes*) *v Abbott*.]

7. We find the following facts:

(a)(i) The taxpayer, during the years of assessment under appeal, was for 1980–81 to 1982–83, a news sub-editor and for 1983–84 to 1985–86, an assistant chief sub-editor of the *Daily Mail*. The duties of these employments involved his attendance d at the offices of the *Daily Mail* from 2.00 p m until 12.15 a m or 1.00 a m, or even later, if required, for four days a week.

(ii) As news sub-editor for particular pages of the newspaper he had to select and check the news reports, rewriting them as necessary, determine the headlines and the page layout, choose pictures, select the type and consider whether any legal problems arose. For this work, he was responsible to the chief sub-editor.

e

(iii) As assistant chief sub-editor he was in charge of a number of sub-editors and had to check and correct as necessary their work (described in sub-para a(ii) above). The paper was published on six days but the staff worked on four so that he often stood in for the chief sub-editor, when he was absent, in which case he would receive material from the 'Back Bench', the section that directs and controls all the news coverage of the newspaper (comprising the night editor and his deputy and two f assistants). He would then plan a page, select the appropriate sub-editor to deal with the particular story, giving him the necessary advice as well as checking and correcting the page. He would sometimes also stand in for others such as the 'Splash' sub-editor (responsible for the front page) or the assistant night editor, when he would have similar duties.

(iv) The various functions of the editor and the editorial staff were explained to g us with reference to a diagram showing the complete editorial hierarchy.

(b) Properly to carry out his duties he needed to have an up-to-date knowledge of all aspects of the news. In order to select copy for the next edition of the *Daily Mail*, he had to know what other newspapers were doing about a particular news item, what stage various issues in a story had reached, judge every story in relation to everything else going on, not repeat stories appearing in other newspapers the h previous day and take the story forward (where it was a continuing event) from what had appeared in the previous day's newspapers, as well as in the *Daily Mail*.

(c)(i) To this end, he purchased on a regular daily basis throughout each of the relevant periods one edition of each of *The Times*, *Daily Mail*, *Daily Express*, *Daily Telegraph*, *Daily Mirror*, *Guardian*, *Daily Star* and the *London Evening Standard*. On a weekly basis he purchased the *Mail on Sunday*, *Sunday Express*, *Sunday Times*, j *Observer*, *Sunday Mirror*, *Sunday People* and the *News of the World*. Together with the *Radio Times* and *TV Times*, he had all the foregoing newspapers delivered to his home in the morning.

(ii) In addition he purchased a number of periodicals including *Time*, *Smash Hits*, *Spectator*, *Economist*, *New Statesman*, *Private Eye*, *Newsweek* and *UK Press Gazette*

from newsvendors as and when he considered it necessary for the purpose of his
a duties. On holiday, he purchased and read the *Daily Mail.*

(d) We accept the evidence of Mr Burden and the taxpayer that the reading of
this material was a necessary part of the duties of sub-editing as described above and
was not merely required to qualify, or maintain the qualifications of, the taxpayer to
do the work.

(e) The newspapers and periodicals were generally read by the taxpayer at home
b in the morning before he left for the office. On the days of non-attendance at the
office he still had to read the newspapers and periodicals as part of his normal duties
but could spread his reading over the whole day. It was necessary for him to do this
work outside the office because: (i) he had to be equipped with the news before he
started operations in the *Daily Mail* offices; (ii) his duties there gave him no time to
read the newspapers or periodicals; he was always working against the clock; (iii) the
c cuttings library at the *Daily Mail* offices was not equipped to provide those daily
reading facilities; and (iv) newspaper reading outside office hours was regarded by
his employer and by the taxpayer as an essential part of his duties.

8. (a) We conclude that the reading of the newspapers and periodicals outside the
Daily Mail offices was in the performance of the duties of the employments,
notwithstanding that this was done at home and outside the hours of attendance at
d the *Daily Mail* offices, and the money expended on them was in each case expended
wholly, exclusively and necessarily in the performance of the taxpayer's duties.

(b) We find also that the taxpayer spent not less than the sums referred to in
para 2 above on newspapers and periodicals, that he purchased them with the sole
object of reading the relative material in the performance of the duties of his
employments and that there was no private purpose in the purchase.

e (c) We hold that the sums expended on newspapers and periodicals by the
taxpayer as indicated in para 2 above were sums expended wholly, exclusively and
necessarily in the performance of the duties of his employments and are therefore
expenses admissible as deductions from his emoluments within s 189(1) of the 1970
Act.

[Paragraph 9 was identical to para 9 of the decision in *Smith (Inspector of Taxes) v*
f *Abbott.*]

Smith (Inspector of Taxes) v Woodhouse

1. At a meeting of the Commissioners for the general purposes of the income tax
for the City of London division held on 20, 21, 28, 29 and 30 June 1989, Mr Gary
Woodhouse (the taxpayer) appealed against assessments to income tax under Sch E,
g Case I for the years 1981–82 to 1985–86 inclusive in respect of his emoluments as a
journalist of the *Mail on Sunday.*

[Paragraphs 2, 3, 4 and 5 were identical to paras 2, 3, 4 and 5 of the case stated in
Smith (Inspector of Taxes) v Abbott.]

6. On 14 May 1990, in accordance with the amounts agreed between the parties
based on the commissioners' decision, the commissioners determined the appeals by
h amending the Sch E assessments to the following amounts:

Year	Assessment	Deductible expenses	Amount determined
	£	£	£
1981–82	20,566	303	20,263
1982–83	27,138	763	26,375
1983–84	32,283	3,581	28,702
1984–85	31,796	790	31,006
1985–86	33,444	750	32,694

[Paragraphs 7 and 8 were identical to paras 7 and 8 of the case stated in *Smith*
(Inspector of Taxes) v Abbott.]

DECISION

1. We have before us appeals against assessments under Sch E, Case I for the *a* years 1981–82 to 1985–86 inclusive on the taxpayer in respect of his emoluments as a journalist of the *Mail on Sunday*, his employer being the Associated Newspapers Ltd.

2. (a) The question for our decision is whether there should be deducted as expenses under s 189 of the 1970 Act, so much of the cost of newspapers and periodicals purchased by him as was reimbursed to him by his employer for the *b* following years of assessment:

Year of assessment	Amount £
1981–82	273
1982–83	733
1983–84	760
1984–85	760
1985–86	720

[Paragraphs 2(b), 3, 4 and 5(a)–(g) were identical to paras 2(b), 3, 4 and 5(a)–(g) of the decision in *Smith (Inspector of Taxes) v Abbott*.]

5. (h) [For the Crown it was contended, inter alia, that:] The expenditure was *d* not deductible because: (i) the newspapers and periodicals could have been provided for the taxpayer to read at the office; the expenditure was personally incurred so that the taxpayer need not spend so much time at the office, being thereby given the opportunity to do reading at home; and (ii) it was not incurred wholly and exclusively in the actual performance of his duties because it was for the purpose of keeping abreast of current affairs as presented and illustrated in newspapers and periodicals *e* or at least in part was incurred to keep up to date, ready and prepared to perform the actual tasks of the day.

[Paragraph 6 was identical to para 6 of the decision in *Smith (Inspector of Taxes) v Abbott*.]

7. We find the following facts:

(a) The taxpayer during the years of assessment was the picture editor of the *Mail* *f* *on Sunday*. His duties involved attendance at the *Mail on Sunday* offices from Tuesday to Saturday (inclusive), his day there being from 9.15 a m to approximately 7.00 p m at the beginning of the week and to 10.00–11.00 p m at the end.

(b) He was directly responsible to the editor for obtaining illustrations for every page in the newspapers and any supplements. The newspaper currently had 64 pages and the supplements 48 pages. He had an assistant picture editor, a sports picture editor and a secretary assistant immediately under him. He had to generate *g* ideas for illustrations and arrange for obtaining them from in-house and freelance photographers or from other sources. He participated in an early conference on Tuesdays with other editors when the overall look of the paper and its contents were considered, usually starting on the features page. There were seven conferences with the editor and specialist editors of sections of the paper during the week. At *h* each of these, the taxpayer was expected to produce a written paper listing his ideas for copy to be discussed. He was expected to suggest to the editors ways in which particular items of news and articles could be illustrated. He was primarily there to put up visual ideas to enhance the look of the paper. He also had mini-conferences with his subordinates who were expected to provide their own ideas which he, in turn, could discuss with the other editors concerned. These were usually held before *j* the daily editorial conference (usually held at about 11.00 a m) although on Tuesdays they were held afterwards. Once ideas were approved, the taxpayer decided who would do the job and delegated the organisation of the work.

(c) To obtain the necessary ideas, the taxpayer always spoke to editors, journalists and specialists in the building because they read publications which he did not read. He always read other publications and to this end he purchased all the daily and

Sunday newspapers, the *Evening Standard* and *Evening News.* The dailies were
a delivered to his home by the local newsagent, the Sunday papers he purchased
himself from that newsagent. He purchased in London each day two or three
editions of the evening newspapers. He also purchased each publication of the
*British Journal of Photography, SLR, Amateur Photographer, Paris Match, Stern,
Creative Camera, Epoca, Punch, Time, Sussex Courier, Life, Express & Star,
Illustrated London News, Tatler, Country Life, Bunte, Cosmopolitan* and *Melbourne*
b *Newsweek.*

(d) The taxpayer gave us many examples of the profitable use to which he put the
reading of these newspapers and periodicals for the purpose of obtaining ideas for
pictures and, in some cases, to obtain copies of the pictures shown therein. We
accept the evidence of Mr Burden and the taxpayer that the reading of this material
was inherent in the process of finding ideas for the illustrations which it was his duty
c to obtain and was not merely required to qualify, or maintain the qualifications of,
the taxpayer to do the work.

(e) He read the newspapers delivered to his house on his railway journey to the
office, lasting usually from 8.30 a m to 9.15 a m, on a selective basis and continued
this at the office for the first three-quarters of an hour. There was no time afterwards
for reading newspapers or periodicals in the office. He also spent time scanning and
d buying from the railway station bookstall periodicals that would be useful for finding
illustrations or ideas for them. He would buy others on the way home and would
read them on the homeward journey and at home in the evenings. He spent three to
four hours on Sunday morning reading the Sunday newspapers. On holidays he
read every newspaper and periodical he could buy, since even then he was on call,
and if a story broke where he was, he was expected to file copy.

e (f) It was necessary for him to do this reading and provide his own reading
material because: (a) he had to be equipped with ideas as soon as he started
consultations with specialist editors and the editor of the *Mail on Sunday*; (b) his
duties in the office except for the first three-quarters of an hour gave him no
time for such reading; (c) the cuttings library available to employees of the *Mail
on Sunday* was not equipped to provide the necessary reading facilities; and
f (d) newspaper reading outside office hours was regarded by his employer and by
the taxpayer as an essential part of his duties.

8. (a) We conclude that the reading of the newspapers and periodicals outside
the offices of the *Mail on Sunday* was in the performance of the duties of the
employment notwithstanding that this was done at home and on the train outside
the hours of attendance at the offices of the *Mail on Sunday*, and the money
g expended on them was in each case expended wholly, exclusively and necessarily in
the performance of the taxpayer's duties.

(b) We find also that the taxpayer spent not less than the sums referred to in
para 2 above on newspapers and periodicals, that he purchased them with the sole
object of reading the relative material in the performance of the duties of his
employment and that there was no private purpose in the purchase.

h (c) We hold that the sums expended on newspapers and periodicals by the
taxpayer as indicated in para 2 above were sums expended wholly, exclusively and
necessarily in the performance of the duties of his employment and are therefore
expenses admissible as deductions from his emoluments within s 189(1) of the 1970
Act.

[Paragraph 9 was identical to para 9 of the decision in *Smith (Inspector of Taxes) v
j Abbott.*]

Alan Moses QC and *Nicholas Warren* for the Crown.
Peter Whiteman QC and *Marion Simmons* for the taxpayers.

Cur adv vult

18 October. The following judgment was delivered.

a

WARNER J. These are appeals by the Crown against five decisions of the General
Commissioners for the City of London concerning liability for income tax under
Sch E. The respondent in each case is a journalist employed by Associated
Newspapers Ltd. Of the respondents (the taxpayers), four worked for the *Daily
Mail*. They are: Mr P J Abbott, a news layout journalist; Mr K P Holt, a staff
photographer; Mr B S Scovell, a sports reporter specialising in cricket and football;   b
and Mr T R Shuttleworth, who was at first a news sub-editor and subsequently an
assistant chief sub-editor. The fifth taxpayer is Mr Gary Woodhouse, the picture
editor of the *Mail on Sunday*. Their appeals to the General Commissioners were
heard together on five days in June 1989, during which all five gave evidence, as did
Mr G P Burden, the deputy managing editor of the *Daily Mail*. The decisions of
the commissioners were given together on 1 December 1989.   c
    Except in the case of Mr Woodhouse, the years of assessment under appeal are
the years 1980–81 to 1985–86. In the case of Mr Woodhouse, they are the years
1981–82 to 1985–86 because, I understand, he did not become employed by
Associated Newspapers Ltd until some time in 1981–82. In each of those years each
of the taxpayers received from Associated Newspapers Ltd an allowance in
reimbursement of the cost of newspapers and periodicals which he bought. In each   d
year the amounts of the allowances received by the taxpayers were identical, except
that Mr Woodhouse received no allowance for 1980–81 and only part of the allowance
for 1981–82.
    The question for determination by the General Commissioners was whether, in
the case of each taxpayer, the amount of the allowance was deductible from his
emoluments as an expense under s 189(1) of the Income and Corporation Taxes Act   e
1970 (the 1970 Act). It was agreed between the parties before the commissioners
(and that agreement holds in this court): (i) that the amount of the allowance was
correctly included in that taxpayer's assessment under Sch E as an assessable
emolument; and (ii) that he had spent on newspapers and periodicals an amount at
least equal to the amount of the allowance.
    Section 189(1) (which is a re-enactment of a provision which has existed in   f
successive Income Tax Acts since the mid-nineteenth century) provides:

> 'If the holder of an office or employment is necessarily obliged to incur and
> defray out of the emoluments thereof the expenses of travelling in the
> performance of the duties of the office or employment, or of keeping and
> maintaining a horse to enable him to perform the same, or otherwise to expend   g
> money wholly, exclusively and necessarily in the performance of the said duties,
> there may be deducted from the emoluments to be assessed the expenses so
> necessarily incurred and defrayed.'

It is notorious that that provision is rigid, narrow and to some extent unfair in its
operation. In order to satisfy its requirements, an office-holder or employee has to   h
show four things. First, he has to show that he has incurred the expenses in question
'in the performance of the duties of the office or employment'. That phrase is to be
contrasted with the more generous phrase, if I may so express it, in s 130(*a*) of the
1970 Act relating to expenditure deductible under Sch D, Cases I and II. That
expenditure needs only to be 'for the purposes of the trade, profession or vocation'.
Second, an office-holder or employee has to show that the expenses he seeks to   j
deduct are expenses that he has been 'necessarily obliged' to incur and defray in the
performance of the duties of the office or employment. Third, he has to show that
those expenses have been 'wholly' so incurred. The better view seems to be that that
goes only to quantum. Last, he has to show that they have been 'exclusively' so
incurred.

a   Each of the cases stated for these appeals has annexed to it the decision of the General Commissioners in the case of the taxpayer concerned. The five cases stated and decisions follow the same pattern and much of the wording is common to them all. The findings and conclusions of the commissioners are expressed in paras 7 and 8 of each decision. I will read first those paragraphs in the decision concerning Mr Holt:

'7. We find the following facts:

b   (a) [Mr Holt] during the years of assessment was employed as a staff photographer for the *Daily Mail*, located in the north of England. He worked at home, at the office or on assignment from Sunday to Friday, there being occasionally an assignment at weekends. He was in telephone contact with the London and Manchester picture desks from home in the morning at between 8.00 a m and 9.30 a m and in the evening at any time. This involved discussions about how assignments were proceeding or forthcoming assignments. He was

c   on call effectively for 24 hours a day.

(b) The duties of the employment were to provide ideas for photographs as well as taking them. He would telephone or be telephoned to discuss ideas gleaned from reading the newspapers and accept the assignment he was to pursue. He would go and do the work, return to the office to develop the film, print it and

d   give the pictures to the picture editor. There was no set time for going home.

(c) [Mr Holt] needed to read newspapers to obtain ideas for stories and photographs and to check that any idea he had was not already dealt with by another newspaper, whether local or national. We were shown a number of examples in which such material had resulted in pictures taken by him. Furthermore, he needed to know the latest news so that he was always ready for

e   discussion of matters raised by the picture editor.

(d)(i) With these objects in view, he purchased . . . [there follows a list of the newspapers, some national and some local, and of periodicals that he bought]. (ii) The newspapers were delivered to his house and he read them from between 7.00 a m and 8.00 a m for three-quarters of an hour to an hour. He scanned them at first and then read the items that interested him in more detail. He

f   made notes and also took cuttings for filing and for future use. When he left home early he bought newspapers in the course of his journey. It was his practice to buy the local newspapers of the town in which he was carrying on an assignment and read them before leaving the town to see whether there was anything of interest to the *Daily Mail*. He did not read newspapers when he was on holiday although he did so on his days off.

g   (e) We accept the evidence of Mr Burden and [Mr Holt] that the reading of this material was a necessary part of the duties of a staff photographer as described above and was not merely required to qualify, or maintain the qualifications of, [Mr Holt] to do the work.

(f) It was necessary for him to do this reading and provide his own reading material otherwise than when he was in the office or on an assignment because:

h   (i) he had to be equipped with the news and ideas as soon as he started discussions for assignments or the assignments themselves; (ii) his duties in the office or on assignment gave him no time for such reading; (iii) there were no adequate provisions at the local offices for such reading; and (iv) newspaper reading was regarded by his employer and by [Mr Holt] as an essential part of his duties.

j   8. (a) We conclude that the reading of newspapers and periodicals was in the performance of the duties of the employment and the money expended on them was in each case expended wholly, exclusively and necessarily in the performance of [Mr Holt's] duties.

(b) We find also that [Mr Holt] spent not less than the sums referred to in para 2 above [those were the amounts of the allowance] on newspapers and periodicals, that he purchased them with the sole object of reading the relative material in the performance of the duties of his employment and there was no *a* private purpose in the purchase.

(c) We hold that the sums expended on newspapers and periodicals by [Mr Holt] as indicated in para 2 above were sums expended wholly, exclusively and necessarily in the performance of the duties of his employment and are therefore expenses admissible as deductions from his emoluments within s 189(1) of the 1970 Act.'   *b*

Paragraphs 7(a) and (b) of the decision in Mr Scovell's case are different. They read as follows:

'7. (a) [Mr Scovell] during the years of assessment was a sports reporter for the *Daily Mail* specialising in cricket and football. He did not work set hours, working at home, in the office or on location. He used the telephone at home to *c* call or be called from the *Daily Mail* offices to discuss his work or to make reports, and to ring people in sport. Occasionally he worked outside the United Kingdom on tour with an English cricket or football team.

(b) He reported football and cricket matches but most of his time was spent writing about events in the sports world rather than reporting what was happening in the field. He developed and explored the information which he *d* acquired from reading other newspapers and followed up ideas obtained from them to provide stories to report for the *Daily Mail*. He reported to the sports editor at 10.00 a m on an average morning and was expected to know what had been going on as reported in other newspapers.'

Sub-paragraph (c) gives details of the newspapers and periodicals bought by Mr Scovell and ends—'. . . together with other periodicals and foreign newspapers which *e* he considered to be relevant to his sports reporting'.

Sub-paragraph (d) corresponds with sub-para (e) of the decision in Mr Holt's case. It reads:

'We accept the evidence of Mr Burden and [Mr Scovell] that the reading of this material was inherent in the process of fact and idea-finding involved in *f* sports reporting as described above and was not merely required to qualify, or maintain the qualifications of, [Mr Scovell] to do the work.'

Sub-paragraphs (e) and (f) read:

'(e) During an average week [Mr Scovell] spent from one to four hours a day reading newspapers and periodicals and on Sundays a maximum of four hours. *g* On days he attended the office he read at home from 8.00 a m to 9.00 a m and then spent 30 minutes on the train continuing his reading. On Sundays, he read the sports pages of newspapers for one-and-a-half hours from 8.00 a m. When abroad, he bought the available English newspapers but continued to have them delivered at home to be skimmed by him on his return.

(f) It was necessary for him to do this work outside the office because: (i) he had *h* to be equipped with the news as soon as he started consultations with the sports editor; (ii) his duties both inside and outside the office gave him no time to read the newspapers; (iii) the cuttings library at the *Daily Mail* offices was not equipped to provide these daily reading facilities; and (iv) newspaper reading outside office hours was regarded by his employer and by [Mr Scovell] as an essential part of his duties.'   *j*

Paragraph 8 of the decision in Mr Scovell's case is, save in one respect, in the same terms as para 8 of the decision in Mr Holt's case. The difference is that in Mr Scovell's case para 8(a) reads:

'We conclude that the reading of the newspapers and periodicals outside the *Daily Mail* [offices] was in the performance of the duties of the employment,

a   notwithstanding that this was done at home and outside the hours of attendance
at those offices, and the money expended on them was in each case expended
wholly, exclusively and necessarily in the performance of [Mr Scovell's] duties.'

There are variants of that formula in the other cases but in each, paras 8(b) and (c)
are in the same terms.

In para 7 of their decision in Mr Shuttleworth's case the General Commissioners
say:

b
'We find the following facts:
(a)(i) [Mr Shuttleworth], during the years of assessment under appeal, was for
1980–81 to 1982–83, a news sub-editor and for 1983–84 to 1985–86, an assistant
chief sub-editor of the *Daily Mail*. The duties of these employments involved
his attendance at the offices of the *Daily Mail* from 2.00 p m until 12.15 a m or
c   1.00 a m, or even later, if required, for four days a week.
(ii) As news sub-editor for particular pages of the newspaper he had to select
and check the news reports, rewriting them as necessary, determine the
headlines and the page layout, choose pictures, select the type and consider
whether any legal problems arose. For this work, he was responsible to the chief
sub-editor.

d   (iii) As assistant chief sub-editor he was in charge of a number of sub-editors
and had to check and correct as necessary their work (described in sub-para a(ii)
above). The paper was published on six days but the staff worked on four so
that he often stood in for the chief sub-editor, when he was absent, in which
case he would receive material from the "Back Bench", the section that directs
and controls all the news coverage of the newspaper (comprising the night
e   editor and his deputy and two assistants). He would then plan a page, select the
appropriate sub-editor to deal with the particular story, giving him the necessary
advice as well as checking and correcting the page. He would sometimes also
stand in for others such as the "Splash" sub-editor (responsible for the front
page) or the assistant night editor, when he would have similar duties.
(iv) The various functions of the editor and the editorial staff were explained to
f   us with reference to a diagram showing the complete editorial hierarchy.
(b) Properly to carry out his duties he needed to have an up-to-date knowledge
of all aspects of the news. In order to select copy for the next edition of the *Daily
Mail*, he had to know what other newspapers were doing about a particular
news item, what stage various issues in a story had reached, judge every story in
relation to everything else going on, not repeat stories appearing in other
g   newspapers the previous day and take the story forward (where it was a
continuing event) from what had appeared in the previous day's newspapers, as
well as in the *Daily Mail*.'

Sub-paragraph (c)(i) begins: 'To this end, he purchased' and then gives details of the
newspapers that Mr Shuttleworth purchased. Sub-paragraph (c)(ii) gives details of
periodicals he purchased 'as and when he considered it necessary for the purpose of
h   his duties'.

Sub-paragraphs (d) and (e) are in the following terms:

'(d) We accept the evidence of Mr Burden and [Mr Shuttleworth] that the
reading of this material was a necessary part of the duties of sub-editing as
described above and was not merely required to qualify, or maintain the
j   qualifications of, [Mr Shuttleworth] to do the work.
(e) The newspapers and periodicals were generally read by [Mr Shuttleworth]
at home in the morning before he left for the office. On the days of non-
attendance at the office he still had to read the newspapers and periodicals as
part of his normal duties but could spread his reading over the whole day. It
was necessary for him to do this work outside the office because: (i) he had to be
equipped with the news before he started operations in the *Daily Mail* offices;

(ii) his duties there gave him no time to read the newspapers or periodicals; he was always working against the clock; (iii) the cuttings library at the *Daily Mail* offices was not equipped to provide those daily reading facilities; and (iv) newspaper reading outside office hours was regarded by his employer and by [Mr Shuttleworth] as an essential part of his duties.'

I do not find it possible fairly to summarise para 7 of the decision in Mr Woodhouse's case. Despite its length I will read it all:

'7. We find the following facts:
(a) [Mr Woodhouse] during the years of assessment was the picture editor of the *Mail on Sunday*. His duties involved attendance at the *Mail on Sunday* offices from Tuesday to Saturday (inclusive), his day there being from 9.15 am to approximately 7.00 pm at the beginning of the week and to 10.00–11.00 pm at the end.
(b) He was directly responsible to the editor for obtaining illustrations for every page in the newspapers and any supplements. The newspaper currently had 64 pages and the supplements 48 pages. He had an assistant picture editor, a sports picture editor and a secretary assistant immediately under him. He had to generate ideas for illustrations and arrange for obtaining them from in-house and freelance photographers or from other sources. He participated in an early conference on Tuesdays with other editors when the overall look of the paper and its contents were considered, usually starting on the features page. There were seven conferences with the editor and specialist editors of sections of the paper during the week. At each of these, [Mr Woodhouse] was expected to produce a written paper listing his ideas for copy to be discussed. He was expected to suggest to the editors ways in which particular items of news and articles could be illustrated. He was primarily there to put up visual ideas to enhance the look of the paper. He also had mini-conferences with his subordinates who were expected to provide their own ideas which he, in turn, could discuss with the other editors concerned. These were usually held before the daily editorial conference (usually held at about 11.00 am) although on Tuesdays they were held afterwards. Once ideas were approved, [Mr Woodhouse] decided who would do the job and delegated the organisation of the work.
(c) To obtain the necessary ideas, [Mr Woodhouse] always spoke to editors, journalists and specialists in the building because they read publications which he did not read. He always read other publications and to this end he purchased all the daily and Sunday newspapers, the *Evening Standard* and *Evening News*. The dailies were delivered to his home by the local newsagent, the Sunday papers he purchased himself from that newsagent. He purchased in London each day two or three editions of the evening newspapers. He also purchased each publication of the *British Journal of Photography, SLR, Amateur Photographer, Paris Match, Stern, Creative Camera, Epoca, Punch, Time, Sussex Courier, Life, Express & Star, Illustrated London News, Tatler, Country Life, Bunte, Cosmopolitan* and *Melbourne Newsweek*.
(d) [Mr Woodhouse] gave us many examples of the profitable use to which he put the reading of these newspapers and periodicals for the purpose of obtaining ideas for pictures and, in some cases, to obtain copies of the pictures shown therein. We accept the evidence of Mr Burden and [Mr Woodhouse] that the reading of this material was inherent in the process of finding ideas for the illustrations which it was his duty to obtain and was not merely required to qualify, or maintain the qualifications of, [Mr Woodhouse] to do the work.
(e) He read the newspapers delivered to his house on his railway journey to the office, lasting usually from 8.30 am to 9.15 am, on a selective basis and continued this at the office for the first three-quarters of an hour. There was no time

afterwards for reading newspapers or periodicals in the office. He also spent
time scanning and buying from the railway station bookstall periodicals that
would be useful for finding illustrations or ideas for them. He would buy others
on the way home and would read them on the homeward journey and at home
in the evenings. He spent three to four hours on Sunday morning reading the
Sunday newspapers. On holidays he read every newspaper and periodical he
could buy, since even then he was on call, and if a story broke where he was, he
was expected to file copy.

(f) It was necessary for him to do this reading and provide his own reading
material because: (a) he had to be equipped with ideas as soon as he started
consultations with specialist editors and the editor of the *Mail on Sunday*; (b) his
duties in the office except for the first three-quarters of an hour gave him no
time for such reading; (c) the cuttings library available to employees of the *Mail
on Sunday* was not equipped to provide the necessary reading facilities; and
(d) newspaper reading outside office hours was regarded by his employer and
by [Mr Woodhouse] as an essential part of his duties.'

I have left the decision in Mr Abbott's case until last because that differs from the
others in that it contains no statement of the kind that is to be found in para 7(e) of
the decision in Mr Holt's case and paras 7(d) of the decisions in Mr Scovell's, Mr
Shuttleworth's and Mr Woodhouse's cases to the effect that the General Commissioners had accepted the evidence of Mr Burden and the taxpayer concerned about
the reading of the material in the newspapers and periodicals bought by that
taxpayer being a necessary part of the duties of his employment, or inherent in the
process of performing those duties, and not merely required to qualify him or
maintain his qualifications to do the work. (I will, for the sake of brevity and
convenience, later refer to those statements in those decisions as 'the Burden
findings'.)

Paragraph 7 of the decision in Mr Abbott's case reads as follows:

'We find the following facts:

(a) [Mr Abbott] during the years of assessment was employed as news layout
journalist for the *Daily Mail*. His duties involved attendance at the *Daily Mail*
offices four days a week. If he was on early shift, he worked from 3.00 pm to
midnight, if on late shift from 5.30 pm to 2.30 am.

(b) His duties were to create a page or series of pages with news stories and
pictures relative to one another and to the advertisements in such a way as to be
attractive and to make people want to read it. He organised illustration with
types, graphs or drawings. He had to work out measures for headlines for sub-
editors to write, the lengths of stories and the sizes of pictures. The creation and
preparation of page layouts were designed for the use of sub-editors in order to
get the stories sorted out. Everything for a particular page had to be carefully
measured for the space available, and [Mr Abbott] was directly responsible to
the night editor or his deputy and was responsible for the last production stage
before the page was published.

(c) [Mr Abbott] needed to read newspapers and periodicals in order to keep
himself informed of current news and how other papers were dealing with it so
that he would know what pictures to place in relation to a story. He had to have
this information so that when he went to the office he did not have to be primed.
As a result, when he was given a series of pictures, he would know from his
reading which were appropriate to a given story. The relative information had
to be known by him before he started work in the office. The pictures had to
suit the stories and it was no use printing pictures which had already appeared
in other newspapers. With these objects in view he purchased all the daily and
Sunday newspapers. In addition he purchased the *New Statesman, Newsweek,
Time, Campaign, UK Press Gazette, Kent Messenger, TV Times* and *Radio
Times*.

(d) [Mr Abbott] collected the newspapers from the local newsagent. He initially spent about an hour at home scanning them, mainly in relation to the news pages and features pages, with special reference to their graphic presentation. The periodicals were read at other times to serve as a source of news and viewpoints in relation to the news. His reading was especially directed to graphic designs and presentation in order to assist him with ideas for layout in the *Daily Mail*. On holidays he read whatever newspapers were available.

(e) It was necessary for him to do this reading and provide his own reading material otherwise than when he was performing his office duties because: (i) he had to be already equipped with the news and ideas as soon as he started his layout and checking work in the office; one, two or even three pages would be waiting for him on his arrival at the office; (ii) his duties in the office gave him no time for such reading after he arrived and the job involved his working throughout the shift period without a break; (iii) the cuttings library available at the *Daily Mail* offices was not equipped to provide those daily reading facilities; and (iv) newspaper reading outside office hours was regarded by his employer and [Mr Abbott] as an essential part of his duties.'

It is common ground of course that I can reverse the decisions of the General Commissioners only if they have erred in point of law. Counsel for the Crown made three submissions in support of his contention that the commissioners had so erred.

His first and main submission was that the expenses that the taxpayers claimed to be entitled to deduct had not been incurred and defrayed by them 'in the performance of the duties of' their respective employments but in preparation for the performance of those duties. It was crucial, he submitted, for the purpose of applying s 189(1) to identify the duties of the relevant employment. This the commissioners had done in each of the present cases at the outset of para 7 of their decision, in the cases of Mr Holt, Mr Scovell, Mr Woodhouse and Mr Abbott in para 7(b) of the decision, and in the case of Mr Shuttleworth in para 7(a)(ii) and (iii). As was indicated in each of the decisions, the purpose of the taxpayer's reading of newspapers and periodicals was to equip him to perform those duties before he actually started performing them. There was, said counsel, as a matter of law a distinction, which the commissioners had disregarded, between the process of making oneself ready and able to perform the duties of one's employment and the process of actually performing those duties. Expenditure incurred by an employee in making himself ready and able to perform the duties of his employment was incurred *for the purpose* of performing those duties but not *in* the performance of them.

In support of that submission, counsel for the Crown relied mainly on *Simpson (Inspector of Taxes) v Tate* [1925] 2 KB 214, 9 TC 314 and *Humbles (Inspector of Taxes) v Brooks* (1962) 40 TC 500.

In *Simpson v Tate* Rowlatt J held that a county medical officer could not deduct from his emoluments his subscriptions to certain professional societies to which he belonged in order to keep abreast of developments and knowledge in his field. The reason was that he incurred that expenditure not in the performance of the duties of his office but in order to keep himself qualified to perform them. It is clear from his judgment that Rowlatt J intended thereby to lay down a principle applicable to 'all subscriptions to professional societies and all taking in of professional literature and all that sort of expense' (see [1925] 2 KB 214 at 219, 9 TC 314 at 318). (In fact Parliament has mitigated the severity of that principle by what in the 1970 Act was s 192, but that is not in point here.)

In *Humbles v Brooks* Ungoed-Thomas J held that the headmaster of a school who was required to teach history could not deduct from his emoluments the cost of attending a course in history at a college for adult education. One reason was that in attending the course he was not acting in the performance of his duties but qualifying himself to perform them.

Counsel for the Crown relied also on dicta in other cases, in particular on a
sentence in the speech of Lord Salmon in *Taylor v Provan (Inspector of Taxes)*
[1974] STC 168 at 190, [1975] AC 194 at 226–227, where he said:

> 'In my view, the decision in *Ricketts v Colquhoun* [see [1926] AC 1, 10 TC
> 118] does no more than confirm the proposition that "in the performance of the
> duties" must be given a strict interpretation and does not mean "in order to
> enable the duties to be performed".'

What Lord Salmon had in mind there is shown by his next sentence: 'Expenses
incurred in travelling to work are not deductible.' Counsel submitted that a duty to
equip oneself with the knowledge necessary to perform the duties of one's
employment was analogous to the duty to get to work on time.

Counsel for the taxpayers accepted that in order to determine whether expenditure
was incurred in the performance of the duties of the relevant employment it was
necessary first to identify what those duties were. He submitted, however, that what
they were was a question of fact for the commissioners and it was not for the court to
reverse their findings. The court could interfere only if, in the words of Lord
Radcliffe in *Edwards (Inspector of Taxes) v Bairstow* [1956] AC 14 at 36, 36 TC 207
at 229, the true and only reasonable conclusion from their findings contradicted
their determination. The findings of the commissioners at the outset of para 7 of
each of their decisions about the duties of the employment were not, said counsel,
intended to be exhaustive, for the commissioners had gone on to find that the
reading of newspapers and periodicals was an essential part of those duties.

Counsel for the taxpayers went as far as to submit that the findings of the
commissioners amounted to findings that, in the case of each of the taxpayers, the
duty to read newspapers and periodicals was part of the terms of his employment
and that the terms of a man's employment were normally conclusive as to what his
duties were. For the latter proposition, counsel relied on a passage in the speech of
Lord Salmon in *Taylor v Provan* [1974] STC 168 at 191, [1975] AC 194 at 227:

> 'When you are considering where the duties of a man's employment require
> him to work, you look first at the terms of his employment. These normally are
> conclusive. A term which may appear to be rather more for the man's benefit
> than for the benefit of his employers is still a term of the employment. The fact
> that you may suspect that the employers might waive it is, in my view,
> irrelevant. I am not suggesting that the terms of employment are conclusive in
> every case. It is easy to imagine a case in which, for instance, an English resident
> employed by an English company as a director to do work unconnected with
> France, has a term inserted in his contract which provides that he shall do part
> of his work in an hotel on the French Riviera and that his employers shall pay
> all the expenses involved, including travelling expenses. This would obviously
> be colourable—a mere device to satisfy his wish to spend some time in the sun
> with his expenses paid tax free. The term could be of no benefit to the company
> which he serves and the job could, no doubt, be filled by persons of no less
> competence but less greed.'

However, Lord Salmon was there dealing with the relevance of a man's terms of
employment in considering where his duties required him to work. I do not think
that Lord Salmon can have meant to say that the terms of his employment were
normally conclusive of the scope of the duties of his employment within the meaning
of the statutory phrase. I was referred to a number of authorities which show that
the terms of a man's employment may impose on him an obligation, or a virtual
obligation, compliance with which requires expenditure on his part, without that
expenditure being incurred by him in the performance of the duties of the
employment (see *Blackwell (Inspector of Taxes) v Mills* (1945) 26 TC 468, *Lomax
(Inspector of Taxes) v Newton* [1953] 1 WLR 1123, 34 TC 558 and *Brown v Bullock
(Inspector of Taxes)* [1961] 1 WLR 1095, 40 TC 1). I do not think that, as was
suggested by counsel for the taxpayers, the present cases can be distinguished from

Simpson v Tate and *Humbles v Brooks* on the ground that the expenditure in question in those cases had been incurred voluntarily. The decisions in *Simpson v Tate* and *a* *Humbles v Brooks* did not turn on that fact.

There is in my judgment no doubt that expenditure incurred by the holder of an office or employment in qualifying himself, or keeping himself qualified, to perform the duties of it—such as expenditure by a professional man in keeping himself informed of developments in his professional field, or expenditure by a teacher in acquiring the knowledge of a subject that he needs in order to teach it—is not *b* incurred by him in the performance of the duties of the office or employment in the statutory sense. On the other hand, it is not in my judgment the law that no reading that is preparatory to the performance of duties of an office or employment can ever itself be part of the performance of the duties of that office or employment. There are manifestly cases where preparatory reading is part of the duties of an office or employment. An example that springs to my mind is that of an employed solicitor *c* reading in preparation for giving advice to a client the papers in that client's case and the statutory provisions or other authorities relevant to it. That reading is just as much in the performance of the duties of his employment as is the giving of the advice itself. What is true is that, where preparatory reading is part of the performance of the duties of an office or employment, it will probably be rare for the undertaking of it to put the holder of the office or employment to expense, but that *d* is not in itself to the point.

That the General Commissioners were aware of the distinction between reading to qualify oneself, or keeping oneself qualified, to perform the duties of an employment and reading in the performance of those duties is apparent from what I have labelled the Burden findings. There was some argument before me about what the commissioners had meant by their reference in each of those findings to *e* the taxpayer's reading being 'not merely' required to qualify him, or maintain his qualifications, to do the work. It seems to me that what the commissioners were doing was adverting to the distinction in question. It is clear from their recital of the arguments of the parties and of the authorities cited to them that they had been made well aware of it. I think that the commissioners were giving expression to a finding of fact that at all events in the cases of the taxpayers other than Mr Abbott *f* the reading of newspapers and periodicals was part of or inherent in the performance of the duties of the employment.

Counsel for the Crown suggested that the commissioners' use of the words 'not merely' showed that in part at least the reading had been undertaken to qualify the reader, or maintain his qualifications, for the employment, in which case the reading had not been undertaken 'exclusively' in the performance of the duties of the *g* employment. I think that, in that respect, the Burden findings are at most ambiguous and that, if they are ambiguous, the ambiguity is cured by the unambiguous findings in para 8(a) of each decision.

In *Edwards v Bairstow* [1956] AC 14 at 33, 36 TC 207 at 227, Lord Radcliffe said:

> 'My Lords, I think that it is a question of law what meaning is to be given to the words of the Income Tax Act "trade, manufacture, adventure or concern in *h* the nature of trade" and for that matter what constitute "profits or gains" arising from it. Here we have a statutory phrase involving a charge of tax, and it is for the courts to interpret its meaning, having regard to the context in which it occurs and to the principles which they bring to bear upon the meaning of income. But, that being said, the law does not supply a precise definition of the word "trade": much less does it prescribe a detailed or exhaustive set of rules for *j* application to any particular set of circumstances. In effect it lays down the limits within which it would be permissible to say that a "trade" as interpreted by section 237 of the Act does or does not exist. But the field so marked out is a wide one and there are many combinations of circumstances in which it could not be said to be wrong to arrive at a conclusion one way or the other. If the

facts of any particular case are fairly capable of being so described, it seems to
me that it necessarily follows that the determination of the Commissioners,
Special or General, to the effect that a trade does or does not exist is not
"erroneous in point of law"; and, if a determination cannot be shown to be
erroneous in point of law, the statute does not admit of its being upset by the
court on appeal. I except the occasions when the commissioners, although
dealing with a set of facts which would warrant a decision either way, show by
some reason they give or statement they make in the body of the case that they
have misunderstood the law in some relevant particular. All these cases in which
the facts warrant a determination either way can be described as questions of
degree and therefore as questions of fact.'

It seems to me that the same applies to the phrase 'in the performance of the duties
of the office or employment' in s 189(1), so that the question for me is whether the
facts found by the commissioners are fairly capable of leading to the conclusion at
which they arrived.

I think that the answer to that question is 'yes' in the cases of the taxpayers other
than Mr Abbott. I do not think that in those cases the findings at the beginning of
each decision (para 7(a)(ii) and (iii) in Mr Shuttleworth's case and para 7(b) in the
other cases) were intended by the commissioners to be exhaustive statements of the
work to be done by each taxpayer in the performance of the duties of his employment.
Otherwise, the Burden findings make no sense. Moreover, I think that on a fair view
of the commissioners' other findings in those cases there was a sufficient nexus
between the daily reading undertaken by each taxpayer and the nature of the duties
for which they were a preparation to make the Burden findings intelligible and
consistent with the law. I therefore think that in the cases of the taxpayers other
than Mr Abbott, counsel for the Crown's first submission fails.

Still dealing only with the cases of the taxpayers other than Mr Abbott, I turn to
counsel for the Crown's second and third submissions.

His second submission was that the findings of the General Commissioners were
insufficient to justify their conclusion that the expenditure that the taxpayers sought
to deduct had been 'necessarily' incurred by them in the performance of the duties
of their respective employments. In particular, there was no express finding that
objectively considered the duties of the employment in each case could not be
performed without such expenditure. Counsel for the Crown relied in that
connection on the familiar proposition that (except perhaps where an office has been
specially created for a person as in *Taylor v Provan*) expenditure is not deductible
unless it is of a kind that any and every holder of the office or employment would be
obliged to incur (see *Ricketts v Colquhoun (Inspector of Taxes)* [1926] AC 1 at 7, 10
TC 118 at 135 per Lord Blanesburgh; see also *Brown v Bullock* [1961] 1 WLR 1095
at 1102, 40 TC 1 at 10 per Donovan LJ). Counsel for the Crown also referred in this
connection (as he had done in support of his first submission) to the observations of
Vaisey J in *Lomax v Newton* (see [1953] 1 WLR 1123 at 1126–1127, 34 TC 558 at
562–563 and of Lord Morris in *Taylor v Provan* (see [1974] STC 168 at 176, [1975]
AC 194 at 210–211) about the need for clear findings of fact by the commissioners.

I do not think, however, that a taxpayer's case is bound to fail unless the appellate
commissioners expressly record a finding that the duties of the office or employment
could not be performed without the holder of it incurring the expenditure in
question. Here again, the Burden findings are to my mind important. In Mr Holt's
case they include a finding that the reading of the material in question 'was a
necessary part of the duties of a staff photographer' and in Mr Shuttleworth's case a
finding that it was 'a necessary part of the duties of sub-editing'. Those findings, the
wording of which shows that the commissioners had in mind the objective test to
which counsel for the Crown referred, seem to me sufficient, read in the light of the
other findings, to support the conclusion of the commissioners that the expenditure
was necessary in the statutory sense. They import a finding that any and every

holder of the employment would have had to incur it. In the cases of Mr Scovell and Mr Woodhouse the commissioners used the phrase 'inherent in the process' rather than the phrase 'a necessary part'. Quite what the difference in language connotes I am not sure. The commissioners may have thought that 'inherent in' was stronger. Be that as it may, I cannot differentiate between the cases on the basis of it.

Counsel for the Crown's third submission was that the expenditure here in question was on any view not incurred by the taxpayers 'wholly and exclusively' in the performance of their duties, because it was in part at least incurred in order to qualify them or keep them qualified to perform those duties. I have already mentioned and rejected counsel for the Crown's argument based on the use by the commissioners of the word 'merely' in the Burden findings. Otherwise, that submission of counsel was based largely on the judgment of Ungoed-Thomas J in *Humbles v Brooks* where (see (1962) 40 TC 500 at 503–504) he drew a distinction between, on the one hand, the preparation by the taxpayer in that case of his own lectures, which was in the performance of the duties of his employment, and, on the other hand, that taxpayer qualifying himself to teach, getting background material and 'even getting information and material which he reproduced in his own lectures' which was not in the performance of those duties. He went on to hold that the expenditure incurred by the taxpayer on his course at the college of further education had not been incurred 'exclusively' in the preparation of his own lectures—a holding which, if I may say so, was manifestly right.

Counsel for the Crown pointed to specific findings in the decisions of the commissioners in the present cases which showed, he said, that in part at least the taxpayers' reading of newspapers and periodicals had been undertaken in order to obtain background information and generally keep up to date, for instance the finding in para 7(d)(ii) of the decision in Mr Holt's case that: 'He made notes and also took cuttings for filing and for future use.' It seems to me, however, that once it is found that preparatory reading of the kind here in question is undertaken in the performance of the duties of the employment the fact that it may yield benefits of lasting usefulness to the employee concerned in performing the duties of that or any like employment is neither here nor there. It is common for knowledge acquired by an employee in performing the duties of his employment to be of lasting usefulness to him. The employed solicitor whom I instanced earlier may well find that his reading in one case has equipped him more promptly and competently to deal with another. That does not mean that his reading in the first case was not undertaken by him exclusively in the performance of the duties of his employment.

For those reasons, I dismiss the appeals of the Crown in the cases of the four taxpayers other than Mr Abbott.

I turn to the case of Mr Abbott. What I have said so far shows the importance that seems to me to attach to the Burden findings in the other cases. The view is tenable that, since the cases of the five taxpayers were heard together by the General Commissioners, the absence of such a finding in Mr Abbott's case is fatal to his claim. However, I think that Mr Abbott is entitled to have his case considered on the basis of the contents of the case stated and decision in his own case without inferences being drawn against him from the contents of the corresponding documents in other cases.

Counsel for the taxpayers naturally pointed to the finding in para 7(e)(iv) of the decision in Mr Abbott's case. That is, however, at best a finding that Associated Newspapers Ltd and Mr Abbott himself regarded his newspaper reading as an essential part of his duties. It is not a finding by the commissioners themselves that it did. Nor is it an express finding that any and every holder of Mr Abbott's employment would have had to incur expenditure of the same kind.

Counsel for the taxpayers also submitted that the absence of such findings was cured by para 8(a) of the decision. That paragraph reads as follows:

'We conclude that the reading of the newspapers and periodicals outside the *Daily Mail* offices was in the performance of the duties of the employment, a notwithstanding that this was done at home and outside the hours of attendance at the *Daily Mail* offices, and the money expended on them was in each case expended wholly, exclusively and necessarily in the performance of [Mr Abbott's] duties.'

At first sight, that paragraph appears to do no more than express a conclusion drawn from what has gone before. But, as counsel pointed out, it is sandwiched between para 7 which contains findings of fact and para 8(b) which contains further

b such findings. It may therefore itself be taken to contain findings of fact, the commissioners' conclusion being that expressed in para 8(c). Paragraph 8(a) is, in part at least, concerned with negativing the contention of the Crown that the duties of Mr Abbott did not begin until he reached the *Daily Mail* offices. What, however, is lacking from para 8(a) is any finding to negative the contention of the Crown that in part at least Mr Abbott's reading was undertaken in order to keep him qualified

c to perform the duties of his employment. That would not, I think, matter were it not for the finding in para 7(d) of the decision that: 'His reading was especially directed to graphic designs and presentation in order to assist him with ideas for layout in the *Daily Mail*.' That conveys to my mind the impression that his reading was directed more to keeping up generally with the techniques and methods being used by other journalists doing the same kind of work than to the handling from day

d to day of the news then current, in other words directed in the main to keeping himself qualified, or better qualified, to perform his duties. There is nothing elsewhere in the case stated or in the decision in Mr Abbott's case to dispel that impression. The findings in para 7(c) of the decision merely convey that to some extent Mr Abbott needed to read newspapers and periodicals in order to be able to handle current news.

e The question in the end is whether the findings of fact of the commissioners are fairly capable of leading to the conclusion at which they arrived or whether, on the contrary, the true and only reasonable conclusion from their findings contradicts their determination. I have, after considerable hesitation, come to the conclusion, for the reasons I have indicated, that in Mr Abbott's case the findings of fact of the commissioners do not justify their determination. Whilst it is to my mind permissible

f to look at para 8(a) of each of the five decisions to resolve an ambiguity in para 7, it is not permissible to invoke it to supply a finding that is made nowhere at all.

I accordingly allow the Crown's appeal in Mr Abbott's case.

Appeal allowed in Mr Abbott's case but dismissed in the cases of the other four taxpayers. Crown to pay four-fifths of the taxpayers' global costs and Mr Abbott to pay one-fifth

g *of the Crown's global costs.*

Solicitors: *Solicitor of Inland Revenue*; *Berwin Leighton* (for the taxpayers).

Rengan Krishnan Esq   Barrister.

Marshall (Inspector of Taxes) v Kerr   *a*

CHANCERY DIVISION
HARMAN J
6, 7 NOVEMBER 1991

Capital gains tax – Death – Variation of terms of will by instrument of variation – Non-   *b*
resident settlement – Assets transferred to non-resident settlement by instrument of
variation – Capital payments from settlement – Whether capital payments taxable –
Identity of settlor of non-resident settlement – Whether testator deemed settlor of non-
resident settlement – Construction of deeming provision – Finance Act 1965, s 24(7),
(11) – Finance Act 1981, ss 80–85.

c

Mr Brooks (the testator) died in Jersey in 1977. He was domiciled and ordinarily
resident in Jersey and neither resident nor ordinarily resident in the United
Kingdom at the time of his death. Under the terms of his will, one-half of the
testator's residuary personal estate was given absolutely to his daughter, Mrs Kerr,
who at all relevant times was resident and ordinarily resident in the United Kingdom.
The testator's personal representative was the Regent Trust Co Ltd (Regent), a   *d*
company incorporated in Jersey and at all relevant times resident there and in no
other place. In 1978, Mrs Kerr and Regent executed an instrument of family
arrangement (the instrument) the effect of which was to settle Mrs Kerr's share in
her father's residuary personal estate on the terms of a settlement of which Regent
was the sole trustee. Capital payments were later made from the settlement to Mrs
Kerr. Estimated assessments to capital gains tax for the years 1983–84 and 1984–85   *e*
were issued in respect of those payments on Mrs Kerr's husband (the taxpayer) on
the grounds that the payments fell within the provisions of ss 80–85*ᵃ* of the Finance
Act 1981 (the 1981 Act) which applied to payments from non-resident settlements if
the settlor was domiciled and either resident or ordinarily resident in the United
Kingdom either at the date of the settlement or during the year of assessment. The
taxpayer appealed. The agreed question of law for the decision of the Special   *f*
Commissioner was whether the capital payments made to Mrs Kerr were subject to
tax under ss 80–85 of the 1981 Act. It was common ground in the appeals that: (i) the
instrument fell within s 24(11)*ᵇ* of the Finance Act 1965 (the 1965 Act) and that the
transactions effected by it therefore did not constitute a disposal for capital gains tax
purposes; and (ii) if Mrs Kerr was deemed not to have been the settlor of the
settlement by virtue of the provisions of s 24(11), the assessments fell to be discharged.   *g*
The Special Commissioner allowed the taxpayer's appeal, holding that Mrs Kerr
was deemed not to be the settlor for the purposes of ss 80–85 of the 1981 Act by
virtue of the deeming provision in s 24(11) of the 1965 Act as affected by the deeming
provision in s 24(7)(b)*ᶜ*. The Crown appealed, contending, inter alia, that s 24(11)
and s 24(7)(b) had been carefully drawn to limit their application as deeming
provisions, that they were for a limited purpose and applied as between limited   *h*
parties and that there were no grounds for extending their application to the question
as to the identity of the settlor of the settlement for the purposes of ss 80–85 of the
1981 Act.

---

a   Section 80, so far as material, provides: '(1) This section applies to a settlement for any year
     of assessment ... during which the trustees are at no time resident or ordinarily resident in   *j*
     the United Kingdom if the settlor or one of the settlors is at any time during that year, or
     was when he made his settlement, domiciled and either resident or ordinarily resident in
     the United Kingdom ... (3) ... the trust gains for a year of assessment shall be treated as
     chargeable gains accruing in that year to beneficiaries of the settlement who receive capital
     payments from the trustees in that year or have received such payments in any earlier year.'
b   Section 24(11), so far as material, is set out at p 694 *j*, post
c   Section 24(7)(b) is set out at p 695 *a b*, post

Held – In considering the extent to which deeming provisions were to be applied,
a the court was entitled and bound to ascertain for what purposes and between what
persons the statutory fictions in those provisions were to be resorted to. Section
24(11) and s 24(7) were deeming provisions. The purpose of these provisions was
simply to deal with computations of gains and to exclude gains which would
otherwise be thought to accrue to a person who made a deed of variation or other
disposal by an instrument. There was no basis for extending the application of these
b subsections to resolve the question as to the identity of the settlor of the settlement
raised by ss 80–85 of the Finance Act 1981. Accordingly, the Special Commissioner
had erred in law and the Crown's appeal would therefore be allowed.
  IRC v Metrolands (Property Finance) Ltd [1981] STC 193 applied.

c **Notes**

  For the scope of deeming provisions, see Simon's Taxes A1.304.
  For liability to capital gains tax on the acquisition of assets as legatee, see ibid,
C1.211.
  For the Finance Act 1965, s 24(7), (11) (now the Capital Gains Tax Act 1979,
s 49(4), (6) (as amended)), see ibid, Part G3.
d   For the Finance Act 1981, ss 80–85, see ibid, Part H1.

Cases referred to in judgment

  East End Dwellings Co Ltd v Finsbury BC [1952] 2 AC 109, [1951] 2 All ER 587, HL.
  IRC v Metrolands (Property Finance) Ltd [1981] STC 193, [1981] 1 WLR 637,
e   [1981] 2 All ER 166, Ch D; *affd* [1982] STC 259, [1982] 1 WLR 341, [1982] 2 All
  ER 557, 54 TC 679, HL.
  Levy, Re, ex p Walton (1881) 17 Ch D 746, CA.

Cases also cited
f
  Macpherson v IRC [1987] STC 73, CA; [1988] STC 362, [1989] AC 159, [1988] 2 All
  ER 753, HL.
  Murphy v Ingram (Inspector of Taxes) [1974] STC 205, [1974] Ch 363, [1974] 2 All
  ER 187, 49 TC 410, CA.
  Russell v IRC [1988] STC 195, [1988] 1 WLR 834, [1988] 2 All ER 405.

g

Case stated

  1. On 2 October 1990, a Commissioner for the special purposes of the Income Tax
Acts heard the appeals of Mr Simon P A Kerr (the taxpayer) against the following
estimated assessments to capital gains tax:
h
                    1983–84   £63,338
                    1984–85   £17,438

  2. Shortly stated, the question for decision was whether the capital payments paid
to Mrs Kerr (at all relevant times the wife of the taxpayer) between 1981 and 1985
were subject to taxation by virtue of ss 80–85 of the Finance Act 1981 (the 1981 Act).
j In order to answer that question it was necessary to construe s 24 of the Finance Act
1965 (the 1965 Act).
  3. No witnesses gave evidence before the commissioner.
  [Paragraph 4 listed the documents placed in evidence before the commissioner.]
  5. The findings of fact and the principal contentions of the parties were set out in
the decision which was issued on 16 October 1990 and a copy of which was annexed
as part of the case.

6. The following cases were cited to the commissioner in argument:

Canada Southern Railway Co v International Bridge Co (1883) 8 App Cas 723.   **a**
East End Dwellings Co Ltd v Finsbury BC [1952] AC 109.
IRC v Metrolands (Property Finance) Ltd [1981] STC 193, [1981] 1 WLR 637.
Macpherson v IRC [1987] STC 73.
Murphy v Ingram (Inspector of Taxes) [1974] STC 205, [1974] Ch 363.
Russell v IRC [1988] STC 195, [1988] 1 WLR 834.

b

7. At the request of the taxpayer's solicitors the commissioner included here a subsidiary argument of the taxpayer's counsel not noted in the commissioner's decision. Such argument was to the effect that since by virtue of s 24(11) of the 1965 Act no disposition made by the instrument (as defined in the decision) was to constitute a disposal for the purposes of Part III of that Act, Mrs Kerr could not, for that reason too, be regarded as being a settlor of the settlement as she was deemed to **c** have disposed of nothing on the occasion of the execution of the instrument and as she in fact disposed of nothing on any other occasion.

8. By his decision the commissioner allowed the appeals and discharged the assessments.

9. The Crown immediately after the determination of the appeals declared its dissatisfaction therewith as being erroneous in point of law and on 25 October 1990 **d** required the commissioner to state a case for the opinion of the High Court pursuant to s 56 of the Taxes Management Act 1970.

10. The questions of law for the opinion of the court were as follows:

(i) whether, on a true construction of s 24 of the 1965 Act, Mrs Kerr was deemed not to be the settlor of an instrument of family arrangement dated 31 January 1978; and **e**
(ii) whether the assessments to capital gains tax on the taxpayer fell to be discharged.

DECISION   **f**

In this appeal I am asked for a decision on a novel point of construction involving the provisions of s 24(11) of the 1965 Act. Although the point at issue is very short it is one which has troubled even the learned authors of legal textbooks.

The nominal appellant in these appeals is Mr Simon P A Kerr (the taxpayer) but the facts of the appeals relate to Mrs Kerr alone. The assessments have been made on the taxpayer pursuant to the provisions of s 45 of the Capital Gains Tax Act 1979. **g** The assessments under appeal are two estimated assessments to capital gains tax. The first is for the year 1983–84 in the sum of £63,338. The second is for the following year in the sum of £17,438. There is no agreement between the parties as to figures but I am asked in the first place for a decision in principle only on the construction of the relevant section in the 1965 Act. Depending on the outcome of these appeals it may be necessary for there to be a further hearing on the question of **h** quantum.

I heard no oral evidence and the facts of the appeal were encompassed in a brief agreed statement of facts supported by a small agreed bundle of documents. Accordingly I can state the facts briefly as follows:

1. Mrs Kerr's father, the late Lionel Horace Brooks (the testator), died in Jersey on 27 February 1977. He was domiciled and ordinarily resident in Jersey and neither **j** resident nor ordinarily resident in the United Kingdom at the time of his death.

2. The testator was survived by his two children, John Brooks and Elizabeth Ann Kerr (Mrs Kerr). Mrs Kerr was at all relevant times the wife of and living with her husband, the taxpayer. On 30 March 1977 the Regent Trust Company Ltd (Regent) proved the testator's will dated 25 February 1974 in the probate division of the Royal Court of the Island of Jersey.

a   Regent is a company incorporated in Jersey and was at all relevant times resident and ordinarily resident there and in no other place.

3. Under the terms of the testator's will his residuary personal estate was given to his two children in equal shares absolutely.

4. On 31 January 1978 Mrs Kerr and Regent executed an instrument of family arrangement (the instrument).

The effect of the instrument was to settle Mrs Kerr's share in the residuary
b personalty of the testator on the terms of a settlement of which Regent was and has remained sole trustee. The settlement was to be in favour of a class of persons, namely Mrs Kerr, her husband or widower, her children and her mother. The trust property was to be held on their behalf for 'a trust period' of 21 years (less one day) after the death of the last surviving descendant of King George V living at the date of the testator's death. In the meantime Mrs Kerr was to have a life interest in the
c trust property and to retain power to appoint capital to any member of the class. Subject to any appointment, at the end of the trust period the property was to vest in Mrs Kerr's children in equal shares.

5. The administration of the estate of the testator was not completed until June 1979. The assets of the estate were at no time vested in Mrs Kerr, but were transferred by Regent (in its capacity as personal representative) to Regent (in its
d capacity as trustee). The assets held by Regent in such capacity were 12 £1 ordinary shares in Brookside Investments Ltd, a company also incorporated in Jersey and at all times resident there and only there.

6. The general administration of the trusts of the settlement constituted by the will of the testator (and varied by the instrument) has at all times been ordinarily carried on outside the United Kingdom.

e   7. The assessments on the taxpayer are raised under the provisions of s 80 of the 1981 Act in respect of capital payments made to Mrs Kerr.

Unusually, the documents placed before me included an agreed statement of law and therefore I set out the following two paragraphs which represent common ground between the parties in these appeals:

1. Pursuant to s 24(1) of the 1965 Act, the personal representative, Regent,
f acquired all the assets of which the testator was competent to dispose (including the testator's residuary personal estate to a share of which Mrs Kerr was beneficially entitled) at market value at the date of the death of the testator on 27 February 1977.

2. The instrument falls within s 24(11) of the 1965 Act being 'a deed of family arrangement or similar instrument' whose effect was to vary (within two years of the death of the testator) the dispositions of the property of which the testator was
g competent to dispose, and that the transactions effected by the instrument did not constitute a disposal for capital gains tax purposes.

It is also common ground in these appeals that the statute which I am required to construe is the 1965 Act, the instrument having been executed before the passing of the Finance Act 1978.

The agreed question for my determination in these appeals is as follows: whether
h the capital payments paid to Mrs Kerr between 1981 and 1985 are subject to taxation by virtue of ss 80–85 of the 1981 Act.

However, the somewhat narrower point on which my decision in principle is required concerns the identity of the settlor of the settlement constituted by the testator's will and varied by the instrument, having regard to the provisions of s 24 of the 1965 Act.

j   Counsel for the taxpayer contended that the settlor of the settlement for the purposes of ss 80–85 of the 1981 Act was the testator, or in the alternative was not Mrs Kerr, and that accordingly those sections cannot apply to the settlement.

Mr Gerald Thirkell, of the Inland Revenue Solicitor's Office, appearing for the inspector made the following contentions:

1. By the instrument, Mrs Kerr disposed of part of her beneficial share in her father's estate on trusts in a non-resident settlement.

2. Sections 80–85 of the 1981 Act applied to the taxation of gains of non-resident settlements which have shares in non-resident companies such as Brookside *a* Investments Ltd. Pursuant to s 85, the gains of Brookside Investments Ltd can be accrued to the gains of the settlement. Payments made and benefits conferred by the settlement to the beneficiaries can be liable to capital gains tax pursuant to ss 80 and 83(5) provided that the settlor was resident in the United Kingdom on the date that the settlement was executed.

3. The settlor for the purposes of ss 80–85 was Mrs Kerr, who was resident in the *b* United Kingdom on the date the settlement was executed in 1978 and has continued to remain so resident. Therefore the payments from the trust are subject to capital gains tax.

Conclusions

It is common ground in these appeals that if Mrs Kerr is deemed not to have been *c* the settlor by virtue of the provisions of s 24 of the 1965 Act, the assessments fall to be discharged. Equally, if I determine that despite the provisions of that section Mrs Kerr remains the settlor, I am to hold accordingly in principle only, leaving the parties to consider whether a further hearing may be required in the absence of agreement between them on quantum. Accordingly there is no need for me to *d* consider at this stage the effect of the charging provisions contained in ss 80–85 of the 1981 Act and I shall not do so.

Section 24 of the 1965 Act, as originally enacted, provided as follows:

'(1) On the death of an individual all the assets of which he was competent to dispose shall for the purposes of this Part of this Act be deemed to be disposed of by him at the date of death, and acquired by the personal representatives or *e* other person on whom they devolve, for a consideration equal to their market value at that date.

(2) Subject to section 34 of this Act, the gains which accrue in consequence of subsection (1) of this section, together with any gains accruing to the deceased by reason of the disposal by him of any asset by way of donatio mortis causa, shall be aggregated and only so much of that aggregate as exceeds five thousand *f* pounds shall constitute chargeable gains.

In arriving at the aggregate—

(a) the respective amounts of the gains shall be computed in accordance with the provisions of this Act (other than this section) fixing the amount of chargeable gains, and

(b) any allowable loss accruing in consequence of subsection (1) of this *g* section, or in consequence of any donatio mortis causa, shall be deducted,

and the provision of this subsection shall not affect the computation of the amount of any allowable loss.

(3) For the purposes of section 20(4) of this Act chargeable gains under subsection (2) of this section shall be included in the gains accruing to the *h* deceased in the year of assessment in which the death occurs.

(4) For the purposes of the said section 20(4) and of the next following subsection allowable losses sustained in consequence of subsection (1) of this section shall be included in the losses sustained by the deceased in the year of assessment in which the death occurs so far as those losses have not been taken into account under subsection (2) of this section. *j*

(5) Allowable losses sustained by an individual in the year of assessment in which he dies may, so far as they cannot be deducted from chargeable gains accruing in that year, be deducted from chargeable gains accruing to the deceased in the three years of assessment preceding the year of assessment in which the death occurs, taking chargeable gains accruing in a later year before those accruing in an earlier year.

(6) In relation to property forming part of the estate of a deceased person the personal representatives shall for the purposes of this Part of this Act be treated as being a single and continuing body of persons (distinct from the persons who may from time to time be the personal representatives), and that body shall be treated as having the deceased's residence, ordinary residence, and domicile at the date of death.

(7) On a person acquiring any asset as legatee—

(a) no chargeable gain shall accrue to the personal representatives, and
(b) the legatee shall be treated as if the personal representatives' acquisition of the asset had been his acquisition of it.

(8) Allowable losses which accrue to the personal representatives of a deceased person in the period of three years from the death, may, so far as they cannot otherwise be deducted from chargeable gains, be deducted from chargeable gains accruing to the deceased in the year of assessment in which the death occurs, or in the preceding three years of assessment, taking chargeable gains accruing in a later year before those accruing in an earlier year.

(9) In this section references to assets of which a deceased person was competent to dispose are references to assets of the deceased which (otherwise than in right of a power of appointment or of the testamentary power conferred by statute to dispose of entailed interests) he could, if of full age and capacity, have disposed of by his will, assuming that all the assets were situated in England and, if he was not domiciled in the United Kingdom, that he was domiciled in England.

(10) For the purposes of this section in its application to Scotland, where the deceased person was an heir of entail in possession of an entailed estate, whether *sui iuris* or not, or a proper liferenter of an estate, he shall be deemed to have been a person competent to dispose of such estate.

(11) If not more than two years after a death any of the dispositions of the property of which the deceased was competent to dispose, whether effected by will, or under the law relating to intestacies, or otherwise, are varied by a deed of family arrangement or similar instrument, this section shall apply as if the variations made by the deed or other instrument were effected by the deceased, and no disposition made by the deed or other instrument shall constitute a disposal for the purposes of this Part of this Act.'

It is thus apparent that in its original form, s 24 was a charging section which imposed capital gains tax on the assets of a deceased individual as provided in s 24(2)–(4). Those subsections were repealed by the Finance Act 1971.

The fact that s 24 was a charging section as originally enacted assumes relevance when comparisons are made, as they have been in these appeals, between the capital gains tax legislation and the inheritance tax legislation. Having said that, it becomes necessary to compare the provision relating to capital gains tax with that relating to inheritance tax (formerly capital transfer tax). The relevant capital transfer tax provision was contained originally in s 47 of the Finance Act 1975 (the 1975 Act) which provided:

'(1) So far as a deed of family arrangement or similar instrument which is made not more than two years after the death of any person varies the dispositions (whether effected by will or under the law relating to intestacy) of the property of which he was competent to dispose—

(a) the variation shall not be a transfer of value; and
(b) this Part of this Act shall apply as if the variation had been effected by the deceased.'

It will be noted that the relevant words in the 1975 Act are 'this Part of this Act shall apply'. By contrast the relevant words in s 24(11) of the 1965 Act are 'this section shall apply'. The gap between the sections has been further widened by s 142 of the

Inheritance Tax Act 1984, which states 'this Act shall apply'. It should be noted however that neither s 47 of the 1975 Act nor s 142 of the Inheritance Tax Act 1984 are charging sections whereas s 24 of the 1965 Act is such a section, or was as originally enacted.

To make the statutory picture complete I must look at s 49 of the Capital Gains Tax Act 1979 (the 1979 Act), whilst bearing in mind that its provisions are not directly relevant to these appeals, the results of which turn, by common consent, on the words employed in the 1965 Act.

Section 49(4) of the 1979 Act re-enacts s 24(7) of the 1965 Act. Section 49(6) of the later Act is an amended version of s 24(11) of the earlier Act, but the vital words 'this section shall apply' reappear in the 1979 Act.

Mr Thirkell submits that the policy behind s 24(11) is that disposals by personal representatives should be relieved from capital gains tax and that the words of this section limit strictly the relief available in contrast to the wide-ranging relief granted by s 47 of the 1975 Act and s 142 of the Inheritance Tax Act 1984. Although the wording of s 24(11) of the 1965 Act was recast in s 49 of the 1979 Act, the vital words 'this section shall apply' were retained in the consolidating Act. The distinction between the reliefs available for capital gains tax and for inheritance tax respectively was maintained.

Although there are no authorities to assist me in construing s 24(11), Mr Thirkell points to the conclusions of learned authors of legal textbooks in support of his contentions. The following appears in *Whiteman on Capital Gains Tax* (4th edn, 1988) p 619:

> 'It was said in the previous edition of this book that in the case of settled property the deceased will be the settlor of the settlement for capital gains tax purposes, and reference was made to section 17 of the 1979 Act. It is now thought, however, that there is a trap here. Section 49(6)(*b*) provides that "this section" shall apply as if the variation had been effected by the deceased, and the same was true of section 24(11) of the Finance Act 1965 (referring of course to that section). This is to be contrasted with section 142(1)(*a*) of the Inheritance Tax Act 1984 which provides that "this Act" shall apply as if the variation had been effected by the deceased. On the basis of this distinction it is now arguable whether the back-dating effect of section 49(6) does or does not extend to anything not strictly within section 49 itself.'

Whilst Mr Whiteman and his learned fellow authors therefore sit on the fence, a more definite statement more helpful to Mr Thirkell is to be found in *McCutcheon on Inheritance Tax* (3rd edn, 1988) pp 266–267. Mr Thirkell submits that Mr McCutcheon and his learned co-authors are clear that in the circumstances similar to those obtaining in relation to these appeals the testator will be the deemed settlor of the purposes of inheritance tax, but not, in their opinion, for the purposes of capital gains tax.

The third edition of Mr Whiteman's book, published in 1980 and entitled *Whiteman and Wheatcroft on Capital Gains Tax* took the opposite view to that of Mr McCutcheon. And I understand that it is only recently that the Revenue has adopted its present stance of denying a backdating effect to variations for capital gains tax purposes, but not for inheritance tax purposes.

Even Mr McCutcheon seems to be somewhat uncertain as to the position for he says, at p 265:

> 'Under section 142 any variation or disclaimer is read back for *all* purposes: by contrast, the CGT legislation merely provides a reading back for the purposes of that section (*i.e.* s.49). This difference in wording may be important, for instance, when it is intended to effect a variation to take advantage of the deemed settlor provisions discussed at 7-92 [see pp 266–267]. For CGT purposes

it is thought [My emphasis] that the person who effects the variation will still be
a   a settlor, *e.g.* for the purpose of the charges imposed by F.A. 1981, s.80.'

It therefore falls to me to put the question beyond doubt and I propose to do so by
reference only to the words of the statute, in the absence of judicial authority.

Counsel for the taxpayer points out quite rightly that the provisions of s 24(11) of
the 1965 Act are governed, inter alia, by the provisions of s 24(7)(*b*). That being so,
b   Regent is deemed to be a legatee of the testator's will, for s 45(1) of the 1965 Act
provides (where relevant): '(1) In this Part of this Act, unless the context otherwise
requires . . . "legatee" includes any person taking under a testamentary disposition or
on an intestacy or partial intestacy, whether he takes beneficially or as trustee . . .'
Both s 24 and s 45 are to be found in Part III of the 1965 Act.

Section 24(7)(*b*) of the 1965 Act is a very wide provision which states that—'. . . the
legatee shall be treated as if the personal representatives' acquisition of the asset had
c   been his acquisition of it'. That wide wording is to be contrasted with the words of
para 20(1) of Sch 7 to the 1965 Act dealing with transfers between husband and wife
which states:

'If, in any year of assessment, and in the case of a woman who in that year of
assessment is a married woman living with her husband, the man disposes of an
d   asset to the wife, or the wife disposes of an asset to the man, both shall be treated
as if the asset was acquired from the one making the disposal for a consideration
of such amount as would secure that on the disposal neither a gain or a loss
would accrue to the one making the disposal.'

It is therefore apparent to me that had the legislature wished to limit the effect of
s 24(11) in the way contended for by Mr Thirkell, it could have done so by the use of
e   appropriate words. As it is, s 24(7)(*b*) operates to place the legatee (in this case the
deemed legatee, namely Regent) in the shoes of the personal representative.
Accordingly, there is not merely a no gain/no loss situation but the acquisition is also
back-dated. I therefore accept the submission of counsel for the taxpayer that the
policy behind s 24(11) is clear, namely that beneficiaries who satisfied its conditions
f   were allowed to rewrite a will and that the consequences for capital gains tax
purposes which flowed from such rewriting were the same as if the rewritten will
had been written originally by the testator.

I cannot accept Mr Thirkell's submissions. He strives to limit severely the effect
of s 24(11) but fails entirely to take into account the effect on that subsection of
s 24(7)(*b*). He also submitted that the deeming effect contended for by counsel for
the taxpayer was limited by the precise words used in s 24(11) but that submission
g   also fails to take into account the effect of the earlier subsection. Mr Thirkell offered
no explanation of the effect of s 24(7)(*b*) in the present case.

Counsel for the taxpayer quoted a long line of authorities in relation to the effect
of deeming provisions in statutes but I think that it is sufficient for me to refer only
to the speech of Lord Asquith in *East End Dwellings Co Ltd v Finsbury BC* [1952]
h   AC 109 at 132–133, where he said, in a unanimous decision of the House of Lords:

'If you are bidden to treat an imaginary state of affairs as real, you must
surely, unless prohibited from doing so, also imagine as real the consequences
and incidents which, if the putative state of affairs had in fact existed, must
inevitably have flowed from or accompanied it. One of these in this case is
emancipation from the 1939 level of rents. The statute says that you must
j   imagine a certain state of affairs; it does not say that having done so, you must
cause or permit your imagination to boggle when it comes to the inevitable
corollaries of that state of affairs. As some of my noble and learned friends have
pointed out, if Parliament had intended the meaning contended for by the
respondents, nothing would have been easier than to provide that the value
should be assessed as if no war damage had occurred. Even, however, if the
meaning of the words to be construed were not plain and the "policy" of the

legislation could legitimately be invoked as an interpretative factor, I am far
from subscribing to the view that the policy in question is that for which the
respondents contend, or that its importation would produce the result which
they desire. But it is unnecessary to develop that argument.'   *a*

Those words, although dealing with s 53(1) of the Town and Country Planning Act
1947, seem entirely appropriate, mutatis mutandis, to the words of s 24(11) and the
facts of the present case.

If reasons are required to explain the difference in wording between the legislation   *b*
applicable to capital gains tax and the legislation applicable to inheritance tax, they
are to be found, in my judgment, in the fact that s 24 of the 1965 Act was a charging
provision, unlike s 47 of the 1975 Act and s 142 of the Inheritance Tax Act 1984.
There was no need for s 24(11) to refer to anything else than the section within
which it was comprised in order to be effective.

I prefer the contentions of counsel for the taxpayer in this case to those of Mr   *c*
Thirkell and I allow the appeals. As a necessary consequence the assessments on the
taxpayer fall to be discharged, as Mrs Kerr is deemed not to be the settlor of the
instrument for the purposes of ss 80–85 of the 1981 Act.

Launcelot Henderson for the Crown.
Robert Venables QC for the taxpayer.   *d*

HARMAN J. This is an appeal by case stated by one of the Commissioners (Mr
Everett) for the special purposes of the Income Tax Acts. The case stated is unusual
in that the facts are agreed and no evidence was given. The sole question which the
Special Commissioner was asked to determine at that stage was a question of law.
The Special Commissioner decided the matter one way. It is now said that he erred   *e*
in his understanding of the law, and it is plainly a proper matter for debate in this
court.

The appeals to the Special Commissioner were appeals by a Mr Simon Kerr (the
taxpayer) against two estimated assessments to capital gains tax: one for the year
1983–84 and the other for the year 1984–85. The amounts of the estimated
assessments are wholly immaterial to this decision, no question of amount having   *f*
yet been considered. The question is stated as being whether the capital payments
made to Mrs Kerr, the wife of the taxpayer, are subject to taxation by virtue of
ss 80–85 of the Finance Act 1981 (the 1981 Act).

The commissioner gave a written decision on the matter, which he described
accurately as a novel point of construction on the provisions of s 24(11) of the
Finance Act 1965 (the 1965 Act). The facts are set out in the case stated and in my   *g*
view do not need repeating now. There is no issue whatever about them and they do
not really affect the question of law to be determined. They merely raise it.

The facts very briefly are that the late Mr Brooks died in Jersey on 27 February
1977. He was domiciled and ordinarily resident there. He was the father of Mrs
Kerr. By his will he left a half-share of his residuary estate to Mrs Kerr absolutely.
By an instrument of variation, not a deed, Mrs Kerr recited that she wished to effect   *h*
a family arrangement and declared that trustees appointed by the instrument were
to hold Mrs Kerr's fund and the income thereof on trusts declared by the instrument.
The trusts were, broadly, that Mrs Kerr was to have the income for life; there was
power to appoint capital to her and, subject thereto, to her children and remoter
issue with a discretionary power limited by a royal lives clause.

That is plainly an instrument within the definition of s 24(11) of the 1965 Act,   *j*
which provides as follows:

'If not more than two years after a death [that is satisfied in this case] any of
the dispositions of the property of which the deceased was competent to dispose
... effected by will ... are varied by a deed of family arrangement or similar
instrument [that is all satisfied], this section shall apply as if the variations made
by the deed or other instrument were effected by the deceased ...'

That is in effect a deeming provision deeming these variations to have effect as if
a they are provisions by the deceased. However, that only provides that 'this section'
shall apply. The section includes the provision in sub-s (7):

'On a person acquiring any asset as legatee—

(a) no chargeable gain shall accrue to the personal representatives, and
(b) the legatee shall be treated as if the personal representatives' acquisition
b   of the asset had been his acquisition of it.'

Again, that is a deeming provision. In particular, sub-s (7)(b) deems the personal
representatives' acquisition, which is at the date of death in the usual case, to be the
legatee's acquisition, notwithstanding that in fact personal representatives hold the
assets of the estate with rights to deal in and dispose of them and the legatee does not
have any vested interest in any of those assets until assent to him by the personal
c representatives. But the provision is that on such an assent—which may in many
cases be two, three or four years after the date of death—the acquisition shall be
treated as if it had been made at the time of acquisition by the personal
representatives.
It is submitted to me that that provision has a double effect. It has the effect of
d deeming the legatee to acquire the assets at their value as at the date of death, and it
has the effect of deeming the legatee to acquire at the date of death, so that nowadays
for purposes of indexation, not extant in 1965 when this Finance Act was passed,
one would compute the indexation from that date.
The commissioner stated in his written decision that the point which required
decision was the identity of the settlor of the settlement. He sets out the argument
advanced before him by a member of the Inland Revenue Solicitor's Office appearing
e for the inspector of taxes. Counsel for the taxpayer has observed to me that the
argument of the Crown here has been somewhat different from the argument
presented to the commissioner. That is probably so, but I do not think it has any
material bearing on the outcome of this matter.
The commissioner set out the proposition that if Mrs Kerr is deemed not to have
f been the settlor for the purposes of ss 80–85 of the 1981 Act, which are in broad
terms a re-enactment (that may not be wholly accurate but will suffice for present
purposes) of s 42 of the 1965 Act, the assessments would fall to be discharged. That
is common ground.
He then sets out s 24 at length and observes that in its original form it was a
charging section. Nobody has asserted before me that that makes any difference
whatever to the construction of the section or the outcome of this appeal. It can
g simply be ignored. It is a true fact that this section was at one time a charging
section. It ceased to be so on an intervening date but the fact that it once was a
charging section is immaterial.
However, the commissioner said that in his view the section's former function as
a charging section was of relevance when making comparisons between the capital
h gains tax and inheritance tax (formerly capital transfer tax) legislation. He cited
s 47(1) of the Finance Act 1975 and noted that the words of that section had
substantially wider effects, in that the provisions of sub-s (1)(b) were that 'this Part
of this Act shall apply' in contrast to the words in s 24(11) of the 1965 Act 'this section
shall apply'. He went on to consider the submission made to him about the policy
behind s 24(11).
It is common ground that there is no authority on the section. There are two
j textbooks which differ in their views of the section, as authors of textbooks are
entitled to do. Judges unfortunately are not allowed to come to an intermediate
decision neither one way nor the other. The textbooks do not seem to me to be
helpful at all.
The submission of the Crown is that since s 24(7) and s 24(11) are both deeming
provisions I should start with the considerations set out by Nourse J in *IRC v
Metrolands (Property Finance) Ltd* [1981] STC 193 at 206–208, [1981] 1 WLR 637

at 645–646 where he went through the cases down to that time and, in particular, referred (see [1981] STC 193 at 208, [1981] 1 WLR 637 at 646) to the famous passage in Lord Asquith's speech in *East End Dwellings Co Ltd v Finsbury BC* [1952] 2 AC 109 at 132–133. Lord Asquith, in that extreme felicity of language for which he is remembered, observes:

> 'If you are bidden to treat an imaginary state of affairs as real, you must surely, unless prohibited from doing so, also imagine as real the consequences and incidents which, if the putative state of affairs had in fact existed, must inevitably have flowed from or accompanied it. One of these in this case is emancipation from the 1939 level of rents. The statute says that you must imagine a certain state of affairs; it does not say that having done so, you must cause or permit your imagination to boggle when it comes to the inevitable corollaries of that state of affairs.'

An observation couched in such striking terms can easily beguile those who read it with admiration into taking it too literally. The temptation to allow one's mind to think that, because judges are bidden not to stop and boggle therefore one must follow a path leading to consequences far beyond those naturally springing to mind, when considering the words of some statutory provision at the outset of a matter is an easy step to take, but to my mind can lead to error. Of course a judge is not to stop and boggle, as Lord Asquith said, at a result which *inevitably* (my emphasis) flows from some provision. None the less, a judge has to consider whether the postulated result does in fact flow from words which inevitably lead to that result.

In terms which I have found a most illuminating guide on the journey from the words of s 24 to the conclusion of this appeal, Nourse J deduced principles for judges to apply in considering deeming provisions. In *IRC v Metrolands (Property Finance) Ltd* [1981] STC 193 at 208, [1981] 1 WLR 637 at 646 he said: 'When considering the extent to which a deeming provision should be applied, the court is entitled and bound to ascertain for what purposes and between what persons the statutory fiction is to be resorted to.'

The learned judge there lays down a principle which I respectfully follow and adopt as my guide on the journey of considering how far the deeming provision should be held to extend. In order to understand how far it should be carried the court in looking at a deeming provision starts off by asking: What is it for, and to whom does it apply? Nourse J went on: 'It will not always be clear what those purposes are.' I regret to say that that observation is a common feeling of all Chancery judges when faced with Finance Act questions. It is very, very rare indeed that the purposes are clear. It is always a question of some difficulty, but it does not mean one does not have to ascertain to whom the purposes apply and what they are. Nourse J went on to say [1981] STC 193 at 208, [1981] 1 WLR 637 at 646:

> 'If the application of the provision would lead to an unjust, anomalous or absurd result then, unless its application would clearly be within the purposes of the fiction, it should not be applied. If, on the other hand, its application would not lead to any such result then, unless that would clearly be outside the purposes of the fiction, it should be applied.'

Thus, he makes an exception for unjust, anomalous or absurd results and says that, whatever the apparent purpose may be, if that is the result one must in some way have misunderstood the purpose or should limit the purpose.

In that context it is commonplace to refer to that great judge James LJ in *Re Levy, ex p Walton* (1881) 17 Ch D 746 at 756, where he observed:

> 'When a statute enacts that something shall be deemed to have been done, which in fact and truth was not done, the Court is entitled and bound to ascertain for what purposes and between what persons the statutory fiction is to be resorted to.'

That is an exact precursor of the observations of Nourse J in *IRC v Metrolands.*
a James LJ went on (at 756)—

> '. . . the bankruptcy law is a special law, having for its object the distribution
> of an insolvent's assets equitably amongst his creditors and persons to whom he
> is under liability . . . That being the sole object of the statute, it appears to me
> to be legitimate to say, that, when the statute says that a lease, which was never
> surrendered in fact (a true surrender requiring the consent of both parties, the
> **b** one giving up and the other taking), is to be deemed to have been surrendered,
> it must be understood as saying so with the following qualification, which is
> absolutely necessary to prevent the most grievous injustice, and the most
> revolting absurdity . . .'

The Lord Justice then construes the statute as if it contained the words 'shall, as
c between the lessor on the one hand, and the bankrupt, his trustee and estate, on the
other hand, be deemed to have been surrendered' to identify between what persons
the deeming provision is to apply.

I therefore take Nourse J's words as the proper basis on which to construe these
deeming provisions. I believe that the contrast which the commissioner found
instructive between s 24(11) and the inheritance tax section is not in truth instructive
d but merely different words to operate for different purposes, so that one section will
have different results from the other and on its true construction operates between
different persons in one case from those in the other. On that basis I turn back to
what I see as the policy of s 24(7) and s 24(11), derived from the terms of the statute
and not from anything else.

It seems to me that counsel for the Crown must be right. The purpose of these
e sections is simply to deal with computations of gains and to exclude gains which
would otherwise be thought to accrue to a person who made a deed of variation or
other disposal by an instrument. The provisions are entirely satisfied, have a clear
purpose and are fully effective if they mean what they precisely say but do not carry
over into any further considerations of deeming than they provide. Subsection (11)
applies as if the variations were effected by the deceased so that the legatee taking
f them and the personal representatives assenting to their vesting and so on are all to
be treated as if the deceased by his will had made the provision which is in the
instrument of variation. That sufficiently takes out of any tax net and any
computations any difference in value between the date of death and the date of the
instrument.

The provision that the legatee shall be treated as if the personal representatives'
g acquisition had been his acquisition is both satisfied and adequately shown to have a
purpose if one treats it as affecting dealings between the legatee (though I do not
have to decide it here, counsel for the Crown suggests it is likely) and persons to
whom the legatee assigns any assets and the personal representatives, so there is no
difficulty in the legatee's acquisition date being the date of death and the legatee's
acquisition value being the value at that date.

h The result of all that is that the deeming provisions can be seen to have limited
purposes and to be limited to certain people. I can see no purpose which would lead
me to consider that the words have wider and more effective results. In particular,
there can be no reason why they should be seen to be applicable in answering the
question posed by, as it then was, s 42 of the 1965 Act, now re-enacted in ss 80–85 of
the 1981 Act. The question which is raised by those provisions is as to whether a
j settlement was made by a person who was domiciled and resident within the United
Kingdom either at the date of the chargeable gain or at the date of the making of the
settlement. In my judgment, the person designated by the answer to that question
is not a person to whom it can be seen the deeming provisions of s 24 are to apply.

The subsidiary point noted by the commissioner in the case stated but not dealt
with in his reasons is to the effect that s 24(11) provides in its tailpiece that no disposal
by virtue of the instrument shall constitute a disposal for the purposes of the 1965

Act. It is not a requirement that one should consider that for the purposes of s 42 of
the 1965 Act. There is no reason to think that the general words have to be applied   *a*
throughout the whole Act to cover provisions which, as far as I can see, were
probably not in the draftsman's mind at all.

Counsel for the taxpayer argued that on the Crown's stated purpose of the deeming
provision, anomalies and absurdities might arise. He instanced two possibilities
where facts could exist which would give rise to anomalous results on the Crown's
construction. I accept that in those somewhat fanciful examples the results would   *b*
be unexpected. I do not accept that those results are properly to be called 'anomalies',
let alone 'absurdities'. It is frequently true that taxing Acts produce results that seem
surprising but that is the inevitable result of very complicated provisions having to
apply to all factual circumstances. In my judgment there is nothing in counsel's
examples to cause me to consider that the construction I have placed on the section
must be erroneous.   *c*

It seems to me that the Special Commissioner did err in his legal conclusions.
That is understandable and natural when dealing with matters which are otherwise
res integra and of some complexity. But, guiding myself by the principles laid down
by Nourse J in *IRC v Metrolands*, I come to the conclusion that the Crown's appeal
in this matter succeeds.

d

Appeal allowed with costs.

Solicitors: *Solicitor of Inland Revenue*; *Wragge & Co*, Birmingham (for the taxpayer).

Rengan Krishnan Esq   Barrister.

a   Gallic Leasing Ltd v Coburn (Inspector of Taxes)

HOUSE OF LORDS
LORD KEITH OF KINKEL, LORD TEMPLEMAN, LORD OLIVER OF AYLMERTON, LORD GOFF
OF CHIEVELEY, LORD LOWRY
28, 29 OCTOBER, 28 NOVEMBER 1991

b

Corporation tax – Group relief – Claim – Claim to be made within two years of end of accounting period – Claim made in notice of appeal and accounts – No specified form for claim – Surrendering companies not identified – Inspector rejected claim as not in identifiable format – Whether valid claim made within two-year period – Taxes Management Act 1970, s 42(5) – Income and Corporation Taxes Act 1970, ss 258,
c   *264(1)(c).*

An estimated assessment to corporation tax was raised on the taxpayer company for the accounting period ended 31 March 1982. The taxpayer company appealed against the assessment and applied for postponement of payment of the full amount of tax on the grounds that the profits would be covered by group relief. That
d   postponement was agreed by the inspector. A copy of the taxpayer company's signed accounts together with a computation of its income assessable to corporation tax for the period were sent to the inspector. The computation was stated to be 'subject to group relief' and the accounts showed the amount of the corporation tax payable on the profits with a deduction of an equivalent amount of group relief. No further information was supplied to the inspector before the expiry of the two-year time
e   limit prescribed by s 264(1)(c)[a] of the Income and Corporation Taxes Act 1970. Following the expiry of the two-year time limit, the inspector agreed the profits for the period and requested 'particulars of any group relief to be claimed' and subsequently a schedule of group relief was submitted. In December 1986 the inspector decided, despite the absence of a prescribed form under s 42(5)[b] of the Taxes Management Act 1970 as to the making of a claim, that no formal claim for
f   group relief under s 258[c] had been made within the time limit. On appeal, the General Commissioners upheld the inspector's decision that the references to group relief in the notice of appeal, in the note on the accounts and in the computation of assessable income did not, either severally or collectively, constitute a valid claim to group relief, but amounted to no more than an intimation that group relief would or might be claimed in the future. Vinelott J allowed the taxpayer company's appeal,
g   holding that in order to make a valid claim, all that was required was for the claimant company to make it clear to the inspector that a claim was being made and that it was unnecessary to identify the surrendering companies or the amount of the relief to be surrendered by each. The Court of Appeal reversed Vinelott J's decision, holding that it was essential to a valid claim for group relief that the surrendering companies be identified and the amount of the relief surrendered by each be
h   quantified. The taxpayer company appealed.

Held – The Revenue had not exercised the power conferred by s 42(5) of the Taxes Management Act 1970 to prescribe the form in which a claim for group relief should be made. Consequently, the validity of a claim to group relief had to be determined by reference to s 258, the section granting the relief. Section 258, however, served
j   no purpose other than that of alerting the inspector to the fact that reliefs were to be sought by the claimant company. A valid claim did not require the claimant

---

a   Section 264(1)(c), so far as material, is set out at p 702 *hj*, post
b   Section 42(5), so far as material, is set out at p 701 *j*, post
c   Section 258, so far as material, is set out at p 702 *c d*, post

company to identify the surrendering companies or the amount of the reliefs to be
surrendered at the time of making the claim. Accordingly, the combined effect of
the taxpayer company's references to group relief in the notice of appeal, the note
on the accounts and the computation of assessable income sufficiently constituted a
valid claim for group relief. The taxpayer company's appeal would therefore be
allowed.

Notes

For group relief, claims and adjustments, see Simon's Taxes D2.648.

For the Income and Corporation Taxes Act 1970, ss 258, 264 (now the Income
and Corporation Taxes Act 1988, ss 402, 412), see ibid, Part G1.

Appeal

The taxpayer company appealed against a decision of the Court of Appeal (Fox,
Balcombe and Stocker LJJ) given on 13 February 1991 (see [1991] STC 151) allowing
an appeal by the Crown against a decision of Vinelott J dated 2 March 1989 (see
[1989] STC 354) allowing an appeal by Gallic Leasing Ltd, the taxpayer company,
against a determination of the General Commissioners upholding the Crown's
refusal of the taxpayer company's claim for group relief for the accounting period
ended 31 March 1982 under s 258 of the Income and Corporation Taxes Act 1970.
The facts are set out in the opinion of Lord Oliver.

Alan Moses QC and *Launcelot Henderson* for the Crown.
David Goldberg QC and *Mrs F Cullen* for the taxpayer company.

Their Lordships took time for consideration.

28 November. The following opinions were delivered.

LORD KEITH OF KINKEL. My Lords, I have had the opportunity of considering
in draft the speech to be delivered by my noble and learned friend Lord Oliver.
I agree with it, and for the reasons he gives would allow this appeal.

LORD TEMPLEMAN. My Lords, for the reasons given by my noble and learned
friend, Lord Oliver, I would allow this appeal.

LORD OLIVER OF AYLMERTON. My Lords, Chapter I of Part XI of the
Income and Corporation Taxes Act 1970 (the 1970 Act) contains provisions enabling
the company which is part of a group of companies to claim reliefs available to other
companies within the group by way of relief from corporation tax for which it is
liable. The question at issue in this appeal relates to the form in which such a claim
requires to be made if it is to be valid.

The appellant company, Gallic Leasing Ltd (the taxpayer company), is a wholly-
owned subsidiary of Gallic Shipping Ltd, a company which had, at the material
time, a number of other subsidiaries and which was itself a subsidiary of Gallic
Management Ltd. On 1 October 1982 an estimated assessment to corporation tax
for the accounting period ended 31 March 1982 was raised on the taxpayer company.
On 31 October 1982 the taxpayer company appealed the assessment and, at the same
time, applied to postpone payment of the full amount of the tax claimed, stating as
the ground for postponement that: 'Profits will be covered by group relief'. On
15 November 1982 the inspector of taxes agreed the postponement. On 30 June 1983
the taxpayer company's accountants sent to the inspector for agreement a copy of
the taxpayer company's accounts for the period to 31 March 1982 duly signed by the
directors together with a computation of its income assessable to corporation tax

which was submitted 'Subject to Group Relief'. Note 6 to the accounts, headed
'Taxation', stated corporation tax at 52% of profits of the year as £167,000 from
which there was deducted the like sum described as 'Group Relief'. At the same
time the accountants submitted accounts for the same period of Gallic Management
Ltd. Thereafter, on 5 August 1983, accounts were submitted for Gallic Shipping
Ltd. On 18 July 1983 the inspector acknowledged receipt of the taxpayer company's
accounts and concluded by saying, 'I have no inquiries to raise and now await details
of the group relief'. Thereafter nothing further appears to have happened for some
18 months save that I infer that accounts of other companies in the group for the
same accounting year—in particular, West Bay Shipping Ltd, Interflow (Tank
Container System) Ltd and Fairmile Construction Co Ltd were submitted to the
inspector for agreement. On 18 January 1985 the inspector wrote to the taxpayer
company's accountants agreeing the taxpayer company's profits for the year in
question at £321,291 and adding, 'I should now like particulars of any group relief
to be claimed'. Subsequently a schedule of group relief was submitted but on
4 December 1986 group relief was formally refused on the ground that 'no claim was
made within the time limit prescribed by s 246(1)(c) [sic] I.C.T.A. 1970'. The
reference to s 246 is plainly a misprint for s 264 which provides a two-year time limit
for making claims. From this decision the taxpayer company appealed to the
General Commissioners who upheld the inspector's decision, holding that the
references to group relief in the notice of appeal of 31 October 1982, in the note on
the accounts and in the accountants' computation of assessable income did not,
either severally or collectively, constitute a valid claim to group relief, but amounted
to no more than an intimation that group relief would or might be claimed in the
future. On appeal to the High Court, Vinelott J, on 2 March 1989, allowed the
appeal (see [1989] STC 354) holding that in order to make a valid claim for group
relief all that was required was for the claimant company to make it clear that a claim
was being made and that it was unnecessary to identify either the surrendering
companies or the amount of the relief to be surrendered by each. On 13 February
1991 the Court of Appeal reversed Vinelott J's decision (see [1991] STC 151), holding
that it was essential to a valid claim for group relief that the surrendering companies
be identified and the amount of the relief surrendered by each be quantified. From
that decision the taxpayer company now appeals to your Lordships' House, leave
for that purpose having been obtained on 9 May this year.

The 1970 Act contains numerous references to the making of claims for reliefs of
various kinds, from relief for small maintenance payments (see s 65(4)) or trade losses
(see ss 168, 177) to relief for copyright payments (see s 389), relief from tax on
delayed remittances (see s 419) and double taxation relief (see s 497(4)). At the same
time, Parliament provided, in s 42 of the Taxes Management Act 1970, a general
code intended to govern the procedure to be employed in making such claims.
Section 42(1) provides that where the Taxes Acts provide for relief to be given on
the making of a claim, the section shall have effect unless otherwise provided for.
Thus every claim is to be made to an inspector (see sub-s (2)) and provision is made
in sub-s (3) for an appeal against an inspector's decision. As regards the form or
content of any such claim, however, the section leaves this to the determination of
the Board of Inland Revenue. Subsection (5) (so far as relevant at all to this appeal)
provides as follows:

> 'A claim shall be in such form as the Board may determine and the form of
> claim—
>
> (*a*) shall provide for a declaration to the effect that all the particulars given in
> the form are correctly stated to the best of the knowledge and belief of the
> person making the claim, and
> (*b*) may require—
>
> (i) a return of profits to be made in support of the claim . . .'

Section 43 provides that, subject to any longer or shorter period prescribed, no claim is to be allowed unless it is 'made' within six years from the end of the *a* chargeable period to which it relates. However, in the determination of how a claim is to be made and when it is to be deemed to be valid or complete, these two sections are in fact totally unhelpful, because, as your Lordships will have been as surprised as I was to learn from counsel for the Crown, speaking on instructions, the power conferred by s 42(5) has never been exercised in the 22-odd years that have elapsed since the Taxes Management Act 1970 was passed. Thus, for the determination of *b* what constitutes a 'claim' in any given case and when it is to be deemed to have been made, we can effectively put this section on one side and are compelled to rely on such guidance as is offered by the individual provision for relief to which any alleged 'claim' relates.

Group relief was, at the material time, regulated entirely for relevant purposes by ss 258–264 (inclusive) of the 1970 Act. Section 258(1) provides: *c*

'Relief for trading losses and other amounts eligible for relief from corporation tax may in accordance with the following provisions of this Chapter be surrendered by a company (called "the surrendering company") which is a member of a group of companies and, on the making of a claim by another company (called "the claimant company") which is a member of the same group, *d* may be allowed to the claimant company by way of a relief from corporation tax called "group relief".'

To find out what constitutes a 'group' for the purposes of the section. reference has to be made to sub-s (5)(a) which provides that two companies shall be deemed to be members of a group of companies if one is the 75% subsidiary of the other or both are 75% subsidiaries of a third company.   *e*

Thus group relief is, by definition, the allowance to one company, the claimant company, by way of relief against its liability for corporation tax of the reliefs by way of trading losses or otherwise of another company to which the claimant company stands in the relation postulated by sub-s (5), which reliefs are surrendered by that other company. That allowance is permitted 'on the making of a claim' by the claimant company (see sub-s (1)) and that expression clearly invokes s 42 of the *f* Taxes Management Act 1970. It tells us, however, nothing more about the procedure for making a claim.

The types of group relief are enumerated in s 259. It covers, for instance, relief for trading losses, capital allowances, management expenses of an investment company and charges on income. This section contains no clues as to the form in which the claimant company's claim may be made, but it does serve to underline the very real *g* difficulties which may be involved in quantifying a claim until not only the accounts of the claimant company for the period in question but also those of all the other companies in a group relationship which may have available reliefs have been finally settled and agreed with the Revenue—a process which, in the case of a large group, may take a very considerable time.

The only other section bearing on the making of a claim is s 264, sub-s (1) of which *h* provides that:

'A claim for group relief—

(a) need not be for the full amount available,
(b) shall require the consent of the surrendering company notified to the inspector in such form as the Board may require, and   *j*
(c) must be made within two years from the end of the surrendering company's accounting period to which the claim relates.'

Again, however, this is not of great assistance. Requirement (a) is purely negative and indicates that where an amount of relief is or becomes available in a surrendering company it does not have to be, though it can be, claimed in toto. The highest that

this can be put is that it indicates what *may* be included in a claim. It goes no
a distance towards indicating what *must* be included. Requirement (*b*) indicates
nothing about the form or contents of the claim but merely that, whatever be the
form of the claim, it requires for its validity a consent of the surrendering company.
Once again, the Board has not laid down any form for a consent, but in any event it
was conceded before Vinelott J (see [1989] STC 354 at 362) that a consent is not a
condition precedent to a claim but only to its acceptance and that the giving of
b consent is not subject to the mandatory time limit in requirement (*c*). The Crown
did not, in the Court of Appeal, contend that consent was required to be given
within the two-year period. As regards requirement (*c*) this indicates, it is true, that
the claim is envisaged as 'relating' to a particular accounting period of the
surrendering company, but that would be implicit in any event since it would be
made in relation to the accounting period of the claimant company and s 259 makes
c it clear that the allowable reliefs are those in the accounting period corresponding
with that of the claimant company.

One is ultimately thrown back to whatever assistance one can derive from s 258
itself. Subsection (1) is simply an enabling provision. It enables available reliefs to be
surrendered and it enables another company in the group 'on the making of a claim'
to set those reliefs off. It is helpful only as containing a definition of 'group relief'
d (i e the relief allowed to a claimant company from reliefs surrendered by another
company with which it is in a group relationship). It does not, however, indicate
any order in which the events leading to such allowance (i e surrender, claim and
consent) are to take place (by suggesting, e g, that surrender must necessarily precede
the claim) and there appears to be no reason why a claimant company should not
make its claim to group relief before it knows the extent of any available reliefs or
e whether the company to which they are available is willing to surrender them. On
this analysis the making of a claim serves no other purpose than that of alerting the
inspector to the fact that reliefs are to be sought by the claimant company.

If that is right, then the documents relied on by the taxpayer company sufficiently
constituted a claim for the purposes of the section. The inspector, who received the
accounts with the references to group relief at the same time as he received the
f accounts of other companies in the group in which the relationships were clearly set
out, cannot have been under any misapprehension as to the existence of a group or
that the taxpayer company was claiming reliefs anticipated to be available within
the group to an extent necessary to extinguish the tax liability on its profits. Indeed
the correspondence shows that he so understood the position and, as Vinelott J
observed in the course of his judgment (see [1989] STC 354 at 362), the combined
g effect of the documents sent to the inspector was precisely the same as if the accounts
had been accompanied by a letter saying, 'We hereby claim group relief under
s 258(1) in respect of the full amount of the profits of the taxpayer company for the
accounting period to 31 March 1982, being the amount shown in the profit and loss
account'. The position subsequently taken by the Revenue, when details were
submitted in response to the inspector's request following the agreement of the
h taxpayer company's accounts, may seem, on the face of it, a little less than
meritorious having regard to the Board's own omission in the 15 years which had
elapsed since the passing of the Taxes Management Act 1970 to specify its own
requirements for a claim. If the Crown is right on the construction of the 1970 Act,
however, that is irrelevant.

The argument advanced by counsel for the Crown starts from an assumption
j regarding the purpose of the two-year time limit prescribed by s 264(1)(*c*). This, it is
said, must have some more specific purpose than that of merely encouraging the
timeous submission of accounts and alerting the inspector to the fact that relief
under s 258(1) is being sought so that he knows, before raising an assessment, that it
may require to be reopened to the extent that relief is ultimately agreed. The
purpose, it is argued, is to ensure that, within the defined period, the inspector has
all the necessary material to enable him either to accept or to reject the claim and, if

he accepts it, to give effect to it. Thus, it is argued, there is an irreducible minimum of information which a claim, to be valid as a 'claim' within the meaning of s 258(1), *a* must contain. This consists of (1) the identification of the claimant company; (2) the amount of profit against which relief is claimed; (3) the identification of each surrendering company; and (4) the amount of the relief of each surrendering company to be surrendered and the origin (e g trading loss, capital allowance and so forth) of the relief surrendered expressed either as a firm figure or as a proportion of the total available relief. As a fall-back from this position, an alternative submission *b* is advanced that the very least that is required is an identification of each surrendering company in respect of which the claim is being made. It may be convenient to label these two alternative formulations as 'the first and second submissions'.

As regards the first submission, this involves ascribing to s 264(1)(c) an assumed purpose which is nowhere expressed in the statute and then arguing backwards from that assumption in order to discover the minimum required to fulfil that assumed *c* purpose. It is an approach which evidently appealed to the Court of Appeal (see [1991] STC 151), but I have not, for my part, found it possible to accept it, for, quite apart from the fact that it involves reading into the statute a very great deal which is simply not there and which cannot be gathered from the words either of s 264 of the 1970 Act or of s 42 of the Taxes Management Act 1970, it seems to me to impose a rigidity on the operation of s 264 for which there is no warrant either in the language *d* used or in the scheme which the section was seeking to effect. The Court of Appeal (at 154–155), having postulated that the claim must be in a form which would enable the inspector to accept it or reject it, nevertheless contemplated both that the claim might not be quantifiable within the time limit allowed and that it might be accepted in an amount different from that claimed. By implication, this would seem to permit acceptance of an amount of relief in excess of that claimed, which must, on this *e* analysis, I should have thought, necessarily involve a new claim so far, at least, as the excess is concerned. Counsel for the Crown, if I understood his submission aright, does not accept this but would contend that the claim must specify in each case the maximum amount claimed by way of relief in the case of each surrendering company and in the case of each source of relief within such company even though a lesser amount may on investigation be actually allowed by the inspector. There is, *f* it is argued—and, in my view, argued correctly—no such thing as 'group relief' in the abstract. The definition of group relief in s 258(1) demonstrates that it is conceived of as a one-to-one transfer of available reliefs involving the claimant company on the one hand and a particular second company with which the claimant company has the group relationship described in sub-s (5)(a). The claimant company may in a single document claim reliefs from a number of different companies with *g* which it has the necessary relationship, just as two or more claimant companies may claim reliefs from a third company in the necessary relationship; but each claim is a separate claim which has to be considered individually and without regard to any other parallel claim which is being made in relation to one or more other surrendering companies. That I find entirely acceptable as a premise, but the conclusion drawn from it that it follows that the claim must contain all the irreducible minima already *h* referred to is one which, in the end, depends on nothing more than the assumed purpose of s 264(1)(c). But the making of that assumption argues, as it seems to me, an ignorance on the part of the legislature of the realities of life. If the purpose is to enable the inspector to have, within the limited period, all the information necessary for him to adjudicate on the claim, then there can be no room for any subsequent adjustment of the figures on which, by definition, the claim has to be based, for that *j* would defeat the object. If on the other hand, the assumption is that the claimant company must, within the period, tie himself to particular amounts in respect of particular reliefs from particular surrendering companies, then the system becomes divorced from practicality. Anyone familiar with company accounts cannot be unaware that it takes a considerable time to prepare and agree group accounts and that their agreement with the Revenue not only may, but very frequently does,

involve correspondence and negotiation over an extended period and also, not
a infrequently, appeals to the commissioners and beyond which are highly unlikely to
be concluded within the two-year time limit. Moreover, the inspector will not in
any event be able to accept any claim unless and until he receives the consent of the
surrendering company provided for in s 264(1)(*b*) and once it is conceded, as I
understand it to be, that the consent does not necessarily require to be lodged within
the time limit prescribed, the assumed object of the time limit is inevitably negatived
b in any event.

In the end, the question is one which depends simply on the proper construction
to be placed on the words which the legislature has used and I find myself unable to
deduce either from the words used or from the scheme of the section the rigid
requirements for which the Crown has contended. I can, of course, see that it would
be convenient for an inspector to have before him timeously such information as to
c the sources and composition of group relief claimed as would enable him at least to
make a start on the process of considering claims to group relief with a view to their
ultimate adjudication, but, as the taxpayer company has pointed out, the remedy
for delay in providing details necessary for adjudication lies in the inspector's hands.
He can make an assessment and require payment of the tax assessed. Moreover, I
can, speaking for myself, see no reason at all why, if the submission of claims in a
d generalised form such as that involved in the instant case is proving inconvenient,
the Board should not exercise its powers under s 42(5) of the Taxes Management
Act 1970 by specifying a form of claim which requires the claimant company to state
from which members of the group reliefs are claimed and to state to the best of its
ability the amounts and sources of the reliefs to which it hopes to establish an
entitlement. In the end, the submission came down to this, that the time limit
e imposes a requirement that before its expiry the claimant company must not only
commit itself to claiming group relief but must commit itself irrevocably to the
precise amounts or proportions claimed from each source of relief in each
surrendering company, albeit it may not know either the extent of the reliefs
available or whether consent to surrender to this extent or at all is going to be given.
I find no warrant in the terms of the section for this requirement.

f As regards the second submission, it is argued that, since group relief postulates
the one-to-one relationship to which I have referred, it follows that a 'claim' to group
relief must, to constitute a claim at all, at least specify that company within the
group by which the reliefs are being or are to be surrendered. Such an argument
might be said to derive some support from s 258(3) which speaks of claims by one or
more claimant companies 'relating to the same surrendering company', thus
g implying that, at least in this subsection, a claim is envisaged as 'relating' to a
particular company. It cannot, it is said—and, indeed this must I think be obvious—
be sufficient simply to say, 'I claim', which is meaningless. By necessary implication
a claim must be made by an identified claimant company and must relate to the
corporation tax liability and thus to the profits of that claimant company. Section
259, which specifies the reliefs available, necessarily ties those reliefs, and thus group
h relief, to a particular accounting period. Thus, a 'claim' by definition has to be the
assertion by an identified company of a right to set against its profits for a defined
accounting period the reliefs available to another group company. A 'claim' cannot,
for instance, consist of a general assertion that for all future years group relief against
whatever profits are made is claimed. Nor equally can a 'claim' be made by an annual
assertion on 1 April in some such form as 'we do not know what (if any) profit we
j shall make during the year now current but, if and so far as we do make any, we
hereby claim group relief'. It is strictly unnecessary for the purposes of this appeal
to decide the point, but, for my part, I do feel able to derive from the 1970 Act that
a claim to have any meaning at all must at least be a claim by an identified claimant
company to relief against identified or identifiable profits for an identified accounting
period. But if this be right, it is asked, must it not also at least identify the company
from which the reliefs are to come more precisely than by saying that they are to

come from some one or more companies within a group? I was at one time attracted by this argument on the ground that, since 'group relief' is defined as the relief allowed to the claimant company for the trading losses and other eligible amounts of a surrendering company, a claim which does not identify the surrendering company, whatever else it may be, is not a claim for 'group relief'. I have, however, felt compelled to reject this. It is pointed out that, on this footing, a claim for group relief in respect of, e g the trading losses (unspecified) of companies A to F inclusive (being all the companies in the group) would be a good claim if one once rejects, as I believe that one must, the minimum criteria propounded by counsel for the Crown in his first submission. It would follow that a claim to group relief from all those companies in the group which are eligible to make surrenders and have reliefs available would be a good claim at any rate in any case where the composition of the group was either known to or made known to the inspector to whom the claim was made. But if one gets to that point, it must equally follow that where the composition of the group is made known to the inspector (as it was in this case) a simple claim by the claimant company in the form 'we claim group relief from the profits shown in our accounts for this period' must have the same effect, for it conveys, although in a different form, exactly the same information. There is nothing in the 1970 Act which requires the composition of the group to be made known to the inspector before or after the claim is made or before or after the two-year time limit for making the claim. In the end, I find myself persuaded by counsel for the taxpayer company's submission that there really is no half-way house between counsel for the Crown's irreducible criteria, which I have felt compelled to reject for the reasons which I have endeavoured to explain, and the acceptance of the validity of a claim in the more generalised form of the claim made in the instant case. I would, accordingly, allow the appeal.

LORD GOFF OF CHIEVELEY. My Lords, I have had the advantage of reading in draft the speech prepared by my noble and learned friend, Lord Oliver. I agree with it and, for the reasons which he gives, I, too, would allow the appeal.

LORD LOWRY. My Lords, I have had the advantage of reading in draft the speech of my noble and learned friend, Lord Oliver. I agree with it and, for the reasons given by my noble and learned friend, I, too, would allow the appeal.

Appeal allowed with costs.

Solicitors: *Cameron Markby Hewitt* (for the taxpayer company); *Solicitor of Inland Revenue.*

Rengan Krishnan Esq   Barrister.

a # Inland Revenue Commissioners v Eurocopy plc

CHANCERY DIVISION
MERVYN DAVIES J
7, 8, 18 NOVEMBER 1991

b *Shares – Share option schemes – Approval – Amendment to scheme so as to reduce the*
period of time which must expire before the option became exercisable – Revenue refusing
to grant approval – Whether amendments could be approved – Income and Corporation
Taxes Act 1988, s 185(1), Sch 9, paras 1, 29.

In June 1987, the company established a share option scheme (the original scheme)
c which was approved by the Board of Inland Revenue. The options granted
thereunder were exercisable after the expiry of nine years from the date of grant.
Subsequently, the company considered that the nine-year time limit was no longer
appropriate and sought approval, inter alia, for an amendment to the original
scheme so as to reduce the time limit from nine years to six years. Under para 1[a] of
Sch 9 to the Income and Corporation Taxes Act 1988 the Board was obliged to
d approve a share option scheme if it fulfilled the requirements of s 185[b] of and Sch 9
to the 1988 Act. On 14 June 1988, the Board approved the amendment in relation to
options to be granted in the future, but refused to approve the amendment to options
already granted under the original scheme taking the view (a) that as a matter of law
it was not possible to vary the terms of an option; (b) that the amendment effected
the creation of a new option; and (c) in the alternative, that if an option was capable
e of variation, the proposed amendment was not a variation but a rescission of the
original scheme contract. The Special Commissioner held that the Board's refusal
was not justified on the grounds that the effect of the amendment to an option
granted under the original scheme was simply to vary the terms on which that option
might be exercised so that the right to acquire shares after the amendment was the
same as that which existed before the amendment. The Crown appealed contending:
f (i) that the existing holder of an option under the original scheme would obtain a
new right to acquire shares if the proposed amendment to the time limit within
which the option might be exercised were to be approved; (ii) that the new right did
not meet the requirements of para 29[c] of Sch 9 because the price at which shares
might be acquired under the new right was manifestly less than the market value of
equivalent shares at the time the new right was obtained ie at the date of the
g amendment; and (iii) that the Board's refusal to approve the amendment in relation
to existing options was therefore justified.

Held – A right to acquire shares under an approved share option scheme had to
meet certain conditions as to the price at which the shares might be acquired (Sch 9,
para 29) and as to the time limit within which that option might be exercised
h (s 185(5)). An alteration in the time limits affecting the right to acquire was an
alteration of the right to acquire. Accordingly in the instant case the existing option
holder's right to acquire shares under the original scheme would not be the same
right if effect were to be given to the amendment, but a new right which would not
satisfy the requirements of para 29. In the circumstances the Board was justified in
refusing its approval to the amendment in relation to the existing option holders.
j The Crown's appeal would therefore be allowed.

---

a   Paragraph 1, so far as material, is set out at p 717 *j* to p 718 *a*, post
b   Section 185, so far as material, is set out at p 717 *g j*, post
c   Paragraph 29, so far as material, is set out at p 718 *b c*, post

Notes

For the approval of share option schemes, see Simon's Taxes E4.511.   *a*

For the Income and Corporation Taxes Act 1988, s 185(1) and Sch 9, paras 1, 29, see ibid, Part G1.

Cases referred to in judgment

British and Beningtons Ltd v North Western Cachar Tea Co Ltd [1923] AC 48, HL.   *b*

United Dominions Trust (Commercial) Ltd v Eagle Aircraft Services Ltd [1968] 1 WLR 74, [1968] 1 All ER 104, CA.

Varty (Inspector of Taxes) v British South Africa Co [1965] Ch 508, [1964] 2 All ER 975, CA; *rvsd* [1966] AC 381, [1965] 2 All ER 395, 42 TC 406, HL.

                                                                                   c

Cases also cited

Bruner v Moore [1904] 1 Ch 305.

Morrell v Studd & Millington [1913] 2 Ch 648.

Morris v Baron and Co [1918] AC 1, HL.

United Scientific Holdings v Burnley BC [1978] AC 904, [1977] 2 All ER 62, HL.

                                                                                   d

Case stated

1. On 5 and 6 March 1990 a Special Commissioner heard the appeal of Eurocopy plc (the company) against a decision of the Board of Inland Revenue dated 9 December 1988 whereby it refused the company's application under para 4 of Sch 9 to the Income and Corporation Taxes Act 1988 (the 1988 Act) for approval of   *e* an alteration to the company's share option scheme (the scheme).

2. The question for the commissioner's determination, his findings of fact on the evidence adduced, the respective contentions of Mr Leigh Sagar for the company and Miss F Saeed-Cockar for the Crown together with the commissioner's conclusions were set out in his written decision which was issued on 12 March 1990 and a copy of which was annexed as part of the case.   *f*

3. The following witnesses gave evidence before the commissioner: Mr Christopher Edward Michael Armitage and Mr John Bedford as witnesses of fact. Mr Nicholas Spencer Tant gave expert evidence.

4. [There followed a list of the documents that were proved or admitted before the commissioner.] In addition, a copy of the Crown's written submissions was annexed to the case.   *g*

5. The following authorities were cited in addition to those considered in the commissioner's decision:

    Dickinson v Dodds (1876) 2 Ch D 463.

    Mountford v Scott [1975] Ch 258.

    United Dominions Corporation (Jamaica) Ltd v Shoucair [1969] 1 AC 340.   *h*

    United Dominions Trust (Commercial) Ltd v Eagle Aircraft Services [1968] 1 WLR 74.

    Halsbury's Laws of England (4th edn) Vol 9.

    Chitty on Contract (26th edn, 1989).

6. At the request of the Crown the commissioner recorded that the six-year option   *j* granted recently by the company and noted at para 11 of the commissioner's decision was granted at the market value of the company's shares then prevailing. That value was higher than the values attached to the scheme options granted to Messrs Bedford, Wood, Goodman and Hall.

7. The Crown immediately after the determination of the appeal declared to the commissioners its dissatisfaction therewith as being erroneous in point of law and on

29 March 1990 required the commissioner to state a case for the opinion of the High
a Court pursuant to the Taxes Management Act 1970, s 56.

8. The question of law for the opinion of the court was whether, on the facts as
found, the commissioner had erred in approving, pursuant to para 5 of Sch 9 to the
1988 Act, the alteration to the scheme as proposed by the company.

Revenue's written submissions annexed to the case stated

b   1. This alteration (whereby the existing options which cannot be exercised for a
period of nine years would be exercisable after a period of six years) results in the
creation of a new option.

2. As a matter of law an option can never be amended except by the rescission of
the old option and the creation of a new option. (See eg *Williams on Title* (4th edn,
1975), p 14, where it is stated that: 'An option must be exercised within the period
c prescribed in the instrument creating it, *though it may be extended by the creation of
a new option*' [emphasis added].

3. An option is an irrevocable offer in the form of a unilateral contract (see eg
Mountford v Scott [1975] Ch 258 at 264–265 per Russell LJ). And: 'In order to be
turned into a binding contract the offer must be accepted in exact compliance with
its terms. The acceptance must correspond with the offer' (see *United Dominions
d Trust (Commercial) Ltd v Eagle Aircraft Services Ltd* [1968] 1 WLR 74 at 81 per
Lord Denning).

4. Even if an option is capable of variation, the amendment proposed here is such
as results not in a variation but in the rescission and replacement of the old option
with a new option.

5. Two of the essential characteristics of a share option agreement are the time
e and conditions of exercise. And therefore any alteration in relation to these terms
will result in the substitution of a new contract because the alteration would go to
the very root of the contract (see *Morris v Baron & Co* [1918] AC 1 at 31 and *British
and Beningtons Ltd v North Western Cachar Tea Co Ltd* [1923] AC 48 at 62 per Lord
Atkinson).

(1) In this case the essential nature of the period of exercise is illustrated, inter
f alia, by the effects of increasing the period during which the option can be exercised
which are considerable eg they become more valuable and there is less chance of
forfeiting them.

(2) Viewed objectively, there is the intention here to extinguish the first option
and replace it with a new one. This can be seen from the purposes intended to be
achieved by the granting of the options. The whole purpose of the first option was
g different: it was seen as a long-term incentive for the directors and employees of a
private company. The company therefore deliberately created a more restricted
period than required by the legislation. The new options, granted post-flotation,
had a different purpose and one of the reasons for making them exercisable earlier
was to make them more advantageous than the old ones.

(3) It is common ground that the new options are more advantageous than the
h old ones and that those with options exercisable after nine years are at a serious
disadvantage to those who are granted options in the future. This further illustrates
the fundamental importance of the exercise period.

6. And if changing the period in which the option can be exercised is a new option
then it cannot be approved because it does not comply with the requirements of the
legislation (see eg para 29 of Sch 9 of the 1988 Act) which provides that the price at
j which shares may be acquired by the exercise of the option must be stated at the
time the right is obtained and must not be manifestly less than the market value of
that time.

7. The Crown further submits that the share option legislation does not envisage
any alteration in the *rights* granted under the scheme but only the creation of new
rights. Only alterations to the scheme which do not affect the basic rights are
permissible eg changes in the person to notify.

8. A number of factors point to this argument being correct:

(1) Paragraph 4 of Sch 9 to the 1988 Act refers to an alteration being made to a *scheme* (not to existing rights).

(2) Paragraph 15 of Sch 9 allows a participant to release his rights under the scheme in exchange for similar rights in a new company and makes specific provision for the new rights to be equivalent to the old rights but only if, inter alia, the new rights will be exercisable in the same manner as the old rights.

If the company's argument is correct then this provision was unnecessary as this could have been achieved by simply varying the scheme.

(3) To allow any variation in the rights granted under an approved scheme could make a nonsense of the legislation. Take the following examples: (a) under s 185(5) of the 1988 Act the time between obtaining the right and exercising it is not to be less than three years. Say that in 1990 under an approved scheme a person is given an option to purchase 100 shares exercisable after three years; and (b) in 1993 the option is altered so that the number of shares is increased to 1000; (c) if Eurocopy's argument is correct, then this is a variation and the option over 1,000 shares is exercisable in 1994 although the right to obtain the shares was granted in 1993, less than three years before.

(4) In this case the company is seeking to effect an alteration which would take place from the date of the grant. If alterations were permissible, then on a true construction of the legislation, *any alteration of an option would result in the creation of a new right being obtained at the date of the alteration* and not at the date of the original grant. This being so, the alteration made in this case would fall foul not only of para 28 but also of para 29 of Sch 9 which provides that no rights should be obtained at a time when they would cause the market value of the shares to exceed the limits, at the time £100,000. In this case when, for example, Mr Goodman first obtained the option he was within para 28 because his rights were worth approximately £60,000. At the time of the alteration the value of the shares was about £1m. Again, if the company is right, variations would take effect from the date of the grant of the original option thus enabling people to avoid provisions of the legislation such as para 28 and para 29.

(5) Paragraph 15(5) of Sch 9 illustrates this further by making specific provision for an alteration to the rights obtained under a scheme to take effect *before the date of the alteration*, thus making it clear that without this provision the alteration could only take effect from the date of the alteration with the resulting consequences.

9. Rule 18 of the approved scheme has given powers to the grantor to amend the *scheme* and make alterations 'which would with material adverse effect abrogate or alter any of the subsisting rights of grantees under Options granted to them . . .' but this does not mean that the Revenue has to approve the alteration and it does not answer the question as to whether this results in creation of a new option or is just a variation.

10. The case of *IRC v Burton Group plc* [1990] STC 242 is clearly distinguishable from this case. In the *Burton's* case the option when granted conferred rights to the specified shares subject to the employee meeting key task conditions set or to be set by the company which could be varied. The issue concerned the right to set key task conditions in the future following the grant of options. Thus the terms of the option (including the power to set in the future or to vary key tasks) were set out clearly ab initio. It was not a case of an alteration after an option had been granted as in this case. Thus if you give yourself a power to vary which sets out specifically the conditions and terms on which you can vary, this would be approved. But a general power to vary would still not be approved.

DECISION

Eurocopy plc (formerly Eurocopy (Great Britain) Ltd) (the company) appeals pursuant to para 5 of Sch 9 to the Income and Corporation Taxes Act 1988 (the 1988 Act) against the decision of the Board of Inland Revenue made on 9 December 1988 *a*   not to approve an alteration to the Eurocopy plc Share Option Scheme made by resolution 8 adopted by the company in general meeting on 14 June 1988. The company's appeal was made on 22 December 1988.

The facts

The evidence in this appeal consisted of a statement of agreed facts and a bundle of agreed documents, supplemented by the oral evidence of the company's group

b   finance director, Mr Christopher Edward Michael Armitage and the company secretary, Mr John Bedford. Mr Bedford is also a director of the company. Expert evidence on behalf of the Crown was given by Mr Nicholas Spencer Tant, an assistant controller at the Inland Revenue Shares Valuation Division.

From the documentary and oral evidence I find the following facts:

1. The company adopted the Eurocopy plc Share Option Scheme (the scheme)

c   on 27 May 1987 and the scheme was approved by the Board of Inland Revenue pursuant to s 38 of and Sch 10 to the Finance Act 1984 (now incorporated in s 185 of and Sch 9 to the 1988 Act) on 22 June 1987.

The following options were granted under the scheme:

Date of grant	Director/employee	Details of option (in each case after adjustment (as agreed with the Board) due to a reorganisation of the company's share capital on 14 June 1988)
21 July 1987	J Bedford	271,440 ordinary shares of 5p each at 10·5p per share
21 July 1987	B Wood	271,440 ordinary shares of 5p each at 10·5p per share
23 July 1987	R Goodman	542,880 ordinary shares of 5p each at 10·5p per share
9 June 1988	D Hall	180,960 ordinary shares of 5p each at 55·25p per share

f   2. The above options are referred to hereafter collectively as 'the scheme options'. Two other scheme options were granted, each on 15 January 1988, to former employees of the company. Those two options lapsed when the employees in question left the employment of the company.

3. At the time of the grant of the scheme options, rule 6(a) of the scheme (which relates to the exercise of options under the scheme) provided that:

g

'Save as provided in Rules 8, 9 and 10 [which Rules relate to termination of the right to exercise options, takeover and winding up] an Option shall be exercisable after the expiry of 9 years from the Date of Grant but not before.'

4. The company, in anticipation of its issued share capital being admitted to the Official List of The Stock Exchange, sought the approval of the Board to a number

h   of amendments to the scheme, including an amendment whereby the period before which options were capable of exercise under rule 6(a) was reduced from nine years to six years. The Board objected to this amendment in so far as it would affect existing options but approved the amendment in relation to options to be granted under the scheme in the future.

Accordingly, it was agreed between the Board and the company's advisers that

j   the amendment, in so far as it related to existing options, should be made the subject of a separate application for approval.

5. On 14 June 1988 the shareholders of the company passed a resolution in general meeting approving various amendments to the scheme including an amendment to rule 6(a) which, following the amendment, now reads as follows:

'Save as provided in Rules 8, 9 and 10, an Option shall be exercisable after the expiry of six years (nine years for options granted on any date prior to 14 June 1988) from the Date of Grant but not before.'

6. That amendment was approved by the Board.

7. Also on 14 June 1988 the shareholders of the company passed another resolution in general meeting reducing the period before which options granted under the scheme before 14 June 1988 could be exercised from nine years to six years and also deleted from the earlier resolution passed on the same date the following words '(nine years for options granted on any date prior to 14 June 1988)'. This second resolution was made subject to the consent of the relevant option holder in each case and also provided that the resolution would not have effect until approved by the Board.

8. Each of Mr Bedford, Mr Wood, Mr Goodman and Mr Hall gave their consent orally on 14 June 1988 as required by the terms of the second resolution passed on that date.

9. The company's business consists of the sale and servicing of photocopying equipment. It trades in a very competitive market in which the poaching of senior staff and successful salesmen in particular is commonplace.

The company introduced the scheme in 1987 in order to assist the retention and motivation of its senior executives. Although it was possible for the company to establish a scheme pursuant to which options could be granted to be exercisable after three years but before the expiration of ten years (see s 38(4) of the Finance Act 1984) a policy decision was reached that such options should not be exercisable until nine years had elapsed, for the following reasons: (a) Although the chairman was hoping to float the company as a public limited company at some time in the future, the time for flotation had not yet arrived. As a private company, the marketing of its shares was difficult and the chairman wished to avoid the complications attendant on the issue to employees and directors of a large number of shares which might prove to be virtually unmarketable in their hands. I infer that he hoped or planned to arrange the flotation of the company as a public limited company before the expiry of nine years from 1987. (b) The scheme was seen as a long-term incentive to participants. (c) The company was advised by its accountants and lawyers that at some later date the period within which options could be exercised could be amended to provide for their exercise at any time between three years and ten years from the date of their grant.

10. Following flotation as a public limited company in 1988, the company has operated in an even more competitive market. It now has institutional shareholders who are very concerned with the company's performance and in particular with its earnings per share. It has become even more important for the company to retain and motivate its senior executives and directors. It has found that competitor companies, having similar share option schemes, grant options exercisable after periods of three, four or five years. It was for this reason that the company decided to amend the scheme to provide for options to be exercised after a period of six years from the date of grant and the resolutions noted above were passed on 14 June 1988. Had the company remained a private limited company, it is probable that the provisions of the scheme would not have been altered to provide for exercise of options granted pursuant to it earlier than nine years from the date of their grant.

11. The refusal of the company's application by the Board has caused dissension and dissatisfaction in the company, for recently a new executive has been granted a valid option pursuant to the scheme exercisable after a period of six years. Options exercisable only after the lapse of a longer period of time than six years are not attractive to potential employees and directors of the company.

The expert evidence

From the evidence of Mr Tant I derive the following propositions:

1. Share prices both rise and fall, but the market at present rates the company well. It views the company as a growth stock.

2. If the options granted to Messrs Goodman, Bedford and Wood become exercisable after six years instead of after nine years, such an alteration would be advantageous to them. It would give each of those gentlemen greater flexibility in deciding when and how to exercise their options, with the prospect of earlier capital profits or a handsome return on savings or both. Such an alteration would be of considerable personal benefit to the employees concerned. Similar factors hold good for the option granted to Mr Hall although since his option was granted at a higher price of 50·25p per share, his capital profits are likely to be less and the prospect of an immediate income benefit less certain.

3. The granting of the options and the proposed change to the terms of the scheme were reasonable things for the company to do if it was concerned about retaining its directors and senior employees.

4. The options granted to Messrs Goodman, Wood and Bedford are designed to be exercisable at a very low price compared with the current price of the company's shares in the market, but the price of 10·5p quoted in their options was approved by the Board at the time, bearing in mind that the company was then a private limited company.

The statutory provisions

Section 185 of the 1988 Act provides, where relevant:

(1) The provisions of this section shall apply where, in accordance with the provisions of an approved share option scheme, an individual obtains a right to acquire shares in a body corporate by reason of his office or employment as a director or employee of that or any other body corporate and he obtains that right ... on or after 6th April 1984.

(2) ... tax shall not be chargeable under any provision of the Tax Acts in respect of the receipt of the right.

(3) Subject to subsection ... (5) below, if he exercises the right in accordance with the provisions of the scheme at a time when it is approved—

(*a*) tax shall not be chargeable under any provision of the Tax Acts in respect of the exercise nor under section 78 or 79 of the Finance Act 1988 in respect of the shares;

(*b*) section 29A(1) of the 1979 Act (assets deemed to be acquired at market value) shall not apply in calculating the consideration for the acquisition of the shares by him or for any corresponding disposal of them to him ...

(5) Subsection (3) above shall not apply in relation to the exercise by any person of a right in accordance with the provisions of a scheme ... if—

(*a*) the period beginning with his obtaining the right and ending with his exercising it is less than three, or greater than ten, years ...'

On the application of a body corporate which has established a share option scheme, the Board is obliged to approve the scheme if it is satisfied that the scheme fulfils the requirements which are referred to in para 1 of Sch 9 to the 1988 Act. However, the Board is forbidden to approve a scheme if it does not meet the requirements of para 2 of Sch 9 which states:

'(1) The Board shall not approve a scheme under this Schedule if it appears to them that it contains features which are neither essential nor reasonably incidental to the purpose of providing for employees and directors benefits in the nature of rights to acquire shares ...'

Conclusions

The point at issue in this appeal can be stated shortly. Miss F Saeed-Cockar of the Inland Revenue Solicitor's Office contends first that it is not possible as a matter of law to vary the terms of an option; second, in the alternative, that if it is possible to vary the terms of an option the amendment proposed by the company results not in variation but in the rescission of the option and its replacement by a new one; and third, that the provisions of the 1988 Act do not envisage any alteration in the rights granted under a share option scheme but only the creation of new rights. Only alterations to a scheme which do not affect basic rights are permissible.

Mr Leigh Sagar for the company takes an opposite standpoint and asks me to approve the proposed amendment to the scheme permitting the scheme options to be exercised after six years from their date of grant.

I will deal first with the effect of para 2(1) of Sch 9 to the 1988 Act. On the evidence of Mr Armitage and Mr Bedford it is clear to me that, commercially, the scheme will be a better scheme if this appeal is successful. Dissension between employees of the company has been caused by the grant recently of an option to a new employee exercisable under the terms of the scheme after a period of six years from the date of its grant. The dissension has reached such a level that in order to attempt to mollify disgruntled employees, unapproved options, outside the terms of the scheme, have been granted to Messrs Wood, Bedford, Goodman and Hall. Those unapproved options, exercisable between 21 July 1993 and 8 June 1995 have been granted as alternatives and not as additions to the scheme options. The exercise by a grantee of his rights under the terms of an unapproved option will extinguish his right to exercise his scheme option.

On the facts in this appeal I hold that the scheme which is the subject of this appeal does not contain features which are neither essential nor reasonably incidental to the purpose of providing for employees and directors benefits in the nature of rights to acquire shares.

I now turn to the question of whether the scheme options are capable of variation to provide for their exercise after a period of six years from the date of their grant, rather than after a period of nine years.

It is common ground in this appeal that if the scheme options are not capable of variation and that the effect of the proposed variation is to determine the scheme options and to replace them by new options, then the appeal must fail. It is also common ground that an option is an offer which cannot be revoked (see *Beesly v Hallwood Estates Ltd* [1960] 1 WLR 549 at 556 per Buckley J). Further it is common ground that in relation to the time during which an option may be exercised, time is of the essence of the contract.

Miss Saeed-Cockar places reliance on *Williams on Title* (4th edn, 1975), p 14 which states:

'Time for exercise of option – An option must be exercised within the period prescribed in the instrument creating it, though it may be extended by the creation of a new option, provided all the above-mentioned requirements are observed in creating the new option. Thus a mere voluntary extension of the period is not enforceable, nor is an oral agreement to extend it. If it is not exercised within the period originally stated, nor duly extended, it will lapse . . .'

My first observation is that the scheme options have not been extended. It seems to me that for the time for exercise of an option to be extended, the closing date for its exercise must be put back and further time, beyond the closing date originally contemplated, granted to the option holder. The granting of further time in those circumstances will in most cases prejudice the grantor of the option. He may have to wait for a longer period in order to discover whether the option holder intends to exercise his rights. In normal circumstances, monetary inflation will further devalue the consideration to be received by the grantor of the option in the event of its valid exercise by the grantee. In this appeal I am asked to consider circumstances enabling the grantees of the scheme options to exercise their rights at an earlier, not at a later date. I believe it to be common ground that such a variation of the terms of the scheme options is likely to be advantageous to their respective holders but I have heard no evidence to the effect that such a variation would operate as a detriment to

the company. The early exercise of the scheme options by their respective holders is
a   much more likely to be of benefit to the company. It may receive its money earlier
than originally contemplated.

My second observation is that there is reference in *Williams on Title* at note 12,
p 14, to the case of *Morrell v Studd and Millington* [1913] 2 Ch 648. In that case
Astbury J accepted that the time limit for acceptance of an option could be extended
by a parol agreement before it expires and in that case the judge was contemplating
b   a later rather than an earlier extension such as is present in this appeal. Although
some doubt was expressed with regard to some of Astbury J's observations in that
case by Morton LJ in *Hill v Hill* [1947] 1 Ch 231 at 239, his criticism was directed to
the operation of the Statute of Frauds and its application to the facts of the case. It
appears that *Morrell v Studd and Millington* is still good authority for the proposition
that the time within which an option may be exercised may be extended by a
c   variation of the terms of the original option.

Mr Sagar also places reliance on *Bruner v Moore* [1904] 1 Ch 305, which case was
referred to by Astbury J (at 656) in his judgment in *Morrell v Studd & Millington*.
It was decided in *Bruner v Moore* that if the grantor of an option leads the other
party to believe that he will not insist on the stipulated time limit, that limit will not
operate.

d   If, as I accept, the terms of an option relating to the time within which it may be
exercised may be varied, the question arises as to whether the variation in the
circumstances of this appeal operated to rescind or vary the terms of the scheme
options.

In *British and Beningtons Ltd v North Western Cachar Tea Company Ltd* [1923]
AC 48 at 62 Lord Atkinson observed:

e   'A written contract may be rescinded by parol either expressly or by the
parties entering into a parol contract entirely inconsistent with the written one,
or, if not entirely inconsistent with it, inconsistent with it to an extent that goes
to the very root of it: *Morris v Baron and Co* ...'

In *Morris v Baron and Co* [1918] AC 1 at 25–26, Lord Dunedin explained the
f   difference between variation and rescission:

'The difference between variation and rescission is a real one, and is tested, to
my thinking, by this: In the first case there are no such executory clauses in the
second arrangement as would enable you to sue upon that alone if the first did
not exist; in the second you could sue on the second arrangement alone and the
first contract is got rid of either by express words to that effect, or because, the
g   second dealing with the same subject-matter as the first but in a different way,
it is impossible that the two should be both performed. When I say you could
sue on the second alone, that does not exclude cases where the first is used for
mere reference, in the same way as you may fix a price by a price list, but where
the contractual force is to be found in the second by itself.'

h   On the facts of this appeal and after due consideration of the authorities and for
the reasons which I have given earlier, I do not accept that the variation of the time
limit within which the scheme options were to be exercised by permitting their
exercise after a period of six years only, amounted to a rescission of the scheme
options, nor do I accept that such a variation was so inconsistent with the original
contract that rescission was presumed to have been intended by the parties. I do not
j   accept that the variation went to the very root of the contracts created by the scheme
options. In coming to that conclusion I take into account the evidence of Mr Bedford
to the effect that he believed by consenting to the variation, the terms of his option
were being improved so that they would become comparable with options granted
by competitor companies.

Miss Saeed-Cockar has placed reliance in her submissions on what she believes
were the motives of the parties in granting the scheme options in the first place and

contends that a different motive operated on the occasion of the scheme options' variation. I do not accept that the parties' motives were relevant to the extent which she contends. It seems to me that motive is only relevant in relation to the operation of para 2(1) of Sch 9 to the 1988 Act.

Miss Saeed-Cockar's concluding submissions were to the effect that the statutory requirements contained in the 1988 Act tend to support her argument that options once granted are not capable of variation. I do not accept her arguments and I draw comfort from the judgment of Vinelott J in *IRC v Burton Group plc* [1990] STC 242 delivered on 31 January 1990 where he said (at 260):

'Put shortly, in my judgment it can make no difference that the number of the shares which the employee may be entitled to acquire on the exercise of the option may be governed not only by conditions set when the option is granted but by conditions subsequently imposed or varied but imposed or varied in good faith in order to ensure that the scheme operates fairly and effectively as an incentive scheme.'

I have no doubt that the terms of the scheme options were varied in good faith and in order to ensure that the scheme operated fairly and effectively as an incentive scheme. On the face of it it is inequitable that employees or directors fulfilling similar roles in the company should not enjoy share options granted on similar terms. In my judgment, if as in *Burton*, the number of shares may be varied, then it is equally certain that the time limits within which the scheme options may be exercised may be varied also.

There remains only Miss Saeed-Cockar's contention that the holders of each of the scheme options did not give consideration for the variation of their terms. On the facts, I reject that submission also. The company received the advantage that it was likely to receive its money earlier, as it was highly likely that the holders of the scheme options would take advantage of the opportunity to exercise their options at an earlier date. In addition there was the collateral advantage to the company that by amending the terms of the scheme options it was removing a cause of dissatisfaction amongst their holders in relation to their terms of employment with the company.

The appeal succeeds and pursuant to para 5 of Sch 9 to the 1988 Act I approve the amendment to the scheme proposed by the company.

Alan Moses QC and *Nicholas Warren* for the Crown.
John R MacDonald QC and *L Sagar* for the company.

Cur adv vult

18 November. The following judgment was delivered.

MERVYN DAVIES J. This is an appeal by way of case stated under s 56 of the Taxes Management Act 1970. The appeal is by the Inland Revenue Commissioners (the Crown). The respondent is Eurocopy plc (the company). The appeal concerns the decision of the Special Commissioner, Mr T H K Everett, dated 12 March 1990. In March 1990 the Special Commissioner heard the company's appeal against the decision of the Board of Inland Revenue dated 9 December 1988 to refuse the company's application under para 4 of Sch 9 to the Income and Corporation Taxes Act 1988 (the 1988 Act) for the approval of an alteration to the company's share option scheme.

The company devised a share option scheme which was approved by the Revenue on 22 June 1987 pursuant to s 38 of the Finance Act 1984 (taken with Sch 10). The current relative provisions are s 185 of the 1988 Act read with Sch 9 to that Act. As I understand, six options have been granted under the scheme but two of them have lapsed by reason of the option-holders having left their employment. The remaining

four options are: (1) on 21 July 1987 to Mr J Bedford, 271,440 ordinary shares of 5p
each at 10·5p per share; (2) on 21 July 1987 to Mr B Wood, 271,440 ordinary shares
of 5p each at the same price; (3) on 23 July 1987 to Mr R Goodman, 542,880 ordinary
shares of 5p each at the same price; and (4) on 9 June 1988 to Mr D Hall, 180,960
ordinary shares of 5p each at 55·25p per share.

At the time of the grant of the options rule 6(a) of the scheme provided—'. . . an
Option shall be exercisable after the expiry of 9 years from the Date of Grant but not
before'.

When the scheme was approved the company was not a listed company. With a
view to listing, approval was sought for some amendments to the scheme. The
proposed amendments included an amendment whereby the time when an option
could be exercised was reduced from nine to six years. The Revenue objected to the
amendment in so far as it would affect existing options but approved the amendment
in relation to options to be granted in the future. In those circumstances there was
an agreement with the Revenue that the amendment in so far as relating to existing
options should be made the subject of a separate application for approval.

On 14 June 1988 the shareholders of the company passed a resolution approving
amendments to the scheme, including an amendment to rule 6(a). Following the
amendment rule 6(a) reads thus—'. . . an Option shall be exercisable after the expiry
of six years (nine years for options granted on any date prior to 14 June 1988) from
the Date of Grant but not before'. As I understand, that amendment has been
approved by the Revenue.

On the same day (14 June 1988) the shareholders passed another resolution
reducing the time for the pre-June 1988 options, that is, those of the four employees
set out above. The reduction in time was from nine to six years. There was also
deleted from the earlier resolution passed on the same date the words in brackets as
set out in rule 6(a) above. The second resolution was made subject to the consent of
the relevant option-holder in each case and was not to have effect until approved by
the Board. The four option holders I have named above have given their consent.
As I have indicated, the Board did not approve the alteration in the scheme that
would arise from implementing the second resolution and the company appealed.

The question considered at the appeal was whether the Board were justified in
refusing to approve the alteration. The Special Commissioner, pursuant to para 5 of
Sch 9 to the 1988 Act, found that the Board were not justified in refusing approval;
and so the alteration in the scheme was approved. In consequence, there is now an
appeal by the Crown by way of case stated.

I set out the more essential parts of the 1988 Act that bear on the matter before
me. Section 185 reads:

'(1) The provisions of this section shall apply where, in accordance with the
provisions of an approved share option scheme, an individual obtains a right to
acquire shares in a body corporate by reason of his office or employment as a
director or employee of that or any other body corporate and he obtains that
right—. . . (b) in the case of any other share option scheme, on or after 6 April
1984.
(2) Subject to subsections (4) and (6) below, tax shall not be chargeable under
any provision of the Tax Acts in respect of the receipt of the right . . .
(5) Subsection (3) above shall not apply in relation to the exercise by any person
of a right in accordance with the provisions of a scheme which is not a savings-
related share option scheme if—(a) the period beginning with his obtaining the
right and ending with his exercising it is less than three, or greater than ten,
years . . .'

One sees from s 187(2) that 'approved' in relation to a scheme means approved
under Sch 9. Going to Sch 9, para 1 reads:

'Subject to the provisions of this Schedule, on the application of a body
corporate ("the grantor") which has established a share option scheme . . . the

Board shall approve the scheme if they are satisfied that it fulfils such
requirements of Part II and this Part as apply in relation to the scheme in
question, and the requirements of Part III, IV or V of this Schedule . . .'

It is common ground that only the requirements of Part IV are for consideration
at present.

Paragraph 4 of Sch 9 reads:

'If an alteration is made in the scheme at any time after the Board have
approved the scheme, the approval shall not have effect after the date of the
alteration unless the Board have approved the alteration.'

It remains to quote para 29 of Sch 9:

'The price at which scheme shares may be acquired by the exercise of a right
obtained under the scheme—(a) must be stated at the time the right is obtained,
and (b) must not be manifestly less than the market value of shares of the same
class at that time . . .'

One notes from the above extracts that tax relief may attend an approved share
option scheme and that an approved scheme is a scheme approved under Sch 9.
Paragraph 1 of Sch 9 enacts that the Board must approve a scheme if the scheme
fulfils the requirements therein mentioned. This case turns on whether or not certain
requirements specified in Part IV have been fulfilled, that is to say, the requirements
indicated in para 29.

Counsel for the Crown submitted that the requirements of para 29 were not
fulfilled as respects the company scheme when read with the proposed alterations
reducing the time for exercising pre-June 1988 options from nine to six years. It was
said, looking at para 29, that it was a requirement that the price at which shares may
be acquired (in exercise of an option) must be stated 'at the time [when] the right is
obtained'. Under the original scheme the time when the right was obtained in the
case of, say, Mr Wood was 21 July 1987. It was accepted that the price stated at that
date was 10·5p per share. That price was not 'manifestly less' (see para 29(b)) and so
the para 29 requirement was fulfilled. But that was not so as to the scheme in its
altered form. The right to acquire that Mr Wood had under the altered scheme was
said to be a new or different right, not the same right that he had under the original
scheme because the new right was exercisable between 1993 and 1997, whereas the
old right was exercisable only after 1996 and before the end of 1997.

Looking again at para 29(a), what has to be stated is the price of the new right 'at
the time the right is obtained', ie 14 June 1988. The proposed alterations in the
scheme do not affect the price stated and the scheme will still state the price of the
right at the figure of 10·5p per share. That price is 'manifestly less' than the June
1988 market value of the shares, the value being then (as was accepted) 55·25p per
share. In this way, said counsel for the Crown, the requirements of Sch 9 were not
fulfilled and the Board was justified in refusing approval.

Counsel for the Crown supported his case by the proposition that there was a
rescission of the original option arrangements in consequence of the introduction of
the new options arrangements. On that footing there was again a new right that had
to be subjected to the test of para 29. I refer to that second submission below.

Counsel for the company drew attention to the fact that the legislation permitted
of an option being exercisable during a seven-year span (see s 185(5) of the 1988 Act)
and that within that span the company had selected the last year and now desired to
come forward so as to enable the option to be exercisable after the sixth year. But
the exercise of the option was, he said, a second stage in the option mechanism. The
first stage took place when the grantee of the option obtained the right to acquire
(see s 185(1)).

Going to para 29, he said that the right to acquire was obtained when the option
was originally granted which in the case of, say, Mr Wood was 21 July 1987. He had

a right to acquire then, he had a right to acquire in June 1988 and he still has that
a right. The only effect of the alteration in the scheme is that the right is to be
exercisable at an earlier date than it would have been before alteration. It was argued
that in this way the requirements of para 29 were fulfilled (post-1987) because (a) the
price at which the shares might be acquired was stated as 10·5p, which was the true
figure at the time when the right was obtained (in 1987), and (b) that price (as is
accepted) was not manifestly less than the market value of the shares at that time,
b that is to say, a right to acquire at 10·5p was obtained in 1987 and the same right
subsists, and the fact that the time for operating the second stage of the option
mechanism has been changed does not alter the nature of the right originally
obtained, ie a right to acquire.

I think it will be apparent from the foregoing that the problem presented in this
case by para 29 is whether Mr Wood will obtain a new right in consequence of the
c proposed alteration in the scheme or whether he will, after the alteration, have the
same right that he had prior to the alteration, ie in 1987. To my mind, it is not
enough simply to say that Mr Wood had a right to acquire shares in 1987 and he
continues to have a right to acquire the shares. One must examine the position a
little further. The number of shares that may be acquired remains the same. I then
take account of the fact that tax relief in respect of shares acquired under an
d approved share option scheme is made dependent on certain requirements as to the
price at which the shares can be paid for (para 29) and as to the time when the shares
may be taken up (s 185(5)). Thus, when a grantee 'obtains a right to acquire shares'
it is important to direct the mind both to the price at which he may acquire and the
time when he may acquire. On that footing the 'right to acquire' spoken of in s 185
cannot be regarded as being independent of any notion of time. For tax relief it must
e be regarded as a right to be exercised within certain time limits. If that be so it
follows that an alteration in the time limits affecting a right to acquire is an alteration
of the right. Put more simply, the Act contemplates a right to acquire as a right to
acquire a specified number of shares at a specified price within a specified time span.
If the time span is altered the right is altered. My view therefore is that the right to
acquire which Mr Wood obtained in 1987 is not the same right as he will have if
f effect is given to the proposed amendment and he can buy in 1993 instead of having
to wait until 1996.

Thus, I conclude with regret that the Special Commissioner erred in law in
approving the alteration in the scheme. The Board is justified in refusing its
approval. I add that the particular Crown submission which I have considered and
accepted was not put at the forefront of the submissions to the Special Commissioner.
g The conclusion I have reached makes it unnecessary to consider the appeal further.

However, counsel for the Crown made a second submission. He said that the
alteration in the rules brought about a rescission of the agreement made in 1987
whereby shares could, after 1996, be acquired for 10·5p a share. This was a point
considered by the Special Commissioner. His decision was that there was no
rescission. Before me counsel for the Crown said there was a rescission because the
h old option (or right) to acquire was done away with and a new option arose. After a
quotation from *British and Beningtons Ltd v North Western Cachar Tea Co Ltd*
[1923] AC 48 at 62, it was said that the test of rescission is whether the contract of
variation (here the alteration) is inconsistent with the 1987 option contract to an
extent that goes to the root of the 1987 contract. The next step was to say that on the
grant of the 1987 option there arose a unilateral contract on the part of the company
j to issue shares conditional on a demand by the employee after the expiry of the time
provided in the contract and tender of the agreed price. That unilateral contract
was of the kind mentioned by Diplock LJ in *United Dominions Trust (Commercial)
Ltd v Eagle Aircraft Services Ltd* [1968] 1 WLR 74 at 83. (See also *Varty (Inspector
of Taxes) v British South Africa Co* [1965] Ch 508 at 522–523, 42 TC 406 at 420.)
From that standpoint and by reference to the *Eagle* case (at 84), rescission of a
unilateral contract is distinguishable from rescission of a bilateral contact, leading to

the conclusion that the alteration of the 1987 unilateral contract by changing nine years to six was such a change in that contract as went to its root.

On that submission counsel for the company took the plain line that the commissioner was right and whether one considered bilateral or unilateral contracts there could not be said to be a change going to the root of affairs if there was a mere reduction in the time before which the right to acquire could be exercised. If it were necessary, I would at present be inclined to accept the company's view, but it is not necessary for me to consider the Crown's intricate argument because I have already concluded the appeal in its favour on its first and principal submission.

Appeal allowed with costs.

Solicitors: *Solicitor of Inland Revenue*; *Simpson Curtis*, Leeds (for the company).

Rengan Krishnan Esq   Barrister.